A GUIDE TO

SHAKESPEARE'S BEST PLAYS

Compiled by the Editors of Monarch Press

MONARCH PRESS
NEW YORK

Published by MONARCH PRESS
A Simon & Schuster Division of Gulf & Western Corporation
Simon & Schuster Building
1230 Avenue of the Americas
New York, New York 10020

MONARCH PRESS and colophon are trademarks of Simon & Schuster,
registered in the U.S. Patent and Trademark Office.
Manufactured in the United States of America
10 9 8 7 6 5 4 3 2 1

Library of Congress Catalog Card Number: 82-61500

ISBN: 0-671-45871-X

CONTENTS

INTRODUCTION

Contrary to popular assumptions, we know a fair number of external facts about Shakespeare's life. We know enough to be sure that the theories that Bacon or Marlowe or someone else wrote the plays are false. William Shakespeare of Stratford-on-Avon certainly wrote most of the plays attributed to him. We do not know intimate personal details of Shakespeare's private life, but we know more about him than we know about most Elizabethan literary men. We know enough to conjecture a reasonably accurate picture of his development.

SHAKESPEARE'S LIFE

In terms of mystery, the life of Shakespeare rivals that of his most celebrated creation, Hamlet. We know little more than the dates of the important events in his life that can be learned from official records. The first date is that of his christening in Holy Trinity Church, Stratford-on-Avon, on April 26, 1564. It is traditionally assumed that he was born on April 23rd of that year. His father was John Shakespeare, a tradesman of Stratford, and his mother Mary Arden, the daughter of a small landowner of Wilmcote. After filling some minor municipal posts, John Shakespeare was elected Bailiff of Stratford in 1568. William was the third child born to his parents, the eldest of four boys and two girls who survived infancy. Although there is no record of his schooling, there seems little doubt that he was educated at the free grammar school maintained by the town of Stratford which offered training in the Classical languages sufficient for university entrance.

At the age of eighteen, he married Ann Hathaway, who was eight years his senior. The license for their marriage was issued on November 27, 1582, and their first child, Susanna, was christened in Holy Trinity Church on May 26, 1583. The discrepancy between their ages plus the fact that their first child was born six months after their marriage suggests that it was a forced marriage, though this is by no means certain. At any rate, he remained with Ann for at least another two years as their additional children, the twins Hamnet and Judith, were christened on February 2, 1585. It is suggested that he left Stratford about 1585 to avoid prosecution for poaching on the property of Sir Thomas Lucy at Charlecote. After such rural beginnings he seems to have also familiarized himself with the tavern life about London, for in the plays which center about the character of Falstaff he writes of such life as from intimate acquaintance.

Whether or not he spent some time as a village schoolmaster, as tradition has it, he seems to have arrived in London about 1586 and thereafter became involved in the theatrical world through which he was to win lasting glory. The first whispers of fame occurred in 1592 when he was mentioned as an upstart playwright in Robert Greene's *Groatsworth of Wit*. The reference there is to his earliest work, the three part *Henry VI*, which probably dates from 1591. When the plague closed the London theatres during the 1593-94 season, Shakespeare wrote the two narrative poems, *Venus and Adonis* and *Rape of Lucrece*. Both were dedicated to the Earl of Southampton, but whether Southampton became his regular patron or enabled him to enter a more aristocratic circle we do not know. In 1594, Shakespeare became a founding member of the theatrical company known until 1603 as the Lord Chamberlain's Men and thereafter as the King's Men. Individual plays by Shakespeare began to appear in print in both honest and pirated editions, and by 1598 he was considered the leading English playwright in Francis Meres's *Paladis Tamia*. His fame as a playwright contributed heavily to the success of his company, and in 1599 the company was able to build the Globe Theatre on the south bank of the Thames to house its performances in London. But he was also active as an actor, appearing in the original performance of Ben Jonson's *Every Man in His Humour* in 1598 and *Sejanus* in 1603. Though he may have acted less in his remaining professional years, he continued as leading playwright and joint owner of the King's Men and their Globe Theatre until his retirement in 1611.

A possible sign of his rising pretensions during the early years of his success may be indicated by the fact that he secured a coat of arms for his father in 1596. This was also the year in which his son Hamnet died. By 1597 he had become so prosperous that he purchased New Place, one of the two most impressive residences in Stratford, at a cost of £60. His other large earnings were also principally invested in Stratford property. In 1601 his father died, and this is also, significantly, the year in which *Hamlet* was written. As for the rest of his family, his mother died in 1608, his daughter Susanna was married in 1607 and his daughter Judith in 1616. In 1611 he retired to live with his family at New Place in Stratford though he continued to visit London until 1614 and purchased a house in Blackfriars, London, in 1613. In March, 1616, he made a will leaving token bequests to members of his theatrical company but the bulk of his estate to his family, including the famous bequest of the second-best bed to his wife. On April 23rd (May 3rd by our calendar), 1616, he died after entertaining the playwrights Jonson and Drayton at New Place.

He was buried in the Stratford church in which he had been christened and within seven years a monument with a portrait bust was erected to his memory there. In 1623, his former fellow actors, John Heminge and Henry Condell (both of whom had been mentioned in Shakespeare's will), edited the first complete collection of his plays, the volume known as the First Folio. The Droeshout engraving on its title page, together with the monument bust by Gerard Johnson, provide the only likenesses considered authentic. Shakespeare's wife also died in 1623 and his last surviving descendant, Elizabeth, the daughter of Susanna, died in 1670, but the immortality of his memory has been assured by the works of his genius, so lovingly collected by his friends. The Stratford scamp who returned to his home town as its most prosperous citizen after having won fame and fortune in London honors Stratford to this day. An endless line of admirers come to pay homage before the surviving landmarks of his personal life: the house where he was born, the house in Shottery where Ann Hathaway lived, New Place, and his grave in Holy Trinity Church, before attending performances of his enduring plays.

SHAKESPEARE'S BEST PLAYS

THE DEVELOPMENT OF SHAKESPEARE AS A DRAMATIST

Shakespeare's Early Reputation on the Stage. In 1582 a dramatist of the time, Robert Greene, wrote on his death bed a work called *A Groat's worth of Witte Bought with a Million of Repentance*. He addresses three of his fellow dramatists, Peele, Marlowe, and perhaps Nashe, as follows:

> Base minded men all three of you, if by my miserie you be not warnd: for vnto none of you (like mee) sought those burres to cleaue: those Puppets (I meane) that spake from our mouths, those Anticks garnisht in our colours. Is it not strange, that I, to whom they all haue beene beholding: is it not like that you, to whome they all haue beene beholding, shall (were yee in that case as I am now) bee both at once of them forsaken? Yes trust them not: for there is an vpstart Crow, beautified with our feathers, that with his *Tygers hart wrapt in a Players hyde*, supposes he is as well able to bombast out a blanke verse as the best of you: and beeing an absolute *Iohannes fac totum*, is in his owne conceit the only Shake-scene in a countrey.

Shakespeare is undoubtedly the "upstart Crow," the "*Iohannes fac totum*" (Johnny do-all), who is stealing the feathers, i.e., the dramatists' art, of the earlier playwrights. Greene was jealous of Shakespeare's success as a dramatist and even parodies a line from one of his earlier plays, for "*Tygers hart wrapt in a Players hyde*" echoes a line from *Henry VI, Part III*, "O tiger's heart, wrapt in a woman's hide." The passage from Greene's *Repentance* shows that Shakespeare was already well known enough as a dramatist to excite the jealousy of another writer for the stage. Greene's friend, Henry Chettle, who saw his friend's manuscript through the press, later apologized for the attack and refers to Shakespeare's good reputation as a man and as a writer.

Shakespeare's Early Poetry. In 1593, Shakespeare's *Venus and Adonis* was entered in the Stationers' Register. It was dedicated to a young noble, Henry Wriothesley, the Earl of Southampton, whom Shakespeare hoped to have as a patron, that is, someone who would reward him financially for his poems. Southampton seems to have been pleased with the dedication of the poem, and Shakespeare's second poem, *The*

Rape of Lucrece, which deals with a chaste Roman matron, was dedicated to him in 1594. Both poems were popular and both contributed to Shakespeare's reputation as a poet.

Probably during this same period Shakespeare began to write his sonnets, on which he continued to work for at least a decade, perhaps up to the time of their publication in 1609. His sonnets employ traditional themes such as the triumph of time, the miseries of sleeplessness, and the fame a poet can win for his mistress. However, Shakespeare deals also with the satisfactions of friendship, the sadness of the death of "Friends hid in death's dateless night," and the limitations of his own abilities as a man and as a creative artist.

Between about 1589 and 1613 Shakespeare wrote about 37 plays, in a great variety of genres. The following datings are based mainly on those of the scholar Edmund K. Chambers in his *William Shakespeare: A Study of Facts and Problems*, published in London in 1930.

The Early Plays 1590–1597. Probably two of Shakespeare's earliest plays were those based on Roman models, *The Comedy of Errors* and the attempt at tragedy, *Titus Andronicus*. This would accord with the theory that he was a schoolmaster somewhere in the country. Other early comedies which belong to this period are *Two Gentlemen of Verona*, a naïve romantic comedy, *Love's Labour's Lost*, a spoof on a group of courtiers intent on study, and *The Taming of the Shrew*, a lively and penetrating farce. Shakespeare's four early history plays, the three parts of *Henry VI* and *Richard III*, also belong to this period. They show Shakespeare's early concern with the evil results of a weak king's rule, with civil war, and with England's attempt to conquer France. *Richard III* shows the evil deeds of this particular tyrant and the final triumph of the House of Tudor. The charming and fanciful *A Midsummer Night's Dream*, the moving tragedy of youthful love, *Romeo and Juliet*, and the theatrical *Merchant of Venice* also belong to this period, as does *King John*.

Histories and Comedies of the Middle Period 1597–1600. To this period belong three of Shakespeare's most enchanting comedies, *Much Ado About Nothing*, *As You Like It*, and *Twelfth Night*. These three "golden" or "joyous" comedies best express the fusion in Shakespeare of the romantic and comic spirit. Shakespeare's great tetralogy, including *Richard II*, the two parts of *Henry IV*, and *Henry V*, was also produced during these years. They show his preoccupation with the realities of politics, the problems of a country governed by a weak king, the nemesis which follows one involved in the murder of a king, the evils of civil wars, and the greatness of an England true to her best instincts. *The Merry Wives of Windsor*, written (according to tradition) because Queen Elizabeth wanted to see the fat knight in love, is the poorest play of this period. *Julius Caesar*, the first of Shakespeare's Roman plays and perhaps the best of his political plays, was probably produced by 1599.

The Dark Comedies and the Great Tragedies 1600–1608. Three so-called "dark comedies" or "problem plays" belong to these years: *All's Well That Ends Well*, *Troilus and Cressida* (more a satire than a comedy), and *Measure for Measure*. All have romantic settings, but all are concerned with serious problems. All contain some elements of satire. All are serious to a degree. In all, as the critic Tillyard observes, a young man gets a shock. None are true comedies in the sense that the "golden" comedies were, but all, particularly the last two, are of interest.

The greatest of the tragedies, *Hamlet*, *Othello*, *King Lear*, and *Macbeth*, were written in this period, when Shakespeare was at the height of his powers. Less great, but of considerable interest, is *Coriolanus*, probably written toward the end of this period, as was the tragedy *Antony and Cleopatra*. *King Lear* was probably written in 1605, when Shakespeare was 41. His poetic and dramatic genius was then at its height. The play is sometimes described as Shakespeare's greatest dramatic poem or "an exalted morality play set against a backdrop of eternity," a "profound commentary on life and its values" (*The Living Shakespeare*, ed. Oscar James Campbell, New York: The Macmillan Co., 1949). The play was performed before the court at Whitehall on the day after Christmas, 1606.

The Tragicomedies 1608–1612. In 1608 Shakespeare's company began to use Blackfriars Theatre for its winter season. To attract the fashionable audience to this indoor, candlelit theater, Shakespeare and his colleagues, Francis Beaumont and John Fletcher, contrived a somewhat new genre, the romantic tragicomedy. It is uncertain which of the three initiated these experiments. Shakespeare's tragicomedies are *Pericles*, *Cymbeline*, *The Winter's Tale*, and *The Tempest*. The first two are unsuccessful experiments, the latter two highly imaginative and successful. All four tragicomedies are set in romantically remote countries and concern a love affair full of catastrophes. All have characters whose innate goodness or badness is easily observed. All but *The Winter's Tale* take place in a court where elements of decadence predominate. All use supernatural devices. In all we can discern a plot pattern which runs from prosperity through sin and destruction to regeneration, and all find the agents of regeneration and of purity in the younger generation. In all these plays, "weeping may endure for a night, but joy cometh in the morning."

THE PUBLIC THEATRE OF SHAKESPEARE'S DAY

Shakespeare's theatre was quite different from our own. It was an octagonal or a round structure with three tiers of roofed galleries around the major part of it. The central portion was an open unroofed yard in which spectators stood. These standing-room-only places cost the least, one penny (later twopence), and the people who went there were often scornfully referred to as "groundlings," and they were believed by the more educated people to like nothing but clowning. This belief is not fully supported by evidence. The roofed galleries, which contained seats, cost more the higher one went. Quite often, young gallants sat on the stage itself. Both men and women went to the theatre, but boys played women's parts in the plays. The stage itself projected almost thirty feet into the yard and was narrower at the front than at the back. Half the stage was roofed with thatch and half left open. There was no proscenium arch and no front curtain, but there were curtains at the back between the two swinging doors placed at an angle to the stage. The curtain at the stage level hid the "inner stage" or "study" in which some furniture properties could be used, such as the bed in *Othello*. Above the "study" was a projecting balcony with a curtain about four feet behind it, and another inner stage. The balcony, or "tarras" was useful for such scenes as the famous balcony scene of *Romeo and Juliet*. Glassless windows were set on this level over the doors, and they too could be used. Above the tarras was a smaller balcony with a railing and a curtain, which was generally used as a musicians' gallery or for the mast of a ship. A collection of three gabled structures, the "huts," was on the very top of all this, creating a fourth level from which sound effects could be produced, and from which things like thrones could be lowered on to the stage. Also on top of the huts was a flagstaff from which the flag of the theatre was flown during a performance. Behind the stage was the "tiring house" or dressing room for the actors, while underneath the stage was the "hell," which had machinery for raising and lowering the stage trapdoors. In all, there were seven separate playing levels on the flexible Elizabethan stage. Performances took place in the afternoon at about two o'clock. They were announced with trumpet calls and generally lasted two hours or a little more. Daylight was the only illumination in the public theatres, though candles were used for indoor performances at court and in the private theatres. The capacity of the theatre varied with the individual building, but it is probable that the Globe, Shakespeare's theatre, could hold between two and three thousand people. The building would, however, rarely be filled to capacity, except for a new play.

There were many advantages to this kind of theatre, and in some ways the physical characteristics of the building and the stage helped to dictate the form of the plays. Since there was no scenery, the stage was whatever place the playwright announced it to be. As a result the action moved quickly from place to place and scene to scene so that alternation of plot and subplot was much easier than it is today. Also, the action could take place on several different levels within the various playing levels. Elizabethan plays were therefore swiftly-moving and enhanced with poetry and ever-changing action rather than scenery. Since there was no attempt at literal, realistic staging, effects of sound and sight were evocative, rather than endeavors to capture the literal truth. Further, the playwright himself, by the use of language, was able to set the stage in the *imagination* of the audience, if not before their eyes.

THE ANTI-STRATFORDIANS

Possibly because of the rather fragmentary evidence concerning the life of Shakespeare, an anti-Shakespeare—or anti-Stratfordian—school of thought has established itself. In general, such critics claim that Shakespeare was too uneducated himself to have written the plays, and a subtle snobbery seems to dictate that any candidate put forward as the "real" Shakespeare must be of superior birth and education to the playwright. Some of the suggestions include Christopher Marlowe, Francis Bacon, The Earl of Southampton, the Earl of Oxford, and Sir Walter Raleigh. The two most popular theories are the Baconian and the Oxford ones; but all but a few scholars prefer to accept Will Shakespeare, however, as the author of the plays.

THE
COMEDIES

All's Well That Ends Well

KING OF FRANCE.
DUKE OF FLORENCE.
BERTRAM, *Count of Rossillion.*
LAFEW, *an old lord.*
PAROLLES, *a follower of Bertram.*
RINALDO, *a Steward* } *servants to the Countess of Rossillion.*
LAVATCH, *a Clown*
TWO FRENCH LORDS, *the brothers Dumain.*
PAGE.
COUNTESS OF ROSSILLION, *mother to Bertram.*
HELENA, *a gentlewoman protected by the Countess.*
An old WIDOW *of Florence.*
DIANA, *daughter to the Widow.*
MARIANA, *neighbor and friend to the Widow.*

LORDS, OFFICERS, SOLDIERS, *etc.*

All's Well That Ends Well

Act I: Scene 1

The play opens in the palace of the Count of Rossillion with the entry of the Countess, the young Count Bertram, her son, Helena, and the Lord Lafew. The people from Rossillion are dressed in mourning for the Count (Bertram's father) and in addition, Helena is still sad for the recent death of her father, physician to the Count of Rossillion. There is also added sadness because Bertram has just been summoned to the court of the King of France who is now the young man's guardian since the death of the old Count.

Lafew, the French lord, speaks consolingly to the Countess, telling her that she has found another husband in the King, and Bertram another father. The King is renowned for his goodness to all his subjects and thus the family is most fortunate because it will be rewarded according to its very considerable virtue. The Countess next inquires after the health of the King and asks whether there is any hope of his recovery. In reply, Lafew says that the monarch has given up all hope and no longer trusts his physicians. The Countess then remembers the skill of Helena's father, a physician of unsurpassed skill and knowledge, wishing that he were still alive to cure the king of his ulcerous sore. Lafew is interested and the Countess identifies the deceased physician as the famous Gerard de Narbon. On hearing this Lafew also recalls the name and says that the King himself had recently spoken admiringly and mourningly of him. Lafew then asks whether Helena is the physician's only child, and the Countess replies in the affirmative, at the same time praising the young lady for all her virtuous qualities, both those she has inherited and those which

she exercises—she is well educated, honest and full of goodness. Since Helena has nowhere to go, the Countess has kindly
let her remain at Rossillion, the only home she has ever known.

Needless to say, these praises and tributes both to herself and
to her father cause Helena to weep. The Countess chides the
young girl for her outward show of grief in case she makes
people think that her sorrow is more affected than real. Lafew
also counsels moderation, even in grief, claiming that excess
in such circumstances can also be an enemy to the living.
Helena replies in an odd way, saying that she affects grief and
also actually feels it.

Bertram then interrupts proceedings to ask his mother's blessing, which she readily gives, wishing that he may be a worthy
successor to his father "in manners as in shape!" She notes
that both "blood and virtue" struggle for rule in him.

The Countess then gives Bertram some advice on behavior
which is reminiscent of that given by Polonius to Laertes in
Hamlet. This kind of moral advice was quite frequently given
to those about to leave on a journey, especially, as in the case
of Bertram, when " 'Tis an unseason'd [inexperienced] courtier." Lafew promises to advise him, and Bertram bids both the
ladies farewell, asking Helena to be a comfort to the Countess.

Left alone, Helena begins to grieve aloud, and in her soliloquy
we find a clue to her earlier riddling remark. She is sad for
the loss of Bertram rather than for her father. In fact she hardly
even recalls her father's countenance, because her love for
Bertram has driven all such memories from her mind. But her
passion for the young count is also impossible of fulfillment
because he is so far above her in rank. Nevertheless, when
Bertram was at home she could at least bask in his presence.
Note here the imagery which Helena uses in speaking of
Bertram: she speaks of her "idolatrous fancy" and of sanctify-
ing "his relics." She has made Bertram into a saint, an object of
worship.

Parolles, a follower of Bertram, then enters and Helena gives
a brief character sketch of him, saying that she dislikes him
because he is "a notorious liar, . . . a great way fool, solely

a coward." She really indicates the attitude that the audience is supposed to have toward Parolles throughout the entire play. Nevertheless, because Bertram apparently enjoys Parolles for his merriment, Helena treats him well. Parolles immediately engages her in a bawdy conversation on virginity, suggesting, however, that loss of virginity is essential for the procreation of the human race. Helena speaks in support of virginity, but she seems very well able to understand Parolles' obscene quibbles on the subject. He goes on to discuss virginity as a barren thing and speaks of procreation in terms of a generous business investment.

Helena then proceeds to list all Bertram's chances in love by using the many overwrought terms for the beloved in Elizabethan and Jacobean love poetry: phoenix, goddess, counsellor, traitress, etc. As Helena wishes Bertram well, she again reveals her love. Then, while Parolles makes ready to depart, Helena makes fun of him for his cowardice. Not a whit discomfited, Parolles condescendingly promises to "return perfect courtier," and in fact he will even educate the ignorant Helena.

Left alone, Helena delivers another soliloquy revealing her innermost thoughts, and she gradually comes to the conclusion that no woman who proved her merit was ever unsuccessful in love. Then with a cryptic hint concerning the King's disease, she leaves.

Act I: Scene 2

This scene takes place in Paris at the palace of the King, who enters with his attendants. The King speaks of wars between the Florentines and the inhabitants of Siena, saying that the Florentines are about to seek aid from France. The King, however, intends to follow the advice of Austria and refuse—officially, that is. After all, as the King and a lord note, this war would be a good training ground in arms for some of the restless gentry of the court.

Bertram then arrives and is greeted warmly by the King who praises the virtues and abilities of his late father. He recalls his wit, his lack of contempt and bitterness, remembering that his pride and sharpness were never shown in an unwarranted manner. He was never arrogant. If he were still living, he would be a model for the men of this present age.

In a rather uncourtly manner, Bertram expresses his thanks for these words, but the King continues, remembering the Count's desire to live no longer than his strength. This is a wish in which the ailing King himself heartily concurs. The reference to his health reminds the King to ask when Gerard de Narbon had died, and on learning that it was six months ago, he comments that if only that physician were living he would call him to the court. Then, calling for the arm of a courtier, the weakened King leaves.

Act I: Scene 3

This scene takes place in the palace of the Countess of Rossillion. The Countess and the Steward try to discuss Helena, but they are continually interrupted by the Clown, who speaks in a thoroughly bawdy manner of his own desire to marry, simply for physical gratification. The Clown has a completely physical view of the matrimonial relationship and seems almost to expect infidelity of his wife. He himself has after all been a wicked creature, and therefore his motive in marriage is repentance. But cuckoldry is most likely, and that state makes all men equal, though they be "Charbon the puritan and old Poysam the papist."

The Clown continues his attack on the virtue of women until the Countess finally dismisses him quite curtly.

Left alone with the Steward, the Countess inquires his business, which concerns the lady Helena. The Countess immediately speaks very kindly of the girl, saying that she is indeed more than worthy of love.

The Steward then informs the Countess that Helena has admitted that she loves Bertram, though he is so far above her, and that he has immediately come to acquaint the young man's mother with the situation. Apparently, this is no revelation to the Countess, who has suspected the matter before, so she says she will speak of it to Helena who enters at this moment. The older woman looks pityingly on the orphan, remembering her own youth.

She then addresses Helena saying that she hopes the young girl regards her as a mother. Helena starts at that statement and the Countess presses the point, asking what has seemed so startling in her use of the word. Helena replies modestly that the Count of Rossillion can never be her brother, since he springs from noble family and she from obscure stock. She will therefore live as his servant and feudal inferior. The Countess then questions Helena further, asking whether she is excluded from taking the place of Helena's mother. The young woman states that such a situation is impossible, just so that Bertram will not be her brother. Finally, the Countess brings the matter into the open and says quite baldly that Helena might be her daughter-in-law, a statement that takes the young girl's breath away. The Countess then asks whether she is right in making the statement that Helena loves Bertram. Helena then confesses her love with great humility, begging that the Countess not blame her for her presumption, speaking of her love in terms of honor and religious faith, while using additional metaphors involving Diana, the chaste huntress, a goddess well fitted to be Helena's patroness.

After further questioning Helena admits that she has been thinking of going to Paris because her father, the late Gerard de Narbon, had left some highly potent prescriptions, one of which seems to be a cure for the disease from which the King is suffering. The Countess then shrewdly asks whether this was the original reason for her wish to go to Paris, and Helena quite honestly admits that Bertram's departure made her think of the cure. Gently, the Countess asks whether Helena believes that the physicians at the king's court will listen to her, unlearned young woman that she is, when the greatest physicians alive have failed. Helena, however, seems very confident, saying that she is prepared to wager her own life on the prospect of the King's cure. The Countess accordingly grants her permission to go to Paris, and says that she will pray for Helena's success.

Act II: Scene 1

This scene is laid in the palace of the King in Paris. The monarch enters with Bertram, Parolles, and a number of young lords who are about to leave for the Florentine war. As the scene opens the King is addressing the young men, exhorting them to be "the sons/ Of worthy Frenchmen," and bidding them "Not to woo honour, but to wed it," in defending the last monarchy.

As for himself, the King sounds as if he does not expect to recover from the illness which is wasting him away. Nevertheless, he warns his young men against the charms of the Italian women whose fame as courtesans was wide in Shakespeare's day.

As the King retires, one of the lords regrets that Bertram must remain behind. The young man immediately launches into an angry tirade against his youth, which forces him to remain at home when he would rather be seeking honor on the battlefield. Parolles and the young lord both try to persuade him to disobey the King and steal away with them, but Bertram merely inveighs against the disgrace of being left at home with the women. Parolles then rather arrogantly tells the lord to give his regards to a certain Captain Spurio who bears a scar on his face from a wound allegedly inflicted by the braggart.

Bertram then announces his intention to obey the King and stay at the court. Parolles promptly offers his master some advice on behavior, telling him exactly how he should behave to those who are older in the ways of the court than he, and informing him that he should take a more extended leave of the departing lords.

Lafew now enters and the King, who has apparently been in the background, now comes forward. The French lord kneels before his monarch who bids him rise. Then, to the King's surprise, Lafew asks whether he wishes to be cured of his malady, going on to say that he has seen a doctor who will reawaken the monarch and even cause the Emperor Charlemagne to write her a love letter. The King is quite amazed to find that this doctor is a woman and asks that Lafew bring her in.

Helena then enters and Lafew introduces her. The King inquires concerning her interest in his illness and Helena explains that she has inherited some medicines from her famous father, including one which he had told her to consider the most precious of his remedies. Needless to say the King is a trifle skeptical, and says that though the disease is considered incurable he still ought not to resort to quackery for a cure. Helena then says that she hopes her offer is not out of place, and if so, she begs pardon. The King graciously thanks her and bids her farewell saying that he knows his peril only too well, and she knows no medical art.

Helena, however, presses her suit a little more strongly, claiming that really the King could not be harmed by trying this medicine; after all, miracles have happened in the past and may do so again. The King once more refuses her offer, but gives her no reward since he has not accepted her help. Helena now pleads with the King, claiming that she is not an imposter, and suggests that the King now place his trust in heaven rather than in the opinion of men. Her own art is honest and she herself places her trust in God. When the King expresses curiosity, Helena speaks an incantatory speech claiming that she can cure the King within two days, and on this result she is willing to stake not only her honor, but also her life. Intrigued, the King says he will try Helena's cure on her terms. The young woman agrees to the bargain, and in reply asks what her reward may be if she is successful. The King offers her anything she may desire that is within his power to grant.

Helena now asks for her payment, the gift of whatever husband she may ask, with one limitation: she will not choose from among the royal family of France. Her chosen husband will be one under the command of the King and he will be free for her to ask. The King agrees and the scene ends.

Act II: Scene 2

The action returns to Rossillion where the Countess and the Clown are talking together. Among other witty comments, the Clown parodies the distinction between nature and nurture found in the main plot when he speaks of himself as "highly fed and lowly taught." In addition, the Clown seems to speak disparagingly of the court, claiming that a man can easily forget his manners there, and also that only the unintelligent can become successful courtiers. He, however, is shrewd enough to have an answer for all questions and all occasions. More witticisms are exchanged and then the Countess calls herself to order for wasting her time with the fool. She sends him to the court with a letter for Helena, asking for a reply, while at the same time asking to be remembered to her son. The Clown departs immediately.

Act II: Scene 3

The scene now returns to the court at Paris. Bertram, Lafew, and Parolles enter and all exclaim at the apparent miracle that has just occurred. Parolles says that the King had been given up by all the doctors, the followers of "both Galen and Paracelsus," yet he is now cured.

Lafew continues to exclaim and Parolles puts in his comments, trying to sound as learned as possible, using more and more high flown language which Lafew seems to ignore.

Helena, the King, and a number of attendants then enter, with the monarch obviously in perfect health. He now intends to keep his part of the bargain and calls before him all the lords of the court, explaining that Helena has the power to choose a husband from among them, and that they cannot refuse her. Lafew looks glowingly on Helena and wishes himself young again so that he could be a candidate. The young lady then announces modestly that though she is not wealthy in terms of money, she is a virgin, and thereby wealthy in virtue. The King then makes it quite clear that any lord refusing Helena will lose his favor.

Moving slowly along the line of young men, Helena finds the first lord willing to grant her suit, and the second also, even though she protests that she is beneath them in rank. She says the same to the third lord, and the fourth, who disagrees with her. Then, on reaching Bertram, she *gives* herself to him:

> I dare not say I take you, but I give
> Me and my service, ever whilst I live,
> Into your guiding power. This is the man.
> (II.iii.102–104)

Bertram is extremely angry at being thus singled out and when the King says "young Bertram, take her; she's thy wife," the young man asks for permission at least to make his own choice of a wife, a reasonable enough request. He does not see why he should pay for the King's cure, and quite frantically seeks a way out of the situation by complaining that Helena is just not good enough to marry him—"A poor physician's daughter my wife!"—and especially a girl who has been brought up in his family as a kind of charity case.

The King counters Bertram's argument by saying that Helena is "virtuous, . . . young, wise, fair," and in respect of these gifts she is noble indeed. Anyway, if Bertram will settle only for a titled lady with a rich dowry, the King is well able to provide Helena with both these things. Then Helena would be a prize indeed, having both the moral and the tangible aspects of nobility.

Finally the King loses his temper with the obstinate young ward and enforces his authority, despite the fact that Bertram declares his flat refusal even to try to love Helena. He turns on Bertram and tells him that he is unworthy of the "good gift" of Helena, that he is angry that the young man will not accept the newly enriched and ennobled Helena. Then he resorts to threats, saying that if he does not accept Helena, Bertram will live out his life under the shadow of the King's displeasure. A trifle afraid, Bertram agrees with very bad grace, saying that since honor goes where the King bids,

> . . . I find that she, which late
> Was in my nobler thoughts most base, is now
> The praised of the king; who, so ennobled,
> Is as 'twere born so. (II.iii.170–173).

The King then tells Bertram to take Helena by the hand and say that she is his, and in turn the monarch will give her a fortune. Bertram does as he is told; the King, acting as witness, gives his consent and wishes that the marriage will turn out well. In addition, he sets the church ceremony for later the same evening, but postpones the feasting until later.

Everyone then leaves the room except for Parolles and Lafew.

The latter says that Bertram was most wise to agree to the King's suggestion, a statement with which Parolles hotheadedly disagrees. Then he tells Parolles to beware of his behavior since he is really a worthless parasite. After he leaves Parolles makes hostile comments concerning the dignified Lord Lafew.

Lafew returns shortly and tells Parolles that Bertram and Helena are now married. Parolles replies in a rude manner, and Lafew orders him to be silent because he is behaving above his station. In addition, the shrewd courtier has already sized up Parolles as nothing more than a vagabond.

Bertram then arrives, complaining that he has been married to Helena against his will. He sees no way out of his trouble, but he declares that even though he has gone through the church ceremony he will not go to bed with the lady. Instead he will go away to the Tuscan wars, a project which Parolles encourages.

Parolles claims that Bertram will be able to pursue honor in the wars, and recommends that he do this rather than stay at home as a husband. Bertram agrees, saying that he will send Helena to his mother at Rossillion with a letter telling her of the hatred he bears toward his wife.

Act II: Scenes 4-5

The first scene takes place in the King's palace where Helena greets the Clown who has been sent from Rossillion, bringing with him the greetings of the Countess. Parolles then enters, greets Helena, and asks the Clown about the Countess' health. After more witticisms, during which the Clown comes off best by showing that he understands the braggart, Parolles comes to the point. Bertram has to leave the court on very urgent business. As a result the newly married pair will have to postpone their wedding night until some future date. Helena herself must also leave the court as quickly as possible, gaining permission for them both and making suitable excuses to the King. Then she should await Bertram's pleasure. Helena, ever obedient to Bertram, agrees.

The next scene between Lafew and Bertram takes place in a room in the King's palace in Paris, where they are both discussing Parolles. Lafew seems most surprised at Bertram's assertions concerning the valor of Parolles, something the shrewd courtier has not in the least expected. What is more, he remains unconvinced that Parolles is as bold as Bertram seems to think. Parolles himself then enters and Lafew makes fun of him by pretending to think him a man sent by a tailor to bring goods to Bertram. This witticism seems to indicate that Parolles is merely the product of his tailor, not of his personal valor.

Bertram asks Parolles whether Helena has gained permission to leave the court and is glad to learn that she has. He himself has written all his departure letters, put his assets into boxes, ordered his horses, and is now ready to leave. Lafew takes more subtle digs at Parolles, and Bertram, puzzled, tries to discover why Lafew dislikes him. Parolles claims ignorance, but Lafew says that the braggart has deliberately gone out of his way to displease his superior, and he warns the young man against his loudmouthed follower. On Lafew's departure Parolles makes a disparaging remark, only to find that Bertram repects the old lord.

At this point Helena arrives bringing news of the King's permission but bearing a message that the monarch would like to see Bertram before their departure. Bertram then gives her a letter to the Countess and tells her to find her own way back to Rossillion. He is sorry, but he must transact some business and therefore he will not see her for a few days. Helena expresses her intention to be obedient to the will of her husband. She states her own unworthiness, and says she is so grateful for having married such a man, so far above her, that she will always take care to obey him promptly. Bertram, a trifle embarrassed, cuts her short, and then she speaks again of her unworthiness, finally summoning the courage to beg for a kiss. Instead Bertram tells her to hurry along, and after her departure swears that he has no intention of returning to his home while Helena is there.

Act III: Scene 1

This very short scene takes place at the palace of the Duke of

Florence. The Duke discusses the reason for the war with the newly arrived French lords. The Frenchmen say that they think the Florentine side of the quarrel seems just, while the opposition seems entirely in the wrong. Needless to say, the Duke of Florence agrees, and says that he cannot understand why the King of France refuses to take a more active part, something another lord finds incomprehensible. The first lord says that he is quite sure that the young lords of France who are tired of doing nothing will come to Florence to fight.

Act III: Scene 2

In Rossillion the Countess tells the Clown that things have happened between Helena and Bertram as she would have wished, except that her son has not come home with his wife. The Clown maintains that Bertram is very melancholy, something that the Countess questions as she opens his letter. While she is reading the Clown laments that he has not felt any liking for Isbel since he has been at the court. Now he begins to love money and he cares less for the satisfaction of his carnal desires.

In his letter Bertram says that though he has married Helena, he has not been to bed with her, and has run away rather than do so. He has sworn never to consummate his marriage, and will forever stay a long way from his wife. The Countess is most displeased with this message, saying that Bertram has acted in an unbridled and rash fashion to fly from the favor of the King, angering his guardian lord simply because he has not cared for a lady who is too virtuous for even an emperor to despise. Just then the Clown, with an obscene quibble or two, announces the arrival of Helena escorted by two soldiers.

The young woman arrives in great sadness to say that Bertram has gone away forever. One of the French lords says that they know he has gone to serve the Duke of Florence, and then Helena produces a letter containing conditions impossible for her ever to fulfill:

> When thou canst get the ring upon my finger, which
> never shall come off, and show me a child begotten
> of thy body that I am father to, then call me hus-
> band: but in such a "then" I write a never.

The letter concludes with a statement that until Bertram has no wife he has nothing in France. So Bertram vows that he will never recognize Helena as his wife until these impossible tasks have been performed.

The Countess is quite shocked at the cruelty of Bertram and immediately takes the side of Helena, whom she calls her child, completely disowning her son. Though one of the French lords endeavors to mitigate the cruelty of Bertram's letter by saying that the young man did not really mean what he wrote, the Countess takes his meaning literally. She claims that Helena is far too good for twenty Bertrams, and when she finds out that Bertram has gone to the wars with Parolles she shows that she also considers him an evil influence, saying that Bertram's noble birth is corrupted by the way the young man permits himself to be led by this evil counsellor. The Countess tells the lords that when they see Bertram they are to tell him for her that his sword can never win him back the same amount of honor that he has lost by his treatment of Helena. She will say more to him in a letter she will give to them.

Left alone, the miserable Helena rehearses the words of Bertram and regrets that she has been the cause that her husband has nothing either in France or at Rossillion. All the shocks which Bertram may encounter, all the charges, indeed, all the dangers of war have been wished upon him unwittingly by Helena. She trembles for Bertram's danger and decides to steal away from Rossillion herself so that Bertram may return to his home.

Act III: Scene 3

This brief scene takes place in Florence with the Duke, Bertram, Parolles, and some soldiers. It serves to indicate the valor of Bertram who has now been appointed general of the Florentine horse. Bertram accepts the weighty responsibility and says that he fights so well and faces danger so boldly because he is a hater of love. Therefore he puts himself among the ranks of Mars, the god of war.

Act III: Scene 4

Again in Rossillion, the Countess has just received Helena's letter from a steward. The young girl has left her home to go on a perpetual pilgrimage to St. Jaques in order to do penance for what she considers her misdeeds. She begs the Countess to write Bertram and call him home from the bloody wars, for his home is once more his own since she has left. She, his wife, has sent him forth to war, and he is too good either for death or for her. She intends to embrace death herself in order to set Bertram free.

The Countess is griefstricken and blames the steward for not giving her the letter sooner so that Helena's flight might have been prevented. She tells the steward, Rinaldo, to write to Bertram, "this unworthy husband," to tell him what has happened to Helena and to try to make him understand her worth. Perhaps he may return to Rossillion when he hears that she has gone, and perhaps Helena too may come back, drawn by pure love. The distraught Lady makes no distinction between her love for her son and his wife; she is bowed down with grief.

Act III: Scene 5

This scene takes place outside the walls of Florence. A Widow enters with Diana, her daughter, Mariana, a neighbor, and Violenta.

They and other citizens of Florence have come to watch the soldiers return from battle. The valor of "the French Count" is praised, and the Widow tells how he took prisoner the opposing commander and also slew the Duke's brother with his own hand. Mariana, the neighbor, warns Diana against "this French earl," saying that "the honour of a maid is her name, and no legacy is so rich as honesty." In other words, a maiden should preserve both her chastity and her good name wherever possible. The Widow then explains that she has told Mariana how Diana has been solicited by the Frenchman's companion. As Mariana speaks of Parolles' filthy nature we realize that the gentleman under discussion is Bertram. The lady warns Diana against Parolles' obscene suggestions to Bertram, and tells the girl to beware of all such people. Diana expresses her steadfastness.

17

Helena then enters, dressed as a pilgrim to the shrine of St. Jaques le Grand, and since the Widow hopes she will lodge at her house she addresses herself to the pilgrim. Helena agrees to stay, and by the end of the scene the Widow reveals that she already has four or five other pilgrims at her house. Helena asks why all the people around her are waiting, and Diana explains that they are awaiting the arrival of the troops, especially the Count Rossillion, a young man who has been most valiant. Diana says that he has made a fine impression on everyone in Florence and goes on to say that he had fled from France because the King had married him against his will to a lady. Helena says that the tale is true, since she knows the lady, to which Diana comments that the gentleman who serves the Count speaks disparagingly of her. Nevertheless, Diana expresses sympathy for the injured lady and the Widow remarks that Diana could indeed do her a service. Upon Helena's questioning, the Widow reveals that Bertram, through Parolles, is soliciting Diana's company for immoral purposes. Just then the procession of returning troops passes by and Helena suffers the irony of having her own husband pointed out to her. Diana praises Bertram, but makes cutting remarks about Parolles, who seems extremely vexed, muttering "Lose our drum! Well!"

As Parolles spies the three women the Widow curses him, and Mariana curses Bertram "for a ring-carrier."

After the procession Helena asks if Diana and Mariana may eat with them at the Widow's house that night.

Act III: Scene 6

This scene takes place in the Florentine camp where Bertram is speaking to two French lords who want to test the bravery of Parolles. Bertram seems to believe in him, but the lords are quite convinced that he is an arrant coward and braggart. They plan to capture Parolles and make him think he is in the enemy camp. Then, if his behavior is as cowardly as the lords expect, Bertram may punish him. The lords suggest that Parolles be sent to recover the captured drum mentioned in the last scene. After all, he has recently been boasting of a stratagem to get it back. The lords think they shall have "Jack Drum's entertainment."

Parolles then enters and the lords and Bertram start discussing the drum. Gradually they push Parolles to the point at which he hints at some fine trick he has to capture it, and eventually he even swears that he will undertake the task. The lords, however, are quite convinced that he will simply return to tell another tall tale, and they agree with Lafew who was the first to doubt Parolles' veracity. The scene concludes with Bertram asking one of the lords to go with him so that he may see where Diana lives. Though she is honest, Bertram nevertheless has hopes of gaining the fair creature for himself.

Act III: Scene 7

This scene takes place in the house of the Widow in Florence. Helena has identified herself and now she tries to persuade the Widow to help her. She does not, however, wish to do anything that might ruin her reputation and that of Diana. Helena then gives the Widow a purse of gold and tells her plan. When Bertram woos Diana she should make an appointment for him to come to her as he wishes, but before she agrees she should ask him for his ancestral ring, passed down in his family for some five generations. Then Diana should arrange for a specific hour for the Count to fulfill his desires, but Helena will take Diana's place to gratify the Count's desires. Afterwards Helena promises Diana a dowry of three thousand crowns. The Widow finally agrees to the plan, and Helena concludes the scene with a riddling comment reminiscent of her double entendres in Act I. There is apparent wickedness in Bertram's visiting the supposed Diana, but in effect the act is lawful, though Bertram's intent is to commit adultery.

Act IV: Scene 1

This scene takes place outside the Florentine camp where a French lord and five or six other soldiers wait in ambush to watch Parolles' attempt to recover the captured drum. They plan to surround and capture Parolles, making him think they are the enemy by speaking all sorts of gibberish. At that moment Parolles enters and he very speedily justifies all the doubts the lords have had concerning his valor. He begins by saying that he plans to wait around without doing anything for another three hours or so and then return. He also seems to suspect that the lords have begun to realize exactly what kind of man he is. He has spoken lately in too foolhardy a manner and he is actually afraid of war. Slowly he begins to puzzle a way out of his dilemma. He must wound himself and pretend that he received his injuries in an attempt to recover the drum. Yet, as he well knows, minor wounds will not be convincing, and he is too cowardly to give himself severe ones. He makes all sorts of suggestions to make his exploit the more plausible, and each time a lord makes a disparaging comment for the benefit of the audience. He wishes that he had a drum of the enemy's which he could substitute. Suddenly the soldiers leap out of their hiding place to capture and blindfold Parolles. As they speak their incomprehensible gibberish, Parolles tries to make himself understood, hoping that someone other than these "Muscovites" may be able to translate some language that Parolles also knows. Finally, a soldier suggests that Parolles might be saved if he were prepared to inform on the Florentines in some way. The coward leaps at the opportunity and promises to tell all the secrets of the camp, the strength of the troops and so on. The lord then bids a messenger go to the Count of Rossillion and his own brother to see exactly how the "valiant" Parolles will fare under pressure.

Act IV: Scene 2

This scene shows the wooing of Diana by Bertram and it takes place at the Widow's house in Florence. The young man speaks of love to Diana, and since she is named for the chaste huntress he speaks to her of the superiority of love over virgin chastity, using an argument very common in Shakespeare's Sonnets and Elizabethan literature, that the only way beauty can be continued is through the loss of virginity. As Diana's mother lost her virginity to conceive the maiden, so should Diana act. The young girl counters by saying that her mother was chaste at the time, and furthermore was married, reminding Bertram of his own matrimonial duty to his wife. Bertram tells her to forget about his wife, whom he was compelled to marry, while he loves Diana unconstrainedly, and will forever be her servant. He has sworn, moreover, never to consummate his marriage with Helena. Diana speaks very realistically, claiming that men swear eternal fidelity, but desert a young virgin after they have done their pleasure with her. She claims that repeated swearing of fidelity does not necessarily mean that the wooer is telling the truth; a single honest oath is quite sufficient. She asks whether Bertram would believe her if she swore by Jove, the amorous god, that she loved him. There is no holding in an oath sworn by the love of God to work against God. Unimpressed, Bertram begs Diana to be gentle to him in his "sick desires."

Diana then asks Bertram for his ring, but he says that he will only lend it to her, since it has been an heirloom in his family, and its loss would be great dishonor. Diana then says that her chastity is like the ring; it too is the honor of a house, and it would be "the greatest obloquy i'th'world/ In me to lose." She echoes Bertram's own words here. Also, the young man has accidentally used honor against his own suit.

Sick with desire, Bertram tears off his ring and tells Diana to take everything of his: ring, house, honor, and even his life. He will do anything she asks. Diana then outlines the plan: at midnight he must knock at her chamber window and she will let him in. Then, once he has had sexual intercourse with her, he must remain only one hour, and he must not even speak to her. Her reasons are very important, and Bertram shall only know them when his ring is given back to him. In the meantime she will put on his finger in bed another ring, as a token in the future of the deeds done that night. In this way, Diana says, "You have won/ A wife of me, though there my hope be done."

Left alone, Diana meditates on the deception of men, saying that her mother was right about their persuasions. She also says that since Bertram has promised to marry her after his wife's death, therefore she will lie with him when she herself is buried. Disillusioned, she says that since Frenchmen seem so deceitful she will live and die a maid, except that in this particular matter she sees no reason not to deceive the man who would win unjustly.

Act IV: Scene 3

The scene now returns to the French camp where two French lords are discussing Bertram's matrimonial difficulties. Apparently the Countess' letter has just been given to Bertram and has greatly affected him. The First Lord says that Bertram is much to be blamed for casting off such an excellent lady as Helena, and the Second Lord comments that he has also incurred the displeasure of the King. Then he goes further, telling his companion that Bertram has seduced a young gentlewoman in Florence, and that this very night he plans to deflower her. Such is his madness that he has even given her his ancestral ring. The First Lord is appalled and the Second Lord speaks of the corruption of such nobility. They wonder about the propriety of discussing this matter, however, and the First Lord asks whether Bertram will return to the camp this evening. Apparently his plan is to return after midnight, and the First Lord is pleased because he wants Bertram to see the proceedings which will reveal Parolles' true nature.

In further conversation the Second Lord tells his companion that Helena has gone on a pilgrimage to the shrine of St. Jaques le Grand, and having accomplished her purpose, died there. It seems that her death was confirmed by the rector of the shrine, and the information passed on to the Count.

The Lords fear that Bertram will indeed be glad of his wife's death; thus the dignity Bertram has gained in battle in Florence will be counterbalanced by the shame he will incur by causing Helena's death, which, in effect, he would seem to have done. Sagely his companion remarks on the "mingled yarn" which makes up the life of man; virtues are counterbalanced by vices, and vice versa. At this moment a messenger enters to say that Bertram plans to return to France the next morning and that he has commendations from the Duke to take to the King.

Bertram soon follows, entirely satisfied with his night's work: he has said farewell to the Duke and his family, buried a wife and mourned for her, written to the Countess that he is coming home, hired his transportation, and in between managed "many nicer needs," here obviously a reference to the assignation with Diana. This last was his greatest achievement, but he does not yet consider that business finished—as he says to a friend, "fearing to hear of it hereafter." Then he wants to get on with the business of "this dialogue between the Fool and the Soldier," or Parolles and the military.

The Second Lord tells Bertram that Parolles has been left in the stocks all night, and he has wept and confessed almost everything possible to a soldier whom he thought to be a priest. The confession will be read aloud to Bertram, and he must have the patience to listen. The soldiers enter with Parolles and one of the men acts as a so-called interpreter. Bertram is a trifle disquieted, but says that Parolles can allege nothing about him. The soldier tells Parolles that an officer has been called to administer the tortures, but that worthy starts to tell all with the mere threat of pain. He lists the strength of the troops, denigrating the ability of the commanders, as well as their soldiers. Parolles swears he is telling the truth and goes on to give a complete account of all the companies, claiming acquaintance with one of the French Lords involved in the trick, Captain Dumaine, about whom he tells a scabrous anecdote.

Then, as a soldier begins reading from a letter the following words, "Dian, the count's a fool, and full of gold," Parolles says that he has written this letter as an enticement to a young Florentine maiden to consider an affair with Bertram, whom he now characterizes as "a foolish, idle boy, but for all that very ruttish," or lusty. He goes on to speak of Bertram as "a dangerous and lascivious boy, who is a whale to virginity, and devours up all the fry it finds." Bertram is totally furious, and then Parolles' poem to Diana is read in which he gives obnoxious advice to the lady. The fury in Bertram's face prompts the soldier to threaten Parolles with a hanging. Then the soldier turns to the subject of Captain Dumaine (one of the plotting lords), and Parolles speaks even more disparagingly of him, finally claiming that in addition to everything else he is not really a good soldier.

Then, on request, Parolles agrees to betray the Florentine army, and Bertram in particular, saying that he regrets having had anything to do with the matter of the drum. But to his horror, the soldier declares that he must die anyway, for having so traitorously betrayed his army. Parolles begs for mercy, but then he is unmuffled and he sees around him the members of his own army. They greet him ironically as "noble captain," and one asks if Parolles has a message for Lord Lafew, while another asks for a copy of his sonnet to Diana, and another remarks that if he could find a land where the only available women were those who had incurred as much shame as he, then he "might begin an impudent nation." Left alone, Parolles makes a speech of self-knowledge. In fact he really steps out of character and says in effect, "braggart, beware," because this is the kind of punishment he will suffer.

Act IV: Scene 4

This scene is again at the Widow's house in Florence where Helena is thanking both the Widow and Diana for their assistance. She says that "one of the greatest in the Christian world," that is, the King of France, will be her surety that she will not wrong either of these ladies. She tells them that she had once done the King a very great favor, and since he is now at Marseilles she wishes to go there, especially since he has convenient transportation. Now that the army is breaking up and Bertram is on his way home, haste is essential. However, Helena asks Diana to help her just a little more, and in return Helena will help the young lady to both a dowry and a husband. Diana agrees to do whatever Helena wishes, while Helena muses upon the strange nature of men who can enjoy the body of a woman they hate, as Bertram has just done with her. So Helena gets ready to depart with a riddling remark that "All's well that ends well."

Act IV: Scene 5

At Rossillion, Lafew tells the Countess that Bertram was misled by the elegant-appearing exterior of Parolles into thinking that the braggart was what he professed to be. The villainy of Parolles was of such a nature that he could have corrupted the immature youth of an entire nation. Also, if Bertram had not listened to Parolles, Helena might still be alive and at home with her husband who would have advanced further in the favor of the King. The Countess laments the supposed death of Helena, as also does Lafew, and even the Clown declares that she was "the herb of grace." The Lord Lafew and the Clown then indulge in witty and somewhat obscene word-play in which the Clown declares that he serves The Black Prince, "alias the prince of darkness, alias the devil."

The Clown goes on with his wittiness until finally Lafew declares himself weary. The Countess says that she too finds his sauciness wearing, but he is in the house because her late husband enjoyed him. Lafew then goes on to the real object of his visit. He has spoken to the King about a possible match between Bertram and his own daughter, something his majesty had raised at some time in the past; now he would like the Countess' opinion. She agrees most heartily, and Lafew tells her that the King will be at Rossillion the next day, in perfect health. In addition, the Countess has had news that Bertram will arrive home this very evening, and she begs Lafew to remain until the monarch and the young count meet. The Clown then reenters bringing news of Bertram's arrival, saying that he has a velvet patch on his cheek, presumably to cover a noble scar.

Act V: Scene 1

This scene takes place at Marseilles where Helena, the Widow, and Diana learn that they have just missed the King who has left in a great hurry for Rossillion. Helena then gives her petition to her gentleman-informant, bidding him to deliver it to the monarch at Rossillion. The Widow is almost prepared to give up, but the resourceful Helena says they must push on to Rossillion.

Act V: Scene 2

In this scene which takes place at the Count's palace at Rossillion, Parolles sends a letter to Lafew asking for an interview. The Clown greets him by holding his nose as if Parolles smells bad.

Then Lafew arrives and treats Parolles in the same contemptuous manner, claiming that he is unworthy of consideration in view of his behavior. Parolles says that since Lafew was the first to see his real nature, so should he try to gain him some grace, or forgiveness. Lafew, after saying punningly that Parolles begs more than "word," the French *parole,* sends him away, nevertheless promising that Parolles shall at least eat, even though he is a fool and a knave.

Act V: Scene 3

Now the scene moves inside the palace at Rossillion, where the King, the Countess, Lafew, the two French lords, and sundry attendants are to be found. The King openly laments the death of Helena, saying that his kingdom is poorer as a result, and similarly that Bertram in his folly failed to esteem her enough. The Countess begs the King to forgive her son, to which the monarch replies that indeed he has already done so, though a short time ago he merely desired the chance to exact vengeance for his disobedience. Lafew also tries to smooth Bertram's path by pointing out that Bertram has been punished enough by losing such a wife as Helena. The King then declares himself reconciled to the young man and bids him come into his presence, but not to beg pardon, since he has put all memory of the offense away from him. Instead he wishes that Bertram approach as if he were a stranger and not an offender.

Bertram then enters to express his repentance to the monarch who cuts him short, changing the subject to the daughter of Lafew. Bertram replies that he remembers her well and in fact had chosen her for himself long ago, before he was bold enough to speak of love. Then, he recalls, contempt made him look harshly on all women. But now he has lost Helena, whom all men praised, and therefore he can see things more clearly. The King then says that because Bertram has come to love the dead Helena he has purged himself of some of the blame for her death. No longer need Bertram be mournful, but instead he should look on Maudlin Lafew, because "the main consents are had." In other words, agreements to marry have been made by Lafew, the Countess, the King, Bertram, and also the lady herself.

The King then gives his blessing and announces that consents have been exchanged and the Countess echoes these sentiments. Lafew then asks Bertram for a token to send Maudlin so that she may come quickly. Immediately Bertram takes a ring from his finger and gives it to his prospective father-in-law who starts with surprise on recognizing it as one that Helena had worn when she departed from the court. Bertram denies that it had belonged to Helena, but then the King recognizes it as his own gift to Helena which he had told her to send him if ever she needed help. Again Bertram denies that the ring was Helena's, but this time the Countess recognizes it.

Finally Bertram is forced into a lie, claiming that a noblewoman in Florence who thought herself engaged to him had thrown it to him from a window and refused to take it back. The King remains unconvinced and believes that Bertram has done away with Helena. He orders Bertram to tell the truth, but the young man stands to his lie, and then the enraged king orders him to be imprisoned while an inquiry is made into the matter. While being taken away under guard Bertram says that it will be as easy to prove the ring Helena's as to prove that he went to bed with her in Florence. He does not know the irony of his statement.

At this moment a letter is brought in, signed Diana Capilet, which accuses Bertram of leaving Florence without fulfilling his promise to marry her after the death of Helena, even though he has been to bed with her on the strength of that promise. Diana has now come to request justice, and she asks the King to force Bertram to keep his vow. The Gentleman who has brought the letter speaks highly of Diana, and explains that she has just missed the court at its last few stops.

Bertram is then returned to the King where he desperately tries to deny everything. Lafew, in the meantime, is totally disgusted and says he wants nothing more to do with Bertram. He would sooner buy a son-in-law at a fair than trust Bertram. The King likewise suspects him of doing away with Helena.

Diana now appears to claim Bertram as her husband, and she produces his ancestral ring as evidence of betrothal. Bertram admits that he knows Diana and the Widow, but he will go no further. Diana next claims that Bertram has in fact married her, an allegation which Lafew is quite prepared to credit, and therefore he withdraws his consent to the marriage with Maudlin. With his back to the wall, Bertram tries to give the impression that Diana had seduced him, and that in fact she was a common strumpet, notorious in the Florentine camp. He is almost babbling with fear by now, and his last allegation is nullified by Diana's observation that he possessed her, not for the "common price" of a whore, but by means of the gift of his valued ancestral ring, something he would not have given to a trollop. The Countess immediately sees that Diana is right and she speaks of the importance of this ring to the family.

The King then asks Diana if she has anyone who will speak in her defense, and she offers Parolles, while wishing that he had a better reputation. Lafew then remembers that Parolles is in the vicinity and the King asks for him to be called. Bertram, now almost hysterical with fear, says that Parolles is "a most perfidious slave," a man who is one of the greatest sinners in the world, and a congenital liar into the bargain, who will say anything for a fee.

At this moment, pressed very hard by the King, Bertram decides to tell the truth, but he slants it to show himself in a good light, implying that Diana had seduced him and demanded his ring, giving him in return something that anyone might have picked up in the market place. In other words, the ring alleged to be Helena's in fact came from Diana. She then asks for the return of her ring, and says in answer to the King that she gave it to Bertram when he was in bed with her. The King now questions Bertram's earlier story of having had the ring thrown to him. Then, as Parolles enters, Bertram agrees that indeed the ring came from Diana.

Parolles now gives some highly confusing evidence, claiming that he frequently went between Bertram and Diana. Lafew on the way manages to interject a little comment concerning Parolles and a drum, which indicates to that worthy that he knows the whole tale of Parolles' unmasking. The King finally becomes most impatient with Parolles and says that unless he has some definite evidence to give he had better step down.

The King now interrogates Diana and asks where she obtained the ring, but she proves most evasive, saying that she neither bought it nor lent it, nor did she find it. Finally, to the complete mystification of everyone, she swears that she never gave it to Bertram. In fury at being so impudently crossed, the King orders Diana to prison saying that she will die within the hour unless she tells the true story of the ring, something she swears she will never do. As she departs under guard, she tells the King that if she has ever known a man physically it was he, himself. In addition, she says that while Bertram knows that she is no virgin, she knows she is, though Bertram does not. She is either a maiden or Lafew's wife. By the end of this puzzling speech the King is quite exasperated and orders her to prison. As this happens, Diana calls on her mother to fetch her bail, and the Widow leaves. Diana says that the jeweller who owns the ring has been sent for, and again she makes a riddling comment:

> He knows himself my bed he hath defil'd;
> And at that time he got his wife with child.
> Dead though she be she feels her young one kick.
> So here's my riddle: one that's dead is quick [alive],
> And now behold the meaning. (V.iii.294–298)

And at the conclusion of the riddle Helena, the answer to it, enters, to everyone's amazement. The King asks whether she is real, and Helena replies that she is but the shadow of a wife, the name and not the thing itself. Bertram is now tremendously relieved to see Helena and says that for him she is both the shadow and the substance, the imitation and the thing itself. Helena then tells Bertram that she has found him "wondrous kind" when she was like "this maid," Diana. She gives him back his ring and says she has fulfilled the conditions set down in his letter. She has obtained his ring and now she is with child by him. Humbly she asks, "Will you be mine now you are doubly won?"

Bertram, who has momentarily thought himself trapped into a marriage contract with Diana, gladly accedes to Helena's plea. Nevertheless, he is still puzzled over some details. Then the King himself, likewise confused, says that if Diana is a maiden, as she claims, then he will give her a large dowry and she may choose herself a husband. And so *All's Well That Ends Well*.

As You Like It

DUKE SENIOR, *living in banishment.*
FREDERICK, *his brother, and unsurper of his dominions.*
AMIENS ⎫
JACQUES ⎬ *lords attending on the banished Duke.*
LE BEAU, *a courtier attending upon Frederick.*
CHARLES, *a wrestler.*
OLIVER ⎫
JAQUES ⎬ *sons of Sir Rowland de Boys.*
ORLANDO ⎭
ADAM ⎫
DENNIS ⎬ *servants to Oliver.*
TOUCHSTONE, *a clown.*
SIR OLIVER MARTEXT, *a vicar.*
CORIN ⎫
SILVIUS ⎬ *shepherds.*
WILLIAM, *a country fellow, in love with Audrey.*
HYMEN, *god of marriage.*

ROSALIND, *daughter to the banished Duke.*
CELIA, *daughter to Frederick.*
PHEBE, *a shepherdess.*
AUDREY, *a country wench.*

LORDS, PAGES, *and* ATTENDANTS, *etc.*

As You Like It

Act I: Scene 1

The scene takes place in the garden of Oliver, eldest son of a deceased gentleman, Sir Rowland de Boys. Oliver's youngest brother, Orlando, is complaining to Adam, the old family retainer, that Oliver has cheated him of his inheritance. Sir Rowland had left Orlando a thousand crowns and charged Oliver to see to it that Orlando would receive a good education. But while Oliver had sent a second brother, Jaques, to school, he had neither given Orlando the thousand crowns which were due him nor done anything at all about his education.

Orlando declares that he will no longer tolerate his brother's injustice. Just then Oliver himself enters, and the two brothers quarrel about the terms of their father's will. Words soon lead to blows, until finally Orlando seizes Oliver by the throat and forces him to listen to his demands. Orlando demands that he receive either an education befitting a gentleman or the money left to him by his father. Grudgingly, Oliver agrees to give Orlando the money, and with a "Get you with him, you old dog," to Adam, orders his youngest brother out of his sight.

Left alone on stage, Oliver reveals in a short aside that he intends to get even with Orlando and that he has no intention of giving him any money. Oliver then calls in Charles, a professional wrestler, who has come to discuss a wrestling match to be held the next day. We learn from Oliver in another aside that he has decided to get rid of his troublesome brother by having Charles kill him in the forthcoming match. However, instead of coming directly to the point, Oliver first asks Charles what news there is at Court. We learn that the rightful Duke of the land (called Duke Senior in the play) has been banished by his younger brother Frederick and has fled with some of his loyal followers to the Forest of Arden. However, he has left his daughter Rosalind behind at the usurper's Court because of her affection for her cousin Celia, daughter of Duke Frederick. According to Charles, the banished Duke and his men are having a very pleasant time in the forest, where they are completely free from all cares, as if they were living in the Garden of Eden.

Charles has come to try to get Oliver to dissuade Orlando from entering the wrestling contest, for fear he will get hurt. Oliver replies that he has already tried to do this very thing, but that Orlando will not listen to him. Oliver goes on to tell Charles that Orlando is a thoroughly evil character, envious and revengeful, who will stop at nothing to hurt someone by whom he imagines he has been injured. In fact, says Oliver, "and almost with tears I speak it," he has even plotted against me, his own brother, so that if you can kill him tomorrow in the match, I shall breathe more easily. Charles is very obliged for the information and promises that Orlando will get what he deserves.

After Charles leaves, Oliver admits in a soliloquy that his brother is really kind and generous, and that it is for these very qualities that he hates him so much. For even Oliver's own servants love Orlando more than they do their master.

Act I: Scene 2

We find Celia and Rosalind on the lawn in front of Frederick's palace. Celia is trying to cheer up Rosalind, who is sad at the banishment of her father. Celia says that Rosalind's sadness shows that she likes Celia less than Celia likes her, for had their positions been reversed, Celia would still have been happy so long as she and her cousin were not parted. In fact, says Celia, when her father dies, she will restore everything to Rosalind that was taken from the banished Duke. Rosalind agrees to try to be cheerful and suggests that falling in love might relieve her sadness. Celia replies that falling in love is a good idea so long as it is done only for fun and does not become serious.

At this point they are joined by Touchstone, the fool or jester of the play. Then comes a fop, Monsieur le Beau, whom Touchstone and the girls make fun of.

Le Beau tells them that if they remain where they are, they will be able to see a wrestling match. This match, which Duke Frederick and his Court have come to watch, is the one between Orlando and Charles. Charles has already defeated three challengers and left them almost dead. Frederick has tried to dissuade Orlando from competing "In pity of the challenger's (Orlando's) youth," but without success. Now he asks Rosalind and Celia to make one last attempt, because he has no doubt that Orlando's fate will be that of the three previous challengers. The moment Celia sees Orlando she thinks he is too young to oppose Charles, and yet he has an air of success about him. The girls call Orlando to them, and Celia urges him to withdraw his challenge, as there can be little doubt of the outcome. Rosalind hits on an idea to preserve the young man's reputation; she will petition the Duke to stop the series of wrestling matches completely. In this way, no one will know that Orlando has withdrawn. But Orlando insists on going ahead with the bout. He gallantly excuses himself to the girls, hoping they will not take it unkindly that he would deny anything to two such beautiful ladies, and asks them for their support. He explains that no matter what happens to him, he could not be worse off than he already is: if he is defeated he will not lose honor or reputation, for he never had any; if he is killed, he will only have lost life, which he has never loved; and he can do his friends no wrong, for he has none. The girls are touched: Rosalind exclaims, "The little strength that I have, I would it were with you," to which Celia adds, "And mine, to eke out hers."

The match begins. Celia and Rosalind enthusiastically support Orlando. After some scuffling, there is a great shout from the audience: the mighty Charles lies prone on the ground. To everyone's surprise, Orlando has won. The Duke is about to praise Orlando for his fine performance, but when he hears that Orlando's father was Sir Roland de Boys, a friend of the banished Duke, he coldly dismisses him. Celia is ashamed of her father's behavior. Rosalind declares that had she known whose son Orlando was, she would have implored him with tears not to risk his life against Charles. Celia decides to make up for her father's unkindness by approaching Orlando and encouraging him. She tells him he has done well and adds that if he keeps his promises in love the way he has exceeded all promises in the match, his lady would be a happy woman.

Rosalind, more and more taken with the young man, gives him a chain from her neck as a keepsake, declaring that she, like Orlando, is "out of suits with Fortune," and would like to give him more, but has nothing else to give. She stops short and asks Celia to leave with her. In an aside Orlando reveals he is very much impressed with Rosalind—so much so that he finds himself speechless and unable to thank her. After a few steps Rosalind pretends to Celia she has heard Orlando calling them back. In an aside she, in her turn, reveals how affected she is by Orlando: "My pride fell with my fortunes,/ I'll ask him what he would." (She refers to her lack of pride because she, the girl, is taking the initiative with the man.) She returns to tell Orlando that he has wrestled well and overthrown more than his enemies (meaning, of course, her heart). In another aside Orlando reveals that he, like Rosalind, has fallen in love at first sight (a typical occurrence in Shakespearean romantic comedy).

Le Beau approaches Orlando to warn him that he should leave the place immediately: because of Orlando's parentage, Duke Frederick might plan to do him harm. Orlando takes the occasion to ask the courtier which of the two girls is Frederick's daughter. He learns about Celia and Rosalind and their affection for each other, which caused Rosalind to remain behind at the usurper's Court. He is told further that Frederick has begun to dislike Rosalind because she is very popular with the common people, who pity her for her father's sake, and that the Duke's anger against Rosalind is likely to come to a boil very soon.

Orlando ponders his plight: "Thus must I from the smoke into the smother [thick smoke]/ From tyrant Duke unto a tyrant brother." However, he comforts himself with the thought: "But heavenly Rosalind!"

Act I: Scene 3

Celia and Rosalind are sitting in a room in Duke Frederick's palace. Rosalind has evidently been sitting in silence for quite some time, for Celia wonders why her cousin is so quiet. Not realizing what has happened between Orlando and Rosalind, Celia thinks Rosalind is still sad about her father's banishment. Rosalind, however, tells her that it is on her own account she is sad: "Oh, how full of briers is this working-day world!" When Celia advises Rosalind to shake herself to make the burrs fall off, Rosalind responds that the burrs are in her heart. "Hem them away" (cough them up), advises Celia. "I would try if I could cry hem and have him," replies Rosalind. Celia now gets the point and wonders how Rosalind could have fallen in love so suddenly.

The conversation between Rosalind and Celia is interrupted by Duke Frederick, who bursts into the room and abruptly orders Rosalind to leave his Court within ten days or suffer death. When the startled Rosalind asks what offense she has committed, the Duke tells her that, as the daughter of the banished Duke, he regards her as a possible rallying point for a rebellion against him. When Celia protests, her father tells her that she is a fool—she should hate Rosalind, for the people pity her and are thus more attached to her than to Celia herself: "She robs thee of thy name." But so strong is Celia's affection for her cousin that she warns her father if he banishes Rosalind he must banish her too, for she "cannot live out of her company." Frederick does not believe Celia will carry out her threat and remains firm in his resolve: Rosalind is to be banished.

Frederick leaves and Celia reaffirms to Rosalind that she, too, considers herself banished and will share her cousin's fortunes. When Rosalind wonders what they should do, it is Celia who comes up with the idea of fleeing to the Forest of Arden to join Rosalind's father. To avoid being molested on the way, they decide to disguise themselves. Celia puts on ragged clothes and dirties her face, while Rosalind assumes men's clothing and carries a spear. No matter what woman's fears I may have within me, says Rosalind, at least I shall have an imposing and war-like exterior—and in this respect I will not differ very much from many cowards of the male sex. Along with the change of clothing goes a change of name: Celia takes the name Aliena; Rosalind calls herself Ganymede.

Rosalind suggests that they take Touchstone along to make them merry on their travels. Celia replies that that will be no problem, as Touchstone is completely devoted to her and will go with her anywhere.

The two girls prepare to set out, Celia with brave and hopeful words on her lips: "Now go we in content / To liberty and not to banishment."

Act II: Scene 1

The scene shifts to the Forest of Arden, where for the first time we meet the banished Duke, or Duke Senior, as he is called. The Duke is extolling the advantages of life in the forest, free from the perils of "the envious Court." He implies that in fact his banishment has been a blessing— "Sweet are the uses of adversity."

When the Duke suggests that they hunt deer, an attendant lord mentions that Jaques, one of the Duke's entourage in the forest, objects to the killing of the forest's lawful inhabitants, claiming that in this action the Duke is a greater usurper than his brother. The lord continues that he overheard Jaques moralize at length at the sight of a wounded deer abandoned by his fellows, comparing the plight of the animal to that of a man down on his luck and consequently deserted by his friends.

Act II: Scene 2

In this very short scene, which takes place in Duke Frederick's palace, the angry Duke discovers that Celia and Touchstone have left the Court with Rosalind. Hearing that all three might be with Orlando, he sends for Oliver, intending to make him find his brother and the others.

Act II: Scene 3

Orlando, however, is not with Rosalind. He returns to Oliver's house, where he is met at the entrance by a very agitated Adam. The old man laments the fact that Orlando is virtuous, strong, brave, and popular. It would have been much better had Orlando not gained such a victory in the wrestling match, he declares, for praise of him has come to the ears of the wrong people. Orlando is completely at a loss and asks Adam what he means. Adam replies that Oliver has heard Orlando's wrestling feat so highly extolled that, stung with jealousy, he intends to set fire to his youngest brother's room that night and burn him to death. Should this fail, Adam has overheard, Oliver plans to dispose of Orlando in some other way.

Orlando is completely at a loss for a hiding place (unlike Rosalind, he has no relatives to flee to in the Forest of Arden), and he is not much helped by Adam's "No matter whither so you come not here." But when he points out that his only alternatives to remaining in his brother's house are to beg or steal, faithful Adam offers his life's savings to his young master, causing the latter to marvel at the kindness of the "good old" world as compared to the cruelty of the present. The two set out into the unknown, convinced that they will be happy, even if poor.

Act II: Scene 4

Ganymede (Rosalind), Aliena (Celia), and Touchstone arrive in the Forest of Arden. They are all exhausted, and Rosalind complains of the weariness of her spirits. Touchstone says that he cares more about weary legs than weary spirits. Rosalind feels like sitting down and having a good cry, but she remembers that she is supposed to be playing the part of a man and pulls herself together. In her role as a man, she even summons up enough strength to encourage her "female attendant" Aliena, who is almost collapsing and who requests the others, "I pray you bear with me, I cannot go no further." Touchstone thinks that he would much rather "bear with" (be considerate to) Celia than "bear" (carry) her. With a weary sigh, Rosalind looks around and says, "Well, this is the forest of Arden." Touchstone is less than impressed: "When I was at home, I was in a better place," he concludes.

Two shepherds approach—Corin, who is an old man, and a youth, Silvius. Silvius is evidently very much in love with a shepherdess called Phebe, whose name he sighs out mournfully; it seems that he has been wooing Phebe for a long time but that she will have nothing to do with him. When Corin tries to sympathize, Silvius tells him that he cannot possibly understand anything about love because he is an old man.

On overhearing Silvius' declaration of love for Phebe, Rosalind is reminded of her own love for Orlando. Touchstone, not to be outdone (and perhaps to cheer up Rosalind), remembers a passion (probably imaginary) he once had for a milkmaid. He too, he declares, like Silvius and Rosalind, was completely overcome by love: with his sword he attacked a stone on which his sweetheart had sat, because he was jealous of anyone else or anything else coming near her; he kissed the udders of the cow her hands had milked; and when he could not be with her he wooed a pea plant instead of her: he took two peapods from the plant and then replaced them, saying, with tears, "Wear these for my sake."

Meanwhile, Celia (who has no love on which to feed) is almost fainting from hunger. She tells her companions to ask the shepherds if they have any food or know of a place to rest. Corin says he would gladly help them but that he is employed by an inhospitable master, who, in any case, is not at home, because he has put his house and sheep up for sale. On hearing this, the girls decide to buy the house and stock for themselves, employing Corin as shepherd.

Act II: Scene 5

In another part of the forest, Amiens, one of the lords attending Duke Senior, sings a song in praise of pastoral life, "Under the greenwood tree." The song makes the conventional statement of pastoral romances: country life is simple and pure, as opposed to the corruption of city and court life.

When Amiens stops, Jaques wants to hear more. Told that listening to more songs will make him melancholy, Jaques replies that he loves to be melancholy. He asks Amiens whether the various parts of a song are called stanzas, and when Amiens replies that they can be called anything one likes, Jaques declares that he really is not interested in the subject at all. Amiens excuses himself from singing any more because he knows that he will never please Jaques, to which Jaques replies that he did not ask Amiens to please him, just to sing. Finally Amiens agrees to sing some more, telling Jaques he does it only because Jaques insists, not because he thinks he sings well. To this Jaques replies that he does not care for people who compliment him or thank him. Amiens says that he will end his song and tells Jaques that Duke Senior has been looking for him all day. And I have been trying to avoid him all day, declares Jaques; I find the Duke too argumentative to enjoy his company. Amiens thereupon finishes his song.

When he is finished, Jaques sings a song of his own composition in reply, which says that only fools would leave the ease of the city for the rigors of the country.

Act II: Scene 6

Orlando and Adam reach the outskirts of Arden, with Adam exhausted and hungry. Orlando decides to go further into the forest to search for food.

Act II: Scene 7

In the forest Jaques entertains the Duke and his followers with an account of his meeting with Touchstone (in spite of the fact that he has just told us he cannot stand the Duke).

Jaques is full of admiration for Touchstone, because he thinks that in the jester he has found a kindred spirit. He is impressed by the fact that Touchstone "railed on Lady Fortune" (criticized life generally). But what he admires most about Touchstone is what Jaques considers Touchstone's philosophical observations on life. Jaques reports that Touchstone took a watch from his pocket, looked at it dully, and proclaimed that it was ten o'clock. Touchstone continued by saying that only one hour ago it was nine, and in another hour it would be eleven, whereupon he concluded that "from hour to hour, we ripe and ripe,/ And then from hour to hour, we rot and rot . . . ." Well, says Jaques, when I heard this man, evidently a fool by his multicolored clothes, thus philosophize on the passage of time in such a deep fashion, I began to laugh heartily for one whole hour, for I timed myself by Touchstone's watch.

So impressed is Jaques by Touchstone and his profession, that he expresses a desire to become a licensed fool too, so that he might criticize whomever he wished without fear of retaliation.

The Duke says that Jaques is the last person who should take it upon himself to criticize the morals of society, for he, at one time or another, has practised most of its vices and he would be more likely to infect the world than cure it. Oh no, replies Jaques, he would do only good, because only the guilty would be hurt by his attacks, since his satire would be general rather than particular; that is, he would not mention anyone by name. In this way the innocent would not feel that they were included in Jaques' exposures of sin and vice, while those who were offended would, by the very fact that they were offended, prove themselves guilty.

Jaques is interrupted by Orlando, who bursts in on the party with drawn sword and demands food. Jaques behaves very coolly in the face of danger. To Orlando's "Forbear, and eat no more," the professional critic Jaques corrects the intruder's statement by saying "Why, I have eat none yet." The Duke (less interested than Jaques in correct forms of speech) asks Orlando whether he has been made to consider robbery by dire necessity, or whether he just naturally despises the laws of ordered society. Orlando replies that the former is his case; he has been well brought up (something of a contradiction to what he says at the beginning of the play) but that circumstances have made him desperate. Orlando is very surprised when the Duke tells him that he is welcome to some food, and that he does not have to demand it at sword-point. "I thought that all things had been savage here," exclaims Orlando, and therefore I was so aggressive. But, he says to the Duke and his followers, I see that you are gentlemen. Whoever you are who in this forest "Lose and neglect the creeping hours of time," if you have ever looked on better days, if you have ever gone to church, if you have ever sat at a good man's table, if you have ever had to wipe a tear from your eyes and know what pity is, forgive me for what I have done and help me. We have experienced all these things you describe, the Duke tells Orlando, and therefore we will try to help you. Orlando thanks him for his kindness and explains that he has left Adam in another part of the forest. He goes to fetch him when the Duke assures him that both are welcome.

Referring to the plight of Orlando and Adam, the Duke turns to Jaques and tells him, "Thou seest we are not alone unhappy," and that in this great theatre of the world there are many people worse off than they.

The Duke's remark causes Jaques to launch into his "Seven Ages of Man" speech, in which (using the imagery of the theatre) he describes the world as a stage, the seven divisions of man's life from birth to death as the seven acts of a play, and man himself as an actor. Just as actors have their exits and entrances, says Jaques, and in the course of their careers, play many different parts, so do men. First there is the part of the infant, whimpering and vomiting, held in his nurse's arms. Then there is the reluctant schoolboy, with his books and his face newly scrubbed clean so that it shines, creeping unwillingly to school at a snail's pace, really not wanting to go at all. Then, when the schoolboy has grown up to be a young man, he begins to play the part of a lover, sighing out his love for his sweetheart with a noise like the bellows of a furnace, and writing endless love poems to win her favor. A little older and the young man becomes a soldier, full of new oaths learned in camp and battlefield, heavily bearded, and concerned about his reputation for courage. He is quick to quarrel with any man from whom he even suspects an insult, and seeks fame, which will last as long as will a bubble, by storming right up to the mouth of the enemy cannon. Having survived the war, the soldier returns to civilian life and becomes a judge in his home town. He becomes fat with bribes brought to him by petitioners and claimants. He assumes a judicial air and dresses to command respect, and now, in place of oaths, his speech is seasoned with proverbs and wise sayings. After this he begins to become senile. He now has to wear spectacles and has lost so much of the weight gained as a judge that his clothes are much too big for him. Even his voice has deserted him or, rather, it has returned to the same pitch it had when he was a child. Last of all, he returns completely to childishness: his powers of reasoning and memory have gone, not to speak of his teeth and eyesight. Thus ends this strange play called life.

Orlando returns with Adam, and the scene ends with another song sung by Amiens in praise of pastoral life, "Blow, blow, thou winter wind," during which Orlando reveals his parentage to the Duke and is welcomed as the son of an old friend.

Act III: Scene 1

Meanwhile, Duke Frederick has summoned Oliver to his palace to ask him the whereabouts of Orlando, whom he believes to be with his daughter Celia and Rosalind. He is furious when Oliver does not know. Oliver is told that if he does not bring his brother back within a year, dead or alive, he will be banished from the Duke's territory and his lands will be forfeit. When Oliver tells the Duke he will be happy to obey his commands since he has always hated his brother, the Duke retorts, "More villain thou."

Act III: Scene 2

Orlando enters with a paper on which he has written a love poem to Rosalind. He calls upon Diana, goddess of the moon and of chastity, to witness his love for the chaste Rosalind, whose name he intends to carve on all the trees of the forest. He exits, and Corin enters in conversation with Touchstone. Corin asks him how he likes a shepherd's life. Touchstone replies (with characteristic realism and wit) that in itself a shepherd's life is a good life, but that insofar as it is a shepherd's life, it is worthless. "In respect that it is solitary," says Touchstone, he likes it very well, "but in respect that it is private [solitary]," he does not like it at all. Inasmuch as it is in the fields, thinks Touchstone, it pleases him very much, but inasmuch as it is not in the Court, he finds it tedious. He concludes by saying that as it is a life of frugality, it suits his disposition, but as there is not more abundance in it, it goes against his grain. Then he turns to Corin and asks, "Hast any philosophy in thee, shepherd?"

Corin answers that his knowledge of philosophy extends no further than knowing that sickness is unpleasant, that it is good to have money and happiness, that rain wets and fire burns, and that the cause of darkness is the lack of light. Touchstone asks Corin whether he has ever been to Court, and when the shepherd says he has not, Touchstone declares that then he must be damned and go to hell. Corin cannot understand this, and Touchstone explains that if he has never been to

Court he has never seen good manners ("good" here bears the double meaning of "morally good" and "socially acceptable"); if he has never seen good manners, then his manners must be wicked (that is, he must be an immoral person); wickedness is a sin, and the penalty for sin is damnation. Touchstone concludes by warning Corin that he is in a very dangerous situation. Corin disagrees and tries to defend himself by pointing out that what are regarded as good manners at Court are not necessarily good manners in the country. For instance, he says, at Court it is the custom to kiss hands on meeting, but for shepherds, whose hands are dirty from handling sheep, this custom would be ridiculous. But Touchstone will not allow Corin's argument; courtiers' hands get just as dirty from sweating, he claims, as do shepherds' from working, and he challenges Corin to produce better proof that he is not bound for eternal damnation. Corin advances several other reasons why Court manners are out of place in the country, but Touchstone mockingly dismisses each of his arguments, so that in the end Corin gives up, saying to his opponent, "You have too Courtly a wit for me, I'll rest." At this the irrepressible Touchstone exclaims, "Wilt thou rest damned? God help thee, shallow man!"

The two are interrupted by Rosalind, who enters reading a love poem. (It is one of those written by Orlando, and it is conventionally extravagant in the fashion of the period): "From the east to western Ind [India],/ No jewel is like Rosalind. Her worth, being mounted on the wind [taken up and scattered abroad by the wind],/ Through all the world bears Rosalind./ All the pictures fairest lined [drawn]/ Are but black to Rosalind. . . ."

Touchstone is not impressed by the quality of the poetry and claims he could write continuously for eight years in that style, "dinners and suppers and sleeping hours excepted" (he hastens to add in his realistic fashion). To prove that his is no idle boast, he then and there rattles off a poem in the same meter as the love poem (but which satirizes rather than compliments Rosalind): "If a hart [male deer] do lack a hind [female deer],/ Let him seek out Rosalind./ If the cat will after kind,/ So be sure will Rosalind. . . ."

Celia enters reading another poem in praise of Rosalind, and the two cousins decide it is time to confer privately about this strange new development, and so ask Corin and Touchstone to leave them alone.

When Celia asks Rosalind whether she knows who might be writing verses in her praise, Rosalind replies that she has no idea. It is obvious that Celia does know who the poet is, and she teases the, by now, very impatient Rosalind by alternately giving her clues and allowing herself to be sidetracked. Finally she reveals the news that it is Orlando. This revelation completely flusters Rosalind, so that she subjects Celia to a barrage of questions, all of which she wants answered immediately: "What shall I do with my doublet and hose her ⌈male attire⌉? What did he when thou sawest him? What said he? How looked he? Wherein went he? What makes he here? Did he ask for me? Where remains he? How parted he with thee? And when shalt thou see him again?" We can sympathize with Celia, who answers that she would need the mouth of a giant to answer all these questions at once. She tries to answer Rosalind's questions, but Rosalind is too excited to listen and keeps interrupting Celia's account of where she saw Orlando with comments on each particular piece of information.

Orlando and Jaques enter, and the two girls hide themselves to overhear the conversation. The men have evidently quarreled over Orlando's carving love poems on the barks of trees. Jaques tells Orlando that he is a fool for falling in love and that, as a matter of fact, he was just looking for a fool when he found him. Orlando tells Jaques that he should look in a brook and there he would find his fool, to which Jaques naively answers that there he would see only his own face. Just so, says Orlando, whereupon Jaques leaves him.

Rosalind, still dressed as a man, comes out of her hiding place and engages Orlando in conversation, which she skillfully steers around to the subject of love. She mentions that she was educated by her uncle who, among other things, taught her a cure for love. She wishes she could meet the man who has been carving *Rosalind* on all the trees, for that man seems to be sadly in need of her cure. When Orlando tells her that he is the man, Rosalind pretends not to believe him, for he has none of the conventional marks of the lover, such as the haggard face, the black marks under the eyes from lack of sleep, the glum appearance, the neglected beard and disordered clothing. When Orlando swears that nevertheless he is very much in love, Rosalind hits on a happy idea of how to cure him of his love and thus relieve him of his misery. If Orlando will pretend that she is Rosalind and come every day to woo her, she, pretending to be his mistress, Rosalind, will act so unreasonably and changeably—as women do—that he will forswear women for the rest of his life. To this Orlando agrees.

Act III: Scene 3

Touchstone has met Audrey, a country wench, whom he is wooing vigorously. He is somewhat hampered by the fact that Audrey usually does not have the faintest idea what he means when he is talking to her. Her vocabulary is even more limited than Corin's. When Touchstone asks her whether she likes his feature, meaning his appearance, she fails to understand him, and when her lover wishes the gods had made her poetical, she confesses her ignorance of that word too. Her own handling of language is no better than her comprehension, so that she innocently says, "I thank the gods I am foul," which in Elizabethan English meant "ugly."

When Jaques, who has witnessed Touchstone's strange wooing, expresses amazement that one of Touchstone's breeding would marry someone like Audrey, Touchstone explains that what motivates him is not love but sexual desire. In fact, he sees some advantage to being married by an incompetent, appropriately called Sir Oliver Martext, on the assumption that a marriage ceremony performed by such a man will be bound to have mistakes in it and therefore not be binding: ". . . it will be a good excuse for me hereafter to leave my wife," thinks Touchstone. However, on the advice of Jaques, the wedding is postponed.

Act III: Scene 4

Rosalind is impatiently awaiting the arrival of Orlando, who is supposed to receive his first lesson in curing love. He is late, and Rosalind, who fears Orlando might be late because he is no longer in love, is at the point of tears. In her frustration she begins to criticize Orlando, but as soon as Celia sympathetically joins in on the criticism, she vehemently defends Orlando in every respect; *she* can criticize him, but no one else can. Celia, however, proceeds with a very cool examination of Orlando and concludes that he is more of a talker than a doer, that he writes and speaks feelingly about love, but fails when it comes to doing anything about it. She confirms Rosalind's own fears by concluding that Orlando may have been in love, but is not any more.

As this point Corin enters and invites the girls to watch the spectacle of Silvius vainly wooing the proud Phebe.

Act III: Scene 5

Silvius feels so unworthy in the presence of his lady Phebe, and she has rejected him so often, that he does not dare beg for her love anymore; he merely implores her not to hate him. Phebe replies that she does not hate him, and certainly has no intention of being the cause of his death, as Silvius has often claimed she would be if she did not take pity on him. But she does not love him. She also does not believe that her eyes have in them the power to kill, as Silvius claims. Frowning on him severely, she asks him to show her the wound her eyes have made. Silvius replies that should Phebe ever fall in love, she will "know the wounds invisible/ That love's keen arrows make." To this Phebe replies that she is content to wait until that time comes, if ever, and that in the meantime she wants Silvius to get out of her sight.

Rosalind, who has been listening to Phebe abuse true love, can stand it no longer and bursts out of her hiding place, followed by Celia and Corin. She turns on Phebe and demands to know why Phebe dares treat Silvius so. Just because you are ugly, she asks, is this a reason to be proud and devoid of pity? Rosalind continues by itemizing Phebe's defects, telling Silvius that he is much handsomer than Phebe is beautiful, so that she really cannot understand why he bothers with her. She advises Phebe to accept Silvius quickly, as, with her looks, she might never get another offer.

While she has been berating Phebe, Rosalind, who, we must remember, is dressed as a man, has noticed Phebe eyeing her intently. She concludes that Phebe must have fallen in love with her, and this is immediately confirmed by Phebe's first words, "Sweet youth, I pray you, chide a year together/ I had rather hear you chide than this man woo." Rosalind warns Phebe against falling in love with her and leaves, along with Celia and Corin.

Left alone with Silvius, the love-smitten Phebe finds that she now likes his company, not because she loves or even likes him for himself, but because he can "talk of love so well," and she hits on a plan of using him. She warns Silvius not to "look for further recompense/ Than thine own gladness that thou art employed." Emphasizing to Silvius that she is not in love with Rosalind, but revealing to the audience by her remarks that she is completely infatuated, she commissions Silvius to carry what she calls "a very taunting letter" to Rosalind.

Act IV: Scene 1

Jaques meets Rosalind in the forest and expresses a desire to become acquainted with her. Rosalind has heard that Jaques has a reputation for being melancholy and asks him if what she has heard is true. When Jaques answers that he loves melancholy rather than laughter, Rosalind answers that any extreme, whether of sadness or of gaiety, is to be avoided. To Jaques' reply that " 'tis good to be sad and say nothing," Rosalind counters, "Why, then 'tis good to be a post."

Jaques now launches into a description of his melancholy which, he claims, is unlike that of any other person; he concludes that his extensive travels have made him sad. Rosalind cannot see the advantage of spending money for foreign travel if the result is to make the traveler sad; perhaps with Touchstone in mind, she concludes that she would rather have a fool to make her merry. Orlando enters and greets Rosalind elaborately, whereupon Jaques, who remembers how Orlando made a fool of him in their last meeting, hastily withdraws. Rosalind bids him farewell and sarcastically reminds him to act like the typical Englishman who has returned to his native country after having traveled abroad: to affect a foreign accent and foreign clothing, to criticize his own country, and to bemoan the fact that he was born an Englishman.

Rosalind turns on Orlando and chides him for being late. He certainly does not act like a lover, she thinks, and warns him that if he is ever late again she will not see him anymore. When Orlando protests that he is only one hour late, Rosalind becomes furious and demands to know how anyone in love can consider an hour's lateness for a tryst to be a trifle. No one, she says, who can be late even a fraction of a minute in an affair of love deserves the name of a true lover. She would rather be wooed by a snail, she concludes, than by a tardy lover, for a snail, although slow, carries his house about with him, so that his wife will not have to look for a place to live; besides, the snail already has horns, saving his wife the trouble of providing him with a pair. To this Orlando answers that when the lady is virtuous the lover will never wear horns, and that his Rosalind is virtuous he knows for certain. At this, Rosalind is evidently so pleased that she almost gives the whole show away, for she says, "And I am your Rosalind." Celia intervenes just in time by saying that of course they are only pretending that Ganymede is Rosalind for the sake of curing Orlando of his love.

Rosalind, still delighted by what Orlando had said about her, gaily instructs him to woo her, for she is in such a good mood that she will probably accept him. Realizing that once again she has allowed herself to be carried away and to forget that she is supposed to be playing a part, she draws herself up and asks Orlando what he would say to her now if he really were his Rosalind. Before I said anything I would kiss her, says Orlando. Rosalind does not think that is a very good approach. Much better, she says, to speak first, and when you have run out of things to say and are trying to think of new material, you should kiss. Yes, says Orlando, but what if she will not let me kiss her? No problem there, says Rosalind, for her denial will give you something else to say; you will plead with her to let you.

Now, says Rosalind, suddenly shifting tactics, as Rosalind's stand-in I say I will not accept you. Then I shall die, Orlando exclaims. Oh, I don't think so, Rosalind says coolly. The world is almost six-thousand years old, and in all that time not a single man has ever died for love. Even such legendary lovers as Troilus, in love with Cressida, or Leander, in love with Hero, died for reasons other than love. "Men have died from time to time and worms have eaten them, but not for love," Rosalind concludes. When Orlando says he would not like his real Rosalind to have such an opinion, for he thinks that even her frown would kill him, Rosalind raises her hand and says, "By this hand, it will not kill a fly."

Rosalind's mood changes again, and she promises Orlando that she will grant anything he asks. He proposes, is accepted, and Celia, officiating in place of a priest, marries Orlando and Rosalind in a mock marriage ceremony. When Orlando swears that he will be faithful to his real Rosalind forever, Rosalind laughs at him and says that both men and women behave quite differently after they are married. Orlando thinks his Rosalind would never behave badly, to which Rosalind replies, "By my life, she will do as I do." Orlando protests that his Rosalind is wise, which prompts Rosalind to say, "Or else she could not have the wit to do this" (referring to the arrangement she has set up, whereby Orlando woos her thinking she is only pretending to be Rosalind).

Orlando tells Rosalind that he must leave her for two hours and that he will be with her again at two o'clock. Rosalind is reluctant to let him go at all and makes him swear that this time he will not be even one minute late. Upon this, Orlando leaves and Rosalind confesses to Celia how deeply in love she is.

Act IV: Scene 2

Jaques enters with some lords and foresters who have just killed a deer. Jaques sneeringly suggests that the deer be presented to the Duke in the form of a trophy of great victory, as captives were presented to victorious Roman emperors. Ironically, he asks one of the foresters if he does not have a song to celebrate this great occasion, adding (in his characteristically bitter fashion), " 'Tis no matter how it be in tune so it make noise enough."

The forester sings a song which discusses what reward would be most suitable for the man who killed the deer. The answer is that he should be given the horns to wear, and the entire company joins in the chorus: "Take thou no scorn to wear the horn,/ It was a crest ere thou wast born./ Thy father's father wore it. . . ."

Act IV: Scene 3

Rosalind and Celia are awaiting the arrival of Orlando for another lesson. Orlando is late. Celia teases Rosalind by saying that Orlando is probably so much in love that he has gone to sleep and forgotten all about his appointment. Silvius enters bearing a letter from Phebe to Rosalind. He says that he does not know what is in the letter, but, judging from how angry Phebe looked when she was writing it, he is sure its contents are not very pleasant. Rosalind looks at the letter and tells Silvius that what it says is so provoking as to be unbearable: Phebe said Rosalind was ugly, lacked manners, was proud, and that she would not fall in love with Rosalind were she the last man on earth. Rosalind angrily turns on Silvius and says Phebe could not have written this, no woman could have written it; the letter is too cutting and cruel to have come from a woman, and she accuses Silvius of having written the letter himself. Silvius protests that he certainly did not write the letter, that Phebe did. Rosalind proceeds to read the letter aloud, commenting on passages as she goes along. The letter opens: "Why, thy godhead laid apart (why did you lay aside your divinity and become a man), Warr'st thou with a woman's heart?' On this Rosalind comments to Silvius that never in her life has she heard such a vicious attack. She continues to read: "Whiles the eye of man did woo me,/ That could do no vengeance to me." The meaning of these lines is, of course, clear, Rosalind declares; Phebe means that I am no human but an animal. She goes go with the rhymed letter, which quite unmistakeably declares Phebe's love for Rosalind, until even Silvius sees that Phebe has taken advantage of him. Celia is sorry for Silvius, but Rosalind thinks he deserves no pity if he loves such a woman as Phebe.

Rosalind tells Silvius to return to Phebe and inform her that if she loves Ganymede, Ganymede commands her to love Silvius. If she will not do this, Rosalind says she will have nothing more to do with her.

The conversation is interrupted by the entrance of Oliver, who has been looking for the owners of the sheep and cottage. He recognizes Ganymede (Rosalind) and Aliena (Celia), for they have been described to him by Orlando, whom he says he has met. Holding out a bloody handkerchief, he says Orlando has asked him to give it to the youth he in jest calls Rosalind. The two girls are puzzled and ask for an explanation. Oliver says he will enlighten them, although the story he is about to reveal will do him no credit. When last Orlando left you, Oliver begins, he promised to return within an hour. As he was walking through the forest thinking about his love, he saw a ragged-looking man sleeping under an oak tree. About the sleeping man's neck a snake had coiled itself and was just about to strike. Seeing Orlando approach, however, it unwound itself and slipped away. But under a nearby bush there lay a lioness watching the sleeping man and waiting for him to wake up, for lions will not prey on anything that appears dead. When Orlando came nearer, he found the sleeping man was his eldest brother. Celia interrupts to say that she has often heard Orlando describe his eldest brother as a monster, completely without any family feeling. Oliver says Orlando was quite right, for he knows very well how that eldest brother behaved. Rosalind urges him to complete the story; she wants to know whether Orlando left his brother there to be killed by the lioness. Twice he turned his back and wanted to do just that, Oliver goes on, but brotherly feeling conquered hate and Orlando attacked the beast, killed it, and with the noise, "From miserable slumber I awaked," Oliver concludes. Are you then that villain who so often tried to kill Orlando, the girls want to know. I was that villain, but I am no longer the same man, answers Oliver, for since then I have converted to a new kind of life. Here Rosalind interrupts him; she wants to know about the bloody handkerchief, and so Oliver continues with his story. After we had been reconciled to each other, he says, Orlando took me to Duke Senior, who treated me very kindly. After that Orlando led me to the cave where he lived, and when he took off his clothes we found that the lioness had torn some flesh from his arm, from which he had been bleeding all the time. Now, after the excitement and with the loss of blood, Orlando fainted, calling the name "Rosalind" as he fell. I quickly got him to come to and dressed his wound. When he was feeling a little better, he sent me here to you to excuse his absence and to give this handkerchief to the youth he in fun calls Rosalind.

On hearing the story and seeing Orlando's blood, Rosalind promptly faints. Celia has the presence of mind to call her by her assumed name: "Why, how now, Ganymede! Sweet Ganymede!" Oliver, who of course is taken in by Rosalind's male attire and knows nothing about her relationship to Orlando, says, "Many will swoon when they do look on blood." When Rosalind comes to, he jokes with her about what happened: "Be of good cheer, youth. You a man! You lack a man's heart!" (which of course is a nice piece of dramatic irony). Yes, Rosalind agrees that she certainly does. She now tries to make it appear that she had only pretended to swoon, and she asks Oliver to tell Orlando that her fainting had only been a joke, but Oliver is skeptical. Finally, after Rosalind insists, he says, all right, you pretended to faint; now pretend to be a man. Why, so I do, says Rosalind.

Act V: Scene 1

Touchstone and Audrey enter, engaged in conversation. Audrey has evidently been asking Touchstone when he is going to marry her, for

Touchstone tells her to have patience; he is just waiting for a suitable time. Audrey (evidently not too convinced) says she cannot understand why they were not married by Sir Oliver Martext; there was nothing wrong with him, she thinks. Touchstone does not agree and then changes the subject by telling Audrey he has heard that a young native of the forest wants to marry her. Audrey says she knows the man he means and maintains that this young man is not really interested in her.

Just then the youth in question enters. He is called William. Touchstone engages him in conversation, beginning by asking his name, age, and place of birth. Evidently impressed by Touchstone, the young man has respectfully taken off his hat, but Touchstone graciously tells him that he may keep it on. Touchstone proceeds with the interrogation of his rival. When William is asked whether he is rich, he says, "soso," which causes Touchstone to compliment him (ironically): " 'Soso' is good, very good, very excellent good. And yet it is not, it is but soso."

Then Touchstone asks William if he is wise, to which William replies yes. Touchstone again commends the answer, although it reminds him of the proverb which says that the fool thinks he is wise but the wise man knows himself to be a fool.

Touchstone then tells William that the heathen philosopher (he does not name him), upon eating a grape, would open his lips when he put it into his mouth, meaning thereby that grapes were made to eat and lips to open. Now Touchstone asks the youth whether he loves Audrey, and Williams says he does. Touchstone asks him whether he is learned, and William says no, he is not. All right, says Touchstone, then learn this of me: "To have is to have; for it is a figure [of speech] in rhetoric that drink, being poured out of a cup into a glass, by filling the one doth empty the other, for all your writers do consent that *ipse* [Latin for "he himself"] is he. Now you are not *ipse*, for I am he.

When the puzzled William asks which "he" Touchstone is talking about, the latter answers, "He, sir, that must marry this woman. Therefore, you clown, abandon—which is in the vulgar [common or simple language] leave,—the society—which in the boorish [common language] is company—of this female—which in the common [language] is woman." Touchstone promises William, in the most ferocious language, that he will murder him if he does not leave Audrey alone. William takes Touchstone's advice and leaves.

Act V: Scene 2

In another part of the forest Orlando and Oliver are discussing the fact that Oliver has fallen in love with Celia. Orlando is astonished at the suddenness of the romance. He asks his brother how it is possible that on so short an acquaintance he could have fallen in love with Celia and Celia with him. Oliver says he cannot explain it; that that was just the way it happened. He asks Orlando to consent to their marriage, declaring that he intends to settle his father's house and money on his youngest brother and remain in the forest with his love to "live and die a shepherd." Orlando consents to Oliver's marriage and thinks the wedding should take place the next day. He will invite the Duke and his followers to the ceremony.

Rosalind joins the two brothers, and Orlando repeats to her his wonder at the suddenness of Oliver's falling in love. Yes, says Rosalind, I know all about it, and indeed it was very sudden. "For your brother and my sister no sooner met but they looked, no sooner looked but they loved, no sooner loved but they sighed, no sooner sighed but they asked one another the reason, no sooner knew the reason but they sought the remedy." And, concludes Rosalind, they are determined to be married.

They will be married tomorrow, Orlando tells her, and adds that while he does not begrudge his brother the happiness, it is a painful thing to have happiness only at second hand, not to have any on your own account. Why, asks Rosalind, will I not be able to take the place of Rosalind tomorrow, as I have done until now? No, answers Orlando, I can no longer be satisfied with make-believe. Thereupon Rosalind tells him that since she sees he is a man of some intelligence, she is going to let him in on a secret. She tells Orlando that she was brought up by an expert magician and from this magician, she says, she learned to do strange things. She now promises Orlando that if he loves Rosalind as much as he claims to, he will marry her tomorrow when Oliver and Aliena are married too. Rosalind continues by saying that she knows all about Rosalind and the difficulties she has passed through, and that, if Orlando wishes, she can set her before his eyes tomorrow, in human form, and without any danger to any of the parties involved. Orlando asks Rosalind if she is speaking in earnest. Rosalind assures him that she is very much in earnest and tells Orlando to put on his best clothes tomorrow and invite all of his friends, for if he really wants to marry Rosalind, there is nothing to prevent the wedding from taking place the next day.

Just then Silvius and Phebe enter. Phebe complains to Rosalind that she has not acted as a true gentleman should, in showing others the contents of the love letter. Rosalind replies that she has no intention of treating Phebe politely, since she does not deserve such treatment. Rosalind reminds Phebe of how much Silvius loves her and orders her not to look at anyone else, but to return his love. Phebe (thinking Rosalind is hard-hearted and does not know what love means) turns to Silvius (the play's expert on romantic love) and asks him to tell "this youth" Ganymede what it means to be in love. (The answer must be quoted in full to be appreciated): "*Sil.* It is to be all made of sighs and tears,/ And so am I for Phebe. *Phe.* And I for Ganymede. *Orl.* And I for Rosalind. *Ros.* And I for no woman. *Sil.* It is to be all made of faith and service [to be ready to do anything one's lady asks],/ And so am I for Phebe. *Phe.* And I for Ganymede. *Orl.* And I for Rosalind. *Ros.* And I for no woman. *Sil.* It is to be all made of fantasy [imagination],/ All made of passion, and all made of wishes,/ All adoration, duty, and observance [of the wishes of one's lady],/ All humbleness, all patience and impatience,/ All purity, all trial [bearing any trial], all observance [devotion],/ And so am I for Phebe. *Phe.* And so am I for Ganymede. *Orl.* And so am I for Rosalind. *Ros.* And so am I for no woman." Then Phebe turns to Rosalind and asks her, if this is so, why do you blame me for loving you? Silvius turns to Phebe and asks her, if this is so, why do you blame me for loving you? Orlando, too, turns to Rosalind and asks her the same question. Startled, Rosalind asks Orlando why he asked her, "Why blame you me to love you?" Orlando explains that he had merely thought of her again as a substitute for Rosalind who, he thinks, is not really present and has not heard him.

By this time Rosalind has had quite enough of chanting refrains about love, which she thinks sound like "the howling of Irish wolves against the moon." She turns to Silvius and tells him that she will help him if she can. She tells Phebe that she would love her if she could and that she will marry her if she ever marries any woman, adding that she intends to be married tomorrow. Lastly, she turns again to Silvius, and promises him that he will be married tomorrow too. She charges all of them to meet her on the next day. They all promise, but the love-sick Silvius is not sure he will live so long: "I'll not fail, if I live," he says.

Act V: Scene 3

Touchstone tells Audrey that the next day will be the joyful occasion of their wedding.

Audrey is looking forward to the event very much, and she hopes that eager anticipation of the marriage will not be regarded in her as any lack of respect for chastity.

Two pages enter, and Touchstone asks them to sing a song for him. They oblige with the famous "It was a lover and his lass," a song praising the beauty of young love and the beauty of Spring in the country. Its theme is the one made famous by the Cavalier poets of the next century—that life is short and that love should be enjoyed in youth.

Touchstone comments (in his usual contradictory fashion) that although the song was not very profound, it was sung very badly. One of the pages defends the singing, claiming they did not lose the time—that is, they kept the proper beat of the music. Touchstone cannot resist a pun on "time," saying, "By my troth yes. I count it but time lost to hear such a foolish song. God buy you [God be with you], and God mend [improve] your voices!"

Act V: Scene 4

It is the next day, and Duke Senior, Amiens, Jaques, Orlando, Oliver, and Celia have gathered to watch Rosalind perform her promised magic. The Duke asks Orlando whether he believes Rosalind can do all she says she can. Orlando answers that sometimes he believes her and sometimes he does not, depending on how optimistic he is feeling at the time. Rosalind, Silvius, and Phebe enter. Rosalind once more reminds the group of their various agreements. She wants to know if the Duke will keep his promise to bestow his daughter Rosalind on Orlando, should she, Ganymede, be able to make Rosalind appear in the forest. The Duke says he would do so even if he had to give kingdoms with her as her dowry. Rosalind asks Orlando if he will marry Rosalind when she appears, to which Orlando answers that he would do so were he king of all the kingdoms of the earth. Now speaking about her assumed personality of the young man Ganymede, Rosalind asks Phebe if she is willing to marry her. Phebe answers she would do so even if she were to die for it one hour later. But, says Rosalind, if for any reason you refuse to marry me, you agree to marry Silvius. Yes, that is the bargain, replies Phebe. Lastly, Rosalind asks Silvius whether he will marry Phebe if she consents, to which Silvius answers that he would do so even if it meant death. All right, says Rosalind, I have promised to make everyone happy; I have to leave for a short time to attend to these matters. She once again charges each member of the group to keep his promise, as she will keep hers.

After Celia and Rosalind leave, the Duke tells Orlando that there is something about Ganymede which reminds him of his daughter Rosalind. Orlando, too, says he has been struck by the resemblance; he says the first time he saw Ganymede he thought he was Rosalind's brother. However, he explains to the Duke, he has learned that Ganymede was born in Arden and tutored in the study of magic by his magician uncle, and so he knows the young man could not be the Duke's relative.

Touchstone and Audrey join the others. This is too much for Jaques, who professes to think that there must be another flood approaching and that all the couples who have gathered to be married have really come to take shelter in Noah's Ark like the animals, two by two. Seeing Touchstone and Audrey (and continuing his comparison of the animals coming to the Ark), Jaques says, "Here comes a pair of very strange beasts, which in all tongues are called fools."

Touchstone greets the company, whereupon Jaques introduces him to the Duke. This is the fool I met in the forest, says Jaques, and he swears he has been a courtier. Why, says Touchstone, let any man who doubts the truth of that claim put me to the test. I have taken part in formal dancing. I have flattered a lady. I have been crafty with my friend, deceptively friendly with my enemy. I have bankrupt three tailors by not paying their bills for the many clothes they have made me. I have had four quarrels and was almost involved in a duel because of one of them. Jaques asks what the outcome was. Touchstone replies that he and his opponent met "and found the quarrel was upon the seventh cause." (Touchstone explains the meaning of this statement a few lines later.)

Jaques is delighted by the way Touchstone is speaking, and the Duke also expresses his pleasure with him, whereupon Touchstone feels compelled to explain why he is present among those waiting to be married: "I press in here, sir, amongst the rest of the country copulatives, to swear and to forswear [to swear the marriage vows and to be forsworn because he has no intention of keeping them—that is, of remaining married to Audrey], according as marriage binds and blood breaks. A poor virgin sir, an ill-favored [ugly] thing, sir, but mine own." He goes on to explain that he is marrying Audrey just because she is ugly and so will have no opportunity to be unfaithful to him.

Jaques now asks Touchstone to explain what he meant by finding the quarrel was on the seventh cause. Touchstone explains that he and his opponent found that the cause of the quarrel was a lie "seven times removed," on which expression he proceeds to elaborate. I did not like the way a certain courtier cut his beard, begins Touchstone, and I wrote to tell him so.

Touchstone continues: He sent me word that if I did not think his beard was cut well, he thought it was; this is called the "Retort Courteous." If I wrote him again that I thought it was not well cut, he would write me that he cut his beard to please himself; this is called the "Quip [sarcastic jest] Modest." If again I said his beard was not well cut, he would say I was unfit to give an opinion on the subject; this is called the "Reply Churlish" [surly, boorish]. If again I said it was not well cut, he would answer that I did not speak the truth; this is called the "Reproof Valiant." If I again said it was not well cut; he would say that I was lying; this is called the "Countercheck Quarrelsome." From here the quarrel would proceed to the "Lie Circumstantial" [an indirect accusation that your opponent is a liar], and finally to the "Lie Direct" [a direct accusation that your opponent is a liar, regarded as a deadly insult, and requiring a duel to redeem the honor of the insulted party]. Well, asks Jaques, and how often did you say that the courtier's beard was not well cut? I did not dare go any further than the "Lie Circumstantial," answers Touchstone, and he did not dare to go as far as the "Lie Direct," so we never did fight a duel.

Jaques is impressed and asks Touchstone if he can once again go over the various degrees of the lie he has just explained. Of course, says Touchstone; I know them by heart, for there are books written on how to quarrel properly, just as there are books to teach good manners. He runs over the stages once again, and then explains that all of the degrees of accusation may be safely indulged in without danger of fighting a duel, except the last one, the "Lie Direct." But even here you may escape safely, adds Touchstone, if you are careful to qualify what you say with an "if." He says he can recall the case of a quarrel which seven judges could not patch up, but when the two opponents actually met face to face, one of them thought of an "if," such as, "If you said so, then I said so," and so they shook hands and swore eternal friendship.

Turning to the Duke, Jaques asks him whether he does not think Touchstone is a wonderful fellow. "He's as good at anything and yet a fool," he points out. To this the Duke replies that Touchstone "uses his folly like a stalking-horse [a horse the hunter would hide behind when stalking game, so that he would not be seen or smelled], and under the presentation [under the cover] of that he shoots his wit."

To the accompaniment of soft music, the figure of Hymen, the god of marriage, enters. With him are Rosalind and Celia. Hymen says that there is rejoicing in heaven when the paths of earthly men run smoothly and all their difficulties are removed.

Hymen then turns to the Duke and tells him to receive his daughter, who has been brought to the forest for the purpose of being joined to the man she loves. (In stage presentations of the play, it is customary to have Rosalind remain heavily veiled in white up to this point, so that no one knows who she is.) Now she removes the veil from her face and reveals herself as Rosalind. She turns to the Duke and says, "To you I give myself, for I am yours." Then she addresses Orlando in the same words. The Duke says that unless his sight is deceiving him, this must be Rosalind, and Orlando echoes what the Duke says. Phebe takes one look at the transformed Ganymede with whom she had been in love and says, "If sight and shape be true,/ Why then, my love adieu!" Hymen now takes charge of the proceedings and addresses the four couples before him. To Orlando and Rosalind he says that no troubles will ever part them. To Oliver and Celia he says that their love will last as long as they live. To Phebe he says that either she must marry Silvius or be married to a woman (Rosalind). To Touchstone and Audrey he says (in a comment on the lack of warmth of Touchstone's love for his wife and on Audrey's looks), "You and you are sure together./ As the winter to foul weather." All join in singing a hymn in praise of marriage, after which the Duke joyfully embraces his daughter and his niece. Phebe suddenly sees Silvius in a new light; she says she will marry him not only because she promised she would do so, but because she finds she has fallen in love with him!

All of a sudden the celebrants are interrupted by the appearance of a new character. He is Jaques De Boys, the second son of Sir Rowland, and brother to Oliver and Orlando. (He was briefly mentioned by Orlando in his speech which opened the play.) Jaques tells the company who he is and announces that he has important news for them. He says that Duke Frederick, having heard that many important men were daily leaving his court and joining his exiled brother in Arden, prepared a mighty army. He led them into the forest with the purpose of capturing and killing his brother, thus removing a source of possible rebellion against his rule. But, reports Jaques De Boys, when Frederick came to the outskirts of Arden he met an old hermit. This hermit prevailed on him not only to abandon his plan of killing his brother, but also to abandon the world and become a hermit, too.

As a result, Frederick has restored to Duke Senior and his followers everything which was taken from them, and they are free to return from exile at any time they wish. Duke Senior welcomes the news on behalf of himself and his company. First, he says, they will proceed with the wedding rites, and then all who have endured bitter exile with him will return to their lands and their former dignity.

But Jaques, when he hears that Frederick has decided to become a hermit and abandon the glitter of the court, resolves to stay with him in Arden.

Jaques bids farewell to Duke Senior and wishes him good fortune in his restored honor. Likewise, he gives his best wishes to Orlando, Oliver, and Silvius, parting from the latter, with, "You to a long and well-deserved bed." Lastly he turns to Touchstone and Audrey; he leaves them to their quarreling and expresses the opinion that their marriage will last about two months. The scene ends with a dance in celebration of the multiple weddings.

As You Like It

When the play is over, Rosalind appears on the stage to deliver an epilogue (a speech by an actor at the end of the play requesting the applause of the audience). Rosalind says that while it is not the custom to have the epilogue delivered by the leading lady, there is nothing wrong with it. She admits that just as a good wine needs no advertisement to make people appreciate it, so a good play should need no epilogue. Yet, she says, people who sell good wines do not hesitate to tell customers how good the wines are, and good plays are improved by good epilogues.

You can see what a position I am in then, Rosalind continues to the audience, without a good epilogue to deliver to you at the end of a good play.

Now, Rosalind says, since I have no intention of getting down on my knees and begging you to be pleased with this play, there is only one thing I can do: I shall win you over by the use of magic. And so I charge you, ladies, to like as much of this play as pleased you. I charge you, gentlemen, for the love you have for the ladies, to like it for their sake.

Now if I were really a woman (the actor, of course, was a boy), Rosalind concludes, I would kiss as many of you men as wore beards which pleased me, had faces I liked, and breath that did not stink. And I am sure that as many as have good beards, faces, and breaths "will, for my kind offer, when I make curtsy, bid me farewell" (by applauding).

The Comedy of Errors

SOLINUS, *Duke of Ephesus.*
EGEON, *a merchant of Syracuse.*
ANTIPHOLUS OF EPHESUS } *twin brothers, and sons to*
ANTIPHOLUS OF SYRACUSE } *Egeon and Emilia.*
DROMIO OF EPHESUS } *twin brothers, and attendants*
DROMIO OF SYRACUSE } *on the two Antipholuses.*
BALTHAZAR, *a merchant.*
ANGELO, *a goldsmith.*
FIRST MERCHANT, *friend to Antipholus of Syracuse.*
SECOND MERCHANT, *friend to Antipholus of Syracuse.*
PINCH, *a schoolmaster.*

EMILIA, *wife to Egeon, an abbess at Ephesus.*
ADRIANA, *wife to Antipholus of Ephesus.*
LUCIANA, *her sister.*
LUCE, *servant to Adriana, also known as Nell.*
A COURTEZAN.

JAILER, OFFICERS, *and other* ATTENDANTS.

The Comedy of Errors

Act I

SCENE 1: The scene opens in a hall of Duke Solinus' palace in Ephesus. Aegeon, an old man from Syracuse, is on trial. He expects "the doom of death" to fall upon him, for, as the duke proceeds to explain, he has unknowingly violated the laws of Ephesus. There is enmity between the towns of Syracuse and Ephesus, and both towns have decided "to admit no traffic to our adverse towns." Syracusans who come to Ephesus are subject to the death penalty or to the payment of a fine of a thousand marks and the confiscation of their property. The duke explains this to Aegeon, observing that this is the law. However, he gives Aegeon a chance to explain his circumstances.

Aegeon expects that his miseries will end with his death, "with the evening sun." The duke, however, gives him a chance to explain why he left home and how it is that he has come to Ephesus.

Aegeon now embarks on a strange and spectacular story which wins the sympathy of his hearers. Many years before in the city of Epidamnum, his wife had given birth to identical twins, of whom she was very proud. At the same inn, a woman of lower class in the same hour also gave birth to twin boys whom Aegeon immediately bought as attendants for his sons. The family set sail, but, when they were a league from Epidamnum, a terrible storm broke out and the ship was in danger. His wife tied one twin and one servant twin to a spar, while Aegeon similarly bound his other son and the other servant twin to another spar. He lashed himself to the latter spar, while his wife tied herself to the former. She and the two children with her were

60

taken up by "fishermen of Corinth," while the father and the two children with him were taken to Epidaurus and later returned to the family home in Syracuse.

When the Syracusan twin became eighteen, he set forth to look for his brother, after whom he had been named Antipholus. He was accompanied by the servant or slave twin. Meantime the father, Aegeon, also set forth to look for his son and unknowingly entered the enemy city of Ephesus, as has been described. His one thought is how to find his lost son, and the slave with him, before his death: "Happy were I in my timely death, /Could all my travels warrant me they live."

The duke is filled with compassion at hearing this extraordinary and pitiful tale. If it were not against the law, he declares, he would certainly take Aegeon's part; but of course he must obey the law.

He does give Aegeon a day to see if from friends in Ephesus he can raise the amount of the ransom which will secure his life. Aegeon does not feel there is much chance of this: "Hopeless and helpless doth Aegeon wend,/But to procrastinate his lifeless end."

SCENE 2: The twin Antipholus of Syracuse, with his servant, the twin Dromio, has arrived in Ephesus. A fellow merchant warns him that as an alien from Syracuse he is in danger from the law in Ephesus which forbids Syracusans to enter. Only today, says the merchant, an elderly Syracusan has been apprehended under this law. He suggests that Antipholus give out that he is of Epidamnum.

Antipholus sends his servant Dromio, with his money, to a house called the Centaur to wait until he comes. He tells the merchant that his servant is a merry fellow who often cheers him and "lightens [his] humour with his merry jests." As the merchant leaves him to attend to other business, Antipholus is planning to explore the city. Left alone, he soliloquizes that he feels always alone, incomplete without his twin: "I to the world am like a drop of water/That in the ocean seeks another drop." He seeks not only his brother but also his mother.

Now the other Dromio, the slave of Antipholus of Ephesus, comes in. He thinks Antipholus of Syracuse is his master. He has been sent to bring him (i.e., his own master) to dinner, for the capon and the pork are already overcooked and it is twelve o'clock, time for dinner. If the clock has struck twelve, his mistress has struck one upon his cheek, for she is angry because her husband has not come home.

Antipholus of Syracuse, of course, thinks that this is his Dromio and that he is fooling. He is concerned as to what Dromio has done with the money he was in charge of. This Dromio insists that his only duty is to fetch Antipholus home to dinner and insists further that the only "marks" (usually money) he has are of whippings from his master and his mistress. Antipholus is baffled by these mentions of a mistress who beats his servant. He has had more than enough of this fooling.

He concludes that his slave has been cheated of his money, but this is not surprising, for Ephesus, he knows, is a town where strange things take place. Cheaters and deceivers are common. "Dark-working sorcerers" and "soul-killing witches," who have power over both mind and body, are common there. He will return to the Centaur to check up on his money and his slave.

Act II

SCENE 1: In front of the house of Antipholus of Ephesus appear his wife Adriana and her sister Luciana. Adriana is anxious because her husband has not yet returned, nor has Dromio, the servant, who was sent to look for his master. It is two o'clock, long past dinner time (usually 11:30 or 12 in Elizabethan households). Luciana suggests that Antipholus may have been invited out. "Good sister," she says, "let us dine and never fret:/ A man is master of his liberty." She thinks a man should be free to come and go as he pleases, since his business takes him abroad in the town. Adriana says her husband does not like it when *she* claims a similar liberty. Luciana on her part says that for a wife to claim such liberty leads to trouble ("headstrong liberty is lashed with woe"). Even in the animal kingdom, among "the beasts, the fishes and the winged fowls," the male is master; so should it be with mankind, who is master of the beasts. Adriana suggests that this viewpoint hinders Luciana from getting married and that if she were married she would assert some power ("bear some sway"). Luciana replies, "Ere I learn love, I'll practise to obey." She would even be patient if her husband sought consolation with other women. Adriana is impatient. She thinks Luciana does not know how a wife can suffer from an "unkind mate." Luciana says soothingly that one day she will test her beliefs out in marriage.

Dromio, the household slave, returns at this point. He has been beaten, by his master he thinks, but he really, of course, has suffered at the hands of the twin Antipholus of Syracuse, whom he reports as "horn mad," i.e., as mad as a beast. When asked to come home for dinner, he spoke only of his money, and denied knowing house or wife in Ephesus. Adriana says he should go back again and fetch his master home, but Dromio says that if he is to be hit from husband to wife in this fashion, he must be clothed with a leather case, like a football.

Adriana is disturbed by the slave's report. She is afraid that her husband is enjoying himself away from her with his "minions" (favorites) and that she is losing the good looks and charm with which she once held him. "I at home starve for a merry look," she claims. Luciana urges her to put jealousy aside, but Adriana asserts, "I know his eye doth homage otherwhere." He has not even brought her the chain he promised. She will "weeping die," to which Luciana exclaims, "How many fond [i.e., foolish] fools serve mad jealousy!"

SCENE 2: Antipholus of Syracuse is mystified. The money Dromio left at the Centaur is safe and "the heedful slave" has gone to look for him. Dromio—his own slave this time, Dromio of Syracuse—enters and his master asks him if his "merry humour" is passed—a humour in which he denied knowledge of the Centaur and the gold and spoke of a mistress waiting with dinner. Dromio of Syracuse, of course, cannot remember making any such statements. Irritated at his denial, Antipholus beats him and declares that while he sometimes allows the slave to act the fool, he is not in the mood for it in his more serious moments. Punning on three meanings of "sconce," Dromio says that as Antipholus is attacking his sconce (fort), he must get a sconce (helmet) for his sconce (head). They joke rather feebly about baldness and allude to venereal diseases which cause loss of hair.

At this point Adriana and Luciana appear. Adriana makes a touching appeal to Antipholus, whom she takes for her husband and whom she thinks has found another mistress. She reminds him that in the early days of their married love he loved to share everything with her—words, things, touch, food. Now he seems to be estranged, although he should be indivisible from her. She reminds him how he would be upset and disturbed if she were unfaithful to him, and she further advances the curious argument that since united in marriage, they are of one blood, any adultery that he commits pollutes her also. She appeals to him, then, to be faithful—"Keep then fair league and truce with thy true bed."

Antipholus of Syracuse, further mystified by what she says, speaks gently and courteously to her: "Plead you to me, fair dame? I know you not:/ in Ephesus I am but two hours old." Luciana thinks he must be joking. Didn't Dromio tell him that dinner was ready? Dromio is the one word that makes sense to Antipholus, but the Dromio with him, Dromio of Syracuse, denies any knowledge of Adriana and her messages, although Antipholus recollects receiving such messages "on the mart." Unfortunately, Adriana misreads Antipholus' conversation with his slave. She thinks they have an understanding with each other to make fun of her. "How ill agrees it with thy gravity/ To counterfeit thus grossly with your slave,/ Abetting him to thwart me in my mood." She will cling to her husband as a vine to an elm.

Antipholus of Syracuse wonders if he was married to her in a dream. At any rate, he decides to play along with her ("I'll entertain the offered fallacy") and agrees to come in to dinner. Luciana orders Dromio to "bid the servants spread for dinner." Startled that she knows his name, Dromio says, "This is the fairy land"—Ephesus is the town of sorcerers and witches—and "I am an ass; else it could never be/ But I should know her as well as she knows me." Adriana still thinks they are making fun of her, but orders Dromio to "keep the gate" while she and her husband dine above in private. Antipholus is mystified, but decides to go along with the events that are taking place around him. He says, "I'll say as they say and persever so/ And in this mist at all adventures go." He, too, directs Dromio to be the porter at the gate.

Act III

SCENE 1: Now Antipholus of Ephesus appears in the street below. He begs the goldsmith, Angelo, to say that he lingered at his shop to watch the bracelet ("carcenet") being finished. "My wife," he says, "is shrewish when I keep not hours," i.e. is ill-tempered when he is late home. He is still annoyed with his slave, who he· says, declared that he had no wife and home in Ephesus and spoke of his owning a thousand marks in gold. Dromio of Ephesus, on his part, feels injured because he has been beaten for making statements which he did not make.

Next, Antipholus, who has invited Angelo and the merchant, Balthazar, to dinner, is startled to find that the door of his own house is locked. Dromio calls to the maids, "Maud, Bridget, Marian, Cicely, Gillian, Ginn," but is answered only by his brother slave, who replies, "Mome [blockhead], malt-horse, capon, coxcomb, idiot, patch [fool]!/ Either get thee from the door or sit down at the hatch." One wench is more than enough—why does he call for so many? "My master stays in the street," cries Dromio of Ephesus, and Antipholus adds that they are waiting for their dinner. Who is keeping him out? Dromio the porter, replies Dromio of Syracuse, prompting Dromio of Ephesus to say that his substitute has stolen both his task and his name. At this point, Luce, the fat serving wench, joins in the dialogue. She tells Antipholus that he has come too late and that he may knock at the door until he hurts it. Even Adriana does not recognize her husband's voice and tells him to get away from the door. She is sure her "husband" is already inside eating with her "above" in full sight of the audience.

Antipholus decides that he will break into his house with an iron crow [crowbar] and is about to send Dromio for this. Dromio puns here on the two meanings of crow—crowbar and the bird. But Balthazar points out to him how he may damage his reputation and that of his wife if he takes such violent action. "Vulgar comment will be made of it," he urges. Antipholus recognizes the good sense of this advice and suggests that instead they dine with the courtezan, who is not only "a wench of excellent discourse," but also "pretty and witty, wild and yet, too, gentle." He decides to spite his wife by presenting the gold chain intended for her to the courtezan and sends Angelo to get it. They plan to meet "some hours hence."

SCENE 2: Luciana makes a moving appeal to Antipholus of Syracuse that he should fulfill "a husband's office." It seems a pity to her that "even in the spring of love," his love should decay. If he married Adriana for love, for this cause he should treat her kindly. If his affections are bestowed elsewhere, he should act by stealth, so as not to offend Adriana. "Be secret-false," urges Luciana, for it is a double sin to be false and to let his spouse know that he is being false. "Comfort my sister," she concludes, "call her wife./'Tis holy sport to be a little vain [insincere]."

Puzzled but gentle, Antipholus of Syracuse replies by asking why she makes his soul "wander in an unknown field." So far as he knows, he owes no loyalty to Adriana. He urges Luciana, "Sing, siren, for thyself . . . Spread o'er the silver waves thy golden hairs,/And as a bed I'll take them and there lie." He would be glad to die under her protection. Luciana is troubled by his romantic appeals to her and urges him to think only of Adriana; but Antipholus insists that his "dear heart" is centered in her, his "sole earth's heaven," his "heaven's claim." He concludes:

> Thee will I love, and with thee lead my life;
> Thou hast no husband yet, nor I no wife.
> Give me thy hand.

Luciana, loyal to her sister, goes to fetch her, "to get her good will."

Dromio of Syracuse—this is Antipholus' own slave—comes in very much disturbed. "Do you know me, sir?" he asks. "Am I

Dromio? Am I your man?" Antipholus assures him that he is, but Dromio still wonders who he is, because he is claimed in marriage by "a very beastly creature," a kitchenwench so fat that Dromio says he could "make a lamp of her and run from her by her own light." She is so fat that if she were burned as a tallow candle she would last "a Poland winter." According to Dromio, she is also very unattractive. In a passage which perhaps was inspired by Rabelais, he compares various parts of her body to countries—her buttocks to the bogs of Ireland, the hard palm of her hand to Scotland, her nose, "embellished with rubies, carbuncles, sapphires," to America, where Spain sent "whole armadas of carracks [ships] to be ballast [loaded] at her nose." The most interesting comparison is to France, "in her forehead, armed and reverted, making war against her hair."

Dromio concludes by saying that the wench laid claim to him and told him what birthmarks distinguished him, such as a mole on his neck and a wart on his arm. This knowledge made him fear she was a witch. Antipholus, too, fears the bewitched atmosphere at Ephesus. He tells Dromio to book a berth on any ship he can get that night. Not only the claims of Adriana but the charms of Luciana alarm him. "Tis high time that I were hence," he says, ". . . and stop my ears against the mermaid's song."

At this moment the goldsmith, Angelo, comes in with the chain ordered by Antipholus of Ephesus. Naturally, he mistakes the brother for his customer. Antipholus of Syracuse is puzzled. "What is your will that I should do with this?" he asks. Angelo, who knows Antipholus has asked for the chain many times, is mystified. "Go home with it and please your wife withal," he advises. He will collect the money later. Antipholus offers to pay him on the spot, but Angelo refuses this from such an old customer. "You are a merry man," he laughs. Antipholus on his part is delighted with his windfall. He resolves to get away from Ephesus as soon as a ship can be found.

Act IV

SCENE 1: Another merchant of Ephesus claims from Angelo a sum he needs to go to Persia. Angelo explains that Antipholus owes him just about that amount and that he expects to collect it at five o'clock. He will then repay his debt to the merchant. At this moment Antipholus of Ephesus (with his Dromio) approaches. He is sending Dromio to buy a rope with which to whip his household for locking him out. Dromio quips, "I buy a thousand pounds [i.e., knocks] a year, I buy a rope." Antipholus also speaks to the courtezan, promising her that he will give her the chain as soon as he gets it from the goldsmith.

Overhearing this and thinking Antipholus must be joking, since he has already delivered the chain to him, Angelo presents his bill and explains that he needs the money to pay the merchant. Antipholus, not having much money with him, asks Angelo to take the chain to his house and get the money from Adriana. Angelo asks for the chain. Antipholus, of course, denies having it. Angelo, who has already given the chain to the other Antipholus, is annoyed, especially as it delays his payment to the merchant who is impatiently waiting. ("Both wind and tide stays for this gentleman,/And I, to blame, have held him here too long.") He insists that Antipholus return the chain which he gave him not half an hour ago. The impatient merchant orders the officer to arrest Angelo in the name of the duke. Angelo in his turn orders the arrest of Antipholus for not paying for the chain he received.

At this crucial moment, the other brother's slave, Dromio of Syracuse, comes in. He has organized the flight from Syracuse, which his master so desired. He has booked passage on a ship, put their luggage aboard, and bought ointment and aqua-vitae (strong brandy). The citizen Antipholus, who sent his slave for a rope to beat his household with, is astounded. However, there is no time to argue this at present. Hastily giving Dromio a key, he orders him to go home and get Adriana to find in his desk a purse of ducats which will deliver him from arrest. Dromio, recollecting that Adriana was the woman with whom they dined at the house where the fat girl claimed him as her husband, sets off against his will.

SCENE 2: Luciana is telling her sister Adriana that Antipholus has made advances to her. Of course, she does not realize that the man who was attracted to her was Antipholus of Syracuse, not her brother-in-law. Adriana, who also thinks her husband has been flirting with her sister, is hurt and wonders if he was really serious. Did he look red or pale? she wonders; sad or merry? She asks Luciana if he blushed, if she saw "his heart's meteors tilting in his face."

Luciana reluctantly says that Antipholus denied that Adriana had any right in him and vowed that he was a stranger. Luciana tried to defend her sister's rights, but Antipholus pursued his suit along lines which, in different circumstances, would be appropriate, for he first praised her beauty, then her manner of talking. Adriana cannot bear to hear this but cries out against her husband, saying "He is deformed, crooked, old and sere/ Ill-faced, worse bodied, shapeless everywhere/Vicious, ungentle, foolish, blunt, unkind." Luciana reasonably asks her if it is common sense to be jealous of such a man and Adriana, her anger collapsing, admits, "Ah, but I think him better than I say . . . ./My heart prays for him, though my tongue do curse."

Dromio of Syracuse enters breathless and gives a confused account of something dreadful that has happened to his master, who has fallen into the hands of "a fiend, a fury, pitiless and rough;/A wolf, nay worse, a fellow all in buff." It is some time before he can collect himself enough to explain that the fellow in buff is a policeman, that his master has been arrested, and that he has been sent for the money to bail him out.

Adriana sends Luciana for the money and asks Dromio if her husband was arrested "on a band [bond]," i.e., because he owed money. Quibbling on another meaning of "band," leash, Dromio says he was arrested on a stronger thing, a chain. Receiving the purse from Luciana, he dashes back with it to his master, leaving Adriana very anxious.

SCENE 3: Antipholus of Syracuse appears. He is much mystified because wherever he goes, someone addresses him by name, offers him money, invites him home, or tries to tell him something. A tailor has just shown him silks and measured him for a suit.

While he is pondering these mysterious happenings, Dromio—his own Dromio—appears with the gold and naturally wonders how his master got away from the police officer. Antipholus says this is enough of his foolery—has he booked passage out of the town tonight? "Why, sir," says Dromio, "I brought you word an hour since that the bark Expedition put forth tonight." He hands over the money. Antipholus is thoroughly confused and disturbed. "The fellow is distract, and so am I," he cries,

> And here we wander in illusions
> Some blessed power deliver us from hence!

Just then the courtezan comes in and asks for the chain. Because she knows his name, Antipholus thinks she is a witch. "Will you go with me?" she asks, "We'll mend our dinner here." Dromio observes that "he must have a long spoon that would eat with the devil," meaning that he who is tempted to sin must be very careful what he does. Antipholus begs the "witch" to be gone, but she asks for the ring she says she gave him or the chain which he took. Dromio thinks she is trying to get something from them in order to carry out her witchcraft. "Some devils ask but the parings of one's nail,/ A rush, a hair, a drop of blood, a pin"—but she wants a chain. He advises Antipholus not to give it to her. Really concerned about her property, the courtezan asks again for her ring or her chain, but Antipholus flees, begging the witch to leave him alone.

The courtezan thinks Antipholus must be mad or he would not act in this way, denying her both chain and ring. She recalls the mad tale he told at dinner of his own doors being shut against him and wonders if his wife, "acquainted with his fits," locked the doors on purpose. She decides to tell the wife that Antipholus, in a lunatic mood, rushed into her house and took her ring away, for, she exclaims, "forty ducats is too much to lose."

SCENE 4: Antipholus of Ephesus assures the officer that he has no intention of breaking away and that he soon expects the money from his wife. She will be upset to hear that he is arrested. Dromio of Ephesus chooses this moment to come back with the rope which his master sent him for. "Where's the money?" asks Antipholus. "Why, sir, I gave the money for the rope." Furious at the thought of five hundred ducats being spent in this way, Antipholus beats his slave until even the officer bids him to be patient, and poor Dromio cries out that he has been beaten all his life: "When I am cold, he heats me with beating; when I am warm he cools me with beating: I am waked with it when I sleep; raised with it when I sit, driven out of doors with it when I go from home; welcomed home with it when I return. . . ." He concludes that when his master has lamed him completely, he will have to beg from door to door.

Now Adriana, Luciana, the courtezan, and one Dr. Pinch assemble. Dr. Pinch is a "conjurer," i.e., a learned man, perhaps a schoolmaster, who knows some Latin and thus could exorcise the demon supposed to be troubling Antipholus. The exorcism, however, is not a success, for Antipholus boxes Dr. Pinch on the ear and declares, "I am not mad." "O that thou wert not, poor distressed soul!" cries Adriana. Antipholus, still smarting at having been shut out of his house, angrily charges Adriana with having entertained Pinch, "this companion with the saffron face," in his stead. Adriana insists that he did dine at home. Antipholus denies it once more and Dromio supports him.

Next Antipholus most unfairly accuses his wife of bribing the goldsmith to arrest him. She insists that, on the contrary, she sent the money to redeem him, and Luciana backs her up. Dromio insists that he fetched not money but a rope. The doctor is sure now that both master and man are mad and must be bound and put in a locked room (the accepted Elizabethan treatment for madness). Once more Antipholus asks why he was locked out and once more Adriana denies it ("I did not, gentle husband, lock thee forth"). Very angry indeed now, Antipholus is sure she has plotted with the others to make him an object of ridicule.

> Disembling harlot, thou art false in all
> And art confederate with a damned pack
> To make a loathsome abject scorn of me.

Frightened, Adriana bids the men bind him and keep him away from her. Her husband struggles but finally both he and his slave are overpowered and led away to be bound in a dark room in their own house. The officer is reluctant to let his prisoner go, but Adriana promises to pay the amount due for the chain, although she does not think Antipholus received the chain. Just as the courtezan is assuring them that she saw the chain when Antipholus took away her ring, Antipholus of Syracuse comes in with a drawn sword, followed by his slave, Dromio of Syracuse. Antipholus, as in the previous scene, is still trying to protect himself from sorcery, but of course Adriana and Luciana think the other pair has escaped. The women and even the officer flee for their lives. Reassured to find that "witches are afraid of swords," Antipholus of Syracuse resolves to fetch their luggage from the Centaur and board the ship. He cannot wait to get away from Ephesus.

Act V

SCENE 1: The concluding scene of the play, which clears up all the mysteries and reunites the family, takes place in "a street before a priory." As the scene opens, Angelo is apologizing to the second merchant for delaying him. He is baffled at Antipholus' behavior, for the latter has a good name in the city, being "of very reverend reputation . . ./ Of credit infinite, highly beloved,/ Second to none that lives here in the city." At that very moment Antipholus of Syracuse comes in with his man, wearing, as Angelo indignantly notices, the very chain which he denied receiving. He now denies denying it, and he and the second merchant dispute and draw their swords. At this moment Adriana, Luciana, and the courtezan come in, Adriana crying out to the merchant not to hurt her husband, for he is mad and must be bound and taken home. In fright Antipholus and Dromio take sanctuary in the priory.

Out of the priory comes the abbess, the head of the priory, and bids the throng of people to be quiet. Adriana explains that they are trying to catch her "poor distracted husband," so that they may bind him and "bear him home for his recovery." Angelo says he was sure his customer was "not in his perfect wits," and the merchant is sorry he drew his sword on him. The abbess asks how long the husband has been possessed and Adriana explains that, while he has been "heavy, sour, and sad" all week, his madness has only broken out into extreme rage this very afternoon. The abbess wonders what is the cause of his distraction—has he lost his wealth in a shipwreck? or has he buried a close friend? or is he involved in an unlawful love? "To none of these, except it be the last," replies Adriana. Now the abbess lays a little trap for Adriana.

> Abbess: You should for that have reprehended him.
> Adriana: Why, so I did.
> Abbess: Ay, but not roughly enough.
> Adriana: As roughly as my modesty would let me.
> Abbess: Haply, in private.
> Adriana: And in assemblies too.
> Abbess: Ay, but not enough.

Adriana replies that it was the subject of all their conversations and that

> In bed, he slept not for my urging it;
> At board, he fed not for my urging it;
> Alone, it was the subject of my theme;
> In company I often glanced it.
> Still did I tell him it was vile and bad.

Having tricked Adriana into admitting that she constantly plagued her husband on this subject, the abbess declares that this is what made Antipholus mad—"the venom clamours of a jealous woman," which are more poisonous than the bite of a mad dog. This nagging must have been the source of his distemper. Luciana speaks up for her sister, saying that Adriana only scolded her husband mildly, but Adriana, much ashamed, admits, "She did betray me to my own reproof."

Adriana wants to fetch her husband out of the priory or have him sent out, for as his wife she wishes to nurse him in his illness, but the prioress insists that she will not release him until she tries whether "wholesome syrups, drugs and holy prayers" will not bring him back to normal. Adriana is inclined to insist on her right to her possession of her husband, but the abbess is firm. At Luciana's suggestion, Adriana determines to appeal for her rights to the duke, whom the merchant points out is expected this way at five o'clock to see "a reverend Syracusan merchant" put to death for unlawfully entering Ephesus.

The duke and his train come in, together with Aegeon and the executioner. As the duke asks once more if any friend has the amount of the fine to redeem the victim, Adriana appeals for justice against the abbess, reminding the duke that it was with his permission that she married her husband, who is now mad, along with his man. In his madness he has been annoying the citizens, rushing out with jewels and rings. She has had him and his man bound once, but they escaped, chased her and her companions with drawn swords, and took refuge in the priory, whence the abbess refuses to release them. She concludes

> Therefore, most gracious duke, with thy command
> Let him be brought forth and borne hence for help.

The duke, who recalls that Antipholus served him well in the wars, sends for the abbess and plans to judge the case before he goes any further. Meanwhile a servant of Adriana's rushes in with the news that Antipholus and Dromio have broken loose, beaten the maids, singed Dr. Pinch's beard, and put out the fire with panfuls of muddy water. He has also threatened to disfigure Adriana in his wrath. The duke tells them not to fear and orders the guard to have their halberds ready. [Halberds were shafted weapons with axelike blades.] Adriana cannot understand why her husband and servant, who just disappeared into the priory, now reappear from the direction of their home. Now Antipholus in his turn cries out for justice, in the name of the scars he has earned to save the duke's life. Seeing him and his servant, Aegeon thinks they are his son and servant from Syracuse, but he does not get a chance to say more because Antipholus of Ephesus is pouring out his grievances to the duke. He says his wife has abused and dishonored him, shut the doors on him "while she with harlots feasted in the house." Adriana and Luciana both insist that, on the contrary, he dined at home with his wife. Angrier than ever, Antipholus declares that if Angelo were not in a conspiracy with the women he could witness that they were locked out. But, he says, the goldsmith, too, is lying, for he insists he delivered the chain although he (Antipholus of Ephesus) knows he has not received it. On his way home with the officer he met his wife with "a rabble more of vile confederates" including the quack Dr. Pinch, who pronounced him mad, whereupon he was bound, together with Dromio. Angelo agrees that his friend was locked out and says that when Antipholus ran into the priory, the chain was seen around his neck. The second merchant remembers hearing him confess to receiving the chain (of course this was the other Antipholus). Antipholus denies that he ever went into the priory. The duke says he thinks they have all drunk of Circe's cup and, like Ulysses and his men in the *Odyssey*, have been turned into beasts. Dromio testifies that his master dined at the Porpentine with the courtezan, and she, sticking to *her* chief concern, says that he took her ring away and that moreover she saw them go into the priory.

Now at last Aegeon is able to get a word in edgewise. "Haply I see a friend will save my life/And pay the sum that may deliver me," he tells the duke, thinking that of course his son will want to free him. He is disappointed, because Antipholus of Ephesus, who has not seen his father since he was a baby, does not recognize him. Greatly distressed, Aegeon exclaims, "O grief hath changed me since you saw me last." He grieves that Antipholus does not even recognize his voice, which must have changed in the seven years since they last saw each other in Syracuse. He for his part, in spite of his aging sight and hearing, does not fail to recognize his son Antipholus. He fears that perhaps Antipholus is ashamed to acknowledge him in his extremity. Antipholus says he has never been to Syracuse, and this statement the duke, his patron for twenty years, supports, saying, "I see thy age and dangers make thee dote."

At this moment of despair for Aegeon, the abbess comes out with Antipholus of Syracuse and Dromio of Syracuse. Everyone crowds around to see the two pairs of twins. Adriana exlaims that she sees two husbands. The duke asks who can distinguish Antipholus from the attendant spirit who duplicates him. Antipholus of Syracuse greets his father (unlike his brother, he recognizes him immediately). Then the abbess has a surprise for everyone. Indicating Aegeon, she says, "I will loose his bonds/And gain a husband by his liberty." She reminds Aegeon that he once had a wife, Aemilia, who bore two sons at one birth. "If I dream not," says the astonished Aegeon, "thou art Aemilia." In reply to his query about their other son, she tells him that, while she and her son and the baby Dromio were all rescued "by men of Epidamnum," the two boys were taken from her by Corinthian fishermen, whereupon she entered the priory.

The duke realizes that this story matches the one Aegeon had told that morning of the two pairs of twins separated in a ship-wreck. Confusing the two Antipholi, the duke asks Antipholus of Syracuse if he came from Corinth. Antipholus of Ephesus explains that *he* is the one who came from Corinth. Adriana asks who dined with her that day and is surprised to hear that it was not her husband. Antipholus of Syracuse admits that she called him husband and that Luciana called him brother and turning to Luciana he promises to fulfill the tender promises he made her earlier in the day. The confusion about the chain is sorted out by the two Antipholi and Angelo, and Adriana realizes that the money she sent to bail her husband out never reached him. Antipholus of Syracuse summarizes the situation:

> I see we still [constantly] did meet each other's man,
> And I was ta'en for him and he for me,
> And thereupon these ERRORS are arose.

Antipholus of Ephesus offers the gold for his father's life, but the duke says, "It shall not need; thy father hath his life." The courtezan, her mind on essentials, demands and gets her ring back. The abbess invites the company to go into the priory, where all explanations shall be made at a "gossips' [friends'] feast."

Even the Dromios cannot tell their masters apart. Dromio of Syracuse asks Antipholus of Ephesus whether he should fetch his baggage from the ship and his own master has to correct him. He tells his servant to embrace his brother and he and *his* brother go out. All go into the priory except the Dromios.

Dromio of Syracuse observes that the "fat friend" who entertained him in the kitchen at dinner will now be his sister, not his wife. Dromio of Ephesus, looking at him approvingly, observes:

> Methinks you are my glass [reflection] and not my brother.
> I see by you I am a sweetfaced youth.

He offers to let his twin go ahead of him into the priory. After an exchange of courtesies, they agree to "draw cuts for the senior." Dromio of Ephesus finishes the play in a jingling couplet:

> We came into the world like brother and brother
> And now let's go hand in hand, not one before another.

Measure for Measure

VINCENTIO, *the Duke.*
ANGELO, *the Deputy.*
ESCALUS, *an ancient lord.*
CLAUDIO, *a young gentleman.*
LUCIO, *a fantastic.*
Two other like GENTLEMEN.
PROVOST.
THOMAS } *two friars.*
PETER
(A JUSTICE.)
(VARRUS.)
ELBOW, *a simple constable.*
FROTH, *a foolish gentleman.*
CLOWN (POMPEY, *a servant to Mistress Overdone*).
ABHORSON, *an executioner.*
BARNARDINE, *a dissolute prisoner.*

ISABELLA, *sister to Claudio.*
MARIANA, *betrothed to Angelo.*
JULIET, *beloved of Claudio.*
FRANCISCA, *a nun.*
MISTRESS OVERDONE, *a bawd.*

LORDS, OFFICERS, CITIZENS, BOY, *and* ATTENDANTS.

Measure for Measure

Act I: Scene 1

In an apartment in the Duke's palace in Vienna at some time in the sixteenth century we find the Duke Vincentio (Vin chen' see oh) speaking to a trusted counselor Lord Escalus (Ess' kuh luss). The Duke says that it would be useless to explain the fine art of government to Escalus since the Lord's science (knowledge) in that field goes beyond any advice the Duke can give him.

The nature of the Viennese, their institutions and laws are well known (pregnant) to Escalus as to any other man in the city. The Duke hands the Lord a commission on the new appointment (the commission appoints Angelo as ruler and Escalus his second in command while the Duke is away on his supposed trip to Poland) and then bids an attendant call for Angelo (An' jell oh). "What figure (representation) of us think you he (i.e. Angelo) will bear?" inquires the Duke of Escalus. This is followed by another question: What does Escalus think of the fact that the Duke has given full power of office to Angelo? Escalus' reply is that if there is anyone in Vienna fit for such an honor it is Angelo.

At this point Angelo enters, and the Duke seizes the occasion to deliver a lecture on the necessity of translating our inner virtue (goodness) from a passive to an active state: "Heaven doth with us as we with torches do, / Not light them for themselves; for if our virtues / Did not go forth of us, 'twere all alike / As if we had them not." He cuts short his lecture and tells Angelo of his new office, saying that "Mortality (death) and mercy in Vienna / Live in thy tongue and heart; old Escalus, / Though first in question, is thy secondary (second in command)." The Duke then hands Angelo his commission in office. Angelo's reply (*Angelo* means *angel* in English) is properly respectful and modest; he doesn't think he will be ready for such a noble position until he has been further tested.

The Duke brushes aside Angelo's objection, saying he has already deeply considered this new appointment: "therefore take your honours." The Duke Vincentio declares he is in great haste to leave and bids them farewell saying he'll keep in touch by letter. He goes on, however, to reassert Angelo's full authority while Vincentio is gone. The Duke is leaving Vienna secretly because as he declares, "I love the people, / But do not like to stage me (publicly show-off) to their eyes: . . . I do not relish well their loud applause and Aves vehement (violent farewells)." Once more the Duke bids Angelo and Escalus farewell and departs.

After Vincentio leaves, Escalus and Angelo withdraw together to consult the extent of the powers of each, and the scene ends.

Act I: Scene 2

On a street in Vienna Lucio (Loo' shee oh) is conversing with two gentlemen. Lucio mentions a league of dukes (city-states) formed against the menacing King of Hungary. In reply the First Gentleman (very often in Shakespeare characters are merely given numbers and class labels: i.e., first and second servants, etc.) tosses off a pun (a play on words with double or even triple meanings: here "peace" is played upon. Shakespeare's favorite humorous device is the pun): "Heaven grant us its peace, but not the King of Hungary's!" Then follows another pun on "steal," on "grace," on "metre." Space does not permit a detailed explanation of each and every pun, but let's take the one on "grace" as a typical example of a Shakespearean pun:

First Gent. . . . There's not a soldier of us all, that, in the thanksgiving before meat, do relish the petition well that prays for peace.

Sec. Gent.   I never heard any soldier dislike it.

Lucio.   I believe thee; for I think thou never wast where grace[1] was said.

Sec. Gent.   No? a dozen times at least.

First Gent.   What, in metre?

Lucio.   In any proportion or in any language.

First Gent.   I think, or in any religion.[2]

Lucio. Ay, why not? Grace is grace, despite of all controversy: as, for example, thou thyself art a wicked villain, despite of all grace.[3]

Explanation: grace[1] = prayer before a meal.

grace[2] = in religion is the special grace of God to man despite his sins.

grace[3] = mercy (no amount of mercy could redeem this wicked villain). Note also that *metre,* meaning time or rhythm, also sounds like *meat* (food) before which grace is said. Note the bawdy puns on *piled* (1. velvet nap 2. bald or hairless as in the French disease, i.e., syphilis, which made one bald). Note too the one on *feelingly* (1. with feeling 2. painful feeling in mouth, as in syphilis). At this point Madame Mitigation (a pun on her sexual function) is sighted, and we have puns on *dolours* (pains) and *dollars* (money) and the inevitable one on the French crown (money; bald head). In short, the humor derives from allusions to the "French" disease.

The arrival of Mistress Overdone (her name is a bawdy pun as are the names of many of the other low-life characters) gives rise to one more venereal joke *(sciatica in the hips* meaning both the disease and the movement of intercourse). Her function is to act as messenger as well as comic butt. She brings news of Claudio's imprisonment for having made his fiancée pregnant. Within three days Claudio's head is to be chopped off for his crime. Lucio, Claudio's friend, shows genuine alarm and hurries off with the other two gentlemen to verify her news.

At this point Pompey, Overdone's servant, enters. He, too, functions as a messenger of news. He tells of a man carried off to prison for "groping for trouts in a peculiar river" (i.e., the sexual act), and he tells all about Angelo's latest proclamation that all "houses (i.e., bawdyhouses) in the suburbs of Vienna must be plucked down." The ones in the city are spared to provide for "seed" as Pompey dryly explains. He mockingly consoles Overdone, assuring her she need not change her trade, and they withdraw at the arrival of the Provost (jailer), Claudio, Juliet, and Officers.

The Provost drags on stage (the street) his prisoner Claudio, who protests being publicly paraded, but his jailor (Provost) replies that the order to make a public display of Claudio came from Angelo. Claudio answers that heaven can choose to punish or not, "yet still 'tis just."

Here Lucio and his two friends enter, and Claudio's close friend (Lucio) asks why he is a prisoner. Claudio says that too much liberty can also be restricting, and man's nature is such (sexual desire?) that he pursues his appetites like hungry rats ("Our natures do pursue, / Like rats that ravin [swallow] down their proper bane [their own poison], / A thirsty evil; and when we drink we die."). Lucio replies that he prefers foolish freedom to moral imprisonment and inquires again the cause. In a long expository speech (speech explaining action before the play began: i.e., background information) Claudio explains that he had gone to bed with Juliet (who, by the way, is with Claudio during the entire scene but remains mute). But their sexual union was legitimate since they were engaged to be married (formal betrothal); all that is lacking is the formal declaration of marriage in public. The reason for the delay in the formal betrothal was that he and Juliet were waiting for friends who were holding the marriage dowry to look more kindly upon the couple, and thus approve a larger marriage settlement (dowry). Friends in Shakespeare's day could also mean relatives. Unfortunately Juliet's pregnancy has produced an obvious bellybulge and the new Deputy (Angelo) has revived an almost forgotten law, which has not been enforced for nineteen years. The law: pre-marital sex is forbidden! Claudio begs Lucio to hasten to Isabella, Claudio's sister, who is about to enter a convent and become a nun, and beg her to use her persuasive arts on the new Deputy. Lucio agrees, commenting that he hopes she'll succeed in the name of both sex and Claudio: ". . . thy life, who I would be sorry should be thus foolishly lost at a game of tick-tack (backgammon = sex)." The scene ends with Lucio's promise to be back within two hours, while Claudio and Juliet are carried off to jail by the warden.

Act I: Scene 3

Scene 3 is a short one of 54 lines. We are in a monastery where Duke Vincentio enters, protesting to Friar Thomas that he is not there to conduct a secret love affair but to learn how to dress and act like a real friar. His purpose: to spy on how good a job Angelo is doing. In long expository speeches the Duke explains how he likes the secluded life away from the madding crowd; how he has yielded the reins of power to Angelo, "a man of stricture (sternness) and firm abstinence"; how for nineteen years he has been most lax in enforcing the strict laws of Vienna and "liberty plucks justice by the nose." Since it was too late to be strict, Vincentio had given power to Angelo and had noised it about that he (the Duke) would be going to Poland. Says the Duke in summary:

"Therefore indeed, my Father, / I have on Angelo imposed the office; / Who may, in the ambush of my name, strike home." The scene ends with this comment by the Duke: "Lord Angelo is precise (puritanical); / Stands at guard (always acts with caution) with envy; scarce confesses / That his blood flows, or that his appetite / Is more to bread than stone: hence shall we see / If power change purpose, what our seemers be."

Act I: Scene 4

Scene 4 is laid in a nunnery; we see Isabella and Francisca in conversation with Lucio joining them later. This too is a short scene of 90 lines, the last scene in Act I. Isabella and Francisca, a nun, enter, and our first glimpse of Isabella, Claudio's sister, is to hear her protesting that the rules of behavior of the nunnery are not strict enough! At this point Lucio calls from without, and Francisca begs Isabella to speak to him, since it is forbidden to the nuns of St. Clare to speak to men unless veiled and in the prioress' presence. So Francisca leaves and Lucio is allowed to enter and deliver his news to Isabella that her brother is in prison for having made Juliet pregnant. Lucio protests that it is so and that he is sincere, though, as he interpolates, it is his habit with maids "to seem the lapwing (a tricky bird) and to jest." He adds that he holds her "as a thing ensky'd and sainted" to be talked to only in sincerity. Lucio goes on to tell her how the Duke has made Angelo Deputy, "a man whose blood / Is very snow-broth; one who never feels / The wanton (lustful) stings and motions of the sense (senses), / But doth rebate (lessen) and blunt his natural edge (of lustful desire) / With profits of the mind, study and fast." He finally tells her why he has come to plead her intervention with Angelo for her brother's sake. She shows doubt as to her powers of persuasion, but he assures her that when "maidens sue, / Men give like gods." She readily agrees to help her doomed brother by speedily seeing Angelo; soon she'll be able to send her brother "certain word of my (her) success." They bid adieu and the scene and Act I ends.

Act II: Scene 1

Scene 1 occurs in Angelo's house and is in roughly three parts: first, Escalus and Angelo; second, Elbow, Pompey, and Froth enter; third, Angelo leaves and the four are left. The scene begins with Angelo explaining that laws are made to be enforced, not violated; otherwise they would be without teeth. Escalus replies, yes, but not to go whole hog and ruin everything. Besides, doesn't Claudio come from a noble family, and cannot an exception be made in his case? Even in your own case, says Escalus, in spite of your most "strait" (narrow, strict) virtue, you must at some time in a headstrong youth have slipped sexually as did Claudio, and then would not the law have been pulled upon you? Angelo's reply is masterful: "'Tis one thing to be tempted, Escalus, / Another thing to fall," but justice must punish the guilty who are caught. The law is a thing apart and must not be identified with the enforcers of it. "When I, that censure (judge) him do so offend, / Let mine own judgement pattern out my death, and nothing come in partial" (i.e., let the law be applied as strictly to me even if I were caught in a similar situation): "Sir, he must die." At this sharp judgment Escalus consents unwillingly, and Angelo orders the execution for nine the next morning. In an aside (to the audience, unheard by Angelo) Escalus asks for mercy from heaven, adding: "Some rise by sin, and some by virtue fall: / Some run from brakes of vice, and answer none: / And some condemned for a fault alone," which seems to mean that some get to the top by being sinful; others fall by being virtuous; some get away with murder, and others get murdered for the flimsiest of sins.

At this point Constable Elbow hauls in his prisoner, Froth, before Angelo and Escalus. "I do lean upon justice, sir, and do bring before your good honour two notorious benefactors" (note the pun on "elbow" and the "malapropism," which is a vocabulary mistake like "benefactor" for "malefactor" [evil-doer]; puns and malapropisms are the two chief forms of humor Shakespeare employs for such low, comic characters like Elbow). Elbow pulls other boners like "precise (puritanical) villains," "profanation" for profession, etc., and Angelo and Escalus, like all of Shakespeare's aristocrats, get a "charge" out of the comic low-lifes by sundry witty comments at the fools' expense. Pompey, who has accompanied Elbow, is called a tapster (barkeep) and parcel-bawd (two trades: tapster and pimp) who works for Mistress Overdone and whose bawdyhouse "was, as they say, plucked down in the suburbs." What follows is a fantastic miscellany of puns, irrelevancies, *non sequiturs,* hair-splitting, and an array of malapropisms like "a woman cardinally given" for a woman carnally given; "detest" for protest, etc. The charge against Froth, or what can be made of it from the comic mélange of accusers and accused, is that Froth has been arrested on the attempted rape of Mistress Elbow in Overdone's bawdyhouse. Hilarious is Pompey's account of how the pregnant Mistress Elbow entered the house longing for stewed prunes (a common dish in Elizabethan bawdyhouses) of which there were only two left, since Froth was busy "cracking the stones" of the rest in a room called "Bunch of Grapes." The circumlocutions (roundabout explanations) and unwitting "boners" of the comics gets to be so tedious to Angelo that he stalks from the room saying, "This will last out a night in Russia / When nights are longest there"; he leaves the case in Escalus' hands.

Pompey defends Froth from the charge, since there is not any harm in his face, which Escalus admits. By inexorable logic, then, Pompey goes on to show that since the worst thing about Pompey is his face, "How could Master Froth do the constable's wife any harm?" Then follows a good deal of humor over the malapropism in Elbow's "respected" (for disreputable?). "Respected" finally comes to mean sexually bedded with, which is the sense Elbow sees in the word: "O thou caitiff! O thou varlet! O thou wicked Hannibal (for cannibal)! I respected with her before I was married to her . . . Prove this, thou wicked Hannibal, or I'll have mine action of battery on thee." Elbow pleads for a decision from Escalus whose judgment is to let Froth continue "in his courses," since no charge has as yet been made because of all the stupidity and confusion. Elbow in his cosmic denseness mistakes "continue" for detained in jail. Then follows Escalus' interview of Froth and Pompey. The reader should consult Eric Partridge's *Shakespeare's Bawdy* for the more obscene allusions on such expressions as "a poor widow's tapster," "Overdone by the last," "Bum, sir" (for Pompey the pimp): "Troth, and your bum is the greatest thing about you; so that in the beastliest sense you are Pompey the great," says Escalus who joins merrily in the grossly sexual game of punning. (Hint: sodomy is hinted at, for example.) In answer to Escalus' comment that the law will not allow a bawd to ply his trade, Pompey's reply is "Does your worship mean to geld and splay (castrate) all the youth of the city," to which Escalus tolerantly replies, "No, Pompey." In fact, says the sage Pompey, if all the sexual criminals were beheaded or hanged, he would be able to rent the best house in Vienna for a mere threepence. Escalus, amused, lets Pompey go with a warning that, if caught again, he shall be whipped. Like Galileo leaving the Inquisitorial Court, Pompey exits muttering that he shall go on as before. Then Escalus instructs Elbow to bring him the names of six or seven men, the most able in his district. The time is now 11:00 A.M. and Elbow makes his exit. The scene ends in Escalus' inviting the Justice to dinner accompanied by an exchange of mutual dislike at Angelo's severe sentence on Claudio.

Act II: Scene 2

Scene 2 takes place in Angelo's house. First, we have Angelo and the Provost; second, the great scene between Angelo and Isabella; in all, a fairly long scene of 187 lines. The scene opens with the Provost in soliloquy (alone and speaking his thoughts aloud) hoping to plead in Claudio's behalf: "All sects (classes), all ages smack of this vice; and he to die for it!" Angelo enters and in reply to the warden's plea for mercy towards Claudio rudely snaps, "Do you your office, or give up your place." The warden meekly informs Angelo of Juliet's birth pains ("She's very near her hour"); Angelo kindly tells the Provost to put her in a better place; this is followed, however, by calling her a "fornicatress" with an added injunction to give her needful but not lavish quarters.

Isabella and Lucio enter; she states her case by baldly asserting first how she abhors the sexual vice of Claudio but, unwillingly, she must make her plea: "At war 'twixt will and will not." Angelo curtly asks her to state her case, and she begs her brother's sin be condemned but not the committer of the sin, Claudio. Angelo rightly ridicules her plea since such a policy would make all laws useless. Isabella's answer is to exclaim, "O just but severe law!" and starts to leave. Lucio, shocked, tells her to try again: "You are too cold; if you should need a pin, / You could not with more tame a tongue desire it: / To him, I say!" Isabella renews her efforts but again she sounds unimpassioned. In turn, Angelo keeps curtly denying her pleas. Again Lucio says to her aside: "You are too cold." Isabella now rises to great heights of passion on the theme of mercy: "No ceremony that to great ones 'longs, / Not the king's crown, nor the deputed sword, / The marshall's truncheon (officer's staff), nor the judge's robe, / Become them with one half so good a grace / As mercy does." After this magnificent plea, Angelo's only answer is to tell her to be gone. She fervently replies that if their positions were reversed, he would feel what it is like to be judged harshly. It is at this point that Lucio shows excited approval: "Ay, touch him; there's the vein." Even Christ himself showed mercy for undeserving sinners says Isabella: "If He, which is the top of judgement (the supreme judge), should / But judge you as you are?" Why then Angelo would show true mercy indeed. But Angelo is inflexible; the law is the law. Isabella rises to passionate heights: Claudio is not in a state of readiness for death; besides, who in the past has been legally murdered for such an offense even though many are guilty of it (i.e., fornication)? Lucio keeps congratulating her at intervals with comments like, "Ay, well said" and, "To him, wench!" Angelo is perfect in his logic: if the first fornicator had been punished as the law requires there would not be this license today and "... now 'tis awake, / Takes note of what is done"; henceforth there will be no progressive violation of the law. Isabella pleads simply: "Yet show some pity." Angelo: "I show it most of all when I show justice"; besides Claudio will not live to corrupt the world still more.

We now reach the emotional height of the play, where Isabella, like Portia in the trial scene of the *Merchant of Venice* ("The quality of mercy etc."), rises to sublime heights in her plea for mercy; it deserves full quotation.

> O, it is excellent
> To have a giant's strength; but it is tyrannous
> To use it like a giant . . .
> Could great men thunder
> As Jove himself does, Jove would ne'er be quiet,
> For every pelting, petty officer
> Would use his heaven for thunder;
> Nothing but thunder! Merciful Heaven,
> Thou rather with thy sharp and sulphurous bolt
> Split'st the unwedgeable and gnarled oak
> Than the soft myrtle: but man, proud man,
> Drest in a little brief authority,
> Most ignorant of what he's most assured,
> His glassy essence, like an angry ape,
> Plays such fantastic tricks before high heaven
> As make the angels weep; who, with our spleens,
> Would all themselves laugh mortal.

Lucio is by now roaring approval from the sidelines, but his use of "wench" belies in part his former vow that he thought her a saint. A captain being noble can err, but the same error in a common soldier would be blasphemy, says Isabella. When asked to explain this statement she replies that true rulers would be aware of their own sinful natures and attempts to acknowledge it; should Angelo search his heart he would find buried in it the same kind of lust shown in Claudio's. At this Angelo confesses in an aside that he is feeling such a lust — for Isabella herself! She even promises to bribe him with heavenly gifts, not with gold or jewels but with prayers that will reach heaven —

prayers given by pure maids like herself and the nuns of St. Clare.
Angelo tells her to come tomorrow to visit him before noon, and
Isabella, Lucio, and the Provost leave. In soliloquy (solo speech)
Angelo confesses himself being sinfully affected by the pure Isabella.
"Can it be / That modesty may more betray our sense / Than woman's
lightness?" he asks himself. Does innocence appeal more to a man's
lust than less innocent women? Does he desire her sexually because she
is pure? Why then, her brother should live, since he is as guilty as
Claudio. "O cunning enemy, that, to catch a saint, / With saints dost
bait thy hook!" A prostitute could never have stirred me (Angelo)
with all her arts of seduction, but "this virtuous maid / Subdues me
quite. Ever till now, / When men were fond (foolish), I smiled and
wonder'd how." With this remarkable soliloquy, the scene ends.

Act II: Scene 3

Scene 3 takes place in a prison with the Duke and Juliet as the chief
participants (total lines = 42). The Duke enters disguised as a
Friar and greets the Provost telling him he has come to console the
prisoners. At this point Juliet enters, and the Duke is told the story and
her pitiable situation by the sympathetic Provost. When Juliet is asked
whether she repents, she replies she truly does; but the Duke-Friar puts
her to the test. Does she truly love Claudio? The act was an act of
mutual love? Finding her repentance, love, and shame adequate, the
"false" Friar bids adieu, saying he is off to console Claudio, who is to
die tomorrow. Juliet: "Must he die to-morrow! O injurious love, / That
respites (prolongs) me a life, whose very comfort / Is still a dying
horror!" End of scene.

Act II: Scene 4

This scene occurs again in Angelo's house, and again the chief combatants are Angelo versus Isabella. The reader will recall that Isabella
was told to visit Angelo on the morrow; this is that morrow. Angelo
enters delivering a soliloquy (his second in the play): he is frustrated
because his prayers were not sincere; the swelling evil of lust kept rising in his heart, and his successes as a ruler he would gladly change for
the idle plumes of the lover; how even the wise are made fools of by
false appearances; how blood (sexual passion) will win out over goodness: "Let's write good angel (note the pun on his own name) on the
devil's horn; / 'Tis not the devil's crest."

When Isabella is announced, the blood surges to Angelo's heart as he confesses; such is true, he observes, of crowds who surge to help a victim, or storm in foolish adoration around a king (note: Shakespeare's habit of philosophizing, even at the height of tense moments; this is a Renaissance proclivity). Isabella enters saying she has come "to know your pleasure," to which Angelo replies that he would be pleased if she did know his pleasure (pun: know = to learn, to have intercourse). At the news that Claudio must die she turns to leave in resignation but urges Angelo to save his soul (Isabella naturally would find the soul more worth saving than the corrupt body). Now Angelo denounces sexual vices again, comparing sexual criminals to murderers; it is all as easy as counterfeiting coins he says. Isabella denies this parallel as being true on earth, even if true in heaven. Angelo quickly seizes upon this defense of sexual vice on earth (she has done this also in their previous interview) to pose a question: "Which had you rather, that the most just law / Now took your brother's life; or, to redeem him, / Give up your body to such sweet uncleanness / As she that he hath stain'd?" Isabella's answer: "Sir, believe this, / I had rather give my body than my soul." But it is not her soul he is talking of says Angelo; besides, sins we do under compulsion ("compell'd") are less serious than those done freely: "Might there not be a charity in sin / To save this brother's life?" Isabella, not understanding his lewd suggestions, says it is no sin to beg for her brother's life, or, if so, she could bear it easily. Frustrated and annoyed, Angelo says she does not get his meaning ("Your sense pursues not mine"); either she is a fool or she is playing a crafty game. He is accusing her of hypocritical "seeming" and compares her to those "black masks / (which) Proclaim an enshield (protected) beauty ten times louder / Than beauty could, display'd," the sense of which is that a masked beauty suggests a beauty ten times more lovely concealed beneath the mask than an openly displayed beauty.

Angelo repeats that her brother is to die but goes on to ask her what would she do if some powerful person could unfetter the manacles on her brother with the proviso that she lay down the treasures of her body to him. She'd gladly be whipped to death ("The impression of keen whips I'd wear as rubies, / And strip myself to death") before consenting to such a shameful proposition: "Better," she says, "it were a brother died at once (physical death) / Than that a sister, by redeeming him, / Should die for ever (death of the soul)." Angelo points out that she is as cruel as the law which condemns her brother. Lawful mercy is not to be compared to foul and evil ransom of the body, is her immediate reply. His counter-argument in this ethics debate is clever: she has called the law tyrannical and her brother's crime nothing but a casual slip (she is contradicting herself). Her lame excuse is that she spoke without thinking, in heat: "I sometimes do excuse the thing I hate, / For his advantage that I dearly love." She did it in her brother's interest and really wasn't being sincere. In reply to Angelo's comment that all are frail in matters of the flesh, she says women are as frail as the mirrors into which they constantly gaze and their sexual virtues as easily broken by men who themselves violate their own divinity by exploiting women: "For we are soft as our complexions are, / And credulous to false prints (easily swayed by false appearances)." From your own testimony on the weakness of women, says Angelo, put on their inner frailty of sex ("the destined livery") and add that to your outer evidence of feminine charm.

Now comes the climactic ending of a great confrontation scene. Angelo puts his proposal in bald terms: "Plainly conceive, I love you." Her brother will not die if she give her love to him. When she expresses disbelief, he assures her it is true: "My words express my purpose." Isabella' s outcry rises to the rafters: "Seeming, seeming! / I will proclaim thee, Angelo; look for 't; / Sign me a present pardon for my brother, / Or with an outstretch'd throat I'll tell the world aloud / What man thou art." His reply to this scream is sharp: who will believe her? His virtue is well known, his reputation high, his power great; she herself will be the only one hurt by such a charge: "I have begun / And now I give my sensual race (sex instinct) the rein: / Fit thy consent to my sharp appetite (sex desires); / Lay by all nicety and prolixious (stupidly delaying) blushes, / That banish what they sue for; redeem thy brother / By yielding up thy body to my will." Should she not yield — her brother dies! Demanding her answer by tomorrow, he stalks out of the room. Isabella in soliloquy cries out against mouths with double tongues ("seeming" again!) that use the law to bow to their will and sexual appetites. She'll hasten to her brother, who, she is absolutely sure, will gladly yield up twenty heads to the executioner's block before he'd allow his sister's body to be polluted. "Then, Isabella, live chaste, and, brother, die: / More than our brother is our chastity. / I'll tell him yet of Angelo's request, / And fit his mind to death, for his soul's rest." These are Isabella's last words as the scene ends.

Act III: Scene 1

The scene, like that of Act II, Scene 3, is a prison cell. The chief protagonists are the Duke, Claudio, and Isabella, and the interest centers on the brother-sister confrontation. The disguised Duke-Friar enters Claudio's prison cell accompanied by the Provost. When Claudio says he has hope to live but is prepared to die, the Duke prepares him for death in a long speech (5-41). Duke: Life and death will be "sweeter" if you concentrate on being cleansed of sin.

> Reason thus with life:
> If I do lose thee, I do lose a thing
> That none but fools would keep: a breath thou art,
> Servile (subject to) all the skyey influences,
> That dost this habitation, where thou keep'st,
> Hourly afflict (i.e., astrology): merely (only this),
>   thou art death's fool;
> For him thou labour'st by thy flight to shun
> And yet runn'st toward him still.

In paraphrase the above quote reads: think on life as trivial, worthwhile only to fools. Man is a puff of air subject to the whims of heaven, a toy of death himself from whom you attempt to flee but merely succeed in running faster toward him. Vincentio continues to preach that Claudio is not really of noble blood since all his comforts and conveniences (accommodations) spring from earthly lowness. Neither is Claudio valiant since he fears the bite of the worm after death. His best rest is sleep, and yet he fears death which is exactly like sleep. He is not really flesh but born from dust; he is not happy because he always wants more, soon forgetting what he already owns. He is not steadfast and reliable, since his temperament changes constantly like the constantly changing shape of the moon. If Claudio is rich, this is not really so, for, like the jackass laden with spoil, he carries his load of wealth but for a short journey only, until death strikes and unloads him of the burden. He has no friends, for his own guts, his born children so to speak, constantly afflict and curse him for bringing in diseases to annoy them; hence they too crave his death:

> Thou hast nor youth nor age,
> But, as it were, an after-dinner's sleep,
> Dreaming on both; for all thy blessed youth
> Becomes as aged, and both beg the alms
> Of palsied eld (tottering old age); and when thou
>   art old and rich,
> Thou hast neither heat, affection (passion, love),
>   limb, nor beauty,

> To make the riches pleasant. What's yet in this
> That bears the name of life? Yet in this life
> Lie hid moe (more) thousand deaths: yet death we fear,
> That makes these odds all even.

In short, youth is short and rich old age is corpse-like, worse than a thousand deaths. Death need not be feared since it will, like a blessing, even the odds.

To this Claudio gives humble thanks: "To sue to live, I find I seek to die; / And, seeking death, find life: let it come on." In short, Claudio agrees that death is the only real life.

Isabella now enters, the Duke leaving only to eavesdrop on the sister and brother interview. This scene between Claudio and Isabella begins by Claudio's eagerly asking whether she brings him comforting news. Yes, she says, she brings comforting news indeed: Lord Angelo, having angelic business in heaven, intends Claudio to be his ambassador in heaven; he should therefore prepare himself speedily, for his new job begins tomorrow.

Again Claudio asks whether she brings comfort (remedy), and she admits there is "none, but such remedy as, to save a head, / To cleave a heart in twain"; at his insistence she reluctantly relates the Duke's proposal; however, for 37 lines we get the following:

Claudio can live and be free, but he will actually be fettered until death, she hints darkly. Should Claudio consent he would find himself in the world's great vastness still in "prison." Should he consent, he would strip himself of all family honor. Claudio, by now exasperated, cries: "Let me know the point."

Isabella, feeling apprehensive, fears that Claudio is hesitating to die, preferring six or seven more years of life to "perpetual" honor. She adds:

> Darest thou die?
> The sense of death is most in apprehension;
> And the poor beetle, that we tread upon,
> In corporal sufferance (body pain) finds a pang as great
> As when a giant dies.

That is, death is only made fearful by our sense of imagination.

When Claudio feels ashamed and resolves to encounter death (darkness) "as a bride" and hug it in his arms, Isabella shows approval: "There spake my brother"; yet, she adds, he must die since he is too noble to save his life through ignoble means ("appliances"). This "outward-sainted deputy" who preys on the folly of youth, she says, is a devil whose filth of evil is hidden like a dark pond. Angelo, like a cunning, hellish devil, wears the uniform of a "prenzie" guard (nobleman? scholars are in doubt as to the meaning of *prenzie*) to hide his inner evil. It is at this point that Isabella comes out with the sex-trade proposal of Angelo's.

Claudio's first reaction is one of disbelief. "O heavens! it cannot be" and "Thou shalt not do't." In reply Isabella says she would readily give her life for him, and Claudio sincerely thanks her. He adds in question whether Angelo has feeling in himself to renovate obsolete laws on fornication, which if it is a deadly sin, is surely the least of them. And as for Angelo, why would he risk eternal burning in hell for a momentary sexual pleasure? "Death," he adds, "is a fearful thing" to which Isabel counters with, "And shamed life a hateful (thing)." Now follows one of the most often quoted of Shakespearean speeches on death uttered by Claudio with quivering apprehension:

> Ay, but to die, and go we know not where;
> To lie in cold obstruction (lifeless corpse) and to rot;
> This sensible (sensitive) warm motion (warm living
>   body) to become
> A kneaded clod; and the delighted (once happy) spirit
> To bathe in fiery floods, or to reside
> In thrilling (shivering) region of thick-ribbed ice;
> To be imprison'd in the viewless winds,
> And blown with restless violence round about
> The pendent world; or to be worse than worst
> Of those that lawless and incertain thought
> Imagine howling? 'tis too horrible!
> The weariest and most loathed worldly life
> That age, ache, penury and imprisonment
> Can lay on nature is a paradise
> To what we fear of death.

The consensus of the above speech is a picture of the soul's torture in a Catholic Hell. Claudio sees his spirit drowned in fiery lakes, locked in ice, blown about by invisible (viewless) winds. The most miserable life

on earth is better by far than the fear of death. Isabella's rejoinder is
scathing in its denunciation of his cowardly vacillation. She calls him a
beast, a coward, a dishonest wretch who will choose life from her sin:
"Is't not a kind of incest, to take life / From thine own sister's shame?"
Claudio cannot be the son of her father, who could not have borne such
a perverse and worthless ("warped slip") son. She cries for him to die,
that she would not even bend down to save him now: "I'll pray a thousand prayers for thy death, / No word to save thee." His sin asks for
no mercy, since such an act of mercy would be vile, like pimping for a
sinful sex-monger. "'Tis best that thou diest quickly."

Now the Duke, who has overheard the entire colloquy, enters to speak
to the desperate Claudio. He tells him that he had overheard the interview
and assures him that Angelo had never intended to really go through
with the "bargain"; it was merely suggested to make a test ("assay")
of her virtue and to test his own power to read character ("to practise
his judgment with the disposition of natures"). Angelo was actually glad
she had spurned his offer, says the Duke, who as confessor to Angelo,
knew all. Therefore, he tells Claudio, "prepare yourself for death." The
contrite Claudio begs to be allowed to ask his sister pardon; he is now
willing to die again. The Duke calls for the warden only to tell him to
leave him alone with Isabella who is still there, off to one side.

The remainder of the scene is prose. The Duke tells Isabella that she is
good, fair, and virtuous. He tells her he knows of Angelo's indecent
proposal (incidentally, Isabella did not hear what the Duke has just said
to Claudio); he has known of others like Angelo, but yet it is surprising.
He poses a question: How will she satisfy the Deputy ("substitute") and
still save her brother? She declares she is going to tell all to the Duke
when he comes back to town (Remember, the Duke is disguised). She
would rather have a dead brother than a live bastard. Saying that the
Deputy will deny her charge and declare he was merely testing her, the
Duke-Friar offers a scheme, a scheme offered out of the goodness of
his heart ("the love I have in doing good"). These are the rewards of
the scheme: it will, if followed and agreed to by Isabella, do good to
"a poor, wronged lady"; it will save her brother; it will preserve her
virginity; it "will much please" the absent Duke, should he ever return.
Isabella agrees to do anything so long as it is not a foul deed. The Duke's
scheme: there is a girl named Mariana, a sister of a great soldier Frederick, who had died at sea. She was to have married Angelo at one time;
indeed, they were engaged and the wedding date set when news came of
Frederick's death. With him went the dowry that was to have been settled

upon the couple. Angelo then deserted his almost-bride, pretending the reason was unfaithfulness on Mariana's part. He left her in great grief ("bestowed her on her own lamentation") and she grieves yet; and he does not relent in his coldness to her. Isabella sympathetically interrupts the scheming Duke to say that death were best for the tragic Mariana and the corrupt Angelo. The Duke continues with his scheme: Mariana still loves Angelo even more passionately than before. Now Isabella is to go to Angelo and seem to agree to his "trade," making only a few minor conditions:

That the stay in bed together be not too long.

That the place be dark and quiet.

That the place be conveniently secret.

This will be granted her; meanwhile the Duke will substitute Mariana for Isabella (the well-known "bed-trick" in which another girl slips into bed with a lover who fondly believes that the original girl who made the date with him is the one next to him in bed. The same "bed-trick" occurs in Shakespeare's *All's Well That Ends Well*). The result is, if the trick works, that Angelo will have done his duty by Mariana, Claudio will be saved from execution, Isabella's virginity will remain untainted and unbroken, "and the corrupt deputy scaled" (revenged upon). The Duke adds that he will now go to Mariana's to prepare her for her part in the trick. If Isabella does her part, the double benefit accruing "defends the deceit from reproof" (prevents the act of deceit from being termed shameful). Isabella heartily assents, and the Duke-Friar urges her to hasten to Angelo and promise to cooperate in the sex-Claudio trade.

Meanwhile the Duke will be off to St. Luke's (a town?) where at "the moated grange" (farm with a moat) resides the dejected Mariana. They bid each other farewell as the scene ends.

Act III: Scene 2

Scene 2 takes place on the street before the prison and is in two parts: first, Elbow, the Duke, and Pompey, and second, the Duke and Lucio (mainly). The disguised Duke enters to see that Elbow has again arrested Pompey for pandering. Elbow complains that if Pompey continues pimping, everyone soon will be drinking sweet Spanish bastard (pun: wine = illegitimate children). Pompey's defense against the charge of pimping is that of two usuries (moneylending and pimping): the merriest was suppressed (pimping) while the worst (usury) allowed by law to flourish (London's moneylenders preyed on many people, especially playwrights; they were dressed in characteristic furred [with fox and lambskin] gowns reaching to the floor). Elbow informs the Duke that Pompey is also a thief, caught redhanded with a picklock in his pocket. The Duke passionately sermonizes to Pompey: You live by causing evil through pimping ("a bawd"). Think closely how you live by means of sexual beastliness. Can you really believe you are really living when your livelihood depends upon stinking sex? Before the bawd can answer the charge, the Friar hastens him off to jail: "Correction and instruction must both work / Ere this rude beast will profit." Elbow adds the information that the Deputy cannot stand a whoremonger and whoremaster (good, clean words in Shakespeare's day). The Duke's reply is garbled in manuscript and hence unclear. Elbow, who loves a pun as well as any comic, says: "His (Pompey's) neck will come to your waist, — a cord, sir." (Pompey will be hanged; cord: hanging rope = rope around Friar's waist.) At this point Lucio enters.

Lucio's first speech is a bewildering array of bawdy. Slangy, casual, and crammed with puns and obscene allusions: "How, now, noble Pompey! What, at the wheels of Caesar? art thou led in triumph?" (Translation: Julius Caesar did defeat Pompey; the custom was to parade the bound victim, while the victor smiled in triumph from his chariot; also, it was the custom to parade bawds and prostitutes down London streets while tied to carts and whipped.). "What, is there none of Pygmalion's images, newly made woman, to be had now, for putting the hand in the pocket and and extracting it clutched?" Translation: In the Greek myth Pygmalion wished that a statue he had fallen in love with (a female nude) would come alive (it did); also, possibly a reference to a very erotic poem entitled "Metamorphosis of Pygmalion's Image (1598)" ordered burned because of obscenity. The "hand in the pocket," etc. is very likely a reference to an obscene action of a prostitute as well as a reference to Pompey's financial take from the sale of sex. Lucio continues taunting Pompey, even calling him an old slut ("trot"). Pompey's reply to Lucio's inquiry about his "dear morsel," the bawdyhouse madam, Mistress Overdone, is to say merely that she has eaten up "all her beef and she is herself in the tub" (overdone = overcooked beef = overdone sexually; tub = pot for cooking = tub for sweat-treatment for victims of venereal disease). Lucio's "ever your fresh whore and your powdered bawd" refers to the practice of salting the venereal tubs; but also *salt* means lascivious, lecherous. Lucio's "you will turn good husband now, Pompey; you will keep the house" means that Pompey is a thrifty household manager, that (by extension) he is a pervert also. Lucio's parting jeers to poor Pompey include a refusal to go bail for Pompey, a wish to increase his bondage in jail, a wish he be more in mettle (mettle: courage = metal irons, or shackles). Pompey is led off stage to jail by Elbow. Lucio is left with the Duke-Friar.

Lucio hails the "Friar" and asks news of the absent Duke. Lucio calls the Duke's sneaking away from his post "a mad fantastical trick of him to steal from the state, and usurp the beggary he was never born to" (to undertake a trick unusual for a Duke). Lucio adds that the Deputy is "Dukeing" it with a vengeance (hard on violators of the law). The Deputy is a little too severe on lechery; lechery is human and "it is impossible to extirp (wipe it out) it quite, friar, till eating and drinking be put down," says Lucio, making an observation made twice before by others. Lucio tells of the rumor that Angelo was born of a sea-maid mermaid); "some, that he was begot between two stock-fishes. But it is certain that when he makes water his urine is congealed ice," a kind of live puppet (two dried codfish begot Angelo — i.e., two stock-fishes; motion = puppet). Lucio then exclaims: "Why what a ruthless thing is this in him, for the rebellion of a codpiece (Elizabethan man's fly = male sex organ) to take away the life of a man!" The absent Duke would never have acted in this way; he never would have hanged a man had he produced a hundred bastards; he was a merciful Duke with some "feeling for the sport" (took pleasure in sex himself). The Duke-Friar defends himself saying the Duke was not inclined that way. But Lucio persists: the Duke put money in the cups of old female beggars (a ducat in her clack-dish = possible obscene allusion?), and he was often drunk too. More than that he (Lucio) knew that the Duke was not as wise as the people thought, but a "very superficial, ignorant, unweighing (thoughtless) fellow."

The Friar's defense of himself to Lucio rises in pitch: Lucio is either envious, stupid, or mistaken. The Duke is known as a scholar, a soldier, and a statesman. And if ever the Duke returns, Lucio is to tell him to his face what he has just told the Friar, who threatens to report this to the Duke. When Lucio brags he is not afraid of the Friar, the disguised Duke replies that Lucio hopes the Duke will not return; or else he thinks the Friar a rather harmless opponent ("too unhurtful an opposite"); the Friar hopes that Lucio will take back (forswear) his slanders, but Lucio says he'll be hanged first. Lucio then abruptly changes the subject and asks whether Claudio will die tomorrow. The Friar asks why should Claudio die; Lucio's reply is brilliant: all Claudio did was fit a funnel (tun-dish) into a bottle and fill it (obscene pun). This sexless Deputy will soon "unpeople the province with continency"; even sparrows are too lecherous for Angelo, and poor Claudio is condemned for "untrussing" (unbuttoning). The good Duke eats mutton on Fridays (violates fast = cohabits with prostitutes), and even would make love with a beggar, "though she smelt (of) brown bread and garlic: say that I said so. Farewell," and Lucio makes his exit. In soliloquy the Duke bitterly comments on how even the great are slandered, no matter how virtuous they have been. "What king so strong / Can tie the gall (bitter slander) up in the slanderous tongue?"

Here enter Escalus, the Provost and Officers with Mistress Overdone in tow. She has been three times warned and still violates the law. "This would make mercy swear and play the tyrant (even the most merciful person would have to be severe with her)." The Provost points out she has an eleven-year record, to which Overdone replies that Lucio has "squealed" on her so she'll inform them that Lucio has a bastard (a good word in Shakespeare's day) by Kate Keepdown (an obscene pun again), a child over a year old. He too had promised to marry her and had reneged. Escalus hails Overdone off to jail and asks for the arrest of Lucio, the "fellow of much license." The officers take Overdone away. The Duke-Friar is introduced to Escalus as the one who has prepared Claudio for death. The Duke tells a gentle white lie that he is in Vienna on special business from the Pope. In answer to Escalus' request for news abroad, the Friar replies that people seek constantly after change and novelty: "There is scarce truth alive to make societies secure; but security enough to make fellowships accurst: much upon this riddle runs the wisdom of the world" (people cooperate just enough to harm each other; there is just enough honesty and virtue in the world to barely keep the world intact); this news is constantly old and new. The Duke then inquires after himself and (unlike Lucio) Escalus has only praise for his virtue. Escalus also hears that Claudio is bravely resigned to death, to which Escalus replies that he has done the best he can for Claudio, but in vain: "my brother justice have I found so severe, that he hath forced me to tell him he is indeed Justice" (note the capitalization for stark justice without mercy). The Duke in soliloquy speaks in dog trot verse now (the effect is almost comic): the Duke delivers a rhymed oration in couplets on knowing one's self before judging others, and shame on the judge who kills for faults he himself possesses! "Twice treble shame on Angelo, / To weed my vice and let his grow!" The Duke closes by denouncing hypocrisy again and goes off to work out his scheme, and the scene ends.

Act IV: Scene 1

The scene is a country house at St. Luke's surrounded by a water-filled trench ("moated grange"). The scene is a short one (75 lines) broken in two parts: a boy singing to Mariana, and the second, Mariana conversing with Isabella and the Duke-Friar. The second opens with the boy singing a lovely song:

> Take, O, take those lips away,
> That so sweetly were forsworn;
> And those eyes, the break of day,
> Lights that do mislead (the eyes mislead one
>   into thinking the morn has already arrived) the morn:
> But my kisses bring again, bring again;
> Seals of love, but seal'd in vain, seal'd in vain.

The lips that "seal" are both kissing lips and the lips that seal a promise, but one which is later broken. The boy stops singing and leaves as the Duke, disguised as a Friar, enters. He begs pardon ("cry you mercy, sir") of the boy for interrupting him, explaining that the music, "my mirth it much displeased, but pleased my woe"; which means the music has removed his present bitterness and replaced it with a pleasant sorrow. Music often has the power "to make bad good, and good provoke to harm," which means, in terms of Renaissance theories on the psychological effects of music, that music can have harmful effects because of its direct effect upon the emotions. Isabella enters now and the Duke craves Mariana's forbearance to leave them alone for a while. They have made an appointment here. The Friar's first question is of the Deputy's reaction to their scheme. Isabella tells him that there is a garden surrounded ("circummured") by a brick wall with a wooden door to which she has a large key, and another smaller door to which she has a smaller key. At midnight she is to meet Angelo in the garden. She assures the Friar she has memorized the way there. Angelo has promised her that she could bring a servant along to wait for her. The Friar, saying Mariana knows nothing yet, calls for her to come forth. Mariana is introduced to Isabella and the two girls exit so that Isabella can acquaint Mariana with the details of the Duke's bed-trick and the role Mariana is to play. They re-enter soon, and Mariana is more than willing to play the substitute bed-partner. Mariana is urged to talk little except to say, when about to leave, "Remember now my brother." The country girl assures the Duke she will not fail in her role, and the scene ends with a justification: "He is your husband on a pre-contract: (see Act I, Scene 2 above) To bring you thus together, 'tis no sin." Her rights in Angelo make the trick a justifiable one ("flourish the deceit").

Act IV: Scene 2

This scene takes place again in prison, a longish scene with the Provost, Pompey, Abhorson, Claudio, Duke. The Provost asks Pompey whether he can cut off a man's head and after an adolescent joke by Pompey, the Provost explains that the executioner needs an assistant; if Pompey accepts, he will be freed of his chains ("gyves"). Pompey gladly accepts and the executioner Abhorson (ab HOAR sun) is called for. He is told to apprentice the bawd for one year, and the shocked and bloody-handed (they cut off heads with one blow of the ax, and if successful, obtain the victim's clothes) executioner complains that a bawd "will discredit our mystery" (trade). Pompey can't resist a pun on *favor* (help, face) and *mystery* (trade, unknown): "whores, sir, being members of my occupation, using painting, do prove my occupation a mystery"; Abhorson replies with a heavy-handed joke. Here the warden re-enters and is told that Pompey accepts the new job; he in turn tells Abhorson to get his ax and block ready for four o'clock tomorrow. Pompey's final thrust: "I do desire to learn, sir: and I hope, if you have occasion to use me for your own turn (that is, use me to cut off your head), you shall find me yare (ready); for truly, sir, for your kindness I owe you a good turn." Here Pompey and Abhorson exit.

Claudio enters and is handed his death warrant by the Provost, who states that the time is "eight to-morrow" for his execution.

Prov. Where's Barnadine?

Claud. As fast (deeply) lock'd up in sleep as guiltless labour / When it lies starkly (stiffly) in the traveller's bones: / He will not wake.

Knocking is heard and the Duke-Friar enters, asking after Isabella and Claudio. When the Provost calls the Deputy cruel ("bitter"), the Friar denies it, saying that Angelo is suppressing sex because he himself is pure: "were he meal'd (stained) with that / Which he corrects, then

were he tyrannous." After a compliment on the gentle Provost a great
noise of knocking is heard. At the re-entry of the warden the Duke hints
there might be some hope for the doomed Claudio, even though no
pardon ("countermand") is dimly in sight from the inflexible Angelo.
The messenger who had knocked so violently finally enters.

The messenger carries a paper which the Duke believes is a pardon from
the now contrite Angelo. Instead, the message calls for Claudio's execution by four o'clock "and in the afternoon Barnardine"; Claudio's
severed head is to be delivered to Angelo by five. The Duke is told
that Barnardine, a prisoner for nine years, has been nine years in getting
reprieves from execution. But with Angelo now in office, his execution
is certain. Vincentio asks whether Barnardine has been penitent.

Prov. A man that apprehends (fears) death no more dreadfully but as
a drunken sleep; careless (without worry), reckless, and fearless of
what's past, present, or to come; insensible of mortality (no fear of
death), and desperately mortal (no hope of afterlife).

Nor will Barnardine listen to advice; he has no desire to escape and
wouldn't if he could; drunk "many times a day, if not many days entirely drunk" with no fear of execution orders.

After a compliment to his own boldness in cunning, the Duke suggests
that Barnardine's execution replace Claudio's and his (Barnardine's) head
be carried to Angelo. If the head is shaved and the beard dyed, Angelo
won't know the difference. The Provost refuses until the Duke shows
him the "hand and seal of the duke" (a letter) stating the Duke's return
in two days; Angelo, however, has received news of the Duke's death,
or perhaps his entrance into a monastery (we are to assume the letter
convinced the Provost). The morning star is already shining, so the
warden is told to call Abhorson to cut off Bernardine's head; but not
before the Friar can give him the last rites preparing him for the next
world, however. The scene ends with the dumbfounded Provost gaping in
amazement.

Act IV: Scene 3

This scene is also in prison with much the same effect and purpose as
the previous scene. First Pompey is in soliloquy, then Abhorson, Barnardine, and the Duke all speaking in prose. Then in blank verse is the
more serious part with the Provost, Duke, Isabella and Lucio. Pompey

feels at home in prison since it is packed with Overdone's customers: Master Rash in for non-payment of debt owed to a hard-fisted usurer (moneylender); Master Caper, in jail and now denounced ("peached") for a beggar, and Dizy, Deep-Vow, Copper-spur, Starvelackey, who affected the upper-class rapier and dagger instead of the good old native English sword and buckler, etc., "all great doers in our trade, and are now 'for the Lord's sake' (the cry of prisoners for alms from passersby)." Abhorson enters now and Barnardine is called for; Pompey: "Master Barnardine! you must rise and be hanged, Master Barnardine!" (Barnardine is offstage.)

Bar. Away, you rogue, away! I am sleepy.

Abhor. Tell him he must awake, and that quickly too.

Pom. Pray, Master Barnardine, awake till you are executed, and sleep afterwards.

Barnardine rustles his straw and comes roaring that he has been drinking all night and is not fitted for hanging. The witty Pompey replies: "O, the better, sir; for he that drinks all night, and is hanged betimes (early) in the morning, may sleep the sounder all the next day." The disguised Duke enters to give Barnardine absolution for his sins, but the unregenerate sinner declines the offer saying he has been drinking all night and requires more time, else they shall have to beat his brains out first: "I will not consent to die this day, that's certain"; he will not die today for "any man's persuasion"; to the Duke's protesting "But hear you" he says scornfully, "Not a word: if you have any thing to say to me, come to my ward; for thence will not I today" and he stalks off stage back to his cell. Says the Duke in disgust: "Unfit to live or die: O gravel (stony) heart! After him, fellows; bring him to the block." Pompey and Abhorson hurry off to fetch him back.

The next section among the Duke, warden, and Isabella is in blank verse. The Provost has conveniently found another prisoner just executed ("One Ragozine, a most notorious pirate"), who resembles Claudio and suggests substituting the pirate's head for Claudio's. Angelo won't know the difference, Claudio will be saved, and Barnardine "must die this afternoon." In addition, the nervous Provost is assured by the Duke that within two days he will be safe from Angelo's wrath, should he discover the trick. The pirate's head is ordered sent to Angelo. The Duke prepares letters to be sent to Angelo announcing his impending arrival in Vienna and telling the Deputy to meet him at the fountain a league (about three miles) below the city, and thence, "By cold gradation and well-balanced form" (without emotion and in good order) he'll soon take care of the Deputy.

The Provost enters with the pirate's head (on a plate like the Baptist's or by the hair like Holofernes?) and hastens off to take it to Angelo. Isabella enters to inquire whether her brother had been pardoned and is told instead that he was executed. The furious Isabella threatens to pluck out the Deputy's eyes but is dissuaded by the Duke. He tells her the Duke comes home tomorrow, as he was told this by another Friar, "And you shall have your bosom (desire) on this wretch, / Grace of the duke, revenges to your heart, and general honour." Isabella's reply is simply, "I am directed by you." He then hands her a letter to give to Friar Peter saying he wants to meet the Friar at Mariana's house that night. It will be the Friar Peter who will accuse Angelo publicly, since Vincentio says he'll be absent from the "trial" of Angelo.

Lucio enters to say that he is pale from sighing at the sight of Isabella's red eyes: "By my troth, Isabel, I loved thy brother: if the old fantastical duke of dark corners had been at home, he had lived." Isabella exits, and Lucio begins again abusing the Duke (who of course is the man he is talking to) by saying he knows the Duke better than the Friar: "he's a better woodman (pun: hunter of animals, of women) than thou takest him for." He even offers to tell "pretty tales" of the Duke, mentioning his own appearance before him by getting a wench with child, which sexual act he denied: "they would else have married me to the rotten medlar (an apple which when mature seems rotten inside). The Duke, offended, bids him farewell, but Lucio offers to accompany him, even apologizing for his bawdy talk. As they walk off, the scene ends.

Act IV: Scene 4

In Angelo's house the Deputy and Escalus are talking about the Duke's contradictory letters to them. Angelo calls him mad; why deliver their authority at the gates? Why the city-wide proclamation for all those with petitions also to show up? Escalus defends that order (on petition proclamation); it is to clear the air of complaints. Angelo alone in soliloquy tells how he has become shaken and dull of intellect from his "date" with Isabella in the garden (really Mariana). He feels guilt over the deflowering of a maid, "And by an eminent body that enforced / The law against it!" How the maid could cry out against him, if it were not for her shame! His reputation for virtue is known everywhere, and his power is such that no one would dare accuse him. Claudio should have lived, but he might have wreaked revenge for his sister; hence, he had to be killed. The scene ends with Angelo's bad conscience showing: "Would he had lived! Alack, when once our grace we have forgot, / Nothing goes right: we could, and we would not."

Act IV: Scene 5

The Duke, without his disguise, instructs Friar Peter on what to do in the showdown scene, and also tells him the Provost is in on the scheme. Peter is sent out to notify various people to help form a cortege for the Duke when he marches to the city gates. Varrius enters and is thanked for his help. Exeunt (they leave).

Act IV: Scene 6

Isabella and Mariana near the city gate are conversing. Isabella tells how the Friar-Duke had told her to make the accusation in public before Angelo. She is loath to do so, but knows that the Duke has some veiled reason for it. She is not to think it strange when at the "trial" the Duke takes up the cudgels against her, "for 'tis a physic (remedy) / That's bitter to sweet end." Friar Peter enters, announcing the arrival of the Duke's cortege, a parade for which the citizens have thronged about the city gates to see. Exeunt.

Act V: Scene 1

The scene is the city gate, the grand showdown scene. The Duke is enthroned, ready to listen to petitioners for aid or favors. We see him pleasantly greeting Escalus and Angelo. "My very worthy cousin, fairly met! / Our old and faithful friend, we are glad to see you." The Duke tells that he had enquired how they had done in his absence and had heard "such goodness of your justice" that he must render public thanks. To Angelo's protest that the Duke make his bonds (of gratitude) still greater, Vincentio replies:

O, your desert (merit *or* deserving) speaks loud;
    and I should wrong it,
To lock it in the wards of covert bosom (to lock it
        deep in the recesses of the heart),
When it deserves with characters (letters) of brass,
A forted (fortified) residence 'gainst the tooth of time
And razure (wiping out) of oblivion.

The Duke asks for Angelo's hand so that the citizens will see that outward show of courtesies indicates the favor felt within. Here Friar Peter
and Isabella come forward from the crowd. At the Friar's urging that the
time is now ripe, Isabella rushes forward to kneel before the Duke. She
calls for justice upon "a wrong'd, I would fain have said, a maid!" She
begs him to hear her and give her "justice, justice, justice!" The Duke
ironically suggests she reveal herself to Lord Angelo who will give her
justice. With loathing, Isabella replies: "You bid me seek redemption of
the devil," and begs the Duke to hear her story: "Hear me, O hear me,
here!" Angelo quickly interrupts to call her crazy from his having
turned her down in her brother's cause; this is why she speaks so bitterly
and strangely. Isabella's gorge rises:

    That Angelo's forsworn (broken his oath); is't not strange?
    That Angelo's a murderer; is't not strange?
    That Angelo is an adulterous thief,
    An hypocrite, a virgin-violator;
    Is it not strange and strange?

Strangely, the Duke calls for the poor soul to be taken away since she
is obviously mad (the "infirmity of sense"). Isabella denies the charge of
madness: "the wicked'st caitiff (villain) on the ground, / May seem as
shy as grave, as just, as absolute / As Angelo." The Duke finds her
madness has a logical coherence beneath it that belies madness. Isabella
asks that the Duke use his reason to uncover the hidden truth and
banish the phony truth of "seeming" falsity. Isabella gives her story
with the somewhat comic aid of Lucio (who is told to shut up until his
turn comes): how Angelo repelled her prayers, how he set a bargain ("to
his concupiscible [lustful] intemperate lust"), how she eventually
yielded to him, and finally, how Angelo had broken his bargain by still
demanding Claudio's head. The Duke treats her story with contempt
("This is most likely," i.e., a likely story) calling her "fond wretch"
(fond = foolish) who doesn't know what she is saying; or else she has
conspired to defame Angelo. The good Deputy is one whose "integrity

stands without blemish"; Angelo is above such pernicious actions: "Some one hath set you on" (she is someone's tool). The Duke ends by telling her to confess she is a tool of some crook. Isabella appeals to the blessed ministers above, crying for self-patience to wait for the time when the present evil will be exposed. The Duke pretending fury calls for an officer to haul her off to prison. He will not let the breath of scandal smear his good colleague Angelo. He again asks for her "putter-on," and Isabella replies, "One that I would were here, Friar Lodowick (the disguised Duke's Friar-name)." "A ghostly (a ghost = a spiritual; a pun) father, belike (no doubt)," and Vincentio asks if anyone here knows the Friar Lodowick. Lucio knows, calling him "a meddling friar" whom he would have swinged (whipped) thoroughly for "certain words he spake against your grace." The Duke calls for this villainous friar to be found. Lucio adds that he had seen her and the friar together at the prison, "a saucy friar, / A very scurvy fellow." At this point the good Friar Peter interrupts to protest these lies. Isabella's charges against Angelo are lies — Angelo "who is as free from touch or soil with her / As she from one ungot (unborn)." As for Friar Lodowick, adds Peter, he is divine, holy, one who never did misreport the Duke. Lucio is a liar, and in time Lodowick will come to clear himself, but not now since he is ill of a strange fever. Peter then explains that he is here at Lodowick's request to uncover the truth. Soon enough, when his witness is summoned, he will clear up all this mess. First, Isabella has vulgarly and wrongfully accused the worthy Lord Angelo; soon she will be forced to confess when his witness turns up. (Here Isabella is carried off by the guards).

Mariana now steps forward wearing a veil. Vincentio tells her to show her face and then speak. He also tells the Deputy to act as judge on this case. She refuses to unveil until her husband bid her; and yet, as she goes on, she reveals she is neither maid (virgin), widow, nor wife! This gives the vulgar Lucio a chance to call her a punk (prostitute) then, "for many of them are neither maid, widow, nor wife." For the second time the Duke is forced to shut Lucio up. Mariana in turn is driven into a set of paradoxes in explaining her case: "I am no maid: / I have known my husband; yet my husband / Knows not that ever he knew me" (knows = the sexual act; see the King James Bible for the same use of this term). Lucio cannot resist another crack at this, and he is again shut up. Mariana goes on with her story: Isabella's charge is wrong since she herself (Mariana) was in bed wtih Angelo at the very time Isabella claims he had possessed her. Angelo believes he never "knew" Mariana's body, and is under the impression he had "known"

Isabella's. When Angelo asks her to remove her veil, she promptly does so, since, as she so archly puts it, it is her husband who has bidden her to do so:

> *Mari:* This is that face, thou cruel Angelo,
> Which once thou sworest was worth the looking on;
> This is the hand which, with a vow'd contract,
> Was fast (tightly) belock'd in thine; this is the body
> That took away the match from Isabel,
> And did supply thee at thy garden-house
> In her imagined person.

Angelo confesses he does recognize Mariana and admits that some five years ago there was "some speech of marriage" which was broken off, partly because her promised dowry had become much smaller, and partly because (this the chief reason) her reputation "was disvalued in levity" (jokes about her purity). Since then he has not seen, heard, or touched her, and this Angelo swears to. Mariana swears to the complete truth of her statements, and if not true, let her forever be as marble in a monument. Angelo, as the Duke previously, calls the women informal (without form or composure) instruments of some "more mightier member / That sets them on: let me have way, my lord, / To find this practice out (to root out this conspiracy)." The Duke readily consents and begins to denounce the foolish Friar Peter and the pernicious Mariana as being in league with the absent Isabella. Does she (Mariana) really think her oaths that sounded so saintly could impugn the worth and credit of the virtuous Angelo? The Duke again calls for the conspiratorial Friar; the Friar Peter agrees that the absent Friar did urge "the women on to this complaint"; the Provost knows where the Friar stays and could fetch him to the city gate. Here the Provost is told to fetch the Friar Lodowick. The Duke tells Angelo to exact stern justice while he (Vincentio) must leave him temporarily, and he exits. Escalus now addresses himself to Lucio: "Lucio, did not you say you knew that Friar Lodowick to be a dishonest person?" Lucio replies that Lodowick was honest in nothing but his clothes and quotes a bit of Latin: " '*Cucullus non facit monachum.*' " (a cowl doesn't make a monk); he adds that the Friar spoke "most villainous speeches of the duke." Escalus: "we shall find this friar a notable fellow (notable = important, full of knowledge, evil)." Lucio agreeing in the last sense (of outstanding evil) adds, "As any in Vienna, on my word." Isabella is called for again, and Escalus begs leave of Angelo to question her: "You shall see how I'll handle her." Lucio with another crack about how she would sooner confess, if she were handled privately (pun: secretly, her private parts).

Escalus says he'll speak to Isabella in private ("darkly to work with her"), and the irrepressible Lucio congratulates him, "for women are light (sexy) at midnight (pun: light = to give light, to be sexy)."

Isabella is brought in by the officers, and at the same time enters the Provost, escorting the Friar Lodowick, whom he was sent out to fetch a while ago. Lucio. as usual. refers to Lodowick as a "rascal," whereupon he is again shushed by Escalus. The Friar Lodowick is charged with having set the women on, as Isabella and Mariana have themselves admitted. The Friar calls the charges false and asks for the Duke: "'tis he should hear me speak." Escalus tells him to speak; his authority is vested in himself and Angelo. The Friar calls the girls "poor souls" who have come to seek justice (the lamb) of the fox (Angelo). He adds that with the Duke gone their cause is also gone. The good Friar even calls Vincentio unjust for leaving the issue in the hands of Angelo: "And put your trial in the villain's mouth / Which here you come to accuse." Escalus now angry tells the unreverend and "unhallow'd" Friar to be taken to the torture rack to be torn joint from joint (touse = tear) until he confesses. Escalus finds the Friar guilty of suborning the girls to slander the good Angelo. The Friar replies:

> Be not so hot; the duke
> Dare no more stretch this finger of mine than he
> Dare rack his own: his subject am I not,
> Nor here provincial (subject to a certain province).
> My business in this state
> Made me a looked on here in Vienna,
> Where I have seen corruption boil and bubble
> Till it o'er-run the stew (pun: food boiling =
> houses of prostitution); laws for all faults,
> But faults so countenanced (tolerated), that the
>   strong statutes
> Stand like forfeits (necklaces of human teeth
>   in barber shops where tooth extracting was
>   also done) in a barber's shop,
> As much in mock (mockery) as mark (in evidence).

The furious Escalus cries, "Slander to the state! Away with him to prison!" At this point Lucio is asked to identify the Friar Lodowick as the man he had seen with Isabella. Lucio does so calling him "goodman baldpate" (a reference to a bald spot. tonsure, worn by all friars in those days), and asking him whether the Friar had not said to him that the

Duke was a "fleshmonger, a fool, and a coward." On the contrary, says Lodowick, you "spoke so of him; and much more, much worse."

> *Lucio.* O thou damnable fellow! Did not I pluck thee
> by the nose for thy speeches?
> *Duke.* I protest I love the duke as I love myself.

Angelo thinks that with this remark the Friar is trying to back down from his charges; Escalus calls for the guards to take him to prison and "Away with those giglots (loose women) too, and with the other confederate companion!" The Duke resists the Provost, but Lucio, getting violently abusive, says:

> Come, sir; come, sir; come, sir; foh, sir! Why you
> bald-pated, lying rascal, you must be hooded,
> must you? Show your knave's visage, with a pox
> (venereal disease) to you! show your sheep-
> biting face, and be hanged an hour (within an
> hour)! Will't not off?

And Lucio pulls off the hood from the Friar's head and face, and Duke Vincentio stands revealed before the entire crowd!

The first thing the Duke says is, "Thou (to Lucio) art the first knave that e'er madest a duke." His next move is to tell the Provost to release the three prisoners (Friar Peter, Isabella, Mariana). Lucio, who is sneaking guiltily away, is seized by officers at the Duke's order. To Escalus his first words are a kind pardon for his abuse of the Duke; to Angelo his demand is for an explanation: "Hast thou or word, or wit, or impudence, / That yet can do thee office (do you some service)?" Angelo immediately confesses because, as he says, he would be guiltier than his own crimes, if he did not immediately recognize that the Duke, "your grace, like power divine, / Hath look'd upon my passes (conduct) . . . Immediate sentence then and sequent (to follow) death / Is all the grace (mercy) I beg." Angelo is told to marry Mariana instantly with Friar Peter officiating. The couple is then to be hurried back into the Duke's presence. Isabella is gently told to come forward: "Your friar is now your prince"; he has not changed his heart with his habit; he will advise ("advertise") and guide her still. Isabella begs pardon for the trouble she has caused to the man she did not know was the Duke. The Duke graciously and immediately pardons her, but in turn begs her pardon for not having saved Claudio's life; he had tried but had arrived too late to save him from the executioner's ax: "But peace be with him! / That life is better life, past fearing death, / Than that which lives to fear: make it your comfort, / So happy is your brother." Isabella's reply is a simple, "I do, my lord." Here Angelo, Mariana, Friar Peter, and the Provost re-enter the scene. The Duke's first words are for the new-married Angelo "whose salt imagination (lustful desires)" had wronged Isabella's "well defended honor"; but since Angelo had committed a double crime, against chastity and breach of promise (his promise to spare Claudio), why then:

> The very mercy of the law cries out
> Most audible, even from his proper tongue,
> "Angelo for Claudio, death for death!"
> Haste still pays haste, and leisure answers leisure;
> Like doth quit (repay) like, and MEASURE STILL
>   FOR MEASURE.

Angelo then is paid in his own coin and condemned to the very block "Where Claudio stoop'd to death, and with like haste. Away with him!" The Duke explains to the protesting Mariana that her honor is saved by marriage to Angelo; and besides after the Deputy's death she is to get all his goods "To buy you a better husband."

Mari. O my dear lord, / I crave no other, nor no better man.

The Duke is relentless even before the kneeling, pleading Mariana, who then pleads with the sweet Isabella to take her part: "Lend me your knees, and all my life to come / I'll lend you all my life to do you service." The Duke replies rightly that should Isabella plead for Angelo's life "Her brother's ghost his paved (covered over) bed would break, / And take her hence in horror." Mariana adds that even the best men are made so through error, and such may be true of her husband. The gentle Isabella kneels alongside Mariana saying that the Duke should judge Angelo as if her brother were not dead. In addition, Angelo had been sincere until he had seen her: "My brother had but justice, / In that he did the thing for which he died." But Angelo's act was different from his intention: "Thoughts are no subjects; / Intents but merely thoughts (that is, one's intentions cannot be as criminal as the deed itself)." The poor Provost comes in for a scolding. He had accepted the word of a private message rather than a special warrant from the Duke in his execution of Claudio. He is told to give up his keys (his job). The good Provost begs pardon and tells of Barnardine whom he had spared in spite of execution orders.

The Duke asks the jailer to fetch Barnardine. Escalus turns to Angelo and laments how such a learned and wise man "should slip so grossly, both in heat of blood, / And lack of temper'd judgment afterward."

> *Ang.* I am sorry that such sorrow I procure:
> And so deep sticks it in my penitent heart
> That I crave death more willingly than mercy;
> 'Tis my deserving, and I do entreat it.

We are now ready for the curtain. The Duke, Escalus, Angelo, Mariana, Isabella and the rest stare at the muffled and mysterious figure who is escorted into the scene along with the notorious Barnardine and Juliet. The Duke addresses Barnardine:

> Sirrah, thou art said to have a stubborn soul,
> That apprehends no further than this world,
> And squarest (you regulate) thy life according.
>   Thou'rt condemn'd:
> But for those earthly faults, I quit them all;
> And pray thee take this mercy to provide
> For better times to come.

Then the Duke turns to the muffled figure and asks, "What muffled fellow's that?" In a dramatic gesture the Provost uncovers Claudio saying he is another prisoner as "like almost to Claudio as himself." The Duke plays along with the good jailer's joke and pardons the prisoner for Claudio's sake. Turning to Isabella he asks for her hand in marriage for her lovely sake, which request he will pursue at some fitter time. To Angelo he says ". . . your evil quits (rewards) you well: / Look that you love your wife; her worth worth yours." The Duke explains he is in a pardoning and forgiving mood. From Lucio he wrathfully wants to know why he had been so slandered, and why had Lucio treated the Duke in this way.

> *Lucio.* Faith, my lord, I spoke it but according to the trick. If you will hang me for it, you may; but I had rather it would please you I might be whipt.
> *Duke.* Whipt first, sir, and hanged after.

The Duke tells the Provost to find any woman wronged by Lucio, and if found he is to wed her and then to be whipped and hanged. Lucio begs not to be wedded to a whore: "Your highness said even now, I made

110

you a duke: good my lord, do not recompense me in making me a cuckold."

The forgiving Duke remits the whipping and hanging, pardons Lucio's slanders; however, the wedding to the whore he has wronged stands. (Mistress Kate Keepdown, the punk (whore) who bears Lucio's child; see Act III, Scene 2, line 210).

Lucio. Marrying a punk, my lord, is pressing to death, whipping, and hanging (pressing to death = killed by placing weights on chest).
Duke. Slandering a prince deserves it.

Lucio is carried off to jail. The Duke's final curtain speech settles so many issues at once that it would be more economical to quote it in full:

> See Claudio, that you wrong'd, look you restore.
> Joy to you, Mariana! Love her, Angelo:
> I have confess'd her and I know her virtue.
> Thanks good friend Escalus for thy much goodness:
> There's more behind that is more gratulate (gratifying).
> Thanks, provost, for thy care and secrecy:
> We shall employ thee in a worthier place.
> Forgive him, Angelo, that brought you home
> The head of Ragozine for Claudio's:
> The offence pardons itself. Dear Isabel,
> I have a motion (desire) much imports your good;
> Whereto if you'll a willing ear incline,
> What's mine is yours and what is yours is mine.
> So, bring us to our palace; where we'll show
> What's yet behind, that's meet (proper) you all should know.

The curtain falls as the actors make their exit. END.

The Merchant of Venice

THE DUKE OF VENICE.
THE PRINCE OF MOROCCO
THE PRINCE OF ARRAGON } *suitors to Portia.*
ANTONIO, *a merchant of Venice.*
BASSSANIO, *his friend, suitor likewise to Portia.*
SOLANIO
SALERIO } *friends to Antonio and Bassanio.*
GRATIANO
LORENZO, *in love with Jessica.*
SHYLOCK, *a rich Jew.*
TUBAL, *a Jew, his friend.*
LAUNCELOT GOBBO, *the clown, servant to Shylock.*
OLD GOBBO, *father to Launcelot.*
LEONARDO, *servant to Bassanio.*
BALTHASAR
STEPHANO } *servants to Portia.*

PORTIA, *a rich heiress.*
NERISSA, *her waiting maid.*
JESSICA, *daughter to Shylock.*

MAGNIFICOES *of Venice*, OFFICERS, JAILER, SERVANTS, *and other* ATTENDANTS.

The Merchant of Venice

Act I: Scene 1

The scene is a street in Venice. Antonio, a prominent merchant, is talking with his friends Salarino and Salanio. He tells them that he does not know why he is so sad nowadays, and that his sadness wearies him as much as it wearies them.

Antonio's companions think that he must be worried about business, since he has several ships out on the ocean where anything might happen to them. Salanio tells Antonio, "Believe me, sir, had I such venture forth,/ The better part of my affections would / Be with my hopes abroad." He says that he would be constantly plucking the grass to test the wind's direction, and peering into maps to chart the routes of his vessels. Salarino pursues this train of thought, declaring that he, for his part, would connect every part of his experience with the thought of possible dangers to his ships. Thus, his breath cooling his broth would make him worry about storms at sea; sand running through an hour glass would remind him that ships can founder on dangerous sandbars; and the stone walls of a church would make him think of the treacherous rocks in the sea.

Antonio denies that he is melancholy because of business. Not all his fortune is invested at one time and, moreover all his capital is not entrusted in a single ship. It is hardly likely that several vessels will come to a bad end simultaneously. Salanio declares that if is not business it must be love that troubles Antonio, but the merchant denies any romantic attachment. With this explanation ruled out, Salanio falls back on the inexplicable ways of Nature, who has made some strange fellows in her time. The best he can say is that Antonio is sad because he is not merry, which, of course, is not to say anything at all.

Three more gentlemen enter, Bassanio, Lorenzo, and Gratiano. Salarino and Salanio leave the newcomers to cheer up Antonio if they can, but before they depart they assure Bassanio that they will be delighted to

114

make merry in his company whenever he is available. When they have gone, Gratiano remarks that Antonio is not looking well, and chides the merchant for worrying too much about worldly matters. Antonio denies this charge, declaring, "I hold the world but as the world, Gratiano / A stage where every man must play a part, / And mine a sad one." Gratiano replies that he, for his part, prefers to play the role of the fool, always gay and laughing. He says that he would rather have his liver heated with wine than his heart cold as the marble on a tomb. (Sixteenth-century psychology held that the liver as well as the heart played a part in emotional life.) From this remark about his own predisposition, Gratiano goes on to criticize those men who keep up an appearance of gravity and silence in order to impress the world with their profundity, as if he thought that Antonio were only pretending to be melancholy.

Lorenzo declares that by associating with the loquacious Gratiano he is afraid he will gain the reputation of the kind of false wise man of whom Gratiano was speaking, for he can never get a word in edgewise as long as Gratiano is around. While Gratiano accepts this rebuke with good humor, Antonio promises to make an effort to talk more. The comical Gratiano is happy to hear this, declaring that silence is only commendable in a dried ox's tail and in an unmarriageable girl.

Lorenzo and Gratiano depart, promising to meet Bassanio for supper. When they have gone, Bassanio declares that "Gratiano speaks an infinite deal of nothing, more than any man in all Venice." His reasons are as obscure as two grains of wheat hid in two bushels of chaff, and worth just as little.

Antonio asks Bassanio to tell him now, as he promised he would, about that lady "To whom you swore a secret pilgrimage." Instead of answering directly, Bassanio talks about the state of his own finances. He reminds Antonio that because he squandered his fortune and lived beyond his means in his youth, he is now heavily in debt, and chiefly to Antonio, his friend and kinsman. Bassanio is deeply distressed at being unable to repay this debt, but now he has an idea of how to win a new fortune. Antonio begs to know how he may be of service to Bassanio and assures him that "My purse, my person, my extremest means / Lie all unlocked to your occasions."

Bassanio hesitates to divulge his plan. By way of introduction he tells Antonio how, when he was a boy, he often lost an arrow by carelessly shooting it without looking to see which way it went. When this happened, he sometimes managed to retrieve the arrow by firing another after it in the same direction, but this time keeping careful watch on its flight. In any case, if he did not find the first arrow, at least he did not lose the second. Turning to the matter at hand, he tells Antonio, "I owe you much, and like a willful youth / That which I owe is lost; but if you please / To shoot another arrow that self way / Which you did shoot the first, I do not doubt, / As I will watch the aim, or to find both / Or bring your latter hazard back again / And thankfully rest debtor for the first."

Antonio chides his friend for this elaborate preparation and tells Bassanio that there is nothing he would not do for him. Thus encouraged, Bassanio reverts to the subject of the lady, which is how their conversation started. He tells Antonio that "In Belmont is a lady richly left;/ And she is fair, and fairer than that word,/ Of wondrous virtues." This lady is Portia, whom Bassanio met some time ago in Belmont and from whose eyes he received "fair speechless messages" that she would not be averse to his suit. Like the Portia of Ancient Rome (daughter of Cato and wife of Brutus), she is an extraordinary woman. Suitors flock to her from all over the world, just as the mythological heroes sought the Golden Fleece. (In Greek mythology the Golden Fleece on the island of Colchis was a precious object for which many men went in quest. Jason finally obtained it after overcoming great danger.) Bassanio tells Antonio that he is sure that if he had the means to return to Belmont he, like Jason, would win the prize so many men seek.

Antonio immediately agrees to help his friend, but, with several ships at sea, he does not have the necessary cash on hand. He therefore asks Bassanio to find someone who will lend the money on the basis of Antonio's.

Act I: Scene 2

The scene is Belmont. Portia and her waiting woman, Nerissa, are talking. "By my troth, Nerissa, my little body is aweary of this great world," sighs Portia, but Nerissa, instead of commiserating with her mistress, declares that Portia's unhappiness can only be the result of an overabundance of good fortune. It is a fact, she says, that superfluity can be as oppressive as insufficiency: "they are as sick that surfeit with too much as they that starve with nothing." The ideal in all things is the mean between two extremes. Portia approves of these "Good sentences and well pronounced," but regrets that it is easier to give good advice than to follow it. I can easier teach twenty what were good to be done," she declares, "than to be one of the twenty to follow mine own teaching. The brain may devise laws for the blood, but a hot temper leaps o'er a cold decree."

The knowledge that one *ought* to be happy is never the same as actually *being* happy, which Portia says she is not. And the reason that she is not happy becomes clear when she adds that all this talk will not serve to choose her a husband. After all, she sighs, it is not up to her to choose a husband for herself. According to her father's instructions laid down just before he died, suitors for her hand must choose which of three caskets contains her picture. Portia finds it hard to bear that she is "curbed by the will of a dead father," that she may neither accept nor refuse any man on the basis of her own inclination, but Nerissa consoles her with the assurance that dying men often have good inspirations. She tells Portia that her father must have devised the lottery in such a way that only a man truly worthy of her would be able to choose correctly.

Nerissa questions Portia about her feelings towards the numerous suitors who have already presented themselves in Belmont and, while she acknowledges that "it is a sin to be a mocker," Portia takes the opportunity to poke fun at them one by one. First there is the Neapolitan prince, who talks of nothing but his horse and of his own expertize in shoeing him. Portia gaily wonders if perhaps "my lady his mother played false with a smith." Next there is the County (Count) Palatine, whose particular characteristic is a perpetual frown. Since he never smiles now in his youth, Portia concludes that he will undoubtedly be "the weeping philosopher when he grows old." She declares she would rather be married to "a death's head with a bone in his mouth than to either of these."

The Neapolitan and the Palatine are Italian noblemen. The next four suitors are French, English, Scottish, and German. Of the Frenchman Portia declares, I know God made him, and therefore let him pass for a man," but she thinks he has no character at all, for he changes mood and behavior from minute to minute. As for the Englishman, Portia cannot really judge, because he knows neither Latin, French, nor Italian (all of which, presumably, she does know), and she has only a smattering of English. Consequently, they cannot carry on any sort of conversation. His appearance, however, she finds decidely peculiar, for he looks as if he bought his coat in Italy, his breeches in France, his hat in Germany, and "his behavior everywhere." The Scottish lord is not worth much comment. Portia merely remarks mockingly that he seems to be generous, for when the Englishman gave him a box on the ear he swore he would pay him back. Finally, as for the German, Portia makes fun of his love of drink, but declares she dislikes him as much in the morning, when he is sober, as in the evening, when he is drunk."

When Portia has run through the list, Nerissa comforts her with the news that she need not fear marrying any of these gentlemen, who have all decided to return home rather than risk the condition imposed by her father's will on all her suitors. (This condition, we will later learn, is that before he may choose among the caskets, each suitor must swear that if he chooses wrongly he will never seek to marry another woman).

Portia, is delighted to hear this, and says. "There is not one among them but I dote on his very absence."

Nerissa asks if Portia remembers one man in particular, "a Venetian, a scholar, and a soldier," who came to visit during her father's lifetime. This man, declares the maid, seemed more deserving than any other of winning a fair lady. Portia does indeed remember him; his name is Bassanio, and he did seem worthy of all praise. At this moment a messenger enters with news that the current batch of suitors is departing and that the Prince of Morocco will arrive shortly as a new suitor. The lady of Belmont wishes she could feel as happy to see the new suitor arrive as she is glad to see the old ones leave.

Act I: Scene 3

The scene is back in Venice. Bassanio has found Shylock, a Jewish moneylender, and is seeking to borrow three thousand ducats for three months, for which Antonio will be bound. As Bassanio tells him the sum of money required and the length of time. Shylock repeats the words in a noncommittal fashion: "Three thousand ducats, well . . . For three months, well . . . Antonio shall become bound, well." Pressed for a decision by Bassanio, who is becoming impatient, the moneylender finally says, "Antonio is a good man." Bassanio, evidently thinking that Shylock uses the word "good" in its moral sense, asks indignantly if he has heard anything to the contrary about his friend, but Shylock assures him that by "good" he simply meant that Antonio has good credit. However, continues Shylock, Antonio is not a very safe risk, since his fortune is bound up in commercial ventures at sea, which is not entirely safe, for "ships are but boards, sailors but men; there be land rats and water rats, water thieves and land thieves—I mean pirates" (pun on pie rats). On the whole, however, Shylock decides that Antonio is sufficient, but he insists on speaking to the merchant himself.

Bassanio invites Shylock to meet Antonio at dinner, a suggestion that Shylock takes very badly. "Yes," he says sarcastically, "to smell pork, to eat of the habitation which your prophet the Nazarite conjured the devil into." He declares that he will do business with Christians, walk with them, talk with them, but he refuses to eat with them, drink with them, or pray with them.

Just at this moment along comes Antonio himself, and Shylock, noticing him out of the corner of his eye, expresses in an aside (that merchant looks like a "fawning publican. "I hate him for he is a Christian; / But more, for that in low simplicity/ He lends out money gratis and brings down/ The rate of usance here with us in Venice. / If I can catch him once upon the hip,/ I will feed fat the ancient grudge I bear him." Shylock goes on to say that Antonio "hates our sacred nation," and concludes, "Cursed be my tribe/ If I forgive him."

While speaking to the audience in an aside, Shylock pretends that he has not seen Antonio but has been thinking about how he can raise the necessary sum of money. He looks up from his revery and says that, although he does not have the ready cash, his friend Tubal can supply the rest, so there will be no problem. Suddenly he notices Antonio (who has been standing there for several minutes) and greets him in sycophantic terms, addressing him as "Your worship," and saying, "Rest you fair, good signoir./ Your worship was the last man in our mouths."

Antonio does not beat around the bush with Shylock but goes directly to the point. Although as a rule he neither lends nor borrows money at interest, he is ready to break his custom in this case in order to help a friend. Shylock justifies his financial practices by citing the story from the Book of Genesis (30:31-43) in the Bible of how Jacob dealt with his uncle Laban. It was agreed between the two men that when Laban's flocks gave birth, Jacob would take as his wages all the multicolored lambs, leaving the solid colored lambs for Laban. While the rams and ewes were mating, however, Jacob used a special magic device to make sure that all the lambs would be spotted and speckled, and in this way he got the best of the bargain. Shylock approves of Jacob's apparent cunning, and declares, "This was a way to thrive, and he was blest;/ And thrift is blessing if men steal it not." Antonio declares that it was beyond Jacob's power to determine the color of lambs before conception, and that their complexion was the work of God, not man. He does not see that this story will justify the practice of usury, and Shylock answers simply that he can make money breed as fast as rams and ewes (which is comic). Antonio remarks to Bassanio apropos of this discussion that "The devil can cite Scripture for his purpose," for Shylock hides his villainous deeds behind the holy words of the Bible, whose meaning he distorts. "O, what a goodly outside falsehood hath!" Antonio observes.

Returning to the matter at hand, Antonio asks Shylock, who has been computing the rate of interest, whether or not he will supply the money. For answer Shylock complains in a long and bitter speech about the hostile and contemptuous way that Antonio has long treated him in public. "In the Rialto you have rated me . . . you call me misbeliever, cutthroat dog, /And spit upon my Jewish gaberdine, / And all for use of that which is mine own." After such words and such treatment, says Shylock, is there any reason why he should be courteous and obliging? "Hath a dog money?" Shylock asks. Is it not too ironical for him to whisper humbly, "Fair sir, you spit on me on Wednesday last, / You spurned me such a day, another time / You called me dog; and for these courtesies / I'll lend you thus much moneys?"

Antonio replies that he is just as likely to call Shylock dog again and to spurn him again. He tells the moneylender that although he holds Antonio as an enemy, Shylock may still lend him money for his own profit. Friends do not charge interest (which Antonio calls "a breed for barren metal"). It is better to lend money at interest to an enemy, in any case, for then one may exact the penalty later with "better face."

After Antonio's outburst Shylock suddenly changes his tone, and declares that he wants to be friends with Antonio, to forget the past, and to supply the three thousand ducats at no interest. "This is kind I offer." Bassanio, suspicious, exclaims "This were kindness," and Shylock goes on to explain that all they need to do is accompany him to a notary to sign a bond "in merry sport" that if Antonio does not repay three thousand ducats in three months he will forfeit a pound of flesh, to be cut off and taken from what part of his body pleases Shylock. Antonio agrees to sign such a bond, "And say there is much kindness in the Jew," but Bassanio is appalled at the proposed condition. Antonio reassures him that the bond will not be forfeited, since his ships will certainly return well before three months with three times the value of the bond. Shylock declares that the bond is just a kind of joke, since he could make no profit from a pound of human flesh, as he would from a pound of mutton or beef or goat flesh. These Christians, he says, suspect the intentions of others because of their own hard hearts. He insists that he is doing this as a favor and in friendship, and says, "for my love I pray you wrong me not." These words settle the matter for Antonio. They agree to meet at the notary's, where Antonio will give instruction for the bond to be drawn up. Shylock returns home to get the money and to check up on his household left in the care of his servant, "an unthrifty knave." When the Jew has left, Antonio cheerfully tells Bassanio, "The Hebrew will turn Christian; he grows kind," but Bassanio, who distrusts Shylock, answers, "I like not fair terms and a villain's mind." Antonio, however, certain that his ships will come home a month before the bond is due, refuses to be dismayed.

Act II: Scene 1

Back in Belmont, the Prince of Morocco (described in the stage directions as a "tawny Moor all in white") is pressing his suit to Portia. He explains that his skin is dark because of the climate of his country and hopes that she will not object to him on that account. The blood that runs in his veins, he assures her, is redder than that of "the fairest creatures northward born," and the most beautiful ladies of Morocco are in love with him. Therefore, he would not change the color of his skin except in order to win Portia's favor.

Portia, for her part, declares that she is bound to abide by her father's order regarding the caskets irrespective of her inclinations. However, she tells him that if the choice were hers to make she would not be led by superficial matters of appearance, and that he would be as likely a choice as any suitor who has yet come to Belmont.

The Prince thanks her for these words and says he is ready to be led to the caskets to make his choice. He only wishes that his fortune depended on his courage rather than on mere luck (it depends on neither), for he swears that in order to win Portia he would stare down the sternest eyes, outbrave the most daring heart, steal cubs from a she-bear, or mock an angry lion (yet he refuses to hazard the leaden box). He brags about having slain the Shah of Persia as well as a Persian prince and about having won three victories over the Sultan Solyman. However, the fact remains that he must take his chance with the caskets, and before doing so, he must go to the temple to swear that if he chooses wrongly, he will never again ask a lady to marry him. The Prince, Portia, and the others go off to the temple.

Act II: Scene 2

The scene is Venice once again. Launcelot Gobbo (the servant whom Shylock, in Act One, Scene Three, called an "unthrifty knave"), enters alone. He is debating with himself whether or not to run away from his master, whom he cannot abide. On the one hand the devil tempts him to leave Shylock, and on the other hand his conscience bids him remain. "Well, my conscience says, 'Launcelot, budge not.' 'Budge,' says the fiend. 'Budge not,' says my conscience." The irony of the situation, says Launcelot, is that conscience counsels him to remain with the Jew, who is a kind of devil, whereas the devil himself bids him run from the Jew. After thinking it over, he decides that "The fiend gives the more friendly counsel. I will run, fiend; my heels are at your commandent; I will run."

At this moment of resolution, Old Gobbo, Launcelot's father, enters, coming from far away to see his son after a long time. Because he is almost totally blind, Gobbo does not recognize his son, and asks him for directions to Shylock's house. The playful Launcelot decides to have some fun with the old man for a while and gives him confusing direction which will cause him to turn and turn and turn. When the old man asks if Launcelot lives there, his son asks if he means "Master Launcelot," but Gobbo says Launcelot is "No master, sir, but a poor man's son." The clown insists they are talking of "Master Launcelot," and the old man maintains it is plain and simple Launcelot. Finally his son says that Master Launcelot is dead. Gobbo is stunned by this piece of news; he says that the boy was the prop and staff of his old age, which causes Launcelot to query the audience, "Do I look like a cudgel?"

At this point Lancelot decides to reveal his true identity. For a while he has a hard time convincing Gobbo, who cannot believe that this young man is really his son. However, Launcelot insists, "I am Launcelot—your boy that was, your son that is, and your child that shall be," and when he wins his point, for old Gobbo acknowledges him as his much-changed son with "what a beard thou got." He tells Launcelot that he has brought a present for Shylock, but the clown objects. "Give him a present?" he asks indignantly. Better "Give him a halter! I am famished in his service." Launcelot tells his father that he is determined to leave Shylock's service and to seek employment with Bassanio, who gives wonderful new liveries to his servants. He asks his father to give the present to Bassanio, whose service he wants to enter (for he is anxious to leave the Jew before he becomes one himself). Just at this moment, as luck would have it, along comes Bassanio in person.

Bassanio enters, accompanied by servants. He asks one of them to make sure that supper will be ready by five o'clock, to do some other errands, and to fetch Gratiano, for Bassanio is preparing to sail for Belmont shortly. Launcelot urges his father to go up to Basanio to request a position for his son. They approach Bassanio, but every time that old Gobbo starts to speak his son interrupts him to explain the situation in his own way. In this fashion and using a number of malapropisms, the two men talk and talk, but Bassanio can make nothing of their meaning. Old Gobbo gives him the present originally intended for Shylock (a dish of doves), and when Bassanio finally understands the nature of the request, he readily agrees to take Launcelot into his service, for Shylock (who had called Launcelot an "unthrifty knave") had unwittingly recommended his servant. Launcelot, for his part, states his preference for working with a Christian who had "the grace of God," rather than the Jew who simply has "enough" (in terms of worldly goods). Bassanio tells the clown to bid his old master farewell and orders that he be given a suit of livery more highly decorated than those of the other servants.

Launcelot is greatly pleased with his success. Looking at the palm of his hand, he pretends to read there a very satisfactory future for himself. "Here's a small trifle of wives! Alas, fifteen wives is nothing; a 'leven widows and nine maids is a small coming-in for one man. And then to scape drowning thrice." In great glee he goes off with his father to take leave of Shylock.

Bassanio gives some final orders to a servant named Leonardo concerning a feast that he will give tonight for his best friends. As Leonardo goes off, Gratiano appears and announces that he has a request. Without the least hesitation and without knowing what the request may be, Bassanio immediately replies, "You have obtained it." Gratiano then explains that he wants to go along to Belmont. Bassanio agrees, but asks his friend to moderate "with some cold drops of modesty" his "skipping spirit," lest his wild behavior give the wrong impression in Belmont of Bassanio's character. Gratiano readily agrees to put on a sober and pious expression and to act with utmost decorum. For this night, however, it is agreed that he will put on his "boldest suit of mirth," for there will be great merriment among the friends who will visit Bassanio at suppertime.

Act II: Scene 3

Launcelot has come to Shylock's house to say goodby to his former master. Jessica, the Jew's daughter, is there alone. She is very sorry that he is leaving. "Our house is hell," she declares, "and thou a merry devil / Didst rob it of some taste of tediousness." In parting she gives him a ducat and asks him to deliver a letter secretly to Lorenzo, who will be at Bassanio's house. Launcelot tearfully parts with her, calling her "most beautiful pagan, most sweet Jew!" He already suspects that a Christian (Lorenzo) has won her heart.

Launcelot leaves and Jessica, left alone, wonders what "heinous sin" it is that she is ashamed to be her father's child. Although she is his daughter by blood, she is completely alien to his way. She is secretly engaged to Lorenzo and, thinking of him, she swears aloud, "if thou keep promise, I shall end this strife, Become a Christian and thy loving wife!"

Act II: Scene 4

Lorenzo, Gratiano, Salarino, and Salanio are making plans for the evening's masque. Gratiano complains that they have not made good preparation, and Salanio declares that it is better not to have any masque at all unless it is "Quaintly ordered." Lorenzo assures his friends that two hours are sufficient time for them to find torchbearers.

Launcelot arrives with Jessica's letter for Lorenzo, who immediately recognizes the fair handwriting. The clown is on his way to "bid my old master the Jew to sup to-night with my new master the Christian." (We already know that Bassanio plans to feast all his best acquaintance this evening.) Lorenzo gives Launcelot some money and asks him to assure

Jessica that he will come by on time, for she is to be his torchbearer in disguise this evening.

Salarino and Salanio exit with Launcelot. Lorenzo, left alone with Gratiano, reveals the plan for his elopement with Jessica that night. Jessica has a page's suit in which she will dress up, and she will take with her gold and jewels from her father's house when she leaves. "If e'er the Jew her father come to heaven, / It will be for his gentle daughter's sake."

Act II: Scene 5

Launcelot has found Shylock just about to enter his house. The Jew warns his former servant that in Bassanio's service "Thou shalt not gormandize / As thou hast done with me," nor sleep and snore all day long. While saying this he has been calling his daughter, but when Launcelot comically echoes Shylock's call for Jessica, Shylock reproves him. "Who bids thee call? I do not bid thee call." And Launcelot remembers that Shylock always told him not to do anything without bidding.

Jessica enters and Shylock gives her his keys, saying that he is going out for supper. He broods about going. "I am not bid for love—they flatter me—/ And yet I'll go in hate to feed upon / The prodigal Christian." He is vaguely uneasy and counsels his daughter to "Look to my house," for last night he dreamt of money-bags, which he superstitiously construes as a bad omen.

Launcelot urges Shylock to go to the dinner. "My young master doth expect your reproach," he says (mistaking the word "reproach" for "approach"). Shylock answers, "So do I his," (meaning "reproach" in its true sense. Parodying Shylock's omen, Launcelot prophesies that there will be a masque, which does not please Shylock at all. He bids Jessica to shut up all the casements of the house when she hears the drum and the "wry-necked fife," and not to look upon "Christian fools with varnished faces." He tells her, "Let not the sound of shallow fopp'ry enter / My sober house." Launcelot leaves, whispering cryptically to Jessica to be on the lookout for a Christian "worth a Jew's eye," that is, Lorenzo. Shylock doesn't catch what he says but asks his daughter, "What says that fool of Hagar's offspring" (that is, outcast), and she replies that he merely had said farewell. Her father declares that Launcelot is kind enough but that he eats too much and sleeps by day, which makes him an unprofitable sort of servant. Shylock is glad that the clown will now help to waste Bassanio's money. Before he departs, Shylock sends Jessica inside and bids her lock the doors: "Fast bind, fast find—/ A proverb never stale in thrifty mind."

Act II: Scene 6

Gratiano and Salarino, disguised for the masque, are waiting for Lorenzo in front of Shylock's house. Gratiano marvels that Lorenzo is so late for a love rendezvous since lovers usually "run before the clock." But Salarino reflects that lovers hasten more when they make a promise than when they must keep it. Gratiano agrees, supporting his thought with the proverbial ideas that the man who sits down eagerly to a feast rises satiated; the horse that first races down a path returns wearily, and the ship that sets out gaily decked like a prodigal son returns again weather-beaten and "beggared by the strumpet wind." Cynically, Gratiano concludes, "All things that are / Are with more spirit chased than enjoyed."

At this moment, Lorenzo appears, apologizing for having been detained by business. He calls up to the window where Jessica appears, dressed in boy's clothing. She recognizes his voice but makes him identify himself anyway. He declares he is "Lorenzo and thy love," and she replies that he is her love, indeed, but is she his? Lorenzo reassures her. Jessica gives Lorenzo the casket she has stolen from her father and expresses embarrassment at being seen in boy's clothes. She objects to bearing Lorenzo's torch, for it will light her shames. Lorenzo assures her that no one will guess her true identity under her boy's disguise. When Jessica leaves the window to collect some more ducats, Gratiano praises her as "a gentile and no Jew," and Lorenzo swears he will love her in his "constant soul," for she is wise and fair and true. Jessica reappears on the street below, and they all exit.

Antonio finds Gratiano and tells him that the masque has been called off, for the wind has changed and the voyagers must board the ship tonight. Gratiano says he is delighted to be able to leave at once.

Act II: Scene 7

Back in Belmont, the Prince of Morocco is about to choose among the three caskets in the presence of Portia and others. The Prince looks over the inscriptions on each casket to determine which one contains Portia's picture. The lead casket reads, "Who chooseth me must give and hazard all he hath." This blunt warning does not appeal to the Prince, who will "hazard" for "fair advantages," not for mere lead. The inscription on the silver casket reads, "Who chooseth me shall get as much as he deserves." The Prince ponders this carefully: "weigh thy value with an even hand," he warns himself. "Rated" by his own "estimation," he deserves the lady by reason of his birth, breeding, fortune, and most of all by reason of the great love he bears her. Turning to the gold casket, however, he reads: "Who chooseth me shall gain what many men desire," and suddenly the puzzle seems very clear to him. What many men desire is the lady, for suitors undeterred by arduous voyages through the desert or over the ocean have come from all over the world to seek her. It would be sacrilege to put her picture in a lead or silver casket instead of a gold one. He recalls that in England there is a golden "coin" with the figure of an angel engraved on it. Here is an angel (Portia) lying on a golden bed (the casket). "Here I choose, and thrive I as I may."

Deciding to unlock the gold casket, the Prince is horrified to discover a picture of Death with a message written in his hollow eye: "All that glisters is not gold; / Often have you heard that told. / Many a man his life hath sold / But my outside to behold. / Gilded tombs do worms enfold." With a grieving heart the Prince takes a hasty leave of Portia, who is quite content to see the last of him, saying, "A gentle riddance . . . / Let all of his complexion choose me so."

Act II: Scene 8

In Venice once again, Salanio and Salarino are talking about recent events, particularly Shylock's reaction to the news that his daughter has run off with Lorenzo and has taken with her money and jewels of great value. Salarino explains that since Bassanio sailed for Belmont the same night that Lorenzo and Jessica eloped, Shylock suspected that the lovers were aboard the same ship. He brought the Duke of Venice down to the dock to search for them. But by the time they arrived it was too late, the ship was already gone. Furthermore, Antonio was there and swore that the lovers were not aboard, and the Duke learned from another source that Lorenzo and Jessica had been seen together in a gondola. Salarino is certain that Lorenzo is not on Bassanio's ship.

Salanio declares, "I never heard a passion so confused, / So strange, outrageous, and so variable / As the dog Jew did utter in the streets: / 'My daughter! O my ducats! O my daughter! / Fled with a Christian: . . . And jewels—two stones, two rich and precious stones, / Stol'n by my daughter! Justice! find the girl! / She hath the stones upon her. . . .'" Salarino adds with enjoyment that all the boys of Venice now follow Shylock, "crying his stones, his daughter, and his ducats."

Salanio recalls Antonio's debt next, and ominously remarks that Antonio will be made to pay for Shylock's loss if he does not meet his bond on time. To which Salarino adds that he had been thinking of Antonio's bond only yesterday, while listening to a report of a Venetian ship that had foundered in the English Channel; he had hoped it was not Antonio's ship.

The two men agree to be gentle in breaking the news of the sunken Venetian vessel to Antonio, for "a kinder gentleman treads not the earth." As proof of Antonio's kindness and generosity, Salarino describes Antonio's parting from his friend Bassanio. Bassanio had promised to return as quickly as possible, but Antonio had urged him not to hurry for his sake and not to worry about the Jew's bond. Bassanio was to take all the time he needed in Belmont for the courtship and "fair ostents of love." Antonio had bidden his friend goodby with tears in his eyes, at which Salanio declares, "I think he only loves the world for him." The two gentlemen go off to seek Antonio to cheer him as best they can.

Act II: Scene 9

In Belmont once again, the Prince of Aragon has taken the oath and is coming to choose among the caskets. Nerissa draws the curtains that conceal the three caskets and, with a flourish of horns, Portia enters with the Prince. He promises never to reveal to anyone which casket he chose and, if he fails, never to woo another maid in marriage, and to leave Belmont immediately. Portia explains that all who seek her "worthless self" take the same oath.

Arragon, like Morocco, quickly passes over the lead casket, saying, "You shall look fairer ere I give or hazard." Then, turning to the gold casket, he reads the inscription: "Who chooseth me shall gain what many men desire." Here, pausing to consider what this may mean, he decides that the "many" are the fool multitude that choose by show, / Not learning more than the fond eye doth teach." He refers to the martlet, a bird that builds its nest on the outer walls of buildings and foolishly imagines itself safe from danger there. He, for his part, will not be deceived by outward appearances like the "barbarous multitudes."

Turning then to the silver casket, he reads: "Who chooseth me shall get as much as he deserves," which strikes him as just and proper, for no one should be granted privileges and titles of which he is unworthy. Pondering over the business at hand, the Prince muses that if all estates and offices were obtained purely on the basis of merit, there would be many reversals of fortune in the ranks of men. "How many then should cover [wear a hat] that stand bare, / How many be commanded that command."

Deciding to pick the silver casket on the basis of his own merit, the Prince unlocks the casket only to find inside the portrait of a blinking idiot. "Did I deserve no more than a fool's head?" he laments: "Is that my prize? Are my deserts no better?" Portia explains that his error was in presuming to judge his own worth, which is only for others to do. Along with the picture of the idiot in the casket is a scroll, which reads in part,

"Take what wife you will to bed, / I will ever be your head. So be gone; you are sped." The Prince exits with his followers, and Portia remarks that these fools think they are so smart when they choose, but in fact have only wit enough to lose; and Nerissa adds that the fate of man is not in his own hands: "Hanging and wiving go by destiny."

A servant (whom Portia addresses as "my lord") enters to announce the arrival of a young Venetian, who precedes his lord with courteous messages and rich gifts. The servant, greatly impressed with the new arrival, says that he has never seen "So likely an ambassador of love. / A day in April never came so sweet / To show how costly summer was at hand, / As this fore-spurrer comes before his lord." Portia pretends to take the news lightly and teases the servant that the Venetian must be a relative of his since he praises him so lavishly, but Nerissa prays that the Venetian will turn out to be Bassanio.

Act III: Scene 1

Salanio and Salarino are discussing Antonio's affairs again. The news on the Rialto (the Venetian marketplace) is that Antonio has lost a rich ship on the Goodwin Sands in the English Channel. Salarino (comparing Report to an Elizabethan gossip who drinks ale and discusses her personal affairs among her cronies, pretending that she regrets the death of her third husband) hopes that Report is as much a liar as the tavern crone. Once more he praises "good Antonio," "honest Antonio," and wishes he had words more worthy of Antonio's name, but Salanio cuts short the eulogy and learns that Salanio is convinced that Antonio has lost a ship. Catching sight of Shylock at this moment, Salarino crosses himself to protect the prayer he has just made for Antonio, for he imagines that the devil incarnate comes "in the likeness of a Jew."

Shylock enters, an catching sight of the two young men, accuses them of being involved in his daughter's elopement. Salarino readily admits that he knew of the plans, and Salanio declares that Shylock himself must have known that Jessica was likely to leave her "dam" (parent). Shylock swears that she is damned for it, but Salarino replies that she will be damned only if the devil (that is, Shylock) is her judge. Outraged at the thought of her disobedience, Shylock exclaims with indignation, "My own flesh and blood to rebel!" at which Salarino taunts him as if Shylock meant by this phrase that he had lustful wishes. Shylock explains that he means that his daughter is his own flesh and blood, but Salarino insists that there is an even greater difference between Shylock and Jessica than there is between jet and ivory or between red and white wine.

Salarino asks Shylock for news of Antonio's ship, and the usurer replies that the merchant is surely bankrupt. He warns that Antonio had better "look to his bond," for Shylock intends to get even with him for the past. "He was wont to call me usurer," says Shylock; "He was wont to lend money for a Christian cursy" (courtesy), but now Shylock intends to get revenge for the past. Salarino declares he cannot believe that Shylock would take a pound of flesh, which is not good for anything, but the Jew insists that he has every intention of doing just that.

In a long and passionate speech, Shylock declares that he will use the flesh "to bait fish withal" if nothing else. In short, it will feed his revenge, for Antonio has disgraced him, hindered his business, laughed at his losses, mocked at his gains, scorned his nation, thwarted his bargains, cooled his friends, and heated his enemies. "And what's his reason? I am a Jew. Hath not a Jew eyes? Hath not a Jew hands, organs, dimensions, senses, affections, passions?—fed with the same food, hurt with the same weapons, subject to the same diseases, healed by the same means, warmed and cooled by the same winter and summer as a Christian is? If you prick us, do we not bleed? If you tickle us, do we not laugh? If you poison us, do we not die? And if you wrong us, shall we not revenge? If we are like you in the rest, we will resemble you in that."

One of Antonio's servants comes seeking Salanio and Salarino, who leave with him just after Tubal, another Jew and Shylock's friend, arrives, but not before Salanio has associated Tubal also with the devil. Shylock eagerly asks his friend, who has just come from Genoa, whether he found Jessica there. Tubal answers that he often heard of her but was unable to find her. Shylock moans, "Why there, there, there, there! A diamond gone cost me two thousand ducats in Frankford! The curse never fell upon our nation till now; I never felt it till now. Two thousand ducats in that, and other precious, precious jewels. I would my daughter were dead at my foot, and the jewels in her ear! Would she were hearsed at my foot and the ducats in her coffin!"

As if it were not enough to have Jessica steal his money, Shylock now bewails the loss of still more money spent in the search for her, "and no satisfaction, no revenge! Nor no ill luck stirring but what lights o' my shoulders, no sighs but o' my breathing, no tears but o' my shedding." Tubal reminds him that this is not really true. Antonio, for instance, has had a ship wrecked coming from Tripolis. Shylock pounces greedily on this news: "What, what, what? Ill luck, ill luck?", and then, "I thank God, I thank God! Is it true? Is it true?" Tubal assures him that he heard the news from one of the sailors in Genoa, and he adds that he also heard that Jessica spent eighty ducats in one night in Genoa. Miserable once more, Shylock exclaims: "Thou stick'st a dagger in me. I shall never see my gold again." Returning to the subject of Antonio. Tubal says that he met several of Antonio's creditors who are convinced that the merchant must be bankrupt. This information cheers Shylock again: "I am very glad of it. I'll plague him. I'll torture him. I am glad of it." Back to the subject of Jessica, Tubal remarks that he saw a ring that Jessica gave for a monkey, and Shylock, horrified, laments, "It was my turquoise; I had it of Leah when I was a bachelor. I would not have given it for a wilderness of monkeys." Tubal reminds him again that Antonio is certainly undone, and Shylock, determined to have vengeance, bids Tubal provide for an officer to arrest Antonio when the bond falls due. "I will have the heart of him if he forfeit, for were he out of Venice I can make what merchandise I will. Go, Tubal, and meet me at our synagogue; go, good Tubal; at our synogogue, Tubal."

Act III: Scene 2

In Belmont again, Bassanio is ready to choose among the caskets. Portia urges him to wait a day or two, for she fears to lose his company if he chooses incorrectly. Too modest to confess her love directly, she remarks, "There's something tell me, but it is not love, / I would not lose you; and you know yourself / Hate counsels not in such a quality." She wishes he could stay a month or two so she could teach him how to choose correctly, but then she would be breaking faith, and this she will not do. She tells him that his eyes have divided her in two: one half is his and the other half is also his, for what is hers is also his. Talking on at length, she is trying to draw out the time before he must choose, but Bassanio begs to be allowed to try his fortune, for he cannot bear the rack on which he lives. Portia teases Bassanio for his use of he word "rack," playfully accusing him of confessing love only in order to end his torture. Taking Portia's suggestion that he "confess and live," Bassanio answers that "confess and love" is all there is to admit. He is pleased that his torturer (Portia) "doth teach me answers for deliverance."

Portia finally bids him choose which casket contains her picture, saying, "If you do love me, you will find me out." She tells the others to stand all apart and orders music to be played while he chooses, so that if he fails he will make a swanlike end, fading in music. If he should win, however, then the music will be like the triumphant flourish when a new king is crowned or like the sweet sounds that a dreaming bridegroom hears at daybreak. She compares Bassanio to the young Alcides (Hercules) of mythology, who rescued the Trojan virgin from a sea monster, and herself to the sacrificed virgin, for her life and happiness depend on him.

While Bassanio comments on the caskets to himself, a song is heard, which begins: "Tell me where is fancy bred, / Or in the heart or in the head? How begot, how nourished? / Reply, reply."

Looking at the caskets, Bassanio first comments to himself that outward appearance is not to be trusted to reveal the inner truth of anything. He will not be duped by ornament, which so often deceives men in all affairs of life. In legal matters and in religion a gracious or learned voice often conceals evil and corruption. "There is no vice so simple but assumes / Some mark of virtue on his outward parts," Bassanio reflects. As if with his sixth sense, Bassanio unwittingly guesses at the contents of the boxes: "Upon supposed fairness, often known / To be the dowry of a second head, / The skull that bred them, in the sepulcher." Bassanio therefore will not put his trust in "gaudy gold" or silver, the "common drudge" used for business transaction. Instead, he chooses "meager lead," which threatens rather than promises anything.

Portia, overjoyed at seeing that Bassanio has chosen correctly, remarks in an aside, "O love be moderate, allay thy ecstacy / In measure rain thy joy, scant this excess. / I feel too much thy blessing. Make it less / For fear I surfeit."

Opening the leaden casket, Bassanio joyfully discovers Portia's picture inside. Amazed at the likeness of the portrait to the original, he wonders with a lover's amazement how the artist could have made the eyes so mobile, the lips so sweet, the hair so like a golden spider's web to trap the hearts of men, without himself falling in love with the sitter. Yet beautiful though the picture is, Bassanio declares it is but a poor shadow of the living Portia.

Together with the portrait is a congratulatory scroll that praises Bassanio for not choosing by external appearance, wishes him all good fortune, and bids him claim his lady with a loving kiss. Bassanio kisses Portia and remarks that he is still giddy with delight, unable quite to believe the reality of his good fortune.

Portia tells him that although for herself she would not be ambitious to be different, yet for his sake she wishes she were "A thousands time more fair, / Ten thousand times as rich," so that she might stand higher in his estimation and bring him greater delight. But, she confesses, the sum of herself "Is an unlessoned girl, unschooled, unpractised; / Happy in this, she is not yet so old / But she may learn; happier than this, / She is not bred so dull but she can learn; / Happiest of all, is that her gentle spirit / Commits itself to yours to be directed, / As from her lord, her governor, her king." She declares that everything she has is now his to command, in token of which she gives him a ring, bidding him guard it always as the symbol of their love. Bassanio swears that he will die rather than part with the ring.

Nerissa and Gratiano now announce that they too wish to be married, and they receive the congratualations of the future Lord and his Lady of Belmont. Just as Gratiano is making a ribald pun on a wager over which couple will have the first son, Lorenzo and Jessica unexpectedly appear, together with Salarino.

Bassanio welcomes his friends, checking with Portia that he does not overstep his bound in thus exerting his newly won rights as a host. Lorenzo explains that although he and Jessica had not intended to come to Belmont, they had met Salarino traveling in this direction, and he had prevailed upon them to change their course. Salarino confirms Lorenzo's story, adding that he had a reason for bringing them along. He delivers Bassanio's greeting from Antonio and a letter, which Bassanio reads immediately. In the meantime, Gratiano urges Nerissa to make Jessica welcome. (Gratiano's engagement has already made him somewhat courteous, for he realizes that Jessica must be feeling shy and awkward and needs urging to feel welcome. Once again he imitates Bassanio, who has just welcomed Lorenzo.) The dismay that overcomes Bassanio as he reads the letter from Antonio prompts Portia to beg her husband to tell her what is the matter, for as his wife, she must share his sorrow as well as his joy.

"Here are a few of the unpleasant'st words / That ever blotted paper," exclaims Bassanio. He explains to Portia that when he told her he was a gentleman with no money, / he was telling the truth, but he had omitted one very important fact, that a very dear friend of his bound himself to his keenest enemy to enable Bassanio to come to Belmont. Is it true, Bassanio asks Salarino, that all Antonio's ships have foundered at sea?

Salarino confirms the truth of the letter and adds that even if Antonio now had the money, Shylock would refuse it. Salarino declares that he never saw a creature so "greedy" to destroy his fellow man. Twenty merchants and the Duke have argued with him but no one can persuade him to relinquish his claim. Shylock threatens the Duke that if the bond is not held valid in court, foreigners will no longer trust in the justice of Venetian courts to uphold the legality of contracts. Jessica adds that when she was with him she had heard Shylock tell his friends "That he would rather have Antonio's flesh / Than twenty times the value of the sum / That he did owe him."

Bassanio explains to Portia that Antonio is not only his dear friend but also the kindest and best-natured man in Italy. When Portia learns that the sum of money in question is three thousand ducate, she exclaims: "What, no more? / Pay him six thousand, and deface the bond. / Double six thousand and then treble that, / Before a friend of this description / Shall lose a hair through Bassanio's fault." She bids him come to church to be married immediately, and then he can haste away to Venice,

"For never shall you lie by Portia's side / With an unquiet soul." After he has paid the debt, twenty times over if necessary, she bids him bring Antonio back with him to Belmont. In the meantime she and Nerissa will live like maidens or widows, awaiting the return of their husbands.

Bassanio reads aloud the letter from his friend, in which Antonio explains that all his ships have been lost and that his bond is forfeit. Antonio is resigned to the fact that in paying his debt to the Jew he must lose his life, and he absolves Bassanio of anything he owes him. His only wish in life now is to see Bassanio once more, but he tells his friend that he must do just as he pleases about coming to Venice. "If your love do not persuade you to come, let not my letter," Portia, deeply moved by these words, urges great haste, and Bassanio promises to hurry to and from Venice as quickly as possible.

Act III: Scene 3

Antonio, guarded by the jailor and accompanied by Salanio, tries to speak to Shylock, but the usurer will not listen to his plea. Warning the jailer to keep a close watch on his charge, Shylock declares, "This is the fool that lent out money gratis." Antonio used to call him dog; well, now let him beware the fangs. "I'll not be made soft and dull-eyed fool, / To shake the head, relent, and sigh and yield / To Christian intercessors."

Antonio realizes there is no use in arguing or pleading any more with Shylock, who is bent on retaliating for all the times that Antonio saved other debtors from Sylock's extortions by lending them money free of interest. When Salanio tries to cheer the merchant by assuring him that the Duke will support him in court, Antonio does not respond. He belives that the Duke will be afraid of losing the confidence of the commercial community if he abrogates this one contract. Worn out by his griefs and losses, Antonio is resigned to his fate, and only hopes that Bassanio will arrive from Belmont in time to see him pay his debt," and then I care not."

Act III: Scene 4

In Belmont once again Lorenzo tells Portia how much he admires her noble conception of love and the dignity with which she bears the absence of Bassanio. He assures her that if she knew all the virtues of Antonio, what a true gentleman and friend he is, she would be even more glad of helping him than of her usual acts of kindness.

Portia replies, "I never did repent for doing good, / Nor shall not now."

She declares that since close friends are generally similar in proportion, lineaments, manners, and spirit, Antonio must resemble Bassanio, who in turn is the reflection of her own soul. Therefore no effort can be too great to rescue such a man from "hellish cruelty." Suddenly embarrassed by this talk which, she says "comes too near the praising of myself," she changes the subject.

Portia tells Lorenzo that she and Nerissa have decided to remain in a neighboring monastery to live in prayer and contemplation while their husbands are away. She asks Lorenzo and Jessica to act as master and mistress of her estate during her absence, and Lorenzo readily agrees. Jessica wishes Portia "all heart's content," and Portia returns the wish.

When Lorenzo and Jessica exit, Portia asks her servant (named Balthasar) to take a message to her cousin, Doctor Bellario in Padua, from whom he will receive certain papers and clothing. She bids him bring these as quickly as possible to the ferry that goes to Venice, where she will be waiting for him. The servant hurries away and Portia tells Nerissa that they will shortly see their husbands without being recognized, for the women will be dressed up as young men. The lady gaily bets her maid that when they are disguised she will be "the prettier fellow of the two." In her imagaination she looks forward to wearing her dagger with a brave grace; to speaking in a high piping voice midway between that of man and boy; to walking with a manly stride; and to bragging of all the women who have died of love for him (her). "I have within my mind / A thousand raw tricks of these bragging jacks / Which I will practice." Nerissa asks if they "'will turn to men," and Portia chides her maid for putting a lewd cast on her intentions. The coach is waiting for them, and Portia promises to explain her plan to Nerissa on the way.

Act III: Scene 5

Jessica and Launcelot are talking together in Belmont some time after Portia has departed from the house. The clown tells the girl that he fears she is damned, for the Bible says that the sins of the father are laid upon the children, and she is daughter to the faithless Jew. He says that he can only think of "a kind of bastard hope" that may save her, the hope that Shylock did not beget her. Jessica replies that then "the sins of my mother should be visited upon me." Launcelet hadn't thought of that; he declares that here can be no hope for her salvation, but Jessica reminds him that she will be saved by her husband, who has made her a Christian. Launcelot is not pleased with this solution, insisting that there are enough Christians already without adding more converts who will eat pork and raise the price of hogs.

At this moment Lorenzo appears and jestingly tells Launcelot that he will grow jealous of him if he gets Jessica into corners, but when his wife explains the nature of their conversation Lorenzo declares that he can answer the charge of raising the price of pork by converting Jessica to Christianity better than Launcelot can answer the charge of getting "the Moor" pregnant. Launcelot does not dispute this charge, merely playing on the words of his sentence: "It is *much* that the *Moor* should be more than reason; but if she be less than an honest woman, she is indeed *more* than I took her for."

Lorenzo throws up his hands at this nonsense, declaring that silence is better than such wit. He bids Launcelot tell the other servants to "prepare for dinner," and Launcelot replies, again with double meaning, that the servants are already prepared for dinner because they all have "stomachs" (sexual as well as eating appetites). He also refuses to "cover" (1. lay the tablecloth, 2. don a hat, 3. mount and impregnate the female), because he knows his duty. There is more punning by Launcelot on Lorenzo's order to "go to thy fellows, bid them cover the table, serve in the meat, and we will come in to dinner." Launcelot twists the words around so that they can be interpreted lewdly, and answers: "For the table, sir, it shall be served in; for the meat, sir, it shall be covered; for your coming in to dinner, sir, why let it be as humors and conceits shall govern."

Launcelot exits, and Lorenzo and Jessica remain on stage. Lorenzo comments that the clown's words show that he has a good memory, even if he makes utter nonsense of his wit. There are many fools "garnish'd like him" in higher social positions who, for the sake of "a tricky word," will obscure the sense of their matter.

Lorenzo now asks his wife what she thinks of Portia, and Jessica replies that she cannot speak too highly of the lady of Belmont. She declares that Bassanio cannot help but live an upright life, "for, having such a blessing in his lady, / He finds the joys of heaven here on earth;" and if he does not deserve it here on earth, he is not likely to get it in heaven. As for Portia, "the poor rude world / Hath not her fellow."

Lorenzo happily remarks that he is just such a husband to Jessica as Portia is wife to Bassanio, but Jessica pertly replies that he must ask her opinion on that matter. When Lorenzo suggests that they go in to dinner, Jessica observes that she had better praise him "while I have a stomach" (the pun here is on her 1. appetite, 2. inclination.) Lorenzo answers this with another pun, saying she had better leave the subject for table talk, and then he will digest her words along with the food, no matter how bad. Finally, Jessica adds the last witty word, "Well, I'll set you forth" (1. lay out a feast, 2. praise you highly).

Act IV: Scene 1

The scene is the court in Venice, where the Duke is presiding over the case of Shylock's claim to his pound of flesh. Antonio, Bassanio, Gratiano, and other Venetian noblemen are already present. The Duke expresses his pity for Antonio, whose adversary he declares is "an inhuman wretch, / Uncapable of pity, void and empty / From any dram of mercy." Antonio replies that he knows that the Duke has done his utmost to persuade Shylock to be merciful but to no avail. The merchant realizes that the law holds him responsible for the bond, and he is prepared to bear with patience and a quiet spirit the brunt of Shylock's fury.

Shylock enters the court and stands before the Duke, who tries once more to soften his heart by telling the creditor that all those present think that he is merely pretending to be cruel until the moment of execution when he will, in fact, show mercy to his victim. The Duke declares that even Turks and Tartars, people known for their savagery and never trained in "tender courtesy," would show greater humanity towards a man such as Antonio who has suffered so many losses all at once. He tells the usurer, "We all expect a gentle answer, Jew," (punning on "gentile" again), but Shylock is unmoved by this as by all other appeals to "human gentleness and love." He declares that he was sworn "by our holy Sabbath" to have his bond, and he warns the Duke of the consequence for Venice if the law is not impartially observed in this as in all cases.

As for why Shylock prefers to have "the weight of carrion flesh" rather than his money, he announces quite simply that it is his "humor" (a physiological and mental disposition) to do so. He compares himself to man whose house is troubled by a rat and who is willing to pay ten thousand ducats to have it poisoned, which it is his privelege to do. "Some men there are love not a gaping pig, / Some that are mad if they behold a cat, / And others, when the bagpipe sings i' the nose, / Cannot contain their urine for affection, / Master of passion, sways it to the mood / Of what it likes or loathes." And just as there is no rational explanation of why one man hates a pig, why another cannot abide a harmless cat, and why a third cannot contain his urine when listening to a bagpipe, so Shylock cannot and will not give a reason for his action other than the deep-seated hatred and loathing that he bears Antonio.

Bassanio heatedly objects that Shylock has given no excuse for his cruelty, for all men do not kill that which they do not love, but the Jew replies that he is not bound to please Bassanio by his answers. He declares that no man truly hates that which he would not kill, and, having once been stung by a serpent (Antonio), he will not give it a chance to sting him again.

Antonio begs Bassanio not to argue with his creditor. "You may as well go stand upon the beach / And bid the main flood bate his usual height; / You may as well use question with the wolf, / Why he hath made the ewe bleat for the lamb. / You may as well forbid the mountain pines / To wag their high tops and to make no noise / When they are fretten with the gusts of heaven," as to seek to soften that hardest of all things, Shylock's "Jewish heart." Accepting his plight, Antonio asks that the court proceed to render judgment, but Bassanio makes one last attempt, offering Shylock six thousand ducats instead of the original three thousand. Shylock, implacable, replies that if he were offered six times the original sum he would not take it but would insist upon his bond.

Intervening once more, the Duke asks Shylock how he can hope for mercy for himself when he shows none to others, but Shylock simply replies: "What judgment shall I dread, doing no wrong?" He tells his listeners that just as they have purchased slaves whom they treat like dogs or beasts of burden, so he is master of Antonio, whom he has bought with his money. And just as the Venetian nobles would never agree to free their slaves, so Shylock declares he will not set Antonio free, but will dispose of him as he pleases. He asks for justice and reminds the Duke that the prosperity of Venice will suffer if the law is not maintained in the city.

The Duke declares that he may dismiss the court unless Bellario, the learned jurist from Padua, arrives to determine the case. Salarino then announces that a messenger from Bellario is waiting outside. While this messenger is being sent for, Bassanio tries to cheer Antonio, swearing that he would rather die than permit Antonio to lose one drop of blood. Antonio, however, protests that he is more ready and more fit for death than his friend: "I am a tainted wether of the flock, / Meetest for death."

Nerissa enters dressed as a lawyer's clerk, and while the Duke reads the letters that she brings from Bellario, Bassanio anxiously watches Shylock whetting his knife for the operation. Gratiano cannot contain himself at this sight. He declares that Shylock sharpens the knife on his very *soul* rather than on the *sole* of his foot, for no metal is as keen as the villain's sharp envy. Gratiano is almost ready to believe with Pythagoras that the souls of dead animals enter the bodies of men, since no other theory can explain Shylock's currish spirit, so "wolvish, bloody, starved, and ravenous." (Pythagoras was an ancient Greek philosopher who believed in the transmigration of souls after death.) Shylock, however, calmly replies to Gratiano that all his anger and harsh words cannot alter the seal upon the lawful bond. "I stand here for law," Shylock asserts.

Having read the letter, the Duke sends Nerissa to fetch Portia, and while she is gone he reads aloud the message from old Bellario, who explains that although he is too sick to come, he is sending in his stead a young and learned doctor of jurisprudence named Balthasar. He begs the Duke not to be apprehensive on account of the lawyer's extreme youth, promising that this Balthasar will bring to bear on the case both Bellario's considered opinion and his own learned judgment.

Portia enters, dressed as a Doctor of Law, and is welcomed by the Duke. Bidding the merchant and the Jew stand forth, she hears Antonio confess that he has signed the bond in question, and she declares, "Then must the Jew be merciful." When Shylock demands to know on what grounds he must be merciful, the young lawyer replies: "The quality of mercy is not strained; / It droppeth as the gentle rain from heaven / Upon the place beneath. It is twice blest; / It blesseth him that gives and him that takes." The sign of true grace in a king, she declares, is not a sceptre in the hand or a crown on the head, but mercy in the heart; for mercy is an attribute of God Himself, and earthly kings are most noble when they temper justice with mercy. "Therefore, Jew," Portia concludes, "consider this, / That in the course of justice, none of us should see salvation. We do pray for mercy / And that same prayer doth teach us all to render / The deeds of mercy." She hopes that he will be moved by these words to renounce his legal claim, but she concludes by saying that if he remains adamant, the Ventian court must pass sentence against Antonio.

Unmoved by Portia's appeal, Shylock still declares, "I crave the law." The lawyer then asks if Antonio is able to repay the bond, and Bassanio replies that he is ready to pay thrice or even ten times the original sum borrowed. Bassanio argues that if Shylock refuses this offer his only motive can be pure malice, and he begs the court to disregard the law just this once in order to save Antonio. Portia, however, denies this request. She refuses to set the dangerous precedent of ever tampering with the law.

Shylock gleefully cries out that the young lawyer is another Daniel come to judge: "O wise young judge, how I do honor thee!" He tells the court that he has sworn an oath to heaven that he will have his bond, and asks whether they think he would risk perjuring himself before God by changing his mind now.

Portia scrutinizes the bond closely and, finding it all in order, declares that the Jew may have his pound of flesh to be cut off nearest the merchant's heart. Turning to Shylock once more, she asks him to accept the sum of three times his original loan and to bid her tear the bond. He refuses. Antonio, anxious to get his ordeal over with, urges the lawyer to proceed to judgment, and Portia tells the victim to prepare his bosom for the knife. "O noble judge! O excellent young man!" cries Shylock, reminding the court that the bond expressly stipulates that he may take the flesh "Nearest his heart." Portia bids him provide a doctor "for charity" to look after Antonio, but the usurer refuses, objecting that " 'Tis not in the bond."

Bidding farewell to Bassanio, Antonio begs his friend not to grieve. He declares that he is well prepared to endure his ordeal, taking comfort in the thought that he will be spared the misery of those men who outlive their wealth and are forced to end their days in cruel poverty. He bids Bassanio convey his greetings to Portia. "Tell her the process of Antonio's end, / Say how I loved you, speak me fair in death / And when the tale is told, bid her be judge / Whether Bassanio had not once a love." In conclusion Antonio swears that as long as Bassanio is truly sorry to see him die, then he for his part does not repent paying his friend's debt "with all my heart."

Bassanio, overwhelmed with grief and frustration, declares that though he dearly loves his wife, he would willingly sacrifice her, or die himself in order to save Antonio. Without revealing her identity, Portia remarks that Bassanio's wife would not be very happy to hear him thus offer her life in sacrifice. Gratiano then declares that he also would gladly see his beloved wife in heaven if she might intercede there for Antonio, and Nerissa remarks that his wife would not take kindly to such an offer. Shylock, who has heard the protestations of these Christian husbands and has taken them literally, declares that he would rather his daughter had married a thief ("any of the stock of Barabbas") rather than a gentile, if this is the kind of love that Christian husbands bear their wives.

Proceeding to render judgment, Portia declares that the court awards Shylock a pound of flesh to be cut off from Antonio's breast. The Jew, greatly elated, praises this "Most rightful judge," Most learned judge." But his joy is short-lived. Portia then goes on to show that although the bond clearly gives him a pound of flesh, it makes no provision for blood. Therefore, if while claiming his pound of flesh Shylock sheds any Christian blood, he will lose all his possessions to the state in accordance with Venetian law. Now it is Gratiano's turn to gloat and to praise Portia "O upright judge! Mark Jew. O learned judge."

Surprised by this turn of events, Shylock declares his willingness to accept Bassanio's offer of three times the original value of the bond, but now Portia will not let the matter rest. She declares that since he asked for justice he shall get nothing but justice, that is, his pound of flesh, and warns him that if he takes either slightly more or less than just a pound he will lose all his property and will be condemned to death. Again

Gratiano crows with delight, imitating Shylock's earlier praise of the lawyer: "A second Daniel! A Daniel, Jew!"

Hoping to salvage at least his original investment, Shylock declares himself willing to accept the original three thousand ducats, but again Portia insists that he shall get nothing but the forfeit. Shylock then decides to abandon his claim, and prepares to leave the court, when Portia tells him of the Venetian law that says if an alien is found guilty of attempting the life of any citizen, his property shall be divided evenly between the intended victim and the state. Furthermore, his life shall be at the mercy of the Duke to dispose of. Shylock is clearly guilty under this law and Portia advises him to bow before the Duke and humbly to seek mercy. Gratiano, delighted by this news, enjoys taunting Shylock in his humiliation.

Before Shylock has a chance to say a word, the Duke pardons his life to show him "the difference of our spirit." He decrees that half the usurer's wealth must go to Antonio, but offers to reduce the debt to the state to a small fine. Shylock, however, is hardly grateful for this concession. "Nay, take my life," he tells the Duke, for without his wealth he cannot earn a living, and he feels he might just as well die now as starve in the course of time.

Portia then asks Antonio what mercy he can render Shylock. Gratiano mutters his hope that Antonio will offer nothing more than a free halter for the Jew to hang himself, but Antonio is a more generous spirit. He asks the Duke to let Shylock keep one half his possessions, allowing Antonio the use of the other half until death, when it will go to Lorenzo and Jessica. The merchant also stipulates that Shylock must convert to Christianity and must make Lorenzo his legal heir. The Duke heartily approves these proposals and declares he will revoke his pardon if Shylock does not agree, whereupon Shylock consents. Portia bids the clerk draw up the deed of gift to his heirs for him to sign. Shylock, feeling ill by now, asks leave to go home and to have the deed sent after for him to sign. The Duke grants this request, and as Shylock leaves, Gratiano declares that if he had been judge he would have sent the Jew to the gallows rather than to the baptismal font.

The Duke invites Portia to dinner, but the "lawyer" politely declines, explaining that "he" must return to Padua immediately. The Duke exists, and Bassanio offers the lawyer a fee of three thousand ducats, which Portia refuses, declaring: "He is well paid that is well satisfied / And I, delivering you, am satisfied." She wants no monetary reward and simply says "I pray you know me when we meet again," (the true meaning of which only she and Nerissa understand). Bassanio, however, insists upon her taking some remembrance, as a gift if not as a fee, and Portia agrees to accept his gloves. When her husband takes off his gloves, she notices his ring and says she will take that. Bassanio, greatly distressed, tries to dissuade her, arguing that the ring is worthless, and offers to find out the most precious ring in Venice instead. When Portia insists on having this one, he finally explains that it was given him by his wife, who made him vow neither to sell, nor to give, nor lose it. The lawyer then accuses Bassanio of selfishness and hypocrisy for refusing to part with the one insignificant trifle she requests. Knowingly, Portia declares that if Bassanio's wife were not insane and if she knew what the lawyer had done for Antonio, she would not begrudge her husband's parting with the ring. With these words Portia and Nerissa exit.

Antonio, chagrined at Bassanio's refusal to give the ring to the lawyer, tells his friend to change his mind: "Let his deservings and my love withal, / Be valued 'gainst your wife's commandments." Bassanio, persuaded, sends Gratiano with the ring after the two young women to request them to come to Antonio's house, where the gentlemen intend to spend the night before setting out early in the morning for Belmont.

Act IV: Scene 2

The scene is another street in Venice, and Portia is bidding her "clerk" bring the deed of gift to Shylock for his signature. Gratiano comes upon them, bringing with him Bassanio's ring for "the lawyer" as well as an invitation to dinner. Portia declines the dinner but accepts the ring with thanks. She asks Gratiano to show her "youth" the way to Shylock's house, and when he agrees Nerissa whispers to Portia that she will try to get from her husband the ring she made him swear to keep forever. Portia replies, also in a whisper, that Gratiano will surely part with his ring too. She predicts that in Belmont their husbands will swear that they gave the rings to men, "but we'll outface them, and outswear them too." Nerissa and Gratiano exit one way, while Portia goes another, having planned to meet her maid shortly.

Act V: Scene 1

Back in Belmont, Lorenzo and Jessica are enjoying a beautiful moonlit night. "The moon shines bright. In such a night as this, / When the sweet wind did gently kiss the trees / And they did make no noise, in such a night / Troilus methinks mounted the Troyan walls, / And sighed his soul toward the Grecian tents / Where Cressid lay that night," Lorenzo muses aloud, and Jessica, following his train of thought, fancies that on such a night Thisbe must have gone to her tryst with her lover Pyramus, when, frightened by a lion, she ran home again. Lorenzo thinks of Dido mourning after Aeneas, and Jessica imagines Medea gathering enchanted herbs to save her lover Jason. Finally Lorenzo says that on such a night, "Did Jessica steal from the wealthy Jew, / And with an unthrift love did run from Venice / As far as Belmont"; to which his wife teasingly replies that on such a night did young Lorenzo swear he loved her well, deceiving her with false vows of faith. Lorenzo replies that on such a night did Jessica slander her love but he forgave her.

The still of the night is interrupted by the arrival of Portia's servant Stephano, who brings words that his mistress and Nerissa are returning from the monastery and will be home before daybreak. Stephano is immediately followed by Launcelot who arrives crying, "Sola, sola! wo ha! ho sola, sola!" (imitating the sound of a post horn) and announces that a post (messenger) has just brought a "horn full of good news" (with a play on "cornucopia") that Bassanio will be home by morning. Lorenzo bids Stephano report these tidings indoors and send out the house musicians to play in the air.

Alone with Jessica again, Lorenzo re-establishes lyrical mood disrupted by the hurried arrival of the messengers, "How sweet the moonlight sleeps upon this bank! / Here will we sit and let the sounds of music / Creep in our ears; soft stillness and the night / Become the touches of sweet harmony." He bids Jessica sit and look at the sky, which he calls the "floor of heaven" inlaid with "patterns of bright gold." He reminds her that "there's not the smallest orb which thou behold'st / But in his motion like an angel sings; / Still quiring to the young-eyed cherubins; / Such harmony is in immortal souls, / But whilst this muddy vesture of decay / Doth grossly close it in, we canot hear it."

The musicians enter and as they play Jessica remarks, "I am never merry when I hear sweet music." This her husband explains is because her soul is attentive. He reminds her that music affects even the wildest of animals, which is why legend tells that Orpheus (son of Apollo and consummate musician) could bend to his spell trees, stones and floods. Nothing in nature is insensible to "the sweet power of music." "The man that hath no music in himself, / Nor is not moved with concord of sweet sounds, / Is fit for treasons, stratagems, and spoils; / The motions of his spirit are dull as night, / And his affections dark as Erebus. / Let no such man be trusted. Mark the music."

While the music is playing, Portia and Nerissa enter. Perceiving the light thrown by the small candle burning in her hall, Portia remarks, "So shines a good deed in a naughty world." When Nerissa observes that the candle was not visible as long as the moon was shining, her mistress answers, "So doth the greater glory dim the less. / A substitute shines brightly as a king / Until a king be by," and then his state seems paltry indeed as does a brook to the "main of waters." The music coming from her house now at night, sounds sweeter to her than it does by day, and she observes that nothing is absolutely good merely in itself, without reference to the circumstances. If the nightingale should sing by day, she would be considered no better a musician than a wren. "How many things by season seasoned are / To their right praise and true perfection!/ Peace! (music ceases) How the moon sleeps with Endymion, / And would not be awakened."

Recognizing Portia's voice, Lorenzo welcomes her home and she explains that she and Nerissa have been praying for their husbands' welfare which, they hope will be "the better for our words." (In fact, their husbands are very much the better for Portia's words spoken in the court of Venice, but Lorenzo thinks she is referring to the efficacy of prayer.) She has just time enough to ask that no one tell Bassanio that she has been away, when trumpets announce his arrival. By now the sky is growing light, and Bassanio greets his wife, saying that as long as she is present it is daylight for him even in the darkest night. To this Portia gayly replies, "Let me give light, but let me not be light / For a light wife doth make a heavy husband / And never be Bassanio so for me." (She is punning on the word "light," which meant "bright" and "unfaithful." She cordially welcomes the new arrivals, especially Antonio, declaring her intention of making him feel welcome more by deeds than by words.

Nerissa and Gratiano have been talking apart when suddenly a quarrel develops, for Nerissa has noticed that her husband's ring is missing. He swears that he gave it to the judge's clerk, and wishes the young man were "gelt" (castrated) rather than that his wife should be so disturbed. Justifying himself to Portia, Gratiano explains that it was just a "paltry ring" engraved with commonplace poetry, "Love me and leave me not." Nerissa, angry that he should speak so slightingly of the value of the ring and of the quality of the poetry, reminds him of his oath to wear it to his grave. She pretends to believe that he gave it to some other woman, but Gratiano swears he gave it to a youth, "A kind of boy, a little scrubbed boy / No higher than thyself."

Portia reproves Gratiano for parting with his wife's first gift and tells him she is positive that not for all the wealth in the world would Bassanio give away the ring she gave him.

At this, Basanio remarks in an aside that had better cut off his left hand to conceal the truth from her, but too late, Gratiano tells all. Bassanio ruefully admits that he too gave away his ring when not other payment would be accepted by the judge. Pretending she is outraged, Portia swears, "By heaven, I will ne'er come in your bed / Until I see the ring," and Nerissa echoes this vow. Poor Bassanio entreats his wife to be reasonable: "If you did know to whom I gave the ring, / If you did know for whom I gave the ring, / And would conceive for what I gave the ring, / And how unwillingly I left the ring / When naught would be accepted but the ring, / You would abate the strength of your displeasure." But Portia will not be so easily reconciled. "If you had known the virtue of the ring / Or half her worthiness that gave the ring, / Or your own honor to contain the ring, / You would not then have parted with the ring." She refuses to believe that any reasonable man would have insisted on being paid with a ring whose chief value was sentimental, and she declares, like Nerissa, that some woman must have gotten the ring. When Bassanio explains that his sense of honor required him to part with the ring for the judge who had saved Antonio's life, Portia warns her husband that she will be just as generous with her favors to the judge as he was. "I'll not deny him anything I have, / No not my body nor my husband's bed"; and Narissa declares she will do likewise. Gratiano, indignant, warns that if his wife plays loose her lover had better watch out, for "I'll mar the young clerk's pen."

Antonio is miserable at being the cause of this quarrel, but Portia reassures him that he is not at all to blame and is most welcome. Ever the loyal friend, Antonio now offers Portia his soul as bond for Bassanio's future fidelity, just as formerly he offered his body as bond to Shylock. This suggestion satisfies Portia, who gives Bassanio the ring he gave away to the judge, asking him to keep it more faithfully than before. Her husband recognizes the ring, and in a last bit of teasing Portia tells him that she got it from the judge who lay with her last night, and Nerissa says the same of the clerk. The men are dumbfounded, but before they have time to become very angry, Portia reveals the truth: that she was the doctor and Nerissa the clerk. Relieved and amazed, Bassanio declares, "Sweet doctor, you shall be my bedfellow. / When I am absent, then lie with my wife."

There are other wonders in store. Portia gives Antonio a letter explaining that three of his ships have unexpectedly come to port and that he is once again a wealthy man. Next she gives Lorenzo and Jessica the deed of gift from Shylock, promising that they will be his heirs. Lorenzo with wonder and admiration declares, "Fair ladies, you drop manna in the way / Of starved people."

It is almost morning. Portia suggests that they all go inside where she will answer their questions. As they all exit Gratiano says that his first question will be whether Nerissa would rather remain with the company or go to bed now that it is two hours to day. "But were the day come, I should wish it dark / Till I were couching with the doctor's clerk. / Well, while I live I'll fear no other thing / So sore as keeping safe Nerissa's ring."

A Midsummer Night's Dream

THESEUS, *Duke of Athens.*
EGEUS, *father to Hermia.*
LYSANDER ⎫
DEMETRIUS ⎭ *in love with Hermia.*
PHILOSTRATE, *Master of the Revels to Theseus.*

QUINCE, *a carpenter.*
SNUG, *a joiner.*
BOTTOM, *a weaver.*
FLUTE, *a bellows-mender.*
SNOUT, *a tinker.*
STARVELING, *a tailor.*

HIPPOLYTA, *Queen of the Amazons, betrothed to Theseus.*
HERMIA, *daughter to Egeus, in love with Lysander.*
HELENA, *in love with Demetrius.*

OBERON, *King of the Fairies.*
TITANIA, *Queen of the Fairies.*
PUCK, *or Robin Goodfellow.*
PEASEBLOSSOM ⎫
COBWEB   ⎪
MOTH   ⎬ *fairies.*
MUSTARDSEED ⎪
Other FAIRIES. ⎭

ATTENDANTS *on Theseus and Hippolyta.*

A Midsummer Night's Dream

Act I: Scene 1

The play opens in the palace of Theseus, Duke of Athens, a legendary Greek hero. He enters accompanied by his bride-to-be Hippolyta, Queen of the Amazons. Theseus tells Hippolyta that although their wedding is only four days away, his impatience makes the time seem long. She answers that the interval will pass quickly. Both measure time by the moon—it is waning now and will be a new crescent on the night of their marriage. Theseus sends Philostrate, who is in charge of entertainment at the court, into the city to organize the public celebration of the wedding, and contrasts this planned merriment with his conquering Hippolyta initially in his war on the Amazons.

Egeus, father of Hermia, comes before the Duke to complain about his daughter. He explains that while Demetrius has his consent to marry her, she has been "bewitched" by Lysander and wants to marry him, thus being disobedient. Accordingly Egeus asks that the law be enforced which provides for either her obedience or her death. Theseus questions Hermia, advising her that her father's authority over her is absolute and likening the relationship between father and daughter to that between a mold and wax. In reply to Theseus' declaration that Demetrius is worthy, she says that Lysander is, too. Theseus says that her father's approval makes Demetrius worthier, whereupon she counters with the wish that her father saw with her eyes. Theseus replies that her eyes must rather be governed by her father's judgment. She asks what may happen to her if she refuses to wed Demetrius. The Duke replies that she must die or become a nun, "chanting faint hymns to the cold, fruitless moon."

She must consider well whether she can undergo a life which, unlike a "rose distilled," rather withers "on the virgin thorn" and "grows, lives and dies in single blessedness." Hermia avows she would rather do thus than marry Demetrius because her father commands it. Theseus says she should think it over and announce her decision on the night of his marriage to Hippolyta. Demetrius and Lysander now exchange sharp words and, in presenting his case, Lysander reveals that there is a further complication. Demetrius has been false to Helena, who is still in love with him even though he has forsaken her by switching his affection to Hermia. Theseus says he's heard of this and he leaves with Hippolyta, taking Demetrius and Egeus with him. Lysander and Hermia are thus left alone on the stage to comment on their situation and plan what to do about it.

Left alone, Hermia and Lysander discuss their situation, and Lysander remarks, "the course of true love never did run smooth." He suggests that they solve their problem by eloping the next night. He will meet Hermia in the woods outside of town and take her to his aunt's house, which is seven leagues away. A league is usually estimated at roughly three miles nowadays. There, free of Athenian law, they may marry. Hermia agrees, swearing "by all the vows that ever men have broke" that she will keep the appointment.

Helena, Demetrius' forsaken but still doting girlfriend, now comes upon the scene. When Hermia addresses her as "fair Helena," her immediate reaction is to tell of her unhappy love for Demetrius. Helena says she herself is not fair since Demetrius loves Hermia's beauty. She wishes appearance were contagious the way sickness is so that she might be just like Hermia and so win back Demetrius.

To comfort Helena, Hermia and Lysander tell her about their plan to meet the next night in the woods by moonlight and elope. After they leave, Helena speaks her mind. She says love has transforming power. Cupid is a blind and winged boy because love does not see with the eyes but with the mind, does not involve the judgment, and is often perjured.

Now Helena refers to Demetrius' inconstancy and resolves to tell him of the planned elopement, betraying her friend so that she may win Demetrius' gratitude and, more important, follow him to the woods and thereby have his company.

Act I: Scene 2

This scene also takes place in Athens, but instead of at the Ducal Palace, we are now among working men. We are now introduced to the following Athenian tradesmen: Quince the Carpenter, Snug the Joiner, Bottom the Weaver, Flute the Bellows-mender, Snout the Tinker, and Starveling the Tailor.

These amiable, simple men have come together to prepare a play to be performed at the wedding of Theseus and Hippolyta. Quince is in charge and he begins by asking if all are present. Bottom, who is the most energetic participator, advises that Quince announce the name of the play and then call each man's name. Their play is, "The most lamentable comedy and most cruel death of Pyramus and Thisbe."

Nick Bottom is the first name called, and Quince says he is to play Pyramus. Bottom asks, is Pyramus a lover or a tyrant? When he finds that Pyramus is a lover who kills himself for love, Bottom declares his fitness for the part, though his "chief humor" is to play a tyrant. He gives a vigorous example of his talent in the latter capacity, reciting a fiery speech impromptu.

After Bottom is named to play Pyramus, Quince names Francis Flute the bellows-mender to play Thisbe. Flute asks if Thisbe is "a wandering knight." Quince answers that Thisbe is the lady that Pyramus loves. Flute objects to playing a woman, saying that he has a beard coming. Quince says that doesn't matter for he shall wear a mask and speak in a falsetto.

Hearing that Thisbe will be played in a mask, Bottom says if he may wear a mask he would like to play Thisbe too. He says he will speak in a "monstrous little voice" and he gives an example of his prowess in this regard. Quince insists, however, that Bottom play Pyramus and Flute, Thisbe. Bottom is temporarily quieted and with an air of injured magnanimity he allows the casting to proceed. We shall see that he is only subdued for a moment. Quince then names Robin Starveling for Thisbe's mother, Tom Snout for Pyramus' father, and himself for Thisbe's father.

Finally, Quince names Snug the joiner for the lion's part. Snug inquires if Quince has the lion's part written out, because if so, Snug would like to begin studying it. He is "slow of study" and wants to be sure to know it on time. Quince assures him that he may do it extempore, for all he has to do is roar. When he hears this, the irrepressible Bottom can no longer contain himself. He has been quiet for all of eleven lines, but the prospect of roaring is too much for him. He must chime in again: "Let me play the lion too." He enthusiastically describes how well he would roar. It will do people good to hear him and the Duke will request an encore. Quince and the others agree that to roar "too terribly" might frighten the Duchess and the ladies, causing them to shriek, and they would all be hanged for it. Bottom won't be stopped. First, he has a joke on the subject —if the ladies are frightened out of their wits, then they may be so foolish (being witless) as to hang them. Second, he has the necessary modification all ready. He will roar as gently as a dove or a nightingale.

Despite the adroitness of Bottom's bid to play the Lion too, Quince insists he can play no part but Pyramus, persuasively citing as reasons that Pyramus is "sweet-faced," handsome ("proper"), and "a most lovely gentle-manlike man." Therefore, says the foxy Quince, Bottom *has* to play Pyramus. Bottom at long last deigns to accept only the one role, little enough for his talents albeit the best part in the play. Having watched his virtuoso performance in this scene, we must share his self-estimate. Once his part has been narrowed to one, Bottom immediately opens up possibilities within it. He asks Quince what color beard he ought to wear and when Quince leaves it up to him, Bottom recites with great relish all the possible colors in beards: "straw-color," "orange-tawny," "purple-in-grain" or "French-crown-color beard, your perfit yellow." Thus he has already embarked with gusto on his theatrical venture. Quince makes a joke on "French-crown-color" saying that some French crowns have no hair at all and then Bottom would be playing bare-faced. Quince hands out the scripts and tells his actors to learn them for a rehearsal the next night. They are to meet in the palace wood a mile outside of town by moonlight. There, Quince states, they will have the privacy and secrecy not possible if they were to meet in the city.

In the meantime, Quince will assemble the necessary properties. Bottom agrees to this on behalf of everybody, saying, "there we may rehearse most obscenely and courageously." His excitement at the prospect carries him away and he uses the wrong word. Quince specifies the meeting place as the Duke's Oak. Naturally it is Bottom who has the last words in the scene as with sporting verve but only hazy meaning he says, "Enough. Hold, or cut bowstrings." We gather the meaning by the energy of the words, but we can only guess at their precise definition.

Act II: Scene 1

This scene takes place in that wood near Athens which has been designated as a meeting place for the characters in each of the two preceding scenes. Puck or Robin Goodfellow and a Fairy enter from opposite sides. Puck inquires about the Fairy's activities. The spirit answers in light and airy song, describing how he wanders everywhere more swiftly than the moon. He serves the Fairy Queen by taking care of the flowers which he calls her "pensioners" (members of the royal bodyguard in splendid uniforms). Specifically, he hangs dewdrops on the gold and ruby-spotted cowslips. The Fairy bids farewell to Puck, saying the Queen and all her elves will come there soon. Puck says the King of the Fairies, Oberon, plans to be there also, and he warns the fairy to keep the Queen out of the King's sight, because King Oberon is very angry at his Queen. Queen Titania has a changeling, a lovely boy stolen from an Indian King, and Oberon is jealous and wants the child for his own. Titania not only withholds the changeling, but makes the little boy her special favorite. And so, Puck continues, every time Oberon and Titania meet, whether in wood or meadow, by a spring or under the stars, they quarrel so fiercely that all their elves are frightened and crawl into acorn cups to hide.

After Puck's description of the frightened elves, so tiny that they can hide in acorn cups, the Fairy asks Puck if he is Robin Goodfellow. In asking the question, the Fairy describes some of the activities attributed to the elf Robin: frightening village maidens, skimming milk so it won't churn, taking the kick out of liquor, misleading people who travel at night, and for those who treat him well, doing work and bringing luck. Puck answers that he is the mischievous Robin Goodfellow, Hobgoblin, and Puck, and he recounts some more of his mischief. Besides being jester to King Oberon, he fools horses by neighing like a filly and he makes old women spill ale on themselves by getting into their cups in the shape of a "crab" and bobbing against their lips. Sometimes he pretends he's a three-foot stool and when a wise, old woman, in the middle of a sad tale, tries to sit down, he moves, she falls, crying "tailor" and coughing, and everybody laughs uproariously.

Puck concludes his speech with the announcement that Oberon is approaching. The Fairy says so is his mistress, Titania, and he wishes Oberon were gone. At this point, the King of Fairies, Oberon, enters with his train at one door and the Queen, Titania, enters with her train at another. Oberon addresses Titania as "proud Titania" and calls their moonlight meeting unfortunate. She replies by calling him "jealous Oberon," and starts to leave, saying she has forsworn his bed and company. Oberon calls her a "rash wanton" (willful creature) and tells her to stay, reminding her that he is her lord. Titania replies that if he is her lord, she must be his lady. Then she begins reciting all his extracurricular romances as an ironical commentary on his claim to being her lord and master. She says he has stolen from fairyland and in the shape of the typical shepherd, Corin, he has played on pipes and sung love poetry to the shepherdess, Phillida. Titania continues by pointing out that he has come from faraway India only because Hippolyta is an old girlfriend who's getting married. The Queen's description of Hippolyta is finely sarcastic: "the bouncing Amazon,/Your buskined mistress and your warrior love." She closes by saying Oberon has come all that way to bless the marriage of Theseus and Hippolyta because he's sweet on the bride. Oberon immediately and indignantly rises in self-defense, saying Titania ought to be ashamed to bring that Hippolyta business up since he knows about *her* love for Theseus. Oberon then neatly rattles off the names of four women whom Theseus abandoned for Titania: the ravished Perigenia, Aegles, Ariadne, and Antiopa.

Titania replies to this onslaught of her past amours with Theseus by accusing Oberon of making them up out of jealousy. She goes on to say that never, since the beginning of midsummer, has she been free of his brawling. Wherever they meet—hill, dale, forest, meadow, fountain, brook or seashore—he disturbs their merrymaking, as they dance with the wind in their hair. Therefore, she continues, since they piped music for the fairy dancing all in vain, the winds took revenge by sucking up contagious fogs from the sea and bringing them to land with disastrous results. These fogs have caused even "pelting" (paltry) rivers to overflow their banks. The resultant flooding has meant wasted labor for both the ox in the yoke and the ploughman driving him. The corn in these flooded fields has rotted while still green and immature. The pens where sheep and cattle should be, stand empty mid the general devastation, and the crows grow fat on the livestock dead of the murrain disease. The areas set aside for outdoor games, such as the nine men's morris (a game played on squares cut in the turf with counters such as pebbles or pegs), or the mazes, are filled with mud and indistinguishable from lack of use.

Titania continues that though men have all the hardships of that season, they have none of the comforts and compensations of winter, no hymns or carols bless the night. Because of Oberon's quarrel with her, says Titania, the moon, who is in control of floods, is pale with anger and keeps the whole atmosphere so drenched that "rheumatic diseases" (colds, grippe, rheumatism) are very prevalent. And as a result of the foregoing disorder in nature ("distemperature"), the seasons are all mixed up. Frosts kill new roses, buds follow fast upon wintry days, none of the seasons act the way they are supposed to. People watching in amazement for the usual indications for each season don't know which is which. Titania concludes by repeating that this string of evil consequences can be traced directly to their quarrel as its cause and origin. They "are the parents and the original" of this evil offspring.

Oberon's answer to all of this is that the solution lies with Titania. There's no reason at all for her to quarrel with him. After all, he *just* wants a little changeling boy to be his "henchman" (page). His wheedling doesn't soften Titania, however. In her most queenly manner she denies him once again: "Set your heart at rest./The fairyland buys not the child of me." Then she explains how she got the boy. His mother was a "vot'ress" (had taken a vow) in the order of which Titania was patroness. They used to sit together on the yellow seashore and gossip. They would watch the trading ships sail out to sea and laugh when the wind made the canvas billow. Being pregnant with this boy, Titania's friend would imitate the ships and go fetch things from inland for Titania. She, being mortal, died giving birth to that boy, says Titania. And for her sake the Queen is bringing him up, and for her sake she will not part with him. After this moving and well-spoken explanation, Oberon asks only how long Titania plans to stay in that wood. Titania replies that she will probably stay till after Theseus is married. The Queen says if Oberon will be patient and participate harmoniously in her activities he should come with her. If not, then he ought to avoid her and she will do likewise. The stubborn King has only one objective. He will go with her if she will give him the boy. But Titania is of an equally firm disposition and she retorts, "Not for thy fairy kingdom." She bids her fairies away, saying she'll only quarrel more if she stays longer. With haughty splendor, she and her train leave. Oberon and Puck are now left to confer on the situation.

Oberon says to the departed Queen, well, if that's the way she wants it. Then he vows that before she leaves that wood, he'll torment her for the injury he considers she has done him. At this point he calls Puck to him. Oberon tells him to recall an occasion when the King sat on a promontory and heard a mermaid's song. His description is a high point in this play's poetry: the mermaid is on a dolphin's back, and she is "Uttering such dulcet and harmonious breath/That the rude sea grew civil at her song,/And certain stars shot madly from their spheres/To hear the sea-maid's music." Puck replies that he remembers the incident. Oberon goes on to says that at that time he saw, though Puck could not, armed Cupid flying between the moon and the earth. Cupid took aim at "a fair vestal, throned by the west." He missed this target however. Oberon saw him shoot the love-arrow from his bow with the force to pierce a multitude of hearts. But the Fairy King could also see that the fiery shaft was "Quenched in the chaste beams of the wat'ry moon," missing the "imperial vot'ress," who went her way "In maiden meditation, fancy-free." Oberon saw where Cupid's arrow did fall. It hit "a little western flower," which had been white but after being hit turned purple. The name of this flower among maidens is "love-in-idleness." Oberon tells Puck to go out and get that flower for him, the one he once showed to him. The King explains that the juice of this flower, when put on the sleeping eyelids of man or woman, will cause the person to fall madly in love with the very first live creature that is seen upon waking, no matter who or what. Oberon repeats his instruction that Puck get this herb, saying the spirit should be back in less time than it takes a whale to swim a league. Puck replies that he will encircle the earth in forty minutes, and leaves to get the little flower. Oberon, left alone, announces his intention in a soliloquy. Once he has this juice, he'll wait for an opportunity to put some on Titania's eyelids while she sleeps. Then, the very first thing she sees when she wakes—whether it's a lion, bear, wolf, bull, monkey, or ape—she shall be madly in love with to the depths of her soul. While she is in this condition of only having eyes for this creature, Oberon will be able to get the little changeling from her. Afterwards, when he has accomplished this goal, he can take the charm off her sight with another herb.

As soon as Oberon finishes explaining his plan to use the love-juice on Titania, he notices two people approaching and wonders who they are. He declares that he will become invisible so that he can overhear their conversation. The two people are none other than Demetrius and Helena, who now enter with her following him. Demetrius is avowing that he does not love Helena and that she ought not to pursue him therefore. He wants to know where Lysander and Hermia are. Recall that Helena has told him of the planned elopement. He says he'll slay Lysander and that Hermia slays him. He reminds Helena that she told him they had stolen into this wood, "And," he says, "here am I, and wood within this wood," because he cannot find Hermia. (Wood means mad.) Demetrius concludes by brusquely ordering Helena off, telling her to follow him no more. Helena answers that he is like a magnet that draws her to him, except that her heart is not iron but steel, which is truer. She says if he'll stop having such magnetism, she'll stop following him. Demetrius asks if he entices her or speaks persuasively, then answers his own rhetorical questions by saying that he has told her straight out that he does not and cannot love her. Helena says she only loves him the more for that. She likens herself to the spaniel, which fawns on him the more he beats her. She asks that he use her only as a spaniel—spurn, strike, neglect, or lose her—only allow unworthy Helena to follow him. She says that's the lowest place she can ask for, to be used as his dog, but high enough for her. Demetrius warns her not to arouse too much hatred in him, and adds that it makes him sick to look at her. All Helena says to such abuse is that it makes her sick *not* to look at him. Then Demetrius points out the immodesty of her following him, leaving the city and putting herself at the mercy of someone who doesn't love her, when the darkness and the seclusion increase the threat to her virginity. Helena replies that his virtue is her protection, that his face lights the night for her, that he is all the world to her so she's not alone.

Demetrius says he'll run and hide, leaving her to the mercy of the wild beasts. She says he may do so, for he is worse than they could be. She adds that all tales of pursuit shall be turned around and the pursuer shall become the pursued—Daphne chase Apollo, the dove chase the griffin, the hind pursue the tiger—and how ridiculous is such a chase where cowardice pursues and valor flies. Demetrius says he won't listen any more, and if she continues to follow him, he warns that he will do some mischief to her in the wood. Helena agrees ironically, saying he does her mischief everywhere: temple, town, field. She concludes by calling his behavior scandalous, since he reverses the role of the sexes, making her do the wooing. Demetrius exits as Helena says, "We should be wooed, and were not made to woo." Then Helena herself leaves, saying she will follow him and that to die at his hand would be making a heaven of hell.

Oberon, who has been observing all that has passed between Demetrius and Helena, now says he will reverse that situation. Before Demetrius leaves the wood, she will flee from him and he will pursue her. At this point, Puck enters, and Oberon asks if he has the flower with him and welcomes him back. Puck says he has it. Oberon asks him for it. Here follows another of the play's noteworthy passages of poetry. Oberon describes the place where Titania sleeps—"I know a bank where the wild thyme blows"—and he names all the flowers that surround her. He adds that there also the snake sheds her skin, a garment big enough for a fairy's outfit. While Titania sleeps there, Oberon will put this juice on her eyes, which will make her "full of hateful fantasies." Oberon then tells Puck to take some juice too, and go looking through the woods for a couple of Athenians. The lady is in love and the youth disdains her, and so, says Oberon, anoint the youth's eyes when the next thing he sees is the lady. Oberon tells Puck he may recognize the youth by his Athenian clothes. He instructs his spirit to be especially careful so that the youth may be more in love with the lady than she with him. Oberon's concluding words instruct Puck to meet him before the cock crows. Puck's reassurance that he will do so closes this scene.

Act II: Scene 2

This scene takes place in another part of the woods. Titania enters with her attendants. She bids them dance and sing and then go perform their various duties. Some will kill worms ("cankers") in flowers, some will fight with bats ("reremice") for their wings out of which elves' coats shall be made, some will keep back the noisy owl that nightly hoots at them. First they must sing her asleep, then do the above jobs. The fairies then sing their song. It is a lullaby, consisting of two four-line tetrameter stanzas and a six-line chorus. In it, snakes, hedgehogs, newts, and blind-worms (small snakes) are told not to come near the Fairy Queen. Then the chorus calls on Philomele, the nightingale, to come and sing in this lullaby for the Queen. The closing lines of the chorus ask that no harm, spell or charm, come near the lovely Titania. The second stanza warns off spiders, beetles, worms, and snails, and is followed by the same chorus as above.

During the second chorus, Titania falls asleep. The fairies depart to perform the tasks she assigned, leaving one of their band as sentinel. When they have left, Oberon enters and squeezes the flower which Puck brought to him on Titania's eyelids. The King incants a charm over her while doing this. Like the fairies' lullaby, it is in rhymed tetrameter lines. It says that whatever she sees upon waking she will fall in love with, whether ounce (lynx), cat, bear, pard (leopard), or bristly boar. No matter what it is, in her eyes it will appear beloved, and Oberon concludes by wishing she wake when some vile thing is near. Then he exits.

After Oberon has left Titania sleeping with the love-juice on her eyelids, Lysander and Hermia enter. They are trying to execute their plan to elope to Lysander's aunt's house. Lysander speaks, remarking that Hermia is weak from wandering in the woods and admits that he has forgotten how to get to their destination. He suggests that if Hermia is agreeable, they'll rest where they are and await daylight. Hermia agrees, says she will rest right there and he ought to go look for a place for himself. Lysander suggests that they sleep on the same turf since their hearts are betrothed to each other. Hermia says no to this, telling him twice to lie further off. Lysander says his intentions are pure and innocent and then he speaks of how their two hearts are really one so she ought not to deny him a sleeping place at her side. Lying thus, he does not lie, says Lysander. Hermia compliments him on his riddling and says she never meant to accuse him of being a liar, but she still insists that he lie further off for modesty's sake. She wants enough space left between them, as society deems proper between a bachelor and a maid. She bids him good night and wishes his love never alter till the end of his life. Lysander adds Amen to that, saying may his life end when his loyalty to her does. He lies down and prays that sleep come to her. Hermia wishes him the same and they both sleep.

While Hermia and Lysander lie asleep, Puck enters. Recall that Oberon had given him some love-juice to remedy the situation Helena was in with the unloving Demetrius, which the King witnessed. He told Puck to look for a youth with Athenian garments on and put the charm on him. Now Puck says he has gone through the forest without being able to find this Athenian to put the magic juice on. Then he spies Lysander and sees his Athenian clothes. He shouts with joy at gaining the object of his search, saying this must be whom Oberon meant, the Athenian youth who despises the maid. Then he sees Hermia, assuming she is the suffering maiden, and remarking how she dare not lie close to this nasty man—this "lack-love," "kill-courtesy," "churl" (boor). Consequently, Puck casts all the power of the love-charm on Lysander, bidding love take over his eyes and that he wake when Puck is gone. The spirit departs to rejoin Oberon. As soon as he has left, Demetrius and Helena enter at a run. She is begging him to stay, even though he kill her. He bids her be off and stop haunting him. She begs him not to leave her in the dark thus. But Demetrius leaves alone, threatening her with peril if she doesn't stay where she is.

Helena is now by herself and she says she is out of breath with this foolish pursuit, and the more she prays the less she gets. She compares herself to Hermia, happy wherever she may be, and speaks of the beauty of her eyes in particular. Helena says that tears did not make Hermia's eyes so bright because her own are more often washed that way. She says she is as ugly as a bear and it's no wonder that Demetrius flees from her, since all the beasts do. It was absurd of her to compare her eyes to Hermia's. At this point Helena sees Lysander on the ground. She cannot tell if he be dead or asleep and to find out, she awakens him. Of course, Lysander has the lovejuice on his eyes so when he awakens and sees Helena he immediately declares his great love for her. He says he will run through fire for her. He calls her "transparent Helena," saying he can see her heart through her bosom. He asks her where Demetrius is, calls him vile, and ends with the fiery statement that such a man is fit to die on his sword. Helena tells Lysander not to talk that way about Demetrius, even though the latter does love Hermia. For, says Helena, Hermia still loves Lysander and that should content him. Lysander forcefully denies that he could be content with Hermia. He says he repents the time he has spent with the latter; he loves Helena, not Hermia, having had the good sense to change a raven for a dove. He then dwells at length on how this change from one love to another is an instance of his reason governing his will. Reason has told him Helena is worthier, his reason was not ripe till now, but now that it is ripe it is governing his will. And *that's* why he loves Helena. His reason leads him to her eyes where he reads love's stories in love's richest book. Helena is quite taken aback by all this and she assumes that Lysander is making fun of her and scorning her. She asks, isn't it enough she has so much trouble with Demetrius, but he should thus torment her for her insufficiency. She says he does her great wrong to woo her thus in jest—she thought he was better bred than that. She says farewell, and leaves lamenting that she should be refused by one man and abused by another because of that refusal.

After Helena's departure, Lysander remarks that she has not seen Hermia. He bids Hermia stay sleeping where she is and he wishes she may never come near him. He likens her to a sweet food of which he has had a surfeit and to a false belief which is hated when no longer held. He says, may she be hated by all, but most of all by him. He concludes by vowing all his love and strength to the honor and protection of Helena, and then leaves. Hermia awakens when he has left and cries to him for help, asking him to pluck a serpent from her breast. She has had a dream that a serpent was eating her heart and that Lysander looked upon the cruelty with a smile. She is still quaking with fear. She calls his name twice, asks where he might be, bids him speak, and finally ascertaining that he is not anywhere near, she leaves to find him or to die if not.

Act III: Scene 1

This scene takes place in the wood near Titania's bower. The Athenian workmen enter: Quince, Snug, Bottom, Flute, Snout, and Starveling. They have come to rehearse their play as they planned to do in Act I, Scene 2. Bottom is the first to speak and he asks if they are all present. Quince says yes and that the spot they're in is a good place for their rehearsal. It has a clear plot to serve as a stage, and a hawthorn hedge to serve as a dressing room. They will do it just as they intend to before the Duke.

A Midsummer Night's Dream

Bottom here addresses Quince, who turns his attention to his friend, "bully Bottom." Bottom wishes to call Quince's attention to certain things in their play which will never please its audience. First, Pyramus must kill himself with his sword—the ladies will not be able to stand that. Bottom wants to know what's to be done about it. Snout agrees that it is a "parlous" (perilous, terrible) fear, and Starveling thinks they'll have to leave the killing out of the final production. But no, the resourceful Bottom has a ready solution. He says he must recite a prologue that explains everything: their swords do no harm, Pyramus is not dead really, and in fact Pyramus is really Bottom the Weaver. In short, the prologue must declare that all the make-believe is merely make-believe. Then, says Bottom, the audience will not be afraid. Quince agrees to such a prologue and suggests it be written in "eight and six" (lines of eight and six syllables alternating, which is the common ballad meter). Bottom cannot resist adding the last touch, so he says it should be written in eight-syllable lines entirely. Snout asks, won't the ladies be afraid of the lion. Starveling, for one, fears just that result. Bottom says very grandly that they ought to consider very carefully bringing in "a lion among ladies." He says, "there is not a more fearful wild-fowl than your lion living," and it requires some attention. Snout unoriginally suggests another prologue. But Bottom again comes up with the solution that works. The lion costume should not entirely conceal the actor wearing it and he must announce that the lion really isn't one; then say his name is Snug the Joiner.

This plan Quince agrees to and he brings up two more production problems. Thisbe and Pyramus are supposed to meet by moonlight, and also they must talk through a wall. First moonlight is discussed. Snout asks if the moon shines the night of the play, and Bottom calls for an almanac to find out. Quince says, yes, it does. Bottom says then they may leave a window open during their performance and the moonlight will come into the chamber that way. Quince says yes to this idea, adding as an alternative that a man may present moonshine with a lantern and a thorn bush.

Then Quince states the second production problem: Pyramus and Thisbe are supposed to talk through a chink in a wall. Snout doesn't see how they can possibly satisfy this requirement and he asks Bottom's opinion. The indomitable Bottom has the answer. It is based on Quince's idea for moonshine—let a man with plaster, loam, or roughcast on him stand for a wall and he can hold his fingers up for Pyramus and Thisbe to talk through as a chink. Quince agrees that in such a fashion they may solve their production problems. He then begins the rehearsal, calling for Pyramus first. After speaking, everyone shall enter the hawthorn hedge on cue.

After Quince has explained the rehearsal procedure and called on Pyramus

157

to begin, Puck enters. He wonders aloud, "What hempen homespuns have we swagg'ring here, / So near the cradle of the Fairy Queen?" He sees it is a play rehearsal and says he'll watch and perhaps act too if he sees the opportunity. He is not seen by anyone. Quince now directs Pyramus to speak and Thisbe to stand forth. In his first line, Pyramus (Bottom) says "odious" instead of "odors" and Quince corrects him. Bottom makes the correction incorrectly, and continues till he must exit to investigate a noise he hears. Puck comments on what a strange Pyramus Bottom makes and he exits too. Thisbe (Flute) asks if it is his turn to speak. Quince explains that it is, Pyramus having just gone to "see a noise that he heard" and that he will be back. Then Thisbe speaks, praising her Pyramus in flower terms and saying she will meet him at "Ninny's tomb." Quince corrects this to "Ninus' tomb," adding that Flute is not supposed to speak that yet—that's supposed to be in answer to Pyramus. Flute has spoken his part all at once, cues and all. Quince calls for Bottom to enter, saying his cue is past. Thisbe repeats Bottom's cue and at this point Pyramus re-enters and lo he has the head of an ass in place of his human one. Puck accompanies him. Quince shouts out his dismay: "O monstrous! O strange! We are haunted." They all flee in terror from the transformed Bottom, leaving him alone. Puck leaves in order to further torment the terrorized tradesmen. The spirit says he'll assume various animal shapes —horse, hound, hog, headless bear, fire too—and lead the deranged Athenians a merry chase through bog, bush, brake, briar, while he makes all the appropriate animal sounds.

Left alone, Bottom, who does not realize what Puck has done to him, expresses his own amazement at the behavior of his fellows. Since he doesn't know his own condition, he wonders why they have run away from him. He decides that they are playing a practical joke on him and trying to make him afraid. Here Snout re-enters and exclaims, "O Bottom, thou art changed! what do I see on thee?" Bottom's answer is that Snout sees an ass-head of his own. Snout leaves and then Quince re-enters and exclaims in turn, "Bless thee, Bottom! bless thee! thou art translated." When Quince has left again and the bewildered Bottom is alone, he resolutely confronts his situation and analyzes thus: "I see their knavery: this is to make an ass of me; to fright me, if they could." He decides that he'll show them he's not afraid—he'll stay right where he is and not run after them. And furthermore, to show most plainly his courage in the face of adversity, he'll walk around and sing so they'll hear that he's not afraid.

Really frightened and bewildered, but resolutely disclaiming this, Bottom bravely "whistles in the dark" to keep his spirits up in the face of such perplexing behavior on the part of his companions. He therefore walks back and forth and sings a song about a "woosel cock," a "throstle," and a "wren with little quill." His singing wakes Titania, who has been sleeping nearby, and she says, "What angel wakes me from my flow'ry bed?"

Bottom continues undaunted, singing another verse about several more birds: finch, sparrow, lark, and cuckoo. (The "plain-song" of the last is noticed by many and they cannot say "nay" to it). Bottom comments on this last fact in his song, saying it is indeed useless to refute a foolish bird, even though he may be wrong. Now Titania is awake, and with eyes enchanted by the love-juice, she has seen Bottom. Consequently she says will he please sing some more, for she loves to hear him. In fact, she continues, she loves to look at him also. Her words are ironical here, because she doesn't know how very true they are, but we do: "So is mine eye enthrallèd to thy shape," says the poor deluded Queen. To this "hempen homespun" crowned with the head of an ass, the Queen of Fairies says that his "fair virtue's force" (the compelling attraction of his manly charms) causes her on first sight to swear she loves him.

Bottom answers her with the same unswerving realism he applied to the last line of his song. He tells her with plain and beautiful truth that she has little reason for that avowal. He adds the comment that reason and love "keep little company together nowadays," and it's too bad they don't get together. He comments on this observation, saying that he can "gleek" sometimes (make biting jests). Titania's response exhibits the superfluity of her passion—"Thou art as wise as thou art beautiful," she proclaims. Her excessiveness contrasts with Bottom's true and solid declarations, and he himself catches her up on this foolishness, saying abruptly, "Not so." But, he adds, if he were wise enough to get out of the wood, that would be wise enough for him. Now the Queen in Titania reasserts itself, as she says with all the authority of her high position, "Out of this wood do not desire to go." She tells Bottom that he will stay whether he wants to or not, and she explains that she is a powerful spirit on whose commands the summer itself depends. And she loves him. Thus he will go with her and she will have fairies wait upon him. Bottom will sleep on flowers while they sing, and, she concludes, she will "purge thy mortal grossness so" that Bottom will become like an airy spirit. At this point she calls her four fairies to attend on Bottom: Peaseblossom, Cobweb, Moth, and Mustardseed.

The four fairies enter at Titania's call and each in turn announces that he is ready, then in chorus ask where she wants them to go. Titania then lists all the services she wants them to perform for her beloved Bottom. They must accompany him courteously and kindly, feeding him with fruits—apricots, dewberries, purple grapes, green figs, and mulberries. They should steal honey from the bumblebees for him, and to light his way at night they will ignite torches from the glow-worm's eyes. She instructs them to pluck butterfly's wings to fan the moonbeams from his eyes as he sleeps. At her behest, each fairy says, "Hail, mortal!" Bottom genteely returns the greeting and courteously inquires each elf's name. He has a friendly comment upon each name. To Cobweb he says he will use him if he cuts his finger (cobweb was used to staunch blood). To Peaseblossom he says he wishes to be commended to Mistress Squash, his mother, and to Master Peascod, his father (a squash is an unripe pea pod and a peascod is a ripe pea pod). To Mustardseed he mentions the well-known patience associated with him and says also that mustardseed has caused his eyes to water (referring to the spice). To all the elves he has said that he looks forward to knowing them better.

Titania now closes the scene by telling her elves to lead Bottom to her bower. She says the moon looks watery and when this happens the flowers weep, lamenting "some enforced chastity" (violated chastity). Bring him quietly, she orders, and they all leave.

Act III: Scene 2

This scene takes place in another part of the same wood. Oberon enters and wonders out loud what it was that Titania fell in love with under the charm he put on her. Puck enters and Oberon asks him what "nightrule" prevails in this "haunted grove." Puck launches right into a description of what he has done to Bottom and the other workmen and how Titania now loves a "monster." He says that near her bower where she lay asleep "a crew of patches, rude mechanicals" came to rehearse a play for Theseus' wedding celebration. Puck describes Bottom as "the shallowest thickskin of that barren sort" and tells Oberon how, when the workman went behind a hedge, he put an ass's head on him. He describes the havoc this caused among the other workmen when they saw their companion, in terms drawn from hunting—they scattered like wild geese or choughs at a gun shot. Puck continues in his characteristically graphic, rough and homey style to paint the disorder he created with his prank. And finally, says he, the "translated" Pyramus (Bottom), thus deserted by his terrified companions, is seen by the enchanted Titania: "Titania waked and straightway loved an ass."

Oberon says he is more than pleased with this result. He goes on to ask if Puck put the love-juice on the Athenian (meaning Demetrius). Puck says yes to this, and that the woman was nearby so he woke in love with her as Oberon intended (but Puck really enchanted Lysander by mistake). At this point, Hermia and Demetrius enter. Oberon says that here is the Athenian he spoke of. Puck, of course, says that this is the woman, but not the man. Then his mistake becomes evident, for, of course, these two discuss their situation. Demetrius left Helena before she awakened Lysander and was beloved of him by the power of the juice, so he knows nothing of that event. Lysander left Hermia sleeping when he set off to follow Helena, so Hermia is also completely in the dark on that score. All Demetrius knows is that Helena told him of the planned elopement and he wants Hermia for himself and has been searching for her. Now he has found her and he protests his great love for her as usual. She, of course, wants to know what has happened to her true love, Lysander, who had been sleeping by her side. He would *never* leave her and she accuses Demetrius of killing him. Lysander was as true to her as the sun to the day, she says, and she would as soon believe that the moon could go through the center of the earth and shine in the daytime on the other side, as believe that Lysander would thus leave her. Demetrius must have murdered him. Demetrius still plays his love game, saying he's the one who's murdered by Hermia's cruelty to him.

Yet she's as beautiful as "yonder Venus in her glimmering sphere," even though she's a murderer. Poor Hermia has no patience with Demetrius' love prattle now. She wants her Lysander, and begs Demetrius for him. Demetrius replies that he would sooner give Lysander's carcass to his hounds than give him to Hermia. She can't stand this and reviles him thoroughly, begging him to speak the truth for once, and not be a double-tongued serpent, killer of a sleeping man. At this passionate outburst, Demetrius ceases his sweettalk and avows he neither killed him nor has any reason to think he is dead. Hermia begs him to reassure her. At her soft plea, Demetrius' designs on her reassert themselves and he callously asks what his reward will be for doing what she asks. Hermia's anger returns at his suggestive, leering remark and she says his reward is to never see her again. No matter how worried she is about Lysander, she'll stand no more of Demetrius' unpleasantness. She leaves and Demetrius remarks that it will do no good to plead his suit while she's in this temper, so he'll sleep there for awhile. Before doing so, he says a few pretty words on the subject. He then lies down and sleeps.

Demetrius now lies asleep, and Oberon has been made fully aware of Puck's mistake. He says as much to him—Puck has turned a true love into a false one and has not turned any false love true. Puck says it's the rule of fate that for every man who keeps his oath, a million break them. Oberon instructs him to go swiftly through the wood and find Helena of Athens, whom he describes as pale and love-lorn. Bring her by some illusion, says Oberon, and meanwhile Demetrius will be charmed with the love-juice in preparation for her appearance so that he will wake and love her. Puck sings that his departure is swifter that an arrow from a Tartar's bow, and he is off on his errand. Oberon then chants the charm over the sleeping Demetrius: the flower that was hit by Cupid's archery shall cause Demetrius to see Helena shining as gloriously as Venus in the sky. Puck re-enters and tells Oberon that Helena is close by. She is accompanied by Lysander, whom he mistook for Demetrius, and the spectacle they present is well worth watching, the mischievous spirit tells his master. "Lord, what fools these mortals be!" is Puck's famous reaction to the sight of Lysander pleading for Helena's love. Oberon says they must get out of the way, for the sound of Lysander's and Helena's voices will awaken Demetrius. Puck is delighted at the prospect of both men loving Helena at once. He loves preposterous things best, and this will really be something.

Lysander and Helena now enter. He is protesting the truth of his love vows, saying his tears prove that he is not wooing in scorn. Helena insists he's just being cunning. His vows belong to Hermia, and when he makes them to Helena they cancel each other out—his vows amount to nothing. Lysander says he had no judgment when he vowed his love to Hermia. Helena wisely observes that he has none now when he gives Hermia up. Lysander's next argument is that Demetrius loves Hermia and does not love Helena. At this crucial moment Demetrius wakes and immediately declares his great love for Helena in the most extravagant language. He calls her goddess, nymph, perfect, divine; he says her eyes are clearer than crystal, her lips more red than cherries, her hand more white than high mountain snow. Helena is understandably confounded by this declaration. In fact, she's outraged. "O spite! O hell!" she exclaims. She's of the confirmed opinion that they have joined together to make fun of her. She had earlier thought Lysander alone was making fun of her when he declared his undying devotion—now she suspects a league against her. She says, can't they merely hate her without so abusing her? It is not manly of them to carry on so as if they loved her when she knows they hate her. They are really rivals for Hermia's love and now they're just trying to outdo each other in mocking Helena. How low of them to make her cry with their derision, she says. No noble person would so torment and offend a young maid just to have the fun of it.

Lysander now takes it upon himself to reprimand Demetrius, saying that since he loves Hermia, Lysander will give over his claim to that girl. In exchange he'll take Helena, whom he now loves till his death. Helena here interjects her opinion of this as idle mockery and a waste of breath. Now Demetrius has his say, which is, of course, that Lysander can keep his Hermia. He only liked her temporarily, and now his affection has returned home to Helena for good. Lysander tells Helena not to believe Demetrius. Demetrius warns him to keep his opinion to himself, and points out to Lysander that his·beloved Hermia is approaching. At this point Hermia, who knows nothing of all the latest goings on, enters. All she knows is that her Lysander disappeared from her side while she was asleep.

Now Hermia, who has been searching for her beloved Lysander, enters. She has seen Demetrius since, but he was no help. He just annoyed her with his usual persistent wooing. When she finds out what's going on, the confusion will reach its hilarious peak. Hermia begins very sedately by observing that in the darkness her eyes didn't help her find Lysander, but her ears were more acute. She concludes by inquiring in a nice way as to why he left her. Since the confusion hasn't touched her yet, she speaks the usual lover-language of nicely turned, somewhat formal phrases. But she won't be left in the dark for long. Or rather, the deeper darkness of the confused situation will soon descend on her, for Lysander immediately answers that he left because love made him leave. Hermia asks what love could possibly make him leave her? Lysander says his love for Helena, who illumines the night more than do the moon and stars above. He asks Hermia why she followed him—didn't she realize that he left her because he hates her? Hermia can only say that Lysander cannot be speaking his real thoughts.

Helena, having heard this exchange between Lysander and Hermia, now thinks she sees what's going on: Hermia is in on the conspiracy against her. Consequently, Helena begins to reprimand Hermia for joining with Lysander and Demetrius in this "foul derision." Helena recounts all the girlhood pleasures and confidences she and Hermia have shared. She speaks of their sitting in the woods together, embroidering flowers, almost as if they were one person, so intimate was their friendship. She accuses Hermia of breaking these long-standing ties, and says she does an injury to the entire female sex in betraying her girlfriend and joining with men against her. Hermia is amazed at this outburst from Helena. To Hermia it seems that Helena scorns her, not vice versa. Helena explains more fully how things look to her. She thinks that Hermia has told Lysander to pretend that he loves Helena, and she has made her other love, Demetrius, do likewise. Why else should Demetrius, who has reviled Helena up till now, suddenly start praising and loving her? And what possible reason is there for Lysander to deny his love to Hermia except at Hermia's own instigation? Helena concludes with the self-pitying observation that since Hermia is so fortunate in love she ought to pity Helena who isn't, not despise her.

Hermia still can only say she doesn't understand what Helena means. Helena is more than ever convinced that Hermia merely pretends innocence, and she accuses them all once again of making fun of her. She says they all lack pity, grace and manners, and she'll just go away to her death somewhere. Lysander begs Helena to stay, calling her his life, his soul, his love. Helena ironically compliments his acting ability, and Hermia asks him not to scorn Helena thus. Demetrius adds his voice, saying he'll force Lysander to stop. Lysander says neither Hermia's entreaties nor Demetrius' threats can keep him from loving Helena more than life itself, and he'll lose his life to prove it. Demetrius says he loves Helena more, and he and Lysander move to fight for the proof. Hermia still asks what Lysander means by all this, and he answers, "Away, you Ethiope!" Demetrius taunts Lysander to follow and fight. Lysander shakes the clinging, loving Hermia off, and calls her a cat, a burr and a serpent. Hermia asks, "What change is this, Sweet love?" Lysander denies her: "Thy love? Out tawny Tartar, out!/Out, loathed med'cine! O hated potion, hence!" The astounded Hermia still can't believe her ears, and she inquires if Lysander is joking. Hearing this, Helena says that he is indeed joking and so is Hermia. Lysander reaffirms the challenge to fight with Demetrius, who replies that he doesn't trust Lysander, since he can't even shake Hermia off to get away for the fight. Lysander answers that even though he hates Hermia, he won't harm her. To this callous distinction, Hermia replies meaningfully. She finally begins to see that Lysander means what he says, and she observes that he can do her no greater harm than to hate her.

The word finally sinks in and she repeats it: "Hate me? Wherefore? O me, what news, my love?/Am not I Hermia? Are you not Lysander?" She points out the obvious fact that she is as fair as ever, that just last night he loved her, and the same night he left her. Heaven forbid that he left her in earnest, Hermia concludes. Lysander says absolutely and positively yes to this question, and swears on his life as well. He says he never wanted to see her again when he left. He mercilessly pounds home the fact that he loves Helena and hates Hermia—beyond a doubt, a hope, a question, for certain, nothing truer, and no joke. At this most fierce and cruel denunciation from Lysander, Hermia turns on Helena. She calls her friend a juggler, a canker blossom, and a thief of love, who came by night and stole her Lysander's heart from her. Helena pretends to compliment Hermia on her acting ability, chides her for her brazen behavior in joking along with the men, accuses her of trying to get a rise out of Helena by pretending thus, and finally Helena calls Hermia a "counterfeit" and a "puppet." When she hears the word "puppet," Hermia thinks she begins to understand what's going on. The shorter Hermia says she now sees that Helena has won Lysander by comparing their heights, and her being taller has won him. She says Helena has grown so high in Lysander's esteem because Hermia is "so dwarfish and so low." Hermia calls Helena a "painted maypole," and says she's not too "low" to reach Helena's eyes with her nails. Helena is afraid of Hermia now, and pleads with the men to protect her, for she is very cowardly and no match for Hermia even though she is taller than Hermia.

Hermia notes this last reference to her lack of height. Helena now pleads with Hermia not to be so bitter, saying she always loved Hermia. But she adds the confession that she told Demetrius of the planned elopement in order to have his thanks and his company. Helena explains how Demetrius mistreated her in the wood, and now all she wants is to go back to Athens without any fuss, taking her foolishness with her. Hermia says that she should just leave then; who's stopping her? Helena replies that she leaves a foolish heart behind. Hermia asks if she leaves it with Lysander: Helena

says she leaves it with Demetrius. Lysander tells Helena not to be afraid
of Hermia, and Demetrius jumps in to be her protector too. Helena now
says how fierce Hermia is when she is angry, and that she was a "vixen"
at school despite her small size. Hermia is very annoyed at this repeated
reference to her short stature and attempts to get to Helena. Lysander
takes it upon himself to revile Hermia in particuarly this way now, calling
her "dwarf," "minimus," "bead," "acorn." Demetrius says Lysander med-
dles too much with Helena, who scorns him. Demetrius says Lysander
will be sorry if he insists on demonstrating his love for Helena. Lysander
says now he's free of Hermia, and he'll fight with Demetrius to see who
gets Helena. Demetrius is eager to do so, and the men leave. Hermia
addresses Helena now and says this whole mess is because of her. Helena
backs off, saying she won't trust Hermia, nor remain in her quarrelsome
company. Hermia's hands are quicker to fight, says Helena, but Helena's
legs, being longer, are good for running away. Hermia can only reply,
"I am amazed, and know not what to say," and both girls leave.

With all four lovers gone, Oberon addresses Puck, and lays the above
havoc at his doorstep. It is Puck's negligence that is the cause, and he
either made a mistake once again, or else did the mischief on purpose.
Puck vows that he made a mistake. After all, he did apply the juice to
someone wearing Athenian clothes as Oberon commanded. However, he
freely admits that he takes great pleasure in the way things turned out—
their "jangling" is a real spectator sport to him. Oberon now says that
since the two men have gone off to fight, he wants Robin to make the
night foggy and lead the rivals astray so they don't ever come at each
other. The King tells him to imitate each man's voice, alternately stirring
them up and leading them on, but always in opposite directions. Keep
them thus separated till they grow very sleepy. Then, says Oberon, crush
another juice on the sleeping Lysander's eyes. This second juice has the
effect of removing the enchantment from his eyes so that he will love
Hermia as before. Thus, Oberon continues, they will all four wake up
and think all that has passed is only a "dream and fruitless vision." They
will go back to Athens, correctly paired two-by-two, and remain so till
death. Oberon concludes by saying that in the meantime he'll go to
Titania and get the little Indian boy. Once he has this object of his desire,
he'll release the Queen from the love charm, she'll no longer love the
monster, and everything will be peaceful. Puck says all this must be done
quickly because the dawn is approaching. He speaks of how ghosts and
damned spirits who have been wandering all night must now return to
their unquiet graves at crossroads or under water. They are too ashamed
to have the light of day shine on them, and they willfully deny themselves daylight and only go out at night. Oberon, says, "But we are spirits
of another sort." And he very beautifully describes how he has enjoyed
the morning. He may stay abroad in full daylight while the red sun turns
the green sea into gold. But, he concludes, let us still be quick with our

business, and we'll get it done before daybreak.

After Oberon speaks of his delight in the morning, he leaves to find Titania. Puck remains to do his job on Lysander and Demetrius. He chants a song in happy anticipation of how he will mislead them. Then he spies Lysander, who enters searching for Demetrius. Puck speaks in Demetrius' voice and Lysander exits again in an attempt to follow the voice he has heard. Now Demetrius enters, having heard Lysander answer Puck, and demands that Lysander show himself, calling him a coward. Puck now speaks like Lysander to Demetrius and eggs him on. Demetrius cannot find his foe and now Puck says he should follow his voice and leads him away. Lysander re-enters when they have gone and complains that as fast as he follows, Demetrius runs away even faster. He says he'll rest till daylight comes to help him find Demetrius, and he lies down and sleeps. Now Puck and Demetrius come back, and Puck is still leading Demetrius on. Demetrius dares him to wait and face up to the fight, and says he just runs away. Puck continues to imitate Lysander, till finally Demetrius is exasperated with the fruitless pursuit and he too says he'll catch his foe in daylight. Then he lies down and sleeps. Now Helena enters, complaining of her weariness, and desiring daylight to come to show her the way back to Athens so she may escape the company of these that hate her. She bids sleep come to put her out of her sorrowful condition for a time. Then she goes to sleep also. Now Puck comments that one more is needed to make up the complete company—two of each kind, he says. He comments, "Cupid is a knavish lad/Thus to make poor females mad." Now Hermia enters, weary and woebegone. She can go no further, she says, and will rest where she is till daylight. Her last words before sleeping ask that the heavens protect her Lysander if there is a fight between him and Demetrius.

Now Puck chants over Lysander and applies the curative to Lysander's eyelids. Puck's song says that when Lysander wakes he will take "True delight/In the sight/Of thy former lady's eye." Puck concludes his song and the scene with a country proverb: Every man should take his own. When every Jack has his Jill all will be well, predicts Puck, and with his pronouncement on life the scene closes.

Act IV: Scene 1

We now return to the situation we left at the end of Act III, Scene 1, where Titania is madly in love with the transformed Bottom. This scene opens with the entrance of Titania, Bottom, and the attendant fairies. Oberon is behind them. Titania is speaking lovingly to Bottom. She wants him to sit down so she can stroke his cheeks, crown him with musk-roses, and kiss his "fair large ears." Bottom, completely at home in his new environment, calls for Peaseblossom. He asks the latter to scratch his head, and then call "Monsieur Cobweb" to him and tell him to bring him some honey, adding considerately that the fairy ought to be careful not to drown in it. Bottom asks "Monsieur Mustardseed" to help "Cavalery Cobweb" scratch Bottom's head. Bottom remarks that he must go to the barber's soon, for he has an extraordinary amount of hair on his face, and he is "such a tender ass" that it tickles him. Titania asks her beloved if he would like some music, and he answers that he would like the "tongs and the bones." The Queen also inquires what he might like to eat, and Bottom replies that he wants provender, oats, and hay. Titania suggests nuts, but Bottom would rather have dried peas. What he most desires right at the moment, however, is to sleep. Titania dismisses all the fairies and, holding Bottom in her arms as the woodbine twists around the honeysuckle or as the ivy encircles the elm, they both sleep. Puck enters and Oberon advances to meet him, pointing out the sight of Titania and Bottom together. Oberon says he is beginning to pity Titania's condition. He met her while she was waiting upon Bottom and he taunted her for it. She begged his patience and he then requested the changeling, which she gave him immediately. Oberon adds the detail that the flowers with which she had crowned Bottom had dew standing in them like tears at the disgrace of being used for such a purpose. Now that Oberon has the boy, he tells Puck, he will take the charm off his Queen's eyes. He instructs Puck to remove the ass's head from Bottom so that the latter may return to Athens with everyone else. Oberon says that Bottom will think his experience to be no more than "the fierce vexation of a dream." Before Puck restores Bottom, Oberon will release Titania. Oberon recites a chant over her that says she will see with her customary eyes, and that "Dian's bud" will overpower "Cupid's flower."

Then he wakes her, and Titania says, "My Oberon, what visions have I seen!/Methought I was enamored of an ass." Oberon points to Bottom and says she loved him. Titania wants to know how that came to be, saying she hates his sight now. Oberon asks her to be silent for awhile, he tells Puck to remove the ass's head from Bottom, and he tells Titania to call for music that will put Bottom into a deep sleep. Titania and Puck do what Oberon has bid, music plays, and the King and Queen dance hand in hand. Oberon says that he and his Queen, in renewed harmony, will dance in Theseus' house the next night and bless it. The two pairs of lovers will also be wedded in all happiness. Puck calls Oberon's attention to the sound of the morning lark. Oberon says they will leave then, adding that they can circle the world "swifter than the wand'ring moon." Titania asks that on their flight she be told how she happened to be sleeping on the ground with all the mortals. All the fairies leave.

Heralded by the sound of a horn, Theseus and all his attendants enter, accompanied by Hippolyta and Egeus. Theseus speaks, saying that now their performance of the May morning ritual is over and while it's still early he'll exhibit his fine hunting hounds to Hippolyta. He commands that the dogs be let loose so that she may hear the music of their barking, and he sends for the forester. The forester is the manager of game and hunting preparations in the royal forest. Theseus tells Hippolyta that they'll go up to the mountain-top to listen to the interplay of barking with echoes. She says she was with Hercules and Cadmus in Crete when they hunted a bear with Spartan hounds. She said she never heard such beautiful sounds—groves, skies, fountains, every place was filled with a concert of sound. "I never heard/So musical a discord, such sweet thunder," Hippolyta says. Theseus is moved by this praise to claim more for his own hounds. The Duke waxes poetic in this famous description. His dogs are of the Spartan breed, and they have the same dewlaps, sandy color, long ears, and thick legs. Though slow, they are "matched in mouth like bells,/Each under each." Theseus' enthusiasm for this latter quality leads him to say that more harmonious sounds never accompanied hunting anywhere, be it Crete, Sparta, or Thessaly, and he tells Hippolyta to decide when she hears. At this moment, Theseus notices the four lovers asleep on the ground, and inquires who they are. Egeus names his daughter Hermia, Lysander, Demetrius, and Nedar's daughter Helena, and he says he wonders what they're all doing there. Theseus says they probably got up early to celebrate May Day and came to the wood because they heard the Duke was celebrating the day in the wood. Theseus asks Egeus if this is the day that Hermia is supposed to announce her choice between Demetrius as a husband on the one hand, and death or a nunnery on the other. Egeus says that it is, and Theseus orders that the huntsman wake the sleeping lovers by blowing the hunting horns. This is done, and they all start up.

Theseus greets them and makes a joke about St. Valentine's Day, when, it was thought, birds began to mate. Lysander asks the Duke's pardon. Theseus requests that they stand up, and he says he knows that the two men are rivals, so how is it that they are here together asleep? Lysander says he can only reply in amazement himself and still half-asleep, but, though he hesitates to say for certain, he thinks he came into the woods with Hermia. Yes, that was it—he came to the woods with Hermia in order to flee the Athenian law. Egeus doesn't let him get any further with his explanation. The enraged father demands the law on Lysander's head, and points out to Demetrius how Lysander was trying to cheat him. Demetrius now speaks and says Helena told him of the planned elopement. He followed them in fury, and she followed him in fancy. But, continues Demetrius, though he's at a loss to say *which* power, some power for sure has dissolved completely his love for Hermia, which now seems just the memory of a childhood toy. Furthermore, he is now completely enamoured of Helena, his heart belongs to Helena, he can see only Helena. Demetrius explains that he was betrothed to Helena before he loved Hermia, and he must have been like a sick man whose appetite is malfunctioning to have ever stopped loving her. Now, he's like a man returned to a healthy state who has his natural appetite again, and he loves Helena and will continue to forever. Theseus says to the lovers that their meeting was fortunate, and he'll hear more of their story later. The Duke tells Egeus that he overrides the father's wishes with respect to his daughter, and the two couples shall be married when he and Hippolyta are. Since the day has grown later, there won't be any hunting and they'll all go back to Athens for a stately feast. Theseus bids Hippolyta come and they leave with Egeus.

After Theseus, Hippolyta, and Egeus have left, the lovers remain behind for a few moments to exchange expressions of amazement at their condition. Demetrius says things seem like mountains seen at such a great distance that they look like clouds. Hermia says it's like seeing double. Helena agrees with her, and says she can't believe she really has her Demetrius—it's like finding a jewel by accident. Demetrius asks the others if they're sure they're all awake. It seems to him that he's still asleep and dreaming. He asks if the Duke came and bid them leave with him. Hermia says yes, and her father, too. Helena adds Hippolyta, and Lysander contributes that they were indeed bid to go with Theseus to the temple. Demetrius says that they must be awake then, and they ought to follow the Duke and tell each other their dreams on the way. The lovers leave.

After the lovers have left, Bottom wakes up. He thinks he's still rehearsing "Pyramus and Thisbe." His first words are that he should be summoned when his cue comes, and he gives his next cue, "Most fair Pyramus." Suddenly he wakes up enough to realize he's alone, and he calls for his companions, Quince, Flute, Snout, and Starveling. He says that they've stolen away and left him asleep, and what a "most rare vision" he's had meanwhile. Bottom's famous reaction to his experience is, "I've had a dream, past the wit of man to say what dream it was. Man is but an ass if he go about to expound this dream." Bottom begins to say what happened to him, but he breaks off and says only a fool would attempt to say what happened to him. None of man's senses can apprehend his dream, he says. In describing this, he confuses all the senses and applies them to the wrong bodily organ: the eye can't hear, the ear can't see, the hand can't taste, the tongue can't conceive, and the heart can't report what his dream was. He says he'll get Peter Quince to write a ballad on his dream. It will be called "Bottom's Dream" because it has no bottom, he says. He will sing it at the end of their play before the Duke, perhaps at Thisbe's death. Bottom's departure here ends the scene.

Act IV: Scene 2

In this scene we are back in Athens with the workmen. Quince, Flute,

Snout, and Starveling enter. Quince asks if anyone's been to Bottom's house to inquire if he's come home yet. Starveling says he hasn't been heard from yet, and that doubtless he's been "transported," meaning either carried off or transformed. Flute says that their play will be spoiled if he doesn't come back. They can't do it without him. Quince agrees with this, saying that no one in all Athens can play Pyramus except Bottom. Flute says Bottom has the best mind of any workman in Athens. Quince agrees and adds that Bottom has the best appearance and voice too. He uses the word "paramour" when he means "paragon" and Flute corrects him saying that a "paramour" is nothing. Snug enters with the news that the Duke has left the temple and that there are "two or three lords and ladies more married." If they had been able to perform their play it would have done them a lot of good. Flute bemoans Bottom's missing the pension the Duke surely would have granted him after seeing his marvelous performance as Pyramus. He would have deserved sixpence a day for sure. At this moment, Bottom enters, inquiring lovingly for his friends. He calls them "lads" and "hearts." Quince exclaims with joy and calls the day "courageous" and the hour "most happy." Bottom tells his friends that he'll tell them wonders, but they mustn't ask what. Then he says he'll tell them everything just as it happened. Quince asks to hear. Now Bottom won't say a word, except that the Duke is through dinner, and they must get ready to perform their play. He instructs them to be clean and well-groomed, except for the lion's long nails, and not to eat onions or garlic. Thus they'll have sweet breath and their play will be considered a sweet comedy. He bids them depart without further talk and they all leave.

Act V: Scene 1

In this scene we are back in Theseus' palace again. Theseus, Hippolyta, Philostrate, lords, and attendants enter. Hippolyta remarks that what the lovers have spoken of is strange. Theseus answers in a famous speech about the lover, the madman and the poet. He says the lovers' story is "more strange than true," and he for one never believes old stories and fairy tales. Lovers and madmen have "seething brains" that grasp more than reason can understand. In fact, he continues, the lunatic, the lover, and the poet all have the same kind of imagination, they just imagine different things. The madman sees more devils than there are in hell. The equally frantic lover imagines a mere gypsy to be as beautiful as Helen of Troy. The frenzied eye of the poet looks back and forth between heaven and earth and whatever the imagination comes up with, he with his pen gives a shape and a name to it. In Theseus' famous words, the poet "gives to airy nothing/A local habitation and a name." He says the imagination has such "tricks" that if it wants to grasp a joy, it can use reason to understand how to bring that joy. Theseus concludes with the example of being frightened at night and thinking that a bush is a bear.

However, Hippolyta still says that the whole story, with everyone's minds "transfigured so together," is more than fanciful imaginings. The story exhibits great constancy, even though it is strange and admirable. Theseus says that the lovers are coming, mirthful and joyous. At this point, Lysander, Demetrius, Hermia, and Helena enter, and Theseus wishes them joy and love. Lysander replies with the wish that the Duke have even more of the same. Theseus asks what entertainment is available to pass the time away between after-supper and bed-time. He calls for Philostrate, the manager of entertainment at court, and the latter says that he is here. Theseus asks him what entertainment is available and Philostrate hands him a list of possibilities which the Duke reads out loud. Out of four choices he selects "Pyramus and Thisbe" and questions Philostrate about it. The description given him interests him by its strange combinations: "A tedious brief scene of young Pyramus/And his love Thisbe; very tragical mirth" is what the tradesmen have called their offering. Theseus comments on the combination of opposites. Philostrate explains that though the play is very short indeed, it is tedious to watch because it is performed so badly; and though Pyramus kills himself, the whole performance made Philostrate laugh.

Theseus asks who the players are and is told about the efforts of the Athenian workmen who are rank amateurs completely unaccustomed to using their minds. Theseus says he wants to see the play. Philostrate tries to dissuade him, saying the only thing amusing about it is how hard they try. But Theseus insists on his choice, saying that if their intentions are good that's all that counts, and he sends Philostrate to get the performers. Hippolyta says she doesn't want to watch these workmen struggle and fail to please. Theseus says she needn't worry, and she replies that Philostrate said they were completely inept. Theseus says that, in that case, more kindness and nobility will be required of the audience. He tells her how he is often confronted with tongue-tied public officials and yet he knows that they mean well. Philostrate comes back and says that the prologue of the play is ready to be spoken. Quince speaks his part and he doesn't punctuate and pause meaningfully, so it comes out all wrong. Theseus, Lysander, and Hippolyta remark how little sense his speech made. Each has a different metaphor for this. Next enter the rest of the actors: Pyramus, Thisbe, Wall, Moonshine, and Lion. Quince continues with the prologue and gives a summary of the story and introduces each character. They all leave except Wall. Theseus says he wonders if the Lion will speak and Demetrius makes the joke that one lion may, since many asses do. Now Wall speaks and introduces himself as Snout, telling what his part is in the play. Through a chink in this wall the lovers whisper. Theseus and Demetrius remark on the wit of the Wall in speaking so. Now Pyramus re-enters, and addresses the black night and the Wall, asking where is his Thisbe. He looks through the chink and cannot see her. Theseus says the Wall should answer, but Bottom tells him that's not the way the play goes. It is Thisbe's cue and she will enter in a moment, he patiently explains.

Thisbe enters and addresses her love-complaint to the Wall that always separates her from Pyramus. Pyramus says that he "sees" her voice and he'll try to "hear" her face. The lovers then greet each other and liken their love to that of famous lovers in the past, only they make their usual errors in doing it. Instead of "Leander and Hero" they mention "Limander and Helen" and for "Cephalus" and "Procris" they say "Shafalus" and "Procrus." This loving exchange is in the form of single, alternating lines of dialogue, rhymed by twos ("stichomythia"). Pyramus and Thisbe arrange to meet at "Ninny's tomb" and Pyramus says he'll be there, come life or death. They exit, and so does Wall, after first saying that he's done his job so he's leaving. Theseus, Demetrius, and Hippolyta exchange comments on what they have just seen. They think it's silly and Theseus says all acting is just "shadows" requiring the audience to use imagination. For this performance, one has to use a little more imagination, that's all. Lion and Moonshine re-enter now, and Lion explains that he's really Snug the Joiner so the ladies won't be frightened. Theseus, Demetrius, and Lysander must comment here too, and they exchange supercilious witticisms about the discretion and valor of Lion. Now Moonshine tries to explain his characterization, but Demetrius and Theseus persist in their disruptive comments. Their joke is that old stand-by about horns, since Moonshine says he is the "horned" (crescent) moon. Hippolyta says she is weary of the moon and wishes it would change. Theseus makes another comment and finally Moonshine gets to speak his whole speech.

But as soon as he finishes, Demetrius must unnecessarily point out that all the objects that Starveling is carrying ought to be inside the lantern since they are inside the moon. Now Thisbe re-enters to keep her appointment at "Ninny's tomb" and she is frightened away by the roar of Lion. Demetrius, Theseus, and Hippolyta compliment Lion, Thisbe and Moon. Hippolyta had said she was weary of the moon, but here she says, "Truly, the moon shines with a good grace." The Lion now shakes the mantle Thisbe dropped before he exits. Theseus, Lysander and Demetrius comment briefly. Pyramus comes in now and, seeing the blood-stained mantle of Thisbe, recites a passionate speech. Theseus says it almost makes a man sad to see this. Hippolyta remarks feelingly, "Beshrew my heart, but I pity the man." Pyramus continues his passionate expression of grief and concludes by killing himself. Moonshine exits and Pyramus dies. Demetrius, Lysander, and Theseus comment once again. Hippolyta inquires how Thisbe will find her lover with the moon gone, and Theseus replies that she will find him by starlight. Thisbe re-enters and Hippolyta says that she hopes she'll be brief. Demetrius and Lysander also comment. Thisbe finds Pyramus and, after first thinking he's asleep, she sorrows deeply over his death. She describes him as having the colors of various flowers: "lily lips," "cherry nose," "yellow cowslip cheeks," and eyes "green as leeks." She calls on the Fates who have killed him to end her life, and she stabs herself to death. Theseus says that Moonshine and Lion are now left to bury the dead lovers. Demetrius adds Wall. At this, Bottom starts up and explains that the wall of hostility between their two families is now no longer. He asks if the audience wishes to see an epilogue or to hear a dance.

Theseus says no epilogue is needed and compliments them on the performance. He requests that they perform their dance instead. Afterwards, the Duke announces that it is midnight and time for bed. It's almost "fairy time" says Theseus and he's afraid they'll oversleep the next morning from being up so late. The performance of "Pyramus and Thisbe" has made the evening pass very quickly. He concludes by saying that they'll continue to celebrate for another fortnight (two weeks), and with these words, everyone leaves.

When everyone has left, Puck enters. He describes the night—the wild animals that roar, howl, and screech; the ghosts that leave their graves to wander abroad; and the fairies like himself that "follow darkness like a dream," and at night make merry. He says nothing shall disturb Theseus' house, and he has been sent with a broom to sweep there. Oberon and Titania enter with their attendants, and the fairies sing and dance. Oberon bids his subjects go about the house blessing everyone. He himself will bless the royal union so that they shall love forever and have perfect offspring. He hands out "field-dew" to be sprinkled in blessing everywhere, and instructs everyone to meet at daybreak. The King and Queen leave with their followers. Puck has the last words in the play. He says that if the play has not pleased but offended, just write it off as a dream. If they're lucky enough to escape being hissed and booed, then he promises they'll improve. And if the audience applauds, then Puck will do good for them. With this, the spirit exits and the play ends.

Much Ado About Nothing

DON PEDRO, *Prince of Arragon.*
DON JOHN, *his bastard brother.*
CLAUDIO, *a young lord of Florence.*
BENEDICK, *a young lord of Padua.*
LEONATO, *governor of Messina.*
ANTONIO, *his brother.*
BALTHASAR, *attendant on Don Pedro.*
CONRADE }
BORACHIO } *followers of Don John.*
FRIAR FRANCIS.
DOGBERRY, *a constable.*
VERGES, *a headborough.*
A SEXTON.
A BOY.

HERO, *daughter to Leonato.*
BEATRICE, *niece to Leonato.*
MARGARET }
URSULA } *gentlewomen attending on Hero.*

MESSENGERS, WATCH, ATTENDANTS, *etc.*

Much Ado About Nothing

Act I: Scene 1

The entire play takes place in Messina, in Italy. Most of the action takes place in and around the house of Leonato, governor of Messina.

A messenger is reporting to Leonato, his daughter Hero, and his niece Beatrice that Don Pedro, Prince of Arragon, will be stopping at Messina that night on his way back from an "action" (that is, a war, presumably the war of rebellion which we later learn has been promoted by his bastard brother Don John). Leonato also learns that a young Florentine named Claudio has received much honor in this war, "doing in the figure of a lamb the feats of a lion." Claudio has an uncle in Messina and, as the messenger reports, at the news of Claudio's valorous deeds he broke out into tears "in great measure." Leonato calls this a "kind overflow of kindness" and adds that "there are no faces truer than those that are so washed."

Beatrice interrupts by asking whether "Signior Mountanto" (by whom she means Benedick, an officer in Don Pedro's army) has returned from the wars. "Mountanto" is a dueling term, and we are to understand here both that Beatrice and Benedick are familiar with each other, and that she is jibing at what appears to be a certain cavalier or boastful quality in his character. The messenger replies that he has also returned, and Beatrice makes some further insulting remarks about his "gallantry," at which Leonato chides her for "taxing Signior Benedick too much," and reminds her than Benedick is her match in witty banter. But she continues, saying that since he is such an excellent "trencher man" (a good man with knife and fork) he ought to have a good "stomach" for fighting. The messenger insists that Benedick is a man "stuffed with all honorable virtues," and Beatrice picks up the messenger's unfortunate word, retorting: "It is so indeed; he is no less than a stuffed man; but for the stuffing—well, we are all mortal."

Leonato mollifies the messenger by explaining that there is a kind of "merry war" which goes on between Beatrice and Benedick and that they never meet without a "skirmish of wit." Beatrice replies that it does Benedick no good, for in their last conflict he lost four of his five wits. Then (perhaps with ill-concealed irritation at Benedick's preference for male friendship) she asks "who is his companion now? He hath every month a new sworn brother."

The messenger observes, "I see, lady, the gentleman is not in your books" (that is, he is not high in your estimation), and she answers, mockingly, that if he were she would burn her study. After a few more jibes their conversation is interrupted by the arrival of Don Pedro, Don John, Claudio, Benedick, Balthazar (Don Pedro's servant), and other supernumeraries. Leonato and Don Pedro exchange compliments, and Benedick gets the worst of a witty exchange with Leonato, which gives Beatrice a chance to gloat. He immediately turns to her and remarks: "What! my dear Lady Disdain, are you yet living?" Here begins the first of the skirmishes in the "merry war" between them. The banter is not easily summarized or paraphrased, but it consists of an exchange of insults and heated denials of love, in which Beatrice claims that Benedick is the very food of disdain, and he claims to have a hard heart and to be in love with no lady. She calls this a "happiness for women" and thanks God for her cold blood, for she "would rather hear her dog bark at a crow than a man swear he loves her." He hopes she never changes her mind, for some gentleman or other will thus escape a "predestinate scratched face." If it were a face like his, Beatrice retorts, it could not be made worse by scratching.

Don Pedro announces that they will accept Leonato's gracious invitation for a month's visit. Leonato even includes Don John in the invitation, since he is now reconciled to his brother. All but Claudio and Benedick leave, whereupon Claudio asks his friend whether he "noted" the daughter of Leonato. He replies, "I noted her not; but I looked on her" (a repetition of the external appearance, inner reality figure). Claudio persists in having Benedick's "sober judgment" of Hero, and he is told:

"Why, i'faith, methinks she's too low for a high praise, too brown for a fair praise, and too little for a great praise. Only this commendation I can afford her, that were she other than she is, she were unhandsome, and being no other but as she is, I do not like her."

And when Claudio insists, "I pray thee tell me truly how thou likest her," Benedick asks (with some sarcasm), "Would you buy her, that you inquire after her?"

Claudio then calls Hero "the sweetest lady that ever I looked on," but is refuted by Benedick, who replies (in another instance of the appearance-reality theme), "I can see yet without spectacles, and I see no such matter." And he chides Claudio for even considering marriage at all.

At this point Don Pedro enters and inquires why they have not followed him to Leonato's house. Benedick asks him to command him to answer truthfully, and when he is thus commanded gleefully reports that Claudio is in love with Hero. Claudio admits it frankly, saying, "That I love her, I feel." And Don Pedro matches this with the remark, "That she is worthy, I know." Both comments are later seen to be ironic in view of the rapidity with which the two of them are taken in by the preposterous allegations against Hero. (Of course, it is the glibness with which some people are prone to use such words as "love" and "worthy" without any really serious analysis of their own feelings which the entire Claudio-Hero plot line illuminates, among other things.) Benedick may be too scrupulous in this respect, but we feel that there is something salutary in his statement immediately following: "That I neither feel how she should be loved nor how she should be worthy, is the opinion that fire cannot melt out of me; I will die in it at the stake." Don Pedro calls him "an obstinate heretic in the despite of beauty."

Benedick expresses gratitude that woman bore him and nurtured him, but declines to have "a recheat winded in my forehead," or to "hang his bugle in an invisible baldrick," apparently a reference to the cuckold's fate which any husband may suffer—he will remain a bachelor. Don Pedro (with the wisdom born of experience) asserts: "I shall see thee, ere I die, look pale with love," but this only provokes Benedick to the vehement promise that if he ever loses more blood with love than he can get back through drinking he will allow them to "hang me up at the door of a brothel-house for the sign of blind Cupid." Don Pedro's sententious quotation, "In time the savage bull doth bear the yoke," leads to some further good-natured raillery centering about "horns" (a symbol of sexual activity); the Prince finally sends Benedick to Leonato with word that they will meet him for supper. After his departure, Claudio tells the Prince that he may be able to help him in his suit and asks: "Hath Leonato any son, my lord?" The Prince replies, "No child but Hero; she's his only heir."

That Don Pedro subscribes to the (courtly love) stereotype of the lover as a spouter of poetic praises of his lady, is indicated by his remark to Claudio: "Thou wilt be like a lover presently, / And tire the hearer with a book of words." He promises, however, not only to intercede with Leonato in Claudio's behalf, but actually to broach his suit to Hero herself—in fact, to woo her for him—an arrangement which only serves to underline the superficiality of the kind of "love" which Claudio imagines he has for Hero. There is to be a masked ball that evening at Leonato's house, and the Prince offers to pretend that he is Claudio in disguise and to "unclasp his heart" in Hero's bosom, and to "take her hearing prisoner with the force / And strong encounter of my amorous tale." "She shall be thine," he promises the young lord.

Act I: Scene 2

In a room in Leonato's house the governor and his brother Antonio are commenting on the preparations for the ball. Antonio reports the "good news" that one of his servants overheard Don Pedro announcing that he loved Hero and intended to ask for her hand in marriage. Leonato decides to be less than optimistic about this, but determines to inform Hero so that she may be prepared in any case.

Act I: Scene 3

In another room in Leonato's house, Don John and his man Conrade are conversing. Conrade wishes to know why his lord is so "sad without measure" and bids him listen to reason. Don John wonders that a man of Conrade's stamp, born under Saturn (planet of malevolent influence) should thus go about to "apply a moral medicine to a mortifying mischief." Conrade advises Don John to bide his time and let the good graces of his brother grow with time. But he is told (in a well-known speech, which shows the motiveless malignity of Don John): "I had rather be a canker in a hedge than a rose in his grace; and it better fits my blood to be disdained of all than to fashion a carriage to rob love from any. In this, though I cannot be said to be a flattering honest man, it must not be denied but that I am a plain-dealing villain."

He ends by saying, "let me be that I am, and seek not to alter me." Borachio enters with news of the projected marriage, which he heard about by concealing himself behind an arras while Don Pedro and Claudio were discussing it. Don John immediately perceives that this may give him the opportunity he wants of practicing mischief. Besides, he hates Claudio for having covered himself with glory in the war of rebellion. Conrade and Borachio both agree to assist him in any plot.

Act II: Scene 1

The first scene opens in a hall in Leonato's house. Leonato, Antonio, Beatrice, and Hero are discussing Don John. To Beatrice he seems to "look tartly," and he gives her heartburn for an hour. Hero describes him (in more conventional terms) as being "of a very melancholy disposition."

Beatrice suggests that a man who should combine in himself the qualities of Don John and Benedick would be an excellent man; such a man could win any woman in the world, provided he also had a good leg (for bowing?), a good foot (for dancing?), and money enough. Leonato calls her "shrewd" (that is, "like a shrew," rather than simply "clever"), and Antonio calls her "too curst." By quoting the proverb, "God sends a curst cow short horns," Beatrice wittily "proves" that by being too curst she will have no "horns" at all; that is, she will have no husband. In any case, she could not stand a husband with a beard on his face, though Leonato suggests that she may find one without a beard. She retorts: "What should I do with him? Dress him in my apparel and make him my waiting gentlewoman? He that hath a beard is more than a youth, and he that hath no beard is less than a man; and he that is more than a youth is not for me; and he that is less than a man, I am not for him. Therefore I will take even sixpence in earnest of the Bear-ward, and lead his apes into hell."

Leonato thinks he can create a witty trap—make her admit she is bound for hell, but she says no, the devil (wearing horns, and hence an "old cuckold") will send her (since she has refused marriage—and therefore "horns") off to heaven where she will sit with the bachelors and live "as merry as the day is long." Leonato, in good humor, expresses the wish that she may someday be fitted with a good husband, but she replies that she will never be mastered by a "piece of valiant dust," a "clod of wayward marl"; besides, Adam's sons are her brethren, and she holds it a sin to marry her kindred.

Leonato then turns to Hero and bids her make a proper answer to the Prince if he should bring up the subject of marriage. Beatrice interrupts, and reminds Hero that "the fault will be in the music" if she "be not wooed in good time." If the Prince seems too lofty for her, she may "tell him there is measure in everything and so dance out the answer."

Beatrice even couches her "marry in haste" warning in the dance figure: "Wooing, wedding, and repenting is as a Scotch jig, a measure, and a cinque-pace"; wooing is the jig, the wedding the measure, and Repentance dances the cinque-pace (by "sinking" into his grave). Leonato compliments her on her "shrewd apprehension" and, in a famous line, Beatrice retorts: "I have a good eye, uncle; I can see a church by daylight." At this point the rest of the revelers enter, all masked. (The usual Elizabethan stage convention provided that disguise was impenetrable, but in this scene we are certainly meant to consider the possibility that the maskers know each other. We know definitely, in any case, that Benedick recognizes Beatrice.)

Don Pedro is first shown walking aside with Hero, and it is apparent that his wooing of her (for Claudio) will now begin. Balthazar, his servant, is shown dancing with Margaret, Hero's lady-in-waiting. There is a slight flirtatious exchange, ending in Margaret's "prayer" to be matched with a good dancer, but to be rid of him when the dance is done. Ursula, another of Hero's maids, is with Antonio; she tells him she knows it is he by the waggling of his head and his dry hands, but he denies it until she admits that she knows him by his "excellent wit." Finally, Benedick and Beatrice are shown conversing. He reports that someone told him she was disdainful and got all of her "wit" out of *The Hundred Merry Tales* (a popular jest book of the day). She says it must have been Benedick who told him, and then describes him as a jester and a dull fool, a slanderer and a villain. When he is introduced to the gentleman, Benedick promises, he will pass the word on to him. Suddenly, hearing the sound of music within, he remarks: "We must follow the leaders" (that is, of the dance), and she adds, "in every good thing."

The maskers dance and then leave, Don John, Borachio, and Claudio remaining on the stage. Don John accosts Claudio as if he were Benedick and asks him to try to dissuade the Prince from marriage with Hero since she is no match for him in social station. When "Benedick" (Claudio) inquires how he knows the Prince loves her, Don John lies, saying that he overheard him swearing his affection. Borachio confirms this, adding that the Prince is eager to marry her that very night. Left alone, Claudio (who believes what he has been told) makes a cynical speech about "all being fair in love," and repents his decision to let the Prince speak for him. "Let every eye negotiate for itself," he declares, "and trust no agent; for beauty is a witch against whose charms faith melteth into blood."

Benedick reenters and starts to congratulate Claudio on his "victory," and adds: "What fashion will you wear the garland of? About your neck, like a usurer's chain? Or under your arm, like a lieutenant's scarf? You must wear it one way, for the Prince hath got your Hero."

Ironically, Claudio, because of Don John's information, chooses to interpret Benedick's news that "the Prince hath got your Hero" as meaning "won her for himself." Benedick rebukes him for thinking that the Prince would have played him false, and Claudio asks to be left alone. His companion accuses him of striking out "like a blind man," and Claudio himself leaves. No sooner is Claudio gone than Benedick begins to lick his own wounds—the slashes that Beatrice delivered under cover of the mask she was wearing. He is particularly incensed at having been called a fool but refuses to think he is deserving of the term merely for his "merry" nature. It is Beatrice's "bitter disposition" that is at fault. Don Pedro reenters at this point, looking for Claudio, and Benedick informs him of the count's melancholy humor and gives the Prince (apparently to see if there is any ground for Claudio's suspicions) an altered version of their recent conversation. He says he offered Claudio a garland as a symbol of "one forsaken" in love or, as an alternative, to "bind him up a rod" as a symbol of one "worthy to be whipped." This last detail he explains by claiming that Claudio is guilty of a schoolboy's fault: being overjoyed with a bird's nest he has found, he shows it to a friend, who promptly steals it. In high spirits, the Prince replies that he "will but teach them to sing, and restore them to the owner."

Don Pedro now explains that Claudio's fears are unfounded, and with merry malice quickly turns the conversation to Benedick. Beatrice, it seems, has been complaining that she was told by her dancing partner that Benedick has been spreading gossip about her. This provokes an outburst from Benedick, who has apparently been cut to the quick by being called the "Prince's jester" and "duller than a great thaw." She fired jests at him so quickly, he complains, that he "stood like a man at a mark, with a whole army shooting at him." She speaks daggers, and every word is a stab wound. He would not marry her, "though she were endowed with all that Adam had left him before he transgressed."

"She would have made Hercules turned spit" and "have cleft his club to make the fire too." She is the "infernal Ate" (a goddess of discord) in good apparel. Hell is her natural place of habitation (Beatrice thinks of it, we remember, as being in heaven with the "bachelors"), and while she is on earth people sin on purpose just to go to hell to escape her.

Suddenly Beatrice appears, and the Prince gleefully points her out. Benedick offers to do any service Don Pedro may have for him—fetch him a toothpick from Asia, find out the length of Prester John's foot, or be an ambassador to the Pigmies—rather than have to converse with this "harpy" (the Harpies were birdlike monsters with heads of women.) The Prince desires only his "good company."

Swearing that he cannot endure "my Lady Tongue," Benedick beats a hasty retreat. The Prince then chides Beatrice for "putting Benedick down" (that is, putting him in a bad humor), and she can only retort that she would not let him "put her down" (on a bed, that is), for she would not like to become the mother of fools. To the Prince's inquiries, Claudio answers that he is neither sad nor sick, and Beatrice adds, "nor merry, nor well; but civil count, civil as an orange, and something of that jealous complexion." The Prince declares openly that Claudio has no need for jealousy; he has wooed Hero in his name, obtained her father's permission, and set the day for her marriage with Claudio. Leonato gives his amen to this, and Claudio, speechless in amazement, is taunted by Beatrice: "Speak, count, 'tis your cue." He can only reply: "Silence is the perfectest herald of joy. I were but little happy if I could say how much." She then turns to Hero, insisting, "Speak cousin, or if you cannot, stop his mouth with a kiss, and let him not speak neither."

The Prince tells her that she has a "merry heart," and Beatrice remarks that she thanks it, "poor fool," for keeping "on the windy side of care" (that is, to the windward side, the side of advantage in a naval engagement). She then cries out, "Good Lord, for alliance! Thus goes every one to the world but I, and I am sunburnt. I may sit in a corner and cry heigh-ho for a husband."

In a jocular tone the Prince offers to "get" her a husband, and Beatrice (punning on the word "get," which also means "to beget a child") tells him she would rather have one of his father's "getting" and asks: "Hath your Grace ne'er a brother like you? Your father got excellent husbands, if a maid could come by them." This might be an intentional slur on the Prince's brother Don John, but Don Pedro pointedly ignores it, replying only, "Will you have me, lady?" He is too costly for daily wear, Beatrice whimsically retorts, and then begs his pardon for her tendency to speak all mirth and no matter. He excuses her on the ground that she was "born in a merry hour," but again reversing direction, she maintains: "No sure my Lord, my mother cried; but then there was a star danced, and under that I was born. Cousins, God give you joy."

Leonato, who apparently thinks Beatrice's forwardness may prove embarrassing to the Prince, dispatches her on some trifling errand, and she leaves, asking her uncle's "mercy" and the Prince's "pardon." In a generous understatement of the case the Prince compliments Beatrice as a "pleasant spirited lady," and Leonato agrees that there is little melancholy in her. "She is never sad but when she sleeps," he remarks, "and not ever sad then," for she frequently dreams unhappy things and "wakes herself with laughing."

The Prince decides that a match between Beatrice and Benedick would be just the thing, and Leonato is tickled by the notion too. "O Lord, my lord, if they were but a week married, they would talk themselves mad." Turning to Claudio the Prince asks him when he wishes to be married, and he replies: "Time goes on crutches till love have all his rites." Leonato, however, wishes a full week "to have all things answer his mind" (that is, to observe all the amenities of ceremony and celebration).

The Prince promises that the time will pass swiftly since, with their help, he hopes to bring Signior Benedick and the Lady Beatrice into a "mountain of affection." Leonato promises his cooperation, and even Hero agrees to perform "any modest office" to help her cousin to a good husband. The scene ends with Don Pedro loudly singing the praises of Benedick. He is noble, valorous, and honest. In spite of his "quick wit and his queasy stomach," he will be made to fall in love. And, the Prince adds, if we are successful in this "Cupid is no longer an archer; his glory shall be ours, for we are the only love-gods."

Act II: Scene 2

In another room in Leonato's house Don John is brooding about Claudio's forthcoming marriage; Borachio says he will "cross" it, and his lord welcomes this offer, remarking glumly that "any bar, any cross, any impediment will be medicinable to me. I am sick in displeasure to him, and whatsoever comes athwart his affection ranges evenly with mine."

Borachio promises to carry out his plot "so covertly that no dishonesty shall appear" in him and reminds Don John of his familiarity with Margaret, Hero's lady-in-waiting. He can arrange it so that she will impersonate Hero and bring her into disrepute by looking out her chamber window during the night.

Don John is not content, however, merely to spoil the marriage; he wants to know what "life" there is in it (presumably, what sort of fuss they can stir up to involve Don Pedro and Claudio). Borachio tells him that "the poison lies in him to temper," that is, that the exact flavor of this unholy brew they are concocting will depend upon the way in which Don John broaches the matter to his brother and Claudio. Borachio advises him to tell the Prince he has wronged his honor in letting Claudio marry a "contaminated stale" (an unchaste woman). This will enable him to "misuse the Prince, to vex Claudio, to undo Hero, and kill Leonato," mischief enough, it would seem, to satisfy even Don John's evil bent. To bring this about he must tell Claudio and the Prince that Hero is in love with him (Borachio), and then bring them to a point under Hero's window where, at a prearranged time, they will observe a woman addressed as "Hero" in what can only be taken as an amorous intrigue. This will take place the night before the wedding, and "jealousy shall be called assurance, and all the preparation overthrown." Don John promises Borachio a thousand marks if he is "cunning in the working this," and the scene ends with the malcontent going off to discover the marriage date.

Act II: Scene 3

Benedick, now in Leonatos' garden, sends a boy after a book which is lying in his chamber window and then delivers himself of a prose soliloquy in which (ironically, as it turns out, since he will himself fall in love in exactly the same way) he laughs at the folly of Claudio, who has formerly scoffed at the "shallow follies" of other young men in love, but is now the victim of his own scorn.

"I have known," he says, "when there was no music with him but the drum and the fife; and now he had rather hear the tabor and the pipe" (love presented once more under the figure of music—and another aspect of the love-war analogy). Claudio, he muses, now lies awake ten nights in a row planning the design of a new doublet, and where his speech was formerly plain and to the point it is now "a fantastical banquet, just so many strange dishes." "May I be so converted," he asks himself, "and see with these eyes?"

But, declares Benedick, he will not be made a fool by love, until love transforms him into an oyster. And he adds: "One woman is fair, yet I am well. Another is wise, yet I am well; another virtuous, yet I am well; but till all graces be in one woman, one woman shall not come into my grace. Rich she shall be, that's certain, or I'll none. Virtuous, or I'll never cheapen [bargain for] her. Fair, or I'll never look on her. Mild, or come not near me. Noble, or not I for an angel [with a pun on the coins, angels and nobles]. Of good discourse, an excellent muscian, and her hair shall be of what color it please God."

Seeing the Prince, Claudio, Balthazar, and musicians approaching, Benedick hides himself in the arbor. Don Pedro invites them all to listen to the music and, following Claudio's comments on the stillness of the evening which seems "hushed on purpose to grace harmony," he calls attention in a whisper to Benedick's concealed presence. The game can now commence. It should be noted that there is no reason for Benedick to hide. Nothing in his character, or in the action so far, makes this plausible; but the exigencies of plot and theme require it. It is one of the more important instances of "overhearing," and it is the necessary means for bringing Benedick and Beatrice together.

The Prince asks Balthazar for a song, but he demurs, asking his lord not to "tax so bad a voice, to slander music any more than once"; Don Pedro, however, overcomes Balthazar's reticence by suggesting that "it is the witness still of excellency, to put a strange face on his own perfection" and, since his servant continues to talk, tells him to speak in "notes." Their exchange at this point is significant:

> "Don Pedro.   Nay, pray thee, come;
>   Or if thou wilt hold longer argument,
>   Do it in notes.
> Balthazar.   Note this before my notes;
>   There's not a note of mine that's worth the noting.
> Don Pedro.   Why these ar very crotchets that he speaks;
>   Notes, notes, forsooth, and nothing. *Music plays.*"

Benedick observes scornfully: "Now, divine air; now is his [presumably Claudio's] soul ravished! Is it not strange that sheeps' guts should hale souls out of men's bodies? Well, a horn for my money, when all is done."

Balthazar now sings his song—"Sigh no more, ladies, sigh no more, / Men were deceivers ever"—and it is, of course, very appropriate, since the Prince and Claudio are about to discourse on Beatrice's passion and Benedick's callous disregard for her feelings. Don Pedro terms it "a good song," while Benedick (and here we are uncertain whether his contumely is provoked by the song's rendition or its import) observes that if it had been a dog that had howled like this they would have hanged him. He would rather have heard the night raven (an ill omen), no matter what evil should follow. The Prince dismisses Balthazar with a command to "get us some excellent music" for a serenade at Hero's chamber window on the following night.

The game now begins in earnest, as Leonato and Claudio express amazement that Beatrice should dote so on Benedick, whom she has always seemed to despise. Laying it on thickly, Leonato insists that she "loves him with an enraged affection; it is past the infinite of thought." The Prince suggests that perhaps she is "counterfeiting," but the governor loudly maintains that "there was never counterfeit of passion came so near the life of passion as she discovers [that is, displays] it" (the appearance-reality theme in still another form). She is proof against all "assaults of affection" save Benedick. Benedick, musing to himself, says, "I should think this a gull [trick] but that the white-bearded fellow speaks it. Knavery cannot, sure, hide itself in such reverence."

Claudio (apparently noticing some look or gesture of surprise on Benedick's part) whispers, "He hath ta'en the infection; hold it up" (that is, "don't stop now!"). They go on to describe in vivid terms how Beatrice spends sleepless nights filling a sheet of paper with affectionate messages to Benedick and then tearing it into a thousand pieces in a fit of pique that "she should be so immodest to write to one that she knew would flout her. 'I measure him,' says she, 'by my own spirit, for I should flout him, if he writ to me, yea, though I love him, I should.' " Claudio then lets his imagination run riot and paints a picture of Beatrice falling, weeping, sobbing, beating her breast, tearing her hair, praying, and cursing. Leonato adds that Hero is afraid she might do violence to herself and, with superb timing, the Prince observes that Benedick ought to be told of this. Claudio replies, however, that it would do no good; he would simply make a joke of it and torment the lady further. For that, he ought to be hanged cries Don Pedro, for she is "an excellent sweet lady," and virtuous. Wise too, says Claudio, in everything but loving Benedick, and he adds that Hero believes she will surely die—she will die if he does not love her, and she will die before she will make her love known; she will die, too, if he should woo her, for she will not relinquish one iota of her usual crossness. This is well, the Prince feels, for Benedick's contemptuous spirit would only make him scorn any of her protestations of love.

They build to a very amusing climax now, as Claudio and Leonato offer grudging compliments to Benedick, and Don Pedro replies to each compliment by "damning with faint praise."

"Claudio.　He is a very proper man.
Don Pedro.　He hath indeed a good outward happiness.
Claudio.　'Fore God, and in my mind, very wise.
Don Pedro.　He doth indeed show some sparks that are like wit.
Leonato.　And I take him to be valiant.

Don Pedro.   As Hector, I assure you; and in the
managing of quarrels you may say he is wise,
for either he avoids them with great discretion,
or undertakes them with a Christian-like fear."

"I am sorry for your niece," the Prince tells Leonato, "shall we tell
Benedick of her love?" "Never," Claudio and Leonato both agree, it
would do no good. I wish Benedick "would modestly examine himself," Don Pedro thinks aloud, "to see how much he is unworthy to
have so good a lady." Then, as they walk out of earshot of Benedick,
the trio congratulate one another on the huge success their imposture
has met with, and they are practically chortling over the scene that
will take place when (after the same deception has been practiced on
Beatrice) the pair will confront each other. It will be a marvelous
"dumb show."

The "conspirators" leave the garden and Benedick emerges from
his hiding place, obviously having been gulled, or taken in by them.
"This can be no trick," he says, "the conference was sadly borne."
And his language here is shot through with suggestions of penitential
remorse. In the "religion of love," he is now a "repentant sinner." "I
must not seem proud; happy are they that hear their detractions and
can put them to mending. They say the lady is fair; 'tis a truth, I
can bear them witness. And virtuous; 'tis so, I cannot reprove it . . .
I have railed . . . long against marriage, but doth not the appetite
alter? A man loves the meat in his youth that he cannot endure in
his age . . . No, the world must be peopled!"

As Beatrice enters (she of course knows nothing of his "reform")
he exclaims, "By this day! she's a fair lady; I do spy some marks of
love in her." Actually, she has merely been sent to summon him to
dinner, which she does with characteristic insults, but Benedick reads
a double meaning into her words which further convinces him of her
love. The scene (and Act II) ends with their departure to dinner.

Act III: Scene 1

The action begins to quicken its pace at the beginning of Act III. In
the first scene Hero, Margaret, and Ursula are seen in Leonato's orchard. Hero sends Margaret off to inform Beatrice that she and

Ursula are walking about in the orchard and discussing her actions. Hero advices Margaret to

> "say that thou overheard'st us
> And bid her steal into the pleached bower,
> Where honeysuckles, ripened by the sun,
> Forbid the sun to enter, like favorites
> Made proud by princes, that advance their pride
> Against the power that bred it."

Margaret goes off to lure Beatrice down, and Hero arranges with Ursula to sing the praises of Benedick and discourse on the love-sickness he suffers for Beatrice. Thus will "little Cupid's crafty arrow" be fashioned.

Beatrice enters from behind and is observed by Hero and Ursula who begin their "angling" for her by dangling their "false sweet bait." They start by reproaching Beatrice for her disdain—for having "spirits . . . coy and wild as haggards of the rock." They then speak of Benedick's great affection for her and of the fact that he has been persuaded never to reveal it. But, Hero remarks, "Nature never framed a woman's heart / Of prouder stuff than that of Beatrice"; she always underrates others and is incapable of love because she is so self-centered. It would be pointless to tell her of Benedick's infatuation, for she would merely make sport of it. No matter how wise, noble, young, or fair a man may be, she always "spells him backward" (that is, speaks the opposite of the truth about him). If he speaks, he is a weathervane, blown by all winds; if silent, he is a block, moved by none.

> "So turns she every man the wrong side out
> And never gives to truth and virtue that
> Which simpleness and merit purchaseth."

But who would dare to tell her this? asks Hero. Not I, certainly, for she "would press me to death with wit." It would be better to let Benedick be consumed by the fire of love than to let him die with mocking, which is no better than to be tickled to death. Hero then announces, for the benefit of the concealed Beatrice, that she will go to Benedick and concoct some harmless slanders which will kill his love for Beatrice, but Ursula interrupts, refusing to believe that

190

a lady of such a "swift and excellent wit" should be "so much without true judgment" as to refuse so fine a man as Signior Benedick.

We are reminded once more of the difference between appearance and reality as Ursula speaks of Benedick's reputation "for shape, for bearing, argument and valor" and, when Hero agrees that "he hath an excellent good name," replies that "his excellence did earn it, ere he had it." The two of them decide that Beatrice by this time has been "trapped" and then go off to discuss Hero's wedding apparel.

Beatrice (deceived by appearances, just as Benedick had been) comes forth bidding farewell to "contempt and maiden pride," proclaiming her love for Benedick:

> "And Benedick, love on; I will requite thee
>   Taming my wild heart to thy loving hand!
> If thou dost love, my kindness shall incite thee
>   To bind our loves up in a holy band;
> For others say thou dost deserve, and I
> Believe it better than reportingly."

Act III: Scene 2

In a room in Leonato's house, the Prince, Claudio, Benedick, and Leonato are conversing. Don Pedro announces his intention of staying until Claudio's marriage has taken place and then starting off for Arragon. Claudio, with more of his astonishing naïveté, offers to accompany the Prince to Arragon and has to be reminded that one who has just married a wife does not go rushing off on trips with his friends: "That would be as great a soil in the new gloss of your marriage as to show a child his new coat and forbid him to wear it."

The Prince (apparently noting a dour look on Benedick's face) begins to chaff him once more. He compliments him on being a man of mirth, one who has "twice or thrice cut Cupid's bowstring," and who has "a heart as sound as a bell and his tongue . . . the clapper, for what his heart thinks his tongue speaks."

Benedick is apparently about to make an open confession of his "conversion," as he admits, "Gallants, I am not as I have been." But Leonato says that he looks even "sadder," and Claudio remarks that he must be in love; when the Prince continues the badinage about his being in love, Benedick draws back. "I have the toothache," he says. This is followed by some punning references to cures for the toothache, and Benedick remarks rather testily, "Well, every one can master a grief but he that has it."

The Prince conducts a mock argument with Claudio, maintaining that Benedick cannot be in love, since there is "no appearance of fancy in him" (that is, his conduct is not strange, as a lover's ought to be). But Claudio points out that he has been brushing his hat in the morning, that his beard has now been shaved off "to stuff tennis balls," and that his perfuming of his body and washing of his face prove unmistakably that he is in love. And he wonders what has become of Benedick's "jesting spirit, which is now crept into a lutestring and now governed by stops." (This means that Benedick, like a typical lover, lets his mood be expressed in ballads sung to the lute, but it is a humorous reminder to the audience of his earlier amazement that the "guts of a sheep" could "hale the soul out of men's bodies." We have to assume that the actions the Prince and Claudio ascribe to Benedick have actually taken place, and that he has begun to conform to the stereotype of the anguished lover.) Benedick finally loses patience with his companions and takes Leonato aside for a few words, which the Prince and Claudio assume will have to do with a marriage to Beatrice.

At this point Don John enters to spring his plot. He asks coyly if Claudio intends to be married on the following day, and the Prince replies that he knows very well he does. Claudio asks if he knows of any 'impediment" (this is a technical term in Canon Law to designate a legal obstacle to a marriage). The malcontent, pretending affection for his brother and Claudio, tells them that Hero is "disloyal"; even that word, he remarks, is "too good to point out her wickedness." He then offers to take them that night to see proof of it at her chamber window. With singular gullibility, Claudio appears to believe him and promises to shame Hero in the congregation on the next day "if I see any thing tonight why I should not marry her tomorrow." The scene ends on a series of parallel comments, aptly suggesting the difference in outlook which distinguishes the three men.

"Don Pedro   O day untowardly turned!

Claudio.   O mischief strangely thwarting!

Don John.   O plague right well prevented!"

Act III: Scene 3

It is at this point that we first encounter the blundering magnificence of Dogberry, Verges, and the Watch. Dogberry is a constable, Verges is a headborough (a lesser officer); the Watch has obviously been specially chosen for the occasion of Don Pedro's visit.

The Watch is not on any specific mission. We see them, as the scene opens, being assigned to their tasks. The farcical antics which the ceremonial "posting" of the Watch (which is, after all, a quasi-military group) turns into carry a faint suggestion of the motif in the main plot by which the soldierly competence of Don Pedro, Claudio, and Benedick turns into the confused "actions" and the "merry war" of the love game. There is no possibility, we see, for manly competence to exercise itself in the love-demented atmosphere of Messina.

It is absolutely impossible to summarize coherently the bumbling *non sequiturs* and disconnected actions of the scene. (With outrageous illiteracy, Dogberry and Verges confuse "salvation" for "damnation," "present" for "represent," and "vagrom" for "vagrant," for instance.) In one sense, of course, it is the typical scene of clownage which, in many Elizabethan plays, was only loosely connected, if at all, with the main action. Shakespeare had already mastered (with notable success in *King Henry IV, Part One*) the technique of making the subplot a symbolic analogy to the main plot, as well as connecting it in narrative terms with the main action; the Dogberry scenes are a wonderful accomplishment in this vein. Dogberry opens by interrogating the members of the Watch on their merits and finally settles proudly on the most "senseless" man (because he can read and write) and makes him the constable *pro tem*. To his question about what is to be done if a suspect will not stand when accosted, Dogberry replies that he is to let him go, "call the rest of the Watch together, and thank God you are rid of a knave." Verges offers the helpful suggestion that in any case, if he will not stand, he is not a true subject of the Prince, and they have been commissioned to apprehend only the Prince's subjects. They are to call at the ale-houses, bid the drunks go to bed, and question them when they are sober. Thieves are no "true men"; the less they have to do with them the better. They should not lay hands on them, for "they that touch pitch will be defiled" (a biblical quotation). If they do take a thief, it would be best to "let him . . . steal out of your company." With a final word to the men to keep watch about Leonato's door on account of the wedding to take place there the next day, and a last admonition to be "vigitant," Dogberry and Verges leave.

Borachio and Conrade now enter upon the scene, engaged in boisterous dialogue. Conveniently, Conrade does not know of Borachio's employment in Don John's nefarious scheme, and this in an occasion for him to be told of it in the presence of the Watch (who are now concealed—this provides another instance of vital information gained through "overhearing"). Borachio says that he will, "like a true drunkard, utter all to thee," and proceeds to relate that he has earned a thousand ducats from Don John. This confession is interrupted, however, by some comic quibbling on "fashions" and "apparel" (like the Prince's reference to Benedick's changes of fashion), loosely related to the idea of the affectations which love brings about in a man, and (very loosely) to the theme of appearance and reality. Finally, he recounts the details of the deception—how he wooed Margaret under Hero's name, how she bid him goodnight a thousand times, and how this "amiable encounter" was witnessed by the Prince, Claudio, and Don John. The "truth" of this scene was confirmed "partly by [Don John's] oaths, which first possessed them, partly by the dark night, which did deceive them, but chiefly by my villainy," Borachio confesses, at which point the Watch rises up and arrests them in the Prince's name (though it is a wonder Borachio and Conrade understand what is happening, considering the fact that they are arrested for "lechery" instead of "treachery," and that the Watch "obeys" them rather than "commands" them to go along with them). The two conspirators cooperate with marvelous resignation, although they realize they may be made laughing stocks by it.

> "Borachio.   We are likely to prove a goodly commodity, being taken up of these men's bills.
>
> Conrade.   A commodity in question, I warrant you. Come, we'll obey you."

Act III: Scene 4

This rather short scene, which deals with the dressing of the bride, shows another set of characters involved ostensibly with "fashions." Margaret praises the "graceful and excellent fashion" of Hero's gown. Hero hopes that God will give her "joy to wear it," for her "heart is exceeding heavy" (presumably, weighted with care at the responsibility she is undertaking). Margaret jests in immodest fashion, saying that it will soon be heavier by the weight of a man, and is chided for this by Hero.

Beatrice enters the room and engages in some light bawdy repartee with Margaret. She then exclaims, "By my troth, I am exceeding ill," and is asked by Margaret: "For a hawk, a horse, or a husband?" She replies, "For the letter that begins them all, H."

For Beatrice's sickness Margaret prescribes "Carduus Benedictus" (the actual name of a medicinal preparation), and Hero, because of the name, jibes, "There thou prick'st her with a thistle." Beatrice accuses Margaret of intending an ulterior meaning, but Margaret enters upon a long disclaimer, denying that she thinks Beatrice is, will be, or can be in love. "Yet," she remarks:

> "Benedick was such another, and now is he
> become a man. He swore he would never marry,
> and yet now, in despite of his heart, he eats
> his meat without grudging; and how you may be
> converted I know not, but methinks you look
> with your eyes as other women do."

To Margaret's unassailable good sense Beatrice can only stammer, "What pace is this that thy tongue keeps?" She replies, "Not a false gallop."

Ursula comes in with the news that all the gallants of the town have come to fetch Hero to church, and the scene ends with Hero urging Margaret and Urusula to help her dress for the wedding.

Act III: Scene 5

This brief scene consists entirely of the unsuccessful efforts of Dogberry and Verges to overcome their insane preoccupation with the sounds of their own voices long enough to tell Leonato plainly what it is that the Watch has discovered. He finally loses patience with them and departs for church, telling them to examine the prisoners and bring the report to him later. There is a good deal of farcical abuse of the language,, and some measure of suspense, as the audience wonders if these two will ever get to the point. We can only utter "Amen" to Leonato's comment: "Neighbors, you are tedious."

Act IV: Scene 1

Most of the major characters are gathered in church for the wedding. After brief preliminaries, Claudio, in a very stagey manner, rejects Hero as a "rotten orange," the "sign and semblance of her honor." He asks:

> "Would you not swear,
> All you that see her, that she were a maid,
> By these exterior shows? But she is none;
> She knows the heat of a luxurious bed;
> Her blush is guiltiness, not modesty."

Leonato at first thinks that Claudio may have deprived her of her virginity and is now trying to reject her as an unchaste woman. But Claudio denies this and rages on about her "intemperate blood" and savage sensuality." Don Pedro also chimes in with appropriately disdainful remarks. Finally, Claudio asks her to answer one question truthfully; he inquires who it was she spoke to at her window the previous night. Hero, of course, absolutely denies having done so, but Don Pedro confirms that she spoke "with a ruffian at her chamber window," who "confessed the vile encounters they have had / A thousand times in secret." Don John is also on hand to bear further witness on the point and there is clearly no chance for Hero to prove her innocence. Claudio, in one last (very precious) bit of verse wistfully condemns her "pure impiety and impious purity," and Hero falls in a faint, while Leonato calls for a dagger to end his life. Only Beatrice, Benedick, and Friar Francis keep their heads, push back the crowds, and give her air. (During the hubbub, Don Pedro, Don John, and Claudio disappear.)

Leonato now launches into an impassioned harangue, expressing the hope that Hero might die, and chiding nature for granting him one child—which proved one child too many. She has fallen into a "salt pit of ink from which she may never be made clean; there is "salt too little which may season give to her foul tainted flesh."

The Friar calls for silence and offers his reading of the lady's character, based on a close scrutiny of her face and eyes. He is willing to swear she has been terribly maligned. "Trust not my age," he insists, "my reverence, calling, nor divinity, if this sweet lady lie not guiltless here, under some biting error." Hero reaffirms her innocence, offering to submit to torture if it can be proved that she even so much as exchanged words with any creature on the previous night. On the level of the sensible characters of the play the crisis occurs at this point. The Friar concludes that "there is some strange misprision [misunderstanding] in the princes," and Benedick puts his finger unerringly on the source of the trouble, declaring:

> "Two of them have the very bent of honor,
> And if their wisdoms be misled in this,
> The practice of it lives in John the Bastard,
> Whose spirits toil in frame of villainies."

Leonato begins to recover himself and to sense the possibility that Hero has been victimized, and he swears to exact vengeance on her accusers if she proves to be innocent. Friar Francis, however, suggests a most practical plan—let it be published abroad that Hero is dead, for by this means we may "change slander to remorse," a good enough result in any case, but it may also be the means of bringing about in Claudio a renewed understanding of his love for her. Some of the best poetry of the play occurs in the Friar's speeches, particularly this description of the probable effect of the news on Claudio:

> "When he shall hear she died upon his words,
> Th' idea of her life shall sweetly creep,
> Into his study of imagination,
> And every lovely organ of her life
> Shall come apparelled in more precious habit,
> More moving delicate and full of life,
> Into the eye and prospect of his soul,
> Than when she lived indeed."

If the plan does not work, the Friar explains, Hero may be hidden away in a convent where she will not be the subject of common gossip. And Benedick offers, in spite of his close friendship with the accusers, to cooperate in this affair. Leonato agrees to this.

All but Benedick and Beatrice leave the church. This is the first time they have had a chance to talk since the deceptions arranged by their friends. Both are obviously closer to mutual understanding, though it is clouded by the Hero affair, a thing which divides Beatrice's heart. Benedick can ignore it temporarily, and he states his love for Beatrice frankly: "I do love nothing in the world so well as you—is not that strange?" But she (always more complex in her self-analysis than Benedick) can only reply: "As strange as the thing I know not. It were as possible for me to say I loved nothing so well as you. But believe me not; and yet I lie not. I confess nothing, nor I deny nothing. I am sorry for my cousin." Her further half-admissions of love only provoke Benedick into ever-stronger protestations of the depth of his affection for her, and he finally asks her to command him to do anything she may desire. "Kill Claudio," she replies, without a moment's hesitation.

Benedick refuses to kill Claudio, and Beatrice retorts, "You kill me to deny it." If she were a man, Beatrice exclaims, she would eat Claudio's heart in the marketplace. Benedick vainly tries to interrupt her as she rants on about the failure of manhood in the world. "Manhood is melted into curtsies, valor into compliment, and men are only turned into tongue, and trim ones too." At length, confused and exhausted, Benedick yields. "By this hand," he swears, "Claudio shall render me a dear account."

Act IV: Scene 2

This short scene, which takes place in prison, is a farcical "interrogation" paralleling the serious interrogation of Hero in the previous scene. Dogberry, Verges, and a Sexton (town clerk) enter, dressed in the formal gowns of office, and put questions to Borachio and Conrade. The Sexton has his head about him and is hard put to keep Dogberry on the track. The First Watch is summoned, and testifies that Borachio admitted that Don John was a villain. To this Dogberry replies: "Write down Prince John a villain," and then, doing a double take, "why, this is flat perjury, to call a prince's brother villain." The examination proceeds this way until even the prisoners lose their patience, and Conrade calls Dogberry an ass. The constable ends the scene with an indignant outburst—"Remember that I am an ass . . . forget not that I am an ass . . . O that I had been writ down an ass!" All leave.

Act V: Scene 1

This scene is lengthy and relatively slow-paced; it shows various characters suffering the effects of the emotional storm of the climactic fourth act. Leonato and Antonio appear, Antonio advising his brother that he is killing himself with grief. Show me another father who has my sorrow, "measure his woe the length and breadth of mine," and I will learn patience from him—but no such man exists. All men counsel patience to those in sorrow, but they never can endure the same themselves. But, Antonio persists, do not take it all upon yourself; make those who have offended you suffer also. He replies:

> "There thou speak'st reason, nay, I will do so.
> My soul doth tell me Hero is belied;
> And that shall Claudio know; so shall the Prince,
> And all of them that thus dishonor her."

Don Pedro and Claudio arrive and are summarily challenged by Leonato, who accuses them of "belying" his innocent child and forcing him to set aside his reverence and gray hair to challenge Claudio to a duel for his "villainy." Claudio, who does not wish to harm Leonato, keeps his patience. Antonio, however, releases a stream of vituperation at Claudio, whom he terms (among other things) one of those "fashion-monging boys, / That lie and cog and flout, deprave and slander, / Go anticly and show outward hideousness." The Prince bears this all tolerantly, saying only that he is sorry for Hero's death and protesting that "she was charged with nothing / But what was true and very full of proof."

Leonato and Antonio storm off, and Benedick storms in, making barbed comments which the Prince and Claudio only gradually realize are uttered in anger. Not wishing to insult Don Pedro, he takes Claudio aside, calls him a villain for having killed a sweet lady, and challenges him to a duel, which Claudio agrees to with good grace. The Prince, catching a few words, imagines Benedick has invited

Claudio to a feast, and Claudio plays along, joking about "a calf's head" and a "capon" which he intends to carve curiously. The Prince continues to jest with Benedick, telling him how Beatrice the other day made disparaging comments about his "wit" and his "double tongue." Benedick maintains a sour attitude, however, and finally informs Don Pedro that they must part company; Don John has fled from Messina, and they have among them killed "a sweet and innocent lady." When he leaves, his companions can only ascribe his odd behavior to his love for Beatrice, and the Prince declares (rather smugly):

> "What a pretty thing man is when he goes in
> his doublet and hose and leaves off his wit."

That his almost dreamlike unconcern is beginning to be dispelled, however, is indicated by his further remark:

> "But soft you, let me be; pluck up, my heart,
> and be sad. Did he not say my brother was fled?"

The Dogberry group now appears with their two prisoners, and the Prince demands to know why they have been arrested. Dogberry, typically, can convey no sensible information—as Don Pedro puts it, "This learned constable is too cunning to be understood." He asks Borachio the nature of his offense and is told the entire story of the plot; Borachio sums it up by saying, "The lady is dead upon mine and my master's false accusation; and, briefly, I desire nothing but the reward of a villain." The speech "runs like iron" through the Prince's blood, and Claudio feels as if he had "drunk poison" while it was being uttered. Ironically, Claudio has only this to say:

> "Sweet Hero, now thy image doth appear
> In the rare semblance that I loved it first."

Leonato, Antonio, and Sexton come on the scene and the governor rejects Borachio's confession of guilt and sarcastically "thanks" the "honorable men" Don Pedro and Claudio for his daughter's death. They both implore him to be patient and offer to perform any penance he might enjoin upon them in expiation of their sin. He commands them to proclaim Hero's innocence to the people of Messina and, if their love "can labor ought in sad invention" (that is, compose a song of mourning), to hang an epitaph on her tomb, and "sing it to her bones." Furthermore, Claudio must marry his niece, who is "almost the copy of my child that's dead," and Leonato's revenge will be complete. Margaret's part in the conspiracy must be determined, he declares, but Borachio insists that she had no knowledge of it, but was herself an innocent dupe. Dogberry interrupts, demanding punishment •of Conrade for calling him an ass. Leonato dismisses him, thanking him for his "care and honest pains." All take their leave, agreeing to assemble the next morning for the wedding.

Act V: Scene 2

Benedick and Margaret are in the garden engaged in a conversation which is marked by the casual wittiness of the first three acts. He sends her to summon Beatrice and then sings one stanza of a love song, following it with a soliloquy lamenting his inability to write love poems. He can find no rhymes but "horn" for "scorn" and "fool" for "school." "No," he declares, "I was not born under a rhyming planet, nor I cannot woo in festival terms." Beatrice arrives and asks Benedick what has passed between him and Claudio. He tells her of the challenge and they proceed to explore once more in dialogue the nature of their loves (which includes some facetious quibbles about the necessity for a man to erect his own tomb [monument] and "be the trumpet of his own virtues"). The old wit is there, but it is strangely subdued.

Ursula appears with the news about Don John and asks them to come to the house. The scene closes with Benedick's comment:

> "I will live in thy heart, die in thy lap, and
> be buried in thy eyes; and moreover, I will go
> with thee to thy uncle's."

Act V: Scene 3

This is a very brief scene in a churchyard. The Prince and Claudio visit the supposed tomb of Hero and carry out their obsequies. They hang a verse epitaph on the monument and sing a dirge, after which Claudio promises to perform this rite yearly. The chief function of the scene is to show Don Pedro and Claudio as victims of a deception (in a way, it is a symbol of their wrong reading of Hero's character).

The transition from night, death, and solemnity to the physical and spiritual daylight of the final scene is also a symbolic equivalent to the main action of the play.

Act V: Scene 4

All the major characters are assembled at Leonato's house for the marriage in this final scene. The ladies are all sent to another room and told to appear wearing masks after the arrival of the Prince and Claudio. Benedick informs Friar Francis that he thinks he will have need of his services and tells Leonato that his niece "regards [him] with an eye of favor." He receives Leonato's permission to marry Beatrice.

Claudio and the Prince arrive; Benedick and Claudio exchange vile insults, but before anything comes of it the ladies enter with Antonio. Claudio, with great aplomb, takes the young "niece's" hand as they stand before the Friar, but he is cast into astonished disbelief, as is Don Pedro, when Hero unmasks. The Friar reflects the mood of this scene very aptly, when he remarks:

> "All this amazement can I qualify;
> When after that the holy rites are ended,
> I'll tell you largely of fair Hero's death.
> Meantime let wonder seem familiar,
> And to the chapel let us presently."

Beatrice next unmasks, and it appears that she and Benedick, by returning to one of their earlier combats of wit, may never bring themselves to utter the necessary words of acceptance. But Claudio and Hero produce sonnets they have written to one another, and they are outfaced by the evidence. Benedick agrees to take her for "pity," and Beatrice agrees to yield in order to "save his life." Benedick calls for a dance and music and turns to Don Pedro, saying:

> "Prince, thou art sad; get thee a wife, get
> thee a wife. There is no staff more reverend
> than one tipped with horn."

A messenger enters to report that Don John has been arrested, but Benedick counsels them to "think not on him till tomorrow." "I'll devise thee brave punishments for him." The play ends with a dance.

The Taming of the Shrew

A LORD.
CHRISTOPHERO SLY, *a tinker.*
HOSTESS, PAGE, PLAYERS, HUNTSMEN, *and* SERVANTS } *Persons in the Induction.*

BAPTISTA, *a rich gentleman of Padua; father of Kate and Bianca.*
VINCENTIO, *an old gentleman of Pisa.*
LUCENTIO, *son to Vincentio, in love with Bianca.*
PETRUCHIO, *a suitor to Katharina.*
GREMIO
HORTENSIO } *suitors to Bianca.*
TRANIO
BIONDELLO } *servants to Lucentio.*
GRUMIO
CURTIS } *servants to Petruchio.*
A PEDANT.

KATHARINA, *the shrew*
BIANCA } *daughters to Baptista.*
WIDOW.

TAILOR, HABERDASHER, *and* SERVANTS.

The Taming of the Shrew

Induction: Scene 1

This scene takes place before an alehouse on a heath. The hostess of the alehouse enters with Christopher Sly, a tinker who is obviously drunk, and demands payment for the glasses that Sly has broken. In reply Sly insults the hostess and boasts of his spurious and inaccurately stated lineage, claiming that his ancestors came to England with "Richard Conqueror." In corrupt Spanish he bids her to keep quiet and go away. After another expression of Sly's impatience, the hostess threatens him with the Thirdborough, the Constable. Sly, however, simply curls up and falls asleep.

The sound of horns is heard and the lord, who has been hunting, appears with his company. He gives orders that his exhausted hounds be looked after, and discusses the progress of the day's hunt. Then he sees Sly lying in a drunken stupor, and comments on the swinishness of the intoxicated man. Suddenly he gets the idea of playing a lively joke on the sleeper. He decides to take Sly, dress him as a lord, and then see whether the tinker will forget his past and accept the new identity offered him. Amused by the possibility, the lord then goes into the details attendant on the deception, saying that the servants must make Sly believe that he has been in a state of lunacy and that his lady has been weeping over his disease. The huntsman agrees wholeheartedly to implement his master's scheme, and Sly is carried out.

At this moment a troupe of strolling players arrives and the lord greets them in a manner that foreshadows Hamlet's greeting to the players. He warns them that at their evening performance there will be a lord who has never before seen a play, and therefore they should not be discomfited by any comments he may make. On receiving the assurance of one of the players that they will remain serious whatever happens the lord sends them to the buttery for refreshment. In addition, he also sends orders to Bartholomew, his page, to dress himself as a woman and pretend that he is Sly's wife when the drunkard awakens.

The actual purpose of the entire induction has been endlessly debated. Certainly it exists in *The Taming of the Shrew,* but Shakespeare has altered its tone considerably. In *A Shrew* the language of the lord is remarkably high-flown and Marlovian, singularly unsuitable for a hunting expedition. In Shakespeare, on the other hand, we have enormous vitality of character and language. Sly is a toughminded Warwickshire peasant and a realistically drawn product of the English countryside. In some ways he is the most "local" and individual character of the entire play, and it is almost easier to believe in him than in some aspects of the Italianate comedy of intrigue which we find throughout the rest of the play. At least one critic has also suggested that the Induction gives the audience a clue to what should be its attitude toward the play of *The Taming of the Shrew,* a farce performed for the delectation of a drunken tinker. But on the other hand, Shakespeare seems to have grown a trifle uncomfortable with the mechanism of the Induction as the play progressed, and perhaps, as he himself became more involved in the development of the play as a series of matrimonial themes rather than as a knockabout farce. As a result we find that Sly disappears after I.i.259, whereas in *A Shrew* he makes various interjections and is finally redeposited, asleep, on the heath where the play opened.

Induction: Scene 2

This scene takes place in a bedchamber in the lord's castle. The folio stage direction also makes it fairly clear that Sly and his attendants would play this scene from the upper level, or "tarras" of the theatre. Sly awakens and calls for ale, but instead the servant offers him "a cup of sack (sherry)," which the tinker refuses rather peremptorily. Similarly, he remains unmoved when he is offered conserves and asked which clothing he will wear. In fact he takes a perverse delight in his unsophisticated tastes and in his lack of material possessions, particularly in his ragged clothing.

Sly asserts his identity in no uncertain manner, refusing at first to accept the evidence of the servants that he is indeed a lord who has been suffering from amnesia. The servants influence him with music and offer him all sorts of esoteric and aristocratic delights, frequently using terms from classical mythology, which are of course quite incomprehensible to Sly. Gradually the tinker is convinced, and when the servants mention his alleged "wife" Sly accepts his new identity and believes that he has indeed been suffering from loss of memory for the past fifteen years. The servants claim that in his sleep he has been calling for persons with strange peasant names, which Sly identifies, but the servants assure him that he does not know any such people.

At this point a young page enters disguised as a woman, and claims to be Sly's wife. Immediately the tinker gets into difficulties with the correct mode of address for a lady. He himself is more used to being called "goodman," but now he must call his "wife" madam, since that is the way lords address ladies. But "madam" or not, Sly comes straight to the point and asks the disguised page to undress and come to bed. Not for him are the indirections of courtly love; physical gratification is the immediate concern. The page refuses his request, claiming that the physicians have as yet forbidden it. A messenger then arrives to inform Sly and his group that a party of players is about to perform an entertainment for their delight, and what is even more interesting, they introduce the play as having medicinal qualities—a curative for Sly's melancholy, since his blood has been congealed with sadness and hence he has fallen into a "frenzy" (madness). Sly then agrees to watch the play, but not until he has asked for the definition of a "commonty." He thinks it is a Christmas farce or a kind of vaudeville, tumbling act.

Act I: Scene 1

This scene takes place in Padua, in a public place. Lucentio and his man Tranio enter, and in an expository speech aimed at the audience rather than the servant, Lucentio explains his reasons for coming to this city. In addition, he identifies himself. He has come to Padua, a university town, in order to study, having left his birthplace, Pisa, with his father's permission. His announced purpose is to study virtue, and particularly the happiness that arises from virtuous philosophy. Tranio, however, sounds a trifle apprehensive that this intention might be just a trifle too serious, and he begs his master not to be stoic. He suggests that Ovid be not forgotten and suggests pleasurable study, not discipline. Love must not be forgotten.

Lucentio tends to agree with his servant, and he wishes that Biondello, his other servant, would come ashore so that they could look for lodgings.

At this moment Baptista, Katherine, Bianca, Hortensio, and Gremio, a pantaloon or foolish old man, enter. Baptista, the father of the two girls, tells Gremio and Hortensio, both suitors to Bianca, that he has no intention of bestowing his younger daughter in marriage until he has a husband for the older girl, Kate. He offers both the suitors leave to court Katherine, if they so desire. Both refuse, and Hortensio insults the girl by claiming that she is too rough. Immediately she offers violence to the young man and objects strenuously to the way her father is trying to get rid of her. Bianca says nothing. Tranio looks with amusement on the incipiently comic situation, but his master, Lucentio, is immediately struck with the "mild behavior and sobriety" of Bianca. In the meantime, Baptista speaks kindly to his younger daughter, showing an obvious favoritism which will be developed throughout the play. While Kate rages on, Bianca makes a humble speech of obedience to her father and goes inside as she is told. Baptista then says that he intends to employ tutors to instruct the tractable Bianca (and incidentally, Kate) until he will allow suitors to court her. As he prepares to leave he tells Kate to remain behind since he has more to say to his younger daughter. Kate promptly flashes back at him, asking if she must be "appointed hours" and she follows her father inside.

On Kate's departure the two suitors of Bianca discuss their unfortunate predicament. Their wooing is stalemated until after Kate is married. Consequently they take the only choice open to them: they temporarily decide to forget about their amorous rivalry and instead work together to procure a husband for Kate. Lucentio during this time has been so completely overwhelmed by the beauty and modesty of Bianca that he has neither noticed Kate nor her violent behavior. He promptly launches himself into conventional transports of romantic passion "I burn, I pine, I perish, Tranio, / If I achieve not this young girl." (I.i.160-161) Love has entered through the eyes and Lucentio is struck to the heart. Tranio tries to explain the situation to Lucentio, but for a while all he can get in reply is a series of speeches praising the beauty and modesty of Bianca. Finally Lucentio understands the situation: that Baptista plans to remove Bianca from society until after Kate's marriage. Then Lucentio remembers Baptista's plan to engage tutors to instruct Bianca; he is not quite deaf and blind with love. He therefore decides to disguise himself as a schoolmaster and present himself as a tutor for Bianca. In the meantime Tranio will disguise himself as Lucentio and Biondello will wait upon the disguised Tranio.

At this moment Biondello arrives and is amazed to discover that Tranio and Lucentio have exchanged clothes. Lucentio makes up a rather pointless cover story about having killed a man and therefore requiring a disguise. The two servants arrange the details of their behavior to each other, and as Lucentio departs he orders Tranio (supposed Lucentio now) to play a part in the wooing of Bianca and offer himself as a third suitor for her hand.

Suddenly we return to Christopher Sly. A servant asks whether the supposed lord is enjoying the play. Sly asks the page if there is any more of it, and on hearing that the performance has barely begun, he wishes that it were already finished. After this remark Sly disappears from the script of the play.

Act I: Scene 2

This scene takes place outside the house of Hortensio in Padua. Petruchio and his man, Grumio, enter. Petruchio orders his servant to knock at the door, and when Grumio takes him literally and knocks his master, he flies into a rage and wrings his servant by the ears.

At the sound of the altercation between Grumio and Petruchio, Hortensio comes out and greets his friend, asking what he is doing in Padua. He also tries to pacify Petruchio. When he hears that Petruchio's father is dead and that the young man is now in quest of a wealthy wife a superb idea strikes Hortensio and he tells the visitor that he knows of a suitable candidate. Petruchio claims that he cares for nothing but money, and declares that sweetness of disposition means nothing to him just as long as his wife is wealthy. After all, he has

> . . . come to wive it wealthily in Padua;
> If wealthily, then happily in Padua." (I.ii.75-76)

Hortensio says that the girl does have some advantages, because she is young and beautiful, and a well educated gentlewoman in the bargain. Her only fault is her "intolerable curst" disposition. Petruchio is immediately most interested and declares himself a match for the girl, particularly when he hears who she is, since he knows of her family. Grumio comments that Petruchio's own evil disposition should make him a match for such a renowned shrew as Kate.

In return for introducing Petruchio to Baptista and Katherine, Hortensio asks his friend to introduce him as a tutor in music for Bianca so that he may gain entrance to the presence of his lady. Hortensio expresses his love for Bianca in the conventional poetic terms, explaining the predicament Baptista has placed him in. Gremio then enters, accompanied by Lucentio, disguised as Cambio, whom he introduces as a tutor in literature who will help to plead his suit to Bianca by reading books of love with her. Lucentio agrees to do so, but of course he has other ideas. Gremio rejoices when Hortensio tells him that Petruchio "Will undertake to woo curst Katherine" and what is more, to marry her if her dowry should prove satisfactory.

Gremio is impressed by the fearlessness of Petruchio who claims that nothing Kate can do will frighten him. Then Tranio, disguised as Lucentio, enters with Biondello and annouces himself as a third candidate for Bianca's hand. He praises the younger girl, but Petruchio expresses interest only in Kate. The three eager wooers of Bianca now offer to finance Petruchio's wooing of Kate in order that they may then compete for Bianca's hand.

Act II: Scene 1

This act is composed of one single scene which is set in a room in the house of Baptista Minola in Padua. It opens with Bianca, whose hands have been tied behind her back by Kate, offering complete obedience to her sister "So well I know my duty to my elders." Kate in reply asks in what appears to be a jealous manner which of all her suitors her sister loves. Bianca, however, declares that she has "never yet beheld that special face" which she prefers above all others. Kate expresses disbelief and since she seems to think that Bianca is lying she runs through the catalogue of wooers, while Bianca begs to be untied. Baptista then enters and scolds Kate for her cruelty. In fury, Kate rushes at Bianca, who flees. Kate, now almost dancing with rage, turns on her father and accuses him of favoritism in wishing to find a husband for Bianca while she, the elder daughter, must dance barefoot on her sister's wedding day, and "for your love to her lead apes in hell."

Gremio, bringing the disguised Lucentio, Petruchio with the disguised Hortensio, and Tranio, disguised as Lucentio and accompanied by Biondello carrying a lute and books, all enter in a body. Petruchio immediately enquires whether Baptista has a daughter named Katherine "fair and virtuous." Taken aback by the bluntness of this enquiry, Baptista hedges, saying that he has a daughter called Katherine, and avoids comment on her advantages. Gremio is at first afraid that Petruchio is coming too fast to the point, but Petruchio begs leave to woo in his own way, and he continues to praise Kate, claiming that he has heard

> . . . of her beauty and her wit,
> Her affability and bashful modesty,
> Her wondrous qualities and mild behaviour. (II.i.48-50)

Consequently he has come to Padua in order to meet her, and as a token of his good faith he presents the disguised Hortensio as an instructor in music and mathematics for Bianca and Kate. Baptista is by now totally confused, and says that Kate is not for Petruchio. The young man deliberately takes him up the wrong way as if he believes that Baptista cannot bear to part with this paragon of daughters, or else dislikes his candidacy, though Baptista is quite impressed when Petruchio identifies himself. Gremio then presents the disguised Lucentio as a literature and language tutor for Bianca. He is promptly followed by Tranio who announces himself as a third suitor for Bianca's hand, and offers as a gift a package of Greek and Latin books for the young lady's edification. The tutors are sent to Bianca's room and the suitors are sent away so that Petruchio and Baptista can talk business alone.

Immediately the conversation starts in a most businesslike manner, because Petruchio says that he is in a hurry to get on with his wooing, and consequently he does not wish to beat about the bush. He announces his financial independence, saying that he has increased the value of the lands and goods which his deceased father had left him. Then he forthrightly asks what dowry he could expect with Katherine if he gains her love. Baptista offers twenty thousand crowns immediately, and on his death half his lands. In return, Petruchio says he will assure Kate of a share in all his lands and leases should she survive him. He then asks that suitable agreements be drawn up so that the verbal covenants may be formalized and fulfilled.

Baptista then says that he wants Petruchio first to gain Kate's "love."

Petruchio, however, replies confidently that he expects no trouble at all from Kate because his temperament is exactly the same as hers. Naturally when two such fiery personalities meet "They do consume the thing that feeds their fury." In this way each will yield to the other, especially since Petruchio is rough and ready in his wooing. Baptista remains sceptical and wishes him good luck.

The father's doubts seem all too justified, because Hortensio enters at that moment with a broken head and an anecdote telling how Kate hit him over the head with his own lute. Petruchio promptly claims that he loves Kate more and more after hearing of this behavior, while Baptista exasperatedly tells Hortensio to concentrate on instructing Bianca. He then leaves, promising to send Kate to Petruchio.

Left alone on the stage, Petruchio takes the audience into his confidence by telling them of his planned wooing approach. He will woo Kate by opposition; the more she rails the more he will praise her gentleness, and the more violent her behavior, the more he will ignore it, praising her for her love of him. Whatever tricks Kate will decide to play he will accept as if she had done their opposite.

On Kate's entrance Petruchio promptly puts his announced plan into practice. He opposes her in every way and praises her in abundance for the qualities that she is famous for lacking. Kate tries out her wit on him, but Petruchio always tops her remarks with equally witty ones, and the humor becomes broad, bawdy, and full of quibbles. In exasperation at being bested in a wit combat (probably this is the first time this has ever happened to Kate), she raises her hand to Petruchio and strikes him. Now in view of Petruchio's earlier enraged and violent behavior to Grumio, his man, we might expect that the young man might reply in kind, but he does not, since he is a gentleman. Instead he overrules all objections and has a good tempered and witty reply to all her insults. Then he praises her beauty, gentleness, courtesy, and slowness in speech, while Kate continues to rail.

Finally, he announces that he alone is a fit husband for her, and he will marry her whether she wishes or not: "For I am he born to tame you Kate."

With the return of Baptista, Gremio, and Tranio, Katherine grumbles about the match, claiming that Petruchio is half lunatic. But she is speedily overruled by Petruchio who gives an amusingly inaccurate account of the wooing, saying that Kate has acted precisely as a well-mannered, well-brought up young lady should. He announces that they have agreed that the marriage should take place on Sunday, a statement which brings forth a protest from Katherine. Gremio and Tranio promptly mock Petruchio for his success in wooing the shrew, but the wooer counters by claiming that he and Kate have agreed that she shall remain "curst" in her public behavior for reasons that seem best to them. Petruchio, however, seems to have hit on the truth some lines earlier when he says, "If she be curst, it is for policy."

Baptista is overjoyed to hear that the wedding will take place.

A difficult daughter is now off his hands, and he can now proceed to the marriage of his favorite daughter. He has Kate and Petruchio join hands as signification of betrothal and the happy wooers of Bianca act as witnesses to the ceremony.

As soon as Petruchio leaves to make preparations for the marriage, Baptista raises the question of Bianca's marriage. It is rather interesting to note the way in which he speaks of it: ". . . now I play the merchant's part, / And venture madly on a desperate mart." Baptista quite cynically sets out to "sell" Bianca's hand to the highest bidder. It does not seem to concern him that Gremio is such a foolish old man that Bianca could hardly find joy in such a match. Baptista does not think of asking Bianca's consent and his approach is quite different from the one he followed in arranging Kate's marriage. Now that he has more than one wooer he acts like an auctioneer and has each suitor bid against the other. The wooers start squabbling among themselves, but Baptista announces that the sole criterion of worth will be the amount of dower, or settlement, that each can make on Bianca. Gremio opens the bidding by offering all he owns, but Tranio (disguised as Lucentio) counters by offering not only his own property, but also that of his father. Hortensio, incidentally, takes no part in these proceedings. He is too busy tutoring Bianca. Gremio admits that he is outbid and Baptista gives his ruling. As a shrewd bargainer he keeps himself covered. The supposed Lucentio's father must ratify the bid that his "son" has made, and if he will not, then Gremio will have the reversion of Bianca's hand. After all, what might happen if "Lucentio" were to die before his father? Gremio as he departs seems to consider his own position more or less secure, for what Italian father would be so foolish as to give his son all before his death and become dependent on his child's goodwill. Tranio, supposed Lucentio, then resolves that there is only one course of action open to him. He must find someone who will pretend to be his father, "supposed Vincentio," and will ratify the agreement that has just been proposed.

Act III: Scene 1

This scene takes place a short time later in a room in Baptista's house. Hortensio and Lucio are shown instructing Bianca in music and literature. The two tutors, however, wrangle over which of them shall have priority in the teaching of the young girl, each pressing the claims of his own discipline. Finally, Bianca settles the argument by saying that she will study the way she prefers and will not be tied down to any set times. She then tells Hortensio to sit down and play his lute while Cambio (Lucentio in disguise) reads to her. The triumphant Lucentio immediately starts with a passage in Latin from Ovid's *Heroides,* and under cover of translating it he reveals to Bianca his own identity and his love for her. Bianca seems intrigued and answers him in the same manner, giving Lucentio some hope of his eventual success.

Hortensio can see quite well what is going on and he determines to watch his fellow tutor. When his turn comes he approaches Bianca in exactly the same way and under cover of teaching her the scale on the lute he contrives to recite her a poem telling of his love. Bianca returns the poem, saying that she does not particularly like it.

At this moment a messenger arrives bearing Baptista's command that Bianca leave her books and help decorate Kate's chamber for the wedding the next day. Without Bianca's presence Lucentio sees no reason to stay, but Hortensio, left alone on the stage, gives vent to jealous suspicion of his fellow instructor. He also speaks in a disillusioned manner of Bianca. If she will cast her glance on every wandering male decoy, then he wants nothing to do with her.

Act III: Scene 2

This scene takes place outside Baptista's house in Padua. It is Sunday, Kate's wedding day. All is ready, and Baptista, Gremio, Tranio, Bianca, Lucentio, Kate and her attendants are dressed and waiting for the arrival of the bridegroom. Baptista is obviously disturbed over Petruchio's tardiness, and he fears that the family will be shamed if the young man does not appear soon. Kate breaks in on the conversation with Tranio, supposed Lucentio, saying that the shame will be solely hers. She is almost beside herself with angry frustration and hurt pride. Weeping, she says that she must give her hand to this madman, Petru-

chio, against her will, and as far as she can see, he does not even
intend to go through with the marriage until he is ready. She
even seems to believe that he has undertaken the entire wooing
as some kind of joke against her so he, Petruchio, will be noted
a merry man. He will go as far as having the banns called, but
he has no intention of going through with the match. Then comes
her crowning indignity: everyone will point at her and say

> "Lo, there is mad Petruchio's wife,
> If it would please him come and marry her!" (III.ii.19-20)

Tranio counsels patience, an ironic suggestion for the impatient,
and indeed the wronged Katherine. Finally she leaves weeping
with anger, and for once even Baptista cannot blame her and he
expresses sympathy for her predicament.

Biondello then rushes in to announce Petruchio's imminent arrival, but then with amusement he goes on to retail the fact that
the bridegroom is coming dressed in the most appalling collection of dirty, ragged old clothes, riding on an old broken-down
diseased horse with half-mended harness. The servant he has
with him is dressed in a similar manner and altogether they
present a most peculiar-looking pair to come to a wedding.
Tranio remarks that Petruchio must be acting thus because of
some odd humor, and anyway he frequently goes about poorly
dressed. The honor of the family, and the reputation of Bianca,
are now saved.

Petruchio then rushes in and calls for Kate. He offers no apologies for his late arrival and brushes aside all suggestions that he
should change his clothes for something more suitable. Baptista
tries to convince him that he is shaming his own rank, as well as
making himself "an eye-sore to our solemn festival." Petruchio
answers by saying that the tale of his tardiness will have to wait
until later, but in the meantime he is impatient to be married to
Kate. Tranio offers him some decent clothes, suggesting that
Petruchio should not go so ill clad to greet his bride. Petruchio,
however, refuses categorically, saying that Kate is marrying him
for what he *is,* not for what he is wearing. After all, it is much
easier to change clothes than to change the essence of a personality, and if the latter were possible, it would be much better
both for Kate and himself. As Petruchio departs in search of

Kate, Tranio comments that "He hath some meaning in his mad attire."

As everyone departs for Kate's wedding, Tranio and Lucentio speak of their plans to have Lucentio marry Bianca. Tranio must find some older man to impersonate Lucentio's father, Vincentio of Pisa, who will make assurance of settling even more money on Bianca than Tranio has promised. In that way Baptista will be tricked into giving his consent to the marriage so that the real Lucentio may marry Bianca in a regular manner. Lucentio, however, is almost in despair, and he even thinks it might be easier to elope and marry secretly than to attempt to overcome all the difficulties facing him and Bianca.

At this moment old Signior Gremio enters to retail to the characters on the stage (and, of course, the audience) the way in which Petruchio has just made a total shambles of the wedding ceremony. The bridegroom is, according to Gremio, "a devil, a very fiend," who is even more curst than Kate herself, who is meek and gentle by comparison. When the priest asked if he would take Kate for his wife, Petruchio answering by swearing "Ay, by gogs-wouns," rather than replying according to the ritual, "I do." Then, when the amazed priest dropped his book, Petruchio struck him so hard that he fell down as well. Needless to say, Kate was so terrified that for once she was speechless, while Petruchio's behavior seems to have grown more and more violent. He stamped and swore at the vicar, quaffed off the ceremonial wine as if he were carousing at a shipboard party after a storm, and threw the winesoaked cakes, the "sops," at the sexton. Lastly, he grabbed Kate around the neck and kissed her with a resounding smack instead of giving her a politely religious peck. Once again Petruchio has gained an advantage over Kate who is too afraid to say anything.

Hard on the heels of Gremio the wedding party returns from the church, and Petruchio says that though he knows that the assembled company had expected to eat a wedding breakfast with him, he and Katherine must leave immediately, despite the fact that the food is already prepared. He bids the guests eat and drink with Baptista, and thanks them for coming to see him married "To this most patient, sweet, and virtuous wife." Tranio and Gremio both beg Petruchio to stay, and Kate adds her entreaties to theirs. She begins mildly, "Now, if you love me, stay," but when Petruchio refuses her she acts true to her shrewish form, defies him openly, and says she will not go with him, commenting that he sounds like a very surly bridegroom in exercising his authority so harshly from the beginning. She stands up for her own rights and tells the company to proceed to the bridal dinner. Petruchio adds his invitation to Kate's, but then says that his bride must go with him, and, acting as if he is about to be attacked by the company, he announces that he will be the master of his wife. He proceeds to state exactly the extent of his power over her as his wife. Legally he is quite right; she is completely within his power. He then draws his sword and orders Grumio to do the same against the alleged opposition of the guests. Since no one offers him a fight, Petruchio then leaves with Katherine and Grumio.

Act IV: Scene 1

This scene takes place at Petruchio's country house just after the wedding of Kate and Petruchio. Grumio enters grumbling and complaining, tired to death, and smarting from a beating. He has been sent ahead to see that preparations have been made for the imminent arrival of his master and mistress. To add to Grumio's discomfort the weather is cold and he is wet through. He calls for Curtis, another servant, and tells him that the master and mistress are about to arrive. Curtis asks whether Katherine is as hot a shrew as her reputation, and Grumio says that indeed she *was* until this frost, in other words, until this cold winter journey. He orders Curtis to see that the fire is made ready and inquires after all sorts of other preparations which should be made to make the house habitable for the newlyweds: the rooms should be clean and fresh, the rushes newly laid down, the carpets on the floor, the serving men in their best livery, and everyone dressed to suit the festive occasion. Curtis says that all these things have been done and then he asks Grumio for his news.

Grumio then proceeds to retail the incidents of the journey, which seems to have been one long accident. First, Katherine's horse fell with her under it in a very muddy place. However, instead of helping his wife up, Petruchio left her lying there and beat Grumio because of the accident. Kate then got herself up and plucked Petruchio off his servant. Petruchio swore, Grumio cried out, and Kate begged her husband to cease beating Grumio, she who had never before begged a favor of anyone. The horses then ran away, Kate's bridle was burst, Grumio lost his crupper, and all sorts of other misfortunes also occurred.

Grumio then calls all the servants together and inspects them. He seems quite satisfied with their appearance, when suddenly the noise of Petruchio's arrival is heard. He shouts for the servants and complains that no suitable preparations have been made for his arrival. He hits out at the servants, who seem to be moving too slowly, and his rage so completely demoralizes them that any natural clumsiness is accentuated. He calls for supper, then changes his mind and demands that his boots be removed. He calls for water and promptly strikes the terrified servant, who lets the vessel fall. Kate begs Petruchio to have patience, telling him that the servant is not deliberately clumsy. The interesting thing to note is that Kate, the impatient shrew, is now the one who counsels patience. Finally, supper arrives, but Petruchio claims that the mutton is burnt and so is all the meat. In a wild rage he flings the meat and everything else about the room and rails madly at the servants. Kate again counsels mildness, saying that the meat was "well enough," if Petruchio had wished to be satisfied. In reply Petruchio claims that the meat was burned and dried up, and he himself is absolutely forbidden to eat it as a result. Anyway, it is bad for the choleric temper of both of them.

The servants see precisely what he is doing, killing her in her own humor. Then, when Kate enters her bridal chamber, we are told by Curtis, the servant, that Petruchio delivers her a sermon on continence, scolding and swearing so that she does not know which way to turn. This is hardly the kind of behavior one would expect of a bridegroom on his wedding night.

While Kate is undressing for bed Petruchio enters and explains his policy of taming to the audience. In so doing he adopts terms from the sport of falconry, something that is extremely important for many reasons. Kate, the falcon, is now hungry, and she will not be fed until she *stoop,* that is, fly to the decoy. Obviously there is a double meaning to the term *stoop* here. In addition, Petruchio says that he will use another approach to tame his wild hawk. He will keep her awake, as falconers keep from sleep those birds that continually flutter their wings and will not learn obedience.

Petruchio then goes on to specific details. Kate has not slept for a couple of nights, and he will make sure that she will not sleep tonight, because he will find some fault about the way in which the bed is made. He will fling the bolster one way and the coverlet and sheets another. But, and this is most important, on all occasions he will pretend that his actions are dictated by his extreme care for Kate's welfare. In short, he will tire her out with his complaining, his rages, and his swearing. In this way he will "kill a wife with kindness," and by following her humor he will speedily make her come to heel.

Act IV: Scene 2

This scene takes place in Padua, before Baptista's house. Tranio (disguised as Lucentio) and Hortensio (disguised as Licio, the tutor) are discussing the progress of their wooing of Bianca. Hortensio has informed Tranio that Bianca is not interested in either of them, and instead is devoting her attention to Cambio, the disguised Lucentio, her literature teacher. Hortensio suggests that he and Tranio watch the progress of Cambio's teaching. Tranio, however, in an amusing double meaning obvious to the audience, claims that he had thought Bianca cared only for Lucentio—as is indeed the case, though hidden by the supposes.

Hortensio then reveals his true identity to Tranio while the two wooers watch Bianco and the disguised Lucentio courting. Lucentio is carefully reading Ovid's *Ars Amatoria (The Art of Love),* and love is what he professes. Hortensio is totally disillusioned with the behavior of Bianca and Tranio claims to feel exactly the same. In fact he is prepared to make an agreement with Hortensio to "Forswear Bianca and her love for ever." Hortensio takes up the suggestion and shakes hands with Tranio to seal the bargain. The two then exchange vows of renunciation, but Hortensio goes one step further. Within three days he proposes to marry a wealthy widow who has loved him for as long as he has loved Bianca. This widow seems in fact to have been pursuing Hortensio, and he claims that he intends this time to woo for kindness in a woman, not for her good looks.

As soon as the forswearing is finished and Hortensio has left, Tranio, Lucentio, and Bianca enjoy the joke at the disappointed wooer's expense. They laugh at Hortensio's plan to marry "a lusty widow," Tranio remarking that certainly Hortensio will tame her, and in order to do so he has gone to the taming school of which Petruchio is the master.

At this point Biondello enters saying that he thinks he has seen a traveler who may be able to fulfill the role of "supposed Vincentio," the father of Lucentio. The old pedant then enters and Tranio enquires after his business, asking where he has come from. On hearing that he has come from Mantua, Tranio feigns horror and tells a wild story, the upshot of which is that the pedant has put his life in jeopardy by coming to Padua. The ships from Mantua are held up in Venice because of a private quarrel between the dukes of each city, and therefore the inhabitants of Mantua are endangered.

The pedant is quite appalled at having blundered accidentally into such a dangerous situation. He has bills of exchange from Florence to deliver, and he wonders how he can carry out his mission. Tranio promptly shows him a way out by asking if the pedant has ever been in Pisa and whether he has heard of Vincentio. The pedant says that he has indeed heard of the "incomparable wealth" of Vincentio, though he has never met the man. Tranio then claims that Vincentio is his father, and that the pedant bears a considerable resemblance to him. Tranio then suggests that the pedant play the part of Vincentio and take up lodgings with his alleged "son." The pedant willingly agrees in order to save his life. Now "supposed Lucentio" has gained a father, "supposed Vincentio." As the pedant and Tranio depart, the servant tells him that Vincentio is expected daily to give assurance of a dower in marriage, something he will explain in detail later on.

Act IV: Scene 3

This scene takes place in a room in Petruchio's house. Kate enters, followed by Grumio. She is hungry, tired, desperate, and totally frustrated by Petruchio's behavior. She asks whether her husband has married her in order to starve her; even beggars at Baptista's door are better treated than she if they entreat char-

ity. She, however, has never had to beg for anything and she
does not know how to do so. And what is the result? She is starving for lack of meat, giddy for lack of sleep, continually kept
awake by Petruchio's oaths, and kept from eating by his quar-
relsomeness and anger at mealtimes. Nevertheless, she cannot
really complain of Petruchio's behavior; her husband has seen
to that and Kate is totally exasperated, because:

> He does it under name of perfect love,
> As who should say, if I should sleep or eat,
> 'Twere deadly sickness or else present death. (IV.iii.12-14)

But though Kate claims that she cannot entreat, she now entreats Grumio to bring her food. Grumio, however, plays the
same tricks on her as his master. He offers a neat's foot (ox's
foot), and when Kate agrees, he suggests that it is too choleric
a meat. Remember that beef was considered to engender bodily
heat and was therefore not good for anyone with a natural inclination toward the hot humors. Grumio then tantalizes her
further by offering her broiled tripe, but again he claims that
might be too choleric, and suggests instead beef and mustard.
Kate almost salivates for joy and agrees, only to have Grumio
contend that the mustard might be too hot. The famished girl
then sinks her pride and says that she'll take the beef without
the mustard, but Grumio says that she must have both. Kate
agrees, but then Grumio offers her just the mustard. At this
point Kate realizes that Grumio has been playing with her, and
sends him away. Petruchio then enters with Hortensio and greets
Kate affectionately, asking why she seems so dejected. He also
asks for a welcome, since he has brought her some food which
he says he has taken pains to prepare for her himself. Kate grabs
for the dish, but Petruchio insists on thanks. Only when he
receives this courtesy does he give the food to her, but then he
tells Hortensio in an aside to try to eat it all up.

Now that Kate seems to have reformed a trifle, Petruchio suggests that they both return to Padua to Baptista's house for a
general celebration. In order to prepare for this journey he has
ordered a tailor to present himself, because, after all, Kate needs
new clothes and he himself wants her to look fine.

The haberdasher first presents himself and offers Petruchio the cap the gentleman had ordered. But Petruchio takes one look at it and refuses it on the grounds that it is ridiculously small. Kate promptly defies him, saying that this is the current style, and gentlewomen wear such caps. To this Petruchio replies that she will then have one when she is gentle. Kate again breaks out in anger, which Petruchio deliberately misunderstands, claiming that it is aimed at the cap and congratulating her on her good taste in disliking it. Almost beside herself with frustration, Kate declares that she will have that cap or none at all—and so the haberdasher leaves, and Kate is left capless.

The tailor then arrives, bringing a gown which Petruchio promptly finds fault with because of the sleeves and the slashes in the material. He excoriates the tailor for botching up good fabric, despite the tailor's claim that he was simply following the orders of Petruchio to make it up in the latest fashion. Again Kate crosses Petruchio, saying that she has never seen "a better fashion'd gown," and further, she fears that her husband is trying to make a puppet out of her. Again Petruchio deliberately misunderstands and blames the tailor. And when the tailor presumes to correct him he flies into a screaming rage. In sheer self-defense the tailor reminds Petruchio that Grumio had been sent to order the styling of the dress. Grumio follows his master's lead and takes everything in its incorrect and literal sense, denying all responsibility for the gown. The tailor counters by reading the notes he had made for the order. No sooner does he begin with "a loose-bodied gown," than Grumio protests.

And so the gulling of the tailor continues with puns, deliberate mistaking of the words, and bawdy double meanings until the tailor is sent packing. But just before the discomfited tailor departs, Petruchio orders Hortensio to see that he is paid, an aside which indicates to the audience that the entire scene is staged for Kate's benefit. This action also helps to salvage Petruchio's character, showing that he is more than a thoughtless and violent prankster.

Finally, then, Kate gets no new clothes, but instead Petruchio lectures her on his favorite theme—the outside is less important than the inside. There is no disgrace in "honest mean habiliments," for " 'tis the mind that makes the body rich," and honor will always be obvious, despite the poverty of the outward apparel.

He then proposes that they set off for Padua to feast at Baptista's house, now that the hour is seven o'clock. Kate assures him, and quite courteously, that he is wrong, and it is almost two. But Petruchio promptly flies again into a rage, claiming that Kate is simply crossing him out of sheer perversity. He then refuses to budge an inch, announcing that whatever he says the time is, that time it will be before he leaves. Hortensio in an aside seems to consider Petruchio utterly mad.

Act IV: Scene 4

This scene takes place outside Baptista's house in Padua. Tranio and the pedant have just arrived, and the pedant is beginning to have doubts about the part he is supposed to play. He is concerned over whether Baptista might perhaps recognize him, because they had lodged together some twenty years earlier in Genoa. Tranio brushes aside this objection as Biondello enters to inform Tranio that Baptista had been told of the arrival of "supposed Vincentio."

Baptista then arrives with Lucentio (supposed Cambio) and Tranio (supposed Lucentio) greets the shrewd merchant, introducing his father (the pedant, supposed Vincentio), begging him to obtain Bianca's hand for him. The pedant plays his part very well indeed, speaking eloquently of the love between "supposed Lucentio" and the lady and praising the worthiness of Baptista. He assures Baptista that he is "ready and willing" to subscribe to a financial agreement to ratify the match. In reply, Baptista says that he is well aware of the mutual affection between Bianca and Lucentio and then turns to business. If Vincentio will assure Bianca of a sufficient dower, then the match can certainly take place, and he, Baptista will be very glad to give his consent.

Tranio very willingly accepts Baptista's consent and asks when and where the agreements will finally be settled. Baptista replies that he prefers not to perform these business arrangements in his house, because too many people, including the servants, might be listening. In addition, old Gremio has not yet lost hope of achieving Bianca and he might interrupt proceedings. Tranio then suggests that the agreements be drawn up and signed at his lodgings where his "father" is staying, an idea which appeals immediately to Baptista. He promptly sends Cambio, the disguised Lucentio, back to inform Bianca that "she's like to be Lucentio's wife." as indeed she is, but not in the sense that Baptista expects.

As Baptista, Tranio, and the pedant, "supposed Vincentio," leave to ratify the financial agreements for Bianca's wedding, Biondello and the real Lucentio, "supposed Cambio," enter. Biondello then informs Lucentio of the arrangements that Tranio has made for his master to marry Bianca. Baptista has asked Lucentio to bring Bianca to him for supper, and Tranio has arranged for a priest at a nearby church to be ready for the arrival of the young couple at any time. At first Lucentio seems a trifle slow, but Biondello spells things out for him. While Baptista and the others are busy over a false financial agreement, Lucentio should marry Bianca before "the priest, clerk, and some sufficient honest witnesses," taking assurances of her *"cum privilegio ad imprimendum solum."*

Act IV: Scene 5

This scene takes place on a public road between Petruchio's country house and Baptista's house in Padua. Kate, Petruchio, and Hortensio have finally embarked on their journey, so presumably Kate has agreed to accept what her husband says about the time of day. Petruchio opens proceedings by remarking "how bright and goodly shines the moon." Kate promptly contradicts him quite flatly by saying, correctly, that the sun is shining, not the moon. The two of them commence to argue about this obvious fact of nature. Petruchio then adopts the same approach that he had previously used (IV.iii.) and threatens to return home if Kate continues to cross him. Consequently, Kate takes Hortensio's advice and agrees with her husband. But even so, she is not completely crushed into blind obedience. Look carefully at the way in which she agrees with Petruchio:

> And be it moon, or sun, or what you please,
> And if you please to call it a rush-candle
> Henceforth I vow it shall be so for me. (IV.v.13-15)

But there is no pleasing Petruchio, because he immediately reverses himself and says "it is the blessed sun." Wearily, Kate decides to humor the man, agreeing with him that it is the sun if he says so, and not if he says otherwise. But she still retains her own private judgment in the matter:

> And the moon changes even as your mind,
> What you will have it nam'd, even that it is
> And so it shall be so for Katherine. (IV.v.20-22)

Hortensio, however, seems to take Kate's apparent capitulation as evidence of Petruchio's success in taming and he congratulates his friend. At this moment the real Vincentio, the father of Lucentio, enters and Petruchio immediately addresses him as if he were a beautiful young gentlewoman, calling upon Kate to agree in praising the beauty of this young lady. Kate replies as requested, going even further than Petruchio in her praise of the "lady," so that Vincentio is utterly bewildered and Petruchio amused. In return, Petruchio pretends to look most puzzled, and solicitously inquires after Kate's sanity in addressing a wrinkled old man as a woman. Kate, however, recovers brilliantly, and completely turns the tables on Petruchio by saying that her "mistaking eyes . . . have been so bedazzled with the sun," an allusion to the previous exchange. This remark now alerts Petruchio to the fact that Kate now fully understands his tricks.

Vincentio now introduces himself and tells the company that he is on his way to visit his son, Lucentio, in Padua. Petruchio is overjoyed and tells Vincentio that Lucentio is either about to marry, or has already married, Kate's sister. He expatiates at length on the beauty, virtue, and dowry of Bianca, and embraces the old man, suggesting that they journey together to Padua. As they depart, Hortensio remarks that he has now learned the way to treat his widow from observing Petruchio in action.

Act V: Scene 1

This scene takes place in Padua in front of Lucentio's house, and it is the climactic confrontation scene and denouement of the subplot. Here all the knots are untied and the disguises are finally stripped from everyone.

The real Lucentio runs off to the church with Bianca to be married, while old Gremio waits outside Baptista's house for him, still supposing him to be Cambio. Petruchio, Katherine, Vincentio, Grumio, and other attendants then enter and Petruchio identifies Lucentio's lodgings to Vincentio, who gratefully invites them in for some refreshment. The father knocks at the door and is answered by the pedant who answers him rudely. Petruchio identifies the inquirer as Lucentio's father, only to be told by the pedant that he is Vincentio. Petruchio, rather puzzled, turns to Vincentio and accuses him of taking another man's name, while the pedant calls for Vincentio's arrest on a charge of false pretenses. Just at this moment Biondello arrives to report that he has just witnessed the marriage of Bianca and Lucentio. His joy, however, is speedily marred by the sight of Vincentio who beats him when Biondello denies knowing him and insists that the pedant is the real Vincentio. Petruchio and Kate retire to watch the confusion which grows with the arrival of Tranio, the pedant, Baptista, and servants. Tranio insists on his identity as Lucentio, and is supported by the others. Vincentio, now nearly frantic, asks the whereabouts of his son, and seems to suspect that Tranio might have done away with him. Tranio calls for an officer and the real Vincentio is placed under arrest, despite the assurances of the man that he is who he claims to be.

Now, when all the confusions and "supposes" seem to have reached their complicated height, Biondello returns with Lucentio and Bianca. Then he, together with Tranio and the pedant, decamp as quickly as possible in order to avoid a beating at the hands of Vincentio. Lucentio kneels before Vincentio and asks his pardon, much to the amazement of Baptista, who still thinks the young man to be Cambio. Lucentio and Bianca together explain the circumstances which caused Lucentio to disguise himself as Cambio and have Tranio change places and clothes with him. They also announce their marriage. But then Baptista realizes that he has been tricked and asks whether the couple have married without his consent. After all, he has now lost a rich mate for Bianca. Vincentio, however, speedily promises a suitable financial agreement—but first he will be revenged on the pedant. Likewise, Baptista wants to get to the bottom of all the trickery. Lucentio assures Bianca that all will be well, and Gremio decides to take part in the feast, even though he has not succeeded in obtaining the lady of his choice.

Katherine and Petruchio then come out from their hiding place and Petruchio suggests that they follow everyone else. But first he asks his wife for a kiss, but she roguishly plays the part of the modest matron wishing to avoid a public display of affection, saying that she is ashamed to kiss in the street. Petruchio promptly starts to play his old tricks and threatens to take her back home again, so she immediately offers him a kiss.

Act V: Scene 2

This last scene of the play takes place in a room in Lucentio's house and represents a gay feast at which every one of the major characters is present, a typical ending for a Shakespearean comedy. As host, Lucentio welcomes all the guests, and when Petruchio declares that "Padua affords nothing but what is kind" Hortensio makes a most interesting comment wishing for both their sakes that his friend were right. Petruchio immediately seizes on the remark and accuses Hortensio of being afraid of his widow. The widow then tries to turn the tables on Petruchio by saying "He that is giddy thinks the world turns round," which means that Petruchio ought not to judge the fate of others by his own. The extremely sensitive Kate understands this meaning perfectly and asks the widow to make her statement more precise. The answer is exactly what she expects: the widow believes that since Petruchio is troubled by a shrew he measures the lot of Hortensio by his own sorrow. The women exchange insults; Katherine becomes angry, and Petruchio offers to bet a hundred marks that she will overwhelm the widow. Even Bianca joins in the wit-combat and makes a couple of bitter remarks to Petruchio.

With the departure of the ladies Petruchio has to accept quite a few insults and considerable commiseration because he married the girl whom Baptista terms "the veriest shrew of all."

Petruchio, however, objects to Baptista's characterization of his wife, and suggests that the three newly married men wager on the obedience of their respective wives. Whichever of the three women will come first when called will win the wager for her husband. Hortensio asks what will be the amount of the wager, and Lucentio suggests twenty crowns. Petruchio, however, appears insulted, saying that he would wager a small sum like that on his hawk or his hound, but twenty times that sum on his wife. Lucentio then suggests a hundred crowns and all agree.

Lucentio confidently opens the wager proceedings by sending Biondello to bid Bianca come to him. Baptista, equally as secure in his own mind, says he is sure she will come. But to everyone's amazement Biondello returns with the news "That she is busy and she cannot come." Petruchio laughs at Lucentio's discomfiture, but Gremio warns him not to be so confident; his wife may send him a worse reply.

Hortensio then sends Biondello to "entreat" the widow to come. The use of the word "entreat" calls forth further witticisms from Petruchio. Hortensio once again insults Petruchio, this time by saying that he is sure that Kate will not be entreated. Biondello, however, soon pricks Hortensio's bubble of self-confidence by returning with a message from the widow saying that she is well aware that Hortensio has some joke in mind, and that he had better come to her instead.

Now it is the turn of Petruchio, and he sends Grumio to Kate with the message that he "commands" her to come. Hortensio, trying to recover his own lost equilibrium, insists that he knows Kate's answer and is certain that she will refuse to come. But he is wrong and Kate appears immediately, inquiring humbly after her husband's wishes, since he has sent for her. Petruchio then asks where the other two wives are, and on hearing that they are simply sitting gossiping in front of the parlor fire he tells Kate to go and fetch them. If they don't want to come, then Kate should whip them to their husbands.

The amazement of all the men in the company is very great indeed, and the most surprised person of all is Baptista who adds another twenty thousand crowns to Kate's dowry. At this point one wonders whether Baptista did not wrong Kate financially in the original negotiations for the match with Petruchio. Baptista is indeed right in saying that Petruchio has really won another daughter, because Kate is so changed.

Petruchio, however, has decided that he wants to test Kate's obedience even further, and the moment his wife appears, driving the other two women before her, he tells her that her cap is most unbecoming and orders her to tear it off and throw it underfoot. Without a word and without hesitation, Kate does as she is told, while Bianca and the widow scoff at her.

Petruchio now asks Kate to tell the other two "headstrong women" the duty they owe to their husbands. Needless to say, Kate is only too willing to comply and she launches into her longest and most important speech in the entire play. It extols feminine subordination, since the station and physical capacities of women are different from those of men. She notes that the husband is the lord of the house and the monarch of the wife, who is his subject, owing to him the same duty that the subject owes the king. The husband is the one who must labor to support his wife, and therefore she should show her appreciation. Finally, she offers to place her hand beneath her husband's foot as a sign of her complete and utter submission, if he should wish it. But Kate has proved herself, and Petruchio does not take her up on that offer. Instead he raises her up and kisses her. And indeed, she has deserved it, because between them they have played an excellent joke on the company. The play concludes with the shrew apparently tamed, although Lucentio remains a trifle sceptical.

Troilus and Cressida

PRIAM, *King of Troy.*
HECTOR ⎫
TROILUS ⎪
PARIS ⎬ *his sons.*
DEIPHORUS ⎪
HELENUS ⎭
MARGARELON, *a bastard son of Priam.*
AENEAS ⎫
ANTENOR ⎬ *Trojan commanders.*
CALCHAS, *a Trojan priest.*
PANDARUS, *uncle to Cressida.*
AGAMEMNON, *the Greek general.*
MENELAUS, *his brother.*
ACHILLES ⎫
AJAX ⎪
ULYSSES ⎪
NESTOR ⎬ *Greek commanders.*
DIOMEDES ⎪
PATROCLUS ⎭
THERSITES, *a deformed and scurrilous Greek.*
ALEXANDER, *servant of Cressida.*
SERVANT *to Troilus.*
SERVANT *to Paris.*
SERVANT *to Diomedes.*

HELEN, *wife to Menelaus.*
ANDROMACHE, *wife to Hector.*
CASSANDRA, *daughter to Priam, a prophetess.*
CRESSIDA, *daughter to Calchas.*

Troilus and Cressida

PROLOGUE: The Prologue first appeared in the 1623 Folio. It gives the locale of the play as Troy. The sixty-nine Greek royal chieftains arrive with their "ministers and instruments of cruel war" in Athens. They vow to ransack Troy to revenge the capture of Menelaus' wife, Queen Helen. When they arrive at Priam's six-gated city, the Trojans are greatly stirred.

The Prologue as a speaker to the audience wishes to note that the play begins in "the middle" of the Greek and Trojan war. One may either "Like or find fault," as he pleases. And whether the play is good or bad, " 'tis but the chance of war."

Act I: Scene 1

The play covers about five days. As the action is often carried on simultaneously in the Trojan and Greek camps, this seems to lengthen the time element.

The opening scene is in front of Ilium, the Trojan palace built by Priam. Its many towers could be seen from a distance so that it appeared to be "wrought up unto the heavens." Troilus, the youngest son of Priam, King of Troy, and Pandarus, a notorious procurer, stand talking outside the gates of the palace. It is early morning and the young warrior is armed for the day's battle. He tells Pandarus that he is not in the humor for battle and declares he will disarm. For what reason should he "go to battle outside Troy's walls when he finds "such cruel battle here within?" If any Trojan is "master of his heart," let him go to battle. He, Troilus, is not. Cressida does not return his love. He has kept his affair with her secret from his father, Priam, and his brothers.

To tease him, Pandarus claims his efforts as go-between have had small thanks. Then he contrasts Cressida's beauty with Helen's. "Because she's kin to me, therefore she's not so fair as Helen." He adds, "And she were not kin to me, she would be as fair on Friday as Helen is on Sunday."

He takes Troilus' impassioned declaration of love calmly, merely saying that he thinks Cressida would be far better off with her father, Calchas, in the Greek camp.

Pandarus, pretending to be disgusted with the young lovers, leaves.

Left alone, Troilus expresses his fears that Pandarus is not urging his "cause" with Cressida. And "he's as techy to be woo'd to woo,/ As she is stubborn-chaste against all suit." He prays to Apollo "for thy Daphne's love" to enlighten him, "What Cressid is, what Pandar, and what me?" He points to an imaginary map, noting where Cressida, a "pearl," lies in India. Between India and the palace, Ilium, there is a wild and wandering "flood." Pandarus is Troilus' convoy, that is, the "bark" that will carry him, the "merchant," to buy the pearl.

As Troilus ambles along, Aeneas, one of Priam's generals, passes by and asks why Troilus is "not afield." Troilus answers, "Because not there." This "womanish" reason he says, explains it. Nevertheless, he is interested in what has happened. On hearing that Paris was wounded by Menelaus, he remarks, "Let Paris bleed 'tis but a scar to scorn; Paris is gor'd with Menelaus' horn."

An alarm sounds, and they both go off to the "sport abroad." Troilus wryly comments that sport is "better at home" if he could do as he wished.

Act I: Scene 2

Later, the same day, in a street near Priam's palace, Cressida strolls along with her servant, Alexander. When Queen Hecuba and Helen pass them, she asks Alexander where they might be going. He replies, to watch the battle still in progress. Alexander discloses that the great Hector was struck down in battle yesterday by Ajax, who, though he is Hector's nephew, is fighting for the Greeks. Ajax is described as a man "into whom nature has so crowded humors that his valor is crush'd into folly." The humiliation of the defeat by such an opponent weighs heavily on Hector and the Trojans.

Cressida notices her uncle Pandarus coming toward them. He stops to ask what "you talk of." Cressida replies that it is of Hector's reported anger at Ajax. Pandarus thinks he knows the cause. But, today, Hector will have his revenge with the aid of Troilus.

For the sake of argument, Cressida refuses to agree with her uncle's praise of Troilus as "a better man" than Hector. She banters sharply with him over the personal "qualities" of the brothers —their "wit" and their "beauty."

Pandarus tries to arouse her jealousy by describing Helen's meeting with Troilus; how she put "her white hand to his cloven chin." Though Troilus is still much too young to have "past three or four hairs on his chin," Helen spied one white hair. According to Pandarus, everyone laughed, even Queen Hecuba so "that her eyes ran o'er." Then Troilus made a joke of it, and there was more laughing.

Pandarus turns the conversation into a serious vein, reminding Cressida to "think" of what he had told her. She promises to.

A retreat is sounded from the battlefield and Pandarus suggests they watch the warriors "as they pass toward Ilium." He calls them by name and gives a quick sketch of each one. First Aeneas, "one of the flowers of Troy"; then Antenor, "he has a shrewd wit," and "He's one o' the soundest judgments in Troy."

When Hector passes by, Pandarus exclaims, "Is't not a brave man!" and "Look you what hacks are on his helmet!"

The next warrior, Paris, is described by Pandarus as "a gallant man"; Helenus follows, "he'll fight indifferent well." When the parade is nearly over Troilus comes by. Cressida, still refusing to agree with Pandarus' extravagant praise of him, asks, "What sneaking fellow comes yonder?" Pandarus replies, "That's Deiphobus." Then he recognizes Troilus, "the prince of chivalry!" He points to his bloody sword and his nicked helmet; these scars show that he is a greater warrior than Hector. Even "Paris is dirt to him; and warrant, Helen, to change, would give money to boot." Cressida appears completely umoved by it all. Her only comment, "Here come more," aggravates Pandarus.

When the common soldiers march by, Pandarus sees them as so

many "asses, fools, dolts! chaff and bran." He stops his tirade to praise Troilus again and places him above Agamemnon. Cressida counters with the remark that Achilles is a "better man than Troilus." Impatient with her, Pandarus declares, "You are such another woman!"

As they banter, Troilus' servant enters with a request that Pandarus go immediately to his house where Troilus is disarming and awaits him. He leaves, promising to bring Cressida a token.

Left alone, Cressida reveals that she is in love with Troilus, but insists she will hold him off. She reasons that, for a woman, it is best to hide her love: "men prize the thing ungain'd more than it is." She resolves that "though my heart's content firm love doth bear,/ Nothing of that shall from mine eyes appear."

Act I: Scene 3

This scene takes place some days later in the Greek encampment in front of Agamemnon's tent. In a long speech, the general regrets that after seven years of seige, "Troy's walls stand." He believes Jove is testing the worth of the Greeks and finds they are lackadaisical. The old general, Nestor, does not agree that blame should be placed on fortune and the gods. Too often, in failure, men take refuge in "chiding fortune." Ulysses brings the discussion to a realistic level, insisting that the generals are busy about other things than war. The system of honor and obedience paid to tradition and authority has weakened, and "when degree is shak'd/ Which is the ladder to all high designs/ The enterprise is sick." He concludes, "Troy in our weakness stands, not in her strength."

When Agamemnon asks for a remedy, Ulysses declares that their most renowned warrior, Achilles, lies in his tent "Upon a lazy bed the livelong day" and "breaks scurril jests" with the effeminate general, Patroclus, whose chief pastime is to burlesque the Greek generals. As Ulysses continues to rail at the misconduct of the generals in the camp, particularly Achilles, Patroclus, and Ajax, a trumpet sounds. Aeneas, the Trojan general, arrives with a challenge. He proclaims that a "prince call'd Hector, Priam is his father," has bid him come with a challenge to the "Kings, princes, lords of Greece." If there is one among them who holds his "honor higher than his ease," then this challenge goes to him. In sight of the Trojans and Greeks, Hector will prove that he "hath a lady, wiser, fairer, truer,/ Than ever Greek did compass in his arms."

The following day, Hector will sound his "trumpet call" between the Trojan and Greek camps. If a Greek lover answers the challenge, Hector will "honor him"; if none appears, he will say, "Grecian dames are sunburnt and not worth/ The splinter of a lance."

Agamemnon promises Aeneas that the challenge will be told "our lovers." If none of the younger warriors will accept, Agamemnon and Nestor jokingly declare they will volunteer. Aeneas and the others depart with Agamemnon. Ulysses and Nestor remain. Ulysses suggests that the challenge is a plot to entice Achilles to fight Hector. In that case, Achilles is already too vain; if he should win, he would crush his comrades with the "pride and salt scorn of his eyes." If he loses to Hector, they have lost their "best man." Ulysses proposes to make a "lottery" and "by device" they would let "blockish Ajax draw/ The sort to fight" with Hector. Whatever the outcome, choosing Ajax will belittle Achilles. Nestor puts it bluntly: the "Two curs shall tame each other." Pride will urge them on "as 't were their bone."

Act II: Scene 1

This scene takes place later the same day in a section of the Greek camp. Ajax enters with Thersites. The latter refuses to tell the content of Agamemnon's proclamation regarding the duel. Thersites, the "cobloaf," is getting a beating from Ajax when Achilles and Patroclus intervene. With his rough jests Thersites belittles their valor and compares them to Hector; he antagonizes both Ajax and Achilles. As he leaves, he says he will see them "hanged" before he comes again to their tents.

After Thersites has gone, Achilles repeats Agamemnon's proclamation: "Hector, by the fifth hour of the sun/ Will, with a trumpet," on the following morning "call some knight to arms." The whole affair is to "maintain" something, but Achilles has forgotten what —"'tis trash." When Ajax asks who the knight will be, Achilles declares it will be decided by lottery, so Hector will not know his opponent beforehand. Ajax declares that would mean Achilles. He leaves to find out more about the duel.

Act II: Scene 2

This scene takes place the same day in a room in Priam's palace. Priam has received a note from the old Greek general, Nestor, asking for the return of Helen and hoping thereby that the "hot digestion of this cormorant war/ Shall be struck off." The king has called a council to ask the opinion of his sons. Hector argues that guarding a thing not theirs has been too costly in Trojan blood. He would "let Helen go." Troilus insists such action would declare the weakness of the Trojan king. Another of Priam's sons, Helenus, complains that although Troilus bites "so sharp at reasons," he has none of his own to answer his father. Troilus tosses off Helenus' comment as stuff for "dreams and slumbers." He scorns all the reasons why Helen should be given back—fear of harm by the enemy and the "sword is perilous." He concludes, "if we talk of reason/ Let's shut our gates and sleep." He sneers that "reason and respect/ Make livers pale and lustihood suspect."

When Hector insists that Helen "is not worth what she doth cost/ The holding," Troilus answers that it depends on how the thing is valued. The worth and dignity of the possessor must be taken into account. It is "mad idolatry,/ To make the service greater than the god."

In a long plea to keep Helen in Troy, Troilus describes the valor of Paris and how he was applauded by the Trojans when he brought home such a "noble prize." They all cried, "Inestimable!" Now, he declares sarcastically, "O theft most base! That we have stolen what we do fear to keep."

A loud cry and shrieks from their sister Cassandra interrupts the discussion. She begs them, "Lend me ten thousand eyes/ And I will fill them with prophetic tears." She prophesies the burning of the city, the "mass of moans to come." But, paid no attention, she leaves.

Paris, who has been silent until now, joins Troilus in arguing against the return of Helen. He calls it treason to the "ransack'd queen" and a "disgrace to your great worths and shame to me" to deliver her now to the Greeks "on terms of base compulsion."

Hector blames the youth of Troilus and Paris for wanting to retain Helen. He compares them to the "young men, whom Aristotle thought unfit to hear moral philosophy." His final plea to release the Greek wife of Menelaus is based on natural law, namely, "Nature craves/ All dues be render'd to their owners: now,/ What nearer debt in all humanity,/ Than wife is to the husband?" Every nation has laws to curb such "raging appetites." However, in the end, though Hector knows his counsel is absolutely correct, he can see the damage that Helen's return would wreak on Trojan dignity.

Troilus claims Hector has at last "touch'd on the life of our design." Since Helen is a "theme of honor and renown," this rises above any other reason why she must be held in Troy.

Troilus continues to play on the vanity of Hector, and the latter succumbs to promises of martial glory. Eager for action, he reveals the "roisting" challenge to a duel that he has sent to the Greeks. He "presumes" it will arouse the sleepy Agamemnon.

Act II: Scene 3

This scene takes place late the same day in front of Achilles' tent. Thersites is alone, mulling over his recent quarrel with Ajax. "He beats me, and I rail at him: O worthy satisfaction!" With a sarcastic gibe at "elephant" Ajax and the "rare engineer" Achilles, he thinks neither will defeat Troy. He asks "vengeance on the whole camp," a good enough curse for those who go to war over a tart. Patroclus enters and invites Thersites to come inside the tent and "rail." Thersites begins at once wishing on him "The common curse of mankind, folly and ignorance." Achilles, hearing the discussion, calls out a welcome to Thersites, "Why my cheese, my digestion," and inquires why he has been so long absent from his table. In the quick and bitter quipping among the three, Thersites shows the juggling for power that goes on in the Greek camp among the generals. He sums it up, declaring, "Agamemnon is a fool to offer to command Achilles; Achilles is a fool to be commanded by Agamemnon; Thersites is a fool to serve such a fool; and Patroclus is a fool positive."

As Thersites continues, he notices that Agamemnon with his commanders is coming toward Achilles' tent. The latter tells Patroclus to say he "will speak with nobody," and asks Thersites to follow him. Thersites again rails at the whole lot and hopes that "war and lechery confound all!" It irks Agamemnon to learn from Patroclus that Achilles is "ill-disposed" and cannot be seen. Ulysses declares that he saw him just now at the door of his tent. Refusing to believe that Achilles is ill, Agamemnon sends Patroclus again to advise him of the general's arrival.

Ajax jokes that Achilles is "sick of proud heart" and demands, "Why, why? let him show us a cause," why he cannot meet with us.

When Patroclus returns with Achilles' regrets that he cannot see Agamemnon, the latter sternly orders Patroclus to advise him that the general "comes to him." Patroclus is to berate him for the "overproud" manner and the "savage strangeness" he assumes. Ulysses goes along to see that the message is delivered. Meanwhile, Ajax uses his chance to disparage Achilles before Agamemnon and his commanders. He "hates a proud man." In a sarcastic aside, Nestor says "And yet he loves himself; is't not strange?"

Ulysses returns with word that Achilles will have no visitors nor will he accept Hector's challenge the following day. When pressed for Achilles' reasons, Ulysses declares that he is "so plaguy proud" that "the death tokens of it/ Cry—'no recovery.' " In a word, he is possessed "with greatness."

Agamemnon is in an embarrassing dilemma over Achilles' haughtiness and disrespect. His proposal to send Ajax "to greet him in his tent" because he "holds you [Ajax] well" is a last pathetic attempt to keep face with his commanders. The proposal is spurned. Ulysses, who has little respect for Ajax's mentality, pretends it would make Achilles even more proud to send him. Ajax is delighted with such praise, but thinks he should go to Achilles. He promises, "I will knead him; I will make him supple." After much discussion, Ulysses, according to the "design" he had proposed to Nestor, quietly remarks that Ajax "can cope the best" though "come knights from east to west." Agamemnon and his commanders leave to discuss further who shall be Hector's opponent in the duel.

Act III: Scene 1

This scene takes place in a room in Priam's palace. Pandarus inquires from the servant of Paris where his master can be found. The servant points to him and his "mortal Venus," who stand nearby, listening to the music Paris has arranged in Helen's honor. Pandarus has a message to give Paris at the request of Troilus. When he sees the pair coming toward him, Pandarus hurries to greet them with "fair words." He especially commends the music, and immediately Paris insists that Pandarus sing for Helen. Despite their pleas for him to sing, Pandarus insists on first giving Paris the message from Troilus; namely, if anyone "call for him at supper, you will make his excuse."

Paris agrees to answer for Troilus, and asks, "What exploit's in hand? Where sups he tonight?" Helen believes it is with "my disposer" Cressida, though Pandarus insists she is "sick." He defends his belief, stating, "I spy." The scene focuses on Pandarus, and with the song "Love, Love, nothing but love" sung at Helen's insistence, he emerges a foolish old man enamored of "tinselled bawdry."

When Pandarus leaves, Helen and Paris stay to watch the warriors return from the day's battle. Paris proposes an honor for Helen, namely, that her "enchanting fingers" unbuckle the "great" Hector's armor. She will be "proud to be his servant."

Act III: Scene 2

The scene takes place immediately in Pandarus' garden. Pandarus enters, expecting to find Troilus there. He arrives shortly. He has not seen Cressida, though he stalks "About her door/ Like a strange soul upon the Stygian banks/ Staying for waftage."

When Pandarus goes inside the house to fetch Cressida, Troilus reveals his emotion in the long speech, "I am giddy; expectation whirls me round."

Pandarus comes back for a moment to give Troilus a few enticing comments on Cressida. When he returns with her, Pandarus is hardly more than the common procurer pleased with his lewd efforts. He hovers about the couple suggesting, urging, then goes off to "get a fire."

When he returns, they "have not done talking." Cressida has delayed her answer, pretending to change her mind. Pandarus vouches that while his "kindred" are hard to woo, "they are constant being won." In a well-calculated rush of emotion Cressida reveals she has long loved Troilus, but refused to woo him. Even now, she fears, "I shall surely speak the thing I repent," and again pretends to change her mind and excitedly decides to leave.

Troilus calms her. He vows the truth of his love. All future lovers shall use the motto "As true as Troilus." Not to be outdone, Cressida promises she will never be false: "Yea, let them say, to stick the heart of falsehood,/ As false as Cressida."

Pandarus, tired of their speeches, urges them to seal the bargain, and he'll be the witness. And taking the hand of each he declares: "If ever you prove false one to another ... let all pitiful goers-between be call'd to the world's end after my name; call them all— Pandars." As they leave, Pandarus calls on Cupid to help "all tongue-tied maidens."

Act III: Scene 3

This scene takes place in the Greek camp the same day. Agamemnon and his commanders, Ulysses, Diomedes, Nestor, Ajax, Menelaus, and the Trojan priest, Calchas, are present.

Agamemnon has called a council to discuss who will oppose Hector in the duel scheduled for the following day. Before the discussion starts, Calchas addresses Agamemnon about the possibility of exchanging his daughter Cressida for the Trojan general, Antenor, recently taken captive. In his petition, Calchas declares that he has "incurr'd a traitor's name" to do service to the Greeks, and now should have a "little benefit." More than that, Cressida's presence "shall quite strike off all service" that he has rendered.

Agamemnon agrees to Calchas's request and sends Diomedes to effect the exchange if Priam is willing. Diomedes is also to find out whether Hector will appear the next day to meet his Greek opponent. He is pleased with his task, a burden he is "proud to bear."

After Diomedes leaves, Ulysses notes that Achilles and Patroclus are standing in front of their tent, a short distance away. He proposes that Agamemnon and the commanders ignore him and walk on to their tents. Ulysses will lag behind them. When Achilles is snubbed, he will likely ask Ulysses why. If he does, Ulysses has "derision medicinable," and it may do some good. He reasons that "pride hath no other glass/ To show itself, but pride; for supple knees/ Feed arrogance, and are the proud man's fees."

They agree and Agamemnon leads the way. As they walk near Achilles' tent and fail to notice him, he calls to them. He thinks Agamemnon is coming to speak with him and calls, "You know my mind; I'll fight no more 'gainst Troy."

When Agamemnon fails to hear the remark, Achilles dismisses it. He notices the cool greetings and is puzzled. He muses at length on "greatness, once fallen out with fortune/ Must fall out with men too." But it is different with him, because "Fortune and I are friends." He enjoys a full life, and it is no great moment that Agamemnon and his commanders pay him no mind. When he notices Ulysses ambling along, he decides to "interrupt his reading" and calls to him. Achilles asks what he is reading. Without looking up, Ulysses replies, "A strange fellow here/ Writes me, that man . . . Cannot make boast to have that which he hath,/ Nor feels not what he owes, but by reflection." Then his "virtues shining upon others" generates "heat" that returns to "the first giver."

The idea is not "strange" to Achilles. He poses an example: one is not able to see his own countenance until it is "mirrored" in another's eye, "where it may see itself."

Ulysses agrees, and he tailors the concept to fit Ajax, whose strength is untried as yet. Now we shall see tomorrow "that by chance" he may gain "renown." To stir Achilles' pride, Ulysses adds, "O heavens! what some men do,/ While some men leave to do!/ How some men creep in skittish fortune's hall/ While others play the idiots in her eyes!" Some are already praising Ajax as if he had his foot "on brave Hector's breast."

Achilles believes him, remarking how they snubbed him just now. When Ulysses sees that his words have been effective, he launches into the longest speech in the play on the folly of resting on one's laurels. He cleverly links a series of proverbs that drive home the idea: "Perservance, dear my lord,/ Keeps honor bright: to have done, is to hang/ Quite out of fashion, like a rusty mail/ In monumental mockery."

When he accuses Achilles of closeting himself and living on his past glory, it is no wonder "That all the Greeks begin to worship Ajax." If he fights against Hector, his glory will live again. Achilles claims "strong reasons" for his "privacy." His love for Priam's daughter, Ulysses declares, is no secret. But it would serve him better "To throw down Hector, than Polyxena." Otherwise, "all the Greekish girls" will be singing, "Great Hector's sister did Achilles win/ But our great Ajax bravely beat him down."

After Ulysses leaves, Patroclus, who has overheard their argument, prods Achilles in the same vein. He attempts to exonerate himself from the charge of keeping the commander from the battlefield because of "your great love to me." Achilles is at last convinced his "fame is shrewdly gored." He asks Patroclus to fetch Thersites. He will send the dwarf to Ajax with an invitation to the Trojan lords to come to his tent after the duel. Achilles has a "woman's longing" to see Hector unarmed—"in his weeds of peace." It will be "A labor sav'd."

Thersites enters and describes Ajax as so excited over being chosen as Hector's opponent that he "stalks up and down like a peacock." When Thersites spoke with him, he replied, "Thanks, Agamemnon." He listens to no one. With Patroclus for a foil, Thersites impersonates Ajax when he received Achilles' message. Thersites plays Ajax as stupid and drunk with pride.

242

Rather than risk a verbal message to Ajax, Achilles will send Thersites with a letter to him. The dwarf quips, "Let me bear another to his horse; for that's the more capable creature."

Achilles leaves with Patroclus. He declares his mind is "troubled, like a fountain stirr'd." When both have gone, Thersites wishes the "fountain" of Achilles' mind would clear up so he could "water an ass at it!" He would rather be a "tick in a sheep" than have "such a valiant ignorance."

Act IV: Scene 1

This scene takes place early in the morning of the following day on a street in Troy. Diomedes has just arrived in Troy with Antenor, the Trojan general, who is to be exchanged for Cressida. He is walking with Paris when they meet Aeneas. While Antenor listens, the three warriors exchange greetings that are full of barbed compliments.

Aeneas tells that he has been sent for by the king but is unaware of the reason. Paris advises him that it concerns the exchange of Antenor for Cressida. Diomedes is charged to bring "this Greek" (prisoner) to Calchas' house where Cressida lives. Furthermore, Paris thinks Troilus may have spent the night there. Though he knows the departure of Cressida will be most unwelcome news to Troilus, Paris attempts to rationalize the unfortunate turn of events for the lovers. He comments, "There is no help;/ The bitter disposition of the time/ Will have it so."

After Aeneas with his servant leaves for Calchas' house, Paris' conscience bothers him over the retention of Helen. He asks Diomedes who "merits fair Helen best,/ Myself, or Menelaus?" Diomedes straddles the question, "Both alike." In elaborating on his remark, he defames Menelaus as "a puling cuckold" who "would drink up/ The lees and dregs of a flat tamed piece." He sees Paris as a "lecher" who "out of whorish loins/ Are pleas'd to breed out your inheritors." Paris complains that he is "too bitter" toward his "countrywoman." Then Diomedes berates Helen as "bitter to her own country." He declares that for every "drop of blood in her bawdy veins" so many Greeks and Trojans have lost their lives. (Compare the arguments given by Hector and Cassandra for the return of Helen in Act II, Scene 2.) Diomedes insists Helen has never expressed any sorrow for the tragedy she has caused. In a clever example of how bargains are made, Paris accuses Diomedes of slyly trying to regain Helen by downgrading her as merchants do when they want to buy. When the Trojans are ready "to sell," they praise their wares.

Act IV: Scene 2

This short scene takes place a few hours later in Pandarus' garden. Troilus and Cressida have spent the night together, and he is anxious to be on his way. Cressida complains, "you men will never tarry." She regrets that she gave her consent too quickly. Pandarus suddenly appears and vulgarly teases Cressida. When a knock comes at the door, Cressida invites Troilus to go inside with her; "I would not for half of Troy have you seen here."

Pandarus answers the knock and is surprised to find it is Aeneas. When the latter requests to see Troilus, Pandarus denies he is there. As they banter, Troilus appears and quickly learns of the exchange of Cressida for Antenor "within this hour." Though he is told that Priam and "the general state of Troy" have agreed to it, Troilus insists on going with Aeneas to meet with him. At Troilus' request, Aeneas promises not to mention that he found him at Pandarus' house.

This sudden change of fortune for Troilus and Cressida greatly disturbs Pandarus. Sensing some grave trouble, Cressida reenters and pleads to know what has happened. Pandarus, finally, tells her that she is "chang'd for Antenor" and must go to her father. Cressida is quite overcome at the news and declares she has "forgot" her father. Her name will stand for "the very crown of falsehood/ If ever she leave Troilus," nor will "Time, force, and death" ever change her. She leaves Pandarus to go in and weep. She will disfigure her "praised cheeks" and "break her heart" by calling Troilus' name. She "will not go from Troy."

Act IV: Scene 3

This very short scene follows immediately on the street in front of Pandarus' house. The hour has come for Cressida's delivery to the Greeks. Antenor, Diomedes, Aeneas, and Paris bid Troilus tell Cressida "what she is to do," and hurry her along. Troilus remains calm and leaves, promising to bring Cressida "to the Grecian Diomedes presently."

After Troilus leaves, Paris expresses his sympathy over the unfortunate turn of Troilus' romance. He muses, "I know what 'tis to love." With Antenor, Diomedes, and Aeneas he enters Pandarus' house.

Act IV: Scene 4

This scene follows immediately in a room in Pandarus' house. In his attempt to comfort Cressida, Pandarus cautions her, "Be moderate, be moderate." But she declares her grief is too violent. Her love "admits of no qualifing dross" nor does her "grief in such a precious loss."

As they talk, Troilus enters and there is a moving reunion of the lovers. Pandarus disconsolately quotes the "goodly saying"—"O heavy heart,/ Why sigh'st thou without breaking?" He quotes the answer, "Because thou canst not ease thy smart/ By friendship nor by speaking."

Troilus declares the purity and sincerity of his love for Cressida. He thinks the gods are angry with him and are taking her from him. Cressida asks whether she must really go. Yes, he tells her, and immediately. Time, "with a robber's haste,/ Crams his rich thievery up, he knows not how." So they must part with "a single famish'd kiss."

Aeneas, waiting outside with Diomedes and the others, calls impatiently to know if Cressida is ready. Troilus tells them to have patience, "she will come."

In the few minutes left, Troilus keeps insisting that Cressida be "true of heart." There is an implication in Troilus' remark that he doubts her fidelity. Cressida shows surprise at his fears. She asks, "what wicked deem is this?" To clarify his meaning, he assures her he does not fear that she will be false, but that she not disclose his plan to see her often. And to see her each night he will "grow friend with danger." As a token of love, he gives her a sleeve to wear. She offers him a glove.

Troilus cautions her a third time to be "true." Cressida is disturbed at it. He defends his qualms on the ground that he has formidable rivals in the young Greeks. They are cultured men, and they love novelty. That is what makes him afraid. Cressida reproves him that he really does not love her. Troilus professes he cannot question her faith, but his qualifications as a lover and husband do not measure up to the Greeks. He cannot dance nor "sweeten talk." Nor can he play "subtle games." Therefore she may be drawn away from him by some "dumb discoursive devil." But she must not be tempted. At Cressida's question whether he thinks she would be tempted, he replies, "No." But he does not discount human frailty.

There is another call from Aeneas to hurry their parting. Before he answers, Troilus embraces her, "Come, kiss; and let us part." At Troilus' bidding, Paris is asked to bring in Aeneas and Diomedes. Meanwhile, Cressida demands of Troilus, "My lord will you be true?" She need not fear, truth is his "vice." In short, he is too simple, "plain and true."

When Diomedes enters, Troilus greets him before the others and introduces Cressida. He asks that Diomedes treat her well. If he does, Diomedes will find mercy at Troilus' sword should they ever meet in battle.

The beauty of Cressida greatly impresses Diomedes. She will "command him wholly." Troilus considers his remark on her beauty as discourteous to him. He declares Cressida is a person of rare moral worth and Diomedes is unworthy to be even her servant. He swears by the "dreadful Pluto" that if Diomedes harms her, he will cut his throat. Diomedes attempts to toss off his remarks as pleasantries. When he has left the Trojan camp, he will answer for his acts. The three leave for the gate.

Aeneas hurries off to keep his promise to escort Hector to the field. He declares the glory of Troy rests that day on Hector's worth and chivalry.

Act IV: Scene 5

This scene takes place the same day around the "fifth hour" in the Greek camp. The "lists" (barriers) enclosing the field of combat are ready for the duel. Ajax is armed and surrounded by Greek commanders, including Achilles. Agamemnon commends Ajax for his "fresh and fair" preparation. He orders the trumpet blown to advise the Trojans to come to the field. With pomp and pride in his ability to defeat Hector, Ajax tosses his purse to the trumpeter. When there is no answer to the call from the Trojans, Achilles suggests it is early.

Agamemnon asks whether the couple coming toward them is not Diomedes and Cressida. Ulysses sarcastically identifies Diomedes peculiar gait. "He rises on the toe; his spirit in aspiration lifts him from the earth."

Agamemnon welcomes Cressida, and each of the generals salutes her with a kiss. She plays the coquette with them, enjoying their fast quipping, until Diomedes steps in to take her to her father. When she leaves, Ulysses who recognizes Cressida for the courtesan she is, gives his scorching vignette: "Fie, fie upon her!/ There's language in her eye, her cheek, her lip;/ Nay, her foot speaks; her wanton spirits look out/ At every joint and motive of her body."

His remarks are cut short with the sound of the Trojan trumpet. Hector enters armed and escorted by the Trojan general, Aeneas, and attendants. Aeneas salutes the state of Greece and requests the rules for the combat. He announces he is agreeable to the wishes of the Greeks. The quick comment of Achilles that "Tis done like Hector; but securely done,/ A little proudly, and great deal misprizing/ The knight oppos'd," is a strong hint of the Greek commander's pent-up scorn for Hector's reputation as a great warrior.

Aeneas recognizes Achilles and hurries to defend Hector as a man in whom "valor and pride" excel themselves. But the duel is a kind of half-hearted thing since the combatants are related (they are cousins). Aeneas declares that only "half Hector comes to seek/ This blended knight, half Trojan and half Greek." Achilles belittles the duel, labeling it a "maiden battle." They are interrupted by Agamemnon, who suggests that Diomedes (returned from taking Cressida to her father) and Aeneas discuss the "order" of the fight, that is, whether it is to be "to the uttermost,/ Or else a breath" (an exercise). Troilus stands near Agamemnon looking downcast. At the general's request Ulysses volunteers a description of Troilus given to him by Aeneas. The "youngest son of Priam" is "a true knight," honest, generous, and endowed with keen judgment. He is as "manly as Hector, but more dangerous," because he is vindictive. The Trojans, according to report, consider him "A second hope."

The duel has barely begun before Diomedes, a second for Ajax, calls a halt. Ajax protests but Hector agrees to the draw. In a long speech, Hector declares his close relationship to Ajax, "my father's sister's son,/ A cousin-german to great Priam's seed," forbids him to take part in a gory contest against him. He embraces Ajax, who falsely flatters him as "too gentle and too free a man." Ajax, remembering Achilles' letter delivered by Thersites (Act III, Scene 3), invites Hector and the Trojans to the Greek tents. Diomedes adds that Achilles' wishes to see "the valiant Hector" unarmed. The invitation pleases Hector. He requests Aeneas to send Troilus to him. Meanwhile he takes Ajax's hand: "my cousin,/ I go eat with thee, and see your knights."

Before they leave, Ajax introduces Hector to the Greek commanders. Agamemnon, with "divine integrity," gives Hector a warm welcome. He greets Troilus, standing beside his brother, "My well-famed lord of Troy." Menelaus gently reproves Hector for mentioning his "quondam wife." Nestor remembers his valor on the battlefield and asks him to let "an old man embrace thee." Hector's responses are most courteous.

When Ulysses invites Hector to his tent, Achilles interrupts, "I shall forestall thee, lord Ulysses." His greeting to Hector is coarse and has a double meaning, though the Trojan is at first unaware of it. In the blunt quipping kept up by Achilles, he reveals the death blow that he has planned for Hector. The latter, unaware of his treachery, is angered at Achilles' bragging how and in what part of his body he will kill him. He tells Achilles, "Henceforth guard thee well,/ For I'll not kill thee there, nor there, nor there;/ But by the forge that stithied [served as an anvil for] Mars his helm,/ I'll kill thee everywhere, yea o'er and o'er." Ajax calms Hector. He rebuffs Achilles for his threats—and insinuates that he is afraid to fight with Hector. The latter chafes under Achilles' blasting and offers to meet him in the field. Achilles accepts the challenge, "Tomorrow, do I meet thee, fell as death; / To-night, all friends."

Then Agamemnon invites "all you peers of Greece" to his tent for a feast to welcome Hector. He orders "Beat loud the tabourines, let the trumpets blow." When they have gone, Ulysses and Troilus stop to chat. The latter asks Ulysses where he can find Calchas. He is in Menelaus' tent and has prepared a feast for Diomedes and Cressida. Ulysses mentions how infatuated Diomedes is with Calchas' daughter. Troilus asks him to take him there after they leave Agamemnon's tent. As they go along, Ulysses is curious about Cressida in Troy. "Had she no lover there/ That quails in her absence?" Troilus insists, "She was belov'd, she loved; she is and doth:/ But still sweet love is food for fortune's tooth."

Act V: Scene 1

This scene takes place the same evening in front of Achilles' tent. Achilles tells Patroclus that he plans to feast Hector and "heat" his blood with wine; tomorrow, he will "cool" it with his sword. Thersites arrives with a letter for Achilles from Hecuba. While he reads it, Patroclus and Thersites indulge in some vulgar scoffing. The dwarf is not content until he ridicules Patroclus as "Achilles' male varlet." Bitter accusations are exchanged.

When Achilles finishes reading his letter he interrupts their bickering to state that his plan to fight in the following day's battle has been impeded by a plea from Hecuba. The Trojan queen has sent him a token from her daughter Polyxena, with whom he is in love. She implores him to keep the "oath" he has sworn not to fight. He is resolved not to break it regardless of the fate of Greece, fame, or honor. His "major vow" is to Polyxena. Thersites is told to "trim" his tent for the banquet to which he has invited Hector. When they have gone, Thersites indulges in a vicious appraisal of the Greek lords—Achilles, Patroclus, Agamemnon, and Menelaus. The first two have "too much blood and too little brain"; Agamemnon is honest but too fond of "quails" (women), and his brother, Menelaus, is both "an ass and an ox."

Thersites is interrupted by Agamemnon and his guests, who have left his tent to find their way to Achilles. The latter comes forward to welcome them, taking care to greet Hector first. Most have excuses for not remaining except Hector. He bids each good night.

When Diomedes leaves because of "important business," Ulysses quietly advises Troilus that the commander will go to Calchas' tent to see Cressida. They follow him.

Ajax, Nestor, and Hector remain to feast with Achilles. When they enter his tent, Thersites remains outside fuming over Diomedes, whom he calls a "false hearted rogue" whose "leer" is as trustworthy as a "serpent's hiss." Whenever Diomedes keeps his word, "the sun borrows from the moon." He has heard that Diomedes "keeps a Trojan drab" in "the traitor, Calchas' tent." He is disgusted that everywhere there is "nothing but lechery! all incontinent varlets!" He follows Ulysses and Troilus to see what is up.

Act V: Scene 2

This scene takes place a short time later before Calchas' tent. Diomedes, returning from Agamemnon's feast, calls to Calchas, asking about his daughter. He answers that she is coming. At a distance, Troilus and Ulysses whisper their comments on what is happening. Ulysses observes that Cressida "will sing any man at first sight." Thersites, an unnoticed onlooker, adds a quick pun, "if he can take her clift [clef]; she's noted." Diomedes in a quick give-and-take with Cressida tries to hold her to her promise to be his mistress. Cressida's plea that he tempt her "no more to folly"

249

prompts Thersites' quiet remark, "Roguery." Diomedes accuses Cressida of being "foresworn" and threatens to have her. She dallies, asking what he would have her do? On the side, Thersites answers "a juggling trick." Diomedes wants her to keep the oath she took, but Cressida asks him not to hold her to it. He threatens to leave, declaring he will be "her fool no more."

Troilus has watched them intently and is greatly disturbed when Cressida whispers something to Diomedes. Ulysses fears that Troilus' anger is so roused by the lovers that he will create a scene. He urges him to leave. He tells Troilus that he "has not the patience." Troilus vows by "all hell's torments" he will not speak a word. He will be patient. But when Cressida becomes more amorous and strokes Diomedes' cheek, Troilus is visibly disturbed, and Ulysses again begs him to leave. Troilus refuses, stating, "There is between my will and all offences/ A guard of patience." Thersites, ambushed nearby, is quietly amused and remarks how the "devil luxury with his fat rump and potato-finger, tickles these two together! Fry, lechery, fry!"

Though Cressida has promised to forsake all others for Diomedes, he wants "some token of surety for it." When she goes to fetch a token, Ulysses reminds Troilus he has sworn to be patient. Cressida returns with the sleeve Troilus had given her and presents it to Diomedes. Immediately, she wants it back. She refuses to tell him who gave it to her, saying, "He loved me."

Diomedes snatches the sleeve from her, and Cressida complains how he who gave it to her now is thinking of the sleeve and her and "gives memorial dainty kisses to it." She asks Diomedes not to snatch it from her because whoever has it has her heart. Diomedes insists he now has her heart. When she still refuses to tell who gave her the sleeve, Diomedes determines to wear it on his shield, and jealously will force the giver to challenge it.

On hearing the dare, Troilus quietly swears he will challenge him. The certainty that he feels over winning Cressida is dashed when she quickly declares, "I will not keep my word." Angered at her frequent change of heart, Diomedes declares he will "not be mocked" nor endure "this fooling." But he relents and asks what hour he must return. "The hour is not important," she says, "Ay, come—Do come—I shall be plagued until then."

After Diomedes leaves, Cressida in a short soliloquy bids Troilus "farewell," though "one eye" still looks on him. She pities her sex, summing up women's difficulties with a bit of ill-hatched logic: "The error of our eye directs our mind:/ What error leads, must err: O! then conclude,/ Minds sway'd by eyes are full of turpitude."

Ulysses, full of sympathy for Troilus, urges him to go: "All's done, my lord." In the quiet of the place Troilus insists he must make a "recordation" to his soul of every word that was spoken. Yet if he tells what he heard and saw, it will be a lie. He has a momentary sort of hallucination that it was not Cressida that he saw with Diomedes. Ulysses calmly and patiently explains that it was, indeed, she. He listens while Troilus declares it a blot on womanhood and on mothers. To say this woman was Cressida gives unscrupulous people a false rule to measure the entire sex. It is better to "think" she was. not Cressida. Ulysses insists that Cressida's infidelity cannot reflect on "our mothers." But Troilus, still deeply moved, tries to persuade himself, "This is Diomedes' Cressida." Reasoning by contraries, "If beauty have a soul, this is not she;/ If souls guide vows," and so on, he declares, "If there be rule in unity itself,/ This was not she." He recognizes the futility of arguing against a thing which has "bifold authority," meaning no validity.

He finally concludes that Cressida is his, "tied with the bonds of heaven," but these bonds by foul means have been "slipp'd, dissolved and loosed." However, in the knot "five-finger-tied" that binds her to Diomedes, there are only fragments of her love. Again Ulysses asks if his love for Cressida is so intense. Assured by Troilus that it is, he vows to regain the sleeve that Diomedes purposes to wear on his helm and kill him. Unable to control his anger, he berates Cressida as false and "all untruths" compared to her "stained name" will seem "glorious."

Ulysses notices Aeneas approaching them and warns Troilus that his "passion" attracts attention. For an hour he has been seeking Troilus to tell him that Ajax waits to conduct him to the Trojan camp. Kind to the last, Ulysses brings Troilus to the gates and receives the latter's "distracted thanks."

Thersites wanders off alone, wishing he "could meet that rogue Diomedes."

Act V: Scene 3

This scene takes place the next morning, in Troy, in front of Priam's palace. A battle is scheduled, and Hector is admonished by his wife, Andromache, not "to fight today." She has had ominous dreams. But Hector swears by the "everlasting gods" that he will go. His sister, Cassandra, comes with a like plea. Both women have dreamt the entire night of "shapes and forms of slaughter." Hector, heedless of their pleas, commands his trumpet be sounded. He declares the gods have heard him swear he will go.

At the appearance of Troilus and ready for battle, Hector tells him to remain away from the battlefield that day. Hector says, "I'll stand today for thee, and me, and Troy." Troilus chides his brother that he has a "vice of mercy" that lets captives live when he should kill them. To Hector, this is savage.

Hector's plea to Troilus to stay out of the battle is overcome when the latter declares, "Not fate, obedience, nor the hand of Mars" nor anyone in his family will keep him from the field. Cassandra, who had left the scene to bring her father, Priam, urges him to use his influence with Hector. He is his father's crutch and without him, Troy will fall.

Priam urges the women's reasons for opposing Hector, but without success. The Trojan general, Aeneas, has Hector's word that he will be in the field, and he cannot break faith. Cassandra is blamed for the forebodings. Her farewell is a series of omens. In a last subtle plea that he is violating honor, she declares, "Thou dost thyself and all our Troy deceive." Priam is disturbed at her words, but Hector cheers his father as they leave together.

Left alone, Troilus hears the battle "alarums" and swears he will overcome Diomedes and regain his sleeve.

When Pandarus enters with a letter from "Yond' poor girl," referring to Cressida, Troilus asks to read it. While he reads, Pandarus pretends he is greatly disturbed with "whoreson tisick" and the turn of affairs with Cressida. He asks to know what she says. Troilus destroys the letter, saying it is full of "words, words, words." He states that "My love with words and errors still she feeds,/ But edifies another with her deeds."

Act V: Scene 4

This scene takes place the same day, on the grounds between the Trojan and the Greek camps. Thersites walks along, musing over the Troilus-Diomedes duel. He sees they have begun their "clapper-

clawing on one another" and indulges in a round of vulgar abuse:
Diomedes is the "dissembling, abominable varlet" wearing on his
helm Troilus' love token to Cressida; Troilus is a "Trojan ass."
He would like to see Troilus return sleeveless to "the dissembling
luxurious drab" Cressida.

Thersites is no kinder to the Greek generals—Nestor is a "stale
old mouse-eaten dry cheese"; Ulysses is a "dog fox" and "not
worth a blackberry"; Ajax is a "mongrel cur" against a "dog of
as bad a kind," Achilles. As Thersites muses, Diomedes hurries
in, followed by Troilus. Troilus declares it is useless for Diomedes
to run away; he will swim even the river Styx to get him. Diomedes
insists "he was only protecting himself against too great odds."
Now he is ready to duel. Thersites, in an aside, urges them on.

When they leave, Hector enters and fails to recognize Thersites.
Unaware that he is a clown, he asks him if he is of noble rank
and thus able to oppose him. Thersites quickly admits to being
only "A scurvy knave; a very filthy rogue." When Hector leaves,
Thersites thanks God, and wishes a plague on him for frightening him.

Act V: Scene 5

Diomedes comes on the field and sees Troilus' horse. He orders
his servant to present it to Cressida with his compliments. He is
to tell her that he has "Chastis'd the amorous Trojan" [which
is a lie] and is now "her knight by proof." The servant does his
bidding. This act shows the length to which Diomedes will go in
treachery and duplicity, as opposed to the honest Troilus.

Agamemnon enters, encouraging his men to fight. He gives the
names of the Greek warriors who have been downed by Trojans,
among them, Patroclus "ta'en or slain." Margarelon, the bastard
son of Priam, waves his beam "colossus wise" over the dead
bodies of kings.

Agamemnon belives the "dreadful Sagittary" was fighting against
them. He urges Diomedes to go with him for reinforcements
before they are all slain.

Nestor enters, urging that Patroclus' body be brought to Achilles
and the "snail-paced" Ajax be told to arm "for shame." There
are, Nestor declares, a "thousand Hectors in the field." He fights

on his horse, Galathe, and afoot. Hector is everywhere, and the Greeks fall before him "like the mower's swath."

A word of encouragement is brought to the Greek commanders by Ulysses, who says that Achilles is finally arming for the battle. The laggard warrior has been roused at the sight of Patroclus' bloody wounds and his mangled Myrmidons. Ulysses says that Ajax, too, has been stirred to fight and is "roaring" to meet Troilus. The latter has had exceptional success in battle and is risking his life with "careless force."

A momentary appearance of Ajax calling for Troilus surprises Diomedes. He calls after him, as does Nestor. The latter is pleased that all the Greek warriors are now together. As he speaks, Achilles enters armed for battle. He is searching for "this Hector." He belittles the latter's strength, calling him a "boy-queller," or murderer. He leaves, declaring Hector will know what it is to meet Achilles' anger.

Act V: Scene 6

In another section of the field, Ajax goes about searching for Troilus. He is joined by Diomedes. At the latter's call, "Troilus, I say! what Troilus," the Trojan enters. He calls Diomedes a traitor and will make him pay with his life for stealing his horse. Both Ajax and Diomedes dispute which one will fight with him. Troilus declares he will "have at" them both. They start to fight.

Hector enters and calls to his brother that he has fought well. At the same moment Achilles enters and offers to fight Hector. He asks the Greek warrior to "pause." Achilles agrees with a curt comment that his "arms are out of use," and therefore his "rest and negligence befriends him." But they will meet again.

When Achilles leaves, Hector muses that if he had expected Achilles he would have saved his strength to fight him. Troilus returns with word that Ajax has captured the Trojan general, Aeneas. Troilus swears to release him if it costs his life. A Greek in costly armor enters and Hector offers to fight, but the Greek refuses. Hector desires his armor and will have it. The Greek hurries off, followed by Hector and Troilus.

Act V: Scene 7

Achilles addresses his Myrmidons (followers), commanding them to follow him wherever he goes. When he finds Hector they are to surround him and "Empale him with your weapons," for it is "decreed that Hector must die."

Act V: Scene 8

Menelaus and Paris enter fighting. Thersites urges them on, with his coarse mocking. They go offstage fighting as the Trojan Margarelon enters. He calls to Thesites, "Turn, slave and fight." Discovering that Margarelon is Priam's bastard son, Thersites reduces the scene to low comedy.

Act V: Scene 9

This scene follows immediately in another part of the field. Hector has just downed the "Greek in sumptuos armor" and rests his sword when Achilles and his Myrmidons enter. His greeting has an ominous note, remarking on the setting sun and "ugly night" hurrying along. He declares that as the day is over, "Hector's life is done." The Trojan warrior pleads that he is unarmed and asks Achilles to "forego this vantage." But Achilles commands his Myrmidons to strike on. As Hector falls, Achilles sends them to spread the word, "Achilles has the mighty Hector slain."

Achilles gloats over his deed. "Stickler-like" he has separated the Greek and Trojan armies. They have fought long enough. He addresses his "half-supp'd sword, that frankly would have fed" but "Pleas'd with this dainty bit thus goes to bed." The Myrmidons are ordered to tie Hector's body to Achilles' horse's tail, and he will ride through the field and humble the Trojans.

Act V: Scene 10

This scene follows immediately elsewhere on the battlefield. Agamemnon and his generals hear the cry, "Achilles! Achilles! Hector's slain!" Diomedes declares rumor has it that Hector was killed by Achilles. It should not be bragged about, according to Ajax. He insists, "Great Hector was as good a man as he" [Achilles].

Agamemnon orders the marchers to continue. A messenger is sent to bring Achilles to Agamemnon's tent. He hopes the gods have befriended them in Hector's death because it will mean the fall of Troy and the end of the war.

Act V: Scene 11

This scene takes place in the field shortly after Hector's death. Aeneas is exhorting the retreating Trojan army when Troilus enters with the word, "Hector is slain." It rouses the Trojans. They listen to Troilus tell how he is being dragged "at the murderer's horse's tail." They hear him beg the gods to be merciful to Troy. Aeneas complains that his news has demoralized the troops, but Troilus insists he does not talk of flight or fear but of a daring resistance to the Greek forces.

Troilus worries greatly how the news of Hector's death can be told to Priam. He fears his father will be greatly disturbed, or, as he says, "turned to stone." The news will terrify Troy. Resigned to his brother's death, he comments, "Hector is dead; there is no more to say." But on second thought, there is. He calls on Troy to revenge Hector's murder. The great coward, Achilles, he will haunt like a "wicked conscience." He urges the troops to march back to Troy "with comfort"—"Hope of revenge shall hide our inward woe!"

The last to leave is Troilus. As he goes, Pandarus calls to him to wait. With a curt, "Hence, broker-lackey," Troilus heaps a heavy curse on him and his kind, wishing that "ignominy and shame/Pursue thy life and live aye with thy name."

Twelfth Night

ORSINO, *Duke of Illyria.*
SEBASTIAN, *brother to Viola.*
ANTONIO, *a sea captain, friend to Sebastian.*
A SEA CAPTAIN, *friend to Viola.*
VALENTINE ⎱
CURIO ⎰ *gentlemen attending on the Duke.*
SIR TOBY BELCH, *uncle to Olivia.*
SIR ANDREW AGUECHEEK.
MALVOLIO, *Steward to Olivia.*
FABIAN.
FESTE, *a clown.*

OLIVIA, *a rich countess.*
VIOLA, *a sister to Sebastian.*
MARIA, *Olivia's gentlewoman.*

LORDS, PRIESTS, SAILORS, OFFICERS, MUSICIANS, *and other* ATTENDANTS.

Twelfth Night

Act I: Scene 1

The play opens in a room in the palace of Orsino, the Duke of Illyria. Orsino is attended by his gentlemen-in-waiting, Curio and other lords.

Grouped about the stage are musicians, who have been entertaining Orsino and his company with airs played on the lute (a Renaissance stringed instrument, very like a large mandolin), recorder (a primitive flute), and other Elizabethan instruments. Orsino's first speech is one of the most famous in the play. "If music be the food of love, play on," he orders his musicians. "Give me excess of it, that, suffering,/ The appetite may sicken and so die." What he's actually saying in this speech is: "If love is nourished by music, play more than enough music indeed, play too much of it so that my appetite for music (and, perhaps, by extension, for love) will become jaded, and I'll no longer be bothered by the romantic longings that plague me now!"

It seems that Orsino is desperately in love with Olivia, a noble-woman of the country, but has so far been rejected in his suit, mainly because Olivia is determined to mourn the recent death of her only brother for a seven-year period. Orsino, in a vain attempt to forget his frustrated courtship, has been listening to music. Hence his comments on the subject. But he almost immediately tires of the tune the musicians play and remarks on how "quick and fresh" is the spirit of love, always longing for change and distraction, always restless and unsatisfied.

Curio asks Orsino if he wants to go hunting—perhaps to distract him further from his romantic melancholy, since music no longer entertains him—but Orsino turns aside the question with a pun on "hart" (a stag) and "heart" and with the comparison of his desires to "cruel hounds." A moment later, Valentine, another of Orsino's servingmen, enters with news that Olivia has refused to hear Orsino's latest message of love, on account of her resolve to mourn her brother for seven years. She's even resolved,

Valentine reports, not to leave her house during this mourning period!

Orsino, surprisingly, is pleased by this. If Olivia is capable of such devotion to a brother, he reasons, how devoted a wife or mistress will she be when her desires are channeled in more romantic directions. And taking heart from this thought, Orsino closes the scene in a manner typical of Shakespeare's early romantic comedies, with an exuberant couplet: "Away before me to sweet beds of flowers! Love-thoughts lie rich when canopied with bowers!"

Act I: Scene 2

We're now at the seashore, where Viola, a nobly-born young girl (who, with Olivia, is one of the play's two heroines) appears with a sea-captain and some sailors. Bewildered, she asks the captain what country they are in, and he tells her that this is Illyria. It turns out that she and her twin brother, Sebastian, had been traveling in this same captain's ship when it was wrecked in a storm off the Illyrian coast. Viola wonders despairingly whether her brother has been drowned, and the captain remarks that since *she* has been saved by chance (in a lifeboat, with the captain and sailors who accompany her now), her brother may also have been saved by chance. In fact, he reports, as the ship was going down he noticed that her brother, being "most provident in peril," had skillfully bound himself to a floating mast, and in his opinion there's every reason to hope that Sebastian may thus have been saved. Viola promptly rewards him for this piece of encouragement with some gold, and then proceeds to cross-examine him about Illyria—who rules it, whether he's married or single, what sort of lady he's courting, etc.

Viola learns from the captain that Orsino, the Duke of Illyria, is hopelessly in love with Olivia, who will not admit his suit because she's in mourning. At first, Viola expresses a desire to serve Olivia. As a well-born young girl, she would obviously be in the safest and most respectable position in the household of a wealthy Illyrian countess. But when the captain tells her that the grieving Olivia will see *no one*, she swiftly decides that her next best sanctuary, while waiting news of her brother, would be Orsino's own court. Prudently, however, she resolves that the captain should present her to Orsino, not as a helpless and unprotected maiden, but as a "eunuch," a boy-singer, who can entertain him "with many sorts of music."

Having already learned of Orsino's fondness for music in scene 1, we can imagine how much of a hit the graceful and talented Viola will be with him, even in the guise of a boy. As the scene closes, she and the captain are setting out, with high hopes, for his court.

Act I: Scene 3

A room in Olivia's house. As the scene opens, Olivia's uncle, Sir Toby Belch, and her serving-maid, Maria (really a kind of lady-in-waiting), enter in the midst of a heated discussion. Sir Toby Belch—as his name suggests, a fat, jovial, middle-aged lover of food, drink, and all the other good things in life—complains about Olivia's excessive grief for her brother. Her insistence on prolonged mourning has cast a pall over the whole household, and Toby is annoyed that anything should interfere with his usual pleasures.

Maria reproves Sir Toby for his wild behavior. Olivia wishes he would come in earlier at night, she tells him, and she herself, Maria, certainly agrees that he should "confine" himself "within the modest limits of order." Moreover, neither she nor her lady, she adds, think very much of his friend, Sir Andrew Aguecheek, a "foolish knight" whom Sir Toby has introduced into the household as a suitor for his niece. "He's drunk nightly, in your company," Maria complains, besides being stupid, quarrelsome, and cowardly, a most unpromising combination!

Sir Toby defends his friend, insisting that he has 3000 ducats a year (a handsome income), plays the viol-da-gamba (ancestor of the modern cello), and speaks three or four languages "word for word without book!" Of course, these last two claims are really outrageous, as Maria knows, and as the audience learns when, a minute later, Sir Andrew himself appears. His behavior during the rest of the scene is so simple-minded that no one could possibly believe in Sir Toby's statements about him

There is much comical word-play, at this point, between Maria, Sir Toby, and Sir Andrew—although the latter's participation is mainly unconscious. For instance, Sir Toby suggests that he should "accost" Maria, meaning that he should flirt with her, but Sir Andrew misunderstands him and, thinking he's introducing Maria by name, addresses her as "Good Mistress Accost!"

Maria finally gets bored with Sir Andrew's idiocy and flounces out, leaving the two knights alone onstage. Sir Toby accuses Sir Andrew of not being cheerful enough, and Sir Andrew, after some further misunderstanding and silly chatter, confesses that he's about ready to leave for home, since Olivia won't receive him as her suitor. With the Duke himself wooing her, Sir Andrew wonders self-pityingly, what chance can *he* have? But Sir Toby—who's anxious to have Sir Andrew and his money around a little longer—quickly flatters him into changing his mind.

In any case, Sir Andrew remarks, he loves "masques and revels" and parties of all kinds, and so he'll stay a month longer. At this, Sir Toby asks him jokingly if he likes to dance, and when Sir Andrew replies proudly that he's an expert dancer, Toby sets the foolish knight hopping and skipping around the stage to show off his prowess, meanwhile cracking a series of punning jokes, all of which are lost on the dancing Andrew. As they exit, Sir Toby is crying, "Let me see thee caper: ha! higher: ha, ha! excellent!" and his friend is executing a series of mad leaps and pirouettes.

Act I: Scene 4

Scene 4 takes place at Orsino's court, where Viola is already well-established in the guise of Cesario, the Duke's favorite pageboy. Wearing man's attire, she enters deep in conversation with Valentine, one of the attendant lords we met in Scene 1. If the Duke continues to treat you so well, Valentine tells Viola wonderingly, "you are likely to be much advanced." It appears that Viola-Cesario, in only three days, has made quite a conquest.

But why do you say "if," Viola asks Valentine? Is the Duke "inconstant in his favors?" When Valentine reassures her that he isn't, she thanks him, and they turn to greet Orsino himself, who has just entered with Curio and some of his other servants.

As if to confirm Valentine's words, Orsino immediately calls for Cesario-Viola, and orders the other servingmen away. Alone with Viola, he reminds her that she now knows everything there is to know about him. To her, in the guise of Cesario, he has "unclasped . . . the book even of [his] secret soul." For this reason, she's most suitable, he thinks, to act as an envoy from him to Olivia, bearing his messages of love and courtship. When Viola protests that if Olivia is so "abandoned to her sorrow" (for her brother) as she's said to be, "she never will admit me," Orsino urges her to be "clamorous" and rude, if necessary, rather than return unheard. He's sure, he continues, that if Viola *is* admitted, his suit will be more acceptable to Olivia if presented by an attractive youth like herself than from an older messenger "of more grave aspect."

Indeed, Orsino tells Viola, unconscious, of course, of the truth of his words, she (Cesario) hardly seems like a man at all. The goddess Diana doesn't have any softer or rosier lips than this "serving boy," he thinks, and even Cesario's voice is like a girl's. But the only lesson he draws from all this is—not that Cesario *is* a girl (he could hardly believe that)—but that since she (he) *seems* so feminine, her youth and gentleness are likely to be quite successful with the melancholy Olivia, whose delicate emotional state might be upset by a coarser, more masculine messenger.

Orsino finishes his speech to Viola by sending "some four or five" attendants with her—a good company—and commenting self-pityingly that "I myself am best/When least in company." "I'll do my best/To woo your lady," Viola promises—and then surprises us by remarking, in an aside to the audience, that here is a "barful strife" (a difficult situation), since, no matter what wooing she does for Orsino, she herself would like to be his wife.

Act I: Scene 5

Scene 5 returns us to Olivia's house, where we're finally going to meet that much talked-of lady. But before her entrance, Maria, her serving-woman, appears in the act of administering a sound scolding to Feste, the household fool, a character now being introduced for the first time.

It seems that Feste, the fool, has been missing from the household more or less "without leave" for some time—and "my lady will hang thee for thy absence," Maria mockingly threatens him. "Let her hang me," replies Feste with good-humored defiance, "he that is well hanged in this world needs to fear no colors." This last sentence embodies a pun on "colors," "collars" and "cholers"—all three of which were pronounced alike in Shakespeare's day, and thus means more or less "Let her do her worst; once she does, I'll have nothing more to fear!"

Maria continues to scold the fool for his unwarranted absence—and Feste continues to turn away her wrath with light answers. After a few more attempts at seriousness, she can't help falling in with his mood, since she herself is an eminently fun-loving creature—and finally he compliments her by saying that "If Sir Toby would leave drinking" she'd be "as witty a piece of Eve's flesh as any in Illyria"—that is, as clever and high-spirited a mistress as Sir Toby, were he so inclined, could hope to find. But this strikes too close to home, and Maria, embarrassed, hushes Feste with an impatient "Peace, you rogue"—and before he has a chance to tease her any more, Olivia herself approaches, with her steward, Malvolio.

As Olivia enters, Feste nervously addresses her—but, deep in her grief, she abstractedly orders her servants to have "the fool" removed. "Do you not hear, fellows? Take away the lady!" Feste remarks—and, before Olivia can repeat her order, he manages to prove that she, and not *he*, is the fool, with his ready wit easily transforming an uncomfortable situation into an apt setting for his light-hearted talents. She's a fool, he points out, in a perfect parody of learned argument, to mourn for her brother's soul being in heaven—the implication being, of course, that she should rather rejoice at her brother's good fortune in being among the blessed.

Olivia is pleased by his "proof"—and turning to her sour-faced steward,

Malvolio, asks what he thinks of the fool. "Doth he not mend?" (that is, mend or heal her sorrow). Malvolio answers with a scornful remark about Feste's abilities, and about fools in general, and there's a rather bitter exchange of words between the two retainers, ending with Malvolio contemptuously calling Feste a "barren" (untalented) "rascal" who could easily be "put down" by "an ordinary fool that has no more brain than a stone."

Olivia, who, as a born aristocrat, is easier with fools and servants than Malvolio can ever be (since she doesn't have such a need to constantly prove how superior she is to them) responds most perceptively to his attack on Feste. "You are sick of self-love, Malvolio," she remarks— sensing instinctively the monstrously inflated egotism that leads him to behave as he does—and goes on to point out that the "generous, guiltless" and innocent mind isn't so sensitive to imaginary insults, or to the kind of barbed witticisms that a fool like Feste specializes in. People like herself, she implies, who are easy with themselves and with their society, understand that there's never any real harm in such fellows.

Feste, relieved, thanks her for her kindness, and a moment later Maria (who had rushed offstage after her last embarrassing exchange with him) re-enters to announce that a young gentleman (Viola-Cesario) has appeared at the outer gate, demanding to see Olivia. Olivia asks if he comes from Orsino, and Maria replies that she doesn't know, but that "Tis a fair young man, and well attended"—so evidently Viola's good looks make an impression everywhere she goes. When Olivia hears that only her "mad" cousin Toby has remained behind to keep this mysterious messenger out, she dispatches Maria to "fetch him off"—and Malvolio, who, for all his arrogance, can be trusted (she thinks) to handle a delicate matter, is sent to dismiss the young "man."

A moment later, Sir Toby, having been called away from the gate by Maria, enters, belching and half-drunk. Olivia, distressed (though good-humoredly so) gently scolds him, and then engages in a bit of dialogue with Feste about the similarity of a drunken man to "a drowned man, a fool and a madman." Finally, she orders Feste to look after her cousin, and he obediently leads Sir Toby off, commenting humorously that "the fool [himself] shall look to the madman [Toby]."

The moment these two are gone, Malvolio reappears with word that Orsino's young envoy will not allow himself to be dismissed. Curious, Olivia asks, "What kind o' man is he?" and Malvolio replies—with hilariously scornful vagueness—"Why, of mankind." But on being pressed by Olivia, he admits in more specific terms that the Duke's messenger is indeed quite young and very good-looking. Really intrigued by now, Olivia decides to "let him approach," and calls for Maria to come in and give her her veil. Thus attired—disguised almost—she prepares to "once more hear Orsino's embassy."

Now Viola enters, in the costume of Cesario of course, and confused by the group of veiled ladies who greet her (Maria and Olivia's other attendants have also veiled themselves) she asks for the lady of the house. Olivia responds—but Viola, still uncertain, asks in the most charming way for further assurance that she's indeed addressing the right person. She's worked hard studying her speech, she tells the ladies frankly, and besides she's very sensitive to "ill usage." When Olivia once again reassures her of her identity, Viola continues her wooing, but with many comically candid asides—such as "I will on with my speech in your praise, and then show you the heart of my message." When both Olivia and Maria grow slightly impatient with the youthful ambassador's long-windedness and urge her to get to the point or "be gone," Viola begs Olivia to dismiss Maria and her other attendants and allow her (Viola-Cesario) to address her (Olivia) in private. Amused—and perhaps more than amused, rather charmed—by this unconventional "fellow," Olivia complies, and the two are left alone onstage.

Now then, Olivia asks, "What is your text?" Viola immediately launches into her prepared speech—"Most sweet lady"—but is interrupted by Olivia. After a moment of witty banter between the two, Viola, overcome by curiosity about Olivia (who is, after all, though she doesn't realize it, her rival for Orsino's love) asks to be allowed to see her face, which has remained veiled throughout the interview. Obligingly (still intrigued by the young messenger), Olivia removes the veil and asks if Viola-Cesario doesn't think her face is "well done." "Excellently done," replies Viola dryly, "If God did all"—that is, if it's natural and not a product of artificial making-up, etc.

When Olivia assures Viola-that her beauty is indeed natural, Viola—perhaps a little bit envious, and more than a little depressed at having to contend with such a rival when the man she loves isn't even aware of her existence as a woman yet—waxes rhapsodic about Olivia's looks. Olivia, she says, is "too proud" but "if you were the Devil, you are fair"—and she goes on to press Orsino's suit, remarking that she can well imagine why her lord and master is in love with such an incomparable beauty.

Olivia, who, by now, is much less interested in the master than in the "man," replies coldly that Orsino knows her mind very well. Though she's aware of all his virtues and advantages, she cannot love him, and "he might have took his answer long ago." But Viola responds that she still understands how her master feels—since if she were in his position *she* wouldn't take no for an answer either. What would *you* do? Olivia asks—and she replies, in a famous speech, that she would make herself "a willow cabin" at Olivia's gate (that is, camp at Olivia's door), and call upon her soul within the house (swear solemn oaths of fidelity); write songs of love, and sing them even in the dead of night; shout Olivia's name to the hills, until all the air re-echoed it, etc.

When Viola has finished speaking, Olivia comments meaningfully that "you might do much"—and then, unable to repress her interest in this mysteriously attractive messenger, asks her briefly about her family background (a sure sign that she's regarding the young envoy as "himself" a potential suitor). Viola replies that her background is even better than her present position as a servant implies (which indeed it is), but that at least she's "a gentleman." Relieved, Olivia dismisses her—remarking that she might as well tell Orsino that there's no hope for his suit—but quickly adding, rather slyly, that of course Cesario (the messenger) might return to tell her how Orsino takes her reply. She then adds insult to injury by offering Viola a purse full of gold, which Viola scornfully rejects, promptly departing with an angry "Farewell, fair cruelty."

Oliva is left alone onstage to meditate aloud, in a short soliloquy, on "this youth's [Cesario's] perfections." With some trepidation, but a basic fatalistic acceptance, she realizes she's fallen in love with the Duke's messenger—and swiftly deciding to take some action, she calls in the trusted Malvolio, and orders him to follow Viola-Cesario with a ring which, she says, "he" left behind as a token from the Duke (though of course Viola did no such thing) and to tell "him" that if "he'll" return the next day, she'll explain in greater detail why she won't accept it. The whole move is plainly a ruse to get Cesario to come again—and it's just as plainly intended as a flirtatious overture from her to "him," since "he" knows as well as she does that "he" left no ring. When Malvolio is gone, Olivia, alone again onstage, closes the scene by commenting that though she fears she's acting hastily, what is destined to be, must be.

Act II: Scene 1

We find ourselves once more at the Illyrian coast, where a sea captain by the name of Antonio enters in conversation with a very familiar-looking young man—familiar because he's none other than Sebastian, the twin brother after whom Viola has patterned her dress, walk and manner, and about whose fate she's still so painfully uncertain. Antonio begs the young man to stay with him longer (Sebastian has evidently found shelter with this kindly captain after being shipwrecked) and then asks where he plans to go, and whether he (Antonio) may not accompany him. Sebastian replies gloomily that the "stars shine darkly over me" and that he thinks Antonio would therefore be better off without him. As for his destination

—he plans merely to wander or, as he puts it, "My determinate voyage is mere extravagancy."

Sebastian goes on to reveal his name and noble parentage to Antonio, and to relate how he thinks his twin sister was drowned "some hours" before he himself was rescued (by this same Antonio) from a similar fate. His sister, he continued, was not only beautiful but also intelligent and good, and though she is (he believes) drowned already "with salt water," he is continually drowning her remembrance still more with his salty tears. Antonio is appropriately sympathetic and offers again to accompany the young man, this time as his servant, but Sebastian adamantly refuses, explaining that he is still too grief-stricken and too near tears to be in company. Finally, remarking briefly that he's "bound to the Count Orsino's court," he takes a fond farewell of Antonio and exits.

Antonio, left alone onstage, speculates aloud that he has many enemies in Orsino's court—as we shall see in the next act—or he would certainly follow Sebastian there at once. But he quickly changes his mind, commenting that this young man is so dear to him "that danger shall seem sport" and he will brave whatever obstacles he may encounter in order to accompany his friend to Illyria (even without that friend's knowledge or permission).

Act II: Scene 2

As this scene opens, Malvolio appears in an Illyrian street near Olivia's house, in hot pursuit of Viola who, as Cesario, has just taken her leave of Olivia in Act 1, Scene 5. Malvolio is bent, as a matter of fact, on carrying out the errand which Olivia assigned to him at the end of that scene. He comes quickly up behind Viola and asks her if she isn't the same messenger who was just now with the Countess Olivia. When she replies that she is, he contemptuously delivers the ring, which Olivia had told him to give Cesario, scornfully remarking that "you might have saved me my pains, to have taken it away yourself," a nasty comment which the love-struck Olivia hardly instructed him to make. He then adds, as Olivia had told him to, that Cesario should assure Orsino that there's no hope for his suit, but that the messenger might return to report "his" lord's reaction. When Viola replies in confusion that she never gave Olivia any ring, Malvolio angrily responds that of course she "peevishly" threw it to her—and then he himself peevishly tosses the disputed token at Viola's feet, remarking that if it's "worth stooping for, there it lies"—and before the bewildered girl can answer him, he makes his usual "grand" exit.

Viola, left alone onstage, exclaims wonderingly that "I left no ring with her. What means this lady?" and then, as the light slowly dawns on her, and she realizes Olivia's romantic intentions, she is by turns amazed, amused, and upset. Obviously, she realizes—despite her own, perfectly cool intentions—her good looks have charmed Olivia, and she recalls that the countess' behavior during their recent interview was indeed rather strange and distracted. Furthermore, since Orsino himself never sent the lady any ring, it's clear, finally, to Viola that the ring is meant as a love gift to *her* in her guise of Cesario. But what a situation to be in! "Poor lady, she were better love a dream," she muses about Olivia's predicament. As for her own, she comments that she can see that disguise itself is "a wickedness," since it can lead to such ruinous deceptions. But further, she recognizes from this incident that woman's frailty is most of all to blame for problems like this—since the fair sex is so readily susceptible to the first charming countenance that comes along.

Confused, and more than a little upset by the emotional tensions of this increasingly complicated situation, Viola wonders how it will all work out. With Orsino in love with Olivia, Olivia in love with Cesario, and Viola herself in love with Orsino, things seem to be in a hopeless tangle. Besides, insofar as she is a "man," Viola has to remain loyal to her "master's love" for Olivia—and inasmuch as she's actually a woman, Olivia's love for her must be doomed to disappointment. Finally, the practical Viola simply shrugs and throwing up her hands in mock despair exclaims "O Time, thou must untangle this, not I! It is too hard a knot for me to untie!" Thus rounding out the scene in typical Shakespearean manner with a neat couplet, she skips offstage.

Act II: Scene 3

This scene returns us again to Olivia's house, this time late at night—well after midnight, in fact. Enter Sir Toby and Sir Andrew, both thoroughly inebriated. Jovially, though a bit sleepily and dizzily too, the two knights stagger about the stage, drunkenly discussing the question of whether being up thus—after midnight—is really being up *late* or being up *early* (since it's technically already morning). Just as Toby is loudly calling for Maria to bring him some more wine, the fool Feste enters—quite sober compared to the other two, but as witty and high-spirited as ever. He greets the two gaily, and Sir Toby proposes that the three of them sing a "catch" (a kind of round). But before Feste can reply, Sir Andrew, in a wandering, befuddled way (when drunk he's even more foolish and incoherent than when he is sober) begins to elaborately compliment the clown on his recent good "fooling." Amused, Feste thanks him—in typical Shakespearean fool's doubletalk. Sir Andrew, still more pleased and vague, calls for a song, and Sir Toby seconds his motion, offering Feste sixpence to perform, which Sir Andrew promptly doubles with a "testril" (sixpence) of his own.

Having agreed to perform for them, Feste asks Sir Toby and Andrew whether they'd prefer a love song or a song of "good life" (that is, a drinking song). Both drinkers hasten to assure him, quite drunkenly, that there's nothing they'd rather hear than a love song. ("I care not for good life," remarks the carousing Andrew foolishly). The clown rewards their enthusiasm with a melodious rendition of the popular Elizabethan song "O mistress mine, where are you roaming?"

When Feste has finished singing, Toby and Andrew join once more to drunkenly compliment him on his sweet voice—and then, a moment later, Toby returns to his original idea that the three revellers should "rouse the night owl in a catch." After some discussion, they decide on a catch known as "Hold thy peace, thou knave," though Feste slyly points out to Andrew that he'll have to call him "knave" (fool) in the course of it. Andrew—who is indeed a knave, or fool—smugly consents, since, as he says, it won't be the first time he's been called a knave. With this, the three set to with a will, singing the noisy and spirited round "Thou knave" at the top of their lungs.

But after just a few renditions of their song, they're angrily interrupted by Maria, who appears in a doorway, arms akimbo, to scold them in outraged tones for their "caterwauling" which, she threatens, is likely to enrage Olivia to the point where she bids her steward, Malvolio, to "turn" all three culprits "out of doors." Unruffled, the offending threesome begin to chaff and "fool" with Maria herself—Sir Toby especially in a rather flirtatious way. But in another moment, just as Maria had predicted, Malvolio himself arrives, wearing his nightshirt and carrying a candle, in a righteous rage at being wakened in the middle of the night.

Indignantly, Malvolio demands to know what these noisy servants and hangers-on think they're doing here "at this time of night." "Are you mad" or what? "Do ye make an alehouse of my lady's house?" he asks, in tones of the deepest outrage. "Is there no respect of place, persons, nor time in you?"

His prissily pompous manner naturally infuriates Toby—himself quite drunk and utterly reckless of consequences—who tells him rudely to be hanged, and that as for time, they kept time in their songs. This reply, in turn, enrages Malvolio even more, and he assures Toby that Olivia herself had told him to inform Toby that, unless he could behave himself, she'd "be very willing to bid him farewell"—a threat with some force in it, since Maria had suggested the same thing in her speech earlier.

Toby's only response to Malvolio's angry warning is to burst still more rudely and clamorously into song. "Farewell, dear heart, since I must needs be gone," he bellows drunkenly, making fun of Malvolio's dire threats, and though Maria tries to restrain him, the clown joins in and together the two dance and sing around Malvolio in a hilariously insulting duet. Finally, Toby stops singing long enough to ask Malvolio the famous question "Dost thou think because thou art virtuous, there shall be no more cakes and ale?"

Feste—who's only been waiting for a chance to express his pent-up resentment to Malvolio ever since the latter insulted him in front of Olivia in Act I, Scene 5—chimes in too. "Yes, by Saint Anne, and ginger shall be hot i' the mouth too," he shouts, meaning that all the spicy luxuries of life are as eternal as merrymaking itself is. Malvolio—furious and frustrated—turns to Maria, as the only one with whom he has any chance of communicating in this company. Angrily threatening to get her in trouble with her mistress and to report the disorderly conduct of the whole group to Olivia as soon as possible, he stomps off.

Maria—from whom he'd evidently expected a little more respect than the others—rudely shouts after him "Go shake your ears," and when Toby exclaims that maybe he ought to challenge Malvolio to a duel (and then disappoint him by not showing up for it) she unfolds another, cleverer scheme for revenge. If only Toby will be patient for tonight, she says conciliatingly, she'll take care of Malvolio herself as soon as possible. Right now, her mistress is "much out of quiet"—rather upset—because of her recent interview with Orsino's messenger.

Excitedly, Toby begs to know Maria's opinion of Malvolio, delighted to have found so sly and quickwitted an ally. Well, he's something of a Puritan, Maria begins, rather understating the case. "Oh, if I thought that," exclaims Andrew feebly, "I'd beat him like a dog!" But not only is he Puritanical, Maria continues, he's also affected, ambitious, hypocritical, cold-hearted, and incredibly egotistical. Her revenge, in fact, is to be based especially on this last trait—his egotism—and a devilishly clever scheme it is, too, as Maria outlines it. What she plans to do is to leave an anonymous love letter in a place where Malvolio can easily chance on it, and in which he'll find what seem to be *himself* described with passion and accuracy. Furthermore, since her handwriting, she explains, is very similar to her mistress', she'll write the letter in such a way that the egotistical steward will believe it to be addressed by Olivia to him. The complications that should ensue from this mistake on his part will, she guarantees, provide "sport royal" for all concerned. Toby and Andrew are delighted, and with a hasty promise to plant them and the fool in a spot where they can observe Malvolio's hilarious "construction" of her letter, Maria rushes off to bed, to "dream on the event."

Left alone onstage, Toby and Andrew remark on Maria's wit and faithfulness to Toby's cause. "She's a beagle, true bred, and one that adores me," comments Toby, not very flatteringly.

Toby seizes this moment of quiet and relative peace to suggest that Andrew must send for more money. When the foolish knight again expresses doubts that Olivia will have him, Toby reassures him and repeats his demand for money.

At last the two go off sleepily to drink some more since, as Toby puts it, "tis too late to go to bed now."

Act II: Scene 4

We find ourselves again at the palace of Orsino, a place we haven't visited now for quite some time. Melancholy as ever, the lovestruck Duke enters, attended by Viola-Cesario, Curio, and others. As usual, he calls for music, explaining that a certain "old and antique song" he heard last night had "relieved" his "passion much." Songs of the present, he continues, are too brisk and giddy. Curio tells him that Feste, who'd sung the song, is not there right now, and a messenger is dispatched to look for him while Orsino's corps of musicians plays the tune alone.

While they wait for Curio to fetch Feste, Orsino calls Viola-Cesario over to him, remarking, ironically enough, that if she should ever fall in love, he hopes she'll remember his example—for all lovers are just like him, tiring easily and easily bored with everything except the subject of love and the beloved.

The Duke goes on to ask Viola how she likes the melody the musicians are playing, and when she replies gravely that it seems to somehow embody the very spirit of love, he's impressed with the genuineness of her tone, and inquires whether she's ever been in love herself, since she seems to know something about it. Viola replies guardedly that she has. With what kind of woman? Orsino asks. A woman rather like himself, Viola answers, with his coloring and about his age. Distressed (since he himself is a good deal older than Viola), Orsino exclaims that in an ideal relationship, the man should definitely be older than the woman, not vice versa.

At any rate, ignorant as he is of the truth of Viola's situation, Orsino goes on to explain that the man should be older than the woman because men are naturally less constant than women, and a man is more likely to grow tired of his wife if she is older than he is. Furthermore, he points out, a woman's beauty, as well as her chastity—the two main traits which make her attractive ·to a man—is a transient and fleeting thing, like a rose "whose fair flower/Being once displayed, doth fall that very hour."

Viola (who knows all too well the truth of Orsino's statements) mournfully agrees, and a moment later Feste is brought in by Curio to sing a sad song of unrequited love called "Come away, come away death," which lyrically reinforces the melancholy tone of this scene.

The song deals with a lover who is "slain" by the failure of a "fair cruel maid" to respond to his amorous advances. Self-pityingly, relishing the tragedy of his love-death (much as Orsino relishes his own love-sickness), the lover asks that no flowers be strewn on his coffin, and that he be buried in an unmarked grave, since otherwise all the other "sad true lovers" in the world would breathe "a thousand sighs" over the spot.

After Feste has finished his song, been paid for his trouble and dismissed, Orsino, inspired by the music to new heights of passion, orders Viola to once more return to Olivia and once more plead his suit. Viola should tell her, he says, that he doesn't care about her lands or fortune, but only about herself—her beauty and her soul. When Viola points out to him that Olivia has already rejected him in no uncertain terms, Orsino responds that he "cannot be so answered." But you must, replies Viola, and she goes on to ask him what he thinks would happen if "some lady, as perhaps there is" (and we know there is—namely, herself) should love him as much as he loves Olivia. Since his heart is already engaged, he wouldn't be able to love her and would tell her so. Wouldn't she then, Viola inquires, have to take no for an answer, just as he must from Olivia?

Scornfully—and rather egotistically—Orsino replies that no mere woman could love as profoundly, passionately, and permanently as he does. A woman's heart isn't big enough for such a grand passion, he asserts extravagantly, and besides, "they lack retention:" that is, they're fickle. But he's contradicting himself, because just a few minutes before he'd told Viola that men are less constant than women.

She responds to Orsino's charges about women by declaring, in a famous passage, that "they are as true of heart as we." "My father had a daughter loved a man," she tells us, "as it might be, perhaps, were I a woman/I should your lordship."

Curious, Orsino asks about the fate of this unfortunate "sister" of "Cesario's." Viola replies that it's "a blank"—since the young lady never told her love, but pined away, concealing her true feelings, and "with a green and yellow melancholy" (a melancholy compounded of jealousy—obviously for Olivia—and hope), "she sat like Patience on a monument" (like a statue of Patience), "smiling at grief."

Still intrigued—and still trying to prove the male's greater vulnerability to unrequited love—Orsino asks Viola if her "sister" died of her love. "I am all the daughters of my father's house,/And all the brothers too, and yet I know not," the little page replies mysteriously—and then abruptly takes her leave of the Duke, departing once again for Olivia's house with a jewel from him and the message that his love will not be denied.

Act II: Scene 5

This scene transports us to Olivia's garden, where Sir Toby, Sir Andrew, and another servant by the name of Fabian are preparing to conceal themselves in order to observe Malvolio's reaction to the trick Maria is going to play on him. As they gleefully anticipate the wonderful sport at hand, Maria rushes in and tells them quickly to conceal themselves behind the "box tree" (a large kind of ornamental hedge much used by Elizabethan gardeners). Then, laughing and excitedly predicting the success of her scheme for mockery, she tosses a letter down on the garden path where Malvolio, who's been strolling and preening himself nearby, is sure to find it.

A moment later, the unlucky steward himself enters, deep in thought, which he expresses aloud in a hilarious soliloquy punctuated by bursts of outraged commentary from Toby, Andrew, and Fabian.

As he strolls by the boxtree, along the garden path, Malvolio is heard speculating that "tis but fortune, all is fortune." And about what subject does he have this great thought? Why—miraculously (Maria obviously understands the arrogant steward to a fare-thee-well)—none other than his mistress Olivia's fancied preference for him. For as the shrewd servingwoman had intuitively known, Malvolio has already, without the aid as yet of the letter, been led by his egotism to imagine that, were he not a member of a lower class, he—and not Orsino, Andrew, or "Cesario" —would be just the man for Olivia.

Speculating thus about his innate suitability as a husband for Olivia, Malvolio walks slowly along. He even indulges in a wild daydream (related out loud, of course) about how, after being married for three months to Olivia and sitting in state, he'd call for "his" cousin Toby in order to chastise him for his wild behavior, as well as for the foolish company he keeps, meaning Andrew. The reactions these remarks draw from Toby and Andrew are furious indeed, and it takes all of Fabian's energy to restrain the two—especially Toby—from leaping out of their hiding place and setting on Malvolio at once.

In another moment, however, Malvolio's fantasy is interrupted. Catching sight of the letter on the path, he picks it up, curious, and begins to read it. He at once identifies the writing as "my lady's hand"—and goes on quickly, with mounting excitement, to examine the text of the letter. Maria has done her work well, as the well-concealed plotters remark, and the whole letter is designed to intrigue a mind like Malvolio's. It begins with a rhymed riddle: "Jove knows I love./But who?/lips do not move./No man must know . . . I may command where I adore,/But silence, like a Lucrece knife,/With bloodless stroke my heart doth gore./M, O, A, I, doth sway my life."

The arrogant steward quickly interprets this obscure utterance as referring on almost every point to himself. After all, Olivia may command him, she is his lady, and all four letters mentioned are in his name. There are, of course, some obstacles: for instance, the letters are out of their proper order. But "to crush this a little," he comments, "it would bow to me" (with a little forcing, in other words, it seems to work better with him than with anyone else).

Jubilantly, he goes on to read the text of the letter, which certainly seems to be addressed to him. Written in a hilarious parody of his own efficiently pompous style (e.g. "Let thy tongue tang arguments of state, put thyself into the trick of singularity..."), this prose passage advises the reader that he should not be "afraid of greatness. Some are born great, some achieve greatness, and some [obviously Malvolio] have greatness thrust upon 'em [by the favor of a great—highly placed—person like Olivia]." The letter writer then goes on to tell him in what specific ways he can show himself to be suited to this greatness which is about to descend on him. He should "be opposite with a kindsman" (Toby), "surly with servants," wear yellow-stockings, go cross-gartered, and continually smile in the presence of his lady.

Malvolio is being advised, in other words, to make a fool of himself. Yellow stockings and cross-gartering are modes of dress more suitable to servants and jesters than to Puritanical stewards; furthermore, as Maria later informs us, Olivia detests the color yellow. As for being surly with servants and smiling to Olivia—the surliness will only antagonize the servants, and the smiles will be most unwelcome in Olivia's predominantly melancholy mood.

At any rate, gullibly believing every word of the false letter, Malvolio is soon beside himself with joy. Resolving to be "strange stout haughty, in yellow stockings and cross-gartered, he exits crying "Jove, I thank thee. I will smile, I will do everything that thou wilt have me." From his point of view, he is already successful.

The plotters, left alone onstage, emerge from behind the boxtree convulsed with merriment. Significantly enough, in view of later developments, Toby exclaims that "I could marry this wench for this device," and when Maria herself appears, flushed with pride in her own cleverness, all three vie with each other to congratulate her. She asks if the trick has really worked, and when they assure her that it most certainly has, she tells them to be sure to see how Malvolio behaves in his next interview with Olivia. In his yellow stockings and cross-gartered, a color and a style the lady can't stand, he's sure to be the very opposite of a hit. As for his smiling, with the melancholy Olivia, it's sure to "turn him into a notable contempt." And "if you will see it, follow me," cries the high-spirited Maria—at which all three rush off in a burst of excitement to gather the fruits of their sport.

Act III: Scene 1

As this scene begins, we are still in Olivia's garden. Viola—apparently in the midst of executing the commission to once more woo Olivia on which Orsino sent her at the end of Act II, Scene 4—enters from one direction and encounters Feste who, carrying a tabor (a small drum), is approaching the house from another direction. She greets him pleasantly and they indulge in a bit of casual banter in order to pass the time more merrily. For instance, when Viola asks Feste if he lives by his tabor—that is, lives on the proceeds of his performances on the tabor—he replies teasingly that he lives by the church, "for I do live at my house, and my house doth stand by [near] the church."

Later, when she asks him if he's the Lady Olivia's fool, which he is, he denies it, remarking that "the Lady Olivia has no folly. She will keep no fool, sir, til she be married,"—and he goes on to show how husbands are like fools. Viola, referring to Act 2, Scene 4, in which Feste had sung "Come away, death" at the Duke's palace, comments that she had seen him at Orsino's—and Feste answers punningly that "Foolery, sir, does walk about the orb like the sun. It shines everywhere."

Viola, pleased with the fool's ready wit, tosses him a coin, and when Feste slyly asks for another ("Would not a pair of these have bred, sir?"), she comments appreciatively on his clever style of begging, and rewards him with another. A moment later he exits and she's left alone briefly to speculate on the nature of such "wise" foolery as Feste's. It is, she decides, "a practice/As full of labor as a wise man's art," for though the fool's remarks seem light-hearted and spontaneous enough, they're almost always ingeniously constructed to express several ideas at once, and they're always carefully chosen to accord as well as possible with the mood and personality of the audience toward which they're directed.

As she finishes her soliloquy, Sir Toby and Sir Andrew enter, and the three exchange courtly greetings. Andrew, especially, trying to show off his reputed facility with languages, addresses Viola in French. But before their witty banter can develop into more than a brief exchange, Olivia enters, accompanied by Maria. Viola salutes her with extravagant courtesy, exclaiming "Most excellent, accomplished lady, the heavens rain odors on you!" Andrew, impressed, remarks to Toby that "that youth's a rare courtier," and when Viola continues elaborately "My matter hath no voice, lady, but to your own most pregnant (receptive) and vouchsafed (condescending) ear," the foolish knight is overwhelmed by the dazzling elegance of her language. Olivia, of course, is also impressed by "Cesario" (she's been pining away with love of "him" for the last few days), and so she quickly dimisses Toby, Andrew, and Maria in order to hear the "youth's" message.

As soon as the two are left alone, Olivia begins eagerly to "make up" to Viola. First, she asks her name—a simple fact which she hasn't been able yet to ascertain. When Viola replies, "Cesario is your servant's name, fair princess," the unhappy lady complains that "Cesario" is unfortunately not *her* servant, but Orsino's. Viola answers courteously that, since Orsino is Olivia's servant, *his* servant must need be *her* servant too. Olivia responds impatiently that she really doesn't want to think about Orsino and, when Viola reminds her that she has only come on his behalf, she impetuously —unable to contain her passionate feelings for "Cesario" any longer— begs the "youth" to "undertake another suit"—his own.

Viola tries to interrupt, but before she can stop her, the lovestruck Countess rushes headlong into a full declaration of her love. She confesses her motives in sending the ring to Cesario, and admits that the "youth" might well have been justified in harshly interpreting the "shameful cunning" of her act. But, she explains, she couldn't help herself. Now her feelings must be obvious to Cesario—and she wonders what "his" reaction to them is. Viola answers frankly, and briefly, that she pities her—and Olivia hopefully remarks that at least pity is a step toward love. But Viola rudely shatters this illusion, commenting that "very oft we pity enemies."

Shattered by Viola's forceful rejection of her romantic advances, Olivia tries to pull herself together, blaming the "youth's" attitude on "his" pride. When she hears a clock striking in the distance, she exclaims distractedly that she realizes she's wasting time, and "be not afraid, good youth, I will not have you." "But still, she adds, when "Cesario" is old enough to wed, his wife is "like to reap a proper man." With this, she dismisses "him" and Viola, relieved, prepares to depart, first asking politely if Olivia has any messages for Orsino.

Olivia, however, though she has made a valiant effort to tear herself away from Cesario, has still not gotten her feelings entirely under control, and she begs Viola to tell her, before leaving, "what thou think'st of me." Viola replies ambiguously "that you do think you are not what you are"—that is, that in loving Cesario and rejecting Orsino, you estimate yourself wrongly.

Olivia responds excitely that the same might apply to Viola—that is, that in rejecting Olivia's advances out of false pride, Viola is undervaluing herself too. To this, Viola replies, "then think you right. I am not what I am"—a remark which is not only mysterious, but also true, since the young messenger is not a man, as she appears, but a woman. "I would you were as I would have you be"—that is, I wish you'd let yourself love me, and stop being so proud—answers Olivia. This annoys Viola, who asks if it would be better than she now is—"I wish it might, for now I am your fool."

Surprisingly, this angry remark only melts the passionate Olivia into a deeper romantic ecstasy. "Oh what a deal of scorn looks beautiful/In the contempt and anger of his lip!" she swoons, and launches into a wild declaration of love, more forthright and emphatic than any yet. By "the roses of the spring/By maidhood, honor, truth and everything," she swears extravagantly, her love for Cesario is so intense that despite all this "youth's" scornful pride, she can't hide her feelings. Therefore she begs "him" at least not to reject her because she, the woman, who should be passive, is actively doing the wooing—but rather, to accept her gift of love freely, since love sought is good, but given unsought is better."

Now Viola is carried away by her feelings too. She sympathizes with the unhappy Olivia, but, of course, she cannot return her love. More than anything she wishes that she could tell this love-lorn Countess the whole truth of the matter, but since she can't do that, at least she can assure her with all the earnestness and solemnity she can summon up, that "no woman" will ever be mistress of her heart "save I alone." She swears this "by innocence" and "by my youth"—and thus swearing bids Olivia emphatically *adieu* (not *au revoir*). "Nevermore," she declares, will I my master's tears to you deplore."

But Olivia, still hopeful despite this clear-cut rejection, begs Cesario to "come again, for thou perhaps mayst move/That heart which now abhors to like his (Orsino's) love"—a possibility which both know is as remote as is the likelihood of Viola's ever returning Olivia's love. And on this note the two depart, in different directions—Olivia to closet herself again within her house, distractedly mourning her brother and pining after the scornful Cesario, and Viola to return, in frustration, to Orsino's palace, where she must herself endure the pangs of unrequited love.

Act III: Scene 2

This scene returns us to the interior of Olivia's house, where Sir Andrew appears with Sir Toby and Fabian. The foolish knight is vehemently expressing his determination to leave at once for home. When Toby and Faby ask him his reason, he bitterly complains that Olivia has bestowed more favors on "the count's servingman [Cesario] than ever she bestowed on me." He's referring to the scene which just occurred in the garden in which Olivia had peremptorily dismissed Toby, Maria and himself from her presence in order to be alone with Viola.

Sir Toby and Fabian cleverly make fun of Andrew's complaints by arguing that Olivia had deliberately shown favor to Cesario in front of Andrew in order to "awake" his "dormouse valor" and try his mettle. In other words, they try to make the gullible knight believe that Olivia is really interested in him and wants to make him jealous by flirting with Cesario. What Andrew ought to have done, they maintain, is shown up the Count's "man" by outshining him on the spot with even more witty and more courtly language than "he" could produce.

Finally, Toby suggests that since he didn't take the opportunity—as he should have—to put Cesario down in Olivia's presence by outdoing "his" wit, the only alternative left Andrew is to challenge the insolent "youth" to a duel. When Fabian agrees, Andrew readily enough sets out to compose an angry letter to Cesario. Toby, egging him on still further, urges him to "write it in a martial hand" and make it as ferocious as possible.

After Andrew has hurried off to carry out Toby's instructions, Fabian and Toby delightedly discuss the sport that will soon be at hand. Fabian remarks that Andrew is a "dear manikin" to Toby—that is, a wonderful puppet for the jolly knight to amuse himself with—and Toby replies punningly that he (Toby) has been "dear" (expensive) to Andrew to the tune of some two thousand ducats. The two agree that Andrew's challenge to Cesario ought to provide some "rare" amusement—and they agree further that the duel itself should be pretty funny since Cesario, too, "bears in his visage no great presage of cruelty"—an understatement if ever there was one, since Viola, as a gently-reared young girl, can hardly dissemble masculinity to the extent of fighting a duel.

Suddenly, however, as the two pleasure-lovers are rapt in contemplation of the hilarious scene to come, Maria enters, convulsed with merriment, with news of further sport. Amid gales of laughter, she notifies them that Malvolio has carried out all the orders in the letter and is even now approaching his mistress in his mad new fashion—smiling, yellow-stockinged, and cross-gartered. "I know my lady will strike him," Maria giggles, and "If she do, he'll smile and take't for a great favor." Overjoyed at the success of their scheme, the three rush off to watch the fun.

Act III: Scene 3

Sebastian and Antonio have just met on an Illyrian street, and Sebastian who—as we recall from Act II, Scene 1—had begged Antonio not to follow him to Illyria, is greeting his friend fondly. He hadn't wanted him to come, he explains, but he's glad to see him now that he's here. Antonio assures Sebastian of his love and loyalty. Despite the danger of being in such hostile territory, he could hardly stay behind, he declares, knowing that Sebastian was "unguarded and unfriended" here, especially since his own experiences with the Illyrians have always been so unpleasant. Sebastian once again thanks him for his kindness and concern, and then, with all the zeal of a young tourist—forgetting his recent troubles—he asks what there is to do in this town, and suggests that the two of them set out to see whatever sights there may be. Antonio tries to put him off, suggesting that they take lodgings first, but Sebastian insists that he's not tired and enthusiastically repeats his suggestion that they do the town.

Finally Antonio is forced to reluctantly admit that he's really in danger on these streets, since "once in a sea fight" he'd inflicted much damage on Orsino's navy, and the Illyrians would be only too eager to revenge themselves on him if they could take him captive. Sebastian remarks that he must certainly have killed a lot of Illyrians to have aroused such hostility, but Antonio replies that the business was more in the nature of a hold-up—not bloody, but costly to the Illyrians in terms of goods and cash. He himself, he claims, performed with the utmost distinction in this battle (and a full-fledged battle it apparently was, between Antonio's unnamed native city and Illyria) and for this reason Orsino's men are especially anxious to lay their hands on him. At this, Sebastian agrees that Antonio should definitely not "walk too open," and they decide to meet at the Elephant, an inn in "the south suburbs" well known to Antonio. The latter is to go there and order dinner while Sebastian tours the town at his leisure.

Finally, before taking leave of Sebastian, Antonio comments that he knows his friend doesn't have much money, and generously offers him his purse, in case he should see any little things he'd like to buy himself while he's wandering about the town. Sebastian gratefully accepts, and the two go off in different directions, agreeing to meet in an hour at the Elephant.

Act III: Scene 4

We once more find ourselves in Olivia's garden, where Olivia herself, still absorbed in romantic thoughts of Cesario, enters with Maria. More to herself than to her solicitous servingwoman, she mentions rather agitatedly that she's sent for the "youth" and "he's" agreed to come. "How shall I feast him?" she wonders, "What bestow of (on) him?" Looking around, she asks Malvolio's whereabouts. Perhaps he can advise her because he is so "sad" and "civil" (serious).

Maria assures Olivia, as demurely as she can—choking back her laughter —that Malvolio is coming, but "in very strange manner." In fact, his manner is so strange that the little attendant declares he must be "possessed," that is, mad. Concerned, Olivia asks why. "Does he rave?" Maria replies gravely that "he does nothing but smile"—and yet Olivia would probably be better off with some kind of guard about her, because the man is clearly crazy. At this, Olivia demands that Maria call him hither, for "I am as mad as he,/If sad and merry madness equal be."

Maria leaves to fetch Malvolio and re-enters a moment later with the crazily costumed steward. He's followed the instructions of his mysterious correspondent to the letter, and he's wearing bright yellow stockings with garters wrapped around them in a zig-zag pattern (cross-garters). He greets Olivia with a cheery "Sweet lady, ho ho." There ensues a long comical exchange between the two, during which Malvolio misinterprets every one of Olivia's remarks in terms of the letter he's purportedly received from her.

When she tells him that she sent for him because she was feeling sad, for instance, he replies that he supposes *he* could be sad too, (since his garters are so uncomfortably tight, but continues with a meaningful leer that "if it please the eye of one" it's all right with him. Again, when she asks if he wants to go to bed (because he's sick) he gleefully misunderstands her solicitude as an invitation to him and exclaims "Aye, sweetheart, and I'll come to thee." Olivia is appalled by this behavior, and she's certainly not enlightened when he answers her repeated questions ("Why dost thou smile and kiss thy hand so oft?" etc.) with knowing winks and references to the letter. Finally, when she's at her wit's end, a servant enters to inform her that Cesario has reluctantly obeyed her summons and is waiting for her in the house. With a few distracted words to Maria— "Let this fellow be looked to . . . Let some of my people have a special care of him"—she rushes off to see Viola, but not without first commending the unfortunate Malvolio to the special care of her cousin Toby.

Alone onstage for a moment, Malvolio soliloquizes jubilantly on the fancied success of his venture. He's so self-deluded and egotistical that he hasn't noticed anything in the least strange about Olivia's response to his amorous advances. On the contrary, he imagines he's a great romantic hit with her. The fact that she's called for Toby to take care of him, for example, strikes him as concurring "directly with the letter." He imagines she's deliberately sent Toby so he can be "stubborn to him," as the letter directed. Excitedly, he repeats whole passages of the letter (which he evidently knows by heart by now) and exclaims that "Nothing that can be can come between me and the full prospect of my hopes."

Now Maria returns with Toby and Fabian (we saw her actually informing them of their plot's success at the very end of Act III, Scene 2). Toby is playing his part well, loudly resolving that even if Malvolio is "possessed" by "all the devils of Hell," he will speak to him. Fabian, as usual, readily goes along with the joke, inquiring of Malvolio in noisily sympathetic tones "How is't with you man?" Malvolio scornfully rejects the trio as, incidentally, the letter had instructed him to. He imagines this is all meant as a test of his mettle on Olivia's part. But they persist in their sport. "Lo, how hollow the fiend speaks within him," Maria cries ominously, and all three melodramatically urge the contemptuous steward to "defy the devil."

By now Malvolio is getting pretty annoyed—but he endures their behavior grimly, convinced that Olivia is on his side. When Toby actually talks babytalk to him, asking insolently "How dost thou chuck?" (as one would humor a sick person) he makes no response but an indignant "Sir!" and when Maria suggests that he say his prayers, he withers her (or so he thinks) with a contemptuous "My prayers, minx!" Finally, however, their remarks are too much for him, and he angrily tells them to go hang themselves, exiting with the scornful statement that they are "idle, shallow things" and *he*, Malvolio, is not of their "element."

The minute Malvolio is gone, Toby, Fabian, and Maria roar with laughter at the wonderful sport they've had with him. Fabian even comments that the whole scheme would be thought "improbable" if it were seen on the stage—a reference such as Shakespeare was fond of making to the fact that the whole scheme *is* being seen on the stage. But when Maria suggests that they "pursue" the unfortunate steward further, lest he come to his senses too soon, the wily Fabian expresses the fear that they may "make him mad indeed." Toby and Maria, however, feel no such misgivings about the prospect, and they agree to "have him in a dark room and bound" before they give up their revenge. When they finally do decide to have mercy on him, Toby flatteringly tells Maria, "we will...crown thee for a finder of madmen."

But before they can discuss their plans for Malvolio's future any more, Sir Andrew Aguecheek appears, flushed and emboldened with his own egotism, carrying the challenge he's just written to Cesario. "I warrant there's salt and pepper in it," he says, handing it to Toby to read.

In its own way, Andrew's letter to Cesario is as much of a masterpiece as Maria's letter to Malvolio—only in this case it's brilliant as a self-parody, not a burlesque of another's style, and notable for its witlessness rather that its wit. Among other things, the "valiant" Andrew informs Cesario that "whatsoever thou art, thou art a scurvy fellow," and goes on to add, however, that Cesario shouldn't wonder at this abuse for he, Andrew, will give him no reason for it. The letter then continues, senselessly, "thou comest to the Lady Olivia, and in my sight she uses thee kindly, but thou liest in thy throat"—a bitter and, in this case, irrational insult, since it has nothing to do with anything else that's been mentioned. Toby and Fabian comment approvingly on all this, evidently having as much fun with the stupidly egotistical Andrew as they did with the madly egotistical Malvolio. Next, the letter threatens that Andrew will "waylay" Cesario on his way home; but warns that if Cesario kills Andrew he'll be doing it "like a rogue and a villain." "Still you keep on the windy [safe] side of the law," remarks Fabian in mock appreciation of Andrew's cleverness. Finally, the letter concludes, feebly, "Fare thee well, and God have mercy upon one of our souls! He may have mercy upon mine, but my hope is better, and so look to thyself. Thy friend, as thou usest him, and thy sworn enemy. Andrew Aguecheek."

Maria, Toby and Fabian join to compliment the foolish knight on his great work and Toby, as usual, leads his protege on to even greater heights of silliness, encouraging him to await Cesario in the orchard and when the unfortunate "youth" appears, to draw his sword at once and "swear horrible." Andrew proudly assures his friends that he's an expert at swearing, and rushes off in a wild fit of what he thinks is ferocity to carry out his mission.

After he's left, Toby tells Maria and Fabian that he certainly doesn't plan to deliver Andrew's idiotic letter to Cesario, since any well-brought-up young man could tell from such a foolish production that its writer is nothing more than a "clodpole" (block-head). He will rather, he declares, deliver the challenge himself, in person, and describe the faint-hearted Aguecheek's courage, strength and fury in such glowing terms that the very young and mild-mannered Cesario will be terrified of him and "they will kill one another by the look, like cockatrices." (A cockatrice was a mythical serpent, able to kill by its mere look).

At just this moment Viola herself enters, with Olivia. The two are still deep in conversation and so Toby, Fabian, and Maria leave to await their farewell. Olivia, miserable, is complaining that Cesario has "a heart of stone" and that she knows she shouldn't persist in her romantic advances to "him" but she can't help herself. Viola replies loyally that her "master's grief" is every bit as intense as the passion Olivia feels—but Olivia ignores this and, offering Viola-Cesario a jewel with her picture in it as a love-token, begs "him" to return again tomorrow. But when she asks Cesario if there's anything else she can give "him" within reason, Viola replies again, adamantly, "your true love for my master." Olivia answers that this request *is* unreasonable, since she's already given her love to Cesario—and so the two ruefully take their leave, Olivia once again begging Viola to return, and Viola, as courteously as possible under the circumstances bidding her goodbye.

As soon as Olivia is gone, Toby and Fabian re-enter and accost Viola, who is herself about to leave the garden. Toby immediately informs her of the challenge Andrew has made to her, and then goes on to terrify her with a vivid description of her "interceptor, full of despite (spite) and bloody as the hunter." Viola, even more frightened than Toby could have imagined she'd be (since he doesn't realize that she's not even a *young* man), assures him that there must be some mistake, since she's never done anyone any harm. But Toby insists that she must have, and "if you hold your life at any price, betake you to your guard." He then goes on to describe Andrew as a skillful knight, "a devil in private brawl," who's already killed three men in duels. When Viola tries to escape, exclaiming that she'll return to the house and get Olivia to provide her with an armed escort, since she's no fighter, Toby restrains her, declaring that her opponent's indignation is well justified in his opinion, and Viola must give him some satisfaction or else take on Toby himself.

Poor Viola, mystified and upset, begs to know what she could have done to offend so powerful a knight. Whatever it was, she didn't do it deliberately, she declares, in her most conciliatory tone. Offering to negotiate for her with her wrathful accuser, Toby leaves her alone for a moment with Fabian, who cleverly takes this opportunity to tell her that though Andrew doesn't look like very much, she's sure to find him the most "skillful, bloody and fatal opposite" that she could find in Illyria. Fabian then slyly offers to make her peace with Andrew, if he can. She gratefully accepts his offer, explaining that she's a gentle person who would rather associate with peaceful priests than bloody knights of this description.

Viola and Fabian leave the stage for a moment, presumably to try to negotiate a peace with Andrew, but a moment later Andrew himself is dragged onstage by Toby. Toby—whose capacity for mischief-making is endless—is now engaged in assuring the terrified Andrew that Cesario is himself "a very devil . . . They say he has been fencer to the Sophy [the Shah of Iran]," he declares. Poor Andrew immediately tries to escape, exclaiming "Pox on't, I'll not meddle with him," but Toby ,who is looking forward to this sport, won't let him go. Frantic, Andrew offers to pacify the supposedly enraged Cesario by giving him his horse. Toby agrees to "make the motion" to the "youth"—and then slyly remarks, in an aside to the audience, that he himself will manage to keep the horse—still further evidence of his unscrupulous exploitation of his friend.

Now Fabian and Viola re-enter, with Viola trailing as reluctantly behind

Fabian as Andrew behind Toby. Though both duellers are straining away from each other, pale with fear, the two plotters—Toby and Fabian—urge them on.

Finally Viola and Andrew draw their swords and are about to have a pass at each other when—of all people—Sebastian's friend Antonio enters, and demands that Andrew put up his sword. "If this young gentleman have done offense," he cries loyally, "I take the fault on me," and before anyone realizes what has happened, he and Toby (who is furious at this interference) are lunging at each other with a will.

Suddenly, however, a group of officers of the law appear, and the fighting immediately stops. (Duelling was illegal in Elizabethan England.) It seems, however, that the officers haven't been summoned to break up a brawl, but rather to arrest Antonio, who's been recognized—as he feared he might be—as a notorious enemy of the state. He protests that the men are mistaken, but they're adamant. "I know your favor (face) well," one of them insists. Evidently he's been on their most wanted list for quite a while. As he's being led away, Antonio turns to Viola and, thinking she's Sebastian, asks for his purse. He's sorry to have to deprive his friend of funds, he explains, but now he'll need some money himself.

Viola, uncomprehending, is dumbfounded, and doesn't answer. Antonio, again—this time with some irritation—asks for his money. Finally Viola's voice returns and she asks him "What money?" She gladly acknowledges his kindness in rescuing her from her trouble with Andrew, she says, but she doesn't know what purse he's talking about. However, because he's been so good to her, she offers to split her own small store of gold with him, since he's obviousuly in need. Outraged by what he thinks is Sebastian's ingratitude, Antonio begins to berate "him" for it.

Viola, still mystified, denies that he's ever done anything else special for her—and is especially upset by the charge of ingratitude, which she says she hates more than almost any other vice in a man. Antonio is almost speechless with rage, but as the officers start to hurry him off he begs to be allowed to tell his story. He just recently rescued this "youth" from "the jaws of death," he declares, and he'd thought the "boy's" charm and attractiveness worthy of much devotion. The officers, indifferent to his anguish, try again to hustle him away, but he won't be stilled. Turning to Viola, he addresses her as Sebastian, exclaiming "Thou hast, Sebastian, done good feature shame"—meaning that he'd loved Sebastian for his good looks, but that the very idea of beauty is debased by Sebastian's immoral and ungrateful denial of friendship. "Virtue is beauty, but the beauteous evil," he cries in bitter rage and disappointment, "are empty trunks, o'er flourished by the Devil"—over-elaborately carved chests, which have nothing inside. At this, "the man grows mad," one of the officers declares, and they lead him forcibly off, leaving Viola behind to ponder wonderingly on his words.

Thinking it all out carefully, she remarks in a brief soliloquy that she knows her brother to be still "living in [her] glass"—that is, the image of herself which she sees daily in her mirror is also her brother's image, since she's deliberately imitated him in her dress, style and manner. If he *should* be alive, as she thinks he is, the supposedly cruel sea has been kind indeed, and she rushes off, completely absorbed in her joyful thoughts.

Toby, Andrew, and Fabian, left behind onstage, discuss sourly what "a very dishonest paltry boy" Cesario must be to have treated his friend (Antonio) so ungratefully. Besides, Toby and Fabian add, he's a coward. This imbues Andrew with the spirit of battle once more, and he vows to follow Cesario and beat him. Delighted at the prospect of a renewal of their sport, Toby and Fabian egg him on, and the three hurry off once again in hot pursuit of poor Viola.

Act IV: Scene 1

This scene takes place in front of Olivia's house, where Sebastian—who's been doing some casual sightseeing in the town, as he told Antonio he would—is waylaid by Feste, the fool, with a message from Olivia. Sebastian, of course, has never laid eyes on this fellow before, and so he can't understand why Feste (who naturally thinks he's Cesario) should have any business with him. Feste, amazed in his turn by Cesario's strange behavior, becomes sarcastic: "No, I do not know thee," he exclaims ironically, "nor this is not my nose neither. Nothing that is so is so." But Sebastian refuses to be intimidated by his sharpness, telling him to go "vent" his "folly somewhere else. Thou knowst not me." Feste, even more annoyed, still can't believe that Cesario doesn't know him, and asks him once more what he should tell Olivia. Sebastian, torn between amazement at this mad mistake and irritation at the fool's persistence, tosses Feste a few coins and tells him threateningly to be off or he'll be paid further in blows instead of coins.

In a moment, before Sebastian has time to make good on his threat to the fool, Andrew, Toby and Fabian enter. They'd left the garden, we recall, at the end of Act III, Scene 4, in hot pursuit of Cesario. Since Fabian and Toby assured Andrew the "boy" was a coward, the foolish knight is determined to challenge "him anew, and punish" him—not only for "his" usurpation of the Countess' affections—but also for "his" ungrateful behavior to Antonio. But now, of course, they've really got the wrong man—for Sebastian is as far from being a coward as his sister is from being a warrior. Trained from birth, like any young nobleman, in fencing and fighting of all kinds, he's mystified by the challenge Andrew shouts immediately on entering, but readily enough draws his sword and lays about him with a will. "Are all the people mad?" he inquires—astonished that everyone seems to take him for someone else—even as he delivers a few well-aimed blows to the unlucky Andrew.

At this point, Toby—who's reluctant to lose his main source of income and amusement (Andrew)—intervenes in his friend's behalf, and begs "Cesario" to hold—that is, put up his sword. But Sebastian is furious mad by now, and keeps right on fighting.

In the meantime, Feste—knowing that Olivia would want to hear of such a battle royal between her kinsman and her "lover"—rushes off to tell her what's going on. Andrew, by now, has managed to get away from Sebastian, and is vowing to "have an action of battery against him, if there be any law in Illyria," though he himself started the fight in the first place, and Toby has taken on the quarrel. In fact, Toby and Sebastian are furiously duelling when Olivia, summoned by Feste, appears on the scene.

Appalled at the bloody sight she sees (and horrified that her beloved "Cesario" should have been so set on by these rascals), she orders Toby to stop fighting and immediately begins to upbraid him for his rude behavior to "Cesario," at the same time begging the really (by now) profoundly amazed Sebastian not to be offended by her cousin's barbarous manners. Andrew, Toby, and Fabian leave in chagrin, and as soon as they're gone, Olivia, still apologizing profusely for their behavior, begs Sebastian to come into the house with her and let her tell him all about the "many fruitless pranks this ruffian [Toby] hath botched up." He should forgive Toby, she says, because the fellow is always in this sort of trouble—and besides, she goes on, once more declaring her love for "Cesario," the whole thing has given her a terrible fright.

Sebastian, completely confused by this—but naturally rather pleased, as any healthy young man would be, by such unsolicited romantic attentions from such a beautiful and elegant woman—wonders whether he's awake or asleep, mad or dreaming. Finally, resigning himself to what's really become, at this point, rather a pleasant situation, he exclaims, "If it be thus to dream, still let me sleep!" Olivia—herself a little surprised to find the formerly reluctant "Cesario" now so eager for her love—asks if he "be ruled by me!" and when Sebastian replies enthusiastically 'Madam, I will," she leads him joyously off, hardly able to believe in her good fortune.

Act IV: Scene 2

This scene returns us once more to the interior of Olivia's house. Maria and the clown enter, apparently deep in some new scheme—which turns out, however, to be merely an elaboration of the old plot against Malvolio. The sly servingwoman gives the fool a priest's gown and a false beard, and instructs him to make poor Malvolio believe he's "Sir Topas," the priest. Then she rushes off to fetch Sir Toby, so he too can join in the fun.

Alone onstage for a moment, the fool makes a few witty remarks about the clergy in an aside to the audience. He says, for instance, that he will not be the first to "dissemble" in a priestly gown. Then, when Maria returns with Toby, he immediately plunges into his act as "Sir Topas." In gravely quavering tones (Feste's performance is a marvelous burlesque of the behavior of a silly priest) he greets the two conspirators with a few learned-sounding remarks, which are, however, no more than nonsense. Then he approaches the "prison" where Malvolio is confined.

Greeting Malvolio in the same portentous clergyman's tones, Feste immediately has the gullible steward believing that he is indeed "Sir Topas," the curate, and Malvolio who, by now, understands that something has gone wrong and that his amorous behavior hasn't brought the results he thought it would, begs for the priest's assistance. "Out, hyperbolical [extravagant] fiend!" is Feste's melodramatic reply. He ignores Malvolio as being a madman, incompetent to converse with anyone, and addresses, instead, the devil that presumably possesses him. When Malvolio bitterly complains that in being charged with lunacy he's been "wronged," the fool again unsympathetically responds with "Fie, thou dishonest Satan!"

When Malvolio complains that the room in which he's confined is dark "as Hell," the false "Sir Topas" responds that on the contrary it has windows "toward the south-north . . . as lustrous as ebony"—and that Malvolio must indeed be mad to say otherwise. Malvolio stubbornly insists that the room is dark (which it is) and Feste then solemnly tells him that the darkness in which he's "puzzled" is the darkness of ignorance. Malvolio begs the priest to "make the trial" of his sanity "in any constant question" (that is, let him prove he's sane by the clarity and force of his mind in logical argument.) This, of course, gives the fool just the opportunity he's looking for, and he quickly makes a hash of Malvolio (who indeed acquits himself quite sanely on the subject) with a lot of double-talk about Pythagoras, concluding with the advice that until Malvolio believes in the Pythagorean doctrine of the transmigration of souls, he must be considered indubitably mad.

When "Sir Topas" has left the unfortunate steward—still unconsoled, in darkness—Sir Toby and Maria, who have witnessed the whole scene, congratulate him heartily on his performance. Then Sir Toby suggests that the fool visit Malvolio in his "own voice" (that is, address Malvolio in his natural voice) and find out without any further clowning how the steward really is. For, says Toby worriedly, he himself is now in so much trouble with his niece (on account of his run-in in the last scene with "Cesario") that he'd rather like to be finally rid of this plot altogether, before it backfires. On this note, he and Maria depart and Feste skips across the stage to Malvolio's prison once more, this time acting only as himself.

Singing a cheerful little song ("Hey robin, jolly robin,/Tell me how thy lady does") the clown pretends to be just casually passing by, with no knowledge at all that Malvolio is confined nearby. When the miserable "madman" woefully calls to him for help—in tones significantly humbler and friendlier than the arrogant ones he'd used at their last encounter— Feste feigns surprise at hearing of his plight. Malvolio confides to him that he's been "notoriously abused" and isn't really mad at all, but just as sane as the fool himself. Feste, who can't resist teasing his old enemy a little longer, replies that "you are mad indeed if you be no better in your wits than a fool," and then goes on to introduce "Sir Topas" onto the scene once more. First he addresses Malvolio in his quavering, priestly voice, and then again in his light-hearted fool's tones. In an exhibition of his virtuosity as a performer, he carries on a little conversation with himself, greeting himself the priest ("God be wi' you, good Sir Topas") and then solemnly warning himself the fool not to carry on any conversation with a dangerous madman like Malvolio ("Maintain no words with him, good fellow").

Finally Feste drops this trickery, and pays a little more attention to Malvolio's pleas for assistance. His friend (and frequent benefactor) Sir Toby has, after all, indicated that he'd like to get the whole business over with, and Feste can help him by at least helping to release Malvolio from his prison. Hence he accedes to Malvolio's request to bring him "light and paper and ink" so that he can write a letter to Olivia explaining just how he's been so abused. (The steward, of course, doesn't know the real authors of the plot against him, but he does think he'd better get the story of the letter straight with his mistress, especially since he still believes it came from her.) Feste promises, further, to convey the finished document to Olivia herself, and the two part with Malvolio extravagantly thanking him for his kindness and promising to "requite it in the highest degree." These words of humble gratitude can't help but be pleasant to the vengeful Feste, who skips merrily offstage, singing an appropriate little ditty about a "mad lad and the Devil."

Act IV: Scene 3

This very brief scene (35 lines) takes place in Olivia's garden, where we discover Sebastian, alone and still puzzling over the strange situation in which he finds himself. He's evidently just come from his tete-a-tete with Olivia "within the house," where she'd taken him at the end of Act IV, Scene 2, and he still finds his good fortune in so quickly winning the love of such a woman hard to believe. But, he concludes, on the evidence of his senses ("this is the air, that is the glorious sun") he's neither mad nor dreaming, so these events must be real. He wonders where Antonio can be, and thinks that his friend's advice might be helpful to him. We, of course, know that the loyal captain has been arrested.

Finally, he concludes that there must be some mistake in all this, or else he's mad, or the lady's mad. But he's already dismissed the idea that he himself might be mad—and as for Olivia being mad, she seems to be able to run her house smoothly enough, and command her servants with authority, things she couldn't do if she were really mad. So he's left again with the notion that something's wrong, but he doesn't know what. ("There's something in't/That is deceivable. . .") Nevertheless, since he himself is by now in love with Olivia, he's quite willing to go along with whatever she may propose, no matter how obscure her reasons are. So when she herself enters with a priest, a moment later, and actually proposes marriage, he accedes gladly enough.

She asks Sebastian to go at once with her and the priest to a nearby chapel, and recite the marriage vows so "that my most jealous and too doubtful soul May live at peace." The clergyman will, she promises, conceal the marriage until "Cesario" is willing to have it publicly announced.

To her surprise and delight, Sebastian readily agrees, promising that "having sworn truth" he "ever will be true." Overjoyed, Olivia calls on the Heavens to "shine" on her act, and the pair go off without further discussion to be wed.

Act V

This final scene of the play, a long and important one, takes place again in front of Olivia's house. Feste the fool and the servant Fabian enter first. Feste is carrying a letter (which, we can infer, is the one Malvolio has just written with his help to Olivia) and Fabian begs the clown to let him see it. Feste, who's promised Malvolio he'll personally deliver the letter to his lady, refuses. He himself is anxious by now to get the whole business over with, and he doesn't trust Fabian's intentions. Before Fabian can do more than mildly protest. Orsino, with his entire retinue —Viola, Curio, and a group of other attendants—appears on the scene.

Orsino addresses Feste and Fabian kindly, asking if they "belong" to the Lady Olivia. They reply in the affirmative and then, after a closer look at the fool, the Duke remembers that he himself is well-acquainted with Feste (who had, in fact, we may recall, been summoned to perform for him in Act II, Scene 4). There follows some light banter between the two, in which Feste shows his wit to good advantage, cleverly proving, among other things, that he's "the better for my foes and the worst for my friends"—because his foes tell him the truth about himself whereas his friends "praise me and make an ass of me." When Orsino shows himself to be well-pleased with this "fooling," Feste redoubles his efforts and with an explosion of dazzling wit manages to beg two separate coins from the Duke. But Orsino refuses to give him a third until he fetches Olivia for him, so Feste hurries off at once to relay the news of this important visitor's arrival to his mistress.

At this moment, Antonio is brought in by the officers who arrested him at the end of Act III, Scene 4. Both Viola and Orsino recognize him immediately, Viola as the man who rescued her from Andrew and Toby, and Orsino as the "salt-water thief" who inflicted so much damage on the noblest vessel of the Illyrian fleet in a recent sea-fight. The officers confirm that the captain is indeed "that Antonio/That took the *Phoenix* and her fraught (cargo) from Candy (Crete)," and they tell Orsino that they caught the fellow brawling without any regard for law or his own safety "here on the streets." Curious, Orsino asks Antonio (calling him "notable pirate" and thief) what "foolish boldness" could have induced him to put himself within the reach of his bitter enemies in Illyria.

Antonio, denying that he's either a thief or a pirate, though (for reasons never given) Orsino's enemy, replies that "a witchcraft drew me hither," and goes on to tell the whole story of his relationship with Sebastian: how he'd rescued the boy from the "rude sea," followed him, purely out of love, into this hostile town, lent him his purse, rescued him from his adversaries (Andrew and Toby), and finally been treated by the youth (who refused to return his money) with the utmost ingratitude.

Viola exclaims that Antonio indeed "did her kindness" by drawing his sword in her defense, but as for the rest of his story, it must be madness. Orsino then asks Antonio when he and and Sebastian had arrived in Illyria, hoping thus to shed some light on the mystery. When Antonio replies that they'd only arrived today, but had been together for three months before this, Orsino concludes that the man must indeed be mad, since the "youth" in question, Cesario—has attended *him* for the past three months.

At this point Olivia enters, and Orsino drops the problem of Antonio (telling the officers to "take him aside") to declare extravagantly that

"Now Heaven walks on earth." Olivia—who is most anxious that the Duke not renew his suit—greets him coldly. Then, catching sight of Cesario (to whom she thinks she was married just a few hours ago), she exclaims "Cesario, you do not keep promise with me." Viola, mystified, starts to reply, but the Duke interrupts her. Olivia, more interested in Cesario's words, tries to silence "his" master, but Viola defers to her lord. ("My lord doth speak, my duty hushes me.") Olivia, annoyed, remarks contemptuously that if what Orsino has to say "be aught to the old tune" his words of love are really quite repulsive to her by now. "Still so cruel?" the Duke asks, rather angrily (he too is becoming annoyed) and "Still so constant" (in her rejection of him) is Olivia's reply. This prompts him to desperately ask her ("You uncivil lady,/To whose . . . altars my soul the faithful'st offerings hath breath'd out") what he should do now. She answers indifferently that he should do what he pleases.

Olivia's coldness is by now too much for Orsino. In a rage of jealousy and frustration at her continued humiliating rejections of him, he swears that he'll revenge himself on her—either, like a famous Egyptian thief (Thyamis, who killed the girl that he'd kidnapped rather than let her fall into other hands) by killing what he loves or, better still, by taking Cesario away from her. Yes, he decides, perhaps it would be best to "sacrifice" Cesario, since he can see that it's really Cesario that Olivia loves. Much as he, too, loves Cesario, he declares, he'd willingly murder "him" to spite the "marble-breasted" Olivia.

Viola—whose own love for Orsino is apparently boundless—then declares that she'd willingly die "a thousand deaths" if that would make Orsino rest easier, and starts to follow him offstage. Olivia, in agitation, asks Cesario where "he's" going, and Viola replies that she's going "after him I love/More than I love these eyes, more than my life,/More, by all mores, than e'er I shall love wife" (a reasonable enough remark, since she could hardly love a "wife" anyway). Olivia, who imagines that she herself is already "Cesario's" wife, exclaims that she's been "beguiled" (deceived) by the "youth", otherwise he wouldn't forget his recent vows so easily. When Viola asks her what she's talking about, she calls him "husband," and at this the Duke, furious, intervenes to ask Cesario what the truth of the matter is. Viola repeats that she doesn't know what Olivia's talking about.

Olivia, rationalizing that Cesario's fear of the Duke's power and importance is making "him" deny "his" recent marriage in such a cowardly way, urges "him" to admit the truth, since "he," as her "husband," will be just as important as Orsino. There's no need for this timidity, she declares, and then calls on the priest (who's been summoned by a servant) to verify that he did, in fact, just marry her to "Cesario." When the priest confirms that such a marriage took place not two hours before this scene, Orsino, enraged, begins to upbraid Cesario for "his" falseness, and finally dismisses "him" forever from his service: "Farewell, and take her," he cries furiously, "but direct thy feet/Where thou and I hence-forth may never meet."

Viola starts to protest, but Olivia, still sure that Cesario is motivated only by fear of the Duke's wrath, tries to stop "him." At just this moment of excruciating tension, Sir Andrew Aguecheek, bloody, battered, and calling loudly for a surgeon, hobbles in.

Distracted from her own troubles for a moment by Sir Andrew's obvious misery, Olivia turns to question him, and he declares that his head has been broken—and Sir Toby's too!—by the "Count's gentleman," Cesario. "We took him for a coward," Andrew complains, "but he's the very Devil incarnate." Orsino, astounded, looks inquiringly at the innocent Viola, who denies all knowledge of the affair. When Andrew sees this gentle Cesario, he immediately confuses him with the other, ferocious "Cesario" (in reality, of course, Sebastian) who's just beaten him up, and begins to bitterly repeat his accusations. Again Viola denies them, remarking that Andrew drew his sword on her "without cause," but that she had treated him politely and not hurt him (in Act III, Scene 4). "If a bloody coxcomb (head) be a hurt, you have hurt me," declares the injured knight indignantly.

At this moment in staggers Toby, supported by the fool, and obviously as much damaged as his friend. Toby's obviously drunk, as usual (and, indeed, Andrew maintains that if he *hadn't* been drunk he would certainly have done more harm to Cesario),and he seems to be bearing his hurt philosophically. He asks for a surgeon to dress his wounds, and the clown merrily tells him that the surgeon has been drunk for an hour and isn't available. "I hate a drunken rogue," comments the drunken Toby.

Olivia—who seems to be fond of her renegade relative despite his awful behavior—orders Feste to help the two knights to bed and get them medical attention, and the three groaningly depart, with Fabian assisting too. As they leave, Toby expresses his pain by heaping extravagant insults on the unlucky Andrew (who is, he says, "an asshead and a coxcomb and a knave, a thin-faced knave, a gull!")

As soon as they're gone, Sebastian himself, the other, ferocious "Cesario," puts in an appearance, apologizing profusely to Olivia for having hurt her kinsman. He sees that she's looking strangely at him (because there are now two Cesarios on stage.) and assuming it's because she's offended by his wounding of Toby, he explains that he couldn't help himself because the two knights struck first. Still, he says he's sorry, especially in the light of the marriage vows he and the Countess so recently exchanged. Dumbfounded, Olivia, Orsino, Antonio, and the others onstage look from Viola to Sebastian, not knowing what to make of this sudden incredible duplication of "Cesario!"

Sebastian now catches sight of Antonio, and with extravagant expressions of love and loyalty, he tells his friend how worried he's been about him since he failed to keep their rendezvous at the Elephant. Antonio, almost speechless with wonder, asks Sebastian how he has "made division of" himself. Pointing to Viola, he remarks that "an apple cleft in two, is not more twin/Than these two creatures." Sebastian now notices Viola for the first time, and he is himself amazed by the sight, since he doesn't of course, know that his sister is alive and, furthermore, dressed as a man. "Do I stand there?" he asks, astonished, and then goes on to declare that he never had a (twin) brother, though he *did* have a sister, recently lost at sea. Who are you? he asks Viola. "What name? What parentage?"

Viola, near tears with joy, explains that Sebastian of Messaline was her father, and that she had a brother named Sebastian who went, looking just like this present Sebastian, to his "watery tomb." Sebastian, now beginning to see the light, tells Viola that if she only were a woman, he "should my tears let fall upon your cheek,/And say 'thrice welcome, drowned Viola!' " And after exchanging a few more pertinent facts about themselves, the two *do* fall weeping into each other's arms, as soon as Viola declares that she *is*, in fact, a woman, and can take Sebastian to "a captain in this town" who has been keeping her female garments for her while she masquerades as Cesario.

Finally, convinced at last that his sister is alive, in the guise of Cesario, Sebastian turns, rather amused, to Olivia, and points out to her that she's actually married the wrong person, but that anyway, in this case the wrong person was really the right person, since the Countess would otherwise "have been contracted to a maid!"

Orsino now decides that he too must "share in this most happy wreck," and turning to Viola (the two couples are finally pairing off in the proper way) he asks her if she meant it when she swore so often that she never would love a woman as she loved him. (He too, is beginning to see the light about Viola, now that her true identity is known.) Viola happily assures him that she did mean it, and will gladly take the same oath again a hundred times over. Touched, and realizing, perhaps, that his Platonic love for the beautiful boy, Cesario, could just as easily become a romantic passion for the lovely, good-humored girl, Viola, Orsino takes her hand and asks to see her in her woman's clothes. Viola explains that the captain who's been keeping them for her has been thrown in jail on some suit of Malvolio's, and so Olivia immediately calls for her steward to explain the matter further and get the captain released as soon as possible.

But now, of course, she suddenly remembers about Malvolio's madness, a problem which she'd completely forgotten for the time being in her absorption with her own romantic madness. At this point, Feste and Fabian coveniently appear, with the steward's letter, which the clown immediately delivers to his mistress, explaining that he wasn't supposed to give it to her yet, but he doesn't really think it matters very much just when "a madman's epistles" are delivered. Olivia orders him to open it and read it to her"—but when he can't refrain from reciting its contents in a melodramatically "mad" tone, she turns to Fabian and asks him to read it. This servant agreeably does his mistress' bidding and in a straightforward manner reads Malvolio's note which proves surprisingly sane. In it, he angrily informs Olivia that he is *not* mad, and that he resents having been put thus into the power of her "drunken cousin" Toby, especially since it was *her own letter* which induced him to behave as he did. Both Olivia and Orsino agree that Malvolio's words don't sound mad, and Olivia orders Fabian to "bring him hither."

While Fabian is gone on his errand, she turns (for the first time) in a friendly way to Orsino, and asks how he'd feel about having her for a sister—which he would if he'd marry Viola as she has married Sebastian. Orsino, nothing loath, at once proposes to the former Cesario, declaring that for all the service she's done him, "so far beneath (her) soft and tender breeding," he will now make her her "master's mistress." Viola is, of course, overjoyed, and Olivia, glad enough now to simply be friends with this original Cesario since she's acquired "his" double, Sebastian, for her very own, exclaims enthusiastically "A sister! You are she."

At this point—now that everything's been settled in the romantic plot— Fabian returns with the long-suffering Malvolio, who immediately begins to protest the injuries he's received at Olivia's hands. When the Countess maintains that she's never done him any wrong, he produces the famous letter, insisting that she can't deny it's in her own handwriting. He then goes on to ask her why she gave him such "clear lights of favor"—bidding him come smiling, cross-gartered and yellow-stockinged to her, etc.—and then allowed him to be imprisoned in a dark room, treated as a madman by the priest, and "made the most notorious geck (fool) and gull" ever.

Olivia, who's been perusing the letter in question throughout Malvolio's recital of his grievances, replies that unfortunately the handwriting is not *hers*, but Maria's, and promises a full inquiry into the whole business, at which the wronged steward can be "both the plaintiff and the judge."

At this point, however, Fabian loyally comes to the little servingwoman's defense. He confesses that he and Toby are solely responsible for the plot against Malvolio (which, of course, isn't really true) and that they were motivated by some just grievances they had against the arrogant steward (which is true). He declares, further, that Maria had written the letter only at Sir Toby's insistence, and then informs the assembled company that as a reward the jovial knight has finally married her.

Olivia hears Fabian's speech sympathetically enough, and then, more amused than not, turns to the hapless Malvolio exclaiming with pity "Poor fool, how they have baffled (disgraced) thee!" This arouses Feste —who still holds a grudge against the steward—to mockingly quote a few lines from Maria's letter and then, worse still, to use his "Sir Topas" voice, revealing the true identity of the "priest" who had so tortured Malvolio in his dark jail. "And thus the whirligig of time brings in his revenges," Feste can't help jeering. "I'll be revenged on the whole pack of you," Malvolio shouts in reply, and rushes furiously offstage.

Orsino—as befits the ruler of this confused kingdom—orders some servants to pursue Malvolio, and try to placate him, especially since the angry steward hasn't yet given them the information they want about Viola's friend, the captain. In the meantime, Orsino declares, he and his party will remain at Olivia's house to celebrate the happy outcome of recent events, and as soon as Viola can be dressed in more feminine clothes, he'll crown her "Orsino's mistress and his fancy's Queen."

On this note, the entire company departs, except for Feste, who remains behind to sing a short sad song, which begins "When that I was and a little boy,/With hey ho, the wind and the rain,/A foolish thing was but a toy,/For the rain it raineth every day." The little balland goes on to outline the progress of the singer's life—from youth, to manhood, to death (always repeating the mournful refrain about the wind and the rain, ballad-fashion, at the middle and end of every stanza), and it finally concludes by informing the audience with sad courtesy that "A great while ago, the world begun,/With hey ho, the wind and the rain,/But that's all one, our play is done,/And we'll strive to please you every day."

Two Gentlemen of Verona

DUKE OF MILAN, *father to Silvia.*
VALENTINE } *the two Gentlemen.*
PROTEUS
ANTONIO, *father to Proteus.*
THURIO, *a foolish rival to Valentine.*
EGLAMOUR, *agent for Silvia in her escape.*
HOST, *where Julia lodges.*
OUTLAWS, *with Valentine.*
SPEED, *a clownish servant to Valentine.*
LAUNCE, *the like to Proteus.*
PANTHINO, *servant to Antonio.*

JULIA, *beloved of Proteus.*
SILVIA, *beloved of Valentine.*
LUCETTA, *waiting-woman to Julia.*

SERVANTS, MUSICIANS.

Two Gentlemen of Verona

Act I: Scene 1

The play opens in Verona, in an open place, with the entry of the two gentlemen of the title. Valentine tells his friend, Proteus, that it is quite useless to try to persuade him to stay at home. "Home-keeping youth have ever homely wits," he says, obviously believing in the educational value of foreign travel and experience. He wishes that Proteus would come with him to Milan, but that young man apparently wishes to live "dully sluggardized at home." The reason for this situation is that Proteus is in love.

Proteus, however, does not seem to consider that Valentine's attitude toward his love is justified, and he sighs forth a sad farewell, bidding Valentine not to forget him, and in fact to recall him to mind whenever he sees something interesting in his travels. Valentine scoffs at the inertia of Proteus and asks if his friend will pray upon some love-book for the success of the traveler. Proteus and Valentine then engage in a wit-combat, the first of many to be found in this play, and Valentine speaks of the tale of Leander as a "shallow story of deep love."

Valentine then gives a description of what being in love means. As he proceeds, one sees that it consists of sighs, groans, and sleeplessness on the part of the lover, with scorn and coyness on the part of the lady. He tries every sensible gambit he can to make Proteus see reason, telling him that Love is his master, and that he is yoked to a fool. Then, when Proteus protests that love can inhabit the finest minds of all, Valentine claims that love destroys wit by turning it toward folly. Proteus remains immovable, and Valentine departs on the appearance of his father. The two friends bid each other an affectionate farewell. Left alone, Proteus laments his sorry state. Valentine is leaving for Milan to seek honor, while he, Proteus, remains sadly at home, pursuing love. He claims that his lady Julia has made him forget his studies and has turned his mind toward folly, leaving him heartsick with thinking of her.

At this moment of Proteus's extreme melancholy, Speed, Valentine's servant, enters and inquires after his master. Proteus tells him that Valentine has just taken ship for Milan.

Speed and Proteus promptly start another wit-combat based on Speed's mistaking of the word "ship" for "sheep" as it was pronounced in Shakespeare's day. The puns- and mistakings continue with jokes on horns, usually indicating the infidelity of a wife, references to mutton, a slang term for courtesan, and so on. However, in the course of conversation we are told that Proteus has used Speed to convey a letter to Julia, who apparently did not even give the messenger a tip for his trouble. Speed therefore claims that Julia is an extremely hard-hearted lady. Rather tired of Speed's wit, Proteus sends the servant away to the protests of that young man that Proteus may in future act as his own messenger.

Act I: Scene 2

This scene takes place in the garden of Julia's house and is between the lady Julia and her witty maid, Lucetta. The two women immediately commence a discussion on love, and Julia asks her maid's opinion of the various suitors who have been visiting the house. Lucetta suggests that Julia mention them all, and as her mistress does so she gives a quick, witty sketch of each. Apparently there are three in all, though Proteus is the only one who actually appears in the play.

Lucetta has used great skill in her comments on the gentlemen to avoid saying anything that might be considered derogatory to Proteus, and she brings with her the letter of which Speed and Proteus had spoken in the preceding scene. Julia immediately flies into a feigned rage, gives the letter back to Lucetta, and tells her to return it. However, when Lucetta has left, Julia begins to feel sorry for acting so rashly. After all, she actually does want the chance to read Proteus's letter. She then calls for Lucetta who very skillfully lets the letter fall. Julia promptly forbids her to pick it up, and another wit-combat ensues, this time centering around music, tunes, burdens [refrains], and the parts of choral harmony. Julia finally accepts the letter, only to tear it across and bid Lucetta leave. The maid, however, shrewdly sees that Julia wants to be left alone in order to read the missive.

Of course she is right. The moment Julia is left alone she crawls around the room picking up the pieces of Proteus's letter, continually lamenting her "hateful hands, . . . [which] tear such loving words." As Julia reads various scraps of the letter one sees that it is a conventionally romantic one, full of the plaints one would expect from Proteus. Each time she reads a few words Julia kisses the letter and castigates herself for her hard-heartedness. But Lucetta enters again, and catches Julia in the act of crawling around after the pieces. Obviously she knows quite well what is going on, but when Julia flies into a rage, telling her to pick up the pieces, Lucetta refuses on the ground that she has already been in trouble for putting them down. Finally the two depart.

Act I: Scene 3

This scene takes place a short time later in the home of Antonio, the father of Proteus. He is speaking with a servant, Panthino, whose advice he apparently trusts. Panthino recounts to Antonio a conversation he has had with his master's brother concerning the future of Proteus. The brother has wondered greatly that Antonio has allowed his son to remain at home, while other men with much less reputation have sent their sons out to seek advancement, some in the wars, some on exploratory expeditions, and some to the universities.

Certainly Proteus was more than adequately fitted for any one of these pursuits, and so the brother bade Panthino beg Antonio that he not allow Proteus to waste his youth at home, because later on his insularity would be a handicap. In reply Antonio says that the situation has also been of great concern to him for this last month. Continually he has been trying to persuade

Proteus that he will always regret not taking up his current opportunities, saying that he cannot hope to be a perfect man unless he has been educated in the great world and has had experience there. Desperately, he asks advice from Panthino, who has his answer ready. Proteus should be sent to join his friend, Valentine, who is currently in attendance at the court of the Emperor (Shakespeare seems to have made a slip here). There the young man may practice in personal combats, in tilts between two parties of knights, and in tournaments, where each knight fights another. In addition, his education would be advanced by hearing suitable conversations among noblemen. Antonio immediately decides to follow this suggestion, and when Panthino reminds him that Don Alphonso, a friend, is journeying to salute the Emperor, the young man's father decides to send his son along also.

Proteus then enters reading a letter which he has apparently received from Julia. Obviously it is full of romantic protestations of love, and Proteus speaks as if he fears parental opposition to their marriage. On seeing his father, Proteus lies very quickly, claiming that the letter is from Valentine. When Antonio asks to see it, Proteus is forced to carry the lie further, saying that his friend is enjoying his life at the Emperor's court, and how much he wishes his friend Proteus were with him. The comment gives Antonio an opening and he says that his wish is the same, and therefore he has planned to send Proteus to Milan the very next day. The young man protests that he has not been given enough time to get things ready, but his father is adamant. As Antonio departs, Proteus laments that in trying to hide his passion for Julia he has fallen into deeper trouble and now must leave his lady.

Act II: Scene 1

This scene takes place in the Duke's palace in Milan. Valentine and his servant, Speed, enter. Speed offers Valentine a glove which the young man has absentmindedly dropped. When Valentine sees it he launches forth into an impassioned address to the glove as "Sweet ornament that decks a thing divine!" and then we discover that the lady's name is Silvia, a name which Valentine breathes with reverence. Speed, following his usual practice of mistaking the word, then calls for Silvia to come, in this way, incidentally, ridiculing Valentine's transports of passion.

Valentine is a trifle taken aback by his servant's casual announcement that his master is in love, and asks how Speed has become aware of his passion. Speed immediately details the obvious signs of love-passion which are evident in Valentine: folded arms (a sign of melancholy), delight in love-songs, a love of solitude, sighing, weeping, fasting, sleeplessness, whining speech. None of these attributes is usual with Valentine.

Valentine promptly interrogates Speed concerning his opinion of Silvia's beauty, and Speed obliges by constantly mistaking his master's meaning, finally claiming that Valentine cannot really know Silvia because he loves her, and love is blind. Then, with a certain malice, Speed reminds Valentine of the way he used to scoff at Proteus for going ungartered.

Valentine attempts to overcome the wit of his servant and is unsuccessful. He then says sadly that Silvia has asked him to write a letter to someone she loves, and in reply to Speed's suggestion that the lines are ill-written, he remarks that they are as good as he can manage because the assignment makes him so sad. At that moment, Silvia, dressed in all her finery, enters, and Speed speaks admiringly of her as an "exceeding puppet."

Valentine greets her with fulsomeness, and Silvia replies in the same manner. He then presents the requested letter, which she approves as "very clerkly done," in other words, as efficiently as a professional might have managed. Valentine protests that the lines are indeed ill-done, and then Silvia returns the letter saying that he should keep it since the word were written unwillingly, and at her request. Valentine is quite stunned and offers to write another such letter. Silvia agrees and suggests that he read his words over once he has written them. As she departs Speed laughs uproariously at the whole exchange. He has perceived what his master has not: Silvia is having Valentine write love letters to himself.

Valentine is somewhat disturbed at Speed's mirth and still seems unable to understand what his servant is trying to say. Finally

Speed very practically suggests that they go to dinner, but Valentine says that he has already dined—on the sight of his lady.

Act II: Scenes 2-3

The first of these scenes takes places in Julia's house in Verona. It is a most touching and tearful farewell between Julia and Proteus. The pair exchange rings "And seal the bargain with a holy kiss." Proteus takes Julia's hand and declares his constancy, promising to remember his lady at every hour of the day.

In Scene 3 Launce enters with his dog, and the empty stage now represents a street in Verona. He then gives a recital covering his farewell from home. Apparently everyone in the entire household was drowning in tears, except for Crab, the dog, whom Launce castigates for his hard-heartedness. With a pair of shoes Launce attempts to replay the entire sad scene before the audience, taking all the parts himself, and again complaining about the dog's lack of emotion.

Panthino then arrives to tell Launce to hurry to embark, otherwise he will miss the boat. This gives Launce the chance to deliver a speech which parodies his master's inflated rhetoric, claiming that he could fill a river with his tears and drive the boat with the wind of his sighs.

Act II: Scene 4

This scene takes place a short time later in the palace of the Duke of Milan. Silvia, Valentine, Thurio, and Speed enter. In the course of the one-line quips traded among the players one finds out that Sir Thurio is a foolish wooer of Silvia and much older than Valentine. A series of wit-combats ensues, in the course of which Sir Thurio becomes angry at his treatment and jealous of the way in which Silvia and Valentine speak together. Valentine compliments Silvia on Sir Thurio's attempts at wit, saying that he has borrowed them from her. Valentine cannot leave the foolish wooer alone and it takes Silvia to keep them from blows, as she speaks kindly to her "servant" Valentine.

The Duke of Milan then enters bringing news to Valentine from his friends. He asks the young man what he knows of Signior Antonio, and then asks after Antonio's son. This question seems to loosen Valentine's tongue and he speaks at considerable rhetorical length concerning the merits of his friend, praising his experience, his judgment, his diligence, and everything about him, claiming that Proteus has every grace becoming to a gentleman. The Duke is a trifle amused at this overwhelming protestation of friendship and comments wryly that he sounds worthy to be an emperor's counselor. Then he tells Valentine that Proteus intends to spend some time at the court of Milan. Valentine is overjoyed and he tells Silvia that this is the young man who would have come earlier with him, but that his eyes were imprisoned by the gaze of his lady Julia. Silvia, with rather charming cynicism, suggests that perhaps the lady has set him free. Valentine says that he is quite sure this is not the case, but Silvia laughs and says that then Proteus must be blind. With an exchange of barbs between Valentine and Thurio this portion of the scene ends, as Silvia tries to keep them at peace.

Proteus then enters and is greeted by both Valentine and Silvia, and after the departure of Silvia and Thurio the two friends are left alone. After an exchange of inquiries Valentine asks after the health of Proteus's lady Julia, and when Proteus seems reluctant to answer, reminding Valentine of how tedious he had previously found love discourses, Valentine announces that he is now a reformed character. He speaks in a highly rhetorical manner of the way that he has fallen in love, just as deeply as his friend, so that he, too, is now a servant of the mighty lord of love. Proteus then asks whether Silvia is the object of Valentine's affections, and on being told that such is the case he speaks of her in a very measured manner. It is now his turn to play the man of common sense and look at his friend's sickness in the same way that Valentine had looked after him. But it is no good; the more Proteus rephrases Valentine's highflown speeches the more Valentine praises his lady and finally he tells Proteus everything about his love affair. He identifies Sir Thurio as the rival lover who, because of his wealth, is the preferred candidate of the Duke.

Valentine is then carried away by his love for Silvia and in an excess of friendship, and probably also from a desire to impress Proteus, he tells his friend of their plans for elopement. He has with him a rope ladder, and that very night he plans to enter the garden of the Duke to let Silvia climb down from her window. Valentine asks the help of Proteus, who refuses, saying that he has other work to do. Left alone, Proteus reveals that he has fallen in love at first sight with Silvia. His love for Julia is completely forgotten in the new passion he feels for his friend's lady. Proteus, however, is not totally blind to the nature and consequences of his act, and in a soliloquy he discusses the nature of his love, and also the central conflict of the play, that of love and friendship. Silvia is fair, but so also is Julia, though now her image is melted like a wax effigy in a fire. Perhaps his friendship with Valentine has cooled, but that is because of the superior claim of his love for Silvia, which has driven all reason from his behavior. As yet he has but beheld her external attributes, but they are sufficient to enslave him. He concludes his speech with a resolution to try to check his errant passion, but if he is unsuccessful he will work as hard as possible to obtain possession of Silvia.

Act II: Scenes 5-6

In the first of these scenes Launce and Speed meet each other on a Milan street. Speed immediately inquires after the progress of Proteus's affair with Julia, but the two become involved in an exercise in mutual lack of communication resulting from deliberate mistaking of the word and attempts as overtopping each other in wit. Speed in return tells Launce that his master, Valentine, has become "a notable lover," a comment which calls forth more wit from Launce. The two finally leave together for the alehouse.

The next scene takes place in a room inside the Duke's palace. Proteus enters and continues the soliloquy he left unfinished at the end of Scene 4. He is still wrestling with his love-problem and assesses the situation in a highly rhetorical speech. First he states the difficulties: shall he leave Julia and be forsworn; or shall he love Silvia and be forsworn; ergo, he will be much forsworn to wrong his friend. But then he speaks of the all-pervading power of love which has driven him to this pass so that he worships the sun (Silvia), instead of a twinkling star (Julia). Gradually he debates with himself until he reaches the position of holding that the claims of self are higher than any other; since love is most precious, then self-love is most important. He will forget all about Julia and will hold Valentine as an enemy, because, according to his rationalizing, he must recognize his loyalty to himself above that of friendship. Therefore he announces his intention of revealing Valentine's plan to the Duke who will, of course, banish the young man, leaving Proteus with no opposition other than Thurio, whom he can easily overcome.

Act II: Scene 7

This scene takes place in a room of Julia's house in Verona. Julia asks Lucetta for help in planning a journey to Proteus, while at the same time safeguarding her honor. Lucetta rather shrewdly suggests that Julia wait until Proteus returns, but her mistress is so lovesick that she cannot wait that long. She speaks as one who is starving for lack of food and says that it would be as easy to "kindle fire with snow" as to "seek to quench the fire of Love with words." Lucetta says that she seeks only to confine the flames of love within reason. Julia says that this is impossible, and finally suggests that she undertake the journey, but dressed in male clothing, the better to avoid encounters with "lascivious men." Lucetta makes considerable fun at the expense of the modest Julia when she decides to travel in page's dress, and though Julia has momentary qualms that her action might be construed as dishonorable, she nevertheless decides to go.

Julia, her mind made up, then speaks with love and complete trust of Proteus's undoubted sincerity and constancy, claiming that everything about the young man is virtuous and good. Lucetta cynically expresses the hope that Julia will not be disillusioned when she arrives. Julia, however, refuses to admit such a possibility and asks Lucetta's help, saying that she will leave all her goods, lands, and reputation in the keeping of her maid.

Act III: Scene 1

This act opens in an anteroom in the Duke's palace in Milan. The Duke, Thurio, and Proteus enter, and Proteus, after stating his duty to the Duke with protestations of virtue, reveals the elopement plans of Valentine and Silvia. In so doing Proteus tells the Duke of the struggle it has been for him to violate the duties of friendship, but he says that loyalty to his lord must come first. The Duke is most impressed with the apparently disinterested honesty of the young man and makes specific inquiries. Proteus then reveals all the details of the plot, including the proposed use of the rope ladder which Valentine has gone to fetch, and he suggests that the Duke intercept him on his return.

Valentine then enters and the Duke waylays him, asking where he is going so fast. Valentine makes some transparent excuse about having to send off some letters, but the Duke insists that he remain to discuss the marriage of Silvia with Thurio. The discomfited lover doesn't quite know what to say, and therefore he praises the wealth and virtue of Thurio, something he would certainly not have done under other circumstances, and then speaks of the worth of Silvia. To his surprise the Duke launches into a diatribe against her, speaking of her as "Proud, disobedient, stubborn, lacking duty." Consequently the Duke claims that he is about to take a wife for himself and disinherit Silvia, turning her away in revenge for her wildness. Valentine asks where he fits into the plan and the Duke tells him that he already has his own candidate for a new wife picked out, but since he has had no occasion to woo for a long time he would like some advice concerning new fashions. Rather nonplussed, Valentine begins to make suggestions, beginning with exchanging gifts, but the Duke claims that he has already found that approach unsuccessful. Valentine suggests sending the lady another gift. Then gradually the Duke begins to put the case so that it closely resembles that of Silvia and Valentine. As a result the young man is slowly led to reveal his plans to abduct Silvia and the Duke discovers the rope ladder that Valentine is carrying under his cloak, and, in addition, a love letter addressed to Silvia. The Duke promptly flies into a rage and banishes Valentine.

Left alone Valentine laments his banishment. He thinks of suicide, because he would prefer death to being parted from Silvia.

At this moment Proteus and Launce enter to greet the distracted Valentine. They inquire whether the news of his banishment is true, and Proteus hypocritically expresses his sorrow at the news. Valentine again grieves over his sentence and Proteus joins him in lamenting. He tells Valentine of Silvia's great sorrow at the news, how she wept and flung herself at her father's feet in supplication.

Proteus and Valentine now trade lamentations, and Proteus offers to see his friend to the city gate, counseling him to hope for better things. Perhaps Silvia will write to him. But Valentine cannot be consoled, and after sending Launce to fetch Speed, he departs with the faithless Proteus.

Left alone, Launce indicates that he considers his master Proteus a knave, and then he reveals that he himself is in love. However, his lady is no romantic, fragile person, but a tough, strong milkmaid, but not a maid, because she seems to have had a child. And as for her qualities, she has more of them than a water-spaniel, including the ability to fetch and carry, and also to milk.

Speed then appears and the two servants commence a wit-combat, Launce following "the old vice still: mistake the word." Launce then admits that he is in love, and Speed commences to interrogate him in a manner which parodies the earlier scenes in which both Proteus and Valentine have praised the virtues of their ladies. Launce's milkmaid is a most unconventional lady, rather like the girl described in Shakespeare's Sonnet 130:

> My mistress' eyes are nothing like the sun;
> Coral is far more red than her lips' red;
> If snow be white, why then her breasts are dun;
> If hairs be wires, black wires grow on her head.
> I have seen roses, damasked, red and white,
> But no such roses see I in her cheeks;
> And in some perfumes is there more delight
> Than in the breath that from my mistress reeks.
> I love to hear her speak; yet well I know

That music hath a far more pleasing sound:
I grant I never saw a goddess go;
My mistress, when she walks, treads on the ground.
    And yet, by heaven, I think my love as rare
    As any she belied with false compare.

Here the situation of the servants makes one take the earlier scenes between Proteus and Valentine less seriously. Finally, Launce remembers to deliver the message from Valentine to Speed.

Act III: Scene 2

This scene takes place shortly afterwards in a room of the Duke's palace. The Duke and Thurio enter, discussing Thurio's suit to Silvia. Apparently the young lady has totally despised him since the banishment of Valentine. The Duke, however, promises that Silvia will eventually come around, and when Proteus enters he proceeds to discuss the matter with him. Proteus claims that Silvia's grief will lessen with time, but the Duke says that Thurio disagrees, and, further, notes that Silvia opposes the will of her father. Proteus then suggests very disloyally that the Duke find a means to slander Valentine "With falsehood, cowardice, and poor descent," allegedly the three things that women most detest. Then Proteus compounds the felony by making the suggestion that these charges would be more believable if they were spoken by a friend. The Duke jumps at this suggestion and tells Proteus to do just that. Proteus then seems suitably reluctant to damage the reputation of a friend, but the Duke quibbles, saying that where Proteus's good word cannot advance his friend, then his ill words cannot in any way operate to his disadvantage. In reply Proteus says that indeed Silvia would thereby lose affection for Valentine, but it does not necessarily mean that she should then love Thurio. The disliked suitor then says that Proteus must see to it that her affection is turned to himself rather than to anyone else. The Duke tells Proteus that they are both depending on him to change Silvia's mind from its current melancholy cast, and further, they both trust him since he is already known to be in love with another lady. Proteus agrees to make an attempt to do as they desire. But then he suggests that Thurio not show himself to be backward; he must write sonnets to

Silvia, saying that "upon the altar of her beauty" he sacrifices his tears, sighs, and heart. In addition, he must endeavor to woo her with music, and Proteus suggests that he visit Silvia's chamber by night with musicians to serenade her. The Duke and Thurio think these to be excellent ideas, and the Duke remarks that obviously Proteus has been in love to be able to think up such stratagems.

Act IV: Scene 1

The exact location of this scene is disputed, but it seems to be in a forest situated either near Milan, or on the borders of Mantua. Outlaws enter and espy strangers, who turn out to be Valentine and Speed. The Outlaws apprehend them and threaten them with harm, but Valentine cries out that he has nothing of value; he is simply a man "cross'd with adversity." The Outlaws then interrogate him and Valentine says that he has been in Milan for sixteen months, but has just been banished for killing a man, an act for which he now feels repentance, but nevertheless, his opponent was killed in a fair fight. The Outlaws are suitably impressed.

Then one of the Outlaws asks whether Valentine understands foreign languages, and when the fugitive says that he does he meets with an unexpected response. The Outlaws are overjoyed and one suggests that he would make an excellent king for them. The Outlaws then try to show that are really rather decent men who were banished for some rather minor crimes: an attempt to abduct a lady, a murder committed in a fit of anger, for instance. Again they ask Valentine to be their king, claiming that they are really not outlaws, but rather a pack of wronged gentlemen.

The Outlaws promise to love Valentine as their commander and king, and they readily accept his stipulation that they "do no outrages/ On . . . women or poor passengers."

Act IV: Scene 2

This scene takes place in Milan, just under Silvia's window.

Proteus enters to tell the progress of his plots against both

Valentine and Thurio. He has been false to both, and even though he has managed to gain access to Silvia he has not been able to change her love and remove it from Valentine. "Silvia is too fair, too true, too holy." No gifts seem able to corrupt her love for Valentine and she continually blames Proteus with falsehood to Valentine and Julia in thinking of wooing for himself. The more she spurns Proteus, however, the more the young man falls in love with her. Sir Thurio's arrival with a troupe of musicians cuts short the meditations of Proteus. The foolish wooer intends to have music beneath the window of his love, Silvia.

At a distance off, the host of the inn appears with Julia, who is disguised as a page. The Host has noticed the young page's melancholy and has suggested that they go to where they will hear music. As they watch, Thurio's consort strikes up a song, the famous "Who is Silvia," one of Shakespeare's best known love songs. Julia looks aghast at the men who have employed the musicians and she draws the obvious conclusion about Proteus. She is even more cast down than before by this evidence of her lover's infidelity. She asks the Host whether Proteus often resorts to the Lady Silvia, and when told that Launce, Proteus's servant, has given abundant testimony of his master's love, she is convinced. The Host claims that Launce has been sent to fetch his dog as a gift for the lady.

After the departure of Thurio all Julia's suspicions are realized, as Proteus woos Silvia with great ardor. Silvia, however, is totally faithful and virtuous. She attacks Proteus for his perjury and disloyalty to Julia, and then to the disguised lady's horror she hears Proteus declare that his love is dead, in order to make Silvia think the better of him. However, Silvia then attacks Proteus for his disloyalty to Valentine, declaring that she is betrothed to him alone. Proteus promptly says that he has heard that Valentine is dead, to which Silvia replies that then her love is buried in his grave. Proteus begs to be allowed to recall that love, but Silvia counters by telling him to recall his lady's love from the grave. As Julia notes, Proteus does not seem to hear this suggestion, and instead begs for Silvia's picture. This favor Silvia grants because it is fitting that a man of his falsehood should worship strange shapes and shadows which are in themselves nothing.

After Proteus's departure Julia awakens the Host and asks where Proteus lodges. By coincidence it is the inn in which Julia is staying. Julia leaves sadly.

Act IV: Scene 3

This scene also takes place beneath Silvia's window, a short time later. Silvia has enlisted the help of Sir Eglamour and asks his help in fleeing from Milan in order to avoid marriage with Sir Thurio, her detested suitor. Sir Eglamour has loved a lady who unfortunately died. He is, however, a true servant of love and swore perpetual chastity upon his lady's grave. He is now a votary of love and spends his life aiding other lovers to the joys which he has forsworn for himself. Silvia asks him to conduct her to Mantua where she expects that Valentine will await her. She begs Eglamour to forget that she is asking aid against her father, but instead to remember that she is escaping from an unwanted suitor. Sir Eglamour agrees, and Silvia makes arrangements to meet him at Friar Patrick's cell in the evening.

Act IV: Scene 4

Like the two preceding scenes, this one also takes place under Silvia's window. It begins with Launce and his dog, the owner blaming the animal for his bad manners in company. He has misbehaved himself in the dining chamber, and rather than allow the dog to be whipped, Launce has himself taken the blame for his offence. But then when given as a gift to Silvia, the wretched mongrel, Crab, has behaved even more shockingly by urinating on the lady's dress.

At that moment Proteus and Julia enter and we find out that Julia has entered Proteus's service as a page named Sebastian. After some discussion the relevance of Launce becomes clear. He has been sent to give a gift of a dog to Silvia, but because the animal bought by Proteus was stolen from him he has given his own mongrel to the lady. This action may be taken both as an example of supreme loyalty and as an expression of fear. Proteus, needless to say, flies into a rage, considering that the gift of Crab was in effect an insult to Silvia.

Proteus then turns to Sebastian/Julia and says that he wishes the page to go to Silvia and present her with a ring, saying that the lady who gave it to Proteus loved him well. Julia, recognizing the ring as the one she had given her lover, mildly remonstrates that Proteus could not have loved the lady well, and asks whether she is dead. Proteus says that the lady lives, to which Julia cries "Alas," and in answer to Proteus's question, says that she pities this lady who has remained faithful while Proteus dotes on Silvia, who does not reciprocate his love. Proteus, who seems a trifle uncomfortable, nevertheless tells the page to give the ring to Silvia, as she has been commanded. Left alone, Julia gives vent to her sorrow; she still loves the undeserving Proteus despite the way he is treating her. Now she must woo Silvia for Proteus, while she herself is almost sick for love of him.

Silvia keeps her part of the bargain, giving Julia the portrait she has promised Proteus. She does not want to listen to Julia's protestations of love sent from Proteus, and she tears up his letter. When she is offered the ring she is horrified. She recalls that it was given Proteus by Julia and therefore she refuses it, saying that she would not wish to do that lady any wrong and charging the page to take this message to her master. Julia says that the lady thanks Silvia for her consideration, and the surprised Silvia asks whether the page knows her. Julia replies that indeed she knows her extremely well, and so Silvia inquires after the lady's state of mind in probably thinking that Proteus has utterly forsaken her. Julia replies that the lady, who used to be as fair as Silvia, is now disfigured with grief and so careless of her appearance that she is sunburned.

Silvia then asks the page to describe Julia, something the lady manages very well indeed, showing up her own personal advantages. Sadly, Silvia leaves, and Julia gazes avidly on the portrait of her rival, comparing herself with the image and concluding that she herself is more lovely, but if something should need alteration, such as hair color, she would cover her "perfect yellow" hair with an auburn wig. Then, to her sorrow, Julia realizes that this picture will be kissed, wept over and adored; still, she will take it to Proteus, partly because of Silvia's sympathy for the unknown victim of Proteus's infidelity.

Act V: Scenes 1-2

The first scene takes place outside an abbey in Milan that

same evening. In accordance with the earlier arrangements, Eglamour is joined by Silvia and the two flee to the wood "not three leagues off." Silvia is afraid that her flight might have been observed.

The second scene takes place in the Duke's palace in Milan. Thurio asks Proteus, who is accompanied by the disguised Julia, how his suit to Silvia is prospering. Proteus claims that the lady is better disposed to Thurio, but that she takes exception to his physical attributes. Thurio questions Proteus closely, and to all his queries the *sotto voce* comments of Julia act as comic counterpoint so that the three-way conversation is reduced by Julia's remarks to its comic essentials. In the midst of the discussion the Duke enters to ask whether they have seen Eglamour and Silvia. On receiving negative replies the Duke jumps to the correct conclusion, that Silvia has fled to Valentine in the company of Eglamour. A friar has seen them in the forest, and she did not appear at Friar Patrick's cell at the time appointed for her confession. The Duke raises a hue and cry and tells the gentlemen to take horse and ride with him to Mantua to apprehend the runaways. Thurio says that he will go to be revenged on Eglamour, rather than for "love of reckless Silvia." Proteus says that he will follow for Silvia's love, and Julia announces that she will go in order to cross that love which Proteus has for Silvia.

Act V: Scenes 3-4

The first extremely short scene takes place in the forest where the Outlaws have captured Silvia. Apparently Eglamour has managed to escape and we hear no more of him. The Outlaws plan to take Silvia to their leader, who is of course Valentine, though Silvia is unaware of the fact.

The second of these scenes takes place in another part of the forest where Valentine expresses his joy in the life of the woods, close to nature and far removed from crowded cities. Here Valentine can luxuriate in love-melancholy and listen to the nightingale's complaint. He wishes sadly that Silvia could be there with him when suddenly he hears the noise of his outlaw band. Immediately Valentine springs to attention. The Outlaws love him well, but he has to keep an eye on them so that they will not perpetrate any outrages on travelers through the forest.

Proteus, Silvia, and the disguised Julia now enter. Obviously Proteus has rescued Silvia from the clutches of the Outlaws, and now in return Proteus begs her for "but one fair look." Valentine, who has concealed himself, is amazed at what he hears and stays hidden in order to see what will develop. Silvia weeps over her unhappy state and says that Proteus's approach has simply made matters worse. She would rather have been devoured by a lion than have "false Proteus" pursue her. She expresses her detestation of "false, perjured Proteus" and tells him to be gone. Proteus again begs for one gentle look, and in reply Silvia bids him remember Julia whom he has forgotten, telling him that he is now totally disloyal and has broken his vows of friendship as well. Now completely insane with lustful desire, Proteus says, "In love/ Who respects friend." Silvia counters by claiming that all men except Proteus do so. Angered, Proteus says he will woo her like a soldier, by force, and he attempts to rape her. This is too much for Valentine. He springs from his hiding place and frustrates the evil designs of Proteus, castigating him for his violation of the rights and duties of friendship. With regret he says that he can never again trust Proteus because his disloyalty is the greatest blow he can bear. "'Mongst all foes that a friend should be the worst." Almost as a reflex action, Proteus expresses his repentance. He is brought to his senses and asks forgiveness.

At that moment Valentine is quite overcome by Proteus's sudden change of heart and forgives him in an astonishing line: "All that was mine in Silvia I give thee." Quite understandably, Julia swoons.

As the disguised Julia awakens, she looks at Valentine and confesses that she has neglected to give a ring to Silvia as Proteus has requested. This is not strictly the truth, because when Proteus looks at the ring he sees that it is the one that he himself had given to Julia. After some general quibbling about how "Sebastian" came into possession of the ring, the page declares that Julia herself has brought it with her. Julia then reveals her identity and begs to be absolved from blame and immodesty because she has come to Proteus in the guise of love. It is, she says, less wicked for women to change their shapes than for men to change their minds.

Proteus promptly looks at Julia with new eyes and quite openly (and rather unflatteringly) starts to wonder what he ever saw in Silvia which Julia does not possess in greater abundance. The two friends are now reconciled and embrace. By his actions toward Julia, Proteus has of course rejected Valentine's offer of Silvia.

The Duke and Thurio, having been captured by the Outlaws, are now brought in, and the Duke immediately calls for Valentine to return Silvia to him so that he can marry her to Thurio. Valentine, however, threatens Thurio with death and the cowardly suitor promptly abandons all claims to Silvia, saying that he would be foolish to endanger his body for a girl who doesn't love him. In other words, Thurio is a coward who will not risk his skin for love. The Duke is enraged at this revelation and promptly praises Valentine as "a gentleman and well derived," while calling Thurio "degenerate and base."

Now the Duke is extremely willing that Valentine take Silvia as his wife because the young man has proved himself more than worthy, and, in addition, the Duke's own eyes have been opened to his false judgment of Thurio. Valentine has now been completely forgiven and nothing is too good for the future son-in-law of the Duke.

Valentine is quick to take advantage of the situation, and he immediately asks the Duke to show clemency towards the Outlaws whom he has led, suggesting that they have now repented of any crimes that they may have committed in the past. Furthermore, after such repentance and long exile they are more than eligible for a second chance. As Valentine puts it, they are "fit for great employment, worthy lord." The Duke is quick to accede to this request and he freely gives his pardon both to them and to Valentine as their leader, telling him to dispose of them according to their worth.

As yet the Duke does not know the identity of Julia, and Valentine tantalizingly offers to tell him the whole story on the way back to Milan. The play ends with Valentine, the erstwhile scoffer at love, in command of the situation, telling Proteus that as a penance he must hear the tale of his loves rehearsed. Then there is the final promise of a double marriage.

THE
HISTORIES

Henry IV Part I

KING HENRY IV.
HENRY, PRINCE OF WALES
PRINCE JOHN OF LANCASTER } *sons to the King.*
EARL OF WESTMORELAND.
SIR WALTER BLUNT.
THOMAS PERCY, EARL OF WORCESTER.
HENRY PERCY, EARL OF NORTHUMBERLAND.
HENRY PERCY, *surnamed* HOTSPUR, *his son.*
EDMUND MORTIMER, *Earl of March.*
RICHARD SCROOP, ARCHIBISHOP OF YORK.
ARCHIBALD, EARL OF DOUGLAS.
OWEN GLENDOWER.
SIR RICHARD VERNON.
SIR JOHN FALSTAFF.
SIR MICHAEL, *of the household of the Archbishop of York.*
EDWARD POINS.
GADSHILL.
PETO.
BARDOLPH.

LADY PERCY, *wife to Hotspur, and sister to Mortimer.*
LADY MORTIMER, *daughter to Glendower, and wife to Mortimer.*
MISTRESS QUICKLY, *hostess of a tavern in Eastcheap.*

LORDS, OFFICERS, SHERIFF, VINTNER, CHAMBERLAIN, OSTLER, DRAWERS, *two* CARRIERS,
TRAVELERS, *and* ATTENDANTS.

Henry IV Part I

Act I: Scene 1

The scene opens at the royal palace in London where King Henry has assembled his courtiers, Prince John of Lancaster (his younger son), the Earl of Westmoreland, Sir Walter Blunt, and others. The purpose of the meeting is to hear Westmoreland's report on a session of the King's council, called to discuss his projected trip to the Holy Land. In measured and formal tones, Henry describes the present moment as a brief period of respite from the ravages of the civil war which has lately been raging. He calls it "the intestine shock, and furious close of civil butchery."

Henry optimistically predicts a period of calm when former enemies shall become allies, giving him the opportunity of visiting the sepulchre of Christ, of organizing a crusade, in fact, to chase the infidels from the holy places.

The King asks Westmoreland for his report, and is immediately told that plans for the voyage have been postponed because word had been received that Edmund Mortimer, Earl of March, has been captured by the Welshman Owen Glendower and a thousand of his men have been butchered. What is more, the Welshwomen had performed horrible mutilations upon the dead bodies. Added to this was a report from the north country that young Henry Percy had engaged Archibald, Earl of Douglas, in combat—as yet, undecided. The King, however, has a later report from Sir Walter Blunt that Douglas has been vanquished, and several of his Scots compatriots taken prisoner by Percy. "And is not this an *honorable* spoil? A gallant prize?" asks Henry. To which Westmoreland thoughtlessly replies: "In faith it is a conquest for a prince to boast of."

The King then angrily declares that "Hotspur" (the surname of young Percy) has refused to relinquish any prisoners to the crown save Mordake, Earl of Fife. Westmoreland attributes this to the prompting of the Earl of Worcester Thomas Percy (Hotspur's uncle). Henry asserts that he has summoned Hotspur, that he has put off the Jerusalem pilgrimage, and that he will hold court at Windsor on the coming Wednesday, since there is much to be said and done.

Act I: Scene 2

The scene is now the Prince of Wales' London apartment. Hal and Sir John Falstaff enter, conversing in prose.

Falstaff asks the time of day, and is treated to an outburst of good-humored abuse by the Prince, who strikes the keynote of Falstaff's character by emphsizing his weakness for sack (wine), capons, and wenches—in short, the pleasures of the flesh. He tells Sir John that he ought to have no interest in the time of day, unless "hours were cups of sack" and "the blessed sun himself a fair hot wench in flame-colored taffeta." Falstaff responds on a note of false rhetoric, saying, "we that take purses go by the moon and the seven stars, and not by Phoebus [the sun], he, that wand'ring knight so fair." He calls the Prince "sweet wag" (a term of easy familiarity) and jests with Hal in a way that shows the intimacy of their friendship.

They continue their mock battle of wit, Falstaff asking the Prince, when he becomes king, to "let not us that are squires of the night's body [his band of cutpurses—with a pun on "knight"] be called thieves of the day's beauty [or "booty"]." Beneath the joking one can discern the Prince's clear understanding of their lawless life, and his realization that society will ultimately judge and punish. He appears to have a genial tolerance of Falstaff's errant ways and a fascinated attraction to the way of life he represents. But Hal never really countenances lawlessness. When Falstaff asks, "But I prithee, sweet wag, shall there be gallows standing in England when thou art king? and resolution [*his* kind of courage] thus fubbed as it is with the rusty curb of old father antic the law? Do not thou, when thou art king, hang a thief," the Prince quickly promises *him* the hanging of thieves. Falstaff immediately takes this to mean a judgeship, but Hal tells him he is judging wrong already—he is to be the hangman.

Being a hangman, Falstaff replies, suits his temperament very well, for he is as melancholy as a gib cat (an altered tomcat), a baited bear, or (the Prince adds) an old lion or a lover's lute, a hare, or Moor Ditch itself (an open sewer in London). More than a mere contest in witty similes, there is here an undercurrent of reference to Falstaff as a man grown old in lechery. He draws back from the combat, saying that the Prince uses the "most unsavory similes," and asks Hal to "trouble [him] no more with vanity." The very word "vanity," the moralist's term for all the transient pleasures of the world, seems to provoke a kind of mock repentance in

Falstaff; he mentions an "old lord" who recently chided him about the Prince, and they both jest (playing on biblical terminology) about Wisdom crying out in the streets and no man regarding it. With whimsical mockery, the fat knight alleges that the Prince has led *him* astray and climaxes this absurd accusation by expostulating: "I'll be damned for never a king's son in Christendom." Hal, refusing to be taken in by Falstaff's pretense of outraged morality, asks where they will take a purse (that is, commit thievery on the high road) on the morrow. Falstaff quickly rises to the bait and agrees to the deed wherever the Prince desires it. With some sarcasm, the Prince comments on Falstaff's "good amendment of life; from praying to purse-taking." With feigned surprise that he should be accused of sinful intentions, Falstaff offers his defense: "Why, Hal, 'tis my vocation, Hal. 'Tis no sin for a man to labor in his vocation."

At this point, Ned Poins, another cutpurse, enters. Falstaff welcomes him, knowing that he will have information about a proposed robbery, and praises him to the Prince as "the most omnipotent villain that ever cried 'Stand!' [in modern parlance, "Don't make a move!"] to a true man. Poins now takes up the good-natured jesting at Falstaff's expense, referring to him as "Monsieur Remorse" (for his pretended melancholy and moral reform) and as "Sir John Sack and Sugar" (for his appetites), and accuses him of selling his soul to the devil on Good Friday for a cup of wine and a cold capon's leg. The Prince then comments that the devil will have his due, for Sir John "was never yet a breaker of proverbs."

Poins reveals the plot. On the next morning at four o'clock a number of rich pilgrims will be riding to Canterbury, and tradesmen will be riding to London, past Gad's Hill (apparently their favorite place for holdups—one of the cutpurses is named "Gadshill", in fact). Poins has masks for all of them and has arranged for their supper in Eastcheap (a district in London). If they will come along, their purses will be stuffed with "crowns," if not, they may stay at home and "hang them all." Falstaff asks the Prince if he will take part in the robbery. He refuses. Sir John abuses him by saying that he has "neither honesty, manhood, nor good fellowship" in him, and that he "cam'st not of the blood *royal*" if he dares not "stand for ten shillings."

Falstaff humorously threatens to retaliate by becoming a traitor when Hal is king, but the Prince says that he does not care. Poins asks Falstaff to leave him alone with the Prince, and the knight exits. Poins then takes Hal into his confidence, revealing that he needs his participation in a jest that he cannot manage alone. They will let Falstaff, Gadshill, Bardolph, and Peto (the last two of the band of thieves) rob the travelers and, once they have the booty, set upon them in disguise and rob them in turn. They will first conceal their horses and then don buckram suits to disguise their easily recognizable clothes. The Prince expresses fear that he and Poins may not be able to overpower the other four, to which Poins replies: "Well, for two of them, I know them to be as true-bred cowards as ever turned back; and for the third, if he fight longer than he sees reason, I'll forswear arms."

The humor of the jest, Poins goes on, will be the "incomprehensible lies" that the fat knight will tell them when they later meet at supper—how many set upon them, how valiantly he fought, and what blows he endured. In the rebuking of Sir John for his lies will be the point of the whole affair. The Prince agrees to take part. Poins leaves, and Prince Hal has the stage to himself for what has become one of the most famous of Shakespearean soliloquies.

The Prince avers that he knows his companions for what they are and will merely tolerate them for a time, just as the sun allows itself to be obscured by clouds so that its beauty will be more wondered at when it is again visible. Holidays are appreciated because they come seldom, and only "rare accidents" are pleasing. So he, when he throws off his wanton ways, something he has never given promise of doing, will shine "like bright metal on a sullen ground," and his reformation will consequently be the more admired for being unexpected.

Act I: Scene 3

The scene is London, the King's palace. The King enters with Sir Walter Blunt and other courtiers, as do the elder Percy (the Earl of Northumberland), his son Henry Percy (Hotspur), and his brother Thomas Percy (Earl of Worcester). The King speaks—in a formal, cold, even overbearing manner—alleging that his blood has been too temperate (that is, his anger too slow to rise) and his patience too long-suffering, considering the indignities the Percies have heaped upon him. He promises to be mighty in the future and feared, rather than smooth and soft and lacking respect as in the past. Worcester demurs mildly, asserting that their house, which has helped Henry to the throne, little deserves to have that very power used against it so ruthlessly.

The King angrily dismisses Worcester, calling his manner bold and peremptory, and informs him that he will send for him when he needs his counsel.

The King then turns to the Earl of Northumberland, who in turn tries to mitigate Henry's wrath by explaining that young Harry's (Hotspur's) denial of the King's demand for the prisoners was not couched in the strong terms which have apparently been reported to him. Either envy or misunderstanding is at the root of the matter, he affirms.

Hotspur then defends himself in a long, impressive, and vivid account of the circumstances under which the King's demand was presented to him. It was on the battlefield, and he was "breathless and faint, leaning on his sword." A lord, the King's messenger, impeccably dressed, shaven and scented, and carrying a dainty perfume box, came smiling and talking even while the dead bodies were being carried from the field. He called them "unmannerly" to bring a "slovenly unhandsome corse" between him and the wind. With many "holiday and lady terms" he demanded the prisoners. Hotspur smarting from his wounds, was infuriated at this "popinjay" and made some negligent answer. He was maddened by this "waiting gentlewoman" with his talk about the virtues of spermaceti for internal injuries, and the "great pity" it was that "this villainous saltpetre [for gunpowder] should be digged out of the harmless earth." Except for these "vile guns" he would have been a soldier himself. Hotspur, finally, implores the King not to let the report of such a namby-pamby be the occasion of their estrangement.

Even Sir Walter Blunt, of the King's party, beseeches Henry to let sleeping dogs lie if young Percy is willing to make amends at this time. But the King reveals that Hotspur still refuses him the prisoners, except on condition that he ransom Hotspur's brother-in-law Edmund Mortimer, Earl of March, who the King says has "willfully betrayed the lives of those that he did lead to fight against that great magician, damned Glendower."

Henry, in any case, refuses to ransom a man he believes to be a traitor and in unequivocal terms gives his opinion of the Earl of March: "I shall never hold that man my friend / Whose tongue shall ask me for one penny cost / To ransom home revolted Mortimer."

Hotspur picks up the King's term, "revolted Mortimer," and in an impassioned outburst, attempts to defend Mortimer's actions before the King. Mortimer, he declares, never gave less than full loyal support to the King, except through the accidents of war. It takes only one tongue to describe the many "mouthed wounds" which he received on the bank of the Severn while he spent the greater part of an hour in single combat with the great Glendower.

Dissimulation (if that is what the King imputes to Mortimer, Hotspur implies) never worked with such deadly wounds, nor could even the noble Mortimer receive as many wounds as he did and take them all willingly.

Without hesitation, Henry accuses him of lying. Mortimer, he declares, would as soon have encountered the devil himself as Owen Glendower. Henceforth, Percy is not to mention Mortimer's name.

Hotspur, without delay, is to send his prisoners to the King, or he will hear about it in a form that will not make him happy, Henry asserts. Turning to Northumberland, he says bluntly: "We license your departure with your son. Send us your prisoner, or you will hear of it." The King then leaves with Blunt and his entourage.

To his father, Hotspur insists that he will not send the prisoners if the devil himself should come for them; he is about to follow Henry to tell him so when the elder Percy restrains him. "Are you drunk with choler [anger]?" he asks. At this point, the Earl of Worcester reenters. Hotspur continues to rant, promising to empty his veins and shed his blood drop by drop if he does not raise the "downtrod Mortimer" as high up as the "ingrate and cankered Bolingbroke."

Northumberland greets Worcester with the explanation that the King has made young Hotspur mad. Young Percy once more explains that the King wishes to have all his prisoners and adds that the mere mention of a ransom for Mortimer caused the King's face to turn pale, as "on my face he turned an eye of death, trembling even at the name of Mortimer."

Worcester remarks that he does not blame Henry, for had King Richard not proclaimed Mortimer the next in line to the throne? Northumberland agrees, adding that he heard the very proclamation made by Richard prior to his setting forth on his expedition to Ireland (following which he was deposed and murdered).

Worcester next laments the fact that their name, rather than Bolingbroke's has been scandalized throughout the world for the murder of Richard. Hotspur (who has apparently discovered for the first time the reason for Henry's fear of Mortimer begins to dwell on the subject. He asks his father if he and Worcester, who "set the crown upon the head of this forgetful man," must suffer the shame of "murtherous subornation" (that is, the reputation of having induced Henry to murder Richard). Will they be cursed as the agents, or worse, the "base second means, the cords, the ladder or the hangman rather?" Then, with a faint suggestion of irony, he asks pardon for stooping to such low themes to evaluate their position.

Hotspur continues his rhetorical questioning and asks if future times will remember them only as men of nobility and power who misused their offices to "put down Richard, that sweet lovely rose, and plant this thorn, this canker, Bolingbroke?" And will you be more shamed than this even, for having been discarded by him when you are no longer of use to him? There is still time to redeem yourselves—to regain honor and reputation in the world. Revenge yourselves upon this proud King, who ponders only the means of your deaths.

Worcester (who, as we soon learn, has been plotting against Henry for some time) tries to calm Hotspur by broaching a "matter deep and dangerous" and "full of peril," but the young man's imagination races far ahead, and he exclaims: "Send danger from the east unto the west, so honor cross it from the north to south, and let them grapple. O, the blood more stirs to rouse a lion than to start a hare." Hotspur then gives vent to a sentiment that has long been regarded by readers of the play as the very key to his character:

> "By heaven, methinks it were an easy leap
> To pluck bright honor from the pale-faced moon,
> Or dive into the bottom of the deep,
> Where fathom-line could never touch the ground,
> And pluck up drowned honor by the locks..."

Completely misunderstanding the import of Worcester's words, he ends with a sarcastic cry of "out upon this half-faced fellowship." Worcester continues to try to mollify the hot-tempered youth, and brings up the subject of the Scottish prisoners, whereupon young Percy interrupts once more, exclaiming, "I'll keep them all! By God, he shall not have a Scot of them." Worcester presses on patiently, attempting to explain his plan for the disposal of the prisoners while Hotspur's imagination takes another tack as he imagines himself training a little starling to shout "Mortimer" in the King's ear to keep his ire burning. He solemnly denounces all studies except the ways and means of harassing Bolingbroke. As for the "sword-and-buckler Prince of Wales," he would have him poisoned except that he believes his father has no love for him and would be glad if he met with an accident.

Worcester sees that he can get nowhere with Hotspur and makes as if to leave. The elder Percy chastises the youth as an "impatient fool," plying his tongue like a woman, but Hotspur continues. Bolingbroke's presence is like a whip, a scourge, a nettle, the sting of ants. He is a "vile politician," a "king of smiles"; on a former occasion, this "fawning greyhound," proffering a "candy deal of courtesy," used such condescending language to him as "gentle Harry Percy" and "kind cousin." "The devil take such cozeners!" he exclaims.

Hotspur's tirade finally at an end, Worcester announces his plan: release all the Scottish prisoners save the son of the Earl of Douglas, who will be a hostage, assuring you of cooperation on the part of the Scots. And you (turning to the elder Percy) shall ingratiate yourself with the Archbishop of York, who "bears hard his brother's death at Bristow."

Worcester goes on to say that the plot is fully hatched and awaits only the opportunity of being put into execution. Hotspur is immediately taken with the idea and predicts its success, saying, "I smell it: Upon my life it will do well." To join the power of Scotland and of York with Mortimer cannot fail. But speed is necessary, Worcester maintains. The King already plans our undoing. But he cautions Hotspur to wait until the time is ripe, which will not be long in coming. We will "bear our fortunes in our own strong arms" (with a pun on "arms").

Hotspur closes the scene in a magnificent epitome of his entire attitude so far:

> "Uncle, adieu. O, let the hours be short
> Till fields and blows and groans applaud our sport."

Act II: Scene 1

The scene is set in an inn-yard in Rochester, where Gadshill has gone to case the prospects for a large haul that night. (We learn in this scene that Gadshill is a "setter" or confederate who lures victims on or sizes them up.) He is in cahoots with the chamberlain (the man who had charge of the bedrooms at the Rochester inn). Two carriers, transporters of goods by horseback, are in the inn-yard at about four in the morning, complaining because their horses are not yet packed for the day's journey. The scene is difficult to understand because of the argot (or slang) that these characters use—slang complicated by more of the sort of riddling and punning observed in Act I. Furthermore, much of what is said appears to have little connection with the main action and themes of the play, though frequently the dramatist uses it to comment ironically or satirically on the poses and actions of characters in the main plot. Of course, the jesting was probably appealing enough for its own sake to the "groundlings" in the contemporary audience for which Shakespeare wrote.

The first carrier enters and bellows a complaint at the ostler (named Tom) for not packing his horse. He then gives the ostler directions for saddling the horse. A second carrier enters at this point, complaining about the horses' feed and remarks that "this house is turned upside down since Robin Ostler died" calling the inn "the most villainous house in all London for fleas."

The two carriers go on with their complaint about being bitten by fleas and attribute the number of fleas to the "chamber-lye" produced by the necessity of answering nature's calls in the chimney, since chamber pots were scarce. They abuse the ostler again for not hurrying, and the first carrier threatens to break his pate, adding, "Come and be hanged! Hast no faith in thee?"

Gadshill now enters and asks one of the carriers for the loan of his lantern; he inquires of them what time they expect to arrive in London. The carriers, apparently seeing skulduggery written all over Gadshill's face, turn him down on both counts. They leave, and the chamberlain enters to inform Gadshill that a franklin (a rich landowner) from Kent, carrying three hundred marks (equal to several thousand dollars today), was up and ready to leave. Gadshill bets his "neck" that they will meet with thieves, but the chamberlain tells him to save it for the hangman. Gadshill says that he will make a "fat pair of gallows" since old Sir John (Falstaff) will hang with him. All puffed up over his familiarity with the Prince, he almost spills the beans about Hal's complicity to the chamberlain by mentioning certain others with him "which for sport sake are content to do the profession some grace," and then, in an amusing catalogue of broken-down thieving types, he adds: "I am joined with no foot land-rakers, no long-staff six-penny strikers, none of these mad mustachio purple-hued maltworms; but with nobility and tranquillity . . ." Gadshill puns on the thieves' habit of "praying to the commonwealth, their saint" (for its "wealth"), and "preying on her" (by making her their "boots" or "spoils"). The chamberlain then matches him in punning by taking "boots" in the sense of "footwear," and asking him if she (the commonwealth) keeps out water. They then jest about the invisibility of thieves (at night) and refer to the popular superstition that fernseed could make a man invisible; finally, with more quibbles about Gadshill's being a "true man" but a "false thief," the scene ends.

Act II: Scene 2

The scene is the highway near Gadshill. The Prince and Poins enter, Poins relating that he has just hidden Falstaff's horse. They retire into the shadows as Falstaff enters, calling for Poins. Hal steps forward, rebuking Sir John for a "fat-kidneyed rascal," and tells him to be quiet. He says that Poins has gone to the top of the hill. Falstaff abuses the "absent" Poins, pretends to be fed up with his antics, and makes a mock threat to kill him, even if he should be hanged for it. He humorously decides that his affection for Poins is the result of a love potion that he has been given: "It could not be else; I have drunk medicines." Crying out on Poins, Hal, Bardolph, and Peto as "stony-hearted villains" for making him walk, he declares "A plague upon it when thieves cannot be true to one another!"

The Prince again steps forward, calls Sir John a "fat-guts," and tells him to lay his ear to the ground to listen for the sound of travelers on the highway. Falstaff refuses, reflecting that there is no lever at hand to raise him up again. He asks Hal to help him find his horse, and the Prince refuses, exclaiming: "Out, ye rogue! Shall I be your ostler" The fat knight then tells the Prince to go and hang himself in his "own heir-apparent garters" and threatens to turn informer and to have ballads composed about the whole lot of them and "sung to filthy tunes." (All of this, of course, with the inimitable flavor of Falstaff's bounding wit.)

Gadshill enters with Bardolph and Peto and cries "Stand!" (a challenge), but Falstaff, unable to take any passing detail with complete seriousness, replies (referring to his size and the absence of his horse): "So I do, against my will." Poins then comes forward, and Gadshill tells them all to don masks, for the victims are approaching. The Prince orders the four to confront the travelers while he and Poins wait below to overtake them if they escape. Peto asks how many of them there are, and Gadshill replies that there are eight or ten. Falstaff wonders aloud who will be robbing whom, and the Prince asks, "What, a coward, Sir John Paunch?" To this, the fat knight (with seeming seriousness) retorts that he is not. The Prince and Poins take their leave.

The travelers now enter and are challenged by the thieves. Falstaff upbraids them with insulting epithets, calling them "whoreson caterpillars," "bacon-fed knaves," "gorbellied knaves," and "bacons," which, considering the glass house in which Falstaff dwells, are most ungracious terms. They rob and bind them and then retire to a quiet place to divide the spoils. At this point, Poins and the Prince, disguised in buckram suits, set upon Falstaff and the others, who all run away—Falstaff, after striking a blow or two. The Prince laughs at the ease with which they took the booty and, in a famous line, says of Falstaff that he "sweats to death and lards the lean earth as he walks along."

Act II: Scene 3

The scene is Warkworth Castle, home of young Hotspur; he enters alone, reading a letter, and making exasperated outbursts concerning the contents. The letter can be reconstructed from his speech, as follows: "But, for mine own part, my lord, I could be well contented to be there, in respect of the love I bear your house . . . The purpose you undertake is dangerous, the friends you have named uncertain, the time itself unsorted [poorly chosen], and your whole plot too light for the counterpoise of so great an opposition."

To this man's objection that the plan is dangerous, Hotspur can only reply (in a famous line), " 'Tis dangerous to take a cold, to sleep, to drink; but I tell you, my lord fool, out of this nettle, danger, we pluck this flower, safety." He calls him a "cowardly hind," a "frosty-spirited rogue," a "pagan rascal" (for lacking *faith* in their plan), and a "dish of skim milk." Hotspur's momentary fear that this lord will now inform the King of their plans is quickly dispelled with the thought, "We are prepared. I will set forward to-night."

Hotspur's wife Kate, enters only to be told by him that he must leave her within two hours. She replies in a rather lengthy speech, ostensibly to ask why she has been in effect banished from his presence lately, but in reality she simply reveals more thoroughly and vividly his monomaniac concern with war and its accouterments. What, she inquires, has taken from him all stomach (desire), pleasure, and even sleep? Why is he constantly fretful, pale, given to melancholy? Even in sleep, she declares, he mumbles tales of war, guides his steed, and makes outcries to his soldiers.

His sweating brow and strange facial expressions have given him, in fact, the appearance of a man whose body and spirit are "at war." These are portents, Kate insists, and she must know what they mean. They are then interrupted by a servant.

Hotspur inquires of the servant if a certain packet of letters has been despatched and if the horses have been brought. One horse has been brought, the servant replies. "That roan shall be my throne," cries young Percy, and then he engages in a witty sally with Kate, who tries playfully to learn his secret, but is finally put off with the comment:

> "... this is no world
> To play with mammets and to tilt with lips:
> We must have bloody noses and crack'd crowns,
> And pass them current too. God's me, my horse!"

Kate asks her husband for a true answer to the question, "Do you love me?" He replies: "When I am a-horseback, I will swear I love thee infinitely." But he refuses to answer further questions. He trusts her "secrecy" to this extent: she will not utter what she does not know. The scene ends abruptly.

Act II: Scene 4

This is unquestionably one of the great scenes of Shakespearean drama. It takes place in Boar's Head Tavern in Eastcheap, where the Prince and Poins have retreated to wait for Falstaff and the others to return. As the scene opens the Prince joins Ned Poins; he has just been consorting for some time with the menial tavern help, the "drawers," or tapster-waiters. The Prince's tone seems a bit stuffy as he laughs at the condescending airs of the tavern lads who have sought to flatter him with such compliments as these: that though he is but Prince of Wales, he is nevertheless a "king of courtesy"; and that when he is King of England he is sure to have the allegiance of all the "good lads" of Eastcheap. Hal lampoons their customs—that, for example, of requiring anyone who pauses for a breath in his drinking to finish off the flagon in a gulp. He remarks to Poins: "I tell thee, Ned, thou hast lost much honour, that thou wert not with me in this action."

Hal has been given a piece of sugar by one of the tapsters (presumably as a gesture of favor). While waiting for Falstaff, and the big joke to be played, he decides to have some fun with the tapster Francis and stations Poins in another room to keep calling for "Francis!" while he detains him, on the pretext of trying to find out why he gave the Prince the sugar. The exchange between Hal and Francis is funny simply for the nonconsecutive absurdity of the dialogue, but it does not lend itself well to summary. The height of nonsense is reached when the Prince asks:

> "Wilt thou rob this leathern-jerkin, crystal-button,
> not-pated, agate-ring puke-stocking, caddis-garter,
> smooth-tongue, Spanish-pouch,—
> [Francis] O Lord, sir, who do you mean?
> [Prince] Why, then, your brown bastard is your only
> drink; for look you Francis, your white canvas doublet
> will sully. In Barbary, sir, it cannot come to so much.
> [Francis] What, sir?"

At this point the vintner-owner enters and rebukes Francis for not answering the calls. He tells the Prince that Falstaff and a half-dozen more are at the door and asks if he should let them in. Hal tells him to let them cool their heels for a while and then to open the door. Poins returns and asks the Prince the point of the jest they have just played on Francis. The Prince makes the enigmatic reply that he is "now of all humours that have showed themselves humours since the old days of goodman Adam to the pupil age of this present twelve o'clock at midnight."

Francis reappears, and the Prince marvels that though he is a man, he should have fewer words than a parrot. His "eloquence [is no more than] the parcel of a reckoning." The Prince's mind turns, by way of contrast, to Hotspur, "he that kills me some six or seven dozen of Scots at a breakfast, washes his hands, and says to his wife, "Fie upon this quiet life! I want work."

"Call in Falstaff," says the Prince, "I'll play Percy, and that damned brawn shall play Dame Mortimer his wife. . . . Call in ribs, call in tallow."

Here Falstaff, Gadshill, Bardolph, and Peto enter—Falstaff swaggering in superiority over the "cowards," Poins and Hal, who have "abandoned" them during the robbery. "A plague of all cowards!" cries Falstaff, "give me a cup of sack, rogue. Is there no virtue extant?" He then complains that there is lime in the sack, another example of the roguery of "villainous man." Yet a coward is worse than that. "There lives not three good men unhanged in England; and one of them is fat and grows old." The Prince eggs him on, and Falstaff scornfully rejects him as "a king's son!" adding, "If I do not beat thee out of thy kingdom with a dagger of lath . . . I'll never wear hair on my face more. You Prince of Wales!" Sir John then calls the Prince a coward, and Hal threatens to stab him, whereupon Falstaff retreats to the safer ground of sarcasm. He says that he will be damned before he calls the Prince "coward," but adds that he would give a thousand pounds to be able to run as fast as he can. "A plague upon such backing! Give me them that will face me. Give me a cup of sack. I am a rogue if I drunk today." At the Prince's insistence, Falstaff explains the reason for his bad temper. They had taken a thousand pounds that morning, and it had been stolen from them through Hal's and Poins' failure to show up at the appointed place.

A hundred men set upon the four of them, Falstaff lies, and they fought for two solid hours. His doublet was pierced eight times, his hose four, his shield "hacked like a handsaw." Gadshill notes that the four of them attacked a dozen men, and Falstaff corrects him—there were sixteen, at least, and when they had finished the sixteen had been bound tight. As they were sharing the loot, another band set upon them (but only after freeing the first sixteen). "What, fought you with them all?" asks the Prince. To which Sir John replies: "All? I know not what you call all, but if I fought not with fifty of them, I am a bunch of radish. If there were not two or three and fifty upon poor old Jack, then am I no two-legg'd creature." To this Hal ironically retorts that he hopes Sir John has not murdered some of them. But the fat knight says it is too late for hopes of that sort, he has certainly killed two of them—two rogues in buckram suits.

The Prince exclaims, "O monstrous! eleven men grown out of two!" Whereupon Falstaff includes an additional "three misbegotten knaves in Kendal green," who came up behind and attacked him in the dark. Hal's vituperation now knows no bounds, and he bursts out: "These lies are like their father that begets them; gross as a mountain, open, palpable. Why thou clay-brained guts, thou knotty-pated fool, thou whoreson, obscene, greasy tallow-catch,—" And he demands of the fat knight a reason for his lies. Falstaff refuses to give a reason "on compulsion," and the Prince attacks him with more outrageous epithets, receiving a string of them from Falstaff in return (including, "you dried neat's-tongue, you bull's pizzle, you stockfish . . . you sheath, you bowcase"—all images of leanness).

Finally, the Prince tells all; how they saw the four of them set on four travelers and rob them; how the two of them then "outfaced them from their prize"; how Falstaff "carried his guts away nimbly . . . and roared for mercy." Hal ends by asking Sir John what dodge he can use now to hide from the shame of this open revelation. And Poins taunts him also: "Come, let's hear, Jack; what trick hast thou now?" Falstaff's reply is one of the most memorable of Shakespearean speeches: "By the Lord, I knew ye as well as he that made ye." And he pretends that out of instinct he was simply unable to turn upon the Prince. He was a coward upon instinct. But he is glad they have the money. Let the doors be locked, and a play be performed extempore. The Prince suggests that the argument (or plot) ought to be Sir John's running away.

"Ah," replies Falstaff, "no more of that, Hal, and thou lovest me!" The hostess enters to tell the Prince that there is a courtier (she calls him "a nobleman of the court") come from his father to speak with him. The Prince jests about him contemptuously, and Falstaff makes a joke about "gravity" being out of his bed at midnight (the courtier is an elderly man), and goes to send him packing. While Sir John is out of the room, the Prince finds out from the others that Falstaff had hacked his sword with his dagger and had made them tickle their noses with speargrass to make them bleed and promise to swear it was the blood of true men.

Falstaff returns, and the Prince wishes to resume the badinage, chiding Falstaff about the number of years that have passed since he was able to see his own knee. But Sir John informs him that the knight who had appeared at the door was Sir John Bracy, who had come to report to the Prince that he must return to court, for young Percy, Glendower, Mortimer, the elder Percy, and Douglas ("that runs a-horseback up a hill perpendicular") have committed themselves to rebellion. And he adds: "thy father's beard is turned white with the news: you may buy land now as cheap as stinking mackerel." The Prince replies in an offhand fashion that in that case, if it should be a hot June they will be able to buy maidenheads by the hundreds. But Falstaff is in haste to change the subject back to the dangers of war, and the threat posed to Hal by three such enemies as Hotspur, Douglas, and Glendower. "Art thou not horribly afraid? Doth not thy blood thrill at it?" he asks. The Prince denies that it does.

The thought of appearing before his royal father seems now to have a sobering effect upon Hal, and he accepts Falstaff's offer to stand for King Henry in a mock interrogation scene so that he may practice his answers. Falstaff calls for a cup of sack "to make his eyes red" so that he may be thought to have been weeping. He must speak in passion, imitating King Cambyses.

The Prince bows, and Falstaff begins, while the tavern hostess sheds tears of laughter. Falstaff includes her in the mock-pageant, saying, in the mechanical prettiness of so much earlier iambic pentameter stage poetry:

"Weep not, sweet queen; for trickling tears are vain . . .
For God's sake, lords, convey my tristful queen;
For tears do stop the flood-gates of her eyes."

Falstaff (as King Henry) now addresses himself to the Prince. He marvels at the way in which Hal spends his time. And he uses an image drawn from natural history to enforce the idea of wasting youth through bad company. "For though the camomile, the more it is trodden on, the faster it grows, so youth, the more it is wasted the sooner it wears."

Much of the humor of the parody comes from Falstaff's mixing it with broadly comic statements, such as, "That thou art my son, I have partly thy mother's word, partly my own opinion but chiefly a villainous trick of thine eye and a foolish hanging of thy nether lip that doth warrant me." He then goes on with another euphuistic comparison—this time of Hal's companions with the substance known as pitch. As pitch defiles, so does bad company. "And yet," he goes on, "there is a virtuous man whom I have often noted in thy company, but I know not his name." He is a "portly man," with a "cheerful look, a pleasing eye, and a most noble carriage . . . his name is Falstaff. . . . Harry, I see virtue in his looks. . . . Him keep with, the rest banish."

In another contest of wit they now exchange places, Falstaff playing the Prince, and Hal playing his father. Of course, the Prince-King's evaluation of Falstaff is quite different. He is a "devil . . . in the likeness of an old fat man," a "roasted Manningtree ox with the pudding in his belly," and so forth. With feigned surprise, Falstaff (as Prince) asks, "Whom means your grace?" He replies: "That villainous abominable misleader of youth, Falstaff, that old white-bearded Satan."

Falstaff (still playing the Prince) defends himself in a magnificent argument. To be old is not to be taken as an indictment but as a cause for pity; and he admits to being old. But as for being a lecher, that he denies. Is sack and sugar a fault? Is to be old and merry a sin? If the fat man is to be hated, then Pharaoh's lean kine are to be loved. "Banish not him thy Harry's company. Banish plump Jack, and banish all the world."

Bardolph enters on the run, to announce that the sheriff is at the door. He is followed by the hostess with the same news, who wishes to know whether she should let them in. The Prince directs Falstaff and the others to hide behind the arras (wall tapestry) while he and Peto remain to greet the sheriff. The sheriff announces that he is looking for a "gross fat man" in connection with the robbery of three hundred marks. Hal, lying, denies that he is there, but promises to send him to the sheriff on the morrow. After the sheriff departs, Peto discovers Falstaff fast asleep behind the arras.

The Prince goes through Falstaff's pockets and finds a paper containing a list of expenditures—a total of 10s. 6d. (ten shillings and sixpence) for sack, capons, and anchovies, but only a halfpenny for bread. The Prince calls it monstrous—this intolerable deal of sack. But his mood changes as he announces to Peto that they will be off to the wars on the next day, and that he intends to procure the captaincy of a troop of foot soldiers for Sir John. The money (that stolen from the travelers) will be paid back with interest. The scene finally closes with Peto's "Good morrow, my lord."

Act III: Scene 1

The scene is Owen Glendower's castle in Wales. Hotspur, Worcester, Mortimer, and Glendower enter, speaking of the prospects for success in their revolt against the crown. Mortimer is optimistic and calm. Hotspur is in his customary choleric humor. They are consulting a map of England, on which they are attempting to trace out an equitable division of the country among Glendower, Mortimer, and young Percy. Glendower invites them all to sit, and calling Hotspur by name, remarks: "For by that name as oft as Lancaster doth speak of you, his cheek looks pale and with a rising sigh he wisheth you in heaven."

Hotspur returns the compliment by telling Glendower that Henry wishes him in hell whenever he hears *his* name. This is the signal for Glendower to embark upon a fantastic recital of the marvelous occurrences which attended his nativity. The brow of heaven was "full of fiery shapes of burning cressets," and the "frame and huge foundation of the earth shaked like a coward."

Hotspur pooh-poohs Glendower's claim and ridicules him, but the Welshman insists that his story is true, whereupon young Percy, in an amusing metaphor, interprets the shaking of the earth not as the result of awe and fear, but simply as a strange eruption of old mother Earth, who was "with a kind of colic pinched and vexed by the imprisoning of unruly wind within her womb." Glendower, still holding to his patience, tells Hotspur that he does not take this sort of rebuke from many men, and once more calmly reiterates his fantastic account, adding that "all the courses of my life do show I am not in the roll of common men." And he asks where the man is who has ever been able to teach him anything. Where is that

> ". . . woman's son
> Can trace me in the tedious ways of art
> And hold me pace in deep experiments?"

Hotspur once more shows his contempt, and Mortimer warns him not to tempt Glendower's rage; Hotspur ignores this advice, and when Glendower goes on to tell him that he has the power to command the devil to appear, Hotspur replies that in that event he himself would have the power to shame him away, and he taunts Glendower three times with the jibe, "Tell truth and shame the devil!" Mortimer tries to terminate the dispute, but Glendower replies:

> "Three times hath Henry Bolingbroke made head
> Against my power; thrice from the banks of Wye
> And sandy-bottom'd Severn have I sent him
> Bootless home and weather-beaten back."

With another quibble (identical with that of Gadshill and the Chamberlain) about "boots" and "foul weather," they begin the serious business of settling the division of the spoils. The archdeacon has arranged three portions. All of England south and east of the Trent and Severn rivers is to go to Mortimer; all of Wales west of the Severn is to be Glendower's; and to young Percy has been assigned all the remainder northward from the Trent. Mortimer, who apparently regards this as a very equitable arrangement, says that they can sign the agreement this very night, and he changes the subject to their eventual meeting at Shrewsbury field with Worcester and Northumberland. "My father Glendower," he says, is not yet ready, but will not be required for a full two weeks. Glendower promises to arrive in a shorter space of time and bids them take their leave of their wives, "For there will be a world of water shed upon the parting of your wives and you."

But all is not to go as smoothly as Mortimer and Glendower would like it; Hotspur has some thoughts of his own about a proper division of the land. The curve of the River Trent, he complains, "cuts me from the best of all my land / A huge half-moon, a monstrous cantle out." He threatens to have it dammed up so that it will not wind so deeply and rob him of so rich a piece of land.

Mortimer defends the division, pointing out that his portion suffers the same sort of bend in the river, and Worcester intervenes to make a slight modification agreeable to both Mortimer and Hotspur. This time Glendower demurs, saying, "I will not have it altered." He and young Percy almost come to blows, particularly since Hotspur taunts him again for speaking with a Welsh accent. With considerable restraint, the Welshman explains that he learned to speak English as a child at the English court where, even at a young age, he had "framed to the harp / Many an English ditty lovely well, / And gave the tongue a helpful ornament." To Hotspur, this makes him nothing more than a "ballad-monger." Nothing sets his teeth so on edge as "mincing poetry." Glendower yields and agrees to have the line altered, but Hotspur cannot accept this with good grace, and he rubs it in, saying that while he would give thrice so much land to a well-deserving friend, "in the way of bargain, mark ye me, / I'll cavil on the ninth part of a hair." After remarking on the manner in which his daughter dotes on her husband Mortimer, Glendower makes his exit.

Mortimer chides Hotspur for crossing Glendower, but Hotspur asserts that he cannot help himself since the Welshman angers him so by telling him

> "Of the dreamer Merlin and his prophecies,
> And of a dragon and a finless fish,
> A clip-wing'd griffin and a moulten raven,
> A couching lion and a ramping cat,
> And such a deal of skimble-skamble stuff
> As puts me from my faith."

Mortimer tries to convince young Percy that Glendower holds himself in check only because he has a high respect for him. He warns Hotspur not to try it too often. Worcester concurs, and admonishes his nephew to "amend his fault." Sometimes, he says, it shows "greatness, courage, blood." Yet at other times it presents "harsh rage, defect of manners, want of government, pride, haughtiness, opinion, and disdain." The least of these things can bring a nobleman into disrepute.

Glendower reenters at this point with his daughter and Kate. Mortimer bemoans the fact that he can speak no Welsh and his wife no English. She is weeping over his departure.

Glendower speaks to her in Welsh, and from his explanation that "she is desperate here. A peevish self-willed harlotry. / One that no persuasion can do good upon," we see still another repetition of the parent-recalcitrant child figure (King-Prince, Northumberland-Hotspur). She speaks in Welsh, and Mortimer makes a very touching speech, explaining that though they are separated by differing tongues they have a mutual understanding of the language of love. But he finally shows his frustration at their inability to communicate, and Glendower translates for him. She is asking him to lie down and rest his head upon her lap, so that she may on his eyelids "crown the god of sleep," and "making such difference 'twixt wake and sleep / As is the difference betwixt day and night."

Hotspur mimics what he considers to be the foolish antics of Mortimer and his wife by saying to Kate: "Come Kate, thou art perfect in lying down; come, quick, quick, that I may lay my head in thy lap." She jibes at him in return, telling him that he is "altogether governed by humours" (we recall that Hal has described himself as being "of all humours"). The lady sings in Welsh, and Hotspur asks Kate to sing also. When she refuses (with a very mild oath), he tells her she swears like a "comfit-maker's wife," and implores her to swear "mouth-filling" oaths, and leave the "pepper-gingerbread / To velvet-guards and Sunday citizens." She still refuses to sing. All leave the stage.

Act III: Scene 2

The scene is London once again—the palace. The King, the Prince of Wales, and several lords enter. The King asks them to leave him alone for a time with Harry, but to remain close by since he will soon have need of them. They go out and Henry immediately begins upon a tongue-lashing of the Prince. Is God punishing him, he wonders, for some sin of his past life? Is God, in His "secret doom," breeding revenge and a scourge for him?

Henry states with some sarcasm that he believes Hal has been appointed by Heaven as an instrument of his punishment. How else, he inquires, "Could such inordinate and low desires, / Such poor, such bare, such lewd, such mean attempts, / Such barren pleasures, rude society," as the Prince is now "grafted to," hold a place in his princely heart?

Hal submissively admits to guilt in some of the things he has been charged with, but alleges that he could doubtless clear himself of many others. In any event, he asks his royal father to excuse these things as the faulty wanderings and irregularity of his youth, and to pardon him for his true submission. "God pardon thee!" rejoins Henry.

The King goes on with his angry spate of words, accusing the Prince of failing to meet the traditions of his ancestors, of allowing his place in council to be taken over by his younger brother, and of being an alien to the hearts of all the King's courtiers. His youthful promise has been dashed, and everyone is predicting his eventual failure. Henry now harks back to the days of his own youth. If he had been so lavish with his company, such a common spectacle, "opinion, that did help [him] to the crown," would have remained with Richard and left him in banishment.

As the King goes on, the serious purpose of his speech begins to take on the coloration of vanity as he speaks of having been wondered at like a comet and of men pointing him out to their children. He evaluates his accomplishments in those days in a speech which in some ways resembles (even while it contrasts markedly with) Hotspur's words about "plucking bright honor from the pale-faced moon":

"And then I stole all courtesy from heaven,
And dress'd myself in such humility
That I did pluck allegiance from men's hearts,
Loud shouts and salutations from their mouths,
Even in the presence of the crowned King."

Only thus, says Henry, did he keep his person unsullied. His presence was like a "robe pontifical" (a pope's ceremonial garment), and his person was seen so rarely that it "showed like a feast" and won "solemnity." Richard II, a "skipping king [who] ambled up and down / With shallow jesters," only succeeded in having his name profaned and scorned. He mingled with the *hoi-polloi*, and became a common sight on the streets of London; he "enfeoffed himself to popularity," and thus like honey, when it is eaten in excess, became an object of loathing rather than love. He began to resemble the cuckoo in men's eyes—heard but not regarded. He was seen only by sick and blunted eyes, such as "afford no extraordinary gaze / Such as is bent on sun-like majesty / When it shines seldom in admiring eyes." In short, the people were "glutted, gorged, and full" with his presence, and that is exactly what the Prince is going to face. He has lost his "princely privilege with vile participation." Every eye is weary of him, complains Henry, save his own, which is now blinding itself with foolish tenderness (he is weeping).

The Prince at this point promises his royal father that he will hereafter "be more myself," and we may take this as the turning point of the play from the standpoint of Hal's progress in reform. But Henry persists in excoriating his son. Even Hotspur has more right to succeed to the throne, he says, for he fills battlefields, rushes into the jaws of the lion, and leads even lords and bishops into bloody battles. He has won undying honor in his conquest of Douglas. Hotspur, a "Mars in swaddling clothes" and an "infant warrior," took the measure of the great Douglas and made a friend of him, "To fill the mouth of deep defiance up / And shake the peace and safety of our throne." But why does he speak of these enemies, the King goes on, when his own son is his nearest and dearest enemy. He is likely, through fear, base inclination, or spleen, to enter Percy's service and fight against the crown. This is the climax and crowning insult of Henry's tirade, and we learn much about the Prince's true character from his calm reply and his impassioned promise to best Hotspur if they should meet in battle.

"When I will wear a garment all of blood
And stain my favors [features] in a bloody mask,
Which, wash'd away, shall scour my shame with it;"

All the honors which are now Percy's asserts the Prince, will then be his. He will call Percy to strict account, and make him "render every glory up," and he swears a solemn oath before his father to die a hundred thousand deaths before he should break the smallest part of this promise. The King is finally convinced of Harry's sincerity, and he applauds his speech with a ringing cry: "A hundred thousand rebels die in this. / Thou shalt have charge and sovereign trust herein." This means, of course, that Hal will be given command of an army. At this juncture, Sir Walter Blunt enters with the news that the Scot Douglas and the English rebels had joined forces at Shrewsbury field on the eleventh of the month and that this betokens foul play for the land. The King replies that the "news" is five days old, that Westmoreland and Lord John (Hal's younger brother) have already been dispatched to the battlefield, and that on the following Wednesday, Prince Hal and the King himself will set out with separate forces to meet twelve days hence at Bridgenorth. He closes the scene with a rhyming couplet: "Our hands are full of business. Let's away; / Advantage feeds him fat while men delay."

Act III: Scene 3

We are once again in the Boar's Head Tavern in Eastcheap. Falstaff and Bardolph enter chaffing one another, Falstaff, as usual, getting the better of it. He is undergoing another bout of mock repentance. His skin is hanging slack about his bones, he says, his strength is lessening, and the need for repentance is upon him. He has practically forgotten what the inside of a church looks like, he adds, and it is nothing but "company, villainous company," that has been his ruination.

When Bardolph tells Sir John that his fretfulness will bring him an early death, Falstaff calls for a bawdy song to make him merry. His life was indeed once virtuous enough, he maintains; he swore only a little, played at dice no more than seven times a week, visited a bawdy house no oftener than four times an hour, and lived well and in "good compass." Now he lives out of all order, out of all compass. To which Bardolph replies that he is out of all compass because he is so fat.

Sir John retorts by abusing Bardolph for his face. It shines so (he is an inveterate toper) that it is like the fleet flagship with its signal lantern (his nose). Still in his "repentance" vein, Falstaff remarks that he can nevertheless make good use of it. As another man might use a death's head or a *memento mori* (reminders of man's final worldly end), he will use Bardolph's face to remind him of hellfire and the suffering Dives (Luke 16:19-31). It is a fiery angel that he might swear by, an *ignis fatuus* or a ball of wildfire, a bonfire which has saved Sir John a thousand marks (which he has not had to spend for torches to light his way at night).

The hostess enters, only to be insulted in her turn by being called "Dame

Partlet the hen," a reference to Chaucer's Pertelote (hence, a garrulous woman). Falstaff wants to know if she has yet discovered who picked his pocket, and she replies that the house has been turned upside-down and not a trace has been found. He insults her further by suggesting that she is a loose woman and that the inn is a place for lewd carryings-on. Accusations fly back and forth. When she asserts that he owes her money, he tells her that Bardolph owes money too; let them coin his face, his nose, his cheeks (they are red, hence like copper). He is outraged at having his pocket picked in his own inn; he has lost a seal-ring of his grandfather's, worth at least forty marks. The hostess claims that the Prince told her it was only a copper ring, and Sir John retorts that the Prince "is a Jack, a sneak-cup," and if he were here he would cudgel him like a dog.

The Prince and Poins suddenly enter, in marching stride, and Falstaff meets them playing on his truncheon (a short heavy stick or club) like a fife. He asks them if that is the way the wind is blowing; will they soon be marching? Bardolph interrupts sarcastically, "Yea, two and two, Newgate fashion" (that is, like prisoners). Falstaff tries to turn the Prince's attention to the picking of his pockets and the ring he has lost, but Hal pooh-poohs it as a trifling "eight-penny matter." The hostess now informs on Sir John, telling the Prince the vile insults he has offered him in his absence and of his threat to cudgel him. She swears by her "faith, truth, [and] womanhood" that she is speaking truly, and Falstaff bursts out, "There's no more faith in thee than a stewed prune; nor no more truth in thee than in a drawn fox; and for womanhood, Maid Marian may be the deputy's wife of the ward to thee. Go, you thing, go."

The Hostess is clearly a pawn for Falstaff. No match for him, she nevertheless continues to badger him. What kind of a "thing" does he mean, she asks. He replies, "a thing to thank God on," and she does not know quite how to take this but, perceiving vaguely that insult is intended, she denies it. She is an "honest man's wife"; and he is a "knave" to call her these things. He then retorts (setting her "womanhood" aside) that she is a beast. What beast? An otter. Why an otter? Because she's "neither fish nor flesh; a man knows not where to have her." The Prince defends her, saying that Falstaff is slandering her outrageously. The hostess matches this by replying that Falstaff has slandered the Prince also, by alleging that he owes him a thousand pounds. In anger (or pretended anger) Hal demands, "Do I owe you a thousand pound?" To which Falstaff, with his amiable dexterity of mind, answers: "A thousand pound, Hal? A million. Thy love is worth a million; thou owest me thy love." To all Falstaff's other boasts, the Prince challenges, "Dar'st thou be as good as thy word now?" Falstaff, of course, backs away from the challenge, but manages it with his accustomed ingenuity. As Hal is a man he dares to meet him, but as he is a prince he fears him—fears him as the "roaring of the lion's whelp." To Hal's question, "And why not as the lion?" Falstaff replies, "The King himself is to be feared as the lion."

The Hostess has a brief moment of triumph as the Prince hurls a spate of abuse at the fat knight: "there's no room for faith, truth, nor honesty in this bosom of thine; it is all filled up with guts and midriff. . . . thou whoreson, impudent, embossed [swollen] rascal, if there were anything in thy pocket but tavern-reckonings, memorandums of bawdy-houses, and one poor penny-worth of sugar-candy to make thee long-winded . . . I am a villain; and yet you will not stand to it; you will not pocket up wrong. Art thou not ashamed?"

With amazing aplomb, Falstaff says to the hostess, "I forgive thee." And he dispatches her to go about her household duties. He then turns to the Prince for a serious account of the news at court.

The Prince informs him that the money has been paid back, and that he is now on good terms with his father. Falstaff tries to continue in a lighthearted vein, joking about Hal's robbing the treasury, but the Prince will not be drawn into humorous flights of wit. He tells Falstaff forthrightly that he has gotten command of a troop of foot soldiers. Falstaff wishes it had been a troop of cavalry (horse), but he claims to welcome the opportunity. The Prince sends Bardolph with a letter to his brother, Lord John of Lancaster, and another to Westmoreland. To Poins he says, "Go Poins, to horse, to horse; for thou and I have thirty miles to ride yet ere dinner time." He directs Falstaff to meet him in the Temple Hall at two o'clock the following day, where he will be given money and orders for equipment.

As the scene closes, the young Prince exits on a stirring rhyming couplet, and Falstaff trumpets another on its heels:

> [Prince]
> "The land is burning; Percy stands on high;
> And either they or we must lower lie." [Exit]
> [Falstaff]
> "Rare words! brave world! Hostess, my breakfast, come!
> O, I could wish this tavern were my drum!" [Exit]

Act IV: Scene 1

Act IV is the shortest act of the play. The first scene opens at the rebel camp near Shrewsbury, and things are happening very rapidly. Hotspur and Douglas, who are very much alike, are conversing, and Hotspur compliments Douglas by remarking that "not a soldier of this season's stamp" goes so "general current through the world," using once more his war-coinage metaphor. Douglas repays the compliment, calling young Percy the "king of honor." A messenger enters with letters from the Earl of Northumberland, who reports that he is "grievous sick" and cannot lead his forces into battle. Hotspur is incredulous at the news, and comments that "this sickness doth infect / The very life-blood of our enterprise."

The Earl has informed them, however, that they must proceed. There is no stopping now. Hotspur, with characteristic verve, quickly recovers from this blow. He refuses to take the Earl's illness as a sign of their certain defeat, to forecast the outcome "on the nice hazard of one doubtful hour." Douglas agrees, and remarks that they should think instead of their future victory and rewards. Worcester, a more reserved and cautious man, is disturbed over the effect this news will have on the armies, for they cannot afford the slightest suggestion of a lack of agreement among the leaders of the rebellion. Some might easily imagine that the Earl's absence is the result of some private reservations about the wisdom of their plan. This is especially dangerous for the "offering" (that is, the rebellious) side. They must stop up all such loopholes before the news begins to breed fear in the soldiers.

Hotspur tells him that he is making a mountain out of molehill. In fact, the Earl's absence gives their enterprise a greater aspect of daring—a greater luster. There is more "honor" to be gained by it. All is yet well. Douglas concurs, adding, "There is not such a word / Spoke of in Scotland as this term of fear."

Sir Richard appears with the news that Westmoreland and Prince John are marching toward them, and that the King himself is on the verge of setting out. Hotspur embraces the challenge with another scornful dismissal of the Prince of Wales, though he asks Vernon for news of him. Vernon's speech in reply is one of the most ironic touches in this act for, in spite of himself, he describes the Prince in glowing terms, in imaginative martial language, the only sort of language that makes any sense to Hotspur. He rose, says Vernon, "from the ground like feathered Mercury, / And vaulted with such ease unto his seat, / As if an angel dropp'd down from the clouds." Hotspur is visibly shaken by Vernon's words, and he cries out, "No more, no more!"

But again Percy recovers, and with an almost maniacal defiance he welcomes the royalist armies as sacrifices marching to the altar of the God of War, to whom they will offer them "all hot and bleeding." Mars will sit on his altar, up to his ears in blood. And the twinlike relationship of the two cousins comes out emphatically in the couplet: "Harry to Harry shall, hot horse to horse, Meet, and ne'er part till one drop down a corse" (corse means corpse).

Vernon has even worse news. Glendower has not been able to muster his forces. Even Douglas is disturbed at this, but Hotspur rises to another romantic pitch, crying out, "Come, let us take a muster speedily. / Dooms-day is near. Die all, die merrily." All leave.

Act IV: Scene 2

This very brief scene begins with Falstaff and Bardolph on a public road near Coventry. Falstaff sends Bardolph off for a bottle of sack and then delivers one of his most impressive soliloquies—amusing, but tinged with pathos. He reveals that he has misused his power of conscription by letting able-bodied men who had enough money buy draft exemptions. He had sought out only those with a good reason for wanting to remain on the home front—landowners, bachelors about to be married, out-and-out cowards—and summoned them. Pocketing the money he then filled up his company with all the broken-down relics of humanity he could find, "the cankers of a calm world and a long peace." One would think he had a hundred and fifty prodigals straight from their swine-keeping; one mad fellow on the road told Sir John that it looked as though he had unloaded all the gallows and pressed all the dead bodies into service. They look either like scarecrows or ex-convicts.

Prince and Westmoreland enter, and after a brief humorous exchange Hal remarks that he has never seen such "pitiful rascals." Falstaff's rejoinder is memorable for its combination of profundity and casualness—it one of the truly affecting and penetrating utterances in the play; even the pos-sibility that Falstaff is posing as he speaks cannot spoil it: "Tut, tut; good enough to toss; food for powder, food for powder; they'll fill a pit as well as better; tush, man, mortal men, mortal men." The Prince bids Falstaff make haste, for Percy is already in the field.

Act IV: Scene 3

We are back at the rebel camp. Hotspur, Worcester, Douglas, and Vernon enter. They are obviously on edge, and they speak in clipped, nervous phrases. Douglas accuses Vernon of fear, and Vernon warns him that he will meet slander with a fight to the death, if necessary; his reply also sug-gests that Douglas has been getting on their nerves with his talk about the bravery of the Scots. Vernon tries to keep a level head, and he rebukes Hotspur and Douglas for not realizing that their men and horses are tired and that certain reinforcements have not yet arrived. But Hospur wants to press the fight. Worcester, too, pleads with him not to engage the superior numbers of the enemy, but to wait for the remainder of their army.

A trumpet sounds for a parley, and Sir Walter Blunt enters. He speaks with dignity and restraint. And Hotspur compliments him, telling him that there are those among them who wish he were ranged with the rebels against the King. Blunt, however, makes the steadfast answer that he will stand against them as an enemy, "So long as out of limit and true rule / You stand against anointed majesty."

Blunt conveys the King's gracious offer to listen to their complaints, his generous promise of redress for their grief, and full pardon for themselves and their followers. But if there had ever been a chance for Hotspur to change his course of action, that time is long past. He speaks disparagingly of Henry when he had just returned from exile as "a poor unminded outlaw sneaking home," and he describes the assistance his father the Earl had given him and how all the lords and barons of the country had flocked to his side, following Northumberland's example. He goes on to analyze what he considers the hypocritical acts of Bolingbroke which won the people's hearts; he ends by noting sarcastically that Henry did not stop at hearts, he

> "Proceeded further; cut me off the heads
> Of all the favorites that the absent king
> In deputation left behind him here,
> When he was personal in the Irish war."

Hotspur now recites a long list of particular acts of the King, directed against the Percies. After deposing Richard and having him murdered, Henry:

1. left Mortimer to languish in Wales without ransom

2. disgraced Hotspur even in his moment of victory

3. had Hotspur spied upon

4. gave Worcester a tongue-lashing and removed him from the council

5. dismissed the Earl of Northumberland from the court

6. broke "oath upon oath," and committed "wrong on wrong"

7. (this is the vaguest of all) "drove us to seek out this head of safety" and to 'pry into his title" (that is, to reexamine the whole question on Henry's legitimate claim to the throne)

Blunt asks if he should return this answer to the King, and Hotspur (in a surprising show of caution) tells him to wait. Worcester will bring their answer in the morning.

Act IV: Scene 4

This exceptionally brief scene takes place at the palace of the Archbishop of York. The Archbishop is dispatching a friend, called only Sir Michael, with letters to unspecified persons urging their support of Hotspur's cause. All we really learn is that Owen Glendower's absence is due to his being "overruled by prophecies," and the Scroop (the Archbishop) is in a panic. There is a slight touch of irony in his reference to the rebel leaders as a "head of gallant warriors" when it is immediately followed by a reference to the King's party as "the special head of all the land." Principally, the scene accomplishes two things:

1. It anticipates the defeat of the rebel army.
2. It creates the illusion of a lapse of time between the conference of Blunt and Hotspur, and the dawning of the day of battle.

Act V: Scene 1

The Fifth Act brings all the groups together on the stage and weaves together the various thematic strands which have threaded through the separate but analogous careers of the rebels, the rioters, and the royalists. The first scene is set in the King's camp near Shrewsbury. The King, Prince Henry, Prince John, Falstaff, and Blunt are present. Henry and the Prince comment on the ominous appearance of the bloody morning sun and the southern wind. A trumpet sounds, and Worcester and Vernon enter with their answer. The King rebukes Worcester as an "exhaled meteor, a prodigy of fear," and asks when he will "move in that obedient orb again / Where you did give a fair and natural light" (tying together once more the images of nature and order). Worcester adopts a somewhat wheedling tone, in his recital of grievances—a catalogue of complaints which is hardly different from what Hotspur has already said. Worcester, however, concentrates on the fact that Henry has violated his *oath* to them (he repeats this several times), and he says that "you yourself have forged [means] against yourself / By unkind usage, dangerous countenance,. / And violation of all faith and troth."

Worcester also portrays Henry's ingratitude in an image which reverberates with echoes of Falstaff's limitless appetite and thus helps to provide a unifying dimension for the two plots. He says that Henry, like the cuckoo,

> " . . . did oppress our nest;
> Grew by our feeding to so great a bulk
> That even our love durst not come near your sight
> For fear of swallowing . . . "

But the King, with dignified contempt, dismisses Worcester's charges as the specious reasons of a wanton rebel. Hal then throws an open challenge to the absent Hotspur, praising him as a valiant, daring, and bold gentleman, but offering to meet him in single combat. Henry refuses to allow this, on the grounds that "considerations infinite do make against it."

Henry displays his true royalty by refusing to bargain, even while he offers his free and unconditional pardon.

The Prince and Falstaff are left alone on stage, and Falstaff complains, "I would 't were bed-time, Hal, and all well." To which the Prince retorts, Why thou owest God a death," and exits, leaving Falstaff to deliver his famous soliloquy on honor. Can honor set a broken arm or leg or take away the pain of a wound? No. Then it has no skill in surgery. Honor is a mere word, and a word is nothing but air. Who has it? The dead hero. But can he feel it or hear it? No. It is therefore insensible to the dead, but can it live with the living? No. Why? Envy will not allow it to. "Therefore I'll none of it."

Act V: Scene 2

We are shown the rebel camp again. Worcester is informing Vernon of his decision not to tell Hotspur of the King's generous offer of truce. Worcester's explanation is one more illustration of the idea than rebellion causes noble minds to degenerate. From a cautious dignified gentleman, Worcester is seen to descend to the level of a defensive, suspicious, and mendacious man. He will not give Hotspur the true word because he is afraid Hotspur might accept the terms, and that Henry will later exact some form of retribution from Northumberland and himself, even while excusing Hotspur for his "youth and heat of blood." So he and Vernon tell Hotspur and Douglas that there was no mercy in the King. Westmoreland, who had been held as a hostage pending their safe return, is released to return their challenge to Henry. Worcester does report accurately the challenge that the Prince has offered, and Hotspur, whose own character is becoming more and more infected with choler and suspicion, asks how the challenge was delivered: "Seemed it in contempt?"

Young Percy defies the Prince and announces that he will "embrace him with a soldier's arm." He calls for speed in arming and shunts aside a messenger with a letter because there is not time:

> "O gentlemen, the time of life is short!
> To spend that shortness basely were too long,
> If life did ride upon a dial's point,
> Still ending at the arrival of an hour."

Percy commands "all the lofty instrumentos of war" to be sounded. The rebel leaders embrace. Trumpets sound, and they leave the stage.

Act V: Scene 3

The long-anticipated battle has finally materialized. The scene is a plain between the camps, and the king's army crosses the stage. Douglas and Sir Walter Blunt then enter.

Blunt proudly refuses to yield to Douglas' challenge. They fight and Blunt is killed. Hotspur enters briefly and tells Douglas about the disguised knights, whereupon he threatens to "murder all his wardrobe, piece by piece." They leave and Falstaff appears, alone. We find out that he has led his men into the thick of it; there are not more than three left alive from three hundred and fifty. The Prince now arrives on the scene, rebukes Falstaff for standing idle, and asks to borrow his sword. Sir John offers him his pistol, but when Hal takes it from the case he finds it contains only a bottle of sack. Crying, "What, is it a time to jest and dally now?" he throws it at Falstaff and leaves. Sir John comments that he does not like the kind of "grinning honor" that Sir Walter Blunt has. "Give me life," he cries. The scene ends.

Act V: Scene 4

Scene four shows us another part of the field. The King, the Prince, Lord John, and Westmoreland enter amidst confused sallies and trumpet calls. The Prince is wounded but refuses to retire. His brother John, impatient for action, returns to the battle and Hal remarks with surprise on his newly matured courage. Westmoreland and the Prince both exit, leaving Henry alone, and Douglas enters and engages the King in a duel. The King is being hard pressed when Hal returns and puts Douglas to flight. Henry acknowledges that this shows that the Prince has some concern for his life, to which Hal replies: "O God! they did me too much injury / That ever said I hearken'd for your death" (this is one of the unspoken bones of contention between the King and his son—Henry's suspicion that Hal was conspiring to overthrow him). The King exits. Hotspur enters. They challenge each other: The Prince, graciously; Hotspur, boastfully. They fight, and the Prince kills Percy, who makes a dying speech in which he bemoans the loss of his "proud titles" more than the loss of his life. While they have been fighting, Falstaff and Douglas have come in. No sooner have they crossed swords than Falstaff falls on the ground playing dead (Douglas, of course, leaves). The Prince now makes a speech over the dead body of Percy which gains an ironic emphasis from the fact that the "dead" body of Falstaff is lying nearby.

The Prince suddenly spies the body of Falstaff lying on the ground, and he makes an equivalent speech over *his* body, the main purport of which is expressed in the couplet: "O, I should have a heavy miss of thee / If I were much in love with vanity." The Prince leaves, and Falstaff rises up and makes another of his famous soliloquies, this time on "counterfeiting." If he had not counterfeited, Douglas would have killed him. But who is truly the counterfeit? It is the dead man, for he is only the counterfeit of a man. Therefore, to counterfeit death is to preserve the "true and perfect image of life itself." He decides to pretend that he himself killed Percy, so he stabs him in the thigh and raises the dead body up on his back. The Prince and his brother enter, astonished to hear Falstaff's claim that he himself killed Hotspur. They were both down and out of breath, he says, but they rose and "fought a long hour by Shrewsbury clock." The Prince, in good humor, says, "Come, bring your luggage nobly on your back. / For my part, if a lie may do thee grace, / I'll gild it with the happiest terms I have." All leave.

Act V: Scene 5

The final scene of the play ties up the remaining loose ends. The rebels have been subdued and prisoners taken. The King sentences Worcester and Vernon to death, but leaves the disposition of Douglas to the Prince. Hal magnanimously frees him—and without ransom—as a reward for the example of his valor.

Prince John has been given the duty of informing Douglas, and he thanks his brother for his "high courtesy."

Henry issues new commands to the armies, since Northumberland, Scroop, and Glendower are still at large, and he puts into words what has been the main theme of the play on both levels (the Prince given over to "riot," and the Percies given over to revolt): "Rebellion in this land shall lose his sway."

Henry IV Part II

RUMOR, *the Presenter.*
KING HENRY IV.
PRINCE HENRY, *afterwards crowned* KING HENRY V.
PRINCE JOHN OF LANCASTER
HUMPHREY, DUKE OF GLOUCESTER } *sons to Henry IV and*
THOMAS, DUKE OF CLARENCE } *brethren to Henry V.*
EARL OF NORTHUMBERLAND
SCROOP, ARCHIBISHOP OF YORK
LORD MOWBRAY
LORD HASTING
LORD BARDOLPH } *opposite against King Henry IV.*
TRAVERS
MORTON
SIR JOHN COLEVILE
EARL OF WARWICK
EARL OF WESTMORLAND
EARL OF SURREY
GOWER } *of the King's party.*
HARCOURT
BLUNT
LORD CHIEF JUSTICE
His SERVANT
POINS
SIR JOHN FALSTAFF
BARDOLPH } *irregular humorists.*
PISTOL
PIETO
PAGE *to Falstaff*
SHALLOW } *both country justices.*
SILENCE }
DAVY, *servant to Shallow.*
FANG *and* SNARE, *two sergeants.*
MOULDY, SHADOW, WART, FEEBLE, *and* BULLCALF, *country soldiers.*
FRANCIS, *a drawer.*

NORTHUMBERLAND'S WIFE.
PERCY'S WIDOW (LADY PERCY).
HOSTESS QUICKLY.
DOLL TEARSHEET.

LORDS, ATTENDANTS, PORTER, *etc.*

Henry IV Part II

Induction

The play opens in Warkworth, before the Castle of the Earl of Northumberland in the northwest of England near the Scottish border. Rumour enters clothed in a suit painted full of tongues. He explains that he has come to announce the victory of King Henry at Shrewsbury against the rebel forces of Northumberland. Harry Percy, the Earl's son, is dead. Douglas of Scotland has been captured in flight, and the whole party of the North has been taken prisoner or routed. According to his nature, however, Rumour must first spread the false report in Northumberland that Harry Monmouth, the Prince of Wales, not Harry Hotspur is dead.

Act I: Scene 1

The scene is still Warkworth. The porter is seen at the gate of Northumberland's castle. Thomas, Lord Bardolph arrives with news and asks for the Earl. The porter keeps Bardolph talking outside the gate until the Earl himself arrives and lets him in.

Bardolph announces the victory of the Earl's party at Shrewsbury, but Northumberland is suspicious of this news and asks for the source of this good report. Bardolph is forced to admit that he has heard it second hand. He believes that the man who gave him the news must have told the truth because he is a gentleman of good family.

Travers, the Earl's messenger arrives next with an equally unreliable although true report that Hotspur is dead. He gives a long and humorous account of how he came by the news from a man who was riding away from the battle. The Earl is inclined to believe the worse report, but Bardolph insists that such bad news could only come from a thief and a liar.

At last Morton arrives. He has actually been at the battle scene and brings an eye-witness account of the events. At first the Earl will not let him speak. He reads in the messenger's tragic face the very news he fears to hear. Moreover, he surmises even worse than the truth, that his brother as well as his son is dead. Morton corrects the Earl's impressions; only the son is dead. Lord Bardolph, still the flattering fool, refuses to accept this. But the Earl trusts Morton's report and bursts into an eloquent speech of grief. He curses heaven and earth and calls for the end of all order. Bardolph is aghast at the Earl's passion and cautions him to "divorce not wisdom" from his honor. Morton adds that the Earl has responsibilities to his people. Moreover, all is not lost. He reminds the Earl that the Archbishop of York, partisan of the deposed and dead King Richard II, is also an enemy of the King. At the moment, he too is calling for revenge, and because he is Archbishop, he justifies his rebellion in the name of God and by displaying the blood of Richard scraped from the stones of Pomfret Castle where the king had been killed.

Morton explains further that the Archbishop is mustering troops to oust the Lancaster King and put a York back on the throne. The Earl is rallied from his passions by this reminder. He had known of these things before. Now he sets aside his words of grief for the action of revenge. He decides to send messengers to York and join the ranks of the King's enemies.

Act I: Scene 2

As the second scene opens, the tall, grey-bearded, fat-bellied knight, Sir John Falstaff, is seen with his recently acquired, dwarfish young page whom he addresses as "Sirrah, you giant." The page delivers three messages to Falstaff: one from his doctor who has done a urinalysis and has found more diseases than he can name; another from Master Dombledon, the cloth merchant, who refuses to give Falstaff credit for his purchases; and a third message concerning his serving man Bardolph who has gone to a disreputable horse market to buy Falstaff a mount. Falstaff is in ill humor over the frustrating reports and rails at the page for each of his three messages. The doctor, Falstaff feels, is making fun of him just as Prince Hal has done by providing him with a diminutive page to set off Falstaff's monstrous size. No one can look at the monstrously corpulent knight followed by the tiny young page without bursting into laughter. The clothier who refuses to give credit without security, Falstaff charges, has none of his own; although a rich man, the clothier's "horn of abundance" is a cuckold's horn (that is, his wife is unfaithful). As for Bardolph, Falstaff moans that he has made as poor a bargain in hiring Bardolph for his servant as Bardolph will make at the horse market. All that is wanting to complete his discomfort, Falstaff reflects ironically, is marriage with a wife from a brothel.

At this point the Lord Chief Justice of the King and his servant enter. Falstaff's page recognizes the Justice as the one whom Prince Hal had struck for his refusal to release Bardolph after the latter's arrest for the Gadshill robbery (in "Henry IV, Part I"). Falstaff had failed to answer a summons for the same crime. In an attempt to avoid an encounter with the Justice, Falstaff turns his back and pretends to be deaf to the servant's call. Told to pluck Falstaff's elbow to get his attention, the servant does so. Falstaff pretends to mistake the servant for a beggar (who would pull a man's sleeve when asking for alms). Falstaff advises the hardy young servant to get a job or join the army rather than engage in an occupation that is even more shameful than rebellion. The servant protests that Falstaff is mistaken; he is not a beggar. But Falstaff insists he would be mistaken only if he called the servant an honest man and urges him to hunt elsewhere for alms.

At this point, the Justice intercedes. Addressing Falstaff directly, he demands to have a word with him. Falstaff pretends to recognize the Justice for the first time. He is overly obsequious, greets the Justice with feigned pleasure, pretends to have heard news of the Justice's illness, asks about his recovery, and warns him to guard his health as he advances in years. The Justice ignores Falstaff's courtesies and gets straight to the point. He demands to know why Falstaff has failed to answer the summons (in connection with the Gadshill robbery) issued before the Battle of Shrewsbury (that is, in "Henry IV, Part I"). Now Falstaff ignores the Justice's questions and comments on a report that the King has returned from Wales in ill health.

The Justice continues to insist on having his word about the summons. But Falstaff embarks on a lengthy medical analysis of the King's condition. Falstaff states that he has read Galen (an ancient Greek medical authority, still respected in Elizabethan days). He concludes that the King's illness is "a kind of deafness." Exasperated, the Justice attributes that disease to Falstaff who immediately contradicts his opponent. His is the disease of not listening which differs from deafness. With threatening wit, the Justice offers to play physician and cure Falstaff's disease by hanging him by the heels. Continuing the play on medical terminology, Falstaff replies, "I am as poor as Job, but not so patient."

At last the Justice is able to make his point. Falstaff has failed to answer to the charges of robbery (which in those days carried the penalty of death). Falstaff explains that he is not legally bound to answer the summons because he is engaged in the King's wars. The Justice concedes this legal point but reminds Falstaff that he is still in "great infamy." Falstaff makes his own obesity the basis of a pun on the word "great"; the Justice retorts with a pun on Falstaff's "great waste." Falstaff takes up the jest on "waste" (waist) and adds one on his "slender means" (limited funds).

The Justice now changes the subject and accuses Falstaff of misleading the Prince. Nevertheless, he is willing to forget the Gadshill robbery because of Falstaff's heroic record at Shrewsbury. He warns him not to incur his wrath in the future, that is, "to wake not a sleeping wolf." Always ready with a rebuttal, Falstaff replies that as a sly fox, he is as dangerous as an angry wolf. Annoyed, the Justice calls Falstaff "a candle, the better part burnt out." Once more Falstaff jokes about his own corpulence, playing on the word "wax" (which had a second meaning of "to increase" or "to grow").

Still angry, the Justice calls attention to Falstaff's white beard, which should give him more "gravity," that is, should make him more serious. But Falstaff thinks of his beard as a trap for "gravy." Next, the Justice calls Falstaff an "ill angel," and Falstaff denies the metaphor. Ill angels (gold coins clipped of some of their content) are light; Falstaff is obviously heavy. But if he had to pass as good coin, Falstaff concedes, he could not, for he has only valor and no financial credit. He reflects on the bitterness of age toward the attributes of youth. Youth is hot-blooded and given to pranks, which age frowns upon. (Falstaff thinks of himself as young, the Justice as old.)

The Justice explodes at the idea of Falstaff's youth. He describes Falstaff's appearance in terms of old age and disease, "every part . . . blasted with antiquity." Falstaff merely replies that he was born as the Justice describes him (implying that old men resemble babies). He adds that, although young, he is old in judgment and has reproved the Prince for slapping the Justice. The Prince, in fact, is doing penance for his misdemeanor "in new silk and old sack."

The Justice dismisses the subject of the Prince with a prayer that he find a better companion than Falstaff. He is pleased to learn that (at his own suggestion) the King has separated Falstaff from the Prince by ordering Falstaff to join Prince John of Lancaster against the rebels. Falstaff replies that he knows the Justice had advised the King to send him into battle. He warns the Justice that heavy exertion in battle might cost Falstaff his life (suggesting that the Justice will be responsible for his death should it occur in the forthcoming battle). Falstaff grants that he cannot live forever, but since the Justice has insisted on Falstaff's old age, he should give him rest not battle. (This is a momentary and subtle plea for respite, but at once Falstaff recovers his composure.) Falstaff comments that the English always take advantage of a good thing. Having proved his bravery before, Falstaff must be tested again and again.

Concluding the interview, the Justice blesses Falstaff's expedition; at which point, Falstaff brazenly applies for and is refused a loan. He decides to turn to "old Mistress Ursula" who has lent him money frequently in the past in return for his false promises of marriage.

Act I: Scene 3

Once more the scene is changed. It is now in rebel territory at the Arch-bishop's palace in York. The Archbishop of York, Thomas Mowbray (the Earl Marshal of the North), Lord Hastings, and Lord Bardolph have met to conspire against King Henry IV. When the scene opens, the conference has already begun. (The Archbishop has stated his reasons for his re-bellion and has described the means by which he intends to conduct it.) The Archbishop now asks the others for their opinions of his plans. Mowbray readily admits that there is just cause to fight, but he wonders whether their armies and supplies are large enough to defeat the King's. Hastings provides some statistics. The rebels now have twenty-five thousand men (a large number for that time), but their supplies are insufficient. For these, they must rely on Northumberland; they cannot conduct the re-bellion without his assistance. Lord Bardolph sensibly suggests that unless Northumberland commits himself to the Yorkists, they would be wise to take no action. The Archbishop agrees and cites as an example Harry Hotspur, Northumberland's son, who was killed at Shrewsbury by the King's son.

Lord Bardolph describes Hotspur's plight at Shrewsbury where he fought with small forces and vainly hoped for supplies and reinforcements from his father. Hastings suggests that hope never hurt anyone. Bardolph replies at some length that hope can be harmful when, for example, hope of a fine harvest is based on the sight of a few early spring buds which will assuredly die in the next frost. Hope, Bardolph says, must be built like a house, first by surveying the plot, drawing up the plans, estimating the costs, then modifying the plans according to one's ability to pay, or giving up the building entirely if it proves too expensive. The rebellion must be planned like the house, Lord Bardolph says, but more carefully, for the undertaking is more important. He recommends a cautious survey of the situation, consultation with those who have experience in battle, analysis of their own strength and that of the opposing forces. The Yorkists must build their rebellion on a sure foundation, or else they are merely making paper plans which can never be carried out or which will only partially be completed before they must abandon the project. Completing the architectural analogy, Bardolph compares an unfinished rebellion to a "part-created" house which is abandoned before completion and stands exposed to the elements, "A naked subject to the weeping clouds / And waste for churlish winter's tyranny."

Hastings submits that the rebel forces which have already been mustered are equal to the King's army. Bardolph is surprised at this remark; surely the King has more than twenty-five thousand troops. Hastings explains that while the King has more men, he also has two other wars to fight. A third of his forces have been sent against the French, another third against

Glendower of Wales, leaving a third or less to direct against the Yorkists. Moreover, the King is running out of funds, "and his coffers sound / With hollow poverty and emptiness." The Archbishop agrees that it would be impossible for the King to send all his troops against the Yorkists.

Satisfied by the assurances of Hastings and the Archbishop, Lord Bardolph now asks who will lead the King's forces to York. Hastings answers that Prince John, Duke of Lancaster, and the Earl of Westmoreland will meet the Yorkists; the King and Prince Hal (Harry of Monmouth) will march against Wales, but he does not know who will lead the English against the French.

The Archbishop announces that it is time to publish their decision to the people. He is sure that the public is ready to depose Henry, and the thought of their fickleness even against his enemy arouses the Archbishop's scorn. He compares the common people to greedy beasts who have fed on Henry and are now ready to vomit him up just as they had disgorged Richard. "What trust is in these times?" the Archbishop asks. Those who wished Richard dead now love his memory; those who followed at the heels of Henry Bolingbroke as he marched through England now wish him gone. This fickleness, which may be of use to him, nevertheless is a source of disgust to the Archbishop. He bemoans the troubles of the times, which are worse than anything in the past or in days to come. The scene ends with a rhymed couplet, spoken by Mowbray and Hastings, announcing that it is time to assemble the troops and start the rebellion:

> Mow. Shall we go draw our numbers and set on?
> Hast. We are time's subjects, and time bids be gone.

Act II: Scene 1

The action now turns from York where the political rebels have completed their conspiracy to a London street where Mistress Quickly, Hostess of the Boar's Head Tavern, seeks a judgment against Falstaff for money he owes her. The Hostess is seen talking with Master Fang, an officer of the law, who is accompanied by another officer. Fang informs the Hostess that he has entered her complaint against Falstaff (indicating that he is prepared to make an arrest). The Hostess asks if he has a lusty yeoman with him (for the arrest of Falstaff requires a strong man). Master Snare is called and is informed that Falstaff is to be arrested. Snare observes that there is danger of their being stabbed if they try to apprehend the dangerous knight. The Hostess agrees that Falstaff is dangerous with his weapon, and admits that he has stabbed her in her own house. In fact, she adds, Falstaff would make a pass with his weapon at any sort of creature.

In a tirade full of malapropisms, mispronunciations, and double meanings,

the Hostess elaborates on her complaint against Falstaff and indicates
where he might be found. His debt to her is "infinitive" (infinite); he
"continuantly" (continually) goes to Pie Corner (which is next to Cock
Lane, a street in London) to buy a saddle (something to ride on), and he
is "indited" (invited) to dinner at the silkman's (among ladies' finery).
He is indebted to her for a hundred marks (in archery, a hundred yards
length), which is "a long one" for a woman to bear.

He has postponed payment repeatedly, she says, in terminology that is
clearly obscene in its second meaning, and (quite accurately) she calls
such dealings dishonest. At last she sees Falstaff and Bardolph coming
down the street and calls attention to Bardolph's red nose, which has been
colored by too much drinking of Malmsey wine. The Hostess demands that
Fang and Snare make their arrest (and again, her request for their services
has a double meaning).

Falstaff, Bardolph, and the page enter. Falstaff immediately notices that
something is amiss. Fang announces the arrest. Falstaff shooes him away
and demands that Bardolph cut off Fang's head and throw the Hostess
in the gutter. A veritable virago, the Hostess looses a stream of curses at
Falstaff, half of which are expressed in fantastic vocabulary. She calls him
a "honeysuckle villain" (homicidal villain), a "honeyseed rogue (homicidal
rogue), and a "man-queller" (man-killer). Without lifting a finger, Falstaff
threatens Fang and the Hostess again. Fang calls for help as the Hostess
continues her invective against Falstaff. Even the little page becomes
involved in the brawl, insults the Hostess, and threatens to beat her.

At this point, the Lord Chief Justice and his men arrive. The Justice calls
for peace and asks Sir John (Falstaff) what he is doing in the midst of
this fracas when he should be on the King's business in York. Meanwhile,
Falstaff has been seized, and the Justice orders him released. The Hostess
explains her suit. When the Justice asks what "sum" is owed her, she
replies not "some" but "all" her money. She vows to pursue Falstaff like a
nightmare until she gets satisfaction, and Falstaff interjects drily that
rather he would ride the mare at night (implying the Hostess is a mare).
The Justice calls Falstaff to task for troubling a poor widow, and Falstaff
asks for an account of his debt.

The Hostess makes an accounting, beginning not with the money owed
her but with his false promise of marriage. She recalls the promise in a
lengthy speech full of seemingly irrelevant details which occurred on the
occasion of the promise and which preceded Falstaff's request for thirty
shillings. Among the details, the Hostess recounts how she had dressed
the wound Falstaff had received from the Prince for insulting the King.
Falstaff answers that the Hostess, Mistress Quickly, is a madwoman distracted by poverty. In fact, she is so mad that she says her oldest son
looks like the Justice.

The Justice is not deceived by Falstaff's innuendo; he is familiar with Falstaff's habit of diverting the cause of truth. He will not be put off by Falstaff's impudence, for it is clear to him that Falstaff has misused the woman's "purse and person." He orders Falstaff to pay the debt and repent his sins. (Falstaff, however, knows and insists on his rights.) He demands that the Justice call off the officers because he cannot be detained while on the King's business. The Justice (recognizing Falstaff's legal right) appeals to Falstaff's moral sense. Immunity to carry out the King's business does not give a man the power to do wrong. Falstaff calls the Hostess aside and begins to talk to her as the messenger Gower arrives on the scene.

Gower announces that the King and Prince Harry have returned from Wales and are now near London. He delivers a written message as well. Meanwhile, Falstaff is pacifying the Hostess with further promises. He asks her to pawn her plate and tapestries to raise the money he needs. When she objects, he tells her that goblets and wall hangings are out of fashion. People are now using glasses and wall paintings instead. Falstaff's affectionate flattery subdues the Hostess' last show of resistance. She agrees to pawn plate and hangings to raise ten pounds for him, invites him to dinner, pathetically extracts still another promise of payment, and offers to procure Doll Tearsheet as his companion at dinner. As she leaves to raise the money, Falstaff sends Bardolph after her to see that she does not change her mind.

As the Hostess leaves, Bardolph and the others follow. Only the Justice, the messenger Gower, and Falstaff remain onstage. The Justice is engaged in conversation with Gower. Falstaff tries to learn the gist of the news being exchanged, but the Justice ignores his inquiries. Gower tells the lord that the King is on his way to London with a part of his troops. Fifteen hundred footmen and five hundred horsemen have been sent to aid Prince John against the Archbishop of York and the Earl of Northumberland. The Justice must now attend to business and asks Gower to accompany him. Meanwhile, Falstaff's inquiries persist and are repeatedly ignored. As the Justice and Gower leave, Falstaff calls to the lord. Then, ignoring the Justice, he addresses Gower and invites the messenger to dinner. Gower politely refuses, but the Justice abruptly intervenes and advises Falstaff to hasten to battle. Again Falstaff ignores the Justice and repeats his invitation to the messenger. The Justice chastises Falstaff for his foolish manners, and Falstaff replies he has learned them from a fool (that is, the Justice, who had previously ignored him). "Thou art a great fool," the Justice states as the scene closes.

Act II: Scene 2

On another street in London, Prince Hal, whose arrival has just been announced by Gower in the preceding scene, appears in the company of Poins, one of his rowdy companions.

Having just returned from battle in Wales, the Prince is extremely tired. He is also depressed by his father's illness. Poins expresses surprise that anyone of royal blood could tire at all. But Hal acknowledges his fatigue even though he knows it is unseemly for a Prince to admit it. He asks Poins if it is not a base thing for a prince to display a taste for the common and trivial occupations of life. Poins replies that it is not proper for a prince to be concerned with the flaws in his own character. Hal suggests that he may have acquired this concern for his defects from some source other than the princely blood (implying that there is a higher morality than that commonly attributed to royalty), for he is, indeed, displeased with his own nature. He is ashamed of his need for such vulgar and trivial matters as concern Poins. He feels disgraced by his own knowledge of Poins' wardrobe, Poins' inability to play tennis because he is short of funds, and the expenses Poins has incurred on account of his illegitimate children who wear his old shirts. These matters are too base to occupy the thoughts of a prince.

Poins finds it out of keeping with the royal nature, as he understands it, for the Prince to talk of such foolish matters after he has just come out of battle and when the King lies ill. Not many princes would behave this way, Poins believes. The Prince, however, feels it would be unseemly for him to show grief for his father at this point after he has disregarded the King's wishes for so long. A show of concern now would be out of keeping with the irresponsible character he has earned from consorting with low companions. Were it not for the opinion of the world, were it not for the fear of being called hypocrite, Hal would display the grief over his father which he really feels. Poins doubts the Prince's sincerity, for he counts him as incurable a reprobate as Falstaff. The Prince warns Poins not to judge him until his career is over; he vows that the end will tell. Poins, however, insists that the Prince's low reputation has been properly earned. His own reputation is much better. All that can be said of Poins is that, as a second son, he is a poor man (the estate having gone to the first son) and that he is a good man in a brawl.

At this point, Bardolph and Falstaff's page enter. The Prince notices the page's new livery which has made the Christian boy look like an ape. Poins, alluding to Bardolph's red nose and face, pretends he is blushing bashfully from having drunk too much ale. The redness is, in fact, a result of too much drinking. The page joins the jesters, adding that Bardolph's face is so red that he could not see it peering through the red lattice of the tavern window and that Bardolph's eyes seemed to be peering through two holes in a red petticoat. The page calls Bardolph "Althea's dream" (mistaking Althea for Hecuba who dreamed she had given birth to a firebrand). Pleased with the boy's wit, the Prince gives him a crown, to which Poins adds sixpence. Bardolph delivers a letter to the Prince from his master, Falstaff, who is in good health according to Bardolph. Poins interjects that Falstaff's sickness is of the soul, but that Falstaff doesn't worry about that because the soul cannot die.

The Prince now looks at the letter and announces with amusement that though Falstaff has been allowed to become familiar with the Prince, the knight insists on maintaining the distance which actually exists between them. Poins notices that the letter begins "John Falstaff, knight" and comments on Falstaff's pride, which makes him use his title at every opportunity just as kinsmen of a king mention their relationship to the blood royal whenever possible. Continuing the letter, the Prince reads the formal greeting from Falstaff to the Prince, which Poins recognizes as the customary opening of a legal document. The letter carries a warning against Poins, who allegedly has spread a rumor that the Prince will marry Poins' sister. It closes with an elaborate signature full of self-praise.

After offering to soak the letter in sack and make Falstaff eat it, Ned Poins denies the charges. Once more the Prince reflects on the folly of his conduct: "Well, thus we play the fools with the time, and the spirits of the wise sit in the clouds and mock us." The Prince inquires after Falstaff and learns that he is to dine at the Boar's Head with Mistress Quickly and Doll Tearsheet. The Prince suggests that he and Poins surprise Falstaff at his amours, to which Poins readily agrees. Before they depart, Bardolph and the page agree to conceal the Prince's plan from Falstaff. Now the Prince expresses an interest in Doll Tearsheet who he imagines is as common as a well-trodden road. Poins suggests that he and the Prince disguise themselves as waiters and spy on Falstaff. The Prince reflects on the lowly part he is to play in the prank by descending from "a prince to a prentice," but he indicates that since the purpose of his misbehavior is important, the folly he commits must also be drastic. He agrees to the plan.

Act II: Scene 3

The scene now shifts to Warkworth Castle in Northumberland where the very first action of the play had taken place. Northumberland, his wife Lady Northumberland, and his daughter-in-law Lady Percy (Kate, widow of Harry Hotspur) are in conversation. Northumberland asks the ladies to accept his decision to join the Archbishop and Mowbray, the Earl Marshal, but they are unwilling to do so. The wife has tired of arguing and tells him to do as he wishes, letting his wisdom be his guide. The Earl replies that he must go to war since his honor is at stake.

Lady Percy reminds the Earl that he has broken his word before to someone more dear to him than the Yorkist rebels are. She reminds him that he had promised Hotspur, his own son, assistance in battle, and that when Harry fought at Shrewsbury, he looked frequently to the North for his father's promised aid, which never came. No one prevented the Earl's going at that time except his own cautious decision. A double honor was at stake at Shrewsbury, Harry's and the Earl's. Harry Hotspur is now dead. The Earl's honor may be redeemed one day, but Harry's is lost forever.

He had been the idol of all the noble youth of England. The valiant young men of the nation copied Hotspur's walk and his heavy speech; they ate what he ate, amused themselves as he did, fought as he did, and imitated his eccentricities. Such was the greatness of the man the Earl had left stranded at Shrewsbury, while now he shows such concern for the Archbishop and the Marshal (Mowbray) who are strong enough without Northumberland's forces. Hotspur with half their troops could have been victorious at Shrewsbury, and Harry Monmouth (the Prince) would now be dead instead of Harry Hotspur.

Northumberland is visibly moved by Lady Percy's argument. She has recalled past mistakes which sorely trouble him, but now he must go to war for fear of worse danger should he hold back. Lady Northumberland suggests that he flee to the safety of Scotland where he can assess the battle before joining it. Lady Percy adds her voice to this suggestion, reminding him that he had done just this kind of thing during the Battle of Shrewsbury. Finally, Northumberland concedes to the ladies. He will go to Scotland until he can estimate the strength of the rebels.

Act II: Scene 4

The action returns to London and the Boar's Head Tavern in Eastcheap where Falstaff is dining with Doll Tearsheet and the Hostess. Francis, a drawer or waiter at the inn, enters with a second drawer to set the scene. Francis upbraids the second drawer for bringing in Applejohns (a type of apple which is not ripe until its skin has withered). The drawer recalls how the Prince had once insulted Falstaff by comparing Sir John to an Applejohn. However, he believes that Falstaff has forgotten that insult by now. Francis orders him to cover the apple and fetch a musician for Mistress Tearsheet. Will, a third drawer, enters to announce that the Prince and Poins are expected at any moment. They will borrow leather jerkins and aprons from the waiters in order to play a prank on Falstaff. Francis is delighted at this news, for it gives promise of the kind of fun that may be had at a festival. The second drawer leaves to find Sneak the musician. Mistress Quickly and Doll Tearsheet enter. The Hostess remarks that Doll seems to have recovered from her excessive drinking of canary wine. In fact, the wine has done her some good; she is now as red as a rose and more cheerful in temperament.

Falstaff enters next, singing an old ballad, but he is interrupted by the odor of a chamberpot which needs emptying. Francis takes out the pot as Falstaff goes on with his song. He stops singing again to ask after Doll's health. The Hostess answers that Doll is sick of a "qualm" (which she pronounces "calm"), and Falstaff comments on the nature of women who cannot abide peace (calm). Doll is immediately insulted and bawls at Falstaff for his unflattering remark. An interchange follows in which each accuses the other of carrying infamous diseases. The Hostess calls for peace, telling Doll that as the weaker vessel, she must bear Falstaff's "confirmities" (infirmities). Doll complains that Falstaff is too gross to bear, but she will make up with him anyway because he is going off to war.

A drawer now enters to announce the arrival of Ancient Pistol, one of Falstaff's men. Doll despises Pistol and identifies him at once as a swaggering rascal who has the foulest mouth in all England. The Hostess refuses to have him admitted. She has an aversion to swaggerers or braggarts. Falstaff exerts his authority in a menacing tone. The Ancient is one of his men, he reminds the Hostess. But the Hostess is persistent; she says her minister has warned her to guard her reputation, which she describes alternately as bad and good, by allowing no swaggerers into her inn. (The Hostess takes the minister's advice literally. Although the tavern is frequented by low persons of every kind, she will not have swaggerers.) Falstaff placates the Hostess by insisting that Pistol is only a cheater not a swaggerer. As long as he is only a cheater, the Hostess consents to have him enter her house. The word "swaggerer" (because the minister had used it) is enough to make her tremble like a leaf, the Hostess confesses.

Pistol, Bardolph, and the page enter. Falstaff offers Pistol a drink. In phrases pungent with double-meaning, Pistol proposes to toast first the Hostess then Doll. Both refuse him, and Doll shows her contempt for Pistol in a stream of invective which mocks his military pretensions. Pistol becomes furious. It takes the combined efforts of the Hostess, Bardolph, and the page to quiet the ranting soldier who is fond of fustian speeches and great shows of anger at slight provocations. At last he quiets down, puts up his sword, and calls for sack. Doll still insists that he be tossed out, and as Pistol shows signs of raging anew, Falstaff orders Bardolph to throw him out.

Now Pistol draws his sword and calls for death in poetic language which is so effusive that the Hostess begins to admire his speech as if she were at a play. At last Falstaff calls for his sword; Pistol retreats. The Hostess is in a tizzy at the sight of drawn weapons. Escorted by Bardolph, Pistol leaves but not before blood is shed. Doll is proud of Falstaff for his valiant show at arms, and the Hostess is fearful that Falstaff has been wounded in the groin. Bardolph returns to report that Pistol has been hurt in the shoulder. Doll, overjoyed at the discomfort of her enemy Pistol, shows her affection for Falstaff whom she compares to the valorous Hector of Troy. She promises to toss with him between sheets if he will have Pistol tossed in a blanket.

With Pistol gone, the music arrives. Falstaff calls Doll to sit on his knee, and she scolds him affectionately for the wild life he leads. Even Doll recognizes that the time has come for Falstaff to reform his ways, to give up fighting and wenching, and to prepare for heaven.

Meanwhile, the Prince and Poins enter in drawers' disguise as Falstaff and Doll continue their conversation. Falstaff asks Doll not to remind him of death. Changing the subject, she asks about the Prince whom she has never met. Falstaff describes him in unflattering terms as a shallow young fellow who should have been born a kitchen-boy. As for Poins, about whom Doll also inquires, he has a thick wit and lacks the power of inventiveness. He claims the Prince likes Poins only because they are the same age and size, which makes Poins an agile and able companion at games and jests. Moreover, the Prince likes Poins' bawdy stories and his skill at swearing.

The Prince and Poins are angered by what they hear. In a whispered conclave, Poins suggests beating Falstaff in front of his mistress, but the Prince is fascinated by the love-making between the fat old man and his mistress. They wonder that such an aged rogue can still show desire. Poins is equally amused at Bardolph who is becoming amorous with Mistress Quickly, Falstaff's confidante.

As the Prince and Poins watch, Doll professes to love Falstaff better than any other, while Falstaff protests that he is an old, old man. Still Doll insists that he is her favorite, and the Flattered Falstaff offers her a present, invites her to bed, and insists she will forget him when he is gone. As Falstaff calls for more sack, the Prince and Poins present themselves before him, still dressed as waiters, of course.

Falstaff recognizes the disguised pair. The Prince scolds Falstaff for the lecherous life he leads, and Falstaff wittily retorts that he lives like a gentleman, while the Prince is but a drawer. The Prince threatens to drag Falstaff by the ears.

The Hostess now recognizes the Prince and greets him respectfully. Falstaff (who pretends to penetrate the disguise for the first time) adds an equally warm but less respectful greeting, which includes an oath on Doll's corrupt body. Poins warns the Prince not to forget Falstaff's insult and their plan for revenge. (He knows how cleverly Falstaff can twist a bad situation to his own advantage.) The Prince vilifies Falstaff and pretends to defend the honor of the "virtuous" Doll. Now Falstaff understands that the Prince has heard his unflattering description. The Prince challenges Falstaff to explain his latest insult, suggesting that Falstaff will rely on the same ruse he had used after the Gadshill episode when he pretended he knew all along that the Prince was disguised as a robber.

Stalling for time, Falstaff insists he meant no abuse to the Prince. He repeats this several times as he considers how to extricate himself from this new difficulty. At last he explains that he dispraised the Prince before a wicked company to insure that these villains would not fall in love with the Prince. Such abuse is a service which the King himself would appreciate. The Prince corners Falstaff with his own reply. Falstaff must denounce his friends as wicked, or he may defend them and duel with the Prince. Falstaff chooses the former course. Bardolph, he says, is irrecoverably lost to the devil. The page, though he has some good in him, is also blinded by the devil. The women are just as bad. Doll is already in hell, and the Hostess to whom he is indebted may or may not be damned for her lending. But that is no matter, for she is guilty of the more serious charge of "serving meat in Lent," that is, of running a house of prostitution. The Prince insists that Doll is a "gentlewoman," but with truth on his side, Falstaff answers that the Prince calls Doll what his flesh rebels against.

At this point, Peto knocks and enters. Breathlessly, he delivers a message to the Prince that his father has returned and lies at Westminster, that twenty battle-weary messengers have come from the North to report on the York rebellion, and that a dozen captains have been sent to fetch Falstaff to court.

Suddenly, the Prince is guilt-ridden for wasting precious time when the whole country is in trouble. He calls for his sword and cloak, hastily bids Falstaff goodnight, and rushes off with Poins, Peto, and Bardolph. Falstaff, left behind, reflects miserably that the best pleasures of the night must be dismissed for the urgencies of the time. Immediately, Bardolph returns with the warning that the captains are at the door waiting to take him to court. With a fine show of bravado, Falstaff bids the ladies goodnight, calling on them to observe how men of merit are constantly sought after, while the undeserving may enjoy their sleep. Tearfully and sincerely, Doll and the Hostess bid Falstaff take care and farewell as Falstaff leaves.

A moment later, Bardolph calls Doll to join his master. Overwhelmed by this turn of fortune, having believed she had seen the last of her favorite knight, the Hostess bids Doll run and join Falstaff.

Act III: Scene 1

As the third act opens, the King is seen onstage for the first time in the play. He is in his dressing gown and is spending a sleepless night in the Palace at Westminster. His first move is to send a page for the Earls of Surrey and Warwick with whom he plans to discuss the rebellion. As soon as he is alone, he voices his troubled thoughts:

> How many thousand of my poorest subjects
> Are at this hour asleep! O sleep, O gentle sleep.

Troubled by his inability to sleep, the King asks the god of sleep why he visits the poor who lie in smoky hovels surrounded by flies, or the shipboy who falls asleep atop the mast in the midst of a stormy racket, and yet fails to visit a king who has all the "appliances and means" for easy sleep. The question must remain unanswered, and the King accepts his fate:

> . . . . .Then happy low, lie down:
> Uneasy lies the head that wears the crown.

Warwick and Surrey enter as the King concludes his soliloquy. (In some versions of the play, Sir John Blunt also enters. Neither Surrey nor Blunt speak in this scene.) The preoccupied King is surprised to learn that it is 1:00 A.M. In reply to his question, Warwick tells the King that the country is affected not by "rank disease" but is merely "distempered" and can easily be cured with a "little medicine." The Northumberland fever will soon be cooled, Warwick states, unaware that the Earl has retreated to Scotland. The King reflects that if youth could foresee the future, a kingdom shaken by revolution, he would not choose to live. He recalls how Northumberland and Richard II, once great friends, soon became enemies, and how his betrayal by Percy (Northumberland), once his dearest ally, was forecast by Richard. The King reminds Warwick (who is mistakenly called Neville; Ralph Neville is Westmoreland's name) that he was present at Richard's prophecy. The King recalls other past events (most of which were enacted in "Richard II"). He swears that he had not intended to usurp the throne, but that circumstances thrust greatness upon him.

Warwick replies that Richard's prophecy was merely a logical guess, not a demonstration of supernatural power. Northumberland who betrayed his king once might be expected to do it again. The seed of rebellion once planted must necessarily come to life. Henry is willing then to face the necessity of rebellion, this predetermined course of events, but he also thinks of another kind of necessity, the need for more troops to meet the fifty thousand of the "bishop and Northumberland."

Again, Warwick assures the King that the number cannot be that great. Rumor always doubles the number of things feared. He urges the King to get some rest, offering the comforting news that Glendower, at least, is dead. He reminds the King that he has been ill more than two weeks and that the late hours he keeps will make him worse. King Henry accepts Warwick's advice and once more voices his desire to make a pilgrimage to the Holy Land.

Act III: Scene 2

The second and last scene of the third act takes place in Gloucestershire in front of the house of Justice Shallow. Gaunt old Shallow offers a cheery greeting to his cousin Justice Silence, a taciturn fellow. In reply to Shallow's questions, Silence remarks with literal precision that his daughter is a "black ousel" (a brunette) rather than "faire" (a blond), and that his son William, although a good scholar at Oxford, is too expensive to maintain. Shallow observes that William will soon be ready to study Law at one of the "Inns of Court" in London and reminisces over his own madcap days when he was a student at Clements' Inn.

Shallow recalls some of his youthful "swashbuckling" companions of the Inn and remarks that Sir John Falstaff was only a boy at that time, a page in the household of Thomas Mowbray, Duke of Norfolk.

Shallow tells Silence that the same Sir John, when still a boy, broke a fellow's head at the court-gate; on the same day Shallow had had a roistering fight with a fruiterer. Now most of these youthful companions are dead, old Shallow reflects. The thought of death induces some reflections on the inevitability of death interrupted by questions and comments on the quality of the cattle being sold at Stamford Fair, the health of Silence's townsman Double who he learns has died, John of Gaunt's (King Henry's father) admiration for Double's skill at archery, and the price of sheep.

Two of Falstaff's men, Bardolph and another, arrive as Shallow once more puzzles over the death of Double. Bardolph announces Falstaff's arrival, and in answer to Shallow's inquiries after Falstaff's wife, informs him that "a soldier is better accommodated than with a wife." Shallow is charmed by Bardolph's unconscious pun and commends his use of the phrase "better accommodated," which includes a newly coined Latinate word. Missing the double meaning of his phrase, Bardolph states that he does not know the phrase but that the word "accommodated," which means "accommodated," is a "soldier-like" term.

Falstaff arrives at this point and is greeted effusively by Justice Shallow. Introduced to Master Silence, Falstaff observes that his name is well-suited to his occupation (implying both that justice is silent, that it cannot be found among men and that peace, which the Justice maintains, is the same thing as silence). Falstaff, sweating as usual, is anxious to get on with the business of drafting troops. Shallow flutters about finding his roll and calling the men. The first to be called is one Ralph Mouldy (whose name like Silence's becomes the subject of Falstaff's wit). Mouldy is described as young, strong, and of good friends. Falstaff accepts him, remarking that it is time he is "used." Shallow is delighted at this show of wit; to show his appreciation, he explains the joke: "Things that are moldy lack use." Disgruntled at having been selected, Mouldy complains about the draft, making bawdy puns using the Elizabethan words "mark down" and "husbandry."

Simon Shadow is called next. His name suggests several puns to Falstaff. The sweating knight remarks that he would like to sit under "Shadow," that Shadow will make a "cold" soldier, that he is probably the illegitimate son of a "shadow" (an unnamed father), that he will serve well for a summer war, and that he may join the list of other "shadows" (mythical names for which Falstaff draws pay) on his rolls.

Next Thomas Wart is called. As his name suggests, Wart is a very ragged fellow. His clothes are so tattered that his bare back shows through, and the rest is held together with pins. He needs no more "pricking" (enrolling), Falstaff decides, and he rejects Wart from his list.

Francis Feeble arrives next. Feeble is a woman's tailor, an occupation which is regarded as effeminate. Nevertheless, he belies his name and job and bravely offers to do good service. Falstaff doubts the value of his valor, but drafts him anyway. In reply to Feeble's aggressive request that Wart be taken along, Falstaff answers that if "forcible Feeble" were a man's tailor, he might sew Wart together and make him fit to be called. But in his present condition, Wart cannot be taken.

Peter Bullcalf is next on the list. A strong lusty fellow, Bullcalf, nevertheless, makes the loudest protest against going to war. He claims he is "diseased" by a cold caught ringing bells on the King's coronation day. Falstaff promises to rid him of his cold and arrange to have bells rung for him too (at his funeral, that is).

His quota of draftees having been met, Falstaff agrees to join Shallow for a drink, but he is too pressed for time to stay for dinner.

Shallow is eager to reminisce over old times with Falstaff. It is not often that he has such a sophisticated visitor from the city. Shallow recalls how he and Falstaff once spent the night at the Windmill in St. George's Field (probably a house of prostitution) and asks after Jane Nightwork who could never abide Shallow. Falstaff seems eager to divert the conversation. "No more of that," he insists; but he answers that Jane Nightwork is still alive and very old. Silence comments that these events occurred fifty-five years ago, but Shallow still takes pleasure in his imagined rogueries and boasts that he and Falstaff have seen things which Silence has not. Falstaff agrees in a poignant sentence heavy with double meaning: "We have heard the chimes at midnight, Master Shallow."

Shallow understands Falstaff's remark only in its literal sense, adds that their watchword used to be "Drink up, boys," and once more invites Falstaff in to dinner.

The stage is now left to Bardolph and the newly enlisted troops. Bullcalf steps forward and offers Bardolph a bribe to withdraw his name from the list. He insists that for his own part, he does not mind going, but that he would rather stay home with his friends. Otherwise, he would be glad to serve. Bardolph accepts the money. Next, Mouldy steps forward to make a similar offer for the sake of his wife who needs him. His bribe is also accepted. Feeble speaks next. Refusing to offer a bribe, he states courageously that a man can only die once and that he owes his duty to the Prince.

Falstaff and the Justices, having finished their drinks, return to the scene. Falstaff asks Shallow which four of the men called ought to be taken. Bardolph quietly informs his master that he has three pounds from Mouldy and Bullcalf. (This is one pound less than he has actually received, indicating that Bardolph has just bilked Falstaff of a twenty-five percent commission.) Falstaff commends Bardolph's activities and again asks Shallow to select the men.

Shallow picks Mouldy, Bullcalf, Feeble, and Shadow as the best men to serve him. Whereupon, Falstaff rejects Mouldy and Bullcalf. When Shallow protests, Falstaff asserts that he cares not for men of large limb and stature and prefers men of spirit instead. Wart, formerly rejected, now promises to be swift of foot, according to Falstaff. Shadow will be a difficult mark for the enemy; Feeble will be fleet in retreats. Again Falstaff insists that he prefers lean, spare men to the great ones. Bardolph and Falstaff next put Wart through a few military paces to demonstrate their point and commend his awkward efforts. Shallow observes that Wart "does not do it right." He imitates a lithe little man he knew many years ago, who could manage a musket with excellent skill. Nevertheless, Falstaff approves of his own selections, bids the Justices farewell, and orders Bardolph to give the men their uniforms.

As the Justices leave, Bardolph marches the recruits offstage, and Falstaff is left alone. He voices his intention to return to Gloucestershire after the battle, for he has seen the bottom of Justice Shallow; an old man who tells lies about his youth should be easy pickings. Falstaff remembers, in fact, that Shallow was a skinny, ungainly fellow who looked like a forked radish on which a fantastic head had been carved. He was so extraordinarily thin that a nearsighted person might easily overlook his presence entirely. He was the "genius of famine," the spirit of starvation itself. Yet his appetite was lecherous, and the prostitutes of the town used to compare him to the mandrake (a plant whose forked roots resembled the torso of a man). He was out of style even then, and when he wooed the decrepit prostitutes, he would sing them workmen's songs and call them serenades. Falstaff compares Shallow to a "Vice's dagger" (a thin wooden sword with which the Vice in morality plays would beat the devil). He marvels over the fact that such a lean ungainly clown has become a rich squire and has put on such airs that he talks of John of Gaunt (Duke of Lancaster, King Henry's father) as if he had been a close acquaintance. Falstaff is willing to bet that Shallow had never seen Gaunt except once at a jousting match where he had had his head smashed for crowding in among his betters. Falstaff himself had been with Gaunt at the time, and he recalls jesting with the Duke for having beaten the "gaunt" fellow who was his namesake.

After a few more remarks on Shallow's skinniness, Falstaff again marvels at his wealth in land and cattle. He vows to renew their friendship later on so that he can use Shallow's gullibility to his own advantage. He will use him as a philosopher's two stones (which presumably could turn metal to gold) and snap up his wealth as a pike snaps up the dace (a small fish used for bait).

Act IV: Scene 1

Scene 1 takes place at a rebel halt in Gaultree Forest, Yorkshire. The Archbishop of York, Thomas Mowbray, Lord Hastings, and others have paused in their march to evaluate their position. For the benefit of the audience, the Archbishop is told by Hastings that they have arrived at Gaultree Forest and that scouts have been sent out to count the enemy. The Archbishop then informs those assembled that he has had a letter from Northumberland, expressing the Earl's regret for being unable to join them. The letter explains that the Earl has been unable to raise a sufficient army and has retired to Scotland until he can increase his numbers. He wishes the rebels good success in overcoming their enemy. Speaking for the rebels, Mowbray states that their hopes in Northumberland are now dashed to pieces.

A messenger arrives announcing that the enemy is approaching from the west, and although they can scarcely be seen, they seem to number thirty thousand. This is exactly the estimate the rebels had made before, Mowbray cries, and he urges immediate action against the royalists.

The Lord Westmoreland, partisan of the King, now arrives at the rebel halt. He greets the Archbishop in the name of Lord John, Duke of Lancaster, General of the King's Army. Westmoreland addresses the Archbishop as the leader of the insurrection and asks the cause of this ignoble action. Westmoreland describes rebellion as an ugly commotion, which might be expected of vulgar mobs, common people, bloody youths, and ragged beggars. A rebellion of this base sort would never have gained the support of the reverend Archbishop and his noble companions. Why then does the prelate now engage in "base and bloody insurrection" when his church itself is maintained by civil peace, Westmoreland asks. He goes on to state that the proper business of a bishop is books not graves, ink not blood, pens not lances. Thus, Westmoreland demands an explanation for the Archbishop's rebellion (which has not yet been stated in the play).

The Archbishop replies that he is afflicted by the disease of the times, the very same disease from which Richard had died—rebellion. But he does not choose to play physician to the disease, nor is he an enemy to peace. Rather, he is the purge itself, which removes internal obstructions and restores the body to health. Dropping the metaphor of disease (which the King and Warwick had used earlier to describe the times), the Archbishop continues his explanation along more explicit lines. He has weighed the harm his rebellion might do against the harm the King has done and has found the King's injuries heavier than his own. He has a long list of grievances to present to the King at the right time—grievances which he had already brought to court. But he had been prevented from seeing the King by the very men who had inflicted the injuries.

The Archbishop continues his reply to Westmoreland. The dangers to the Yorkists of Richard's time are not yet out of memory. At this very moment new dangers present themselves to those who defended Richard. It is wise, therefore, for the Archbishop to take up arms, not to break peace, but to establish a peace that is real as well as nominal.

Westmoreland finds the Archbishop's charges incredible. He asks him to verify the complaints, to be more specific about the occasions on which his appeals were denied, or the King was insulting, or an audience refused. He accuses the Archbishop of inventing injuries in order to justify his rebellion. The Archbishop replies (in a difficult passage which seems to mean) that he has made Henry's injuries against the commonwealth in general and against his own brother in particular his personal causes for grievance against the King.

Westmoreland answers that King Henry's actions cannot be regarded as crimes requiring redress, or if they are crimes, the redress would not belong to the Archbishop personally. Mowbray asks why the Archbishop should not receive redress for Richard's overthrow, since that action affected all of Richard's adherents, who have been thrown into royal disfavor and have been deprived of honors which were rightfully theirs under Richard.

Westmoreland argues that the conditions of the times, not the King himself, should be blamed for these injuries. Even so, he knows certainly that the King does not wish any of the lords of the kingdom to have cause for grievance. As proof of the King's honorable intentions against his former enemies, Westmoreland reminds Mowbray that all his father's properties and rights have been restored to him.

Mowbray, however, is still angry about his father's lost honor, which he feels had been brought about by Henry Bolingbroke (now King Henry IV). He recalls how his father and Bolingbroke were mounted on chargers ready to fight, how his father could have defeated Bolingbroke in single combat, and how he could have cleared himself of Bolingbroke's charge of treason.

But King Richard had suddenly halted the contest and banished both the disputants. Richard, thus, sealed his own doom, Mowbray says, when he prevented his father from killing Bolingbroke.

Westmoreland deflates Mowbray's filial boasts. He says Mowbray does not know what he is talking about, for Hereford (that is, Henry Bolingbroke) then had the reputation throughout the realm as the most valiant of Englishmen; his chances of victory were as good as Norfolk's. Westmoreland adds that no one will ever know what the outcome of that contest might have been. Furthermore, if Norfolk had defeated Henry Hereford, the people would never have let the victor get out of Coventry (the scene of the dispute), for Henry was then more beloved by the people than King Richard himself.

All this is beside the point, Westmoreland continues, anxious to get on with his mission. He has come to announce that Prince John and the King himself wish to know the rebels' grievances, to give them audience for their wrongs, and to set right whatever injuries have been done without regard for any of their acts which might be construed as rebellious.

Mowbray replies that the King is being politic, shrewd rather than kind; he suggests that the King is afraid to engage in battle. Once more Westmoreland finds Mowbray presumptuous; the King offers mercy not policy. He is not afraid to fight; his army is well-trained, well-equipped, close by, and ready to do battle. He is not compelled by weakness to make this offer of peace. Still Mowbray refuses the truce, and Westmoreland attributes the refusal to the unsoundness of his cause. Mowbray's arguments would fall apart under discussion, Westmoreland taunts.

Hastings, however, is interested in Westmoreland's proposal. He wants to know if Prince John has his father's proxy to make binding agreements with the rebels. Assured that he does, the Archbishop turns over his list of grievances to Westmoreland, and speaking for all the rebels, promises to sign a peace if each of the complaints is answered satisfactorily.

Westmoreland accepts the bill of particulars, says he will show them to Prince John, and takes leave of the rebels, promising to meet them again in peace or in battle.

After Westmoreland's departure, Mowbray expresses the belief that even if the King accedes to their demands, he would soon withdraw his concessions and break the peace again. Hastings opines that if terms as hard as theirs were accepted at all, the peace would rest on a foundation as solid as a rocky mountain. But even if the King kept the terms, Mowbray argues, he would never trust the insurgents again, and any slight deviation from his will, which they might make in the future, would be cause to remind the King of their rebellious action. Even if they died martyrs for the King, their loyalty would always be doubted, and the very essence of their best deeds would be regarded as mere chaff.

The Archbishop, on the other hand, defends the King's integrity. Apparently eager to settle on a peace, he states that the King has learned his lesson and that he now knows that the consequence of killing one enemy is to arouse the wrath of two new ones. The Archbishop believes the King is now willing to redress their wrongs and forget the past and has learned that he cannot kill a man every time he doubts his loyalty. The Archbishop compares England to an erring wife whom the King is prevented from striking because she holds up the child she has borne him.

Siding with the Archbishop, Hastings adds that the King's forces are depleted, so that even if he threatened action later on, he would be powerless to execute it. The Archbishop, confirming Hastings' argument, assures the doubtful Mowbray that if the peace is accomplished, it will be stronger than ever because of the rebellion. He compares the hoped-for peace to a broken limb which becomes stronger after mending than it was before its break. "Be it so," Mowray yields as Westmoreland returns.

Westmoreland requests that the Archbishop meet Prince John in the field midway between the two armies. Mowbray urges the Archbishop to set forward, and the latter agrees to go at once.

Act IV: Scene 2

Prince John greets Mowbray, who has arrived first. Then he turns to the Archbishop whom he calls Lord of York. The Archbishop had made a more fitting appearance, Prince John states, when he assembled his people with church bells rather than war drums. A man who is favored by the King may work great mischief when he decides to betray his patron, and this is what the Archbishop has done, John asserts. Speaking for the King, Prince John states that everyone has known with what high regard his father has held the Archbishop. The King considered the Archbishop "the imagined voice of God himself," the intermediary between heaven and earth. That the Archbishop should abuse the King's high trust, that he should use his divine powers to dishonor the King, is unbelievable to John. The Prince accuses the Archbishop of betraying his divine office by using its powers to rebel against the King who is God's substitute on earth.

The Archbishop answers that it was not the wish to betray King Henry's peace which made him take on his monstrous form (that is, the wearing of armor, an unnatural and monstrous kind of apparel for a priest). He has been forced by the disorders of the time to fear for his own safety and to put on armor in self-defense. The docket of grievances which he has sent the Prince has previously been presented at court, where it was ignored and dismissed with scorn, the Archbishop states, repeating and elaborating on the complaint he had previously made to Westmoreland. For this reason, the many-eyed "Hydra son of war" has been born. But those dangerous martial eyes may be lulled to sleep if the rebels' requests are granted by the King.

Aggressively, Mowbray interjects that the rebels are prepared to fight if the concessions are not granted. He is seconded by Hastings who promises that the rebellion will go on generation after generation even if the present insurgents are vanquished. Prince John answers that Hastings is too "shallow, / To sound the bottom of the aftertimes," that is, to foretell the future.

Once more Westmoreland displays his ability to get to the point; he asks the Prince to discuss the articles of complaint with the rebels and to tell them what he thinks of the grievances stated therein. At once, the Prince answers that he likes all the particulars and will honor all the complaints. He swears "by the honor of my blood" that the King has been misunderstood, that his advisers have presumed too much in barring the rebels from his presence. He swears upon his soul to redress all the grievances speedily. Finally, the Prince asks the rebels to disband their armies if they are satisfied with his answer so that they might all rejoice and drink in friendship.

The Archbishop is pleased with Prince John's reaction to his list of complaints; he trusts the Prince's word and believes in the sincerity of his oaths. At once, Hastings orders one of his captains to announce the peace, to pay the soldiers, and to disband the army.

The Archbishop has been given a cup of wine with which he toasts the Earl of Westmoreland. Westmoreland pledges a toast in return, adding that he has worked hard for this peace and promising to show his love for the Archbishop more openly hereafter. (Notice that Westmoreland has been hiding something which he will soon show openly.) The Archbishop expresses his faith in Westmoreland, which greatly pleases the Earl. The Earl now turns to toast Mowbray's health, and Mowbray ironically welcomes that particular pledge, for he is suddenly feeling very ill. The Archbishop, now extremely cheerful, suggests that Mowbray's gloom, as in the familiar proverb, forecasts a good event, while ill chance is preceded by merriment. Whereupon, Westmoreland cryptically urges the rebels to be merry because sorrow forecasts good things. The Archbishop insists he is feeling very gay, and gloomy Mowbray remarks: "So much the worse, if your own rule be true."

Shouts of joy are now heard from afar. Prince John explains that the rebel army has just learned of the peace. Mowbray wishes the shouts had been induced by a victory in battle rather than by peaceful entente. But the Archbishop reasons that a peace arranged before battle is a conquest too, although of another sort, in which both parties are victors. Prince John now commands Westmoreland to discharge the royal army. At John's request, the Archbishop sends Hastings to present the rebel army before they disperse so that the Prince may review the men he would have encountered in battle. As Hastings departs, Prince John addresses the remaining leaders: "I trust, lords, we shall lie tonight together."

Westmoreland now returns with a strange message. Although he has ordered the royal army to disperse, the leaders (by a prearranged agreement) will not move until they have the order from John himself. "They know their duties," the Prince remarks.

Hastings returns to report that he cannot muster the men for a military review, for as soon as they heard of the peace, they scattered in all directions. Westmoreland, without further delay, pronounces Hastings' report "Good tidings" and announces the arrest of Hastings, the Archbishop, and Mowbray as traitors.

The rebels are startled at this turn of events, which they regard as a betrayal. Is this arrest just and honorable, Mowbray demands. "Is your assembly so?" Westmoreland asks by way of reply. Prince John asserts that he has broken no faith, for he intends to keep each of his promises. He will redress each of the grievances listed in the bill of particulars. As for the rebels' personal safety, he had made no pledge; he will deal with them in accordance with their crime. Dramatically, John closes the scene with three final couplets: The rebels have acted foolishly by beginning the insurrection and have compounded their folly by dispersing their armies. John orders the drums to be struck up in pursuit of the scattered forces and attributes the victory of the day to God. Finally, he calls for the guards to lead the traitors "to the block of death, / Treason's true bed and yielder up of breath."

Act IV: Scene 3

In another part of Gaultree Forest, Falstaff is still laboring to join the royalist party. He comes upon a Yorkist partisan who identifies himself as Sir John Coleville of the Dale. Punning on his enemy's name, Falstaff informs the rebel that his title will be changed to traitor, although his name will remain Coleville and his abode a dungeon, which because it is deep is merely another kind of dale. Coleville, recognizing Falstaff, asks if it is he. Falstaff asks in turn whether the rebel will yield or fight. With words rather than action, Falstaff attempts to cow the rebel into submission, but Coleville insists on knowing his opponent's name. Falstaff finally replies that his enormous belly is answer enough. It is full of tongues which reveal his identity. Were it not for the size of his belly, Falstaff asserts indulging in characteristic self-praise, he would simply be taken for the most active (and courageous) fellow in all Europe.

Before Coleville has a chance to state whether he will surrender or fight, Prince John, Westmoreland, and other royalists (possibly including Blunt) appear on the scene. A retreat has been sounded calling off the royal troops who have been pursuing the rebels. Westmoreland is sent to order the men to follow no further, and Prince John confronts Falstaff, demanding an explanation for his delayed arrival at York. He warns the knight that his tardy tricks will one day lead him to the gallows.

Always ready with an answer, Falstaff replies that rebuke has ever been the unjust reward for valor. After all, Falstaff complains, he is not as swift as a swallow, an arrow, or a bullet, nor has he the speed of thought (which having no substance can fly like the wind). He is an old man, slow in motion. Nevertheless, Falstaff says, he has come as quickly as possible. Moreover, along the way, he has captured Sir John Coleville, a furious and valorous knight, who was subdued at the mere sight of Falstaff.

John suggests that Coleville's surrender was owing more to his courtesy than to his fear. But Falstaff insists that as long as Coleville is captured, he would have that fact recorded with the rest of the great deeds performed that day. If not, Falstaff warns, he will have a personal ballad written to describe his feats and will have engraved upon the broadside a picture of Coleville kissing Falstaff's feet. If he is forced to publish such a poem, Falstaff continues, he will make Prince John look far less worthy in it than Falstaff himself.

Prince John quibbles with Falstaff over his claim to reward. He says his deserts are too heavy to mount and too thick to shine. Falstaff concedes that the Prince may use what words he likes so long as they do him good. The Prince next addresses Coleville as a "famous rebel," and Falstaff reminds John that a "famous subject" took him. Coleville answers the Prince, saying he is no better than his leaders, but had he been in charge, the Prince would have paid more dearly for his victory than he had. Falstaff comments meaningfully that he does not know how the rebel leaders sold themselves, but Coleville gave himself away free of charge (that is, without a fight), for which Falstaff thanks him.

Westmoreland returns to announce that the royal toops have been called back. Sir John Blunt is ordered to take Coleville to York where he is to be executed for treason; Westmoreland is to report to the sick King who will be comforted by the news of victory. Falstaff is allowed to pass through Gloucestershire on his return to London, and Prince John will follow Westmoreland to court, where, he promises Falstaff, he will speak better of him than he deserves.

As the royal leaders depart, Falstaff is left alone onstage to air his annoyance with Prince John in the famous soliloquy in praise of sack. Falstaff realizes that Prince John despises him and that the Prince has no sense of humor at all. He attributes John's cold-blooded demeanor to the fact that he does not drink heavy wine and that he eats sparingly. Men like that lack virility; they generally suffer from an anemia or thin-bloodedness of the sort that afflicts young girls, and when they marry they are capable only of producing girl children. Abstemious men are generally fools and cowards as most men would be were it not for the drinking of sack. Falstaff praises the effects of sherry sack on his own constitution; it ascends to his brain, dries up all foolishness and makes him quick-witted; it warms his blood, reddens his liver, and produces courage. In Falstaff's case, sack illuminates his face and musters up his spirits so that he is capable of valorous deeds.

Continuing his soliloquy, Falstaff praises the valorous Prince Hal whom he contrasts with Prince John. Although born with his father's cold blood as was his brother John, Prince Hal has worked assiduously to heat it by the drinking of sherry. In this way, he has managed to acquire courage despite his inherited handicap. The soliloquy concludes with Falstaff's assertion that if he had a thousand sons, he would forbid them diluted drinks and addict them to sack.

Bardolph's return interrupts Falstaff's reflections. He reports that the troops are all gone. Falstaff resolves to visit Master Robert Shallow in Gloucestershire, for he has been itching to carry out the scheme for bilking the Justice, which Falstaff has been hatching ever since their last meeting.

Act IV: Scene 4

The action now moves to the Jerusalem Chamber in Westminster. (This is a guest room adjoining the southwest tower of Westminster Abbey; it took its name from the tapestries of Jerusalem hung on its walls.)

The King addresses Warwick, his sons Thomas Duke of Clarence, Humphrey Duke of Gloucester, and others gathered around him. Referring to his projected crusade to the Holy Land, the King announces that his navy is ready, his army assembled, and his substitutes (the men who will take over the government during his absence) are instructed. The only things that keep him from the crusade now are the rebellion at York and his own ill health. As soon as these obstacles are overcome, Henry vows to engage in a nobler sort of endeavor and do no more fighting unless it is a holy war (that is, he will join in the centuries-old effort to wrest Jerusalem from the Turks).

Warwick assures the King that he will soon be able to enjoy both the end of the rebellion and improved health. But the King is too preoccupied with other thoughts to answer Warwick. His mind is on his prodigal son, Prince Hal. In reply to the King's question, Humphrey says that he believes his brother Harry has gone hunting at Windsor (a royal park not far from London). He does not know who his companions are, but his brother Thomas of Clarence is not among them, for he is here with the King now. With a humble show of filial respect and princely obedience, Clarence asks his father's wishes. Affectionately, the King replies that he wishes nothing but well to Clarence. But he wishes he were with his brother Harry, for Prince Hal loves Thomas of Clarence best of all his brothers. The King advises Clarence to return Hal's affection so that he may mediate between the Prince and his other brothers when Hal becomes King.

The King tells Clarence that Hal is gracious, that he is merciful and charitable, but that when he is angered, he is as hard as flint, cold as winter, and as quick-tempered as "flaws" (blades of ice) which form at dawn on a winter's day. Therefore, his temper must be watched; he is to be chided for his faults, but respectfully, when he is inclined to mirth. Hal is also a moody fellow, and his passions must be given time to work themselves out. The King entrusts Clarence with the unity of the family after he is dead. He compares the brothers' blood to wine in a keg bound by Thomas of Clarence who will be like a hoop of gold preventing the wine from leaking out even if it is mixed with poison as strong as aconite or gunpowder (discord), which is likely to happen in these troublesome times.

Clarence promises to accommodate his brother Hal and protect the interests of his family. He informs the King that he is not at Windsor with the Prince because Prince Hal is presently in London accompanied by Poins and others of his "continual followers."

Distressed by this information, the King compares Hal's noble and versatile nature to rich and fertile soil which is most subject to weeds because of its richness. Hal, who is the image of the King in his own youth, is infested with undesirable growths. Therefore, the King grieves for his kingdom after his death. He mourns the irresponsible rule and corrupt government which he envisions under Hal's future reign. He fears that Hal will be dominated by angry and hot-blooded "humours," and that when he inherits the means to support his extravagant habits, he will indulge them to the point of peril and decay.

In an attempt to comfort the King, Warwick protests this picture of the Prince. The King misunderstands his son, Warwick insists; he "looks beyond him," missing the real man. The Prince is only studying his companions as if he were studying an indecent language, so that he might learn what it is and come to hate it. Warwick appeals to the King's own knowledge of human nature; the King knows that it is necessary to learn about immodest things in order to judge what modesty is. He assures the King that at the right time, the Prince will discard his low companions and remember their extravagances only as a guide for his own moderation.

Despite Warwick's protests, the King remains unconvinced. " 'Tis seldom when the bee doth leave her comb / In dead carrion," the King insists (alluding to the natural fact that when a bee deposits her comb in dead flesh, she seldom leaves it. Hal like the bee will not leave his companions, the King believes).

Westmoreland arrives at this point, announces the defeat of the Archbishop, Hastings, and all the rebels, and hands the King a bill of particulars detailing the action of the day. Overjoyed, the King calls Westmoreland "a summer bird" who brings tidings of spring at winter's end.

Harcourt arrives next to announce that Northumberland, Lord Bardolph, and a great power of Scottish troops have been overthrown by the Sheriff of Yorkshire. He also presents a written report of these events.

Suddenly, the King is overcome. Perhaps the good news is too much for his weakened health. The King blames Fortune, the ironical goddess who never comes with both hands full, for his sudden weakness. She gives the poor man a sound stomach but deprives him of food; she gives the rich the means for feasting but takes away the health with which to enjoy it. His sight failing, his brain reeling, the King falls to the floor.

There is a flurry of excitement and great show of concern among the noblemen present. Warwick, always the levelling force, assures the lords that the King is habituated to fits of this kind and will recover shortly. But Clarence insists that the King has been so weakened by the strains of royal labors that the wall of his mind has broken and his life is ebbing through the breach. Humphrey of Gloucester voices his fear of the people should his father die, for they have their eyes on certain illegitimate claimants to the throne. He fears they will usurp the Lancaster reign and, like the year that sometimes skips a season, they may choose to overlook the direct line of succession to Henry's throne. Clarence, still concerned over the King's condition, interprets as an ill omen the fact that the river Thames has overflowed three times as it had done just before the death of their great-grandfather King Edward III (d. 1377).

The King recovers from his swoon and asks to be conveyed to another room.

Act IV: Scene 5

The King now lies in another room in the palace at Westminster. Thomas of Clarence, Humphrey of Gloucester, Warwick and others are in attendance.

At the King's request, Warwick sends for soft music to comfort the weary sovereign. The King places his crown on a pillow near his head. In the background, Clarence comments on the King's waning strength, and Warwick hushes him as the King falls asleep.

Prince Henry now enters the King's room seeking his brother Clarence who is heavy with grief. "How now!" jests the Prince, alluding to his brother's tears, "Rain within doors, and none abroad!" The Prince learns that the King is extremely ill, that he has already heard of the royal victory against the rebels, and that his health had altered greatly upon hearing it. The Prince remarks that the King will recover without medicine if he is only sick with joy. At this point, Warwick quiets the princes so that the King may sleep undisturbed.

Clarence, Gloucester, and Warwick withdraw from the room, but the Prince prefers to sit by the King. Left alone with the sleeping King, the Prince notices the crown set upon the pillow and addresses it. He calls the crown a "troublesome . . . bedfellow," "polished perturbation," and a "golden care," which keeps its wearer from many a peaceful night's sleep. Turning to the silent King, the Prince observes that he sleeps with the crown now, yet his slumber is not so peaceful as the common man's. The humble nightcap is to be preferred above the crown.

Ending his reflections on sleep, the Prince next compares the crown to armor, which both protects and scalds its wearer on a hot day. Then the Prince notices a feather lying still on the King's pillow; he believes it would be stirring if the King were breathing. Addressing his father, who he believes is dead, the Prince reflects that death at last has separated him from his crown. Now he sleeps soundly enough in the final repose which has divorced so many kings from their crowns. Tearfully, he tells the supposed corpse of the King that he will pay him with the sorrow and love that is natural for a son. In return, he will take the crown which is due him from his father.

Removing the crown from the pillow, the Prince places it on his head. Expressing the belief that God will protect his right to it, he vows that none shall take the crown with which his father has honored him. He promises to pass it on to his heirs as his father had passed it to him. Taking the crown with him, the Prince leaves his father's room.

As the Prince exits, the King awakens and calls for his lords. Warwick, Gloucester, and Clarence hastily respond. Clarence informs the King that they had left the Prince to watch at his bedside. The King asks for the Prince. Then he notices that his crown is missing. Still inclined to believe the worst of his son, the King concludes that the Prince has mistaken his sleep for death because he wished it to be so. As Warwick leaves to find the Prince, the King groans that the Prince's latest deed will hasten his death. Addressing his two other sons, the King exclaims, "See, sons, what things you are!" How quickly even sons will discard natural filial loyalty when gold is the prize. For this betrayal, the King complains, over-loving fathers spend sleepless nights, work their fingers to the bone, save their gold, and thoughtfully educate their sons. He compares fathers to the male bee who, when he fills his mouth and thighs with honey for the hive, is murdered for his pains. Ruefully, the King states that the dying father has only bitterness from the honey he has gathered for his sons.

Still speaking, the King turns to Warwick, who has returned to his bedside, and demands to know "where is he that will not stay . . . / Till his friend sickness" finishes his work.

Warwick informs the King that he found the Prince in the next room weeping so bitterly that Tyranny himself, who drinks only blood, would have bathed his knife in tears of sympathy. The King still cannot reconcile this report to the Prince's removal of the crown. When the Prince enters at this point, the King asks that they be left alone. The lords leave the King and his heir together.

Astonished to see his father still alive, the Prince exclaims that he never expected to hear his voice again. This exclamation seems to confirm the King's surmise. "Thy wish was father, Harry, to that thought," the King accuses. Ironically, he regrets that his life lingers so long, tiring his son who is so hungry for the throne that he has taken the honor of the crown before the King has relinquished it in death. He chides Harry for his foolish haste in seeking the power which will ultimately overcome him. The King informs Harry that his breath is weak and he will die momentarily. Yet the impatient Prince cannot wait to acquire the crown by legal means. At the very hour of the King's death, Harry seems to have confirmed his father's worst judgment of him. The King now claims that Harry's wild life suggested he never loved his father; now the removal of the crown has proved his hatred.

His anger increasing, the King charges that Harry cannot wait the half-hour till his death. He challenges his son to dig the grave himself, to ignore the mourning period, and to have the "merry bells ring" for his coronation rather than toll the King's funeral knell. Impassioned with grief, the King tells Harry to bury and forget him, for now that Harry will be King, rules of decorum need no longer be observed "For now the time has come to mock at form. / Harry the Fifth is crowned," the King cries desperately.

Working himself into a state of unleashed fury, the King imitates the riotous king he fears Harry will be. He calls for the rise of vanity, the fall of the royal state, the dismissal of the wise counselors, the assembly of apes and idlers. He pretends to address the people as Harry the Fifth: Send me your scum, your ruffians, your revelers, and I shall gild their guilt and give them high office. Restraint, like the wild dog, has been unleashed, and every innocent shall become a victim.

Spent with emotion, the King drops the role of Harry the Fifth and groans for his kingdom. When Harry is king, it will return to wilderness, and wolves once more shall roam the land. Weakened by his tirade, the King falls into silent grief as Harry begins to speak.

The Prince earnestly begs his father's pardon. He would have stopped this deep rebuke, which he knows has been spoken only out of grief, but he was too overwhelmed by tears to interrupt. He returns the crown and humbly prays that God may spare the King to wear it longer. He swears that he did not take the crown out of disrespect for the King. Actually, he was deeply stricken by the sight of his father who he supposed was dead. Repeating his oath, the Prince prays that he may never live to show the doubting world his noble change if he is not speaking the truth.

The Prince explains how he came into the room, thought the King dead, almost died at the thought, and then upbraided the golden crown for destroying his father. He tells the King how he philosophized on the paradox of gold. The crown, made of fine carat, symbol of the highest office in the kingdom, is presumed to be the best of gold but is really the worst. Coarser gold, such as that used in medicines, is more precious because it preserves life, while the fine golden crown destroys it.

Thus, states the Prince, he put the crown on his head as if he were encountering an enemy who had murdered his father. He swears once more that he did not take the crown with joy or pride or welcome.

Moved by the Prince's plea, which he esteems for its wisdom, the King forgives his son. He reinterprets the act of removing the crown as a divine inspiration designed to bring about the reconciliation of father and son. Affectionately, the King invites Harry to sit on his bed and hear his last words of advice.

The King confesses to his son that his means of achieving the crown were indirect and crooked and that he has never been able to wear it in peace. He believes, however, that Harry will be better received than Bolingbroke was, for the memory of the father's crimes will be buried with him. The King goes on to tell Harry that his rule had been troubled by many who lived to regret their part in raising him to the throne and who eventually rebelled against him. In fact, the King states, his entire reign was but one single long argument over his accession. He warns Harry that although he will be better received as an heir than a usurper, yet his position is not completely firm. The rebels, who had helped Henry to the throne before turning against him, have been put down, but only temporarily. They may still decide to turn against his son. To avoid plots hatched by idle minds, the King had planned a holy crusade. Thus, by keeping his lords busy in Jerusalem, he had hoped to forestall further rebellions. He advises Harry to follow his example and keep his noblemen busy in foreign wars so that present action will cause them to forget past grievances.

His strength waning, the King begs God's forgiveness for taking the crown from its rightful owner and prays that Harry may wear it in peace.

The Prince assures the King that because he had won the crown, worn it, protected it against insurgents, and now gives it to his son, the crown rightfully belongs to that son. He promises to guard it against all the world. Prince John of Lancaster and Warwick interrupt the conversation between the King and his heir. Pleased to see John, the King says he can die now that he has seen him. He asks Warwick where it was that he was first stricken fatally. When he learns it was the Jerusalem Chamber, he asks to be carried there so that he can fulfill a prophecy made many years ago that he would die in Jerusalem. The King had thought it would be the Holy Land; now he sees the true meaning of the oracle and is determined to die in the fated chamber. The scene ends as the lords carry the King away.

Act V: Scene 1

The scene is now Gloucestershire. Shallow, Falstaff, Bardolph, and the page are seen in a room in Justice Shallow's house. In response to Falstaff's pretense that he must hasten away, Shallow insists over and over again that he shall not be excused.

Shallow calls for Davy and asks him to fetch William the cook. But Davy is preoccupied with other duties and informs the Justice that certain writs cannot be served. He asks whether or not a field (usually left unplowed to mark the bounds of the property) should be sowed with wheat. He gives the Justice the blacksmith's bill, tells him the bucket needs a new link, asks if deductions are to be made in William's wages for some missing sack, and whether or not Falstaff will stay overnight.

The Justice answers each of his inquiries rapidly and adds requests of his own, which Davy disposes of quickly. In this rapid exchange between master and servant, it is decided that the field will be plowed with red wheat, the cook will serve pigeons for dinner, the smith is to be paid, William shall be charged for the missing sack, and hens, mutton, and dainties are to be served with the pigeons.

Finally, Davy learns that Falstaff will stay overnight. The guest and his men are to be treated well because Shallow is anxious to make a friend at court. Shallow warns Davy that Falstaff's men may backbite if ill-used, and he is pleased at Davy's witty rejoinder that the men themselves are backbitten (by lice), for their clothes are remarkably filthy. Taking advantage of the Justice's pleasure with his wit, Davy inserts a plea for his friend William Visor, whose suit will be heard in Shallow's court. The Justice reminds Davy that Visor is an arrant knave against whom many complaints have been lodged. But Davy argues that he has given the Justice good service for eight years. As a show of appreciation, the Justice ought to allow Davy to suborn him once in a while. After all, Davy pleads, an honest man can speak for himself, a knave cannot. Ambiguously, the Justice replies, "He shall have no wrong."

Shallow returns to Falstaff, Bardolph and the page, whom he calls my "tall fellow," and urges them to feel welcome. Shallow leaves with the promise that Falstaff will follow him shortly; Bardolph and the page are sent to look after the horses, and Falstaff once more is left alone on the stage.

As in their previous encounter, Falstaff is impressed by Shallow's gauntness. He remarks that four dozen Shallows would make one Falstaff. He is also amused at the similarity between Shallow and his men; they watch him and imitate his follies, while Shallow, from long association with his servants, has come to imitate their servile manners. Both wisdom and ignorance are as catching as disease, Falstaff philosophizes. Therefore, men ought to guard the company they keep. Falstaff maintains that he would praise the servants to the master if he wanted a special favor from the serving-men. Falstaff anticipates the sport he will have at Shallow's expense, which he will later relate for the amusement of the Prince. He observes that it is an easy thing to amuse a fellow like the Prince, who has never done a hard day's work in his life, by lying with an oath or jesting with a sad face. Shallow calls from within, and Falstaff departs.

Act V: Scene 2

The location of the action shifts to the palace at Westminster. Warwick greets the Lord Chief Justice who has come to see the King. The Lord Justice learns that the King is dead and wishes he had been called to join his departed liege. He fears that the King's enemies will now repay him for the loyal service he has given the dead King. Warwick agrees that the young King (that is, the former Prince Hal) does not love the Lord Justice. But the Lord Justice states that he is resigned to his fate, which he believes will be worse than anything he has been able to imagine.

As John of Lancaster, Thomas of Clarence, Humphrey of Gloucester, Westmoreland, and others arrive, Warwick expresses his preference for the worst of the three brothers over Henry the Fifth. If Henry were like any of his brothers, the lords who had been his father's friends would not now fear the disfavor of the new King. Echoing his former King, who had grieved for the country under young Harry's reign, the Lord Justice cries, "O God, I fear all will be overturned!"

John remarks about the short greetings that are being exchanged among the lords. The lords are behaving like men who have forgotten how to speak. Warwick replies they are too heavy with grief to say very much. Humphrey and John next comment on the Lord Justice's show of despair and confirm Warwick's opinion that among those present the Lord Justice stands to receive the coldest reception from the new King. Thomas remarks that he will have to recant his attacks against Sir John Falstaff, but the Lord Justice courageously asserts that he had spoken in justice then and will uphold the truth now. If he is executed for his righteousness, he will join his master the dead King and tell him who sent him.

The Prince, now King Henry the Fifth, arrives at this point, accompanied by Blunt. Addressed by the Lord Justice as "your Majesty," Harry remarks that he is uneasy in his new role. He perceives at once that the lords' grief for their dead King is mingled with fear of the new one. He assures them that he intends to follow English not Turkish tradition; he is not Amurath succeeding Amurath, but Harry Harry.

The new King commends his brothers on their sorrow, which becomes them well (that is, he believes it proper for sons to mourn their father) and tells them that he shares their grief. As for their fears, they are to be discarded. The living Harry seeks only his brothers' love, for which he, in turn, will act as father and brother and protect their interests. Therefore, he exhorts them, weep for the dead Harry. But the living Harry, he promises, will convert those tears to happiness.

Still unconvinced, the brothers answer courteously that they hope for no more than Harry has promised. Harry turns next to the Lord Chief Justice, whose suspicious glance shows that he still fears the young King's disfavor. The Justice asserts that he believes Harry has no "just cause" to hate him. Harry reminds the lord of the indignities he heaped upon him when he was Prince, how he rebuked him and sent him to prison. The young King demands to know if this treatment can be easily forgotten.

Yielding no ground, the Justice replies that Harry had struck the Justice at a time when he represented the King his father. In doing so, Harry had dishonored his own father. For this, he had been imprisoned. If this was a misdeed, the Justice argues, then Harry must be content to let a son of his disobey the very laws that Harry will make to guard his own security. Better still, Harry must be content to let his son insult his person by mocking his representatives. He tells the young King to imagine, before he passes sentence, that he was the father mocked and disdained and that the Justice was taking his part against the son. He charges Harry to state in what way the Justice has acted contrary to his duties of office, his personal position, or the King's laws.

In a decision startling to those present, the young King rules that the Justice is right and commissions him to continue in office, balancing the scales of justice and brandishing the sword of law until Harry's own son commits youthful offenses and also learns to obey. Then will Harry echo his father's praise of a lord justice bold enough to curb a king's son and a son great enough to submit to the curb. He urges the Lord Justice to continue his bold, just, impartial administration of law and order. Offering his hand, the young King promises to treat the Lord Justice as his father, whose wisdom he seeks to guide his rule.

Turning to his brothers, Harry beseeches them to believe that his wildness has been buried with the King their father. But the spirit of their father, which is also his, survives to belie the low opinion of him which the world has formed as a result of his raucous behavior. Indeed, he has yielded to vanity until now; henceforth, he will behave with majesty. As if anxious to fulfill this promise immediately, Harry calls for an assembly of the High Court of Parliament so that counselors to the state may be selected at once. Harry plans to make England one of the best-governed nations in the world by learning the art of government in peace and in war and by following the advice of his counselors, chiefly the Lord Justice. Once his coronation is over, he will meet with the High Court and begin a rule so great that no man will wish for the early death of King Henry the Fifth.

Act V: Scene 3

The scene now shifts to the fertile green countryside of Gloucestershire. Accompanied by Silence, Davy, Bardolph, and the page, Shallow takes Falstaff on a tour of his apple orchard. Falstaff is impressed by the richness and comfort of Shallow's domain, but Shallow insists that the land is barren and they are all beggars. Falstaff next remarks what a good servant and manager Davy is, and Shallow agrees. (Clearly, Falstaff is trying to ingratiate himself with both master and servant by following the plan of flattery described in his soliloquy in V.i.)

Shallow announces that he has drunk too much at supper. Silence, who has said almost nothing in his previous appearance, now bursts into a merry drinking song, and Falstaff, also flushed with wine, commends Silence's good cheer. Meanwhile Davy bustles about supplying Bardolph and the page with drink, and Shallow like his servant urges all to be merry. Silence is reminded of a Shrovetide song which also urges men to be merry, and he tells the surprised Falstaff that this is not the first time he has been gay. There were three other times before in his long life.

Davy produces a dish of apples and offers Bardolph a cup of wine. This offer reminds Silence of another song praising the merits of a cup of wine. Pleased by Silence's high spirits, Falstaff toasts the old justice, who continues to sing snatches of song suggested by the conversation. Shallow drinks to Bardolph and the "caballeros" of London, and Davy expresses a desire to see London before he dies. Bardolph and Davy agree to drink a quart or two together should they ever meet in London, and Shallow promises that Davy will keep up with Bardolph's drinking. As Davy goes to answer a knock at the door, Silence sings a Bacchanalian song in which he asks to be dubbed knight for emptying a large bumper of wine.

Having answered the door, Davy returns to announce the arrival of Pistol, who has just come from the court. Pistol informs Falstaff that the latter is now the greatest knight in the realm. Silence, more than a little nearsighted, thinks he recognizes Pistol as a man named Puff. A puffer, indeed, Pistol is not Silence's man. Insulted by the honest error, Pistol calls Silence a base coward. Turning to Falstaff, he reports that he has hastened helter-skelter from court to bring good tidings. Falstaff urges Pistol to deliver his news, but Pistol disgresses into one of his ludicrous and highly figurative rants: "A foutra for the world and worldings base; / I speak of Africa and golden joys." Perceiving that he will get nowhere with his direct line of questioning, Falstaff addresses Pistol in his own rhetorical style: "O base Assyrian knight, what is thy news? / Let King Cophetua know the truth thereof."

Meanwhile, Silence begins to sing of Robin Hood, Scarlet, and John, angering Pistol who resents the introduction of such base heroes into his high-flown conversation. Moreover, he is being prevented from delivering his message in his own way. Shallow next inquires after Pistol's breeding and is told to lament if he does not recognize it at once. Shallow asserts his authority as Justice, which is derived from the King, but when questioned by Pistol, he admits that his authority is derived from Henry the Fourth. Triumphant, Pistol spurns Shallow's authority as no longer valid now that Henry the Fifth is king.

The news of the old King's death spurs Falstaff to action. He orders his horse saddled and promises Shallow and Pistol high office and dignity. Bardolph rejoices on his own good fortune, which will come to him through his master Falstaff. By this time, Justice Silence has succumbed to wine; Falstaff orders that he be carried to bed, while Shallow is told to put on his boots and ride with Falstaff to London.

Elated by the news of Harry's succession, Falstaff offers rewards to all who have been his friends and promises woe to the Lord Chief Justice his enemy. He suggests that they take anyone's horses, for now the laws of the land are his to command. Extravagantly, Pistol consigns the Lord Chief Justice to the vultures and cries welcome to the pleasant days ahead.

Act V: Scene 4

Hostess Quickly and Doll Tearsheet in the charge of two Beadles are being dragged along a street in London as the scene opens. The Hostess bawls at the Beadle who has had her arrested, charging that he has pulled her shoulder out of joint. The Beadle promises she will have a whipping now that she is arrested, for there have been too many men killed in her establishment, the last one beaten to death by the Hostess, Doll, and Pistol. With her usual scurrility, Doll now adds her invective to the Hostess' and claims her pregnancy may be interrupted as a result of this mistreatment.

The Hostess expresses the wish that Falstaff were present to defend her; he would make someone's blood flow. At the same time she hopes that Doll will miscarry. The Beadle promises that Doll may have a dozen cushions to replace those she is now using (to feign pregnancy and escape punishment). Referring to his slender appearance, Doll calls the Beadle a "thin man in a censer" (a container used for burning incense) and a "filthy famished correctioner." She swears she will give up wearing skirts if the Beadle is not beaten.

Doll demands that she be brought to justice at once, and the scuffle continues as the two women are dragged across the stage, shouting vile names at the scrawny Beadle.

Act V: Scene 5

The scene is now a street in London near Westminster Abbey where the Prince is to be formally crowned Henry the Fifth. Two grooms strew rushes on the muddy street to prepare it for the coronation procession that is to pass at two o'clock.

At the sound of trumpets, King Henry and his entourage pass across the stage on their way to the Abbey. Following behind are Falstaff, Shallow, Pistol, Bardolph, and the page.

Falstaff arranges his friends along the sidelines to watch the procession. He tells Shallow to look for the King's leer of recognition when Falstaff catches his eye. He wishes he had had time to buy new clothes with the thousand pounds he has just borrowed from Shallow.

With characteristic optimism, Falstaff decides that it would be a greater mark of his zeal to make a poor show before the King. Shallow agrees to this and to the fact that Falstaff's poor appearance will also show his affection, deep devotion, and selfless concern for the Prince, which has caused him to hasten home without pausing to change clothes. Falstaff fantasizes on the impression his travel-stained, sweaty appearance will make on the new King. He imagines Hal will see him as a devoted subject who cares for nothing but his liege. Pistol quotes two irrelevant Latin phrases and proceeds to mistranslate them. (The phrases seem to have some bearing on his announcement of Doll's arrest.) Pistol utters a poetic rage as he reports on the mistreatment and imprisonment of Doll Tearsheet by vulgar men with dirty hands. He urges Falstaff to call up revenge from its dark abode with Alecto, the snake-haired fury. The over-confident Falstaff promises to do so, and Pistol applauds this promise by comparing it to the roar of the sea and "trumpet-clangor sounds."

Trumpets actually do sound at this point, but none marking Falstaff's pledge. They announce instead the conclusion of the coronation and the advent of the King and his lords, among them the Lord Chief Justice.

Overly familiar in his choice of address, Falstaff shouts his blessings to "King Hal, my royal Hal!" Pistol addresses the new King as "imp of fame." Falstaff ignores the Lord Chief Justice, who has been sent over to chide him, and continues to address the King without decorum or leave.

"I know thee not, old man. Fall to thy prayers," the King frigidly replies. He proceeds to lecture Falstaff on the impropriety of such foolish conduct in a man with white hairs. He refers to their earlier association as a dream from which he has awakened and which he now despises. He rebukes Falstaff for his gluttony, his neglect of his soul and reminds him to think of his end, which is rapidly approaching. He warns Falstaff not to answer him with some foolish jest, nor to presume that the King is the man he was. God knows the King has reformed, and the world shall soon know it too, Harry says. He gives Falstaff leave to see him only if he hears that the King has returned to his former, riotous ways. Until then, Falstaff is banished from London and is forbidden to approach the King within ten miles.

The banishment pronounced, the merciful King now endows Falstaff with a pension so that lack of means will not lead him into new evils. He promises additional rewards according to the progress Falstaff makes in improving his morals. The King charges the Lord Chief Justice to see that his pronouncements are carried out, and his procession leaves the stage.

Distressed by this unexpected turn of events, Shallow calls in his loan. Falstaff assures him that the King did not mean a word he said in public, and he is personally convinced that the King will send for him in private later. He repeats his promise to make Shallow great. But Shallow no longer cares to curry Falstaff's favor and replies that the only greatness Falstaff will be able to provide is a gift of one of his doublets stuffed with straw. Once more he requests the return of the loan, reducing the amount by half in despair of getting all of it back. Another pledge from Falstaff and the repeated assurance that the King's words were but a "color," induces Shallow to pun on "color" (collar, a hangman's noose), which he predicts Falstaff will "die" (dye) in. As a rejoinder, Falstaff tells Shallow to "fear no colors" (enemy standards), and invites him to dine with him, Pistol, and Bardolph as they await the King's call.

The King's messengers are not long in coming. At this very moment, the Lord Chief Justice, Prince John, and their officers appear. The Justice peremptorily places Falstaff and all his company under arrest, promising to hear them soon. The officers lead away the entire group as Pistol, with dramatic bravado, utters the Italianate phrase: "Si fortuna me tormenta, spero contenta."

Left alone onstage, Prince John tells the Lord Justice that he is pleased with the King's proceedings. He informs the lord that King Harry plans to keep his former companions well provided but has banished them until they learn more wisdom and modesty.

Prince John next informs the Lord Justice that the King has called his Parliament and that he believes the swords of domestic strife and civil dissension will soon be directed against France. "I heard a bird so sing, / Whose music, to my thinking, pleased the King. / Come will you hence?" John asks the Lord Justice. And so ends the play.

Epilogue

In some editions of the play, the directions read that the epilogue is spoken by a dancer, who promises to do three things: express his fear of the audience's displeasure, curtsy as it is his duty to do, and beg the audience's pardon for the play. He says the speech will not be a good one, for it is of his own making. Getting on with his business, the dancer apologizes for the bad play which has just ended, begs the audience to have patience with it, and (speaking for the author) promises a better play next time. Indeed, the author had meant to pay the patience of the audience with a good play this time too, but like the perennial debtor to his gentle creditors, he continues to break his promises. When dunned for money, he pays a little of the debt and for the rest offers infinite promises.

If this promise is insufficient, the dancer urges the audience to command him to dance so that, in good conscience, he will pay in the best way he can. He adds that the ladies have already forgiven him for the bad play. If the gentlemen have not, they are in disagreement with the ladies, a thing unheard of at such an assembly.

He announces that the author will continue the story of Falstaff if the audience is not too cloyed with the taste of fat meat and that a new character, fair Katherine of France, will appear in the next play. He suggests that Falstaff may die in the next play, if he has not been killed already by audience opinion. Finally, the dancer assures the audience that John Oldcastle, who died a martyr, is not the prototype of Falstaff.

His speech concluded, the dancer promises to leave the stage when his dance is over and his legs are weary. Bidding the audience good night, he kneels and offers a prayer for the Queen.

Henry V

KING HENRY V.
HUMPHREY DUKE OF GLOUCESTER
JOHN DUKE OF BEDFORD } *brothers to the King.*
DUKE OF CLARENCE
DUKE OF EXETER, *uncle to the King.*
DUKE OF YORK, *cousin to the King.*
EARL OF SALISBURY.
EARL OF WESTMORLAND.
EARL OF WARWICK.
ARCHBISHOP OF CANTERBURY.
BISHOP OF ELY.
EARL OF CAMBRIDGE.
LORD SCROOP.
SIR THOMAS GREY.
SIR THOMAS ERPINGHAM
GOWER
FLUELLEN } *officers in King Henry's army.*
MACMORRIS
JAMY
BATES } *soldiers in the same.*
COURT
WILLIAMS.
PISTOL.
NYM.
BARDOLPH.
BOY.
HERALD.

CHARLES VI, KING OF FRANCE.
LEWIS, THE DAUPHIN.
DUKE OF BURGUNDY.
DUKE OF ORLEANS.
DUKE OF BERRI.
DUKE OF BOURBON.
DUKE OF BEAUMONT.
DUKE OF BRITAINE.
CONSTABLE OF FRANCE.
RAMBURES
GRANDPRÉ } *French lords.*
GOVERNOR OF HARFLEUR.
MONTJOY, *a French herald.*
AMBASSADORS *to the King of England.*

ISABEL, QUEEN OF FRANCE.
KATHARINE, *daughter to Charles and Isabel.*
ALICE, *a lady attending on her.*
HOSTESS *of a tavern in Eastcheap.*

LORDS, LADIES, OFFICERS, SOLDIERS, CITIZENS, MESSENGERS, *and* ATTENDANTS.

Henry V

Act I: Scene 1

The play opens with a Prologue introducing the action. The Prologue is delivered by the Chorus, who begins by invoking a "Muse of fire."

The Chorus goes on to wish for a stage as large as a kingdom, for princes as actors, and for ruling kings as audience. Only under these conditions will the hero, King Henry, truly appear like a god of war before an audience worthy of him. The Chorus apologizes for daring to tell such a great story with mere actors on a small stage. Comparing the limited area at his disposal with the great expanses of France, he realizes that the entire theater has not room enough to hold even the helmets used in the great battle of Agincourt, which is the climax of the play, so this mere play will represent in the imagination the vast areas and mighty personnages of history.

The Chorus asks the spectators to imagine the two great kingdoms of England and France, separated by the narrow English Channel. He asks them to imagine that each man on the stage represents a thousand men and to believe that real horses are visible when horses are talked of by the actors. The imagination of the audience must clothe the actor for his role and must leap from place to place and from event to event with the story. The Chorus offers to help the audience in this process by commenting on the action. He concludes by requesting patience and a favorable judgment of the play.

The first scene is a dialogue between two bishops, the Archbishop of Canterbury and the Bishop of Ely, at the court of King Henry V of England. They are discussing a bill designed to strip the church of much of its possessions. This bill had come up before the previous king, but had been neither approved nor disapproved because of the continuous civil disorders besetting the government. Canterbury is deeply perturbed by the proposal, which would take from the church all lands bequeathed to it in the wills of devout men. The value of the lands is sufficient to support fifteen earls, fifteen hundred knights, six thousand two hundred squires, and a hundred almhouses caring for the sick and aged, as well as contributing a thousand pounds a year to the King. This is a great deal of money. The two bishops fear that the church will be left with almost no revenue at all.

When Ely asks what can be done to prevent the bill, the Archbishop sidesteps the question and enters into a lengthy speech praising the King. As a prince, he says, Henry (Hal) spent his days among the common people in a life of lighthearted amusements, banqueting and drinking in the taverns and playing at sports. Yet this giddy and self-willed young man underwent an amazing transformation when he ascended the throne. It was as if death had killed his father and his own youthful wildness at one stroke. Canterbury praises King Henry as a "true lover of the holy Church," a scholar, a man with rare ability to argue theology, debate affairs of state, and discuss the complicated art of war. In addition to a keen understanding of many subjects, Henry has the power to charm and to persuade with his sweet and honeyed sentences.

Because as a prince Henry did not spend his time in study and solitude, the Archbishop marvels at his grasp of affairs and his general maturity. Ely replies by comparing Prince Henry to a berry growing beneath a covering of nettles or to summer grass springing up at night unseen. Similarly, the young prince must have been maturing unobserved by those around him.

Returning to the subject at hand, Canterbury says that the King has not yet made up his mind about the bill regarding the church lands. In an effort to dissuade him, the Archbishop has urged Henry to press his claim to the French throne by making war on France. By way of encouragement, he has promised the greatest sum of money ever given by the church to a monarch to aid the English effort. The Archbishop did not have time to explain in detail to Henry his legal right to the French crown. Now the French ambassador is about to have an audience with the king, and Canterbury and Ely go off to hear it.

Act I: Scene 2

The second scene opens with the entry of the King into a room in the palace, accompanied by several prominent noblemen, Humphrey, Bedford, Clarence, Warwick, Westmoreland, and Exeter. Henry intends to hear the Archbishop before the French ambassador. Canterbury enters and blesses the King, who asks him to explain "justly and religiously" the grounds for his claim to France. Henry emphasizes that he will only press a legitimate and honorable claim and warns the Archbishop against distorting the truth in his interpretation of law and history. The King's advisor will be responsible for every drop of innocent blood shed in a war that results from his faulty counsel.

The Archbishop proceeds to deliver a lengthy and complicated refutation of the French contention that Henry is not the rightful heir to France. The French argument is based on Salique Law, which states that no woman shall succeed her father in Salique land. The French say that the Salique land is France and, therefore, Henry's claim is invalid. However, the Archbishop proves that the Salique land is really a part of Germany. Moreover, he cites historical examples of French kings who came to power on the basis of female rights of succession. Since the French do not apply Salique Law among themselves, they are merely using it as a pretext to keep Henry away.

When Henry again asks if he may "with right and conscience" make this claim, Canterbury assures him that if it is a sin, he will accept full responsibility. Quoting the biblical injunction that the daughter shall inherit from her father, he urges Henry to fight for his right, and to model himself upon his ancestors who led the victorious English in France during the previous century.

Ely, Exeter, and Westmoreland second the arguments of the Archbishop. They remind Henry that he is heir to the blood and courage as well as to the crown of his ancestors. He owes it to them and to himself to make use of his youthful vigor. They declare that the other kings of Europe expect great things of him, that his cause is just, and that no English king ever had richer nobles or more loyal subjects anxious to serve his cause. Finally, Canterbury repeats his promise that the church will raise a greater sum of money than ever before to support the war effort.

The King has one final scruple. He remembers that every time his great-grandfather invaded France, the Scots came down upon defenseless England and ravaged the land. This fear is assuaged by Canterbury and Ely, who declare that with careful preparation England can both fight abroad and maintain security at home. Canterbury emphasizes this point in a speech comparing the government of men with that of bees, both of which are based on the principle of obedience. Like men, bees live in a highly organized society ruled by a king (we may wonder why Shakespeare did not know that the chief bee is a queen). Arguing by analogy, the Archbishop declares that just as the bees can coordinate their many different activities, so can men. He suggests that Henry leave three-quarters of his forces at home for the defense of England and take one-quarter with him to fight in France.

The King's mind is made up. Sending for the ambassador, he tells his nobles that with their help and God's he will make France his in fact as it is in right.

At the conclusion of this speech the ambassador of France and his attendants enter. Henry expresses his readiness to know the "pleasure" of the Dauphin (heir apparent of France), who has sent a message. The ambassador begins by asking whether he may speak freely and fully or should merely hint at his meaning. Henry replies with dignity that he is not a tyrant but a "Christian King" who can control his passions. The ambassador may therefore speak without fear.

The message from the Dauphin is in reply to Henry's claim to certain dukedoms in France. The French prince taunts the King with references to his youthful wildness, saying that France cannot be won by dances and revels. (The galliard, specifically mentioned by the Archbishop, was a gay dance popular in the sixteenth century. This is one of many anachronisms in the play.) Therefore, rejecting the English claim, the Dauphin sends a present, which is revealed to be a barrel of tennis balls.

Henry cooly thanks the ambassador and says he is glad the Dauphin is "so pleasant with us." Then, waxing impassioned, he declares that when he has tried out these tennis balls in England, he will play a set in France with the French crown at stake. These tennis balls will turn to cannon balls, and France will have cause to weep more than to laugh at the outcome of this jest. The Dauphin does not realize that Henry may be a wiser and a more powerful king because of that very youthful wildness. Henry warns that he is coming on as King of England and of France. And now his object is not only to win his rightful inheritance but to wreak vengeance on the Dauphin for this insult.

The French ambassador exits with a safe conduct pass from the King, and Exeter remarks ironically that the Dauphin has sent a "merry message." Henry replies that he hopes to make the sender blush for it. Turning to the business at hand, he orders preparations for the war to be completed as quickly as possible.

Act II: Scene 1

The first scene begins with an introductory speech by the Chorus, describing the changes that have taken place in England since the last act. The whole country, especially the youth, is excited at the prospect of winning honor by following Henry to France. Across the channel, the French tremble at the news of the English preparation. Seeking to avert the invasion, the French resort to conspiracy by bribing three

Englishmen to kill the King in Southampton before he sails for France. The three are Richard, Earl of Cambridge; Henry, Lord Scroop of Masham; and Sir Thomas Grey, a knight of Northumberland. At this moment they have been paid, and the King is on his way from London to Southampton, where we will next see him. The Chorus promises the audience a safe and comfortable journey to France in the final scene and an equally easy return to England later in the play. No one will be made seasick by this journey in imagination. The first scene, however, still takes place in London.

The action of the first scene involves the characters of the comic subplot of the play and takes place in London. Bardolph (a lieutenant) and Nym (a corporal) meet on stage and greet each other. We learn that Nym and Ancient Pistol (Ancient was the title of a standard bearer in the army) are no longer friends because Pistol has married Mistress Quickly, the Hostess, to whom Nym had been engaged. The conversation consists mainly of Bardolph's questions and Nym's laconic replies, which reveal his morbid and fatalistic view of the world. Nym is a coward; he tells Bardolph that he doesn't dare to fight Pistol and that he prefers to use his sword for toasting cheese. When Bardolph says he hopes to reconcile Nym and Pistol so that the three of them can go to France together, Nym merely replies that he will live until he dies and do as he may. Things are what they are; knives have edges; and men may be killed when they sleep.

These gloomy generalizations are interrupted by the entrance of Pistol, and the Hostess. Bardolph addresses Pistol as "mine host" (because his wife has kept a tavern), at which Pistol becomes furious (he is given to sudden bursts of anger) and declares that his wife will keep boarders no longer. She agrees to this, affirming that people say she is keeping a brothel merely because fourteen gentlewomen lodge with her. (In *Henry IV* Mistress Quickly did run a tavern that was also a bawdy house. That is why we must laugh at her remark.)

Suddenly the Hostess notices Nym, and he and Pistol draw swords. Bardolph intervenes, thinking to stop them, but this is unnecessary; the two prefer name-calling to fighting. Pistol calls Nym an "Iceland dog" and a "viper vile." When the corporal tells the Hostess that he wants her "souls" (meaning both alone and unmarried), Pistol delivers some flashing verbal retorts but still does nothing. Bardolph again bids them put up their swords and they comply, but Pistol still cannot control his tongue and renews his insults. He is interrupted by the arrival of the Boy, who asks them to come to his master, Falstaff, who is lying very ill upstairs. The Hostess goes off, declaring that the King has surely killed poor Falstaff's heart.

Bardolph again tries to reconcile Nym and Pistol, who now quarrel over eight shillings that Nym won from Pistol in a bet. Pistol refuses to pay, "Base is the slave that pays;" Nym insists and again they draw swords. At this point Bardolph intervenes with an oath and the two quarrelers come to terms. Pistol will give Nym a noble (a coin worth about six shillings), liquor, and his friendship. This friendship is worth something, for Pistol has been appointed provisioner to the army and offers to share with his companions the benefits of this profitable position. On this basis Nym agrees and peace is restored.

Now the Hostess rushes in, begging them to come to Falstaff, who is dying upstairs. All grieve that the King has broken poor Falstaff's heart, but Pistol complacently remarks that though Falstaff die, "we will live."

Act II: Scene 2

The second scene takes place in Southampton, where the King and army are ready to embark for France. Bedford, Exeter, and Westmoreland enter, discussing the conspiracy against the King's life, which Henry has discovered. They marvel at the traitors' powers to dissemble, and they are amazed at the participation in the plot of one man particularly dear to the King.

Henry comes on stage accompanied by various lords, including the three conspirators, Scroop, Cambridge, and Grey, who do not yet know that they have been found out. They assure Henry that no King was ever better loved or more feared than he. Grey says that even those who were his father's enemies have been won over to his side. Henry replies that he is completely confident of the loyalty of all his subjects, both those who will accompany him to France and those who will remain in England. Turning to Exeter, Henry bids him set free a man recently imprisoned for speaking ill of the King while drunk. All three conspirators protest against this leniency, urging Henry to make this man an example for others. When the King says, "O, let us yet be merciful," they declare that allowing such a man to live after severe punishment is mercy enough. But Henry is determined to free the prisoner. If slight misdeeds committed under the influence of wine are not forgiven, how shall we react to more serious crimes, he asks. Then, turning to his three false friends, he hands each one a paper which he says is his commission for the army, but is really a warrant for arrest. Reading the papers, the three grow pale, confess their fault, and throw themselves upon the mercy of the King.

The King delivers a long speech, reproaching his former friends for planning to commit treason and murder. How do they dare, for very shame, to ask for mercy! They themselves have just warned Henry against showing clemency to a man who merely attacked the King with words. *They* would have taken his life. By their own advice, then, he ought not to show mercy and he will not do so.

What makes their plotting most cruel is that Henry has loved and trusted these men, particularly Scroop, whom he now calls an "Ingrateful, savage, and inhuman creature." Henry cherished, trusted, and confided in this man above others. Scroop ought to have been the last man in England to turn traitor, for he seemed serious, scholarly, and religious, moderate in his passions and prudent in his judgment. In the light of what Scroop seemed to be, his fall seems to Henry like another fall of man. Henceforth the King will suspect even the most virtuous men of secret duplicity. Ordering the arrest of the traitors, he commits them to the mercy of God.

Exeter pronounces each man under arrest and, one by one, Scroop, Cambridge, and Grey express their repentance. Scroop declares that God has justly revealed their evil purpose and begs Henry to forgive his fault but not his body. The two others share his feelings.

In pronouncing sentence, the King declares that he seeks no personal revenge. As guardian of the country, however, he must sentence to death men who would have subjected lords and commons alike to foreign oppression and contempt. He hopes that God in His mercy will give the traitors true repentance and endurance to bear their death.

As the three traitors are taken off-stage by guards, Henry turns his attention to the expedition against France. He interprets the discovery of the plot as a sign of God's favor. With no other hindrance, they may commit themselves to the hands of God and put to sea. Henry will be "No King of England if not King of France."

Act II: Scene 3

Pistol, Bardolph, and Nym are leaving London for Southampton to embark with the army. The Hostess asks her husband if she may go part of the way with them, but he says no, for he is still grieving over the death of Falstaff (which has taken place since the first scene of this act). The conversation then turns to the subject of Falstaff's death. Bardolph wishes he were with him in heaven or in hell. The Hostess quickly replies that Falstaff is in heaven, for his death was as peaceful as any innocent child's. She relates how she could tell he was dying by the way he fumbled with the sheets, and toyed with flowers, and smiled at his fingers. His nose looked sharp and pinched and he babbled about green fields. At one point he cried out "God, God, God" until she tried to comfort him by saying that there was no need yet to think of God. But his body was cold as a stone, and he died.

Nym says that Falstaff cried out a warning against sack (the Rhine wine he had loved to drink), and Bardolph adds that he also cried out a warning against women. This second point the Hostess tries to deny, although she admits that it may be so, for he talked of the Whore of Babylon. (The Hostess, who kept a brothel herself, does not want to think that the devil will have Falstaff on account of women. In that case she would be partly responsible. The Whore of Babylon is a religious reference, which the Hostess and the others probably do not understand, although the audience should. In the *Book of Revelation* in the New Testament the Whore of Babylon stands for the antichrist.) The Boy remembers how Falstaff thought a fly on Bardolph's nose was a soul burning in hell. Bardolph (who is known for having a fiery red nose) says that "the fuel is gone that maintained that fire" (meaning that Falstaff is dead, for Bardolph was in his employ and got the money to pay for his wine and therefore his red nose indirectly from Falstaff).

The men prepare to leave. Pistol bids farewell to his wife, kissing her and telling her to guard his property, to give no credit to customers, to trust no one, and to be cautious in all things. They are off to France, he says, to suck like leeches the enemy's very blood (which the Boy remarks is a very unwholesome food). They exit.

Act II: Scene 4

The scene now shifts to France, where the French King is discussing the threatening state of affairs with his chief advisors, the dukes of Berri and Britaine, the Constable of France, and the Dauphin. Concerned about the condition of the French defenses, the King asks the four dukes and the Dauphin to mobilize the men and supplies necessary to fortify the towns along the path of the approaching English. The Dauphin replies that although a nation should at all times be in a state of preparedness, there is no present cause to fear England, for her king is "a vain, giddy, shallow, humorous youth." The Constable objects to this evaluation of Henry and bids the Dauphin heed the reports of the French ambassadors who have just returned from England. These ambassadors have great respect for the English King, and particularly for the calm determination with which he is pursuing his present course of action. The Constable compares Henry to the Roman Brutus (Lucius Junius Brutus pretended to be stupid in order to avoid suspicion while plotting against Tarquin, the King) and to a rose bush that is covered with manure before it yields the sweetest flowers.

The Dauphin is unimpressed by these arguments, but he grants that it is wiser to overestimate than underestimate the power of the enemy. His father, however, thinks King Henry strong, and not only because of what the ambassadors report. The French King remembers Edward the

Black Prince, who led the victorious English in the battle of Crecy, and he fears that Henry has inherited the prowess and courage of his warlike ancestor.

At this point a messenger announces the arrival of an ambassador from Henry. The King remarks that the English are advancing quickly. Urging his father not to show weakness, the Dauphin compares the English to "coward dogs," who yell loudly when their prey runs away, but who dare not stand and fight.

Exeter enters accompanied by attendants. His message from Henry to the King is a demand for the crown of France, which he claims by right of his descent from Edward the Third. The laws of God, of nature, and of nations confirm this right. If France will not yield peacefully, Henry intends to compel assent by force of arms. "Therefore in fierce tempest is he coming." He bids the French King resign the crown and spare the widows, orphans, and bereaved sweethearts who will otherwise mourn for husbands, fathers, and lovers slain in battle. This is Henry's message to the King. He has sent another for the Dauphin.

The French King promises to consider his answer carefully and to have it ready by the following day. Then the Dauphin asks for his message from England, and Exeter conveys Henry's scorn, defiance, contempt, and everything in the way of slight regard that is not unbecoming a prince to express. If the Dauphin's father does not grant the English demands, a fierce and bloody war will answer the mock the French prince sent. To this the Dauphin replies that nothing will please him more than war with England, and that he sent the tennis balls on purpose to engender animosity. Exeter warns that the French will learn to their sorrow that Henry is a far different man as King than he seemed to be as Prince. He announces that the English have already landed in France and urges the French King to prepare an answer as quickly as possible.

Act III: Scene 1

The Chorus introduces this act as he introduces the others, by describing the events that have intervened between the last act and the following scene. We must imagine that we have seen the King's majestic fleet embark at Southampton. He bids us see in our mind's eye silken streamers flying from the masts and shipboys climbing on the rigging. In our mind's ear we must hear the shrill sound of the ship's whistle, issuing commands to the crew as the invisible wind draws "the huge bottoms through the furrowed sea." The Chorus bids us magine that we are on the shore and watching a veritable city dancing on the waves, for this royal armada is like nothing so much as a city afloat on the water.

As the King holds his course for the French port of Harfleur, we shall follow him, leaving behind a silent England guarded only by grandfathers and infants. Every Englishman of strength and honor is determined to prove his manhood by the side of the King and his noblemen in France. Now we must imagine the English arrived at Harfleur, their cannon trained on the town. Exeter returns to Henry from the French court with an offer of Katherine, the French princes, in marriage together with several minor dukedoms. These peace terms are unacceptable. The English cannons open fire on Harfleur.

The action of the first scene is very brief. It takes place during the siege of Harfleur and consists entirely of Henry's speech rallying his men: "Once more into the breach, dear friends, once more, / Or close the wall up with our English dead." (Medieval towns were surrounded by walls for protection. An attacking army therefore had to lay siege to the town either by scaling the walls or by making an entry way with their cannons. Such an entry point was called the breach and there the fighting was fierce.) Henry urges his men forward again, bidding them imitate the ferocity of the tiger. The gentle qualities that become a man in peacetime should be exchanged in time of war for savagery and violence. Instead of looking calm and mild, the warrior must assume a terrifying appearance to suit the fierceness of his actions.

Continuing his oration, the King reminds the lords of their noble ancestors and bids them not dishonor their fathers and mothers in this encounter. He tells them to be models to the other soldiers ("men of grosser blood") and teach them how to war. Then, turning to the yeomen (farmers), he urges them to prove the quality of their rearing, for no one on this battlefield, however low his rank, lacks a "noble lustre" in his eyes. Comparing his army to greyhounds straining at the leash before the hunt, he declares, "The game's afoot!" and orders the charge with the cry "God for Harry! England and Saint George!"

Act III: Scene 2

Bardolph, Pistol, Nym, and the Boy pause to rest during the siege. Bardolph urges the others back to the fighting, but they know him well enough to realize that he is as content as they are to remain safely away from the fray. Nym remarks that he has only one life, and the battlefield is no place to preserve it. Pistol agrees, and breaks into a little song telling how immortal fame is won on the battlefield. The Boy says he does not care about fame. He wishes he were safe in a London alehouse and he joins in Pistol's song. At this light-hearted moment, Captain Fluellen enters and orders the shirkers back to the breach. They go off, but only after Pistol begs Fluellen in absurdly comic terms to "abate thy rage."

Left alone on the stage, the Boy reveals in a soliloquy what he knows of the other three. Although he is their servant and younger than they, he is more honorable than three such buffoons put together. Bardolph, he says, is white-livered (cowardly) and red-faced; therefore he never fights. Pistol's words are fierce enough to kill, if words could kill, but his sword hurts no one. Therefore he breaks his word (because he never performs the deeds he promises) and keeps his sword intact. Nym, on the other hand, is a man of few words, but the few he does say are as bad as most of his actions. These three rascals will steal anything. Bardolph, for example, stole the case of a lute (a popular stringed instrument resembling a guitar), carried it a great distance, only to sell it for a few pennies. They want the Boy to steal also, but this villainy goes against his nature, and he determines to seek some other service.

Captains Fluellen and Gower enter separately and Gower summons Fluellen to come to the Duke of Gloucester at the mines. Fluellen declares that the mines are no good, that they are not deep enough. Gower maintains that Macmorris, chief advisor to the Duke of Gloucester who is in charge of the siege, is a valiant Irishman. Fluellen disagrees. He believes that anyone who does not know or care about Roman military science must be a fool, and the Irishman is such a one.

At this point Macmorris himself comes in with Captain Jamy, a Scotsman whom Fluellen praises for his valor and for his knowledge of the ancient wars. Macmorris begins to lament that his mines have not been used to blow up the walls of the town as they could have done. Fluellen, preoccupied with his one overriding interest, asks Macmorris to enter into a discussion of the Roman wars. Captain Jamy appears to share Fluellen's interest, but Macmorris does not. The middle of a siege is no time for discourse, he declares, especially with the trumpet summoning them to the breach. "Tis shame for us all," he asserts, to be standing here when "there is throats to be cut, and works to be done." Captain Jamy is torn, for he would have liked to hear the debate; but he swears that before the day is over he will do good service or lie dead on the ground. Fluellen, however, is not yet ready to abandon his argument with Macmorris and, therefore, with excessive politeness, refers to the Irishman's "nation." A regular quarrel is brewing, when the trumpet sounds a parley (for talks between the opposing sides), thereby putting a stop to the controversy, although Fluellen manages to get in a last word about the "disciplines of war."

Act III: Scene 3

Speaking to the governor of Harfleur, who is standing upon the walls of the city, Henry offers the French one last chance to surrender. If they refuse, the King declares upon his honor as a soldier that he will not cease the onslaught until the city lies buried in her ashes. As yet, Henry can still restrain his men, but he warns that if the battery is resumed and the city taken, he will be as powerless to control them as to command a leviathan (a mythical sea monster). He prophesies destruction, pillage, and slaughter if the fighting begins again. The common soldier, he warns, "In liberty of bloody hand shall range / With conscience wide as hell, mowing like grass / Your fresh fair virgins and your flowering infants." Mercy will then be out of the question. And "What is't to me," he asks, when the citizens of Harfleur have, by their obstinacy, brought this scourge upon themselves. He bids the governor take pity on the young girls, the old men, and the infants, and yield to the clemency offered by the King.

The governor agrees to yield the town, for he has received word from the Dauphin that reinforcements cannot arrive in time. Henry gives his uncle Exeter command of Harfleur with orders to fortify it and to treat its citizens with mercy. With winter coming on and sickness spreading among the troops, Henry will spend only one night in Harfleur before withdrawing with the army to Calais.

Act III: Scene 4

This short scene takes place in a room in the French palace and is mainly in French. Princess Katherine tells her lady in waiting, Alice, that she would like to learn to speak English, and asks Alice, who has been in England, to teach her some words. Repeating after her maid, Katherine learns to say hand, fingers, nails, elbow, neck, chin, foot, and gown. Each time she learns a new word she reviews all the others. Both teacher and pupil make comical mistakes in pronunciation. Alice, for example, says "nick" for "neck" and Katherine says "bilbow" for elbow and "sin" for "chin." At one point, after Katherine has just mispronounced five words in a row, Alice compliments her for speaking like a native. At the end of this short lesson the princess has mastered nine words of English.

Act III: Scene 5

The King of France, the Dauphin, the Constable, the Duke of Britaine (called Bourbon in some editions), and others are in conference in Rouen (a city not far from Harfleur in northern France). The King declares that Henry has surely passed the river Somme by now. The others, angry and humiliated at the recent developments in the invasion, begin reviling England and the English. What are these upstarts but "Norman bastards," asks Britaine. (In 1066 the Normans under William the Conqueror defeated the Saxons and took control of England. Gradually the ruling Normans mixed with the native Saxons to produce a new race of Englishmen.) The duke declares that if the English are allowed to advance unopposed, he will buy a dirty farm in the shabby isle of Albion. (Albion was another name for England, generally derogatory.) The Constable wonders where the English get their daring spirit, since the English climate is raw and foggy and the English sun rarely shines. How can a people whose national drink is beer compare with the wine-drinking French. "O for the honor of our land," he cries, let us show ourselves the equal of these "frosty English." The Dauphin and Britaine say that the French ladies mock their lords as cowards, and bid them learn to dance in English dancing schools, since the only step they seem to know is how to run away.

After hearing these speeches, the King sends for his herald, Montjoy, that he may send a message of sharp defiance to the English. Ordering the dukes, princes, barons, lords, and knights to the field, he bids them wipe away the stain of the English invasion and bring Henry prisoner to Rouen. This royal declaration satisfies the Constable. He declares that he is only sorry that the English army is so small and its soldiers sick and hungry, for he is sure that Henry will shrink with fear and offer ransom instead of fighting. Seizing upon this idea, the King orders the herald to ask Henry what ransom he will voluntarily offer to avoid a battle. Then, commanding the unwilling Dauphin to remain with him in Rouen, the King sends the Constable and other lords to meet the English.

Act III: Scene 6

The scene is near Agincourt, the day before the battle. Captains Gower and Fluellen meet on stage. Fluellen, who has just come from the bridge which he calls the Pridge), expresses his admiration for the excellent discipline maintained there by the Duke of Exeter, who is in charge. At the bridge he noticed in particular one soldier named Pistol, who seemed as valiant as Mark Anthony. Just at this moment, in comes the same Pistol, looking for Fluellen. Bardolph, it seems, has stolen a pax from a church (a pax is a holy tablet kissed by communicants during Mass) and is sentenced to be hanged. In his usual absurd way, Pistol declares that fortune has turned against Bardolph. Fluellen, who likes the sound of his own voice quite as much as Pistol does his, gives his own account of the fickle goddess fortune and the moral that she holds for men. However, when Pistol begs Fluellen to use his influence with the Duke of Exeter to save Bardolph, the Welshman refuses outright. Even if the culprit were his own brother, says Fluellen, "discipline ought to be used." Pistol answers by cursing Fluellen, and repeating the vulgar expression "figo" and "the fig of Spain" before he exits. (These terms were accompanied by a gesture of contempt, putting the thumb between two closed fingers or into the mouth.)

Despite Fluellen's assurance that he heard Pistol speak brave words at the bridge, Gower declares that Pistol is a notorious rascal, pander, and thief, the kind of man who follows the army during a war in order to play the part of a hero when he returns to London. Such a man will avoid all danger and concentrate upon learning the names of the generals, and who fought at which places in order to impress his gullible friends in the tavern at home. Fluellen sees that he was taken in by Pistol's bravado, but he promises to unmask the rascal at the first opportunity. At this point the King enters. Fluellen must give him news of the bridge.

Fluellen tells the King that after some fighting the French have withdrawn and the brave Duke of Exeter is master of the bridge. Whereas the enemy suffered numerous casualties, the English lost only Bardolph, who is to be executed for robbing a church. The King declares, "We would have all such offenders so cut off." He gives orders that in the course of the English march through the countryside nothing is to be taken without being justly paid for and none of the French are to be abused in word or deed. When gentleness and cruelty contend for a kingdom, he says, lenience is the more likely winner.

Montjoy, the French herald, enters with his message for Henry. The French King sends word that up to now he has been biding his time. He could have stopped Henry at Harfluer if he had wanted to, but he chose to wait and make deliberate preparations. Now he bids Henry consider what ransom he will offer, although all the wealth of England cannot compensate for the loss of French blood and the stain on the French honor. Sending his defiance, the French King warns that the fate of the English is sealed.

After complimenting the herald on the ability with which he performs his office, Henry answers that although he would willingly march on to Calais without a battle, he will not avoid one. His few men are so weak and sickly, he says, that they are "almost no better than so many French." When they were in health, he declares, he thought one Englishman the equal of three French. Stopping himself short for bragging, the King asks God to forgive him. It is the French air that has blown this vice in him, he affirms, and he must repent. Rejecting the very thought of ransom, he bids Montjoy tell his master: "My ransom is this frail and worthless trunk; / My army but a weak and sickly guard; / Yet, God before, tell him we will come on, / Though France herself and such another neighobr / Stand in our way." He gives the herald a purse for his labor, and Montjoy, promising to deliver the message, departs. When he has gone, the Duke of Gloucester says he hopes the French will not seek a battle now, to which the King replies, "We are in God's hand, brother, not in theirs." He orders that the army camp for the night across the bridge.

Act III: Scene 7

It is the eve of the battle. Several French lords are whiling away the hours in desultory conversation. The Constable brags of his armor, Orleans of his horse, and all long for morning. The Dauphin begins to praise his horse with romantic fervor: "He trots the air. The earth sings when he touches it. The basest horn of his hoof is more musical than the pipe of Hermes." Once the Dauphin wrote a sonnet to his horse beginning, "Wonder of nature." The others remark that such language is usually reserved for one's mistress, and the Dauphin replies "my horse is my mistress," a statement that gives his companions a theme for puns and double meanings. For example, the Constable says he would just as soon have his mistress a jade (jade means both a horse and a loose woman). Deriding the English, Rambures offers to go hazard with anyone for twenty prisoners. At midnight the Dauphin goes off to arm himself, and the others, who remain behind, make him the subject of conversation. The Constable has a low opinion of the Dauphin, for he brags too much about his horse and his valor and about what he will do to the English. Orleans defends the Dauphin as a gallant prince, but the Constable insists that no one ever witnessed his bravery except his servant (whom he can treat with impunity anyway).

The French lords are in the midst of matching proverbs with one another when a messenger comes in to tell the Constable that the distance between the enemy camps is fifteen hundred paces. The Constable thinks "Poor Harry of England" does not long for the morning as the French do, and Orleans agrees that if the English had any sense at all, they would run away. Rambures declares that the English mastiffs are very brave, but Orleans maintains that it is foolishness and not bravery to fight against overwhelming odds. The Constable agrees that the English must have left their wits at home with their wives. Now it is time to arm. By ten o'clock, he prophesies, "We shall each have a hundred Englishmen."

Act IV: Scene 1

The Chorus sets the scene by describing the sights and sounds of the army camps the night before the battle of Agincourt. The two armies are so close to each other that each sentinel can almost hear his opposite whispering the password. In the light of the flickering fires, each side glimpses the faces of the enemy. Sounds are heard through the night of horses neighing and of armorers closing up the rivets on the knights (who had to be encased in ponderously heavy battle armor). Cocks crow. It is three in the morning. The French, confident of victory, are impatient for the day to begin. The haggard English, fearfully sitting by their fires, "Sit patiently and inly ruminate / The morning's danger." Henry, "The royal captain of this ruined band," walks throughout his camp to inspect and to cheer his soldiers. He "Bids them good morrow with a modest smile / And calls them brothers, friends, and country-men. / Upon his royal face there is no note / How dread an army hath enrounded him." Henry appears so unwearied and untroubled that the apprehensive soldiers are heartened by the "little touch of Harry in the night."

The Chorus concludes with apologies for presuming to represent the great battle of Agincourt with a handful of actors on a stage.

Conferring with his two brothers, Gloucester and Bedford, during the grim night, the King tries to persuade them that good can sometimes be derived from the worst of situations. He encourages them to think of the enemy as unwittingly doing them a service, by making them rise early, which is healthful and prudent, and by causing them to summon up their reserves of courage. Moreover, the French threat results in the English preparing their souls for death and examining their con-sciences, which is also very good to do and all too often neglected.

Sir Thomas Erpingham, a loyal and white-haired captain, enters. Cheer-fully he tells the King that he is quite content where he is, "Since I may say, 'Now lie I like a King.' " These brave words please the King greatly. Telling the others that he wishes to be alone for a while, he borrows a cloak from the good old man, and the others leave him.

Pistol enters and, noticing the king (who is disguised by his cloak) he demands, "Qui va la?" (In French this means: who goes there? In Elizabethan England thieves commonly used this phrase among them-selves.) Henry identifies himself as a Welsh gentleman named Harry le Roy. (Le roi, in French, means the King; and Henry, born in Monmouth, was therefore Welsh by birth.) When Pistol asks the stranger if he knows Fluellen, the King answers that he not only knows Fluellen but is his friend and kinsman. Pistol then bids him warn Fluellen of his intention to knock his leek about his head upon Saint Davy's day.

After Pistol exits, the King remains on stage and overhears Gower and Fluellen, who pass by. Fluellen is reprimanding Gower for speaking in a loud tone of voice. He declares in his usual longwinded sentences that it is strictly against the ancient rules of warfare to make such noise, and that Pompey would never have allowed it. Gower objects that the enemy is very noisy, but Fluellen replies indignantly, "If the enemy is an ass and a fool and a prating coxcomb, is it meet, think you, that we should also, look you, be an ass and a fool and a prating coxcomb?" Gower agrees to speak lower, and the two captains exit. The King is pleased with Fluellen's carefulness and valor, even though the Welshman is "a little out of fashion."

Three soldiers enter next: John Bates, Alexander Court, and Michael Williams, all worried about the coming battle. The King tells them that he belongs to the company of Sir Thomas Erpingham who, he says, in answer to their question, has refrained from telling the King his fears. This is as it should be, continues Henry, for "I think the King is but a man, as I am. The violet smells to him as it doth to me; all his senses have but human conditions. His ceremonies laid by, in his nakedness he appears but a man." Since the King is as liable to fears as any man, it is important that no one should encourage his appreheneion, "lest he, by showing it, should dishearten his army."

Bates declares that no matter what courage the King may display, he probably wishes himself anywhere else than here. Henry denies such a suggestion. He thinks the King would not want to be anywhere else. Speaking for himself then, Bates wishes he were safely out of this trap. Henry affirms that he would gladly die in the King's just and honorable cause. Bates replies that subjects cannot know and should not seek to judge the merits of a King's cause. Then, if the King be wrong, he alone is responsible for the misdeeds committed in his name.

Williams ponders this question. If the King leads men to their death in battle for an unjust cause, he will have a heavy responsibility to fear, especially for those who die with souls unshriven and unprepared for the last judgment. Henry strongly objects to this argument. He declares that the King is no more responsible for the state of his subjects' souls when they die in battle than the father is responsible for the soul of his son who drowns at sea while on his father's business. The King does not intend his subjects' death while they are in his service. Besides, no army is without soldiers who have sinned, and in some cases war is God's way of catching and punishing the guilty. "Every subject's duty is the King's, but every subject's soul is his own." Therefore, every soldier should settle his account with God and his own conscience before a battle, just as a sick man should do. Then, if he dies, he will die well, and if he lives, he will enjoy an easy conscience and a state of grace. Williams and Bates are convinced by this argument, and they resolve to fight lustily for the King. Henry declares that he heard the King say he would not be ransomed, but Williams is sceptical about the durability of that promise. It is all very well for the King to say what he pleases before the battle, but when the soldiers' throats are cut he may be ransomed all the same. At this Henry becomes indignant. He vows that if he lives to see it, he will never trust the King's word after. Williams becomes even more scornful at this remark. What can it injure a monarch, he demands, if a subject does not trust his word? A monarch is impervious to the displeasure of a commoner. The King, angry at this reproof, exchanges a glove with Williams as a gage. After battle, if they are living, Williams will wear Henry's glove in his hat and Henry promises to challenge it, warning that he may "take thee in the King's company." Bates urges the two adversaries to be friends. The English have enough quarrels with the French, he says, without squabbling among themselves. The soldiers depart, leaving Henry alone on the stage.

Left to his thoughts, Henry soliloquizes on the burdens of the kingship, "We must bear all." Musing upon his conversation with the soldiers, he notes that subjects try to lay all their responsibilities upon the King for their lives, souls, debts, wives, children, and sins. The King can never enjoy privacy such as the ordinary man knows, for his name, his words, and all his actions are the task of every fool. "And what have kings that privates have not too, / Save ceremony, save general ceremony?" And what, after all, is the value of ceremony? It brings in no rents. In fact, it is nothing but "place, degree and form / Creating fear in other men." And those other men are more happy fearing the King than he is in being feared, for he can never be sure that friendship will not turn to betrayal (we recall Scroop). Ceremony and all the accoutrements of royalty (the balm, the sceptre, the sword, the crown, the royal robes, the throne) cannot cure the sick nor even teach the king to sleep as soundly as a wretched peasant who, toiling from sunrise to sunset, "Sleeps in Elysium." Except for ceremony the peasant has the advantage over the king. His days occupied with profitable labor, the peasant never guesses what work it is for the King to maintain the country's peace.

Sir Thomas Erpingham enters and, finding Henry, tells him that the English nobles are seeking him throughout the camp. The King agrees to meet them at his tent. When Erpingham leaves, the King prays to God to keep his men free from fear when they will see the numbers of the enemy. He beseeches God not to remember on this day that his father Henry IV, acquired the crown by deposing Richard II. To atone for his father's crime, the son has given Richard new burial and has built two chapels where priests sing mass for Richard's soul. Moreover, the King keeps in his service five hundred paupers to pray for forgiveness of his father's sin, and he himself sheds contrite tears of penitence for that deed. Gloucester comes upon the King at this moment and Henry goes off with him, declaring, "The day, my friends, and all things stay for me."

Act IV: Scene 2

It is morning. Several French lords, including the Dauphin, Orleans, and the Constable, are preparing to mount their horses. They are in high spirits and joke about the tears the English soon will be shedding. A messenger arrives to tell them that the enemy is already on the battlefield. Surveying the poor and ragged English army, the Constable declares that the French lackeys and peasants could defeat such a rabble. Grandpré agrees, for the English banners are so shabby, their horses so sickly, and their general appearance so lifeless that he refers to the English as "Yond island carrions, desperate of their bones." Finally, after the Dauphin laughingly suggests giving the enemy fresh suits and a decent meal, the French depart for the battlefield.

Act IV: Scene 3

The English lords are gathered together, awaiting Henry's return from inspecting the battlefield. Westmoreland says that the enemy has 30,000 men, or about five times as many as the English. The lords bid each other farewell. A spirit of harmony and friendship pervades the somber group, as they wish each other good luck and praise each other for valor and kindness.

As the King enters he overhears Westmoreland wishing for 10,000 more English soldiers, a wish that Henry does not share. Turning from Westmoreland to address all his troops, the King declares that he does not wish a single additional man. "If we are marked to die, we are enow / To do our country loss; and if to live, / The fewer men, the greater share of honor." He says that though he is not greedy for money, he is covetous of honor and, therefore, he does not want to share the honor of this glorious battle with a single additional man. Moreover, he does not want anyone to fight with him who does so in fear and against his will. Henry tells Westmoreland to proclaim throughout the army that any soldier who wants to leave will be given a passport and money for the journey. "We would not die in that man's company / That fears his fellowship to die with us." This day is the Feast of Saint Crispin, he reminds his listeners. Looking into the future, he foresees that on the anniversary of this day each soldier who survives the battle will celebrate, feasting his neighbors and telling them what feats he did on Crispin's day. Each man shall tell his son, and the sons will tell their sons, so that throughout history this glorious day will live in the minds of men. "We few, we happy few, we band of brothers; / For he today that sheds his blood with me / Shall gentle his condition; / And gentlemen in England now abed / Shall think themselves accursed they were not here, / And held their manhood cheap while any speaks / That fought with us upon Saint Crispin's day."

Salisbury re-enters with news that the French are ready. Westmoreland, fired by the King's rousing words, declares that he wishes he and Henry could take on the enemy by themselves. Henry's speech has clearly infused the English with courage and enthusiasm.

Trumpets sound and Montjoy appears on behalf of the Constable to ask Henry once more if he will offer ransom and prevent certain defeat. The Constable also bids him remind his troops to settle the state of their souls, for they will surely die upon this field. Henry's answer is defiance and refusal to offer ransom. Why should they mock me thus? he wonders. "The man that once did sell the lion's skin / While the beast lived, was killed with hunting him." Henry tells the herald proudly that he and his men are tried and tested warriors. Their uniforms, once fresh and new, are now soiled from days of marching through French fields. Managing to joke in this trying hour, he says that the lack of feathers in their headgear should be a sign that they will not fly (double meaning: they will neither fly like a bird nor run away). Inside these ragged uniforms, he tells the herald, "our hearts are in the trim," for the English have determined to wrest new clothes from the defeated French. Henry tells Montjoy never to come again on such an errand, for the King will offer no ransom but his own dead body. The herald departs, promising not to return. The Duke of York begs Henry that he may lead the vanguard of the troops and the King agrees, bidding his soldiers march away, "And how thou pleasest, God, dispose the day."

Act IV: Scene 4

This short and comparatively lighthearted scene takes place in the middle of the battle of Agincourt. Pistol has captured a French soldier. The soldier begs for mercy in French, and Pistol demands money in English, and neither one understand the other. Finally, the Boy undertakes to translate. He discovers that the soldier's name is Mr. Fer, that he comes from a good family, and that he will give Pistol two hundred crowns for his ransom. This offer satisfies Pistol, and the soldier expresses his thankfulness for having fallen into the hands of one whom he calls, "them sot brave, valorous, and thrice-worthy seigneur of England." Pistol and his captive exit. The Boy, left alone on stage, declares that he never heard so much noise come from such an empty heart as Pistol's. Nym and Bardolph, who have both been hanged, at least had more courage than Pistol. The Boy says that he must stay with the other lackeys with the baggage of the camp, which the French could easily capture, since it is guarded only by boys.

Act IV: Scene 5

The Constable, the Dauphin, Orleans, Bourbon, and Rambures, realizing that they have lost the battle, cry shame upon themselves. Is this the king we sent to for his ransom, they ask. Are these the English for whom we played at dice? Determined to make one last attempt to save their honor if not the battle, they return to the field in the same disorder as before. "Let life be short; else shame will be too long."

Act IV: Scenes 6-7

Although the English have done well, the fighting is not yet over, the king tells his followers, for the French are still in the field. Exeter brings word that the Duke of York died in battle. He describes how the fatally wounded York stretched out bedside the Earl of Suffolk, who had just died, and embracing his friend, declared that he was glad that their two souls would fly to heaven together, "As in this glorious and well-foughten field / We kept together in our chivalry!" York's last words were, "Commend my service to my sovereign." Exeter admits that he was moved to tears by this scene, and the King is equally touched by this description.

An alarm announces that the French have reorganized their scattered men to make a last stand. Henry orders all prisoners to be killed.

Fluellen and Gower are aghast that the French have attacked the English baggage train, killing all the boys and burning the king's tent. It is certain that there is not a boy left alive. Therefore, says Gower, the King, in reprisal, has caused his soldiers to kill their prisoners. He praises the King for this, "O, 'tis a gallant King."

Fluellen compares Henry to Alexander the Great, whom he calls Alexander the Pig (it is one of his peculiarities to say "p" for "b"). Macedon, Alexander's birthplace, and Monmouth, Henry's birthplace, are almost identical, says Fluellen. At Monmouth there is a river called the Wye and at Macedon there is also a river, although he cannot remember its name. "But 'tis all one; 'tis alike as my fingers is to my fingers." Then, comparing Henry's life with Alexander's, he says that Alexander, when he was drunk and angry, killed his best friend Cleitus. Gower interrupts to deny any similarity between Henry and Alexander on that score, for Henry never killed any of his friends. But Fluellen explains that he meant to compare the way that Alexander in a drunken rage killed Cleitus with the way that Henry, "being in his right wits and good judgements, turned away the fat knight with the great belly doublet." Fluellen admires Henry for rejecting Falstaff.

Henry enters with several English lords and French prisoners. He declares that he was not angry since he came to France until this instant, and bids a herald ride to the French horsemen on the opposite hill and tell them either to come down and fight or yield the field. Otherwise, the English will come after them.

At this moment Montjoy appears to ask permission for the French to seek through the bloody battlefield to count and bury their dead. Henry says that he does not know whether the English have won, for French horsemen still gallop over the field. "The day is yours," Montjoy answers. Henry's next words are, "Praised be God and not our strength for it." Learning that the castle nearby is called Agincourt, Henry names this the field of Agincourt, fought on the day of Crispin Crispianus. Fluellen reminds the King that his ancestors Edward III and Edward the Black Prince fought brave battles in France and that Welshmen did very good service in those wars, wearing leeks in their caps. Henry says that he does not scorn to wear the leek in his cap on Saint Davy's day, "For I am Welsh, you know, good countryman." Fluellen declares that all the water in the Wye cannot wash out the King's Welsh blood from his veins. He says he is proud to be Henry's countryman. "I care not who know it. I will confess it to all the world. I need not to be ashamed of your majesty, praised be God, so long as your majesty is an honest man." Henry replies soberly, "God keep me so."

Henry sends his heralds to go with Montjoy and bring him word of the French and English casualties. Then, noticing Williams, who has entered, he calls the soldier over and asks him why he wears a glove in his cap. Williams answers that the glove belongs to a man with whom he quarreled the previous night. If the stranger wears Williams' glove in his cap, the soldier promises to box his ear. Henry asks Fluellen if he thinks that Williams should keep his oath even if his adversary should turn out to be above his station. Fluellen replies that Williams is honor bound to fight the man, whoever he may be. Bidding the soldier keep his oath, Henry sends him off to fetch Gower. When he has left, the king asks Fluellen to wear a certain glove in his hat, which he says he got from the Duke of Alencon (while fighting him), but which really belongs to Williams. Henry tells Fluellen that anyone who challenges the glove must be a friend of Alencon's and an enemy of Henry's. The Welsh captain is honored to be allowed to show his devotion to the king by wearing the gage. Henry then sends Fluellen after Williams. When he has gone, the King explains the situation to Warwick and Gloucester, and asks them to follow Fluellen to see that no harm results from his encounter with Williams.

Act IV: Scene 8

Fluellen encounters Gower and Williams returning to the King. Williams, noticing his glove in Fluellen's cap, strikes him and Fluellen seizes the soldier as a traitor to the king. Williams hotly denies the accusation, and the two men are scuffling when Warwick and Gloucester enter, followed closely by Henry himself. The King restores peace by revealing that he was the unidentified man of the previous night with whom

Williams exchanged gages. He rebukes the soldier for the words he spoke in abuse of the King, but Williams replies with steadfast dignity, "Your majesty came not like yourself. You appeared to me but as a common man; witness the night, the garments, your lowliness. And what your highness suffered under that shape, I beseech you take it for your own fault, and not mine; for had you been as I took you for, I made no offense." The King is contented with this answer. He fills Williams' glove with money, and bids Fluellen make friends with the man. Impressed with the soldier's courage, Fluellen gives him a shilling (which Williams grudgingly accepts) and counsels him to avoid future quarrels.

An English herald returns with the list of casualties. He reports that the English have taken fifteen hundred French noblemen as prisoners (including Orleans and Bourbon), and a number of common soldiers as well. French dead number ten thousand, of whom one hundred and twenty-six are noblemen and eight thousand four hundred are lesser gentry. The French dead include the flower of the army: the Constable, Rambures, the Admiral of France, and several others whose impressive titles Henry reads aloud. The English losses are, by comparison, amazingly few: two noblemen (York and Suffolk), two gentry, and twenty-five others. Henry is moved and declares, "O God, thy arm was here! / And not to us, but to thy arm alone, Ascribe we all!" He orders that no man take the praise from God by boasting of this victory. When Fluellen asks wistfully if they may tell the number of men killed, the King consents on condition that divine aid be acknowledged at all times. Henry commands that religious services be sung and the dead buried. Then the army will set out for Calais and for England, "Where ne'er from France arrived more happy men."

Act V: Scene 1

The Chorus once again fills us in on the events not presented on stage. We must imagine the King's arrival at Calais and embarkation for England, where an ecstatic throng of men, women and children awaits him at Southampton. His lords want to have his injured sword and helmet displayed along the road to London, but Henry refuses to permit such ostentation. "Being free from vainness and self-glorious pride," he gives all honor to God and disclaims any for himself. His arrival in London is as triumphal as Caesar's return to Rome. The mayor and all the citizens turn out to greet him, as they would greet the English general were he to return now from Ireland. (In 1599, at the time Shakespeare was writing *Henry V,* Lord Essex was in Ireland, quelling a rebellion against the queen.) Henry remains in London until an emissary comes on behalf of France to try to arrange peace terms. Then the King crosses the Channel and we must follow him back to France.

It is one day after Saint Davy's day. Gower asks Fluellen why he is still wearing a leek in his hat, and Fluellen explains that on the previous day Pistol impudently brought him bread and salt and ordered him to eat his leek. At that time and in that place a fight was out of the question, but Fluellen intends to wear the leek until he meets the cowardly braggart again. At this moment Pistol enters "swelling like a turkey cock," and Fluellen, ignoring Pistol's protests that he hates the taste and smell of leek, forces him to eat every morsel of the vegetable. As "sauce" for the leek and by way of encouragement to the reluctant Pistol, the Welshman rains blows upon him. When he has finished, Fluellen compels him to accept a groad (a small coin), threatening to make him eat another leek if he refuses to accept the money. Warning the rascal to keep out of his way, Fluellen exits.

Once his enemy is safely out of earshot, Pistol boldly threatens revenge, declaring that "All hell shall stir for this." Gower reproves the "counterfeit cowardly knave" for mocking an ancient and honorable Welsh tradition. Fluellen's Welsh manner of speech diminishes neither his valor nor his skill with a good English cudgel, as Pistol has learned by experience.

Gower exits and Pistol, left alone on the stage, ruminates that Fortune has turned against him. He has received news that his wife is dead. Suddenly he feels old and weary. But he still has thoughts for the future. He decides to become a bawd and a cut-purse. "To England will I steal, and there I'll steal; / And patches will I get unto these cudgelled scars / And swear I got them in the Gallia wars."

Act V: Scene 2

The scene takes place in the French court. Henry and his chief lords (Exeter, Bedford, Warwick, and others) enter from one side, while the French King, Queen, Princess, the Duke of Burgundy, and others enter from the other side. Henry's first words immediately reveal the purpose of this assembly, "Peace to this meeting, wherefore we are met!" He wishes health and joy to his "brother" and "sister," the French King and Queen, and to his "most fair and princely cousin," Katherine. Turning to Burgundy and all the French peers, he salutes them with royal dignity. The French King welcomes Henry and the English princes in equally formal but briefer terms. "Right joyous are we to behold your face." The Queen expresses her hope for a happy settlement of the present griefs and quarrels.

The Duke of Burgundy is intermediary between England and France. (At that time Burgundy was an independent land, and its duke at least as powerful as the King of France.) He has done his best to bring the two parties together, and now he asks what hindrance can there be to restoring peace to France. In a lengthy speech he tells how the "naked, poor, and mangled Peace" was driven from fertile France, where ruin and desolation ensued. Gardens, vineyards, and meadows, once carefully tended, are neglected and grow wild. Moreover, he adds, the French children, like the gardens, run wild, for all their experience is of bloody and fearful deeds. In conclusion, he asks the princes here assembled to restore the natural harmony and order to this "best garden of the world" that is France.

Henry replies that the French may buy the precious gifts of peace by acceding to the English demands. The French King requests a conference with Henry's counselors so that he may deliberate and pronounce his final answer on the spot. Henry appoints his uncle Exeter, his brothers Clarence and Gloucester, and two other lords to negotiate the peace terms with the French. The Queen declares her intention of attending the conference in the hope that a woman's voice may prove soothing to stubborn men. Henry asks that Katherine be left with him, since she is first among his demands. The Queen agrees, and all exit except Henry, Katherine, and Alice.

Left to woo Katherine (chaperoned by Alice), Henry does so with the high spirits of a plain-talking soldier. He starts by asking her to teach him the soft terms that will move a lady's heart. For he is unused to the gentle ways of court society. Katherine thinks he must be mocking her, since she cannot speak English well, but Henry answers that he will be happy to hear her declare her love in broken English. When he asks, "Do you like me?" she answers that she does not know what is "like me," and Henry, punning, tells her that an angel is like her. Katherine understands his words, declaring, in French, that men are full of deceits. As if in answer to her charge, Henry vows that he can woo only in plain and simple speech. As if addressing a comrade in arms, he asks her to consent and shake hands on the bargain. He has neither verses nor dances to win a lady's favor, but if fighting, or leaping on his horse could win her approval, he would quickly win a wife. "But before God, Kate, I cannot look greenly nor grasp out my eloquence, nor I have no cunning in protestation, only downright oaths which I never use till urged, nor never break for urging." If she will have him, good. If she refuse, he will not die of grief, and yet he loves her. He advises her that he is sure to be constant in his affection. Lacking the ability to win the favors of other ladies, he cannot then be false to her. "A good leg will fall, a straight back will stoop, a black beard will turn white, a curled pate will grow bald," he tells her, "but a good heart, Kate, is the sun and the moon." Therefore, he urges, "If thou would have such a one, take me; and take me, take a soldier; take a soldier, take a king."

Henry V

Katherine asks if it is possible that she should love the enemy of France. He answers that he is not the enemy but the friend of France, for he loves France so well that he will not part with a single village. And, he adds, "When France is mine and I am yours, then yours is France and you are mine." Because she cannot follow this in English, he repeats it in halting French. Becoming more confident, he tells her that he knows she loves him, and at night, with Alice, will dispraise those parts she likes best in him. He asks her to be merciful, "because I love thee cruelly." Still more jovial, he tells her that between them they will produce a boy, half-English and half-French, who will defeat the Turks.

Reverting briefly to the traditional language of the wooer, he calls her, in French, "the most beautiful Katherine in the world" and "my dearest and divine goddess." She declares that his false French could deceive the wisest maiden in France, but Henry, unabashed, continues both to dispraise his own ability as a lover and to swear his love for her. Finally he demands outright, "Wilt thou have me?" She replies that she will have him if it pleases the King, her father. Henry declares that it certainly shall please the King, and Katherine says that then it shall also content her. Upon these words Henry calls her his queen and silences her objection that it is not the custom in France for girls to kiss before they are married by telling her that customs are made by kings and therefore may be broken by kings. Kissing her, he declares, "You have witchcraft in your lips, Kate." One kiss from her, he says, would have more effect on him than the French Council or a petition of monarchs.

The French and English lords return. Henry and Burgundy exchange slightly bawdy remarks about the progress of the wooing. The jokes turn mainly on the fact that Cupid, the god of love, is traditionally represented as a naked and blind boy, whom a sheltered maiden would be embarrassed to look upon. Finally Henry says that the French may be thankful that his love for Katherine has made him blind to many French cities. He is told that the French king has agreed to all the English demands, including Katherine, except for the form of address which he will use in writing to his son-in-law. Henry has insisted upon being addressed in French and in Latin "Our very dear son Henry, King of England, inheritor of France." The French King readily concedes this point now. He bids Henry take his daughter, and with her raise a son who will unite the two countries, plainting peace "In their fair bosoms, that never war advance / His bleeding sword t'wixt England and fair France." To this all present cry amen, and Henry kisses Katherine as his queen. The French Queen invokes the blessing of God on the couple, that their two hearts and two realms may be united and Englishmen and Frenchmen may be as brothers. Again all cry amen. Henry orders that preparations be made for the wedding, on which day he will ask Burgundy and all the peers to guarantee the peace terms. "Then shall I swear to Kate, and you to me, / And may our oaths well kept and prosp'rous be!" All exit.

The Chorus returns to deliver an epilogue. For the last time he apologizes for the "rough and all unable pen" of the author, and for the temerity of trying to represent the glory of such great historical personnages. He concludes by reminding us that though Henry left his infant son lord of England and of France, in the reign of that son (Henry VI) France was lost and England witnessed the beginning of a long and bloody civil strife.

Richard II

KING RICHARD II.
JOHN OF GAUNT, *Duke of Lancaster* ⎫
EDMUND OF LANGLEY, *Duke of York* ⎬ *uncles to the King.*
HENRY, *surnamed* BOLINGBROKE, *Duke of Hereford, son to John of Gaunt, afterwards* KING
   HENRY IV.
DUKE OF AUMERLE, *son to the Duke of York.*
THOMAS MOWBRAY, *Duke of Norfolk.*
DUKE OF SURREY.
EARL OF SALISBURY.
LORD BERKELEY.
BUSHY ⎫
BAGOT ⎬ *favorites to the King Richard.*
GREEN ⎭
EARL OF NORTHUMBERLAND.
HENRY PERCY, *surnamed* HOTSPUR, *his son.*
LORD ROSS.
LORD WILLOUGHBY.
LORD FITZWATER.
BISHOP OF CARLISLE.
ABBOT OF WESTMINSTER.
LORD MARSHAL.
SIR STEPHEN SCROOP.
SIR PIERCE OF EXTON.
CAPTAIN *of a band of Welshmen.*

QUEEN *to King Richard.*
DUCHESS OF YORK.
DUCHESS OF GLOUCESTER, *widow of Thomas, Duke of Gloucester.*
LADIES *attending on the Queen.*

LORDS, HERALDS, OFFICERS, SOLDIERS, GARDENERS, KEEPER, MESSENGER, GROOM, *and other*
   ATTENDANTS.

Richard II

Act I: Scene 1

The play begins in the year 1398, at the court of the medieval English King Richard II. This first scene is angry in mood and ominous. Richard is seated on his throne surrounded by courtiers. Peremptorily, he asks his uncle, John of Gaunt, Duke of Lancaster, if Gaunt has brought to court, as he had promised to do, his son and heir, Henry Bolingbroke. Bolingbroke has accused Thomas Mowbray, Duke of Norfolk, of treason.

This accusation is of the type called an "appeal," a very serious charge which the accuser must stand ready to back up with a duel to the death. Assured by Gaunt that Henry will be there, Richard probes deeper. Has Gaunt discovered Bolingbroke's reason for the accusation? Does he have good grounds? Or is he moved by personal malice and hatred? Gaunt answers respectfully enough, but rather tersely, that he believes his son does have evidence of treachery—treachery threatening the King himself.

Richard orders that both Bolingbroke and Mowbray be called before him. He wants to see them confront each other, "frowning brow to brow," and to hear them speak their grievances freely. He knows that they are both haughty, strong-willed men. They enter together, each making a brief, complimentary speech to the King. Richard is not a good judge of character, but neither is he a complete fool. He, therefore, thanks them for the praise but reminds them that one must be insincere, since each has accused the other of high treason, which would be an offense against the King. (Shakespeare ignores the possibility that they might both be mistaken in their charges and that, therefore, neither would be guilty of treason.)

Both noblemen show themselves to be indeed haughty and high-spirited as they repeat their accusations in the presence of the King. Bolingbroke, who speaks first, is the more aggressive. He calls on Heaven to witness that he is motivated solely by a true subject's love for his ruler's safety and by any "misbegotten hate." Turning to Mowbray, he says he is willing to make good with his body (in combat) the charge he prefers against him. He will even stake his immortal soul on the truth of his words. Then, in indignant tones, he labels Mowbray "traitor" and "miscreant" (criminal). With a verbal cleverness of the type that will be shown many times in this play, he says Mowbray is "too good to be so [too high in rank to be evil], and too bad to live." In pompous righteousness he declares that the higher the title, the more disgraceful any misdeeds that becloud it. He winds up by repeating "traitor," which he says he stuffs down the throat of Mowbray. He then challenges his opponent to single combat. "What my tongue speaks, my right drawn sword may prove."

Mowbray is by no means cowed. His words, he says, may be cold and few, but this is not a woman's war, a verbal squabble. This is a quarrel that must be settled by combat and bloodshed. But he is not so tame as to be completely silent. Only the restraint imposed upon him by the royal presence prevents him from flinging back at Bolingbroke the name of "traitor." He is well aware of the advantage Bolingbroke has in his royal connections and close relationship to Richard. Nevertheless, "I do defy and spit at him / Call him a slanderous coward and a villain." He is glad to accept the challenge of Bolingbroke. In fact, he would "allow him odds," or travel far to meet him, even to the "frozen ridges of the Alps." Mowbray then grasps the pommel of his sword. With this weapon will he defend his loyalty and prove Bolingbroke a most false liar. Bolingbroke immediately throws down his "gage."

Bolingbroke says he'll disavow, in connection with this controversy, all his royal connections and any help they might be to him. He taunts Mowbray with cowardice and dares him, if he isn't too weak with fear, to pick up the gage. Mowbray, of course, snatches it up and declares that he is ready to stand the knightly trial. If he *is* a traitor or if he fights unfairly, let him perish in the encounter.

Richard, who has not been able to get in a word for some time and who finds the situation going far beyond his plans for it, demands that Bolingbroke recite his specific charges against Mowbray, who, Richard points out, has a good record. Thereupon, Bolingbroke supports his statement that Mowbray is a traitor with two specific charges and one general one. The first is that Mowbray misappropriated eight thousand nobles (a gold coin which had the purchasing power of about fifteen dollars today) which he had been instructed to pay to English soldiers fighting in France in a campaign of the Hundred Years War. The second specific charge is that Mowbray had plotted and accomplished the murder of the King's uncle, Thomas of Gloucester (pronounced Glos' ter), uncle also of Bolingbroke himself.

Gloucester was as guiltless and as well-meaning as Abel of the Old Testament, and Bolingbroke is determined to avenge him. The general charge is the extravagant claim that all the treasons of the last eighteen years (the period of Richard's effective reign) can be traced back to "false Mowbray."

The King takes a long look at this cocksure Lancaster cousin of his and mutters to himself, "How high a pitch his resolution soars!" But without delay, he turns to Mowbray and invites him to speak out freely and answer the charges. He assures Mowbray that he will not allow his family connection with Bolingbroke to prejudice him; they are both subjects of equal status in his eyes. He swears this by his "sceptre's awe," and he refers to his "sacred blood."

Mowbray vehemently and circumstantially denies both charges. He is not an embezzler. Three-quarters of the money given him to take to Calais he distributed to the King's soldiers. The remaining quarter he kept by consent (apparently of Richard). The King owed him that amount for the expenses Mowbray suffered when he went to France to escort Richard's present Queen to England for her marriage. So Bolingbroke can just swallow that lie! Furthermore, he did *not* kill Gloucester, although he *should* have. He must admit, however, that he did once attempt to kill Bolingbroke's father. This he does repent; he has confessed it; he has also begged Gaunt's pardon and, with a look at the listening Gaunt, believes he has received it. Otherwise Bolingbroke's charges are the "rancor of a villain . . . and most degenerate traitor." Contemptuously, he throws down his own glove. He asks Richard to assign their trial day.

The King with some help from John of Gaunt, who with the other courtiers has been observing in silence the heated progress of the quarrel, attempts to persuade the two enraged nobles to withdraw their challenges. They should "forget, forgive, . . . and be agreed." He even tries to make a little joke about it. The doctors, consulting the astrology that influenced such medieval medical practice, have said it is not a good month for blood-letting! But the "wrath-kindled gentlemen" do not smile. They remain obdurate, scornful of each other, and, although outwardly respectful, quite unintimidated by the King. Each protests that he cannot in honor withdraw his gage.

Mowbray says that he would give up his life in the King's service, but he cannot, even for his monarch, allow a blemish on his name. He has been wounded by a slanderous attack. The only balm that can heal the wound is the heart-blood of his accuser. A man who has lost his good reputation is but "painted clay." Take away his honor, and he might as well be dead. He implores his liege to let him defend his honor.

Getting nowhere with Mowbray, Richard turns around to Bolingbroke who has already firmly resisted his father's attempts to sway him. He is just as unyielding to Richard. "Oh, God defend my soul from such deep sin!" To withdraw his challenge would shame his family and his noble rank. Before he would agree to forgive Mowbray, he would bite out his tongue and "spit it bleeding . . . / Where shame both harbor, even in Mowbray's face." This violent defiance discourages Richard. He admits defeat and emphasizes his failure with a memorable line, "We were not born to sue, but to command." In obvious displeasure, he orders them to appear on St. Lambert's Day, September 17, at Coventry (in central England) for their single combat.

Act I: Scene 2

The quarrelsome tone of the first scene continues, but in a quieter way. John of Gaunt is talking in his palace to his sister-in-law the Duchess of Gloucester, the widow of the murdered Thomas. Gaunt's first words show that she has been urging him to revenge the murder of her husband. He protests that since he is Gloucester's own brother, he is even more eager than she to see justice done against the murdering butchers. But he hints that the guilt is Richard's, and only Heaven can punish the King. He adds, however, that he is confident that Heaven will, in due time, "rain hot vengeance on offenders' heads."

The Duchess is too upset to find much solace in the vague chance of divine intervention. Bitterly, she accuses Gaunt of lack of family feeling. Is his blood too old to feel the fire of brotherly affection? The former King, Edward III, had seven sons, seven vials of his blood, seven branches of his paternal root. Some have already died naturally; but Gloucester's vial has been spilt, his branch has been hacked by unnatural and murderous malice. His blood was one with Gaunt's. The same bed conceived them; the same womb molded their bodies. Gloucester's death is, in fact, Gaunt's own death. Patience in a situation like this is a poor, mean thing —and dangerous policy, too. Gaunt may be the next to be slaughtered. To safeguard his own life, he should avenge her husband's death.

Somewhat more stern after this harangue, Gaunt replies that the quarrel is God's and that he will never approve of any attack, direct or indirect, on Richard, whom he regards as an anointed ruler, God's deputy, whose wrongdoing should be punished by God alone.

To whom, then, cries the Duchess, can she complain, if Gaunt won't help. "To God," replies Gaunt, "the widow's champion and defense." The Duchess accepts this and says farewell to "old Gaunt." (By her repeated references to both Gaunt and his brother Edmund of York as being "old," the Duchess repeats a theme already introduced by Richard and also implies that Gaunt's failure to act may be partly due to the weakness of old age.) After expressing her hope that she will at least have the satisfaction of a Bolingbroke victory at Conventry, the Duchess concludes this scene with a speech in which she wallows in considerable self-pity. She hates to let Gaunt go. She will be left with her long, heavy sorrow, she says. For a moment she thinks she has no more to say; but then she calls him back to give him a message for his brother, the "old" Duke of York. Gaunt should tell him to visit her at her estate at Plashy (pronounced Pla' shee). But, no—he'll find it very lonely. She withdraws her invitation; let him not come. She'll go home to die. Weeping, she leaves. In her final speech she emphasizes the word "desolate." It tolls out not only the sadness of her personal bereavement and loneliness but also a kind of threat of universal affliction.

Act I: Scene 3

It is now September 17, and we move to Coventry for the judicial combat between Bolingbroke and Mowbray. There is much colorful pageantry and careful observance of protocol in this event. These ceremonies afford welcome, if temporary, relief from the foreboding events of the earlier scenes. The formalities proceed correctly. The Lord Marshal, who is in charge of the combat, ascertains that both combatants are ready and armed, awaiting only the arrival of the King to make their appearance. To the sound of trumpets, Richard enters, escorted by John of Gaunt, Bushy, Bagot, Green, and other attendants.

Mowbray appears with his herald. Richard directs the Lord Marshal to interrogate and swear in this first contestant. In response to the request of the Marshal, Mowbray states his name and titles,* and then his status here as the defendant knight challenged by Bolingbroke. He announces that he intends to prove Bolingbroke "a traitor to my God, my King, and me." He asks that Heaven defend him if he fight truly, as he intends to do.

Bolingbroke now appears, "plated in habiliments of war." The same formula of interrogation is followed with him. He repeats his charge of treason against Mowbray and, like the other man, prays for Heaven's favor if he fights fairly. The Marshal orders all spectators to stay well away from the combat field, called the "lists." Bolingbroke and then Mowbray request permission, through the Lord Marshal, to do homage to Richard. Boling-

---

*This identification is necessary because the contestants ride in full armor with visors down. It was essential that each knight know for sure whom he was fighting. The armor in this period is the heavy plate armor that replaced the earlier chain mail.

broke says they are like two men starting a long pilgrimage. They wish to take formal and affectionate leave of their King and friends. Richard not only acquiesces but actually descends from his open-air throne to embrace first one and then the other. He says good-by to each, reminding Bolingbroke that if he is the one who is killed, Richard will mourn him as a cousin but will not be able to avenge him. Bolingbroke is blithe enough and says no one should weep for him if he is punctured by Mowbray's spear. He takes leave of his father and of his first cousin, the Duke of Aumerle (pronounced O merl'), who is the son of Edmund, Duke of York. He asks his father to pray that he will succeed in adding new luster to the name of Gaunt. Gaunt urges him to be "swift like lightening" and to hammer the helmet of Mowbray with thunderous blows. Bolingbroke calls on St. George and his own innocence to protect him. Mowbray asserts that his soul is dancing into the combat, happier than a freed captive. In fact, he goes to the fight as eagerly as to a jest. Richard reserves his final word and encouragement for Mowbray. He says he relies on the virtue and valor he sees in that knight's eyes.

Then, finally, the moment is at hand in which all these fine words will be put to the acid test. The two heralds march forth: the first to identify Bolingbroke again and to state his challenge; the second to identify Mowbray and to accept his challenge. The Marshal orders the sounding of the trumpets that will signal the commencement of the combat.

At this point of high suspense, even as the two mounted warriors wheel their horses and poise their spears, all this measured, punctilious formality is shattered by a small but significant action on the part of Richard. He throws down his "warder," a gilded staff symbolizing his authority over the proceedings. "Stay!" barks the startled Lord Marshal. Combatants and spectators alike freeze, their eyes riveted on Richard.

Relishing the melodrama of the moment, the King commands the two fighters to put aside their helmets and weapons and approach his throne. Then Richard announces that he and his Council have decided to exile both Bolingbroke and Mowbray. They do this in the interests of civil peace. They fear that the pride, envy, and ambition shown in this quarrel will plunge the country into civil war, and "fright fair peace" away from England. Bolingbroke's sentence is a ten-year exile. With a surprisingly mild "Thy will be done," Bolingbroke accepts the decree. He goes on to declare smoothly and hypocritically that he will be able to rejoice during his banishment in the fact that he will be warmed by the same sun that shines on his liege lord Richard.

Mowbray's is a life sentence. He may never return to England. He is more disturbed and outspoken than Bolingbroke, declaring in sadness rather than in anger that he has deserved better from Richard. He grieves because in exile he will no longer be able to use his familiar English language. His tongue will be like an "unstringed" harp or other useless musical instrument. It will be a prisoner "enjailed" behind the heavy grating of teeth and lips. He is too old to learn a foreign tongue. Richard's sentence is, in effect, a speechless death for him.

Richard, although he has said that he reluctantly gave Mowbray so heavy a sentence, shows him no pity now, but tells him it is too late for complaining. He then summons both sentenced men before him and makes them swear on his royal sword that they will never meet, correspond, or conspire together during their banishment. They both so swear.

Bolingbroke, still trying to get the upper hand, tries to force a confession out of Mowbray. "Since thou hast far to go, bear not along / The clogging burden of a guilty soul." But Mowbray, far from admitting guilt, protests his innocence as he leaves. He halts his departure momentarily to turn back toward Bolingbroke, "But what thou art, God, thou, and I do know, / And all too soon, I fear, the King shall rue." These lines restore with emphasis the ominous tone of the first two scenes.

Richard gives his attention to his uncle and his cousin. Moved, he says, by Gaunt's grief, he reduces Bolingbroke's sentence to six years.

Bolingbroke, perhaps to avoid humbling himself by thanking Richard, comments flatteringly on the power of a King who is able in one breath to cancel out four long years. Gaunt does thank the King for this reduction in punishment, but he asserts that he won't live to see his son return. Richard brushes this off with his irritating mannerism of disposing of a serious situation with a joke or pleasantry. Gaunt gravely reminds Richard that even royalty can't lengthen life. Richard can kill Gaunt, but, wealthy though he is, he could not buy one breath for the dead Gaunt. Richard, with considerable acuteness, sees that Gaunt is really shaken up by his son's sentence. So he, in turn, reminds Gaunt that Gaunt himself participated in the Council's decision to impose the sentences of exile. Gaunt admits this, but says his official action was an offense to his feelings as a father. Actually he was more harsh in judging his son than he would have been with a stranger. He blames Richard for allowing him to be betrayed into this excessive strictness. Richard does not respond to this except to say good-by to Bolingbroke and to advise Gaunt to do the same.

After the King's withdrawal, Aumerle tells Bolingbroke to write from his exile and let them know where he is staying. The Lord Marshal says he'll ride along with Bolingbroke to whatever seaport he will use for his departure. Gaunt, like a good parent, submerges his own grief and tries to cheer up Bolingbroke. He tells him six winters are not so long and urges him to look upon the exile as an opportunity for travel and new experiences. He can pretend that he has left the court of his own will—banishing it instead of it banishing him. Or he might tell himself that he has left England for a while to avoid an outbreak of the plague. At any rate, sorrow has less power to "bite" the man who resolutely keeps his chin up. Bolingbroke protests that pretending never really works. If one's hand is being burnt by fire, does it ease the pain to think of the snows on the Caucasian Mountains? No! To think of good when one is enduring evil just aggravates the suffering.

As they depart, Bolingbroke, like Mowbray before him, stresses his love of England.

Act I: Scene 4

King Richard is again at his court with two of his followers, Bagot and Green.* Aumerle enters, and Richard chides him rather peevishly for his attendance on the departing Bolingbroke. Aumerle protests that he rode only to the highway junction with Bolingbroke. Any tears that he shed at their separation were caused by the strong northeast wind blowing into his face, not by sympathy for the exile.

Seeing that the King is suspicious of him, Aumerle tries even harder to clear himself. He explains that he didn't answer to Bolingbroke's final "farewell"; he pretended to be too choked up with sorrow at the parting to get a word out. This trick, says Aumerle, was to avoid wishing Bolingbroke the good luck that "fare well" would mean. However, if the word "farewell" could have extended Bolingbroke's exile, Aumerle would have been glad to shout it repeatedly after the departing figure of Bolingbroke. Richard ignores this foolish exaggeration, but his mind does linger for a moment on what *will* happen when Bolingbroke's comparatively brief exile is over. He tells Aumerle that this cousin of theirs probably will not consider them his friends.

Richard then comments sourly on the throng that watched Bolingbroke's departure and on Bolingbroke's irritating playing-up to them. This is a vivid passage that takes you right into a medieval working-class crowd lining the roadway to see a popular hero. Bolingbroke is the hero, and he has the true politician's touch and charm. He smiles at them as a group. But, better than that, he makes them feel he is aware of them as in-

---

*Although described as servants, these two men, and also their friend Bushy belong to the minor nobility. They have considerable authority and are closer to Richard than most of the high-born nobles.

dividuals. He takes off his cap with a flourish to a girl who sells oysters, and he makes a deep bow to two carters who call him a greeting. In a master stroke he wins both their admiration and their sympathy by convincing them that under his cheery manner his heart is broken by the banishment sentence. No wonder Richard's teeth are on edge as he describes this scene and comments at the end that Bolingbroke acted as if he were the acknowledged heir to the throne.

In response to a reminder from Green, Richard announces that they must now depart for Ireland to subdue the rebellion there. (The English claim to sovereignty over Ireland dated from the twelfth century, but rebellions recurrently challenged that claim.) Suddenly Bushy enters. He brings word of John of Gaunt's serious illness. Richard immediately sees advantage for himself in this and frankly hopes for Gaunt's quick death. He indicates that he will delay his departure to the Irish wars to visit Gaunt at Ely House. With the revoltingly insensitive "Pray God we may make haste, and come too late" (that is, too late to find Gaunt alive), Richard leads his retinue off stage.

Act II: Scene 1

We are now in Ely House in London. Gaunt, sick and weakened, awaits with his brother Edmund, Duke of York (usually referred to as "York"), the visit of the King. Gaunt's first words reveal that he intends to tell the King flatly how wrong and dangerous some of his policies are. York, although he shares his brother's opinion that Richard is a weak, unsteady, and willful King, advises Gaunt to save his breath "for all in vain comes counsel to his ear."

Gaunt says that the words of a dying man should have a special force and should "undeaf" Richard's ear. Small chance, believes York. In his opinion, the kingly ear is far too busy listening to flattery, to the latest popular poetry, and to fashion reports from Italy. This reminder of Richard's frivolous and expensive interests serves only to stiffen Gaunt's determination and to rouse him to one of the most famous speeches of the play. In this speech he praises England, "this other Eden, . . . this precious stone set in the silver sea, . . . this dear, dear land." He praises her for her power and majesty, for her military might ("seat of Mars"), for her closeness to perfection (a "demi-Paradise"), for the fortunate sea-protected position, for her royalty ("feared" and "famous") who have traditionally been true to Christian and chivalric ideals.

And "this blessed plot" is now, because of Richard's shaky financial arrangements, bound in by "inky blots and rotten parchment bonds." England is virtually enslaved by his questionable money deals. They hear the approach of the King, and hastily York urges Gaunt to be mild and to avoid antagonizing Richard.

The King is accompanied by his Queen, various courtiers, and attendants. Gently the Queen inquires for Gaunt's health; but before she can be answered, Richard asks brusquely, "How is't with aged Gaunt?" Again the dig, the gratuitous insistence on Gaunt's age. Gaunt picks up the cue for the pun and plays on the meanings of the word "gaunt" with a virtuosity that makes us echo Richard's "Can sick men play so nicely with their names?"

Gaunt's point, however, stands out clear enough from all the luxuriance of the language. Richard's misgovernment of England has made Gaunt gaunt with worry. Richard, too, is on the point of death—political death, because of his financial policies. If his grandfather, King Edward III, could have foreseen the nature of Richard's rule, he would never have agreed to Richard's succession.

This stings Richard to threaten Gaunt with execution. Only their close relationship saves him, says the King. Even that did not protect Gloucester, retorts Gaunt. But now the dying man has no more strength and no more desire for talk. He orders his servants to bear him to bed—and then to his grave. After he leaves, York tries briefly and to no avail to assure Richard of the loyalty of the Lancasters (Gaunt and Bolingbroke). They are interrupted by the Earl of Northumberland's report that Gaunt will speak no more; "his tongue is now a stringless instrument"; he is dead.

So much for that, says Richard in effect. Then he announces that he is seizing "the plate, coin, revenues and movables" of Gaunt to finance his Irish expedition.

York objects on three scores. Such wrongdoing is a disgrace to Richard's upbringing; his father, the Black Prince, would never have sunk so low. It is completely unjust to Bolingbroke, the heir to the Lancaster properties. It is extremely dangerous to Richard himself. Richard ignores York's advice (as does almost everyone that York attempts to advise), says he's off to Ireland on the morrow, and appoints York his deputy or representative in his absence. Then he departs. With him go the Queen and most of the courtiers. Three noblemen linger, however. They are the Earl of Northumberland. Lord Ross, and Lord Willoughby.

After some preliminary sparring to feel out their individual opinions, they find that they are agreed in strong opposition to the King. They have long resented the burdensome taxation, and now they see an additional threat in the injustice to Bolingbroke. If the King can do this to Bolingbroke who is a member of the royal family and the strongest nobleman at court, what defense would they in their less protected positions have against him? Northumberland then confides to them the startling news that Bolingbroke is returning from exile, accompanied by several important noblemen. They have, in fact, already sailed from Brittany in "eight tall ships," well manned and equipped. They are to land at Ravenspurgh (pronounced Ray'ven sperg) in Yorkshire, far to the north of London. With Bolingbroke back, Northumberland hints, the days of real kingship may return. His excited invitation to the other two to join him in a speedy trip north to the Channel port where Richard is to land is enthusiastically accepted. They hasten away to mount their horses for the long ride.

Act II: Scene 2

In the interval between this and the first scene of the act, Richard departs for Ireland.

In effective contrast to the excitement and rush at the end of the previous scene, this scene opens on a subdued, sad note. The mood is set by the Queen who talks with Bushy and Bagot at the royal palace of Windsor (a short distance up the Thames from London). She is in low spirits. Her sadness is explained in part, of course, by the departure of her "sweet Richard." But she is also deeply disturbed by a vague, nameless fear. Bushy tries to persuade her that it is just that she is lonesome for Richard. "It may be so," she admits "but yet my inward soul / Persuades me it is otherwise . . . . / I cannot but be sad, so heavy sad." She does not have to wait long for the vindication of her feminine premonitions.

First, Green enters with the "hope" that Richard has not yet left for Ireland, as we, however, know full well he has.

The word has come that Bolingbroke has landed at Ravenspurgh. The three conspirators of the previous scene have joined him, as have also a Lord Beaumond, and two of the Earl of Northumberland's relatives. These relatives are his son Henry (Harry) Percy, and his brother the Earl of Worcester (pronounced Woos' ter). The last named was an official in Richard's court, but broke his staff of office and defected. All have been proclaimed traitors, but to subdue the revolt an energetic and firm leader is required. In ironic contrast to that emphatic need, the King's deputy, the aged York, enters, too old, as he laments, to support himself, let alone underprop all England. He confirms the report Green has given, and, in a distraught fashion, tries to attend all at once to the demands of the emergency—summoning any nobles still loyal (most have fled, he says, and the common people are uninterested), mustering forces, raising money, notifying the King, attending to the shocked Queen. His intentions are good, but he is unable to execute them in any effective way. Also, he is deprived of two supports that he counted on: His son, Aumerle, has disappeared; and, in the midst of the flurry, he hears that the Duchess of Gloucester is dead. Eventually he mentions the problem that is probably more responsible for his confusion than any debility of old age: "Both are my kinsmen. / The one is my sovereign, whom both my oath / And my duty bids defend. The other again / Is my kinsman, whom the King hath wronged, / Whom conscience and my kindred bids to right."

York orders Bushy and the others to assemble soldiers and meet him at Berkeley (pronounced Bark' lee) Castle in western England. He deplores the fact that he has no time to go to pay his last respects to the dead Duchess of Gloucester. Then the old man fussily leads out the Queen, to "dispose" of her, as he rather tactlessly puts it.

Bushy, Bagot, and Green remin behind. They very gloomily assess their personal prospects, as well as the national distress. Bushy has learned that the winds on the Irish Channel will favor the ship bringing Richard the bad news, but will delay the ship which should return him to England. He is pessimistic about the chances of raising an army large enough to stop Bolingbroke. They all agree that the populace is antagonistic to Richard because of the tax burdens. They themselves, as well-known confidants of the King, are very vulnerable. They pay no attention to York's final order to them. Bushy and Green resolve to go west to Bristol Castle to join the loyal Earl of Wiltshire. Bagot, however, decides to take off for Ireland. He hopes to join Richard before Richard embarks for the return to England. They bid each other farewell. Bagot and Green are fatalistically sure that it is for the last time. They have no confidence in York, the "poor Duke."

Act II: Scene 3

This scene proves that the reports that so alarmed Richard's followers in the last scene were by no means exaggerated. It also provides a good mood relief in its contrasting optimism and vigor. It satisfies, too, our curiosity about the activities of the rebels. We find Bolingbroke leading some forces through a wild countryside in Gloucestershire (pronounced Glos' ter sheer). He is accompanied by Northumberland. They have marched southwestward across central England from the English Channel port where Bolingbroke had landed. Bolingbroke asks wearily how far they are from their destination, which turns out to be the same Berkeley Castle that York mentioned in the previous scene. Northumberland says that he doesn't know. It's all strange territory to him. Its very roughness makes the miles seem longer, but he counts himself lucky to have had the pleasant company of Bolingbroke to shorten the way. Northumberland's son, Harry

Percy, enters and reports that his uncle, the Earl of Worcester, has deserted the court of Richard to ally himself with Bolingbroke. Worcester had sent his nephew to spy out York's strength at Berkeley.

The young man's father then introduces him to Bolingbroke, and the youth promises the rebel his service, which he says will become more valuable as he grows to manhood.

Young Harry gives them the good news that Berkeley Castle is actually within sight. He tells them also that it is held by York and Lord Berkeley, and just then the Lords Ross and Willoughby join the group. Immediately afterward Lord Berkeley and then York himself appear.

Bolingbroke salutes York with "My noble uncle" and kneels before him. But York is for the moment proof against such flattery. "Grace me no grace, nor uncle me no uncle," he says testily. Bolingbroke may be his nephew, but he is also a detestable traitor who has alarmed his country and defied his king in the person of his deputy.

Bolingbroke pleads the special injustice to him of Richard's seizure of his possessions. If York had died first, Gaunt would have aided Aumerle, York's son. York does not deny that Bolingbroke had plenty of provocation, but he insists that Bolingbroke's armed rebellion is wrong. But with that bit of plain, forthright speaking, the old man's fire is suddenly spent.

He announces his intention of remaining neutral since he does not have power to sudue the rebels. He even offers them the hospitality of Berkeley Castle. Bolingbroke accepts the offer and says he hopes to persuade York to advance with them on Bristol Castle to crush Bushy and Bagot. (It is these two whom he mentions. Actually Bushy and Green are at Bristol. Bagot, as we know, intended to make for Ireland.)

York is now frankly out of his depth. "Things past redress are now with me past care." But he clings to a small foothold of independence. Bolingbroke has to be satisfied with "It may be I'll go with you. But yet I'll pause, / For I am loath to break our country's laws."

Act II: Scene 4

This very short scene adds still another item to the catalog of catastrophe that is accumulating for Richard. The action takes place in a military encampment in Wales. In an abrupt farewell speech, the Captain of a Welsh fighting force informs the Earl of Salisbury, a nobleman still loyal to Richard, that his troops are departing. They have waited ten days beyond the appointed date for the King, and still he has not appeared.

Salisbury's reply is very brief and mechanical, as if he were drained of hope. He does ask the Captain to remain another day, for in this Welsh force "the King reposeth all his confidence."

In contrast to Salisbury's emotional flatness and lack of conviction, the Captain's firm reiteration of the Welsh intention is colorful and charged with assurance. His men will leave because they are sure Richard is dead. They have "evidence" in the form of Welsh trees unnaturally withered, a bloody hue observed on the moon, sinister warnings from lean prophets, and other omens of disaster. So, fortified with "reasons," the Welsh Captain stalks off.

Salisbury, alone for his final speech, laments the decline of Richard's fortunes with a much freer flow of language than he could muster to talk of Richard's plans. He associates Richard with the setting sun. It is a bad weather sun, a weeping sun foreseeing "storms to come."

In his final lines, Salisbury speaks of the defections to Bolingbroke and of the general worsening of Richard's fortunes.

Act III: Scene 1

Bolingbroke, York, Northumberland, Ross, Percy, and Willoughby all troop onto the stage. Soldiers also lead in Bushy and Green, fettered, obviously prisoners. In the background looms Bristol Castle which the unfortunate Bushy and Green had sought as a refuge. It has, however, fallen to Bolingbroke, and their doom is sealed. This Bolingbroke makes clear immediately. He says he must rehearse their crimes to justify his execution of them, but he will not stress their sins since that could be disturbing to men so soon to die. He does not want to be guilty of that kind of offense against charity.

His general accusation is that they have been an evil influence on the King. Then he states rapidly the particulars of his case against them.

1) They have established an unnatural relationship with Richard which has alienated the King and Queen.

2) They have "misinterpreted" Bolingbroke to the King and so caused Bolingbroke's exile.

3) During his exile they grabbed as many of his possessions as they could. He could, he says, double the list but this is sufficient to warrant their condemnation. He orders their immediate execution.

Each condemned man indicates, whether in bravado or in sincerity (it is difficult to tell for the speeches are very brief), that Bolingbroke is evil and unjust. Each affirms that he goes with a calm mind to his death. They are led out to execution by Northumberland.

Bolingbroke takes a minute to ask York to give the Queen, who is sheltered in York's house, a message of regard and commendation. With that the energetic Bolingbroke summons away the other lords "to fight with Glendower and his complices."

Act III: Scene 2

Again we have a castle scene, and again the locale is western England. We are on the Welsh coast. Nearby is Barkloughly (pronounced Bar klaw' klee) Castle, a fortress as stark and grim as Bristol Castle. But this time our eyes and ears have some diversion. Drums beat a royal flourish, and there is a show of flags and standards. Richard has finally made it to England. He is accompanied in his entrance by the Bishop of Carlisle,* Aumerle, and a small detachment of soldiers. Apparently he has had a rough as well as slow crossing of the Irish Channel. The King's ship has been "tossing" on "breaking seas," according to Aumerle. (We never discover just where Aumerle joined the King, but presumably it was at the Welsh port where Richard landed.)

But for more reasons than the difficulty of the sea voyage, Richard is very, very happy to be once again on his native English soil. (Again the theme of patriotism, of love of England, is stressed.) He addresses that dear native earth, and he bends to salute it with a caress of his hand. Like a child after a separation from its mother, he says he both weeps and smiles to be restored to the security of his own land. He weeps because of the hardships of the separation, and smiles because those hardships are now no more. Like a child, he immediately has a petition. He asks that fostering English earth to do what it can to thwart Bolingbroke. It should withhold from the rebel forces its pleasant scents and sights, and instead annoy their marching feet with venomous spiders, toads, and stinging nettles. He suggests that it hide a poisonous adder (the only poisonous snake native to England) in every flower they stoop to pick. Conscious of his followers' stares and perhaps grins at the strangeness of this address to the insensible earth, Richard tells them not to mock him. This very earth and its stones would indeed rise in defence of any rebellion

---

*The high churchmen, such as bishops, of medieval England were often large landowners and practiced politicians. They also were lords of the realm and ranked with the higher nobility. As such they could be deeply involved in many political and even, in a noncombatant fashion, military actions.

against their true King. Carlisle agrees that the Divine Right of Kings will operate to help Richard, but emphasizes that Heaven helps him who helps himself, that Heaven expects him to take advantage of every means to maintain his rule. Aumerle eagerly seconds Carlisle, pointing out that they have been at fault in letting Bolingbroke make so many uncontested advances.

Richard is moved to one of his most poetic speeches. Doesn't his cousin Aumerle know that it is when the sun is absent from our world and night descends that wrongdoers lurk and flourish? But when the sun returns, its rays search out all the dark corners to expose and shame the criminals. So Bolingbroke, "this thief, this traitor," has been making the most of Richard's absence and of England's resulting darkness to hatch his wicked schemes. But with Richard's return, like the sun's eastern rising after its "trip" through the regions on the other side of the globe, light begins again to flood England. Bolingbroke himself will be shamed by the exposure of his infamy. The language of this speech up to this point is very flowery and very confident. Richard now moves on to the reason for his confidence. It is the theory we already know to be basic to his political philosophy. "Not all the water in the rough rude sea / Can wash the balm [consecrated oil used in coronation ceremony] off from the anointed king. / The breath of worldly men cannot depose / The deputy elected by the Lord."

Richard's final lines show how very high above the practicalities of the situation his confidence in his divine right to rule has floated him. For every rebel Bolingbroke raises, God, he declares, has an angel to fight for "His Richard." And as his imagination plays with that fascinating picture of opposing ranks of men and angels in battle array, he arrives at the conclusion that is so obvious to him, and so comforting—if angels fight men, the issue can only be victory for the angelic hosts.

Richard interrupts himself as Salisbury, who, we know, is one of the few lords still loyal to him, enters. "How far lies your power?" inquires Richard. Despite his fantasies, he realizes he must attend to some practical issues. He wants to know the location of the Welsh force that Salisbury was responsible for contacting. "Nor near nor farther off, my gracious lord, / than this weak arm," puns Salisbury wryly. Actually, he now commands no other power than the might of his own muscle. He tells Richard of the shift of the Welsh troops, twelve thousand fighting men strong, to the side of Bolingbroke. By one brief day Richard missed the rendezvous that would have convinced them that their omen lied and their king still lived. Small wonder that Salisbury warned Richard that he brought a message of despair. Richard pales. When Aumerle comments on this change, Richard says he has good reason to be pale. The blood of thousands of fighting men has been drained from his cheeks. He expects to continue to look pale—and dead—as his supporters defect.

Aumerle tries to prevent this despondent reaction, and Richard does attempt to recover his spirits. Is he not a King? Isn't his very name a power? What if a "puny subject" strikes out at him? Who can really harm majesty on its heights? And anyway York has plenty of troops.

Another lord loyal to Richard, Sir Stephen Scroop, strides in. He *wishes* his king happiness, but says he can *bring* him none. Hearing this, Richard again changes his attitude. He says he is prepared now for the worst. Has he lost his kingdom? So what—it was a heavy care. Is Bolingbroke trying to be his equal? Well, they'll serve God together, and so be fellows. Do his people rebel? He can't prevent it; let them defy God, if they dare. Let Scroop cry whatever calamity he likes; the worst is death, and death is bound to come some time. Scroop says it is well the King is so philosophical. A mighty flood is moving over England, the flood of the revolt loosed on the land by Bolingbroke.

People of all ages and conditions are joining the rebel ranks. Old men, boys, clerics, and even women choose unaccustomed weapons and join the regular soldiers.

Richard inquires with rising anger for Bagot, Bushy, Green, and the Earl of Wiltshire. Why did they let Bolingbroke get such a start? They'll pay for their failure to do their duty. "I warrant they have made peace with Bolingbroke." Scroop, a little nettled by Richard's failure to appreciate the difficulties of those who were on the home front, says that they have indeed done just that. Richard flies into a real rage. They are villains, vipers, turncoats, dogs, snakes. Still the stream of verbal attacks flows. They are triple-dyed Judases. "Terrible Hell make war / Upon their spotted souls!"

Dryly, Scroop suggests that Richard "uncurse their souls." These men have lost their lives in fidelity to Richard and lie now in their graves. All at Bristol Castle met this fate.

Aumerle inquires for his father and the army they think York must be leading. This is apparently to give Richard something more encouraging to think about. Richard interprets it that way, anyway. But Richard is now as low and depressed as he was exhilarated before the arrival of Salisbury. Let no man speak to him of comfort. "Let's talk of graves, of worms, of epitaphs." And he does just that, at some length but with great effectiveness. This is one of the most famous speeches of the play. His words are rather morbid, and he is again playing a role suggested by his imagination. But he does, nevertheless, stir us with his reflections on the transientness and hollowness of earthly glory. They and their possessions are in the hands of Bolingbroke. Nothing of their own can they claim, except their bodies. They can pass the time telling "sad stories of the death of Kings"—usually assassinations. Within the very "hollow crown" of monarchy Death grins and mocks, and at the appointed moment strikes. And he? Well, after all he is only flesh and blood like themselves, subject to the same afflictions. Indeed, he is a *subject* and no king. Let them no longer reverence him.

Carlisle can stand no more of this reaction which seems maudlin self-pity to him. He urges Richard to buck up. He is a worse enemy to himself than is Bolingbroke; let him make some plans. After all, in such a situation to fight and die is better than not to fight at all. Changeable as a weathercock and as responsive to influence, Richard *is* stimulated by Carlisle, and turns again to Scroop for the report on York.

But the unfortunate Scroop has to admit that he plays "the torturer by small and small." His last and worst message is "Your uncle York is joined with Bolingbroke, / And all your northern castles yielded up, / And all your southern gentlemen in arms / Upon his party." "Thou hast said enough!" is Richard's sober acknowledgement of this report. Although momentarily shocked into that sober brevity, Richard again speaks emotionally as he leaves. He says they had been wrong in trying to raise his spirits. He now will yield himself completely to despair, pining away in Flint Castle. He gives orders for his followers to be discharged. Let them go join Bolingbroke's dawning day. Richard's sun sinks under night's blackness.

Act III: Scene 3

Flint, another of the many castles that topped Welsh hills in those days of frequent petty warring, is the setting for this great scene. In under its ramparts march the Bolingbroke party—Bolingbroke himself, York, Northumberland, and a good show of military strength behind them. Bolingbroke and Northumberland are jubilant about the feebleness of the forces that rallied to Richard on his return from Ireland.

York is still holding aloof from them, psychologically if not physically. He reproves Northumberland for omitting Richard's title. When that arrogant Earl shows little concern about this breach of respect, York, in a fine flash of word play, reminds the Northerner of the time when such an offense would have brought Northumberland to the executioner's block.

Bolingbroke and York exchange rather unfriendly warnings. Each cautions the other not to go too far. They are interrupted by young Harry Percy who had been sent ahead to demand the castle's submission. To their great surprise, they learn the King is there before them, and the castle, as Harry says, is "royally manned."

Bolingbroke, although taken quite off guard by this news, is able after only a minute's reflection to take the situation in hand. He orders that a message stating his allegiance be delivered to Richard. But attached to this promise of loyalty is a big "if." He will submit to Richard if Richard will repeal the exile sentence and restore the Lancaster lands and money. And there is a big "if not." If Richard will not come to terms, Bolingbroke will lay waste Richard's domain. He suggests that while the message is being delivered his men and equipment should be put through some military exercises on the plain below the castle. "Our fair appointments [strength] may be well perused [examined]" by the occupants of the castle. In the next breath after that hostile suggestion and even as he eyes with satisfaction his efficient troops, he says that he is quite willing to have Richard play the fiery, raging, dominant part. He himself would be content in a mild, unmenacing role.

Trumpets play the notes that indicate a parley or conference is to take place. The King appears on the ramparts.

The Bishop of Carlisle, Aumerle, Scroop, and Salisbury stand around him. Bolingbroke points out the King to his friends. York gazes upward and comments, probably to himself, how kingly Richard *looks*. "Behold his eye / As bright as is the eagle's . . . . Alack, alack . . . / That any harm should stain so fair a show!"

In accord with the appearance York noted, Richard does begin in fine kingly fashion. Bolingbroke and his aides have not made the ceremonious bow and genuflection demanded by the presence of royalty. And why not? Richard is stern and premptory. Is he not their king? If not, "who hath dismissed us from our stewardship?" He has, because of Bolingbroke's treachery, few earthly supporters. But "my master, God Omnipotent, / Is mustering in His clouds on our behalf / Armies of pestilence." The rebels will be punished and their sons and their sons' sons. Bolingbroke is trifling with "the purple testament of bleeding war." If he is not careful, he will cause the deaths of thousands of Englishmen.

Bolingbroke remains silent and at a distance from the castle. Northumberland moves to the base of the castle walls and replies for his chief. Looking up at Richard, Northumberland speaks according to his instructions. Bolingbroke swears by his close relationship to Richard and by the ancestral blood they have in common that all he wants is the cancellation of the exile sentence and the restoration of his property. Granted these two requests, he will become the peaceful, faithful servant of the King.

Richard's reply is very strange. He instructs Northumberland to tell his "noble cousin" that "all the number of his fair demands / Shall be accomplished without contradiction." Is this the amazing capitulation to Bolingbroke that it sounds like? We soon learn positively that it is. Richard turns to Aumerle and says he feels that he debases himself by talking so mildly. He is tempted to call back Northumberland and send the other possible reply to Bolingbroke—a message of defiance and battle challenge. Aumerle counsels that it is best to stick to the friendly line and bide their time. Northumberland withdraws to confer with Bolingbroke.

Richard bewails his fate. That he should actually stoop to revoking the exile sentence! He wishes he could be as great as his title. Or failing that, that he could forget his past prestige, that he could ignore what he must now become. He does not give the returned Northumberland time to indicate Bolingbroke's decision. Instead he fires a barrage of questions, all showing that he expects Bolingbroke to dominate, perhaps depose him. He claims that he doesn't care. He is ready to relinquish all the symbols of his privileged position—his jewels, palace, robes, scepter, subjects. He is ready to exchange them all for humble substitutes—ready in fact to exchange his kingdom for a grave. He rambles off into a ridiculous image of himself and Aumerle weeping away until their tears have dug out their graves. Finally, he brings himself to attend to Northumberland's message that Bolingbroke awaits Richard in the lower court of the castle (probably an open air courtyard). Richard descends to "King Bolingbroke" (note that Richard himself is the first to crown, as it were, Bolingbroke), to the "base court, where kings grow base."

As they wait for Richard to make his progress down inside the castle, Northumberland warns Bolingbroke that Richard, in his sorrow and grief, has been talking like a frantic (insane) man.

Now, his will having prevailed, Bolingbroke is punctilious in his respect to Richard. He drops to his knees as Richard advances into the courtyard. But Richard urges him to rise. "Your heart is up, I know, / Thus high [and here Richard levels his hand with his crown] at least, although your knee be low." Bolingbroke, in wounded tones, objects that he wants only what belongs to him. Richard passes over this obvious falsehood and on to the hard political fact that justifies Bolingbroke's usurpation. "They well deserve to have / That know the strongest and surest way to get." He then turns to comfort the weeping York. He tells Bolingbroke that he will do what he wants "for do we must what force will have us do."

Act III: Scene 4

At last we get relief from the succession of grim castles and fighting men in armor that are so conspicuous in the first three scenes of this act. We discover the Queen and her ladies in a garden at Langley (pronounced Lang' lee), York's estate a short distance north of London. The ladies try unsuccessfully to divert the Queen whose mind is naturally with her husband Richard and his fortunes. She has had no recent news of him. When a gardener with two assistants starts to work in one corner of the garden, the Queen moves over near him. Everyone, she says, is discussing the political situation. She will eavesdrop to hear what this trio has to say. The gardener gives his orders to his two helpers. One assistant should bind up the "unruly" branches of the apricot tree; they are bending down the tree with the weight of their Fruit. The other man is told to cut back "too fast growing" sprigs. The head gardener will himself pull up the weeds that "suck the soil's fertility." One of the assistants remarks that the three of them are doing a better job of keeping law and order in their domain than the King and his aides are doing on the national level. These rulers have let the "sea-walled garden" that is England become rank with weeds and undisciplined growth, "swarming with caterpillars." (The weeds, the wild growth, the caterpillars all refer to abuses that Richard has promoted or tolerated in his government and his officials.)

The gardener tells this assistant not to worry about the country's situation; some of the worst weeds have already been pulled up. Bolingbroke has disposed of the Earl of Wiltshire, Bushy, and Green. Furthermore, the King, who has been so neglectful of the garden (kingdom) entrusted to his care, so remiss in trimming and dressing his orchard of fruit trees (nobility), is now in the hands of Bolingbroke. It is likely that he will be deposed in favor of Bolingbroke.

The Queen can contain herself no longer. She bursts from her listening place and bitterly tongue-lashes the gardener. How does he "a little better thing than earth" dare suggest that the great Richard has fallen? Where did he hear such a report?

The gardener is apologetic. He does not like to bring bad news, but he insists that what he said is true. Richard is indeed in "the mighty hand of Bolingbroke." On the scale of fate, Richard's fortunes descend and Bolingbroke's rise. Let her hasten down to London. She will find that his words are true, common knowledge, in fact.

With a natural resentment that she seems to be the last to know of Richard's unhappy state, the Queen calls her ladies, telling them to prepare for the London trip. As she hurries away, she flings back at the gardener a spiteful remark: she hopes that the plants he is working on will all wither. He does not retort in kind, even inwardly. He wishes only that her unhappiness might be removed by so simple a thing as an effective curse. Then he transplants a seedling of rue. (Rue is a fragrant herb. In the symbolic language of flowers, it is associated with sorrow.) It marks the place where the Queen's tears fell—"in the remembrance of a weeping Queen."

Act IV: Scene 1

Assembled in Westminster Hall is a group of high prelates, noblemen and magnates of the realm.

The Bishop of Carlisle, the Abbot of Westminster, Bolingbroke, Aumerle, Northumberland, his son Harry Percy, and Bagot are all there. Other less important personages swell the attendance at this meeting which is presided over by Bolingbroke. Bolingbroke has already assumed some political and administrative powers. As the first business of the meeting, he is trying to discover the truth about the death of the Duke of Gloucester.

First, he urges Bagot to tell what he knows. Not at all loath and probably primed, Bagot accuses Aumerle. He actually claims to quote a boast that he says he heard Aumerle make about his ability to murder Gloucester. He then caps that with the assertion that he heard Aumerle also wish for the death of Bolingbroke. Aumerle is hot in his denial and calls Bagot a liar. He throws down his glove as challenge to mortal combat, despite the fact that Bagot's blood is not noble. Ordinarily a nobleman would disdain to stain his knightly sword with base blood. Aumerle considers that the provocation excuses his breach of etiquette. But Bolingbroke will not let Bagot pick up the gage. Fitzwater, who *is* of noble blood, repeats the accusation of Aumerle and throws down his gage. Fitzwater and Aumerle exchange appropriately slanderous reflections on each other's integrity. Apparently Aumerle throws down his other glove to respond to Fitzwater's challenge. Harry Percy chimes in, on the other side of Fitzwater, of course; and another lord does also.

Then the Duke of Surrey, an older man who has been silent so far, berates Fitzwater for giving a false report to Aumerle's words prior to the assassination of Gloucester. Surrey heard them, too. According to him, they were quite different from Fitzwater's version. A private but lively quarrel develops between Surrey and Fitzwater. Mowbray's name is dragged in as one who had held the opinion that Aumerle was really the assassin. Aumerle, having used up both gloves, asks someone to lend him one. He wants to throw one down now as a challenge to the absent Mowbray. Bolingbroke announces that Mowbray will be summoned home to give his testimony against Aumerle. Mowbray will also, says Bolingbroke, be reinstated in his property. (He had lost this at the time of his exile.) But Bolingbroke, who has been faring very well in this attack on Aumerle since Aumerle is a supporter of Richard, cannot have everything his way. The Bishop of Carlisle announces that Mowbray has concluded an honorable career as a valiant warrior. He has died in Italy, at Venice, and has been buried there. So Bolingbroke tells the accusers and the accused that they will be assigned days for their single combats.

York enters and informs Bolingbroke that "plume-plucked Richard" wishes to abdicate and to hand over the sceptre to Bolingbroke. Long live King Henry IV! Bolingbroke accepts. "In God's name I'll ascend the regal throne."

The Bishop of Carlisle rises and addresses Bolingbroke and the others. He admits that he is not the gifted speaker that some of them are, but his office demands that he assert the truth. There is no one there good enough in character or high enough in rank to judge "the noble Richard." They are subjects of Richard and therefore not eligible to judge him. Also they are judging Richard in his absence, an injustice they would not inflict on common thieves. Their deed is "heinous, black, obscene." King Hereford (Bolingbroke) is a traitor to Hereford's King. Then the great prophecy rolls out that brings us back to the play's beginning, back to that other far-seeing, experienced old man, John of Gaunt. Although Carlisle speaks against Bolingbroke and Gaunt spoke against Richard, both really make the same point—that the welfare of England is being endangered, and that these present policies will cause trouble in the future. Carlisle fore-tells that if Bolingbroke proceeds with his usurpation of the throne, English blood will "manure" English ground, "future ages will groan for this foul act," "kin with kin" will war, and England will become another Golgotha.

Northumberland, apparently silently directed by Bolingbroke, promptly arrests the churchman for treason. This arrest, however, does not entail his imprisonment at this time. Bolingbroke orders that Richard be brought to the hall to make a public "surrender."

York reappears with Richard and officers who carry the royal crown and other symbols of sovereignty. Richard is in a distressed and a distressing state when he enters. His self-control improves as the scene progresses. At this point, he complains that he hasn't yet learned to act like a subject, especially to those men who, Judas-like, did him reverence so short a time before.

Anyway, why has he been sent for? York, firmly, as if speaking to a peevish child, reminds Richard that he has come to resign his state and crown to Henry Bolingbroke. Richard has himself indicated that he wants to do this.

Richard II

Richard picks up the crown. He looks at Bolingbroke and tells him that the crown is like a deep well which has two buckets, his and Bolingbroke's. His is the one that is submerged, "full of tears." (This is another water image. Richard, now associated with water, is no longer symbolized by fire or sun.)

Richard says that he does intend to yield his crown, but he is keeping his griefs. Bolingbroke points out that Richard is handing over heavy cares with his crown. Richard plays with the word "care"; then he plays with Bolingbroke's feelings when the latter tries to pin him down. "Are you contented to resign the crown?" "Aye, no—no, aye," retorts Richard, unhelpfully. In a litany type of list Richard enumerates what he is relinquishing—the crown's "heavy weight," "the unwieldy sceptre," the balm that consecrated him at the time of his coronation, pomp, majesty, manors, rents, decrees, statutes. They all go to Bolingbroke "that hast all achieved." And now, he inquires, what else do they want him to do? Northumberland presents him with a prepared statement of guilt which they want him to read. Richard says Northumberland has his own guilt. It includes the deposing of a king. He and the other onlookers are so many hand-washing Pilates. But theirs is a guilt no water can wash away.

Richard delays and delays, by no means daunted by Northumberland, "thou haught, insulting man." He suggests again, as he does early in the scene, his wish for death. This time it is in another fire-water image. He wishes he were a king of snow who could melt away to water drops before the sun of Bolingbroke. Then he startles them all by asking for a mirror to study his face; has it changed since he gave up his sovereignty? Bolingbroke orders the mirror to be brought, and Northumberland again offers the paper for Richard to read, while the glass is being fetched. Richard turns on Northumberland in real anger and calls him a tormenting fiend. Bolingbroke, who probably agrees, tells Northumberland "to urge it no more." Richard examines his face in the mirror and marvels that it is the same face that he had in his days of power. "Was this the face / That, like the sun, did make beholders wink?"

His scrutiny ended, Richard smashes the glass as a sort of symbol of the destruction he at least half-wishes for himself. The prosaic Bolingbroke, moved perhaps more than he had expected to be by the pathos of the occasion, makes a poetic and perceptive observation: "The shadow of your sorrow hath destroyed / The shadow of your face." This states very well Richard's fatal addiction to pretense, to living with shadows instead of substance and fact. Its particular reference is to his breaking of the mirror (the shadow of his face) in a flashy theatrical gesture (the shadow of his sorrow). Richard is generous enough to admit both the beauty and the truth of his rival's remark. His "external manners" are "merely

shadows to the unseen grief / That swells in silence in the tortured soul."
He asks the new King one boon, and Bolingbroke promises to grant it.
Richard wants to depart—any place so long as he is out of their sight.
Bolingbroke gives an order that he be taken to the Tower of London.

Bolingbroke sets the following Wednesday as his coronation day and
sweeps out, followed by most of the others. But the Bishop of Carlisle, the
Abbot of Westminster, and Aumerle linger. They are ripe for revolt
against Bolingbroke, and the Abbot divulges that he already has plans
afoot. But they must assure him of their good faith by receiving the sacrament of the Eucharist. Then he will disclose his plot "that will show us
a merry day."

Act V: Scene 1

The Queen and her ladies have arrived in London. They have stationed
themselves in one of the narrow streets that lead to the Tower of London.
They await Richard who, they have learned, will be taken this way to his
imprisonment. Soon the Queen sees Richard approaching. She finds him
much altered, a withered "rose."

Richard speaks tenderly to the Queen. He asks her to refrain from grief.
He says she must learn to look back on their former life as a happy dream.
They are to be parted: he must walk alone now, with "grim necessity,"
towards death. He counsels her to seek refuge in a convent in France.
The Queen protests that he cannot be so completely transformed. Has
Bolingbroke deprived him of his intellect as well as everything else? Will
he really take all this injustice mildly and without resistance?

Richard does not respond to her effort to shame him into action. He
repeats his advice that she go back to her native France, leaving him, in
effect, on his deathbed. In years to come, as people tell sad tales of an
evening by winter firesides, she will be able to cap all their stories with
her "lamentable tale" of "the deposing of a rightful king."

Northumberland brusquely interrupts. The orders for Richard's imprisonment have been changed (probably because rumors of the conspiracy
have reached the ears of Bolingbroke). He is to go to Pomfret (Ponte-
fract) Castle in northern England. The Queen is ordered to depart immediately for France. As on earlier occasions, Richard shows a strong
aversion to Northumberland. This Percy, says Richard, is the ladder by
which Bolingbroke has climbed to the throne. But this collaboration will
not persist. They will quarrel; each will become jealous and fearful of the
other; each will have learned from this Richard episode the extent of the
villainy of which the other is capable.

Northumberland is not alarmed and orders the husband and wife to part. Richard says he is twice divorced—of his crown and his wife. He must leave her to go to the chill North. She will return to her homeland, France, from which she came a girl, sweet as Maytime. She returns to it touched by the frosts of autumn.

Lovingly, the couple kiss and try to make their farewells. Her request to share Richard's banishment is refused by Northumberland. Richard gives additional evidence of his new grasp of reality, for it is he who moves to terminate the painful conversation. He is even able to see that their repeated endearments make their love and grief seem frivolous.

Act V: Scene 2

The Duke of York and his Duchess discuss at their Langley estate the recent political events. The Duke has been telling his wife of the entry of Bolingbroke and Richard into London, at the end of the trip from Flint Castle. His tearful reaction to the situation still persists, and his recital has been interrupted by a fit of weeping. The Duchess, however, is naturally eager to hear the news. She implores him to get control of his feelings and to continue. She reminds him that he broke off at the description of the crowd's insolence toward Richard. They threw dirt and rubbish on his head as he rode along. York does resume. Bolingbroke had the crowd's hearty applause as he spurred his fiery but well-controlled horse through the streets. So alive were the buildings with onlookers and so noisy and hearty their welcome to Bolingbroke that it seemed the very windows and walls were saluting him. Bolingbroke acknowledged the greetings with low bows from his saddle.

But what about poor Richard, the lady inquires. Her husband rejoins that he suffered the fate of the second-rate actor who follows a star act.

He received contempt and mistreatment. But he bore the hostility with patience and with smiles despite his tears. So pitiful was he that the only explanation of the crowd's enmity toward him must be that Heaven so designed it. At any rate, York is accepting that convenient explanation; he reminds his wife that he has sworn allegiance to Bolingbroke.

Aumerle approaches, and York informs his wife that Aumerle must be now called Rutland. Bolingbroke has reduced him from Duke of Aumerle to Earl of Rutland because of Aumerle's association with Richard. York has become pledge for his son's loyalty to Bolingbroke. The father and mother try to get Aumerle to talk court gossip, but he is not interested. York spies a seal, the type used on important documents, sticking out of the young man's shirt and asks what it is. Aumerle hastily conceals it with "My lord, 'tis nothing." Suspicious, York insists on seeing the paper. The more the father insists, the stronger the son's refusal to show the paper. Finally, York is able to snatch it, takes a rapid glance down the page and cries, "Treason! Foul treason! Villain! Traitor! Slave!" A servant is sent posthaste to get York's riding boots and to saddle his horse. The Duchess receives no answer to her startled queries as to what's wrong except "Peace, foolish woman!" "I will not peace!" she rejoins and appeals to her son for an explanation. She gets nothing from him except a frightening "It is no more than my poor life must answer." York is still yelling for his boots. He must ride immediately to the King. The Duchess tries to remonstrate with her husband.

Surely, he isn't going to publicize his own son's errors? And his only son, too. They have no others and, of course, cannot expect more children at their age. Will he injure her by taking away her "fair son"—the son who so resembles himself?

York calls her "mad" and "fond" (which meant "foolish"). Would she conceal this conspiracy, sworn on the sacrament of the altar, this conspiracy to kill the King (Bolingbroke now) when he arrives at Oxford? The Duchess does not take a stand about the conspiracy; it doesn't much interest her. But Aumerle does, and, she says, they can just keep him at home at Langley so he can't go to Oxford. This plan is just further evidence to York of her "fondness." He declares that if Aumerle were twenty times his son, he'd accuse him. The Duchess tries another approach. She knows why York is so pitiless; he suspects that Aumerle is not his son, but a bastard. "Sweet York, sweet husband, be not of that mind!" He is the image of York, obviously his son; he doesn't resemble her or her family. But this trick of pretended hurt fails. York pushes her aside and leaves.

The mother turns to Aumerle. She urges him also to ride off to London, if possible, to outride his father and get to King Henry first with a confession of whatever crime he has committed. And she herself will follow. She's old, it is true, but she can still keep pace with York. She will throw herself at the feet of Bolingbroke and not rise until Aumerle is pardoned.

Act V: Scene 3

King Henry (Bolingbroke) complains to his lords at Windsor Castle about his spendthrift son, Prince Hal. He says he hasn't laid eyes on him for three months. He hears reports that the young man hangs out in the London taverns; and "they" say that he and the low dissolute companions he has taken up with amuse themselves by beating the patrolling watch-men and robbing pedestrians. The youthful Harry Percy tells the King of a chance conversation he had a couple of days before with the Prince. They had talked about the tournament scheduled for Oxford.

The Prince flippantly announced his intention of entering the competition wearing a common prostitute's glove as his token. The King shakes his head and says that the Prince is as bold as he is dissolute: but there have been evidences of real worth in the young man's character, and on these the father pins his hopes for the future.

All of a sudden, Aumerle rushes in with a distraught look immediately noted by his cousin the King. He begs the King for a private conference. The others withdraw, and Aumerle throws himself on his knees insisting that he will never rise until he has Bolingbroke's pardon. Bolingbroke says he'll get the pardon if the crime, whatever it is, has not actually been committed. He agrees to Aumerle's suggestion that they lock the door while Aumerle explains. But there comes a frantic pounding at the door, and York's voice warns the King: "Thou hast a traitor in thy presence. . . ./ Open the door, or I will break it open." Bolingbroke draws his sword and admits York who hands him the incriminating document. Aumerle reminds the King of the pardon (or so he interprets it) just extended. Bolingbroke and York take turns in berating Aumerle. The father's indignation is just as hot as the King's. "Forget to pity him, lest thy pity prove / A serpent that will sting thee to the heart!" cries York, and "Mine honor lives when his dishonor dies." "Oh loyal father of a treacherous son," compliments Bolingbroke.

Now, there is more hammering on the door and more shouting. It is the redoubtable Duchess. She implores the King to admit her, a "beggar." The melodramatic aspects of the situation begin to amuse the King, who tells Aumerle, "my dangerous cousin," to let his mother in. As she enters, York is still urging the "cutting off" of Aumerle. Immediately, the Duchess begs the King to ignore York, really a dangerous man to everyone since he can be so unnatural to his own son. The family tempest surges around the King. Soon all three, father, mother, and son, are on their knees before him. Aumerle, as usual, is almost silent. But his parents, especially his mother, are abundantly vocal. The chief line of argument of the Duchess is that York must be only pretending, and she is in dead, dead earnest. But probably her most effective weapon against Bolingbroke is her refusal to stand up. Bolingbroke doesn't try to say much, but three times he does beseech her, "Rise up, good Aunt." "Do not say 'Stand up,' / Say 'Pardon' first," she interjects between two stages of her verbal barrage.

So Bolingbroke says it: "I pardon him, as God shall pardon me." The Duchess rejoices in the superiority, as she puts it, that her inferior kneeling position has given her. But she demands that Bolingbroke repeat his pardon to make it "strong." And the King does: "With all my heart / I pardon him." But there will be no pardon for the other conspirators. York is empowered to raise a force to seize them at Oxford or wherever else they are hiding out. The King then bids the whole family farewell with a compliment to the Duchess for her maternal love and a charge to Aumerle to try to be loyal.

Act V: Scene 4

Sir Pierce (Peter) of Exton, a nobleman who has not previously figured in the play, is consulting with his servant. They are in Windsor Castle and are discussing recent remarks of King Henry. As quoted by Exton, Bolingbroke had said twice, and with some urgency, "Have I no friend will rid me of this living fear?" The servant agrees that these were the King's exact words. After these words were said by Bolingbroke, Exton had then felt that the King's eyes, ranging over the listening group of courtiers, had settled meaningfully on him, as if he were saying, "I would thou wert the man / That would divorce this terror from my heart." Exton supplies the explanation of what the King meant by "terror." He says that Bolingbroke is referring to that other "King," the man who lies imprisoned at Pomfret. And I am, indeed, "the King's friend, and will rid his foe," declares Exton. "Come, let's go."

Act V: Scene 5

Richard, in solitary confinement in dismal Pomfret Castle, begins this dolorous scene with a long soliloquy. He says he has been considering how he can compare his prison cell to the world. Of course, the world is thronged with people, and his cell is empty save for himself. But he won't be thwarted. By the combined labor of his mind and soul, he will produce thoughts and ideas to people his lonely room. Thoughts are like people— complex, everchanging, full of humors.

The highest kind of thoughts, those concerned with religion, usually are accompanied by disturbing scruples. He thinks of the Bible's reassuring "Come, little ones."* But then comes the memory of the stern warning that it is easier for a camel to go through the eye of a needle than for a rich man to enter heaven.**

*He probably has in mind the words of Jesus in Matthew, Chapter 19: "Suffer little children, and forbid them not to come to me."

**Shakespeare's eye is still on Matthew, Chapter 19: "And again I say unto you, it is easier for a camel to go through the eye of a needle, than for a rich man to enter into the kingdom of heaven." The fact that the two passages come from the same chapter accentuates the contrast that Richard feels in them.

Richard II

Richard continues tracing his thoughts. Sometimes he thinks of escape, of tearing out his prison walls with his fingernails. This brave thought dies of frustration. Next come thoughts intended to soothe: he is not the first to suffer in this way, nor will he be the last. In his present mood, Richard regards this kind of thinking as weak, fitting for a beggar in the stocks, perhaps; but a king should not transfer his burdens to the backs of others who may have endured the same punishment.

In entertaining these thoughts, he is, as he says, playing "many people." But actually his development of this idea shows that what he ponders is two people: Richard, the monarch; and Richard, the subject. Which is better off? When he thinks of himself as King, the fear of treason makes him prefer to be a beggar. But the fear of poverty swings back his preference to the throne. Then he recollects that in point of fact he is "unkinged," and unkinged by Bolingbroke. This makes him feel very depressed —"and straight am nothing." But the climax of his meditation is the realization that no human being will ever be content "till he be eased / With being nothing," until death has released him.

Richard hears music, or rather dissonance produced by an untalented player. He hates this ugly distortion of good music. Equally hateful, he says, is the distortion of a human life. He, although he has a fine delicate ear for music, did not hear soon enough the grating distortions in the music of his own life. He failed to "keep time" in his living. And then, switching to another meaning of time (note, again, the Elizabethan introduction of puns into very serious material), he laments, "I wasted time, and now Time doth waste me." He indulges next in a complicated, too-clever image, comparing his thoughts to minutes, his eyes to watches, his finger to the watch hands on the dial, his groans to chimes, and his heart to the bell itself. It all adds up to the point that time drags for him and that it is punctuated by his sighs, groans, and tears.

Again the music sounds, and he shouts out "let it sound no more." He has heard that music is sometimes used therapeutically to cure the insane, but the kind that he is hearing now will have just the opposite effect. Yet, he reminds himself that he should really appreciate this sound, for the playing is well-intentioned. Someone is trying to alleviate his loneliness. It is a gesture of love, and he gets little love these days "in this all-hating world."

Someone enters the dark cell and salutes Richard. "Hail, royal Prince." Richard retorts ironically, "Thanks, noble peer." The man's dress shows that he belongs to the servant class, but Richard wants to express his new philosophy that all men are about equal. Richard inquires who the man is. A visitor is most unusual. Ordinarily Richard sees only "that sad dog (his jailer) / That brings me food to make misfortune live." The new-comer explains that he had been a groom in Richard's royal stable. He is on a trip north to York and had gone to great difficulty to get the necessary permission to visit Richard. He wants to look again on Richard's face.

As he talks to Richard, the groom relates how unhappy he had been on the recent coronation day to see the new king riding the very "roan Bar-bary" horse* that Richard used to ride. Often had this groom curried and prepared him for Richard. Richard inquires with interest how the horse acted with his new rider. The groom has to admit that the Barbary pranced as "proudly as if he disdained the ground." Richard is hurt. The horse might have shown more gratitude for Richard's kindness to him, the treats of tasty food, the rewarding pats. Couldn't he at least stumble and break Boilngbroke's neck? But good sense reasserts itself. Why blame the horse whose nature it is to bear burdens? Why not blame himself? Contrary to what is right for his royal nature, he has allowed Bolingbroke to load him like an ass, to spur and weary him.

As the keeper enters, the groom leaves. The jailer wants Richard to eat some food he has brought. Richard tells him to taste it first, their usual procedure to assure Richard that he is not being poisoned; but the keeper refuses. He has been commanded not to by Sir Pierce of Exton, just arrived "from the King." Richard flares up. "The Devil take Henry of Lancaster and thee! / Patience is stale, and I am weary of it." He beats the jailer, who yells for help.

Exton and at least two followers, all armed, come pounding in. Richard immediately understands his danger. He seizes an axe out of the hands of one of the men and promptly kills the fellow with it. He then turns on the other follower and kills him, but in so doing he exposes himself to Exton, who gives him a mortal blow. Richard, dying on the flagstones of his cell, tells Exton his murderous hand will burn in Hell, for that mur-derous hand has stained England with royal blood.

Richard dies quickly. His last words are a prayer that his soul mount up-ward even as his body collapses on the cold floor.

Exton can't help paying the dead man a tribute. Richard, he says, was as full of valor as of royal blood. He hopes he has done the right thing, but he has some misgiving. "For now the Devil, that told me I did well, / Says that this deed is chronicled in Hell." But, at any rate, he will bring Rich-

*Horse of one of the admired, spirited breeds produced in the Arabic world, brown or brownish red in color.

ard's body to Bolingbroke. The other two who lie dead nearby shall be buried at Pomfret.

Act V: Scene 6

Preceded by a ceremonial flourish of trumpets, King Henry enters attended by York and other noblemen. The King remarks to York that late reports indicate that the rebels have burnt the town of Cicester (pronounced Si' sis ter; Cirencester in western England). But he has not yet had report about the fate of the rebels themselves. He turns from York to greet the entering Northumberland. Northumberland has encountered and overcome four of the chief insurgents, the Lords Oxford, Salisbury, Blunt, and Kent. He has beheaded them, and their heads are now on the way to London. Bolingbroke thanks Northumberland and promises him a reward for his diligence. Lord Fitzwater strides in. Two more rebels fell into his hands, and their heads have met the same unhappy fate. Hard on the heels of Fitzwater comes young Percy. He has captured the Bishop of Carlisle and has brought the prelate with him. He reports the death, whether from natural causes or by execution is not clear, of the arch-conspirator, the Abbot of Westminster. But at least he has the Bishop "to abide thy kingly doom [judgement]." The doom that Bolingbroke pronounces for Carlisle is that the Bishop should select some suitable but secluded residence. There he should live in quiet comfort. So long as he lives peaceably, he will not be disturbed. It is true, says Bolingbroke, that Carlisle has always been his enemy. Nevertheless, he admires and respects the churchman for the "high sparks of honor" he has seen in him.

Exton enters. Several men follow him bearing the burden of a coffin. Exton tells Bolingbroke that he brings King Henry's "buried fear." In the coffin lies Richard of Bordeaux, "mightiest of thy greatest enemies, . . . by me hither brought." Bolingbroke, with his customary rapid adjustment to surprise and rapid power of decision, turns on Exton. "I thank thee not, for thou hast wrought / A deed of slander." The offense, as Bolingbroke sees it, is not to Richard but to Bolingbroke himself and "all this famous land." Exton protests that he thought Bolingbroke said that he wanted Richard disposed of. Bolingbroke admits that he did wish Richard dead; but that does not prevent him from despising Exton, just as the poisoner can loathe the poison. "I hate the murderer, love him [Richard] murdered." He will give Exton no reward nor sign of favor. Rather let him roam in dark and nameless obscurity, blood brother to Cain. Bolingbroke tells the nobles around him that he is saddened that his rise to power was attended by the shedding of Richard's blood. He asks them to lament with him and to put on mourning clothes. He also announces his intention of making a pilgrimage to the Holy Land "to wash this blood off from my guilty hand." All depart from our sight, following in solemn procession the "untimely bier."

Richard III

KING EDWARD IV
EDWARD, PRINCE OF WALES }
   afterwards KING EDWARD V } *sons to the King.*
RICHARD, DUKE OF YORK. }
GEORGE, DUKE OF CLARENCE }
RICHARD, DUKE OF GLOUCESTER } *brothers to the King.*
   afterwards KING RICHARD III }
A young son of Clarence, (EDWARD PLANTAGENET, *Earl of Warwick*).
HENRY, EARL OF RICHMOND,
   afterwards KING HENRY VII.
CARDINAL BOURCHIER, ARCHBISHOP OF CANTERBURY.
THOMAS ROTHERHAM, ARCHIBISHOP OF YORK.
JOHN MORTON, BISHOP OF ELY.
DUKE OF BUCKINGHAM.
DUKE OF NORFOLK.
EARL OF SURREY, *his son.*
ANTHONY WOODVILLE, EARL RIVERS, *brother to Elizabeth.*
MARQUESS OF DORSET *and* LORD GREY, *sons to Elizabeth.*
EARL OF OXFORD.
LORD HASTINGS.
LORD STANLEY, *also called* EARL OF DERBY.
LORD LOVEL.
SIR THOMAS VAUGHAN.
SIR RICHARD RATCLIFFE.
SIR WILLIAM CATESBY.
SIR JAMES TYRREL.
SIR JAMES BLUNT.
SIR WALTER HERBERT.
SIR ROBERT BRAKENBURY, *Lieutenant of the Tower.*
SIR WILLIAM BRANDON.
CHRISTOPHER URSWICK.
TRESSEL *and* BERKELEY, *gentlemen attending on the Lady Anne.*
KEEPER *in the Tower.*
LORD MAYOR OF LONDON.
SHERRIFF OF WILTSHIRE.

ELIZABETH, *Queen to King Edward IV.*
MARGARET, *widow of King Henry VI.*
DUCHESS OF YORK, *mother to King Edward IV, Clarence, and Gloucester.*
LADY ANNE, *widow of Edward Prince of Wales, son to King Henry VI;*
   afterwards married to Richard.

Richard III

Act I: Scene 1

According to history the play covers about fourteen years—from the death of Henry VI, the last of the Lancastrians, in 1471, to the death of the Yorkist, Richard III, formerly Duke of Gloucester, in 1485. The latter's elder brother, King Edward IV, usurped the throne from Henry VI and reigned until 1483. But for dramatic purposes Shakespeare has crowded the events of these years into a few months.

When the play opens, Richard, Duke of Gloucester, is walking along a London street. He is musing on the peaceful times that have followed the Civil War between the House of Lancaster and the House of York.

Richard's thoughts turn to his ambitions to be King. It will take more bloody work and he is eager for it. Before the play opens he has determined to create hatred between his brothers, King Edward IV and George, Duke of Clarence. He has invented a prophecy and had it relayed to the King. It mentioned a traitor and assassin whose initial is "G". As Richard muses, he admits his villainy is prompted by his deformity—he is a hunchback and lame. He is so ugly that even the dogs on the street bark at him. Since he "cannot prove a lover" he is "determined to be a villain."

His thoughts are interrupted by the Duke of Clarence who walks toward him on his way to the Tower. Richard pretends surprise that Clarence has an armed guard. He is pleased at his brother's answer—the fault of the King's belief in an old prophecy given him by a fortune teller. The prophecy portends that the King's life is endangered by a person whose name begins with the letter "G". As the Duke's full name is George, Duke of Clarence, the King will feel more secure if his brother is imprisoned in the Tower. Richard insists that his imprisonment is not the King's doing, but that the King's wife, Lady Elizabeth Grey, and her family are to blame. He is supposedly sympathetic with Clarence, and advises him that as things are in the kingdom both are in danger. They had best keep the King's favor and the Queen's. Most especially he recommends keeping in favor with the King's friend, Mistress Jane Shore. He mentions how she has just obtained Lord Hastings' release from the Tower and may do the same for him. As the brothers part, Richard falsely promises Clarence to work for his release or take his place in the Tower.

Before Clarence is out of sight Lord Hastings, just released from the Tower, enters. He is greeted by Richard who pretends his distress over sending such worthy subjects as Clarence and Hastings to the Tower while lesser subjects remain free.

Hastings has news of the King's health. He "is sickly, weak and melancholy." Richard, swearing with his usual oath "By Saint Paul," pretends that he is greatly grieved at hearing such bad news.

He bids Hastings a hurried farewell. The news of the King's illness disturbs him since the King may die before Clarence. Clarence *must die before* the King! Otherwise he could be released from the Tower and proclaimed King.

Richard decides to visit the King at once and stir up more hatred and fear against Clarence. If he fails to move the King, then a murderer for Clarence must be found the next day.

He gambles that Edward will die shortly of natural causes and leave "the world for him to bustle in," but not alone. He will marry Lady Anne, the widow of Edward, Prince of Wales, son of King Henry VI. He admits as his thoughts ramble that he killed Anne's husband and her father-in-law. Cold and callous about it, Richard decides the only way to compensate Anne is to marry her and "become her husband and her father." He would not do it for love, but for a "close intent," which was likely the great wealth left her by her father.

As the scene ends he realizes his thoughts are racing ahead of him, and he determines that before anything else can be accomplished his two brothers, Edward IV and Clarence, *must* die.

Act I: Scene 2

This long scene opens several days later on a London street. A funeral procession is moving slowly along: an open coffin containing the body of King Henry VI is carried on attendants' shoulders and two gentlemen with swords are guarding it. The body is being transferred from a tomb in St. Paul's Cathedral to Chertsey. The only mourner is Lady Anne, the widow of Edward, Prince of Wales, son of Henry VI.

Anne speaks to the bearers of the coffin, telling them to put it down, that she wishes to rest and lament the untimely death of the King. She denounces most bitterly the murderer of her father-in-law and her husband, and declares the same murderer killed both. She wishes curses on him and any children he may have. Though she never names the murderer, it is evident that she is referring to Richard, Duke of Gloucester, who she knows slew her husband.

After this long lament, she orders the men to take up the coffin. As the procession starts again the Duke of Gloucester enters from a side street, and at his command the bearers again put down the coffin. Immediately Anne upbraids the men for obeying him. She violently denounces Richard and accuses him of the murder. Professing his love for her, Richard asks her not to be too bitter toward him. But this only infuriates her more. She asks the bearers of the coffin to see how the King's wounds are bleeding!

Anne's ravings continue, and she heaps abuse on Richard as a "lump of foul deformity," and begs God to revenge the King's death. Richard, patient in his declarations of love, gently chides her that she knows "no rules of charity." He begs her to let him make excuse for what he has done. Finally, he insists that it was her beauty that caused him to commit the murders. But Anne continues to revile him and even spits at him. He insists that he is going through "a living death."

Even the story of his own father's death, when often repeated by her father, the famous Duke of Warwick, never brought tears to his eyes; but her beauty has made him blind with weeping and if she is so vengeful —he hands her his sword, and, kneeling, bares his breast that she may stab him. On his knees he admits he killed King Henry, and also that he "stabb'd young Edward," her husband. It was her "heavenly face" that made him do it.

Anne lets the sword fall and calls him a "dissembler." He takes it up and offers to stab himself if she will bid him do it. Anne's attitude toward him softens, but she fears he is not truthful. She tells him to put up his sword. Richard asks if she has then forgiven him. She answers that she will tell him later. He offers her a ring and she accepts, saying "to take is not to give," meaning she will not give her word to marry him.

Richard offers to see to the burial of the King and suggests she return to her house. He asks her to bid him farewell, but she tells him "Imagine I have said farewell already."

When Anne has gone Richard orders the coffin to be taken to *White Friars* and await his arrival.

Alone on the stage, in a long soliloquy Richard ponders his strange wooing of Anne. He boasts he will have her but immediately declares, "I'll not keep her long."

Richard is amazed at his ability to overcome her extreme hatred for him in one short meeting. He questions whether she has forgotten her husband whom Richard very decently praises as a gentleman. He compares his own misshapened figure with the gallant and handsome Prince. Perhaps he has understated his own looks if Anne can find him "a marvelous proper man." Highly pleased with himself, he will begin at once to study fashions, employ "a score or two of tailors" to make him costly garments. But his business at hand is to get the body of King Henry in a tomb. Then he will report to Anne. Meanwhile, he bids the sun keep shining until he can purchase a glass and see his shadow as he passes.

Act I: Scene 3

The scene opens in a reception room in Whitehall Palace. It serves to bring Richard face to face with two avenging members of the royal family: Queen Elizabeth, wife of Edward IV, and Queen Margaret, the bitter-tongued widow of Henry VI.

Queen Elizabeth, Lord Rivers, her brother, and the Queen's son by a former marriage, Lord Grey, are discussing King Edward's illness. The Queen fears for her own safety and that of the young princes, sons by her marriage to Edward IV, if he dies. As they talk, the Duke of Buckingham and Lord Stanley enter. They report that the King's health seems improved. Moreover, he has sent for his brother, Richard, Duke of Gloucester, and the Queen's brothers, to try to bring peace to the royal household.

Richard, Duke of Gloucester, enters with Lord Hastings and the Marquis Dorset, brother of Lord Grey. He is angry that the King has sent for him because people have been complaining that he is too stern. The Queen openly accuses Richard of disliking her and her children and of being envious of her advancement at court.

In turn, Richard accuses the Queen of imprisoning the Duke of Clarence, which she swears is not true. Lord Rivers denies that she caused Lord Hasting's term in the Tower. The Queen is distraught at Richard's "bitter scoffs" and she threatens to tell the King how he has treated her. As she mourns over the "small joy" that she has had "in being England's Queen," Margaret, the widowed Queen of Henry VI, enters back stage. She comes slowly forward making asides on the sharp dispute between Richard and the Queen. (Asides are comments intended to be heard only by the audience.)

In the first of these asides she declares that the Queen should not be on the throne since Edward IV has usurped the Crown. Margaret claims that it belongs to her. She is deeply stirred when she hears Richard tell the Queen that she can report what she pleases about him to the King and that he is not afraid of being sent to the Tower. To Margaret Richard is a "devil" who killed her husband and her son. Unaware of her presence on stage, Richard continues to antagonize the Queen, inferring how as a nobody she had made subtle use of her widowhood to get on the English throne. He claims his one difficulty in dealing with the tangled affairs at Edward's Court is that he is too soft-hearted. He is "too childish-foolish for this world."

When Lord Rivers remarks that if Richard might one day be "our lawful King" the realm would be loyal, Richard denies any such ambition and declares that he "had rather be a pedlar."

Impatient with their glib remarks over the lawful occupant of the throne, Margaret advances and demands they listen to her. She angrily claims to be their lawful Queen. Richard denounces her and reminds her how his father, Richard, Duke of York, cursed her when she killed his son (Richard's brother) Edmund, Duke of Rutland, on the battlefield.

Cassandra-like, Margaret dominates the scene, heaping curses on Richard and taunting those who call her a "lunatic." Before she leaves she warns Buckingham, for whom she professes some friendliness, to beware of Richard. "Sin, death, and hell have set their marks on him:/ And all their ministers attend on him."

When Margaret goes, Richard, contrary to the others, pities her and repents the wrongs that he did to her. The Queen denies having ever wronged her, though Richard jibes that as Queen she is enjoying the wrongs done to Margaret. His mistreatment of her as well as that of his brother Clarence was to aid their brother Edward to gain the throne. He sneers that Clarence is nicely "frank'd up" (imprisoned) for his pains. Lord Rivers gives a caustic reply, taunting Richard for his "Christian-like conclusion."

Sir William Catesby, a gentleman of the King's household, enters with word that the Queen and the nobles have been summoned by the King.

Left alone, Richard takes deep satisfaction in his "secret mischiefs" that include the imprisonment of Clarence and placing the blame on the Queen. He comments how neatly he has clothed his "naked villany." He has done it "With old odds and ends stol'n out of Holy Writ/ And seems a saint, when most I play the devil."

He pauses to greet the two hirelings whom he has engaged to kill Clarence. They agree to "dispatch this thing" and ask him for the warrant. Richard gives the warrant he had gotten from Edward IV for the death of Clarence.

But the order which the King had subsequently sent to the Tower countermanding the warrant Richard has intercepted and kept.

Among the instructions that Richard gives them is a warning to act quickly and not listen to the pleas of Clarence: he speaks well and may provoke their pity. When they have done their work they are to go to his palace, Crosby Place, for their fee.

Act I: Scene 4

This scene, which takes place the same evening, is laid in a room in the London Tower. Brackenbury, the Keeper of the Tower, listens patiently to the Duke of Clarence relate the ghastly dream he has had. He dreamed he had escaped from the Tower and with his brother Richard was on a ship bound for France. At the suggestion of Richard they walk on deck. Clarence tells that his brother "stumbled" and knocked him overboard.

While he floundered in the sea he wished to die, though the thought of dying terrified him. As he sank into the waves he imagined he saw the old wrecks of ships, fish gnawing on the bodies of the crew, great jewels, "heaps of pearls" and gold "scatter'd in the bottom of the sea." Brackenbury twits him on having time to think of riches when he was so close to death.

Clarence relates that when the waves finally engulfed him he did not wake but thought that he crossed the River Styx and came to the lower world, the "kingdom of perpetual night." There he saw the souls of those he had wronged: his father-in-law, Richard, Duke of York, who accused him of treason: and Prince Edward, heir of Henry VI, who cried to the Furies to avenge his murder by Clarence. A legion of fiends tormented him with their howling.

After relating the dream Clarence admits to Brackenbury that he had committed wrong deeds, but that he had done them for the King, his brother, Edward IV. He is grieved that his brother has been so cruel as to imprison him. But Clarence prays to God to avenge him alone for his crimes, and he asks Him to spare his wife and children.

Wearied from recounting his frightening dream, Clarence falls asleep. As Brackenbury muses on the dangers and trials that beset royalty, two murderers enter with a warrant, signed by the King, to deliver Clarence to them. He gives them the keys, points to the sleeping Clarence and retires to tell the King he has discharged his duty.

The First and Second Murderers, as Shakespeare refers to them, discuss the murder they are about to commit. The Second Murderer has a "kind of remorse." His companion accuses him of being a coward and reminds him of the reward Richard has promised them. The Second Murderer blames his hesitancy on conscience, and he rattles off all the times in a man's life when it makes "a coward" of him; "A man cannot steal, but it accuseth him": and "if a man swears, it checks him." And so on.

Fighting off the pricks of conscience, they discuss how they will murder Clarence. They decide to knock him unconscious, then stab him and throw him into an outer room where he will be taken for a drunk. The Second Murderer suggests killing Clarence while he sleeps, but the First Murderer objects. He thinks they should reason with him.

Clarence is finally awakened by their talk and demands to know who they are. He suspects their intent is to murder him, and they admit they are to kill him by the King's order. Making a desperate plea for his life Clarence insists he has committed no wrong; he has had no trial at court and the deed will bring eternal damnation on those who commit it.

The Murderers accuse him of Prince Edward's death. Clarence insists that was done for love of his brother, Edward IV. While they banter with him, the murderers reveal to Clarence that his brother Richard has sent them there "to destroy" him. Clarence insists it cannot be true, and recalls how Richard promised to have him freed from the Tower.

When the Murderers bid him make his peace with God, Clarence asks, "A begging prince what beggar pities not?" The First Murderer answers "Ay," and stabs him. He carries the body off stage. The Second Murderer is remorseful over the "bloody deed," and like Pilate would wash his hands "of this most grievous murder." He tells the First Murderer to keep the fee and he repents that Clarence is slain. The First Murderer calls him a coward. He declares that as soon as he collects his "meed" he must get away from London.

Act II: Scene 1

In a room in the Palace of King Edward IV a colorful gathering of the nobles at his Court is awaiting him. Among those present are the Queen, her sons, Dorset and Grey, Rivers, Hastings and Buckingham. Showing signs of his grave illness, Edward enters, leaning on the arm of an attendant.

The King happily greets those present, mentioning his "good day's work" in bringing a semblance of union among the factions in his kingdom. He feels his death is imminent and wishes to depart leaving his friends in peace. He insists that Lord Hastings, a firm Yorkist, embrace Earl Rivers, brother of the Queen and, like her, unfriendly to him. Each swears "perfect love" for the other.

Feeling that the display of affection he is witnessing could be insincere, he asks the Queen to let Lord Hastings kiss her hand and do it without pretense. The Queen promises to forget their former hatred, and to seal it the King calls on the Marquis of Dorset, son of the Queen by her first marriage, to embrace Hastings. Then the Duke of Buckingham, friend of Richard, swears fealty to the Queen and her allies.

As the King is voicing regret over the absence of Richard, he enters and wishes the King and Queen "a happy time of day." He is pleased to hear that the King has made "peace of enmity, fair love of hate" among those gathered about him.

Immediately, Richard claims he loves peace. To those present he feigns true friendship, asking forgiveness if he committed a wrong, and declares it is "death to me to be at enmity." He closes a long speech thanking God for his "humility."

The Queen takes him at his word and would celebrate this peaceful union with a holiday. She quickly remembers the King has not mentioned his brother Clarence. All present are aghast when Richard tells that Clarence is dead. He pretends to think they knew it. The King insists that his order was reversed but Richard lies to him, saying that a cripple bore the "countermand" and it arrived too late.

Emotionally overcome by the tragic news of his brother's death, which instantly blights his bright hopes for peace, King Edward has scarcely time to answer Richard when Lord Stanley, Steward of the King's household, hurries on stage. He begs a "forfeit" (an acquittal) from a charge of homicide against his servant. The request disturbs the King—he can help a servant, but is now unable to help his brother. He feels stinging remorse for Clarence's death. He tries to shift the blame to those around him. Why, he asks, did they not come to him and remind him of all the kind things Clarence had done in helping him to the throne? They knew he was in prison, yet none "would once plead for his life." Edward goes off stage lamenting that he and each of them will feel God's justice.

As the scene ends Richard and the Duke of Buckingham are left alone on the stage. Richard pretends he is indignant at the rash murder of Clarence. He notes that the "guilty kindred of the Queen look'd pale" when they heard it. He is quite satisfied that "God will revenge it." Buckingham goes with him to offer "comfort" to Edward.

Act II: Scene 2

This scene takes place several days later. In a room in the King's palace the Duchess of York, mother of King Edward and Richard, is talking with her young grandchildren, the son and daughter of Clarence. She tries to conceal from them that the actual cause of her tears is their father's death, not King Edward's illness.

With the suspicion common to children they think something has happened to their father, or why does she keep saying: "O Clarence, my unhappy son!"

When the Duchess says that their father is "lost" the son is quick to interpret her remark as meaning death, and he declares that King Edward is responsible for it. He knows God will revenge it and will pray daily that He does. Though the Duchess tries to shield the King's guilt the children disbelieve her. They have it on the word of their Uncle Richard that the King ordered it and "was provoked to't by the Queen." He says their Uncle Richard has been very gentle with them. He had wept as he kissed them and promised he would be a father to them. Saddened that Richard should stoop so low in his deceitful ways, the Duchess calls him at once "her son and her shame."

She is interrupted by the loud weeping of the Queen who enters with her brother, Rivers, and her son, Dorset. She reveals that the King has died. The Duchess is deeply moved and complains how death has now left her only "one false glass" for her comfort, and Richard is her shame.

The children of Clarence are harsh toward their aunt, the Queen. Steeped in Richard's lies to them, they feel that she showed no sorrow for their father's death. In turn, they have none for her.

Dorset and Rivers try to comfort the two women by urging them to accept God's will in the case of Edward's death—a natural one. They also remind the Queen to look to the care of her son, who must be sent for immediately and crowned.

As they are talking Richard enters with Buckingham, Stanley, Hastings, Ratcliff and others. Richard greets the Queen as "Sister," telling her to "have comfort," weeping will not cure her woe. Pretending he had not seen his mother, the Duchess, he kneels for her blessing. When she asks God "to put meekness in thy breast," he mockingly adds in an aside, "and make me die a good old man!"

Buckingham had been prompted by Richard to take the initiative in urging the coronation of Elizabeth's son, Edward, Prince of Wales.

Hastings and Stanley agree with Buckingham that the Prince should have a small train accompany him. The Duchess and the Queen are asked by Richard to help decide who shall fetch the Prince from Ludlow.

Alone with Richard on the stage, Buckingham declares that it is essential that both of them go to Ludlow if they are to begin the project "we late talk'd of/ To part the Queen's proud kindred from the Prince." Playing the sycophant, Richard agrees to all Buckingham proposes. He calls him "My oracle, my prophet! my dear cousin,/ I, as a child, will go by thy direction." They are off for Ludlow.

Act II: Scene 3

This scene takes place some few days later. Two citizens on a London street pass the time of day and exchange the latest news—the King's death. The Second Citizen has a very gloomy outlook for the state of the nation. A Third Citizen joins them. He and the Second Citizen see only trouble ahead. The First Citizen has faith in Edward's young son: "By God's good grace," he will rule well. The Third Citizen is not convinced, and his fears rest on the Scriptural text, "Woe to that land that's govern'd by a child!" The Second Citizen admits a council under him might rule well. This was the case "when Henry the Sixth/ Was crowned in Paris but at nine months old." The Third Citizen remarks that the infant French King had "virtuous uncles to protect His Grace," but that this is not the case at present. Young Edward has uncles, but Richard is "full of danger" and his mother's sons and brothers are too proud.

The First Citizen's comrades are too pessimistic. The Third Citizen feels certain that times will be troublesome; one can sense it, as he does the change of seasons: "When the great leaves fall, then Winter is at hand." The Second Citizen agrees that every one is apprehensive. But the Third Citizen warns that men always fear a change: they had best place it all in God's hands. With this final word they go their way to the Justices.

Act II: Scene 4

This is another short, homey scene (comparable to Act II, sc. 2). It takes place in a room in the palace; the Queen, her younger son Richard, Duke of York, and the Duchess of York listen as the Archbishop of York tells the latest news of the arrival of the Duke's brother, Edward, Prince of Wales. He has travelled by way of Northampton and Stony Stratford and should be in London the next day. The Duchess is anxious to see him and wonders if he has grown. When the Queen says "no," that her "son of York/ Has almost overt'aen him in in his growth," the young Duke, a delightfully precocious youngster, declares he is not at all pleased to outgrow his brother. Quite innocent of its poignancy, he describes an incident at supper one night with his uncles Rivers and Richard, who were remarking on his quick growth. He was very impressed with the old saying that his uncle Richard quoted, "Small herbs have grace, great weeds do grow apace." And since then the young Duke had wanted to grow slowly. The Duchess is quick to apply the saying to *her* son, Richard, noting how slowly he grew, and yet she implies he is not gracious.

A messenger enters to give the disturbing news that Richard and Buckingham have imprisoned in Pomfret Castle the Queen's brother, Lord Rivers, and her elder son, Lord Grey, and with them Sir Thomas Vaughan. Both the Queen and the Duchess fear massacre and "domestic broils" will be the outcome.

As suggested by the Archbishop, the Queen and her son are escorted by him to Westminster sanctuary to take refuge.

Act III: Scene 1

The scene is late in the day following the flight of the Queen and her son to Westminster for sanctuary.

We are on a London street watching the triumphal return of Edward, Prince of Wales, who is to be crowned King of England. Trumpets sound as the young heir approaches, accompanied by his Uncle Richard, Buckingham, Cardinal Bouchier, Catesby, and others.

Buckingham is the first to welcome Edward to the city. Before he can reply, his uncle remarks that he seems "melancholy." The Prince bluntly replies that he wanted "more uncles here to welcome" him. Richard describes them as too "dangerous." They have "sugar'd words" but poisoned hearts. He turns quickly to proclaim the arrival of the Lord Mayor and his train.

After a short greeting the Prince complains that his mother and brother should have arrived to greet him and wonders that Hastings has brought no news of them. As he speaks, Hastings arrives with word that the Queen and her young son have taken refuge in Westminster sanctuary. He would have brought the Duke, but his mother forbade him. Buckingham, secretly anxious to separate both sons from their mother, thinks the Duke should be seized as he has no right of sanctuary. This starts a discussion with the Cardinal during which Richard offers no opinion. Buckingham convinces the Cardinal that as a child the Duke has neither the "dealings" to deserve the place nor the wit to claim it. Accompanied by Hastings, the Cardinal agrees to fetch the Duke.

Richard III

While they await his arrival, Richard convinces the Prince that the Tower is the fit place for his brother and him to await the coronation. The Prince objects to the Tower—all towers. He questions whether Julius Caesar really built the London Tower, as it is said. Buckingham assures him that Julius Caesar began it. In an aside, Richard remarks that "so wise so young, they say, do ne'er live long." To satisfy the Prince's curiosity he had to repeat the jingle but he quickly changed it to "without characters, fame lives long." If the Prince lives to be a man, he intends to emulate Caesar. He will "win our ancient right in France again." Richard's only comments are in asides that foreshadow the tragedy closing in on the young Prince.

When the Cardinal and Hastings arrive with the young Duke, Richard has a more difficult time with him—"a parlous boy/ bold, quick, ingenious, forward, capable:/ He's all the mother's, from the top to toe."—so Richard, later, describes him. He reminds his Uncle about fast growth of weeds, seeing how the Prince has grown. He asks for his Uncle's dagger and gets it with the promise of "a greater gift"—a sword, the young Duke guesses. When the Prince taunts him for his sharp bantering with his Uncle, who has called him "little lord," the Duke makes an unfortunate reference to his uncle's deformity: "Because that I am little, like an ape,/ He thinks that you should bear me on your shoulders."

In an aside Buckingham tells Hastings "to be so cunning and so young is wonderful." Richard sharply stops the banter and without any ado manouevers the Princes into the Tower against the childish fears of the Duke that he would be haunted by his Uncle Clarence's "angry ghost." His Grandam, the Duchess, had told him he had been murdered there. With a "heavy heart" the Prince leads the way.

When the Princes are safely locked up, and Buckingham and Richard are alone except for the attendant, Catesby, the former reverses his compliments about the young Duke. He fumes that the "prating" youngster must have been coached by his "subtle mother/ To taunt and scorn you thus approbiously." Richard agrees it was "no doubt" his mother's influence, but he lists a string of good qualities which suggests that he admires the Duke more than his brother, the Crown Prince.

He leaves to Buckingham the task of instructing Catesby how to sound out the allegiance of Lord Hastings to Richard's cause. Catesby doubts Hastings' affection for the Prince can be alienated. If he proves obstinate, Catesby is not to push the matter. As Catesby departs, Richard sends a greeting to Hastings to let him know his ancient enemies, Grey and Rivers, will die the next day. Still twitting him about Mistress Shore, this news is so good he should give her one more "gentle kiss." Catesby leaves, promising to bring news to Crosby Palace before they retire for the night.

Buckingham wonders what they will do if Hastings will not yield to their "complots." Richard's answer is direct, "chop off his head, man." And, when he is King, Richard promises Buckingham for his loyalty "The Earldom of Hereford and the movables" of his brother, the late King.

Act III: Scene 2

The scene takes place about four o'clock the following morning. The house of Lord Hastings is the setting. A messenger from Lord Stanley has arrived there ahead of Richard's messenger. His message is urgent, hinging on a dream that Richard "had rased off" Stanley's helmet. Also, Stanley has learned that there are to be two Councils which he thinks may force enmity between him and Hastings. One way to shun the danger he foresees is for both of them to race north on horseback.

Hastings makes light of Stanley's worries. They will be together at one of the Councils; Catesby, whom he trusts, at the other, so they will know what goes on at each. As for dreams, Hastings is amused that he would "trust the mockery of unquiet slumbers." He bids the messenger tell his master to rise and come to his house. They will both go to the Tower and Stanley can see that the "boar" will be gentle towards them.

Catesby enters as the first messenger leaves. Hastings is in a buoyant mood: he does not suspect the loyalty of this assistant of the late King. Hastings doubts Catesby's word that Richard wants to be crowned King. He is pleased to learn of the imminent execution of his enemies, Rivers and Grey, at Pomfret Castle. But he tells Catesby that he will lose his own head before he will give his "voice on Richard's side." He feels so secure that he prophesies that he will send others "packing," even some who are dear to Richard and Buckingham. Catesby mentions that Hastings is quite highly thought of by them, but, in an aside, it is his head on the Bridge they really want.

As they are talking Stanley arrives. Hastings jests about his dream of the "boar." But Stanley, who has a keen judgment regarding Richard, does not trust him. Rivers and Grey, he reminds Hastings, "had no cause to mistrust." When Hastings glibly tells him they are to be beheaded that day Stanley's reply is stern and portentous, "They, for their truth, might better wear their heads/ Than some that have accused them wear their hats."

It nettles Hastings when he realizes that the implication is a jibe at him. He bids Stanley go along toward the Tower, that he will follow.

Hastings pauses to talk with a State Messenger who is passing. The last time they met, Hastings recalls, he was on his way as a prisoner to the Tower by "the suggestion of the Queen's allies." He cautions the messenger not to tell that on "This day those enemies are put to death;/ And I'm in better state than e'er I was." For the messenger's good wishes he tosses him his purse, saying "There, drink that for me."

A priest passing by stops to greet Hastings. The latter remembers he is in debt for the Priest's ministrations to him in the Tower. On "the next Sabbath," Hastings will "content" him. As they talk, Buckingham arrives on his way to the Tower. He jests that while Hastings' friends at Pomfret need a priest, Hastings has no shriving work in hand. As both Hastings and Buckingham go along their way to the Tower, Hastings remarks that he will "stay dinner there." In an aside Buckingham sneers, "And supper too, although thou know'st it not."

Act III: Scene 3

This scene takes place the same day (not historically) in front of Pomfret Castle. Ratcliff, a noble henchman of Richard, is overseeing the execution of Rivers, Grey and Vaughan. The three nobles are conducted by a guard. Each of the men is vengeful. Rivers proclaims. he is dying "For truth, for duty, and for loyalty." Pomfret he calls a "bloody prison"— the place where Richard II was "hack'd to death." Grey repeats Margaret's curse on them "For standing by when Richard stabb'd her son." Rivers corrects the order of the names of those Margaret cursed; he places Richard next to themselves, then Buckingham and Hastings.

Act III: Scene 4

The Tower is the setting for this scene. It completes the action of Scene 2 in which Stanley, Hastings and Buckingham are on their way to the Tower.

The members of the Council of which Hastings spoke in Scene 2 are sitting around the table. Those present are Buckingham, Stanley, Hastings, John Morton, Bishop of Ely, Ratcliff, Lovel, and others.

Hastings, in an exuberant mood, opens the Council with a terse statement of its business, namely, to set a date for the coronation of young Edward. Everything is ready for the occasion, according to Stanley. All that is needed is to name the day, and the Bishop suggests the following day. They realize that Richard, now Protector, must be consulted and will have the final say when he arrives.

Who present knows Richard's mind in the matter? Buckingham contradicts the Bishop that he does. Rather it is Hastings who should "soonest" know the Protector's mind—they are closer friends. Pleased with Buckingham's false flattery, Hastings denies he has had any word with Richard regarding the coronation.

Richard enters apologizing for being "long a sleeper." He learns from Buckingham the prominent part Hastings is taking in the Council. In fact, he is ready to act in Richard's stead and "Had pronounced your part—I mean your voice,—for crowning of the King." Richard says that he knows Hastings loves him well. He turns to the Bishop and remarks that he would like some of the fine strawberries he saw in his garden. The Bishop gladly orders his servant to fetch some.

As the Bishop leaves the room, Richard draws Buckingham aside to give him Catesby's report on Hastings. He repeats that Hastings said he "will lose his head e're he give consent" to crown any one king but the son of Edward IV. At Buckingham's suggestion they leave the council room to talk it over. While they are gone, Stanley, still suspicious of Richard despite his affable manner, thinks the coronation should be postponed for a time.

Just then the Bishop returns and asks for Richard. He is anxious to tell him that he has sent for the strawberries. Hastings gaily remarks how happy the Protector looks—he must have some plan that pleases him. He thinks Richard's face always betrays his heart. Stanley asks Hastings, "What of his heart perceive you in his face," today? Hastings, never suspecting that Catesby had betrayed his opinions concerning the Crown Prince to Richard, answers that the Protector's looks show that "with no man here he's offended."

Hastings barely finishes when Richard, in an angry mood, returns with Buckingham. He has discovered there are "devilish plots" and "damned witch craft" working against him. (See Hastings' remarks to Catesby in Act III sc. 2.) Richard asks what should be done with the perpetrators of them. In a display of loyalty, Hastings declares "they have deservéd death." Richard bares his withered arm, which, he says, was caused by witchcraft—the consorting of Edward's wife, the Queen, that "monstrous witch," with the "harlot strumpet Shore."

Hastings fumbles again, saying "If they have done this thing, my gracious lord—" Brusquely interrupting, Richard points to *him* as the traitor, declaring "Off with his head! Now, by St. Paul, I swear/I will not dine until I see the same." Telling his henchmen Ratcliff and Lovell to "look that it be done," Richard asks the others who "love" him to follow.

Left alone, Hastings realizes his mistakes. He blames himself for not heeding Stanley's warnings. He was too vengeful on hearing of the beheadings of Rivers and Grey, and now Margaret's curse has fallen on him. As he is led off stage he pities England, and prophesies dire times for the nation under "bloody Richard."

Act III: Scene 5

This scene takes place the same day, outside the Tower and a short time after the execution of Hastings.

As the scene opens, Richard and Buckingham are seen on the Tower walls wearing rusty armor and looking harassed and bedraggled. They are staging a mock duel with an imaginary foe who is avenging Hastings' death. Richard coaches Buckingham how to be "mad with terror." But Buckingham declares he "can counterfeit the deep tragedian" and is as adept at "ghastly looks" as he is with "enforcéd smiles."

Catesby has been sent to bring the Lord Mayor and his train. When he arrives, a crowd has gathered outside the Tower. Richard and Buckingham are racing back and forth shouting commands as if they are warding off blows from an attacker. Buckingham starts to tell the Lord Mayor why they have sent for him, but Richard interrupts with a plea to be careful, there are enemies nearby.

Lovell enters with Hastings' head, holding it up so all can see "that ignoble traitor." Richard, pretending he is overcome by grief, weeps as he eulogizes Hastings as "the plainest harmless creature/That breathed upon the earth a Christian." Richard tells how he loved him as a confidant until he found that Hastings was consorting with Mistress Shore and covering his vice with a "show of virtue."

Buckingham sees him only as a "subtle traitor." He accuses Hastings of plotting this day in the council house to "murder me and my good Lord of Gloucester."

Richard assures the Mayor except for "the extreme peril of the case,/ The peace of England and our person's safety," they would never have proceeded so rashly. The Mayor praises them. It will be a warning to others. But he was not surprised at Hastings after he had taken up with Mistress Shore.

The death sentence was carried out with greater haste than they intended, Buckingham declares. They wished that the Mayor might have heard, him confess the purpose of his treason. Then the Mayor could have informed the citizens, and they would not have blamed them and would not "wail his death."

The Mayor is satisfied with the justice of the case. Having so neatly hood-winked the Mayor, they politely bid him farewell.

He is scarcely out of hearing when Richard reveals Buckingham's next task. He must overtake the Mayor on the way to the Guild Hall and get across to him,

(a) That Edward's children are likely bastards.

(b) That Edward had an insatiable and indiscriminate lust.

(c) That Edward himself was likely illegitimate: (his father was away at the wars and by computing the time found the child was not his, nor did he resemble Warwick, Richard's father).

(d) Buckingham must be guarded in pressing this last issue because Richard's mother, the Duchess, is still alive.

Buckingham assures Richard he will "play the orator." If he is successful, Richard will await him at Baynard's Castle "with reverend fathers and well-learnéd bishops."

To be certain that at least two prominent clergy are on hand, Lovel is sent to fetch Dr. Shaw, the Mayor's brother; Catesby, to bring Friar Penker, Provincial of the Augustinian Friars. Meanwhile Richard, alone now, muses that he will give a "privy order" that will keep "the brats of Clarence out of sight." No one will be allowed to see them.

Act III: Scene 6

This very short scene is on a London Street.

A scrivener muses over an indictment pertaining to the beheading of Lord Hastings. The original draft took eleven hours to draw up. The scrivener remarks that it also took him eleven hours to copy it. He will post it in St. Paul's.

The scrivener is not satisfied with the accusations against Hastings. He notes that Hastings was "untainted, unexamined, free, at liberty," within five hours of his death. No one is so "gross" as to not mistake it for a device, yet no one is so bold to say so. It is a bad world, he thinks, when "such ill dealing" is concealed.

Act III: Scene 7

This scene follows a few hours after Scene 5 in Baynard Castle.

Richard and Buckingham are alone in the courtyard. When Richard learns that "The citizens are mum, say not a word," regarding the Crown, he demands if Buckingham mentioned the illegitimacy of Edward's children. Buckingham declares he did, and gives him a point by point resumé of his harangue to the crowd. He made much of Edward's supposed engagement to Elizabeth Lucy, of his unbridled lewdness in London, and of his bastardy.

As a boost to Richard's pride Buckingham had also added that Edward did not resemble their father, Richard, Duke of York, as Richard did. The latter was the image of his father, both in "form and nobleness of mind." Buckingham told also how victorious Richard had been in the Scottish wars, and the wisdom he had in peace. When he had shown Richard as bounteous and full of virtue and "fair humility," he called on those that did love their country's good to cry *God save Richard, England's royal King!*

Richard asks if the citizens responded. Buckingham replied, "They spake not a word." They stared and looked deadly pale, he said. He upbraided them. The Mayor explained that the crowd was unaccustomed to being spoken to directly: a recorder always relayed the Court's message. But the recorder was no more successful. A few of Buckingham's hirelings threw their caps in the air and about ten cried, "God save King Richard!" Then, Buckingham said, he took "vantage of those few" and thanked the citizens for their applause. It proved, he said, their wisdom and love for Richard.

It is hard for Richard to believe that these "tongueless blocks" would not speak. Anxiously, he asks if the Mayor and his train will meet him. Buckingham had at least interested the Mayor who is on his way now to the Castle.

Buckingham ventures some suggestions how Richard should receive him: he should pretend some fear; be difficult to gain access to; it would look well for him to be reading a prayer book and stand between two churchmen; and not be easily won over. Richard must "Play the maid's part; still answer nay, and take it."

Before he can say more, the Mayor knocks, and Richard hurries out of sight. Buckingham welcomes the Mayor and advises him that it is difficult to get an audience with the Duke. Catesby brings word that

Richard asks Buckingham to come to see him the following day. He is in meditation with two right reverend fathers and no worldly business can interrupt him. Catesby is sent back to urge a meeting with the Mayor and Alderman. There are "matters of great moment" that touch the general good to be discussed.

While Catesby is about his errand, Buckingham uses the interim to compare Richard's holiness with the vices of his late brother, the King, though the latter is not named. But Buckingham feigns great fear that Richard will not accept the "sovereignty of the nation." The Mayor prays God that he will.

Catesby brings word that Richard is worried that Buckingham has "assembled" so many citizens. The latter sends back word that he, as well as all present, "come to him in perfect love." Buckingham moralizes how devout men, like Richard, are loathe to leave their "zealous contemplation."

In a gallery just above them, the Mayor spies Richard with the two clergymen. Buckingham is quick to point to the prayer book in his hand—a true sign of a holy man. He addresses Richard as "Famous Plantagenet" and regrets interrupting his devotions. Richard begs him not apologize but tell him the purpose of the visit. He is afraid he has done "some offense." Buckingham assures him he has in *not* becoming King. In a long speech Buckingham musters all the reasons why he should accept. Richard's answer is a cleverly devised rejection, coming finally to the point that Edward has left "royal fruit" in the young Crown Prince, "The right and fortune of his happy stars:/ Which God defend that I should wring from him!"

Buckingham praises Richard's nicety of conscience. Later, in his long speech, he implies that the father, Edward IV, of this young prince is illegitimate.

The House of York, he claims, is in great danger unless Richard accepts the crown. Richard cannot see why he should take on such a burden. Buckingham declares the young Prince will never reign. He pretends to be out of patience with Richard and starts to leave with the Mayor and the citizens.

At Catesby's urging Richard calls them back. Since they "buckle fortune" on his back, he will accept the Crown. Buckingham is the first to salute him, "Long live King Richard, England's worthy King!" Then all answer "Amen."

Buckingham asks when he wishes the coronation. It is settled for the following day. With the clergymen, Richard leads the way "to our holy work again."

Act IV: Scene 1

This scene takes place in front of the Tower, shortly after Richard has been crowned King.

Queen Elizabeth, her elder son Dorset, and the Duchess of York come forward to greet Lady Anne, accompanied by Lady Margaret Planta-genet, the young daughter of the murdered Clarence. The latter are on their way "to gratulate the gentle Princes" in the Tower.

As they talk Brackenbury, the Keeper of the Tower, enters, and the Queen inquires about the health of the Princes. He assures her that they are well, but gives the disturbing news that the King has forbidden anyone to see them.

The Queen, and those with her, are unaware of the events of the previous day. They are amazed at the word "King." "Who's that?" she asks. Brack-enbury corrects himself—he means, the "Lord Protector." Despite the ardent pleas of the three women Brackenbury declares he is bound by oath to refuse anyone admittance to the Princes.

As he finishes, Lord Stanley enters to summon Lady Anne to West-minster to be "crowned Richard's royal Queen." It is disturbing news. When Dorset tells his mother to be of good cheer, she pleads with him to flee to France and join Lord Stanley's step-son, Richmond. She fears for his life remembering Margaret's curse that she will die "Nor mother, wife, nor England's counted Queen."

Stanley agrees that Dorset should leave immediately for France and will give him letters to Richmond. He cuts short the lament of the Duchess of York for the "cockatrice" that she has "hatch'd to the world" in Richard. He bids Lady Anne make haste to the coronation; but she will not leave until she has declared her folly in marrying Richard. She recalls how she repulsed Richard's affection for her; she repeats the curse that she wished for him and whoever would be his wife, namely, that she be more "Miserable by the life of thee/ Than thou hast made me by my dear lord's death!" Since her marriage to Richard, she has always felt her own curse, and now, she believes, he "will shortly be rid" of her.

The Queen and the Duchess bid Lady Anne farewell. The Queen asks her to wait a bit and look back with her to the Tower. She gives what amounts to a tender eulogy for her young sons. She addresses the Tower as "Rude ragged nurse, old sullen playfellow/ For tender princes, use my babies well!" She implies their fate in her remark, "So foolish sorrow bids your stones farewell."

Act IV: Scene 2

This scene is in a room of state in the palace. Richard enters, already crowned. With him are Buckingham, Catesby, a Page, and attendants.

He is delighted with the pomp and ceremony and asks Buckingham to help him ascend the throne. His first words as King are in praise of Buckingham, "Thus high, by thy advice/ And thy assistance, is King Richard seated." Almost immediately he begins to test Buckingham's loyalty. He wants to know whether Buckingham "be current gold indeed."

Though all may call him King, Richard is troubled because "Young Edward lives." Buckingham's reply, "True, noble Prince," nettles Richard. He reprimands him for being so dull. Richard wants "the bastards dead," and he wants it done quickly. Further, he wants Buckingham's opinion on it. When the latter begs time to think it over, Richard is at once suspicious. Catesby, in an aside, observes "The King is angry; see, he gnaws his lip."

When Buckingham leaves the room, Richard remarks he has no time to waste on "iron-witted fools," and none are for him who look at him with "considerate eyes." He comes down from the throne musing, "High-reaching Buckingham grows circumspect." Then, without more ado, Richard plans the death of the Princes. Through his Page he learns of Tyrell who will kill for "gold."

While the Page goes to fetch Tyrell, Richard, alone on the stage except for Catesby, declares if Buckingham has grown weary keeping up with him and must stop for breath, "well, be it so." As he is speaking Stanley enters with news that Dorset has gone to France to help Richmond.

The news brings the play to a climax. Richard is keenly aware that Richmond will be hard to conquer. His mind races on to defend himself. To prepare the public for Lady Anne's death, Catesby must rumor it about that she is "very grievous sick." When Catesby is slow to go Richard is impatient. To safeguard the throne, he must marry his brother Edward's daughter, or else the "Kingdom stands on brittle glass." He must also marry off Clarence's daughter to a "mean-born gentleman." As to Clarence's son, "the boy is foolish, and not to be feared."

But the Princes must be disposed of first. He recognizes the end of it all is uncertain. In a kind of desperate nonchalance he acknowledges, "I am in/ So far in blood, that sin will pluck on sin." But he remarks none of it creates pity or tears in him.

When the Page reenters with Tyrell, Richard loses no time engaging him to dispatch "those bastard brats in the Tower." Tyrell, fortified with a token, agrees to the task. When it is done, Richard wants immediate report. He promises Tyrell his love and preferment.

Buckingham returns to the room as Tyrell leaves, and tells Richard he has been considering the "question," meaning the murder of the children. But Richard is deaf to his remarks. He is completely engrossed in the knowledge that Dorset has joined Richmond. He implies to Stanley that serious consequences can result since Richmond is his wife's son. Stanley makes no reply.

Buckingham again tries to get Richard's attention, reminding him of the kingly gifts he had promised—the earldom of Hereford and "the movables." Richard ignores him. Stanley listens to Richard recount the prophecy of Henry VI, that Richard would be King when he was yet a "little peevish boy." He wonders why Henry was not able to prophesy his own death by Richard's hand. Richard repeats the word "Richmond." He tells Stanley how during a visit to Exeter the Mayor showed him the castle and mispronounced it "Rouge-mont." It startled him because an Irish bard had long before told him he would die soon after he saw Richmond.

During Richard's musing Stanley never interrupts. Buckingham interrupts the King several times to ask about his promised earldom. Exasperated with him, Richard demands the time of day. He compares Buckingham to a jack, the iron figures of men on the outside of old clocks that struck the hours, because "thou keep'st the stroke/Betwixt thy begging and my meditation." Richard declares he is "not in the giving vein today." Boldly, Buckingham asks for a definite "yes" or "no" about the earldom. Irritated by his persistence, Richard walks off stage with Lord Stanley, fretting, "Thou troublest me; I am not in the vein."

Left alone, Buckingham sees his folly in placing confidence in Richard's promises. To avoid the same fate as Hastings, he leaves immediately for his castle in Wales.

Act IV: Scene 3

This scene, full of tragedy and pathos, takes place in a room in the King's palace.

Tyrell enters alone. In a long soliloquy he laments "this ruthless piece of butchery"—the murder of the young Princes. Though inured to crime, even the two assassins whom he hired, Dighton and Forrest, wept like children as they told him. He relives the scene, repeating the assassins' exact description of the murder. Dighton told that the boys were asleep with their arms around each other. A prayer boòk lay on the pillow. Forrest said *that* "almost changed my mind/ But O, the devil—" Dighton continued, "We smotheréd/The most replenishéd sweet work of Nature,/ That from the prime creation e'er she framed." When they were dead, Tyrell went to look at them and has come to report the deed to the "bloody King."

When he hears the King's step, he goes to greet him as "my sovereign Lord!" Richard inquires if he will be happy over the news. Tyrell assures him he has done the "thing" he had been charged to do. Did he see them dead and buried? Tyrell did see them dead, but a priest buried them secretly. Richard dismisses him with the charge to return after supper and give him the details of the murders. Meantime, Tyrell was to think how Richard may do him "good."

Alone on the stage, Richard reviews what he has accomplished in blocking any challenge to his right to the Crown:

> 1—He has imprisoned Clarence's young son. Clarence's daughter he has "matche'd marriage to a nobleman." (Clarence's daughter married Sir Richard Pole. She became the mother of the great Reginald Cardinal Pole. During the Reformation she was beheaded by King Henry VIII.)
>
> 2—Edward's sons "sleep in Abraham's bosom."
>
> 3—Richard's wife, Lady Anne, has already "bid the world goodnight."

Now young Richmond wants to marry Edward's daughter Elizabeth to unite the Yorks and Lancasters on the throne. But Richard, "a jolly, thriving wooer," will go to her first.

His jubilant mood vanishes when Catesby hurries in with the news that John Morton, Bishop of Ely, has gone to the aid of Richmond; Buckingham, with a battalion of Welshmen, has also turned against Richard. Ely's defection disturbs Richard more than Buckingham's. But he concludes that discussing what tactics to pursue only causes delay. Catesby is ordered to "muster men;" Richard will prepare for battle at once.

Act IV: Scene 4

This very long scene takes place within a few days in front of the palace.

Queen Margaret is alone on the stage. She is as vengeful as in her first appearance (Act I, sc. 3). She sees prosperity on the wane among her enemies. Soon she will return to France, and she leaves with the hope that the future for them will be as "bitter, black, and tragical as it promises."

As Queen Elizabeth and the Duchess of York arrive, Margaret keeps out of their sight. The Queen sighs over the deaths of her "tender babes." In an aside, Margaret picks up her plea that the "gentle souls" of the children will hover about her. She would have them tell their mother that Divine Justice has now avenged them both—each has lost a son. When the Duchess mourns for her son, Edward IV, the scene becomes almost an antiphonal as the two mothers, and, later, Margaret, indulge their sorrows in bitter lamentations over their bereavements.

Elizabeth asks when did God ever "sleep while such a deed was done?" In an aside Margaret answers: when her husband and son died. The Duchess, referring to the "world's shame" and to herself as a "living ghost," sits on the ground. Elizabeth sits beside her, wishing that the earth would as easily afford a grave as this "melancholy seat." She asks "Ah, who has any cause to mourn but I?" Coming forward, Margaret pleads, "If ancient sorrow be most reverend" that her sorrow be given "seniory." Addressing her remarks to the Queen, Margaret matches murder for murder in the two families.

The Duchess draws attention to her own sorrows. Like Margaret and Elizabeth she has lost a husband and a son by the assassin's knife. But her remark brings a heap of vicious invective on her for bringing Richard into the world, "That dog, that had teeth before his eyes." The old Duchess begs Margaret not to triumph in her woes; she has often wept for Margaret's. But her plea is unavailing and Margaret admits that she is "hungry for revenge." Now she is enjoying a surfeit of it. One by one those who wronged her have been mowed down by Richard. Now her only prayer is that she may live to say of him, "The dog is dead."

Elizabeth remembers Margaret's prophecy (Act I, sc. 3) that the day would come when she would wish her nearby to help her curse Richard. The remark launches Margaret's long speech—a veritable diatribe on Elizabeth for usurping her place as Queen. Half of the yoke that Margaret has long borne, Elizabeth now bears. But soon Margaret will leave it all to her.

Moved by her speech, Elizabeth asks her to wait and teach her how "to curse" her enemies. She must learn, Margaret counsels, to "Compare dead happiness with living woe." Then her own woes will sharpen her curses, and they will "pierce" as do Margaret's.

As Margaret leaves the Duchess impatiently asks, "Why should calamity be full of words?" They help nothing, Elizabeth replies, but "they ease the heart." If so, the Duchess urges Elizabeth to come with her, and with bitter words "smother/My damnéd son, that thy two sweet sons smother'd."

The Duchess warns that the drums announce Richard's approach, and tells Elizabeth they must "be copious in exclaims."

Richard and his train are starting off to war and asks who it is that "intercepts" him. The Duchess says it is she who might have "intercepted" him by strangling him in her "accurséd womb." Both women ply him with questions where their loved ones are. Richard is irked by their railing on "The Lord's anointed." He orders a flourish of trumpets to drown their "exclamations."

A bitter dispute follows between Richard and his mother who detains him despite his refusal to listen to her. She quickly sketches his life from his birth to now—every moment of it has made earth a hell. If he so offends her, Richard asks to be let go his way. The Duchess pleads for a word more—"For I shall never speak to thee again." She places on him her "most heavy curse," which in the day of battle will tire him more than his "complete armour." Prophesying "bloody will be thy end," she leaves. Richard murmurs, "So."

Elizabeth, with more cause to curse Richard but "less spirit" to do it, says "Amen." She follows the Duchess, but Richard asks to have a word with her. Instinctively, Elizabeth believes he means more harm to her family. When she learns it is her daughter Elizabeth he wants to marry, she vehemently denounces the idea. If necessary, she will swear that she is illegitimate and not Edward's daughter.

Like the wooing of Lady Anne (Act I, sc. 1) Richard is repulsed by Elizabeth at every promise he makes and every explanation of his cruelty to her family. When he asks her how he might best woo her daughter Elizabeth mocks him. She suggests sending a letter with "a pair of bleeding hearts" engraved "Edward and York": a handkerchief that he could say had been dipped in their blood to wipe her eyes.

But Richard is patient. In a long speech he describes how she can live again in honor and happiness through her daughter as Queen. He cannot recall the dead, but he can make her again mother of a King and "the ruins of distrustful times/ Repair'd with double riches of content." And he bids her, "Go, then, my mother, to thy daughter go." Elizabeth must prepare her for marriage, and when he has chastised "dull-brain'd Buckingham," he will marry her. Then "she shall be sole victress, Caesar's Caesar."

Richard III

Elizabeth tantalizes him with her questions and objections. She loses no opportunity to taunt him for the children "Thou hast butcher'd." After a long speech promising "to prosper and repent," he calls on heaven and fortune to refuse him happy hours and the planets of good luck to oppose him if his love for Elizabeth's daughter is not a holy love. His final plea shows how desolation and ruin to the nation will be avoided by his marriage to her daughter.

Elizabeth, questioning herself if she can be so tempted by the devil, leaves, promising to win her daughter for Richard. As she goes, she utters a last reproach for his murder of her children. Accepting Richard's "true love's kiss" for her daughter, she states that he must write to her "very shortly," and she will give her daughter's answer.

If Elizabeth is deceiving Richard, he seems unaware of it. To him she is a "Relenting fool, and shallow-changing woman!" He turns immediately to the news brought by Ratcliff and Catesby. A "puissant navy" has been seen on the west coast. It is reported that Richmond is the Admiral.

Richard tells Catesby to go immediately to the Duke of Norfolk; but, as if dazed for a moment, he forgets to give him the message. He quickly remembers. Catesby is to tell Norfolk to meet him at Salisbury with the "greatest strength and power he can make." Richard confuses a command to Rutland. When the latter complains that he has been given no errand Richard remarks, "My mind is changed." He turns abruptly to greet Stanley who has just entered the room.

Stanley's news is not good. He is twitted by Richard for delay in telling it. In a blunt statement he reveals that "Richmond is on the seas."

Richard hopes Richmond is a victim of the seas. He asks what the "white-liver'd renegate" is up to. Stanley can only "guess." Pressed for his "guess" Stanley replies, "Stirr'd up by Dorset, Buckingham and Ely,/ He makes for England, here, to claim the Crown."

Stanley's blunt "guess" roils Richard, and he tosses a string of questions at Stanley: "Is the King dead? the empire unpossess'd?/ What heir of York is there alive but we?/ And who is England's King?" *Why* should Richmond be on the sea? Unless it is that he wants to be King, Stanley "cannot guess."

Richard snarls, "Unless for that he comes to be your liege." He fears Stanley will revolt and aid Richmond. Firmly denying that he would be disloyal, Stanley can, however, offer no immediate army. The reason he gives is that his "friends are in the north." If given leave to go there, Stanley will "muster" them and meet Richard when and where it pleases him. But Richard refuses to trust him, despite Stanley's avowal that he has never had cause to find him disloyal; that he "never was nor never will be."

It is arranged that Stanley can leave, but Richard demands his son, George Stanley, as a hostage. And he warns, "look your faith be firm,/ Or else his head's assurance is but frail." Stanley's parting remark, "So deal with him, as I prove true to you" is equivocal, but Richard is too engrossed to notice it.

Richard is beset by messengers, each bringing news of uprisings. Sir Edward Courtney of Devonshire, with his brother the Bishop of Exeter, is in arms; the Guildfords in Kent have raised an army and are moving against him; Buckingham's army is marching. Deeply disturbed, Richard orders the messengers to leave—"Out on ye, owls!" who have only "songs of death." He interrupts the third messenger and strikes him, "take thou that, till thou bring better news." But his message is good: Buckingham's troops have been scattered and he has fled alone. Richard begs pardon for the blow and tosses his purse to the messenger. He learns that word has already been given to capture Buckingham.

The fourth messenger brings news that Lovel and Dorset are heading an army in Yorkshire. He also says that Richmond's fleet has been dispersed by storms; the Commander doubted the loyalty of the army ashore that claimed to follow Buckingham and now the fleet is sailing back to France.

Richard commands his train to "March on," but halts when Catesby arrives with the word that Buckingham has been captured. He contradicts the news of Richmond's fleet. The young Admiral has landed "a mighty power" in Milford Haven. Immediately Richard with his troops starts for Salisbury, and gives an order that Buckingham is to be brought there.

Act IV: Scene 5

This scene takes place in Lord Stanley's house. It is scarcely more than a short conversation between him and Sir Christopher Urswick.

Since his son George is held by Richard as a hostage, Stanley's position at the Court is extremely precarious. He is anxious that Richmond understand the situation. Except for the danger to his son, Stanley would send Richmond aid immediately.

Urswick tells him that Richmond is either at Pembroke, or in nearby Haverford West in Wales. He satisfies Stanley that men of "noble fame and worth" are aiding Richmond. All the troops of his allies are now on their way to London, unless stopped by battle. Without comment Stanley gives Urswick letters for Richmond that will "resolve him of my mind." He sends greetings to Richmond, also the Queen's word that her daughter, Elizabeth, will marry Richmond.

Act V: Scene 1

This scene takes place in an open space in Salisbury.

Buckingham is led to execution by the Sheriff and a guard. The scene is almost a soliloquy interrupted twice by short retorts from the Sheriff.

Buckingham has asked to speak with Richard, but the request has been denied. He tells of Richard's victims, mentioning Hastings first. If those "moody, discontented souls" are peering at him through the clouds and mocking him—Buckingham doesn't finish. He remembers it is All Souls Day.

It was this day, years before in the time of King Edward IV, that he wished would mark his death if he were found disloyal to Edward or "False to his children or his wife's allies." He recognizes he "dallied" with God who has turned his "feignéd prayer" on his head and given him what he "begg'd in jest." So man uses his free will to punish himself. Margaret's curse (Act I, sc. 3) comes vividly to Buckingham's mind. He quotes her words; Richard "shall split thy heart with sorrow." *Now* he can say "Margaret was a prophetess." He asks to be led to execution, moralizing as he goes that wrong begets wrong and "blame the due of blame."

Act V: Scene 2

This scene takes place on a plain near Tamworth. Like the preceding two scenes, it is almost a soliloquy by Richmond. Accompanied by the Earl of Oxford, Sir James Blunt, Sir Walter Herbert, and others, Richmond appears in the play for the first time.

His address to his forces is a sincere plea for loyalty. He bases their allegiance to him on the necessity to rid themselves from the "yoke of tyranny" imposed by Richard, the "wretched, bloody and usurping boar." Richmond tells of the comfort and support he is promised by his father, Stanley (Act IV, sc. 5). Word is brought that Richard and his troops are near Leicester, a day's march away. With one battle they can "reap the harvest of perpetual peace." Each of Richmond's friends offers a word of encouragement: they are fighting against "bloody homicide" in an honest cause; Richard's friends are bound to him by fear; in the hour of need they will forsake him.

Richmond closes the scene exhorting them to march "In God's name." He declares that "true hope is swift." It reduces kings to idols and makes "meaner creatures kings."

Act V: Scene 3

This scene is laid on Bosworth Field, a battle ground near Liecester in central England. (Shakespeare disregards the actual date of the battle, August 22, 1485.) It is evening. Richard's troops are encamped on one end of the field, and Richmond's troops at the other. The action shifts from camp to camp.

Richard enters with his troops, accompanied by the Duke of Norfolk, the Earl of Surrey, and others. Orders are given to pitch his tent. He banters with Surrey and Norfolk, complaining the former looks sad; agreeing with the latter that they must give and take. Norfolk advises Richard that their opponents' power numbers "six or seven thousand."

Three times as many are fighting for Richard, who remarks "Besides, the King's name is a tower of strength." After taking every precaution for success by ordering men recognized for their military skill to survey the battle ground, Richard leaves with Norfolk and Surrey.

The action shifts immediately to Richmond's camp. He enters with Sir William Brandon, Oxford, and others. Soldiers are readying his tent.

Richmond comments on the sunset as predicting fair weather. He appoints Brandon as his standard bearer. Then calling for ink and paper, he will begin to sketch the plan of battle and assign each leader his particular duty. All the nobles leave except Oxford. Brandon, Herbert and Blunt, who remain for consultation.

Blunt is sent to tell the Earl of Pembroke to visit Richmond at "the second hour in the morning." He is also to deliver a letter to his step-father, Lord Stanley, whose forces are encamped a half mile away. With his leaders, Richmond enters his tent to plan the next day's battle.

In Richard's tent he talks with Norfolk, Ratcliff, Catesby and others.

Richard III

It is nine o'clock and "supper-time." but Richard will not dine. He is anxious about his armor.

Norfolk is bid goodnight and told to "stir with the lark tomorrow." Catesby is sent to Lord Stanley who must bring his troops before sunrise or his son, George, will forfeit his head. Richard's attendants bring him wine and a "watch," as he demands.

His horse, Surrey, must be readied for the field. Ratcliff allays his fears about the "melancholy Lord Northumberland": with the Earl of Surrey he has been "cheering up the soldiers." Richard asks for another bowl of wine, and complains that he has not the "cheer of mind" that he was wont to have. Ratcliff has procured ink and paper for him, and is told to return at midnight to help Richard arm. Richard retires alone into his tent and sleeps.

We return now to Richmond's tent. He is seen talking with his officers as Lord Stanley enters. Richmond greets him warmly as his "noble father-in-law."

Stanley brings greetings from Richmond's mother and tells of her prayers for him. It is a brief visit. He advises Richmond to fight a "mortal-staring war." He cannot shift his troops immediately to Richmond's side because his young son, George Stanley (Richmond's stepbrother), would be executed by Richard "in his father's sight." Expressing a fond farewell, Stanley leaves. Richmond sends his officers as an escort to see him safely to his regiment.

Richmond says that he will try "to take a nap." When all have left, before he retires, Richmond prays that God "whose captain I account myself" will look on his cause with a gracious eye. And "sleeping and waking," he asks for divine protection.

Both Richard and Richmond retire for the night. While Richard sleeps, he has a troubled dream.

In the center of the field between their tents there arise, one by one, ten ghosts, the souls of those whom Richard has murdered. Prince Edward, son of Henry VI, is the first. The others follow in the order of their demise. Each ghost speaks to him, identifies itself and accuses him of its murder. The last word of each is almost the same, "despair and die!" As each of the ghosts leaves Richard, it appears to Richmond bidding him, "live thou, and flourish!"

Richard awakens from his dream startled. He thinks he has lost his horse, and asks that his wounds be bound up. When he realizes that he has been dreaming, he upbraids his "coward conscience," aroused at long last, for so afflicting him. The candle burns blue so he knows it is midnight.

In a long soliloquy Richard reveals a tortured mind looking at itself—one moment he condemns himself for his crimes and the next, proclaims "Richard loves Richard." But his conscience "has a thousand several tongues." Each tongue accuses him at eternity's court and cries "Guilty! guilty!" No one loves him, no one will *ever* pity him. Despairing, he should have no pity because he exclaims, "I myself/ Find in myself no pity to myself."

Ratcliff interrupts him to say his friends are buckling on their armor. Richard confides the details of his "fearful dream" to Ratcliff. The terror they roused in him was greater than ten thousand troops fighting against him under "shallow Richmond." He leaves with Ratcliff to go eavesdropping around the soldiers' tents to find if they are disloyal to him.

Richmond is awakened in his tent by Oxford and other lords. He tells them he has had "The sweetest sleep, and fairest-boding dreams." He thought that the souls "whose bodies Richard murder'd" came to his tent and cried, "On! victory!" His heart is "very jocund." When he discovers it is four in the morning, Richmond remarks "then 'tis time to arm and give direction."

Richmond advances toward his troops and addresses them as "loving countrymen." He asks them to remember their cause is good and God is on their side, as are the saints and the wronged souls. He describes Richard's tyrannical climb to the throne. His deeds proclaim him God's enemy and He "will, in justice, ward you as His soldiers;/ If you do sweat to put a tyrant down." Richmond's speech rises to a climax as he proclaims the spiritual and material benefits their victory will bring to their country, wives, and children. If Richmond wins they will share his glory.

The scene changes to Richard's sector of the field. He talks with Ratcliff, who brings reports from Northumberland and Surrey. The first belittles Richmond as he "was never train'd up in arms"; the latter considers that a boon. Richard is satisfied with the report. The weather is dull, and he believes it a bad omen; "A black day will it be to somebody."

Norfolk enters with the news that the foe is already in the field. Richard calls for his horse. He commands that Lord Stanley's forces be brought up. The general plan of the battle, as he has sketched it, is disclosed by Richard to Norfolk and Surrey. They will command the "Foot and Horse," and Richard will follow in "the main battle."

Norfolk commends Richard's plan. Casually, he shows him a scroll that he found "on his tent." Richard reads the rhyme: "Jockey of Norfolk, be not too bold,/ For Dickon thy master is bought and sold."

Richard, aware of the traitorous meaning, declares it was "devised by the enemy." He urges his leaders to victory and cautions them not to be disturbed by "babbling dreams," nor by conscience, a coward's word. "Our strong arms be our conscience, swords our law."

Richard turns to address his soldiers. In a long speech he does little else than disparage Richmond and his troops—"A sort of vagabonds, rascals, and runaways." They are the "scum of Bretagne" who are vomited forth to seek venture and destruction. Richmond, he claims, is a "paltry fellow" and "a milk-sop" who has been held a political refugee in France.

As Richard finishes his talk, the sound of drums is heard, and he again exhorts his men to victory. A messenger hurries in to say that Stanley refuses to bring up his troops. Richard immediately orders Stanley's son, George, beheaded. Norfolk suggests he wait—the battle is more important at the moment as the enemy has crossed the marsh. At once, Richard commands his troops to advance and fight "like fiery dragons." With the war cry, "Victory sits on our helms," they march into battle.

Act V: Scene 4

This brief scene takes place in another part of the field. Norfolk enters leading his troops. Catesby hurries on stage to tell him of Richard's plight —his horse has been killed, and he is fighting on foot. He races about looking for Richmond.

Richard enters calling for a horse. Catesby offers to help him. Crazed with the desire to kill Richmond, he declares he has already killed five men, mistaking each for Richmond. Offering his kingdom for a horse, he goes back to the field of battle.

Act V: Scene 5

This scene follows immediately. Richard and Richmond enter from opposite sides of the stage and engage in a duel. They continue fighting as they move off stage, and Richard is slain.

Richmond returns to give "God and your arms" praise for the victory.

Then he announces (curiously enough, in Margaret's terms, see Act IV, sc. 4) "the bloody dog is dead."

Stanley is the first to congratulate him. He has taken the crown from Richard's head and places it on Richmond, telling him to "Wear it, enjoy it, and make much of it." Richmond is grateful when he learns George Stanley's life has been spared. He orders that the nobles who were slain on Richard's side be given burial "as becomes their births." He proclaims a general pardon for deserters who fought for Richard, provided they submit to his rule.

When he has received the Sacrament he will wed Elizabeth and so "unite the white rose and the red." His last address to his troops laments the scars left on England by the long civil war. It made enemies of brothers, fathers, and sons.

He hopes the union of the Houses of Lancaster and York will bring peace.

He calls "Richmond and Elizabeth,/ The true succeeders of each royal House." He hopes God will bless them with issue and secure the future with "smooth-faced peace." He hails the end of war—now "peace lives again:/ That she may long live here, God say Amen!"

THE
TRAGEDIES

Antony and Cleopatra

MARK ANTONY ⎫
OCTAVIUS CAESAR ⎬ *triumvirs.*
M. AEMILIUS LEPIDUS ⎭
SEXTUS POMPEIUS.
DOMITIUS ENOBARBUS ⎫
VENTIDIUS ⎜
EROS ⎜
SCARUS ⎬ *friends to Antony.*
DERCETAS ⎜
DEMETRIUS ⎜
PHILO ⎭
MAECENAS ⎫
AGRIPPA ⎜
DOLABELLA ⎜
PROCULEIUS ⎬ *friends to Caesar.*
THIDIAS ⎜
GALLUS ⎭
MENAS ⎫
MENECRATES ⎬ *friends to Pompey.*
VARRIUS ⎭
TAURUS, *lieutenant-general to Caesar.*
CANIDIUS, *lieutenant-general to Antony.*
SILIUS, *an Officer in Ventidius' army.*
A SCHOOLMASTER, *Ambassador from Antony to Caesar.*
ALEXAS ⎫
MARDIAN, *a Eunuch* ⎬ *attendants on Cleopatra.*
DIOMEDES ⎭
A SOOTHSAYER.
A CLOWN.

CLEOPATRA, *Queen of Egypt.*
OCTAVIA, *sister to Caesar and wife to Antony.*
CHARMIAN ⎫ *attendants on Cleopatra.*
IRAS ⎭

OFFICERS, SOLDIERS, MESSENGERS, *and* ATTENDANTS.

Antony and Cleopatra

Act I: Scene 1

The play opens upon the following political situation: Rome has extended
its empire over most of the known world, from the British Isles to Parthia
and Mesopotamia in the east, and from the African shore of the Mediterranean to Germany in the north. Much of its eastern empire has been
conquered by Mark Antony who, together with Octavius Caesar and
Lepidus,.makes up the Triumvirate or ruling body of the empire. Octavius
Caesar rules over Rome and the northern provinces, Lepidus over Africa,
and Mark Antony over the east. Supposedly to govern his conquered
territories, Antony has set up headquarters and remained in Egypt.
Actually he has fallen in love with Cleopatra, queen of Egypt, which is
one of his conquered kingdoms. Their love is the story of the play. It
begins in Cleopatra's palace in Alexandria, the Egyptian capital. Two of
Antony's lieutenants, Demetrius and Philo, are complaining in one of the
rooms of the palace.

Philo condemns Antony's infatuation with Cleopatra outright. Their
general, he tells Demetrius, has lost his manliness and given over his
pursuit of war and conquest to pursue his lust instead. He "is become
the bellows and the fan/ To cool a gipsy's lust."

Almost as if to give proof of Philo's speech, Antony, Cleopatra, and her
servants enter, in a procession marked by oriental luxury and splendor.
Philo, in an aside, promises Demetrius he shall see Antony, "the triple
pillar of the world" (i.e., one of the three rulers of the world), become
the plaything of a whore. And, indeed, Antony at once begins to
exchange extravagant vows of love with Cleopatra. "There's beggary in
the love that can be reckoned," cries Antony, expressing not only his love
for Cleopatra but his contempt for the sound commercial account-keeping
that has made Rome a great power. He is obviously annoyed when an
attendant interrupts to announce a messenger from Rome. Antony refuses
to see him. The business "grates" him, he says, and he demands "the sum"
of it, quickly, so that he can turn back to Cleopatra. She, however, now

begins to taunt him for being under the thumbs of Fulvia, his wife, and the boyish Caesar. (Octavius Caesar is in his early twenties. His youth, as compared to the other Triumvirs, is alluded to throughout. Despite his age, he is the leader of the Triumvirate.) Antony's reply is a ringing speech in which he renounces Rome's claims upon him, and determines to stay in Egypt with Cleopatra.

Cleopatra, however, ignores Antony's grand rhetoric and continues to tease him. She wonders why Antony married Fulvia, since he does not love her, and whether, perhaps, the same fate will someday be hers. She urges him to see the messengers, although of course it is to her interest for Antony not to be in contact with Rome. Antony, who feels that he merits her praise for refusing to see them, talks only of love and pleasure; when Cleopatra interrupts with "Hear the ambassadors," he chides her for being so difficult: "Fie, wrangling queen." He is determined to fill every minute of their lives with pleasure, "for the love of Love"; there is no time to waste. They exit without hearing Caesar's messenger, and Demetrius, realizing that this is a grave insult, tells Philo that he is convinced that the rumors which have reached Rome of Antony's debasement are true.

Act I: Scene 2

In another room of the palace an Egyptian soothsayer (a kind of fortune-teller) is revealing what life holds in store for Cleopatra's various attendants: Alexas, her male servant; Mardian, her eunuch; Charmian and Iras, her maids. Silently looking on and listening to the revelry and lewd joking are a group of Roman soldiers: Enobarbus, Antony's trusted lieutenant and close friend; Lamprius, Rannius, and Lucilius. Occasionally Enobarbus adds his rude voice to the coarse exchange. But for the most part their silence represents a sober Roman reprimand to the loose conversation.

Alexas seems to have been teasing Charmian by predicting for her a husband whom she will cuckold. Charmian hopes he is right: "O that I knew this husband, which, you say, must charge his horns with garlands!" (A cuckold is a man whose wife has committed adultery. As a sign of her infidelity he is jokingly said to grow horns.) She asks the soothsayer to confirm the good fortune Alexas has promised. He replies that he cannot change her fate, only foresee it. She hopes for several husbands and many children; what he tells her, however, is that she will outlive Cleopatra, and that the part of her life which is to come will be less pleasant than that which she has already lived.

Much sexual joking follows. The women wish for many children; because of the pleasure of begetting them, the soothsayer implies. Enobarbus knows what their fortunes will be at least that night: "drunk to bed." Iras, turning to palmistry, claims that hers is a palm which shows that she is nothing if not chaste; Charmian retorts ironically that if she is chaste, then the overflowing of the Nile is a portent of famine, when in fact it is just the opposite. The soothsayer claims simply that the fortunes of Iras and Charmian are alike, and refuses to give particulars. Charmian begs for news of a husband who is sexually well-endowed, and, in mock-spite, wishes for Alexas a wife who is not, followed by one who will cuckold him. She begs the goddess Isis to grant her this wish, even if she denies her something more important later on.

Enobarbus says, "Hush, here comes Antony," but it is Cleopatra who enters.

Cleopatra asks for Antony; when last seen, she says, "He was disposed to mirth; but on the sudden/ A Roman thought hath struck him" (that is, either a thought of Rome, which sobered him, or a thought such as a Roman might have, implying that Romans are sour and incapable of mirth). Antony enters with a messenger from Rome, possibly the one he would not hear before. The messenger is afraid to tell Antony some bad news, and Antony magnanimously assures him that he, the messenger, will not be blamed for it.

Actually the messenger brings a military dispatch from the eastern frontier where Labienus and his Parthian armies have invaded Antony's territory. Antony thinks he is withholding his real message out of deference and fear. He thinks it is that his reputation in Rome is suffering, and that Fulvia is angry. Before he can learn the truth, another messenger enters with news from Sicyon; Antony, caught up in this whirl of portentous activity and excited by all the comings and goings, muses: "These strong Egyptian fetters I must break/ Or lose myself in dotage." A third messenger enters and announces, without preamble, that Fulvia, Antony's wife, is dead.

Antony takes the news stoically and chides himself for desiring Fulvia's death, as he obviously did, because it would leave him free to marry or live with Cleopatra. The effect of the news is to strengthen his resolve to break off from Cleopatra, and resume his rightful place as leader of the world; his idleness, he thinks, is responsible for this and many other ills. All business, he summons Enobarbus and bids him make ready to leave without telling him why; Enobarbus retorts in a jocular tone, and makes what, under the circumstances, is an unfortunate joke about Cleopatra dying of grief if Antony leaves. He begins a mocking description of Cleopatra: "Alack . . . her passions are made of nothing but the finest part of pure love," but Antony cuts him short with the news that Fulvia is dead. Stunned at first, Enobarbus recovers and tells Antony that this is cause for rejoicing; now Antony can have Cleopatra. Antony, however, is resolved to leave, and sternly admonishes Enobarbus to stop joking. He will break

with Cleopatra and return to Rome, despite Enobarbus' warning that
Cleopatra will never survive it. Another reason for returning, Antony
explains, is that Sextus Pompeius (usually referred to in the play as
Pompey) is threatening to fight a sea-war against Rome; the Roman
people are wavering in their allegiance to the Triumvirate, partly because
of his, Antony's, refusal to meet his responsibilities.

If he does not act, says Antony, the situation may become dangerous, and
he compares it in seriousness to the venom of a serpent.

Act I: Scene 3

The place is the same, a room in Cleopatra's palace. We break in on a
tactical discussion between Cleopatra and Charmian, who suspect that
Antony is about to leave, but who do not know of Fulvia's death. Cleopatra reveals her feminine tricks and wiles; she sends Charmian to Antony
with these instructions: "If you find him sad,/ Say that I am dancing; if
in mirth, report/ That I am sudden sick." Charmian counsels her to give
in to him, but Cleopatra's strategy is to battle him. Antony enters, and
Cleopatra rails at him, simultaneously feigning illness. She postures heroi-
cally: "O, never was there a queen/ So mightily betrayed!" She is alternately eloquent—"Eternity was in our lips, and eyes,/ Bliss in our brows'
bent," and waspish—"I would I had thy inches," (i.e., his great strength
and size, so that she might beat him). Antony vows to go, giving
Cleopatra all the reasons except the most important; he speaks of
Pompey's rebellion and the civil unrest in Rome. Finally he tells her of
Fulvia's death. This provokes from Cleopatra a perverse and unlooked-for
reaction: Because Antony is not weeping for his wife, she calls him false,
exclaiming, "Now I see, I see,/ In Fulvia's death, how mine received shall
be." She then affects illness once more, but continues to rise from her
fainting-spells to berate Antony energetically. She accuses him of lying
pretense; of using Fulvia's death as a pretext to desert her; and of trying
to make his action thus seem honorable. Antony grows angry, and begins
to swear, "Now, by my sword—" but Cleopatra interrupts the oath to
chide him further, scornfully calling him "this Herculean Roman."

"O, my oblivion is a very Antony," she sighs, and then, sarcastically, bids
him a conventional Roman farewell, to which he, missing the irony, replies
in kind.

Act I: Scene 4

Now the scene shifts abruptly from Cleopatra's court in Alexandria to

the house of Caesar in Rome (where Antony is going): the first of many
such far-ranging movements in the action of the play. Caesar has received
a letter from the attendant to whom Antony refused to listen in Scene 1.
The agent writes that he was unable to deliver the message which Caesar
had sent from Rome, and that Antony had shown no concern for his
two partners in the Triumvirate. Besides this insult, the agent reports,
Antony's idleness and luxury and his constant round of pleasures have
taken away his manliness and made him as womanly as Cleopatra. Caesar
quotes the letter as evidence to convince Lepidus that their partner in the
east has grown soft and rotten. But Lepidus will not be convinced by
Caesar's bad opinion. He thinks too highly of Antony to blame him. He
says these faults are really only minor compared to his virtues; they are
weaknesses which Antony has inherited, not evil habits that he actually
chooses.

Caesar will not be put off. Even if Antony's wantonness and carousals
are not terrible in themselves, he argues, he has chosen a terrible time to
indulge in them. It would be a small matter if Antony were only ruining
himself by running around with Cleopatra, but the whole empire is at
stake, and he knows it. He is putting his own sensual satisfactions before
the welfare of the whole state.

Their conversation is here interrupted by a messenger, a kind of scout
that Caesar has sent out to gather news. The information which he brings
to the two Triumvirs picks up the subplot of Pompey's growing naval
strength. Earlier, Antony had used Pompey's threat as an excuse to leave
Cleopatra and return to Rome. We learn that Antony was correct when he
estimated the loyalty of the common people. For, the messenger relates,
those who never loved Caesar but merely followed him out of fear, are
flocking to the seaports to join arms with Pompey when his ships attack.
Caesar comments that the loyalty of the crowd is a fickle and a contrary
one. They wish for something only until they have it; they do not value
a great man until they've lost him.

The messenger also brings information that Pompey has joined forces
with two famous pirates of the Italian coasts, Menecrates and Menas.
These two, trafficking in Pompey's name and fearful reputation, have been
raiding the maritime provinces of Italy and plundering the coastal trade.
This is too much for Caesar. Overcome with distress, he calls aloud on
Antony to leave the base pleasure of the Egyptian court and come to
Rome's aid. In doing this he tells how, in the old days, Antony was the
strongest, manliest soldier of them all.

The scene ends as Caesar and Lepidus prepare a council of war to decide
how best to defeat Pompey.

Act I: Scene 5

Scene 5 returns to Cleopatra's palace in Alexandria. The Egyptian queen, surrounded by her attendants, complains of how much she misses her lover. She asks Charmian to give her a sedative, a kind of sleeping potion, so she can forget her loneliness in sleep. But she is not so sad that she cannot joke with her eunuch, Mardian, about his sexual impotence. She tells him to be glad he has no sexual desires which would make him long for someone as she does. He replies that while he might never perform the sexual act, he can dream about it. He has erotic thoughts about the adultery of Venus (goddess of love and wife of Vulcan) and Mars (god of war). Cleopatra tries to picture Antony in his absence, recalling his physical presence when he made love to her.

Her thought of Antony's strength and manly prime leads her to contrast her own aging charms and she begins to doubt she can hold so great a man. She sees her Egyptian skin as burnt black from the sun and wrinkled with age. (Shakespeare obviously thought of Cleopatra as negroid, rather than the Greek she actually was.) She recalls, almost nostalgically, how her youthful beauty had conquered the hearts of the great Roman conquerors Julius Caesar and Pompey the Great (the father of the Sextus Pompeius of this story).

Here Alexas, another of Cleopatra's attendants, enters with a message from Antony. The joy of hearing from him reassures her, lifts the gloom which had begun to thicken about her. She is impatient to hear his greeting and to find out how he looked when he gave it. Alexas hands her a pearl which Antony had kissed before sending, as his token of the kingdoms he will conquer for her. She is not surprised to hear that his disposition and demeanor were temperate when he sent it.

Immediately the queen, like a young girl in love again, sits down to answer Antony's message. Her mind goes back to her former Roman lover for a second, and she asks her maid, Charmian, "Did I . . ./ Ever love Caesar so?" And the maid taunts her by mimicking her former praises of Caesar when she was in love with him: "O that brave Caesar!" and "The valiant Caesar!" At this Cleopatra threatens to bloody her teeth. For she praised Caesar in her "salad days," when she was young and ignorant, she says: "green in judgement: cold in blood."

Act II: Scene 1

From Cleopatra's court in Alexandria we move back to Messina, in Sicily, where Pompey has his headquarters. (Remember, there were originally no act divisions in the play.) There, in Messina, Pompey with the pirates

Menecrates and Menas (mentioned earlier in Act 1, Scene 4) plan his rebellion against the Triumvirate. Pompey is unhappy because of the delay in their plan. He feels that the longer they wait, the worse will become the Roman state for which they are going to fight. Menecrates, however, calms him by saying that the delay may all be for the best; it is in the hands of the gods. Then Pompey analyzes their chances in the forthcoming battle and describes the characters and weaknesses of their foes. His chances are good, he estimates. His navy holds mastery of the sea, and the common people of Italy have swung to his side. Besides, Mark Antony is away in Egypt, too caught up in court pleasures and intrigues to care about larger affairs. Octavius Caesar controls the purses of the citizens, but cannot control their love. And Lepidus is a weak sister: he keeps in the others' good graces, and they in his, but there is no love lost among them. Pompey realizes that the success of their plan depends upon the great warrior, Antony, remaining in Egypt; so much so that he apostrophizes (as Caesar did to Antony in Scene 4 of Act 1) to Cleopatra to keep Antony with her by means of her witchcraft and beauty. Pompey hopes that Antony, with his sense of honor dulled by sensual indulgence, will not come to aid his friends.

So Varrius' entrance at this point is very dramatic. Just as Pompey finishes wishing that Antony would stay in Egypt to insure their success, Varrius brings news that he has already left Egypt and is expected at any moment in Rome.

At first Pompey cannot believe it; but immediately he tries to take courage by saying that their conspiracy must be a grave threat indeed if Antony will leave Cleopatra just to fight against them. Menas is also shaken up by the news. He tries to find some comfort in the hope that Caesar and Antony may fall out with one another, since both Antony's wife and brother had formerly warred with Caesar. Pompey agrees that all is not right among the Triumvirs, but fears they might be able to overlook their own petty squabbles long enough to unite against the conspirators. At any rate, he will not fall victim to wishful thinking. Laying the outcome in the hands of the gods, he nevertheless bluffly counsels his friends "to use our strongest hands."

Act II: Scene 2

In the house of the third and weakest of the Triumvirs, Lepidus, Antony's and Caesar's arrival is expected. Lepidus opens the scene by trying to persuade Enobarbus to use his influence on his friend and captain to greet Caesar with "soft and gentle speech," so as not to offend him and stir up ill-feeling among the Triumvirs. For Lepidus realizes that the three leaders must suppress their own quarrels with each other in order to pursue their common quarrel against Pompey successfully: only in their unity is their strength. Enobarbus has just refused Lepidus' request absolutely, when the two disgruntled leaders enter with their parties. With Antony is his lieutenant, Ventidius; with Caesar, his shrewd and politic adviser, Agrippa, and the wealthy patron of the arts, Maecenas. Both parties are absorbed in conversation. Lepidus immediately tries to buffer and soften the collision beween the two by admonishing them not to let passions or hard words turn their trivial differences into a bitter fight, lest "we do commit murder in healing wounds."

Antony is the first to agree; he embraces Caesar, who welcomes him to Rome. But their show of friendliness is only on the surface; beneath it the old resentments rankle. Antony opens the conversation by telling Caesar, in effect, to mind his own business. What he, Antony, does in his own province (the East and, therefore, Egypt) is his own affair and no concern of Caesar's. Caesar denies having meddled, says that he does not criticize Antony's conduct in Egypt, but his conspiracy in Rome. He accuses his partner of having an interest in, or at least being the excuse for, the wars which his late wife, Fulvia, and his brother, Lucius, had waged against the Roman state. Antony pleads innocent to the charge, and claims he has reports from among Caesar's own troops that Lucius, in challenging Caesar's authority, challenged his own brother's as well. He put himself on Caesar's side of the dispute and assured his partner of it by means of letters at the time. To question his loyalty now, at this late date, is only to pick a fight: any old stick will do to beat a dog, as it were. Antony's accusation hurts Caesar—"You praise yourself,/ By laying defects of judgment to me," Caesar says—and when the dispute threatens to break down into a personal squabble, Antony tries to keep the atmosphere cool. He first flatters Caesar with a gentle compliment on his good judgment of men and events, and then turns Fulvia's indiscretion into a joke at his own expense. Caesar is too astute not to be confident of Antony's loyalty, he says. And even Caesar himself, master of a third of the world, would have had his hands full taming Antony's spirited wife. After this note of humor Caesar breaks off and tries a new line of argument. He accuses Antony of disregarding his official letters and insulting his messenger.

Antony admits the incident but claims innocence of any insult intended, for two reasons: (1) the messenger overstepped himself by entering his chamber uninvited; and (2) he had a hangover that morning that soured his disposition. Besides, the next day he as much as asked the fellow's pardon. Again he accuses Caesar of patching a quarrel out of trivial slights that do not really matter. Get to the point, he says. This time Caesar is hurt by the accusation into his sharpest attack so far. Before, he had questioned, first, Antony's loyalty, and then his manners; now he attacks his honor by accusing Antony of having broken his promise to lend arms and aid when Caesar needed them to fight Fulvia and Lucius. This is the heart of Caesar's grievance, and Lepidus is alarmed, for it is a most serious charge. But Antony answers it calmly. He had not denied Caesar's requests but only neglected them, because he was so caught up in the pleasures of Cleopatra's court. It was to lure him out of Egypt and away from Cleopatra that Fulvia instigated the war against Rome. He asks Caesar's pardon, not for having intended any injury, but for having been "the ignorant motive" of it. At this concession the entire company is relieved and relaxes a bit. Lepidus praises Antony's nobility; Maecenas begs them to break off their dispute; even Enobarbus (despite what he said to Lepidus at the beginning of the scene) oversteps his place and advises the two leaders to turn their quarrel toward Pompey. Antony promptly rebukes him for it. Now it is Caesar's turn for concession, and he backs out of the argument neatly by claiming that he does not so much dislike *what* Antony says, as the *way* in which he says it. He would adopt any means, he vows, to strengthen their friendship and insure the unity of their dominion over the entire world. This is the cue for Caesar's calculating adviser, Agrippa, to put forth his plan for bringing the two quarreling leaders back together again. Caesar has a sister, Octavia, he says, and Antony is now a widower.

Let their marriage, Agrippa urges, be the knot that ties the two Triumvirs perpetually together. The match would be perfect: She is beautiful and virtuous; he is "the best of men." Their marriage would cool all jealousies, squelch all fears, scotch all rumors that threatened to divide the Triumvirate, while, as Caesar's sister, she would be the intercessor and mediator between the two. They receive his suggestion cautiously at first. Caesar is unsure whether Antony considers Cleopatra his mistress or his wife. But after they are sure of each other's acceptance their enthusiasm grows. Antony grasps Caesar's hand in friendship and swears brotherhood and loyalty, which Caesar returns. Then the two immediately fall to talking about the conspiracy of Pompey. Antony is awkward about defying the rebel leader. He feels obliged to repay certain "strange courtesies" which Pompey has lately lavished on him before he can openly quarrel with the rebels.

But time is pressing, Lepidus urges. Pompey's naval strength is second to none, and his land forces grow stronger daily. The three Triumvirs decide to seek a meeting with Pompey at his camp near Mt. Misenum, but first proceed to Caesar's house to settle the business of Antony's marriage to Octavia.

When they depart, Enobarbus, Agrippa and Maecenas remain alone on stage. The two Roman statesmen welcome the soldier back from Egypt and pump him for information and descriptions of Cleopatra's fabulous court. He not only vouches for the truth of their most fantastic stories about its luxury, but goes them one better in his sumptuous description of Cleopatra's arrival in Cilicia to appear before Antony's tribunal.

Called before Antony to answer charges that she had supported Cassius and Brutus against him in the battle of Philippi, Cleopatra plans to escape his inquisition and reprisals by making him fall in love with her. That accounts for her spectacular arrival by boat on the River Cydnus. And what a boat! Its poop (a partial deck raised above the main deck in the rear) was fashioned of solid gold. The oars which propelled it were of silver, and they kept stroke to the music of flutes on board (as soldiers, for example, march to the sound of drums and martial music). The sails were purple and perfumed so that the very breeze languished and grew lovesick in breathing on them, and their scent assailed the spectators who lined the river banks to watch.

The rigging and tackle were of silk, as befitted the softness of the ship's "hands," Cleopatra's attendants, who resembled so many mermaids or nereids (mythical water nymphs, daughters of the sea-god Nereus) as they managed the ship and fawned over its cargo, Cleopatra. Cleopatra herself was stunning beyond description. She neither stood nor sat, but reclined (probably on the golden poop deck), shaded by a sumptuous silken canopy into whose tissue were woven threads of purest gold. She resembled a painting of the goddess of love herself (probably the lost *Venus Anadyomene*, or "Venus Rising out of the Sea," painted by the Greek, Apelles, in the 4th century B. C.), only more lovely, surrounded by pretty young boys, who stirred the perfumed air about her with many-colored fans, like so many little cupids (Cupid was the son of Venus by Mars, god of war).

Word of the spectacle soon emptied the city as the people flocked to the river banks to watch, leaving Antony by himself in the market place, enthroned for his tribunals, "whistling to the air." He sent word to invite the queen to dinner with him: she refused his offer but returned the invitation, which he accepted. And there at the banquet Antony lost his heart to her.

Agrippa and Enobarbus then exchange stories of Cleopatra's fabulous beauty which could bewitch great (Julius) Caesar, and which is made even more perfect by every defect in it. So when Maecenas says that Antony, pledged to Octavia, must give up Cleopatra for good, Enobarbus answers: "Never; he will not."

The scene ends on Maecenas' earnest, but somewhat hollow, hope that Octavia's "beauty, wisdom, modesty, can settle the heart of Antony," and reform the notorious rogue.

Act II: Scene 3

The conversation among Enobarbus and Caesar's counselors provides the time needed between the departure of the Triumvirs from Lepidus' house and their arrival at Caesar's. (Although Antony insisted upon Lepidus' accompanying them to visit Octavia, Lepidus does not appear with them in this scene at Caesar's house.) The scene opens with Antony's saying good-bye to Caesar and Octavia. In parting, he forewarns his prospective wife that, after their marriage, he will be away from her often on military and political adventures. She accepts this and promises that she will be on her knees all the while he is gone, praying constantly for him.

No sooner are the sister and brother gone, when the soothsayer, who comes from Cleopatra's court and who reminds us of the magic and the mystery of the East, appears to tell Antony's fortune and to prophesy how his new friendship and alliance will turn out. Badly, the wizard tells him, and urges Antony to return at once to Egypt. For Antony's guiding spirit or guardian angel is greater than Caesar's when he is alone, but when they are together, it is overpowered; he suffers always by comparison with the younger man. His luck always deserts him; in games with Caesar, he is sure to lose.

Antony is so struck by the soothsayer's advice, that he makes him promise not to repeat his prophecy to anyone else. He sends the soothsayer off to tell Ventidius, his lieutenant, that he wants to see him. When the wiseman is gone, Antony confirms his prophecy as true in a short soliloquy (a speech in which a character, usually alone, speaks his thoughts aloud to the audience, no one else on stage overhearing him). In his gambling with Caesar, Antony admits, the dice have always betrayed him; in sports, luck has been with his rival. He then makes a startling decision: he will follow the soothsayer's advice, and even while tying the marriage knot with Octavia, he vows he will return to Egypt to continue his affair with Cleopatra. "I make this marriage for my peace," he says, "In the East my pleasure lies."

Antony's business with Ventidius is short: he gives his lieutenant orders to report to Parthia to check the enemy invasion there.

Act II: Scene 4

Scene 4 is very short, ten lines of dialogue between Lepidus, Maecenas, and Agrippa to show the Romans marshalling their forces for the confrontation, several days later, with Pompey at Mt. Misenum.

Antony and Cleopatra

Act II: Scene 5

This scene whisks us back to Cleopatra's palace in Alexandria. The queen is restless, love-sick, longing for her absent Antony. To pass the time she first calls for music, "the food of love," but when Mardian, her eunuch, enters to play for her, she dismisses him and challenges her maid, Charmian, to shoot a game of billiards with her instead. Charmian declines, but Mardian takes up the challenge, and Cleopatra, with an obvious sexual jest, says she may as well play games with a eunuch as with a woman. She never gets to the game, however, for already her quicksilver mood has shifted again, and she wishes to go fishing. With every fish she catches she will pretend she is drawing home her roving lover. Charmian reminds her of a trick she once played on Antony.

And Cleopatra reminisces about the wonderful times she had with Antony, including one in which, both drunk, she dressed him in her woman's garments while she "wore his sword Phillipan."

But her laughter is suddenly stilled by the appearance of a messenger from Italy. Immediately she jumps to conclusions: "Antonius dead!" she screams, and alternately threatens and cajoles the messenger to give her good news, as though by promising gold or threatening death she could make his message any different from what it is. Continually interrupted by her gifts and threats, the messenger can only give his news piecemeal. Antony is well, he says, and friends with Caesar, and adds darkly, "Caesar, and he, are greater friends than ever"—but does not yet reveal the reason and seal of this friendship. Cleopatra is overjoyed, and over-generous—"Make thee a fortune from me"—until the messenger's "But yet, madam . . ." gives her her first real reason to suspect something is wrong. She snatches at it immediately, but still does not catch the messenger's drift when he says, "he's bound unto Octavia." Why? For what purposes, she asks, and only slowly does the shock of despair overcome her when he replies, "Madam, he's married to Octavia." Once the truth is clear and out in the open, she reacts immediately and violently. Suddenly she is upon him, knocks him to the ground, cursing him and, despite his protests, kicking and scratching. She threatens to put out his eyes, tear out his hair, have him whipped with wire and boiled in brine. Then in an instant she relents, all softness again, begging him only to say it is not so to make his fortune. When he sticks by his message, she is at his throat once more, this time with a knife, and would have his life but that he runs away. Charmian tries to calm her when he is gone, and succeeds enough to have Cleopatra call the boy back again.

But the boy is afraid to come before the "fury of a woman scorned," and his fear awakens a spark of nobility and self-respect in Cleopatra.

499

She regrets having struck the messenger for two reasons: (1) he is socially inferior to her and therefore she demeans herself by hitting him; (2) it is not his fault, but rather her own that Antony's marriage upsets her. In a sort of half-apology, she advises the boy when he reappears, to tell good tidings but let bad tidings tell themselves, and asks him again if Antony is married. When he confirms the news once more, once more she flies into a rage, over and over demanding that he repeat the bitter news and then cursing him for it when he does. However, she will not lay hands on him again, but banishes him from her presence. Her panic recedes with her violence. She begins to recover her wits, and though her heart is breaking, she is already weaving the snares and trammels that will snatch her lover out of his new wife's arms and fetch him back to hers. But first she must size her rival up. She sends Alexas to speak to the messenger to find out what Antony's wife looks like: how old she is, her temperament or disposition, the color of her hair, how tall she is. Then she asks her waiting-woman Charmian to pity her in silence and lead her to bed.

Act II: Scene 6

Now comes the long-expected confrontation between the Triumvirs and the conspirators near Mt. Misenum in Naples. The two sides have exchanged hostages as pledges of their good intent, and the Triumvirs have sent Pompey terms for an armistice before the armies start to fight. Now Caesar starts negotiations by asking Pompey if he will accept their terms for a truce. Pompey replies by stating the reasons for his rebellion. Just as the Triumvirs—Caesar's adopted son Octavius and close friends— avenged Julius Caesar's murder by defeating Brutus and Cassius, his murderers, at the battle of Philippi: so he, Sextus Pompey, with his friends, will overthrow the Triumvirs in order to avenge his father, Pompey the Great, whom Julius Caesar had overthrown.

That is his personal grudge against the Triumvirs; his public purpose is to do what Brutus did in killing Julius Caesar: to rid Rome of an oppressive tyranny and return the people to their freedom. His aggressive statement puts Antony's hackles up, who challenges him to a sea contest, since he will not face the Triumvirs' superior forces on land. Pompey replies with a sarcastic jibe that Antony had bought his father's house (Pompey the Great's) at auction and then refused to pay for it.

As the exchange becomes heated, Lepidus, the peacemaker, steps in to cool the atmosphere. He asks Pompey to answer Caesar's question—does he accept the truce or not? Antony is quick to remark that they are not begging him, and Caesar adds that it will be for his own good. Then Pompey repeats the terms of the treaty: In return for rule over Sicily and Sardinia (another large island in the Mediterranean off the west coast of Italy), he must promise to rid all the Mediterranean Sea of pirates and to pay an annual tax to Rome in the form of wheat.

This agreed upon, the two armies will pull back without fighting. "Know, then," he says, "I came before you here a man prepared/ To take this offer. But Mark Antony/ Put me to some impatience." He feels he deserved better from the Roman general because he had welcomed Antony's mother and given her protection in Sicily when she was forced to flee from Italy, after her son Lucius' rebellion was defeated. Antony acknowledges the debt of friendship, and Pompey, grasping his hand, says he is surprised to see Antony at all, this far from Egypt. "The beds in the East are soft," Antony acknowledges, but duty has called him away from pleasure, "thanks to you." Then Pompey concludes the business of their meeting by asking that the terms of the treaty be written up and sealed.

The pact will be sealed with a celebration party thrown by each of the four signers. Pompey offers to choose lots to decide who will begin. Antony wants the honor of being first, but Pompey repeats that they must choose lots. But whether first or last, he taunts Antony, your "fine Egyptian cookery shall have/ The fame." Did not Julius Caesar get fat on it? Antony stiffens at the remark. But Pompey assures him, disarmingly, "I have fair meanings, sir."

Pompey continues to rib Antony. Now he includes Cleopatra in the joke by referring to a famous episode, in which one of her friends, Apollodorus, carried the queen to Caesar wrapped in a mattress.

Enobarbus finishes the story that Pompey starts and draws from the rebel leader a handshake, an offer of friendship, and praise for his qualities as a fighter. The straightforward soldier returns the compliment, though not thé love, he says, and this openness even further ingratiates him with Pompey. Then Pompey with a flourish invites everyone at the parley to celebrate their treaty aboard his flagship, and all leave but Enobarbus and Menas, the pirate. Menas first speaks an aside in which he shows his apprehension over the new treaty: "Thy father, Pompey, would never have made this treaty."

Then Menas addresses Enobarbus before he can leave with the rest and falls into conversation with him. There is no pretense between the two: each recognizes the other for what he is: a thief. Menas makes his living as a pirate; Enobarbus as a mercenary (a soldier of fortune, who sells his services to the highest bidder and fights for pay, not patriotism). They shake hands and exchange roguish pleasantries until the conversation gets around to the present situation. "We came hither to fight with you," Enobarbus says, and Menas answers that he is sorry the battle did not come off. He distrusts the truce, he confides to his erstwhile enemy, and feels that "Pompey doth this day laugh away his fortune." Then Menas, surprised at seeing Antony back in Italy, brings up the subject of Cleopatra. This is Enobarbus cue to blurt out the marriage plans between Antony and Octavia. But he does not agree with Menas that this will insure the continued friendship of Caesar and Antony. Just the opposite, this nuptial band that was supposed to bind the two together will turn out to be the rope that strangles their friendship. "Octavia is of a holy, cold, and still conversation (behavior)": Antony is not. And Enobarbus predicts that Antony "will to his Egyptian dish again: then shall the sighs of Octavia blow the fire up in Caesar," and the marriage which was intended to bind the Triumvirate together will break it apart. Menas then suggests they go on to the party to drink each other's health, and Enobarbus accepts, saying, "we have used our throats in Egypt."

Act II: Scene 7

This scene takes place soon after the last. Everyone has gone aboard Pompey's galley for the feast; they have eaten and drunk, and now it is time for the "banquet" or dessert. Two or three servingmen bring it on stage and chat and joke for a minute to set the scene. Their joking reveals that the party has been a success; the revelers are in different stages of drunkenness, and Lepidus in particular is flushed with his drinks. As the peacemaker, he tried to relax the tension building up between the two groups at the party and did this by encouraging them to drown their enmity in wine. When they became quarrelsome he would break it up by offering them a drink—and having one himself. Since he cannot hold his liquor as well as the others he has succeeded only in losing all sense of discretion. One of the servants observes that Lepidus has a name only among his companions; he is not their equal or fellow as a man. As useless to be too small for a job as too great; a reed is as useless in battle as a sword that is too heavy to wield, he reflects. His friend agrees: to have a job that one cannot do is like having empty sockets where eyes should be.

Suddenly a trumpet sounds a sennet. (A "sennet" was a group of notes or a tune which was used to identify a particular person, a kind of musical signature.) The music introduces the great men and their advisers and captains, Caesar, Antony, Pompey, Lepidus, Agrippa, Maecenas, Enobarbus, Menas, and others. Antony is describing some Egyptian farming customs to Caesar. The farmers can gauge their crops according to the height to which the River Nile rises in flood season. "The higher Nilus swells,/ the more it promises," because the farmers plant their crops in the rich "slime and ooze" left behind when the waters recede. Lepidus pipes up, "You have strange serpents there?" and when Antony answers yes, the tipsy Triumvir ventures a foolish explanation of how Egyptian serpents are bred. "Your serpent of Egypt is bred now of your mud by the operation of your sun: so is your crocodile."

The other leaders take advantage of Lepidus' condition to bait him. Pompey calls for another round of drinks, and offers a toast to him, and though he is sick and would rather not, Lepidus drinks with the rest and goes on talking about Egypt. While Lepidus is running on about the pyramids, Menas catches Pompey's attention, unnoticed by the others. He wants to speak to his chief alone for a minute, but Pompey, too much enjoying his spoofing of Lepidus, puts him off and pours the groggy general another drink. When Lepidus asks "What manner of thing is your crocodile," Antony takes up the teasing with as nonsensical an explanation of the crocodile as Lepidus had given him of the serpent. "It is shaped, sir, like itself, and it is as broad as it hath breadth: it is just so high as it is, and moves with its own organs. It lives by that which nourisheth it." This seems to satisfy Lepidus, who only asks, "What color is it of?" and learns that it is "of its own color too." " 'Tis a strange serpent," he reflects, apparently forgetting that he had asked about crocodiles.

Again, Pompey's fun is interrupted by Menas, but this time the pirate's persistence succeeds in separating the host from his guests. The two go apart and, after pledging his loyalty to his chief, Menas asks bluntly, "Wilt thou be lord of all the world?" Pompey thinks he must be mishearing him and has Menas repeat the question. "How should that be," he asks. Menas assures him, "though thou think me poor, I am the man/ Will give you all the world." Now Pompey doubts his friend's sobriety: "Hast thou drunk well?" But Menas denies it: "No, Pompey, I have kept me from the cup"; and assures him again that he can make his chief the master of the world. "Show me which way," Pompey demands, and Menas reveals his scheme. "These three world-sharers, these competitors,/ Are in thy vessel. Let me cut the cable,/ And when we are put off, fall to their throats." Pompey's reaction is surprising. "Ah, this thou shouldst have done" on your own, he says, "and not have spoke on it first." For Menas, his lieutenant, his henchman, it would have been good service to ambush his enemies and kill them; but it would be dishonorable for Pompey himself to allow it. "Being done unknown,/ I should have found it afterwards well done,/ But must condemn it now."

Menas sees the weakness of Pompey's character through this speech and grows wary of him. He says aside, as if to himself, that he will pull out of his alliance with Pompey because Pompey's good fortune is on the wane; he has the world in his hand and will not take hold of it. "Who seeks and will not take, when once 'tis offer'd," Menas predicts, "Shall never find it more." Pompey turns back to his guests, the genial host once more, to raise another toast to Lepidus. But by this time the tipsy general is under the table.

So Antony drinks Lepidus' pledge for him and the wine jug goes round again. Pompey fills his cup; Enobarbus toasts Menas and jokes of the servant who is carrying out the unconscious Lepidus, that he "bears the third part of the world." (Lepidus as a Triumvir rules Africa, approximately one-third of the then known world.) Menas replies that "the third part, then, is drunk: would it were all/ That it might go on wheels!" Again the wine is poured around; again the cups are raised. Pompey complains that the party has not yet reached the frenzy and orgy of an Alexandrian feast at Cleopatra's court. But we're trying, Antony adds, and raises a toast to Caesar to draw him into the drunken revelry.

Caesar declines another drink at first, but Antony urges him to comply for the sake of the party, and Caesar reluctantly raises his cup to answer Antony's toast. Enobarbus has no such reserve. Already in his cups, he carouses familiarly with Antony, whom he calls "my brave emperor," and suggests they climax their celebration with "the Egyptian Bacchanals," a' dance in honor of Bacchus, the god of wine in classical mythology. Pompey is enthusiastic, and Antony bids them all to drink "Till that the conquering wine hath steep'd our sense/ In soft and delicate Lethe." (Lethe was believed by the Greeks to be a river in Hades which caused forgetfulness to those who drank from it.) Enobarbus then officiously places everyone in a ring, joining their hands, and gives instructions for the chorus. The men will carry the burden or refrain of the song, while the boy sings the descant. Then the musicians strike up and the drunken leaders reel through their song and dance to an orgiastic climax of their "Alexandrian feast." Their song invokes Bacchus, who is both the god of wine and the wine itself they are drinking. They bid him come, with his "pink eyne" (eyes) and his vats of wine, with clusters of grapes to crown their heads and make them all drunk "till the world go round." Hardly have they finished their tipsy song and dance when Caesar breaks off impatiently, chiding his drunken fellows with "What would you more?" He bids a hasty goodnight to Pompey, the host, and begs out with a none too gentle reprimand: "our graver business/ Frowns at this levity." They have all drunk so much, "the wild disguise" (drunkenness) "has almost/ Antick'd us all" (made clowns of us all).

At Caesar's urging the party breaks up; the revellers prepare to go ashore. Pompey, however, has no intention of letting the party die, so he offers to "try" Antony once more "on the shore." "And shall, sir" Antony accepts, "give's your hand," and the two erstwhile enemies grow maudlin over their boozy friendship. The stage is empty now but for Menas and Enobarbus, who decline to go ashore to continue the party and stagger off to Menas's cabin instead.

Act III: Scene 1

This scene takes us to Syria where Ventidius, Antony's lieutenant, has accomplished his mission and defeated the Parthian hordes who had swept across the frontiers of the eastern provinces of the Roman Empire.

Ventidius enters in triumphal procession behind the slaughtered body of his enemy, Pacorus, the Parthian general. He claims that his victory over "darting Parthia" and the death of Pacorus revenge the defeat and death of Marcus Crassus.

When Silius urges Ventidius to follow up his victory by pursuing the routed Parthians through Media and Mesopotamia, Ventidius is cautious. "I have done enough," he says. Rather than praise and honor, he would win Antony's displeasure for his pains. "For learn this, Silius;/ Better to leave undone, than by our deed/ Acquire too high a fame, when him we serve's away." He is afraid that if he makes too good a showing, defeats the enemy too soundly, Antony will be jealous of his renown. He quotes the example of Sossius, like himself one of Antony's lieutenants, in Syria, whose victories gained him renown and lost his captain's favor. "Who does i' the wars more than his captain can,/ Becomes his captain's captain . . ." (There is no authority in Plutarch for the story of Sossius' dismissal.) Paradoxically, the soldier's ambition is better served by gaining less than he might, than by gaining more. "I could do more to do Antonius good,/ But 'twould offend him. And in his offence/ Should my performance perish." Silius acknowledges the wisdom of Ventidius' words; without such wisdom a soldier is no better than his sword. Then Ventidius tells how he will inform Antony of his victory, making it seem Antony's victory, disclaiming any credit for himself. Silius asks where their captain is now, and we learn from Ventidius' reply that Antony is on his way to Athens and that they plan to meet him there. With that the victorious lieutenant disappears from the play.

Act III: Scene 2

Ventidius' mention of Antony's going to Athens is the cue for this shift back to Rome. Here we shall see the newly-married Antony and Octavia taking leave of Caesar and Lepidus. Shakespeare introduces their farewells with the farewell conversation between the outspoken Enobarbus (leaving with Antony) and the politic Agrippa, which comments on the scene about to take place. We learn from their exchange that the "brothers" —an ironic description of the new accord between Pompey, Caesar, Antony, Lepidus—are parting. Pompey is already gone (back to Sicily) and Antony is preparing to leave for Athens. "Octavia weeps/ To part from Rome;" Enobarbus says, and "Caesar is sad." However, they direct most of their sarcasm at Lepidus, who "since Pompey's feast . . . is troubled with the green-sickness." (Green-sickness was a kind of anaemia believed to affect love-sick young girls. Here it may be used sarcastically to describe Lepidus who is "in love" with Caesar and Antony.) They mimic Lepidus' fawning adulation of his two partners: "O, how he loves Caesar!" "But how dearly he adores Mark Antony!" If Caesar is "the Jupiter of men," then Antony is "the god of Jupiter." (Jupiter was father of the gods; high praise indeed to be god of Jupiter.) If Caesar is "the nonpareil" or utterly incomparable, then Antony is the "Arabian bird!" (The phoenix bird, a fabled creature, only one of which existed at any time.) And so on. Lepidus plies "them both with excellent praises," yet can praise neither enough. "Hoo! hearts, tongues, figures, scribes, bards, poets, cannot/ Think, speak, cast, write, sing, number, hoo,/ His love to Antony," Enobarbus parodies the sonneteers.

Their fun is interrupted by a signal for Enobarbus to mount, and they exchange farewells.

Perhaps they are about to leave but are detained by the entrance of Caesar, Antony, Lepidus, and Octavia. These four have come, like Enobarbus and Agrippa, to say goodbye. But the light note of wit and banter changes now to one of sadness as brother and sister take their leave. Caesar gives each a final admonition: to his sister to "prove such a wife as my thoughts make thee"; to Antony to "let not the piece of virtue which is set/ Betwixt us, as the cement of our love/ To keep it builded, be the ram to batter/ The fortress of it . . ."

Antony's back goes up at this advice, and he protests that Caesar has no grounds for such a fear. When Caesar turns to Octavia for a last goodbye, the tears start from his sister's eyes. She is so broken up emotionally, "her tongue will not obey her heart, nor can/ Her heart inform her tongue," and she must whisper her goodbyes in Caesar's ear.

Here Enobarbus is so surprised by any show of tender emotion in Caesar that he questions Agrippa aside, "Will Caesar weep?" (Obviously they have not left the stage; furthermore, their presence is unknown to the others.) Agrippa believes he may, because "He has a cloud in his face." Enobarbus replies that a cloud in the face is a bad sign in a horse and in a man as well.

Agrippa disagrees and accuses Antony of similar softness. (Enobarbus is almost taunting Agrippa with Caesar's tender youth; Agrippa cites Antony because he is old and battle-hardened.) Did he not weep when he found Julius Caesar dead, and when he found Brutus slain after Philippi? But Enobarbus cynically dismisses Antony's tears as hypocritical —so much water, "a rheum." He wept over sorrow that he himself had caused; he wept until even the cynical Enobarbus wept with him. The two interlopers retire again to the background; Antony and Caesar embrace; Octavia bestows a final parting kiss on her brother and, trumpets sounding, the newlyweds start on their journey.

Act III: Scene 3

Back in Alexandria we find Cleopatra where we left her in Act II, Scene 5, although considerable time has elapsed. Recovered from her original shock and despair at Antony's marriage, she summons the messenger again before her to learn more about Antony's new wife. Naturally he is terrified and reluctant to appear, but the queen is in good humor and soon puts him sufficiently at his ease. When she is sure he has actually seen Octavia with his own eyes, she pumps him for information about her appearance. "Is she as tall as me?" she asks, and learns she is not. "Didst hear her speak?" she asks; "Is she shrill-tongu'd or low?" "She is low-voic'd," the boy replies, and Cleopatra reflects, "That's not so good: he cannot like her long."

Charmian is quick to agree with her queen, and that little bit of encouragement is all she needs. Cleopatra wants desperately to believe the worst reports about her rival, so wishful thinking soon turns all Octavia's felicities to faults. Her soothing voice and petiteness become "dull of tongue, and dwarfish." Heartened by her "discovery," Cleopatra moves onto surer ground with "What majesty is in her gait?" and adds the naked threat, "Remember if e'er thou look'dst on majesty." The messenger takes the hint, falls in with Cleopatra's self-deception. "She creeps," he answers, and from now on his enthusiasm for the game will feed hers. "He's very knowing," she says, "The fellow has good judgment," because he has told her what she wants to hear. So when she asks him how old Octavia is, he starts by saying, "She was a widow," because that will soften the fact that she is considerably younger than the aging Cleopatra. When he admits that Octavia is thirty, Cleopatra does not even acknowledge it but rushes on to question him about Octavia's looks. Is her face long or round, she asks, and of course he replies, "Round, even to faultiness." Not only is she moon-faced, which signifies foolishness, but her forehead is extremely low as well.

Charmian, out of pity for her queen and happy to see her happy, continues to flatter Cleopatra's mood, after the messenger leaves with a handful of gold for having been so obliging. She agrees that Octavia is nothing to lose sleep over and that the messenger's report is to be trusted. "The man hath seen some majesty," Cleopatra vaunts of herself, "and should know." Charmian agrees, a little too effusively, and leads her mistress off to write letters to Antony.

Act III: Scenes 4-5

Antony and Octavia have arrived in Athens. Already the rift between the two emperors has begun to widen, and Octavia finds herself left in the breach. The scene opens in the middle of their conversation. Evidently Octavia has been defending her brother against Antony's charges, but has been fighting a losing battle. Now he raises his bitterest complaint. Caesar (1) has waged new wars against Pompey in violation of their agreement; (2) has made his will and read it; (3) has attacked Antony's honor and reputation indirectly by speaking grudgingly of him.

Octavia defends her brother by claiming that perhaps these reports are not all true, or if true, perhaps not as offensive as they sound. She laments her position in the quarrel, abandoned between the two, her love and prayers equally divided. Antony woos her to his side of the quarrel, telling her that if Caesar succeeds in destroying his reputation she would as well be not married at all as married to him. He will be like a great tree left branchless. But he urges her to mediate between them as she has requested, and informs her that in the meantime he is raising an army which will eclipse her brother's. Scene 5 also takes place in Antony's house in Athens. When these two leave, Enobarbus and Eros come on to gossip about the latest news. They disclose that Caesar, after joining with Lepidus to defeat Pompey, turned on his erstwhile partner and denied him an equal share of the victory. Besides this, under the pretext of some "treasonous" letters which Lepidus had formerly written to Pompey, and with no other proof than his own accusation, he threw his former partner into jail to await execution.

Enobarbus responds to Eros's news with a flippant metaphor that pictures the world as so much food, ground between "a pair of chaps," i.e., the upper and lower jaws (Antony and Caesar). Antony has heard the news also and is upset by it, Eros reports. He is also outraged that one of his own officers has murdered Pompey.

The backstairs gossip continues. We are informed that a great fleet has been equipped, ready to sail against Caesar. Eros finally gets around to the point of his errand: Antony wishes to speak with Enobarbus. Enobarbus shrugs the message off: the meeting will be pointless. Then he asks Eros to lead him to Antony, and the two go off.

Act III: Scene 6

As Scene 4 opened in the middle of Antony's denunciation of Caesar, this scene, back in Rome, finds Caesar denouncing Antony before his two advisers, Agrippa and Maecenas. He immediately reveals a new

Antony and Cleopatra

development in the story: Antony has left Athens a while before and has gone to Alexandria—to his mistress there.

In Alexandria Antony has resumed his former life in the Egyptian court and has cast further insults on Rome. Caesar enumerates them: (1) He has had, or allowed, himself and his mistress to be publicly enthroned amidst extravagant display in the market place. (2) He has given public recognition and a place of honor to Caesarius, Cleopatra's son by Julius Caesar, and all of their own "unlawful" offspring. (3) He has conferred independence on Egypt and made Cleopatra absolute queen over it and several other conquered territories: Lower Syria, Cyprus, and Lydia (Shakespeare follows North's confusion here, giving Lydia for Plutarch's Lybia, but corrects himself later, when North does, in line 69, "Bocchus, the king of Libya"). (4) He has proclaimed his sons kings of kings. (5) He has given outright the conquered territories of Media, Parthia and Armenia to his son Alexander. (6) To his son Ptolemy he has assigned Syria, Cilicia and Phoenicia. (7) His mistress, Cleopatra, appeared that day, and often in audiences, dressed as the goddess Isis (chief Egyptian goddess; patroness of motherhood and fertility).

Caesar's advisers urge him to make these complaints public, so as to turn popular opinion, which is already "queasy," completely against Antony.

"The people know it" already, Caesar replies, and have even heard Antony's accusations in turn. They are: (1) That Caesar took Sicily from Pompey but did not cut him in on the spoils. (2) That he loaned Caesar some ships and never got them back. (3) That Caesar despised Lepidus, then never split his confiscated property with Antony. And Caesar in turn has answered Antony's accusations. He has told him: (1) That Lepidus was put down because he had grown too cruel and abused his high position. (2) That he is perfectly willing to give Antony a share of all the spoils he has conquered, but in return demands a share of Armenia and all the other kingdoms Antony has conquered on his own.

They realize, of course, that Antony will never agree to the conditions. Suddenly, unexpectedly, Octavia walks in on the three conversing men. Caesar is first of all shocked to see her back in Rome, then pleased, then angry. He is shocked because he had no inkling she was not still in Athens, even though Antony had left for Egypt. He is pleased to see her because of the great affection he bears for his sister: "That ever I should call thee castaway!" he gently chides her. He is angry that she should arrive so quietly, so unannounced, almost so stealthily. She, Caesar's sister, wife of Antony, "should have an army for an usher," and their marching feet should have beaten a cloud of dust "to the roof of heaven" to tell of her approach. But she has come, he chides, like "a market-maid to Rome," and in coming so quietly has prevented a mammoth welcome and demonstration of love on their part. They would have given her the red-carpet treatment.

But Octavia dismisses his objections and defends her husband. She was not forced to travel thus unaccompanied, but chose to do so for swiftness' sake. Antony agreed to her journey when he heard of Caesar's war preparations. Rather to get rid of you, Caesar answers, because you stood " 'tween his lust and him."

"Where is he now?" he tests her. And when she replies "in Athens," he breaks the news ungently to her, "No, my most wronged sister, Cleopatra/ Hath nodded him to her." "He hath given his empire/ Up to a whore," he says, and then goes on to rehearse the list of kings and kingdoms that Antony has marshalled for his war against Rome (Shakespeare's list follows closely that of North). Octavia's heart is broken by this threatened break between the emperors, for she loves both men. Caesar tries to win her to his side. He has held back from openly attacking Antony thus far, he says, until he could be sure of two things: (1) that Antony in any way abused or mistreated Octavia; (2) that his own empire was in danger of attack. Now that he has evidence of both, the break must come. But, he says, think of this war as justice, who "makes his ministers of us, and those that love you." Again he welcomes her warmly to Rome; Agrippa and Maecena join him in extending their welcome, and the scene closes for the last time on a bewildered and broken-hearted Octavia.

Act III: Scene 7

This scene is set in Antony's camp near Actium (on the west coast of Greece, across the Ionian Sea from the heel of the Italian boot). Enobarbus is arguing with Cleopatra that she should not take a personal part in the battle that is brewing. She claims that since the war was declared against her, she should be there in person. Enobarbus answers with a metaphor under his breath. If they were to use both stallions and mares in battle, the stallions would be so distracted by the mares that their services would be lost altogether: "the mares would bear/ A Soldier and his horse." Cleopatra does not hear what he says, so he explains his objection aloud. Her presence, he says, will only distract Antony's attention from the battle and prevent him from doing his best. They cannot afford that now. Already in Rome they are laughed at because it is joked "that Photinus, an eunuch [Mardian] and [Cleopatra's] maids/ Manage this war." But Cleopatra disdains Rome and its rumors. She has contributed heavily to Antony's forces and she *will* be present at the battle as head of her kingdom. Enobarbus breaks off the argument as Antony enters with Canidius, one of his captains. They are discussing Caesar's rapid maneuver, by which he has already transported his armies from the southwest coast of Italy across the Ionian Sea, to take Antony by surprise at Actium. Antony decides to meet his enemy by sea. Cleopatra agrees, "By sea, what else?" but Canidius asks him why. And Antony's only answer is because "he dares us to't." So you have dared him to single combat, Enobarbus objects, "Ay, and to wage this battle at Pharsalia . . ." Canidius seconds him; but Caesar has shrugged off both dares because neither is to his advantage. "And so should you," Canidius advises. Enobarbus argues against a naval encounter for several reasons: (1) Antony's fleet is less experienced than Caesar's. Caesar's navy fought against Pompey; Antony's ships are manned by landlubbers—captured mule drivers and farmers—pressed into service quickly to fill the need. (2) Caesar's ships are light and maneuverable, built for warfare; Antony's, mainly borrowed, are heavy and built for display. (3) Antony holds the absolute advantage over Caesar's land army, in numbers and experience, and is himself the master strategist. He sacrifices his advantages and lays himself open to chance and hazard by choosing a sea battle. Still, Antony is firm: "I'll fight by sea." And we know the real reason for his firmness when Cleopatra joins in: "I have sixty sails, Caesar none better." So, committed to a sea encounter he is ill-prepared for, Antony draws up his strategy. He will burn all the ships he cannot fully man and meet Caesar's invasion head on as it approaches the headland of Actium from Toryne. "But if we fail," he second-guesses himself, "We then can do't at land," hoping to destroy the enemy forces on the beaches. When a messenger arrives to confirm the presence of Caesar's army at Toryne, the battle is joined. Antony is dumbfounded by Caesar's swiftness, but issues orders for Canidius to command his nineteen legions and twelve thousand cavalry on the beaches while he takes to his flagship to command the fleet. But before he can leave, an old soldier comes before him to raise his seasoned voice to beg Antony to avoid a naval engagement. "Trust not to rotten planks," he begs, but all he gets for his pains is Antony's brusque "Well, well, away!" He is eager for his doom. Now the stage is left to the old soldier, who spills out his anguish to the more receptive ears of Canidius. "So our leader's led," the latter agrees, "And we are women's men," referring to Cleopatra's power over Antony. But at least they have salvaged a sizable land contingent; all may not be lost. The two soldiers exchange news; Canidius learns that Caesar's lieutenant is an old acquaintance of his, Taurus. And then their gossip is interrupted by a messenger who summons Canidius to Antony.

Act III: Scenes 8-10

These three brief scenes keep us informed of the battle's progress. In Scene 8 Caesar gives orders to his lieutenant, Taurus, leading his troops. Caesar tells him not to attack Antony on land until after the naval battle is over, and hands him a scroll containing further orders and battle plans. Scene 9 shows the same thing happening on the other side. Antony gives

Enobarbus instructions where to station his troops for the coming battle so they can watch the developments at sea (and, incidentally, so that Enobarbus and Scarus will have a good vantage from which to describe the battle in the next scene). Scene 10 is the actual battle scene, but of course we do not see it directly. First, Canidius marches across the stage with a group of Antony's soldiers, then Taurus does the same with some of Caesar's, and when they are gone, the noise of a sea fight is heard offstage. Suddenly Enobarbus rushes onstage to spread the alarm. Cleopatra's flagship, *The Antoniad*, has turned and run from the battle! And behind her, following in full retreat, fly all sixty of the Egyptian ships. He cannot believe his eyes. But there is no mistake about it. On rushes Scarus to verify the defeat. "We have kiss'd away/ Kingdoms, and provinces," he cries in despair. How does the battle look now, Enobarbus asks, and Scarus answers, "On our side, like the token'd pestilence,/ Where death is sure."

Antony's defeat is sure, because when his ships were beginning to get the upper hand, that worn-out jade, Cleopatra, like a cow stung by a gad-fly in the heat of summer, hoisted a full sail to the wind and scurried off in fright. This Enobarbus already knows; but there is worse still to come. For, seeing his mistress' ships in flight, Antony hoisted his sails and took off after her, leaving the battle at its very height, and still un-decided. "I never saw action of such shame," Scarus adds.

Canidius enters, full of the tragic news, and complains bitterly that the defeat is all Antony's fault. He echoes Scarus' opinion that Antony is not himself, hinting that Cleopatra holds some magic power over him. And Canidius adds, "O! he has given example for our flight . . ." He intends to surrender his legions of soldiers and cavalry to Caesar. Already six other kings have done the same and fled to the Peloponnesus. Scarus has half a mind to join him; but he decides to wait and see what will happen. Enobarbus decides against his better judgment to stick by Antony.

Act III: Scene 11

Some days have passed since the defeat at Actium. We find Antony back in Cleopatra's palace in Alexandria. He is off by himself, moody and crest-fallen over his cowardly performance. Only a few attendants are with him, and even them he urges to "fly,/ And make your peace with Caesar."

He is terribly ashamed and depressed over his recent defeat; he feels his cowardly example has instructed others to do likewise, "To run, and show their shoulders"—referring to those kings who have gone over to the enemy. Evidently contemplating suicide in his despair, he urges his friends to follow the others to Caesar's ranks. He offers them gold and letters of introduction to smooth their path and make their betrayal easier. Only, he prays, "look not sad,/ Nor make replies of loathness." He begs, not commands, them to leave him to himself, for he feels he has lost all right to command. Just as he slumps to his seat in utter dejection, Cleopatra is led on by her attendants Charmian and Iras, and Antony's lieutenant, Eros. Eros has evidently brought her to try to comfort his lord. The others second his urgings. But despite them, the two estranged lovers remain aloof at first. Antony reflects aloud how Caesar at Philippi wore his sword merely for show, "like a dancer," while he did the actual fighting. "Yet now . . . ?" he adds wistfully. Moved by this speech and by the entreaties of her attendants, Cleopatra relents and goes to comfort him. "O, whither hast thou led me Egypt?" he addresses her, and confesses that he has been avoiding her out of shame. But she blames herself. "Forgive my fearful sails!" she begs, "I little thought/ You would have followed." You knew I would, he replies, for I was bound to you by my heart strings. You knew you had me completely in your power. Then he complains that he is reduced to grovelling before the youthful Caesar, begging favors—he who once ruled half the world. All because he loves her. "Pardon, pardon!" Cleopatra cries through her tears, overcome by sorrow. Instantly the scolding soldier is dissolved and goes to comfort his comforter. "Fall not a tear," he soothes her, for "one of them rates [is worth]/ All that is won and lost." When she is quiet again, he asks if "our schoolmaster" has come back.

Then Antony calls for wine to lift their spirits and cries his defiance to fortune as the scene ends.

Act III: Scene 12

Antony mentioned "our schoolmaster" at the end of the last scene; now his reference is explained. At Caesar's camp in Egypt the schoolmaster (Euphronius) comes before Caesar and his advisors—Agrippa, Dolabella, Thidias, and others—as Antony's ambassador to ask for terms of surrender. Dolabella takes it as a sign of Antony's weakness, who before could make his conquered kings errand boys, to send a lowly schoolteacher. The ambassador delivers his message. Antony surrenders and acknowledges Caesar as his lord in exchange for two requests: (1) That he may remain in Egypt, or if that is too much to ask, that he be allowed to live out his days as a private citizen in Athens. (2) That Cleopatra may keep the crown of Egypt for her heirs while recognizing Caesar's supremacy. Caesar turns down Antony's request outright. As for Cleopatra, he tells the messenger, she can have whatever favor she chooses on one condition: that she drive Antony out of Egypt or kill him there. The schoolmaster bows himself out to deliver his message. Then Caesar calls Thidias before him, to entrust him with an important mission.

He dispatches this smooth diplomat to seduce Cleopatra away from Antony by eloquence and flattery and extravagant promises. He hopes that her marred fortunes with Antony will make her more receptive to a new lover. Caesar cautions Thidias also to observe how Antony's spirit is bearing up under his misfortunes and disgrace.

Act III: Scene 13

Gloom is thick in the halls of Cleopatra's palace. Through it Cleopatra, Enobarbus, Charmian and Iras try to see some brightness in the future. "What shall we do," the queen questions Enobarbus, and he answers bleakly, "Think, and die." But he reassures the queen that she is not to blame for the defeat at Actium; Antony is man enough and soldier enough, or should be, not to let "the itch of his affection" spoil his judgment in battle. He should have known better than to follow her ships in flight. It is the old conflict in Antony between reason and passion. Cleopatra silences him suddenly as Antony enters, speaking loudly with his returned ambassador, Euphronius. He repeats Caesar's offer to Cleopatra: her kingdom for Antony's head. With four words she shows it is unthinkable: "That head, my lord?"

So Antony sends the ambassador back with his refusal and a challenge to cap it. He accuses Caesar of cowardice and ineptitude: His captains win his battles for him. And he dares his brother-in-law to a duel, single combat, "sword against sword," as he leads the schoolteacher off to write it out in a letter.

Enobarbus shakes his head at this. Antony has lost his sense along with his sovereignty if he seriously believes Caesar will accept such a ridiculous challenge. Would ever the winner, riding high, give up his advantage and descend to fight on foot with the loser? "Caesar," he exclaims aside, "thou hast subdued/ His judgement too." A servant enters to announce a messenger from Caesar (the messenger is Thidias, dispatched by Caesar at the end of Scene 12). Cleopatra notices that he does not show any of the deference or forms of courtesy which servants are accustomed to use when they address their queen.

The servant's impertinence causes Enobarbus to consider again whether he should get out while there is still time. If we are loyal to a fool, he reflects, our loyalty is mere folly. But the man who can endure "To follow with allegiance a fall'n lord," conquers his conqueror "and earns a place i' the story."

Thidias enters on his errand of seduction. At first, Cleopatra is brusque with him. Naturally he wants to speak to her alone; but she will not dismiss her friends. So he starts by mentioning Caesar's generosity and leniency. Immediately he gives Cleopatra a ready-made excuse by saying that Caesar realizes she did not choose to consort with Antony out of love, but out of fear. Therefore, Caesar pities her frailties rather than blames them. Cleopatra falls in with the scheme. She accepts Caesar's out and denies she ever yielded her honor willingly. She was conquered by Antony. Enobarbus, overhearing their exchange, is disgusted by her disloyalty, for he believes Cleopatra is turning against Antony and accepting Caesar's overtures of friendship. Outraged, he storms out to look for Antony and warn him of Cleopatra's treachery. He reflects again that Antony is like a sinking ship; even his dearest friends abandon him. With Enobarbus gone, Thidias presses his advantage. Caesar is generous as well as forgiving. If Cleopatra will quit Antony and put herself under Caesar's protection, she may have whatever she desires from him. To show her willingness, she grasps Thidias hand and kisses it, in proxy for Caesar's feet to hear his judgment. Thidias commends her wisdom and nobility in choosing Caesar above Antony and bends to kiss' her hand. As he does so, Enobarbus rushes back in with Antony just in time to witness what seems to both the emblem of her perfidy and the besmirching of her honor. Antony is furious: The storm breaks.

But Antony has seen just enough to convince him of the opposite. He berates Thidias severely as a "kite," but does not yell at Cleopatra in public, while any underlings are in the room. Then he sends Caesar's personal emissary out to be whipped like a common hoodlum because he dared to grow too familiar with Cleopatra's hand.

When the servants have dragged Thidias off, Antony turns on Cleopatra. He reflects bitterly on all that he has given up for her sake: his place in Rome; his wife Octavia, a "gem of women"; and the lawful children she would have borne him. And for what? To be made ridiculous by a queen who flirts with her servants! He shouts over her protests; he accuses her of always having been shifty and calculating, but says his better judgment has been so blinded by his passion that he has adored her for the very tricks and wiles by which she has deceived him. His anger rages like a fire: what he says, instead of damping it, feeds it. He dredges up old grievances against her: he picked her up after she had been dirtied and dropped by others. "I found you as a morsel, cold upon/ Dead Caesar's trencher: nay, you were a fragment/ Of Gnaeus Pompey's . . ." (Remember Cleopatra boasted of her youthful conquests in Act 1, Scene 5). She does not know the meaning of chastity, he says. While she can only ask in bewilderment, "Wherefore is this?"—what have I done to deserve this? Antony does not mention what Enobarbus must have told him, only accuses her of what he has actually seen: letting a lackey, an errand boy, kiss her hand. But he feels like a cuckold.

Feeling so wretched and betrayed, he cannot speak civily to her who caused it any more than a condemned man can thank the hangman for being handy with his noose. A servant interrupts the violent scene, bringing in Thidias who has been soundly whipped. Antony sends him back to Caesar to make his report and insultingly tells his rival to whip, or hang, or torture Hipparchus, one of Antony's freed slaves in exchange.

When they are gone, he turns back to Cleopatra, but the fire has died down now. He can reflect that, as our heavenly moon's eclipses portend disasters on earth, so the change in Cleopatra, his earthly moon, "portends alone/ The fall of Antony!" She is all patience, waiting for the fire of his anger to burn itself out. When it has died, she reassures him. If her heart is cold toward him, she swears, let it freeze into hailstones of poison and the first of these kill her slowly as it dissolves; and the second her cherished son Caesarion; and so on till all her children and the people of Egypt be dead and covered with flies. "I am satisfied," he says as she finishes. And with his restored faith comes back some of the old optimism and bounce: "There's hope in't yet," for him. But though his army is pretty much intact and his navy back in shape, he knows he will be battling against odds, so he will give no quarter on the battlefield. And since it may be his last night alive he determines to make it a gaudy, festive one. It is Cleopatra's birthday and they will celebrate it without stint, as in earlier, better times. Off they go, Antony bluffly boasting that next time he fights, he will deal death like the plague itself. Enobarbus remains behind; this scene has decided him. Hesitant before how to act, now he sees his path clear before him. Antony's optimism, he feels, is unwarranted; his courage, foolhardy. "In that mood/ The dove will pack at the estridge [hawk]." He can foresee only doom in Antony's action, for it is based on passion rather than reason. So Enobarbus follows the council of prudence and makes his decision: "I will seek/ Some way to leave him."

Act IV: Scene 1

Caesar, with Agrippa and Maecenas, receives Antony's letter of challenge in his camp and laughs it to scorn. Maecenas estimates Antony's anger to be desperation and urges Caesar to attack his enemy in the heat of it. Caesar concurs that the time is ripe; with so many deserters from Antony's ranks he feels he can win at the odds. He orders a huge celebration feast.

Act IV: Scene 2

Antony and his confidants receive Caesar's rebuke. Antony seems honestly perplexed by Caesar's refusal of a duel. Enobarbus explains that his advantage is in numbers, and Antony replies that he will beat him in open battle, too. Then he asks his most loyal lieutenant, "Woo't [Wilt] thou fight well," and Enobarbus says, "I'll strike, and cry 'Take all.'"

Antony is pleased by his response and calls for the feast to celebrate Cleopatra's birthday. As his servants answer his summons, he takes each by the hand in what seems a farewell embrace. Cleopatra wonders at it; Enobarbus attributes it to his sorrow. Antony grows maudlin, asking his servants to tend him well at that night's feast for it may be the last time they serve him at all. He may be wounded or killed in tomorrow's battle. So he speaks to them as one who says goodbye, and asks them to tend him in the same spirit. The servants are discomforted by these remarks; they grow uneasy and start to weep, and even Enobarbus says through his tears, "for shame,/ Transform us not to women." This jostles Antony out of his mood; bluff and confident again, he disclaims any sadness. "For I spake to you for your comfort," he says. He hopes well for tomorrow, he claims, for victory not death, and on that rising note bids them to supper and to drink.

Act IV: Scene 3

This is another short prelude to the battle that is brewing. A company of Antony's soldiers, standing guard before the palace, are frightened in the middle of their watch by strange music under the earth. At first, they do not know what it signifies, but one of them says it bodes no good. He interprets it to mean that Antony's patron god, Hercules, is leaving him.

They are much agitated and disturbed by this explanation and confer with some other soldiers who also marvel at its strangeness. Then they all cautiously follow to investigate its source.

Act IV: Scene 4

The night is no more peaceful inside the palace. Antony, anxious for the dawn, cannot sleep. He rises early and calls for Eros to help him put on his armor. When Cleopatra cannot coax him back to bed, she goes to help him dress. But she does not understand the complicated contraption and fumbles with the buckles. Good-naturedly he puts her off; it is not for his body she provides the strength, but for his heart. But she insists on taking a hand, so he shows her the proper way to do it.

When she succeeds with the stubborn buckle, he half-seriously complains to Eros that his queen makes a defter squire than he. He tries to reassure her about the coming battle. A soldier enters, armed, to fetch the general; and Antony warms to his day's task. The men are ready; trumpets flourish. On come the captains and soldiers; they greet their general. He finishes donning his armor; it is time to go. He turns a moment to say goodbye to Cleopatra. No formal farewell; no "mechanic compliment." With a brief "soldier's kiss" he leaves her "like a man of steel." Then he bids her that gentlest of goodbyes: "Adieu." She turns to Charmian; "he goes forth gallantly," she says and is sure that were he to fight Caesar alone, he would win. "But now . . . ?" she worries, as she leaves the scene.

Act IV: Scene 5

Trumpets sound through Antony's busy camp. He greets the old soldier who advised him against a naval engagement at Actium (Act III, Scene 7). Antony regrets not having taken that advice. The soldier reveals that one more has deserted from Antony's ranks: Enobarbus. The general is dumbfounded. Although Eros claims his property and gear are still in camp, the old soldier insists that he has fled. Antony's reaction is surprising. He does not blame his lieutenant, but himself: "O, my fortunes have/ Corrupted honest men." He asks Eros to write a letter to Enobarbus saying "that I wish he never find more cause/ To change a master." Then he sends it along with Enobarbus' abandoned treasure, after him.

Act IV: Scene 6

Caesar's camp is no less busy; no fewer trumpets flourish. Caesar enters with Agrippa and Dolabella and the deserter Enobarbus. Caesar gives orders to his troops to take Antony alive. He foresees victory that day and following it a period of universal peace.

A messenger announces the arrival of Antony in the field. Caesar gives his battle plan. He orders Agrippa to place all those who have come over from Antony's army in the front ranks so that he will be confused and seem to destroy his own men. They leave Enobarbus alone on stage. He ponders the fate of the others who have deserted to Caesar's side.

Alexas, sent by Antony to confer with Herod, betrayed his master and persuaded the Jewish king to join him in Caesar's service; and for this Caesar hanged him. Canidius and the rest of the deserters have been given tasks but no trust. "I have done ill," Enobarbus concludes of his betrayal; "I will joy no more." At this moment of moral crisis, he hears that a messenger has arrived with his abandoned treasure and equipment, bearing Antony's farewell note and a bounty besides. Enobarbus thinks he is being mocked at first, but then he is plunged even further into dejection. He contrasts the kindness and generosity with which Antony repays his own treachery, and his heart swells almost to bursting with the thought. "If swift thought break it not, a swifter mean/ Shall outstrike thought," Enobarbus vows, but feels sure that "thought will do't."

Act IV: Scene 7

The stage now represents the battlefield between the two camps, contended for by both armies. First a contingent of Caesar's troops, commanded by Agrippa, retreats across the stage. The battle is not going well for them. Then Antony helps the wounded Scarus to cover.

Though concerned over Scarus' wounds, the men are able to joke about their victory. Scarus says that his wound "was like a T,/ But now 'tis made an H."

"We'll beat 'em into the bench-holes," Scarus boasts.

Eros comes on to rally them after the retreating foe as the scene closes.

Act IV: Scene 8

The battle is over; Antony's formations return victorious to their camp under the walls of Alexandria. Antony congratulates them and gives them encouragement for the next day's battle, when they will annihilate the enemy. They have fought like Hectors, he compliments them.

Cleopatra rushes on to greet her victorious husband. He addresses her as "Thou day o' the world," and sweeps her into his embrace, harnessed in iron though he is. "Leap thou," he commands her, "to my heart . . ." His high spirits spill over into jokes about his age and prowess, and he even offers to Scarus' lips the hand he was so jealous of the day before. He orders his men back into formation; calls to the trumpeters for a flourish, and a roll from the drums, and marches his army off in triumph through the city.

Act IV: Scene 9

The triumphal clamor of Antony's camp dies into the gloomy watchfulness of Caesar's. A group of sentries on the outskirts of the camp come upon Enobarbus spilling the last torment of despair from his soul. He calls upon the moon — "the sovereign mistress of true melancholy" — to witness his remorse for having betrayed his beloved lord. He wishes that the damp night air will poison him and be his death, a punishment for his infamous revolt against Antony.

Then begging Antony's forgiveness, he dies of a broken heart with his friend's name upon his lips. The watchmen of the guard, approaching to question him, are puzzled to find him dead. Suddenly they hear reveille mustering the troops; it is the signal that their tour of duty is over. They carry the dead man off to the guard-room.

Act IV: Scenes 10-12

Again we are on the battlefield between the two camps. A new day is breaking; the generals draw up their battleplans. First Antony and Scarus march across with their army. Antony says that Caesar, frightened to meet him again on land after yesterday's defeat, prepares for a naval engagement. Antony orders his foot-soldiers to take up positions on the hills commanding the city, from which they can follow the progress of the sea battle. His ships have already put to sea.

When they have gone to find their vantage point, Caesar leads his army on. He resolves that, unless he is attacked on land, he will depend that day on his seapower to win the advantage. With Antony already in command of the hills, he orders his soldiers into the valleys. When they have gone, the stage remains empty for a few moments, while an alarm, "as at a sea-fight," rises in the distance and then dies down again. When all is quiet once more, Antony comes on with Scarus.

Antony spots a good vantage point further up by a tall pine tree and leaves Scarus alone onstage while he goes off to observe the battle. When he is alone, Scarus reveals that all is not well; he expects disaster that day, for "swallows have built/ In Cleopatra's sails their nests," and that is an evil omen. Although the augurers (soothsayers who could predict the future from signs and omens) say they do not know what this means, they show by their grim looks and their silence that it bodes no good. Antony too is moody, shifting unsteadily from hope to fear, from courage to dejection. Scarus' soliloquy is interrupted by a frantic Antony: "All is lost," he exclaims, and immediately accuses Cleopatra of betraying him. For his men, when they had sailed out of the harbor, instead of attacking the enemy fleet joined them, surrendered themselves, tossed their caps in the air and caroused together "like friends long lost." Antony's defeat is complete; he gives over utterly to thoughts of despair and death. But he promises to get even with the "triple-turn'd whore" who has sold him out "to this novice," as he contemptuously refers to Caesar.

He cares for nothing now—loyalty, friends, nothing—but revenging himself on the enchantress who has cast her charm over him; and then his own death, for he no longer wants to live. The friends (or rather those he thought were friends, and Cleopatra chief among them) who were as slavishly devoted as spaniels to him when he was master, now abandon him: to "melt their sweets on blossoming Caesar." He is like a great pine tree that once towered over the forest and now is stripped of its bark and branches and left to decay.

Again he blames "this false soul of Egypt," this "right gipsy," who has cheated and beguiled him.

He calls for his faithful lieutenant; but Cleopatra answers his call. He is repulsed by the sight of her, but she does not understand his anger. In a torment of rage he sweeps over her, drowning her in abuse. Let Caesar take her back to Rome in his triumphal procession, a shameful mockery, a whore, to be displayed like a monster in a cage. Let Octavia have her for awhile to dull her nails on Cleopatra's face. The frightened queen runs before this wave of hatred which threatens to engulf her.

She is gone, but he cannot reconcile himself. The rage upon him is like Nessus' legendary shirt of fire which tortured Hercules to his destruction.

Hercules is Antony's patron among the gods, so in his misery the defeated general prays to him for strength. Then the accumulated anger and humiliation overcome him and he swears "the witch shall die." Thus sworn, he leaves to find Eros.

Act IV: Scene 13

Meanwhile Cleopatra is frightened for her life by Antony's furious attack. She does not understand the reasons for it, and runs to her attendants for protection. "He's more mad/ Than Telamon for his shield," she laments.

Charmian devises a plan. Cleopatra will go to the mausoleum she has already prepared for her entombment and lock herself in. Meanwhile she will send Mardian, her eunuch, to tell Antony she is dead. She does so, saying she has killed herself.

Act IV: Scene 14

Back in Cleopatra's palace, empty now but for Eros and himself, Antony's passion has subsided. His dejection is still profound—he will not come out of it again—but he is more reflective than furious now. He opens his conversation with a strange question: "Eros, thou yet beholds't me?" "Ay, noble lord," his bewildered friend replies. Antony is comparing himself and his fortunes to clouds that race across the evening sky. As we watch, the clouds assume various shapes, one looks like a dragon, another like a bear, a lion, a turreted castle, a cliff, a mountain, "a blue promontory with trees upon't."

The clouds no sooner take a shape—say, a horse—when they dissolve again back into nothing, "as water is in water." So, the defeated Antony reflects, am I "even such a body." He too will dissolve, like so much vapor. He went to war for Egypt's queen, because he loved her and thought she loved him. He thought he had a million loyal friends: all gone, dissolved. She has dealt from a stacked deck and played his cards into Caesar's hand. Now he is trumped. But, he comforts the weeping Eros, they still have a way out; "there is left us/ Ourselves to end ourselves." Upon this quiet scene comes Mardian with Cleopatra's false message to shock Antony back into anger. "O' thy vile lady!" he exclaims upon seeing him, "She has robb'd me of my sword."

Mardian denies it, protests his mistress's love and loyalty: he uses the past tense. Antony vows Cleopatra's death before Mardian lies that she is already dead. Not only dead, but by her own hand, and in despair for having lost Antony, with his name the last thought in her heart. When he hears this false message, all the life goes out of him. He has been living only to punish Cleopatra; now that he thinks she is dead, there is no more reason for him to go on. He starts to remove his armor, as if for sleep.

Eros helps him; he cannot get it off fast enough. Finally, the uniform of his soldiery stripped, he sends Eros out with the "bruised pieces," while he prepares for death. Now he will be reconciled with his queen in that world beyond death "where souls do couch on flowers." Hand in hand they will walk like lovers so as to steal the show even from Dido and her Aeneas.

He calls Eros back into the room. Remember, he says, you have sworn, when the need should come, when death is the only alternative to disgrace and horror, you would kill me. "Do't, the time is come . . ." he commands. Eros turns pale at the thought; but Antony shows him the alternative: to see his master brought back to Rome disgraced, a captured slave behind Caesar's chariot. Again he exacts Eros's oath to kill him, and this time Eros complies. He draws his sword; he tells Antony to turn his face aside, and when he has done so Eros plunges the sword into—himself! "Thus I do escape the sorrow/ Of Antony's death," he exclaims. This is Antony's second example: Cleopatra and Eros have both shown him the way. Without more delay he draws his sword and falls on it, but the wound is not immediately fatal. A guard comes in followed by Decretas, and he begs them to finish the job. But they are all frightened to see their leader fallen, and refuse. Decretas, when the guard has fled, pulls the bloody sword from Antony's wound but not to answer his prayer. He intends instead to use it as his passport into Caesar's good graces. Diomedes enters looking for Antony. Decretas, hiding the bloody sword beneath his cloak, points to the dying man and leaves. And now, too late, Diomedes reveals that Cleopatra is not dead but locked in her monument and fearful that just this would happen as the result of her lies. With the last of his ebbing strength Antony summons his guard and as his last command bids them take him to Cleopatra. Weeping, they take him up and carry him off.

Act IV: Scene 15

Locked in her monument, Cleopatra complains to Charmian; she fears she will never leave her tomb. Charmian is attempting, unsuccessfully, to comfort her, when Diomedes returns with the dying Antony, borne by his guards. Cleopatra had feared he was dead, but how much more fearful is the reality of a dying Antony to the mere thought of a dead one. Surely the sun must burn up the heavens at this calamity and leave the world in darkness.

Her lover's name breaks from her lips in anguish when she sees him wounded; she cries to those around her to help her lift him up into the monument. But he puts her fears at naught: it was not Caesar's hand produced this wound, but his own.

"I am dying, Egypt, dying," he tells her, and begs one final kiss, but she is afraid to leave her sanctuary, lest she become Caesar's "brooch," or trophy. She has already decided to die there by knife, drugs, or, significantly; serpent. So with the help of her maids and his guards, she manages to lift Antony into the monument.

Again in his lover's arms, Antony repeats, "I am dying, Egypt, dying." "Die when thou hast lived" again, she says, brought back to life by her kisses. But he has not much strength left. He must use it to admonish her. He gives her three cautions. First, that she should not sacrifice her honor to Caesar in order to secure her safety. Second, that she should trust none of Caesar's advisers and lieutenants but Proculeius. She replies that she need not trust even him: her own hands and resolution will be enough. Third, that she ought not to mourn over his death, but glory in the nobility of his life who was "the greatest prince o' the world . . ." For he did not die basely, nor cowardly, but nobly by the hand of another Roman— "valiantly vanquished." That is all: three words of advice and he is dead in his mistress's arms: thus "the crown o' the earth doth melt." And in the almost superhuman eloquence of her grief she exclaims, "O, wither'd is the garland of the war,/ The soldier's pole is fall'n: young boys and girls/ Are level now with men: the odds is gone,/ And there is nothing left remarkable/ Beneath the visiting moon." With that she swoons.

Iras is thrown into a violet agitation by her mistress's fainting spell. She calls upon her as "Royal Egypt: Empress!" until Charmian cries "Peace, peace, Iras!" Cleopatra revives saying, "No more but e'en a woman," like any, the simplest of her sex. What meaning is there left in titles or distinctions when Antony is dead? "All's but nought . . ." Patience or impatience to bear such suffering are equally meaningless. "Then is it sin," she asks herself, "To rush into the secret house of death/ Ere death come to us?"

Act V: Scene 1

The scene shifts from the still depths of a doomed love to the efficient bustle of Caesar's camp, flushed with his recent triumph. A council of war is in progress. Caesar cockily dispatches Dolabella to demand Antony's surrender as Decretas enters, carrying the blood-stained sword of Antony. He passes himself off as Antony's loyal follower: "I wore my life/ To spend upon his haters." Now he offers his services—and his loyalty—to Caesar and promises to do the same for him: "As I was to him/ I'll be to Caesar." For, he explains, "Antony is dead." Caesar is surprised and genuinely moved. So great a catastrophe, he says, "should make a greater crack," should cause some similar catastrophe in "the round world."

For Antony's death is not just his personal tragedy; it alters that entire part of the world which he ruled. Caesar is saddened to hear it, and exchanges reminiscences of Antony's exploits with his advisors. "Say nothing of the dead but what is good," the Roman aphorism admonished, and their remarks are in keeping with its spirit. Agrippa reflects stoically that the gods who make men make them flawed so they will not challenge their supremacy. What makes the news specially poignant to Caesar is the knowledge that he has hounded Antony to this deed. He has cut Antony off as he would a diseased part of his body, not in despite or hatred, but to keep the sound part wholesome. It was him or Antony; the world held not room enough for both. Then Caesar launches into a stirring eulogy of his defeated "brother," "competitor" (friendly rival), "mate in empire," "friend and companion in the front of war,/ Arm of mine own body and the heart where mine his thoughts did kindle." He blames their falling out, which has led them to this moment, on the influence of their guiding stars, doomed to opposition.

Caesar abruptly breaks off his sorrowful praise of Antony to question an Egyptian messenger, sent by Cleopatra to learn of Caesar's intentions and accept his instructions. Caesar tells her not to worry: he will act honorably toward her and kindly. "For Caesar cannot live to be ungentle." Immediately he turns to Proculeius and orders him to reassure the Egyptian queen of his good intentions, "Lest, in her greatness, by some mortal stroke/ She do defeat us."

Evidently concerned by this last thought he sends Gallus along to back up Proculeius and bids them a speedy return. Then he invites those closest to him who remain to hear the story of how and why this war came about.

Act V: Scene 2

Just as Antony, before he commits suicide, reflects upon the insecurity of life that changes so quickly from prosperity to disaster, so Cleopatra opens the scene in which she will die. Since life is full of treacheries, hopes which are never fulfilled, misfortunes without meaning, changes for the worse—then suicide, which puts an end to all uncertainty, is a "better life." And so she seeks "that thing that ends all other deeds": death.

Antony and Cleopatra

Proculeius breaks in upon her morbid reflections with Caesar's message. This is the man Antony told her to trust; but she has no use for him now. She asks her price: "Give me conquered Egypt for my son . . ." But her attitude toward her conqueror is hostile and aloof: she treats his messenger coldly with a "take-it-or-leave-it" tone. Though defeated, she will not give in. Proculeius tries to win her confidence. He tells her, in effect, she will catch more flies with honey than with vinegar. "Let me report to him/ Your sweet dependency," he says, and you'll find him begging you for suggestions how best to please you.

She softens somewhat, shows her obedience to him, and asks to see him. Proculeius, gladdened by her change of tone, is about to deliver her request when a troop of soldiers, led by Gallus, surprises them from behind and surrounds the monument. He tells Proculeius and the soldiers to guard her till Caesar comes.

Immediately upon seeing the soldiers, Cleopatra's waiting women, Iras and Charmian, panic. Cleopatra is cooler-headed. She is determined not to be taken alive. She draws a concealed dagger and is about to kill herself when Proculeius lunges for her arm and manages to wrest the knife away before she can use it. He insists again that she mistakes Caesar's intentions: he means her no harm. Nor does death, she replies, that puts injured dogs out of their misery. Proculeius tone becomes firmer; he reprimands her for jealously trying to deny Caesar an opportunity to show his generosity. For if she is dead, to whom can he show it? But Cleopatra is distraught. Her accumulated misery breaks out in an anguished cry for death to comfort her. She *will* have death, she vows, if not from a dagger, then from hunger and thirst and lack of sleep. "This mortal house [her body] I'll ruin,/ Do Caesar what he can." She would prefer the vilest, most painful death to that which she could never tolerate: the mockery and censure of Rome's vulgar mobs. Dolabella, another of Caesar's diplomats, arrives to relieve Proculeius, whom Caesar wants to see. Proculeius, genuinely concerned for Cleopatra, asks if he may not deliver some message from her. "Say, I would die," she answers. When he is gone, Dolabella tries to break the ice by introducing himself as an old acquaintance. But Cleopatra could not be less inclined to social amenities. She treats him like any uncouth ruffian who will "laugh when boys and women tell their dreams . . ." For life seems like a sleep to her now, and the past all a dream, Antony a dream. "O such another sleep," she exclaims, longing for death, "that I might see/ But such another man!" This exclamation loosens a landslide of emotion; words of love and praise for her dead lord pour from her mouth around the bewildered Dolabella. He was like a constellation of stars in the heavens, she says; he was like the great Colossus bestriding the ocean; "his rear'd arm crested the world"; his voice was like the music of the heavenly spheres to those he loved, but to those he hated, like "the rattling thunder." His generosity knew no barrenness of winter; he gave like an autumn harvest. Even his delights were so enormous they raised him out of the common sea of pleasure, as dolphins show their backs above the element they live in. He had kings for servants, and kingdoms and islands were like small change "dropp'd from his pocket."

Dolabella is both perplexed and annoyed by her running on. He interrupts her several times but cannot stop her. Finally she asks him if he thinks such a dream could come true. When he says no, she protests loudly. If ever Antony lived, he was greater than her dream. Nature cannot produce men as great as we imagine them, she says, but Antony was nature's masterpiece, greater than any dream or imagination. Dolabella tries to quiet her. He tells her the greatness of her grief not only argues the greatness of her loss, but makes even him grieve deeply over Antony's death. This does quiet her; she trusts Dolabella. "Know you what Caesar means to do with me?" she asks. This puts him in an awkward position: He hates to have to tell her, but he thinks she should know. He starts by defending Caesar's honor; but she saves him embarrassment by saying it for him: "He'll lead me then in triumph." Dolabella admits she is right, as a flourish sounds announcing Caesar's arrival. With him are Proceuleius, Gallus, Maecenas, and some other attendants. Caesar enters, asking, "Which is the Queen of Egypt?"

Cleopatra, playing along with his stratagem, falls to her knees in respect and obedience. He protests that she should not kneel; they are equals. He holds no grudges against her for the war, he says, though injured by it. She does not try to defend her actions or excuse them; she blames them on the frailities of her sex. Caesar reassures her of his kind intentions, if she cooperates. But if she tries to defeat him by taking Antony's course of suicide, he will destroy her children. He prepares to leave. Anxious to create a good impression, Cleopatra hands him an account of her wealth before he goes. In it are listed all the major items of her wealth: money, silver and gold plate, jewels. She summons Seleucus, her treasurer, to swear it is accurate. But he does not! He claims the account is fraudulent; she has kept back as much as she has made known. Cleopatra blushes—from shame or rage we cannot tell. But Caesar takes it in good spirit and even approves her business acumen. This does not subdue her anger. She lashes out at Seleucus as an ingrate, a slave she has raised to a position of trust, who now turns on her and curries favor with Caesar because she has been defeated by him. Seleucus recoils from her as she lunges for his eyes. Caesar comes between the two to restrain her. She turns to him, all apology and explanation. She has kept out a few trifles, she admits, unimportant things of no value to give as presents to her common followers and servants, and a few more expensive things to win the friendship of Octavia and Livia, Caesar's wife.

But Seleucus exaggerates out of envy for her, she petulantly accuses him. He should rather have pity on me, she says, as she banishes him from her sight. For the leader is blamed for what his underlings do, and when he falls from grace he is punished for others' faults.

Caesar tells her to put her account away; he wants none of her treasure. She continues to wrong him in estimation, he objects; he is no merchant; he will treat her as she herself dictates. "Feed and sleep," he counsels her, having in mind her threat to Proculeius earlier to starve herself. She goes to kneel once more in respect as he leaves, but he restrains her and bids her "adieu." As soon as Caesar is out of sight, Cleopatra drops the mask of meekness and subservience. She has seen through his kindness to the evil design behind it, and she rejects both in the only way left open to her.

Cleopatra whispers instructions to Charmian and sends her off on an errand.

Charmian passes Dolabella on the way out. He has come back secretly to tell her Caesar's plans. The conqueror intends to return to Rome by way of Syria. In three days he will send her and her children before him. Then this last man bows out of the life of a woman who has charmed many men.

Cleopatra rehearses again for Iras's sake the fate that awaits them in Rome. She reminds her servant of the vulgar rabble who will witness their disgrace, the foul breaths that will mock and jibe at them, the venal officers of the law who will snatch at them like strumpets, the dirty songs that will be sung about them. Comedians will make jokes about them, little scenes will be performed to mock them.

With Iras now in a state of near-panic at the prospect of being taken alive to Rome, Charmian returns from her errand. She is no sooner back but Cleopatra sends her with Iras to fetch her royal robes, and her sign of office—the crown of Egypt. She wants to look as beautiful and seductive for this last meeting with Mark Antony as she had her first on the river Cydnus (Act II, Scene 2). Now Shakespeare interrupts Cleopatra's morbid preparations with a humorous exchange, between the queen who is bent on death and a rustic clown who brings her a basket of figs in which are concealed the poisonous asps by whose bite she will die.

The clown gives up his burden reluctantly and with many warnings and cautions about the "worm of Nilus," the asp. He says that he heard all about how deadly and painful its bite is from a lady who had died from one. Cleopatra is rather impatient with his inane joking. She tries to get rid of him quickly. But he is either too stubborn or too stupid to take her none-too-gentle hints.

The clown leaves, wishing the queen "joy of the worm." Charmian and Iras reenter, bearing Cleopatra's robes, royal crown, and jewels. She bids her maids attire her as for a state occasion; she is impatient at their slowness.

For she imagines Antony waiting for her, praising her courage, and laughing from the other side of death at the fickle "luck of Caesar." "Husband," she cries out, "I come," claiming for the first and last time in the play the sanction of that title for their guilty love. She is entitled to use it, she says, because she is willing to die for it.

She gathers her faithful serving-women into a last farewell embrace. The moment is too charged with emotion for poor, fragile Iras: She dies on the spot of a broken heart. Almost playfully Cleopatra chides her; if she is the first to meet Antony beyond the grave, he will bestow on her "that kiss/ Which is my heaven to have." She takes one of the deadly snakes from the basket and pulling open her robe, applies it to her breast.

Impatient still at the asp's slow work, she takes another and applies it to her arm. But none is needed; in the middle of a question that expects no answer, she dies. "What should I stay . . ." she begins, and Charmian finishes, "In this vile world?" Then the loyal maid closes her queen's eyes, straightens her royal crown, and applies an asp to her own arm. The guards come noisily in. When they see that "Caesar's beguiled," they call Dolabella. Just as he enters, Charmian dies. He precedes Caesar by only a moment. The conqueror and his train of followers march into a peaceful scene, not one of carnage. The queen, in full regalia, reclines on her couch, her maids dead at her feet, but nowhere a sign of blood. They seem asleep rather than dead. "She looks like sleep," the moved Caesar says, "As she would catch another Antony/ In her strong toil of grace." He wonders how death was caused; there are no usual signs of poisoning. Then Dolabella discovers the tell-tale swellings on her breast and arm, and a guard notices the trail of the asp on her skin and on the fig leaves in the basket. Caesar is resigned; "She shall be buried by her Antony." He is even moved by her death to some nobility of sentiment. "Their story is/ No less in pity than his glory which Brought them to be lamented."

And as his final act of the play, Caesar orders Dolabella to make arrangements for a state funeral and to observe "high order/ In this great solemnity."

Coriolanus

CAIUS MARCIUS, *afterwards* CAIUS MARCIUS CORIOLANUS.
TITUS LARTIUS ⎫
COMINIUS ⎭ *generals against the Volscians.*
MENENIUS AGRIPPA, *friend to Coriolanus.*
SICINIUS VELUTUS ⎫
JUNIUS BRUTUS ⎭ *tribunes of the people.*
MARCIUS, *son to Coriolanus.*
ROMAN HERALD.
NICANOR, *a Roman.*
TULLUS AUFIDIUS, *general of the Volscians.*
LIEUTENANT *to Aufidius.*
CONSPIRATORS *with Aufidius.*
ADRIAN, *a Volscian.*
CITIZEN *of Antium.*
TWO VOLSCIAN GUARDS.

VOLUMNIA, *mother to Coriolanus.*
VIRGILIA, *wife to Coriolanus.*
VALERIA, *friend to Virgilia.*
GENTLEWOMAN, *attending on Virgilia.*

Roman and Volscian SENATORS, PATRICIANS, AEDILES, LICTORS, SOLDIERS, CITIZENS,
 MESSENGERS, SERVANTS *to Aufidius, and* ATTENDANTS.

Coriolanus

Act I: Scene 1

Though this play is entitled *The Tragedy of Coriolanus,* the hero does not appear immediately. The first scene is laid in a street of Rome, where a great deal of the action takes place. A company of mutinous citizens, armed with staves, clubs, and other weapons, enters. The First Citizen comes in inciting the people to riot, asking them if they are prepared to die rather than starve. Needless to say, the crowd affirm this resolution. The First Citizen then claims that Caius Marcius is the "chief enemy to the people." The crowd all agree with him and the First Citizen suggests that they should kill Caius Marcius so that they can get corn at their own price, which is not specified.

The First Citizen then proceeds to give a list of grievances against the patricians, the aristocratic class of ancient Rome. He claims that the citizens are despised while the patricians are by contrast considered good. In his anger he accuses the aristocrats of having plenty to eat, while the common people starve, and he wishes that the ruling class would at least let the people have the stored crop surplus before it goes bad. The First Citizen is really quite a demagogue too, because he incites his listeners by telling them that the suffering of the common people is actually useful to the aristocrats, who wish to keep things that way because the people, being weak from hunger, will thus be easier to control. The First Citizen suggests, however, that the common people "revenge this with our pikes ere we become rakes." His motive, he says, is to gain food, not just revenge.

Finally the Second Citizen manages to get a hearing; he has been trying for some time to get the attention of the crowd. Now he asks the First Citizen whether he plans to turn particularly against Caius Marcius, to which question the First Citizen retorts indignantly that Caius Marcius acts like a dog to the common people.

The Second Citizen, who seems more moderate than the First Citizen, then recalls Caius Marcius' services to his country, and suggests that these should not be forgotten. The First Citizen says that he knows them very well indeed and would take them into consideration, but for the fact that Caius Marcius repays himself for this valor by being proud. Despite the rebuke of the other speaker that such a remark smacks of malice, the First Citizen continues his attack by claiming that, whatever men may say to the contrary, Caius Marcius has acted valiantly in order to gain personal glory. In addition, the desire for glory, the Roman *virtus*, or "valiantness," was not so much for the service of his country, but in order to please his mother and also to gratify his own overpowering pride. The Second Citizen tries to calm his compatriot by saying that one cannot blame a man for acting according to his nature. After all, Caius Marcius is not a vicious man, and certainly one thing is in his favor: no one can accuse him of personal greed. But the First Citizen is too angry to listen and says that Caius Marcius is absolutely full of faults. The debate is then interrupted by a new noise of rioting. Apparently the other half of the city has risen in rebellion against the patricians.

At this rather chaotic moment Menenius Agrippa enters. He is an elderly man, a patrician, but "one that hath always loved the people," and even the First Citizen admits that "He's one honest enough." Immediately Menenius addresses himself to the crowd, calling them "my countrymen," and asking why they are armed with staffs and clubs. The First Citizen is not long in replying, and very insolently too. He says that the Roman Senate knows very well what the matter is, and what is more, it has known for the past two weeks. The people are now out of patience so they're about to make the patricians listen by force of arms. The poor petitioners have strong arms as well as strong breaths.

Menenius, however, seems unlike the typical patrician as drawn by the First Citizen. He tries to ingratiate himself with the citizenry of Rome by addressing them as "masters, my good friends, mine honest neighbors." Then he questions the wisdom of their decision to rebel against the patricians. He tries reason and tells the mutinous citizens that the patricians take most loving care of them, and far from blaming the patricians for the scarcity they should recognize that they are wrong in raising a rebellion against the Roman state. It, like heaven itself, will simply proceed on its appointed course whatever happens. Anyway, the gods are responsible for the dearth, not the patricians. The citizens would therefore be better advised to kneel and offer sacrifice to the gods rather than to raise a rebellion against their political rulers.

Menenius also takes care to give the citizens a way out by claiming that he can of course see that they are almost out of their minds with the calamity that has befallen them. Naturally that is the reason they are making such totally false allegations against the heads of the state who care for the common people the way fathers care for their children. This last comment provokes a derisive snort from the First Citizen, who launches into a recital of the real and imagined woes of the populace. Again he claims that the patricians don't care about the starving people of Rome. They are letting the common people die while they themselves have grain stored away for their own use. They repeal acts which are against the interests of the rich, while at the same time passing others to make life harder for the poor. Menenius listens patiently to this outburst and then starts to tell a very homely tale in order to pacify the rebellious crowd.

Menenius then begins his most famous speech, the anecdote on the revolt of limbs against the belly. As the elderly statesman tells the story the people listen to the way in which the members began openly to complain of the uselessness of the belly sitting in the middle of the body merely absorbing all the food put into it, and unlike the limbs and senses, playing no active part and doing no work. All the other bodily functions seem to contribute to the general welfare of the body, except the lazy belly. By now Menenius is having a very good time with his captive audience and starts to act out his part with artistic embellishments. He will make the belly smile as well as speak, for instance. In this approach he shows not only a good sense of humor, but also a firm grasp of the principles of telling a good story. Having claimed that the belly will speak, he resorts to a rhetorical device and digresses, or turns aside, from his apparent desire to entertain and goes on to his main purpose, comparing the fictional situation with the attitude of the citizens towards the senators of Rome.

By this time the impatient First Citizen interrupts and tells Menenius to hurry up, but he has fallen into a trap set rather adroitly by Menenius, because he immediately starts praising the limbs and the other functions of the body at the expense of the belly. The patrician cuts in with a joking "tut, tut," because the First Citizen seems to be taking the floor away from him. Nevertheless, the citizen continues with his thesis, calling the belly a cormorant, as though it were the greedy bird that would eat anything.

The old storyteller, Menenius, still bides his time and then, when he has everyone's attention, he continues with his tale. He, of course, takes the side of the belly, and demolishes the argument of the First Citizen. Certainly the belly agrees that he receives all the food, and so he should as the storehouse and shop of the body. But then, he continues, his task is to send all this nourishment throughout the various nooks and crannies of the body in order that every portion should receive its proper nourishment. In fact the entire body lives off the belly, which sends forth nothing except what is good and useful, while it is left with only the waste products.

Menenius now zeroes in on the citizens and applies this parable specifically to the current situation in Rome. The senators of Rome, he claims, are the belly, while the citizens are the "mutinous members." And like the belly, the Senate has nothing but the public welfare as its aim.

He continues by asking the First Citizen what he thinks and then humorously insults him by calling him the "great toe" of the assembly, since he is "one o' th' lowest, basest, poorest/ Of this most wise rebellion." Here, of course, Menenius is using irony, saying the opposite of what he believes about the insurrection. But then he rounds on the First Citizen and the crowd saying that Rome and her rats (obviously he means the mob) are at the point of civil war, in the course of which one or the other must be destroyed.

Just at this inopportune moment Caius Marcius enters, and he promptly lives up to the derogatory remarks that have been made about him. He insults the citizenry and in his opening image betrays his attitude towards them. They have made themselves scabby by "rubbing the poor itch" of their "opinion." Their minds and their policies are therefore diseased. The First Citizen comments ironically "We have ever your good word," and in reply Marcius begins a tirade against the crowd, calling them *curs, hares,* and *geese* rather than lions and foxes.

According to Marcius the mob of citizens is fickle, and no more to be depended on than "the coal of fire upon the ice."

In other words, the favor of the people soon melts away, the way the fire melts the ice, or the way a hailstone melts in the sun. The commons are so lacking in virtue that they taint any man who trusts them so that anyone who thinks himself great is better advised to gain their hate than their love. They cannot be depended upon, and making use of them would be like trying to swim with fins of lead or trying to cut down an oak tree with rushes. In short, the people are a useless lot, quite capable of turning upon their former heroes and destroying them. Were it not for the careful government and control of the Senate the populace would probably destroy itself.

He then asks Menenius what on earth the people want and is told that they want corn at their own price.

Caius Marcius is enraged at the audacity of the populace in daring to question the nobles and their policies. He again expresses his contempt for the people and claims that their conduct weakens the general structure of the government. He wishes aloud that the nobles would cease to feel pity for the starving common folk and instead permit him to inflict physical punishment on them.

But Marcius has some strange news to bring to Menenius from the council chamber of the Roman Senate. The other group of the common people had presented a petition to the Senate, playing upon the sympathy of the patricians and saying that the gods did not send corn only for the good of the rich. The patricians then granted the petition, but its strangeness still puzzles and angers Caius Marcius. Indeed, it does seem irrelevant to the alleged purpose of the riots—corn gratis. The people have been granted a kind of political representation, five tribunes to be chosen by them to present their wrongs to the nobles. Junius Brutus and Sicinius are two who have been chosen, and they are the only ones we meet in this play. Caius Marcius is disturbed by the precedent and looks ahead to a time when this policy will cause greater revolution than at present. He sees it as a weakening of the central authority and wishes that he had been allowed to crush this particular rebellion by military force.

Almost with disgust Caius Marcius orders the populace to go home, and at that moment the two new tribunes Sicinius and Brutus enter along with some unnamed senators and two generals, Cominius and Titus Lartius. This group brings the news to Marcius that the Volsces, enemies of Rome, have taken up arms against the city. Immediately Marcius is all warrior and he rejoices in the possibility of war. After all, as he says, the Volscians have a leader named Tullus Aufidius who is a thoroughly noble man and a good soldier. In fact he is the only person with whom Marcius himself would change places. Cominius, the general, asks if the two have fought each other, and Caius Marcius generously replies "He is a lion/ That I am proud to hunt." So great a warrior is this Aufidius that he would wish to make war only with him, and would even change sides to fight against him should they chance to be on the same side.

The senators then tell Marcius to go with Cominius to this war against the Volscians. Titus Lartius, though an old man, promptly declares his intention of throwing away his stick and going along as well. The senators then order the people home and Sicinius and Brutus are left alone on the stage discussing the events. Within a moment they start pulling the character of Caius Marcius to pieces. Sicinius sees him as a totally proud man, and Brutus agrees, adding the hope that the war will rid Rome of him. The man has become so proud through his valor that he cannot be borne. Sicinius then wonders aloud how such a proud man can bear to work under the command of Cominius. Brutus in reply gives an explanation which in some respects tells us more about the tribune himself than about Marcius.

He claims that Caius Marcius actually prefers the subordinate position in order to preserve his own personal reputation for complete success. Consequently the general will be blamed whenever anything goes wrong, and public opinion will praise Marcius more and wish that he had been in command.

Sicinius agrees with the incorrect assessment, and Brutus goes on to say that Cominius in fact deserves half the honor that the general reputation gives to Caius Marcius, who does not really merit the high opinion in which he is held.

Act I: Scene 2

The scene now shifts to the senate chamber of the Volscian town of Corioles (sometimes called Corioli), where a discussion is taking place among Tullus Aufidius and the assembled senators. Obviously both the Romans and Volscians have their spies, because Aufidius notes that the Romans always seem to have advance knowledge of the Volscian plans. He himself has also received a letter from Rome telling of the famine riots and giving news of the Roman mobilization, probably against Corioles. The letter even names the generals, Cominius, Titus Lartius, and of course Marcius, who is listed to Aufidius as "your old enemy." The Volscian general regrets that the premature discovery of the plans means that the army can no longer proceed with its original intention to capture many smaller towns before Rome awakened to its danger. Then, in a situation parallel to that of the preceding scene, Aufidius looks forward to a meeting with Caius Marcius, saying that they have sworn to fight to the death at their next meeting. The senators wish Aufidius well and all withdraw.

Act I: Scene 3

This scene takes place in the house of Caius Marcius, and it is totally different in tone from the preceding hurly-burly of the play. Volumnia and Virgilia, the mother and wife of Caius Marcius, enter, and setting down two low stools, they start sewing. This action immediately indicates the domestic nature of the scene. Volumnia commences by trying to cheer up the preoccupied Virgilia, begging her to sing, or at least to sound more cheerful. She claims that if she were married to Caius Marcius she would rejoice more in an absence by which he gains honor than in his loving presence in bed. Then, in what may be an attempt to shame her daughter-in-law, Volumnia recalls how she sent her son to the wars when he was but a young boy. To her delight he returned with a garland of oak leaves on his head in token of having saved the life of a Roman citizen in battle. She claims that she was just as elated at this sight as she had been when she had learned that she had borne a boy child.

Virgilia, however, asks Volumnia what her reaction would have been had Marcius been killed. To this question Volumnia proudly replies that then the honor he had gained in the engagement would have been sufficient to take the place of her son. She says that if she had had a dozen sons she would prefer that eleven should die nobly for their country rather than that one should avoid battle because of softness and overindulgence.

This contrast is enhanced by the way in which the timid and shrinking Virgilia wishes to retire when the lady Valeria is announced. Volumnia, of course, will not permit her to do so, and proceeds with a speech which recreates in her imagination what is probably going on in Corioli, with Caius Marcius defeating Aufidius and urging his troops on to action though he himself is covered with blood. The mention of blood is too much for Virgilia, who shudders with fear, "O Jupiter, no blood!" This comment seems to Volumnia to be a confession of weakness and she scornfully tells Virgilia that blood becomes a warrior better than the gilt on his monument. Then she goes on to declare that the forehead of Hector when it spouted forth in blood from a Grecian sword looked lovelier than the breasts of Hecuba when she suckled her son. Virgilia is almost overcome by the savagery of Volumnia's denial of the primacy of a mother's love and utters a prayer that Caius Marcius may be protected from

Note: In some sources of the story of Caius Marcius the name of the wife is given as Volumnia and that of the mother as Veturia. Shakespeare follows Plutarch for his assignment of names.

Aufidius. The dauntless Volumnia only replies contemptuously that Marcius will utterly defeat his enemy.

A third contrast is then supplied with the arrival of the lady Valeria. She is a merry person who seems to have come visiting with the avowed purpose of cheering up the ladies whose man is away at the war. Incidentally, she represents a third kind of Roman lady, a noble and virtuous maiden, as opposed to Volumnia the stern matron, and Virgilia the gentle, loving wife.

As soon as she enters, Valeria, with consummate tact, asks Virgilia after the health of her son. Virgilia merely replies in a few words, but Volumnia takes over the conversation and insists on the warlike proclivities of her grandson. Valeria laughs merrily and tells of the way she saw the child run after a butterfly which he caught and accidentally let go. In its pursuit he fell down and when he caught it he tore it to pieces with his teeth. The reactions to this cruel act, reminiscent of the tales of the Emperor Nero, are indeed interesting. Volumnia is immediately reminded of one of Caius Marcius' moods, something that informs us about both Volumnia and her son. Valeria thinks the incident indicates nobility and seems amused, but Virgilia says that he is "a crack" (an imp) to act so. She is disapproving.

Valeria, however, has not come merely to be sociable. She invites the ladies to go with her to visit a woman who has recently given birth. Virgilia says that she cannot go, and indicates that she is waiting for news of her husband, which Valeria promptly mentions now that she is reminded. She tells how Marcius and Titus Lartius are encamped outside the walls of Corioli waiting for something to happen. Once again Valeria begs Virgilia to go with her and Volumnia, but finally the wife's gentle stubbornness wins the day, and she stays home.

Act I: Scenes 4-5

The scene takes place outside the walls of Corioli. Marcius and Titus Lartius, the old general, are trying to discover whether Cominius has yet begun an engagement with the Volsces. The Romans then sound a parley, but the people of Corioli say that their armies are about to sally forth to fight the Romans for whom they have no fear. Like Aufidius himself, not a single man is intimidated by the reputation of Caius Marcius.

Marcius then exhorts his own troops to fight bravely, but it is no use and the Romans are beaten back to their trenches. Then, at the moment of what seems like defeat, Caius Marcius turns on his troops with a flood of invective like that of a non-commissioned officer cursing his troops back into the battle. He wishes plagues and diseases upon his cowardly soldiers, calls them geese with the souls of geese, and then threatens to destroy them himself. He calls on them to follow him through the gates of Corioli, but no one does, and the gates close, leaving Marcius alone inside the enemy city. The troops naturally consider that he is finished, and tell Titus Lartius accordingly. The old general speaks of the valor of Marcius as though he were already dead, but suddenly the man himself appears, bleeding profusely, but still fighting. Heartened by the sight, the entire army enters the city.

Roman soldiers now appear, but they are discussing booty, not the glory of war, when Marcius and Titus Lartius appear. Marcius expresses his disgust with this attitude when he suddenly catches sight of Aufidius. Leaving Titus Lartius to make sure of the city, he sets off to help Cominius, followed by those soldiers who still have spirit left. Titus tries to dissuade him by saying that he is in no condition to continue fighting, but Marcius refuses to withdraw. The blood he has shed is "physical" (healthful) for him rather than anything else. He says he is hardly even warmed to the fight and so he sets out to find Aufidius. Titus remains behind and calls for a trumpet sound in the market place to summon the town officials of Corioli to speak with him.

Act I: Scene 6

The scene now shifts to another part of the battlefield where Cominius has been hotly engaged with the enemy. He has temporarily retired to regroup his forces and he speaks words of courage to his soldiers, telling them that their comrades are supporting them elsewhere. This speech is interrupted by the arrival of a messenger who says that he has had a very difficult time avoiding Volscian pursuers. He gives the impression that things are in a very bad way, that Caius Marcius and Titus Lartius have been driven to their trenches. But before Cominius can fully digest this bad news, a bloody apparition comes into view and is recognized as Caius Marcius.

The opening words of Marcius are typical, "Am I too late?" Such a speech from a man literally covered with blood indicates unusual courage. Cominius greets him with relief, but is disturbed about his wounds. The two soldiers then embrace and Marcius' speech bears careful examination:

O, let me clip ye
In arms as sound as when I wooed, in heart
As merry as when our nuptial day was done,
And tapers burned to bedward!   (I.vi.29-32)

Marcius tells how Titus Lartius is busy meting out justice in
Corioli, but Cominius enquires about the apparently false information brought by the messenger. Caius Marcius then tells of the
course of the battle and starts to insult his troops again, saying
that they don't deserve political representation, because they have
shown themselves so cowardly in action.

Marcius, never one to waste time in battle, then asks where the
enemy's most trustworthy troops are located, and hearing that the
Antiates under Aufidius are in the vanguard, he asks to be set
opposite them. Cominius suggests that perhaps Marcius needs a
bath and medical treatment, but the young man hotheadedly refuses. He calls for troops to follow him and rouses the men to a
frenzy of patriotism by asking which of them are worth four of
the enemy and equal to Aufidius in valor. The troops shout and
cheer him, and Marcius picks four companions.

Act I: Scenes 7-8

The seventh scene takes place inside Corioli where Titus Lartius sets
a guard on the city and goes to join Cominius and Caius Marcius.

The next scene begins with the entry of Marcius and Aufidius from
different doors. The two valiant soldiers insult each other verbally
at first—a common convention of epic single combat. Next, each
boasts of his own military prowess, and then they fight. Some
Volscians come to Aufidius' aid, but Marcius fights with all of
them and finally drives them away. Disconsolate, Aufidius retires.

Act I: Scene 9

This scene is laid in the Roman camp and opens with a flourish
of trumpets, and the sounding of a retreat. Cominius enters, and
then Marcius, from another door, with his wounded arm bound up
in a scarf. Cominius joyfully congratulates Marcius on his success
and claims that Rome will thank the gods she has such a brave
soldier once he, as Marcius' superior officer, reports the brave
deeds of the young man. Titus Lartius then enters with his troops
and Cominius begins to tell him of the valorous behavior of Caius

Marcius. Almost rudely Marcius interrupts to say that he can't bear praise, even from his mother. He has done his duty towards his country, and any man who has done that has acted in a more praiseworthy manner than he. Cominius refuses to allow such modesty, but Marcius demurs, saying that his wounds hurt him when anyone speaks either of them or of his valor. Nevertheless Cominius persists and assigns Caius Marcius a tenth of the total treasure taken in the capture of Corioli. The young warrior refuses this offer, saying that it would merely be a bribe to pay for his sword; he will simply accept what would normally be due to him. At this the trumpets blare; the army shouts his name; the soldiers throw their caps in the air; and Titus Lartius and Cominius stand bareheaded in tribute.

Marcius almost rudely brushes aside all this pomp and circumstance, saying that all this praise of him is mere exaggeration, even hypocrisy. Cominius repeats that he is too modest and then crowns him with a garland of victory, announcing at the same time that he gives Marcius as a free gift his own war horse, complete with harness. In addition, because of the deeds done at Corioli, he suggests that in the future the young man be known as Caius Marcius Coriolanus. There is another flourish of trumpets; the army shouts; and Caius Marcius says "I will go wash." He affirms that he is blushing with embarrassment, but says he will accept the horse, and of course, the title.

After Cominius has transacted some business, Coriolanus begs a favor of his general. He recalls that a poor man in Corioli had treated him kindly, but the Romans had taken him prisoner. He asks that the poor man be given his freedom. Of course Cominius agrees, but then Coriolanus cannot remember his name.

Act I: Scene 10

This last scene of Act I takes place in the camp of the Volsces. Aufidius, bleeding from battle, enters with a few soldiers. He is distraught and depressed because Corioli has been taken, and although the Romans will return it after suitable peace negotiations, Aufidius' pride is hurt. He has now been beaten five different times by Caius Marcius and is beginning to think this will always be the case. In defeat Aufidius is less noble and valiant than he has seemed before. He now speaks rather meanly of the way in which he will be revenged on Caius Marcius by the use of craft, even if Marcius were a guest in his own house. Instead of generously respecting his opponent's prowess, Aufidius now actively hates him.

Act II: Scene 1

If the last act was mainly one of exposition, largely devoted to showing Caius Marcius Coriolanus as a soldier, this act shows Caius Marcius the triumphant warrior and the unsuccessful politician. Act II is mainly political.

The scene is a public place in Rome, and Menenius enters with the two tribunes, Sicinius and Brutus. They await news from the battlefront, and Menenius remarks that the common people will be unhappy to hear of Caius Marcius' success since they dislike him so much. Sicinius says that nature teaches beasts to know their friends, a remark which seems to indicate unexpected dislike for the commons from one of their representatives. Brutus and Menenius then engage in a witty exchange about Coriolanus, but then the patrician goes on to ask, in a characteristically ironic way, whether there is any vice in which Caius Marcius is weak and which the tribunes do not possess in abundance. Brutus claims that Caius Marcius has all possible vices, and Sicinius returns to Marcius' pride above all else, and Brutus speaks of his boasting. Menenius then turns the tables on the two tribunes by asking them if they know what people think of them in the city, and then telling them that they really have no right to call Marcius proud. They ought to look at themselves to see a pair of meritless, proud, perpetually angry magistrates, in other words, fools.

The tribunes are a trifle taken aback and try to retaliate in kind, claiming that Menenius himself is known quite well in the city for what he really is. But Menenius is too quick for them and he seizes the advantage by giving a character sketch of himself as a "humorous (whimsical) patrician" who likes to drink his hot wine straight and whose judicial weakness is taking the side of the first person to see him about a complaint. Sometimes too he is a trifle hasty about minor things and he loves night life. But his worst fault, as he sees it, is his uncompromising frankness. Rather than do anything underhanded he lets his dislike be known in his speech. He now rounds on the tribunes and tells them, quite frankly of course, that they are no Lycurguses.

In addition they are not good statesmen and have put their case badly; in fact, they have sounded like a pair of asses most of the time. Since they are the people's representatives he must put up with them, but he cannot say they have good faces, a deliberately ambiguous remark: (1) virtuous faces which bespeak virtuous hearts; (2) handsome faces. Now if the tribunes can see such faults in him, then what can their blinded eyesight see in their own characters?

Brutus, overwhelmed by this flow of words, simply stammers "We know you well enough," but again Menenius seizes the advantage and says that the tribunes have never known anything, neither themselves nor anyone else. He sees them as ambitious for the respect, the uncapping and the bowing of poor men. They love to exercise their tiny bit of authority, spending a whole morning on a trivial case, and then adjourning another. They worry more about their personal comfort than about the administration of justice, and if they should get a stomachache they raise a great cry and adjourn the lawsuit.

At last Brutus manages to get in a gibe and claims that Menenius is better known for his wit at a banquet than for his ability as a judge in the Capitol. But again Menenius lets fly: the speech of the tribunes is worthless, yet they claim that Caius Marcius is proud when he is worth the sum total of all the tribunes' ancestors since the legendary great flood. He disgustedly bids them farewell as "herdsmen of the beastly plebeians."

Volumnia, Virgilia, and Valeria then enter to greet Menenius, who is now alone. The mother greets him with the news that Marcius is on his way home, having sent letters to her, to the Senate, to Virgilia, and, she thinks, to Menenius. The old patrician almost goes into an ecstasy of joy and says he will hold a feast. He enquires whether Marcius is wounded, as is customary with him. Virgilia fearfully protests, but Volumnia joyously announces that indeed he is, and that he is returning for the third time with the oak garland for having saved the life of a Roman citizen in battle. Further, he has beaten Aufidius again. Menenius rejoices and asks whether the Senate has been informed, and Volumnia says that the general has written to them and praised Marcius most highly. As Valeria says, "wondrous things" are spoken of him. Virgilia hopes they are true, but Volumnia interrupts with an exclamation of disgust. Of course they're true.

Again Menenius enquires after the wounds of Caius Marcius, and Volumnia says that he is wounded in the shoulder and the left arm. As a result he will have great scars to show the people when he becomes a candidate for public office. He now has a total of twenty-seven different wounds received in all his war expeditions, each one of which, says Menenius, meant death to an enemy.

At this moment the trumpets sound and Cominius and Titus Lartius, the Roman generals, enter, followed by Coriolanus, wearing the oak leaf garland, with a train of soldiers behind him. A herald

announces the new title of Coriolanus in virtue of his valor inside
the gates of Corioli. Everyone rejoices, but again Coriolanus rejects empty praise, and as soon as he sees his mother he kneels
before her in respect. He has done what she would have wished
him to do in battle. This kneeling is very important because in
the last act Volumnia kneels to her son in a totally different situation. Coriolanus then addresses himself to Virgilia as "My gracious
silence, hail" and he chides her for appearing as sad as the widows
of Corioli.

Volumnia and Menenius interrupt this tender interlude with rejoicing and Coriolanus says he must visit the patricians to thank
them for his promotion. Volumnia joyfully proclaims that she has
seen all but one of her wishes fulfilled in Coriolanus—and she has
hopes of the last.

As they set off for the Capitol, Sicinius and Brutus enter to tell of
the tumultuous reception Coriolanus is receiving from all ranks and
conditions of people. The tribunes are therefore most unhappy, and
Sicinius fears that Marcius will be elected consul, one of Rome's
two chief magistrates. Brutus tacitly agrees, and says he fears that
during his term of office (which would be one year) the power
of the tribunes may be weakened, if not altogether destroyed.
Sicinius suggests that since Coriolanus cannot bear his honors
without showing his contempt for the populace, he will be unsuccessful in his candidacy and will lose public regard. If the tribunes
work hard on recalling the old hostility between the commons and
Coriolanus, the people will probably forget his services to the state.
Brutus, musing aloud, remembers that Coriolanus had once said
that if he were to stand for consul he would never go through with
the custom of standing in the market place in humble clothes,
showing his wounds to the people to ask their approval.

Brutus gives his opinion that Coriolanus would sooner miss out
on the office if he could not gain it merely by the request of the
gentry. The two tribunes, of course, wish nothing better than that
Coriolanus should keep to that particular policy. They then start
thinking about strategy, and Brutus suggests that they recall Coriolanus' hostility to the people and his desire to treat them like
beasts of burden, taking away all their political rights. Sicinius
heartily agrees, and remarks that they should suggest these things
when Coriolanus will have made the people angry at him, something that is sure to happen. At this moment a messenger arrives
to summon the tribunes to the Capitol. He confirms the tribunes'
suspicions by saying that everyone now expects Caius Marcius to

be consul, and adds that his valor has everyone at his feet. The tribunes leave.

Act II: Scene 2

This scene takes place within the Capitol where two officers, who are laying cushions for the senators, are discussing the selection of a consul. Apparently there are three candidates, but the Second Officer seems fairly sure that Coriolanus will be the successful one. The First Officer recalls his pride and dislike of the common people, but the Second Officer says that he's not the first who hasn't loved them, but out of his noble indifference to public opinion he has let the people see his attitude. The First Officer notes that Coriolanus seems to seek their hate rather unwisely, but the Second Officer declares that he has deserved so much recognition from his country that it would be an act of ingratitude to deny him this office.

At that instant there is a flourish of trumpets and the entire senate enters. Sicinius and Brutus, as the tribunes of the people, are present, though they sit separately. Menenius opens the proceedings by announcing that the Senate has sent for Titus Lartius, who had been left to administer Corioli. He then asks Cominius, the present consul, to speak of the valorous deeds of Caius Marcius Coriolanus. A senator seconds the request and asks the support of the tribunes in influencing the people to ratify the Senate's decision. Sicinius answers civilly, but Brutus declares that Coriolanus will need to value the common people a little more than he has done in the past. Menenius, rather embarrassed, rules Brutus out of order, but the tribune presses the point. In reply Menenius says that Coriolanus doesn't have to act as the "bedfellow to the commons," at which point Coriolanus offers to leave, saying that he can't bear to listen to a recital of his personal exploits. Brutus, with heavy irony, hopes that he is not sending Coriolanus away, but the soldier replies that his dislike of praise is sending him away.

Cominius then begins a recital of all of Coriolanus' bold deeds, and here we get a full account of the young man's first battle against the forces of the Tarquins when he was a mere sixteen years old. There he did more than was expected of a grown man, wounding Tarquin himself in the knee, and obtaining the first of his oak leaf garlands.

Cominius then continues to tell of Coriolanus' gallant exploits at Corioli. Menenius and the senators are overwhelmed by this account of valor, and are even more amazed when Cominius says that Coriolanus would take no reward for his deeds, considering his performance sufficient glory in itself.

Coriolanus is then called for and Menenius announces to him that the Senate has decided to make him Consul. In reply Marcius says that he owes the Senate his life and service. But when Menenius tells him he must stand in the market place to speak to the people Marcius requests that this custom be omitted. Sicinius promptly insists on the people's rights in this matter and says that they will not allow any abridgement of the custom. Menenius tells Coriolanus to go along with the custom, but the new Consul protests that he will be extremely embarrassed, and further, he thinks that the ceremony could well be dispensed with. Brutus notes this comment. Despite the protests of Coriolanus, Menenius insists, and asks the tribunes to speak to the plebeians in favor of the Senate's decision. As the Senate departs, the tribunes comment on Coriolanus' conduct.

Act II: Scene 3

This scene takes place in the Roman Forum, where Coriolanus must stand to ask the approval of the people. Seven or eight citizens enter discussing what they should do when Coriolanus asks for their voices. Four separate attitudes are obvious: (1) the people ought not to deny their approval; (2) the people have the right to withhold their voices if they wish; (3) the people would be ungrateful if they refused to accept the evidence of Coriolanus' many wounds; (4) the people ought to remember Coriolanus' attitude over the corn as well as the fact that he called them a "many-headed multitude."

Finally, after more discussion, the Third Citizen comments that if only he would lean a little toward the people, Coriolanus would be a worthy man.

Coriolanus then enters in the garb of humility, accompanied by Menenius, who warns him to be mild. The Third Citizen in the meantime has told his followers to come up to Coriolanus in twos and threes so that he will have to make his request for voices to specific persons. Coriolanus still protests to Menenius; how can he ask his wounds to speak for him when he really wants to say that the citizen-soldiery had run away from the same battle in which he had distinguished himself. Menenius begs him to be temperate, but Coriolanus in reply tells him to make the people wash their faces and clean their teeth.

Three citizens then enter, a "brace" as Coriolanus calls them, using a term used for game birds and animals rather than people. He cannot humble himself and claims that his worth and not his wish has brought him to the market place to ask for voices. When the First Citizen says that he must ask kindly for the office, Coriolanus goes through the motions of doing so. But he does not show his wounds, saying that he'll do so in private. The first two citizens give their voices, but the Second Citizen is a trifle dubious. The Fourth Citizen claims that Coriolanus has not always deserved nobly of his country because he has not loved the common people, even though he has been successful in war. In reply Coriolanus argues that his refusal to be "common" in his love is really a recommendation, but if the people desire, he will take off his cap to them, and so he asks for their voices. The Third and Fourth Citizens gladly give their approval, but Coriolanus again avoids showing his wounds. As the group departs, he grumbles against the custom of begging from the plebeians. He would rather not have the position than do so, but he will continue since he is halfway through the business. Three more citizens appear and Coriolanus asks for their voices after speaking of his wounds and his battles. Again he does not actually show his wounds, and his rage at his humiliation is barely suppressed.

Immediately after, Menenius, accompanied by the tribunes, enters and says that Coriolanus has stood in the market place as long as the custom requires and he can now go. Sicinius and Brutus have also given their approval, which is of course that of the people. Coriolanus can hardly wait to get out of his humble clothes and the two patricians arrange to meet at the Senate.

Left alone, Sicinius and Brutus await the arrival of the people, and they speak of the pride with which Coriolanus wore his humble garments and begged voices. The plebeians then come in and the tribunes ask if they have given their voices. They say that they have, but express misgivings: Coriolanus seemed to be mocking the people when he asked for their voices; he didn't actually show his wounds; his manner seemed insulting. Sicinius seizes on these comments and says that the people were very foolish to have approved under such circumstances. Brutus agrees and asks why on earth the plebeians didn't do as they were told. After all, Coriolanus has always been their enemy, even when he lacked power; what will he do now that he has power, since he has always opposed the political rights and liberties of the plebeians? Sicinius suggests that they should have extorted a promise of support from him as their price; then Coriolanus would probably have become angry and they could legitimately have refused him. Brutus builds on his suggestion and harps on the fact that Coriolanus mocked them even as he asked their support, and Sicinius feigns amazement that the plebeians gave their voices under such circumstances. The Third Citizen says that since the appointment is not yet confirmed the plebeians can still revoke their voices; the First and Second Citizens agree and claim that they can raise a thousand voices hostile to Coriolanus.

Sicinius and Brutus then give the citizens a list of the arguments they should use in raising this opposition: say that the people have chosen a consul who will take away their civil liberties; emphasize the pride of Coriolanus, his contempt for the people, and especially the mockery with which he asked for their voices. Then, with a political master stroke, Brutus suggests that the three citizens blame the tribunes for agreeing to the appointment of Coriolanus. Sicinius picks up the argument, telling them to say that they agreed because of the insistence of the tribunes, while Brutus adds specific detail saying that the tribunes had told the people of Coriolanus' past valor and noble lineage.

Sicinius repeats Brutus' argument and says that the people now ought to claim that they have discovered from Coriolanus' current behavior and from recollecting his past attitudes that the new consul is an enemy of the people. Therefore they wish to revoke their approval. Again Brutus repeats the same argument and suggests that when a sufficient crowd has been gathered the citizens ought to go to the Capitol. The people agree enthusiastically and depart to carry out the plan.

Brutus and Sicinius remain behind to contemplate their handiwork, Brutus remarking that this new mutiny will so provoke the anger of Coriolanus that he will reveal himself in his true colors. Sicinius, with an eye for appearances, suggests that the two of them ought to hasten to the Senate so that they will arrive before the crowd. In this way the revocation will seem to be wholly the idea of the populace, and not instigated by the tribunes.

Act III: Scene 1

This act opens in a Roman street to the sound of cornets as Coriolanus, Menenius, the nobility, Cominius, Titus Lartius, and some senators enter. Titus Lartius informs Coriolanus that since Tullus Aufidius had raised another force against Rome a speedy agreement had been concluded in Corioli. Coriolanus seems disappointed that the Volscians have not been totally crushed and thinks it a matter of time until they rise again. Cominius disagrees and doesn't think Rome will have any further trouble from them in the current generation. Titus, in answer to a question by Coriolanus, says that Aufidius was angry at his followers for surrendering the town in such a cowardly manner. In addition, Aufidius had spoken of his rivalry with Coriolanus and his hatred toward Rome. He has now retired to his town of Antium, and Coriolanus wishes he could find an excuse to meet him there.

Sicinius and Brutus now enter, and Coriolanus says how much he despises them as the "tongues o'the'common mouth."

The tribunes warn the troop of patricians, and Coriolanus in particular, not to proceed any further, because the new consul has not received the approval of the people. Coriolanus promptly blusters "Have I had children's voices?" The senators wish to force a passage to the market place, but the tribunes advise against this policy, claiming that the people are so enraged that it would provoke open battle. Coriolanus then turns on the tribunes asking what is the matter with their "herd" if they can now disclaim what their tongues had just spoken. He asks rather shrewdly whether the tribunes might not have led the people on, and disregarding Menenius' warnings to keep calm, he claims that the tribunes are here plotting to circumvent the wishes of the nobility. If such a limitation is permitted, Coriolanus sees Rome as actually being ruled by a mob who cannot and will not be ruled by their betters.

Brutus promptly returns to the root of the argument: Coriolanus' opposition to giving free corn to the people and his attack on those who had supported their cause.

Sicinius then adopts a fatherly tone and suggests that Coriolanus should be humbler and gentler to the people. Menenius tries to calm everyone down, and Cominius tries to act as a moderate voice, saying that Coriolanus has not really deserved this insult from the people. Coriolanus, however, is not to be stopped. He offers to make exactly the same speech against free corn once more. He won't beg pardon of the changeable, smelly crowd because he would rather they regarded him as honest enough not to flatter. He is opposed to making peace with the people on this matter of the consul's office. Giving in would encourage the weed of rebellion to grow in the state which the nobles have so carefully cultivated.

One of the senators now tries to silence Coriolanus, but it is impossible. He will not be stopped and goes on to say that he would be untrue to his valor if by his silence he permitted the spread of "those measles [leprosy]," that hidden disease in the otherwise healthy state.

By now Coriolanus is in a full-blown rage and he insults the tribunes. But what really angers him beyond all measure is the comment of Sicinius that the mind of the new consul "shall remain a poison where it is" and not corrupt anything else. This imperative *shall* is of course totally disrespectful to the nobles, and Coriolanus sees red. He calls Sicinius the leader of a bunch of minnows and tries to show the patricians their folly in granting any political power to the mob. He rages on and warns that chaos can be the only result when two authorities, each equal in rank, attempt to rule the state.

Then he returns to the matter of the free corn and blames all the later trouble in the state on the weakness of the Senate in acceding to the demands of the mutinous mob on that occasion. And again he attacks the populace, claiming that they deserve nothing because of their cowardice in battle. They spend more time and energy in mutiny against their leaders than in fighting the enemy. As Coriolanus sees things, the Senate ought not be courteous to the populace unless it intends to lose its own authority. After all, the populace is in the majority and is likely to insist on the rights of mere numbers. The result would be the overturning of the established order, and crows would peck at eagles.

Coriolanus continues to plead with the senators to get rid of the voice of the populace and to rule them as members of the state who don't really know what is good for themselves. He supports the principle that the integrity of the senators is worth preserving even at the risk of abolishing all the political representation of the populace. Such a remedy is strong medicine for the body politic, but the senators should not hesitate to administer it for the health of the state.

Sicinius explodes at this series of comments and says that since Coriolanus has spoken like a traitor he shall be forced to answer as a traitor. Note that imperative again. The tribunes are indeed exceeding their authority. Then Sicinius calls for an aedile to come to arrest Coriolanus as a traitor to the state.

Sicinius repeats his charge of traitor and lays hands on Coriolanus who calls him an "old goat." The patricians promise to pledge themselves for Coriolanus, but more aediles enter with a group of citizens. The plebians call for Coriolanus' destruction and the senators vainly try to restore order. Sicinius then addresses the mob, claiming that Caius Marcius desires to take away the people's liberties. Menenius remonstrates with him for inflaming the passions of the mob instead of trying to quench them, but Sicinius speaks for government by the many: "What is the city but the people?" This sentiment meets with support from the multitude, who give the tribunes their vote of confidence. Cominius claims that this kind of divisive attitude is the way to destroy the city physically and politically, but by now Sicinius and Brutus are really playing upon the fickle mob and Sicinius calls for Caius Marcius to be taken to the Tarpeian Rock.

Menenius tries to temporize once more, Brutus calls on the crowd to arrest Coriolanus, who draws his sword, and all is confusion. Again Menenius calls for order and asks the nobles to help Coriolanus. This they do and the people are driven off.

Menenius immediately tells Coriolanus to flee, but naturally he wants to stay and fight. A senator, however, supports Menenius, and finally Cominius adds his voice. Protesting that he could beat forty of the populace at once, Coriolanus is at last persuaded to leave while the politicians are left behind to treat the sore of rebellion. Note again the image of disease for the condition of the state.

Left alone with Menenius, a patrician regrets Coriolanus' policy, but Menenius pleads in extenuation that Coriolanus is too noble and too honest to flatter anyone for anything. Further, he is accustomed to speaking his mind frankly. Nevertheless, even Menenius wishes that he had spoken more gently to the people.

The tribunes, together with the rabble, now return and call again for Coriolanus' blood. A citizen, speaking for all, claims that as the tribunes are the mouths of the people so the citizens are the tribunes' hands, and therefore they wish to cast Caius Marcius from the Tarpeian Rock for his treason. Menenius tries to calm them down, but the tribunes continually inflame the mob. A debate then ensues between Menenius and Sicinius. Menenius claims that to destroy such a man as Coriolanus would be an act of ingratitude, but Sicinius claims he is a disease which must be cut out of the body politic. Menenius counters by saying that he is simply a diseased limb that needs treatment rather than possibly fatal amputation. The tribunes are not to be convinced because they see Coriolanus as a gangrened foot, and Brutus says that he must be cut off to halt the spread of the disease.

Menenius warns of the dangers of civil war and destruction if the tribunes follow their proposed course, and suggests that they proceed according to the established rules of legal practice. He promises that Coriolanus will appear at a properly constituted legal trial. At this point the tribunes, somewhat mollified, order the people to lay down their swords, but threaten open war if Caius Marcius fails to appear.

Act III: Scene 2

This scene takes place in a room of Coriolanus' house and is concerned with attempts to make him see political reason. Caius Marcius enters, still in a rage, and claims that he will stand firm against any kind of torture the mob may propose. One noble agrees with him, but Coriolanus is puzzled that Volumnia, his mother, who had never said anything good of the populace, seems to disapprove of his action. Just at this moment she enters, and Coriolanus asks why she wishes he had acted more mildly. Here Volumnia shows a more astute political sense than that of her son; she wishes he had made more certain of his power before he attempted to exercise it so openly. Again, Coriolanus is amazed, but Volumnia says that he acted too soon. He should have waited until the people were powerless to cross him. Menenius and a senator support Volumnia's plea for moderation as she goes on to say that she hates the idea of apologizing to the people and begging their help as much as he does. Nevertheless, her intellect tells her that at the moment this is good policy.

The suggestion of admitting to the people that he had been wrong galls Coriolanus, who says that he couldn't bring himself to apologize to the gods, therefore how can he apologize to the people. Again, Volumnia tries to tell him that he is too inflexible, and uses one of his own arguments: since honor and policy grow together in time of war, in this case he must grant that they should also work together. Coriolanus at first refuses to listen, but she goes on with an analogy; it is no more dishonorable to talk kindly to the mob than it is to capture a town with fair words to save the lives of his soldiers. She herself would certainly dissemble in this case because the end is good, the preservation of the internal peace and stable government of the city of Rome. Menenius naturally agrees with this argument from expediency, and so she goes on to tell Coriolanus that he should take off his hat to the people, and even kneel before them. He must be as humble as a ripe mulberry; in other words a ripe mulberry is easily bruised with the touch and he must be extremely soft in his appearance and manner. Then, when he has the attention of the people he he should say that since he has been brought up as a soldier he simply doesn't have the honeyed words they are accustomed to hear. Then, of course, he must say that he will arrange his behavior so that it will please them. Volumnia almost orders Coriolanus to do as she suggests, despite his dislike of flattering anyone.

Cominius then arrives with the news that people are expressing their anger against Coriolanus in the market place, and suggests that he had better come with a strong force or make a good case for himself. The consensus is that fair speech is the only answer.

But Coriolanus protests that he cannot act as his mother suggests because it is totally against his nature. Volumnia then appeals to his affections, as she later does in Act V, saying that she made him a soldier through her praises, and now he must perform a new role, even if it is foreign to him. Coriolanus is shocked by the suggestion that he must prostitute himself to the people in order to achieve office, and he refuses. At this point Volumnia castigates him openly, telling him to do just as he pleases and let Rome go to ruin. She denies cowardice in herself and takes responsibility for his valor, but says that his pride comes completely from himself. She has no part of such dangerous obstinacy. Almost immediately, Coriolanus backs down. He cannot bear his mother's contempt because her good opinion is all-important to him. Therefore he agrees to go to the market place and insinuate himself into the love of the people by artful speeches. He sends greetings to Virgilia, and says that he will return as consul or never trust his tongue in flattery again. With a curt "Do your will" Volumnia leaves. Significantly, the last lines of the scene show Coriolanus echoing Menenius' advice—"Mildly!" This is to be the watchword for the next scene.

Act III: Scene 3

The scene now returns to the Roman forum. Sicinius and Brutus enter and Brutus suggests that Coriolanus be charged with a desire to gain tyrannical power over the people. But if he should wriggle out of that charge they should accuse him of hating the people, and claim in addition that the booty captured during the war with the Antiates was never distributed. They are planning here to charge Coriolanus with deliberate dishonesty, and by having all their charges ready they are trying to nullify the legal process under which they have agreed to try him.

Coriolanus

An aedile then brings the news that Coriolanus is coming, accompanied by Menenius and some of the senators who have always been in his favor. Sicinius then asks whether a voting list of those against Caius Marcius has been prepared, and he arranges that the people will follow whatever he says in terms of passing sentence on Coriolanus. They will repeat his pronouncement of fine or death, and support the truth of the charges. Brutus then tells the aedile to make sure that the noise will continue so that the people will insist upon immediate execution of whatever sentence the tribunes decree. As the aedile leaves, Brutus says that the first thing to do will be to anger Coriolanus. Once enraged, he will be incapable of controlling his tongue and will let his true self be shown. Thus he will play into the hands of the tribunes and bring about his own destruction.

At this point Coriolanus, Menenius, Cominius and others arrive, Menenius all the while counselling calmness. Coriolanus rather bitterly agrees to act as though he were the poorest stable boy in an inn. After all, the end is the preservation of peace and justice in Rome.

The two groups then confront each other, and the aedile gathers in the people to listen to the exchange. The audience is most probably hand-picked, to judge from what has gone before. First Coriolanus asks whether everything is to be settled right at this time and place. Sicinius doesn't really answer the question and demands that Coriolanus here submit himself to the judgment of the people after the charges have been heard. Caius Marcius agrees.

Menenius then takes over and asks the people to consider the wounds Coriolanus has received in battle against the foes of Rome, something the young man laughs off as a collection of mere trifles. In addition, the patrician says that Coriolanus is trained as a warrior, not as an orator or wordspinner, and therefore he sounds more brusque than he really is. Coriolanus then interrupts and asks what is the matter: since once having been accorded the approval of the populace he is now dishonored by its retraction.

Sicinius promptly rules Coriolanus out of order and says that the tribunes will do all the questioning. Coriolanus apologizes, and Sicinius charges him with conniving to abolish established political offices in Rome and become the wielder of tyrannical power. For this allegation, which Sicinius seems to accept as proven, he calls Coriolanus a traitor. This word gets under Coriolanus' skin and he repeats it, asking for further details. Menenius counsels calmness, but it is no use. Coriolanus has fallen completely into the trap baited by the astute, and dishonest, tribunes. He is angry, and immediately consigns the entire populace to "The fires i'th'lowest hell," and accuses the tribune of lying.

Without delay Sicinius appeals to the people, who yell "To th' Rock." Sicinius then sums up the case, laying emphasis on Caius Marcius' contemptuous attitude toward the people in the past, and also on his current defiance of the legally constituted judges, the tribunes who are there to try him. Thus Sicinius calls for the "extremest death," but Brutus here interrupts and for the record pleads Coriolanus' services to Rome. This is a very shrewd move, for Coriolanus knows how to deal with insolence and defiance, but not with what would at first appear to be pity and sympathy, especially from inferiors. Thoroughly enraged now, Coriolanus challenges the people to pronounce the penalty of execution by means of the Tarpeian Rock, or banishment. Whatever they want, he will not lower himself one jot in order to plead for mercy from those he despises.

Again Sicinius sums up, and pronounces sentence. Since Coriolanus has hated the common people and has sought to remove their political power, and since he has physically attacked those whose duty it is to dispense justice, his sentence is to be perpetual banishment from Rome under penalty of execution as a traitor should he return. This decision is, of course, ratified by the voices of the populace as the tribunes had planned. Cominius tries to speak for Coriolanus and starts by pleading his own wounds and service, but the tribunes cut off all discussion.

They cannot, however, prevent Caius Marcius Coriolanus from having just about the last word. With scathing contempt he goes further than merely accepting the sentence of the populace. Instead he expresses his hatred of the people as a common pack of mongrel dogs with foul breaths. With superb pride he announces "I banish you." He claims that he doesn't wish to remain in a city filled with such a fickle, rumor-ridden mob. He wishes the ultimate doom upon the city that, not perceiving the mob as its real enemy, will banish its defenders. May Rome be captured without defence by another nation. Then he proudly announces that Rome is not everything, "There is a world elsewhere."

The scene ends with the aedile calling for cheers of rejoicing; the people oblige, praising the "noble tribunes," and the stage is left empty.

Act IV: Scene 1

This act opens in Rome before a gate of the city. Coriolanus enters, accompanied by Volumnia, Virgilia, Menenius, Cominius, and members of the young nobility of Rome. All are sad and some are weeping. Coriolanus is the only one who seems remotely cheerful as he tells his followers to wipe their eyes. He gives the impression that he expects his banishment to be only brief, and again he refers to the Roman mob as "the beast/With many heads."

Above all, Coriolanus seeks to console his mother, Volumnia. He tells her to take her own advice and remember that the worst situations are the occasions when a noble spirit best reveals itself. To behave like a gentleman when wounded requires a special knowledge. These are some of the precepts she had taught him.

Virgilia weeps at her husband's attempts to cheer up everyone, and Marcius has begun to comfort her when Volumnia lashes out verbally against all the tradespeople of Rome. Coriolanus, however, seems to have more confidence than anyone else and claims that the populace will love him once they miss him. He compliments his mother on her strength, saying that she is capable of performing half the labors of Hercules.

And so Coriolanus says goodbye to the sorrowing Cominius and the weeping Menenius, begging Cominius to put some courage into the other members of the company. He promises his mother, too, that though he is leaving Rome without any companions, he is going like a lonely dragon into his marshy lair where he will be even more feared than when he is seen. He insists that he will still do better than the normal run of humanity, or else be destroyed. Volumnia begs her son to make specific plans before he leaves, and Cominius offers to go with him until he is settled in exile so that communication between him and his friends will not be broken. After all, if the possibility of his recall should arise, his friends would want to know where to find him. Caius Marcius refuses the kind offer of the aged general and asks his friends to escort him to the gate, saying that they will hear about him, and that he will always remain true both to himself and to his ideals. Then, alone, he leaves the city.

Act IV: Scene 2

As Coriolanus and his supporters leave the stage, Sicinius and Brutus enter with an aedile and start discussing the departure of their enemy. Now that he has left Rome they arrange for the aedile to disperse the crowd. Between themselves they discuss the manner of their future behavior, now that they have achieved their purpose in getting rid of Caius Marcius. Sicinius notes that they have incurred the hostility of a considerable proportion of the nobility, and Brutus suggests that now they have shown their power they ought to lie low and seem most humble in order to ingratiate themselves again.

Then, in this moment of their success, they catch sight of Menenius and the three ladies of Coriolanus' party, whom they naturally want to avoid, particularly Volumnia, who they say is mad. They are too late, and Volumnia utters imprecations on their heads, wishing that all the plagues of the gods be visited on them. Even Virgilia speaks up in this situation when she forces Sicinius to listen to Volumnia's speeches. Sicinius tries the technique of ironic insult, which has succeeded so well against the ever-touchy Coriolanus, but it is a poor weapon against Volumnia, who turns the tables on him, saying that he has craftily banished a man who has done more service to Rome than Sicinius has ever spoken words. Sicinius, thinking himself secure in his position as tribune, and seeing Volumnia as a mere distraught female, then asks Volumnia what would happen if she were to get her wish and Coriolanus were to confront him in the Arabian desert. But to our amazement and that of the tribunes, the answer comes from Virgilia and it is surprisingly bloodthirsty. Coriolanus would kill the two tribunes and destroy their posterity, a suggestion Volumnia promptly takes up.

Sicinius and Brutus then engage in some of the most hypocritical conversation of the play when they piously wish that Coriolanus had continued to do Rome the same service he had done her in his earlier life. Volumnia in reply tells them that she knows who set the populace against her son, and says that they, the tribunes, are totally unfit to judge the great warrior. By this time even the hardened politicians are a trifle embarrassed and they leave, pursued by Volumnia's angry words. Then the four supporters of Coriolanus leave as well, Volumnia declaring that she nourishes herself on her anger.

Act IV: Scene 3

This next scene, which takes place on a highway between Rome and Antium, gives another kind of reaction to the banishment of Coriolanus when a Roman and a Volscian meet. The Roman, Nicanor, is obviously part of the Volscian spy network, and the Volscian,

Adrian, has been sent to meet him. Nicanor tells of the strange insurrection of the Roman people against the patricians and the rulers. Adrian is surprised to hear that the riots are now over and says that the Volscians are in full warlike preparation to move against Rome now that she is distracted with internal troubles. Nicanor remarks that the conflict has continued to smoulder, even since the banishment of Coriolanus. The announcement totally amazes the Volscian, who tells Nicanor that this news will indeed be welcome to his masters. Nicanor agrees and says that Tullus Aufidius will now have an excellent chance to prove his mettle as a soldier since his great opponent will be out of the competition. The two spies depart merrily, happy in the knowledge that Rome is now vulnerable to an assault by the Volscian force.

Act IV: Scene 4

This scene is set in Antium. Coriolanus enters, poorly dressed and muffled as a disguise. He admires the city and remembers the havoc he has wrought in it by causing the deaths of many young men. Hiding his identity for obvious reasons, Coriolanus accosts the first citizen he sees and asks the way to the house of Tullus Aufidius, if he is in Antium. Left alone in front of Aufidius' house, Coriolanus meditates upon the fortunes of the world and of life in general which turn things so topsy-turvy that friends are found duplicitous and hostile while those formerly thought to be foes are now sought out as friends. Chance is indeed a strange thing, and Coriolanus finds that he now hates his birthplace and loves instead this enemy town. He makes up his mind to enter the house of Aufidius and take the risk that the Volscian general may slay him. Should this happen, it will be nothing more than he deserves in the way of justice, but should Aufidius give him the chance, then Caius Marcius can do the Volscians some service.

Act IV: Scene 5

The scene now shifts to the interior of the house of Aufidius where a banquet is in progress. Coriolanus enters and realizes that he certainly cannot pass as a guest, something that the two serving men make quite clear as they tell him brusquely to leave.

Coriolanus tells the serving men to get out of the way and leave him alone, something that rather confuses them. The servants try politeness to get him to leave, but Coriolanus, with the arrogance of one accustomed to command, overcomes all objections. Intrigued by this odd stranger, the serving men question him, and when asked where he lives, Coriolanus replies that he dwells under the heavens, in the city of birds of prey, kites, and crows.

The serving men take up this last remark and ask if he dwells with jackdaws, foolish birds, as well. To this question Coriolanus replies that he does not serve Aufidius.

After this display of bitter wit Coriolanus rather arrogantly beats one of the servants. In the meantime another serving man has gone to fetch Aufidius to order this importunate stranger out of his house. The general comes quickly and asks the muffled figure to identify himself. Coriolanus does not answer immediately, trying to see if Aufidius will recognize him, and giving him a hint that his name is unpleasant to Volscian ears, and harsh in Aufidius' own. Aufidius is still puzzled, but he notes both Coriolanus' grim appearance and the commanding air of his face, and is perceptive enough to note that beneath the threadbare clothing this stranger seems to be noble.

Coriolanus now takes off his scarf and reveals himself, telling Aufidius that the only thing he has left to him from his valorous days in Rome is the title *Coriolanus*, which is not of course a diplomatic one to use in Antium. Everything else has been taken from him by the cruelty of the Roman populace, and what is more, the nobles have permitted this to happen. They too have forsaken him and have allowed the voices of slaves to shout him out of Rome.

Caius Marcius then goes on to explain his motives in coming to the house of Aufidius. Certainly he doesn't fear death, otherwise he would hardly have come to the house of his deadliest enemy. No, his motives proceed from pure desire for vengeance on all those who banished him. In other words, Coriolanus has a proposition to make. He wants to work with Aufidius, and he will fight like an infernal spirit against his own people.

Coriolanus concludes by saying that if Aufidius is not agreeable to the suggestion then he, Coriolanus, offers his unprotected throat to his enemy, telling Aufidius that he would be a fool not to take the opportunity. He almost dares him to slit his throat.

Aufidius' reply is almost immediate and it shows a different side of his character from that of the disgruntled, hate-ridden, defeated warrior of Act I. Seeing his enemy in such an unfortunate situation brings out the natural generosity of Aufidius. He cannot forbear a noble action. If he cannot outdo Marcius by force of arms, then he will outdo him in generosity. He embraces his erstwhile enemy and claims that every word Caius Marcius has uttered has weeded another root of malice from his own heart. He greets the Roman in terms which recall the words of Caius Marcius himself in the first act. He felt no greater joy when his beloved wife first entered his house than he did in seeing Caius Marcius here in his house.

Aufidius then speaks of the immense Volscian army, and says that he had planned to do battle once more with Coriolanus.

Fighting with Coriolanus seems to have become almost an obsession with Aufidius because he speaks of dreaming about doing battle with him. Even if the Volscians had no other quarrel with Rome than that the city had banished Coriolanus, Aufidius says that he would raise an army to avenge him. Joyfully he invites Coriolanus into the banquet chamber to meet the Volscian senators who have come to feast his departure. Incidentally, Aufidius says that his army had been made ready for attacks on Roman *territories* rather than on Rome itself.

As Coriolanus thanks Aufidius for his kind reception, the Volscian makes an astonishing gesture of generosity. He calls the Roman a most perfect man, treats him with respect, and offers him half of his own command. After all, the Volscian can make use of Caius Marcius' specialized knowledge of the strengths and weaknesses of the Roman territories and the city fortifications as well. The two warriors go into the banquet hall.

So far everything seems to be going well for Caius Marcius, and now the serving men comment on the strange happenings they have just witnessed. They all congratulate themselves on not treating the unknown visitor too roughly, and now they all seem to remember something notable about him. Then they start to compare the relative military prowess and reputation of Coriolanus and Aufidius. The First Servingman even seems to claim Coriolanus as greater than Aufidius.

An even more important hint about coming events is given by the Third Servingman in calling Caius Marcius "he that was wont to thwack our general." Then a further debate ensues concerning the merits of the two warriors, the First Servingman supporting Aufidius and the Second Servingman, Coriolanus. The Third Servingman expresses his astonishment at seeing the Volscian senators bareheaded before Coriolanus, while Aufidius was hanging on his every word. Lastly, Aufidius has divided his power with Coriolanus and everyone at the table has approved.

Apparently Coriolanus has said that he will destroy Rome. The serving men realize that war is about to begin and, unthinking, foolish men that they are, they rejoice in the fact. After all, peace is dull, and they look forward to the day when Romans are held as cheaply as Volscians. With a shout they opt for war as preferable to peace.

Act IV: Scene 6

The scene now returns to Rome, where Sicinius and Brutus are congratulating themselves on their actions in getting rid of Coriolanus. Sicinius comments that no one in Rome hears anything about him, and obviously any counter measures that his friends might take will have no effect on such a peaceful city. The people are now happy and quiet, where before they had been in turmoil.

Sicinius claims that Coriolanus' friends are really rather embarrassed that everything is going so well in Rome, alleging that the patricians actually prefer to see the populace in a state of confusion instead of working peacefully in their shops. Brutus agrees with his fellow tribune and says that they took their stand at just the right time. At this moment Menenius enters and Sicinius remarks that he has grown very kind and tolerant lately. The tribunes greet him and Sicinius cannot forbear the gibe that Coriolanus is not missed much in Rome at large, only by his friends. Further, the Commonwealth is carrying on very peacefully; the rage of Coriolanus has absolutely no effect on it. Menenius replies moderately that things are going well, and would have gone better if Caius Marcius had been of a more compromising mind and tongue. And in reply to the tribunes' question he says that not even Coriolanus' wife and mother hear anything from him.

A few citizens then enter and greet the tribunes with respect, and the reaction of Sicinius and Brutus is almost royal in its paternal condescension. Brutus sanctimoniously wishes that Coriolanus had loved the common people as much as their tribunes had. The grateful citizens depart and the tribunes continue to preen themselves on their success, Sicinius saying how much better things are now than when "these fellows" (the crowd) were in rebellion. Brutus again returns to the subject of Coriolanus, saying that he was a good warrior, but insolent, self-centered, too proud, and too ambitious, while Sicinius adds the charge that he wanted to rule alone. Menenius, of course, disagrees, but the tribunes remain secure in their self-satisfaction.

The contentment of the tribunes is suddenly dispelled with the entrance of an aedile bringing news that a captured slave claims that the Volscians with two separate armies have entered Roman territories to lay them waste. Menenius jumps to the conclusion that Aufidius must be emboldened by the news of Caius Marcius' banishment. The tribunes, however, react blindly and stupidly. Sicinius tells Menenius not to talk about Marcius, while Brutus gives orders that the rumor-mongering slave should be whipped. They are obviously disturbed, but ostrichlike they refuse to admit that the Volsces "dare" break peace with Rome; after all, that would show the defeat of their policies. Menenius, on the other hand, sees only too clearly the possibility of a Volscian attack; he has already seen three in his lifetime. Wisely, he recommends against whipping the slave, who might not then reveal the source of his information. After all, he may be telling the truth, and this may be a timely warning. The tribunes refuse to listen.

A messenger then arrives to say that all the nobles are congregating at the Senate and that they seem to expect bad news. Sicinius now orders the whipping of the slave only to be told that the rumor has been confirmed with an addition. Menenius then reveals what he has apparently known all along, that Caius Marcius is said to have joined with Aufidius to lead an army against Rome in order to inflict the ultimate vengeance on the city. The tribunes treat this news with contempt, Brutus saying that it is merely a trick to bring the vacillating citizens to wish Caius Marcius home again. Menenius optimistically tends to discount news of the alliance because of the great enmity between the two warriors. But then another messenger confirms that part of the rumor as well.

Cominius now enters and promptly begins to attack the tribunes, ironically telling them that they are really responsible for the ravishing of their own daughters and the coming destruction of the city, which he pessimistically sees as unavoidable. Then in answer to Menenius, Cominius says that Coriolanus is almost the god of the Volscians and leads them like a superhuman being. In turn, they follow him against "us brats" of Rome with the same confidence that children chase summer butterflies, and less thought than butchers give to killing flies.

Menenius now turns on the tribunes and ironically congratulates them on the success of their work and that of the stinking, garlic-eating mob. Coriolanus will shake Rome down about their ears as Hercules shook down ripe fruit.

Brutus, suddenly a trifle humbled, for the first time in the play uses an address of respect to a patrician in enquiring after the truth of the rumor. Cominius confirms it, saying, in addition, that the territories revolt happily against Rome and that resistance to the forces of Caius Marcius is considered valiant, but utterly foolish and hopeless.

Menenius remarks that Rome is lost unless "the noble man," Coriolanus, has mercy. Cominius asks who can possibly beg him for it, and indeed he is right. The tribunes cannot ask, because of their part in the banishment, and neither can the people, because their voices banished him. His friends are just as bad because they permitted the tribunes and the mob to have their own way, and therefore they are the equivalent of enemies. Menenius agrees and says he couldn't even plead with Caius Marcius to save his own house. Then, ever the rhetorician, he turns on the tribunes with a devastating remark:

> . . . You have fair hands,
> You and your crafts! You have crafted fair! (IV. vi. 118-119)

The tribunes now show themselves wretched cowards who refuse to accept the responsibility for their actions. Menenius denies the guilt of the nobles for the current state of affairs, but admits their cowardice in permitting the mob their will, while Cominius shrewdly comments that he is afraid the fickle mob will "roar him in again." In other words, they will look out for their own self-interest, not the good of Rome. The only thing the city can do is fight against the alliance—and even Tullus Aufidius obeys Coriolanus.

A troop of citizens now enters, and Menenius castigates them for their part in exiling Coriolanus. Now he is coming back to exact reparation, and Rome deserves what is coming to her. The citizens try to shift the blame and say that many of them thought it was a pity that Coriolanus was banished, and after all, they only acted for the best, as they thought. Cominius taunts the mob as mere voices, "You and your cry," an ironic reminder of Coriolanus' farewell, "You common cry (pack) of curs." The patricians then leave for the Capitol, while Sicinius tries to control the situation by claiming that the patricians are trying to make political capital out of it. They really want this rumor to be true. The citizens leave, grumbling that they had never been fully committed to the idea

of banishing Coriolanus. Left alone, the tribunes admit that they
don't like the sound of the news and hope it is untrue.

Act IV: Scene 7

The scene now shifts to the Volscian camp, just outside Rome,
where Aufidius is speaking with his lieutenant and asking whether
his troops still fly to follow Coriolanus. The lieutenant says that
he doesn't quite understand the "witchcraft" or superhuman power
of the Roman, but his soldiers treat him as a god, invoking him
as the grace before meals and speaking constantly of him. In this
expedition Aufidius' own valor is denigrated, even among his supporters. In reply Aufidius says that he doesn't want to disturb
things at the moment while the expedition is going on, but he is
disturbed by the proud bearing of Coriolanus, even to himself.
But as he says, one cannot expect a man of Caius Marcius' nature
to behave differently.

The lieutenant wishes that Aufidius had either run the whole
expedition himself, or else left it solely to Coriolanus. The mistake
was to invite comparison. Aufidius sees the point, but hints that he
will find something to accuse Coriolanus of, when he must give an
accounting of his policy and behavior toward Rome. At the moment he is doing good service for the Volscian state and is fighting
like a dragon. Sooner or later Aufidius will have the chance to
destroy him. The lieutenant then asks his general if he expects
Coriolanus to capture Rome, and Aufidius says that he has no doubt
of his success. His personality is magnetic, the nobles and gov-
ernors of Rome are his supporters, the tribunes have no military
ability, and the populace will recall him just as hastily as they
banished him. He will devour Rome as an osprey, a fish-hawk,
devours a fish.

Aufidius then recapitulates Coriolanus' career, commenting that he
served Rome well, but could not carry his honors with suitable
humility. He wonders about the reason. Was it personal pride
arising from too frequent success, was it faulty judgment in failing to seize opportunities, or was it inability to be other than the
warrior trying to rule peace and war in the same way? Certainly
one, or all, of these possibilities made Coriolanus feared, hated,
and finally brought about his exile.

Aufidius then shows himself appreciative of the merits of Coriolanus, which almost outweigh his faults, but then in a few proverbs he indicates his intention to drive out his opposing fire,

Coriolanus. The concluding couplet of the scene states his future policy more directly: he will attack Coriolanus after he has captured Rome.

Act V: Scene 1

This last act opens in a public place in Rome. Menenius and Cominius, together with Sicinius, Brutus, and other Romans, come in. Menenius says that he will not go to plead Rome's cause with Coriolanus since the warrior has refused to talk to Cominius, the general. Certainly he has been very close to Coriolanus, but that won't help. He suggests that the tribunes and those who banished him go to the Volscian camp to kneel as petitioners before Coriolanus. He himself will just stay at home. Cominius seems almost heartsick that Caius Marcius would not even deign to recognize him, though once he did say his name. At that point Cominius had urged the claims of old acquaintance and fellowship in arms, but Caius Marcius would not even answer to the proud name of Coriolanus. In fact he forbade all names for him, saying that he was a nameless nothing until he had made a reputation by burning Rome.

Menenius again upbraids the tribunes as Cominius tells of the unsuccessful arguments he used in an attempt to soften the resolve of Coriolanus. He suggested that granting pardon when it was least expected was a noble, a royal act, but Coriolanus refused to grant his petition from a state that had punished him as a subject. Cominius then suggested that surely Coriolanus did not wish to destroy his friends, but Coriolanus replied that he didn't have the time to sort out a few good grains from a heap of smelly chaff. This last remark touches Menenius to the quick; he himself is one of those few grains, as also are Virgilia, Volumnia, Valeria, and Young Marcius. They must all be destroyed for the sake of the majority.

Sicinius still begs Menenius to try his luck with Coriolanus and says that he is the person most likely to get Coriolanus' ear because of his close relationship to him. Brutus adds his appeal to that of his fellow tribune.

At this point Menenius agrees to go, and he really thinks that he has a chance of success. Incurably optimistic to the last, he suggests that possibly Coriolanus needed a good meal when he sent Cominius away. He is much more likely to accede to a request after a good dinner.

Act V: Scene 2

This scene takes place in the Volscian camp before Rome. Menenius arrives, and is challenged by the watchmen. He states his business and identifies himself as "an officer of state" come to speak with Coriolanus. When refused admission he gives his name, confidently expecting it to be recognized and insists on seeing the young general. He tells the watchmen of his admiration for Coriolanus, and even orders them to let him pass, but of course the guards tell him to return to Rome. Nothing seems to put Menenius off, and finally the watchmen start baiting the old man with tales of what they will do to Rome, and when that does not work, they threaten him with physical violence. Even then Menenius persists.

At this moment Coriolanus and Aufidius enter, and significantly Coriolanus speaks first, asking the watchmen what is the matter.

Menenius seizes the opportunity, and with a combined gibe and threat to the watchmen, he throws himself at the feet of his "son" Coriolanus, wishing for his prosperity, and offering his own tears as water to quench the fire that Coriolanus is preparing for Rome. He begs Coriolanus to pardon Rome and assuage his wrath on the watchmen, if necessary. Coriolanus, however, simply tells him to go, and in answer to Menenius' question, he says he knows no ties of affection, not even to the members of his own family. His personal power to pardon Rome now resides in the hearts of the Volscians, whose cause he has espoused. He tells Menenius to forget their past friendship rather than poison it by his present ingratitude. Nevertheless, since he did once love Menenius, he gives him a letter to take back to Rome, but he refuses to listen to his pleas.

As Menenius prepares to leave, Coriolanus turns to Aufidius, almost as if asking for congratulations on his singlemindedness, and says that the old man had been one of his most beloved friends in Rome. Aufidius replies dryly that Coriolanus is indeed steadfast in his purpose. Left alone with the watchmen, Menenius is taunted by them and he leaves brokenhearted, with barely enough strength to insult them. The watchmen express admiration for the strength of "our general," Coriolanus, who, like a rock or an oak, will not be shaken by the wind of Roman petitions.

Act V: Scene 3

This scene takes place within the tent of Coriolanus, where he is busy arranging last details of battle strategy with Aufidius. Again one wonders who is really commanding the army, since Coriolanus refers to Aufidius as "my partner in this action," and then tells him that he *must* report to the Volscian lords telling them how well he, Coriolanus, has performed in the action.

Aufidius offers testimony to the loyalty of Coriolanus, saying that he has shut his ears to the pleading of Rome, and has held no private conversations with Romans, not even his friends. Warming to the subject, Coriolanus tells what it meant for him to send away beloved old Menenius, who had almost made a god of him. Obviously, by sending him, the Romans indicate their desperation. Once again Coriolanus has offered Rome the same peace conditions which they had already refused. The only reason he offered them once more was to soften the blow of his refusal to the old man. From now on, he declares, he will not listen to any private suits from Rome, no matter who comes. This remark is punctuated by a shout outside, but Coriolanus declares that he will not break his vow.

Virgilia, Volumnia, Valeria, and Young Marcius, with attendants, now come into the tent. Coriolanus is a trifle taken aback, but he speedily fights down the affection that wells up in his heart, and also any feelings of duty that he may have. Then, as he looks on them, his resolution begins to melt, and he muses aloud that for his mother to bow to him is as if Olympus, the abode of the gods, should bow to a molehill. Even Young Marcius seems to beg his father not to deny him. But this weakness is a passing one, and he says that he will never be such a young goose as to obey his affectionate instincts. No, he will stand firm as though he were self-begotten and had no family.

Then Virgilia speaks to him as "My lord and husband!" and Coriolanus melts with affection for her. He greets her with sadness for her sorrowful face, and realizes that he has forgotten the part he has set himself to play. He begs her to forgive his tyranny, but tells her not to ask forgiveness for Rome. Oblivious of everything else he kisses her passionately, and then realizes that he has forgotten to greet his mother, so he turns and kneels before her.

Volumnia tells him to stand, and then she kneels before him in supplication, deliberately reversing the roles of child and parent. This is too much for Coriolanus, who raises her. For a mother to kneel before the child she has chastised is a total violation of the natural order of things. When such an occurrence comes to pass, order is destroyed in the universe and impossible things happen:

pebbles snap their fingers at the stars, and winds strike the cedars against the sun.

Volumnia greets Coriolanus as the warrior she has helped to make and introduces Valeria to him. Respectfully he speaks to the beautiful and chaste maiden.

Coriolanus greets his son fondly and wishes that he may prove invulnerable to shame and that his thoughts may always be noble. At Volumnia's order the child kneels before him. But Coriolanus cuts his mother short and says he doesn't want to listen to any petitions because he has already made up his mind to deny mercy to Rome. He won't dismiss his troops and he won't treat with the Roman multitude; he doesn't want to be told that he is unnatural, and he doesn't want anyone to try to assuage his wrath.

Volumnia, on hearing these terms, says that they have come to ask precisely what he has just denied, but nevertheless, they will speak so that their failure, if they fail, will be laid at the door of Coriolanus rather than blamed on their own inefficient pleading. Trapped, Coriolanus asks Aufidius and the assembled Volscians to remain and listen, because he wants to have no private conversations with Rome.

Following up her advantage, Volumnia tells Coriolanus to look at the shabby dress of his family and to ask what their lives have been like since his banishment. Their misfortunes are such that the very sight of him makes them weep rather than rejoice. From this emotional plea she moves skillfully to one combined with patriotism, asking him to think how it must be for them to see him, a son, a husband, and a father, destroying his country. And how can they pray for their country's welfare when their loyalty is divided? If they pray for their country, then they are in effect praying for the death of the man they love most, and to whom they owe their first loyalty. If they pray for him, they must lose their country. In either case he will be ruined: he will either be led as a foreign criminal through the streets of his native city, or else will be congratulated for destroying both his city and his family. She then offers him defiance. If she has anything to say, he will march on Rome only over her body, over the womb that bore him, something that she will not permit. And Virgilia adds her defiance to Volumnia's. Marcius also defies him—just like a younger edition of his father. He'll run away until he's old enough to fight back.

Volumnia, however, presses her advantage. She is not asking her son to save Rome by destroying the Volsces. That would run counter to his personal honor. She is merely asking him to use his influence to *reconcile* the opposing forces so that the Volsces may take pride in the mercy they have shown, while the Romans will be both humbled and grateful for the mercy they have received. Then he will be praised for his part in arranging this peace. After appealing to his pride in achievement, she returns to the matter of personal honor and reputation, saying that if he allows Rome to be destroyed, posterity will say that his last act wiped out all the nobility of his former valor and service. His name will be forever accursed. She asks whether it is noble to hold a grudge, and calls upon Virgilia and Marcius to speak in her support, but they remain silent, Virgilia in tears.

Then Volumnia tries another approach, one not shown elsewhere in the play. She begs Coriolanus to remember the love she has shown to him and appeals to his filial affection, upbraiding him because he has never in his life shown her any special consideration, although he has been her only son, to whom she has given up her entire life. Let him spurn her and deny her request; she is simply doing her duty as a mother. This thrust strikes home, and Coriolanus turns away. Quickly Volumnia falls to her knees and bids the other suppliants do likewise.

But since that seems to have no effect, Volumnia plays her last card, one that she has used before—contempt. Coriolanus is so proud of his valiant title that he has no pity left. Very well, they will go back to Rome and die. She tries to use Young Marcius, saying that the child argues the rightness of their petition more than Coriolanus has strength to refuse. Then she throws out her last insult; Coriolanus, "this fellow," had a Volscian for his mother, he is married in Corioli, and Young Marcius is like him only by accident. She then asks leave to depart. She will remain silent until the city is burning, and then only will she speak.

At the end of the speech Coriolanus "holds her by the hand, silent," according to a stage direction that sounds like Shakespeare's own. Then he speaks, claiming that the gods must be laughing at this unnatural scene of a mother pleading with her son. He congratulates her on having won a happy victory for Rome, but he foresees that it will be fatal for him. The course she has set him on can only lead to his death. But with a sudden shift, Coriolanus is again the soldier. Death is inevitable, and so he turns to Aufidius and says that though he cannot make good wars, at least he can make a suitable peace. Then, almost as if asking for support, he asks Aufidius if he would not have done the same thing, to which Aufidius replies grudgingly, "I was moved withal." Now that he has made a decision Coriolanus is almost jovial, and remarks that it is no small thing to make him weep. He asks Aufidius to decide the terms that he, Coriolanus, should make with Rome. Then he sends his family and Valeria back to Rome, saying that he will not return with them, but asking their support in the whole business.

Aufidius in an aside hints at what will happen and also sums up the nature of Coriolanus' dilemma. Mercy and honor are now opposed within his rival so that out of this conflict and the resultant decision Aufidius will be able to restore his own power.

Coriolanus finally dismisses the women and says that they deserve to have a temple built in their honor. No one else in all Italy could have arranged this peace.

Act V: Scenes 4-5

The scene now turns to a public place in Rome, where the pessimistic Menenius speaks as though the ladies' mission to Coriolanus is a hopeless gesture. Caius Marcius has grown from a man to a dragon.

Sicinius objects that Coriolanus had always loved his mother dearly, but Menenius says that will be irrelevant. Coriolanus is nothing more than a hard, tough, efficient fighting machine, totally without mercy. Sicinius utters a brief prayer to the gods, but Menenius says that he doesn't expect help from that quarter, since in banishing Coriolanus Rome had no thought of the gods.

A messenger then bursts in, telling Sicinius to flee immediately because the plebeians have offered violence to Brutus, swearing that they will kill him by inches if the Roman women are not successful.

The first messenger is immediately followed by another announcing that the ladies have been successful, the Volscians have retired, and Caius Marcius has left. Immediately rejoicing breaks out and music sounds. Menenius sets off to meet the women, saying that Volumnia is worth the entire city, including such tribunes as Brutus and Sicinius, who is lucky to have saved his wretched neck. Sicinius offers thanks to the messenger and all withdraw.

Straight away a procession of senators and lords enters, bringing with it the Roman women. The senators call for cheers. Another senator then calls for a shout of welcome to Coriolanus' mother to repeal the sentence of banishment on her son.

Act V: Scene 6

This scene returns to Antium, where Tullus Aufidius enters with some attendants.

Aufidius sends a package by his attendants to the lords of the city of Antium. Obviously it is a letter of accusation against Coriolanus, and Aufidius says that he will vouch for its truth in public. Coriolanus, in the meantime, has entered the city gates and intends to absolve himself of blame with words.

Three or four conspirators who support Aufidius now enter, and a guarded conversation takes place. One of the conspirators offers to deliver Aufidius from the danger they had formerly discussed, if he still has the same purpose. Aufidius says they will have to wait until they see the behavior of the people, and the conspirator remarks that the people will always remain uncertain while there's a difference of opinion about the two (Coriolanus' name is not mentioned, but it is obviously implied), but the fall of either one will leave the other in sole command. Aufidius then proceeds to a recital of his own grievances, claiming that he has endured enough to justify his hostility. After all, he raised Caius Marcius to be a commander in the Volscian army, and pledged his own honor for his trustworthiness, only to have his protege flatter his way into new friendships. Again, the vaguest language is used: "He watered his new plants with dews of flattery." He alienated Aufidius' friends from him, and even bent his previously unbowed head for that purpose. The conspirator recalls that Coriolanus had been notably stiffnecked in Rome.

Aufidius goes on to detail the ways in which he befriended Coriolanus, making him equal with himself, giving him his own way in everything, even allowing him to choose the best men from his own troop, and in return his men seem to have considered the glory of the expedition to be solely that of Coriolanus. Finally, Aufidius has been repaid by arrogant treatment, for Coriolanus has chosen to patronize where he should have given respect. The First Conspirator says that the entire army has wondered at Aufidius' patience. But the last straw for Aufidius was the way in which he sold a perfect chance to sack Rome for the tears of a few women. Aufidius therefore vows that Coriolanus shall die, and he will regain his own lost power with the fall of his enemy.

The conspirators feed Aufidius' anger by telling him of the jubilant reception Coriolanus has received from the people while Aufidius, their legitimate leader, entered his own town unnoticed. The Second Conspirator speaks of the stupidity of the crowd, who shout for the man who caused such slaughter among their children. The Third Conspirator therefore advises Aufidius to seize the advantage before Coriolanus has the chance to open his mouth to move the people with speech. Then, since the only version known will be that of Aufidius, anything in favor of Coriolanus will be buried with him.

The lords of the city enter at that point to welcome Aufidius, at the same time regretting to hear the charges that he has written against Coriolanus. The earlier faults might have been punished with small fines, but the unpardonable offence was to give up just where he should have begun (with Rome, in other words), not returning by way of spoil the expenses of the expedition. Making a treaty where he could have made a victory is not to be condoned.

Coriolanus now enters with drum and flags, followed by the people. He tries to put a good face on things, saying that he has returned a loyal soldier of the Volscians, still uninfected by love of country. He speaks of leading an army to the very gates of Rome and says that he has managed to defray one third of the expedition's expenses with captured booty. Then he offers the argument that the peace with Rome brings as much honor to the people of Antium as humiliation to the Romans, and with a flourish produces the agreement, signed and sealed by the Roman authorities.

Aufidius then calls on the lords, telling them not to read the agreement, but instead to tell the traitor that he has abused the powers granted to him. Coriolanus immediately picks on the word traitor and asks what is meant. Aufidius makes the application quite specific with "Ay, traitor, Marcius." Coriolanus picks up the name Marcius questioningly, and Aufidius asks if he expects to hear his "stol'n name / Coriolanus in Corioles."

Aufidius then flings the principal charge at Coriolanus: he has traitorously betrayed the cause and given up the city of Rome for a few tears from his wife and his mother. He makes great emotional play with the words "your city" of Rome, impressing the fact on the Volscians that the city was so nearly theirs. Enraged, Caius Marcius invokes Mars, but Aufidius tells him not to call on the god of war, "Thou boy of tears."

This insult from the slightly older man infuriates Coriolanus, as Aufidius had intended, and so he sallies forth to attack the Volscian with words, calling him a slave, and claiming in the vernacular of the duel that he will give him, "this cur," the lie. He impugns the courage and military prowess of Aufidius and recalls his own military superiority to him. One of the lords tries to get in a word, but Coriolanus is now in full cry and shouts defiance at the entire assemblage of Volscians, daring them to cut him to pieces. He repeats Aufidius' insult of "boy," and calls him in reply a "false hound," taunting him and the company with his own superlative exploits right inside their own town of Corioles.

Aufidius makes the most of the situation, claiming that Coriolanus had merely been lucky in Corioles, and anyway, why should the Volscians listen to such a braggart who tries to shame them. The conspirators call for his death, and the expectedly fickle multitude join in the cry, now remembering the slaughter that Caius Marcius had wrought on the Volscian forces in earlier wars. But even here there is a man of moderation, a lord who calls for peace, saying that Coriolanus is a noble man and justly famous throughout the entire earth. He deserves a fair trial, and therefore the lord orders Aufidius to stand firm and not trouble the peace. Coriolanus, however, is in a blind rage after his military prowess has been insulted, and he offers to fight six Aufidiuses at once. This last insult gives Aufidius his chance, and all the conspirators call "Kill." They draw and kill Caius Marcius who falls to the ground dead. Aufidius stands on his corpse to use it as a platform in defense of his action.

The lords are horrified at what has happened and tell Aufidius not to tread on Coriolanus. Aufidius is quite surprised at the hostility the killing has caused and finds himself forced to justify his action. He claims that Coriolanus was a danger to the state, and offers to defend his conduct before the Senate, or else endure the censure of the lords.

The First Lord then orders that the body of Coriolanus be removed and decrees that the city will mourn for him as the noblest corpse that ever a herald followed to his burial urn.

In extenuation of Aufidius' conduct, another lord draws attention to Coriolanus' own impatience and insulting anger, contributing factors which ought to lift some of the blame from Aufidius.

Then Aufidius pronounces what is in effect an epic funeral oration over the body of the hero, his former enemy. He says he is "struck with sorrow," and we should probably believe him. He then asks three of the highest ranking soldiers to take up the body and bear it from the place with the sound of the drum and with the trailing pike customary for the funeral of a great soldier. Despite the slaughter that Coriolanus caused among the young men of the Volsces, he will nevertheless be given a noble memory.

Hamlet

CLAUDIUS, *King of Denmark.*
HAMLET, *son to the late King Hamlet, and nephew to the present King.*
POLONIUS, *Lord Chamberlain.*
HORATIO, *friend to Hamlet.*
LAERTES, *son to Polonius.*
VOLTIMAND
CORNELIUS
ROSENCRANTZ
GUILDENSTERN } *courtiers.*
OSRIC
GENTLEMAN
PRIEST, *or* DOCTOR OF DIVINITY.
MARCELLUS
BERNARDO } *officers.*
FRANCISCO, *a soldier.*
REYNALDO, *servant to Polonius.*
PLAYERS.
Two CLOWNS, *grave-diggers.*
FORTINBRAS, *Prince of Norway.*
CAPTAIN.
ENGLISH AMBASSADORS.

GERTRUDE, *Queen of Denmark, and mother to Hamlet.*
OPHELIA, *daughter to Polonius.*

LORDS, LADIES, OFFICERS, SOLDIERS, SAILORS, MESSENGERS, *and other* ATTENDANTS.
GHOST *of Hamlet's father.*

Hamlet

Act I: Scene 1

The play opens at a sentry post before the castle of Elsinore, Denmark, during legendary times. It is midnight and Francisco, a sentry, is at his post awaiting his relief. Bernardo enters and asks, "Who's there?" But Francisco challenges him for the password, saying, "Nay, answer me; stand, and unfold yourself."

Horatio and Marcellus, who are to share Bernardo's sentry duty this evening, now enter. Horatio is not a regular sentry but has been especially asked by Marcellus to spend this watch with them because of something unusual which has occurred on the two previous nights for which they wish his opinion and help. When Bernardo greets Horatio with the question whether it really is he, Horatio replies, "A piece of him." Marcellus now tells Bernardo that Horatio has rejected their story as "fantasy" and will not allow himself to believe it.

Marcellus proceeds to explain the "dreaded sight" that has appeared before them the last two nights, but, before he and Bernardo have half begun their tale, the Ghost enters. Horatio agrees with the two sentries that the Ghost, who is dressed in armor, has a form like that of the dead King Hamlet. Marcellus suggests that, since Horatio is a "scholar," he should be the one to know how to speak to the Ghost. Horatio does this, beginning by asking the Ghost, "What art thou?" and closing with the challenge, "by heaven I charge thee, speak!" But Marcellus notes that "It is offended," and Bernardo that "it stalks away." Now that his own eyes have seen the Ghost, Horatio admits that it is "something more than fantasy" and that it forbodes "some strange eruption to our state," some coming disaster.

Marcellus now asks Horatio whether he knows why there is such a strict watch and why the country is so busy building armaments.

574

Hamlet

Horatio replies that, as they know, the late King Fortinbras of Norway, jealous of the martial conquests of the late Danish King Hamlet, challenged the Danish King to combat, staking all his possessions on the outcome, and that the late Hamlet killed Fortinbras and took over his forfeited lands as had been agreed. Recently, however, young Fortinbras, son of the slain King, had raised an unlawful army with the apparent aim to recover by force of arms the territories his father had lost to the Danes. It is against such a possibility, Horatio thinks, that the present Danish military preparations have been undertaken. Bernardo agrees with this and further suggests that it may be in connection with these wars, with which the late King Hamlet is still so involved, that his Ghost has now been aroused. Horatio is not so sure of this as he is troubled by the remembrance of similar supernatural occurrences before the murder of Julius Caesar: ghosts in the Roman streets, comets, bloody dews, ominous signs in the sun, and a lengthy eclipse of the moon. He suggests that "heaven and earth" are demonstrating a similar "omen" to "feared events" for their own country.

At this point the Ghost re-enters and Horatio, recognizing the danger involved, vows to cross it even if it destroys him. He challenges the Ghost to speak to him, but only on certain conditions. He first proposes "If there be any good thing to be done/That may to thee do ease and grace to me,/Speak to me." The second condition under which Horatio will permit the Ghost to speak to him is if he has some secret knowledge of his country's fate which his country might avoid by being told of it; and the third condition is if the Ghost wishes to reveal the hiding place of any treasure he may have buried. Before the Ghost can answer, however, the cock crows and, as the three characters try vainly with their swords to force the Ghost to stand and answer the questions, the Ghost fades away. Horatio notes that he has often heard that at the cock's warning of the approach of day the "erring spirit" must return "to his confine" and that the present disappearance of the Ghost seems to confirm the truth of this saying. Marcellus agrees, but further notes that there are those who say that at the Christmas season,

> Wherein our Saviour's birth is celebrated,
> The cock crows all night long.
> And then, they say, no spirit dare stir abroad,
> The nights are wholesome, then no planets strike,
> No fairy takes, nor witch hath power to charm.
> So hallowed and so gracious is that time.

As it is now morning, Horatio suggests that they break up their watch and go to Hamlet to tell him what they have seen, for he suspects that "This spirit, dumb to us, will speak to him." Marcellus agrees and they depart from the stage.

Act I: Scene 2

The second scene opens on the following day with the entrance of King Claudius and the important members of his court into a room of state in the castle at Elsinore. Claudius begins the scene with a formal public address to his court which touches on the important matters of state before him.

The first item which Claudius takes up is his hasty marriage to his brother's widow, Queen Gertrude. He explains that, as she has an equal right to the throne and as his own desires also favored her, he has married her even though it is less than two months since the death of her husband and his brother, the late King Hamlet. He admits that it might have ben more fitting for him and the whole kingdom to remain in mourning for the late King rather than to celebrate a marriage, but he states that he has only proceeded in this matter because his chief counselors of state had freely advised him to do so, for, which he thanks them.

The second item of state, and the real reason for this meeting, is concerned with the activities of young Fortinbras, of which we have already learned something in the first scene. We are now told that Fortinbras, believing Denmark to be disorganized and weak as a result of the death of King Hamlet, had sent several messages to Claudius demanding the surrender of the lands lost by his father. Claudius' response is to send an envoy to the King of Norway, the uncle of young Fortinbras, who, old and bedridden, has scarcely heard of the unlawful activities of his nephew. In the letter he is sending to the King of Norway, Claudius demands that he suppress the unlawful activities of his nephew, further suggesting that the cost of rearming Norway is all coming out of the King of Norway's own revenues and that he had better look into this matter. Claudius now dispatches Cornelius and Voltemand to carry this letter to the King of Norway as quickly as possible.

The third item is the personal request of Laertes, son of the Lord Chamberlain, Polonius, to be permitted to return to Paris, from which he had come to attend Claudius' coronation. Before Claudius allows Laertes to make his request, he tells him how willing he is to grant him any request because of the great respect the throne of Denmark holds for his father. Upon learning the nature of the request, he refers the decision to Polonius, who gives his consent to his son's leaving, which is then seconded by Claudius.

Claudius now turns to the last item of business, the desire of his nephew, now step-son, Hamlet, to return to his studies in Wittenberg. But, as Claudius addresses him with the words "my cousin Hamlet, and my son," Hamlet says to himself, "A little more than kin, and less than kind!"

Claudius now asks Hamlet how it is that he is still in such a downcast state of mourning, and Hamlet quickly retorts that his mourning is not sufficient. His mother begs him to put off his mourning attire and gloom and look with more friendliness upon Claudius, to seek in him rather than in the dust for his father, and, finally, to accept the fact of his natural father's death since he knows " 'tis common. All that lives must die." Hamlet agrees: "Ay madam, it is common." Gertrude next asks why it then "seems" so special to him, not understanding that the very commonness of death may increase rather than diminish Hamlet's despair. Hamlet picks up her innocent use of the word "seems" to disclaim any such false appearance: "Seems, madam? Nay, it is. I know not 'seems'." His full mourning is not simply an outward show which a man might play since his inner feelings go beyond all such external appearances: "I have that within which passeth show." Claudius says that it is good for a son to give such mourning duties to his father as long as it is held to some prescribed term but that to continue beyond such a time is impious and unmanly; "It shows a will most incorrect to heaven" since it stubbornly refuses to accept the will of heaven. Claudius begs Hamlet to put aside his mourning, to think of him as his father for he does feel towards Hamlet as a father, and to make him happy by remaining beside him in Denmark rather than returning to Wittenberg. The Queen seconds this desire on her own account and Hamlet replies that he will obey her. Claudius is so delighted with this unforced reply that he vows to spend the evening toasting Hamlet's apparent reconciliation with him. With this, the formal audience is over and the King and court depart from the stage, leaving Hamlet alone.

We have now arrived at Hamlet's first "soliloquy," a term for the Elizabethan stage convention which permits a character to speak directly to the audience his inner, silent thoughts. Hamlet begins with the anguished wish that his "solid" (some scholars, following Kittredge, would substitute "sullied" here as the word Shakespeare originally intended) "flesh would melt" away by itself. Since this cannot be, he wishes that God had not given a direct law forbidding suicide. He continues with an anguished general cry against the will of heaven: "O God, God, / How weary, stale, flat, and unprofitable / Seem to me all the uses of this world!" He is led to this cry of despair by his recent recognition that justice does not rule the world, that "things rank and gross in nature possess it merely." The world appears to him in this light because his "excellent" father has died and Claudius, so far inferior to his father, has succeeded to his place, not only to his father's throne but also to his wife. But it is his mother's behavior which has most disillusioned him. His father had been "so loving" and gentle to his mother and she had seemed to return his affection, "would hang on him" as if the more she was with him the more her "appetite" for him would grow. (Note that Hamlet expresses his father's feelings for his mother as "love" but his mother's feelings for his father as "appetite," a sign of his new awareness of the "grossness" of nature in general and of his mother in particular.) Not only that, she had seemed genuinely overcome by grief at his father's funeral. "And yet within a month" she had married. The thought is so horrifying to him that he tries to close it out from his mind, "Let me not think on't," for as soon as he does think of it he must condemn his mother and, with her, all women: "frailty, thy name is woman." (The fact that the happy marriage of his parents, in which he had believed all of his life, now seems to have been a delusion—that his mother could not have loved his father as much as she appeared to since she now acts the same way with another man, and that man her brother-in-law—shows Hamlet that he did not know the true nature of the person closest to him, his mother, and that, if he cannot even trust his own mother, there is no one he may trust. In the past two months, then, two terrible facts of human existence have been brought personally home to him through his loved ones: the fact of death and the fact of human imperfection and falseness, and these have so disillusioned him with the value of life that he has sunk completely into a suicidal state of mind.) He is particularly heartbroken over the behavior of his mother and over the fact that there is nothing he can do about it: "It is not, nor it cannot come to good./But break my heart, for I must hold my tongue."

At this point Horatio enters with Marcellus and Bernardo. Hamlet quickly rouses himself from his suicidal reflections and is delighted to see Horatio, a fellow student of his at the University of Wittenberg whom he holds in high respect. Asked what he is doing in Elsinore, Horatio, who for some unexplained reason has not previously greeted Hamlet, replies that "I came to see your father's funeral." Hamlet ironically returns: "do not mock me fellow student./I think it was to see my mother's wedding." When Horatio agrees that it followed quickly upon the funeral, Hamlet replies with further satiric bite: "Thrift, thrift, Horatio The funeral baked meats/Did coldly furnish forth the marriage tables." And then he more seriously expresses his displeasure.

Horatio now tells Hamlet that a ghost with the appearance of his father has three times appeared before the midnight sentries at their guard post and that he had been present at the last visitation. Hamlet questions Horatio minutely as to the appearance of the spirit and, convinced of its similarity to his father, resolves to appear at the watch that night. He vows: "If it assume my noble father's person,/I'll speak to it though hell itself should gape."

Hamlet asks the guards to tell no one of the appearance of the ghost, saying that he will reward them for their silence, and, appointing a meeting for that night, bids them farewell. They leave and, alone, Hamlet expresses his suspicion that there has been "some foul play," a reechoing of his earlier, half thought suspicion.

Act I: Scene 3

The scene is set in Polonius' rooms within the castle at Elsinore later that day. Laertes is about to leave for Paris and is bidding his sister, Ophelia, farewell. In a long speech, he warns her not to trust Hamlet's intentions towards her and to protect her chastity, for even though Hamlet may say he loves her and perhaps now does, he cannot marry as he wishes since he is of royal birth and is thus far above her. She answers that she will follow his advice but that he should not simply preach strictness to her and then act like a libertine himself. At this point Polonius enters surprised that Laertes is still there since the wind is up and he is waited for at the boat. He hurries him to go, gives him his blessing, and then delays his departure with moral commonplaces: he should be discreet in words and action; devote himself to true friends rather than every new acquaintance; avoid quarrels but, once involved, bear himself strongly; listen to all but reserve his true thoughts only to a few; accept other men's criticism but refrain from criticizing others; dress with an elegance that is not gaudy, for appearance is often used as a guide to the nature of a man; neither borrow nor lend; "This above all, to thine own self be true,/And it must follow as the night the day/Thou canst not then be false to any man."

Laertes now leaves, bidding Ophelia to "remember well what I have said to you." Polonius questions Ophelia as to what this is and is told that it concerns Hamlet. This reminds Polonius that he has been told of the meetings between Hamlet and Ophelia and asks her what there is between them. To her reply that Hamlet has recently given her many signs of his "affection", Polonius expresses disgust: "Affection? Pooh!" He tells her that she is just an innocent girl if she believes Hamlet's intentions. When she says that he has spoken to her of "love in honorable fashion," Polonius says that this is just a trap to seduce her. To protect his daughter's honor and his own, he tells her first that she should not see Hamlet so often, in fact, should play harder to get. But as he continues to explain the ways of men to his innocent daughter, he becomes more and more convinced of her danger until he suddenly decides that she must not see him again and so commands her. She is an obedient daughter and agrees to obey him, at which they leave the stage.

Act I: Scenes 4-5

Hamlet, Horatio and Marcellus enter the platform before the castle where the sentry post is situated. It is midnight, as they note, and some trumpets are heard to sound. Horatio asks Hamlet what it means and Hamlet replies that the King and court are spending the evening drinking and that every time Claudius makes a toast, the trumpets and drums sound. Horatio asks whether this is a Danish custom and Hamlet says that it is, but that though he is a native here "and to the manner born," he thinks it better not to keep this time-honored custom which has given Denmark a reputation for drunkenness among other nations.

Hamlet continues that, just as Denmark's positive achievements are overshadowed by its reputation for drunkenness, so it can happen in the case of particular men. A personality defect with which they are born, and for which they cannot be held guilty, may so develop that it leads to irrational behavior, or a habit may similarly overcome the control of their reason. Then such men, carrying "the stamp of one defect," though they have all other virtues, will come under general condemnation for this one fault.

At this point the Ghost enters. Hamlet calls upon the angels to defend him and then addresses the Ghost. He says that whether he is an angel come from heaven with charitable intent, or a damned spirit come from hell with wicked intent (the only two possibilities he considers), the question is so uncertain that he will speak to him

Hamlet

as though he were the true spirit of his father. He asks him why he has returned from death, but the Ghost, rather than answer him, silently beckons Hamlet to follow him. Horatio and Marcellus advise Hamlet not to follow the Ghost, but Hamlet says he has nothing to fear since "I do not set my life at a pin's fee." Horatio says that the ghost might tempt him to the edge of the cliff, drive him mad, and then cause him to commit suicide (possibilities which might follow if the Ghost were a devil). But Hamlet answers, "My fate cries out," and, breaking away from Horatio and Marcellus who are now physically holding him back, he follows the Ghost to another part of the platform, leaving the stage. Though Marcellus now says, "Something is rotten in the state of Denmark," Horatio hopes the coming of the Ghost may have a blessed effect. He says, "Heaven will direct it." In any case, they decide it is not fit to leave Hamlet alone and follow him.

The fifth scene begins with the entrance of the Ghost on another part of the platform. Hamlet follows but then tells the Ghost to stop and speak because he will follow him no further. The Ghost turns and now finally reveals that he is the true spirit of Hamlet's father, doomed for a certain term to purgatory; he has returned to earth to tell Hamlet that if he ever loved his father he should "Revenge his foul and most unnatural murder."

Upon learning of his father's murder, Hamlet is anxious to learn the name of his murderer that he may be "swift" in his revenge. But when the Ghost reveals that the murderer is Claudius, Hamlet exclaims, "O my prophetic soul!" (This indicates that Hamlet had dimly suspected as much, as was earlier shown.) The Ghost now reveals something else, that Claudius had seduced his "most seeming-virtuous queen" to "shameful lust" before his death. And the Ghost agrees with Hamlet as to the relative merits of Claudius and himself when he says: "O Hamlet, what a falling-off was there." Though he considers Claudius "a wretch whose natural gifts were poor to those of mine," he also understands that lust will leave "a radiant angel" to "prey on garbage." He then explains how he was killed, that he was sleeping in his orchard in the afternoon when Claudius poured poison in his ear which quickly killed him. "Most horrible" of all, Claudius' murder deprived him of the opportunity of confession and of the Sacraments before death. He now tells Hamlet that if he has any natural feeling for his father he should not allow his murderer to live and, what is even worse, turn his royal bed into a couch for incestuous lust. Whatever he does, however, he should not "taint" his mind by even contemplating anything against his mother but "leave her to heaven" and to her own conscience. As morning is coming, he bids Hamlet a quick farewell with the words, "remember me."

Hamlet's immediate response is to call for help upon all the host of heaven and the earth, and then he has the terrible suspicion that perhaps he had better also call upon the help of hell in remembering his father. But he immediately rejects this suspicion that the Ghost may come from hell; "And shall I couple hell? O fie!" Taking hold of himself, he vows to wipe everything from the tablet of his memory except his father's commandment to revenge his murder. But as he thinks of his evil mother and still more of Claudius, a "villain, villain, smiling, damned villain," he suddenly begins to lose control of his reason. He feels he has discovered a wonderful truth that he must write down in the notebook he carries with him to record memorable sayings, and he writes "that one may smile, and smile, and be a villain." Such a statement is, of course, neither a brilliant discovery nor an especially well phrased observation and so would not normally be written down. But that Hamlet is not in a normal frame of mind is immediately shown when he responds to his friends' calling to him with a falconer's cry used for summoning his hawk: "Hillo, ho, ho, boy! Come, bird, come." They ask him for his news and, after pledging them to secrecy, reveals that any "villain dwelling in all Denmark" is a thorough "knave" or scoundrel. To this Horatio well responds: "There needs no ghost, my lord, come from the grave to tell us this." Hamlet agrees and somewhat hysterically says that they should part, the others to their business and he to pray. Horatio notes: "These are but wild and whirling words, my lord," again indicating that Hamlet is not in a rational state.

Hamlet collects himself for a moment and tells them that "it is an honest ghost," that is, the true spirit of his father rather than a devil who has assumed his form, but that he cannot tell them what they said to each other. He now asks them once again to swear that they will never reveal what they have seen tonight, but they feel insulted that Hamlet should ask them again what they have already promised him. Hamlet continues that he wants them now to formally swear to this upon his sword and, as they continue to hesitate, the ghost cries from under the stage, "swear." This once again unsettles Hamlet's reason and he becomes hysterical, saying to the ghost: "Ha, ha, boy, say'st thou so? Art thou there, true-penny." He tells them to swear as they "hear this fellow in the cellarage." They shift ground but the Ghost continues to follow them under the stage, repeatedly telling them to "swear by his sword." At this point Hamlet exclaims to the Ghost: "Well said, old mole! Canst work i' th' earth so fast? O worthy pioner!"

Hamlet once more returns to rationality, but his unsettling experience with the supernatural causes him to tell Horatio: "There are more things in heaven and earth, Horatio, / Than are dreamt of in your philosophy." Though the supernatural appears mysterious to Hamlet, his experience with it causes him to grant it a validity which Horatio's earlier scepticism would have denied. He now tells them that they should be careful not to give any indication, whether by look or word, that they know anything about this night as he may later think it necessary "to put an antic disposition on," that is, to act as though he were insane.

Horatio and Marcellus now formally swear to keep Hamlet's two secrets, the meeting with the Ghost and Hamlet's assumed madness, and they now prepare to part. Before leaving, however, Hamlet says, "The time is out of joint. O cursed spite / That ever I was born to set it right!"

Act II: Scene 1

We are once again in the rooms of Polonius, and Polonius is seen sending off his servant, Reynaldo, to Paris with money and letters for his son, Laertes. He tells Reynaldo that he should inquire about the behavior of Laertes before he visits him. Reynaldo, who seems to know his master's ways very well, tells Polonius that he had already intended to do this and is well praised for this in turn. Polonius now instructs him in some of the refinements of spying. He is to find some Danish acquaintances of Laertes and casually bring up the subject of Laertes. He is then to suggest that Laertes is a libertine, that he gambles, duels, swears and goes to brothels. Reynaldo objects that this would dishonor Laertes, but Polonius explains that this will draw out, either by agreement or denial, the truth about Laertes' behavior as it has been seen by these other Danes. In the middle of this explanation, Polonius forgets what he wants to say and has to be reminded of what he had just said by Reynaldo. Polonius then concludes with a generalization about his tactics, that it is wisdom to be devious in approaching one's target for one can best "by indirections find directions out." Satisfied that Reynaldo has learned his lesson, Polonius bids him goodbye but with a final order to make sure that Laertes is keeping up his musical studies.

Ophelia now enters in a very frightened condition. She explains that, as she was sewing alone in her room, Hamlet had entered in a very disordered state, his jacket unlaced, without a hat, his stockings dirty and hanging down ungartered to his ankles, his knees knocking together, "And with a look so piteous in purport / As if he had been loosèd out of hell / To speak of horrors." He had taken hold of her wrist and held her hard at arm's length with one hand while his other hand was held over his brow. Staying a long time in this position, he observed her face with the intense concentration of one who would draw it. At last, shaking her arm a little and nodding to himself three times in silent agreement with something, he made such a pitiful and deep sigh that it seemed capable of ending his life. He then let her go and went out of the room, but as he left his head was turned over his shoulder and he continued to stare at her until he was out of the door.

Polonius decides that Hamlet is suffering from frustrated love and, forgetful once more, asks Ophelia whether she has quarrelled with him. She replies: "No, my good lord; but as you did command / I did repel his letters and denied / His access to me." Polonius, having forgotten all about his hasty command, now concludes that this is the source of Hamlet's madness. He now makes an unusual admission about his own character; he admits that she showed poor judgement with regards to Hamlet's intentions but excuses this on the grounds of old age: "By heaven, it is as proper to our age / To cast beyond ourselves in our opinions / As it is common for the younger sort / To lack discretion." Old age, he says, is given to authoritarian presumption of its wisdom while having lost the power of true judgement. He now decides to take Ophelia to the King with this discovery as to the source of Hamlet's madness.

Act II: Scene 2

The scene shifts to a room in the castle where Claudius and Gertrude are greeting Rosencrantz and Guildenstern. These gentlemen are boyhood friends of Hamlet whom Claudius has recalled to Denmark in the hope that they may be able to help him investigate the nature of Hamlet's increasing mental disorder. His "transformation," earlier described by Ophelia, seems to Claudius to have resulted from more than simply his father's death, and he hopes that by discovering the reason for this these friends may help him to restore Hamlet's health. The Queen seconds this with the promise of an ample reward, and they agree to help the King.

Polonius enters with the news of the return of the ambassadors to Norway. He then says: "And I do think—or else this brain of mine / Hunts not the trail of policy so sure / As it hath used to do —that I have found / The very cause of Hamlet's lunacy." (If

Hamlet

Polonius was forced in the last scene to admit that his lack of judgment was a symptom of old age, he now hopes to dispel any similar doubt that Claudius may have about his continuing usefulness.) Claudius is more anxious to hear of this than of the results of his ambassadors: "O, speak of that! That do I long to hear." But Polonius asks that the ambassadors be attended to first and Claudius agrees. While Polonius goes to bring in the ambassadors, Claudius tells his "dear Gertrude" that Polonius thinks he has discovered the source of her son's disorder, but she is convinced that she already knows the reason: "I doubt it is no other but the main / His father's death and our o'er-hasty marriage."

Voltemand now enters with the news of his successful mission to Norway; the King of Norway, upon investigating Fortinbras' activities, had found Claudius to be correct and, very grieved by this, had restrained his nephew from attacking Denmark. He has, however, decided to deploy Fortinbras and the force he has raised against Poland, and now asks Claudius' permission for the safe passage of these troops through Denmark on their way to Poland. Claudius' immediate reaction to this is positive but he is far too impatient to hear Polonius' theory about Hamlet to give his full attention to this matter now. Telling the ambassadors that they will feast together at night, he bids them retire now and turns to Polonius.

Although saying that "brevity is the soul of wit," Polonius is so long-winded about getting to the point that the Queen finally interrupts him with the words, "more matter, with less art." But Polonius continues awhile with comically pretentious rhetoric until he finally gets to the point: his daughter has obediently given him a love letter to her from Hamlet. He now proceeds to read this letter which almost rivals his own comic speeches in its over-wrought, conventional love melancholy. Claudius, satisfied with Hamlet's love for Ophelia, asks Polonius how she has received his love, and he replies his duty towards the King led him to tell his daughter that, as the Prince was so far above her, "she should lock herself from his resort, / Admit no messengers, receive no tokens." She had done this and the result of this rejection of his love, Polonius concludes, has led to Hamlet's progressive madness. Claudius asks Gertrude whether she thinks this is the reason, and she replies, "It may be, very like." Polonius claims that his advice has always been correct and that they should behead him "if this be otherwise."

Claudius now asks him what they might do to further investigate his theory and Polonius suggests a plan with which he had evidently come prepared. He says that there is a spot near where they are standing where Hamlet often walks for four hours at a time. "At such a time I'll loose my daughter to him," he suggests, while the King and he observe from behind a hanging tapestry the nature of their encounter. If this does not prove his case, he concludes, "Let me be no assistant for a state / But keep a farm and carters." The King agrees to try Polonius' plan, whereupon Hamlet enters.

The Queen notes how "sadly the poor wretch comes reading," and Polonius begs them to leave him alone with Hamlet. He tries to make conversation with Hamlet but Hamlet counters everything he says with apparently mad but actually quite satiric thrusts. He calls Polonius a "fishmonger," which also meant a pimp, and tells him that he had better not let his daughter walk in the sun as she may conceive spontaneously like maggots.

Polonius, further convinced by this that Hamlet's madness has resulted from his disappointed love, now asks him what he is reading. After bandying about with this for a while, Hamlet finally says that he is reading slanders against old age by a "satirical rogue" who says that "old men have grey beards, that their faces are wrinkled" and "that they have a plentiful lack of wit, together with most weak hams," all of which, though he agrees with it, he does not think it decent to write down since Polonius, himself, is old. At this Polonius silently comments, "Though this be madness, yet there is method in't." After a few more lines in which Hamlet shows a disconcerting wit, Polonius decides to leave and says, "I will most humbly take my leave of you." Hamlet begins to return this satirically but then his mood abruptly changes: "You cannot, sir, take from me anything that I will more willingly part withal— except my life, except my life, except my life." After Polonius starts to leave, Hamlet expresses his final disgust with Polonius: "These tedious old fools!"

Rosencrantz and Guildenstern now enter and are happily greeted by Hamlet as "My excellent good friends!" After some introductory kidding with them about the state of their fortune, he asks them what they have done to deserve being sent here to "prison." When they question Hamlet's reference to Denmark as a prison, he replies: "Why, then 'tis none to you, for there is nothing either good or bad but thinking makes it so. To me it is a prison." Seizing this opportunity to begin their investigation, they suggest, "Why, then your ambition makes it one." After arguing this point, he asks them again, in the "way of friendship," what they are doing at Elsinore. They reply that they have come simply to visit him. Hamlet thanks them for this but then immediately asks whether it is a free visit or whether they were sent for by the King and Queen. They hesitate to answer him; he asks them again; and, as they finally confer on an answer, Hamlet says to himself, "Nay then, I have an eye of you." They finally do admit, "My lord, we were sent for," but it is too late—Hamlet's trust has been alienated. In one of the most beautiful speeches in the play, Hamlet now explains to them why they were sent for: "I have of late—but wherefore I know not—lost all my mirth." In his depressed state the good earth seems to him "a sterile promontory," the majestic heavens appear "nothing to him but a foul and pestilent congregation of vapors," man, himself, with his noble reason, infinite faculties and beauty, seems to him the "quintessence of dust."

Rosencrantz and Guildenstern now tell Hamlet of the coming of a company of actors and there is some discussion between them of acting companies which reflects the conditions in the Elizabethan theatre at the time, Before the players enter, however, Hamlet tells Rosencrantz and Guildenstern that they are welcome to Elsinore. More than this, he also tells them that Claudius and Gertrude are deceived about his madness, that he is only mad when he feels like it and can otherwise be perfectly sane, as indeed has been shown in this scene with them.

Polonius now enters with the players. He introduces them with comical pretentiousness which leads Hamlet once again to make fun of him in the role of madman. Hamlet now welcomes the players and asks them as a proof of their quality to recite a speech from one of their plays about the death of Priam, the old King of Troy, which he begins. Hamlet's delivery is praised by Polonius and then the player continues: Pyrrhus drives at Priam but "in rage strikes wide." Nonetheless, Priam, the "unnerved father," falls from the wind of Pyrrhus' sword. Instead of killing him then, however, "his sword, / Which was declining on the milky head / Of reverend Priam, seemed i' the' air to stick" and, against his own will, "did nothing." Finally however, "aroused vengeance sets him new awork" and never did blows fall like those now on Priam. He now continues with an impassioned speech on Hecuba's grief over the death of her husband, Priam. Hamlet is delighted with the player's recitation and asks him whether the company could play "The Murder of Gonzago" that night with an insertion of a speech of "some dozen or sixteen lines" which he would write himself. The player agrees to do this and Hamlet tells Polonius to see that they are well looked after, upon which they all depart, leaving Hamlet alone.

We now come to Hamlet's second soliloquy. Hamlet begins with the exclamation: "O, what a rogue and peasant slave am I!" It seems monstrous to him that the player could so work himself up "for nothing, / For Hecuba! / What's Hecuba to him, or he to Hecuba, / That he should weep for her?" He wonders "what would he do /· Had he the motive and the cue for passion / That I have?" Though the player, with such real motivation would "make mad the guilty," he, "a dull and muddy-mettled rascal," moans about in a dream without any real feeling for his cause and "can say nothing," no, not even for a dear King who was cursedly murdered. He then asks himself whether he is a "coward." At first he is horrified by such a humiliating suggestion, but then he concedes that it must be so, that "I am pigeon-livered and lack gall / To make oppression bitter" since he has not yet fattened the vultures with Claudius' guts. He then tries to work up a passion against Claudius by yelling: "Bloody, bawdy villain! Remorseless, treacherous, lecherous, kindless villain! / O, vengeance!" But then he immediately realizes, "Why, what an ass am I!" This is some bravery, that the son of a dear murdered father, "prompted to my revenge by heaven and hell," must release the feelings of his heart simply with words rather than with action.

He now finally puts his brains to work upon the revenge. He remembers having heard "that guilty creatures sitting at a play" which represented their own crime have been so struck by guilt that they have confessed their crime. He decides (apparently having already forgotten that he had just instructed the players to do the same thing) that he will "have these players / Play something like the murther of my father / Before mine uncle. I'll observe his looks" and if he but flinches "I know my course." This is the first time we have seen Hamlet express any doubt about his course, but the reason he gives is one that he may well have entertained:

> The spirit that I have seen
> May be a devil, and the devil hath power
> T' assume a pleasing shape, yea, and perhaps
> Out of my weakness and my melancholy,
> As he is very potent with such spirits,
> Abuses me to damn me.

He decides that he needs further objective proof of Claudius' guilt and that "The play's the thing / Wherein I'll catch the conscience of the king."

Act III: Scene 1

The scene is set in the room in the castle where the planned encounter of Hamlet and Ophelia is to take place. The King and Queen are present surrounded by Polonius, Ophelia, Rosencrantz, Guildenstern and other lords. Claudius is in the midst of asking Rosencrantz and Guildenstern whether they have discovered anything concerning the cause of Hamlet's madness, but they answer that Hamlet "with a crafty madness" has kept from "confession of his true state." Gertrude asks them how he received them and whether they have been able to interest him in any pastime. They reply that he treated them like a gentleman and was overjoyed by their news of the arrival of a company of players whom he has already ordered to appear this night before him. Polonius says that Hamlet has also asked the King and Queen to attend the performance, and Claudius says that he is happy to hear of Hamlet's new interest and to support it by attendance.

Rosencrantz and Guildenstern now leave and Claudius suggests that Gertrude leave also as he has secretly sent for Hamlet that he may accidentally meet Ophelia. Claudius and Polonius mean to spy on the encounter to test whether Polonius' theory of the source of Hamlet's madness, disappointed love, is correct. Gertrude tells Ophelia that she hopes Ophelia is "the happy cause of Hamlet's madness" and that, if her virtues are able to cure him, there would be a hope for their marriage. As Ophelia seconds her hope, Gertrude leaves. Polonius now instructs Opelia that, while the King and he hide themselves, she is to walk there by herself reading a pious book since this would serve to explain her lonely presence. He now reflects, as well he might, that people are often to blame for covering evil behavior with a show of "pious action." In an "aside" (a speech spoken to the audience and meant to indicate silent thought), Claudius reveals that Polonius' words have stung his conscience, for he too covers his deed with behavior as false as a harlot's painted charms. The maintenance of this falsehood has become so difficult for him that he must cry out, "O heavy burden!"

As Hamlet is now heard approaching, Claudius and Polonius withdraw behind the painted tapestry to watch his encounter with Ophelia.

Hamlet enters so involved with his own thoughts that he does not at first see Ophelia. We now hear the famous "To be or not to be" soliloquy. He begins by questioning which is the "nobler" code of behavior, that which bids one "to be," to live even though this means "to suffer" from "outrageous fortune," or that which bids one "not to be," to commit suicide and thus "end" one's suffering through the act of "opposing" the outrage which fortune would do him. "To die," he reasons, is "to sleep—no more," and by such a sleep it is possible to "end the heartache, and the thousand natural shocks" that human beings inherit in the process of being born. Such an end to human troubles, he concludes is "a consummation devoutly to be wished." "To die," he repeats, is "to sleep," but in sleep, he now remembers, there is also the possibility of dreams and this creates a new difficulty. For when we have cast off the difficulties of life "in that sleep of death," we do not know "what dreams may come," and this must cause us to hesitate before commiting suicide. This is what causes people to endure the "calamity" of a "long life." For who would bear the injuries of existence, the wrongs and humiliations of oppression, "the pangs of despised love," the delay in both law and position which those with merit must patiently bear from the unworthy and insolent people who do receive high office, who would bear the general burdens of "a weary life,

> But that the dread of something after death,
> The undiscovered country, from whose bourn
> [confinement]
> No traveller returns, puzzles the will,
> And makes us rather bear those ills we have
> Than fly to others that we know not of?

This consciousness of the religious problem involved with suicide, the dread of eternal punishment, "does make cowards of us all," and "the pale cast of thought" sickens the power of "resolution," and this not only with regards to suicide but to all great "enterprises," whose force is similarly turned away into inaction through overconsideration. He now sees Ophelia at her prayers and tells her to include in them "all my sins."

The meeting between Hamlet and Ophelia begins politely as Ophelia asks Hamlet how he has been feeling these past days and he replies that he has been feeling well. She then tells him that she has with her some things he had given her which she has long desired to return to him and prays him now to receive them. He denies having given her anything and she, apparently hurt by this, says that she knows very well that he did and with his presents added such sweet words "as made the things more rich." Since this sweetness is now gone, she bids him take back his presents, for "rich gifts wax poor when givers prove unkind." He then laughs out hysterically and asks her whether she is "honest," and again whether she is "fair" (that is, "white" as is the color of purity and virtue). She does not understand what he is driving at and asks him what he means, to which he answers, "That if you be honest and fair, your honesty should admit no discourse to your beauty," that is, if she were truly virtuous, she would not admit anyone to approach her beauty. She takes his verbal quibble in another sense and asks him whether beauty could do better than to go with honesty. He becomes ever more hysterical and says that she is right, for beauty has such power that it can "transform honesty from what it is to a bawd." Though this seems a paradox, it has recently been proven. He then abruptly claims, "I did love you once." She, still hurt though now apparently vindicated, answers, "Indeed, my lord, you made me believe so." To this Hamlet lashes out at her that she should not have believed him since his stock is so sullied that it is incapable of virtue. He now as abruptly claims, "I loved you not," and she even more sadly replies, "I was the more sadly deceived." He then cries out to her in a long, bitter speech: "Get thee to a nunnery. Why wouldest thou be a breeder of sinners? I am myself indifferent honest, but yet I could accuse me of such things that it were better my mother had not borne me: I am very proud, revengeful, ambitious, with more offenses at my beck than I have thoughts to put them in, imagination to give them shape, or time to act them in. What should such fellows as I do crawling between earth and heaven? We are arrant knaves all; believe none of us. Go thy ways to a nunnery." He then abruptly asks her where her father is and, when she replies that he is at home, he says that Polonius should be locked in there "that he may play the fool nowhere but in's own house." He bids her "farewell," but, as she prays to heaven to help him, he continues that if she should marry she can take this curse with her that however chastely she may behave she will still gain a bad reputation. He tells her again to go to a nunnery, says farewell again, and then continues that if she must marry she should marry a fool, "for wise men know well enough what monsters you make of them." He sends her to a nunnery again, says farewell again, and, as she prays again to heaven to restore his sanity, he continues his outburst against her, this time directed against women's cosmetics, "paintings." He charges, "God hath given you one face, and you make yourselves another." As he continues against the seductive movements, tones and nicknaming habits of women, he finally cries out, "Go to, I'll no more on't; it hath made me mad." He demands that there be no more marriages, though, "all but one" of those who are married "shall live." He tells her to go to a nunnery a final time and leaves without another word. Ophelia is left in a state of shocked despair at the behavior of her former lover. In a return to poetry after the prose of the last section, she exclaims, "O, what a noble mind is here o'erthrown!" He who was the ideal courtier, soldier and scholar, the hope of the state, the model of fashion and manners, and of a most noble intelligence, is now completely disordered by madness, while she who received the sweetness of his love is the most wretched of ladies.

Claudius and Polonius now come out from their hiding place each convinced of the truth of his own theory as to Hamlet's condition. Claudius begins by rejecting outright Polonius' theory about love. He also notes that "what he spake, though it lacked form a little, was not like madness." He believes that there is something in Hamlet's soul which is causing him to brood and which will finally "hatch" into some "danger." To prevent this eventuality, Claudius immediately decides to send Hamlet "with speed to England" with the covering excuse that he going to demand of England the tribute it owes to Denmark. He tells Polonius that he hopes the change of surroundings "shall expel this something-settled matter in his heart," and asks Polonius what he thinks of the plan. Polonius agrees to it though he still believes "the origin and commencement of his grief / Sprung from neglected love." He asks Ophelia how she is but immediately turns from her to continue his discussion with Claudius despite his daughter's grief. He now suggests a new spying plan to Claudius, that after the play Gertrude should send for Hamlet and ask him to come alone to her room. She should then ask Hamlet plainly to explain to her what is troubling him. Polonius will himself be hidden in the room to overhear their conference. If Gertrude does not discover the source of his melancholy, then Claudius should send Hamlet to England. Claudius agrees with Polonius' new plan, concluding "Madness in great ones must not unwatched go." They leave and the scene ends.

Act III: Scene 2

Hamlet enters a hall of the castle explaining to the players how they are to perform. They are to pronounce the words easily rather than mouth them broadly; they are not to "saw the air too much" with their hands "but use all gently"; their passion should be controlled and smooth, for it is offensive to hear a "fellow tear a passion to tatters, to very rags, to split the ears of the groundlings, who for the most part are capable of nothing but inexplicable dumb shows and noise." But neither should they be too tame. He tells them to "suit the action to the word, the word to the action, with this special observance, that you o'erstep not the modesty of nature," for the purpose of drama from its origin to the present "was and is, to hold, as 'twere, the mirror up to nature." Though overacting may cause the uneducated to laugh, it "cannot but make the judicious grieve," and one of these outweighs a whole theatre of the others. He has seen actors who "have so strutted and bellowed that I have thought some of Nature's journeymen had made men, and not made them well, they imitated humanity so abominably." This should be completely reformed as well as the license for improvization given to clowns; these should "speak no more than is set down for them" so that they do not obscure "some necessary question of the play" through the laughter of "barren spectators." The players agree and leave to prepare themselves for the performance.

Polonius, Rosencrantz and Guildenstern now enter to tell Hamlet that the King and Qeen will attend the performance, and Hamlet sends them out again to hurry the royal couple.

He now calls Horatio over to him and tells him that he considers him the most just man he has ever met and that, ever since he has been able to distinguish between men, his soul has chosen Horatio to be his truest friend. It is Horatio's Stoicism which most attracts him:

> . . . for thou hast been
> As one in suff'ring all that suffers nothing,
> A man that Fortune's buffets and rewards
> Hast ta'en with equal thanks; and blest are those
> Whose blood and judgement are so well commeddled
> That they are not a pipe for Fortune's finger
> To sound what stop she please.
> Give me that man who is not passion's slave, and
>   I will wear him
> In my heart's core, ay, in my heart of heart,
> As I do thee.

Hamlet reveals that he had earlier confided in Horatio about the circumstances of his father's death. He now continues this by confiding in Horatio his plan about the play soon to be performed. He asks Horatio to help him observe the way Claudius reacts to the part of the play which reenacts his crime and then to compare these observations with his own. He concludes that if Claudius' guilt does not reveal itself under these circumstances then "It is a damned ghost that we have seen, / And my imaginations are as foul / As Vulcan's stithy [smithy]." Horatio agrees and, as the court is now approaching, he tells Horatio to part from him as he must now be "idle." This may refer to the resumption of a madman's role.

The King and court enter with a flourish of trumpets and drums. Claudius asks Hamlet how he is and Hamlet answers somewhat obscurely that he is not satisfied with eating promises (a suggestion of his disappointed ambition), but Claudius says he cannot make sense of what he is saying. Hamlet now turns to Polonius and asks him about his university acting. Polonius says that he once played Julius Caesar and was killed in the Capitol. (This remark serves as a dramatic foreshadowing of Polonius' fate in the next scene.) The players are now ready to appear and Gertrude asks Hamlet to sit by her. He rejects her, however, saying he prefers the more attractive Ophelia. This supports Polonius' theory as he is quick to point out to Claudius. Hamlet now lies at Ophelia's feet but he treats her with no respect, making several lewd sexual puns (particularly one on "country matters" in which a pun is intended on the first syllable of "country"). These, however, seem to escape Ophelia's understanding. She notes simply that he is "merry." Hamlet replies: "O god, your only jig-maker! What should a man do but be merry?" Since God's creation is a farce, man can do nothing better than to laugh. Both of these points are proven by his mother's behavior: "For look you how cheerfully my mother looks, and my father died within's two hours." When Ophelia objects that "'tis twice two months, my lord," Hamlet ironically returns, "O heavens! die two months ago, and not forgotten yet? Then there's hope a great man's memory may outlive his life half a year." (This is the reference to the time lapse between the first and second acts earlier referred to, at which place the significance of Hamlet's slip that it is two rather than four months since his father's death was explained as revealing that for Hamlet time has really stopped since his encounter with the Ghost.)

At this point the players put on the kind of "dumb show" that Hamlet just recently disapproved of in his discussion with them. This "dumb show" silently enacts the plot of the play: a king and queen embrace lovingly; then he lies down in a garden and she leaves. Another man comes in, takes off his crown and kisses it, pours poison in the sleeper's ear and leaves him. The Queen returns to discover that the King is dead, at which she displays passionate grief. The poisoner returns with some others and they try to comfort her. When the body is carried out, the poisoner woos the queen who, after some harshness, accepts his love.

The Player King and Player Queen now enter to begin the play and we are surprised to learn that the major emphasis of the play is not to be on the murder of the King but the infidelity of the Queen. The King begins by remembering how long they have been married and the Queen hopes they may continue married just as long, though she is very worried by his recent sickness. He replies that he shall not live long and hopes that she may find as kind a husband as he has been after he dies. She interrupts him, horrified by such a treasonous thought: "In second husband let me be accurst! / None wed the second but who killed the first." In a long reply, the king says that though she may feel that way now, such purposes "like fruit unripe sticks on the tree, / But fall unshaken when they mellow be." In time many things may change her present purposes, for, he concludes: "Our thoughts are ours, their ends none of our own." Nonetheless the queen now makes a powerful vow that she will never remarry, and Hamlet exclaims: "If she should break it now!" He then asks his mother how she likes the play and Gertrude, perhaps with fellow feeling for woman's frailty, replies: "The lady doth protest too much, me thinks." To Hamlet's more serious charge against her in the play, complicity in the murder, she seems, however, quite innocent.

Claudius, apparently aroused by the connection Hamlet seems to be intimating between the Player Queen and Gertrude, now asks Hamlet whether he knows the plot of the play and whether there is any offense in it. Hamlet answers that there is "no offense i' th' world," and, when asked the play's name, that it is called "The Mousetrap." We remember that he had said, "The play's the thing / Wherein I'll catch the conscience of the king," and he now continues to play his little cat-and-mouse game with Claudius by saying that it is the story of a murder committed in Vienna. He then continues: "'Tis a knavish piece of work, but what o' that? Your majesty, and we have free souls, it touches us not." The Player Murderer now enters and Hamlet announces that it is "Lucianus, nephew to the king." When Ophelia comments that he is as good as a stage narrator of the action, Hamlet turns to her and continues his earlier sexual joking with her. He finally calls to the actor playing Lucianus and tells him to begin. The Player King, having in the meantime gone to sleep, Lucianus approaches him, notes the fitness of all things and carefully describes the properties of the poison he is to use. As he pours the poison in the Player King's ear, Hamlet once again starts to explain the story, but Claudius has already risen very upset, as indicated by Gertrude's concern for him, calls for more light, and quickly leaves the hall followed by all except Hamlet and Horatio.

Hamlet reacts to Claudius' breakdown with hysterical glee. He begins to sing and asks Horatio whether this play would not win him a share in a company of players. Horatio calmly answers that he would only earn "half a share" which Hamlet heartly disputes and then continues to sing. As he ends the verse poorly, Horatio again calmly notes, "You might have rhymed." This finally has the effect of dampening Hamlet's high spirits long enough to discuss Claudius' reaction with Horatio and to conclude, "I'll take the Ghost's word for a thousand pound."

In continued high spirits, Hamlet calls for some music, asking the players to bring in the recorders, simple flute-like instruments. At this point Rosencrantz and Guildenstern enter and desire to talk with him. They tell him that the King is extremely upset and, as Hamlet jokes about this with great gaiety, Guildenstern urges him: "Good my lord, put your discourse into some frame, and start not so wildly from my affair." Hamlet becomes tamer and Guildenstern continues his message, that Hamlet's mother "in most great affliction of spirit" has asked him to come to her room to speak with her before he retires. Hamlet had interrupted this message several times in the telling until even he apologizes that he cannot make "a wholesome answer; my wit's deceased."

Rosencrantz now asks him, in virtue of the love Hamlet formerly had for him, to open his heart to him and tell him the cause of his diseased mind. Hamlet quickly returns the answer Rosencrantz has been fishing for in their earlier meeting: "Sir, I lack advancement." When Rosencrantz asks how that can be since he has "the voice of the King himself for your succession in Denmark," Hamlet replies with half a proverb which obscurely intimates dissatisfaction with a long delay. A player enters with the recorders and Hamlet takes one. He now asks his friends why they are trying to drive him into a snare. Guildenstern objects that it is just the result of excessive love. Hamlet then asks Guildenstern to play the recorder for him. Guildenstern says he is unable to play the instrument. After repeated entreaties, Hamlet finally says: "Why, look you now, how unworthy a thing you make of me! You would play upon me, you would seem to know my stops, you would pluck out the heart of my mystery, you would sound me from my lowest note to the top of my compass; and there is much music, excellent voice, in this little organ, yet cannot you make it speak." Polonius now enters to tell Hamlet again that his mother wishes to speak to him and immediately. Hamlet, however, proceeds to have fun at his expense. He asks Polonius whether he sees a cloud shaped like a camel. When Polonius agrees, Hamlet changes his mind and says he thinks it looks first like a weasel and then like a whale with Polonius agreeing each time. Finally, he tells Polonius that he will come to his mother soon. In an "aside" he says, "They fool me to the top of my bent," and then asks them all to leave him.

Worn out by all the "fooling" with Rosencrantz, Guildenstern and Polonius and committed to visit his mother, Hamlet's mood now changes. Left alone in depressed spirits after his recent hysteria, he notes:

> 'Tis now the very witching time of night,
> When churchyards yawn, and hell itself breathes out
> Contagion to this world. Now could I drink hot blood
> And do such bitter business as the day
> Would quake to look on.

As he is going in this murderous mood to visit his mother, he tells his heart not to lose its natural feelings for her however cruelly he may act: "I will speak daggers to her, but use none." He then exits.

Act III: Scene 3

The King is seen talking to Rosencrantz and Guildenstern in a room of the castle about the danger which Hamlet's madness poses to him. He informs them that he is dispatching them to go with Hamlet to England. Guildenstern says that the danger of regicide represents a "most holy and religious fear" to the very many people who depend upon the King, who "live and feed upon your majesty." Rosencrantz continues that a king is more obligated to protect himself than a private person since the welfare of many lives depend upon him. He compares the death of a king to a whirlpool which draws "what's near it with it," then to a huge wheel fixed on the summit of the highest mountain "to whose huge spokes ten thousand lesser things" are joined which attend "the boist'rous ruin" when it falls. He concludes: "Never alone / Did the king sigh, but with a general groan." The King now tells them to hasten their preparations for the journey which will imprison the cause of "this fear" and they leave to attend to this.

Polonius now enters to tell Claudius that Hamlet is going to his mother's room and that he is now also going there to hide himself in her room.

Left alone, Claudius gives way to the guilt which is beginning to torment him despite all his practical efforts to protect himself. We saw it earlier in his reaction to a chance remark by Polonius about hypocrisy and then in his reaction to the play. Now he cries out: "O, my offense is rank, it smells to heaven; / It hath the primal eldest curse upon't, / A brother's murther." The curse of Cain, who killed his brother Abel in the first biblical murder, was alienation from God. This is now the condition of Clauduis, for he says: "Pray can I not, / Though inclination be as sharp as will. / My stronger guilt defeats my strong intent." But then he asks himself what the purpose of divine mercy is if not to forgive the guilty. Feeling more hopeful, he now asks himself what form of prayer he can use. He realizes that he cannot simply ask God to "forgive me my foul murther," since he still possesses the results "for which I did the murther, / My crown, mine own ambition, and my queen." Though it may be possible in this "corrupted" world to be pardoned while still retaining the fruits of crime, he is fully aware that " 'tis not so above. / There is no shuffling; there the action lies / In his true nature." Aware that he cannot be divinely pardoned and so be relieved of his guilt while he still enjoys the fulfillment of his royal ambition and the possession of his beloved Queen, he realizes that his only remaining possibility of pardon is to "try what repentance can," though such repentance would involve his giving up of the worldly happiness he has derived from his crown and Queen. He knows that such repentance could effect his pardon, yet is still in despair because he is too much in love with his crown and Queen to give them up: "Yet what can it when one cannot repent? / O wretched state! O bosom black as death! / O limèd soul, that struggling to be free / Art more engaged!" And yet the despair of his guilt is so great that he finally does pray to receive the grace which would enable him to give up the beloved effects of his crime and achieve true repentance: "Help, angels! Make assay. / Bow stubborn knees, and heart with strings of steel, / Be soft as sinews of the new-born babe. / All may be well." He kneels in such a deeply engrossed state of desperate prayer that he does not hear Hamlet's entrance.

When we last saw Hamlet, his mother's invitation to visit her had put him in a murderous rage against her which he was trying to control. Now on his way to his mother's room, as Polonius has recently informed us, he accidentally comes upon Claudius alone and in prayer. He realizes that this is a perfect opportunuity to perform the revenge, especially as his conscience is now clear as to Claudius' guilt (based on Claudius' reaction to the play) and as he has already been informed (as he tells his mother in the next scene) that he must leave immediately for England. His threatening behavior to the King, both in the scenes with Ophelia and with the the play, have thoroughly aroused Claudius to take precautions against him so that, if he does not perform the revenge now, he may never again have as good an opportunity. Seeing his opportunity, Hamlet says: "Now might I do it pat, now 'a is a-praying, / And now I'll do't." But his use of the word "might" already shows his lack of inclination to kill Claudius now, for his whole spirit is eagerly bent on his coming confrontation with his mother, and so he finds an immediate excuse to delay his revenge: "And so 'a goes to heaven, / Am so am I revenged. That would be scanned." It is not religious scruples which prevent him from killing a man in the pious act of prayer, but the thought that, as Claudius is purging his soul, he would go to heaven upon death whereas his father's soul was unprepared for death and so went to purgatory. Unsatisfied simply to perform earthly justice, Hamlet wants his revenge to have eternal effects and he therefore wants to ensure Claudius' damnation as well as death. It is with this thought that he puts away his drawn sword:

> Up, sword, and know thou a more horrid hent
> [occasion].
> When he is drunk asleep, or in his rage,
> Or in th' incestuous pleasure of his bed,
> At game a-swearing, or about some act
> That has no relish of salvation in't—
> Then trip him, that his heels may kick at heaven,
> And that his soul may be as damned and black
> As hell, whereto it goes.

Looking forward to this more horrid occasion and also to seeing his mother who has been waiting for him during this unfortunate delay ("My mother stays"), he leaves the room. Claudius now rises to reveal that his prayer has not been effective, that he has not been truly able to repent: "My words fly up, my thoughts remain below. / Words without thoughts never to heaven go."

Act III: Scene 4

We are now in Gertrude's room in the castle. Polonius, alone with Gertrude, tells her that Hamlet will be there immediately and that she should be very forceful with him, should tell him that she has protected him as much as she could but that his behavior has been too unrestrained to be endured any longer. Polonius now withdraws behind a hanging tapestry as Hamlet is heard approaching.

He enters and immediately asks his mother "what's the matter?" She answers: "Hamlet, thou hast thy father much offended." Offended by this reference to Claudius as his father, he sharply returns: "Mother, you have my father much offended." The conversation quickly proceeds with Gertrude objecting to Hamlet's "idle tongue" and Hamlet objecting to her "wicked tongue," until she finally asks, "Have you forgot me?" Though she is asking Hamlet whether he has forgotten the respect due to a mother, he answers with a bitter identification: "You are the Queen, your husband's brother's wife, / And (would it were not so) you are my mother."

Seeing that she will not get anywhere with him, she proposes to end their meeting, but Hamlet is not going to let this longed for opportunity to speak his mind to his mother get away from him so easily. Forcing her angrily to sit down, his expression must appear to her so murderous that she is forced to cry out in terror for help: "What wilt thou do? Thou wilt not murther me? Help, ho!" At this the startled Polonius also begins to cry for help and Hamlet, quickly drawing his sword, drives it through the tapestry killing the figure behind it with the words: "How now? a rat? Dead for a ducat, dead!" The Queen cries out to ask him what he has done and Hamlet replies, "Nay, I know not. Is it the King?"

The Queen well describes the act when she exclaims: "O, what a rash and bloody deed is this!" But Hamlet is still more concerned to attack his mother than to care about what he has done, and he immediately replies with his worst accusation against her: "A bloody deed—almost as bad, good mother, / As kill a King, and marry with his brother." The Queen is innocently shocked and confused by the meaning of such a suggestion—"As kill a King?"—and so Hamlet, simply repeating "Ay, lady, it was my word," drops the subject. He then lifts the tapestry and, seeing it is Polonius, reacts only with a casual coldness which becomes a bit mocking: "Thou wretched, rash, intruding fool, farewell! / I took thee for thy better. Take thy fortune. / Thou find'st to be too busy is some danger." Then, imediately dismissing the whole subject, he returns to his primary object of attacking his mother with verbal daggers and says to her: "Leave wringing of your hands. Peace, sit you down / And let me wring your heart."

When the Queen asks what she can have done to deserve such rudeness from him, Hamlet begins to describe in fierce terms the immodesty, hypocrisy and irreligiousness with which she has debased her "marriage vows." He then tells her to compare the pictures of her two husbands and asks: "Have you eyes? / Could you on this fair mountain leave to feed, / And batten on this moor?" Not only was his father far superior to Claudius but she cannot even excuse her change as resulting from love since she is too old, he claims, to be capable of such romantic feelings. Her behavior is so lacking in sense that it must be the work of a "devil" who has so blinded her that she has lost all sense of shame. And as he continues to cry out against her lack of shame, she finally begs him to "speak no more" for he is turning her eyes inward to look upon

Hamlet

the guilt in her soul which she cannot erase. The admission of her guilt only inspires Hamlet to make his most revolting description of her act: "Nay, but to live / In the rank sweat of an enseamèd [greasy] bed, / Stewed in corruption, honeying and making love / Over the nasty sty—" Once more she interrupts him to beg him to stop tormenting her with "these words like daggers." But he continues until he forces a third anguished cry, "No more."

At this point the ghost reappears, this time dressed in his nightgown rather than his armor, and Hamlet is stopped from the relentless and increasing fury of his attack upon his already crying mother. Calling for angelic protection, he asks the "gracious figure" of the ghost if he has come to "chide" his "tardy son" for having let his "dread command" become "lapsed in time and passion." The Ghost agrees that this is why he has had to return: 'This visitation / Is but to whet they blunted purpose." But, as Gertrude is looking upon Hamlet's conversation with "amazement," having already said, "Alas, he's mad," the Ghost tells Hamlet to "speak to her." To his question as to how she feels, she responds with concern for him since he seems to be talking to nothing. Hamlet points to the Ghost and describes for her his pitiful expression but she can neither see nor hear anything unusual. At this point the ghost "steals away" out of the door and, as Hamlet continues to describe the Ghost's last motions, Gertrude concludes that what he has seen must have been a hallucination produced by his own brain, such hallucinations being a special effect of madness. Hamlet denies that he is mad and, as proof, says that he can repeat everything he has said. Then, fearing he is to lose the whole effect of his earlier tirade, he tells her that she should not flatter her soul that it is his madness which has magnified her sins for this will only increase her corruption.

Attempting to turn his mother's spirit back to her former purity, he advises her to do what Claudius had earlier himself attempted: "Confess yourself to heaven, / Repent what's past, avoid what is to come, / And do not spread the compost on the weeds / To make them ranker." Calmer now and feeling sorry for his former rudeness to her, he asks her to "forgive me this my virtue." But then, excusing himself by the needs of a corrupt time, he again shows a touch of self-righteous disrespect when he concludes that "Virtue itself of vice must pardon' beg, / Yea, curb and woo for leave to do him good."

But Hamlet has achieved his wish; he has caused his mother to contritely admit her guilt to him as she now does in saying, "O Hamlet, thou hast cleft my heart in twain." Happy with his success,

601

he tells her to "throw away the worser part of it" by never again
going to his uncle's bed. By way of farewell, he says: "Once more,
good night, / And when you are desirous to be blest, / I'll blessing
beg of you."

In this moment of harmonious reconciliation with his mother, Hamlet achieves a sense of general well-being and harmony with the
universe which enables him to view his murder of Polonius in a
new light. Noticing the dead body of Polonius for the first time
since the murder, he says:

> For this same lord, I do repent; but heaven hath
>   pleased it so,
> To punish me with this, and this with me,
> That I must be their scourge and minister.

Hamlet excuses the fatal effects of his new role by saying, "I must
be cruel only to be kind." He says that he will take the body from
the room and "will answer well the death I gave him." Aware that
"worse remains behind" for him as a result of this killing, he prepares to say goodnight again but then remembers to tell his mother
that she should not "let the bloat King" for "a pair of reechy
kisses" cause her to confess that Hamlet is not truly mad "but mad
in craft." Gertrude promises this and then Hamlet reminds her
that, as she knows, he must leave for England. He now confides
in her that he neither trusts the sealed letters Claudius is sending
nor his "two schoolfellows," Rosencrantz and Guildenstern, whom
Claudius is also sending along with him: "They bear the mandate;
they must sweep my way / And marshall me to knavery." With his
new sense of divine mission, however, Hamlet is not worried for
his own safety and success:

> Let it work.
> For 'tis the sport to have the enginer
> Hoise with his own petar [mine], and't shall go hard
> But I will delve one yard below their mines
> And blow them at the moon. O, 'tis most sweet
> When in one line two crafts directly meet.

So far from being worried, Hamlet is elated with the thought that he
will somehow turn against his former friends the evil that they are
now helping Claudius to work against himself. He feels no sympathy for any of Claudius' accomplices. Seeing Polonius only as
a means of getting himself shipped off to England, he says most
crudely: "This man shall set me packing. / I'll lug the guts into

the neighbor room." Then, calling Polonius "a foolish prating knave" and saying a final goodnight to his mother, he leaves the room tugging the body of Polonius after him.

Act IV: Scenes 1-3

The King and Queen, with Rosencrantz and Guildenstern, enter another room of the castle soon after the killing of Polonius. Claudius asks Gertrude why she is sighing so heavily and, after asking Rosencrantz and Guildenstern to leave them alone a while, she answers with a description of Hamlet's "mad" killing of Polonius.

After a brief statement of sorrow, "O heavy deed!," Claudius immediately sees the danger Hamlet's action poses to him:

> It had been so with us, had we been there.
> His liberty is full of threats to all.
> To you yourself, to us, to every one.
> Alas, how shall this bloody deed be answered?
> It will be laid to us.

Not only might Hamlet have killed either himself or Gertrude in place of Polonius, but he might yet do so if he is not immediately restrained. Even as it is, he is afraid that he, himself, will be blamed for the murder and rightly so, for it was his "love" which prevented him from truly recognizing the danger earlier. Asking Gertrude where Hamlet is, she tells him that he has gone to draw away the body and, now sorry for his deed, "weeps for what is done." Claudius now tells Gertrude that he must ship Hamlet away by dawn and then must use his utmost skill to excuse the dead. He calls back Rosencrantz and Guildenstern, tells them of Hamlet's action and that they should find him, speak politely to him and bring the body into the chapel. After they leave, he tells Gertrude that they must also go and tell the council what has happened and what he means to do with Hamlet so as to offset any possible rumors that may arise. Very disturbed by this situation, he says as they leave, "My soul is full of discord and dismay."

In the second scene, Rosencrantz and Guildenstern come upon Hamlet just after he has hidden the body of Polonius. Hamlet's attitude throughout the next two scenes is viciously satirical, though his satire is primarily a reaction to his renewed awareness of death through contact with Polonius' body. To their question as to what he has done with the body, Hamlet replies that he has "compounded it with dust." As they insist upon knowing, Hamlet objects to being "demanded of a sponge," and he explains this reference by saying: "Ay, sir, that soaks up the king's countenance, his rewards, his authorities. But such officers do the king best service in the end. He keeps them, like an ape, in the corner of his jaw, first mouthed, to be last swallowed. When he needs what you have gleaned, it is but squeezing you and, sponge, you shall be dry again." Hamlet satirically tells them that they have lost all human identity by selling their services to the King and that the only reward they may expect for selling their souls is to be destroyed by the King who uses them, but they claim not to understand him. After continuing his contemptuous satire against both them and the body for a bit longer, he demands to be brought to the King and they all leave to go to Claudius.

The third scene begins with Claudius' explanations to some of his advisers. He tells them that he has sent for Hamlet since it is dangerous to let Hamlet continue to go about "loose" but that he must not "put the strong law on him" and "he's loved of the distracted multitude." All he can do, therefore, is to send Hamlet immediately away while giving the impression that this has been done with much deliberation. Rosencrantz now enters to say that they have been unable to find where Hamlet has put the body but that they have brought him guarded to the King and that he is waiting outside the room. Claudius orders Hamlet's appearance and, when he enters, immediately demands of Hamlet to be told where Polonius is. Hamlet satirically answers that Polonius is "at supper," and then, when questioned about this, explains that this supper is "Not where he eats, but where 'a is eaten. A certain convocation of politic worms are e'en at him. Your worm is your only emperor for diet. We fat all creatures else to fat us, and we fat ourselves for maggots. Your fat king and your lean beggar is but variable service—two dishes, but to one table. That's the end."

Hamlet continues to discuss the conversion of men to worms to fish to men again until Claudius finally demands of him "Where is Polonius?" To this Hamlet flippantly answers: "In heaven. Send thither to see. If your messenger find him not there, seek him i' th' other place yourself. But if indeed you find him not within this month, you shall nose him as you go up, the stairs into the lobby."

After sending attendants to find the body of Polonius, Claudius informs Hamlet that "for thine especial safety," he is to leave immediately for England. To this Hamlet says "Good," and Claudius adds, "So is it, if thou knew'st our purposes." Hamlet does see through Claudius' false mask of goodwill, however, as he indicates by his ambiguous reply, 'I see a cherub that sees them." Feeling heaven to be on his side, he is not overly worried, and, after another bit of verbal quibbling, he leaves to prepare himself for England.

Left alone, Claudius reveals that his letter to the King of England demands "the present death of Hamlet." This alone can cure the feverish anxiety which Hamlet's free raging produces in him and which prevents his enjoying his fortune. The scene now ends as Claudius leaves the stage.

Act IV: Scene 4

The scene opens the following morning on a road near the Danish border. Fortinbras enters with his army and stops to talk to his Captain. He tells the Captain to go to the Danish King with his greetings and to remind him of the permission he had earlier granted Fortinbras to transport a Norwegian army over Danish territory. The Captain agrees to do this and is left alone on stage after the departure of Fortinbras and the army. Hamlet now enters with Rosencrantz, Guildenstern and others on their way to the ship which is to bear them to England. He questions the Captain as to the nature and purpose of the army and is told that it is a Norwegian army commanded by Fortinbras on its way to conquer a small piece of Polish land "that hath in it no profit but the name." When Hamlet suggests that the Poles then "never will defend it," he is told that "it is already garrisoned." Hamlet now comments that the expenditure of "two thousand souls and twenty thousand ducats" over "the question of this straw" is the sick result of "much wealth and peace." He now tells the men with him to go on a little before him and is left alone on the stage.

We now come to Hamlet's last soliloquy, his fourth (unless his speech over the praying figure of Claudius be considered a soliloquy, in which case the present soliloquy would be numbered his fifth, or his speech about the "witching time of night" be so considered, in which case this would be his sixth). The sight of this army going out to fight a worthless war for a point of honor serves to stir Hamlet's shame once more at his own dishonor in having allowed revenge to be so long delayed: "How all occasions do inform against me / And spur my dull revenge!" He now asks himself "what is a man" if his chief value and occupation be "but to sleep and feed." In line with his recent contemptuous view of man as engaged solely in eating and being eaten, he answers himself that such a man is "a beast, no more." Referring now back to the subject of his earlier speech to Rosencrantz and Guildenstern about the wonderful qualities of man, he reasons that the Creator did not give man "that capability and godlike reason" so that it would grow mouldy with disuse.

Realizing that man was given his abilities to accomplish something more worthy than mere bestial feeding, he now asks himself whether it was "bestial oblivion" (the forgetfulness of an unaware animal) or some cowardly "scruple" produced by "thinking too precisely on th' event" which explains his lack of action on his revenge. But he finally must conclude: 'I do not know / Why yet I live to say, 'This thing's to do,' / Sith I have cause, and will, and strength, and means / To do't."

In comparison with his own shameful lack of action, he now must witness the behavior of Fortinbras "whose spirit, with divine ambition puffed," exposes his own "mortal and unsure" existence "to all that fortune, death, and danger dare" for nothing more valuable than "an eggshell." He concludes from this that to be truly "great" one must not simply be ready to fight for a sufficient and worthy cause "But greatly to find quarrel in a straw / When honor's at the stake." As he had said in the second soliloquy, the man of true honor is he who has sufficient "gall to make oppression bitter," who is willing to fight a duel at the slightest excuse. Once again he must compare himself with this model of honor, here represented by Fortinbras who is going out to battle to regain his father's lost territories and thus restore the family honor. With both his reason and his natural feelings excited by his father's murder and mother's dishonor, Hamlet can "let all sleep" while, to his "shame," he sees "the imminent death of twenty thousand men" for a merely imagined point of honor. Having shamed himself into renewed commitment to his revenge at a time when such revenge is almost impossible, he concludes strongly: "O, from this time forth, / My thoughts be bloody, or be nothing worth!" With this he leaves to rejoin his companions and the scene ends.

Act IV: Scene 5

This scene returns us to the castle at Elsinore after a lapse of perhaps a month in time. (This is the first lapse in time since the end of Act I, for all of Act II, Act III, and the first four scenes of

Hamlet

Act IV took place in a very crowded twenty-four hour period.) The Queen enters with Horatio and another gentleman. They have been trying to persuade her to see Ophelia, but Gertrude insists: "I will not speak with her." The Gentleman says that Ophelia is very desirous of seeing Gertrude and that her state should be pitied. When Gertrude asks what Ophelia wants with her, the Gentleman only describes her behavior, that "she speaks much of her father" and of the deceit of the world, that she acts and speaks in a disordered way which observers construe in a lascivious way, though Ophelia's "winks and nods and gestures" seem to support such an interpretation. Horatio urges that " 'Twere good she were spoken with" for she is giving malicious minds unfortunate ideas. Gertrude now relents and tells them to admit Ophelia; the two gentlemen leave and, left alone, Gertrude admits that her "sick soul!" has dreaded to confront any new misfortune because of her already agitated sense of "guilt" (thus showing that Hamlet's efforts to arouse her conscience have had a permanent effect).

Ophelia now enters in a distracted state of insanity. She first asks, "Where is the beauteous majesty of Denmark?" (This is the only objective statement in the play that Gertrude is a beautiful woman and it helps to explain Claudius' love for her, the tender concern of the ghost and, perhaps, even Hamlet's oversensitivity to his mother's sexual activities. Clearly she is a woman fully in her prime.) Though Gertrude addresses her, Ophelia does not seem to know her but starts to sing two snatches of song: the first asks how one is to know her "true-love" from another, and the answer is by his clothes, which are those of a pilgrim; the second snatch of song announces, "He is dead and gone, lady," buried under grass with a stone at his heels. She continues to sing of a burial as Claudius comes in, and he concludes that her insanity was caused by thoughts of her father. Ophelia does not wish to hear of this and, by way of explaining the meaning of her state, sings another song. This is a rowdy ballad about a girl's loss of virginity on St. Valentine's day: her lover opens his chamber door to "Let in the maid, that out a maid / Never departed more"; when she later tells him, "Before you tumbled me, / You promised me to wed," he answers that he would have done so had she "not come to my bed." She now returns to weeping at the thought of her father's death and that "they would lay him i' th' cold ground," reminds them that her "brother shall know of it," and, calling for her coach, departs saying "Good night, ladies." Claudius sends Horatio to look after her and again concludes that her insanity "springs all from her father's death."

Claudius now tells Gertrude that Ophelia's insanity is not their only sorrow: first Ophelia's father was slain; next Gertrude's son was justly exiled; thirdly, the people are confused by Polonius' death since no explanations were given and he was hurriedly and secretly interred; lastly, Laertes has secretly returned from France and, since no true information has been provided, has been filled with rumors of Claudius' own responsibility for Polonius' death. This last fact makes him particularly fearful. At this a noise is heard and a messenger enters. Claudius is so unnerved by this that he calls for his "Switzers," his hired Swiss guards. The messenger tells him that he must act to save himself since Laertes at the head of a riotous rabble has overcome the King's officers. The rabble mob, having forgotten the ancient hierarchy and customs of society "cry, 'Choose we! Laertes shall be king!'" At this point another noise is heard; the King cries "The doors are broke;" and Laertes with some followers enters demanding the King. Laertes tells his followers to leave him alone but guard the door, and then he says to Claudius, "O thou vile king, / Give me my father." The Queen tries to calm Laertes but he replies: "That drop of blood that's calm proclaims me bastard." Claudius now asks Laertes the cause of his rebellion. Gertrude has tried to physically restrain Laertes, but Claudius tells her to let him go since "There's such divinity doth hedge a king / That treason can but peep to what it would, / Act little of his will." Laertes answers with the question, "Where is my father?" Claudius answers, "Dead," and Gertrude immediately interjects, "But not by him." Since Claudius now tells him to demand whatever he wants to know from him, Laertes answers:

> How came he dead? I'll not be juggled with.
> To hell allegiance, vows to the blackest devil,
> Conscience and grace to the profoundest pit!
> I dare damnation. To this point I stand,
> That both worlds I give to negligence,
> Let come what comes, only I'll be revenged
> Most thoroughly for my father.

Claudius now tells Laertes that he will not hinder his revenge but asks whether Laertes means to include in his revenge "both friend and foe." When Laertes answers that he is only opposed to "his enemies" and is willing to learn the true circumstances of his father's death, Claudius says that he will prove to Laertes that he is guiltless of his father's death. At this point Ophelia reenters and Laertes is shocked and grieved to discover his sister's mental state. As Ophelia proceeds to sing of her father's funeral and offer flowers to the various people there, Laertes tells her, "Hadst thou thy wits, and didst persuade revenge, / It could not move thus." Continuing to sing of her father's death as she departs, she leaves a grief-stricken Laertes whom Claudius now turns to comfort. He tells Laertes that he should choose his wisest friends to judge between them as he explains the circumstances of Polonius' death. If they still find him guilty, Claudius is willing to give Laertes his crown and life, but if they find him innocent he says that he will be willing to help Laertes to accomplish his revenge against the truly guilty party. Laertes agrees to this and says that he wishes a full explanation of his father's "obscure funeral" with "no noble rite nor formal ostentation." Claudius says that he shall be satisfied and then "where th' offense is, let the great axe fall." They now all leave to attend to this inquiry.

Act IV: Scenes 6-7

The sixth scene takes place in another room of the castle immediately following the last. Horatio has been called to this room to meet some sailors who have asked for him. He is given a letter from Hamlet which describes Hamlet's adventures at sea as follows: after they were two days at sea, a pirate ship chased and then came alongside of his ship. Some fighting ensued during which Hamlet alone boarded the pirate ship. (This shows his customary quickness to undertake physical activity when not related to his revenge and refutes the idea of Hamlet as a simply intellectual man.) Immediately the pirate ship got clear of the Danish ship with the result that Hamlet became their prisoner. They have treated him well, however, and Hamlet now means to reward them for the freedom they have given him. He tells Horatio to see that they get to the King with the letters he has sent to Claudius and then that Horatio should come with these "good fellows" to where he is as he has "words to speak in thine ear will make thee dumb." Horatio now leaves with them immediately to go to the King.

The scene now shifts to another room in the castle where the King has been in conference with Laertes. The seventh scene begins with Claudius' conclusion to the inquiry: Laertes must now acquit him since he understands "That he which hath your noble father slain / Pursued my life." Laertes grants him the appearance but asks him why he did not proceed to take justice against the offender who so threatened his own life. Claudius responds that it was "for two special reasons" which might not seem as strong to Laertes as they do to him. The first reason he states as follows:

> The queen his mother
> Lives almost by his looks, and for myself
> My virtue or my plague, be it either which

> She is so conjunctive to my life and soul
> That, as the star moves not but in his sphere
> I could not but by her.

Claudius now tells Laertes that the second reason he did not prosecute Hamlet was that he was afraid the "great love" the common people bear for Hamlet would cause his plans to backfire against himself "and not where I had aimed them." Laertes complains that this does not satisfy his need to revenge the death of his father and mental breakdown of his sister, but Claudius calms him with the assurance that he will help him accomplish his purposes.

At this point a messenger arrives with the letters from Hamlet. Claudius is shocked at this event but he then proceeds to read the following letter to Laertes: "High and mighty, you shall know I am set naked on your kingdom. Tomorrow shall I beg leave to see your kingly eyes; when I shall (first asking your pardon thereunto) recount the occasion of my sudden and more strange return. HAMLET."

While both Laertes and Claudius are confused by this turn of events, as well they might be, they are quick to see advantage for themselves in it. Laertes says "it warms the very sickness in my heart" that he will be able to return his injury back to Hamlet. Claudius immediately conceives a new plan which will so cleverly dispose of Hamlet that "for his death no wind of blame shall breathe, / But even his mother shall uncharge the practice / And call it accident." Laertes says that he will only be fully satisfied with the plan if he might be its instrument, and Claudius replies that this is in line with his thoughts.

He now tells Laertes about the visit of a Norman two months earlier who astonished the court with his horseback riding. This Norman had known and praised Laertes extravagantly, particularly for his skill in fencing. This had made Hamlet so envious that he had kept wishing for Laertes' sudden return so that he could have a sporting fencing match with him. It is from this fact that Claudius now means to work Hamlet's destruction. Before explaining his idea, however, Claudius asks Laertes how much he loved his father and then, very much like the Player King, reminds him that the passage of time can weaken any purpose and that one should quickly accomplish his will. To his final question as to what he would do to prove himself his father's true son, Laertes replies that he would "cut his throat i' the' church!" And Claudius agrees: "No place indeed should murther sanctuarize; / Revenge should know no bounds." (Here we see most clearly the damnable nature of revenge in its essential opposition with religion. It is ironic that Claudius seconds Laertes' willingness to do that which Hamlet refrained from doing, that is killing a man in prayer, though it is also to Hamlet's discredit that his reason for not then killing Claudius was not Hamlet's reverence for piety. In any case, Laertes' statement underscores his eagerness to "dare damnation" to effect his revenge, and in this he is in marked contrast to Hamlet. Claudius now explains that his plan is to propose a fencing match between Hamlet and Laertes. Since, as just markedly shown by his letter, Hamlet is "remiss, / Most generous, and free from all contriving," he will not examine the foils and Laertes should easily be able to choose a sharply pointed rather than practice foil with which, during the course of the match, he can kill Hamlet. Laertes agrees and, not to be outdone in villainy, adds that he will also dip the tip of his foil in poison so that a mere scratch will prove fatal. Claudius now suggests that if even this should fail there had better be a reserve plan so that their failure would not be apparent. He now suggests that he will prepare a poisoned chalice for Hamlet to drink when he becomes thirsty during the match so that "if he by chance escape your venomed stuck, / Our purpose may hold there."

Gertrude now enters with the sorrowful news that Ophelia has drowned and beautifully describes the scene of her death. Ophelia had attempted to hang a wreath of wild flowers on the bough of a willow tree which had grown over a brook and the bough on which she was climbing broke, throwing her into the water below. There she lay for a time, bouyed up by her clothes while she sang snatches of old songs and was incapable of recognizing her danger. At last her drenched garments pulled her down to death.

Laertes tries to restrain his tears at the recounting of his sister's death but finally is forced to quickly leave the room. Claudius and Gertrude quickly follow to try to comfort him as the fourth act ends.

Act V: Scene 1

The scene takes place in a graveyard near the castle at Elsinore on the following day. Two gravediggers, who are to be played by clowns, are discussing the funeral rites of the lady for whom they are preparing a grave. It appears that she is to have a Christian burial though, to their way of thinking, she was clearly a suicide and they resentfully see this as a result of her high position: "And the more pity that great folk should have count'nance in this world to drown or hang themselves more than their even-Christen. Come, my spade. There is no ancient gentlemen but gard'ners, ditchers, and grave-makers. They hold up Adam's profession." Here a more democratic Christian gentility is asserted in the face of the false aristocratic notion of honor, and the proof of this is in their profession, for their graves serve all and must "last till doomsday."

The chief gravedigger now sends the other for some liquor and, after he leaves, continues to dig while singing a song of youthful love: "In youth when I did love, did love, / Methought it was very sweet." At this point Hamlet and Horatio enter and Hamlet is surprised that the gravedigger is so lacking in "feeling of his business, that 'a sings at grave-making." Horatio explains this as a product of "custom" and Hamlet agrees. The gravedigger now throws up a skull and Hamlet reflects on the vanity of human wishes: "How the knave jowls it to the ground, as if 'twere Cain's jawbone, that did the first murther! This might be the pate of a politician, which this ass now o'erreaches; one that would circumvent God, might it not? . . . . Or of a courtier, which could say 'Good morrow, sweet lord!'" (Here Hamlet seems to be thinking of Claudius and such courtiers as Polonius, Rosencrantz and Guildenstern. Claudius has tried to "circumvent God" through a brother's murder like that of Cain and yet all he shall finally gain is a death like that which Hamlet has already awarded to Claudius' courtiers, as we shall soon see. Hamlet's readiness to identify the skull he sees being rudely thrown about with that of Claudius shows us that Hamlet has Claudius' coming death very firmly in mind.) As Hamlet continues to reflect on the generality of death, however, he becomes upset by it: "Did these bones cost no more the breeding but to play at loggets with 'em? Mine ache to think on't." After continuing to reflect on the losses of the grave's occupant, whether lawyer or great landowner, he finally asks the gravedigger whose grave it is. When the gravedigger answers that though "I do not lie in't, yet it is mine," Hamlet replies in as humorous a vein, "Thou dost lie in't, to be in't and say it is thine. 'Tis for the dead, not for the quick; therefore thou liest." (Here we see Hamlet once more moving quickly from melancholy to punning wit and still very upset by the fact of death as at the first. But his mood is more controlled, his melancholy brief, his wit more playful. He is not a different Hamlet, but he seems to have himself in better control.) After finally being told that the grave is being prepared for a woman, Hamlet asks him how long he has been a gravedigger, and the gravedigger replies that it has been thirty years, that he began on "that day that our last king Hamlet overcame Fortinbras" which was also "the very day that young Hamlet was born." (Here we have our first indication of Hamlet's exact age. Shakespeare has refrained from informing us that Hamlet was a man rather than a boy until Hamlet had matured to his full thirty years. As Hamlet is soon to reach his tragic end, it is important to fully establish his significance as a grown rather than young man whose actions are not motivated by youthful disillusionment but mature consideration.)

The gravedigger now comes upon the skull of one he knew, Yorick, the king's jester, who had died twenty-three years before. Hamlet takes the skull and says to Horatio: "Alas, poor Yorick! I knew him, Horatio, a fellow of infinite jest, of most excellent fancy. He hath borne me on his back a thousand times. And now how abhorred in my imagination it is! My gorge rises at it. Here hung those lips that I have kissed I know not how oft. Where be your gibes now?" (In his disturbance over Yorick's death, Hamlet may also begin to fear his own since he is also "a fellow of infinite jest, of most excellent fancy." Indeed, the gravedigger's mention of Hamlet's age reminds him that he has already lived a full generation, and he is soon to leap into this very grave dug by one who has been preparing graves. since the day Hamlet was born. If death is waiting for Claudius, it may also be waiting for him.) When Hamlet now begins to wonder whether one's imagination can "trace the noble dust of Alexander till a find it stopping a bunghole," Horatio sanely advises him that " 'Twere to consider too curiously, to consider so." Hamlet, however, continues to elaborate this subject, just as he had after Polonius' death, until he is interrupted by the approach of a funeral party led by the King. He notes that the "maimed rites" indicate the funeral of a suicide and he decides to withdraw with Horatio to observe the event unseen.

After the entrance of the King, Queen, Laertes, a Doctor of Divinity, and other lords following the corpse, Laertes suddenly cries out: "What ceremony else?" The Doctor of Divinity explains that since "her death was doubtful," they have enlarged her funeral rites as much as they could and are at least burying her with prayers in sanctified ground rather than throwing rocks on her unsanctified grave. The disgusted Laertes is forced to agree to the funeral but tells the Doctor, "A minist'ring angel shall my sister be / When thou liest howling." At this the shocked Hamlet says, "What, the fair Ophelia?" Gertrude now scatters flowers on Ophelia's grave with the sad mother's reflection: "I hope thou shouldst have been my Hamlet's wife. / I thought thy bride-bed to have decked, sweet maid, / And not have strewed thy grave." But her mention of Hamlet enrages Laertes with the remembrance of Hamlet's guilt for all his family's woes, and he exclaims: "O, treble woe / Fall ten times treble on that cursed head / Whose wicked deed thy most ingenious sense / Deprived thee of!" At the thought of her fate he longs to embrace her once more and, leaping into the grave, calls upon the gravediggers to bury him with her under such a mountain that it "o'ertop old Pelion" or Olympus itself. (This refers to the mythical war in which the Titans attempted to pile the mountain Ossa upon the mountain Pelion in order to reach the heaven of the Olympian gods.)

At this point Hamlet (aroused, as he later says, "into a tow'ring passion" by the ostentatious display of Laertes' grief and perhaps by his sense of guilt at Laertes' accusation of his responsibility for Ophelia's death) comes forward, questions Laertes' right to such grief when he, "Hamlet the Dane" is there, and leaps into the grave after Laertes. Laertes begins to fight with him, saying, "The devil take thy soul!" But Hamlet objects to this prayer and his reply further indicates his self-awareness of his dangerous tendency to rashness: "Thou pray'st not well. / I prithee take thy fingers from my throat, / For though I am not splenitive and rash, / Yet have I in me something dangerous, / Which let they wisdom fear." Though he has leaped belligerently into the grave, he tries to control himself from fighting with Laertes and especially right there in Ophelia's grave. After they have parted and leave the grave, however, Hamlet says that he is willing to fight Laertes to the death on the subject of his love for Ophelia. Though Laertes holds him guilty of her death, he proclaims: "I loved Ophelia. Forty thousand brothers / Could not with all their quantity of love / Make up my sum." Hamlet is willing to match any attempt on Laertes' part to prove his love for Ophelia. If Laertes wishes "to outface me with leaping in her grave," so will he and will call down as much earth to cover them as will "make Ossa like a wart!" He concludes his unseemingly harangue with the words "I'll rant as well as thou," at which point his mother explains to Laertes that "this is mere madness." She continues her explanation by saying that for "a while the fit will work on him" and then, "as patient as the female dove," he will silently "sit drooping." Upon hearing his mother's words, he does calm himself sufficiently to ask Laertes: "What is the reason that you use me thus? / I loved you ever." With no apparent awareness of his responsibility for the deaths of Laertes' father and sister and for his present disruption of Ophelia's funeral, he self-righteously concludes: "But it is no matter. / Let Hercules himself do what he may, / The cat will mew, and dog will have his day." Believing that no amount of heroic endeavor would keep a low animal like Laertes from making noises at him, he abruptly turns from them and leaves.

Claudius tells Horatio to follow Hamlet and then tells Laertes to keep his patience in the memory of the previous night's conference and in the assurance that very soon "this grave shall have a living monument," that is, the life of Hamlet. Upon this note of discord between Hamlet and Laertes, the scene ends.

Act V: Scene 2

The final scene takes place in a major hall of the castle at Elsinore soon after the funeral. Hamlet enters in the act of explaining his recent behavior to Horatio. He immediately comes to the important events on shipboard which, in his letter to Horatio, he had said would make Horatio "dumb." In all of his soliloquies, he precedes his discussion of events with generalizations he has drawn from them. What he did on shipboard was rash and, in what is probably the most significant speech in the play, he now explains the culminating insight of his experience:

> And praised be rashness for it—let us know,
> Our indiscretion sometime serves us well
> When our deep plots do pall, and that should learn us
> There's a divinity that shapes our ends,
> Rough-hew them how we will—

Shakespeare has Horatio underscore the significance of these statements by saying, "That is most certain."

Hamlet now explains that one night on shipboard he felt so extremely restless that he "rashly" left his cabin, found his way in the dark to the cabin of Rosencrantz and Guildenstern, discovered their package of letters, and returned to his own cabin. Once there, he was "so bold" as to "unseal /Their grand commission; where I found, Horatio—/ Ah, royal knavery!—an exact command" that without any loss of time, "No, not to stay the grinding of the axe, / My head should be struck off." Hamlet gives this important piece of concrete evidence against Claudius into the care of a shocked Horatio. He then continues his story. Surrounded as he was "with villainies," he again acted upon impulse without any prior planning of this course of action: "Or I could make a prologue to my brains, / They had begun the play." Although he had earlier considered fine penmanship the mark of a lower mind and had tried to forget his early training in fine handwriting, this training now served him well for it enabled him to write a formal state document. He immediately "devised a new commission, wrote it fair," and demanded of the

English King that without any debating of this order "He should the bearers put to sudden death, / Not shriving time allowed."

When Horatio asks him how he was able to seal this forged commission, Hamlet replies, "Why, even in that was heaven ordinant. / I had my father's signet in my purse." That he was able with this model of the Danish seal to make a perfect forgery Hamlet sees as a sign of the shaping hand of heaven in these events. And further, the whole exploit by which he discovered Claudius' villainous designs against himself, was able to convert this plan so that it would lead to the destruction of Claudius' accomplices, and then return the forged commission so that the change was never known, finally led him to his grand conclusion that "There's a divinity that shapes our ends, / Rough-hew them how we will."

Horatio now notes in what must be a faintly disapproving tone, "So Guildenstern and Rosencrantz go to't." But Hamlet strongly justifies his actions with words:

> Why, man, they did make love to this employment.
> They are not near my conscience; their defeat
> Does by their own insinuation grow.
> 'Tis dangerous when the baser nature comes
> Between the pass and fell incensed points
> Of mighty opposites.

Horatio's next comment, "Why, what a king is this!" enables Hamlet to come to the real issue on his conscience, the question of regicide:

> Does it not, think thee, stand me now upon—
> He that hath killed my king, and whored my mother,
> Popped in between th' election and my hopes,
> Thrown out his angle for my proper life,
> And with such coz'nage—is't not perfect conscience
> To quit him with this arm? And is't not to be damned
> To let this canker of our nature come
> In further evil?

Horatio now stresses the practical need of speedy action since Claudius will undoubtedly be soon informed of the result of his mission to England. Hamlet blandly agrees: "It will be short; the interim is mine, / And a man's life no more than to say 'one.' "

But now that his own revenge seems so close to accomplishment, he suddenly becomes aware of Laertes' just grievance against himself and feels "very sorry" that "to Laertes I forgot myself." Although he excuses his treatment of Laertes on the grounds that "the bravery [ostentation] of his grief did put me / Into a tow'ring passion," he hopes to be able to gain Laertes' forgiveness and vows, "I'll court his favors."

At this providential moment of Hamlet's concern to regain Laertes' goodwill, the courtier Osric enters with a message of welcome from Claudius. Turning aside to Horatio and finding that he does not know "this waterfly," Hamlet tells Horatio that he is the better for not knowing such an ostentatious, land wealthy fool, and it is characteristic of Claudius that, though "a beast be lord of beasts," he allows him to eat at his own "mess." Osric doffs his hat before Hamlet as he is about to deliver his message, but Hamlet democratically tells him to return his hat to his head. When Osric refuses on the grounds that "it is very hot," Hamlet begins to make fun of him as he earlier had with Polonius, insisting first that it is cold and then hot, Osric agreeing to everything Hamlet says, until Hamlet finally prevails on Osric to wear his hat. Ostric now tries to get to the point of his coming, the "great wager" the King has placed on Hamlet's head. When he begins to extol Laertes merits in the most ridiculously affected manner, however, Hamlet cannot restrain himself from imitating Osric's absurd manner of speech. But Osric is too foolishly vain of his own accomplishments to realize that Hamlet is making fun of him and replies: "Your lordship speaks most infallibly of him." Hamlet continues his marvelous caricature of Osric, to the delight of Horatio, until he finally gets the bewildered Osric to come to the point of the wager. Regaining his speech with all its affection, Osric now explains that Claudius has wagered six Barbary horses against six French rapiers and poniards that in a fencing match between Hamlet and Laertes, of a dozen passes, Laertes would not exceed Hamlet by three hits. The odds are laid twelve to nine in Hamlet's favor. He now wishes to know whether Hamlet is willing for this match to come "to immediate trial," and Hamlet answers that he is willing to have the foils brought immediately to this very hall and to begin the match, that Osric can deliver this message "after what flourish your nature will." After Osric leaves, Hamlet and Horatio continue to comment on the comic absurdity of courtiers like Osric until another lord enters from Claudius to know whetner Hamlet still wishes to play immediately with Laertes or would "take longer time." As Hamlet says that he is ready if the King so wishes, the lord informs him tnat the King, Queen and court are coming to the match and that the Queen desires Hamlet to greet Laertes in a gentlemanly fashion before they start to play. Hamlet says that he will follow this instruction and the lord leaves.

When they are once more alone, Horatio suggests that Hamlet will "lose this wager," but Hamlet disagrees as he has been "in continual practice" since Laertes went to France and should be able to "win at the odds." Nonetheless, he feels a premonition of danger in his heart, though he rejects such "foolery." Horatio advises Hamlet to obey his intuitions and says that he will delay the match on the grounds that Hamlet is not well. But Hamlet replies:

> Not a whit, we defy augury. There is special providence in the fall of a sparrow. If it be now, 'tis not to come; if it be not to come, it will be now; if it be not now, yet it will come. The readiness is all. Since no man of aught he leaves knows, what is't to leave betimes? Let be.

The King and court now arrive to the accompaniment of trumpets and drums. While the hall is being prepared for the fencing match, Claudius places Laertes' hand into Hamlet's in an apparent bid for their reconciliation. Hamlet begins in the most cordial terms by saying: "Give my your pardon, sir. I have done you wrong, / But pardon't, as you are a gentleman." As Gertrude had done twice before, he now attempts to excuse his behavior on the grounds of madness, a madness which, as he also said over the corpse of Polonius, punishes him as much as his victims: "His madness is poor Hamlet's enemy." If Hamlet "when he's not himself does wrong Laertes," he can at least offer in his own defense: "Let my disclaiming from a purposed evil / Free me so far in your most generous thoughts / That I have shot my arrow o'er the house / And hurt my brother."

Laertes admits that he is "satisfied in nature" though it is this which should stir him most to his revenge, but he is not willing to make a formal reconciliation with Hamlet until "some elder masters of known honor" can show him by precedents that his honor will not be stained by such a peace. Until that time, however, he says that he will "not wrong" Hamlet's offering of love. Hamlet embraces Laertes' reply and is ready to begin "this brother's wager." They call for the foils and, making a pun on the word "foil," Hamlet generously tells Laertes, "I'll be your foil," his own poor performance making Laertes' skill shine the more brightly. As they go to choose the foils, Hamlet seems to convince Laertes that he does not "mock" him. Hamlet is satisfied with the foil he chooses but Laertes is not and goes to choose another foil while Claudius explains to Hamlet once more the terms of the wager. As they prepare to play, Hamlet asks whether the foils are all alike, that is, have dulled ends, and Osric replies, "Ay, my good lord."

Hamlet

Claudius now calls for wine to be placed on a table and says that if Hamlet hits Laertes in the first three exchanges "the king shall drink to Hamlet's better breath." He will then drop a rich "union" or pearl into the cup for Hamlet while "the kettle to the trumpet speak, / The trumpet to the cannoneer without, / The cannons to the heaven, the heaven to earth." They begin to play and on the first exchange Hamlet scores, as Osric says, "A hit, a very palpable hit." The drum, trumpets and cannon sound and the King stops the play to drink to Hamlet, drop the pearl into the cup and offer the ceremonial cup to him.

Hamlet, however, unceremoniously refuses to join Claudius in a toast and asks that the cup be set by awhile until he finishes the next bout. He calls for the beginning of the second bout and immediately makes "another hit," as Laertes confesses.

Claudius now tells Gertrude "our son shall win." In apparent delight over his son's good performance, she goes to wipe Hamlet's brow with her handkerchief. As this brings her close to the table near the fencers on which the cup has been placed, she picks up the cup and tells Hamlet that she too is going to toast his fortune. To this action Hamlet exclaims "Good madam!" but Claudius calls out to her imperiously, "Gertrude, do not drink." She insists, however, "I will, my lord; I pray you pardon me." In silent agony, Claudius reflects: "It is the poisoned cup; it is too late." Hamlet still does not wish to interrupt his fencing and says to her, "I dare not drink yet, madam—by and by." She then goes to wipe his face once more before he starts to play again.

As the third round is about to start, Laertes tells Claudius that he will hit Hamlet in this bout. Claudius replies that he doubts it and Laertes admits to himself, "And yet it is almost against my conscience." Hamlet now playfully taunts Laertes about his poor performance, "You but daily," to which Laertes responds, "Say you so? Come on." Playing now to his best ability, Laertes can only bring Hamlet to a draw by the end of the bout. Enraged, he lunges at Hamlet after the close of the round—"Have at you now!"—and manages to wound Hamlet. When Hamlet realizes by his wound that Laertes has been fencing with an illegally sharp sword, he returns the attack with such fury that he gains control of the poisoned weapon in exchange for his own with which he seriously wounds Laertes.

Though Hamlet is anxious to continue his fight with Laertes despite

Claudius' attempts to have them parted, the fight is finally stopped by the fall of the Queen. Horatio also notes that "they bleed on both sides" and asks Hamlet how he is. Osric also asks Laertes how he is and Laertes replies: "Why, as a woodcock to mine own springe [trap], Osric. / I am justly killed with mine own treachery." Hamlet, not as seriously wounded as Laertes, is more concerned about his mother, but Claudius answers his query by saying that Gertrude is only swooning at the sight of their blood. When she hears Claudius' false words, the dying Gertrude cries out: "No, no, the drink, the drink! O my dear Hamlet / The drink, the drink! I am poisoned."

With the Queen's full confession of Claudius' villainy before the assembled court, the enraged Hamlet attempts to assume control of the state and begin an immediate inquiry into Claudius' guilt: "O villainy! Ho! let the door be locked. / Treachery! See it out." But Laertes now falls with the words, "Hamlet, thou art slain." He explains that the sword in Hamlet's hands is not only sharp but poisoned and that Hamlet has no more than "half an hour's life." Laertes is also doomed, for his "foul practice / Hath turned itself on me." For both their deaths and for the poisoning of the Queen, he cries out to all, "The king, the king's to blame." Hearing that his life is now forfeit, Hamlet turns his poisoned sword on the King with the words, "The point envenomed too? / Then, venom, to thy work." But though Claudius is apparently convicted by the reigning Queen and by Laertes of the "treacherous" murder of themselves and of the crown prince, so great is the court's horror of regicide and reverence for a King's life that they all cry out "Treason! treason!" against Hamlet's murderous act. At this cry of support from his court, the fatally poisoned Claudius speaks his last words, "O, yet defend me, friends, I am but hurt."

But Hamlet quickly dispatches him with the poisoned drink he had prepared. Forcing this down his throat, he cries: "Here, thou incestuous, murd'rous, damned Dane, / Drink off this potion. Is thy union here? / Follow my mother." As the King dies, Laertes says that "he is justly served" by the poison he had prepared for Hamlet. He now turns to Hamlet with his last words: "Exchange forgiveness with me, noble Hamlet. / Mine and my father's death come not upon thee, / Nor thine on me!" The dying Hamlet accepts the dead Laertes' wish as he says: "Heaven make thee free of it! I follow thee."

Hamlet wishes he could more fully explain his act to the horrified spectators but, "as this fell sergeant, Death, / Is strict in his arrest,"

he tells Horatio that he must "report me and my cause aright /
To the unsatisfied."

For once, Horatio attempts to go against Hamlet's wishes. Objecting that he is "more an antique Roman than a Dane" (that is, a
Stoic who believes in suicide rather than survival with shame),
Horatio attempts to emulate Hamlet's nobility, as he understands
it, by drinking the remaining poison and following his beloved
friend to death. But with his last strength Hamlet forcibly wrests
the poisoned cup from Horatio's hands: "Give me the cup. Let go.
By heaven, I'll ha't." Death may provide final happiness, but if
Horatio truly loves him he would better follow his example by
continuing the painful process of living and justifying Hamlet's
name: "If thou didst ever hold me in thy heart, / Absent thee from
felicity awhile, / And in this harsh world draw thy breath in pain,
/ To tell my story."

Hamlet now hears a "warlike noise" and is informed by Osric that
it is the greeting of Fortinbras, returned from his conquest in
Poland, to the ambassadors from England whom he has met on his
way to Elsinore. The poison has so overcome him, however, that
Hamlet fears he will not live long enough to hear the result of his
substituted commission to the English King. As his death will also
mark the end of the Danish royal line, he now turns his last thoughts
to the question of the Danish succession, for he is now *de facto*
ruler of Denmark and must attend to the good of his state: "I do
prophesy th' election lights / On Fortinbras. He has my dying
voice." Horatio is to tell Fortinbras of this and of all that has
happened because for Hamlet "the rest is silence." As Hamlet dies,
Horatio bids farewell to his noble friend in the full confidence of
his spiritual salvation: "Now cracks a noble heart. Good night,
sweet prince, / And flights of angels sing thee to thy rest!" Immediately upon the death of Hamlet, Fortinbras enters with the ambassadors from England.

As Fortinbras views the royal deaths he can only ask, "O proud
Death, / What feast is toward in thine eternal cell" (reminding us
thereby of the equal validity of Hamlet's earlier if less graced vision
of death's universal feeding upon man). To complete death's feast,
the ambassador from England informs us "that Rosencrantz and
Guildenstern are dead." Horatio now suggests that the bodies be
arranged in state and placed on view after which he can tell them
"Of carnal, bloody, and unnatural acts, / Of accidental judgments,
casual slaughters, / Of deaths put on by cunning and forced cause,
/ And, in this upshot, purposes mistook / Fall'n on th' inventors'

heads." Fortinbras is anxious to hear of this but also takes the opportunity to state his claim to the throne of Denmark. Horatio says that he has cause to speak of this as well but that first the funeral arrangement should be made to quiet "men's minds." Fortinbras now orders four captains to "bear Hamlet like a soldier" to a high platform accompanied by the rites of a military funeral, "For he was likely, had he been put on, / To have proved most royal." As the soldiers bear Hamlet upwards to the sounds of cannons, the tragedy comes to a fitting end.

Julius Caesar

JULIUS CAESAR
OCTAVIUS CAESAR
MARK ANTHONY } *triumvirs after the death of Julius Caesar.*
M. AEMILIUS LEPIDUS
CICERO
PUBLIUS } *senators.*
POPILIUS LENA
MARCUS BRUTUS
CASSIUS
CASCA
TREBONIUS
CAIUS LIGARIUS } *conspirators against Julius Caesar.*
DECIUS BRUTUS
METELLUS CIMBER
CINNA
FLAVIUS *and* MARULLUS, *tribunes.*
ARTEMIDORUS OF CNIDOS, *a teacher of Rhetoric.*
SOOTHSAYER.
CINNA, *a poet.*
Another POET.
LUCILIUS
TITINIUS
MESSALA
YOUNG CATO } *officers under Brutus and Cassius.*
VOLUMNIUS
FLAVIUS
VARRO
CLITUS
CLAUDIUS } *soldiers in Brutus' army.*
DARDANIUS
STRATO
LUCIUS } *servants and slaves to Brutus.*
PINDARUS, *servant and slave to Cassius.*

CALPURNIA, *wife to Caesar.*
PORTIA, *wife to Brutus.*

SENATORS, CITIZENS, GUARDS, ATTENDANTS, *etc.*

Julius Caesar

Act I: Scene 1

The play opens in a street in Rome. Two tribunes, Flavius and Marullus, are dispersing the crowds that have gathered there. The tribunes have trouble extracting an explanation from a cobbler who appears to be leading the mob, for the cobbler gives equivocal answers to the direct questions of the officials. He claims to be a "mender of bad soles," "a surgeon to old shoes," and one who lives by the "awl." Finally, he admits that the workingmen have left their shops and have assembled "to see Caesar and to rejoice in his triumph."

Marullus is incensed by the reason he is given. He rebukes the commoners for gathering to honor Caesar. What territories has Caesar conquered for Rome, the tribune asks; what prisoners has he led home? He reproaches the people for their hard hearts and senseless cruelty in forgetting Pompey so soon after they had cheered him. He reminds the mob of how they had lined the streets and climbed the battlements of buildings, sitting there all day with babes in arms to get just a glimpse of Pompey when he returned after a victory. "And do you now strew flowers in his way/That comes in triumph over Pompey's blood?" Marullus harangues. He warns the unfeeling mob that their ingratitude will be repaid by plague if they do not disperse immediately and pray mercy of the gods. Flavius enjoins the people to run to the Tiber and weep for Pompey until the river is filled with tears up to its highest bank.

When the commoners leave, Flavius remarks, "They vanish tongue-tied in their guiltiness." Then he instructs Marullus to go through the city and "disrobe the images," that is, remove the decorations intended to honor Caesar. Marullus asks if it would not be sacrilege to remove the decorations for the Feast of Lupercal, which is being celebrated on this same day, but Flavius replies that it does not matter. He also orders Marullus to drive the vulgar from the streets so that the absence of the people (who grew like feathers on Caesar's wing and enable him to fly higher than he otherwise could) will keep Caesar's ambitions in check.

Act I: Scene 2

Shortly after the crowds have been dispersed by the tribunes, a procession arrives. There is music and pageantry as Caesar, Antony, Calpurnia, Portia, Decius, Brutus, Cicero, Brutus, Cassius, and Casca, dressed in elegant attire, march through the street. A large crowd follows the procession which is on its way to the race traditionally held on the Lupercal.

Caesar calls to his wife, Calpurnia, and tells her to stand directly in Antony's way, as he runs through the streets. He orders Antony to strike her since "the barren touched in this holy chase, / Shake off their sterile curse." Antony replies to Caesar's command, "When Caesar says 'do this,' it is performed."

From the crowd a Soothsayer emerges and cries to Caesar, "Beware the ides of March!" Caesar asks the Soothsayer to come forward and repeat what he has just said. He peruses the man's face, hears the warning again, and decides, "He is a dreamer; let us leave him."

As Caesar and his followers go off to the feast, Cassius and Brutus remain behind. Brutus tells Cassius that he will not follow the course of the young men (as they race around the city), for he is not "gamesome" and has not Antony's "quick spirit." Cassius expresses his fear that his good friend Brutus disapproves of him, for his looks no longer show his former love. Brutus assures Cassius that he is not vexed with his friend but with himself. He is, in fact, "with himself at war" and "forgets the show of love to other men."

Relieved to learn that he is still in Brutus' favor, Cassius tells his friend that he had misunderstood his emotional state and had refrained from discussing important matters with him. He asks Brutus if he can read his own character, which shines in his own face, revealing that Brutus is a just man. Many men, "except immortal Caesar," are now enslaved by Caesar's rule and wish that Brutus had Caesar's eyes so that Brutus could see his own nobility as Caesar sees his own.

Having thus complimented Brutus, Cassius prepares to tell Brutus the subject of his argument. But first, he testifies to his own honest character, his veracity, his sobriety, his loyalty to friends.

Shouts are heard and a sennet is sounded (a series of bars played on a trumpet, symbolizing sovereignty). Brutus blurts out his fear that the people have chosen Caesar for their king. Cassius latches on to Brutus' expression of fear: "Ay do you fear it / Then must I think you would not have it so." Briefly, Brutus answers that he would not have Caesar king, and yet he loves him. Then he urges Cassius to go on with his message and promises that if it concerns the general good, even the fear of death will not permit him from doing what is honorable.

Returning to his speech and taking his cue from Brutus' remark about honor, Cassius announces his subject is honor. He cannot tell what other men think, but speaking for himself, Cassius states his preference for death to subjugation under a man who is no better than he. Caesar is just another such man, Cassius argues. He and Caesar were born equally free, were nurtured equally and endure the cold in the same way. In fact, Cassius claims, Caesar cannot swim as well as he, for once in a swimming contest, Cassius, like Aeneas (founder of Rome, who bore his father Anchises on his shoulders to save him from the flaming city of Troy), bore Caesar to safety on his shoulders. Another time, when Caesar was afflicted by fever in Spain, he cried for water as a sick girl might. Cassius is angered at the thought that a man of such "feeble temper" should now rule the majestic world alone, while Cassius, his equal, must bend to Caesar's slightest nod.

The crowd roars and the trumpet flourishes a second time. Brutus surmises that some new honors are being heaped on Caesar. Cassius compares Caesar to a Colossus and calls Brutus and himself "petty men," who walk under the legs of this giant. "The fault, dear Brutus, is not in our stars./But in ourselves, that we are underlings," Cassius states. Then he asks: "Why should that name be sounded more than yours." Once more he alludes to Caesar's physical attributes and asks by what virtue he has become great: "Upon what meat doth this our Caesar feed/That he is grown so great?" The reputation of Rome rests in the fact that it does not esteem "one only man." He ends his exhortation to Brutus by reminding him of his namesake, Lucius Junius Brutus (a Roman hero who had expelled Rome's last king, Tarquin, five hundred years earlier).

Brutus replies to Cassius' argument point for point. He assures Cassius that he is not suspicious of his love and that he is somewhat inclined toward Cassius' sentiments. But exactly what he thinks of conditions in Rome must be discussed at another time. Brutus promises to consider what Cassius has already said, to listen to him further and to answer him at a later time. For the present, Brutus tells Cassius, "chew upon this: Brutus had rather be a villager/Than to repute himself a son of Rome/Under these hard conditions as this time/Is like to lay upon us."

The conversation is concluded by Caesar's return from the race. Brutus detects anger on the face of the dictator; he notices the paleness of Calpurnia's cheeks and the fires that burn from Cicero's eyes as if he had been "crossed in conference by some senators." Caesar, on his part, spies Cassius standing by, and turning to Antony, he tells him that he trusts fat men above lean ones. "Yond Cassius has a lean and hungry look! /He thinks too much, such men are dangerous." Antony urges Caesar not to fear Cassius, for he is a noble Roman of excellent disposition. Caesar asserts that he has no fear, "for always I am Caesar," but if he had, he would avoid Cassius more than any other man. He contrasts Cassius with Antony, who loves plays and music and laughter. Cassius, on the other hand, is never entertained; he reads a great deal, watches men, and penetrates the motives behind their deeds. He rarely smiles, except as if in self-mockery. Such men are dangerous, Caesar warns Antony, insisting that he says this by way of instructing Antony in the ways of men and not because he is expressing his own fear. As Caesar leaves with his train, he bids Antony come to his right side, because he is deaf in the left ear, and tell him what he really thinks of Cassius.

When Caesar leaves, Brutus grasps Casca's cloak and asks the cause of Caesar's anger. Casca replies that Antony had offered him the crown three times and that three times Caesar refused it. Each time Antony held out the crown, Caesar fingered it, but discerning the mood of the mob which rejected monarchy, he put it aside. To Casca's thinking, however, he refused the crown more reluctantly each time. Then, Casca relates, Caesar fainted. Brutus remarks that Caesar has the falling-sickness (epilepsy). Cassius ironically replies that it is not Caesar, but they, who have the falling-sickness (that is, the Republic is falling). Having thrice refused the crown and thrice seen how glad the people were at his refusal, Casca continues, Caesar opened his doublet and offered them his throat to cut. Casca admits that if he had had a weapon, he would have taken up Caesar's offer. Casca goes on to say that when Caesar recovered from his fainting spell, he blamed his actions on his infirmity, and the mob forgave him. Casca ends his description with the words: "If Caesar had stabbed their mothers, they would have done no less."

In reply to Brutus' question on Cicero's reaction to the events at the Lupercalia, Casca answers that Cicero spoke Greek to his friends, but "it was Greek to me." He states further that Marullus and Flavius have been "silenced" for pulling garlands off Caesar's statues.

Seeing that Casca feels the same way toward Caesar as he does, Cassius invites him to dinner. After Casca leaves, Brutus comments that Casca is unpolished, but Cassius explains that Casca's rudeness is a mask behind which he can speak the truth freely. Repeating his promise to talk more the next day, Brutus leaves.

Alone on the stage, Cassius states that Brutus is a noble man, but that he sees Brutus can be diverted from his natural inclinations. Reflecting that noble minds should always keep company with other noble minds lest they be seduced, Cassius also observes that no one is so firm that he cannot be persuaded to change his course. He acknowledges that he is in Caesar's disfavor and that Brutus is loved by Caesar, but if he were Brutus, Cassius asserts, he would not let Caesar's love prevent him from following his principles. Cassius then announces his plan to win over Brutus completely. He will forge letters from leading citizens in which he will praise Brutus' name and hint covertly at Caesar's dangerous ambition to overthrow the Republic. After the letters have been thrown into Brutus' window and he has read them, Caesar should beware, for "We will shake him or worse days endure."

Act I: Scene 3

It is the eve of the ides of March. Lightning flashes through the sky and thunder roars. On a street in Rome, Casca is seen with drawn sword, frightened out of his wits by the storm. He meets Cicero on the street and tells him that either there is "civil strife in heaven" or else men have offended the gods. He then describes other prodigies he has seen that night. A common slave's left hand was burned with flame, yet remained unscorched; a lion roamed loose near the Capitol; a hundred women have sworn they saw men walk in fire up and down the streets, and the birds of the night hooted and shrieked at noonday. Cicero philosophically replies, "Indeed, it is a strange-disposed time," but men interpret things absolutely contrary to the meaning of the events themselves. He asks Casca if Caesar is coming to the Capitol tomorrow, and Casca says he will be there. Declaring that "this disturbed sky/ Is not to walk in," Cicero departs.

Casca hears someone coming and issues a challenge. It is Cassius, who recognizes Casca by his voice. Casca asks why the heavens are so menacing. Cassius replies that he has been walking through the storm, exposing himself to the lightning, and asserts that these unnatural events are heaven's instruments of fear and warning that something unnatural is happening on earth. Then he compares the storm to a man no mightier than himself or Casca, a man who roars like a lion in the Capitol. Casca replies, " 'Tis Caesar that you mean."

Casca remarks that on the morrow the senators plan to establish Caesar as king over all lands of the empire except Italy. At this Cassius delivers a tirade against tyranny and hurls abuse at the servile Romans for following "so vile a thing as Caesar!" Cassius declares that he is armed and ready to fight Casca should he turn out to be one of Caesar's men. But Casca gives his hand as a pledge of his cooperation, telling Cassius he will join his cause. Cassius then tells Casca that he has already enlisted some of the "noblest-minded Romans" to join him in the deed, "most bloody, fiery and most terrible."

As Cassius and Casca conclude their pact, Cinna, a member of the conspiracy, arrives. He begins to talk of the storm, but Cassius cuts him short, anxious to know if the conspirators are waiting for him. Cinna says they are and adds how beneficial it would be to their cause if Cassius could "but win the noble Brutus to our party." Cassius orders Cinna to put one of the forged letters on Brutus seat of office, to throw another in his window, and to place a third on the statue of Lucius Junius Brutus (the ancient and heroic namesake of Marcus Brutus). Then Cinna is to meet him at Pompey's theater. Cassius then tells Casca that Brutus is three-parts won to his cause, and at their next encounter he will be entirely persuaded. Casca remarks that Brutus "sits high in all the people's hearts," and that what would appear to be evil if done by them, would appear virtuous if done by Brutus. Cassius agrees with Casca's judgment that Brutus is of great worth and is much needed for their cause, and he bids Casca join him in securing Brutus for their party.

Act II: Scene 1

Brutus is seen in his orchard at three o'clock in the morning of the ides of March. He cannot sleep because he is troubled by the conflict between his love for Caesar and his love for freedom and Rome. He bids his servant, Lucius, to bring him a candle, and muses over what must be done. He resolves that the only way to stop Caesar is to kill him. Brutus has no personal motive for murdering him; he believes that Caesar must die for the general good. Since he can find nothing in Caesar's past conduct which would justify murder, Brutus projects his thoughts into the future. He considers the possibility of Caesar receiving the crown, changing his nature, and becoming a tyrant. It would be better not to give Caesar this opportunity, not to give the adder its chance to strike. Brutus resolves to "think him as a serpent's egg/Which, hatch'd, would as his kind grow mischievous,/And kill him in the shell."

Lucius reenters with a letter he has found while lighting the candle in Brutus' study. It is the forged note which Cinna has tossed into the window and bears the cryptic message, "Brutus, thou sleepst. Aware, and see thyself!/Shall Rome, etc. Speak, strike, redress!" Brutus interprets "Shall Rome, etc." to mean "Shall Rome stand under one man's awe?" Lucius returns to report that tomorrow is the fifteenth of March. When the servant leaves to answer a knock at the gate, Brutus continues his thoughts. He says that since Cassius has "whet" him against Caesar, he has not slept a wink. His wakefulness has been a nightmare of conflict between "the genius and the mortal instruments" which work on the human condition as insurrection does on a kingdom.

The word "insurrection" still rings on the stage as Lucius enters to announce the arrival of "your brother Cassius" (Cassius is married to Brutus' sister). Others are with him, but their hats are pulled low over their ears and their faces are buried in cloaks so that they cannot be identified. Brutus comments on the shamefulness of conspiracy that fears to show its monstrous face even in a state full of evil. But he quickly overcomes his sense of shame by reasoning that even if the conspirators continued in their normal ways, the blackness of Erebus (the path to hell) could not hide them from Caesar's tyranny ("prevention").

Cassius, Casca, Decius Brutus, Cinna, Metellus Cimber, and Trebonius enter. Before introducing these men, Cassius tells Brutus that each one is acquainted with and honors him. Brutus and Cassius whisper to each other as the rest of the conspirators engage in small talk, disagreeing over the direction in which the sun is rising. The conclave finished; Brutus takes their hands one by one as fellow conspirators. Cassius proposes that they swear an oath, but Brutus says it is unnecessary, since "the sufferance of our souls, the time's abuse" are strong enough motive to assure their good faith. Honesty and the promise of a Roman is enough, Brutus patriotically asserts.

The oath rejected, Cassius then proposes that Cicero be included in their group. Casca and Cinna agree, and Metellus Cimber reasons that Cicero's dignity and age will win them the good opinion of the masses. "It shall be said his judgment rul'd our hands," Cimber states. Brutus rejects Cassius' second proposal, arguing that Cicero "will never follow anything/ That other men begin." Cassius grudgingly agrees to leave Cicero out. Decius proposes to kill Antony as well as Caesar. Cassius readily agrees, on the grounds that Antony is a "shrewd contriver" and may well harm them later. For a third time, Brutus opposes Cassius on the grounds that "Antony is but a limb of Gaesar. / Let us be sacrificers, but not butchers." As for Caesar, "Let's carve him as a dish fit for the gods,/ Not hew him as a carcass fit for hounds." Naively, Brutus adds, "We shall be call'd purgers, not murderers. And for Mark Antony, think not of him;/ For he can do no more than Caesar's arm/ When Caesar's head is off."

The clock strikes three, and Trebonius says it is time to part. Cassius finds it doubtful that Caesar will come forth because of the "apparent prodigies" and unaccustomed terrors of the night, "for he is superstitious grown of late." But Decius promises to get Caesar to the Capitol by flattering him with praise of his hatred for flatterers. Cassius proposes that, instead, all the conspirators go and fetch Caesar. Metellus Cimber bids them include Caius Ligarius in the plot, and Brutus assents, asking that Caius Ligarius be sent to him. Their plans concluded, the conspirators adjourn. Brutus calls his servant, but finding him asleep, he tenderly wishes him sweet dreams and reflects on the sound slumber of those unburdened by care.

When the conspirators have gone, Brutus' wife, Portia, comes to inquire why Brutus is up in the middle of the night. She wants to know what has been absorbing him so much of late. Brutus replies that he is not well. Portia retorts that Brutus is not acting like someone sick in body but like someone with a troubled spirit. She implores him on her knees to tell her what is wrong and asks about the visitors who had come in with their faces hidden. She declares that by failing to share his secret, Brutus excludes her from part of the marriage and makes her his harlot rather than his wife. Brutus insists she is his honorable wife, but Portia continues to protest her good repute, by virtue of her father, the noble Cato, and by her own act of courage, a self-inflicted thigh wound that was intended to prove her worth as Brutus' wife and the sharer of his secrets.

Brutus is touched by his wife's devotion and is about to tell her his plans when he is interrupted by the entrance of Ligarius. Ligarius has been ill but is ready to throw his bandages aside if Brutus proposes some exploit worthy of the name of honor. Brutus says such an exploit is planned, and at these words, Ligarius throws aside his bandages and presents himself ready for action. Brutus says that the plot is one which will make sick men whole and that he will tell Ligarius of it as they walk. Ligarius replies that even though he is ignorant of the plot, it is enough for him that Brutus leads it.

Act II: Scene 2

The storm is still raging as the scene shifts to Caesar's house. It is three A. M. in the morning of the ides of March. Caesar, like Brutus, is spending a restless night. He exclaims that neither heaven nor earth is peaceful on this night; even Calpurnia, his wife, is having disturbed dreams and has cried out three times in her sleep, "Help, ho! They murder Caesar!" Caesar sends a servant to the priests and orders them to make a sacrifice and send him the results. Calpurnia enters and begs Caesar not to stir out of the house that day, but Caesar fatalistically replies, "What can be avoided Whose end is purposed by the mighty gods?"

Calpurnia says that she is not normally upset by prodigies, but that the **unnatural** occurrences of the proceding night have disturbed her: a lioness was seen giving birth in the streets; the dead rose from their graves; and fiery warriors fought in the clouds so fiercely that blood drizzled upon the Capitol. There were also reports that horses neighed, that dying men groaned, and that ghosts shrieked and squealed along the streets.

Calpurnia interprets the comets in the air, also seen during the night, as a prophecy of the death of a prince, for comets are never seen when beggars die. Caesar firmly encourages his wife with the now famous lines, "Cowards die many times before their deaths;/The valiant never taste of death but once." He finds it strange that men should have fears, since death is a necessity which "will come when it will come."

The sacrifice Caesar had ordered earlier has been done, and the servant returns to report that the priests advise Caesar to stay at home, for the beast, when opened, was found to have no heart. Caesar defies this answer of the gods sent by the priests, and like Cassius and Calpurnia, he gives his own interpretation of the sacrifice, which is colored by his personal predilections. The heartless beast, Caesar asserts, is a chastisement of the gods against cowardice. If he should stay at home this day, Caesar would be a beast without a heart. (The heart was regarded as the seat of courage in Renaissance physiology and philosophy.) He calls himself the brother of danger; metaphorically, he and danger are two lions born on the same day, and of the two, Caesar is the more terrible. (The lion, the king of the beasts, traditionally represented the king of men, the masculine spirit, and male courage.) "Caesar shall go forth," the intemperate ruler declares.

When Caesar declares himself braver than danger itself, Calpurnia exclaims that Caesar is losing sight of his wisdom in his overconfidence. She implores him to send Mark Antony to the Senate to say Caesar is not well. According to her "humor," Caesar agrees to send the message and to remain at home.

Decius Brutus enters to fetch Caesar to the Senate. Caesar asks Decius to bear his greeting to the senators and tell them that he will not come today. He adds that to say he cannot come is false, and to say he dares not come is even falser. Calpurnia tells Decius to say that Caesar is sick, but Caesar insists that he will not send a lie. He bids Decius again to say simply that he will not come. Craftily, Decius asks Caesar to give him some cause so that Decius will not be laughed at when he delivers the message. Arrogantly, Caesar answers that it is enough to tell the Senate that Caesar will not come, but because he loves Decius, for his personal satisfaction, he will give him the reason: Calpurnia keeps him at home because she dreamed she saw his statue like a fountain with a hundred spouts, pouring forth blood in which smiling Romans bathed their hands.

Decius protests that Calpurnia's dream has been misinterpreted, that it really means that Rome sucks reviving blood from Caesar and through him regains its vitality. Decius adds that the Senate has decided to give Caesar a crown this day. If he does not come, the Senate may change its mind. Decius argues that the dream as a reason for his absence "were a mock/Apt to be rendered for someone to say/'Break up the Senate till another time,/When Caesar's wife shall meet with better dreams." That is, Caesar's excuse might be interpreted as an insult by one of the senators. Furthermore, if Caesar does not appear, senators will say that Caesar is afraid. Caesar is persuaded to see that Calpurnia's fears are foolish ones and tells his wife to get his robes, for he will go.

Publius, Brutus, Ligarius, Metellus, Casca, Trebonius, and Cinna enter to escort Caesar to the Senate, and Caesar graciously welcomes them. Alluding to their former enmity, Caesar also notes that Ligarius' illness has made him lean. The clock strikes eight as Antony enters. Caesar remarks that despite the fact that Antony revels all night, he is able to get up in time for his duties in the morning. Caesar apologizes for keeping his escorts waiting and bids Cinna, Metellus, and Trebonius to sit near him in the Senate. Trebonius replies in an aside that he will be so near Caesar that Caesar's best friends will wish he had been further away. Caesar invites the men to drink wine with him and then "like friends," they shall be off together. In response to Caesar's show of trust, Brutus mourns, in an aside, that every "like" is not the "same."

Act II: Scene 3

In a street near the Capitol, Artemidorus appears reading a paper. Artemidorus places himself in a spot where Caesar must pass on his walk to the Capitol, and rereads the letter he plans to thrust into Caesar's hands. The letter warns Caesar to beware of Brutus, Cassius, Casca, Cinna, and other members of the conspiracy because they are plotting against his life. It warns Caesar that unless he is immortal, overconfidence opens the way for conspiracy. His letter ends, "If thou read this, O Caesar; thou mayst live;/If not, the Fates with traitors do contrive."

Act II: Scene 4

On the morning of the ides of March, Portia stands before the house of Brutus, directing her servant Lucius to run to the Senate House. Having been informed of the assassination plot by Brutus, she is visibly distraught over the possible danger to her husband should his plans miscarry. The boy asks what errand he is to perform at the Senate, and Portia realizes that she cannot tell. How hard it is for a woman to keep a secret, Portia reflects, for although she has a man's mind, she has only a woman's might. The bewildered servant asks if he must run to the Capitol and back again and do nothing else, but Portia, now composed, orders him to bring her word if Brutus looks well, for he seemed sick when he left.

Portia imagines she hears a "bustling rumor" (uproar, report) from the Capitol, but it is only the Soothsayer who arrives on his way to the Capitol. Hoping to get news of him, Portia asks the Soothsayer which way he has been, but when she learns that he has just come from home, she asks him the time and inquires whether or not Caesar has gone to the Capitol. The Soothsayer replies that Caesar has not gone yet; he adds that he himself is going to find a place to see Caesar pass on the way to the Senate. Portia wants to know if he has a suit with Caesar, to which, he replies that he is going to "beseech him to befriend himself." Fearfully, Portia asks if the Soothsayer knows of any harm intended toward Caesar, and she is told that the Soothsayer *knows* of no harm intended but *fears* there will be some. He excuses himself, saying that he must find a good spot before the crowds gather.

After he leaves, Portia complains about the weakness of the woman's heart, "O Brutus!/The heavens speed thee in thine enterprise." Fearing that the boy has overheard her prayer, she adds that "Brutus hath a suit /That Caesar will not grant." She grows faint and, forgetting her former errand, tells the boy to run to Brutus, inform him that she is well, and return with word of what he says.

Act III: Scene 1

Brutus, Cassius, Casca, Decius Brutus, Metellus, Trebonius, Cinna, Antony, Lepidus, Popilius, Peblius, and others accompany Caesar through the streets to the Capitol. A crowd has gathered to watch the procession, among them Artemidorus and the Soothsayer. As Caesar and his train pass, Caesar sees the Soothsayer in the crowd and confidently reminds him that "the ides of March are come." "Ay, Caesar," replies the Soothsayer, "but not gone." Artemidorus then comes forward and begs Caesar to read his note, but Decius hastily intervenes with another note, asking Caesar to read Trebonius' suit at his leisure. Impetuously, Artemidorus demands that Caesar read his first, for it is of personal importance to Caesar. Magnanimously, Caesar replies, what concerns

Caesar himself will be read last. When Artemidorus insists again, Caesar indignantly exclaims, "What! is this fellow mad?" Cassius steps in and chides Artemidorus for presenting petitions in the streets; the Capitol is the proper place for such things.

Caesar goes up to the Senate House, followed by the crowd. Popilius whispers good luck to Cassius on his enterprise, but when the startled Cassius asks, "What enterprise, Popilius?" the senator simply replies, "Fare you well" and advances toward Caesar. Cassius tells Brutus of Popilius' ambiguous remarks and expresses his fear that their conspiracy has been discovered. He vows that if the plot is unsuccessful, he will kill himself. Brutus tells Cassius to be calm, for Popilius is smiling as he talks to Caesar and Caesar's face shows no sign of change.

Cassius notices that the plan is beginning to work, for Trebonius is drawing Antony out of the way. Antony and Trebonius leave as the senators take their seats. Cassius asks for Metellus Cimber so that he can present his suit to Caesar, while Brutus urges the conspirators to press near Caesar and aid Metellus. Cinna tells Casca that he is to be the first one to strike Caesar. As Caesar calls the Senate to order, Metellus kneels before Caesar and begins a flattering address. Caesar cuts him short with a lengthy reply in which he asserts that Caesar is not like ordinary men who succumb to flattery and make childish decisions. He cannot be melted by praise from the "true quality" of a suit. He says that if Metellus is pleading for his brother who has been banished, Caesar will "spurn thee like a cur out of my way." Metellus asks if anyone else will aid his suit for his banished brother. Brutus comes forward and kisses Caesar's hand, saying that he does this not in flattery, but out of desire for Caesar to repeal the banishment of Publius Cimber. Next, Cassius humbly entreats Caesar, falling "low as to thy foot." But Caesar remains adamant.

In a piece of over-extended self-eulogy Caesar asserts, "I am constant as the Northern Star,/Of whose true-fixed and resting quality/There is no fellow in the firmament." Among men on earth, Caesar continues, "men are flesh and blood, and apprehensive;/Yet in the number I do know but one/That unassailable holds on his rank,/Unshaked of motion; and that I am he." Publius Cimber shall remain banished, for Caesar cannot be moved. Cinna and Decius implore Caesar, but he dismisses them, uttering the most arrogant statement of all, "Hence! Wilt thou lift up Olympus?" Casca signals the attack, "Speak, hands, for me!" He stabs Caesar, and one by one, the other conspirators add their blows. Seeing Brutus among their number, the stricken Caesar cries, *"Et tu, Brute? Then fall, Caesar."*

As Caesar dies, the senators and people retreat in confusion. Cinna cries out, "Liberty! Freedom! Tyranny is dead!/Run hence, proclaim, cry it about the streets." Cassius bids the conspirators to run to the common pulpits and call out "Liberty, freedom, and enfranchisement!" Casca encourages Brutus to go to the pulpit, and Decius urges Cassius to go also. Brutus and Cassius advise the senator Publius to leave, lest the people attack the conspirators and harm the aged senator. Brutus adds that no man should bear the consequences of the deed, except the conspirators themselves. Trebonius returns and tells his fellows that Antony has fled to his house amazed and that "Men, wives, and children stare, cry out, and run,/As it were doomsday."

Brutus asks the Fates what is in store for the assassins now. Agreeing with Cassius that life involves the fear of death, Brutus declares that they are Caesar's friends for having cut off his life from years of fearing death. Then Brutus exhorts the conspirators to bathe their hands and arms in Caesar's blood, and with their swords besmeared with the blood, to walk into the market place, shouting "Peace, freedom, liberty!" Cassius envisions that in ages to come this noble scene will be enacted by nations yet unborn and in languages yet unknown. Brutus wonders how many times plays will be held portraying the bleeding of Caesar, who now lies by Pompey's statue, "No worthier than the dust!" And Cassius adds that in these plays of the future, they will be remembered as the men who gave liberty to their country.

The conspirators have decided to leave the Senate House with Brutus at their head when a servant of Antony's arrives. The servant says that Antony instructed him to kneel before Brutus and deliver the message that Antony loves and honors Brutus, that he feared, honored, and loved Caesar, and if Brutus can show him why Caesar deserved to die, "Mark Antony shall not love Caesar dead/So well as Brutus living; but will follow/The fortunes and affairs of noble Brutus." Brutus at once replies that his master is a wise and valiant Roman. He instructs the slave to fetch Antony to the Capitol to learn the cause of Caesar's murder and to tell him that by Brutus' honor, he will depart unharmed. While the servant runs to get Antony, Cassius tells Brutus that he fears Antony and that his fears very often prove correct.

Antony arrives, and ignoring Brutus, he addresses Caesar's body, "O mighty Caesar! Dost thou lie so low?/Are all thy conquests, glories, triumphs, spoils,/Shrunk to this little measure?" Then Antony asks who else must die and says that if he is marked for death, he will never be more ready than now. If he lived a thousand years, he would find no place, nor hour, nor weapon more pleasing than those which have accompanied Caesar's death, nor would he find executioners more fitting than those who are now "the choice and master spirits of this age."

Brutus tells Antony not to beg for death, for although the conspirators appear to be bloody and cruel, their hearts are actually filled with pity for the general wrong done to Rome by Caesar. Antony is welcome to join their ranks. Cassius adds that Antony will have as much power to dispense favors in the new state as the conspirators do. Brutus asks Antony to await an explanation patiently until the people, who are beside themselves with fear, have been appeased; then he will explain why he who loved Caesar struck him down.

Pretending to be satisfied with the assassins' wisdom in overthrowing Caesar, Antony takes the bloody hand of each of the men. Antony realizes that to the conspirators he must appear to be either a coward or a flatterer, and turning to the dead body of Caesar, he begs its forgiveness for befriending Caesar's enemies. He declares how unbecoming it is to the love he bore Caesar to make peace with the assassins in the very sight of the corpse; it would be more fitting to weep at the fall of Caesar, whom Antony now compares to a noble deer, run down and killed by a pack of hounds.

Cassius interrupts Antony's apology to Caesar, at which Antony begs his pardon for praising the dead man before his slayers. Still, Antony points out, his praise is slight; Caesar's enemies will do him as much credit. In a friend, however, Antony's words are merely passionless understatement. But Cassius is not prepared to blame Antony for praising Caesar; what he wants to know is can Antony be counted on as one of his allies, or shall the conspirators go along their way without depending on Antony's support. Antony explains that he shook their hands in order to indicate his alliance with their cause, but the sight of Caesar did indeed sway him from that resolution. Therefore, Antony qualifies his pledge of friendship; he will join their ranks if they are able to supply reasons why and in what way Caesar was dangerous. Brutus promises that the reasons he will give Antony would satisfy him even if he were the son of Caesar himself.

Antony asks if he can deliver the funeral oration over Caesar's body in the market-place. Without any hesitation, Brutus agrees to Antony's request. Cassius pulls Brutus aside and cautions him not to allow Antony to speak. "You know not what you do," Cassius warns. Antony easily may stir up the people. Convinced of the justice of his crime, Brutus answers that he will speak first and tell the people the reasons for the murder of Caesar, and that Antony speaks with their permission, since they want Caesar to have "true rites and lawful ceremonies." Brutus is sure "it shall advantage more than do us wrong." Cassius says he still doesn't like it. Brutus then orders Antony not to blame the conspirators during his oration, but to speak good of Caesar without condemning his killers. Furthermore, he is to say he speaks with the insurgents' permission, and he must agree to speak after Brutus. Antony assents, and Brutus bids him to prepare the body and follow them. The conspirators go off, leaving Antony alone with the body.

Alone with the body, Antony speaks his true feelings to the corpse. He begs pardon for being so meek and gentle with Caesar's butchers. "Thou art the ruins of the noblest man/That ever lived in the tide of time," Antony declares. He swears an oath so strong that he calls it "prophecy" over the gaping wounds of Caesar which "like dumb mouths, do ope their ruby lips/To beg the voice and utterance of my tongue." The limbs of men shall be cursed for Caesar's death, domestic fury and civil strife shall spread through Italy. Blood, destruction, and other monstrosities of war will become such a familiar sight in the land that mothers will merely smile when they see their infants cut up by the hands of war. Caesar's spirit, with Ate (the hellish god of discord) at his side, shall range through the land and "Cry 'Havoc.'" And "this foul deed shall smell above the earth/With carrion men, groaning for burial."

Antony's harangue is ended by the arrival of a messenger who Antony recognizes as the servant of Octavius Caesar. The messenger begins to relay his message, but when he sees the body of Caesar, he cries out. Tears welling in his eyes, Antony asks the slave if his master is coming and learns that Octavius is only seven leagues from Rome. Antony orders the slave to tell his master what has happened and to warn him that Rome is not safe for entry. On second thought, Antony decides to have the servant wait until after the funeral oration. After they see how the people react to the murder, the slave may report to Octavius on the state of things. Then Antony and the servant carry Caesar's body off.

Act III: Scene 2

Later on the same day, the ides of March, throngs of citizens crowd the Forum of Rome. They are angry and fearful at Caesar's death. When Brutus and Cassius arrive, some among them cry, "We will be satisfied! Let us be satisfied." Brutus divides the crowd so that some stay to hear him speak, while others go off to listen to Cassius. Brutus begins to speak in a dry, emotionless prose. Logically and coldly, he appeals to the wisdom and judgment of the crowd, asking them to trust his honor so that they may believe his reasons. First he addresses "any in this assembly, any dear friend of Caesar's," to whom Brutus says that his own love for Caesar was no less than his. If then that friend demand why Brutus rose against Caesar, this is the answer: "Not that I loved Caesar less, but that I loved Rome more." He declares that

Caesar would have enslaved them if he had lived, and asks them if they would rather be slaves and have Caesar alive or be free men and have Caesar dead. He tells the mob: "As Caesar loved me, I weep for him; as he was fortunate, I rejoice at it; as he was valiant, I honor him, but as he was ambitious, I slew him." He asks any so base as to be a slave to speak up, or any so rude as to be other than a Roman, or any "so vile as will not love his country?" Brutus then asserts that the reason for Caesar's death is a matter of official record in the books of the Senate.

As Antony appears with the body of Caesar, Brutus announces that Antony, although he had no part in the slaying, will receive all the benefits of Caesar's death, a place in the commonwealth, as shall all the crowd. Finally, he closes his speech with the words, "As I slew my best lover for the good of Rome, I have the same dagger for myself, when it shall please my country to need my death." Moved by Brutus' oratory, the crowd cries, "Live, Brutus! Live, live!" Some of the citizens suggest that they build a statue of Brutus. Another exclaims, "Let him be Caesar." Brutus silences the mob and asks them all to stay and hear Antony praise Caesar. Before he leaves, he orders that none depart before Antony finishes his speech, save himself.

As Antony makes his way to the pulpit, one citizen exclaims, " Twere best he speak no harm of Brutus here," while another cries out, "This Caesar was a tyrant," and another answers, "Nay, that's certain,/We are blest that Rome is rid of him." Antony mounts the pulpit and begins his speech: "Friends, Romans, countrymen, lend me your ears;/I come to bury Caesar, not to praise him." Antony declares that the evil which men do lives after them, not their good; "So let it be with Caesar." Pretending thus to agree with Brutus, Antony continues, "The noble Brutus/Hath told you Caesar was ambitious: If it were so, it was a grievous fault." (He does not state it was so.) Antony repeats again and again that Brutus has called Caesar ambitious, "and Brutus is an honorable man." The speech continues to relate how Caesar wept when the poor cried out. "Ambition should be made of sterner stuff: /Yet Brutus says he was ambitious;/And Brutus is an honorable man." Antony reminds the crowd that Caesar had refused the crown three times at the Lupercal. "Yet Brutus says he was ambitious;/And sure, he is an honorable man." Antony reminds his listeners that they all loved Caesar once and not without cause. What keeps them from mourning him now, Antony exclaims, crying, "O judgment, thou art fled to brutish beasts,/And men have lost their reason!" Bursting with emotion, Antony mourns, "My heart is in the coffin there with Caesar, /And I must pause till it come back to me."

As Antony weeps, the plebeians comment on his remarks. There is reason in them, one plebeian observes. "He would not take the crown;

Therefore 'tis certain he was not ambitious." Another, totally converted to Antony's cause, asserts, "There's not a nobler man in Rome than Antony."

Having composed himself, Antony begins to speak again. He says that he means not to inflame them against the conspirators, for they are all honorable men. Then he produces Caesar's will from his cloak, and holds it up for the people to see. Antony says he cannot read the will, since if he does, "they would go and kiss dead Caesar's wounds,/ And dip their napkins in his sacred blood." A citizen shouts out for Antony to read the will. He refuses again, saying that if he reads the will, they would find out how much Caesar loved them, and the knowledge would inflame them and make them mad. The same citizen cries out again for the will to be read. Antony calls for patience and ironically says that he has gone too far: "I fear I wrong the honorable men/Whose daggers have stabbed Caesar: I do fear it." Another citizen cries, "They are traitors. Honorable men!" Still another shouts, "They were villains, murderers. The will! Read the will!" Antony finally consents to read the will and tells the crowd to make a ring about Caesar's body so that he can show them him who made the will.

Antony descends from the pulpit and comes down to Caesar's body. He takes Caesar's cloak in his hand and begins to speak. He says that Caesar first put on this cloak on the day he conquered the Gallic tribe, the Nervii. He points to a tear in the cloak and says, "Look in this place ran Cassius' dagger through./See what a rent the envious Casca made." Then he points to the wound that Brutus made and explains, "Brutus, as you know, was Caesar's angel:/Judge, O you gods, how dearly Caesar loved him!/This was the most unkindest cut of all;/For, when the noble Caesar saw him stab,/Ingratitude, more strong than traitors' arms,/Quite vanquish'd him. Then burst his mighty heart,/And, in his mantle muffling up his face,/Even at the base of Pompey's statue/(Which all the while ran blood), great Caesar fell." Then Antony openly calls the bloody deed treason. The crowd is weeping now over Caesar's mutilated clothing, and Antony asks why they weep over mere clothing. "Look you here! Here is himself, marred as you see with traitors." Dramatically, Antony reveals Caesar's corpse to the horror-stricken view of the public.

At the point when Antony drops his irony and openly calls the conspirators traitors, the crowd becomes angry and ugly. The citizens shout, "Revenge! About! Seek! Burn! Fire! Kill! Slay! Let not a traitor live!" But Antony cries halt and, resuming his irony, he says this murder was the deed of honorable men. He adds that he is not an orator like Brutus and that he speaks with the leave of the conspirators, who know very well that Antony has "neither wit, nor words, nor worth,

/Action, nor utterance, nor the power of speech to stir men's blood."
He only tells the crowd what they already know and shows Caesar's
wounds so they can speak for him. He adds, "But were I Brutus,
/And Brutus Antony, there were an Antony/Would ruffle up your
spirits, and put a tongue/In every wound of Caesar, that should move
/The stones of Rome to rise and mutiny." The suggestion planted, the
citizens shout out, "We'll mutiny." One citizen suggests, "We'll burn
the house of Brutus." As the citizens are about to leave the Forum
and begin the pillaging of the murderers' houses, Antony calls halt
again, for they have forgotten the will which Antony was going to
read. Antony then reads: "To every Roman citizen he gives/To every
several man, seventy-five drachmas" (about one hundred fifty dollars
in modern purchasing power). A citizen calls out, "Most noble Caesar!
We'll revenge his death." Antony continues, "Moreover, he hath left you
all his walks,/His private arbors, and new-planted orchards,/On this
side Tiber; he hath left them you,/And to your heirs for ever—common
pleasures,/To walk abroad, and recreate yourselves./Here was a Caesar!
When comes such another?"

The citizens are now wild with fury; they pile up benches, tables, and
stalls from the Forum to use as fuel for Caesar's funeral pyre, which
they plan to erect in a holy place. The crowd leaves with the body
of Caesar to bring it to the holy place for cremation. Antony muses
to himself over the results of his speech, "Now let it work. Mischief,
thou art afoot,/Take thou what course thou wilt."

A servant enters with a message that Octavius has already arrived in
Rome. He and Lepidus are at Caesar's house. Antony replies that he
will come at once, that Octavius' arrival is like the granting of a wish.
"Fortune is merry," Antony remarks, and so is Antony. The servant
reports that he has heard that Brutus and Cassius "are rid like madmen
through the gates of Rome." To this, Antony remarks, "Belike they
had some notice of the people,/ How I had moved them." Antony and
the servant leave for the house of Caesar where Octavius awaits them.

Act III: Scene 3

Later that day on the ides of March, Cinna the poet is seen on a street
near the Forum. As he walks along, he muses over a dream he has had
in which he feasted with Caesar. Now omens of evil are charging his
imagination. He does not wish to go out of doors, but something leads
him forward. A band of citizens suddenly appears and question Cinna;
asking his name, where he is going, where he lives, and if he is married
or a bachelor. Wittily Cinna replies that he is "wisely . . . a bachelor."

An enraged citizen interprets this as an insult to married men and promises to beat Cinna for calling him a fool. Cinna then reports that he is going to Caesar's funeral as a friend. When he answers that his name is Cinna, one citizen cries; he is a conspirator, tear him to pieces. Cinna protests that he is Cinna the poet, not Cinna the conspirator. But another citizen, completely unreasonable, shouts, "Tear him for his bad verses." When Cinna again pleads that he is the poet, still another plebeian answers, "It is no matter; his name's Cinna! Pluck but his name out of his heart, and turn him going." Madly they set upon the helpless poet, and when they have finished rending him, they charge off to burn the houses of Brutus, Cassius, Decius, and the rest.

Act IV: Scene 1

The scene now shifts to a room in Antony's house where Antony, Octavius, and Lepidus are holding council. They are found in the middle of their discussion, deciding who is to be killed in the reign of terror which they are about to begin. Octavius tells Lepidus, "Your brother too must die. Consent you, Lepidus?" Lepidus consents "upon condition that Publius shall not live,/Who is your sister's son, Mark Antony." Antony calmly agrees to this. Antony then sends Lepidus to Caesar's house to fetch Caesar's will in order to see if they can eliminate some of the heirs.

As Lepidus leaves, Antony tells Octavius that Lepidus has little merit as a man and is only fit to do errands. He asks if it is right that this man should get a third part of the world. Octavius answers that Antony seemed to think well of Lepidus when he asked his advice about the proscription lists. But Antony replies he has been using Lepidus as a scapegoat on whom the blame for the murders may be placed later on. Lepidus follows where they lead, or leads where they tell him to go. He will be discarded like an ass set to pasture when it has delivered its burden. Octavius leaves these plans up to Antony, but interjects that Lepidus is a tried and valiant soldier. Antony insists once more that Lepidus can only be regarded as property like a horse. Then he reports that Brutus and Cassius are beginning to gather their forces and that now is the time for unity and for taking council. Octavius assents and they leave to make plans.

Act IV: Scene 2

The scene now shifts to a camp near Sardis where Brutus' army has pitched its tents. Drums are sounded as Brutus arrives before his tent

accompanied by Lucilius, Titinius, and other soldiers. Lucius, Brutus'
servant, is also present. Lucilius has just returned from a visit to Cassius' camp, accompanied by Pindarus. Brutus tells Pindarus that his
master Cassius has given him some cause to wish "things done, undone." Pindarus replies that his master will appear "such as he is, full
of regard and honor." Brutus then asks Lucilius how he was received
by Cassius, and Lucilius explains that he was received with courtesy
and respect, but not with the old familiarity that Cassius used to show.
Brutus tells Lucilius that he has witnessed a "hot friend cooling," and
he compares Cassius to a horse which seems spirited at the start but
quickly falls under trial of battle. He then learns from Lucilius that
Cassius' army will be camping at Sardis that night.

Cassius enters with several soldiers and greets Brutus with the words,
"Most noble brother, you have done me wrong." He accuses Brutus
of hiding his wrongs under "this sober form of yours." Brutus reminds Cassius of his hasty temper and tells him not to wrangle in
front of their two armies. Both armies are led off some distance as
Brutus and Cassius enter the tent where Brutus regally promises, "I
will give you audience."

Act IV: Scene 3

Inside the tent, Cassius tells Brutus he has been wronged because Brutus
has condemned Lucius Pella for taking bribes from the Sardians, even
after Cassius had sent letters entreating him not to dismiss Pella.
Cassius adds that this is not the time to scrutinize and rigidly censure
every petty or trifling offense. Brutus reproaches Cassius for selling
offices to undeserving men for gold. At this, Cassius becomes infuriated and says that if anyone but Brutus had told him this, he
would have been killed on the spot. Speaking of corruption, Brutus
says that Cassius himself has set the example among his men and
has escaped punishment only because of his high position. Brutus
reminds Cassius of the ides of March, how they had struck down
Caesar, the foremost man of all the world, for the sake of justice.
He asks if they should now "contaminate our fingers with base
bribes." Brutus argues, "I had rather be a dog, and bay the moon,
/Than such a Roman." "Brutus, bait not me;/I'll not endure it,"
Cassius warns. He adds that Brutus forgets himself when he attempts
to restrain Cassius' actions, for Cassius is a more experienced soldier
and more able "to make conditions," that is to make bargains with men
and officers. Indignantly, Brutus retorts that Cassius is not more
able; Cassius insists he is; Brutus contradicts. Cassius warns Brutus
to provoke him no farther, but Brutus insists that Cassius had better
listen, since he will not be silenced by Cassius' rash temper. When
he asserts that he cannot be frightened by a madman, Cassius ex-

claims, "O ye gods, ye gods! Must I endure all this?" Viciously, Brutus warns Cassius that he will defy him until "you shall digest the venom of your spleen," and he promises that Cassius will be the object of his ridicule from this day forth. Sarcastically, Brutus urges Cassius to prove he is a "better soldier," for he is anxious to learn from "noble men." Cassius protests, "I said, an elder soldier, not a better." He asserts that Caesar dared not treat him so, and Brutus replies that Cassius had not dared to provoke him as he dares Brutus now. Now at the peak of his anger, Cassius threatens, "Do not presume too much upon my love;/I may do that I shall be sorry for." Brutus replies arrogantly that Cassius has already done what he should be sorry for and that his threats have no terror for Brutus, "for I am arm'd so strong in honesty/That they pass by me as the idle wind." Next Brutus complains that Cassius did not send him any of the gold which he had badly needed, for he cannot raise money by vile means, that is, by extorting it from local peasants. Cassius claims that he did not deny Brutus the gold but that the messenger who delivered his reply was a fool. Cassius charges that Brutus no longer loves him, for he refuses to tolerate Cassius' weaknesses and makes them even greater than they are. Cassius unsheathes his dagger, and, handing it to Brutus, he says, "I, that denied thee gold, will give my heart:/Strike, as thou didst at Caesar, for, I know,/When thou didst hate him worst, thou lovedst him better/Than ever thou lovedst Cassius."

Seeing Cassius with his bosom bared and his dagger offered for his death, Brutus apologetically tells Cassius to sheathe his dagger and "be angry when you will." Brutus compares himself to a lamb that carries anger only briefly as a flint afire one moment is cold the next. Brutus is sorry he has laughed at Cassius' weakness of temperament, promises to tolerate it in the future, and the friends are reconciled.

Suddenly, there is a disturbance outside the door. A poet is trying to gain admittance to the tent on the grounds that he must stop the quarrel within, for the two generals should not be alone at such a time. Lucilius, who has been guarding the entry, refuses to admit the poet, but the poet insists, "Nothing but death shall stay me." Cassius appears and inquires the poet's errand and learns, through some doggerel verses, that someone who is older than either of the generals knows it is not fitting for them to fight. Cassius laughs at the poet and at the inferior quality of the rhymes, but Brutus is annoyed and says that foolish poets are out of place in war. Although Cassius is tolerant of the new fashion of taking poets to war, Brutus orders the poet to be gone. Then Brutus orders Lucilius and Titinius to bid the officers to make camp for the night, and Cassius adds that Messala is to be brought to them immediately.

The poet gone, Brutus asks Lucius, his servant, for a bowl of wine.

Julius Caesar

Cassius remarks that he did not think it was possible to make Brutus so angry. But Brutus explains that he hears many griefs. Cassius reminds Brutus to make use of his philosophy in facing evil events. Then calmly Brutus tells Cassius that Portia is dead. Amazed at this news, Cassius wonders how Brutus prevented himself from killing Cassius when he had crossed him so. He asks of what sickness Portia had died. Brutus replies that, impatient of his absence and seeing Mark Antony and Octavius grow strong, she killed herself by swallowing fire. Appalled, Cassius cries, "O ye immortal gods!"

Lucius reenters with wine and tapers. Brutus says he buries all unkindness in a bowl of wine, while Cassius says, "I cannot drink too much of Brutus' love." Titinius and Messala arrive and are told that Brutus has received letters saying that Octavius and Antony are marching with a mighty force toward Philippi. Messala says he has had letters to the same effect and adds that Octavius, Antony, and Lepidus have murdered a hundred senators. Brutus remarks that their letters differ in this point, since his report says seventy senators had been killed, Cicero among them. Messala asks if Brutus has received any news from his wife. Brutus replies he has not and asks Messala if he has heard anything. Messala reports that Portia is dead. Brutus, with philosophic quietude, states, "With meditating that she must die once, /I have the patience to endure it now."

Messala compliments Brutus on his stoical acceptance of Portia's death; this is the way great men should endure their losses, he says. Cassius states that he knows as much about the theory of Stoicism as Brutus does, but his nature (rash and choleric) could not bear grief with the resistance of the Stoic.

Anxious to leave the subject of Portia's death, Brutus suggests that they march to Philippi with their armies, but Cassius is against this plan. He feels it is better to let the enemy come to them, wearying their troops in the long march, while Brutus and Cassius' men are rested and ready to defend themselves. Brutus counters Cassius' suggestion by asserting that the enemy will gather fresh troops along the way among the people Brutus and Cassius have antagonized by extorting their money. Silencing Cassius, Brutus argues further that the morale of their troops is at its highest, and that if they wait, the morale will decrease. Cassius reluctantly agrees to march to Philippi. Brutus announces that it is time for rest, and Cassius begs Brutus that such a disagreement as had begun that night may never again come between their souls. Brutus replies, "Everything is well," and as Cassius, Titinius, and Messala leave, each in turn addresses him as "my lord" or "Lord Brutus."

Preparing for rest, Brutus calls for his gown and asks Lucius to find his instrument (lute). Paternally, he notes that Lucius is drowsy from hav-

ing served all day. He sends for Varro and Claudius to sleep in his tent
in the event that messengers to Cassius are needed during the night. The
two soldiers offer to stand guard all night, but Brutus considerately insists that they sleep until they are called. From the pocket of his gown,
Brutus produces a book he had blamed Lucius for misplacing and apologizes to his servant for being so forgetful. Still apologetic, Brutus asks
the tired boy to play a tune and promises to reward him if Brutus lives.
Music and a song follow before Lucius falls asleep. Tenderly, Brutus
removes the lute from Lucius' hands. Then, finding his book, Brutus
begins to read.

As Brutus picks up his book to read, the ghost of Caesar, unnoticed by
Brutus, appears in the tent. Brutus observes that the taper burns poorly.
Then, suddenly, he sees the apparition, which he tries to attribute to the
weakness of his eyes. As the spirit draws closer, Brutus asks, "Art thou
some god, some angel, or some devil,/That mak'st my blood cold and my
hair to stare?/Speak to me what thou art."

The ghost answers, "Thy evil spirit, Brutus." Brutus asks why the spirit
has come, to which the ghost replies, "To tell thee that thou shalt see
me at Philippi." Then I shall see you again? Brutus asks. "Ay, at
Philippi," the ghost replies. The ghost disappears as suddenly as it has
come. "Now that I have taken heart, thou vanishest," Brutus exclaims.

Brutus wakes Lucius, Claudius, and Varro. Lucius, dreaming he is still
playing, says, "The strings, my lord, are false." Brutus asks him if he
had dreamed and cried out in his sleep, but Lucius says he did not know
he cried out and that he saw nothing in the tent. Brutus asks the same
questions of Varro and Claudius, and their replies are as negative as
Lucius'. Immediately, Brutus sends Varro and Claudius to tell Cassius to
set out with his forces promptly and that Brutus will follow close behind.

Act V: Scene 1

The action now shifts to the plains of Philippi where Antony, Octavius,
and their armies are encamped. Octavius tells Antony that their prayers
are answered since the enemy is coming to meet them on the plains
rather than keep to the hills as Antony had imagined. Antony replies that
he knows why the conspirators do this. They are trying to make a show
of courage, which Antony does not believe they really have. A messenger
enters to announce the enemy's approach. Antony tells Octavius to take
the left side of the field, but Octavius demands the right. Antony asks,
"Why do you cross me in this exigent?" Octavius ominously replies, "I
do not cross you; but I will do so."

At the sound of the drum, Brutus and Cassius lead their army to the field. Lucilius, Titinius, and Messala join them. Brutus notes that Antony and Octavius stand as if to invite a parley. Antony, observing the same hesitation on Brutus' part, decides to answer the enemy's charges before doing battle. Cassius and Brutus advance to meet Antony and Octavius, while the armies wait for a signal from their generals to begin the fray. The rivals exchange insults over Brutus' love of good words and Octavius' penchant for giving bad strokes (in fighting). A master of the discourteous retort, Antony tells Brutus, "In your bad strokes, Brutus, you give good words;/Witness the hole you made in Caesar's heart,/Crying 'Long live! Hail, Caesar!' " Antony gets as good as he gives when Cassius reminds him that Antony is yet untried in battle, although his speech is gifted and his honeyed words rob the bees of Mount Hybla. Parrying Cassius' thrust neatly, Antony replies, "Not stingless too." Antony becomes angry as the insults continue, and his taunts become more venomous. "Villains!" he cries. "You did not waste words when your daggers struck Caesar while some of you smiled like apes, fawned like hounds, bowed like bondmen, kissing Caesar's feet, while damned Casca". . . stabbed him in the back. "O you flatterers!"

Failing an answer, Cassius turns to Brutus, arguing that if his advice had been followed instead of Brutus', they would not now be listening to Antony's abuses. Octavius draws his sword and swears that he will not sheathe it, "Never, till Caesar's three-and-thirty wounds/Be well aveng'd; or till another Caesar/Have added slaughter to the sword of traitors." Brutus replies that Octavius cannot die by traitors' hands unless he himself brought those hands with him. When Octavius says that he was not born to die on Brutus' sword, Brutus replies that he could not die more honorably if he were the noblest of his strain, that is, if he were his uncle, Julius Caesar. In a final insult, Octavius bids Cassius and Brutus to come to the field if they dare to fight that day; if not, they may come when they have the stomachs for a fight.

As Antony, Octavius, and their armies leave the field, Brutus and Lucilius, his lieutenant, go aside to talk, while Cassius and Messala confer in the foreground (downstage). Cassius says that this day is his birthday, and he calls Messala to witness that he is compelled, against his will, to risk everything on one battle, just as Pompey was. Cassius confides that although he had formerly believed in Epicurus, he has now changed his mind and believes, to some extent, in portents and omens. He relates how, on their way from Sardis, two eagles swooped down, ate from the hands of the soldiers, and followed them all the way to Philippi. Now, however, the eagles have flown away, and in their stead, ravens, crows, and kites look down upon them as if they were sickly prey. Advised not to believe in the omen, Cassius admits that he only partly believes in it, for at the same time, he is "fresh of spirit and resolved/To meet all perils very constantly."

Brutus and Cassius finish their conversations with their respective lieutenants and rejoin each other. Cassius suggests that although the gods are favorable, he and Brutus might hold a final conversation before battle. If the worst befalls them, this conversation will be their last, Cassius states; therefore, he asks Brutus what he proposes to do should they lose the day. Brutus replies that he would arm himself with patience and live by the same rule of philosophy he had followed when he had condemned Cato for his "cowardly and vile" suicide. Cassius asks if this means Brutus would be content to be led captive through the streets of Rome, and Brutus arrogantly replies, "No, Cassius, no. Think not, thou noble Roman,/That ever Brutus will go bound to Rome./He bears too great a mind." Without revealing how he could escape humiliation and still avoid suicide should he be defeated and taken prisoner, Brutus asserts, "But this same day/Must end that work the ides of March begun." He bids a final farewell to Cassius and the two part friends. As they go off to battle, Brutus impatiently wishes, "O that a man might know/The end of this day's business ere it come!"

Act V: Scene 2

On the battlefield at Philippi, Brutus and Messala exchange hasty words. Brutus orders Messala to ride to the legions on the other (right) side of the field to deliver written orders to Cassius. He is to make an immediate attack on Antony's wing. Then Brutus observes that Octavius' wing shows signs of weakening and orders a sudden attack to overthrow it completely.

Act V: Scene 3

Cassius and Titinius appear on another part of the field of Philippi. Cassius, seeing his men deserting, tells Titinius how he slew his ensign who was turning to run. Titinius cries that Brutus gave the word to attack Antony too early. Meanwhile, Brutus' men, having overcome Octavius, were busy plundering the enemy's camp instead of assisting Cassius' flank, which was surrounded by Antony's soldiers. Pindarus enters to warn Cassius to flee, for Antony and his men have reached his tents. Cassius answers that he has retreated far enough. Looking across the plain, he asks, "Are those my tents where I perceive the fire?" Titinius replies, "They are, my lord."

Cassius sees a body of horsemen in the distance and asks Titinius to ride to them and learn whether they are friends or foes. As Titinius

Julius Caesar

rides off, Cassius orders Pindarus to climb higher on the hill to watch what is happening to Titinius, for his own "sight was ever thick" (near-sighted). As Pindarus climbs the hill, Cassius expresses his complete resignation to death: "This day I breathed first; time is come round,/And where I did begin, there shall I end;/My life is run his compass." Pindarus yells back to Cassius that Titinius has been surrounded by horsemen and exclaims, "He's ta'en! And hark! They shout for joy." Cassius bids Pindarus to come down, grieving that he is a coward to live so long and to see his "best friend" captured before his face. When Pindarus returns, Cassius reminds him how he had spared his life in Parthia when he had taken him captive on the condition that Pindarus swore to do whatsoever Cassius demanded. Cassius declares Pindarus a free man and orders him to take his sword, the same which ran Caesar through, and strike him in the bosom. As Pindarus guides the sword into his heart, Cassius cries, "Caesar, thou art reveng'd/Even with the sword that kill'd thee." And with these words, Cassius dies. Pindarus sighs, "So I am free; yet would not so have been,/Durst I have done my will. O Cassius!/Far from this country Pindarus shall run,/Where never Roman shall take note of him."

As Pindarus leaves the Roman world for good, Titinius returns with Messala. Messala tells Titinius that they have exchanged Brutus' victory over Octavius for Antony's victory over Cassius, leaving the situation the same as at the start of the day. Titinius remarks that these tidings will comfort Cassius. Messala asks where Cassius is and learns that he is on that same hill, just as he discovers a body on the ground. When Titinius sees that it is Cassius', he cries, "Cassius is no more. O setting sun!/As in thy red rays thou dost sink to night,/So in his red blood Cassius' day is set;/The sun of Rome is set. Our day is gone;/Clouds, dews, and dangers come; our deeds are done./Mistrust of my success hath done this deed." Messala, however, blames Cassius' suicide on his lack of confidence in their victory for Rome and on the imaginary fears produced by Cassius' melancholy and despondent nature. Titinius then asks where Pindarus is. Messala tells him to look for Pindarus, while he returns to tell Brutus the bad news.

When Messala leaves, Titinius addresses the body of his noble lord Cassius, mourning, "Alas, thou has misconstrued everything." He takes the victory garland which Brutus had given him for Cassius and places it as a sign of honor on the head of the corpse. Then, asking leave of the gods (for ending his time before their appointed hour), he expresses his duty as a Roman, picks up Cassius' sword, and kills himself.

Messala returns bringing Brutus, young Cato, Strato, Volumnius, and Lucilius. Brutus asks where Cassius' body lies, and Messala points to where Titinius kneels in mourning. Brutus discovers that Titinius is dead and cries, "O Julius Caesar, thou art mighty yet!/Thy spirit walks abroad, and turns our swords/In our own proper entrails."

In a final tribute to his dead friends, Brutus exclaims, "Are yet two Romans living such as these?/The last of all the Romans, fare thee well!" Brutus then orders that Cassius' body be sent to Thasos for the funeral, lest his funeral at Philippi destroy the morale of the soldiers. He bids young Cato, Lucilius, Labeo, and Flavius prepare for another battle before the night, since it is only three o'clock.

Act V: Scene 4

Brutus, Cato, Lucilius, Messala, and Flavius are seen on another part of the battlefield of Philippi. In the midst of battle, Brutus passes quickly across the stage, encouraging his men to fight bravely.

As Brutus goes off, young Cato stoutly proclaims he is the son of Marcus Cato, "a foe to tyrants, and my country's friend."

Enemy soldiers appear and engage Cato and Lucilius in single combat.

Echoing young Cato's cries, Lucilius shouts, "And I am Brutus, Marcus Brutus, I." The fighting continues. Lucilius sees young Cato fall. As he continues to fight, Lucilius pays tribute to his comrade, "O young and noble Cato, art thou down?/Why now thou diest as bravely as Titinius."

Commanded to yield, Lucilius ceases to do battle and offers his captors gold to kill him instantly and to be honored by having slain Brutus in battle. The soldier declines the bribe, for it is a far greater honor to take the noble Brutus prisoner.

Antony arrives at this point and is told that Brutus is captured. Addressing Lucilius, Antony asks where Brutus is. Loyally, Lucilius answers, "Brutus is safe enough." He adds, "When you do find him, alive or dead,/He will be found like Brutus, like himself" (that is, as noble as ever).

Antony informs his men that Lucilius, although he is not Brutus, is a worthy prize. He orders them to take Lucilius prisoner and to treat him kindly, for Antony would like to have him as a friend. Then others are ordered to pursue Brutus and to report to Antony at Octavius' tent.

Act V: Scene 5

Brutus, Dardanius, Clitus, Strato, and Volumnius appear in another part of the field. Brutus and the remnants of his army rest on a rock. Clitus reports that Statilius has sent a signal, but since he did not come back he has evidently been captured or slain. Pessimistically, Brutus replies, "Slaying is the word;/It is a deed in fashion." Leaning closer, Brutus whispers into Clitus' ear, and Clitus responds to the message, "What, I, my lord? No, not for all the world!" Brutus then turns to Dardanius, who replies, "Shall I do such a deed?"

Clitus and Dardanius compare notes and reveal that Brutus has requested each of them to kill him. They watch him as he meditates quietly apart. "Now is that noble vessel full of grief,/That it runs over even at his eyes," Clitus observes.

Brutus calls Volumnius to him and tells him about the ghost of Caesar, which has appeared to him twice, once at Sardis and again last night at Philippi. "I know my hour is come," Brutus declares. Volumnius tries to argue Brutus out of his depression, but Brutus is convinced that the enemy has beaten them to the pit like wild beasts. It is better, he decides, "to leap in ourselves/Than tarry till they push us."

An alarm is sounded and Clitus warns Brutus to fly. Brutus bids his men farewell, declaring, "My heart doth joy that yet in all my life/I found no man but he was true to me." Now he is tired and his bones crave rest. The alarm is sounded again, and warnings to fly are shouted from within. Brutus sends the others off, promising to follow. Only Strato is asked to remain.

Brutus confronts his servant Strato with the same request he had made of his friends, and Strato agrees to hold the sword and hide his face, while Brutus ends his life.

Servant and master take hands and say goodby. Then, with the words "Caesar, now be still;/I killed not thee with half so good a will," Brutus runs upon his sword and dies.

A retreat is sounded as Brutus dies. Antony and Octavius arrive on the scene. They have with them Messala and Lucilius who have been taken prisoner. Octavius speaks first, "What man is that," he asks, pointing to Strato. Messala identifies Brutus' servant and asks Strato where Brutus is. "Free from the bondage you are in, Messala," Strato replies. Brutus has killed himself, "and no man else hath honor in his death." Lucilius praises Brutus' suicide, which proves to him that Brutus was as honorable· as he had thought.

651

Octavius offers to take Brutus' men into his service, and Strato agrees to go if Messala gives him a recommendation. Learning that Strato held the sword for Brutus, Messala urges Octavius to take this good servant as his follower.

Antony, who has been silent all the while, speaks now over the body of Brutus: "This was the noblest Roman of them all./All the conspirators save only he/Did that they did in envy of great Caesar;/He, only in a general honest thought/And common good to all, made one of them." Antony concludes his eulogy of Brutus by describing his nature as gentle "and the elements/So mixed in him that Nature might stand up./And say to all the world, 'This was a man!' "

It is Octavius who has the last words in the play. He orders that Brutus be given "all respect and rites of burial" and that within Octavius' tent "his bones tonight shall lie,/Most like a soldier, ordered honorably."

King Lear

LEAR, *King of Britain.*
KING OF FRANCE.
DUKE OF BURGUNDY.
DUKE OF CORNWALL, *husband to Regan.*
DUKE OF ALBANY, *husband to Goneril.*
EARL OF KENT.
EARL OF GLOUCESTER.
EDGAR, *son to Gloucester.*
EDMUND, *bastard son to Gloucester.*
CURAN, *a courtier.*
OLD MAN, *tenant to Gloucester.*
DOCTOR.
FOOL.
OSWALD, *stewart to Goneril.*
CAPTAIN *employed by Edmund.*
GENTLEMAN.
HERALD.
SERVANTS *to Cornwall.*

GONERIL
REGAN   } *daughters to Lear.*
CORDELIA

KNIGHTS *of Lear's train,* CAPTAINS, MESSENGERS, SOLDIERS, *and* ATTENDANTS.

King Lear

Act I: Scene 1

The play opens in a room in the palace of King Lear, a legendary ruler of Britain in the time before Britain became fully Christianized. Two noblemen, the Earl of Kent and the Earl of Gloucester (pronounced Glos'ter), are chatting about court politics. From this gossip we discover that Lear—who we later learn is about 80 years old—has decided to divide his kingdom and give up his throne before he dies. He intends to divide Britain among his three daughters, who are named Goneril, Regan and Cordelia.

Kent expresses surprise to Gloucester that the kingdom is to be evenly divided. He had thought that Lear liked Albany, Goneril's husband, better than he liked Cornwall, Regan's husband.

In the middle of the discussion between Kent and Gloucester, Kent notices that Gloucester has Edmund, the younger of his two sons, with him. Gloucester tells Kent that Edmund is a bastard whom Gloucester begot with a mistress a year after his legitimate son, Edgar, was born. Kent barely recognizes his friend Gloucester's son, because Edmund has been away from court for nine years. Gloucester jokes lewdly about the fun he had the night Edmund was conceived. He tells Kent that although his property will go by law to the older, legitimate Edgar, he loves Edmund no less, and "the whoreson must be acknowledged."

The worldly, realistic tone changes abruptly when a trumpet flourish announces the entrance of Lear accompanied by his three daughters, his two sons-in-law, and various courtiers, or nobles who serve the king in his palace. Lear reaches for a map of Britain and announces his intention to divide the kingdom so that he can "Unburthen'd crawl toward death." (This is ironic, as the play turns out, because the division of the kingdom increases, rather than decreases, Lear's burdens.)

Lear announces the way in which he will divide his lands. There is a catch to it, although he doesn't think of it as a catch. Before Lear gives each daughter her third of the kingdom, she must tell him how much she loves him. Goneril, the oldest daughter, is called on first. She has no trouble making a glib, hypocritical speech. She tells Lear that she loves him "Dearer than eyesight, space and liberty," and, indeed, "no less than life" itself. Regan makes a similar speech. But while Lear is lapping up Goneril's and Regan's praise of him, Cordelia is nervously wondering what will be left for her to say when her turn, as youngest daughter, finally comes. (Her problem stems not from lack of love for Lear, but from her embarrassment at making flowery, ceremonial speeches.)

Finally Lear turns to Cordelia, and calling her his joy (she has always been his favorite daughter), asks her what she has to say about her love for her father. Can her speech draw the richest third of Britain? But all Cordelia says is "Nothing, my lord." Lear is thunderstruck at this blow to his ego. "Nothing?" he asks. "Nothing will come of nothing," he warns her. In other words, she will be disinherited if she can't find some praise for her father.

Cordelia, wretched, says she can't make flowery speeches the way her sisters do. She loves her father as much as daughters are supposed to love their fathers: no more, no less. This perfectly reasonable answer infuriates the proud old king. He warns Cordelia that she will lose her dowry: he will disinherit her. (It is interesting that he assumes that without a money settlement on her marriage, Cordelia won't be able to get anyone to marry her.)

At this point Kent tries to butt in, but Lear warns him not to come "between the dragon and his wrath." Lear banishes Cordelia from his sight, and announces that the third of Britain that was supposed to go to her will instead be divided between

Goneril and Regan. Lear, accompanied by a retinue of 100 knights, will spend one month alternately with each daughter.

Again Kent intervenes. He has always loved Lear and been faithful to him, and now that Lear is acting rashly and foolishly in disinheriting the daughter who loves him most, Kent feels he must warn the King. Lear furiously orders him out of his sight. Kent replies, "See better, Lear."

Driven to a peak of anger by Kent's blunt reply, Lear gives him five days to pack his belongings and leave England. Lear warns him that if on the sixth day Kent is found anywhere in his realm, he will be executed on the spot. Kent answers that as long as Lear is going to be so unreasonable, freedom is outside England and banishment is in England. (Normally banishment was considered a very severe punishment.) Kent asks for blessings on Cordelia, warns Goneril and Regan that they had better live up to their words of love, and leaves the court.

Now Gloucester enters with the two suitors for Cordelia's hand, France and Burgundy. Lear announces to Burgundy that if he wants to marry Cordelia, he will have to accept her without a dowry.

When he hears that Cordelia has been disinherited, Burgundy quickly backs out. But the King of France is made of better stuff. He tells Lear he is shocked at this disinheriting of Cordelia, and then announces that he will be glad to marry her even if she comes to him without a penny, for she is "most rich, being poor." In other words he sees that her spirit is rich, and her spirit is what counts. He will bring her back to France with him to live. Lear agrees to the marriage, and leaves.

Cordelia now says goodbye to Goneril and Regan. She tells them that she hopes they will be as good as their words to Lear. Regan's answer is that, being disinherited, Cordelia had better worry now about satisfying her new husband, France, who has taken her without a cent of dowry. (The catty cruelty of Goneril and Regan to Cordelia is very much like the behavior of the older sisters to Cinderella.) Cordelia and France leave. Now that they and Lear are gone, Goneril and Regan discuss the situation cynically and selfishly. Goneril points out to Regan how unreasonable Lear's behavior has been. She is shrewdly worried that everyone in court will notice how peculiar his action was in disinheriting his favorite daughter. Regan answers that their father is probably senile, but, in fact, she says, he never really knew his own mind. Both sisters are worried by Lear's "unruly waywardness" and "unconstant starts," in short, his eccentricity. They talk clearheadedly and unsympathetically about him, as the scene ends.

Act I: Scene 2

We are now in Gloucester's castle. Edmund enters carrying a letter which he has forged as part of a plot to get his brother, Edgar, disinherited. Before we find out the contents of the letter, however, Edmund reveals himself to the audience in the first soliloquy of the play.

Edmund calls Nature his goddess, saluting her here as the divinity of lust and as one who would crown his efforts (illegal) to get his brother's land away from him. This is not the nature to whom Lear later appeals and whom Cordelia, Edgar, and Kent obey, but a naked, selfish individualism, given over to lust and greed. Edmund renounces both religion and the laws of human society, seeing nature in opposition to them. Also, as a bastard, Edmund is a "natural child," meaning he was not born as a result of marriage, a social convention. Edmund is haunted in this soliloquy—and later in the play—by the fact that he is a bastard. He tells himself he is as good a man as his brother, Edgar, and probably a better man. The reason he gives is that more energy is required in an adulterous affair than in normal marriage, so that he was conceived when his father, Gloucester, was really lusty.

"Well then,/ Legitimate Edgar," Edmund sneers, "I must have your land." The letter Edmund has just forged should get it for him. Filled with evil confidence he shouts, "I grow, I prosper;/ Now, gods, stand up for bastards!"

Now Gloucester enters, musing distractedly about the speed of the unhappy events in the previous scene. Edmund cleverly pretends to hide the letter that is in his hand, knowing that doing so will only make his father more curious to find out what is in it. Edmund refuses to hand the letter over, saying it isn't fit for his father to read. The more Edmund refuses, the more Gloucester insists. Finally Edmund gets his real wish—the counterfeited letter is read by Gloucester, who is horrified at its contents.

The letter, supposedly written by Edgar to Edmund, says that Edgar wishes his father would die soon so that he could inherit his estate. Edmund adds fuel to the fire now raging in his father's breast by saying he has often heard Edgar complaining about this point. Gloucester gullibly believes him, and Edmund's plot is well-launched.

Gloucester, shouting that Edgar is an "Abominable villain," asks Edmund where he is. Edmund says he doesn't know, but will search Edgar out, and bring him to Gloucester.

Gloucester blames some recent eclipses of the sun and moon for the divisions between parents and children and between friend and friend that he has just seen in the court and now in his own life. First, Lear has been alienated from his daughter, Cordelia, and his friend, Kent. Second, Gloucester himself is now alienated from his son, Edgar. Gloucester says the best part of his life is now over: all that awaits him is "hollowness, treachery, and all ruinous disorders." When Gloucester leaves, shaking his head sadly, Edmund, in another soliloquy, makes fun of his father's gullibility and superstition.

Edgar now enters, and Edmund asks him if he can remember offending their father recently. Edgar says no. Then Edmund, playing a cat-and-mouse game with his naïve brother, says that apparently someone has slandered Edgar to his father, because Gloucester is furious with him. He warns Edgar that he had better fly for his life; if Gloucester sees him, he will kill him. Edgar doesn't understand what Edmund is talking about, but being as credulous as his father, he agrees to flee for his safety.

Act I: Scene 3

The scene shifts to the palace of Albany and Goneril. Goneril is complaining to her servant, Oswald, that Lear's retinue of 100 knights is annoying her and upsetting her household. Lear is apparently spending the first month after abdicating the throne with his eldest daughter and her husband. He has brought with him a band of knights to serve him, and they are not getting along well with the regular household staff. At the moment, Lear is out hunting. Goneril takes this opportunity to tell Oswald that she's had enough of her father and his "riotous" followers. When Lear comes back from his hunting expedition, Goneril wants Oswald to tell him that she's sick and can't speak with him.

Calling Lear an "idle old man," Goneril furthermore tells Oswald that in the future the steward is to ignore any requests her father may make. If the old king objects to this treatment, he can go visit with Regan for a while. Also, she tells Oswald, "let his knights have colder looks among you." In other words, Lear and his retainers are to be totally ignored, if not actually snubbed by Goneril's own servants.

Act I: Scene 4

Lear returns from the hunt, and finds Kent, disguised, waiting to see him. Lear does not recognize his old friend and retainer, whom he banished from England in Scene 1. He asks Kent what he wants, and Kent replies that all he wants is to serve Lear. Kent says he recognizes "authority" in Lear's face and would like to be a loyal retainer. He tells Lear he is 48 years old, much younger than he really is. Lear accepts his services.

One of Lear's knights says that he has noticed "a great abatement of kindness" to the old man lately. Lear agrees that he, too, has perceived "a most faint neglect of late," but blames it on his own jealousy and desire for attention. He cannot believe that he is being purposely neglected by Goneril. Then he adds that he "will look further into" the matter.

Then Lear calls for the Fool, or court jester, to cheer him up. The knight tells him, however, that the Fool has been keeping to himself lately, pining for Cordelia, whom he loved, and who is now in France with her husband. The Fool never really recovers from the blow of Cordelia's banishment.

Now Oswald enters. He speaks insolently to Lear, and Kent trips him up and sends him sprawling on the floor for his insolence. This act immediately draws Lear together in a new bond with his old, wronged friend, even though he still does not recognize him. He gives Kent some money as a kind of tip. At this point the Fool enters the room.

In this scene the Fool's jests with Lear all come to one thing: Lear, not the Jester is the real fool. For Lear has upset the natural order of things by putting himself in his daughters' care. He did the opposite of what Nature intends parents to do with their children. For upsetting this balance of Nature, in which children must obey their parents, and not vice versa, Lear will suffer. For instance, when Lear asks the Fool if he is calling his master "fool," the Fool answers: "All thy other titles thou hast given away; that thou wast born with." Kent recognizes the truth behind this remark, and tells Lear, "This is not altogether Fool, my Lord." (This is like Polonius, saying of Hamlet that if he is mad, there's a method to his madness.)

Now Goneril enters, in a bad mood. She upbraids her father for what she considers the wild and boisterous behavior of his retainers. Lear cannot believe his own daughter could be so harsh with him. He asks, with tragic irony, "Who is it that can tell me who I am?" In other words, if Goneril is talking to me in this manner, can I possibly be the King and her father? The Fool answers, appropriately enough, "Lear's shadow." Goneril persists in her scolding. She complains that Lear's followers have made her palace into a "tavern or a brothel" by "not-to-be-endured riots." This is the final touch. Calling his daughter "Degenerate bastard," Lear orders that his horse be saddled. He will leave the house before his month is up and stay with Regan.

Albany enters and tries to calm down the enraged king, but succeeds only in making Lear even angrier. Lear shouts at Goneril that she is lying about his knights; they are "of choice and rarest parts." He begins to regret his impatience with Cordelia for a relatively small fault. Beating at his head with his fists, Lear cries, "Beat at this gate, that let thy folly in, / And thy dear judgment out!" Then in tones like those of an Old Testament prophet, he denounces his daughter, at first praying that she be childless. But then he changes his mind and asks Nature to make her bear a child, so "that she may feel / How sharper than a serpent's tooth it is / To have a thankless child!"

Lear has rushed out of the room after making his great speech. While he is out, he evidently learns that Goneril intends for him to dismiss 50 of his knights—half his retinue—for he returns in an even greater rage.

This time he even weeps, although in the speech just before he had begged Nature to make Goneril weep with a parent's sorrow. Instead, against his will, the tears start rolling down his cheeks. Goneril, still unmoved, stands coldly by while Lear threatens that he will get Regan to right the wrong that has been done to him. He keeps saying "I have another daughter" who will be kind to him.

After Lear storms off, accompanied by Kent and some retainers, Goneril sends Oswald with a letter to her sister, Regan, informing her of the day's events, and warning her of the temper she will find her father in when he arrives at her house.

Act I: Scene 5

In this brief scene, Lear asks Kent to deliver a letter explaining to Regan what has just happened at Goneril's house. The letter also says that Lear will be arriving to visit Regan soon. Lear very fair-mindedly tells Kent not to add any details about Lear's miserable reception at Goneril's house to whatever is already in the letter. He warns Kent that if he doesn't hurry, the letter will get to Regan only after Lear arrives.

Kent rushes off with the letter, and the Fool continues his riddles and jokes. Typically, he asks Lear if he knows why a snail has a shell. The answer is that a snail has a shell to keep his head safe, and not to give it to his daughters. Lear is distracted with grief, mixed with a tinge of self-pity. He says of himself, "So kind a father!" The Fool says that if Lear were his fool, he would have him beaten for being old before he was wise. In the midst of this joking, Lear prays tragically: "O! let me not be mad, not mad, sweet heaven."

Characteristic of Shakespeare's love for mixing the tragic with the comic, after this solemn prayer, the scene ends with the Fool making a lewd joke.

Act II: Scene 1

We are now in Gloucester's castle. Edmund meets the courtier, Curan. Curan tells him that Cornwall and Regan will be visiting Gloucester tonight. Curan adds that Cornwall and his brother-in-law, Albany, are feuding, and open war between them is likely to break out.

Now Edgar appears. Edmund warns him that Cornwall and Regan are due to arrive at any moment, and rumor has it that Edgar has spoken against them. Gullible as ever, Edgar doesn't understand how this rumor could have gotten started. He still doesn't realize that Edmund is plotting against him. Edmund hears Gloucester approaching, and fools Edgar into drawing his sword and entering a mock duel. Then he tells Edgar to leave, and scratches his own arm with his sword. Now, when Gloucester appears, Edmund complains to him that he just got the wound from Edgar. He thus further angers Gloucester against his one good son, Edgar. Gloucester says that Edgar may have escaped just now, but swears he will be caught and punished.

At this point, Cornwall and Regan arrive at Gloucester's castle. Gloucester appeals to them for sympathy, crying that his "old heart is crack'd" about his son's "treason."

Edmund has joined with Regan and Cornwall. He uses every means to frighten Edgar and make him flee. Also, he turns his father still more against Edgar by reporting that he was "mumbling of wicked charms"—which would especially alarm the superstitious Gloucester. Gloucester actually believes that Edgar wanted to kill him and is ready to catch and "dispatch" him.

Regan asks Gloucester if Edgar had been keeping company with her father's "riotous knights." Gloucester says he doesn't know, but Edmund quickly butts in and says yes, "he was of that consort." (This seals Edgar's doom as far as Regan and Cornwall are concerned.) Cornwall compliments Edmund on his devotion as a son in uncovering Edgar's "plot" against his father. Edmund answers smugly and hypocritically, "It was my duty." Neither Regan nor Cornwall show much sympathy for Gloucester's misery as a father, although Regan, calling Gloucester her "good old friend," tells him not to worry. She and her husband will take care of his treacherous son, Edgar.

Act II: Scene 2

This scene takes place before dawn, in front of Gloucester's castle. The two servants, Lear's Kent and Goneril's Oswald, enter separately, each carrying a letter for Regan. Oswald, pretending not to recognize Kent as the man who tripped him for his insolence to Lear in Act I, suavely asks him where he may leave his horse. But Kent, who can't stand Goneril's hypocritical servant, replies with a torrent of abuse, calling Oswald, among other names, "A knave, a rascal . . . a lily-livered whoreson" and a "beggar, coward, pandar, and the son and heir of a mongrel bitch." Kent demands that Oswald draw his sword and fight like a man. When Oswald refuses, Kent starts beating him. Oswald's cries of "murder, murder!" bring Edmund, rapier drawn, to the scene. Edmund asks what the matter is, and Kent offers to teach him a lesson in swordsmanship, too.

By now the whole castle is aroused by the commotion. Cornwall, Regan and Gloucester come out to learn what the matter is. Cornwall asks Kent why he is so furious, and he answers that he is angry that "such a slave as this (Oswald) should wear a sword, / Who wears no honesty." Cornwall's answer is that Kent is the kind of insolent boor who disguises his bad manners as blunt honesty. He calls for the stocks, a device which locks the prisoner's feet so that he cannot move, and makes him an object of mockery to all who see him. He says that Kent will be locked in the stocks until noon, but Regan, typically even more vicious than her husband, changes this order to night. Kent protests that he doesn't mind for himself, but that it is an insult to the King to put his servant in the stocks, which are usually reserved for petty criminals and offenders. Gloucester also begs Cornwall not to punish Kent this way, but to no avail. Kent resignedly whistles himself to sleep in the stocks, bidding "Fortune, good night; smile once more; turn thy wheel!"

Act II: Scene 3

This very brief scene (only 21 lines long) consists of a soliloquy by Edgar. He is alone in a wood. He reveals that he knows he is being pursued and decides to adopt a disguise. He will pretend to be a harmless idiot beggar, named Tom Turleygood, or Tom of Bedlam.

Act II: Scene 4

We are in front of Gloucester's castle again. Lear, accompanied by the Fool and an unnamed Gentleman, comes upon Kent in the stocks. At first Lear assumes that Kent is just playing a joke by sitting there. When Kent assures him that he was placed in the stocks by Cornwall and Regan, Lear can't believe what he hears. He is sure that they wouldn't dare treat his own servant in this shameful manner.

Kent, however, tells Lear about his encounter with Oswald, and how Goneril's messenger got a much more welcome reception than he did. Lear, in his anguish on hearing this, cries out, "Hysterica passio! down, thou climbing sorrow!" (Hysterica passio is a disease marked by suffocation or choking.) Lear goes into the castle to find out what has happened, leaving the Fool and the Gentleman to comfort Kent in the stocks. Lear soon comes out of the castle again, amazed that Regan and Cornwall have left word they do not wish to be disturbed. They've said they are tired from their journey to Gloucester's castle and aren't feeling well. At first, Lear is angry, but then is willing to accept the excuse. Still, he is furious that Kent is in the stocks and wants some explanation.

Finally, Gloucester emerges from the castle with Cornwall and Regan. A servant sets Kent free. Lear immediately begins unburdening himself to Regan. He tells her that Goneril "hath tied / Sharp-tooth'd unkindness, like a vulture here," pointing to his heart. Regan's answer is that Lear should be patient; she can't believe her sister would "scant her duty" to him. She tells her father that he is old, and should be more discreet. He should return to Goneril and let her take care of him. Lear again can't believe what he hears. Should he return and ask Goneril's forgiveness? Should he kneel before her and say "Dear daughter, I confess that I am old; / Age is unnecessary: on my knees I beg / That you'll vouchsafe me raiment, bed, and food"? Never!

He begins to curse Goneril, and Regan rightly says that someday he will curse her too, "when the rash mood is on." Lear says he never would, because Regan is kind where Goneril is cruel. He is about to ask her again why Kent was put in the stocks when he is interrupted by a trumpet announcing the arrival of Goneril. When she enters, Lear asks her if she is not ashamed to look upon his old white beard. But Regan takes her sister's hand, and Lear feels completely betrayed. He gets Cornwall to admit that he was responsible for putting Kent in the stocks. Regan pleads with her father to dismiss half his retinue and return to Goneril. Lear cries out that rather than do that he would live out in the open air, or even beg France for a pension.

Lear tells Goneril that he will stay with Regan, and keep his 100 knights. But now Regan tells him he can't. She isn't prepared to receive him yet, as he wasn't supposed to come to her until the end of the month. Again she urges him to return to Goneril. She asks him why he needs even 50 knights. If he stays with her, he'll have to do with 25. Lear answers tragically, "I gave you all." Regan cruelly counters that he certainly took his time about it. She and Goneril keep arguing with him and finally doubt that he needs even one attendant, and Lear cries, "O! reason not the need."

Lear cries to the heavens for patience: "You see me here, you Gods, a poor old man, / As full of grief as age; wretched in both!" He vows that he will not weep; instead he'll take revenge on both daughters.

For the first time, from a distance, we hear the storm which will unleash all its fury on Lear in the next act. Crying again to the Fool that he will "go mad," Lear leaves, followed by Gloucester, Kent and the Fool.

Cornwall, hearing the storm, asks Regan and Goneril to come back into the castle with him. Regan says the castle is too small to house Lear and all his retainers. She will receive him gladly, "but not one follower." Goneril agrees that he has only himself to blame if he is left outdoors in the storm. Gloucester returns, and tells the sisters that their father is in a towering rage. Regan cooly answers that this will teach him a lesson: "He is attended with a desperate train" who would abuse her hospitality. Regan orders the doors of the castle to be shut as the storm finally breaks, and the act ends.

Act III: Scene 1

Kent and a Gentleman meet out on the heath. The storm by now has reached full fury. Both men are searching for Lear. The Gentleman tells Kent that he last saw the King "contending with the fretful elements." Lear was shouting that the wind could blow the earth into the ocean, as far as he cared, if only the world as it now exists would change or cease to be. The Gentleman also tells Kent that Lear is accompanied only by the Fool, who is trying to keep his spirits up. Kent, in turn, informs the Gentleman of two important developments:

1. Albany and Cornwall are vying for power and are bringing England to the brink of civil war.

2. France, hearing of the mistreatment of his father-in-law, has launched an invasion of England.

Kent tells the Gentleman to make his way to Dover, where he will find the invasion force. Giving him a ring which will identify him to Cordelia, he tells the Gentleman to inform her of recent developments.

Act III: Scene 2

On another part of the heath, we find Lear raging against the storm. He defies the winds to crack their cheeks with blowing and calls out for cataracts to drown the earth and for thunderbolts to singe his white head. In this great speech, interrupted only briefly by some sardonic remarks by the Fool, Lear says that Nature, even at her most violent, is not so cruel as his daughters. The elements, indeed, are merely "servile ministers," because they combine with Lear's daughters to make him wretched. If the storm could accomplish just one thing—destroy the mould of Nature from which "ungrateful man" comes, it would be justified in Lear's eyes, even though he suffers in the process.

As Lear raves, the Fool keeps trying to comfort him with jests and snatches of song. Then Kent enters. He is shocked to see his sovereign out in this weather, bareheaded and accompanied only by his Fool. Even "things that love night / Love not such nights as these," Kent says. Since he reached manhood, he has not seen "Such sheets of fire, such bursts of horrid thunder, / Such groans of roaring wind and rain."

To Lear, however, the storm represents a kind of wild justice taken by the "great Gods" against sinful man. Nevertheless, he himself, he feels, is a man "more sinned against than sinning." (Ironically, the real sinners, of course, are comfortably indoors.) Kent tries to persuade Lear to take temporary shelter in a hovel or hut nearby, while he attempts to force Regan and Cornwall to open their gates to Lear. The King, in his misery, feels his "wits begin to turn"—in other words, he is going mad. However, he agrees to find temporary shelter, even in a peasant hovel, because necessity "can make vile things precious." He goes off with the Fool, who sings an adaptation of the popular Elizabethan song, "The rain it raineth every day," which Feste also sings in *Twelfth Night*.

Act III: Scene 3

We move, in this scene, from the heath to a room in Gloucester's castle. Gloucester is bemoaning to Edmund the fact that he was forced by Regan and Cornwall to lock the doors of his own house against Lear. In addition, they warned Gloucester "on pain of perpetual displeasure, neither to speak of (Lear), entreat for him, or any way sustain him." Edmund hypocritically calls this behavior "most savage and unnatural."

Then Gloucester makes a fatal mistake. He tells his son the news that there is a rift between Albany and Cornwall, and, more important, that he has a letter announcing the invasion of England by France to "revenge" the "injuries the King now bears." Realizing how dangerous it is to have such a treasonable letter in his possession, Gloucester has locked it up for safekeeping. He then tells Edmund that he is going out to search for Lear, even if he is killed for doing so. If Regan and Cornwall should ask Edmund where Gloucester is, Edmund is to tell them that he is ill and has gone to bed.

No sooner does Gloucester leave than Edmund decides to retail the information he has received to Cornwall. Gloucester will be a double traitor in Cornwall's eyes, because:

1. Cornwall has forbidden him to help the King.

2. Gloucester has a treasonous letter in his possession telling about the invasion from France.

Edmund soliloquizes after his father leaves that "the younger rises when the old doth fall." In other words, he is perfectly cold-blooded about betraying his father. If Gloucester is executed for "treason," Edmund will inherit his property.

Act III: Scene 4

We are now in front of the hovel to which Kent has led Lear and the Fool. The storm is still raging. Kent tries to persuade Lear to enter, saying "the tyranny of the open night's too rough / For nature to endure." But Lear answers that it would break his heart to take shelter from the storm because then he would be free to think about his ungrateful daughters. He prefers to endure the storm, he says, because at least that keeps his mind off Goneril and Regan. "Pour on," he defies the storm, "I will endure." But then his resolution begins to weaken, and he cries, "O Regan, Goneril! Your old kind father, whose frank heart gave all. . . ." He then breaks off, realizing that brooding about how his daughters have wronged him will lead him directly to madness.

Lear tells the Fool to go into the hovel first, while he waits outside. He will pray and then sleep. After the Fool enters the shack, Lear voices a magnificent prayer for all the "poor naked wretches," wherever they are, who must "bide the pelting of this pitiless storm." He realizes now, in his own wretchedness, that when he was King, he had taken too little care of his poverty-stricken subjects. Now he has learned true compassion for the physically miserable of the world. "Take physic (medicine), Pomp," he cries, "Expose thyself to feel what wretches feel."

Lear's meditation is abruptly broken by Edgar, who, dressed as the madman, Tom of Bedlam, shouts from within the hut. Apparently he had taken shelter there before Lear arrived. In a minute the Fool comes rushing out shouting that he's seen a ghost inside the hut. Kent takes command of the situation, calling into the hut for whoever it is to come out. Edgar finally emerges, and, pretending to be mad, cries, "Away! the foul fiend follows me."

Lear's immediate reaction to the spectacle is that Edgar, too, must have given everything he had to his daughters. Otherwise he couldn't have fallen into such a sorry state. Edgar answers Lear's questions about himself with mad gibberish, frequently referring to the fact that "poor Tom's a-cold." Again Lear comments, with tragic irony, "What! has his daughters brought him to this pass?" He cannot imagine that there could be any other reason for going mad than the ingratitude of children. When Kent assure Lear that Edgar has no daughters, Lear refuses to believe him.

The Fool rightly comments that "this cold night will turn us all to fools and madmen." Indeed, a good deal of the eerie atmosphere of the scene is produced by the fact that Edgar is pretending to be mad, Lear is really going mad, and the Fool, speaking as usual in puns, riddles and snatches of songs, often seems to be mad. Only Kent miraculously retains his sturdy sanity. Lear, listening to Edgar's prattle and seeing him in rags, asks, "Is man no more than this? . . . unaccommodated man is no more but such a poor, bare, forked animal as thou art." (By "forked," Lear means two-legged, like a two-pronged fork.) Again he thinks of the puniness of man in a hostile, or at best indifferent universe. The sheep at least has wool to keep it warm, but without clothing man is a miserable, exposed animal. Indeed, as if proving his point, Lear starts tearing his clothes off, to identify himself with all suffering humanity. The Fool prevails on him, though, to keep some clothing on, because it's "a naughty night to swim in."

Now Gloucester, who has been searching for Lear, enters carrying a torch. Edgar pretends to think he is the devil, because of the eerie light which surrounds him. Actually, of course, he is afraid his father will recognize him. It is so dark, though, that at first Gloucester does not see who is there. Nor does he ever recognize Edgar, his own son, in the wretched disguise he has assumed. When Edgar treats him to a typical raving monologue, Gloucester sadly asks Lear, "What! hath your Grace no better company?" He explains to Lear that he is disobeying Regan's and Cornwall's orders to keep his doors barred against the King. He has come to bring Lear to "where both fire and food is ready."

Lear, however, ignores Gloucester's offer, even though Kent, too, urges him to accept. Instead, Lear keeps questioning Edgar, as if he were a learned man. Kent notices this, and asks Gloucester to repeat his offer, because Lear's "wits begin t'unsettle." Gloucester says he can't blame Lear for going mad; his daughters seek his death. Then he thinks of his own situation, and says he is almost mad, too, because he has a son, who though Gloucester loved him dearly, sought his life.

Seeing that he can't get Lear to stir, Gloucester at last persuades him to take shelter inside the hovel, and they all go in as the scene ends.

Act III: Scene 5

We shift back to the "sane" world of a room in Gloucester's castle. Edmund and Cornwall are alone together. Edmund has just told Cornwall that his father, Gloucester, has been plotting treason. The scene opens with Cornwall saying "I will have my revenge ere I depart this house." (Notice that it never strikes Cornwall as poor behavior for a guest to have "revenge" on his host while in the host's own house.)

Edmund hypocritically says that he is afraid that his loyalty to England will bring him the censure of people because it has been at the expense of his natural loyalty as a son. Edmund shows Cornwall the letter telling of the invasion plans from France. (This is the letter Gloucester had foolishly told his son about in Act III, Scene 3.) "O Heavens!" Edmund hypocritically cries, "that this treason were not, or not I the detector!" Cornwall assures Edmund that whether the report of the invasion in the letter is true or false, Gloucester is still guilty of treason for receiving the letter and, as a traitor, has forfeited his earldom. Cornwall makes Edmund the new Earl of Gloucester and tells him to find his father so that Cornwall can arrest him. In an aside, Edmund says that he'll try to catch his father in the act of comforting Lear, which will make Gloucester even more treasonous in the eyes of Cornwall. But aloud to Cornwall all he says is that he will "persever in my course of loyalty, though the conflict be sore between that and my blood." In other words, he will be loyal to Cornwall, even though his blood, or natural filial loyalty, tells him not to be. Cornwall assures him that he will find "a dearer father (than Gloucester) in my love," and the scene ends with each hypocrite giving assurances of loyalty to the other.

Act III: Scene 6

We are now in a room in a farmhouse near Gloucester's castle. Gloucester and Kent enter. Gloucester tells Kent that he will try to get some food and additional supplies to make the room more comfortable for the King, and off he goes. Now Lear,

Edgar and the Fool come in. Edgar is still muttering gibberish and warning everyone to "beware the foul fiend." The Fool asks Lear one of his typical riddles: "Tell me whether a madman be a gentleman or a yeoman (a farmer)." Lear's answer is that a madman is a king. He is getting good at solving the Fool's riddles.

For a moment Lear thinks of taking military revenge on his daughters ("red burning spits / Come hissing in upon 'em"). Then he abandons this idea and decides to try his daughters for their cruelty. This is another and more pathetic way of revenging himself on his daughters. Calling Edgar "most learned justicer," and the Fool "sapient (wise) sir," he tells them to be seated, for the trial is about to begin. Kent tries to bring him to his senses, begging him to lie down and rest, but Lear insists on holding his "trial" first. The first to be arraigned is Goneril, about whom Lear says that "she kick'd the poor King her father." Then Lear "tries" Regan. Meanwhile Kent is appalled at Lear's madness, and Edgar is so much moved by the spectacle of the old man trying two daughters who aren't even there that he begins to weep. He fears his tears will be noticed and his disguise discovered. Lear asks tragically in his "anatomizing" of Regan, "Is there any cause in nature that makes these hard hearts?"

Tiring finally of the mock trial, Lear prepares to go to bed, asking Kent to "draw the curtains." (Evidently in his madness he thinks he is back in his own castle, not in a rude farmhouse.) Then he says, "We'll go to supper i' the' morning," because Gloucester has not yet returned with food, and Lear must go without eating that night. The Fool adds, "And I'll go to bed at noon."

Now Gloucester finally gets back. He asks Kent where Lear is. Kent answers that he's there in the hut, but asks Gloucester not to trouble him, because "his wits are gone." Gloucester replies that he has overheard a plot to kill the King. He tells Kent to place the sleeping Lear on a stretcher and carry him to Dover, where he will meet Cordelia and France. He warns Kent to hurry. If he wastes even half an hour, Lear's life, as well as Kent's "stand in assured loss." Kent regrets that Lear can't be allowed to rest undisturbed, but he orders the Fool to help him carry the stretcher away. Kent, Gloucester and the Fool all leave, bearing the King and leaving Edgar alone in the hut to soliloquize that because Lear's sufferings are even greater than his own, they help him to bear his own better. (Because Edgar is alone, his soliloquy is spoken in his own voice, not in the disguised voice of Tom of Bedlam.)

Act III: Scene 7

This is the most terrifying and blood-curdling scene in the play. It opens in a room in Gloucester's castle on the morning after the storm, with Cornwall telling Goneril to deliver a letter to her husband, Albany. The letter, which is the same one Edmund had stolen from Gloucester, informs Albany that the army of France has landed at Dover. Cornwall is obviously anxious to end the feud with his brother-in-law, and unite with him against France. Cornwall also orders a servant to find the "traitor," Gloucester. On hearing Gloucester's name, the bloodthirsty Regan cries, "Hang him instantly." Goneril adds, "Pluck out his eyes." But Cornwall tells the vicious sisters to let him handle the matter in his own way. He asks Edmund to accompany Goneril on her trip home, because the punishment he is about to mete out to Gloucester is "not fit for your beholding"; in other words, it will be too horrible for the victim's son to witness.

Now Oswald enters and Cornwall asks him where Lear is. Oswald tells him that the King has been spirited away by Gloucester. Followed by some of his loyal knights, he is now headed for safety in Dover, where France and Cordelia are. Saying hasty farewells to Goneril and Edmund, Cornwall orders some servants to capture Gloucester and bring him back to the castle. He reflects to himself that although he can't give Gloucester a fair trial, his power in the land is so great that while men may blame what he is doing, they can do nothing about it.

In a minute the servants re-enter, bringing in Gloucester as a prisoner. Cornwall orders his arms bound, and the servants tie Gloucester into a chair. The old man cannot understand why he is being treated this way. He reminds Cornwall and Regan that they are his guests in his own castle. Regan's reply is to call Gloucester a "filthy traitor," and to pluck his beard in a traditional gesture of contempt. Gloucester protests his innocence and tells Regan that the white hairs she has just plucked from his beard will come to life and accuse her. Cornwall and Regan now question Gloucester viciously about his alleged treachery, and demand to know why he has sent Lear to Dover.

Gloucester answers that he has sent the King to safety because he "would not see thy cruel nails / Pluck out his poor old eyes." (Ironically, this is just what is about to happen to Gloucester himself.) He tells Regan that if wolves had howled at her gate for shelter from the storm the night before, she would have given it to them, yet she turned out her own father. Gloucester takes comfort in the thought that he "shall see / The winged vengeance overtake such children." But Cornwall, ordering his servants to hold fast the chair to which Gloucester has been tied, assures him he will never see anything again, and proceeds with his thumbs to gouge out one of Gloucester's eyes. The bloodthirsty Regan insists that he gouge out the other eye, too. But before Cornwall can do so, one of his servants, unable to stand the spectacle, begs him to cease. He tells Cornwall that he served him since childhood, but the best service he can do him now is to beg him to let Gloucester alone. Cornwall and the servant now draw swords and begin to fight. The servant wounds Cornwall seriously, but before he can finish him off, Regan grabs a sword and stabs the servant in the back, killing him instantly. Then Cornwall, even though he is in mortal pain, cries, "Out, vile jelly!" and gouges out Gloucester's other eye.

In the depths of his agony, Gloucester cries out for Edmund. But with vicious satisfaction Regan informs him that Edmund hates him and that it was Edmund who let them know of his treachery. Suddenly Gloucester perceives the whole plot against him and cries out at his folly. He begs the gods to forgive him for abusing his one good son and begs them to bring Edgar to prosperity. Regan orders the servants to thrust Gloucester out of his castle, and, since he is now blind, to "let him smell / His way to Dover."

When a servant leaves, leading Gloucester with him, Regan asks her husband how his wound is. Cornwall first orders Gloucester to be turned out of the castle grounds and the servant who revolted against him to be thrown on a dunghill. Then he replies that he is bleeding badly. Regan helps him out of the room. The two remaining servants comment on the viciousness of their lord and lady and vow to help Gloucester. One of them will find Tom of Bedlam, who will lead Gloucester to Dover, and the other will apply some ointment to his bleeding wounds.

Act IV: Scene 1

This scene, one of the most philosophically rich in the play, takes place on a heath near Gloucester's castle, immediately after the barbaric events of the preceding scene. Edgar enters alone, still disguised as Tom of Bedlam. He philosophizes in a soliloquy that since he has reached the lowest ebb in his fortunes, things can only improve for him. Normally a hopeful and active young man, Edgar refuses to despair. Having hit bottom, he feels he can only rise: "the lamentable change is from the best," he says, "The worst returns to laughter."

But Edgar's hopeful philosophy is shattered by the sight of his father, the blinded Gloucester, who enters at this point. Gloucester, whose eyes are still bleeding, is led by a humble old man, who has been a tenant on the Gloucester estate for 80 years. When Edgar sees the pathetic pair, he cries, "World, world, O world! / But that thy strange mutations make us hate thee, / Life would not yield to age." This is an extension of the philosophical position which he had just taken in his soliloquy. Here Edgar feels that it is only the changes in fortune that chance brings to our lives which reconcile us to growing old and dying. These changes make us hate life so bitterly that we do not mind leaving the world when our time has come. Meanwhile Gloucester, who of course cannot see his son and who doesn't recognize his voice, which Edgar has disguised, tries to get rid of his old tenant. He tells the old man that he can no longer comfort him, and to be seen with Gloucester would be dangerous to him. When the old man protests that Gloucester cannot see his way alone, Gloucester bitterly replies, "I have no way, and therefore want no eyes; / I stumbled when I saw."

Gloucester pathetically wishes he might live just long enough to "see" his son Edgar, if only with his sense of touch. (The irony is that he is standing right before Edgar, but doesn't know it. Edgar wants to retain his disguise until he is able to set things right again in his family. It is the only chance he has to defeat his unscrupulous brother.)

The sight of his father plunges Edgar into the depths of pessimism. He has just said that his fortune could only improve. Now he realizes that it has taken a turn for the worse, and may get worse still. In fact, he says, "the worst is not / So long as we can say 'This is the worst.' " In other words, as long as we still have the power of mind to say anything like "this is the worst that can happen," our fortunes can still take a plunge. We can still go mad, or die, and above all, we are not yet entirely without hope.

The old man asks Edgar where he is going, and Gloucester asks whether this stranger (Edgar) is a beggar. When the old man tells Gloucester that Edgar is both a madman and a beggar, Gloucester replies that he must still have some shred of sanity left, or he wouldn't be able to beg. He says he saw a man the night before, in the storm, who reminded him of his son, and who reminds him too of this beggar. Gloucester says that the mad beggar he had seen in the storm (who was, of course, Edgar) was so miserable that he "made me think man a worm." Then Gloucester makes one of the most crushing philosophic statements in the play: "As flies to wanton boys, are we to th' Gods; / They kill us for their sport." The point is that man is destroyed not merely because the gods are indifferent to him; he is destroyed because the gods take a cruel, sadistic glee in crushing him, just as boys enjoy tearing a fly to pieces. This is the most pessimistic religious position taken in the play because it states that evil and suffering in the world are not merely the result of passive indifference, or of chance, but are the result of active, positive cruelty on the part of the gods.

Gloucester again asks the old man to leave him. If he likes, Gloucester says, he may rejoin him further along the road to Dover. But first he asks the old man to procure some clothes for the poor Tom of Bedlam. Meanwhile Gloucester will entrust himself to Tom's care. When the old man protests that the beggar is mad, Gloucester bitterly comments that it is typical of the times that "madmen lead the blind." Finally the old man consents to find some clothes for the almost naked, shivering Edgar. Left alone with his father, Edgar resumes the "mad" patter that he used to disguise himself in the hovel during the storm. Gloucester asks him if he knows the way to Dover and, out of pity for Edgar's mad replies, gives him some money. Gloucester, contemplating suicide, asks Edgar to lead him to one of the high cliffs of Dover. Beyond that point he will not need to be led any further. The pathetic pair leave the stage together.

Act IV: Scene 2

This scene takes place the following day, in front of the Duke of Albany's palace. Goneril and Edmund have just arrived after their trip from Gloucester's castle. Goneril welcomes Edmund to her home, but expresses surprise that Albany is not on hand to greet them. She asks Oswald, who enters at this point, where his master is. Oswald tells her that a great change has come over Albany. When Oswald told him that France had landed an army at Dover, Albany merely smiled at the news. When told that Goneril was coming home, Albany had curtly commented, "the worse." In short, Oswald complains, "What most he should dislike seems pleasant to him; / What like, offensive."

Goneril's response to this news is that her "mild husband" is probably too frightened to fight against the French invasion. She scornfully tells Edmund about the "cowish terror" of her husband's spirit, and asks Edmund to return to Gloucester's castle and hasten Cornwall's war preparations. Hinting that she would not take it amiss if Edmund were to murder Albany some day, she gives him a "favor," or souvenir, and a kiss, and speeds him on his way.

As soon as Edmund is gone, Albany enters. Goneril sarcastically comments on his delay in greeting her, sneering, "I have been worth the whistle." Albany, however, loses no time in upbraiding her for her behavior. "O Goneril!" he cries, "You are not worth the dust which the rude wind / Blows in your face." He accuses her and Regan of being "Tigers, not daughters" for their behavior to their father. He is amazed that Cornwall allowed them to lock Lear out in the storm (obviously he doesn't know Cornwall), and foretells that if the heavens don't tame such wild offenses, then "Humanity must perforce prey on itself / Like monsters of the deep." (This, of course, is precisely what is happening throughout the play.)

Goneril's only reply to this richly deserved tongue-lashing is to accuse Albany of being a "milk-liver'd man," in short, a coward, for not arming against France. The argument heightens in intensity, with Albany finally shouting that if he were not a man and Goneril were not a woman, he would tear apart her flesh and bones. Goneril sneers at this statement, coolly and contemptuously like a great cat, "Marry, your manhood—mew!"

At this point a messenger enters with the news that Cornwall has died of the wounds inflicted on him by his servant. It is the first Albany has heard of the putting out of Gloucester's eyes. He is torn between horror at that monstrous act and relief at the swift justice that overtook Cornwall for committing it. "This shows you are above, / You justicers," Albany exults, "that these our nether crimes / So speedily can venge!" In other words, to him the stabbing of Cornwall by the servant is a demonstration (1) that the gods are just, and (2) that they act speedily to punish the criminal, even if, ironically, they do it through a mere servant. This is one of the more optimistic statements of belief in the play.

The news of Cornwall's death has a very different effect on Goneril. To her, it is both good and bad. The good part is that with Cornwall dead, she may be able to usurp his and her sister's part of the kingdom. The bad part is that now Regan as a widow may be able to marry Edmund. To make matters worse, Goneril herself has just sent Edmund to Regan, thus allowing them plenty of opportunity to scheme against her, while she is stuck with her now distasteful husband, Albany. She must have time to think; hence, she takes a letter the messenger has brought her from her sister and retires within the palace with the excuse that she must read and answer it.

Albany asks the messenger where Edmund was all the time that Gloucester was being tortured. The messenger replies that Edmund was escorting Goneril home and has since departed again. Did he know what was being done to his father, Albany asks? Not only did he know, the messenger replies, but it was Edmund who betrayed Gloucester in the first place. Albany swears to "revenge" Gloucester's eyes and to thank him for the love and loyalty he showed to King Lear.

Act IV: Scene 3

This scene provides necessary relief and contrast from the squabbling between Albany and Goneril in the preceding scene. It consists of a quiet conversation between Kent and a Gentleman in the French camp near Dover. Kent learns from the Gentleman that the King of France has had to return home on urgent business which required his personal attention. He has left behind him in Dover Cordelia and a Marshal of France, one Monsieur La Far, to conduct the campaign in his absence. The Gentleman is the same one who was sent by Kent to Cordelia in Act III, Scene 1, bearing letters telling her of the mistreatment of Lear. Kent now asks him what her reaction was to the news of Lear's suffering. The Gentleman reports that she simultaneously wept with sorrow and smiled with patience, shaking "holy water from her heavenly eyes." Kent, marvelling at the difference between Cordelia and her sisters, muses that "It is the stars, / The stars above us, govern our conditions; / Else one self mate and make could not beget / Such different issues." In other words, man is ruled by an unalterable destiny which he cannot understand. Otherwise how can one explain a Cordelia and a Goneril or Regan being born to the same parents?

Kent then tells the Gentleman that although Lear has arrived in Dover, he refuses to see Cordelia for shame at having given "her dear rights / To his dog-hearted daughters." The Gentleman says that Albany's and Cornwall's armies are on the march, and the scene ends with Kent begging the Gentleman to put up a little longer with his disguise—he will reveal himself when the time is ripe.

Act IV: Scene 4

Amid a flourish of drums and flags in the French camp, Cordelia enters, accompanied by a doctor and some soldiers. Apparently some time has elapsed since the last scene. In that time, Cordelia has received a distressing report about her father. Lear has managed to wander away, in his madness, from the attendants who were supposed to guard him. Cordelia tells the doctor that her father was seen, completely mad, singing aloud and dressed with a variety of flowers. She tells a soldier to send out a hundred troops to look for the King and bring him back to the camp. Then she asks the doctor if there is anything he can do to restore Lear's senses to him. Whoever can do that, Cordelia says, can have all her possessions. The doctor replies that the only treatment he can prescribe for Lear is rest, the "foster-nurse of nature." Cordelia again begs the troops to go in search of Lear, lest, in his insanity, he come to some harm.

Now a messenger arrives with the news that the armies of Albany and Cornwall are fast approaching. Cordelia answers that she is prepared for them. She stresses the point that if there is war, it will be to save her father, not because of any "blown ambition" on France's part. With a prayer that she may soon see her father again, the scene ends.

Act IV: Scene 5

We are back in Gloucester's castle, where Regan has remained after Cornwall's death. She is questioning Oswald, who has just arrived with Goneril's letter for Edmund. Regan asks Oswald if Albany's troops are on the move, and if Albany is leading them.

Oswald snidely tells her that while the army is indeed marching, with Albany at the head, Goneril is "the better soldier" than her husband. Then Regan tries to pry loose from Oswald some information about the letter which was given him in Act IV, Scene 2. Oswald pretends ignorance out of loyalty to his mistress. Regan tells him he can't deliver the letter to Edmund there anyway, because Edmund has gone off to kill Gloucester and to find out how strong the French army is. Letting Gloucester live after blinding him, she tells Oswald, was a great mistake. Wherever he goes in his wretchedness he arouses "all hearts against us." According to her, however, Edmund's motive in killing his father will be "pity of his misery."

Then Regan tries desperately to keep Oswald at the castle, thus making sure that he can't deliver the letter from her sister. She tells him that the roads are dangerous now, with all the troops marching about, but Oswald remains loyal to Goneril and insists on leaving in search of Edmund. Regan then tries to win Oswald over to her side by assuring him that she knows what is going on in the Albany household anyway. "I know your Lady does not love her husband," she tells Oswald. (How much she loved her own husband is shown by her running after Edmund the minute Cornwall is dead.) She assures Oswald that it is "more convenient" for Edmund to marry her, now that she is a widow, than for him to wed the still-married Goneril. Finally, despairing of ever getting Oswald over to her side, Regan tells him he will benefit greatly if he should happen to encounter Gloucester and kill him, and she sends him on his way.

Act IV: Scene 6

This is one of the most crucial and difficult scenes in the play. We are in the countryside near Dover where Edgar, disguised as a peasant in the clothing Gloucester's old tenant had found for him in Act IV, Scene 1, is leading his blind father. Gloucester's only thought now is of suicide. He wants Edgar to lead him to the top of one of the steep cliffs of Dover, where he will leap into the sea below. But Edgar has other plans. He will tell his father they have reached the cliff's edge when, in fact, they are on level ground. Then, when his father jumps, and, of course, doesn't die, Edgar will tell him that he has been spared because the gods want him to live. Given Gloucester's superstition, Edgar hopes that this "miracle" will give him the strength to continue existing and to recognize his son.

As father and son progress, though, Gloucester's suspicions are aroused. Edgar tells him that they are climbing a "horrible steep" hill, but Gloucester rightly maintains "the ground is even." Edgar asks him if he can't hear the sea roaring below them, and when Gloucester says he can't, Edgar replies that his sense of hearing must be affected by his loss of sight. Then Edgar paints a most ingenious picture of how tiny everything below them is. The crows seems as small as beetles; the fishermen on the beach look like mice, and so forth. Gloucester finally seems convinced and bids Edgar leave him there, giving him his purse as a reward for leading him this far.

Then Gloucester kneels and prays to the "mighty Gods," renouncing the world and saying he cannot bear to be in it any longer. He throws himself forward and falls, fainting with the thought that he has leapt off a cliff. Edgar rushes up to him, awakens him, and says he has fallen "many fathom down." It is a miracle he is still alive, Edgar says. He should have been broken like an egg. Gloucester is merely disappointed that he hasn't in fact died. Edgar helps him to his feet, saying that the beggar who led him to the edge of the cliff was some fiend so that Gloucester can attribute his life to the fact that the gods wished to preserve him. Gloucester vows to bear his affliction until the end and not try to commit suicide again.

At this point Lear enters, dressed in wild flowers, as Cordelia had described him in Act IV, Scene 4. He has eluded his attendants, and is wandering madly about, claiming at one point to be a counterfeiter, at another a recruiting officer, then an expert bowman and a sentry. Beneath all his incoherent babble, however, there is a good deal of sane comment on the state of the world. Edgar and Gloucester are struck with horror at the spectacle of the mad King. Gloucester seems to recognize Lear's voice, and asks, "Is't not the King?" Lear answers magnificently, "Ay, every inch a King." But then he ironically adds, "When I do stare, see how the subject quakes." Again, as in Act III, Scene 6, he holds a kind of mock trial, but this time all nature, not merely his daughters, is arraigned. No one shall be executed for adultery from now on, Lear maintains, because the whole natural world, down to the tiniest wrens and flies, is promiscuous. Besides, Lear says bitterly, "Gloucester's bastard son / Was kinder to his father than my daughters / Got 'tween lawful sheets."

Then Lear rages against women and sex in general; the "riotous appetite," as he calls it. In sex, he says, is "hell, there's darkness, / There is the sulphurous pit." He is totally revolted by the constant sexual maneuverings throughout all nature, and holds women especially responsible for them. Gloucester, moved deeply by Lear's words, cries, "O! let me kiss that hand." But Lear replies, "Let me wipe it first; it smells of mortality."

Calling Lear a "ruin'd piece of Nature," Gloucester asks if the King recognizes him. Lear says that Gloucester must be blind Cupid, and warns Gloucester that he will never make him love.

Lear adds that Gloucester doesn't need eyes to "see how this world goes." The law of the world, Lear explains, is that there is no difference between judge and criminal. It is just a matter of who is in the more powerful position, for we are all guilty. In his disgust with the world, Lear catalogues all the injustices, all the ways in which people in power get away with the same crimes for which they savagely punish the less powerful. Such is the eloquence of his speech that Edgar turns aside and comments, "O! matter and impertinency mix'd; / Reason in madness."

Then Lear tells Gloucester that he really does know him, and says he must be patient about dying; we can no more control the time of our death than the time of our birth, and "when we are born," Lear adds, "we cry that we are come / To this great stage of fools." Lear then abruptly thinks of his sons-in-law (he doesn't yet know of Albany's sympathy for him) and cries, "kill, kill, kill, kill, kill, kill!"

At this point Lear's attendants catch up with him and try to reason with him to go to Cordelia. But Lear thinks he is being taken prisoner and tells them that if they treat him well, they will get ransom. Then he mockingly bids them catch him and dashes off, leading the attendants quite a chase. Edgar asks the Gentleman who has come with Lear's attendants how near the armies of Albany and Cornwall are. The Gentleman says that they are very close and are about to engage in battle with the French army.

Suddenly Oswald enters, overjoyed that he has found Gloucester, so that he can kill him and gain the prize Regan promised him. But Edgar steps forward in defense of his father and speaks insultingly to Oswald in broad peasant dialect. Oswald is infuriated that a lowly peasant should interfere with his killing of Gloucester, and he begins to duel with Edgar. But Edgar quickly knocks him down, fatally wounding him. Before Oswald dies, he begs Edgar to deliver his letter to Edmund. But, once Oswald is dead, Edgar of course rips open the letter and discovers in it that Goneril is proposing to Edmund that he kill Albany and then marry her. Suddenly the drums of war are heard in the distance, and Edgar leads his father off the stage.

Act IV: Scene 7

This great scene of the reunion of Cordelia and Lear takes place in Cordelia's tent in the French camp. Lear has evidently been recaptured by the attendants and has been returned to the camp, put to sleep, and dressed in fresh clothes while he slept. Cordelia tells Kent of her deep gratitude to him for all he has done for her father, begging him to come out of disguise and reveal himself to the others. Kent, however, asks her to wait until he thinks it is the proper time to show himself. Then Cordelia asks the doctor how her father is doing. The doctor says that since he has been sleeping soundly for a long time, they might wake him now. So Lear is borne in on a chair and placed before Cordelia, Kent and the doctor. Music is played to wake Lear as gently as possible, and Cordelia, staring at her father's sleeping face, reflects in wonder that her two sisters could have mistreated him. "Was this a face / To be oppos'd against the warring winds?" she asks, and makes the observation, made so often before in the play, that "Mine enemy's dog, / Though he had bit me, should have stood that night (of the storm) Against my fire." Cordelia is amazed that her father was able to survive the experience at all.

As Lear begins to awaken, the doctor bids Cordelia speak to him. She asks her father how he is, but Lear, still half asleep, thinks she is "a soul in bliss" descended from heaven to mock him in hell, where he is "bound / Upon a wheel of fire, that mine own tears / Do scald like molten lead." When Cordelia asks him if he knows her, Lear repeats that she is a spirit, and asks in turn when she died. Finally Lear is fully awake. He is overcome with guilt when he confronts the daughter he had wronged and who, he thinks, still hates him. He tries to kneel before her for forgiveness, but Cordelia begs him to get up. Lear confesses tragically that "I am a very foolish fond old man, / Fourscore and upward, not an hour more or less; / And, to deal plainly, / I fear I am not in my perfect mind." He begs Cordelia not to weep, but says that if she has poison for him, he will drink it. He is sure she does not love him, because he has wronged her, and her sisters, who benefited from him, hate him. "You have some cause" to hate me, Lear says, "they have not." But with simple nobility Cordelia assures him, "No cause, no cause." Then Lear asks her if he is in France, and Cordelia assures him he is in his own kingdom. Again Lear thinks he is being mocked. The doctor intervenes, telling Cordelia that Lear ought to rest again; he is still too weak to learn the whole history of where he is and how he got there. Lear, repeating that he is "old and foolish," leaves with Cordelia, the doctor and some attendants.

This immensely touching scene ends with a brief discussion between Kent and the Gentleman about the death of Cornwall and Edmund's taking the title of Earl of Gloucester. The Gentleman, not knowing who Kent is, mentions a rumor that Edgar and Kent are together in Germany. Kent evasively answers that rumors are not to be trusted; what is to be done now is to arm properly against the oncoming armies of Albany and Cornwall.

Act V: Scene 1

After the brief interval of affection and forgiveness in Act IV, Scene 7, we are plunged once again into a scene of monstrous plotting and intrigue. The scene shifts to the British camp near Dover, where Edmund and Regan enter, accompanied by soldiers and a flourish of drums. Edmund asks an officer to find out whether Albany is still on their side or if he has deserted them, since "he's full of alteration / And self-reproving." When the officer leaves on his errand, Regan comments that Albany certainly is untrustworthy. Then she gets to the matter which most closely concerns her: does Edmund in fact love her sister? Edmund answers cagily that he loves Goneril honorably, but to think that he has seduced her is unworthy of Regan. He assures her that they have not had an adulterous affair. Regan begs Edmund not to be "familiar" with Goneril, and Edmund reassures her that he cares equally little for Goneril and "the Duke her husband."

Albany and Goneril themselves arrive, also accompanied by soldiers, drums and flags. Goneril's first remark (made aside) on seeing Edmund once more, is that she would rather lose the battle than that Regan should get Edmund for herself. Then Albany informs Regan and Edmund that he has heard that Lear and Cordelia are reunited, along with "others whom the rigour of our state / Forc'd to cry out." He points out that the only reason he is there to help out in the fighting is that "France invades our land." Goneril and Edmund are all for making peace with Albany because they need his army. A council of war is decided upon, but Edmund holds back a moment. Then Goneril and Regan argue about who is going to remain outside with Edmund. Neither is willing to trust the other alone with him for a second. Meanwhile Edgar, still disguised, enters. He asks Albany if he may have a word with him alone. The others all leave the stage for their council of war.

Edgar now hands Albany the letter which was given him by Oswald. "Before you fight the battle," Edgar tells Albany, "ope this letter." The letter, we remember, contains the plot between Goneril and Edmund to slay Albany and then get married. If Albany should be successful in battle, Edgar tells him, he is to let a trumpet sound, and a champion will come who will give proof of what is in the letter. If Albany falls in the battle, of course, it won't matter. Albany tries to get Edgar to stay until Albany has read the letter, but Edgar says he must leave, and he does.

Edmund re-enters and tells Albany that he has been successful in his spying on the French camp, but that they must hurry off to battle. When Albany leaves to rally his troops, Edmund remains behind for another of his cynical, witty and unscrupulous soliloquies. He has sworn his love to both Goneril and Regan, he says, and each is madly jealous of the other. "Which of them shall I take?" he asks himself. "Both? one? or neither?" One thing is certain; he can enjoy neither sister if the other remains alive. Coldly and cynically he weighs the advantages and disadvantages of each sister in his mind. The chief obstacle in his way right now is Albany. He will let Albany fight in the impending battle because he can use his army. If Albany is killed, then all is well. If he survives, let Goneril kill him. In any case, one thing is clear: the merciful treatment which Albany intends for Lear and Cordelia must be vetoed after the battle. Edmund is concerned only with defending his state, not with debating about it. No enemies can be left alive, and Lear and Cordelia, although they are not active enemies, would be a rallying point for the now numerous people in Britain who hate Edmund.

Act V: Scene 2

This brief scene takes place on a field between the British and

French camps. Lear, Cordelia and the French forces enter and quickly leave the stage for the battle, amid flourishes of trumpets and drums. Then Edgar enters, leading Gloucester. He tells his father to rest in the shade of a tree until the battle is over. All Gloucester can do for the cause is "pray that the right may thrive." Then Edgar also races off for the battle. Suddenly the trumpets sound again to announce the retreat of the French forces. Edgar dashes in to tell his father the bad news that Lear and his daughter have lost the battle and are taken prisoner. He begs Gloucester to seek shelter with him, but the old man hasn't the heart to wander any further. Gloomily he tells Edgar that "a man may rot even here." Why keep running from death when that is all he wants? But Edgar tries to cheer him up again, in terms of stoic philosophy: "Men must endure / Their going hence, even as their coming hither": he tells his father, "Ripeness is all." He convinces Gloucester of this truth, and together they leave for safety.

Act V: Scene 3

The final scene of the play takes place in the British camp near Dover. Edmund enters, bringing with him Lear and Cordelia as prisoners. He orders a group of officers to take them away until it is decided what to do with them. Cordelia tells Lear that she doesn't care what happens to her, but is unhappy for him. She tries to comfort the old man by telling him that now they will be reunited with Goneril and Regan, but this is slim comfort, indeed, for Lear cannot bear to see his two evil daughters again. Instead, he is quite content to live out the rest of his days in prison with Cordelia, where, he says, "We two alone will sing like birds i' the' cage: / When thou dost ask me blessing, I'll kneel down, / And ask of thee forgiveness." In the prison they will gossip about court life, "and pray, and sing, and tell old tales." They will be utterly removed from the cares of the world, from "who's in, who's out" in court politics.

Edmund harshly breaks in on Lear's idyllic picture of prison life, and again orders a guard to take the prisoners away. Lear finally comforts Cordelia, telling her that "Upon such sacrifices, my Cordelia, / The Gods themselves throw incense." (In other words, when human beings have suffered and sacrificed as nobly as they have done, the gods must worship them, instead of their worshipping the gods. There are two major interpretations of what Lear means by "sacrifices." A. C. Bradley says he means his own and Cordelia's renunciation of the world. G. L. Kittredge thinks Shakespeare means specifically the sacrifices Cordelia has made for Lear's sake.)

As Lear and Cordelia are taken away to prison by the guard, Edmund hands one of his captains a secret note to bring to the jail with them. The note orders that Lear and Cordelia be executed in prison. Even that last bit of happiness is to be denied them. Edmund feels he has the authority to issue this death warrant because he is commander-in-chief of the British army, in place of the dead Cornwall. Cordelia is to be hanged, and then the rumor will be spread that she committed suicide out of despair. Edmund is quite aware of the bloodthirstiness of his order. He prepares the captain for this cruel mission by telling him that "to be tender-minded / Does not become a sword." These are hard times, Edmund says, and a man must be prepared to act ruthlessly in them if he hopes to get ahead. The officer promises to carry out the order, and Edmund sends him off, asking him to "write happy" when the execution has been carried out.

Now, amid a flourish of trumpets and drums, Albany, Goneril, Regan and some soldiers enter. Albany congratulates Edmund on his "valiant strain" which won the day's victory. But then he asks him for the royal prisoners he has taken, "so to use them / As we shall find their merits and our safety / May equally determine." Edmund tells Albany that he has sent them to prison, but holds back the information that he has secretly ordered their execution. Instead he says they will be ready for trial tomorrow. He and the rest of the army are too tired from the battle to think about Lear and Cordelia right now.

Edmund's high-handed behavior in sending Lear and Cordelia to prison without consulting him irritates Albany, who reminds Edmund that he is merely a commander in the war, but not really Albany's equal as far as civil authority is concerned. Albany is, after all, a duke, while Edmund, even if he has a right to his father's title, which is dubious while Gloucester is still alive, would only be an earl. But Regan intercedes for the man she loves and tells Albany that since Edmund led the army in the dead Cornwall's place, he has every right to order things as he pleases. Now open warfare breaks out between Regan and Goneril over Edmund. So inflamed is Goneril at her sister's standing up for Edmund that she forgets that her own husband is present, and she passionately begins to insult Regan. Unaware that Goneril has secretly poisoned her (this happened offstage), Regan begins to feel the first symptoms in her stomach. She defiantly gives Edmund all her "soldiers, prisoners, patrimony," and calls him her "lord and master." Relations between the sisters and Edmund and Albany become very tense. Enjoying the onset of Regan's death agony, Goneril bitchily asks her, "Mean you to enjoy him (Edmund)?" Albany angrily reminds his wife that it is not up to her to decide whom Regan shall marry, and Edmund, who all this time has been cynically enjoying the fuss made over him, sides with Goneril and tells Albany it isn't up to him to decide either.

Finally, Albany can stand the squabble no longer. He has read the letter given him by Edgar in Act V, Scene 1, and his fury at the treachery of Goneril and Edmund has been growing ever since. Now he breaks into the argument to inform Edmund and Goneril that they are both under arrest for "capital treason." With bitter humor he tells Regan that her claim on Edmund is barred: Edmund is apparently already promised to Goneril. If Regan wants to marry again, Albany tells her, she will have to marry him, for his lady has first claim on Edmund. Goneril laughs off Albany's bitter sarcasm, calling it "an interlude," i.e., a little bit of farcical drama, like a short comedy. Ignoring his wife, Albany challenges Edmund to a duel. He calls for the trumpet to sound, as Edgar had told him to do when he gave him the letter. Then, throwing down his glove in the standard gesture of challenge, he tells Edmund that if a champion does not appear to fight him, he will lower himself to duel with him. Edmund throws down his glove, too, and replies that he will maintain his "truth and honour firmly" against anybody. Meanwhile the effects of the poison Goneril gave Regan have been increasing, and now, feeling mortally sick, Regan is led into Albany's tent.

A herald enters, sounds the trumpet, and reads the following proclamation: "If any man of quality or degree within the lists of the army will maintain upon Edmund, supposed Earl of Gloucester, that he is a manifold traitor, let him appear by the third sound of the trumpet." Three times the trumpet is blown, and on the third call it is answered by Edgar's trumpet. Edgar enters, fully armed, his face concealed behind a visor. The herald asks him who he is, what his rank is, and why he has come to answer the summons. Edgar replies that his "name is lost" but that he is of noble blood, as noble as his adversary's. Then, calling Edmund "False to thy gods, thy brother and thy father," Edgar challenges him to combat as a "toad-spotted traitor." Edmund replies cooly that according to the rules of knighthood, he ought to demand his challenger's name, but since the stranger seems well bred and warlike, he will consent to fight him.

The two brothers duel, and Edmund eventually falls, mortally wounded. Albany calls for a doctor to save him (because he wants Edmund to live long enough to be tried for treason), and Goneril cries out that he should not have fought because the laws of chivalry do not require a noble to fight "an unknown opposite." But Albany abruptly tells her, "Shut your mouth, dame," or he will stuff it with the incriminating letter he has. He even tries to get the dying Edmund to read the letter. After exchanging insults with her husband, Goneril leaves the stage, followed by an officer sent by Albany because he fears what she may do in her desperation.

Now Edmund, in his death agony, confesses to all the charges brought against him. Indeed, he says he is guilty of "more, much more; the time will bring it out." (Presumably Edmund means his secret order to execute Lear and Cordelia. Why he doesn't send a messenger to stop the execution at this point, when he does later, is a mystery in the play.) Then Edmund asks Edgar again who he is, saying that he forgives him if he is a nobleman. Now is the time that Edgar decides finally to reveal himself. "My name is Edgar," he says proudly, lifting the visor, "and thy father's son. / The Gods are just, and of our pleasant vices / Make instruments to plague us." He adds that Gloucester had to pay with his eyes for begetting Edmund in a "dark and vicious place," i.e., illegitimately. Albany embraces Edgar, and wants to know where he managed to hide himself all this time, and how he knew of the miseries of his father. Edgar tells the story of his disguise as Tom of Bedlam and of his nursing the blinded Gloucester. He didn't reveal himself to his father until just a half hour ago, he says, and he did it then only because he wasn't sure that he would survive the combat with Edmund. When he told Gloucester who he was, and asked for his blessing, the old man's "flaw'd heart, / Alack, too weak the conflict to support! / Twixt two extremes of passion, joy and grief, / Burst smilingly." Albany and even Edmund are moved by the story of Gloucester's final reconciliation with his son and his ensuing death. Edgar goes on to tell how he met with the banished Kent and joined forces with him.

Edgar's tale is interrupted by the frantic entrance of a Gentleman, carrying a bloody knife. The Gentleman tells Albany that the knife is hot from the heart of Goneril, who stabbed herself after poisoning her sister. Both are now dead. Edmund comments, with typical wit, even in his death throes: "I was contracted to them both: all three / Now marry in an instant." Edmund also expresses here perhaps the only genuine emotion he has had throughout the play: "Yet Edmund was belov'd." This suggests that his whole vicious career may have been caused by his feeling that he wasn't loved, a feeling relieved here by the death of the two sisters for love of him. Albany's attitude, however, is that their death was the judgment of heaven, for which he can't feel any pity. At this point Kent enters, seeking Lear. Albany remembers that he doesn't know where Lear and Cordelia are. But before anything can be done about it, the bodies of Goneril and Regan are brought onstage. Edmund tells Kent what happened, and then decides, since he is dying, to do at least one good deed in his life. He tells Albany of his secret execution warrant, and bids him send a messenger to prevent the deaths of Lear and Cordelia. Albany does so, and the dying Edmund is borne offstage.

But Edmund's last bit of mercy comes too late, for now Lear enters, with the dead Cordelia in his arms. Howling with horror, Lear begs for a looking glass to see if Cordelia has any breath of life left in her. He places the glass to her lips, and convinces himself that she does still breathe. He is too absorbed in trying to revive Cordelia to notice that Kent has knelt by his side to reveal himself to his King at last. Although later he does recognize Kent, at this moment Lear has no mind for anything but his Cordelia, whom he begs to "stay a little." Of her he says, "Her voice was ever soft, / Gentle and low, an excellent thing in woman." (And very different from the shrill, grating, fishwife voices of Goneril and Regan heard earlier in this scene.) Then Lear remembers that in a last surge of royal power he had killed the executioner who was hanging Cordelia. An officer confirms this story of Lear's last heroic action. Kent, Albany and Edgar try to tell Lear the bits of the story that he doesn't know, but his mind has completely gone now, in sorrow for Cordelia. Even the announcement by an officer that Edmund has just died, causes Albany to say, "That's but a trifle here," in the face of the overwhelming tragedy of Cordelia's death and Lear's final suffering. Lear gazes raptly at his daughter, trying to convince himself that there is still a stir of life in her. "Why should a dog, a horse, a rat, have life, / And thou no breath at all?" he asks bitterly. Finally the majestic old King begs someone to undo a button that is constricting him, and, with a final hope that Cordelia may yet be alive, dies of a broken heart.

Edgar tries to revive him, but Kent wisely says: "Vex not his ghost: O! let him pass; he hates him / That would upon the rack of this tough world / Stretch him out longer." The wonder, Kent says, is that he managed to endure so long. Albany commands that the body of Lear be borne away, and asks Kent and Edgar to rule the kingdom. But Kent refuses: he is too broken-hearted at the death of his master, who he says calls him. Edgar will rule alone. The final words of the play, given in some editions to Albany, and in others to Edgar, aptly summarize, whoever speaks them, the feelings of the survivors:

> The weight of this sad time we must obey; / Speak what we feel, not what we ought to say. / The oldest hath borne most: we that are young shall never see so much, nor live so long.

Then the survivors leave the stage, to the solemn music of a funeral march.

Macbeth

DUNCAN, *King of Scotland.*
MALCOLM ⎫ *his sons.*
DONALBAIN ⎭
MACBETH ⎫
BANQUO ⎭ *generals of the King's army.*
MACDUFF ⎫
LENNOX
ROSS
MENTEITH ⎬ *noblemen of Scotland.*
ANGUS
CAITHNESS ⎭
FLEANCE, *son to Banquo.*
SIWARD, *Earl of Northumberland, general of the English forces.*
YOUNG SIWARD, *his son.*
SEYTON, *an officer attending on Macbeth.*
BOY, *son to Macduff.*
ENGLISH DOCTOR.
SCOTTISH DOCTOR.
CAPTAIN.
SOLDIER.
PORTER.
OLD MAN.
Three MURDERERS.

LADY MACBETH.
LADY MACDUFF.
GENTLEWOMAN *attending on Lady Macbeth.*
HECATE.
Three WITCHES.
APPARITIONS.

LORDS, GENTLEMEN, OFFICERS, SOLDIERS, ATTENDANTS, *and* MESSENGERS.

Macbeth

Act I: Scene 1

The play opens with a meeting of three witches in some sort of deserted place. The witches tell us that the next time they meet it will be with Macbeth. The meeting will take place when the tumult ("hurlyburly") is ended, when a battle has been "lost and won," and that this will occur before the sun goes down.* After having said this, the witches hear the cries of their "familiar spirits," (two of whom are called Graymalkin and Paddock), recite an ambiguous couplet ("Fair is foul and foul is fair: / Hover through the fog and filthy air"), and exit.

Act I: Scene 2

This scene takes place in a military camp. The following characters enter: Duncan, who is king of Scotland; Malcolm, Duncan's elder son; Donalbain, Duncan's younger son; Lenox, a nobleman of Scotland; and a number of attendants. They meet a wounded man referred to by Malcolm as "the sergeant." The sergeant has been wounded apparently in the battle referred to by the witches in the last scene, and Duncan decides that because the sergeant has been wounded he must know how the fight has been going. We also learn from Duncan's remarks that the battle is part of a revolt against Duncan. Malcolm asks the sergeant for news of the battle, and the wounded man tells this story. The fight was such that it was difficult to tell which side would win, the rebels' troops headed by Macdonwald or the forces loyal to Duncan, which, we learn in the course of the scene, are headed by Macbeth and Banquo. Added to Macdonwald's troops were Irish foot soldiers

* The ability of the witches to predict that the battle will be over before "the set of sun" tells us that they are able to predict the future. This ability has an important effect on Macbeth and on the meaning of the play.

694

and horsemen ("kernes and gallowglasses"). Fortune seemed to be all on the rebels' side, but to no avail. For "brave Macbeth" despite fortune, made a passage for himself to Macdonwald by killing everyone between him and the leader of the rebels. When Macbeth came face to face with Macdonwald, he immediately ripped the rebel open from the navel to the lips, cut off his head, and placed it on the roof of the loyalists' castle. Unfortunately, continues the sergeant, that did not end the difficulties. No sooner did Macdonwald's Irish soldiers run away than the king of Norway, whose name is Sweno, in league with the rebels, took advantage of the situation, and "began a fresh assault," with new supplies of men and guns. But this did not make the loyalist leaders, Macbeth and Banquo, despair. They redoubled their strokes upon the enemy. As the sergeant is about to continue, he finds he cannot, for he feels faint. When Duncan sends off the sergeant to the doctor, Ross and Angus, two more noblemen of Scotland, enter. They have come from the battlefield, and Ross proceeds to finish the story broken off by the sergeant's weakness. The king of Norway (referred to simply as "Norway") with his great number of troops was assisted by another traitor, the Thane of Cawdor. (Thane is a Scotch title approximating that of earl). Ross says the conflict was "dismal." However, the conflict was dismal only until "Bellona's bridegroom" (almost certainly meaning Macbeth) with equal strength met the strong king of Norway and beat him. Now Sweno, the king of Norway, wishes to come to terms with Duncan. Duncan says that the Thane of Cawdor will no longer deceive him, for Cawdor will be sentenced to death. And Macbeth, Duncan announces, will be the new Thane of Cawdor. Duncan sums up the situation in the last line, "What he (the Thane of Cawdor) hath lost, noble Macbeth hath won."

Act I: Scene 3

The scene opens with the appointed meeting of the three witches. The first witch gives an account of what she has been doing since their last meeting. She tells us that she has met a sailor's wife munching on chestnuts. When the witch asked the wife for some nuts, the latter refused them to her. The witch will therefore soon take revenge, the revenge to be taken through the wife's husband, the sailor, who is the captain of the ship *Tiger*. She will cause the wind to blow so that he will never be able to sleep. He will be so weary that he will "dwindle, peak, and pine." However, the witch, much as she can cause the captain of the *Tiger* to suffer, cannot make him lose his ship ("his bark").

The witches then hear the sound of a drum, which announces the arrival of Macbeth and Banquo, who now enter. Macbeth's first words, spoken to Banquo, apparently comment on the weather, "So foul and fair a day I have not seen." They then see the witches, who greet Macbeth with three titles, those of the Thane of Glamis, the Thane of Cawdor, and the future king. We learn from Banquo's speech immediately following the witches' greeting that Macbeth is visibly shaken by the witches' words, for Banquo says, "Good Sir, why do you start, and seem to fear / Things that do sound so fair?" But Macbeth is not only shaken; he is so involved with his thoughts that he does not hear Banquo and therefore does not answer Banquo's question. Returning to the witches, Banquo asks them whether they have any predictions for his own future. They reply that he will be "lesser than Macbeth, and greater" and "not so happy, yet much happier." They also tell him that, although he himself will not be a king, he will be the father of kings. Macbeth, coming to himself, asks the witches questions, but they vanish. As Macbeth and Banquo are speculating about the witches, Ross and Angus enter to tell Macbeth that he has been granted the title of Thane of Cawdor. "The Thane of Cawdor lives," says Macbeth, "why do you dress me in borrow'd robes?" That is, Macbeth asks why the title should be given him when the man to whom it belongs is still alive. Macbeth is told the story of Cawdor's disloyalty; he then privately asks Banquo whether Banquo does not hope for the fulfillment of the prophecy for Banquo as the prophecy for Macbeth has in part been fulfilled. Banquo indicates a distrust for the witches. He tells Macbeth that the tools of Satan ("instruments of Darkness") often fool us in the final result ("betray's in deepest consequence") by first telling us truths as thereby appearing honest.

As the other characters are involved in conversation, Macbeth speaks an aside. (An aside is a speech spoken by one character and heard by no one else on stage except those actors whom he may be addressing. In this case Macbeth is speaking to no other characters.) Macbeth tells himself that this beckoning him on (to greater things) by beings who know more than ordinary men ("supernatural soliciting") is ambiguous. That is, it is difficult to decide whether it is good or evil. The fact that he is made Thane of Cawdor seems to indicate that they tell the truth, and that appears to show that the beings are good. On the other hand, how can they be good when he allows himself to see a picture so horrible that it makes his hair stand on end and his heart beat unusually hard. Macbeth goes on to say that immediate dangers ("present fears") are less frightening to him than horrible things which he imagines. Exactly what makes his hair stand on end and heart beat wildly becomes a bit clearer in the following line: "My thought, whose murder is but fantastical . . . " Apparently he has been thinking of murdering someone. The picture of himself as a murderer has been so vivid that he has been throughly shaken and caught up completely by his inner thoughts. He is incapable of seeing anything around him. Banquo remarks to his companions on Macbeth's self-absorption. But Macbeth continues his speech. If fortune ("chance") wants him to be king, he says, fortune may find a way to make him king. The implication is, of course, that Macbeth then will not have to do anything. (Almost certainly, he is thinking of the murder he has just been imagining.) Banquo still watching Macbeth remarks that Macbeth apparently is not yet accustomed to his new honors; they fit him "like our strange garments, [which] cleave not to their mold." Macbeth ends his deliberations with "Come what come may, / Time and the hour runs through the roughest day." Banquo tells Macbeth that the group is waiting for him, and Macbeth begs their pardon. He also tells them that he appreciates the trouble they have taken to inform him of his good fortune. Then in an aside to Banquo, Macbeth advises Banquo to think about what has occurred, which they will sincerely discuss at their leisure. Banquo replies, "Very gladly."

Act I: Scene 4

We have here another short scene (58 lines) but one of great significance. Duncan, his two sons, Lenox, and some attendants enter. In the first two speeches we learn that the rebellious Thane of Cawdor has been executed. Malcolm tells us that a witness of the execution has reported that Cawdor confessed his treason and repented of it. He therefore died well: "Nothing in his life / Became him like the leaving of it. . . ." Duncan talks of the difficulty of knowing from a man's face what is going on in his mind. Cawdor, Duncan says, "was a gentleman on whom I built / An absolute trust." He breaks off because Macbeth enters.

Banquo, Ross, and Angus enter with Macbeth. Duncan greets Macbeth with an elaborate speech, the essence of which is that Macbeth has done more for Duncan than Duncan can ever repay. Macbeth replies courteously and formally, saying in effect that the services that he, Macbeth, has given Duncan are their own reward and need no thanks from Duncan, for Macbeth owes these services to Duncan since Macbeth is a subject and Duncan a king. Macbeth states his reply thus in part: " . . . our duties / Are to your throne and state, children and servants," and Macbeth is only behaving properly "by doing everything / Safe toward [for the safety of] your love and honor."

Duncan now turns to Banquo and says, "I have begun to plant thee, and will labor / To make thee full of growing." That is, Duncan is comparing a Banquo latent with honors to a seed Duncan would plant. Just as he would cultivate the seed and make it grow, so he would cultivate a Banquo latent with honors and make him grow into a Banquo flowering with honors. Duncan ends with " . . . let me infold thee, / And hold thee to my heart." That is, "Let me embrace you," which, of course, tells the actors what to do. Banquo replies, "There [in your heart] if I grow, / The harvest is your own." He says, in other words, "If I grow in your esteem, you will have the results of the growth, for I will return your love."

Duncan says that his joys are so many that he is beginning to weep. Apparently when he recovers from weeping, he makes an important announcement. Malcolm, his eldest son, will hereafter have the title of Prince of Cumberland. But Malcolm will not be the only one newly honored. Other nobles will also receive greater honors. He then says that he will proceed to Inverness, Macbeth's castle. By becoming Macbeth's guest, he tells his host-to-be, he will put himself in even greater debt to Macbeth. Macbeth replies to Duncan that he, Macbeth, will now put forth an effort which is not for Duncan's pleasure but for Macbeth's. Macbeth will hurry forth and he himself will be the messenger who will announce the news of Duncan's arrival, which will make Lady Macbeth, Macbeth's wife, "joyful." "My worthy Cawdor," says Duncan, thus at once thanking Macbeth and giving him permission to leave. But before Macbeth exits, he has an aside. "The Prince of Cumberland!" he says, "that is a step / On which I must fall down, or else o'erleap. / For in my way it lies." What he means is that Malcolm's having been named the Prince of Cumberland is a block in his acquisition of the kingship. If he wishes to become king, he must leap over it. The reason Malcolm's becoming the Prince of Cumberland is an obstruction in Macbeth's way to the kingship is explained by George Steevens, the eighteenth century Shakespearean scholar. "The crown of Scotland was originally not hereditary. When a successor was declared in the lifetime of a king, as was often the case, the title of Prince of Cumberland was immediately bestowed on him as the mark of his designation." Malcolm, therefore, in being given the title of *Prince of Cumberland* is being designated as the next king of Scotland. It is this obstruction that Macbeth must overcome. Macbeth continues the aside by telling the stars to hide their light ("fires") so that their light will not discover Macbeth's "black and deep desires"; nor must their light show the eye shut in refusal to see [the action of] the hand. Yet he wants that deed to be done which, having been committed, the eye would be afraid to see.

After the speech Macbeth exits. During the speech Duncan had been talking with Banquo, and we hear the last part of their conversation. They have been apparently discussing and praising Macbeth, for Duncan agrees with Banquo that "he" is extremely brave. Duncan also says that when Macbeth is praised, Duncan is "fed." Commendations of Macbeth are "a banquet to me." And they exit to follow Macbeth. Duncan's last words are that Macbeth "is a peerless kinsman."

Act I: Scene 5

The scene takes place at Macbeth's castle at Inverness. Lady Macbeth enters reading a letter from Macbeth. The letter itself is the first piece of prose in the play. Lady Macbeth's comments following the letter and the ensuing dialogue return to poetry. Lady Macbeth is reading apparently the last part of the letter. Macbeth has been writing her about the witches, who, he says, met him on "the day of success," that is, the day of victory. He has learned dependably that they have more knowledge than ordinary mortals. Macbeth wanted very much to question them further, but they dissolved into air. As he "stood rapt in the wonder of it," the news came that he was the Thane of Cawdor, by which title the witches had previously greeted him, and they also greeted him with "Hail, King that shalt be!" that is, hail, future king. Here the letter ends its account of his meeting with the witches and addresses Lady Macbeth directly. This news of the meeting with the witches, he thought it "good" to tell her so that her ignorance of her future greatness would not keep her from rejoicing at the prospect of her greatness ("that thou might'st not lose the dues of rejoicing, by being ignorant of what greatness is promised thee"). Immediately before the last remark Macbeth calls Lady Macbeth his "dearest partner of greatness." He ends by telling his wife to put the letter to her heart, and he bids her farewell.

Lady Macbeth now comments on the letter. She says that Macbeth shall attain the goal he has been promised, that is, the kingship. But she is afraid that his character is "too full o' the milk of human kindness, / To catch the nearest way." That is, she is afraid that he is too soft-hearted to attain the kingship in the quickest possible fashion. She continues by saying that although he is ambitious, he does not have that evil in his character that will permit him to reach his great goal. She continues, " . . . what thou wouldst highly, / That wouldst thou holily", in other words, the great things Macbeth desires, he wishes to gain virtuously. She continues in this latter vein for a short time, the point of her remarks being that Macbeth wants the greatness which it would take an evil deed to win; yet he refuses to commit the evil deed. Then, as though she were addressing him directly, she says, "Hie thee hither. . . ." She says, in other words, "Come here quickly." She wants him to come quickly so that she can fill him with her spirit and disperse with a tongue lashing all of his character which prevents him from attaining the crown ("the golden round") promised him by fate and supernatural help ("metaphysical aid").

A messenger interrupts Lady Macbeth's thoughts to inform her that the king will arrive at Inverness that night. "Thou'rt mad to say it," cries Lady Macbeth. Would not Macbeth, who is with the king, have warned them beforehand so that the castle could be prepared for the king's arrival? The messenger replies that one of his fellow servants had indeed been sent beforehand and is completely out of breath from rushing with the news. He precedes Macbeth, who will arrive before Duncan. When the messenger leaves, Lady Macbeth has a soliloquy of some fifteen lines. In the first line and one-half she imagines a raven greeting the "fatal" arrival of Duncan to her castle ("my battlements"). She says that a raven greeting this arrival would have a voice even more harsh than usual (obviously because the entrance will be "fatal" to Duncan). She then invokes (calls on for aid) "Spirits / That tend on mortal thoughts. . . ." That is, she asks the spirits that are the servants of murderous ("mortal") thoughts to come to her aid. She wants them to "unsex" her, that is, to take away her womanliness, which makes her soft-hearted. And she wants these spirits to fill her from head to toe with the worst sort of cruelty. She wants the spirits to make it so that nothing in her nature will prevent her from carrying out her "fell" (cruel) purpose. She continues the invocation, "Come to my woman's breasts. . . ." She now wishes the servants of murderous thoughts (whom she this time calls "murdering ministers") to act as her children sucking at her breasts. But instead of taking milk from her breasts as children normally would, the "murdering ministers," she hopes, will take milk and inject in its place gall (bitterness). She now invokes "thick night" and tells night to cover itself with the gloomiest smoke of hell. She wants this done so that her knife (she means, of course, the eye that is guiding her knife) will not see the wound it makes and heaven will not be able to peep through the dark to tell her to stop.

The entrance of Macbeth brings us to the first dialogue between the play's two main characters. Lady Macbeth greets her husband with his two current titles, Glamis and Cawdor. He will have a title, she continues, greater than both in the future. His letters have made her feel the future in this moment. She obviously means that she feels now like the queen. Macbeth replies with a statement that apparently does not follow logically, "My dearest love / Duncan comes here tonight." Lady Macbeth asks her husband when Duncan is leaving, and he replies, "Tomorrow, as he purposes [intends]." Her response is that the sun will never see the morning (when Duncan leaves their castle). Macbeth apparently looks disturbed at his wife's remark, for she says, "Your face, my Thane, is as a book, where men / May read strange matters." She tells him, in other words, that his face shows a disturbed mind. Then in a series of images which mean more or less the same she advises him not to give away his thoughts by the expression on his face: "To beguile [cheat] the time [that is, the men of the time], / Look like the time . . . / . . . look like the innocent flower, / But be the serpent under't." She adds ironically, "He that's coming / Must be provided for [prepared for]. . . ." She concludes by saying that he shall turn over to her the management of the affair, the results of which shall give to the rest of their days "sovereign sway and masterdom," that is, complete dominion. Macbeth answers only, "We will speak further." She tells him again to keep a face that indicates an undisturbed mind, "Only look up clear . . . ." To change one's face (an indication of disturbance in the mind) is always to be afraid. Lady Macbeth ends by saying, "Leave all the rest to me."

Act I: Scene 6

The scene occurs in front of the castle at Inverness. Duncan and his party enter. The characters in the party whose presence interests us are Malcolm and Donalbain (Duncan's two sons), Banquo, Lenox, Macduff, Ross, and Angus, all of whom are Scotch noblemen, or thanes. The scene is a formal one consisting in large part of the elaborate and courteous language used in ceremony, in this case the ceremony of greeting the arrival of a guest. Here, of course, it is a special guest, the king. When Duncan enters, he remarks upon the pleasantness of the air around Macbeth's castle. Banquo agrees with Duncan by saying that the presence of a martlet's nest in every possible corner of the face of the castle proves that "the heaven's breath / Smells wooingly here," that is, that the air smells enticingly here. The presence of so many martlets' nests shows the air's pleasantness because the martlet is "temple-haunting." That is, the martlet ordinarily nests in churches. If he chooses to rest elsewhere, it is because the air is as soft and pleasing as the air about the churches. Banquo ends his speech by saying that he has observed that where "they most bred" the air is "delicate," that is, soft.

Lady Macbeth enters, and Duncan greets her in an elaborate and complicated way. The point of the speech is that Lady Macbeth really does not mind the extra pains she takes in having Duncan as a guest, because she loves Duncan. Lady Macbeth replies as elaborately as Duncan has spoken. She says that double all of the service which Macbeth and Lady Macbeth have done for Duncan does not compare to the "honors deep and broad" which Duncan has given their house. For both the old honors and the recent honors Macbeth and Lady Macbeth will pray to God for him ("We rest your hermits"). Duncan asks for Macbeth, who, he says, has ridden faster than Duncan. Duncan had hoped to precede Macbeth. Duncan concludes with "Fair and noble hostess, / We are your guest tonight." The hostess replies that everything in the house is really Duncan's. He asks her to conduct him to Macbeth, whom he loves and whom he will continue to honor; and they exit.

Act I: Scene 7

The scene opens with various servants obviously serving dinner; passing back and forth across the stage. It is, of course, the dinner in honor of Duncan's visit. Macbeth then enters and speaks a soliloquy, which begins, "If it were done when 'tis done, then 'twere well / It were done quickly. . . ." *It*, of course, refers to the murder, and the statement as a whole means: if the murder were completed when it was accomplished, then it would be a good thing if it were committed quickly. He continues in a series of images the essence of which is: If the murder should be successful here on this earth and have no dangerous consequences, the risk of punishment in the next world would be worth it. But in cases such as the murder of Duncan, Macbeth goes on to say, we are sentenced for our crime in this life. The sentence is this: when we commit an assassination, we in effect teach others to commit the same act. It is "even-handed justice." Macbeth now turns from the practical reasons why he should not kill Duncan to the moral reasons. He says that Duncan is in his house "in double trust." First, Macbeth is both Duncan's relative and Duncan's subject. Both of these ties to Duncan make the murder reprehensible. Second, Macbeth is Duncan's host; as Duncan's host Macbeth should shut the door against Duncan's murderer, not carry the murder knife himself. Macbeth then goes on to a political reason why he should not murder Duncan. Duncan, he says, has been so mild and guiltless as king that Duncan's virtues will cry out like a trumpet against

Macbeth

his murder ("taking-off"). And pity, as though it were "a naked new-born babe," or some member of an order of angels ("heaven's cherubins") riding the wind, "Shall blow the horrid deed in every eye"; there will then be a tremendous amount of weeping ("tears shall drown the wind"). Macbeth continues with an image from horsemanship, which says that he has no reason to murder Duncan except ambition.

Lady Macbeth interrupts Macbeth's thoughts with her entrance. We learn that Duncan has almost finished supper and that he has wondered why Macbeth has disappeared from the table. Macbeth then says that he and his wife will no longer continue with the business of killing Duncan. The reason is that Duncan has recently honored Macbeth, and Macbeth has "bought / Golden opinions from all sorts of people, / Which would be worn now in their newest gloss, / Not cast aside so soon." Macbeth means that not only has Duncan honored him but also all kinds of people have come to think of him highly, and their "golden opinions" ought to be thoroughly enjoyed; they are not to be tossed aside by the assumption of the new roles of king and queen, in which roles they will have to work hard for new golden opinions. At Macbeth's remarks Lady Macbeth pours out a torrent of contempt, the main idea of which is this: you do not really love me when you are not man enough to go out and get what you want. Macbeth replies, "I dare do all that may become [is appropriate to being] a man. . . ." To this his wife says, "What beast was't, then, / That made you break this enterprise to me?" That is, as she explains in the next line, when you dared to the murder, you were a man; so that if you dare do all that is appropriate to being a man, you would dare do the murder. By breaking the promise to commit the deed you are behaving like a creature lower than a man, which is a beast. She goes on to say that when Macbeth promised her to kill Duncan the best possible occasion for the murder had not presented itself ("Nor time, nor place, / Did then adhere"; and in fact he had said that he would have created a good occasion for the deed. But now that the best possible occasion has presented itself, he is unmanned. She then follows with one of the most blood-curdling images of the play. She knows, she says, "How tender 'tis to love the babe that milks me [feeds at my breast]." But rather than break the kind of promise that Macbeth wants to break now, she would, while the baby at her breast was smiling up at her, pull her nipple from the baby's mouth and crush out the baby's brains. Macbeth has no answer to this and turns to the practical problem of possible failure. Lady Macbeth tells him that as long as he has courage, they will not fail. She then recounts the plan for the murder. When Duncan is sound asleep, as he will be after his hard day of travel, she will so fill with drink his bedroom attendants that they will sleep as though they were dead. Then Macbeth and his wife can do anything they wish to Duncan, who will be unwatched. And they can put the guilt upon the drunken ("spongy") guards. Macbeth says that his wife ought to bear only boys because her courageous spirit should go into the making of men. He then turns back to the murder plan and, as though he had not heard his wife's last words, he repeats in the form of a question what she had said about the guilt being put upon Duncan's drunken attendants. She replies that since she and Macbeth would be loudly grief-stricken over Duncan's death, no one would dare put the blame anywhere but on the drunken attendants. Macbeth says that he has decided to go through with the deed. And now Macbeth repeats his wife's advice of a previous scene: the expression on the face must be innocent although the heart intends murder.

Act II: Scene 1

The scene is still Macbeth's castle at Inverness, this time, the stage directions tell us, a court of the castle. Banquo is talking with his son, Fleance. We learn from their first lines that the night is dark. "There's husbandry in heaven"; says Banquo as a mild joke, "Their candles are all out." He means there must be economy in heaven because the lights of heaven (the stars) are shut off. Banquo goes on to say that, although he is very tired, he does not want to sleep because of the "cursed thoughts," that is, bad dreams, he has in his sleep. Apparently because he hears someone coming, he asks Fleance for his sword. With his sword in hand he shouts, "Who's there?" Macbeth enters and answers, "A friend." Banquo wonders why Macbeth is not yet asleep. The king, Banquo says, has already gone to bed having had "unusual pleasure," and he has bestowed many gifts in Macbeth's servants' quarters ("your offices"). Banquo also shows Macbeth a diamond that Duncan has left for Lady Macbeth because she has been such a "kind hostess." And, Banquo says, Duncan is "shut up in measureless content," that is, has concluded the day with a satisfaction so great that it cannot be measured. Macbeth says courteously that he and his wife were unprepared, and therefore they could not do as much for the king as they would have liked. Banquo then tells Macbeth that he dreamt last night of the "three weird sisters," whose predictions have partially come true for Macbeth. The latter replies, "I think not of them. . . ." However, he continues, Banquo and he, when they have leisure and if Banquo wishes to give the time, might talk about the matter. Banquo agrees. Macbeth goes on, "If you shall cleave to my consent, when 'tis, / It shall make honor for you." That is, if you go along with me when the time comes, you will be rewarded. Banquo picks up the word *honor* from Macbeth's remark and uses it first in another one of its senses. (Actually, he does not use the word *honor;* rather he uses none in reference to Macbeth's using the word, and Banquo means, no *honor.*) He changes its meaning from *reward* (Macbeth's usage) to *honorableness,* or *uprightness.* Banquo's reply, therefore, signifies: As long as I lose no uprightness in trying to add to my rewards ("it" referring to *honor*) and keep myself guiltless and innocent, I shall listen to you. They wish each other good night, and Banquo and Fleance leave.

Macbeth is left alone with his servant to whom he gives instructions for Lady Macbeth. She is to ring a bell when his "drink" (his bedtime drink, his nightcap) is ready. Left alone, he speaks another soliloquy. "Is this a dagger, which I see before me, / The handle toward my hand?" He thinks he sees a dagger in the air, the handle toward him. He wishes to take hold of the dagger, but since it is an hallucination, he cannot do so. He sees it still as vividly as the one which he now actually draws. He asks himself whether it is real or a creature of his mind, and he says that it leads him the way that he was going (that is, to murder Duncan). And the dagger he sees in the air is the very one he was going to use for the murder. Now he can see drops of blood on the dagger. "There's no such thing," he cries. "It is the bloody business which informs / Thus to mine eyes." That is, there is no such dagger in the air; the fact that I am going to do the murder ("the bloody business") causes me to imagine I see it. Macbeth goes on to give his impression of the atmosphere of the night. He says that over half the world all activity seems to have stopped, and evil dreams are disturbing sleep. Witches are celebrating the rites of the moon ("Hecate," another name for Diana, the goddess of the moon; but Hecate was considered also the goddess of witchcraft). And "withered murder," that is, murder personified as wrinkled and shrunken, awakened by his guard, the wolf, strides secretly and quietly toward his purpose, like Tarquin. (Tarquin is Sextus Tarquinius, the son of the last Roman king. Tarquin's rape of the virtuous Lucrece caused the expulsion of his family from Rome and the establishment of the Roman republic.) Macbeth then addresses the stones of the earth asking them not to make noise as he walks, for the noise will take from the current occasion the horror which is appropriate to it. The bell sounds which Macbeth had the servant tell Lady Macbeth to ring. Apparently, it is a pre-arranged signal between them, the signal which summons Duncan to heaven or to hell. That is, it is the signal that tells Macbeth that he is to murder Duncan.

Act II: Scene 2

The setting is the same as the one in the previous scene. The beginning of this scene occurs as Macbeth is in Duncan's room committing the murder. Lady Macbeth enters in a state of high excitement In the last scene of Act I she had said that with "wine and wassail" she was going to make Duncan's two attendants drunk. Apparently, she has not only done so, but she has also taken some of the drink herself, for she says when she enters, "That which had made them drunk hath made me bold. . . ." But despite the daring given her by drink, she is nervous. "Hark!" she cries when she hears a sound, which turns out to be nothing but the shriek of an owl. "He is about it," she then says; that is, Macbeth is committing the murder. She recounts her preparations: the doors are open (so that Macbeth can get in): the attendants ("grooms") are snoring, for she has drugged their nightcaps ("possets"). Macbeth suddenly cries from inside, "Who's there?" Lady Macbeth is afraid that Macbeth's shout means that the grooms have awakened and that the murder has not been committed. The attempt at the deed, she says, not the murder itself will cause their failure. She grows increasingly nervous. She thinks she hears a noise again, for she cries once more, "Hark!" She must now be thinking that Macbeth cannot find the daggers she had prepared: she says, "I laid their daggers ready; / He could not miss 'em." Then she says, "Had he not resembled / My father as he slept, I had done't." That is, if Duncan in his sleep had not looked like Lady Macbeth's father, she herself would have murdered Duncan. At this point Macbeth enters, and his wife calls to him, "My husband!"

When Macbeth enters, he tells his wife that he has "done the deed." But they are both obviously nervous, for they ask each other a series of quick questions about noises they have heard. The exchange ends with Macbeth's "Hark!" and they both apparently listen, hearing nothing. Then Macbeth asks who was sleeping in the "second chamber," that is, the bedroom behind Duncan's. "Donalbain," Lady Macbeth replies. Macbeth apparently looks at his bloody hands, for he says, "This is a sorry sight." His wife tells him that he is foolish to think so. Macbeth then goes on to recall an incident that occurred while he was in Duncan's chamber. In telling of the incident Macbeth talks of two men who were sleeping in a room. It is difficult to know whether he is talking of Malcolm and Donalbain who were apparently sleeping in the room behind Duncan or the two grooms who were in Duncan's room. It hardly matters which of the two groups he is talking about. It is the story that Macbeth tells that counts, not the participants. In any case, one of the men laughed in his sleep and the other cried out, "Murder!" The sounds each made woke the other, but they said their prayers and returned to sleep. During their prayers one said, "God bless us!" and the other responded with "Amen." The men expressed these wishes as though they had seen Macbeth with his "hangman's hands," that is, with his hands full of blood. Macbeth listened with fright. When the first man said, "God bless us!" Macbeth wanted to reply, "Amen," but he was unable to do so. Lady Macbeth tells him not to think about it. But Macbeth wants to know why he could not say, "Amen." He wants to know why the word stuck in his throat. She says that if they keep thinking that way they will go mad. But Macbeth continues in the same vein. He thought he heard a voice cry, "Sleep no more! Macbeth does murder sleep. . . ." In recalling what the voice had said Macbeth is reminded of the importance in life of "innocent sleep." Sleep, Macbeth says in a series of images, nightly soothes the spirit made sore by the difficulties of daily life. After a short interruption by Lady Macbeth, to which her husband seems to pay no attention, he continues to talk of the voice he thought he heard. The voice continued to cry, "Sleep no more! . . . Glamis hath murdered sleep, and therefore Cawdor / Shall sleep no more, Macbeth shall sleep no more!" Lady Macbeth is rattled by this and asks Macbeth who cried out in that way. But she recovers her composure and tells Macbeth that he makes himself weak-spirited to think in this way; he must get some water and wash away the blood from his hands which would reveal his having done the murder. She now notices for the first time the daggers he has brought with him from the scene of the crime, and she tells him to return them and to smear the faces of the grooms with blood. Macbeth refuses to return. It is bad enough that he is afraid to think of his crime; he dares not look at it again. His wife derides his weakness ("Infirm of purpose!"), takes the daggers, tells him that sleeping and dead people are like pictures feared only by children; if Duncan is bleeding, she herself will smear the grooms' faces with blood. And she goes to perform her task.

Macbeth is left alone. A knocking can be heard. Macbeth has turned so many ordinary night noises into frightening ones that he thinks the knocking is another ordinary night noise his imagination has turned into a dangerous one. He looks at his hands. They are so bloody, he thinks, that they are blinding him. He wonders whether the ocean can wash his hands clean. They cannot, he says; rather, his bloody hands will make all the seas of the world red. Lady Macbeth re-enters and tells him that her hands are also red, but she is ashamed to have a coward's heart ("a heart so white"). She hears the knocking, which is at the south gate. She tells her husband that they must go to their bedroom. "A little water clears us of this deed: / How easy is it then." That is, once they have washed their hands, how easy it will be not to feel guilty and to fool people into believing that they have not committed the deed. Macbeth apparently remains immobile, for his wife says, "Your constancy / Hath left you unattended." That is, your firmness has deserted you. The knocking is heard once more, and she urges Macbeth to move so that he can appear as though he has just awakened. He finally exits showing his regret, "Wake Duncan with thy knocking: I would thou couldst!"

Act II: Scene 3

The scene is really a continuation of the previous one. The knocking at the gate heard by Macbeth and his wife is still heard after they leave the stage, and soon after the porter, whose job it is to open the gate, enters. His speech is in prose. "Here's a knocking, indeed!" he says. "If a man were porter of hell-gate, he should have old turning the key." That is, if a man were assigned the job of opening the gate of hell for the dead people who were sent there, he would have plenty to do ("should have old") turning the key. He hears the knocking again, and his remark about the porter of hell-gate apparently prompts him to play a game. He imagines himself to be the porter of hell-gate, and he thinks of types for whom he would be opening the gate and the reasons why these types would be coming to hell. The first is "a farmer, that hanged himself on the expectation of plenty. . . ." The farmer, the porter means, hanged himself because he had stored up grain originally expecting bad crops and high prices; but it now appeared as though the crops would be good and the prices would therefore be low; so, on the "expectation of plenty" he hangs himself. The next man is "an equivocator, that could swear in both scales against either scale; . . . yet could not equivocate to heaven. . . ." An equivocator is a man who purposely says something that has one meaning for most people hearing it but another meaning for himself. That is why he can swear on either side of the scale of justice against the other side. The third type is "an English tailor come hither for stealing out of a French hose. . . ." The English tailor had copied what he thought was the current French style just as that had changed. Since Englishmen followed the French style, he thought the copying would make him popular. But he outsmarted himself. The porter hears the persistent knocking at the gate. "Never at quiet," he says. He is about to continue with another type when he remarks, "But this place is too cold for hell. I'll devil-porter it no further: I had thought to have let in some of all professions, that go the primrose way to the everlasting bonfire." That is, he was

Macbeth

going to show those in each profession who cheat and make it easy
for themselves and therefore go to hell. He opens the gate for the
men who have been knocking and asks them for a tip ("I pray you,
remember the porter").

Macduff and Lenox are the men who have been knocking. Macduff
asks whether the porter's sleeping late is a sign that he had gone
late to bed. The porter answers that the people of the house had
gone to bed at 3 a.m. ("the second cock") because they were up
drinking. An exchange of shady dialogue about lechery and equivocation follows until Macbeth enters.

Macbeth enters and there follows some courteous greeting between
him and the two thanes. It is Macduff's duty to wake the king, and
he goes off to do so. Lenox talks about the stormy night that has
just past. Among other things, chimneys were blown down, "strange
screams of death" were heard as well as "lamentings . . . i' the air."
Macbeth replies, " 'Twas a rough night." Macduff then rushes out
shouting the news of Duncan's murder: "Most sacreligious murder
hath broke ope / The Lord's annoited temple. . . ." Macbeth and
Lenox go out to confirm Macduff's report. Macduff rings the alarm
bell and wakes the house. Lady Macbeth and then Banquo enter.
Hearing of Duncan's murder, Lady Macbeth cries, "What! in our
house?" When Macbeth re-enters with Lenox, the former says that
if he had died an hour before the accident of Duncan's murder he
would have thought of his life as blessed. He goes on to say, "The
wine of life is drawn, and the mere lees / Is left this vault to brag
of." That is, the best part of life is over. Malcolm and Donalbain
enter and discover what has happened, and Malcolm asks who has
done the deed. Lenox replies that because the grooms were covered
with blood it seems as though they had done it. Macbeth says that
he is sorry he has killed the grooms. To Macduff's question as to
why he did so, Macbeth replies that in the cross-current of violent
emotions he felt upon seeing Duncan dead he had killed the attendants "to make's love [for Duncan] known." When Macbeth
finishes telling his story about the killing of the grooms, Lady Macbeth faints (indicated by "Help me hence, ho!"). During the excitement brought on by Lady Macbeth's fainting Malcolm and
Donalbain decide that in the currently dangerous situation they had
better leave in a hurry. Lady Macbeth is carried out, and Banquo
says that as soon as they are all properly dressed they will confer
as to what to do. They all agree. Everyone but Malcolm and Donalbain exits. The latter decide that, in the situation as it stands, the
false man easily shows false sorrow. Malcolm will go to England;
Donalbain to Ireland. They will be safer if each goes a different

way. Malcolm concludes by saying that, since there is no mercy left, there is good reason to steal oneself away.

Act II: Scene 4

The scene occurs outside Macbeth's castle. Ross and an old man enter. The old man says that he can remember things for seventy years back, but he cannot remember a night as stormy as this has been. Ross replies by saying that the heavens are behaving as though they are troubled by "man's act," that is, last night's murder, and are threatening man. He goes on to say that, although the clock says that it is daytime, yet it is as dark as night. The old man answers, " 'Tis unnatural, / Even like the deed that's done." And the old man and Ross talk of other unnatural events that have recently occured, which fit with last night's event and the present day's darkness. For example, Duncan's horses, previously tame, turned wild and ate each other. Macduff now enters and tells the two who have been on stage the common belief concerning the murder. Malcolm and Donalbain, who have fled, hired the grooms to kill Duncan. He continues with the news that Macbeth has already been named king and has gone to be crowned at Scone, where Scottish kings are crowned. Duncan has been taken for burial. Ross asks Macduff whether he is going to the coronation at Scone, and Macduff replies, "No cousin; I'll to Fife." (Fife is Macduff's home; he is the Thane of Fife.) Ross says that he will go to Scone, and Macduff replies, "Well, may you see things well done there . . . / Lest our old robes sit easier than our new!" And each leaves on his own way.

Act III: Scene 1

The scene takes place in the palace of the king of Scotland at Forres. As we learned in the last act, Macbeth is now king. Banquo enters and speaks a soliloquy. As though he is talking to Macbeth, he says, "Thou hast it now, King, Cawdor, Glamis, all / As the weird women promised. . . ." That is, you now have all the titles promised you by the witches. And Banquo goes on to say that Macbeth attained the titles "most foully." But Banquo remembers the rest of the prophecy. No descendents of Macbeth would be kings; yet Banquo himself would be the forebearer of a line of kings. If the prophecy for Macbeth came true, why should not the prophecy for Banquo come true and make him hopeful. But he sees Macbeth, Lady Macbeth and their party enter and he must be quiet.

Macbeth

Among the attendants of the king and queen are Lenox and Ross. Macbeth's first words refer to Banquo, "Here's our chief guest." Lady Macbeth adds that to forget Banquo is to have "a gap in our great feast." Macbeth formally announces the "solemn supper" they will hold tonight, and he formally invites Banquo. Banquo accepts the invitation. In the course of apparently casual conversation, Macbeth finds out from Banquo that Banquo and his son, Fleance, are going horseback riding and that they will not be back until after dark. During this conversation we also learn that Malcolm and Donalbain, whom Macbeth calls "our bloody cousins," are in England and Ireland. They do not confess "their cruel parricide," that is, the murder of their father, and they make up strange stories. Banquo leaves and Macbeth tells everyone to do as he wishes until the feast that evening. Macbeth commands a servant to bring in some men who are waiting for him. While he waits for the men, Macbeth is left alone on the stage, and he speaks a soliloquy.

"To be thus is nothing, but to be safely thus . . . ," says Macbeth. That is, to be king has no meaning unless one is securely a king. Macbeth is afraid of Banquo. Banquo has the character of a king, which contains something to be afraid of: Banquo is daring, fearless, and wise enough to act safely. Macbeth is afraid of no one but Banquo, for Macbeth's angel ("My Genius") is always put down by Banquo. Banquo chastized the witches when they first called Macbeth king and asked them to speak to him, Banquo. They told Banquo that he would be the forebear of "a line of kings" and upon Macbeth's head they placed "a fruitless crown, / And put a barren sceptre in my gripe. . . ." That is, no descendants of Macbeth would be kings. If this is so, Macbeth has given up his immortal soul ("eternal jewel") to the devil ("the common enemy of man") only to make kings of Banquo's descendants. Rather than allow this to be the case, Macbeth challenges fate. But he is interrupted in his thoughts by the entrance of the servant bringing his two visitors.

The servant enters with the two men whom the stage directions call murderers. In the course of Macbeth's conversation with them we learn that they have had a previous interview with him. He told them in that interview that where they had thought it was Macbeth who had deceived them with false promises, it was in actuality Banquo. Macbeth then goes on to the point of the current meeting. He tries to persuade them that if they are men, they will not take their betrayal lying down. The first murderer has answered only very briefly until this point. Now he says in a speech of three lines that his luck has been so bad that he is desperate and does not care what he does. The second murderer in a speech equally long agrees with the first. Macbeth tells them that Banquo is also Macbeth's

711

enemy. Although he could kill Banquo "with bare-faced power," yet he dare not do it because of the mutual friends that he and Banquo have, whose love he is afraid to lose. Therefore, he asks the two men to take care of his business privately. They give their consent. Macbeth will advise them as to the place. And they must kill Fleance also, for Fleance's death is as important to Macbeth as Banquo's. The murderers agree and leave. Macbeth concludes with "Banquo, thy soul's flight, / If it find Heaven, must find it out tonight."

Act III: Scene 2

We are still in the king's castle at Forres. Lady Macbeth enters with a servant. Lady Macbeth asks the servant whether Banquo has as yet left the court, that is, has he yet gone riding. The servant replies that he has but that he will be back in the evening. The mistress sends her servant for Macbeth, and Lady Macbeth is left alone. She has a short speech before Macbeth enters. "Naught's had, all's spent / Where our desire is got without content . . . ," she says. That is, when one has attained one's goal without mental ease and satisfaction, all the effort used to attain the goal has been put forth for nothing. She continues by saying that it is safer to be the murdered person ("that which we destroy") than to be the murderer living in uncertain happiness ("dwell in doubtful joy").

Macbeth enters, and his wife berates him. Why, she asks, does he isolate himself with his unhappy thoughts? Those thoughts about the dead should have died with them. Things that cannot be helped should not be thought about. "What's done is done." Macbeth replies that they have slashed the snake in two; they have not killed it; the snake will re-form into a whole. Macbeth uses figurative language to say that in killing Duncan and his two grooms Macbeth and his wife have not completely eliminated their danger; because the danger has not been completely eliminated, it will again be as great as once it was. He goes on to tell Lady Macbeth that he will let the entire universe disintegrate before he and his wife "will eat our meal in fear, and sleep / In the affliction of these terrible dreams, / That shake us nightly." It is better, he says, to be with the dead whom they have killed to gain peace (for their ambitions) than to be in constant mental anguish. Duncan is dead, and nothing in this life can hurt him any more. Lady Macbeth tells her husband to take it easy and to be happy at the feast that evening. He says that he will be happy and that she should be happy too. She ought to pay special attention to Banquo: while they are unsafe, their faces must mask their hearts. "You must leave this," says Lady

Macbeth. "O! full of scorpions is my mind, dear wife!" answers her husband. That is, my mind is full of evil thoughts. Macbeth adds, "Thou know'st that Banquo, and his Fleance, lives." She replies that they do not live forever. "There's comfort yet," says her husband. He tells her that Banquo and Fleance are vulnerable. He adds that before night a dreadful deed shall be done. "What's to be done?" she asks. "Be innocent of the knowledge, dearest chuck, / Till thou applaud the deed." That is, you do not have to know about the deed, darling, until it is over, at which time you can praise me for it. Macbeth now makes an invocation to night. He asks night to come and to blindfold the eye of day, which is full of pity; and night, he continues, with its "bloody and invisible hand," will then destroy "that great bond / Which keeps me pale!" (the lives of Banquo and Fleance). Apparently, night once more answers Macbeth's command, for he now says, "Light thickens," and he goes on to describe the onset of night, which again reflects the state of his mind: " . . . night's black agents to their preys do rouse." Lady Macbeth evidently gazes at her husband in astonishment, for he remarks to her, "thou marvell'st at my words. . . ." He goes on to observe that things begun badly improve themselves by continued evil. "So, pr'ythee, go with me," says he as they exit.

Act III: Scene 3

The scene occurs in a park near the palace. Three murderers enter. Two of them we know; they are the men who had the interview with Macbeth in the first scene of this act. The third one is known neither to us nor to the first two murderers. The first murderer asks, "But who did bid thee join us?" The first murderer is apparently suspicious of the third. The latter says that Macbeth told him to come. The second murderer says, "He needs not our mistrust. . . ." That is, we need not mistrust him. The reason why they need not distrust the third murderer, he says, is that the third murderer gives them all the directions Macbeth had promised they would receive. The first murderer agrees and then describes the coming of night in lovely language. When he ends, the third murderer hears their victims. Banquo enters with Fleance, who is carrying a torch. Banquo says, "It will rain tonight." The first murderer responds with "Let it come down." The first murderer apparently then puts out the torch being carried by Fleance. The murderers attack Banquo, who cries, "O, treachery! Fly, good Fleance, fly fly, fly!" He dies, and Fleance escapes. The third murderer asks who put out the light. The first murderer returns with the question, "Was't not the way?" That is, was not that the arrangement. They realize that Fleance has escaped, and the second murderer says, "We have lost/Best

713

half of our affair." The first murderer says that they ought to report to Macbeth, and they exit.

Act III: Scene 4

This scene takes place in a room of the palace set for a banquet. Macbeth, Lady Macbeth, Ross, Lenox, other lords, and attendants enter. Macbeth says, "You know your own degrees, sit down . . . ." He tells them, in effect, that since they know their proper ranks, they can seat themselves according to rank without the formality of Macbeth's having to place them. After being thanked Macbeth goes on to say that he himself will mingle with the guests while the hostess (Lady Macbeth) remains on the throne. As the formalities of welcome continue, the first murderer appears at the door. Macbeth continues talking but meanwhile making his way to the door. Presumably, the guests cannot see the first murderer. Macbeth says to him, "There's blood upon thy face." The first murderer replies that it is Banquo's blood. To this Macbeth says that he prefers Banquo's blood on the murderer's skin than inside Banquo's body. The first murderer assures Macbeth that Banquo is dead. Macbeth asks whether Fleance is also dead. The murderer replies that Fleance has escaped. "Then comes my fit again: I had else been perfect . . .," says Macbeth. That is, because Fleance has escaped, I am once more in a fit of fear; if he had not escaped, I would now be healthy. He continues in the same vein in a series of images, which are climaxed by "But now, I am cabin'd, cribb'd, confin'd bound / To saucy doubts and fears." He means that he is not to act normally at ease but subject to doubts and fears. "But Banquo's safe?" he adds. That is, is Banquo safely dead? The murderer assures him that Banquo is "safe in a ditch . . ./With twenty trenched [cut] gashes on his head . . . ." Macbeth thanks the murderer. Then in a metaphor in which Banquo and Fleance are compared to a grown serpent and the child serpent ("the worm") Macbeth says in effect that, although Banquo is dead, Fleance, who has escaped but offers no threat now, will one day present a threat. Macbeth tells the murderer to leave, that they will have another interview tomorrow. The murderer exits.

Lady Macbeth now calls to her husband, who has been absenting himself from the table. She tells him that the feast without Macbeth's ceremony of good cheer is like a feast not given. Macbeth becomes aware of his surroundings and begins to act hearty. Lenox asks Macbeth to sit at the table. Macbeth says that all of the men of distinction of the country would be here now if Banquo were present. And Banquo's absence, Macbeth tells his listeners, is due

Macbeth

to Banquo's unkindness rather than to accident. While Macbeth has been speaking, Banquo's ghost enters. Now Ross asks Macbeth to be seated at the table. As Macbeth approaches the empty place at the table, the place reserved for him, he sees the place occupied by Banquo's ghost. "The table is full," says Macbeth. The others cannot see the ghost. They tell Macbeth that there is a place for him. "Where?" asks Macbeth. "Here, my good lord," replies Lenox, who then asks Macbeth what is troubling him. Macbeth shouts at his guests, "Which of you have done this?" That is, who has killed Banquo? The guests do not know what Macbeth is talking about. Macbeth now shouts at the ghost, "Thou canst not say, I did it [the murder]; never shake / Thy gory locks at me." Ross tells the other lords to leave; Macbeth, he says, is not well. Lady Macbeth, however, intervenes. She tells the lords to sit. She says that Macbeth has had momentary fits since his youth and any attention paid to them extends the fit. She then whispers to Macbeth, "Are you a man?" He says that he is a bold man, for he dares "look on that / Which might appal the devil." Lady Macbeth pours contempt on her husband. What he claims to see is the same as the dagger he saw before Duncan's murder, nothing but an hallucination. He insistently points at the ghost, "Behold! look! . . . ." He then becomes desperate: "Why what care I?" And he challenges the ghost to speak. The ghost disappears. Lady Macbeth continues to berate him, "What! quite unmann'd in folly?" Macbeth insists that, as he is alive, he saw him. We know of course that him is Banquo; Lady Macbeth, since she does not see the ghost, cannot be certain whom Macbeth sees. Whoever it is, she must set things in order again. "Fie! for shame!" she tells him. Macbeth says that in former times, when a man was murdered, he would stay dead; "but now, they rise again, / With twenty mortal murders on their crowns [heads], / And push us from our stools." Apparently the ghost of Banquo has the "twenty trenched gashes on its head" about which the first murderer told Macbeth. The ghost, then, is all cut and bloody. Seeing that Macbeth is coming to himself again, Lady Macbeth says, "My worthy lord, / Your noble friends do lack you." That is, the guests miss him. Macbeth replies, "I do forget." He goes on to give for himself the same excuse Lady Macbeth had previously given for him, that he has a strange illness which, when it shows itself, does not surprise people who know him. He now offers a toast to everyone at the table, "And to our dear friend Banquo, whom we miss; / Would he were here!" Of course, at this point the ghost of Banquo re-appears. Macbeth sees it and shouts for it to leave his sight. He says, in effect, that since the ghost is only a ghost it ought to let itself be buried. Lady Macbeth tries to smooth things over again. She repeats that Macbeth's peculiar behavior is not extraordinary. "Only it spoils the pleasure of the time." Macbeth continues speak-

715

ing to the ghost. He dares do anything a man would do: let the ghost appear in any form but that in which it now appears; let it appear in the form of a bear or a tiger or even the live Banquo, and Macbeth would fight with him. "Unreal mockery, hence!" That is, get away, you parody of reality. The ghost disappears. Since it has done so, Macbeth says, he is "a man again." He turns to his guests and tells them to sit still. Lady Macbeth says that he has destroyed everyone's good time. Macbeth, who thinks that the guests have also seen the ghost, cannot understand how they could have looked at such a sight without fear. Ross asks him what he has seen. Lady Macbeth intervenes and requests the lords not to speak; questions will make Macbeth only worse. "At once, good night": she says to them, "Stand not upon the order of your going, / But go at once." And all the lords leave.

Macbeth and Lady Macbeth are left alone. Macbeth says that no matter how secretly done, murder will out. He asks his wife the time, and she tells him that it is almost dawn. He now asks her what she thinks of Macduff's refusal to present himself at Macbeth's command. To her question as to whether he had sent for Macduff, Macbeth replies, "I hear it by the way... / There's not a one of them, but in his house / I keep a servant fee'd." He goes on to tell her that he is going to see the witches the next day. Then he says, "For mine own good, / All causes shall give way...." He feels that he is so deep in blood "returning were as tedious as go o'er." He has strange things in his mind, he continues, which must be accomplished before they are thought about. Lady Macbeth tells him that he lacks what everyone has, sleep. "Come we'll to sleep," he says. His peculiar self-punishment, he goes on, is the fright that comes from first doing an evil deed. Evil has not yet become customary for them. "We are but young in deed," he says as the scene ends.

Act III: Scene 5

Almost no one believes this scene to be by Shakespeare: the verse is not as good as Shakespeare's, and the content adds nothing to our understanding of the play. This scene and part of Act IV, Scene 1, were probably added after Shakespeare's retirement or death apparently because the witches were popular. The company would have wished to capitalize on their popularity and had these sections added. These parts of the play also permit the witches to sing songs, which undoubtedly heightened the interest the witches held for the audience. These songs are from a play, *The Witch*, by

Shakespeare's contemporary, Thomas Middleton. Because the company used the songs from Middleton's play, some critics think that Middleton also wrote the insertions for this play. However, a number of scholars who know Middleton's work well are inclined to think otherwise.

As far as content goes, the point of this scene seems to be that the witches will make Macbeth feel secure, and his sense of security will lead him to destruction. Beyond this, discussion appears to be irrelevant.

Act III: Scene 6

Most editors locate this scene in the king's palace at Forres. In the original edition of the play it is unlocated, and some critics believe that this conversation could not occur in the king's palace filled with spies. On the bare Elizabethan stage probably no one would have thought about where the scene takes place; only important was the fact that the scene developed the play's plot, atmosphere, and idea. The surface reality did not matter: the scene obviously occurs somewhere in Scotland, and we learn something about Macbeth and something about Scotland.

Lenox and an unnamed lord enter. Apparently, they are either in the midst of a conversation or they have previously discussed matters. For Lenox says that in his "former speeches" he has said what the lord had been thinking. Lenox then becomes obviously ironic. Macbeth pitied Duncan, and Duncan died. Banquo stayed out too late; it is possible to say that Fleance killed him because Fleance ran away. One must also think how terrible it was for Malcolm and Donalbain to kill their father. This made Macbeth very unhappy that in religious anger he killed the murderers. He was wise to do it, too, for it would have made anyone angry to hear them deny the deed. Lenox thinks, therefore, that Macbeth has managed things well. And he also believes that if Malcolm, Donalbain, and Fleance were in Scotland, they should know what it is to kill a father. Lenox now changes the subject. He has heard that Macduff is not in the king's good graces because he has spoken "broad words," that is, Macduff has spoken too obviously—of course, too obviously against the king; and because he did not appear at the "tyrant's feast" (Macbeth's banquet). He wishes to know whether the lord can tell him where Macduff is.

The lord replies that "The son of Duncan, / From whom this

tyrant holds the due of birth, / Lives in the English court...."
The lord must be talking about Malcolm, because we know that
Malcolm said that he was going to England; and because we know
that with Duncan's death, Malcolm should be on the throne. The
lord then says that Malcolm lives at the English court of "the most
pious Edward" (Edward the Confessor) who treats Malcolm very
well. Macduff has gone there to ask Edward to encourage Siward,
the Earl of Northumberland, to help Malcolm in an undertaking
to overthrow Macbeth. This undertaking (if successful) would
once more "Give to our tables meat, sleep to our nights, / Free
from our feasts and banquets bloody knives . . . ." The report of
all this has prompted Macbeth's sending for Macduff. Macbeth
sent for him, continues the lord, but Macduff replied in a definite
negative. When Macduff thus answered the messenger looked threateningly at him. Lenox says that Macduff should be cautious enough
to retain a distance. He hopes that Macduff does well in England
so that "a swift blessing / May soon return to this our suffering
country / Under a hand accursed."

Act IV: Scene 1

The scene occurs in a cavern in the middle of which is a boiling
cauldron. The three witches enter. As they speak a charm, with
which they hope to secure Macbeth, they throw into their boiling pot
such parts of repulsive animals as the eye of a newt, the wool of
a bat, and a lizard's leg. The refrain of their charm is "Double,
double toil and trouble: / Fire, burn; and, cauldron, bubble." When
they are finished, Hecate, the queen of the witches, enters together
with three other witches. The lines Hecate recites and the song the
witches sing are considered by most scholars to be non-Shake-
spearean.

After Hecate and the other three witches leave, Macbeth enters.
He insists that the witches answer his questions. It makes no
difference to him, he says, whether or not the universe is totally
destroyed in the process; he will have his answer. They agree, but
first they inquire as to whether he would have the answer from
them or from their masters; Macbeth prefers the latter. The witches
then throw into the boiling cauldron some appetizing liquids: the
blood of a sow who has eaten her young and the sweat that fell
from a murderer as he was being hanged. This addition to the
witches' brew brings forth the apparition of an armed head. Macbeth is about to ask a question when the first witch informs him
that the apparition knows his thought. The apparition tells Mac-

beth to beware of Macduff, the Thane of Fife. The head then disappears. Macbeth thanks the armed head for cautioning him about Macduff and adds that this warning supports his own fear. Macbeth wishes to inquire further, but the first witch tells him that the apparition will not respond again. However, a stronger power will now appear.

The second apparition comes forth, and it is in the form of a bloody child. The second apparition advises Macbeth to be "bloody, bold, and resolute," for no one who was born of a woman can harm him. The apparition disappears. Macbeth's comment on this information is that he need not fear Macduff (for Macduff is a man and all men are born of women). Macbeth, however, wishes to make "double sure"; he wishes to obliterate any trace of fear, and he says that he will kill Macduff anyway.

The third apparition now comes forth in the form of a crowned child with a tree in his hand. Macbeth asks who the apparition is, but the witches merely tell him to listen. The third apparition advises Macbeth to be courageous ("lion-mettled") and proud, not to care about those who are dissatisfied or those who consipire against him, for Macbeth will never be defeated until the woods (called Birnam wood) around his castle Dunsinane march toward the castle. The third apparition disappears. Macbeth says that it is impossible for a forest to move; the prediction is a good one. Macbeth now feels that he "Shall live the lease of Nature, pay his breath / To time, and mortal custom." That is, he feels he will die a natural death. However, he wishes to know one more thing: will Banquo's descendants ever rule Scotland. The witches try to dissuade him from inquiring further, but Macbeth insists, whereupon the witches call for a show; a show, they say, which will "grieve his heart."

There follows a procession of eight kings. The last of them holds a mirror. To anyone watching the procession from the front, the mirror makes it seem as though the line of kings stretches endlessly. Some of the kings carry "two-fold balls and treble sceptres." All of the kings in the procession resemble Banquo, and Banquo himself comes behind the line of eight, his hair caked with blood ("blood bolter'd"). He looks at Macbeth, smiles, and points at the procession; Macbeth takes these actions to mean that Banquo's descendants will, in fact, rule Scotland. Macbeth calls this pantomime a "horrible sight." To cheer him up the witches perform a wild dance (an "antic round") and disappear. After they disappear, Macbeth says, "Let this pernicious hour / Stand aye accursed in the calendar!"

He calls for his attendant, who turns out to be Lenox. Macbeth asks Lenox whether the latter has seen the witches. Lenox replies that he has not. Macbeth says that he heard a horse's gallop, and he wishes to know who went by. Lenox informs Macbeth that word was brought of Macduff's flight to England. "Time, thou anticipat'st my dread exploits," says Macbeth to himself. From now on, he continues, he will immediately do whatever his heart desires. And to turn his current wish into an act, he will make a surprise attack on Macduff's castle at Fife, kill Macduff's wife, children, and any relative that might succeed him. Macbeth says that he will no longer boast. He will commit this act before his intention diminishes in strength. "But no more sights!" he says, apparently referring to what the witches have shown him. He then asks to be led to the messengers, and Lenox and Macbeth exit.

Now, all this appears to be foolish quibbling on the part of the witches; for Macduff was certainly born of a woman, and Birnam wood will never really move. Why, then, did Shakespeare resort to this silly dodge? Of course, this is not a dodge at all. Like everything else in this play, it is well-planned and fits in with the play's structure and idea. Macbeth himself had been a quibbler; he had been able to fool people to gain his end by saying one thing and meaning another, thus making fair foul and foul fair. He had been, as we saw earlier, an equivocator. Ironically, he is now fooled by the "equivocation of fiend, / That lies like truth . . ." (Act V, Scene 5). But because he has so completely entrusted himself to evil, evil has found it so easy to equivocate with him. Instead of learning from past experience to be more careful of evil, because his own complicity in evil has led to a desperate desire for confidence, he is less careful. And when in the fifth act we discover the silliness of the equivocation, we are made to realize that the devil is laughing; the devil is laughing at the seriousness with which we take ourselves and the ease with which we can be defeated once we have succumbed to evil. It is as though the play were suggesting, "Instead of using your cleverness to be yourself equivocal, try to understand the devil's equivocation."

The ease with which the satanic forces can now further engage Macbeth in their designs for his destruction can also be seen by the very fact that they give Macbeth advice and by the reckless nature of their auspicious predictions for him. That these predictions excited evil thoughts in Macbeth caused him to be leery of them. The witches dared not tell him then to murder Duncan in order to gain the kingship. He had to work himself into the evil deed and the evil thoughts that followed. However, having succumbed to temptation, his conscience now hardened against any crime he may commit,

720

Macbeth

increasingly driven by desperation, Macbeth accepts advice given him in this scene without a thought that it might lead him to utter destruction. And what advice! It is the kind almost anyone would be at least a little put off by, for the witches tell Macbeth to be "bloody, bold, and resolute" and to take no care of the location of the conspirators. The devil can now lead Macbeth to destruction with the greatest of ease.

Other ironies of Macbeth's situation may be observed from Macbeth's own words and from the refrain of the witches' charm. For example, when Macbeth tells the witches that he does not care if the universe is destroyed as long as his questions are answered, Shakespeare re-emphasizes an irony we noticed before. In the second scene of the third act Macbeth had told his wife, "But let the frame of things disjoint, both the worlds suffer, / Ere we will eat our meal in fear . . . ." In the fourth scene of the same act he again speaks to his wife, "For mine own good, / All causes shall give way . . . ." In the scene we are currently discussing, he says essentially the same thing: in order to gain his end he would destroy the universe. But his goal has been to gain complete mastery in Scotland. Yet what good is complete mastery if the universe is destroyed? We see here the absurdity to which Macbeth's original action has inevitably led him.

"Double, double toil and trouble: / Fire, burn; and cauldron, bubble" also reminds us of the irony of Macbeth's situation. As the play proceeds Macbeth appears to be working harder and harder. His toil is at least doubled. However, instead of attaining desirable results, he keeps acquiring more and more trouble; his trouble has at least doubled. The second line of the refrain reminds us inevitably of hell and the results of Macbeth's double toil and double trouble, which will be hell.

Now, when Macbeth has been given the predictions and the advice, he is instilled with confidence, which we at this point suspect is a false confidence. However, although the predictions and advice have the effect upon Macbeth that the witches desire, he cannot fully enjoy even his false confidence. He is impelled to ask about Banquo's descendants' ruling Scotland. He discovers, of course, that the previous prediction is correct. "Horrible sight!" he calls it; for even if the other predictions be true in exactly the way Macbeth wishes them to be, all of his toil will have been for nothing: Macbeth's descendants, if he should have any, will never inherit the kingdom. Nothing, however, can make Macbeth turn back from his desperate course. Finding that Macduff has escaped, he now plans to kill Macduff's entire family. And in general, he decides to turn his

721

every wish—and each is probably bloody—immediately into act.

But there have been indications throughout the play that he will not be king for long. For example, Macbeth has killed Duncan, but he has not succeeded in murdering Malcolm; he has killed Banquo, but Fleance escaped. Malcolm is now in England trying to obtain aid from King Edward for an invasion of Scotland; Macduff is in England with the intention of aiding Malcolm. But this scene can assure us, if we were not certain before, of Macbeth's imminent defeat, for the form of the three apparitions presented to Macbeth may symbolically picture for us the course of the entire play. The armed head may very well stand for the aggression of Macbeth's rebellion and murder. The ruin Macbeth has brought upon himself and his country may be symbolized by the bloody child, for Macbeth wishes and turns out to be a child killer, thus stopping the very life source of his kingdom. Finally, the third apparition, a crowned child with a tree in its hand, confronts us once more with the growth theme, which we have noticed throughout the play. We may take this to mean Macbeth's defeat and the consequent re-assertion of God's plan and God's plenty. Trees and children will be born, mature, decay, and die.

Before we leave the commentary on this scene, we must look at something extraneous to the understanding of the play, which requires at least mention because it is so frequently discussed. James I, king of England when Shakespeare wrote *Macbeth*, was a descendant of the historical Banquo. James I of England was also James VI of Scotland and therefore one of Banquo's descendants, who, it was predicted, would rule instead of Macbeth's descendants. It is believed by many critics that the show of kings presented to Macbeth is a compliment to King James. We may remember that the last of the eight holds up a mirror which makes the line of eight stretch endlessly. This is a pictorial way of saying to King James that his line shall go on forever. Other references to James have been observed. For example, the two-fold balls and the treble sceptres that some of the kings carry are supposed to be indications that this line of kings will rule England as well as Scotland. The theory that Shakespeare had James in mind as he wrote this play and the thought of James had an effect upon the play is probably true. But the knowledge of his theory is unnecessary for the understanding of the play. For example, Shakespeare was probably being courtly in pictorially saying to James that his descendants will rule for a long time. But how does this concern the meaning of *Macbeth?* Not at all. Is the show in the play a compliment to James? Of course not. We explained one reason why the show was in this scene. Another reason is obvious. The fact that the good Banquo's line will flourish endlessly contrasts with the barrenness of Macbeth.

Act IV: Scene 2

This scene takes place in Macduff's castle at Fife. Lady Macduff, her son, and Ross enter. Lady Macduff is speaking to Ross. She does not understand why her husband has run away from Scotland. "His flight was madness," she says. She implies that even though Macduff is not a traitor, his fear makes him look like one. Ross tells Lady Macduff that she cannot know whether it was fear or wisdom that made her husband run. But, she questions, how can his flight be wise when he leaves his wife and children in a place from which he himself runs away. "All is the fear, and nothing is the love . . . ," she comments. Macduff's flight, she insists, was unreasonable. Ross tells Lady Macduff that her husband is a wise and trustworthy man. He understands the cruel times in which men "float upon a wild and violent sea . . . ." Ross, however, breaks off the conversation to say that he must leave. But he will soon be back. He comforts Lady Macduff by saying that things at their worst will either come to an end or improve. He gives his blessing to young Macduff, whom Lady Macduff calls "fatherless." Ross feels he cannot prevent himself from weeping, and so he departs at once.

An amusingly pathetic dialogue now ensues between Lady Macduff and her son. Lady Macduff says to her son that his father is dead. "How will you live?" she asks. He will live as the birds do, he replies. "Poor bird!" she calls him, and she hopes that he need never fear a trap as birds fear it. The son now reverts to their former conversation and says that he does not believe that his father is dead. His mother insists that his father is dead, and they joke a bit about a consequent search for another husband. The son then asks, "Was my father a traitor, mother?" Lady Macduff replies that his father was. The son now asks, "What is a traitor?" "Why, one that swears and lies," she answers. The question arises whether all that swear and lie must be hanged. To Lady Macduff's affirmative response, the son says that "the liars and swearers are fools." They are fools because there are more of them than there are honest men. If the liars and swearers were smart, they would band together and hang the honest man. Lady Macduff now returns to her former theme: "But how wilt thou do for a father?" The boy still does not believe that his father is dead. If his father were really dead, the boy insists, she would weep for him. A messenger suddenly enters. He is not known to Lady Macduff, he tells her, although he is looking out for her honor. He warns her to run away, for danger is fast approaching her. He blesses her, says that he dare not stay longer, and exits. Lady Macduff exclaims that she does not know where to run. "I have done no harm," she says. But, she reflects, in this world it is often praiseworthy to do harm; to do good is often thought to be "dangerous folly." Why, then, does she bother saying that she has done no harm?

Murderers suddenly interrupt her. "Where is your husband?" one murderer asks. Lady Macduff replies that she hopes that he is in no place so unholy that he can be found by the murderer (who, she implies, would ordinarily frequent only places that are damned). The murderer says that Macduff is a traitor. Macduff's son cries, "Thou liest, thou shag hair'd villain!" At this the murderer stabs the boy, who tells his mother to run away. The scene ends with Lady Macduff running off the stage crying "Murder!" followed by the murderers.

Act IV: Scene 3

The scene takes place at the palace of King Edward of England. Malcolm and Macduff enter. To Malcolm's remark that Macduff and he go to a deserted spot and weep out their sadness, Macduff replies that they ought rather to hold in their hands their deadly swords and conquer their native land. There every morning "New widows howl, new orphans cry; new sorrows / Strike heaven on the face . . . ." Malcolm replies in effect that he does not trust Macduff. He [Macbeth] hath not touch'd you yet," (that is, he has not hurt you yet) continues Malcolm. He suggests that perhaps Macduff is looking for a reward from Macbeth by luring Malcolm to Scotland. Macduff answers, "I am not treacherous." "But Macbeth is," says Malcolm: a good man may not be able to resist orders from a king. But Malcolm then begs Macduff's pardon. Malcolm says that his thoughts cannot change Macduff's nature. Even though some good people may change, not all good people change. Macduff (seeing that Malcolm is hesitant about his proposals) says that he Macduff, has lost his hopes (for an invasion of Scotland). But it is in Scotland that Malcolm finds his reasons for doubting Macduff. Why did Macduff suddenly leave his wife and children, asks Malcolm. Malcolm begs Macduff not to take the question as implying Macduff's dishonor but rather Malcolm's caution for his own life. Apparently feeling the hopelessness of persuading a suspicious man of one's innocence, Macduff says that his country must continue in its ruin. He adds that he would not be suspected as a deceiver for all of Scotland and the rich Orient combined.

Macduff is about to leave but Malcolm tells Macduff not to be offended, for Malcolm has spoken not merely in fear of Macduff. Malcolm believes his country is suffering, that there would be Scotsmen who would come over to his side. From "gracious England" he has received offers of help. But despite all of this, when he has conquered the tyrant Macbeth, Scotland would suffer more from Macbeth's successor than it is suffering now. To Macduff's question, "What should he be?" Malcolm replies that he is talking about himself, who, in the course of time, would make Macbeth appear pure. Macduff replies that no one could be worse than Macbeth. Malcolm says that he knows Macbeth is "Luxurious [lustful], avaricious, false, deceitful, / Sudden [violent], malicious, smacking of every sin / That has a name . . . ." However, he continues, not all the women of Scotland can ever satisfy *his* lust; it would be better for Macbeth to reign. Macduff replies that such lust is tyrannical and has caused the fall of many kings; but Malcolm should not hesitate to take the kingdom that belongs to him. For undoubtedly enough women will find the greatness of kingship sufficient lure so that he will be satisfied. But Malcolm goes on to speak of another fault. He is so avaricious that he would invent quarrels with his good and loyal subjects only to obtain their wealth. This is worse than lust, says Macduff; but Scotland has riches enough to quench Malcolm's desire. Lust and avarice are bearable when other virtues ("graces") are taken into account. But, Malcolm answers, he has no other virtues. He has no desire for the virtues which are fit for a king; such virtues as "justice, verity, temperance, stableness, / Bounty, perseverance, mercy, lowliness, / Devotion, patience, courage, fortitude." Instead, if he had the power, he would "Pour the sweet milk of concord into hell, / Uproar the universal peace, confound / All unity on earth."

Macduff replies that the kind of man that Malcolm describes is not only unfit to govern but also unfit to live. He wonders when his nation will once more see "wholesome days." Now a bloody usurper is on the throne and the rightful occupant is self-accused in villainy. Macduff goes on, apparently trying to understand how it came about that Malcolm is so evil, for he talks of Malcolm's parents who were very holy. Macduff bids good-bye to Malcolm and adds that what he has learned of Malcolm's character has in effect banished him from Scotland (for no invasion will occur, and he cannot otherwise return).

Malcolm once more holds back Macduff. Malcolm says that Macduff has shown himself to be a man of integrity and has erased Malcolm's suspicion of him. Macbeth, Malcolm says, had tried to trick Malcolm into returning to Scotland by sending men who acted as Macduff did at first. Malcolm has had to use "modest wisdom" to discern the true man from the false. But he knows now that Macduff is honest, and he says that all the evil character he has given himself is untrue. The first lies that he has ever told have been about himself. His true self is ready to obey the commands of Macduff and of his country. Also, Old Siward, the Earl of Northumberland, has already started for Scotland with ten thousand men. "Now," continues Malcolm, "we'll together . . . ." Malcolm asks Macduff why the latter is silent. Macduff replies that he is confused by the quick reversal of things.

A doctor enters and Malcolm stops the discussion with Macduff; they will continue it later, he says. Malcolm now addresses the doctor, asking him whether the king (King Edward) is coming out. The doctor replies in the affirmative: a group of sick people are waiting to be cured by the king. Their illnesses cannot be cured by the art of medicine, but King Edward's hand has been given such holiness that when the sick people are touched by him, they are cured. Malcolm thanks the doctor, who then exits. Macduff asks Malcolm what illness the doctor is talking about. Malcolm replies that the illness is called the evil. He has often seen the good King Edward perform this miraculous cure. How Edward has asked heaven for this miraculous power only Edward knows. All Malcolm knows is that people sick with the evil, a disease that causes swelling and ulcers, are cured by Edward and cannot be cured by doctors. It is said that this healing power will be inherited by Edward's successors. With this ability to heal he has the "heavenly gift of prophecy; / And sundry blessings," which indicate that he is "full of grace."

Ross enters. Macduff recognizes him immediately, but Malcolm has some difficulty in doing so apparently because Malcolm has not seen Ross for a long time. Macduff asks Ross how things are going in Scotland. Ross replies that things are very bad; the country cannot "Be called our mother, but our grave." Violence and death are commonplace. Malcolm asks what has given the most recent cause for grief. Ross answers that anyone attempting to report a crime an hour old as the newest cause of grief would be ridiculed, for every minute brings new ones.

"How does my wife?" inquires Macduff. "Why, well," replies Ross. "And all my children?" is Macduff's next question, to which Ross answers, "Well, too." Macduff then asks whether Macbeth has not harassed Macduff's family. "No," says Ross; "they were well at peace, when I did leave 'em." Macduff tells Ross not to be so stingy in details about the family; he wishes to know how they are. Instead of answering him, Ross says that when he came here to bring his sad news, a rumor went about that many good men had taken up arms against Macbeth. Ross believes this to be true, because Macbeth had his army mobilized. "Now is the time of help," he says. Malcolm's appearance in Scotland would cause many, including women, to fight and rid themselves of their troubles. Malcolm tells Ross about the forthcoming invasion, which will be aided by Siward, than whom no older nor better soldier can be found in Christendom. Ross says that he wishes his news were as good. Macduff asks whether the news concerns all of them or one of them. Ross says that all virtuous men must share the grief of his news, but mainly the news concerns Macduff. The latter requests that it be given to him quickly. After apologizing for the necessity of bringing Macduff such a report, Ross tells him that his wife and children have been "savagely slaughtered."

Probably because he is weeping, Macduff pulls his hat over his eyes. After an expression of shock, Malcolm tells Macduff that the latter should not have pulled his hat over his eyes. If a man does not speak out his grief, Malcolm continues, his heart breaks. Macduff merely asks, "My children too?" To this question Ross replies, "Wife, children, servants, all / That could be found." Macduff cries, "And I must be from thence!" That is, he is exclaiming over the bitterness of his absence from his castle at the time of the attack. Evidently unable completely to absorb the situation, he once more inquires, "My wife kill'd too?" Ross tells Macduff that what he has said is true. Malcolm tells Macduff to cure his grief with revenge upon Macbeth. "He has no children," says Macduff, probably referring to Macbeth. Still unable to accept the terrible facts, Macduff now asks whether all of his children were killed. "O Hell-kite!" he exclaims. "All?" Were all the children were killed. "O Hell-kite!" he exclaims. "All?" Were all the children and their mother killed at once? Macolm tells Macduff to fight against his grief like a man. Macduff says that he will do so; "But I must also feel it as a man . . . ." He then says, "Sinful Macduff!" All his family were killed, he feels, not for their original sin (for they were so innocent, it would seem, they had none) but for his. Having cried out his grief, he can accept the horrible facts: ". . . heaven rest them now!" he says. Malcolm tells Macduff to "let grief / Convert to anger." Macduff says that he could weep now and brag. Instead, he prays to heaven to bring him as soon as possible face to face with the "fiend of Scotland." If Macbeth escapes, may heaven forgive Macbeth. Malcolm says that Macduff's words are manly. Malcolm now tells his countrymen to come along to the king (King Edward); "our power [army] is ready," he says, all they require is leave from the king. "Macbeth is ripe for shaking," Malcolm says in the concluding lines of the scene, "and the powers above / Put on their instruments." (The last words mean that the forces of heaven are arming themselves.)

Act V: Scene 1

The scene occurs in a room at Dunsinane. Except for the last nine lines the scene is in prose. A doctor and a lady-in-waiting of Lady Macbeth enter. The doctor addresses the lady-in-waiting. He has stayed awake with the latter for two nights, but he has not seen what she reported to him. He asks her when Lady Macbeth last walked in her sleep. The lady-in-waiting replies that, since Macbeth ("his majesty") went into the field to fight, she has seen Lady Macbeth get up from bed, put on her dressing-gown ("night gown"), write on some paper, seal it, and return to bed. All the time she did this, Lady Macbeth was fast asleep. The doctor says it is a disturbance of nature when one is simultaneously awake and asleep. He then asks what Lady Macbeth has said. The lady-in-waiting refuses to tell, even to the doctor, because she has not witness to support her statement.

As the lady-in-waiting speaks, Lady Macbeth enters holding a lighted candle, which light, the lady-in-waiting informs the doctor, Lady Macbeth has at her bedside all the time. From the conversation of the two observers, we learn that the queen is sleep-walking; her eyes are open "but their sense are shut." She is also making the motion of washing her hands. The lady-in-waiting has seen her mistress do this sometimes for a quarter of an hour.

Until she exits, Lady Macbeth speaks a number of disconnected phrases and sentences. The latter cannot be summarized; they can only be repeated, and therefore they can as well be read in the text of the play. But we can say now that most of Lady Macbeth's remarks refer to incidents which have been dramatized in the play; and that a listener might infer from her remarks a soul tortured by the guilty acts of its owner. The two listeners do make the inference about Lady Macbeth and express their shock at what they have been forced to conclude. When Lady Macbeth leaves, the doctor indicates that rumors are flying about of "unnatural deeds" committed by the ruling couple. Guilty minds, he says, will relieve themselves of their secrets by telling them to their pillows, which do not really hear. He asks God to forgive them all. He tells the lady-in-waiting to look after her mistress and to remove from the latter any means of self-harm. He ends with "I think but dare not speak." The lady-in-waiting bids the doctor good night, and they exit.

Act V: Scene 2

The scene is the country near Dunsinane. Menteth, Cathness, Angus, Lenox, and their soldiers enter. They are Scotch rebels, who have not left their native land, the "many worthy fellows that were out" of whom Ross had told Malcolm and Macduff in the previous act. Menteth reports that the English forces, led by Malcolm, his uncle Siward, and Macduff, are near. They are burning for revenge, and their righteous cause would raise the dead to do battle. Angus says that the native rebel army will meet the English near Birnam wood. A short discussion follows as to who makes up the English army. Donalbain is not there, but Siward's son is there and many other young men. Menteth asks about Macbeth's situation. Cathness replies that Macbeth is strongly fortifying Dunsinane. Cathness continues, "Some say he's mad; others, that lesser hate him, / Do call it valiant fury: but, for certain, / He cannot buckle his distempered cause / Within the belt of rule." Angus says that Macbeth can no longer escape from his crimes; every minute ("Now minutely") "revolts upraid his faith-breach." His men obey him only by command, "Nothing in love: now does he feel his title / Hang loose about him, like a giant's robe / Upon a dwarfish thief." Menteth adds in a rhetorical question that Macbeth cannot be blamed for being frightened "When all that is within him does condemn / Itself for being there." Cathness says that they will march ahead "To give obedience where 'tis truly owed." And it is agreed that they will pour out as much blood as is necessary for their country's cure.

As for Macbeth "He cannot buckle his distempered cause / Within the belt of rule." We have not had the space to look at the clothing imagery since the early part of the play, but it is important that we do so now. In the image drawn in the quotation at the head of this paragraph, Macbeth's cause is seen as an illness which swells his stomach. His power to rule is seen as a belt around clothing with which Macbeth tries to pull in his morbid cause. However, he cannot do so. Macbeth cannot pull in the swelling revolt inside his country with the "belt of rule," his power of command. In the next speech another clothing image is used. Angus says, " . . . now does he feel his title / Hang loose about him, like a giant's robe / Upon a dwarfish thief." Here the title of king, that is, the kingship, seems to be too big for Macbeth. Although the pictures of Macbeth in the two images contradict each other, for in one clothing is too small for Macbeth and in the other clothing is too large for him, the intentions of the two images are not contradictory. The implication of both images is that Macbeth is incapable of wielding the powers of the kingship. At the beginning of the play Macbeth was in his place under Duncan. Although he was not at the pinnacle of worldly power, he was nevertheless loved and respected by all as the defender oi his native land. He was aiding a land to flourish in God's order, and he therefore had significance. When he became Thane of Cawdor, Banquo noticed that "New honors come upon him, / Like our strange garments, cleave not to their mold, / But with the aid of use." If Macbeth had waited to grow into his new honors, perhaps he might have become king and grown properly into that honor. In any case at the beginning of the play he has stature. But the fact that he has ruined his country, caused sterility instead of growth, caused his men to "move only in command, / Nothing in love" shows that he has not had the largeness of soul for the kingship. Macbeth's egotism, has ironically caused a shrinkage in him. However, not only do others hate him; "all that is within him does condemn / Itself, for being there." He himself despises the "dwarfish thief" he has become. He may have a "valiant fury," but how insignificant that is in a "dwarfish thief"! In Macbeth's quest for self-aggrandizement he has ironically shrunk from a man of honor and respect to a "dwarfish thief" frantically trying to protect his ill-gotten gains.

Act V: Scene 3

The scene is in a room at Dunsinane. Macbeth, the doctor, and attendants enter. Macbeth speaks. He wants to hear no more reports of men deserting him. He cannot fear, for the prophecy had been that no man born of woman will defeat him, and Malcolm has been born of woman. A servant, white-faced with fear, enters. The servant informs Macbeth that ten thousand soldiers of the English power are approaching. Macbeth keeps interrupting his servant's report with scornful remarks because the servant looks frightened and undoubtedly speaks in a frightened way. After the servant leaves, Macbeth speaks a soliloquy, which he twice interrupts with calls for his armor-bearer, Seyton. In the soliloquy he says that he is "sick at heart" when he sees . . . and we do not learn what makes him sick at heart, for he interrupts by crying once more for Seyton. Then he says that this attack "Will cheer me ever" or topple him from the throne now. He has lived long enough, he feels; " . . . my way of life / Is fall'n into the sere, the yellow leaf." All that one ordinarily expects of old age, such as "honor, love, obedience, troops of friends," Macbeth must not expect to have. Instead he will receive "Curses, not loud, but deep, mouth-honor, breath"; these who give the mouth-honor know in their hearts that they do not want to give it but dare not withhold it. Seyton enters and says that all reports (probably of the approaching English and of the desertions) are true. Macbeth says that he will fight until his "flesh is hacked" from his bones. Macbeth wishes Seyton to help him on with his armor. Seyton tells him that it is not necessary yet. Macbeth insists. He gives orders to send out men, who will hang those who say they are frightened. He interrupts his talk and addresses the doctor, of whom he inquires about his wife. The doctor tells Macbeth that Lady Macbeth is not so much physically ill as she is bothered by illusions which come one after the other and keep her from sleep. "Cure her of that . . . ," Macbeth tells the doctor. He then asks the doctor whether the latter can help a person sick in his mind. The doctor replies that in that situation a person must help himself. "Throw physic [medicine] to the dogs . . . ," replies Macbeth. Macbeth, talking at once to the doctor and to Seyton, tells the latter to help him on with his armor, to send out . . . for something—the order is never completed; to take off his armor. To the doctor he says that his nobles are leaving him; and then he says that he would greatly applaud the doctor if the latter could find a cure for his sick country. Has the doctor heard that the English are coming? The doctor replies in the affirmative. But Macbeth is now back to Seyton, commanding him to follow Macbeth with the armor. Macbeth exits saying that he will not be frightened "Till Birnam forest come to Dunsinane."

Act V: Scene 4

The scene occurs in the country near Birnam wood. With drum, colors, and soldiers marching enter Malcolm, Siward, Siward's son, Macduff, Menteth, Cathness, Angus, Lenox, and Ross. Malcolm addresses the native rebels, saying that he hopes that soon bedrooms will be safe. (Duncan was murdered in a bedroom.) Menteth replies that his group does not doubt that at all. Siward asks for the name of the wood which they are near. He is told that it is Birnam wood. Malcolm announces that every soldier is to cut off a bough from the tree so that the army may fool the enemy by camouflage. Siward says that "the confident tyrant" (Macbeth) remains in Dunsinane and will sit out his antagonists' siege in the palace. Malcolm adds that that strategy is Macbeth's principal hope for victory. For whenever Macbeth's soldiers have the opportunity to do so, they revolt against him. Macduff and Siward agree that they should not speculate on such matters; rather they should do their jobs as good soldiers, and time will tell whether or not their speculations are right. The group exits marching.

Act V: Scene 5

The scene takes place within Dunsinane castle. Macbeth, Seyton, and Macbeth's soldiers enter with drum and colors. Macbeth cries out that he and his soldiers will remain in the castle because the castle's "strength / Will laugh a siege to scorn." He will be able to endure until his enemies are depleted by famine and illness. If his enemies were not reinforced with men who have deserted him, his army might have gone out and met the enemy and beaten them back.

A cry of women interrupts Macbeth. Seyton goes off to discover the cause. "I have almost forgot the taste of fears," says Macbeth aside. At one time, he continues, he would have had chills on hearing a cry in the night; and at a horrible story his hair would have stood on end. "I have supp'd full with horrors: Direness, familiar to my slaughterous thoughts, / Cannot once start me," he concludes. Seyton re-enters to tell Macbeth that Lady Macbeth is dead. "She should have died hereafter . . . [at a later time]" says Macbeth. He then speaks one of the most famous Shakespearean speeches, which begins, "Tomorrow, and tomorrow, and tomorrow . . . ." The main idea of this speech is that all the future and all the past have no significance. The speech ends with Macbeth's saying that life "is a tale / Told by an idiot, full of sound and fury, / Signifying nothing."

A messenger enters and tells Macbeth of something that seems unbelievable: ". . . . I looked toward Birnam, and anon, methought, / The wood began to move." Macbeth cries, "Liar, and slave!" The messenger insists upon the truth of his statement. Macbeth says that if the messenger is lying, the latter will hang on a tree alive. If the messenger is telling the truth, Macbeth would be indifferent to the messenger's hanging him. Macbeth says that he begins "To doubt the equivocation of the fiend, / That lies like truth." He had been told not to fear until Birnam wood came to Dunsinane, "and now a wood / Comes toward Dunsinane." Macbeth gives the order to fight outside the castle, for if what the messenger said be true, it does not matter whether or not his army outwait the siege in the castle or wait outside. "I 'gin to be aweary of the sun," reflects Macbeth, "And wish the estate o' the world were now undone." Then he cries, "Ring the alarm bell! Blow wind! come, wrack! / At least we'll die with harness on our back."

Act V: Scene 6

The scene takes place on a plain before the castle. Enter Malcolm, old Siward, Macduff, and their armies, with boughs. Malcolm says that they are now near enough (to the castle) to put down the branches of Birnam wood, which they have been using as camouflage. Malcolm then makes the arrangements for battle. Siward, who is to leave the group, bids it goodbye. Macduff gives the order for the trumpets to sound, which announce the coming of "blood and death."

Act V: Scene 7

The scene occurs on the field of battle. Macbeth enters. He feels like a bear tied to a stake in the spectator sport of bear-baiting. (In that game the bear is tied to a stake and dogs are sent out to fight him.) Macbeth then refers to the prophecy that is his last hope. He does not believe a man exists who was not born of woman. "Such a one / Am I to fear, or none," he says. Young Siward enters. When he asks Macbeth for the latter's name, Macbeth replies that Siward will be afraid to hear it. "No; though thou call'st thyself a hotter name / Than any is in hell," answers the young man. But on hearing Macbeth's name, young Siward says, "The devil himself could not pronounce a title / More hateful to mine ear." Macbeth adds, "No, nor more fearful." But the remark only incites the young man to call Macbeth a liar and to start the fighting. Macbeth kills young Siward, and this leads Macbeth to the grimly humorous conclusion that Siward was born of woman.

Macbeth leaves the stage. Macduff enters. Macduff has been looking for Macbeth. Macduff feels that if Macbeth dies without Macduff's having a part in killing Macbeth, he, Macduff, will be haunted by the ghosts of his family. He does not want to fight with the hired Irish foot-soldiers ("kerns"); he will either fight with Macbeth or not at all. He hears a great noise and believes that should denote the presence of a great person. He exits saying, "Let me find him, Fortune! / And more I beg not."

Macduff's exit is followed by the entrance of old Siward and Malcolm. Perhaps because his son's body has been in one way or another removed from the stage; perhaps because the stage arrangement is such that the audience can see his dead son and he cannot, Siward is unaware that his son has been slain. He is telling Malcolm that the castle was surrendered without much fight; that Macbeth's men fight on Macbeth's enemy's side as well as on Macbeth's. Malcolm almost has the victory clinched, says Siward. They exit as Siward shows Malcolm into the castle.

Act V: Scene 8

The scene occurs in another part of the field of battle. Macbeth enters and says that he will not behave like the Roman soldier who would commit suicide before he allowed himself to be captured and killed by his enemies (like Brutus or Antony in other plays of Shakespeare). As long as Macbeth sees others alive, he would rather give others wounds than himself. Macduff enters and cries, "Turn hell-hound, turn!" Macbeth tells his pursuer that he has been avoiding Macduff more than he has avoided any other man, for "my soul is too much charged / With blood of thine already." He tells Macduff not to fight him. But as an answer Macduff does little more than show his sword ready for battle. In the midst of the fight Macbeth warns MacDuff that the latter is wasting time fighting, for Macbeth leads "a charmed life" and cannot be defeated by "one of woman born." Macduff tells his adversary to give up hope, because "Macduff was from his mother's womb / Untimely ripped." Macbeth cries, "Accursed be that tongue . . .," for it frightens him. Macbeth continues, "And be these juggling fiends no more believed, / That palter with us in a double sense; / That keep the word of promise to our ear, / And break it to our hope." And Macbeth refuses to fight with Macduff. In that case, Macduff says, Macbeth must surrender and must submit to being displayed as a monstrous rarity in the side-show. Macbeth refuses to surrender. He will neither serve Malcolm nor "be baited with the rabble's curse." Despite the fact that the conditions of his defeat as foretold in the prophecies have arrived, he will fight to the end. Placing his shield before him, Macbeth challenges Macduff, ". . . lay on, Macduff; / And damned be him that first cries, 'Hold, enough!' "

Act V: Scene 9

The scene occurs within the castle. Malcolm, old Siward, Ross, and their army enter victoriously. Malcolm says that he wishes that their friends who are not present were safely here (that is, not dead). Old Siward replies that (in war) some must die. Yet, from all he can tell, the great victory of this day was achieved at the expense of few lives. Malcolm says that Macduff and old Siward's son are missing. Ross tells old Siward that young Siward "paid a soldier's debt." That is, he died as a man should. After old Siward is assured that his son had indeed died as a man should and had wounds on his face before he died, the father says, "Why then, God's soldier be he!" If old Siward had as many sons as he has hairs on his head, he would not wish them better deaths than this one. Malcolm says that he will give the young man more grief than his father has given, for the young man deserves it; but old Siward insists otherwise: "They say he parted well and paid his score: / And so, God be with him!" (The idea in "paid his score" is that each man owes God a life, and we pay God our debt when we die.)

Macduff now enters carrying Macbeth's head. He hails Malcolm as king, points to Macbeth's head, and announces that now "the time is free." He then asks the nobility (the "kingdom's pearl") to shout with him, "Hail, King of Scotland!" This the nobility does. Malcolm says that he will not permit a long time to pass before he pays his debt to those present. The thanes shall become earls, the first earls ever named in Scotland. Whatever else remains to be done, "which would be planted newly with the time," such necessities as recalling Scotland's exiles, finding out the agents of the cruel Macbeth and his "fiend-like queen," who, it is thought, committed suicide—such necessities, Malcolm says, he "will perform in measure, time, and place." Giving thanks to all and inviting them to his coronation, Malcolm leads the actors off the stage in their final exit.

Othello

OTHELLO, *the Moor.*
BRABANTIO, *father to Desdemona.*
CASSIO, *an honorable lieutenant.*
IAGO, *a villain.*
RODERIGO, *a gulled gentleman.*
DUKE OF VENICE.
SENATORS.
MONTANO, *Governor of Cyprus.*
LODOVICO *and* GRATIANO, *two noble Venetians.*
CLOWN.

DESDEMONA, *daughter to Brabantio, wife to Othello.*
EMILIA, *wife to Iago.*
BIANCA, *a courtezan.*

GENTLEMEN *of Cyprus*, SAILORS, MESSENGER, HERALD, OFFICERS, MUSICIANS, *and*
ATTENDANTS.

Othello

Act I: Scene 1

The scene opens on a street in Venice. It is night. Roderigo and Iago are engaged in a heated discussion over the latter's failure to perform the services he has been paid for, that is, to keep Roderigo informed of Desdemona's affections. Her elopement with Othello the Moor has just come to Roderigo's attention.

Roderigo implies that Iago has abetted the elopement and does not really hate the Moor as he had said. Iago protests. His hatred for the Moor is a very real one, especially since the general has refused to appoint him lieutenant, despite the humble suits made in his behalf by three great men of the city. Iago complains of Othello's pride and "bombast circumstance" and is angered by the appointment, in his stead, of Michael Cassio, an educated military theoretician of Florence, who has had no practical experience in war. Iago himself has shown his courage fighting with the Moor at Rhodes, at Cyprus, against Christians and heathens, but the ungrateful Moor has made Cassio lieutenant, while Iago remains "his Moorship's ancient."

At Iago's outburst of grievances, Roderigo expresses surprise that the ancient continues to follow the general whom he hates so much. Iago assures his companion: "I follow him to serve my turn upon him." In following the Moor, Iago follows himself and serves neither for love nor duty, he asserts. "Whip me such honest knaves," he says of those who after long and faithful service are cashiered when they are old and useless. He expresses his admiration for the man who appears to perform his duties, but actually attends unflinchingly to his own interests, using his masters only for his own gains. The self-interested man has "soul," Iago declares, and such a man of "soul" is he.

Roderigo seems inclined to brood over the good fortune of Othello (whom he calls "thick-lips") in winning Desdemona, but Iago calls for action. Rouse Brabantio, Desdemona's father, Iago advises. Let her enraged kinsmen poison Othello's joy and spread plague on his delight. Roderigo agrees.

Immediately, the unseemly pair arrive at Brabantio's house. Iago urges Roderigo to raise a horrible cry as if the whole town were on fire, and he joins him by shouting, "Thieves!" A sleepy and confused Brabantio appears at the window. Roderigo and Iago ask him the condition of his house, knowing that he will be unable to answer their questions. Vulgarly, Iago informs him that his "white ewe" has gone off with a "black ram," meaning, of course, that his daughter has eloped with a dark-skinned Moor or a Negro. (Elizabethans made no distinctions between the two.) More respectfully, Roderigo identifies himself, but he is prevented from speaking further by Brabantio's charges of drunkenness and his reminders that Roderigo is unwelcome both to his house and to his daughter.

Patiently, Roderigo attempts to convey his information, but Iago breaks in and, alluding to Othello's race, warns Brabantio that his daughter is being covered by a "Barbary horse" (named from "Barbary" on the coast of North Africa) and that his grandchildren will be "gennets" (black horses).

Brabantio, shocked at this report, asks the "profane" (foul-mouthed) wretch to identify himself. Receiving another virulent report about his daughter and the Moor, Brabantio himself identifies the speaker as a "villain."

Iago starts to retaliate the name-calling, but as if out of respect to Brabantio, he cuts himself off and replies, "You are—a senator." Infuriated, Brabantio promises to make Roderigo answer for the insults of the unidentified villain. Still patient and respectful, Roderigo at last gets the opportunity to deliver his message. In a speech ornamented with rhetorical flourishes, Roderigo informs the senator that his fair daughter has been transported by a common knave, and that, if he knows of this elopement and has consented to it, his informants are guilty of "bold and saucy wrongs." If he does not know of the elopement, then he has wrongly rebuked the informants. With much civility, Roderigo assures Brabantio that he would not trifle over so serious a matter and advises the father to confirm the report of his daughter's revolt.

Addressed in the only language to which he is capable of responding, Brabantio becomes alarmed. He calls for lights, arouses his retainers, and admits that he has had a dream not unlike Roderigo's report. Then he repeats his cry, "Light, I say! light!"

As Brabantio departs to rouse his household, Iago takes his leave of Roderigo. It is unwholesome, he explains, to be discovered in an action against the Moor, his general. Besides, he tells Roderigo, Brabantio's action against

Othello will only "gall him with some check," for Venice needs the Moor to protect its interests in Cyprus. Othello's equal as a military leader cannot be found, Iago maintains, and although he hates the Moor, he must follow and pretend to love him "for necessity of present life." He tells Roderigo to lead Brabantio and his party to the Sagittary (apparently an inn) where Othello can be found.

As Iago departs, Brabantio returns still wearing his dressing gown; he is attended by servants whose torches light the night. He has checked Desdemona's room, and, indeed, she is gone. Between outbursts of grief for the fate of father, Brabantio questions Roderigo for details. Where did you see her? Was she with the Moor? What did she say? Are they married? When Roderigo expresses the belief that they are married, Brabantio's grief is augmented considerably. How did she get out! he wails. Without waiting for an answer, he accuses his daughter of betraying her blood. Clutching at straws, he seeks an explanation for her betrayal in stories he has read of young girls who have been deceived by charms. Roderigo agrees that he has read stories of such enchantments. Now Brabantio sends for his brother, and in the next breath bemoans the fact that he had refused her to Roderigo.

At last Brabantio asks where he can find the Moor, and Roderigo agrees to show him the way. Calling for officers and promising to reward Roderigo, Brabantio goes off to find Othello.

Act I: Scene 2

On another street in Venice, Othello, Iago, and several attendants bearing torches appear. Iago is in the middle of a description of his encounter with Brabantio. He tells Othello that Brabantio's remarks so angered him that he felt like killing him but was restrained by the fact that, apart from war, he has never "contriv'd murther," that is, he has never murdered in the heat of passion or for personal reasons. Othello approves of Iago's restraint, but Iago continues to insist on the enormity of the provocation. Brabantio spoke so disparagingly of the Moor's honor that it took all the "godliness" within Iago to refrain from harming the man. He warns Othello that Brabantio is extremely powerful in the government of Venice and, like the Duke, has two votes in the senate. (Historically, this would be impossible.) Brabantio will certainly try to divorce the couple and seek every legal means of redress against Othello.

Othello replies that Brabantio may do his worst; he is assured that his military services to the government will outweigh Brabantio's complaints. Furthermore, Othello asserts, although he does not like boasting, he will make known the fact that he is descended from a royal line. In all due humility, Othello states, his family is equal in honor and rank to the house of Brabantio. He informs Iago that he would not have given up his "unhoused free condition," his bachelor freedom, for anything in the world, except the deepest love.

Lights are seen in the darkness as Cassio and several officers with torches arrive. Iago, who is expecting Brabantio, warns Othello to retreat and hide. Othello proudly refuses. Standing his ground, he states confidently, "My parts, my title, and my perfect soul/ Shall manifest me rightly."

Othello now recognizes his lieutenant Cassio and his officers, whom he calls "servants of the Duke" and "friends." Cassio delivers the Duke's summons to Othello. Messengers have been arriving one after the other from the Venetian galleys, and many of the Duke's consuls are already assembled to discuss the emergency. They have sent three times for Othello, who could not be found at his usual lodgings. Othello replies, " 'Tis well I am found by you," and promises to join Cassio after he has spent a moment in the house.

Perplexed at Othello's delay, Cassio asks Iago what is going on. In a vulgar periphrasis, Iago explains that Othello is married. He is interrupted by Othello's return before he can tell Cassio the name of the bride.

At this point, Brabantio, Roderigo, and armed officers with more torches arrive on the scene. Again, Iago warns Othello of Brabantio's malice. Denouncing Othello as a "thief," Brabantio signals his retainers to draw their swords. An incurable fighter, Iago singles out Roderigo as his special opponent.

Contemptuously, Othello refuses to respond to Brabantio's violence. "Keep up your bright swords, for the dew will rust them," he advises. Diplomatically, he informs Brabantio, "Good Signior, you shall more command with years / Than with your weapons."

The outraged father looses a stream of invective against Othello. He damns him, calls him an enchanter, insists that the "tender, fair, and happy" Desdemona was so shy of marriage that she shunned the "curled darlings of our nation," that is, the foppish and elegant suitors of the Venetian courts. He insists that Desdemona has been intimidated; why else would he lay her fair head on his "sooty bosom?" The answer must lie in Othello's use of poisonous drugs or black magic, offenses under the law. Brabantio demands Othello's arrest and orders the officers to subdue him if he resists.

Patiently, and with great dignity, Othello assures Brabantio that he has no intention of resisting and agrees to go wherever Brabantio chooses in order to answer his charges. Brabantio chooses prison, where he plans to keep Othello until court convenes to hear the case. Othello then informs Brabantio that he has' been summoned by the Duke on business of state and asks how he shall obey both men at the same time. An officer confirms Othello's assertions, and for the first time during this troubled night, Brabantio learns that the Duke is in council. Although he surmises that the state is in danger if the council is assembled at this late hour of the night, Brabantio asserts, "Mine's not an idle cause." He decides to bring his complaint against Othello before the Duke immediately.

Act I: Scene 3

It is still the same night. The scene now shifts to the Duke's council chamber where the Duke and senators discuss and assess various conflicting reports of the size of the Turkish fleet and its whereabouts. Although they do not fix the enemy's number, the despatches confirm that the enemy fleet is bearing up to Cyprus. The Duke too becomes convinced that Cyprus is in danger, just as a sailor arrives with a message that the Turks are really heading for Rhodes. One senator argues that this is a Turkish trick Cyprus is more important to the Turks than Rhodes, and it should not be presumed that they would attempt to conquer Rhodes when Cyprus is both easier to win and more profitable to possess. The Duke confirms this belief that Cyprus is the real target. Another messenger arrives hard upon this decision to report that Turkish ships do, indeed, head for Rhodes, but that a second fleet follows behind and steers for Cyprus. The Duke is certain, then, that Cyprus is in danger.

At this point, both parties, Othello's and Brabantio's, enter the chamber. Breaking protocol, the Duke first greats Othello with the news that he must be employed at once against the "Ottomans." Then, noticing Brabantio, the Duke apologizes for not seeing him at first. He welcomes Brabantio to court, expressing regret that he had lacked the senator's help this night.

Barely returning the Duke's greeting, Brabantio proceeds to outline his daughter has been "abused, stol'n . . . and corrupted." He is so anxious to stress the illegal means by which she was taken, that is, the "spells and medicines" of witchcraft by which she was deceived, that he neglects to name the defendant at first. The Duke promises that Brabantio himself will be allowed to pass judgment on the miscreant, that is, Brabantio will read "the bloody book of law" against his daughter's deceiver "though our proper son / Stood in your action."

Much to the regret of the Duke and all the senators, Brabantio points to Othello, the man whom state affairs have brought to court. Although the Duke has believed the charges made by the noble and trusted senator, he

Othello

now turns to Othello and asks him what he has to say in his own defense. Impatiently, Brabantio insists that Othello has nothing to say but to agree. Nevertheless, Othello speaks. Showing the same tact he had employed with Brabantio before, he does, indeed, begin by agreeing that he has taken Brabantio's daughter. So much is true and no more. Humbly (and eloquently), he asserts his rudeness of speech and his inability to defend himself with the polished smoothness of the civilian. His skill is in "broil and battle," he cleverly reminds the court, and he must rely on the "gracious patience" of the Duke to listen to the "unvarnished tale" of his courtship and by what magic he won Brabantio's daughter.

Brabantio, however, mistakes Othello's reference to "magic," and passionately interrupts again, repeating the reasoning by which he has concluded that fair, gentle Desdemona must have been drugged. She was a quiet maiden, never bold, and so bashful that she blushed at her own emotions. It is unthinkable that such a timid young lady should oppose her own nature, the modesty befitting her youth, the manners of her country, the honor of her name, and everything else, and fall in love with a man whose very aspect she feared to look at.

The Duke responds to Brabantio's outburst by informing him that assertions are not proofs. (He is beginning to suspect that Brabantio's case is unfounded. Notice the parallel situation later when Othello demands proof from Iago of Desdemona's infidelity.) One of the senators asks a direct question. Did he or did he not use drugs? Still, Othello avoids a negative answer and suggests that Desdemona be called to speak before her father. While she is being fetched, Othello offers to recount their courtship.

In a long autobiographical account, Othello then reveals his romantic and adventurous life. He had been a frequent guest in Brabantio's house where he had told his adventures in Desdemona's hearing. For many years, he has been a soldier and has engaged in "battles, sieges, fortunes." He has repeatedly risked his life without question. He had once been captured and made a slave, but had managed to escape. He had been in all sorts of dangerous and mysterious places, vast caves, vacant deserts, high mountains. He has known Cannibals, the "Anthropophagi," and "men whose heads / Do grow beneath their shoulders."

Continuing his narrative, Othello tells how Desdemona was attracted by fragments of his tales, which she had overheard as she came and went about the house. Privately, she requested that he repeat them to her in full. As she listened, she wept over his trials and hardships. Finally, she stated that she would welcome such a man as her suitor. Thus encouraged, Othello proposed marriage. "She loved me for the dangers I had pass'd /

743

And I lov'd her that she did pity them." This was Othello's only witchcraft, he concludes; "Let Desdemona witness it."

At the conclusion of Othello's narrative, Desdemona appears, attended by Iago and several others. The Duke declares that Othello's story would win his daughter too. Before hearing Desdemona's testimony, the Duke asks Brabantio to reconcile himself as best he can to "this mangled matter," to this irregular marriage. Brabantio, however, insists that Desdemona be heard before a decision is made. Gently, he asks his daughter if she knows where her obedience lies. He is clearly unprepared for the answer she gives him. Desdemona replies that her duty is divided. She owes obedience and respect to her father because he gave her life and education, but even for this reason does she now owe obedience to her husband, for her mother had showed her that a woman, once married, must prefer her husband to her father.

Desdemona makes it abundantly clear that she married Othello through her free choice, and, with this declaration, Brabantio's case collapses. Brabantio makes the best of what he considers a bad situation and gives Othello Desdemona apparently with all his heart. But he admits that if Othello did not already possess her, he would do everything in his power to keep her from him.

In a conciliatory speech, the Duke asks Brabantio to smile at his loss, for, in smiling, he prevents the thief from enjoying his discomfort. Wryly, Brabantio suggests that Venice, if it loses Cyprus, may also smile and thus deprive the Turks of their victory. He accepts the Duke's decision reluctantly and finds no ease to his grief in the Duke's words. "I never yet did hear / That the bruised heart was pierced through the ear." Thus, still unreconciled to his daughter's marriage, he asks the Duke to move on to the business of the state.

The Duke appoints Othello Commander-in-Chief for the military defense of Cyprus. In no way embarrassed or upset by what has happened, Othello courteously but firmly requests that the state make living arrangements for his wife in accordance with her rank and education. Brabantio refuses to quarter his disobedient daughter, although the Duke has suggested it. Desdemona interposes in her quiet and unaffected way to ask that she may accompany Othello to Cyprus. In doing so, she makes an important declaration about the kind of love she has for this man:

> That I did love the Moor to live with him,
> My downright violence and storm of fortunes,
> May trumpet to the world. My heart's subdu'd
> Even to the very quality of my lord.
> I saw Othello's visage in his mind,

And to his honours and his valiant parts
Did I my soul and fortunes consecrate.
So that, dear lords, if I be left behind,
A moth of peace, and he go to the war,
The rights for which I love him are bereft me,
And I a heavy interim shall support
By his dear absence. Let me go with him.

Othello adds his own request to Desdemona's. He does not ask that Desdemona be with him simply to satisfy his rights as a husband, "but to be free and bounteous to her mind." Love will not interfere with Othello's responsibilities for the conduct of the war.

The request of the newly wedded couple is granted by the Venetian senate, and the Duke affirms to Brabantio that "Your son-in-law is far more fair than black."

As the senate adjourns, Othello is given meaningful advice by the first senator and by Brabantio. The senator urges Othello to use Desdemona well, while Brabantio warns: "She has deceived her father, and may thee." Othello answers, "My life upon her faith!"

When the Duke and senators leave, Othello entrusts Iago with Desdemona's safe voyage and asks him to have Emilia, his wife, wait on her. Then, with only an hour left to attend to love and business, Othello departs with his bride.

Roderigo has witnessed the entire action and when the council chamber is cleared, he turns to Iago and announces that he is going to drown himself. To live without Desdemona would be torment, and although he is ashamed of his foolishness, he admits that he has not the "virtue" (an inherent power of character) to amend the foolishness.

Anxious to save his dupe, Iago responds heatedly. In all twenty-eight years, he has never met a man who knew how to love himself. Personally, Iago argues, he would rather be an ape (a creature without reason) than kill himself for a woman. As for "virtue" (the naturally endowed powers Roderigo says he lacks), we are what we *will* ourselves to be, Iago asserts. If we had not this will, we'd be nothing more than beasts, subject to "carnal stings" and "unbitted lusts." Fortunately, however, man has reason to cool his lusts. Love is only a form of lust, Iago tells the incredulous Roderigo; it is a condition that exists only with the permission of the will.

Iago's cold philosophy makes little impression on Roderigo, but when Iago tells the foolish lover again and again to put money in his purse to follow the wars, and to wait for Desdemona to tire of the Moor, Roderigo's hopes begin to rise. Iago asures him that love which begins violently ends in the same way, and that Desdemona, finished with the old Moor, will begin to look for a young lover. He promises that Roderigo will enjoy Desdemona yet, if Iago's wits and "all the tribe of hell" (which apparently serves as inspiration to his wit) are any match for the barbarous Moor and the "supersubtle" (sophisticated) Venetian, Desdemona. Once more resolved to live, Roderigo agrees to follow Iago's advice and sets off at once to sell his land.

Left alone, Iago utters the first soliloquy of the play. He states that he has only saved Roderigo for the sake of his purse and for the fun that the foolish man gives him. Otherwise, he would not waste his time expending his hard-earned knowledge of human nature on such a "snipe" as Roderigo. Reaffirming his hatred for Othello, Iago then says rather strangely that he suspects the Moor of having relations with his own wife (Emilia), yet he doesn't know or seem to care whether or not his suspicion has any foundation.

Next, Iago works out a plot against Othello, which he formulates as he speaks. Since the Moor has faith in his ancient (Iago), he will be inclined to believe Iago when he suggests that Cassio is too familiar with Desdemona. According to Iago, Othello is an "ass" because he has a "free and open nature." Othello thinks others are as honest as he "that but seem to be so." Delighted by the plan he has just devised, Iago exclaims, "Hell and night / Must bring this monstrous birth to the world's light."

Act II: Scene 1

Some weeks have passed. The action moves on to Cyprus. Montano, a leading citizen of Cyprus, discusses the war with two gentlemen. Montano is satisfied that the Turkish fleet has either sought refuge somewhere or has been destroyed in the course of a terrific storm that has been raging. A third gentleman brings news that the Turkish fleet has, indeed, suffered serious losses and that Cassio has arrived in Cyprus. Othello, who has been given the full powers of governor of the island, is still at sea. The gentleman reports that Cassio is worried about Othello's safety. Montano expresses his hope for Othello's safe return, for he once served under the Moor and found him to be a perfect commander.

Cassio now joins the group. Having heard Montano speak of Othello, he thanks him for his praise. He assures Montano that Othello's ship is a strong one and his pilot well-skilled; he has good hopes for the governor's safety. A second ship is sighted, and, as Montano and Cassio await a report on its passengers, Cassio tells his companion that the Moor is married to "a maid / That paragons description and wild fame; / One that excels the quirks of blazoning pens."

Desdemona's ship has arrived. She is accompanied by Iago, Roderigo, and Emilia. Desdemona thanks Cassio for his effusive welcome and expresses her fear over Othello's delayed arrival. A bantering conversation ensues when Cassio kisses Emilia's hand in greeting and renders her speechless. But she finds her tongue when Iago describes her as a chiding wife and she warrants that *he* shall never write her praise. Iago goes on to defame the female sex in general. Encouraged by the company, he recites several proverbial jests about the frailty of women. Everyone takes them in good humor, including Desdemona, who calls Iago a "profane and liberal counsellor." Cassio is forced to admit that Iago speaks truthfully and to the point, and suggests that Desdemona will find greater merit in Iago as a soldier than as a scholar. Cassio next extends the courtesy of aristocratic hand-kissing to Desdemona, as Iago looks on. In an "aside" (a stage whisper, another convention of the Elizabethan theater, in which the speech is intended only for the audience's hearing), Iago comments: "He takes her by the palm. Ay, well said, whisper! With as little a web as this will I ensnare as great a fly as Cassio."

At last Othello arrives. He embraces Desdemona and expresses his supreme happiness at this moment of reunion. She is his "soul's joy." "If after every tempest come such calms / May the winds blow till they have waken'd death!" Othello then expresses the fear that such great contentment as he feels just now cannot come twice in a single lifetime.

Desdemona replies with a hopeful picture of a future full of tenderness and love. Othello responds by putting his hand upon his heart which has almost stopped beating through the weight of emotion. Kissing her, he says that kisses ought to be the greatest "discords" they may ever be forced to experience. Iago, looking on, reveals his satanic thoughts in another "aside." Grimly jesting on his undeserved sobriquet, "honest Iago," he picks up Othello's musical metaphor: "O, you are well tun'd now! / But I'll set down the pegs that make this music / As honest as I am." Prattling happily about the victory, the good people of Cyprus, and his joyous reunion with his bride, Othello leads Desdemona off to his castle.

We now have a long chorus-like dialogue between Iago and Roderigo, in which Iago assures his dupe that Desdemona loves Cassio. Iago pours out his envy, spleen, and disdain for the marriage of Othello and Desdemona. He again reveals his contempt for sex, and he reduces all human relationships to the lowest common denominator. Iago pictures Desdemona as an animal of aggressive sexuality. Dulled by the "act of sport," and obviously promiscuous as all women are, she will seek a handsome man to renew her interest in love. Othello, according to Iago, is not physically attractive, and Desdemona, who already showed her imbecility in choosing such a braggart, will soon be bored with him. Here is where Cassio will come in, for he has what women of "folly and green minds look after." In fact, Iago declares, "the woman hath found him already." Roderigo objects; he cannot believe any such thing; Desdemona is "full of most blessed condition." "Blessed fig's end!" Iago shouts; "the wine she drinks is made of grapes." (She is only human.) Besides, she indulges in courtesies, which are prologue to lust.

Next, Iago broaches his plan to get Cassio out of the way by having Roderigo provoke an incident which will put Cassio in a bad light as an undisciplined officer. With Cassio ruined, Roderigo will be better able to effect his purposes (Iago's actually).

When Roderigo departs, Iago, in a second soliloquy, reviews his accomplishments of the day and his plans for the future. He reveals his belief that Cassio actually loves Desdemona. He decides that her love for Cassio will make a likely and credible story (but it will only be a story). Whatever else Iago feels about the Moor, he does admit that Othello will make a good husband, for he "is of a constant, loving, noble nature." Iago then restates his self-induced idea that Othello may have committed adultery with Emilia and decides to seduce Desdemona himself in order to be "even'd with him, wife for wife." Considering the possible failure of his plan to seduce Desdemona, Iago devises an alternate plan. If the seduction fails, he will make Othello incurably jealous of Cassio. Of course, the fool Roderigo must play his part properly if Cassio is to fall into Iago's power, an idea which appeals to Iago. Next Iago expresses his belief that Cassio (if he tried) could seduce Emilia. Finally, Iago gloats over the thanks he will receive from Othello "for making him egregiously an ass," that is, he envisions how Othello will thank him for falsely informing on Desdemona and Cassio.

These are the evil conceptions formulating in Iago's mind. Iago realizes that his plan for revenge is only roughly outlined, but he states his intention of working out the details as the events occur: "'Tis here [in his head], but yet confus'd." Knavery is unpredictable, Iago says; its course becomes clearer only after it is put into effect.

Act II: Scene 2

This is scarcely a scene at all. On a street in Cyprus, an official messenger or "herald" reads a proclamation that there is to be a public festival, with free food and drink for all, to celebrate the utter destruction of the Turkish fleet. Moreover, Othello's marriage is to be honored with dancing, bonfires, and other sport.

Act II: Scene 3

Othello, Desdemona, Cassio, and attendants are present as the scene opens in a hall of Othello's castle. Othello admonishes Cassio in "honourable step" (moderation). The festival should not outrun discretion, Othello cautions, and guard duty is to be observed as usual. Cassio promises to instruct Iago accordingly and to supervise the frolics personally. Othello concludes the interview, observing that "Iago is most honest," a good man for the job.

Iago reports to Cassio just after Othello leaves with his wife and attendants. At Cassio's suggestion that they begin their watch, Iago protests it is too early to renew their duties; it is only ten o'clock. Othello's departure should not be a sign that the feast is over, Iago states; the general has left early because he is anxious to enjoy his wife. "He hath not yet made wanton the night with her," Iago explains, "and she is sport for Jove."

Cassio responds to Iago's vulgar description of Desdemona with several courtly phrases of his own. She is "exquisite"; she is "a most fresh and delicate creature"; she is "perfection." Iago, on the other hand, finds her "full of game," "a parley to provocation," "an alarum to love."

Pleading with Cassio not to hurry to the military watch, Iago invites him to a "stope of wine" with "a brace of Cyprus gallants." Cassio declines, saying he has already had one watered glass of wine tonight and that it has not agreed with him. Iago insists; it is a "night of revels," and besides, the gallants are waiting outside for his company. With characteristic politesse, Cassio goes at once to greet the gallants, leaving Iago alone momentarily.

In a brief soliloquy, Iago expresses his belief that if he can succeed in getting Cassio to take one more drink, the lieutenant will become as quarrelsome as a young lady's dog. Now Roderigo (who cannot always be counted on to play his part properly) is already drunk (and thus, oddly enough more reliable) and has been appointed to guard duty that night. In addition, Iago has plied with wine three Cypriots, mettlesome young men, sensitive to "honor," who are also to keep watch. Amid this "flock of drunkards," it would seem easy to provoke Cassio to some offensive action, which would arouse all of Cyprus against him (and make his dismissal mandatory). As Cassio returns with Montano, several gentlemen, and a servant with wine, Iago's reflections break off with the lines:

If consequence do but approve my dream,
My boat sails freely, both with wind and stream

Montano now insists that Cassio should have a drink, and Cassio, caught up by the spirit of the feast, accepts. Iago swings into action, singing two boisterous songs, which he has learned in England, a country of expert drinkers. Iago has skillfully turned the social occasion into a drinking party.

Cassio begins to show the effects of wine and is very self-conscious about it. He begins to talk about religious salvation. Inadvertently, he throws a barb at Iago (who has suffered by Cassio's promotion) when he says "the lieutenant is to be saved before the ancient." (This is, ironically, also true.) "Do not think, gentlemen, I am drunk. This is my ancient; this is my right hand, and this is my left," Cassio raves, as he staggers away from the party.

Montano (who holds his liquor well) suggests that the party return to duty and mount the watch. Assuming a pitying air, Iago tells Montano that Cassio, "this fellow that is gone before," is really a fine military man. Unfortunately, his drinking vice is as great as his virtue as a soldier. Othello puts too much trust in him, Iago fears. Some day, Cassio's drunkenness will cause the whole isle of Cyprus to shake.

Alarmed over the safety of his island, the Cypriot gentleman Montano asks, "But is he often thus?" With mock reluctance, Iago replies that Cassio frequently drinks himself to sleep, for if he is sober, he will stay awake all day and night. Montano, now more concerned, suggests that Othello be informed of Cassio's habits; perhaps the general takes his lieutenant too much on appearances and does not penetrate his real deficiency.

Roderigo appears briefly, and Iago secretly orders him to follow Cassio. He departs at once. Meanwhile, Montano continues his ironic commentary on the Moor's favored officer. It is dangerous for Cassio to be in command; the Moor ought to be informed, Montano decides. With his usual duplicity, Iago asserts that he loves Cassio and would not inform on him for all "this fair island."

Noise suddenly erupts from "within" (offstage), and Cassio appears, driving Roderigo before him. Angrily, Cassio tells Montano that this rogue, this rascal (Roderigo), has tried to teach him his duty. Roderigo and Cassio come to blows. Montano intervenes and Cassio threatens him roughly. As Montano and Cassio tussle, Iago slyly directs Roderigo to run off and rouse the town. Iago next turns to the combatants and makes a feeble effort to break up the fight. Hearing bells in the distance,

Othello

Iago pretends to wonder who rang them. Belatedly, Iago warns Cassio to desist or he will awaken the town and be disgraced forever.

Having heard the bells, Othello arrives at once. Montano exclaims that he has been wounded. (Some editions of the play indicate that Montano faints at this point, but in view of Othello's subsequent line, "Hold for your lives," it is apparent that Montano, although wounded, is still on his feet and doing battle. "Faint" may be a misreading for "feint"—(a movement with a sword.)

His sense of military propriety shocked, Othello cries, "Hold"; Iago echoes his command. Are we like the Turks, to kill ourselves when heaven has prevented our enemies from killing us? Othello demands. He reminds the combatants that they are Christians, not barbarians, and warns, "He that stirs next . . . / . . . dies upon his motion." Acting swiftly and decisively, Othello orders that the bells be silenced, for it will frighten the inhabitants of Cyprus out of their senses. Next, he turns to "honest Iago," whose face he finds "dead with grieving." He charges Iago "on his love" for his general to identify the trouble-maker.

Iago replies that he cannot identify the miscreant. Only moments ago, he reports, Montano, Cassio, and all were as friendly as bride and groom undressing for bed. (Iago slyly alludes to what he supposes Othello and Desdemona were doing before the bells sounded, hoping to infuriate the Moor all the more because he has been disturbed at such a moment.)

With feigned innocence, Iago disclaims any knowledge of the cause of this "opposition bloody." Turning to the others, Othello pursues his inquiry. Cassio asks pardon; he cannot speak. Next, Othello asks Montano, reputed in his youth for his serious and peaceful nature, why he has suddenly turned "night-brawler." But Montano, who has been seriously wounded in the fight, finds it difficult to speak. He refers Othello to Iago for the explanation and intimates that he has fought only in self-defense.

Othello is annoyed with everyone's reticence and warns them not to anger him further. Echoing the Duke's promise to Brabantio to punish his own son if it is required by justice, Othello promises to punish the offender though he turned out to be his own twin brother. The crime of disturbing the peace is a serious one, for Cyprus is still a "town of war," and its people are still anxious and fearful over the dangers they have just escaped. To hold a private quarrel "in night, and on the court and guard of safety? 'Tis monstrous," Othello declares. "Iago, who began 't?" the Moor demands.

Montano, too, urges that Iago tell the truth, reminding him that if he shows partiality to Cassio because of personal friendship or official ties, he is no soldier. Iago admits that Montano has hit home. He would rather lose his tongue than use it against Cassio. However, he is convinced that speaking truth could not injure the lieutenant. He describes how he and Montano were engaged in conversation when Cassio came running in with sword drawn, pursuing some fellow (Roderigo, whom Iago pretends he does not know). Montano interposed, attempting to restrain Cassio, while Iago pursued the other fellow to prevent his cries from terrifying the town. The fellow eluded him, but hearing sword-play and Cassio's swearing (as he had never heard him do before), Iago returned to find Montano and Cassio at blows. This is all he knows, Iago states. Damning Cassio finally in a pretended defense, Iago suggests that surely Cassio must have endured from his victim some "strange indignity, / Which patience could not pass." Othello acknowledges Iago's desire to ameliorate Cassio's guilt. Turning to Cassio, Othello informs him that though he loves him, he relives him of his duties as an officer forever.

Desdemona (who has heard the disturbance) arrives to inquire about the matter, but Othello puts her off and sends her back to her room. Advising Montano that he personally will attend to his wounds, he has him taken away. Next he orders Iago to placate any Cypriots who have been disturbed by the commotion. Such is the soldier's life, he tells Desdemona.

Iago and Cassio are now left alone. Apparently Cassio has begun to groan, for Iago now asks him if he is hurt. Cassio replies that he is hurt past all surgery and begins to confide in him at once. Cassio is distraught by the public loss of his reputation. What's reputation, asks Iago, but nothing at all? (He is going to tell Othello in a later scene that reputation is practically everything.) Cassio is being punished as a matter of military policy; there is no hard feeling behind it. To his satisfaction, Iago learns that Cassio cannot identify Roderigo. The drinking had blurred his mind, and he can remember the events of the night only as "a mass of things." Iago tells Cassio to stop worrying about his drunkenness: "You or any man living may be drunk at a time." He advises him to try to get his post back through Desdemona's influence, "for she holds it a vice in her goodness not to do more than is requested." Cassio is very grateful to "honest" Iago for his constructive advice and leaves Iago, who must attend to his guard duty.

Once alone, Iago expresses his thought in another soliloquy. Alluding to his conversation with Cassio, he gloats, "And what's he then that says I play the villain?" Doesn't he give Cassio the most probable advice, freely and honestly showing him the way to win Othello's approval again? Desdemona can easily be made to support a cause, for she is as bounteous as the four elements (fire, air, earth, and water), which are free to all. In turn, Desdemona can win over Othello, for his "soul is so enfetter'd to her love," that he will grant her every wish. "How am I then a villain?" Iago asks again with melodramatic heaviness and malicious delight. He addresses himself to the "Divinity of hell" and compares his methods to those of devils, who, when they wish to entice a soul to "blackest sins," first put on "heavenly shows" of virtue.

Planning his next move, Iago decides that, while Desdemona appeals to Othello to recall Cassio to his post, Iago will pour the libel into Othello's ear that she is motivated to aid Cassio by adulterous lust. Iago's eventual triumph will be the destruction of all his enemies through Desdemona's *virtue*: "And out of her own goodness make the net / That shall enmesh them all."

Roderigo enters, interrupting Iago's reflections, and declares his impatience to win Desdemona. He has been sorely beaten tonight, Roderigo complains, but he fears that all he will get from his pain is the experience of it, a depleted purse, and not much more wisdom than he had before. Iago scolds the impatient suitor: everything takes time; wounds, for example, must heal by degrees. He reminds Roderigo that he works by wit, not witchcraft, and that wit must await the proper moment. He reviews the plan to Roderigo, pointing out that things are going as scheduled. Even though Roderigo has been slightly hurt in the action, Cassio has been dismissed. The rest will follow in good time, just as fruits must blossom before they can ripen. Be patient a little longer, Iago advises. Then, observing that the sun is rising, Iago remarks, "Pleasure and action make the hours seem short."

Dismissing Roderigo, Iago continues his cogitations. Two things must be done next, he decides: his wife, Emilia, must arrange a meeting between Cassio and Desdemona, and the Moor must be brought to witness their encounter.

Act III: Scene 1

It is morning now. Cassio is seen in the court before the castle in the company of musicians whom he has engaged to play for Othello. He bids them play briefly, and when the General appears, they are to wish him "Good morrow."

As the musicians begin to blow their tune, a Clown emerges from the castle and asks them if their instruments have been to Naples.

The musicians identify their noise-makers as "wind instruments," which incites the Clown to several ribald puns on "wind," "tale," and "tail." The Clown delivers a gratuity from the General and tells them that he only admires music that cannot be heard. Unable to comply with this request, the musicians depart.

Cassio next addresses the Clown, and curbing his "quillets" (word-play) with a piece of gold, he asks him to entreat Emilia to have a word with him.

Iago arrives and is surprised to see Cassio stirring so early. Cassio informs the ancient that he has taken the liberty to send for Emilia in order to ask her to arrange an interview with Desdemona. Iago promises to send her down immediately and offers to assist further by drawing the Moor out of the way so that the interview can be held privately. As Iago leaves on his errand, Cassio remarks, "I never knew / A Florentine more kind and honest."

Emilia arrives promptly, greets the "good lieutenant," and expresses her sympathy for his misfortune. She informs Cassio that the General and his wife are discussing his misadventure at this very moment. Desdemona is already defending his cause, but the Moor has replied that Cassio's victim, Montano, is a very prominent man in Cyprus and has important connections. It would be bad policy to reinstate Cassio, Othello feels, even though he loves his former lieutenant dearly. In fact, Othello "needs no other suitor but his likings," and were it not for political prudence, he would reappoint Cassio at the first opportunity. Despite Emilia's report, Cassio importunes an interview with Desdemona, and Emilia agrees to arrange one.

Act III: Scene 2

This scene of less than ten lines takes place in a room in the castle where Othello is conducting business with Iago and several gentlemen. Concluding his affairs, Othello hands over some letters to Iago which are to be given to one of the pilots of the fleet and delivered to Venice. He tells Iago he will be inspecting the "works" (fortifications) and asks the ancient to report to him there on his return. The gentlemen accompany Othello as he departs to make the inspection.

Act III: Scene 3

The third scene of Act III shifts to a garden in the castle where Desdemona, Cassio, and Emilia conduct the interview, which was originally suggested by Iago. Cassio implores Desdemona to take swift action in his behalf, for he fears that long delays and postponements may cause Othello to forget him. Desdemona promises to act at once. She will watch Othello and "tame" and "talk him out of patience." She assures Cassio that she will plead his cause as if it were her own, "for thy solicitor shall rather die / Than give thy cause away."

Toward the end of the conversation, Othello and Iago are seen approaching. The forthright and uninhibited Desdemona bids him stay to hear her speak in his defense, but Cassio is too embarrassed to face the General he has offended and abruptly takes his leave of the ladies.

When he sees Cassio leave Desdemona, Iago mutters, as if to himself, "Ha! I like not that." Believing Iago has addressed him, Othello inquires, "What doest thou say?" Assuming reluctance to speak, Iago replied, "Nothing, my lord; or if—I know not what." Casually, Othello turns to another subject, "Was not that Cassio parted from my wife?" Affecting surprise, Iago answers evasively, "Cassio, my lord? No sure, I cannot think it, / That he would steal away so guilty-like, / Seeing you coming."

Now Desdemona greets Othello and her first words are about Cassio, who "languishes in your displeasure." She pleads for "present reconciliation" between Othello and Cassio, for the latter has "erred in ignorance and not in cunning." But Othello, still curious to identify the "guilty-like" figure, wants to know if Cassio has just departed. He has, Desdemona replies, adding that Cassio has been humbled by grief and urging that Othello call him back at once.

Othello wants to postpone his forgiveness. (He is probably hoping that Cassio's misconduct will be forgotten presently, and the reinstatement can then be made without raising the objections of the entire town.) Desdemona, however, becomes insistent. In fact, she nags. She wonders what Othello would ask her to do that she would deny "or stand so mammering on." She reminds him how Cassio came wooing with him and defended him when Desdemona had disdained him. Finally, Othello yields, saying that he will deny her nothing. He beseeches her, in return, to leave him alone. Whereupon, Desdemona grants his wish immediately, calling upon Emilia to witness what an obedient wife she is. Upon her departure, Othello remarks: "Perdition catch my soul / But I do love thee! and when I love thee not, / Chaos is come again."

Iago asks Othello whether Cassio knew of his love when he first wooed Desdemona. Told that he did, Iago affects surprise at learning this. "Indeed," he exclaims and refuses to explain his surprise. He claims the question was asked only "for a satisfaction of my thought," and when probed for further explanation, he evasively parrots Othello's words:

Iago: I did not think he had been acquainted with her.
Othello: O, yes, and went between us very oft.

Iago: Indeed?
Othello: Indeed? Ay, indeed! Discernst thou aught in that?
Is he not honest?
Iago: Honest, my lord?
Othello: Honest? Ay, honest.
Iago: My lord, for aught I know.
Othello: What dost thou think?
Iago: Think, my lord?
Othello: Think, my lord?
      By heaven, he echoes me. . . .

Othello declares that Iago is playing echo "as if there were some monster in his thought / Too hideous to be shown."

His curiosity excited, Othello appeals to Iago's love for him to reveal his thoughts. Iago answers this appeal indirectly. He asks if Othello is assured in his love for him; to which Othello replies he is convinced that Iago loves him. He adds that the delaying tactics Iago is using are tricks commonly employed by false, disloyal knaves. In "honest" Iago, however, these evasions indicate that Iago is a man who weighs his words carefully before speaking.

Thus assured, Iago states that he thinks Cassio is honest, and Othello agrees. Slyly, Iago next suggests that he has no basis for his belief in Cassio's honesty except the fact that "men should be what they seem." Infected by the suspicions Iago has successfully planted so quickly, Othello demands that Iago speak what he thinks no matter how horrible his thoughts may be. With a sense of timing and pace, Iago refuses to utter his thoughts at first. He pretends to be uncertain about his ideas. Suppose they are "vile and false"; after all, the best of men is subject to an occasional unclean thought. In a long, carefully measured preamble which says nothing definite, Iago points out his own tendency "to spy into abuses"; often his "jealousy" (suspicion) "shapes faults that are not." He cautions Othello against prying into his thoughts, for they are "not for your quiet nor your good." (This is the truth, of course, but Othello has no way of knowing that Iago is speaking with conscious irony.) Then, his famous speech on reputation in which he reverses the position he took when discussing the subject with Cassio (in II.iii), Iago asserts:

> Who steals my purse steals trash; 'tis something, nothing;
> 'Twas mine, 'tis his, and has been slave to thousands;
> But he that filches from me my good name
> Robs me of that which not enriches him
> And makes me poor indeed.

Finally, Othello demands, "By heaven, I'll know thy thoughts." But Iago, adopting an air of rugged independence and injured integrity, replies firmly, "You cannot . . . / Nor shall not." "Ha!" cries Othello. This "Ha!" is open to two interpretations. One is that the image of Desdemona's infidelity has sprung into the mind of Othello. Iago has been able, by subtle insinuation, to bring it to a monstrous birth. The other interpretation is that the "Ha!" merely expresses Othello's impatience with Iago's reluctance to be straightforward. In an case, Iago now assumes that suspicion has taken hold of Othello and warns, "O, beware, my lord, of jealousy! / It is the green ey'd monster." Othello still fails to catch the drift of Iago's meaning. Is Iago trying to advise his master against a jealousy which he does not feel? Does Iago think that "blown surmises" and "inference" will make him jealous? Othello asks. Desdemona's behavior cannot be misinterpreted; though she is fair, enjoys feasts, loves company, has all the graces of speech, song, play, and dance, yet she is virtuous. Confidently, Othello states, "She had eyes, and chose me. No, Iago; / I'll see before I doubt." Furthermore, if he were ever furnished with proof, still he would not be jealous, for he would discard love and jealousy simultaneously.

Iago expresses pleasure at learning that Othello is not a jealous man, for this will give him leave to prove his loyalty with "franker spirit." At the moment he has no proof, but he suggests that Othello keep his eye on Desdemona and Cassio. He informs Othello that he knows the ways of Venetian women very well. Their conscience on matters of adultery "is not to leave it undone, but keep't unknown." He reminds Othello of Desdemona's former duplicities: she deceived her father by marrying the Moor, and when she pretended to fear Othello's looks, she loved them most.

Having gone as far as the situation will permit, Iago now apologizes for imparting his suspicions to the General. Othello protests that he is deeply indebted to Iago for unburdening his thoughts. He insists they have not troubled him, as Iago continues to apologize for expressing such unsettling thoughts and as he cautions the Moor not to misunderstand him. Iago has only expressed his suspicions, nothing more. This is understood, Othello claims, "And yet, how nature erring from itself—"

Seizing on the idea of "erring nature" in Othello's moment of doubt, Iago pounces, "Ay, there's the point!" He submits that "her" (Desdemona's) unwillingness to accept the numerous matches her father proposed to her with men of similar "clime, complexion, and degree" (which it was natural for her to do) marks her as a woman with "a will most rank," in which "foul disproportion, thoughts unnatural" are harbored. With all due apologies to Othello, Iago adds, he is not speaking of Desdemona in particular. Even so, Iago fears, "her" will, on reconsideration, may cause her to compare Othello with her own countrymen and to repent her original choice of husband. Othello has heard enough. He bids Iago farewell, asking him to report if he perceives anything more and to set his wife Emilia to observe Desdemona.

As soon as Iago leaves, Othello gives vent to the grief that has been building up. "Why did I marry," he groans. He is certain that Iago knows more than he is willing to tell.

Iago returns with an afterthought. Making another plea for moderation, he suggests that Cassio should not have his place back yet, so that Othello can be watchful and note whether or not Desdemona goes out of her way to support him. With that Iago takes his leave once more.

A soliloquy of Othello's follows; it is indignant and pathetic at the same time. Iago, he thinks, is "exceeding honest" and really knows what life is about. He himself is a black man, on the older side ("declin'd / Into the vale of years") and has not the gift of making sweet love-talk as "chamberers" (wanton gallants) do.

Some unpleasant images of life with an unfaithful wife pass ominously through Othello's mind. Then, as he sees her coming, the nightmare lifts and gives way to the heavenly image of Desdemona: "If she be false, O, then heaven mocks itself! / I'll not believe it."

But the psychological stress to which Iago has submitted him now has its physical effects. Faintly, he accuses himself of harboring evil thoughts. Then Othello attributes his mutterings to a severe headache. Desdemona offers him a handkerchief (later we find that it is a special heirloom) with which to bind his forehead. In his agitation, Othello drops it, and it is retrieved by Emilia, who recalls that Iago has tried to persuade her to steal it for quite some time. Now that she has the opportunity, she decides to have the "work" (embroidered design) copied and given to Iago, though she has no idea what he wants it for. But then Iago enters and forcibly takes it from her, refusing to return it, although Emilia complains that Desdemona, "Poor lady, she'll run mad / When she shall lack it." Iago summarily orders Emilia away.

Left alone, Iago works on his plot again. He will plant the handkerchief in Cassio's lodging. Something may come of it. The Moor is already inclined toward suspicion, and Iago is sure it will soon grow into a belief.

In several sad, melodious lines, uttered like an incantation, Iago observes the approaching figure of Othello:

Othello

> . . . . Not poppy, nor madragora,
> Nor all the drowsy syrups of the world,
> Shall ever medicine thee to that sweet sleep
> Which thou ow'dst yesterday.

Othello greets Iago with the violent accusation: "Ha! Ha! fálse to me?" When Iago inquires the reason for Othello's wrath, Othello replies that before Iago had given him reason to suspect Desdemona, Othello had enjoyed her company freely. Now his pleasures are tainted by doubt. Hitherto, Othello says, "I found not Cassio's kisses on her lips." If only he knew nothing at all, Othello complains. Othello is deeply depressed. Empassioned by despair, Othello bids farewell to "Pride, pomp, and circumstance of glorious war." Finally, he turns against Iago again: "Villain, be sure thou prove my love a whore!" (For once, Othello has correctly identified the character of "honest" Iago, but, ironically, he does not know it.) He demands that Iago bring him "ocular proof" of Desdemona's treachery. If Iago has lied, he will wish he had been born a dog rather than answer to Othello's "wak'd wrath."

Owing to his lack of self-control, the result of his tortured state of mind, Othello is here no match for the calculated hypocrisy of Iago. Iago answers Othello's demands with a complaint to the world at large. After all, what has he done but be "honest" and demonstrate his love for Othello? "Take note, take note, O world," Iago cried, "To be direct and honest is not safe."

(There is grim humor in Iago's complaint, for we know that he means exactly what he is saying. Since Othello does not, this is another instance of dramatic irony.) Othello recants his threat; Iago must continue to be honest. By way of apology, Othello explains his agorizng conflict: "I think my wife be honest, and think she is not." He describes his new hateful image of Desdemona; her face is "now begrim'd and black as my own face." Othello now changes his threat to a humble request for satisfaction; then, his determination returning, he asserts that he *will* be satisfied. (Othello has played right into Iago's hands; the villain has a handkerchief, we may recall.) "But how? how satisfied, my lord?" Iago asks. Do you want to see the actual act of adultery being committed? This would be hard to bring about, but "imputation and strong circumstances" are easily produced. Othello bites. "Give a living reason she's disloyal," he asks Iago. Now Iago tells how he has recently slept in the same bed with Cassio and has heard him mutter various compromising things about Desdemona in his sleep. Othello reacts violently to this tale: "O monstrous! monstrous!"

Affecting moderation, Iago says, "Nay, this was but a dream." (He has something more tangible to offer.) Iago now introduces the matter of the handkerchief "spotted with strawberries," which, luckily, he has acquired only a few moments ago. Cleverly improvising, Iago claims that he has seen Cassio wipe his beard with it. (Apparently, Othello has not noticed that it was this same handkerchief which Desdemona had offered him for binding his forehead.) Iago declares that "it speaks against her with other proofs." Utterly convinced for this moment Othello completely loses control: "All my fond love thus do I blow to heaven . . . / Arise, black vengeance, from the hollow hell!" Agitated by his terrible passion, he is reduced to calling for "blood, blood, blood," as Iago prods him to further depths by urging patience, and by suggesting that he may change his mind.

In the heat of anger, Othello swears never to change his mind and, like the icy currents of the Pontic sea, never to change his course, never to look back, never to cease till he has had his revenge. Kneeling, he takes a sacred vow on these words. Iago kneels beside the crazed Moor and adds his own oath, swearing to serve the wronged Othello in "what bloody business ever."

Othello accepts Iago's fellowship in revenge and consigns Cassio to Iago's sword. Iago now agrees to exchange Cassio's friendship for the Moor's, but he sustains his role as "honest" Iago by asking that Desdemona be spared. Passionately, Othello denies this request, damning Desdemona as a "lewd minx." He retires to devise a means of killing her, but not before appointing Iago his new lieutenant.

Act III: Scene 4

The scene takes place in front of the castle. Accompanied by Emilia, Desdemona asks the Clown where Cassio "lies" (1. lodges, dwells; 2. speaks falsely, "stabs"). The Clown replies equivocally with puns on "lie," "stab," and "lodge." He fails to produce the information, for he really does not know. In periphrastic terms of a comic nature, the Clown agrees, however, to search out Cassio.

Desdemona tells Emilia that she is disturbed by the loss of her handkerchief; she would rather lose a purse full of money. But she consoles herself (with the dramatically ironic), "And but my noble Moor / Is true of mind and made of no such baseness / As jealous creatures are, it were enough / To put him to ill thinking." (Attention is called here to the importance of the handkerchief in the plot and to Othello's usually unsuspecting nature. Desdemona will be unable to recognize Othello's jealousy when she sees it, for she has a decidedly different view of his character.) Surprised that a wife can so describe her husband, Emilia inquires, "Is Othello not jealous?" Emphatically, Desdemona replies, "I think the sun where he was born / Drew all such humours from him."

Othello enters and takes Desdemona's hand. Dissembling affection, he says her hand is moist. Desdemona interprets "moist" to mean that she has not been dried by age and sorrow, but Othello says that it is a sign of "fruitfulness and a liberal heart" (wantonness is suggested). In pretended jest, he prescribes loss of liberty, fasting, and prayer as a remedy for the "sweating devil" (sprit of sexual desire), which he finds in her hand. It is a noble hand, Othello continues, and a "frank" one. Desdemona replies that her hand is indeed a "frank" one (meaning "generous, magnanimous"), for it was this hand that gave her heart to Othello.

Following this mingled conversation in which Desdemona playfully reverses Othello's insinuating diagnosis, Desdemona informs her husband that she has sent for Cassio to speak to Othello. Othello ignores this piece of information and, claiming a cold in the head, asks for her handkerchief. Desdemona expresses regret that she does not have it with her. Othello reproves her for not having it and then gives an account of why the handkerchief is so important. Since the handkerchief plays so important a part in the plot machinery of the play, the description is repeated here.

> That handkerchief
> Did an Egyptian to my mother give.
> She was a charmer, and could almost read
> The thoughts of people. She told her, while she kept it,
> 'Twould make her amiable and subdue my father
> Entirely to her love; but if she lost it
> Or made a gift of it, my father's eye
> Should hold her loathly, and his spirits should hunt
> After new fancies. She, dying, gave it me,
> And bid me, when my fate would have me wive,
> To give it her. I did so; and take heed ont';
> Make it a darling like your precious eye.
> To lose't or give't away were such perdition
> As nothing else could match.

"There's magic in the web of it," Othello assures the distressed wife. It was sewn by a two-hundred-year-old Sybil in "prophetic fury" and "dy'd in mummy which the skilful / Conserv'd of maiden's hearts."

Desdemona's surprise and distress mount as she listens to this tale. She cannot produce the handkerchief, but she denies that it is lost. (This is Desdemona's first deception, and, as we shall see, it will contribute to her ultimate destruction.) Artfully, she refuses to fetch the handkerchief, claiming that Othello has used the story as a trick to dissuade her from discussing Cassio.

Repeatedly, Othello insists on seeing the handkerchief, while Desdemona answers each of his demands with a plea for Cassio. Othello leaves in a rage.

As Othello departs, Emilia repeats the question she had asked prior to this angry interview, "Is not this man jealous?" (This time, however, the question is rhetorical.) Desdemona confesses, "I ne'er saw this before." (His wife is the first to note that Othello has changed.) She repeats her concern for the lost handkerchief, but Emilia, still wondering over Othello's strange behavior, merely reflects on the fickleness of men, "They eat us hungrily, and when they are full, / They belch us."

Iago and Cassio now join the ladies. Iago has been insisting that Cassio importune Desdemona once more. Cassio asks Desdemona for a final decision; he does not want to keep pleading. If his reinstatement is denied, he will seek some other fortune. Regretfully, Desdemona explains her situation. She has been pressing his suit, but Othello is not in a good mood, his "humour" has altered. In reply to Iago's question, Emilia says that Othello has just gone away "in strange unquietness." Iago pretends to be surprised at the news. He has seen Othello maintain his calm in the fiercest heat of battle, even when his brother's life was destroyed. "Something of moment" must be disturbing the Moor. Desdemona urges Iago to see Othello.

Latching on to Iago's suggestions that something important is disturbing her husband, the humble Desdemona decides it is some business with Venice or some matter of state. Apologizing for her husband, Desdemona explains to Emilia that men frequently mistreat their wives when they have great worries on their minds. "We must not think men are gods," she cautions Emilia, blaming herself for thinking unkindly of Othello before Iago's suggestion clarified his outrageous behavior. Emilia, more realistic, prays to heaven that state-matters are truly the cause of Othello's conduct, and not some jealousy of Desdemona. Thinking of her own husband, Emilia asserts that wives need not give their husbands cause for jealousy, for " 'tis a monster / Begot upon itself, born on itself."

Despite her awareness of Othello's ill-humor, Desdemona decides to find him and once more advance Cassio's cause, this time "to my uttermost." Cassio is asked to await her return.

As Desdemona and Emilia leave, Cassio is left alone onstage. Bianca arrives and is greeted with much familiarity by Cassio, who states that he was planning to pay her a visit very shortly. Bianca too was just on her way to Cassio's lodgings, for, she complains, he has not been to see her for an entire week. This is a long time for lovers. Cassio explains that his absence was owing to the pressure of "leaden thoughts," but he promises to make up for his absence when he can do so without interruption. As if to turn the conversation, Cassio gives Bianca a handkerchief and asks her to copy its pattern. Bianca is immediately suspicious that the handkerchief has come from some new mistress. Cassio explains that he found it in his chamber and does not know its owner. Before he must return it, he would like to have a copy of the design, which he finds most attractive.

Cassio asks Bianca to leave him, for he is awaiting the General and does not want to be found with a woman. Bianca is reluctant to go; she asks Cassio to walk her a bit of the way and presses him to dine with her that night. Anxious to get rid of her, Cassio promises to see her soon, and Bianca takes her leave as the scene ends.

Act IV: Scene 1

The scene is again the yard before the castle. Iago and Othello are in the midst of an earnest conversation. (Their opening remarks are somewhat ambiguous, but they may be interpreted in terms of the lines which follow.) Iago asks Othello if he will think a kiss in private an "unauthoriz'd" (unwarrantable) thing, and Othello insists that he does not think but knows it to be so. Next, Iago asks if it is possible for Desdemona to spend an hour in bed with a lover and mean no harm. Othello, of course, asserts that this is impossible. Iago contends that as long as they do nothing, they are merely committing a minor sin, "But if I give my wife a handkerchief—"

Reminded of the handkerchief, Othello compares it to a "raven o'er the infected house." Iago pretends to make light of the handkerchief (implying that he has more incriminating evidence to report). Cassio has admitted his intimacies with Desdemona. Othello is thoroughly shaken. His mind gives way, and he utters a series of disjointed and confused thoughts (all highly relevant to the situation, but without syntax) before falling into a trance. Chanting diabolically, Iago gloats, "Work on / My medicine, work! Thus credulous fools are caught."

Cassio enters at this point. In reply to his question, Iago states that the Moor has "fall'n into an epilepsy." Refusing his assistance, Iago asks Cassio to withdraw, promising to speak to him after the General recovers. Cassio leaves.

As soon as Othello recovers, Iago asks about his head. Othello imagines he is being mocked (that an allusion has been made to the horns on his head, traditionally ascribed to cuckolded husbands). Iago denies having made such an allusion. He wishes Othello would behave like a man, or, if he feels like a beast (with cuckold's horns), then he should be comforted in the knowledge that the city is full of such beasts. In fact, Othello is better off than millions of men who do not know they are being deceived. No, Iago asserts, he personally would rather know the truth about his wife, and knowing his own nature (vengeful), he knows what she would be (punished). Othello is impressed by Iago's wisdom.

Next, Iago informs Othello that Cassio had been there and that he will come back. Othello is to conceal himself, and he will overhear the truth from Cassio's own lips. Othello hides.

Cassio returns, and Iago begins to question him not about Desdemona, as Othello has been led to believe, but about Bianca, the local prostitute.

Iago starts a stream of rough banter, alleging, among other things, that Bianca has spread the rumor that Cassio intends to marry her. Cassio thinks this is a hilarious joke. Meanwhile, Othello in his hiding place interprets the laughter as Cassio's exultation over his conquest. Bianca returns at this point and angrily shakes Desdemona's handkerchief in Cassio's face. On second thought, she has decided that Cassio has been unfaithful to her, that the handkerchief is "some minx's token," and that she would be a fool to "take out" (copy) its work. When Bianca leaves in a huff, Iago sends Cassio after her to quiet her down, learning first that Cassio will dine at Bianca's that night. Othello comes out of hiding prepared to murder his former officer.

Othello claims his heart has turned to stone, yet when he thinks of Desdemona's sweetness, her skill in embroidery, in music, her plenteous wit and invention, he is deeply moved, "But yet the pity of it, Iago! O Iago, the pity of it, Iago!"

Othello is now totally convinced of Desdemona's guilt. Determined to kill her, he asks Iago to get him poison. But Iago suggests a more symbolic revenge: "Strangle her in . . . the bed she hath contaminated." Othello is pleased with the justice of this method. Iago undertakes to dispose of Cassio.

A trumpet sounds. Desdemona enters in the company of her cousin Lodovico, the Venetian ambassador, and other attendants. As Othello reads the letter he has received from Venice, Desdemona explains to Lodovico that there has been a misunderstanding between Othello and

Cassio, in which she hopes her cousin will clear up. Othello listens to her conversation, interjecting ominous remarks, which he pretends are commentaries on the letter. Angered by Desdemona's reference to "the love I bear to Cassio," Othello asks her if she is wise (that is, to admit her love publicly). When she expresses her pleasure at Cassio's appointment as Othello's deputy-governor, he becomes violently angry and publicly strikes her. Everyone in the distinguished assembly is shocked. Othello's private torture is now public property. He deepens the effect of his barbarous conduct by hinting at her promiscuity: "Sir, she can turn, and turn, and yet go on / And turn again." Lodovico can make no sense of the behavior of the "noble Moor," the man of undaunted courage and monumental dignity, whom he had hitherto known.

After Othello storms out, Iago insinuates that Othello is often brutal and could get worse. But after arousing Lodovico's curiosity, he puritanically asserts: "It is not honesty in me to speak / What I have seen and known." The innuendo strikes home at once. Urged to observe the Moor himself, Lodovico departs, convinced that he has been "deceived in him [Othello]."

Act IV: Scene 2

In a room within the castle, Othello questions Emilia about Desdemona's activities. She assures him that Desdemona is honest. Cassio has been with her, of course, but never alone. Emilia was never sent to fetch a fan, gloves, mask, or anything else. In short, Emilia insists, she is ready to wager her soul on Desdemona's virtue. "That's strange," Othello reflects, as he sends Emilia to call Desdemona. But as soon as Emilia leaves, Othello decides that, although Emilia has made an adequate defense of her mistress, it is no more than any bawd would do. Besides, Emilia is a subtle whore, who keeps a private room full of villainous secrets on the one hand, and on the other, she will kneel and pray with the most virtuous. Othello says he has seen her do it (that is, pray). And with that, he dismisses her testimony.

Emilia returns, escorting Desdemona. Gently, Othello invites Desdemona to ". . . come hither." Then, dangerously, he tells her to look into his eyes, to show her face. Turning to Emilia, he bids her get to work, close the door, attend to her "mystery" (duty, the function of a madam of a brothel).

He urges Desdemona to damn herself by swearing (falsely, he presumes) that she is his wife, and to be "double-damned" by swearing she is honest.

At last Desdemona realizes that the Moor is jealous. She swears she is faithful but to no avail. Othello is a pathetic sight. He shooes her away and bursts into tears. (Desdemona is thoroughly perplexed; she cannot believe he means his accusations and still thinks "something of moment" is the cause of his suffering. But what connections has that with her?) She asks if he suspects her father, Brabantio, to have been behind his recall to Venice. If so, she implores, he must not blame her, for she too has lost Brabantio's favor. Moved by self-pity, Othello says he could have endured the most painful afflictions, but to be discarded by the woman he has loved or to keep her "as a cistern for foul toads / To knot and gender in" —this is beyond endurance. (The image of adultery as a cistern full of toads is particularly foul and conveys precisely the horror Othello felt for this act. Other horrific images and outrageous epithets follow.) He compares Desdemona's chastity to "summer flies in the shambles"; she is a "fair paper" inscribed with "whore," a "public commoner," an "impudent strumpet," and "heaven stops the nose" at her rank smell. Desdemona asserts her innocence time and again, but she can do nothing with this madman. Sarcastically, Othello apologizes for mistaking her for "cunning whore of Venice, / That married with Othello," and he calls for Emilia with several equally unsavory epithets. Concluding his fantastic conception (the pretense that he is visiting a brothel), he pays Emilia the madam's fee and asks her to unlock the door and keep secret his visit.

Othello leaves Desdemona totally dazed; she describes her condition to Emilia as "half-asleep." (She has been through a nightmare and has not yet fully awakened.) In a grotesque bit of word-play on "my lord" and "thy lord," Desdemona pathetically argues with Emilia that since "my lord" is the same man to both of them, Emilia's lord, Iago, is Desdemona's lord too. She orders that her wedding sheets be put upon her bed and that Iago be called.

Emilia returns promptly with Iago. Desdemona is too full of self-pity at this point to state her wishes clearly. Emilia tells Iago that Othello has abused and "bewhored" Desdemona. Desdemona asks, "Am I that name, Iago?" (Delicately, she refuses to use the word "whore.") Covering his malicious delight, Iago innocently asks, "What name, fair lady?" But Desdemona is evasive, "Such as she says my lord did say I was." Emilia, suffering from fewer inhibitions, bluntly states. "He call'd her whore." A fine thing, indeed, Emilia broods, to call a woman whore who has refused fashionable marriages, and has left her father and her country to be with her husband. With sarcastic virulence, Emila repeats all the inquiries Othello had made of her. Finally, Emilia states her suspicion that some slanderer has been at work. She tells Iago that it was some such "base notorious knave" that caused him to suspect her with the Moor.

In another piece of dramatic irony, Desdemona asks Iago for advice. How can she win her lord again, she asks the villain. Iago tells her not to worry; it is some business of state that has caused him to act this way. Trumpets sound, announcing dinner which the Venetian envoys are to attend. Desdemona and Emilia leave for it.

The scene concludes with a conversation between Roderigo and Iago. Roderigo has begun to suspect Iago. He tells him that "your words and performances are not kin together"; Iago's words and deeds do not correspond. Roderigo has given Iago enough jewels for Desdemona to corrupt a nun. (Obviously, the jewels have been pocketed by Iago.) Roderigo threatens to demand them of Desdemona. If they are forthcoming, he will repent his "unlawful solicitation," if not, he will demand satisfaction of Iago. Iago devises another impromptu scheme. Othello will be leaving with Desdemona, unless some accident causes him to stay. Now, if Cassio were removed, if he were incapable of taking Othello's place, the Moor and his wife would have to stay on Cyprus. If Roderigo, will undertake to knock out Cassio's brains, Iago will be there to second him. It is high supper time as the scene ends.

Act IV: Scene 3

Othello, Lodovico, Desdemona, Emilia, and attendants are assembled in another room in the castle. As the scene opens the supper has ended and Lodovico is taking his leave. Othello offers to walk with his guest part of his way. He orders Desdemona to go to bed for the night, to dismiss Emilia, and await his return.

When the ladies are left alone, Emilia remarks that Othello looks gentler than he did before. (This is the calm before the next storm.) Desdemona asks for her nightclothes and hurriedly prepares for bed, for fear of displeasing her husband. As she undresses, she expresses her love for the Moor even though he is stubborn, scolding, and angry. Emilia reports that she has laid the bed with the wedding sheets as Desdemona had ordered. As if presaging doom, Desdemona's thoughts fly to death. She asks Emilia to shroud her in her wedding sheets should she die before her attendant. Then she tells Emilia about a song she once learned from her mother's maid—a girl called Barbary—whose lover went insane and forsook her. The song is called "Willow." It is an old song, Desdemona recalls, "but it express'd her fortune, / And she died singing it." That song has been in her mind all night. She has all she can do to keep from singing it, Desdemona says, and she tries to forget her troubles with idle chatter about Lodovico. But the diversion doesn't work, and Desdemona sings poignantly: "The poor soul sat sighing by a sycamore tree, / Sing all a green willow."

Desdemona asks Emilia whether there actually are women who commit adultery; she would not do such a thing for all the world. Emilia replies,

"The world's a huge thing. It is a great price for a small vice." She would not do such a thing for a trifle, but "who would not make her husband a cuckold to make him a monarch?" In a more serious vein, Emilia argues that it is the indifference and misbehavior of husbands that lead women to sin. Emilia's thesis is that women have the right to live by the same moral standard as men.

Act V: Scene 1

The scene shifts to a street in Cyprus near Bianca's house. Iago and Roderigo are preparing to ambush Cassio. Roderigo has misgivings about murdering Cassio, but he reasons that death is merely the departure of a man, and this murder may bring him satisfying results. Iago is also uncertain about the outcome, but he sees enormous gains no matter what happens. Roderigo is to do the actual killing; if Roderigo survives, Iago will have to restore the jewels intended for Desdemona and which Iago has misappropriated. It is to Iago's advantage that Roderigo dies in the encounter wtih Cassio. Cassio's death is also desirable, for "he hath a daily beauty in his life / That makes me ugly." Besides, Cassio would expose Iago's lies to Othello if he ever learned of them. No, Iago must have them both out of the way.

Cassio arrives; Roderigo attacks. As he feared, Roderigo's onslaught is unsuccessful. In fact, Cassio is protected by a coat of mail and succeeds in wounding Roderigo. Iago now emerges from concealment, wounds Cassio in the leg, and flees. Othello, hearing Cassio's cries, is delighted with Iago's work ("O brave Iago, honest and just / That hast such a noble sense of thy friend's wrong"). He leaves without examining Cassio's supposed corpse.

Both wounded men lie on different parts of the stage, calling for help. At a distance, Lodovico and Gratiano hear their shouts. Iago returns with a light and finds Cassio. "What villains have done this?" he asks. Iago calls Lodovico and Gratiano to help Cassio and goes off in "search for the bloody thieves." Finding Roderigo, Iago stabs him to death. Lodovico commends Iago on his timely action, and all turn to assist Cassio. Roderigo's last words have been, "O damned Iago! O inhuman dog!"

Bianca rushes out of her lodging and is terribly distraught. On the spur of the moment, Iago decides to implicate Bianca in the ambush of Cassio. He tells the gentlemen that he suspects "this trash / To a part in this injury." Next, he feigns the discovery of Roderigo, whom the Venetians, Lodovico and Gratiano, know. Through artfully phrased questions, Iago continues to cast suspicion on Bianca for engineering the death of Roderigo. Cassio is put in a chair, and the General's surgeon is called.

Emilia arrives and learns from Iago that Cassio's misfortunes are "the fruits of whoring." There is a brief exchange between the two women in which Bianca claims (perhaps with justice) to be as honest as Emilia. Bianca freely admits that Cassio "supp'd" at her house, and Iago uses this statement to charge her with the crime. Emilia is sent to inform Othello and Desdemona of the disaster, and Iago (once more foreshadowing his own fall) privately expresses doubt: "This is the night / That either makes me or fordoes me quite."

Act V: Scene 2

The final scene of the play shifts to a chamber in Othello's castle. Desdemona is in bed. Carrying a candle, Othello enters. He sees Desdemona asleep and beings to speak: "It is the cause, it is the cause, my soul."

Othello declares that he will not name the "cause" to the "chaste" stars. Looking down on fair Desdemona, he declines to shed her blood or scar "that whiter skin of hers than snow / And smooth as monumental alabaster." (He plans suffocation, which leaves no marks.)

Murder must be done, and darkness is needed for the crime. "Put out the light, and then put out the light," Othello says, addressing the candle. Playing on two meanings of the word "light" (1. candlelight; 2. light of life), Othello says, "If I quench thee / the taper /. . ./ I can again thy former light restore." But the light of Desdemona, once extinguished, is out forever. He addresses Desdemona as a "pattern of excelling nature" and compares her to a rose, which, once plucked, must wither. Moved by his reflections, he kisses his sleeping wife. So affecting is that kiss that Othello is tempeted to break his sword of "justice." He is even brought to tears, cruel tears, but he soon regains his former resolve.

Desdemona wakens and timidly asks, "Will you come to bed, my lord?" (Stern in his sense of justice, Othello does not want to damn Desdemona's soul.) "Have you pray'd?" he asks. He urges her to confess her sins before being killed. "Talk you of killing"? Desdemona asks, apprised for the first time in the play of Othello's full intentions. "Heaven have mercy on me," Desdemona cries. She expresses her hope that he does not mean this, but she sees the rolling of his eyes and is reduced to terror. At last Othello tells her the cause of his anger: "That handkerchief which I so lov'd and gave thee / Thou gav'st to Cassio." Sensibly, she tells him to send for the man and ask him. She pleads with Othello, telling him that she never did offense to him in her life, never loved Cassio "but with such general warranty of heaven / As I might love." Angrily, Othello responds that he himself saw Cassio with the handkerchief in his hand. His fury increasing, he blames Desdemona for turning his sacrifice into a murder, that is, for making him angry so that he will kill in passion and not in cool justice. (He regards the calculated killing as a "sacrifice" to the God of justice.) As for Cassio, he is dead. Ambiguously, Desdemona cries, "Alas! he is betray'd and I undone." She bursts into tears, which Othello interprets as grief for Cassio: "Out, strumpet! Weep'st thou for him to my face?" Smothering her pleas for mercy, he kills her before she has prayed.

Suddenly, there is a knocking at the door. It is Emilia coming to report Roderigo's death and the attack on Cassio. The knocking continues as Othello tries to make sure that Desdemona does not linger in pain. "By-and-by," Othello calls, assuring himself that Desdemona is dead. He surmises correctly that Emilia has come to report on Cassio: "If she come in, she'll sure speak to my wife." Suddenly, the awful realization occurs. "My wife! my wife! I have no wife." (These words recall Desdemona's grim jest on the loss of "my lord" and echo hollowly in the death chamber.)

Emilia continues to call. In a moment, Othello answers, drawing the curtains around Desdemona's corpse. Emilia enters with the news, that foul murder has been done. Before she can finish her message, Othello sums up the deeds of the night:

> . . . It is the very error of the moon;
> She come more nearer earth than she was wont,
> And makes men mad.

A death cry comes from Desdemona, "O, falsely, falsely murther'd." Emilia discovers her dying mistress; "O who hath done this deed?" she cries. "Nobody, I myself," Desdemona gasps before she dies. Othello feigns innocence momentarily, then passionately charges, "She's, like a liar, gone to burning Hell! /'Twas I that kill'd her." Then her lie makes her more than the angel and Othello the blacker devil for killing such a one, Emilia retorts. They exchange their judgments of Desdemona's virtues and remain deadlocked on either side of the question until Othello says, "Thy husband knew it all." Emilia is stunned. "My husband?" she repeats over and over again. "I say thy husband. Dost understand the word?" Emilia curses Iago's soul and turns her fury against Othello, whom she now calls Desdemona's "filthy bargain."

Emilia yells for help and, at the same time, spits abuses at the Moor: "O gull! O dolt! / As ignorant as dirt!" Montano, Gratiano, Iago, and others respond to her cry. At once Emilia demands that Iago explain and clear himself. Iago equivocates at first, but he is forced to admit that he accused Desdemona. Emilia discloses the murder to the shocked assembly.

Gratiano, Desdemona's uncle, finds some consolation in knowing that Brabantio has died before this calamity. Othello explains the cause of the murder and mentions the handkerchief. Now Emilia understands the whole plot. Stricken with shame and remorse, Emilia insists on speaking. Iago draws his sword, threatening to quiet her forever, but Emilia shows the episode of the dropped handkerchief in its true light.

Othello runs at Iago when he hears the truth, but he is restrained by Montano and disarmed. Iago stabs Emilia and flees. Now dying, Emilia asks to be buried by the side of her mistress. Montano takes off after the villain, and Gratiano goes to guard the door, leaving Othello and Emilia alone.

Othello castigates himself for losing his sword to Montano. He feels there is no point in loving now that Desdemona is dead. Meanwhile, Emilia has become delirious and addresses her dead mistress. Singing snatches of the "Willow" song, Emilia defends her mistress to the "cruel Moor" with her dying breath.

Recalling that he has another sword in his chamber, Othello finds it and calls for Gratiano, whom he addresses as "Uncle." When Gratiano enters, Othello shows him the weapon, boasts of his skill in using it, and in a torrent of self-recrimination, mourns for his dead wife.

He delivers a long, heart-rending speech. He knows that he has come to the "very sea-mark of my utmost sail"; it is his "journey's end." "Where should Othello go?" he asks. He looks upon the corpse of Desdemona—"O ill-starred wench! / Pale as they smock!" On judgment day the look that she bears in death will send his soul to hell. His surge of wild rhetoric ends in a moan; "O Desdemona! Desdemona! dead! O! O! O!"

Iago is brought back, a prisoner who has in part confessed to his "villainy." Othello succeeds in wounding him on his next try. Then, Othello asks forgiveness of Cassio, who has been brought in on his chair. He wants to know why "that demi-devil," Iago, has ensnared his body and soul. Intractable to the end, Iago replies, "Demand me nothing; what you know, you know / From this time forth I never will speak word." What is not confirmed about Iago's plot by various witnesses is supplied by letters found on the person of Roderigo. The details of the story are clarified but the tragedy cannot be undone.

Othello is to be relieved of his command; he will be returned to Venice as a prisoner until his case is disposed of. But Othello has other plans. In his final speech, he says Venice is aware of the service he has rendered her. Lodovico and the others are to report to him as he truly is, exaggerating nothing, casting malice on nothing: "then must you speak / Of one that lov'd not wisely but too well." Othello punctuates the end of his speech by stabbing himself to death: "Set you down this; . . . / I took by th' throat the circumcised dog / And smote him—thus."

Before dying, Othello addresses the body of Desdemona: "I kiss'd thee ere I killed thee. No way but this— / Killing myself, to die upon a kiss." He falls upon her bed. In the briefest of eulogies, Cassio says, ". . . He was great of heart." Lodovico expresses the feelings of all when he calls Iago, "O Spartan dog / More fell than anguish, hunger, or the sea!" and consigns the "censure of this hellish villain" to Cassio.

A fitting conclusion to this summary of the tragedy of *Othello* is Dr. Samuel Johnson's evaluation of the play as a whole. No one can say more in a few words: "The beauties of this play impress themselves so strongly upon the attention of the reader, that they can draw no aid from critical illustration. The fiery openness of Othello, magnanimous, artless, ardent in his affection, inflexible in his resolution, and obdurate in his revenge; the cool malignity of Iago, silent in his resentment, subtle in his designs, and studious at once of his interest and his vengeance; the soft simplicity of Desdemona, confident of merit, and conscious of innocence, her artless perseverance in her suit, and her slowness to suspect that she can be suspected, are such proofs of Shakespeare's skill in human nature, as, I suppose, it is vain to seek in any modern writer. The gradual progress which Iago makes in the Moor's conviction, and the circumstances which he employs to inflame him, are so artfully natural, that, though it will not be said of him as he says of himself, that he is *a man not easily jealous,* yet we cannot but pity him when at last we find him *perplexed in the extreme.*"

Romeo and Juliet

ESCALUS, *Prince of Verona.*
PARIS, *a young nobleman, kinsman to the Prince.*
MONTAGUE } *heads of two houses at variance with each other.*
CAPULET
OLD MAN, *cousin to Capulet.*
ROMEO, *son to Montague.*
MERCUTIO, *kinsman to the Prince, and friend to Romeo.*
BENVOLIO, *nephew to Montague, and friend to Romeo.*
TYBALT, *nephew to Capulet's wife.*
PETRUCHIO, *of the house of Capulet.*
FRIAR LAURENCE } *Franciscans.*
FRIAR JOHN
BALTHASAR, *servant to Romeo.*
SAMSON
GREGORY } *servants to Capulet.*
CLOWN
PETER, *servant to Juliet's nurse.*
ABRAHAM, *servant to Montague.*
APOTHECARY.
Three MUSICIANS.
PAGE *to Paris; another* PAGE; *an* OFFICER.

MONTAGUE'S WIFE.
CAPULET'S WIFE.
JULIET, *daughter to Capulet.*
NURSE *to Juliet, called* ANGELICA.

CITIZENS *of Verona; several* MEN *and* WOMEN; MASKERS, GUARDS, WATCHMEN, SERVINGMEN, *and* ATTENDANTS.

Romeo and Juliet

Prologue

The play opens with a sonnet spoken by a chorus. (Actually, the prologue was probably spoken by a single actor, the same actor who will speak the sonnet at the beginning of Act II.) These fourteen lines outline the action of the play and its effect on the lives of the characters. In Verona, a pleasant Italian town, two equally important families which have long harbored grudges against each other break out into open feud. Romeo, son of the Montague family, and Juliet, daughter of the Capulet family, fall fatally in love, and it is only through their love and their death together that the long strife between the two families can also die. This "death-mark'd" love is the subject of the play.

Act I: Scene 1

Sampson and Gregory, two of Capulet's servants, armed because of the long-standing feud, are joking with each other as they walk in Verona. Sampson declares that he will "not carry coals," that being the work of laborers. He means that he will not submit to being humiliated by the servants of Montague. Gregory retorts that if they did carry coals, they would be colliers, and colliers had the reputation of being dirty and of cheating. Sampson returns the pun so as to clarify his meaning: if "we be in choler [anger], we'll draw [swords]." Gregory continues to banter, deliberately misunderstanding Sampson, and implying that he is a coward who is slow to draw his sword and quick to run when faced with danger. Sampson enjoys being teased and finally gets the upper hand by announcing that he will either cut off the heads of the maidens of Montague, "or their maidenheads, take it in what sense thou wilt." Gregory quibbles and the two exchange a few more bawdy jokes, until they find themselves actually drawing swords, because Abraham and Balthasar, servants of the Montague family, appear.

Facing the Montague family servants with drawn swords, Sampson and Gregory continue to joke with each other, but more furtively. Sampson again makes a phallic reference by saying "My naked weapon is out," and Gregory still implies that Sampson will run away with fright. Yet it is Sampson who takes up the challenge and shows his bravado first by provoking a fight. At this moment Gregory, who has been urging the fight, sees Tybalt, a Capulet, coming, and tells Sampson to assert that his master is better. What Gregory has not seen is Benvolio, a Montague, coming from the opposite direction. The four servants draw swords and begin to fight.

Coming quickly upon the fighting men, Benvolio tries to stop them, saying, "Put up your swords; you know not what you do." But Tybalt, seeing Benvolio with his sword unsheathed, derides him for fighting among cowardly menials. Although Benvolio wants only to stop the fight and "keep the peace," Tybalt is furious, and declares that he hates peace as much as he hates hell and the Montagues. Benvolio and Tybalt fall to fighting and are joined by more Capulets and Montagues. The sound of clashing swords is joined by the clubs of Officers of the Peace, who call out for the downfall of both the feuding houses that disturb Verona's peace.

Lord Capulet and Lord Montague now come on the scene. Both are anxious to join the fight but are restrained by their wives. It is only when Escalus, Prince of Verona, arrives with his followers that fighting ceases. Prince Escalus scolds both families bitterly, calling them "enemies to peace" and therefore "beasts" instead of men, who have three times broken the peace of their town and its people, making even old men take sides. He declares that the penalty for another fight shall be death.

Only Lord and Lady Montague and Benvolio remain as the others depart. Benvolio explains how the feud began again. But Lady Montague is more concerned about her son, Romeo, whom she has not seen that day. Benvolio did see him, walking at dawn without company and clearly preferring to be left alone. Montague comments that Romeo has been in such a mood for quite awhile, weeping and mooning, staying out all night but going in as soon as the sun rises, locking himself in his room with the curtains drawn as if to make "himself an artificial night." Montague tells Benvolio that he does not know the cause, but "would as willingly give cure as know." At this point they see Romeo coming, and Benvolio tells the Lord and Lady to "step aside" while he attempts to find out what is bothering Romeo.

Yes, Romeo is in love, but the lady does not "favour" him, so he mourns, and the hours seem long. Romeo would like to change the subject away from Benvolio's questions, but when Benvolio presses him, he pours out his heart in a series of paradoxes: "O brawling love! O loving hate! . . . O heavy lightness! O serious vanity!/ Misshapen chaos of well-seeming forms!/ Feather of lead, bright smoke, cold fire, sick health!" Romeo is miserable, forlorn, and hang-dog, because he is in love, and he tells Benvolio that he accepts this change in himself as part of love: "This is not Romeo, he's some other where." He loves a woman who does not love him, and who insists on remaining chaste. Romeo refuses to say who she is. Benvolio suggests that Romeo try to forget her and begin looking at other pretty girls, but the young lover insists that he cannot, that such a thing is impossible. They leave, and Benvolio goes to report to Lord Montague.

Act I: Scene 2

Having met the Montagues, we now meet Lord Capulet, walking through Verona's streets with Paris, a relative of Prince Escalus. They are returning from visiting the Prince, and as they walk they discuss the recently imposed penalty for further feuding. Capulet feels that men of their age should be able to keep peace. Paris agrees, but soon turns the conversation to a matter closer to his heart: his wish to marry Capulet's fourteen-year-old daughter, Juliet. They have discussed the suit of marriage before, and Capulet maintains that she is yet too young. He urges Paris to wait two years, when she will be "ripe to be a bride." Capulet hesitates. His words reveal that he loves his daughter deeply, and has placed all his remaining hope on earth in her. Still, he favors the marriage, and if Paris can win Juliet's consent, Capulet will not oppose it. He invites Paris to a party to be held at his house that evening. At the party will be many pretty young girls, "Earth-treading stars that make dark heaven light," and Lord Capulet would have Paris see them all in comparison with Juliet before he makes up his mind.

Capulet has given to one of his servants a list of people whom the servant is to see are invited to his party. The servant cannot read the list, however, and after puzzling over it a bit, he stops two strangers in the street and asks them to read it to him. The strangers are none other than Romeo and Benvolio, still discussing Romeo's love-sick state and what to do about it. Benvolio again tells his friend, in a series of images, that a new love affair alone will cure old love-sickness. Again Romeo tries to turn the conversation and, in the next breath, bewails his state. The servant then interrupts and Romeo, after jesting with him, reads the list of guests to be invited, as the servant reveals, to Capulet's party that evening. The servant adds, before departing, that if they are not Montagues, they will surely be welcome. One of the guests whose name Romeo read out was the fair Rosaline.

Romeo and Benvolio promptly decide to "crash" the party. It suits the purposes of both. Kindly Benvolio sees it as a chance for Romeo to compare Rosaline with other young ladies. He hopes she will not withstand the comparison, and that this romance will be cured by a new one. Of course, Romeo protests fervently, again claiming that this could never be. His language is loaded with contraries and comparisons of his love to religion. But he would be happy to go, just to see her. They depart.

Act I: Scene 3

The scene changes now from Verona's streets to the house of the Capulets, where Lady Capulet is telling the old Nurse to call Juliet. The Nurse swears by the purity she had when she was a twelve-year-old that she *has* called Juliet, and calls again. Juliet comes, obediently. Lady Capulet has something to tell her daughter, and at first tells the Nurse to go, then lets her stay, as she has known Juliet since birth. The mere reference to how long she has known Juliet starts the Nurse onto a string of repetitive memories that both mother and daughter are hard put to bring to a halt. The Nurse knows Juliet's age to the day (two weeks younger than fourteen years), because her own daughter, Susan, was born on the same day and died soon after. Because of these circumstances she had become Juliet's wet nurse, which she remained for three years, until the earthquake. Rambling through her memories, the Nurse remembers the very day when Juliet was weaned from her milk. (This was accomplished, as was the custom in Elizabethan times, by rubbing wormwood, a bitter herb, on the breast. From this the child recoiled.) Even the day before the weaning, the Nurse remembers Juliet had been able to walk by herself, had fallen, and bumped her head. The Nurse's husband had picked up the crying child and jokingly said, "Dost thou fall upon thy face?/Thou wilt fall backward when thou has more wit." At this colorful reference to her own yet far-distant puberty, the baby had stopped crying, as though she had understood and agreed. The Nurse, delighted at the old joke, especially as Juliet is now of age, repeats it twice, with vigor and laughter. She relishes all the details and the appropriateness of the sexual reference. She is enjoying herself so well, that not until Juliet has reminded her does she begin to run down, and only adds that she wants to see Juliet married once.

Marriage is indeed the subject that Lady Capulet has called Juliet to discuss, and she promptly asks her daughter how she feels about marrying. Juliet replies, "It is an honour that I dream not of." The nurse, from her own point of view, praises Juliet for that answer, saying marriage is definitely an honor. Lady Capulet takes Juliet's reply as it was meant, with the emphasis on the word "dream," and encourages her to think about marriage, as Paris wishes to marry her. Both the Lady and the Nurse consider Paris a flower of manhood, and Lady Capulet launches into a long rhymed speech, comparing Paris to a book which is beautiful to see and to read, and which only lacks a binding: that is, a wife. She wants Juliet to see him at their party this very evening, and she urges Juliet to consider marrying him. Juliet answers, "I'll look to like, if looking liking move." A servant comes to announce that the party is about to begin without them, and the scene ends.

Act I: Scene 4

Romeo and Benvolio, along with a retinue of masked entertainers and torchbearers, are on their way through Verona's streets to Lord Capulet's party. With them is Mercutio, who is objective, as he is not a member of either of the feuding families, but is a relative of the Prince. He is also Romeo's close friend and confidant. It was traditional that masked gate-crashers should deliver a humorous "apology" for their intrusion, but to Romeo's question about what their apology shall be, Benvolio replies that there should be none. "Let them measure us by what they will,/We'll measure them a measure [dance out a formal dance pattern], and be gone." Benvolio prefers to overlook such usual frivolities, perhaps because they are going among enemies. Romeo, still keeping his love-sick attitude, declares that he does not even want to dance, and would rather carry a torch, as torchbearers do not dance. Mercutio chides him and Romeo replies with wit, though still on the same theme, that the "soles" of others' shoes are light for dancing, but his "soul" is too heavy. Mercutio again prods him, and, extending his wit with words still further, Romeo continues to protest that he is so "bound" by love that he cannot "bound," that is, jump and dance about, or rise above the boundaries of ordinary conduct. When Mercutio "cracks" that at this rate, Romeo will be such a burden on love that it will be crushed, Romeo retorts that love is not tender, but rough, and "it pricks like thorn." Mercutio crowns the word-play with his words to the effect that if Romeo would treat love as it treats him, he'd have the better of it.

Mercutio, for one, is exhilarated at the prospect of the party, and although he has been invited—as we know from hearing his name read off the servant's list (see Scene 2 of this Act)—he calls for a mask, then decides his face is ugly enough to serve as a mask, and puts the real one aside. Romeo still wants a torch so that he won't have to dance, and can give over the game and be a spectator. "Dun's the mouse" ("Keep still!") replies Mercutio, and again takes up the game by teasing Romeo for being a stick-in-the-mud. But the raillery slows, for Romeo has had a fore-boding dream.

At Romeo's mention of a dream, Mercutio launches into an extended (forty-two lines) speech of great fantasy and virtuosity, beginning with, "O, then I see Queen Mab hath been with you." It is a real flight of the imagination, and is well-known as the "Queen Mab speech". He calls Queen Mab "the fairies' midwife," and describes her as being as small as a figure carved in the stone of a ring. She comes in a cart made of an empty hazel nut, fitted with parts made of grasshopper wings, spider webs, and moonbeams, and drawn by tiny creatures across the bridges of sleeping men's noses. When she rides through the brains of a lover, he dreams of love. She visits all sorts of people, and whomsoever she visits dreams that night of his greatest desires, or of the chief occupation of his life. Nor are they all good dreams. She is mischievous, Queen Mab, and sometimes she puts knots in horses' manes, a bad omen. She does much, and all that she does is fabulous. Mercutio is cut short by Romeo, who says "Thou talk'st of nothing." Mercutio assents, "True, I talk of dreams,/Which are the children of an idle brain,/Begot of nothing but vain fantasy,/Which is as thin a substance as the air,/And more inconstant than the wind." Benvolio reminds them that they are making themselves late to the party, and before they leave, Romeo adds that for him, they will not be too late, but too early, for he is still filled with premonitions of something about to happen that can only end in his death.

The Queen Mab speech has been used to speed up the mood, but Romeo's foreboding continues too strongly, and he says, before he leaves, "My mind misgives/Some consequence, yet hanging in the stars,/Shall bitterly begin his fearful date/With this night's revels, and expire the term/ Of a despised life closed in my breast/By some vile forfeit of untimely death." This is a crucial speech. It is not spoken in the conceits we have come to associate with Romeo's attitude of love. Indeed, it is a real premonition, for at this festival he meets Juliet, and their love leads directly to their deaths. It is "hanging in the stars", as foretold in the prologue's reference to "star-crossed lovers." (See the discussion of the influence of stars in the Introduction.) Stars are also significant later in the love imagery which Romeo and Juliet will share. The very quality of Romeo and Juliet's love contains its own destruction, and in that sense is fated to end in untimely death.

Act I: Scene 5

After two scenes of preparation, we have come to the party at Lord Capulet's. We must remember that Romeo is here to see Rosaline, and Juliet to consider Paris as a future husband. The scene opens with bustling servants, cheerily fetching and carrying, calling to each other and cursing each other good-naturedly as they complete preparations for the party. As the servants go off, Lord Capulet with Juliet and his household comes to meet the entering guests and the maskers, Romeo among them. Capulet is in a jovial mood as host, a role he clearly enjoys. He threatens to accuse any lady who does not dance of having corns, and he remembers with the men the last time when he came masked to parties and courted ladies. He calls for music, which is struck up, and merrily calls orders to the servants. Again, he comments on the unexpected fun of maskers, and wonders with a cousin at the years passed since they played at such a role. This talk of maskers brings our attention to Romeo, who, amidst the gaiety, has called a servant apart from the crowd, and now asks, in a hushed voice, "What lady is that." The lady is Juliet, whom he sees across the hall, and although the servant cannot answer his question and the room between them is alive with activity, it is as though no one else were in the room besides the two of them. He stands apart, and rapturously praises her: "O, she doth teach the torches to burn bright .... Beauty too rich for use, for earth too dear." His speech is simple, but full of graceful images, and in one word, he foreswears any love he has ever felt before.

Tybalt overhears Romeo speaking, becomes immediately furious at hearing a Montague's voice, calls for his sword, and inventing the excuse that Romeo has come to scorn the traditional Capulet feast, prepares to fight. He is restrained by Capulet himself, who was chastized by the Prince just this morning for feuding, and who now prefers peace. Besides, Capulet is the host, and he does not want his hospitality marred. Forcefully stating, "It is my will," and "He shall be endured," Capulet flies into a small temper himself, and even calls Tybalt "a saucy boy," only to be distracted away by his duties to his guests. Tybalt, fuming at having to be patient, and promising that Romeo's intrusion will end bitterly, retreats.

In the commotion, Romeo has stolen across the room to where Juliet stands, and the two are alone together at one side of the hubbub. There is a precious silence around and between them. Romeo removes his mask, steps toward her, and their first words to each other form a sonnet. In his previous speech about her, Romeo hoped to touch Juliet's hand, and so bless his own hand. Now his first words are, "If I profane with my unworthiest hand/This holy shrine." His lips, "two blushing pilgrims," he offers, as a gentler sin than the touch of his rough hand, but Juliet replies, "Good pilgrim, you do wrong your hand too much," and with natural sweetness tells Romeo that saints and pilgrims kiss by clasping hands. (It is stage tradition that Romeo's masking costume is that of a pilgrim.) If hands kiss, then Romeo's lips will pray, and he prays for a kiss to purge his sin. They kiss, and the feeling between them is so strong that Juliet's only defense against her own heart is to remark, lightly and playfully, "You kiss by the book." The Nurse interrupts them to tell Juliet she is wanted by her mother.

Juliet having gone to her mother, Romeo takes the opportunity to ask the Nurse who her mother is. The reply—that she is Lady Capulet—so astounds Romeo that he cannot answer before the Nurse adds her humorously pedestrian comment that whoever marries Juliet will be a rich man. Romeo responds "My life is my foe's debt." It is a stark reply. Already Romeo feels he would die without Juliet, and so he is in debt for his life to a family enemy. Benvolio, probably noticing his friend's agitation, urges that they leave, but as he is herding Romeo out they are stopped by the hospitable Capulet, offering them food. This they refuse. As they depart, the party ends, and Capulet, satisfied, heads for bed.

Juliet, returning as the guests depart, is more subtle about finding out who Romeo is. She asks her Nurse the names of several departing guests before she asks Romeo's. As her Nurse goes to find out who he is, she comments to herself, "If he be Married,/My grave is like to be my wedding bed." She, too, feels that separation from this new-found lover would be her death. Her Nurse returns with far worse news, that he is a Montague, to which Juliet responds, as bravely and as stricken as Romeo, "My only love sprung from my only hate!" When her Nurse asks her what she is telling herself, she covers it up, saying it is only a rhyme she has just learned. The guests have all gone, and Juliet and the Nurse retire.

Act II: Chorus

The chorus, like the prologue, is a sonnet. The two poems were probably both spoken by the same actor. Here, the important events of the first act are reiterated. Rosaline did not stand as beautiful in comparison with Juliet, and a new affection has replaced the old desire in Romeo's heart. But now, when both Romeo and Juliet are in love, they are prevented from natural courtship by the feud between their families. Only because their passion is so strong will they find the strength and means to carry on their secret courting.

Act II: Scene 1

Romeo, fresh from meeting Juliet at Capulet's party, has ducked away from his comrades in search of solitude in which to contemplate this new state of events. Passing Capulet's orchard, he cannot find heart to take final leave of Juliet's house quite yet. It is as though he were made of the same earth as the orchard, and that earth were recalling him. He jumps over the wall, and fast on his heels come Mercutio and Benvolio, in search of him. Instead of continuing to call Romeo, Mercutio tries to conjure him up like a ghost from the grave. First he invokes Romeo by the image of his love-sickness: sighs, rhymes, and Cupid. When this brings no response, he tries by conjuring an image of Rosaline, whom he supposes, naturally enough, that Romeo still loves. Even playfully sensual images bring no angry stirring in the bushes. Benvolio relents, remarking that since Romeo is blind with love, dark fits him best, and they had best leave him alone. Mercutio now seems half angry, as he laughingly deals his last blows, a few coarse sexual remarks, and then he, too, gives up. They go away, Benvolio commenting that there is no use in looking for someone who does not want to be found. As they leave, Romeo, who has overheard it all, and must be thankful for Benvolio's characteristic tact, mutters to himself a retort to Mercutio's derision: "He jests at scars that never felt a wound." This completes the rhyme scheme of the sequence, and puts a poignant end to the jocose indecencies.

Act II: Scene 2

No sooner have Mercutio's raucous laughter and jokes echoed down the street for the last time, than Romeo sees a window illuminated in Capulet's house, and a girlish figure standing there. "But soft! what light through yonder window breaks?/It is the east, and Juliet is the sun." These words break from him, and begin his famous soliloquy (a speech spoken by one person to himself alone). The conceits of romantic love return, but with new life and vigor. The moon, he thinks, is sick and pale with jealousy at Juliet's brilliance. As she steps full into view on the balcony, Romeo can at first do little but exclaim "O, it is my love!" and wish to tell her so. He feels that she is speaking, and he wants to answer, but falls back shyly. Instead he becomes enraptured with her eyes, calling them stars, and her cheeks, which would make real stars dim in comparison, and again her eyes, which, if they were set in heaven, would make birds think it was daylight by their brightness.

Juliet, high on her balcony, is so filled with emotion at their recent meeting that all she says is "Ay, me!" She does not know her lover is in the garden below, and she is lost in remembering. Romeo, delighted to hear her voice, breathes out praises. To him, she is a "bright angel," a messenger from heaven before whom mortals fall thunderstruck. She lights up the whole sky. But when Juliet speaks again, she is mournful: "O, Romeo, Romeo!" Why must her love be Romeo, a Montague and an enemy? She wishes she could deny her name, and offers, if he loves her, to give up her own name, presumably by marrying him. For only the name is an enemy, not anything that is an inseparable part of Romeo, the man. She vows that if he will give up his name, he shall have all of her in exchange. Romeo, stepping from the shadows, takes her at her word, and declares aloud that he will be Romeo no longer.

782

Hearing Romeo speak up to renounce his name, Juliet is startled, and demands to know what man has overheard her. But he cannot tell her his name, as he has just given it up for love of her. She knows his voice, and when she asks if he is Romeo, a Montague, he replies that he is *not*, if she dislikes the name. In reality, this giving up of names is a token of love, and the pair know that they cannot renounce what they have been born to. Juliet first fears for Romeo's safety, but he brushes this aside, declaring that no walls or danger could daunt his love. He fears more from one hostile glance of her eyes than from the swords of her relatives. Eased by Romeo's assurances, Juliet softens to shy, gentle coquetry: If it were not for the "mask of night," he would see her blush at having been overheard. "Fain would I dwell on form," she says, and withdraw what was spoken, so that they might pursue a formal courtship. But it is too late for that. In the profusion of her love, she asks first that he swear he loves her, and then, if he thinks she is too quickly won, she promises she will deny her love, so that he may court her. Otherwise, she would never deny it.

Romeo wants only to swear his love, and he swears by the moon. Juliet does not want that, as the moon is not constant, but has its phases. If he must swear he must swear by himself, but when he starts to do so, she again cuts him short. She wants no swearing. Their love making has been so beautiful to her that she is afraid it will end as suddenly as it began, like a fateful flash of lightning. Juliet would prefer that the bud of their love have time to blossom. To allow for that, she would say good night now, but Romeo detains her. He wants to exchange vows, but Juliet has given hers, and more would just be extra. Still, when she hears her Nurse calling her, she finds she can't bear to leave Romeo, and tells him to wait until she can come back. While she is gone, Romeo speaks to the night: "O blessed blessed night! I am afeared,/Being in night, all this is but a dream,/Too flattering-sweet to be substantial."

Juliet returns to her window, and whispering hastily to her lover while her Nurse calls to her from the room behind, she says that if he wishes to marry her, Romeo should send word the next day by her messenger. If not, she pleads that he leave her alone. Again she vanishes within, while Romeo finds the night impossible without her light. Yet one last time she reappears, just as he is going, and calls him. She wants only to ask what time she should send her messenger tomorrow. She has forgotten her real purpose in calling him back. Perhaps it was just to linger a bit longer with him. The two do not want to say good night yet, and Juliet embroiders their lingering with her playfulness: She would like him to go, but no farther than a pet bird on a string who can be tugged back when its mistress wants, "So loving-jealous of its liberty." Only she knows that if he were her bird, she might kill him with too much loving. At last, calling "Good night, good night! parting is such sweet sorrow/That I shall say good night till it be morrow," Juliet goes in for the last time, and Romeo stands a moment in the darkness, then departs himself for a visit to his priest and confessor.

Act II: Scene 3

It is early morning, and Friar Laurence, the monk who is Romeo's confessor, is up and about already. He is educated in the lore of herbs and their powers, and since herbs, if they are to keep their full potency, must be gathered before the sun has dried the dew from their leaves, he goes out at dawn to fill his "osier cage," or basket, "With baleful weeds and precious-juiced flowers./The earth that's nature's mother is her tomb;/ What is her burying grave, that is her womb." The good Friar comments on the cycle of life, on plants growing from the earth and decaying back into it. All things in nature, even the most vile, have a special function and good use on earth. At the same time, the Friar knows that even the best things on earth can be misused for the purpose of evil. Both properties can exist in the same plant; for example, an herb can be beneficial to the health if smelled, but poisonous if eaten. Everything lies in how we use what nature gives us, and this is true even of men, who can use or misuse their own inherent qualities, so causing themselves to be good or evil.

Romeo, who has been up all night wooing Juliet, now comes to see the Friar. The Friar is surprised to see him, feeling that a youth, with no cares to make him sleepless, should still be sleeping at this hour, or else must be disturbed in mind or body. He feels this is not so in Romeo's case, and guesses that he had not been to bed at all. Romeo acknowledges the truth of the guess, while quickly assuring the Friar that "the sweeter rest" he had was not with Rosaline, for he has forgotten her and the sadness she brought him. Romeo riddles the Friar a bit, saying he has been with his enemy, who has wounded him and been wounded by him, but that the cure for both their wounds is within the monk's "holy physic," or sacred healing power. He quickly clarifies things, however, telling the Friar that he and Juliet have pledged their love for each other, and that it only remains for the Friar to join them forever in marriage this very day.

Friar Laurence is bowled over by this abrupt change, and comments on the changefulness of youth. Only yesterday Romeo cried salt tears for a love that did not even last long enough to be seasoned by that salt. The Friar's ears still ring with Romeo's groans, and while he had encouraged Romeo to bury that love, he didn't intend that another love should spring up instantly. Still, he admits that he felt that Romeo was loving according to a book he could scarcely even read yet. Apparently, the Friar senses from Romeo's elation that this is not love by the book, but the real thing. Also, he hopes that the love and marriage of a Montague to a Capulet might force an alliance between the two feuding houses, and change the hate between them to love. On hearing this approval, Romeo cries, "O, let us hence; I stand on sudden haste." To this impetuousness the monk replies, "Wisely and slow; they stumble that run fast."

Act II: Scene 4

Mercutio and Benvolio, abroad in Verona this morning, wonder where Romeo is. They know he has not been home, and fear Rosaline will drive him mad. Tybalt, angered by Romeo's uninvited appearance at the Capulet festival, has sent him a challenge to duel. Benvolio feels sure Romeo will answer not just the letter, but the man and the dare; but Mercutio says Romeo is already dead, slain by a woman's eye, a love song, and Cupid's arrow, and not in the manly state necessary to fight Tybalt. "Why, what is Tybalt?" asks Benvolio. In lore, Tybalt is the name for the prince of cats. Mercutio punningly states that this Tybalt is more than prince of cats, but a master of the laws of ceremony, one who fights with a sense of timing as natural to him as keeping time to music is to those who sing. Yet Mercutio clearly despises Tybalt, despite his skill with a sword, and goes on to make fun of him as a silly dandy who is at least as concerned with having fashionable manners and clothes as he is with fighting like a true gentleman.

Just now, Romeo comes into view, and the two men begin a chanting tease. Mercutio calls him a dried herring, without its roe. He means that without Rosaline, Romeo is like a herring without its mate: he dries up and becomes "fishified." Running through all the heroines of literature, Mercutio states the faults Romeo must find in them in comparison with Rosaline. But he is glad to see Romeo, and ribs him about having slipped away the previous evening. Romeo, just come from the Friar, is in a fine, delighted frame of mind, and he warms up to the fast-flying witticisms immediately. He scores many good returns over Mercutio as their conversation skips from courtseys and courtesy to dancing pumps, the singularity of jests, and finally runs a "wild goose chase" around itself. Periodically Mercutio, who is delighted at Romeo's return to free-spirited word play, protests that Romeo is in excellent form: "Thy wit is very bitter sweeting; it is a most sharp sauce." Romeo retorts that Mercutio is a "broad goose," using "broad" to mean obvious, indecent, and unrestrained all at once. Mercutio is pleased beyond answering, and bursts out: "Now art thou sociable, now art thou Romeo; now art thou what thou art, by art as well as by nature," and adds the sexual pun that love had made Romeo "hide his bauble (the stick carried by a fool or jester) in a hole."

Benvolio stops Mercutio there, to prevent his tale from becoming "large" (meaning both long and licentious).

As the men conclude their jest, the Nurse and her servant Peter arrive. The Nurse is the messenger Juliet promised to send to Romeo. She is on an errand of courtship and is about to speak with highly-bred gentlemen. It is a role she enjoys, and to play it to the full, she affects the airs of a lady of breeding, holding a fan before her face in modesty as she approaches. After one quip to the effect that her fan is prettier than her face, Mercutio falls in with the play-acting and greets her as a gentlewoman, only to instantly affront her assumed gentility by saying, "The bawdy hand of the dial is now upon the prick of noon." Romeo, and even gentle Benvolio, fall in with this spirit of raillery for and at the Nurse. Mercutio even breaks into song, intimating that the Nurse is a prostitute now gone stale with age. He and Benvolio depart, leaving Romeo to share the confidence the Nurse has requested.

The Nurse asks who that rogue was, referring to Mercutio. True to the role she has chosen, her sense of dignity is offended by him. She must express this to Romeo, and in the vigor with which she does so she lets her demure facade drop, breaking out into, "Scurvy knave! I am none of his flirt-gills"; that is, not one of Mercutio's loose, flirtacious wenches. Resuming the role, she chides Peter for not defending her, then turns to Romeo and gets down to business. First, she gets in her warning that Romeo had better not be playing double with her young mistress. Romeo protests, and tells the Nurse of his hopes to marry Juliet that very afternoon in Friar Laurence's cell. He urges that Juliet find a means to be there. He also promises to send a ladder, which shall be his means for reaching Juliet tonight so that they may consummate their marriage. All this the Nurse promises to relay to her mistress. True to herself, she must prattle away a bit about Paris, his suit for Juliet's hand, and how Juliet turns pale when the Nurse teasingly says that Paris is the more handsome. She tells him that Juliet has some small verse about Romeo and rosemary. (Rosemary is the flower of remembrance, used at weddings and, what is ironical in this case, also at funerals.) Romeo breaks this off, and leaves.

Act II: Scene 5

Juliet is alone in her father's orchard, waiting impatiently for her Nurse to return with Romeo's message. The Nurse promised she would be back in half an hour, but for three long hours Juliet has waited. It is now noon, and the young girl is in a small frenzy. She wishes her messengers to Romeo could be thoughts, which would fly like doves or the wings of the wind, driving back the shadows of the hills as they fly. It seems a long journey that the sun has traveled from morning to midday. If the Nurse were as young and full of passion as Juliet, she would move between the two lovers like a tossed ball, carrying their messages. Though Juliet knows the Nurse is old and slow, this much delay seems to her to result from someone pretending to be dead.

The Nurse and Peter now come, and Juliet greets the Nurse with high excitement. Peter is sent out, and she questions the Nurse urgently. But the Nurse, as if in answer to Juliet's previous remark on old people, only complains about her weary joints. Juliet has no sympathy at present; she wishes the Nurse had her young bones, and she had the Nurse's news. The Nurse only retorts that her mistress can wait till she has caught her breath. Juliet is getting irritated. The Nurse has spent more breath complaining than the answer to the question, "Is thy news good or bad?" would take. In answer, the Nurse takes a tone of derision, and uses it to praise highly Juliet's choice of a husband. Juliet knows Romeo's value, all she wants to hear is whether or not they will be married. Again the Nurse returns to patter about her aches and pains. Driven to distraction, Juliet has been unsympathetic to the ailments of old age, and the Nurse, partly out of perversity and partly from desire to be pitied and given attention, will play this game until her young mistress shows some response to her complaints. Seeing this at last, and regreting her own unresponsiveness, Juliet softens, and caresses her Nurse. But when the Nurse teasingly starts to relinquish her news, only to interrupt herself with a question about the whereabouts of Lady Capulet, it is the last straw. Juliet speaks crossly and abruptly, with real irritation. Then only does the Nurse answer, in a short, concise, and surprisingly accurate speech, describing the plans for the marriage this afternoon at the Friar's, and for the ladder which will let Romeo come to his bride and consummate their marriage that evening. Juliet joyfully departs for Friar Laurence's cell.

Act II: Scene 6

It is the time and place of the wedding. Romeo and Friar Laurence speak quietly to each other as they wait for Juliet. The Friar asks for heaven's smile on the marriage, so that it may not be followed by sorrow. Romeo adds his "Amen," but for him, no amount of sorrow can weigh more strongly than the joy of a moment with his bride. If the Friar only joins their hands in holy marriage, he will dare "love-devouring death" to do whatever it might. He will have named her for his own, and that is enough. The Friar answers with his moderation and wisdom: "These violent delights have violent ends,/And in their triumph die, like fire and powder,/Which as they kiss consume." He enjoins Romeo to love moderately, so that he may love long.

Juliet comes, and her step is so light that Romeo fancies it would not break the gossamer of summer air. She greets the "ghostly," meaning spiritual, Friar. The imaginations of both Romeo and Juliet are on fire. If her joy leaps up as high as his, Romeo bids her to sweeten the air with the music of her imaginings about the love they will share. Her answer is that she must speak of substance, not ornament, but that the substance of her love is so great that she cannot add up half the wealth of it. The Friar then takes them to his inner chamber, where he will by "Holy church incorporate two in one."

Act III: Scene 1

The afternoon has drawn on after the wedding, and has become hot. Benvolio, who is with Mercutio, observes that hot weather makes hot tempers, and since the Capulets are about, he pleads that they go home and escape more fighting. Mercutio, who feels mischievous, jestingly accuses Benvolio of really wanting a fight, and of being quick to pick one over slight excuses, such as a man cracking nuts when Benvolio has hazel eyes. Benvolio maintains that if he were as soon moved to quarrel as is Mercutio, his life would not be worth a "fee-simple." At this juncture the Capulets do appear, with Tybalt leading them. Mercutio cares not, and at Tybalt's request for a word with them, tauntingly suggests that he ask for a word *and* a blow. He dares Tybalt to find a reason for fighting him. He pretends that Tybalt has called himself and Benvolio "minstrels," a faintly derogatory word implying vagabonds, and he draws his sword as a fiddler draws his bow, to make Tybalt dance. He is deliberately provoking the antagonistic Capulet. When Benvolio suggests that the two of them should either keep their quarrel rational or go some place private, Mercutio retorts that men can stare, but he is not going to budge.

Romeo, newly married an hour since, appears just at the crucial point. It is Romeo that Tybalt wants to fight and for whom he has been waiting, despite Mercutio's jabs: "Here come my man." But Mercutio is angered at Tybalt's resistance to his gibes, and he takes this remark of Tybalt's in its lowest sense, that of calling Romeo a servant. Tybalt deliberately insults Romeo, trying to entice him to a duel. But Romeo's state of mind has transcended the sarcastic irony of such name-calling as "The love I bear thee can afford/No better term than this—thou art a villian." No one knows of the marriage but Romeo and the audience, and Romeo's suspenseful pause, and the riddling response he gives is perplexing to everyone on the stage. Tybalt refuses to be forgiven for slandering, and has no intention of missing his chance to revenge the grudge he holds. But Romeo continues his mysterious talk of loving the Capulet name as well as his own. His comrades are astonished.

Mercutio, livid, cries out, "O calm, dishonorable, vile submission!" and draws on Tybalt, saying that he means to have one of the nine lives of the king of cats. Tybalt answers by drawing and, ignoring Romeo's cry to Mercutio to stop, they fight. Romeo then draws himself, calling to Benvolio to help him, and rushes to break up the fight. As he tries to separate his cousin and his friend, he blocks one of Mercutio's parries. Tybalt and his followers withdraw, and as they do, Mercutio clutches his side, saying, "I am hurt,/A plague o' both your houses. I am sped," a cry which he repeats more than once while the scene lasts, "Ay, ay, a scratch, a scratch; marry, 'tis enough." Romeo is stricken, and to his inquiries Mercutio replies that the cut is "not so deep as as a well, nor so wide as a church door," but that it is enough to make him a "grave" man by tomorrow. An abusive torrent bursts from Mercutio, vilifying Tybalt, "a dog, a rat, a mouse, a cat, to scratch a man to death! a braggart, a rogue, a villian, that fights by the book of arithmetic!" Why did Romeo try to come between them? It was this, says Mercutio, that caused the fatal wound. Romeo did what he thought would be best, but Mercutio again curses both houses, and turns to Benvolio to be carried out. Romeo stands stunned, muttering painfully to himself at the indignity he feels over what has happened, and confirming Mercutio's thoughts in a simpler and stronger speech than he has yet used: "O sweet Juliet,/Thy beauty hath made me effeminate,/And in my temper soften'd valour's steel." Almost immediately Benvolio returns. Mercutio, the "gallant spirit" that scorned the earth, is dead. Romeo can see nothing but the blackness of this day, and many more to come. He bows his head to this new fate.

Suddenly, furious Tybalt shows himself again. This is too much for Romeo. Abruptly he casts away the "respective lenity" that had resulted from his marriage. He calls to Tybalt that Mercutio's soul is waiting, and one or both of their's must accompany it. Tybalt's answer rings: it will have to be Romeo's soul. The two fall to furious, earnest fencing, and Romeo kills his new cousin. As Tybalt falls, Mercutio is avenged, and Romeo has at last stood for his own honor. Benvolio cries to him, "Away, away" for the citizens are aroused and the newly established penalty for such fighting is death. Romeo groans "O, I am fortune's fool!" and forces himself to run off.

Citizens come running and close on their heels come both the feuding households and Verona's Prince. Amidst cries for vengeance, Benvolio explains to Prince Escalus what has occurred. He perhaps exaggerates Romeo's humility, and in the exaggeration lie the tones not only of desire to protect Romeo, but of annoyance at Romeo's conduct. The tale is otherwise vivid and true to the facts. Lady Capulet accuses him of natural prejudice in favor of the Montagues, and asks for Romeo's death. Lord Montague's answer is that Romeo only gave Tybalt the punishment coming to him. The Prince ponders, weighing both sides. His conclusion is that Romeo shall be exiled, and that for the pointless loss of Mercutio, one of his own family, he shall exact heavy fines from both the feuding households. Romeo must leave Verona immediately. If he is caught first, he will be put to death. The Prince can have no more mercy, for his past leniency has seemed only to give license to more murdering.

Act III: Scene 2

Juliet, unaware of what has just happened, waits out the passing of the day in her father's orchard. She is more impatient than ever, for tonight Romeo is to come to her as her husband. At the opening of the scene, she delivers an impassioned soliloquy, well known as "Juliet's invocation to the night." Beginning with the words, "Gallop apace, you fiery-footed steeds," she urges the sun on to its setting in the west, so that night may arrive sooner. "Spread thy close curtains, love-performing night." She longs for the shelter of darkness, when Romeo can come to her unseen. The dark suits lovers, for love is blind and the beauty of lovers is enough light for them. Juliet compares night to a "sober-suited matron, all in black," who will teach her how to lose the game of love to her lover. Only by losing can she win. Changing the image to one of falconry, this tender girl compares herself to a falcon: a hawk or bird of prey used by hunters for catching pheasants and quail. Until released for the kill, a falcon is kept quiet by having its head enclosed in a small black hood. When nervous or anxious for the kill, a falcon will "bate," or beat its wings rapidly. So Juliet hopes that night will "Hood my unmann'd blood, bating in my cheeks." With the word "unmann'd" she had used the language of falconry to refer to her own virginity. She invokes night, and she invokes Romeo, the lover who is "day in night," and who will glide on the wings of night like "new snow on a raven's back." All she asks is that this night bring Romeo to her. After that, if he dies (which Juliet does not imagine) the night may take him back, may set him in the heaven with stars. Then "All the world will be in love with night, And pay no worship to the garish sun." For love belongs to Juliet now that she is married, but she does not own it, and she can't own love until Romeo posesses her. Because of that she is waiting now, as impatiently as a child waits for a festival.

Now the Nurse comes, carrying with her the very cords Romeo has prepared to let him come to his wife tonight. They are to be thrown over the balcony so that he may climb up. To Juliet these ropes, as well as any word connected with Romeo, are harbingers of joy. But the Nurse flings the ropes to the ground and with shocking sorrow, begins to mourn, saying "He's gone, he's killed, he's dead." Juliet, assuming the nurse means Romeo, can only say, "Can heaven be so envious?" By envious she means not only jealous of their happiness, but malicious. The nurse takes the latter meaning and retorts that Romeo can be envious. This is more than Juliet can bear, and she bursts out, "What devil art thou that dost torment me thus? This torture should be roar'd in dismal hell." She demands to know if Romeo has killed himself, and playing on the various meanings of "I," "aye," and "eye" she makes it clear that her misery hangs on the Nurse's answer. The Nurse, who is never straight-forward enough to give a simple answer, does not answer yes or no, but launches into a gory description of how she saw the wound with her own eyes. Juliet, beside herself with dismay, cries "O break, my heart!" and, "Vile earth, to earth resign, end motion here." The only interpretation that she can give to the Nurse's words is that Romeo is dead, and that is Juliet's own death sentence.

At last, the Nurse begins to clarify her news. She reveals that it is Tybalt for whom she mourns. Juliet, convinced of Romeo's death, now thinks that both are dead: "Then, dreadful trumpets, sound the general doom!/ For who is living if these two are gone?" But the Nurse finally lets the full blow fall, and reveals that Tybalt was killed by Romeo, and that Romeo himself is banished. Juliet, by now utterly confused by one reversal after another and worked up to an extreme emotional pitch by the Nurse's playful devices, lets loose a torrent of words reviling the Romeo she loves: "O serpent heart, hid with a flowering face!" and "Despised substance of divinest show!" Using all the opposites of evil and good at her command, she curses her lover as a fiend who hides evil in sweet and even holy trappings. The Nurse picks up this cry, and, claiming that all this sorrow is making her old, she says, "Shame come to Romeo!" But hearing her curses in the mouth of another brings Juliet to her senses. She retorts with all her spirit, "Blister'd be thy tongue/ For such a wish! he was not born to shame:/ Upon his brow shame is ashamed to sit." Realizing what she herself has just done, Juliet adds, "O, what a beast was I to chide at him."

When the Nurse asks Juliet how she can praise a man who killed her cousin, Juliet retorts that she cannot speak badly of her own husband, and is overcome with remorse that she, a newly wedded wife, could mangle her own husband's name. She realizes that had Romeo not killed Tybalt, Tybalt would surely have killed him. She should shed tears of joy that her husband still lives, not of sadness at her cousin's death. But she still finds herself crying uncontrollably, no matter what comfort she tries to offer herself. Why? Gradually she begins to remember the word she would rather forget, a word that was worse than news of Tybalt's death: "Banished!" If Tybalt's death wants another grief to keep it company, Juliet would rather it were anything than this. To her, the news of Romeo's exile is worse than news that everyone, including herself, is dead. "There is no end, no limit, measure, bound, In that word's death." The Nurse tells Juliet that her parents are mourning Tybalt, but the girl's tears are all for her lover's banishment. Seeing the cords which Romeo had sent as a "highway" to her bed, and with which the Nurse began this long telling of sad news, Juliet picks them up. She will take them to her wedding bed, "And death, not Romeo, take my maidenhead!" The Nurse finally sees what true depth of misery she has caused Juliet. She is remorseful. Feeling that her mistress might really kill herself, she offers what comfort she can. She will go find Romeo, who is hiding in the Friar's cell, and make sure that he will come tonight. Juliet brightens at this, and hands the Nurse a ring to give to Romeo, so that he will know that she is still true to him, and wants him to come.

Act III: Scene 3

Romeo, fearful because he has killed Tybalt, has fled to the safety of Friar Laurence's cell. The Friar, coming from a quick stroll around Verona where he has found news of Romeo's punishment, calls Romeo out from the inner room where he is hiding. The Friar speaks of Romeo as "wedded to calamity," and Romeo asks him what doom the Prince has pronounced. The young lover only hopes it is less than "dooms-day." Confident that his news will be of some comfort, the Friar tells Romeo that he is not sentenced to death, but is instead banished from Verona. At this, Romeo cries out abruptly "Ha, banishment! be merciful, say 'death.'" To him, as to Juliet, banishment is worse than death. The world beyond Verona seems to offer nothing but hell, and to be exiled to hell is surely not less than being dead. To say that banishment is less than death is, for Romeo, as cruel as smiling while delivering the death sentence. But to the Friar's way of thinking, Romeo is being rudely unthankful in refusing to see the mercy with which the Prince has ignored the rule that death shall be the punishment for killing.

Romeo is not to be so quickly dissuaded from his grief. He has said that any place but Verona is hell. He feels this, just as he feels that wherever Juliet strays is heaven. Dogs, cats, mice, even the flies that feed on decaying flesh will have the honor and "courtship" (that is, the chance at courtliness and the courting) of gazing at Juliet's hands and at her blushing virgin lips. But he, Romeo is banished. He would rather be killed by poison or knives, for the very word kills him. "Banished" is a word for the damned who howl in hell. Romeo wonders how his spiritual confessor, the Friar, can have the heart to use it. The Friar does not want to use the word; he wants to give Romeo the armor to ward off the stings of banishment: the armor he offers is philosophy. "Hang up philosophy" says Romeo, unless it can reverse these misfortunes. The Friar wants to discuss Romeo's state philosophically, but Romeo stops him by saying, "Thou cans't not speak of that thou dost not feel." If the Friar were young, in love, just married, had just killed a man and been banished, then Romeo feels he might have a right to talk. But, Romeo also feels sure the Friar would not talk; instead he would tear his hair and fall to the ground. So saying, Romeo does throw himself to the ground in a frenzy of despair, "Taking the measure of an unmade grave."

As Romeo throws himself to the floor in despair, there is a knocking at the Friar's door. The Friar is concerned at the idea of the young exile being discovered. He tells Romeo to get hold of himself and hide before he is found. Romeo refuses, saying that if his love hides him then he will be hidden. When the Friar finally gives up and asks who is there, we hear with relief the voice of the Nurse, saying that she comes on an errand for Juliet. The Friar is as relieved as the audience, and lets the Nurse enter. When she sees Romeo, for whom she is searching, lying on the ground in a fit of distracted grief, she declares that her mistress is in the same pitiful state, "weeping and blubbering." She tells Romeo that for Juliet's sake he must stand up like a man. To this persuasion Romeo responds and recovers himself. His first words are of Juliet. Does she think he is a murderer now that he has killed her cousin? Where is she? How is she? What is she thinking? The Nurse answers that Juliet only cries, falls on her bed, and calls out first Tybalt's name, then Romeo's. Romeo is afraid that his name can only mean death to his young wife. He draws his sword, and is ready to plunge it into whatever part of his body houses his own name.

Seeing Romeo draw his sword is too much for the kind Friar. He jumps to prevent the act, and in doing so lets loose a torrent of invective at such impetuosity, and, as it seems to him, lack of maturity in Romeo. "Art thou a man?" he asks. Romeo's form is a man's but his tears have been those of a woman and his acts those of a wild beast. The Friar is amazed; he had thought Romeo's disposition was "better temper'd," that is, more moderate. So Romeo has killed Tybalt; does he now want to kill himself, and by doing so, kill Juliet too? The Friar declares that Romeo is shaming his own shape, love, and wit. When the Friar's speech reaches this point, his anger begins to subside and the philosophy he has been wanting to encourage replaces it. The Friar's language and the structure of his speech become more formal. Using the three aspects of shape, love, and wit, he cautions Romeo. The misuse of these three things in a man changes his shape into mere wax, lacking in manliness; his love into a lie that can only kill itself; and his wit into a blaze of ignorance. Romeo has been doing this to himself. But the Friar encourages his young friend also, reminding him to be happy: for Juliet is alive; Romeo himself, instead of being dead by Tybalt's sword has killed his would-be killer; and the law which would have had him executed has softened and only exiled him. The Friar sees all this as a "pack of blessings," which Romeo mistakenly ignores. He warmly advises the young lover to go to his new wife, to comfort her, and only to be cautious and leave for the town of Mantua early enough to escape detection. Turning to the Nurse, the Friar sends her back to Juliet with the news that "Romeo is coming." The Nurse praises the Friar's good advice, and the Friar tells Romeo that he will find a time when he can joyfully call him back to a reconciled family, his marriage with Juliet, and a pardon from the Prince. The Nurse promises to deliver her message. Romeo, completely restored at the prospect of seeing Juliet, tells the Nurse that Juliet should prepare to "chide" him. He accepts the ring his beloved has sent, and as the Nurse bustles out, Romeo's "comfort is revived" by it. The Friar, feeling his old genial self again, says goodbye to Romeo, and adds his warning that Romeo take care when leaving Verona. The Friar will keep him posted as to what is happening in his absence. Romeo, who values the Friar highly, leaves to go to his bride, saying, "But that a joy past joy calls out on me,/It were a grief so brief to part with thee."

Act III: Scene 4

Abruptly we find ourselves at the Capulet house, where Lord and Lady Capulet are talking to Paris about his proposal of marriage to Juliet. Capulet explains that, due to the misfortune of Tybalt's death, they have had no time to pursue the matter of Juliet's marriage. She and her parents loved Tybalt, and Capulet sighs philosophically, saying "Well, we were born to die." Juliet will not be down tonight, and Lord and Lady Capulet themselves would have been in bed by now, if it were not for their visit with Paris. Paris is sympathetic to these things, and prepares to take his leave. Lady Capulet promises to speak to her daughter about this marriage tomorrow, but her husband is even more anxious to seal the match. He breaks in, saying that he feels he is on firm ground in promising Juliet's assent to the proposal: "I think she will be ruled/In all respects by me." He is sure that Juliet will do as he tells her. Turning to his wife, he tells Lady Capulet to go to Juliet tonight, immediately after Paris leaves, and tell her that Paris loves her and that she is to marry him.

Lord Capulet is anxious to have the marriage as soon as the proper time for grief has elapsed. He settles on Thursday, three days from now, and hopes that Paris will approve of this haste. In view of Tybalt's recent death, and so that no one will think his own family didn't love him, the wedding will be kept small and sober, with only a few guests. Paris agrees to all this readily; for him, tomorrow would not be too soon. Everything settled, Capulet calls for a servant to light his way to bed and tells his wife to give Juliet the news and prepare her for the marriage. With a comment that it is so late it might even be called early morning, he bids "Goodnight."

Act III: Scene 5

It is Capulet's orchard at night. Again we find Juliet high aloft on her balcony, with the light from the room behind her setting her off. But this time, Romeo is not below her; he stands with her on the balcony. They have spent one glorious night together, but the time has come for them to part, and for Romeo to go into exile. As the scene opens, Romeo has apparently begun to take his leave, and the first words we hear are Juliet's "Wilt thou be gone? It is not yet near day." The lovers have heard a bird singing. Juliet says it is the nightingale, a bird known for serenading in the night. She denies that it is the lark, a bird which sings at the break of day, and insists sweetly on the fact that there is a nightingale in her garden who sings each night from a certain tree, saying it was his call they heard. She wants Romeo to believe her so he will not leave yet. But Romeo knows "It was the lark, the herald of the morn," and he points to the malicious light that is beginning to cut through the clouds in the east, where the sun will rise. "Night's candles are burnt out," he says, "and jocund [jolly] day/stands tiptoe on the misty mountain tops:/I must be gone and live, or stay and die." Despite his consciousness of the anguish of departure and the sure death that will find him if he stays, Romeo's images are permeated with the joy of the night he has just spent. Juliet refuses to recognize what she knows to be true. She hopefully insists that the light is a meteor sent as a torch to guide Romeo to Mantua, and that he can linger still a while longer.

Romeo is vulnerable to the persuasions of his beloved. He will stay and be put to death if she wishes. He will say that the grey of dawn is only a reflection of the moon (Cynthia), and that the calling of that bird in the sky is not that of the lark. "I have more care to stay than will to go" he says, and he welcomes death because Juliet seems to prefer it to parting. But Juliet does not want him to die, and she immediately changes her tune, says that it is day, and that he must leave quickly. That bird is the lark, but instead of making "sweet division"—that is, singing a series of short lyric notes instead of one long one—its song seems to her to be "harsh discords," because it pronounces the "division" of herself from Romeo. As the lark "hunts up" the day, that is, arouses it, so it hunts Romeo out of town and away from her. The light of dawn increases as she speaks, and she wails, "O now be gone; more light and light it grows." Romeo answers, "More light and light, more dark and dark our woes!" The Nurse entering Juliet's room (from which they are curtained off as they stand on the balcony), interrupts gruffly with "Madam." She warns that Juliet's mother is coming to her room, and adds, "The day is broke; be wary, look about." Juliet can only answer in dismay, "Then window, let day in, and let life out." Romeo kisses her, and climbs down from the balcony.

The lovers part. Juliet, calling to her "love-lord" and "husband-friend" begs that she hear often from him, for in the space of a minute of their separation, days will seem to pass. Romeo assures her that he will let no chance of sending her news escape him. He is sure they will be together again, to talk over joyfully the pains of their separation. But even as he says this, Juliet is startled by what seems an evil vision. As she looks down at him in the grey light below, he seems to resemble a corpse, and she cries: "O God! I have an ill-divining soul:/Methinks I see thee, now thou art below,/As one dead at the bottom of a tomb." Romeo, seeing her pallor, has the same sensation, but comforts her by saying, "Dry sorrow drinks our blood," meaning that their sadness at parting has drawn the blood from their faces. Calling "Adieu," he leaves quickly.

As Romeo disappears into the growing morning, Juliet speaks of fortune, and hopes it will be as fickle as men say it is, for then it will turn the misfortune of this parting back to good fortune, and the lovers will be together again. Just then, Lady Capulet enters, and Juliet, wondering what unusual happening causes her mother to be up this late or to have arisen this early, goes in to her. Seeing her daughter's tear stained face, Lady Capulet expresses surprise. Juliet says she is not feeling well, but the Lady, assuming the tears have been shed over Tybalt's death, chides her daughter. Even if she washed her cousin's grave with tears, she could not make him alive, and while much grief indicates great love, too much grieving is a sign of stupidity. Juliet takes up this cue as a way to keep her secret from her mother and still not have to restrain her own excessive feeling of grief at parting from Romeo. She speaks on two levels, and referring within herself to Romeo, she says, "Yet let me weep for such a feeling loss." Trying to console her daughter, Lady Capulet says she should try to feel her friendship for Tybalt, not her loss. If Juliet must cry, it should be over the fact that the man who killed Tybalt is alive. Juliet senses fully the irony of this conversation, and whispers to herself that she pardons that man, and yet no man gives her more grief. Overhearing the last of this, the Lady says that of course Juliet grieves that the murderer lives, to which Juliet replies ironically that her grief is that he lives too far from her hands. Then, fearing that she will be discovered in her word-tricks, she adds what her mother assumed she meant, that she wants vengeance. To soothe the girl, Lady Capulet promises to send someone to Mantua to poison Romeo. At this Juliet is frightened, but replies with great presence of mind, that if this is to be done, she must "temper" the poison. She means, of course, not to make it stronger, but to make it completely ineffectual. She goes so far as to say that she can't bear to hear Romeo named, when she cannot even go to him and "Wreak the love I bore my cousin Tybalt/ Upon his body." She truly means "love" but again her mother assumes she means revenge. But the Lady's visit has another purpose; she changes the subject, saying she brings "joyful tidings," and Juliet only answers that she needs some joyous news.

Lady Capulet tells Juliet that her father, out of concern for her grief, has arranged for her an especially happy day in the near future. On Thursday she is to marry the gallant young nobleman, Paris. Juliet retorts abruptly that Paris will not make her into a joyful bride, then covers this over by protesting at this haste in the midst of Tybalt's loss, and at being married without even being courted. She swears she will not marry, and to make her mother feel the finality of this as well as to give vent to her feelings, she swears she'll first marry Romeo (whom they know she hates). At this point, Lord Capulet comes himself, with the Nurse, to see how his daughter responds. He is in high spirits, and makes jokes about the dew, the rain, the shower of tears his daughter has cried out. He compares Juliet to a ship in the midst of a storm, shaking her own body with winds of sighing and tides of crying. He turns to ask his wife if she has delivered "our decree," and Lady Capulet tells him Juliet refuses, adding "I would the fool were married to her grave." Capulet can't believe his ears, and asks if Juliet is not thankful, proud and blessed to be given such a husband. Juliet answers that she is not proud of what she hates, but she is thankful to her parents even for this hateful thing they have done out of love for her. Capulet is extremely irritated. He calls his daughter's answer "chop-logic," that is, a mere bargaining with twisted logic. He imitates her manner offensively. Growing more infuriated as he speaks, the Lord says "Thank me no thankings, nor proud me no prouds," meaning he will have none of either. Ranting, he declares in vivid language that Juliet will dress and get herself to Paris at the church on Thursday, or he will drag her there. By this time he is beside himself with rage at being opposed by Juliet, and referring to her great pallor, he calls her a waxy-faced "baggage," another word for a slut. At this, both Juliet and her mother call out in protest, but Capulet is going full blast. He repeats his demand that Juliet marry on Thursday, making it an ultimatum by adding that if she doesn't, he'll never look at her again. He wants no answers; in his rage his fingers itch to slap his daughter, and he calls her a curse on his life.

Lady Capulet and Juliet can offer no retort to the Lord's stream of invective. It is the Nurse who breaks in and tells him he must blame himself for so losing his temper. He snaps back sarcastically, suggesting that "my lady wisdom" save her tongue for gossiping. The Nurse persists, and when Capulet calls her a "mumbling fool," Lady Capulet at last finds words. "You are too hot," she says. His anger subsiding only a bit, the Lord finds he must defend his rashness. He says he has thought much about whom he will match with his only daughter, and now he has found the perfect match, a man against whom no objections can be made. After all this, he cannot abide his daughter, "wretched, puling fool," having the nerve and stupidity to say no. With menace, but comparative calm, he delivers his last word: Juliet may think it over, and if by Thursday she still refuses to marry, he will turn her out of house and home forever, and let her "Hang, beg, starve, die in the streets." This is his final warning, and he leaves.

Juliet begs for pity first from the clouds, then from her mother. If the marriage cannot be delayed for a month or a week, Juliet asks that they "make the bridal bed in that dim monument where Tybalt lies." But Lady Capulet refuses even to discuss the matter, and leaves as abruptly as her husband did. Clearly, the marriage must be prevented. Juliet is caught; her husband is alive on earth, and her religious faith forbids her to have two husbands. She cannot break such a stern law of the Church, but the only way she can see of preventing such a sin is for Romeo himself to die, leave earth, and go to heaven. The misery of such a prospect, and indeed of all that lies before Juliet, makes her turn and beg for comfort from her Nurse. The Nurse can only offer one solution. Since Romeo is banished, it is unlikely that he would return to challenge Juliet's marriage to Paris, and even if he dared, he could not do it openly. Considering this, the Nurse gently advises her mistress to marry Paris. Hoping to win Juliet to this, she begins to extol Paris's virtues, calling him an eagle, he is so quick and handsome. She says Romeo is a "dishclout," meaning he can't compare with Paris, and that this second marriage will be better than the first. Even if Juliet doesn't agree to this comparison of the two, the Nurse thinks Romeo is as good as dead, being permanently absent, and therefore he is of no use to Juliet. Juliet, astounded, asks the Nurse if she means this. The Nurse curses herself if she doesn't. Juliet's answer, "Amen," indicates that she too curses the Nurse for these thoughts. But she only says mildly that she is comforted, and that she will now go alone to Friar Laurence, where she will make her confession to having displeased her father. The Nurse goes to tell Lady Capulet this encouraging news. The moment she is out of sight, Juliet bursts forth, "Ancient damnation! O most wicked fiend." She curses the Nurse furiously, and cannot even decide whether the Nurse sins more in suggesting that she have two husbands, or in hypocritically degrading the Romeo she has so often highly praised. She severs herself forever from the Nurse: "Go counsellor; /Thou and my bosom henceforth shall be twain." She resolves to go to the Friar for advice, and if he can give none, to find the strength to die.

Act IV: Scene 1

The act opens, as we might have expected, in Friar Laurence's cell. But it is Paris, not Juliet, who is visiting the good Friar. Apparently, Paris has asked him to perform the coming marriage between himself and Juliet. The Friar realizes as fully as we do the dangerous implications of such a union. His first words are full of perplexity and hesitation: "On Thursday, sir? The time is very short." Paris answers that this speed is Capulet's wish, and that he, too, is anxious to marry soon. The Friar then raises the objection that Juliet has not yet given her consent, but Paris can explain that also. He did not wish to speak of love in a house full of grief, and Lord Capulet urges the speedy marriage specifically so that his daughter will not mourn herself into oblivion over Tybalt. The Friar mutters to himself that he wishes he could think of a reason that he was free to tell, which would explain why this marriage should be put off.

At this point, Juliet arrives at the cell. Paris greets her as "my lady and my wife" and although Juliet must be taken aback to see him, she answers demurely, "That may be, sir, when I may be wife." Paris says she shall be his wife, as of Thursday, to which Juliet makes a noncommittal, but assenting, reply. Their conversation proceeds in single-line remarks and replies. Paris presses her to declare her love for him, but she sidesteps his efforts with coy modesty. Paris comments that her face is abused with tears, and she answers that her face was bad enough before the tears. When he admonishes her not to slander her face, for it is now his, she only replies cryptically that perhaps it is his; at any rate, it is not hers. What she means is that it belongs to Romeo. To escape further conversation, she turns to the Friar and asks if she may see him now, or should she come later? The Friar asks Paris to leave them alone and he does so, but not before promising to come for Juliet early Thursday and taking a parting kiss as he goes. When she is alone with the Friar at last, Juliet's composure leaves her, and she breaks into cries of grief. The Friar tries to comfort her, saying that he knows what has happened, and that it strains his wits to fully grasp the awfulness of it. Juliet wants only to know how to prevent the marriage. If the Friar has no answer, she only asks his blessing on her suicide. Her hand and heart have been joined to Romeo's in holy wedlock, as the Friar knows. Before her hand could clasp another's or her heart perform such treachery as another marriage, she would use her dagger to end the life in both hand and heart. Can the Friar restore her to true honor? She urges him to answer, for if he cannot, she will kill herself.

The Friar quiets her, for he sees some hope. It is a desperate hope, but in the face of the threat of another marriage, better than none. If Juliet is desperate enough to kill herself, perhaps she will be willing to undergo something very close to death, but not death itself, which could free her from her shame. Juliet is all eagerness, declaring she would jump off a battlement, go among thieves and serpents, be chained among bears, and even allow herself to be shut into a sepulchre of the dead (a "charnel-house"). On this last her headstrong imagination catches, for it holds the greatest horror. She says she would let herself be covered with stinking, rattling, yellow bones, or even hide in the shroud of a newly dead man. She has trembled at hearing her own descriptions, but she would do any of these, "Without fear or doubt, To live an unstain'd wife" to Romeo.

The Friar, convinced by Juliet's desperation that she has the strength to do this, begins slowly to outline his plan. She is to go home, act cheerful, and pretend to agree to the marriage. Tomorrow night, Wednesday, the night before the wedding, she is to get into bed, and drink the liquid from a small vial or container which the Friar will give her. She will feel her veins grow cold, and her pulse slow to a standstill. She will sleep—cold, pale, and without breath—and it will be a sleep "Like death, when he shuts up the day of life," stiff and corpse-like. This will last forty-two hours, and then she will awaken pleasantly. The bridegroom, in the meantime, will find her and think her dead; and as is customary, she will be placed in full dress on an open bier or platform, and taken to the Capulet family tomb. While this happens, the Friar will send letters to Romeo explaining it all. Romeo will come to Verona and meet the Friar; and at the time that Juliet awakens they will be standing watching her in the tomb. Then Romeo will take Juliet with him to Mantua, and she will be free from shame. The Friar only hopes she will not lose her valor and be afraid to take the drug. Juliet's response is, "Give me, give me!" The Friar gives her the little flask and wishes her well, saying he will send to Romeo immediately. "Love give me strength! and strength shall help afford," are Juliet's words as she leaves the Friar's cell.

Act IV: Scene 2

The scene is the Capulet house, and the mood is merry, in contrast to the previous one. Capulet sends out one servant with a list of guests to be invited to the wedding feast. Another servant he sends to fetch twenty cooks, and the servant promises to bring back only cooks who enjoy licking their own food from their fingers. The Nurse tells Capulet that Juliet is with the Friar, and he comments that he hopes the visit will do his peevish, self-willed daughter some good. Juliet appears at that moment, and the Nurse notices that she looks merry. "How now, my headstrong! where have you been gadding?" calls her father in jolly tones. Juliet answers that she has repented her opposition to him, and has been told by the Friar to beg her father's pardon. She does so now, with a nice gesture. At this Lord Capulet is delighted, sends out a servant to tell Paris, and decides to hold the wedding tomorrow, Wednesday, instead of Thursday, as was planned.

Juliet tells her father how she met Paris at the Friar's and gave him as much love as her modesty would allow. Capulet is even more pleased. Now he wants Paris brought to him, and praises the Friar for having so well directed his daughter. Juliet goes off with the Nurse to prepare clothing for the wedding. When Lady Capulet protests that they cannot be ready by tomorrow, Capulet says he'll handle things. His wife may go help Juliet; he intends to stay up all night, and even play housewife. He calls for a servant, then realizing that they are all running errands he decides to go himself to see Paris and prepare him for the wedding. His heart is "wondrous light," now that his wayward Juliet has come back to him.

Act IV: Scene 3

In her bedroom, Juliet and her Nurse have finished preparing the dress she will wear tomorrow. Juliet asks that the Nurse leave her alone tonight; she pleads that she has many prayers ("orisons") to make, so that heaven will forgive the sinfulness she is about to begin. Lady Capulet comes to offer help, but Juliet has nothing more to do. She asks her mother to take the Nurse, who could help the Lady with her own preparations, as Juliet wishes to be alone. Telling the young girl to rest well, the Nurse and Lady Capulet leave.

"God knows when we shall meet again" Juliet says to herself as her Nurse and Mother depart. She faces a great trial, and although she feels alien to them, she is not sure when she will again see any humans at all. Already, fear makes her blood run cold and she cannot feel the heat of her own life. She is tempted, and starts to call the Nurse back for comfort. But there is nothing the Nurse can do to help: "My dismal scene I needs must act alone." She considers the flask of liquid, "Come vial," and wonders what will happen if the drug does not work. She will not marry, and to assure herself of that she puts her dagger within easy reach. Again she questions, fearfully, whether perhaps the Friar has not given her real poison, to avoid the dishonor that would fall on him if it became known that he had performed her marriage to Romeo. She fears this, but she knows better, for the Friar has always proved himself a holy man.

Yet another fear occurs to the young girl, the fear that she will wake in the tomb too early, before Romeo comes to "redeem" her. This she accepts as a justified fear, and she begins to imagine herself stifling and suffocating in the foul air of the vault, and dying of slow strangulation before Romeo arrives. And if she doesn't die for lack of air? If she lives, she will find herself in the midst of night, death, and the terror of "an ancient receptacle," containing the bones of ancestors hundreds of years old, "Where bloody Tybalt, yet but green in earth,/Lies festering in his shroud." This image of decaying flesh brings to her mind a worse terror, that of the un-dead spirits whom she has heard frequent tombs of the dead. Juliet's imagination races and riots with these dreadful visions, and she sees herself, waking early to hideous odors and "shrieks like mandrakes torn out of the earth." (Mandrakes were roots grown from the bodies of criminals who had been executed and buried; when torn up, they were supposed to omit wild shrieks that would drive insane whoever uprooted them.) Picturing this, she sees herself driven distraught with fear, playing madly with the bones of her ancestors; pulling Tybalt's mangled body from beneath his shroud; and finally, in crazed desperation, knocking out her own brains with some old bone. Wrought to a pitch of terror by her own frightened imaginings, Juliet now thinks she sees Tybalt's ghost vengefully attacking Romeo, his killer. She tries to stop the ghost, she seems to fail, and in her frenzy, she believes Romeo to have been killed. Without another thought, she swallows all the potion and tries to join her Romeo in death, crying, "Romeo, I come! this do I drink to thee." Juliet now falls, senseless, on her bed.

Act IV: Scene 4

It is early morning now, and the Capulet household is alive with the bustle of wedding preparations. The Nurse is sent to get spices. Dates and quinces are needed. Capulet is going about, arousing all those not yet busy, and making sure no cost is spared on the baked meats. The Nurse scolds him playfully, calling him "cot-queen," a derogatory term for a man who is acting as a housewife, and telling him to get some rest. Lord Capulet refuses to sleep, saying he has been up all night before with less reason. Even Lady Capulet is in good spirits, and says his previous all-night vigils were mouse-hunts; that is, chases after women. Capulet only ribs her in turn for being jealous.

Servants go to and fro, one with something the cook needs, one in search of dry logs. Lord Capulet hurries them, and they make jokes for his benefit. He awaits Paris, who will come with the musicians. Presently music is heard, and Capulet calls the Nurse. She must go wake Juliet and dress her up properly, while the Lord chats with the bridegroom. Capulet calls, "Make haste, I say."

Act IV: Scene 5

We come, with the Nurse, to Juliet's chamber. Juliet lies hidden from sight on the curtained bed. Calling and scolding cheerfully, the Nurse bustles about, perhaps drawing the curtains from the windows. She believes her mistress is fast asleep in bed, and as the Nurse hurries around she tries to rouse Juliet with cries of, "lamb," "lady," "slug-a-bed," and "bride." She admits that Juliet has need of a bit of sleep now, for surely Paris plans to keep her sleepless these coming nights. Still, she is surprised that Juliet sleeps so deeply, and finally the Nurse is moved to pull the curtains of the bed apart. There lies Juliet, fully dressed, which seems strange. The Nurse starts to shake her, but the body beneath her hands feels stiff and chill. Horrified, the Nurse wails, "Lady! Lady! Lady!" and "Help, help! my lady's dead," in a crescendo of despair. Lady Capulet, hearing this commotion, comes in quickly to see what is the matter. The Nurse can only point and cry, "O lamentable day!" and "O heavy day!" Seeing for herself how her daughter lies, Lady Capulet moans, "My child, my only life,/Revive, look up, or I will die with thee," and calls for help. Now comes Lord Capulet. Paris is waiting, and the Lord, annoyed at this delay, has come to see that his daughter come quickly. He is greeted by both his wife and the Nurse, crying the word "dead" over and over. His first reaction is close to anger: "Ha! let me see her. Out, alas!" He feels how cold and stiff she is, and sees how pale, and it seems to him that death has come "like an untimely frost" to this sweet flower. The Lady and the Nurse can say little; they mourn the sadness of this day and time. And for the first time, Capulet himself can find no words, not even a wail, for death "Ties up my tongue."

Hurrying in come the Friar and Paris with the bridal musicians. The Friar asks, "Is the bride ready to go to church?" This prompts Capulet to regain his words. She is ready, he says, to go to church and never return. On the eve of the wedding, Death has slept with Paris's bride, and she, the flower, lies deflowered (robbed of her virginity) by death. It is Death who has married Juliet and is now Capulet's son-in-law and heir. Capulet can only die and leave all he has, including life, to Death. Paris, for whom this day promised much, stands bewildered. Lady Capulet now curses the day, this miserable hour in the pilgrimage of time, for having taken her one poor cause for joy out of life. The talkative Nurse finds no coherent thought, and can only curse repeatedly the black day, the hateful day. Now Paris finds words: He has been divorced by death, and now can only love in death. And again Lord Capulet cries out. His child was his soul; his soul lies martyred, and all joy is dead for him.

The Friar knows the true state of things, and he only has retained his composure. He interrupts them now, and tries to calm their grief with chiding philosophy, saying, "Peace, ho! for shame! confusion's cure lives not/In these confusions." He explains that these friends and relatives shared Juliet with heaven, and now heaven has all of her, and keeps her from death by giving her eternal life. This is an honor and a joy far greater than any of them could have offered her, and they are selfish not to be happy for her sake. He adds, "She's not well married that lives married long,/But she's best married that dies married young." Juliet had once kept rosemary for Romeo (Act II, Scene 4, line 225), and we noted then that this evergreen herb, symbolizing eternal life and remembrance, was used at both weddings and funerals. Appropriately, the Friar mentions the herb now, bidding the mourners to put their bridal rosemary around the corpse, dress her in the robes in which her wedding was to be celebrated, and carry her to the church. Juliet indeed seems to have married Death. Capulet adds his directions: everything that was to be used for the wedding festival will now be used for the funeral. The wedding dinner will be a burial feast, the hymns will be dirges, "And all things change them to the contrary." The Friar tells them all to prepare to accompany Juliet's body to the grave, and adds his warning: heaven has punished them for something, and they must now stop all disobedience to heaven's will. All leave, except the Nurse, to do the Friar's bidding.

As the mourners go to church, the musicians remain behind, preparing to leave also. Most likely they are the same musicians who played at Capulet's party, when Paris was to consider his proposed bride, and when Romeo and Juliet fell in love. The Nurse tells them to pack up their instruments, commenting how pitiful is the state of things, and goes herself to mourn. Peter, one of Capulet's servants, comes in. He asks for the song "Heart's ease" to ease his heart, for, he says, his heart itself is playing the tune, "My heart is full of woe." Peter is sad, but it is the musicians who feel that music would be inappropriate. Yet gaiety gets the best of them, and instead of making music, they exchange witticisms about music and the money they hope to earn by it. Finally, they go off, planning to wait until the mourners return, so that they may have a free dinner.

Act V: Scene 1

The scene is Mantua, where Romeo is in exile. Surprisingly, he is in a light-hearted, elevated frame of mind. If he may trust the flattery of dreams, joyful news must be coming to him. He relates his dream: "I dreamt my lady came and found me dead." Juliet came to him and revived him by breathing kisses of life on his lips, and when he regained life, he found he was an emperor. Romeo sighs happily, reflecting that love is so sweet that even its shadows and sorrows, such as this separation from Juliet, are "rich in joy."

At this point, the messenger, whom Romeo's dream has led him to expect with happiness, appears. It is Balthasar, a servant of the Montague household, come fresh from Verona. Romeo welcomes him heartily, showering him with questions: is there a letter from the Friar? How is Juliet? And his parents? Before Balthasar can answer any of these, Romeo asks again about Juliet, "For nothing can be ill if she be well." In that case, nothing goes ill, answers Balthasar, but he speaks more slowly, and with a marked difference of tone. Juliet is well, for her body is in the tomb and her soul is with the angels. The servant watched her being placed in the Capulet vault, and then hurried to Mantua to tell Romeo. At this point, Balthasar breaks his somber tone and begs Romeo's pardon for bringing him such news. Romeo's first words come slowly. He is stricken and almost unbelieving as he says, "Is it even so?" And then, in a burst, in one short, ringing phrase, he expresses his reaction: "Then I defy you, stars!"

Immediately, with headlong speed, Romeo begins to act. He asks Balthasar to go to the place where Romeo has been staying, get a pen and paper, and hire horses; for Romeo intends to leave tonight. The good servant, seeing his master looking "pale and wild," fears that Romeo is about to do something rash, and cautions him to have patience. Romeo protests that Balthasar is mistaken, and should hurry away on these errands. Almost as an afterthought, he asks whether there are no letters for him from the Friar. When the servant assures him that there are none, Romeo shrugs and hastens him on, saying he will join Balthasar soon.

Romeo's intention is promptly clarified. His first words after Balthasar's departure are, "Well, Juliet, I will lie with thee to-night." Without wasting a second, he begins to consider how he will carry out his intention. The thoughts of desperate men quickly find a way to do whatever mischief they set their wills to. Romeo remembers an apothecary (a druggist) situated not far from where he is now. The man was obviously poor: dressed in rags, thin, miserable, and worried. His shop had looked shabby, its shelves bare except for what trifles he had managed to put on them for the sake of appearances. As Romeo had passed by, the pathetic poverty had caught his eye, and the thought had come to him that only from such a person could one buy poison. (The penalty for selling poison in Mantua was death, and only a man desperately in need of money would take the risk.) Romeo finds the shop, and calls the apothecary to him.

Romeo now talks to the apothecary, offering him forty ducats (a large sum of money, as ducats were made of gold) in exchange for a dram of the quickest-acting, most fatal poison the man can provide. Romeo describes graphically the effects he wishes this poison to have. The apothecary admits that he has "such mortal drugs," but adds that the penalty for selling them is death. "Art thou so bare, and full of wretchness,/ And fear'st to die?" Romeo points out that starvation, oppression, and contempt are clearly shown in the apothecary's appearance. Clearly, no one in such an extreme of misery can think that the world and its laws are his friends, or that such laws will make him rich. Break the law, Romeo urges, and by breaking it, get rid of this poverty. The apothecary consents because of his poverty but against his will, to sell the poison, and Romeo says he pays the man's poverty, not his will. The apothecary gives him enough poison to kill twenty men instantly. Romeo pays him, and as he does so he comments that the gold is a worse poison and kills more men than this liquid. He says goodbye, adding kindly to this man that he should buy food and get some flesh on him. The poison is, for Romeo, a cordial or sweet liquor to be used at Juliet's grave.

Act V: Scene 2

Once again we find ourselves in Verona, and at the cell of Friar Laurence. Someone is knocking and calling at his door, and the Friar answers eagerly. Upon conceiving the desperate plan to help Juliet and giving her the potion, he had sent, as promised, a message to Romeo in Mantua explaining the plan. Two days have passed, and he expects that his messenger, a monk named Friar John, will be returning now with Romeo's reply. It is indeed Friar John at the door, and Friar Laurence welcomes him, pressing him for Romeo's answer. But Friar John has another story to tell, and one that bodes no good. He had gone to find yet another monk to accompany him to Mantua. This third friar had been visiting the sick, and as Friar John spoke to him of the journey, searchers came. The job of searchers was to roam through Verona and seal up houses where people with infectious diseases lived, thus preventing such sickness from spreading. These searchers sealed up the house where Friar John and his companion were talking, suspecting it to be some such house of disease. Friar John could not get out, and never got to Mantua. Fearfully, Friar Laurence asks who did take the letter to Romeo. The sad answer is that no one did. People were so afraid of catching the disease that Friar John could persuade no one to take the letter to Mantua, nor even to return it to Friar Laurence.

Friar Laurence is shocked, and cries out, "Unhappy fortune." He explains that the letter was not trivial, but concerned directions of great importance. He asks Friar John to help him now by finding an iron crowbar and bringing it to the cell quickly. Friar John, seeing he has inadvertantly had part in causing some calamity, is all too willing to be of help, and leaves immediately. Friar Laurence then expresses his own intention to go to Juliet's vault alone. She will be awakening within three hours, and he is sure that she will blame him severely for not having notified Romeo. The Friar's plan is to take the young girl from her tomb and hide her in his cell while he sends yet another message to Romeo, telling him to come for his wife. Feeling very sorry for Juliet, who is "closed in a dead man's tomb," the Friar leaves.

Act V: Scene 3

We come now, at night, to the place on which all the action converges. It is a graveyard and the vault of the Capulet household. We expect various people, but the man we see there now was not expected. It is Paris, come with flowers to the tomb of the girl he loved and intended to marry. He has a young boy with him, a page who carries his torch. Paris tells the boy to put out the torch, so that they will not be discovered. The boy is to lie down under the nearby yew trees, and put his ear to the ground. As the earth of the churchyard is loose from the constant digging of graves, the boy will be able to hear the approach of any footsteps, and can whistle a warning to Paris. The page is a bit afraid, all alone in a graveyard, but he goes off to obey his master. Turning to face the closed vault where Juliet lies, Paris mourns, "Sweet flower, with flowers thy bridal bed I strew."

The bridal bed is made of dusty stone, for it is a tomb, and Paris intends to come each night to water it with his tears and strew it with flowers, as he does now. The page's whistle pierces the air, and Paris wonders "what cursed foot" has come to interrupt this ritual of love's grief. Seeing a torch, he begs the night to hide him from view, and goes off a way.

It is Romeo who approaches. He is just arrived from Mantua, and with him is his servant, Balthasar, carrying the torch, and a hammer and crowbar. Romeo, unaware that he is being watched, takes the tools and torch from Balthasar and gives him a letter. The letter is to Romeo's father, and Balthasar is to deliver it early next morning. Romeo instructs the faithful servant not to try and restrain him. He explains that he is going to "descend into this bed of death," that is, enter the tomb, partly to see his lady's face, but mostly in order to take from her finger a precious and important ring. Balthasar must leave immediately, and if he is suspicious and returns, Romeo threatens to tear him limb from limb and cast his remains all over the churchyard. "The time and my intents are savage-wild,/More fierce and more inexorable far/Than empty tigers or the roaring sea." Balthasar promises to leave his master alone, and Romeo assures him that only by doing so can Balthasar show his friendship. Romeo gives the servant money and wishes him well in life. Despite all this, Balthasar mutters to himself as he leaves that he fears his master's looks and doubts his intentions. He will hide nearby.

Romeo approaches the tomb he is about to open, and addresses it, calling it a "Womb of death," and an awful mouth which has filled itself with Juliet, "the dearest morsel of the earth." With his tools, he pries open the "rotten jaws," that is, the door of the vault, declaring that to spite this mouth of death for taking Juliet, he will cram it with more food, meaning his own dead body.

Paris has been watching all this, infuriated by what he sees. As he understands it, Romeo has murdered Juliet's cousin, and, since it is believed that Juliet died of her grief over Tybalt's death, Romeo is indirectly her murderer. Now the banished man has the nerve to come and threaten to shame the bodies he has killed. Paris emerges from his hiding and shouts at Romeo, commanding him to stop this unholy action. Does Romeo really think he need carry revenge further than death? Paris wants to arrest Romeo, and take him to his death sentence for breaking his exile. "Thou must die," cries Paris, to which Romeo replies, "I must indeed; and therefore came I hither." Romeo does not know who cries at him from the darkness. He pleads to this young man not to tempt him, for he is desperate, and easily urged to a fury that would bring the sin of another killing on his head. Romeo begs Paris to leave, saying, "By heaven, I love thee better than myself,/For I come hither armed against myself." Romeo does not wish to fight, and his madman's advice to this unknown challenger is to flee. But Paris refuses, and continues to try to arrest Romeo. It is almost with a sigh that Romeo, seeing no other alternative, begins to fight. The page sees them, and runs to call the guards. Romeo kills Paris, whose dying request is to be laid beside Juliet in the tomb. Hearing the request, Romeo looks at the face of this young man he has killed and sees it to be Paris, cousin of his friend Mercutio. Vaguely he remembers that, on the swift ride from Mantua, Balthasar told him Paris was to have married Juliet. Romeo's mind was so distracted during that ride that he is not sure whether he heard this, dreamed it, or just madly assumes it because of Paris's last request. But he will fulfill the request, and he carries dead Paris to "a triumphant grave" in Juliet's tomb.

As he carries Paris into the tomb, Romeo hears himself calling it a grave. It is not a grave, he says, but a lantern, for Juliet's beauty transforms it to a "feasting place full of light." He lays Paris down, commenting that this dead man has now been buried by another dead man, and how, before death, men are known to make merry. Such merriment is called the "lightning before death," and he wonders if that is his present state. He sees Juliet fully now, and exclaims, "O my love! my wife." Death has not lessened her beauty and Romeo, seeing how the color still remains in her face, says, "Thou art not conquer'd; beauty's ensign yet/Is crimson in thy lips and in thy cheeks,/And death's pale flag is not advanced there." Seeing Tybalt's sheet-covered corpse, Romeo thinks that by killing himself, he will be killing Tybalt's enemy and murderer, and avenging his death. "Forgive me, cousin!" he says, and turns back to Juliet, puzzling that she has remained so beautiful. To his distracted mind, it seems that "unsubstantial Death" is in love with Juliet, and keeps her here in the dark to be its beloved. Romeo can't allow that: he will stay in this "palace of dim night" with Juliet forever, taking his eternal rest, and will "Shake the yoke of inauspicious stars/From this world-wearied flesh." He takes his last look at his beloved, his last embrace, and with his kiss he seals finally "A dateless bargain with engrossing Death." Drawing the vial of poison from his pocket, he invokes it as the bitter and desperate pilot which will guide the boat of his body, sick and tired of this sea of life, onto the rocks of death. With the gesture of a toast, "Here's to my love!" Romeo drinks down the poison he calls a cordial. The drug is quick. His lips move from the kiss of the poison to Juliet's lips, and "With a kiss I die."

At this point the Friar, who has hurried so much that he has managed to stumble over every grave in his path, appears. He carries tools for opening the vault, but sees, to his surprise, that the Capulet tomb is open and lit from within by a torch. Meeting Balthasar, he asks whose torch it is in the tomb. The servant replies it is Romeo's and that he has been there a full half an hour. Balthasar has sworn at the threat of death not to stay, so he fears to accompany the Friar and show himself to Romeo. But he does tell the holy man that he has had a dream that Romeo fought and killed another man before entering the tomb. The Friar is filled with fear that something has gone badly amiss. He advances to the tomb, calling Romeo's name, and soon finds blood stains and swords to witness the truth of Balthasar's dream. In a moment the Friar sees Romeo, all pale, and with him a bloody Paris. No sooner has he taken this in than he sees Juliet stir and waken. She sees the Friar, but she is yet oblivious to the head that lies heavily on her breast. Remembering everything in a flood, she asks, "Where is my Romeo?" Approaching noises are heard, and the Friar urges Juliet to quickly leave this "nest/Of death, contagion, and unnatural sleep:/A greater power than we can contradict/Hath thwarted our intents." He tells her that on her bosom lies her dead husband, that Paris is dead too, and he promises to find a place for her in a convent of nuns. Only she must come now, without questions, for the watchmen are coming and the Friar does not dare stay. As Juliet refuses to move, he flees.

Juliet is left alone, to do what she must. Her mind is clear about her love for Romeo, so much so that she scarcely has time to express it or her overpowering grief at his death before she goes to join him. She sees a cup in his hand, and knows that he has poisoned himself only moments too soon. She chides him, in her gentle way, at having left no poison for her. She feels so close to him and to death that she can scold sweetly for a moment before she kisses his lips to see if any poison is left there. Having kissed Romeo she murmurs, "Thy lips are warm," and the pathos of that cry brings down on us like a bludgeon how this accelerated action has doomed the love, how the lovers' happiness hung on a few fateful minutes. It was lost because Juliet had not quite awakened and Romeo had not been able to waste a moment in joining her. Juliet now hears the voices of the watchmen; she, too, senses the need for speed. She takes Romeo's dagger and stabs herself, saying, "This is thy sheath; there rust, and let me die."

The watchmen, led by Paris's page-boy, enter abruptly. Seeing blood, some leave to search the grounds. It is clear that Juliet is newly dead. Messengers are sent to Prince Escalus, the Capulets, and the Montagues, and the watchmen are puzzled. They cannot comprehend from this slaughter what has happened. Balthasar and the Friar have been found, and are brought in and held for questioning. Now the Prince enters, with Lord and Lady Capulet close behind him. All have heard cries of fear in the streets, and gravely the watchman tells them of the three deaths. Balthasar and the Friar are being brought forward for questioning, but this is interrupted by the Capulets, both of them overcome with horror at the sight of Juliet's fresh blood and the Montague dagger "mis-sheathed" in her breast. Lord Montague enters on this cue. His wife has died, during the night, of grief at her son's exile. What other grief awaits him? With something akin to resignation, Montague sees his son and heir, dead before his time. The Prince now calls a halt to all mourning, in order that the ambiguities and complications of this triple death may be clarified. He calls the suspects, and the Friar steps forward, "both to impeach and purge" himself of all this murder. He tells, as quickly and simply as he can, the story of the love and marriage of Romeo and Juliet, Tybalt's death, Romeo's exile, the bethrothal of Juliet to Paris, his own plan to save her from dishonor, the accident of the letter failing to reach its destination, and the inevitable end. The Nurse will bear witness of the marriage, says the Friar, and adds that, if it is judged that any of this is his fault, he will accept the death penalty. Prince Escalus pardons him. Balthasar now speaks, and gives to the Prince the letter Romeo had meant for his father. The letter supports the Friar's statement, and the story has been put back together.

Calling the two feuding families to him, the Prince admonishes, "See what a scourge is laid upon your hate,/That heaven finds means to kill your joys with love." The Prince himself has lost two relatives by not punishing the feuders harshly enough to make them stop. Capulet and Montague, each pledging gold statues of the other's child, shake hands and vow to feud no more. The play ends on a note of "glooming peace," "The sun for sorrow will not raise his head." The Prince challenges everyone to think this over, and closes the play with the words, "Never was a story of more woe,/Than this of Juliet and her Romeo."

Timon of Athens

TIMON OF ATHENS.
LUCIUS and
LUCULLUS } *two flattering lords.*
SIMPRONIUS, *another flattering lord.*
VENTIDIUS, *one of Timon's false friends.*
APEMANTUS, *a churlish philosopher.*
ALCIBIADES, *an Athenian captain.*
FLAVIUS, *steward to Timon.*
POET, PAINTER, JEWELER, *and* MERCHANT.
FLAMINIUS
LUCILIUS } *Timon's servants.*
SERVILIUS
CAPHIS
PHILOTUS
TITUS } *servants to usurers (Timon's creditors).*
HORTENSIUS
A PAGE. A FOOL. *Three* STRANGERS.
PHRYNIA
TIMANDRAA } *mistresses to Alcibiades.*

CUPID.
SENATORS, LORDS, OFFICERS, SOLDIERS, THIEVES, SERVANTS *and* ATTENDANTS.

Timon of Athens

Act I: Scene 1

The scene is Athens. It is late afternoon and a group of hangers-on
—a poet, a painter, a jeweler, a merchant, and others—are conversing in the hall of a stately mansion that belongs to a wealthy Athenian, Timon. They await his arrival.

The poet and painter remark on the number of people who live on
Timon's bounty. Each displays what he has prepared to offer him.
The merchant has come to find whether Timon will buy the pearl
he has loaned him.

A trumpet sounds, and Timon enters with attendants. The usual
line of petitioners wait their turn to plead for a favor. One needs
money to free his master imprisoned for debt. Another, Timon's
servant, Lucilius, needs money to marry a wealthy Athenian's
daughter. Both receive their requests. The poet and the painter are
commended for their works and will be rewarded. They are invited
to stay to dinner, as is the jeweler. The latter finds he has more bargaining to do with Timon.

The cynic Apemantus enters and begins his usual bantering with
Timon. He censures the falsity of flatterers. Though part and parcel
of human dealings, flattery promotes evil. In a spiteful mood,
Apemantus refuses Timon's invitation to dinner.

When the trumpets announce the Greek general Alcibiades, and
his attendants, Timon welcomes him. Apemantus, in an aside, is
amused at all this courtesy "between these sweet knaves" who have
"small love" for each other.

The general goes along to dinner with Timon. Apemantus changes
his mind and goes to dinner with several lords who arrived late.
They joke with the cynic and praise Timon's generous ways. One

declares Timon has the "noblest mind" that "ever govern'd man."

Act I: Scene 2

This scene follows immediately in Timon's sumptuous banquet hall. Musicians are playing. While the steward and servants prepare the banquet table, Timon enters with his guests. Among them are Alcibiades, Ventidius, lords, senators, and Apemantus. As they stand talking with Timon, Ventidius offers "doubled" thanks for the "talents" that brought him liberty. Though he wants to reimburse Timon, the latter refuses because "there's none/ Can truly say he gives, if he receives."

When his guests are seated, Timon welcomes them. He is annoyed at the curt remarks of Apemantus, who recognizes the deceit of those enjoying Timon's bounty. Apemantus gives a long speech on human ingratitude—"O you gods, what a number of men eat Timon, and he sees 'em not!" He is grieved "to see so many dip their meat in one man's blood." The "madness" of the whole thing is that Timon "cheers them up to 't." Apemantus would have invited these people "without knives." It is "safer for their lives."

When wine is served, Apemantus offers a toast, "Here's that which is too weak to be a sinner, honest water, which ne'er left man i' the mire." He declares people at feasts "are too proud to give thanks to the gods," and he offers "grace": "Immortal gods, I crave no pelf;/ I pray for no man but myself:/ Grant I may never prove so fond,/ To trust man on his oath or bond;/ Or a harlot, for her weeping;/ Or a dog, that seems a-sleeping;/ Or a keeper with my freedom;/ Or my friends if I should need 'em./ Amen. So fall to 't:/ Rich men sin, and I eat root."

No attention is paid to the remarks of Apemantus. Timon is pleased at his guests' compliments. Whatever he has done, they will in return do for him. Friends would be "needless creatures" if one never had use for them. Apemantus injects cutting remarks as the lords revel in Timon's love for them.

A trumpet sounds to announce "certain ladies most desirous of admittance." Their "forerunner" Cupid declares the "five best senses" acknowledge Timon as their patron. Four of the senses have been well replenished at his table. These ladies come "but to feast thine eyes." They are cordially welcomed.

Music sounds and Cupid reenters with "a Masque of Ladies," dressed as Amazons, dancing and playing the lute. Apemantus chides "vanity," and the dancers he calls "mad women." As the dinner ends, each guest rises from the table very ceremoniously and thanks Timon. Each then chooses a lady and dances with her.

When they have danced a while, Timon thanks the dancers, declaring they have added "worth" and "luster" to his banquet. Timon sends his steward to fetch him his "little casket." In an aside, the steward laments Timon's foolhardy generosity. He foresees the end of his fortune.

Before the lords leave, Timon distributes rare jewels to several of them. A servant announces to Timon that "certain nobles of the Senate" have come to visit him. Even though it "concerns him" deeply, he will see them later. They are first to be entertained. Another servant announces that Lord Lucius has presented Timon with "four milk-white horses, trapp'd in silver." A third servant announces the gift of "two brace of greyhounds" for the next day's hunt. He accepts each of the gifts but "not without fair reward."

In a long aside, the steward, Flavius, reveals that Timon has exhausted his treasury. He is hopelessly in debt. His land will soon be seized by the state. The steward wishes he were gently relieved of his job before he is forced to go. His heart bleeds "inwardly" for his master.

Before the lords leave, Timon offers a second round of trifles and "a bay courser" which one of the lords had admired a few days before. They are grateful. Timon answers that he "could deal kingdoms" to his friends and "ne'er be weary." Timon turns to Alcibiades and notes that as a soldier, he is not rich. "It comes in charity" to him. All of his success is "'mongst the dead."

When the guests have left, Apemantus scowls on the whole lot. "Friendship's full of dregs," he declares. "Methinks, false hearts should never have sound legs." Timon answers that he would be "good" to Apemantus if he were not so "sullen." But Apemantus wants nothing because he, too, would be bribed and no one would be left "to rail" upon Timon. "What need," he asks, "these feasts, pomps and vain glories?" Timon refuses to listen when Apemantus begins "to rail on society" and leaves, telling him to return when he has "better music." After he has gone, Apemantus laments, "So; thou wilt not hear me now." He regrets that "men's ears should be/ To counsel, but not to flattery!"

Act II: Scene 1

This very short scene takes place the following morning in the room of a senator's house in Athens. The senator enters carrying a handful of papers and muses as he reads the sums of money that Timon owes his creditors. He owes "five and twenty thousand" in all. This includes Timon's debt to the senator. The generosity of Timon borders on the ridiculous. He calls his servant Caphis and bids him to importune Timon for money. The servant is not to accept any excuses. While the senator professes to "love and honor" Timon, he himself needs money. Caphis leaves, taking "the bonds along," so as to have the "dates in compt."

Act II: Scene 2

This scene opens in a hall in Timon's house later the same day. Flavius enters carrying a sheaf of bills. He deplores Timon's "senseless expense." He determines to be plain spoken with him when he returns from hunting. Three servants of Timon's creditors enter to present their masters' bills. Timon arrives with Alcibiades and lords. At Timon's question, "What is your will?" each servant presses his master's request for payment. Timon appears amazed at their insistence. Alcibiades and the lords leave, and Timon calls his steward to explain why these bills are unpaid. Flavius manages to put the servants off until after dinner. Timon promptly commands, as they leave with the steward, that they "be well entertained."

The servants of the creditors wait in the hall to have some "spirit" with Apemantus and a Fool who enter. Quick banter follows Apemantus' discovery that the three servants are "usurers' men! bawds between gold and want."

When Flavius tells Timon the enormous sum he owes, it is a shock to him. His accusation that the steward may not be honest prompts the latter to ask that his books be audited. The steward declares that he has spent restless nights worrying over the expenses of his master's great banquets. Timon demands that the steward "sermon him no more." He has not given "unwisely, not ignobly." He is certain that friends will come to his aid. In a sense, "his wants" can be called "blessings." He can now "try" his friends.

Immediately, three of Timon's servants are called and told to commend him to Lord Lucius, Lord Lucullus, and Sempronius. Timon is "proud" that the occasion has come when he can "use 'em toward a supply of money; let the request be fifty talents." By another servant Timon sends word to the senators, "of whom" he has "deserved this hearing," to send him "o' the instant/ A thousand talents."

After the servants are gone, Flavius reports to Timon that he has had no luck standing off the servants of his creditors. They repeat the usual apologies to a debtor—they "need treasure"; "they are sorry"; "'tis pity."

Timon is not disturbed. Ingratitude is "hereditary" in his creditors; "Their blood is cak'd, 'tis cold, it seldom flows." He sends a servant to Ventidius. He will remember how Timon "clear'd him" from prison with five talents. Now in "good necessity," he needs "those five talents." "Ne'er speak, or think,/ That Timon's fortune 'mong his friends can sink." The steward wishes he "could not think 't."

Act III: Scene 1

This scene takes place in Athens shortly after Timon's servants leave. Flaminius, one of Timon's servants, is waiting in a room in Lord Lucullus' house to speak with him. When he enters, he wonders (in an aside) what gift Timon has sent—it could be "a silver basin and ewer" that he dreamt about. He inquires about Flaminius' "bountiful good lord and master" and asks what the servant hides under his cloak. It amazes him to hear Timon's request for fifty talents, and "nothing doubting" that Lucullus will assist him.

But Lucullus is amused: "La, la la la, nothing doubting, says he?" He says he has often warned Timon of too great expenditures. But declares, "Every man has his fault, and honesty is his." Lucullus insists, "this is no time to lend money; especially upon bare friendship without security." He bribes Flaminius with three solidares (small coins) to deny having seen him. Angry at such "damned baseness/ To him that worships thee!," the servant flings the money at Lucullus. Calling him a "fool," Lucullus leaves. Flaminius wishes that "molten coin" be the damnation of Lucullus. Why should food from Timon's table nourish him when he "is turn'd to poison?"

Act III: Scene 2

This scene, in a public place in Athens, follows immediately. Lord Lucius and three men (identified in the play as Strangers) are discussing the report that Timon is in severe financial difficulties.

Lucius says it is only gossip. The Second Stranger insists Timon's servant had been sent to Lucullus to borrow fifty talents; he "urged extremely for 't," but was denied. Lucius claims it is wrong to deny "that honorable man." While he has received only "some little kindnesses" from Timon, such as "money, plate, jewels, and such like trifles," he would never have denied him so few talents.

Lucius is then accosted by Timon's servant, Servilius, who gets his attention by stating, "My lord has sent—." Pretending that he expects Timon has sent a present, he jokes at a request to borrow fifty talents. He feels like a "beast" in saying no to Timon. The three Strangers can bear witness that he was about to ask Timon for a loan. It is one of his "greatest afflictions" that he is unable to help him. Lucius asks the servants to use these very words to Timon.

After both Lucius and Timon's servants go their ways, the Strangers talk over the deceitful way Lucius treated the Athenian. One of the men recalls all that Timon had done for Lucius—he had been a "father" to him, "supported his estate; nay, Timon's money/ Has paid his men their wages." His house is full of silver gifts from Timon. Man is monstrous when "he looks out in an ungrateful shape." The Third Stranger remarks that "Religion groans at it." The First Stranger declares that, though he had no favors from Timon, he admires "his right noble mind; illustrious virtue,/ And honorable carriage." If he had asked him, he would have given half of his estate, "So much I love his heart." But men should "learn with pity to dispense;/ For policy sits above conscience."

Act III: Scene 3

This scene takes place the same day in a room in Sempronius' house. He is the third person whom Timon asks for a loan. Sempronius is annoyed that he has sent his servant to ask him for money. He might better have asked Lucullus, Lucius, and Ventidius, the latter having recently inherited his father's fortune. Each of them is beholden to him. Timon's servant declares that they have all been asked and "found base metal; for they have all denied him."

Sempronius offers as his excuse that he is the last to be asked and people would think him a "fool." If Timon had sent first to him, he would have given three times what he asked. As Sempronius leaves, he bids the servant say to Timon, "Who bates mine honor, shall not know my coin." The servant muses that Sempronius is "a goodly villain." He declares, the Devil thwarted himself "when he made man politic." Sempronius was Timon's last hope. He has only "the gods" left. Now, he must stay home and ward off his creditors.

Act III: Scene 4

The scene takes place the following morning in a hall of Timon's house. Servants of his creditors are gathered, discussing the prospects of collecting money. The servant of Lucius declares Timon resembles a prodigal whose "course/ Is like the sun's; but not, like his, recoverable." Another servant is repelled at his master's demand for money from Timon, when he is wearing jewels that were his gifts. Such "ingratitude makes it worse than stealth." Servants reckon that altogether Timon owes eight thousand crowns.

Flaminius, Timon's servant, enters and reports that Timon is not ready to meet with them. As he leaves, the steward, his face hidden, enters but pays no attention to them. He finally stops and asks why they failed to ask for their money when they enjoyed Timon's bounty. Then, they smiled and would "fawn on his debts,/ And take down the interest into their gluttonous maws." But now he pretends that he is no longer employed by Timon, and so it is useless for him to talk with them. They jeer at the steward, but decide they have their revenge—he is poor and has no place to go. Timon's servant Servilius enters to ask them whether they will return later because his master is quite disturbed and "out of health and keeps" to his room. Lucius' servant thinks that if he is so ill, he had better "make a clear way to the gods."

As they chatter, Timon enters in a rage. He is followed by his servant Flavius. He protests that he is a prisoner in his own house. The place where he has feasted, "does it now,/ Like all mankind, show me an iron heart?" In quick succession the servants of his creditors rush toward him, each presenting his bill. Timon is helpless and cries at them to cut his "heart in sums"; and "may the gods" fall on them.

Hortensius, one of the creditors' servants, declares they will never be paid; they are dealing with a "madman." The steward returns while Timon is still raving at the servants, calling them "slaves." He sneers, "Creditors? devils!" Timon advises his steward to "bid all my friends again/ Lucius, Lucullus, and Sempronius; all:/ I'll once more feast the rascals." Flavius tries to dissuade him, as there is nothing left even for "a moderate table." Timon is adamant—he and his cook will provide.

Act III: Scene 5

The scene takes place in Athens in the Senate House: the senate is sitting. Two of the senators are discussing the death penalty for a "bloody" crime. One of them opposes leniency, declaring, "Nothing emboldens sin so much as mercy." Alcibiades and his attendants enter. He greets the senators and proceeds at once to plead for a soldier who is guilty of murder. In several long pleas for mercy, Alcibiades weighs the soldier's virtues as a man, his courage on the battlefield, and his willingness to sacrifice his life for his country. According to Alcibiades, the unpremeditated murder of which he is guilty does not deserve the death penalty.

A senator attacks these arguments, declaring that Alcibiades is "striving to make an ugly deed look fair." He declares that a man is "truly valiant that can wisely suffer" even the worst wrongs and "wear them like his raiment, carelessly." Alcibiades declares that if the soldier owes his life for a crime, war will claim it in "valiant gore." The senate, however, rules that he must die. Believing that his position in the army gives him the right to seek clemency from the senate, Alcibiades declares that in their dotage they have forgotten his rank. The daring accusation angers the senators, and they banish him "forever." He answers them, "Banish your dotage; banish usury/ That makes the senate ugly." Without more ado he leaves, vowing to return and conquer the city.

Act III: Scene 6

This scene takes place in one of the magnificent rooms of Timon's house. The table is set for dinner. There is music, and servants are waiting for the guests to arrive. The lords Lucius, Lucullus, Sempronius, the senators, Ventidius, and others enter and chat among themselves. Each tells how insistently Timon urged him to come, or otherwise he would have refused the invitation. There is a general feeling of pity over not being able to help him.

The conversation stops as Timon enters with attendants. He is cordial, hoping they will enjoy the music until dinner is served. Several mention their "shame" in not honoring his request for a loan. One mentions the banishment of Alcibiades but keeps details for another time.

When the feast is brought in, Timon asks them to be seated, and not to observe protocol. He offers thanks to the gods. The address is full of concealed hate.

A covered dish is placed before each guest. Timon tells them, "Uncover, dogs, and lap." The dishes contain warm water. Several guests are dismayed. Timon declares it is his last feast. He "stuck and spangled you with your flatteries" and now "sprinkles in your faces/ Your reeking villainy." He throws the water in their faces, and keeps reviling them. He pelts them with stones and drives them out of the house, crying, "Burn, house! sink, Athens! henceforth hated be/ Of Timon, man, and all humanity!"

Act IV: Scene 1

This very short scene takes place within a few days outside the walls of Athens. Timon is walking alone and stops to look back at the city. He vents his anger on the government and all the citizens. He calls to the "slaves and fools" to take over the senate, and everywhere "let confusion live"; he wishes diseases of every kind to plague Athens. As for himself, "Nothing I'll bear from thee/ But nakedness, thou detestable town!" Timon declares he will go to the woods. He begs the gods to grant his prayer that "as Timon grows, his hate may grow/ To the whole race of mankind, high and low! Amen."

Act IV: Scene 2

This scene takes place in Athens in a room in Timon's house. The steward and several servants enter and are disturbed to find the house empty. They are loyal to Timon. The steward divides what little money he has with them and hopes for Timon's sake they will always be friends. He bids them remember, "We have seen better days." The steward professes his affection for Timon and feels that he has been brought "low by his own heart,/ Undone by goodness." His "worst sin" is, "he does too much good." The steward declares that he will always be Timon's friend. Now he will go and find him.

Act IV: Scene 3

This scene is in a wood some distance from Athens. Timon has found a cave and, noticing the sunshine, calls on it to "draw from the earth/ Rotten humidity!" He begins to muse on the inhumanity of man. He declares that every person who is successful in life is flattered by those less fortunate. Thus there is nothing natural in "our cursed natures,/ But direct villainy." He abhors all gatherings of men for any reason—he even "disdains" himself. He urges that "Destruction fang [poison] mankind!—Earth, yield me roots!" He begins to dig.

In lifting the first spadeful of earth, to his disgust he discovers gold, not the roots he needs for food. He attributes all of man's woes and crimes to gold. Even a small piece "will make black, white; foul, fair;/ Wrong, right; base, noble; old, young; coward, valiant." He covers up the gold, keeping it in the earth as nature intended. A small piece is kept as a token.

As he works there is a sound of drums, and Alcibiades enters with his two mistresses. He speaks to Timon, but gets a surly reply. Wishing he were a dog that he might love him, Timon tells him to go and "With man's blood paint the ground." He heaps abuse on the two women with Alcibiades, telling them to spread disease. Alcibiades attempts to soften Timon's harshness. He regrets "how cursed Athens" has forgotten his aid to the city and his bounty to its citizens. Timon refuses the small gold he offers him. "Keep 't, I cannot eat it." There is no need to give him gold. He offers Alcibiades gold. If he has more gold, one of the women asks for some. Timon admits he has, and enough to make her kind "forswear her trade." While he gives them some, he rails at the women, urging them, "Paint till a horse may mire upon your face:/ A pox of wrinkles!" Anxious to be alone, he tells them to go.

When Alcibiades conquers Athens he will visit him again. But Timon hopes never to see him. Left alone, he begins digging in the earth. He begs the earth to "yield him, who all thy human sons doth hate," just "one poor root."

He finds a root as Apemantus enters. The sight of him annoys Timon. When Apemantus accuses him of copying his "manners," Timon replies that he imitates a dog. As in the time of Timon's affluence, they banter. Apemantus tells him not to turn flatterer and gain back all he has lost. Timon insists Apemantus never knew the wealth that begets flatterers. Why then should he hate men? If Apemantus had not been born the "worst of men" he would have "been a knave and a flatterer."

Timon begins to eat the root he found, and refuses the food which Apemantus offers him. He wishes him to tell Athens he has gold, but it "sleeps" and "does no hired harm." Timon does not give the cynic gold, as he would spurn it. In his blunt way Apemantus regrets that Timon has not known "the middle of humanity," but "the extremity of both ends." Ignoring his lack of comment, Apemantus asks what things in the world can he "nearest compare to thy flatterers." Women, Timon thinks, are "nearest; but men, men are the things themselves." Apemantus sees "a parcel of soldiers" coming toward them and after another exchange of abuse, Timon throws a stone at him. When he goes, Timon ponders over the need to prepare a grave for himself near the sea. He looks at the gold despairingly, calling it a "sweet king killer" that "speak'st with every tongue/ To every purpose." He begs the gods that gold confound men, "that beasts/ May have the world in empire!"

Apemantus hears him and returns briefly, calling to him, "Live, and love thy misery." Timon sends him away, wishing him to "long live so, and so die!"

As soon as Apemantus leaves, three banditti enter, looking for Timon. They have heard he has "a mass of treasure." Timon suspects that they are thieves, though they call themselves paupers. With all nature to feed them (berries, grass, grapes) Timon cannot understand why they should be in want. He is thankful that they are "thieves profess'd" and do not work "in holier shapes." With the gold he finally gives them, Timon "examples" them about thievery. All things in nature are thieves—the sun "robs the vast sea"; the moon snatches "her pale fire from the sun," and so on. If they must be thieves, they should do it "like workmen." So he bids them to go to Athens and "break open shops" and "gold confound you/ howsoe'er! Amen." As the banditti leave, unable quite to understand Timon, the steward arrives. He is disturbed at Timon's appearance. He greets him as "my dearest master."

Timon has forgotten him—he has "forgot all men." Flavius convinces Timon of his identity and tells him that while his money lasts, he wishes to be his steward. The request moves Timon deeply. He would fain "have hated all man-kind," but now the steward has redeemed himself. The rest of the world Timon would "fell with curses."

To be certain of the steward's loyalty, Timon asks if his could be a "usuring kindness," as when rich men "deal gifts" and expect "twenty in return for one." Flavius is straightforward. He declares, "Heaven knows" his offer to serve is "merely love/ Duty and zeal" for Timon's "unmatched mind." His only one wish is that Timon could "requite" him by making himself rich.

Timon quickly notes his wish is already granted. He declares "The gods out of my misery,/ Have sent thee treasure." He gives Flavius gold on which he can live and be happy, but "thus conditioned": he must hate men, curse them, and "show charity to none." Let the flesh fall from a beggar's bones, rather than help him—"give to dogs,/ What thou deny'st to men."

When the steward begs to be let stay and comfort Timon, he refuses him unless he wants curses. Flavius should go while he is "blest and free." But he must never return.

Act V: Scene 1

This scene takes place several days later in front of Timon's cave. He overhears the painter and poet, whom he had befriended in Athens, discussing the report that the Athenian now has great wealth. They want a share of it, but have nothing to present to him. Timon overhears this and muses on what a "god" gold is. The temple where he is worshipped is more base "Than where swine feed." He comes out to meet them. He sarcastically praises them for not coming to see him for gold. But for past services, he gives them some. Then he draws them out, declaring, "You came for gold, ye slaves." As they leave, the steward and two senators arrive. The senators have made a "pact and promise" with the Athenians to talk with Timon. Flavius tells them it is quite useless. Nevertheless, he calls Timon, who enters. He spurns their greetings from Athens and "would send them back the plague/ Could he but catch it for them." He is not interested that the Athenians would make amends for their offense and give him "such heaps and sums of love and wealth" as to "blot out what wrongs were theirs."

Feigning sorrow, Timon will "beweep these comforts." The "captainship and absolute power" in Athens will be his when Alcibiades is conquered. In a bitter reply, Timon "cares not" whatever atrocities Alcibiades commits in Athens, for soldiers' knives do nothing but good when there are throats to cut. Timon advises that he is writing his own epitaph. Tomorrow, it will be seen. His "long sickness of health and living begins to mend."

With the hope that Alcibiades will be their plague, he greets his loving countrymen and he wants to do a kindness for them—

"teach them to prevent wild Alcibiades' wrath." The preventive for all of high or low degree is to come speedily to his cave where a tree grows but soon will be cut down. Each one can hang himself from it. "I pray you," he says, "do my greeting."

Though ready to leave, Timon holds the senators for a final word. They are to say to Athens that he "hath made his everlasting mansion/ Upon the beached verge of the salt flood." His grave-stone is to be their oracle: "Lips, let sour words go by and language end:/ What is amiss, plague and infection mend!/ Graves only be men's works, and death their gain!/ Sun, hide thy beams! Timon hath done his reign." Despondent over their failure to entice Timon back to Athens, the senators and the steward leave. They must be swift to find other ways to protect the city against Alcibiades' armies.

Act V: Scene 2

The scene takes place the following day, outside the walls of Athens. Two senators and a messenger are discussing the great threat that Alcibiades has made against the city. Their only hope is that Timon will forget his hostility toward the city and come to their rescue. The messenger says he has just seen a courier hurrying to Timon's cave with a message, begging his help.

The senators who had just left Timon arrive in Athens. They report that he refused to accept their offers. Athens must prepare for war.

Act V: Scene 3

The scene is the woods near Timon's cave. A crude tomb is close by. A messenger enters looking for Timon. He calls, but there is no answer. He notices the tomb and realizes Timon is dead. Unable to read the inscription he takes a wax impression of it for his captain Alcibiades. He is "an aged interpreter, though young in days."

Act V: Scene 4

This scene takes place outside the walls of Athens. Alcibiades and his forces are ready to invade the city. Trumpets sound and Alcibiades declares they are a warning "to this coward and lascivious town/ Our terrible approach." He reviles the city for its injustices and indifference to the public welfare.

The senators of the city take their stand on the walls of Athens. In their plea to Alcibiades to spare the city, they remind him of their proposals for peace; nor should the city—its walls, its taverns, its schools, built by ancient forebears—be the victim of his wrath against contemporary enemies. Alcibiades is invited to enter the city and take his tenth, but spare his "Athenian cradle." They will open the gates of the city to him if he will send his "gentle heart before/ To say thou'lt enter friendly." As a "token" of his honor they ask him to throw down his glove. Alcibiades agrees to their request and throws down his glove. The enemies of both Timon and himself, whom the state will "set out for reproof," he will punish, but no others. His soldiers will not pillage; if they do, they shall be subject to Athen's public laws.

The senators accept his word. As the city gates are opened, a courier hurries in to report to Alcibiades that Timon is dead. He gives him the wax impression he made of the inscription. Alcibiades reads it aloud, "Here lies a wretched corse [corpse], of wretched soul bereft;/ Seek not my name; a plague consume you wicked caitiffs left. Here lie I, Timon; who, alive, all living men did hate:/ Pass by and curse thy fill; but pass, and stay not here thy gait."

Alcibiades' tribute to Timon closes the play. He understands Timon's change of heart—his hatred for humanity, their eloquent apologies, and their affected tears. "Rich conceit" (imagination) prompted Timon to make the ocean weep "On thy lowe grave, on faults forgiven."

To bring about peace, Alcibiades promises "to use the olive" with his sword: "Make war breed peace; make peace stint war; make each/ Prescribe to other, as each other's leech."

Titus Andronicus

SATURNINUS, *son to the late Emperor of Rome, and afterwards declared Emperor.*
BASSIANUS, *brother to Saturninus; in love with Lavinia.*
TITUS ANDRONICUS, *a noble Roman, general against the Goths.*
MARCUS ANDRONICUS, *tribune of the people, and brother to Titus.*
LUCIUS
QUINTUS
MARTIUS } *sons to Titus Andronicus.*
MUTIUS
YOUNG LUCIUS, *a boy, son to Lucius.*
PUBLIUS, *son to Marcus the Tribune.*
SEMPRONIUS
CAIUS } *kinsmen to Titus.*
VALENTINE
AEMILIUS, *a noble Roman.*
ALARBUS
DEMETRIUS } *sons to Tamora.*
CHIRON
AARON, *a Moor, beloved by Tamora.*
CAPTAIN, TRIBUNE, MESSENGER, *and* CLOWN.

TAMORA, *Queen of the Goths.*
LAVINIA, *Daughter to Titus Andronicus.*
NURSE, *and a black* CHILD.

ROMANS, GOTHS, SENATORS, TRIBUNES, OFFICERS, SOLDIERS, *and* ATTENDANTS.

Titus Andronicus

Act I

During the decline of the Roman Empire, the death of the Emperor leaves his two sons Saturninus and Bassianus in dispute over the succession. As the play opens a crowd has gathered in front of the capitol to hear each of the sons plead with the Roman people to support his rights to the throne. Marcus, a tribune of the people and brother of Titus Andronicus, the great warrior, interrupts to tell the people that Titus is returning to the city as conqueror of the Goths. Of his twenty-four sons, all but four have died in battle. To honor Titus, Marcus asks Saturninus and Bassianus to dismiss their followers and plead their "deserts in peace and humbleness." Both heed Marcus' request. Bassianus, the younger brother, is loud in his praises of Titus, his sons, and his daughter, Lavinia, with whom he is in love.

Titus is announced and enters with his sons, an array of prominent Goths who have been taken prisoners, and a coffin that contains his sons killed in battle. In his address to the Romans, Titus repeats what his brother Marcus has told of his sacrifices to extend the Roman Empire. His son Lucius asks him to name the proudest prisoner he has taken among the Goths. Titus names Alarbus, son of Tamora, Queen of the Goths. Lucius and his brothers will sacrifice him to honor their slain brothers. Alarbus is marched offstage as his mother and brothers ask vengeance from the gods for his death. When Lucius returns to announce his death, it is a signal for Titus to have the trumpet sounded and lower the coffin containing the bodies of his sons in the grave. He declares, "Here lurks no treason"; there are "no storms" only "silence and eternal sleep." His daughter Lavinia enters to welcome him and kneels for Titus' blessing with his "victorious hand."

Marcus asks his brother to become a "candidatus" for Emperor. He deserves it after his victories in battle. Titus declines, feeling himself too old after having spent forty years on the battlefield. At the mention of his name, Saturninus is angry. As the late Emperor's eldest son, he feels he has the right to the Crown. Bassianus is not disturbed when Titus agrees with Saturninus and asks the tribunes to permit him to name the Emperor. They agree, and he chooses Saturninus. With a request for "voices and applause of every sort," Marcus announces Lord Saturninus as "Rome's great Emperor."

His first act is to choose Titus' daughter, Lavinia, to be his Empress. She does not appear to be too happy because of her betrothal to Bassianus. But she accepts without any ado. Saturninus' next act is to set free all the prisoners of war.

After a flourish of trumpets Saturninus courts Lavinia in a dumb show. When it is over Bassianus steps forward and seizes Lavinia. He declares, "This maid is mine." Marcus quickly settles the dispute, declaring that according to Roman justice Bassianus "seizes but his own." Lavinia's brothers come to Bassianus' defense and go offstage with the lovers, leaving one of their number, Mutius, to guard the door. When he refuses to permit his father to pass, Titus stabs him. Lucius chides him for killing his own son. But Titus feels that he has been dishonored by his sons for aiding Lavinia against the Emperor. Saturninus takes the view that he does not need her nor Titus nor his "treacherous haughty sons." If he tried to regain the favor of Titus, Titus could then say that Saturninus "begg'd the empire at his hands." In a quick move Saturninus asks Tamora, Queen of the Goths, to be his bride. She gladly accepts. Titus is left alone to muse on his strange fate—it is a new role for him to walk alone and in dishonor.

His three sons and Marcus disturb his reverie, denouncing him for killing Mutius. When they want to bury him with his other brothers, Titus refuses, calling Mutius a traitor. Marcus intervenes to demand burial for his nephew. In unison Titus' sons declare he will be buried with their brothers or they "will accompany him." Marcus bids his brother "be not barbarous" and remember that he is a Roman. Titus gives in, and Mutius is buried in the family tomb. The sudden rise to favor by Tamora puzzles both Marcus and Titus. They agree it is probably "by device." As they talk, Saturninus and Tamora return, and with them Bassianus and Lavinia. Saturninus is still jealous of his brother because of Lavinia, and he promises vengeance. He blames his loss of Lavinia on Titus' "dishonorable sons." Bassianus begs Saturninus to remember that Titus killed his own son in his "zeal for you." Tamora brings about a false peace between Saturninus and Titus. In an aside she prevails on the Emperor to make peace with Titus or the people may accuse him of ingratitude, "a heinous crime" in Rome, and put him off the throne. One day she will massacre father and sons in revenge for killing her son. Saturninus and Tamora leave after accepting an invitation from Titus to a hunt the following day.

Act II

Aaron, a Moor, brought to Rome as a prisoner by Titus, is a paramour of Tamora. Her marriage to the Emperor does not affect their liaison. He is planning a way to have a rendezvous with her when her two sons enter. They are in love with Lavinia though she is married to Bassianus. He tells them a scheme whereby they may have their wish. They can hide in the forest where Titus will have his hunt. There will be a chance to seize Lavinia, and then both can revel in their desires. The palace has "tongues," but the woods are "deaf and dull." The hunt begins as a charming outing, but fades when the scene shifts to the Moor hiding a bag of gold. It "must coin" a strategem.

As he finishes, Tamora comes to meet him and pretends to be enraptured with the beauty of the Roman forest. But Aaron, in a vengeful mood, reveals his vicious plan against Titus. He has plotted the death of Bassianus, and her sons will carry off Lavinia. They will rape and maim her. He will give Tamora "a fatal plotted scroll" to give Saturninus. It will throw suspicion on Titus' sons. They see Bassianus and Lavinia approaching. Tamora is told by Aaron to quarrel with him and her sons will come to her aid. He has already warned them. When Bassianus accuses her of meeting the Moor for "a foul purpose," she calls for vengeance and her sons rush in and stab him. They throw his body into a pit and carry off Lavinia as Aaron planned.

When Tamora leaves, Aaron enters with Quintus and Marius, sons of Titus. He takes them close to the pit where Bassianus' body has been thrown. One of them falls in and while his brother attempts to help him, Aaron quietly leaves. They are appalled to discover Bassianus' body. They are still struggling when Aaron returns with Saturninus, who sees them. It is then that he learns of Bassianus' death. Tamora gives him the letter that throws suspicion on Titus's sons. When Titus joins the group, he admits that he found the letter. But he asks that until the suspicion be removed from his sons that he "be their bail." Saturninus refuses and says that if there were a worse punishment than death, they would have it. The Emperor orders the body of Bassianus carried back to the palace and the murderers to accompany it. The erstwhile happy hunting party turns into a weird funeral march.

The sons of Tamora enter, with Lavinia maimed. They mock her in sadistic glee and then leave her alone in the forest. Her uncle Marcus discovers her plight. He bemoans her hideous disfigurement and is sorry for Titus. Such a sight will "make thy father blind."

Act III

When Titus and his sons are brought before the judges, senators, and tribunes, he pleads for their lives. It is to no avail. As he argues Marcus enters with Lavinia. Seeing her tortured body, Titus becomes "numb from grief." While his son Lucius and Marcus try to comfort him, Aaron enters. He declares that the senate will spare Titus' sons if he cuts off his hand and sends it to the king. Titus is willing to do it and is grateful to Aaron. The latter cuts off his hand. In an aside, the Moor reveals he has deceived Titus and his sons will be executed. Shortly, a messenger enters with the heads of his two sons. Titus goes into a laughing fit and pretends insanity. With Marcus and Lavinia he will go bury the heads. Before he goes, he directs Lucius, the last surviving son, who has been sent into exile by the Emperor, to raise an army of Goths. He must return and conquer Rome. As Titus leaves, he embraces Lucius, "Let's kiss and part for we have much to do." Lucius vows vengeance on the Emperor.

Murder and revenge continually haunt Titus. He keeps up his pretended insanity. Marcus notes how grief has "wrought on him" until he "takes false shadows for true substances." He goes off with Lavinia to read "sad stories."

Act IV

In Titus' garden his grandson, young Lucius, fears his aunt Lavinia because of her disfigurement. The boy likes to read and runs from her with an armful of books. Titus and his brother, Marcus, enter and quiet him. As the four sit talking, Titus and Marcus discuss who the villain could be that maimed Lavinia. She takes a staff and writes on the ground the names of Tamora's sons. Titus and Marcus on their knees vow vengeance.

Young Lucius, fond of playing warrior, goes with his grandfather to his armory. Titus gives him a bundle of weapons with messages attached, and they go off to the palace to deliver them to the

Emperor, Tamora, and her sons. The latter accept the "presents" from Lucius. The boy declares they are from his grandsire and "the goodliest weapons from his armory." Tamora's sons, Demetrius and Chiron, consider the weapons as a display of Titus' insanity. Aaron, who is with them, is told by a nurse that the Empress has given birth to a "blackamoor" child. She has sent it to him with word that he is to kill it. Instead of the child, Aaron kills the nurse. He explains that if three saw it—the midwife, the Empress, and the nurse—"Two may keep counsel when the third's away." He orders Tamora's sons to bury her in the field. The infant is "the vigor and picture" of his youth, and he will flee with it to the Goths.

When Lucius returns from the palace, Titus and Marcus take him to a public place to practice archery. To each arrow, Titus ties a message. He tells Lucius to shoot some of the arrows into the Emperor's courtyard. When a clown with a basket of pigeons passes by, Titus claims he has "news from heaven." He sends him with a "supplication" to the Emperor. He folds a knife inside the scroll.

Before the clown arrives, Saturninus has gathered up the arrows Lucius had shot into the palace courtyard and read the strange messages attached to them. These, together with the clown's "supplication," begin to worry Saturninus. He knows the "mad" Titus has sent them. It is best to have him killed, and he will be the "slaughterman."

A servant brings Saturninus word that the Goths are marching on Rome. With Lucius at the head of the army, the Emperor fears his popularity with the Romans will make him Emperor. Tamora offers to talk with Titus and "enchant" him. She leaves to fill him with "golden promises." A servant is sent to know what "hostage" Lucius asks.

Act V

As Lucius nears Rome with his army, a soldier hears a child cry and discovers Aaron in a hideaway. Lucius forces from him the horrors that he plotted Bassianus, Lavinia, and her brothers. He begs that Lucius spare his infant and send it to Tamora. He wants it silently to accuse her before the Emperor. Lucius intended to hang Aaron but now reserves a worse fate for him.

In answer to the Emperor's request regarding a "pledge," Lucius asks for Titus and Marcus. Meantime, Tamora and her sons, in disguise, visit Titus. She believes he is insane, especially when he names her sons as Rapine and Murder. With his one arm, he will embrace her. She is pleased that she can manage him despite his "brain sick" fits. Titus agrees to send for Lucius. While he is away from the troops, she can destroy the army.

Marcus is sent to summon Lucius and his chief generals. They must come to Titus' house to a banquet that he will give for the Emperor and Tamora. When the Empress leaves Titus, her sons stay to "watch" him. He quickly orders them bound and with the aid of Lavinia murders them.

The banquet turns into a scene of horrors. Titus, dressed as a cook, serves Tamora the bodies of her sons. After he tells her, he quickly stabs her. In the general slaughter only Lucius, his young son, and Marcus are left alive. Aaron, the Moor, has been imprisoned in Titus' house. He is sent for and his intrigues exposed to the people. Lucius condemns him to a lingering death. Marcus goes up to a balcony in Titus' house and asks the Romans to accept Lucius as governor. Titus' son tells of all the atrocious deeds done to his family. The Romans overwhelm him with shouts of "Rome's gracious governor!" Lucius thanks them and he hopes to govern so, "To heal Rome's harms, and wipe away her woe!"

THE
ROMANCES

Cymbeline

CYMBELINE, *King of Britain.*
CLOTEN, *son to the Queen by a former husband.*
POSTHUMUS LEONATUS, *a gentleman, husband to Imogen.*
BELARIUS, *a banished lord, disguised under the name of Morgan.*
GUIDERIUS } *sons to Cymbeline, disguised under the names of*
ARVIRAGUS } *Polydore and Cadwal, supposed sons to Morgan.*
PHILARIO, *friend to Posthumus* }
IACHIMO, *friend to Philario* } *Italians.*
CAIUS LUCIUS, *general of the Roman forces.*
PISANIO, *servant to Posthumus.*
CORNELIUS, *a physician.*
PHILARMONUS, *a soothsayer.*
ROMAN CAPTAIN.
TWO BRITISH CAPTAINS.
FRENCHMAN, *friend to Philario.*
TWO LORDS *of Cymbeline's court.*
TWO GENTLEMEN *of the same.*
TWO JAILERS.

QUEEN, *wife to Cymbeline.*
IMOGEN, *daughter to Cymbeline by a former Queen.*
HELEN, *a lady attending on Imogen.*

LORDS, LADIES, ROMAN SENATORS, TRIBUNES, DUTCHMAN, SPANIARD, MUSICIANS, OFFICERS, CAPTAINS, SOLDIERS, MESSENGERS, *and other* ATTENDANTS.

Cymbeline

Act I: Scene 1

This scene takes place in ancient Britain. It is summer. In the palace garden of Cymbeline, King of Britain, two gentlemen attached to his court are discussing the King's great discontent over the marriage of his daughter Imogen with the poor commoner Posthumus Leonatus. The first gentleman explains to his comrade that Posthumus Leonatus was a ward of the King and in this way fell in love with his daughter. The first gentleman praises Posthumus Leonatus and Imogen as a virtuous couple deeply in love with one another. He implies that another lover was spurned by Imogen. It is Cloten, son of the Queen, Cymbeline's second wife.

The Queen, Imogen, and Posthumus enter the garden. The Queen pretends she has the good of the young couple at heart. She jests that Imogen is her "prisoner," and she will attempt to "quiet" the "rage of fire" in the King. Meanwhile, he should accept his exile with patience. She leaves them for a "turn about the garden." When the Queen leaves, Imogen deplores her "dissembling courtesy." Though she fears her father's wrath, she promises to be faithful while he is away. Posthumus promises absolute fidelity. He will go to Rome and stay with a friend of his father's. Imogen gives him a jewel and a diamond ring that was her mother's. He clasps a bracelet, "a manacle of love," on her arm.

The Queen returns for a moment. As she leaves, she says in an aside that she will send the King into the garden. He comes as the couple finish their protestations of love. Cymbeline curses Posthumus, "Thou art poison to my blood." Posthumus leaves quickly with a gracious farewell to the King. Cymbeline then scolds Imogen for marrying a poor commoner who would debase his throne.

Daring her father's wrath, Imogen declares it is his fault that she "loved Posthumus." The King "bred him" as "her play fellow." As the Queen enters, he demands that she "pen" up Imogen. Pretending to take Imogen's part, the Queen sends Cymbeline to reflect and meditate. Posthumus' servant Pisanio brings news to the Queen that her son Cloten and Posthumus have fought a duel. She is glad that neither was injured. He has come from Posthumus, who is ready to sail, and he gives Imogen "notes," telling what his duties are toward her. The Queen remarks Pisanio's faithfulness to Imogen. She suggests the latter walk for a while in the garden. Imogen says she will see the Queen in half an hour. She tells Pisanio to "Go see my lord aboard: for this time leave me."

Act I: Scene 2

In a public place in the same (unnamed) town in Britain, Cloten and two gentlemen discuss his duel with Posthumus. Cloten cannot understand why blood was not drawn. In an aside one of the gentlemen attributes it to his clumsiness with his sword. Cloten questions why Imogen should "love this fellow, and refuse" him. He wishes "there had been some hurt done" in the duel. It would have shown his valor.

Act I: Scene 3

Later the same day in a room in Cymbeline's palace, Imogen asks Pisanio to give her the details of Posthumus' departure. He obliges with a graphic account how he stood on the deck waving his handkerchief and "kiss'd it, madam." And until he was out of sight, he waved "with glove, or hat, or handkerchief." To her question, when she would hear from him, Pisanio declares as soon as he can find means to send a letter. Imogen bemoans the fact that she had no chance to say "goodbye." She had many "pretty things" to say. She would warn him against "the shes of Italy," that they "should not betray her interest and his honour." Three times a day—morning, noon, and night—she would have reminded him she is at her "orisons," and then she is "in heaven for him." She complains that her father came in just as she was ready to give "a parting kiss" and like the tyrannous north wind, "Shakes all our buds from growing."

A lady-in-waiting enters to say the Queen desires "your Highness' company." She leaves Pisanio with "things" to tend to for her.

Act I: Scene 4

The scene is some days later, in an apartment in Philario's house in Rome. He and his friend, Iachimo, with several others (designated only as a Frenchman, a Dutchman, and a Spaniard) are discussing the recently arrived Posthumus. The impression of him that Iachimo gives is not glowing. He had seen him casually in Britain. Philario defends him. The Frenchman knew him in Orleans, but was not particularly impressed. Then there is the question of his unhappy marriage to "his King's daughter." Philario comes to Posthumus' defense. The latter's father and he were soldiers together, and Philario owes his life to him.

Posthumus enters and is introduced to the group by Philario. The Frenchman remembers a duel the young Briton, some years before, had fought over the virtues of women. Only the night before, he adds, there was a similar discussion, wherein it was declared that there were no women as virtuous as those of France.

It is Iachimo's belief that no woman is as moral as these duels indicate. The statement starts a harsh quipping on the subject between Iachimo and Posthumus. It ends in a wager by the Italian that he can seduce Imogen. He stakes "ten thousand ducats" to Posthumus' ring that after two meetings with her he "will bring from thence that honour of hers which you [Posthumus] imagine so reserved."

Posthumus is willing to give his diamond ring if Imogen is proved unfaithful. But if she is faithful, then Iachimo will have to "answer" with a duel for his ugly remarks about her. It is agreed, and they go to have the wager duly recorded.

Act I: Scene 5

The scene takes place some few days later in Britain in a room in Cymbeline's palace. The Queen with her ladies and a physician, Cornelius, are discussing a box of drugs that he has brought her. Desirous to know for what use the Queen intends them, she appears surprised he would ask her. As his pupil, has he not taught her how "to make perfume? distill? preserve?" Even the King likes her "confections." This is answer enough unless he thinks she is "devilish." Now she intends to try some potions on animals —"but none human."

When Pisanio arrives, the Queen dismisses the physician. In an aside, she declares he will be her first "work." He is an enemy to her son and a "factor" for Posthumus. Cornelius, in a long aside, reveals that he knows what she is most likely up to. He has given her some harmless drugs that at most produce only a deep sleep. The person's "spirits" are deadened for awhile but are "more fresh" when they waken.

After the physician leaves, the Queen questions Pisanio about whether Imogen seems to be more resigned to Posthumus' absence. She charges the servant to talk against his master. If he can bring her word that Imogen loves Cloten, "he will receive great preferment from the King. The confections that the doctor brought are an "earnest" to Pisanio of all the Queen will do for him. While he goes to call her "women," she muses that the drugs will kill Pisanio, "a sly and constant knave." Her next victim will be Imogen. The Queen's women come with flowers they have gathered for her, and she goes off happily, reminding Pisanio to "think" on her words. He declares that he will. But when she has gone, he swears that before he will prove untrue to Posthumus, he will "choke" himself.

Act I: Scene 6

The scene follows a day later. Imogen is alone in her room in the palace. She sighs over her predicament—hated by her father and stepmother, her husband banished. She wishes she had been kidnapped along with her two brothers in infancy. However miserable their state, at least they are not imprisoned like herself.

She answers a knock at the door. Pisanio introduces Iachimo, who gives her a letter from her husband. She welcomes him. In an aside, Iachimo is much impressed by her beauty, and if her mind is "so rare," then she is "alone the Arabian bird."

He worries that he has already lost the wager. He sees that he must be bold to win her.

Imogen opens the letter and reads only the first two sentences. It introduces Iachimo as a friend of "noblest note." She is to "reflect on him as you value your trust." The rest of the letter "warms" her heart. Iachimo is very welcome. He praises her beauty, comparing it to nature. Imogen nicely pretends she is at a loss to know what he is really talking about. After a while she inquires about Posthumus' health. Iachimo declares he is well and happy. He is called the "Briton reveller."

The false account he gives of Posthumus' gay life in Rome disturbs Imogen. Iachimo suggests that she take revenge and have an affair with him. The suggestion angers her. He immediately apologizes for his false report. It was just to test her love for Posthumus. She readily forgives him. He asks a favor—that she store a trunk for him, containing a present he was commissioned to purchase for the emperor. Imogen will be glad to keep the trunk. He must send it to her. She is sorry that he is leaving the next day. At Iachimo's suggestion, she will give him a letter to take to Posthumus.

Act II: Scene 1

This scene follows a few hours later. Cloten and two lords stand in the palace courtyard discussing their luck at bowling. Cloten has not been successful and wishes he might have answered his opponents who "take him up" for swearing. He would like a fight, but as a noble he dare not. His mother also keeps too close a watch on him. The First Lord questions if Cloten has heard about the newly arrived Italian "stranger." No, but he is anxious to meet him. He will win back from him at "bowls" what he lost. With the Second Lord, he leaves.

The First Lord muses that "such a crafty devil as is his mother/ Should yield the world this ass!" He feels sorry for Imogen. She is afflicted on every side with hatred and duplicity. He hopes she can "keep unshak'd/ That temple, thy fair mind," and live to enjoy her "banish'd lord and this great land."

Act II: Scene 2

The scene takes place near midnight in Imogen's room in the palace. She is reading in bed. A lady is attending her. Iachimo's trunk is in a corner of the room. Imogen complains that she is weary of reading. She asks the lady "to fold down the leaf" of the book to mark the place. She wants the taper left burning. If the lady wakes at four in the morning, she is to call her. Asking the gods to protect her "from fairies, and the tempters of the night," she falls asleep.

Iachimo crawls from the trunk. He steals over to her bed. Looking at Imogen, he breaks into a long rapturous praise of her beauty.

But he remembers his "design" is to write down a description of the room. He takes the bracelet from her arm and notes a mole on her left breast. This will be the strongest proof that he has seduced her. He notes she has been reading the tale of *Tereus*. Iachimo has taken sufficient notes, and goes back to the trunk and shuts the "spring of it." Fear comes over him. "Though this [is] a heavenly angel, hell is here."

Act II: Scene 3

This scene occurs a few hours later in an antechamber adjoining Imogen's apartment. Cloten and several lords are discussing his losses at cards. He appears "patient" over it. Things would be right if he could win "this foolish Imogen." He has ordered musicians to play outside her room. Friends have advised him "to give her music o' mornings; they say it will penetrate."

The musicians enter and tune their instruments. In answer to his request for a "wonderful sweet air," they play and sing, "Hark, hark! the lark at Heaven's gate sings."

Whether or not the song moves Imogen, Cloten declares he will "never give o'er." When the musicians finish, Cymbeline and the Queen enter and comfort Cloten's impatience with Imogen's aloofness. The Queen suggests ways of attracting her attention. A messenger brings the King word that ambassadors from Rome have arrived. One is Caius Lucius. After Cloten has spoken with Imogen, he is to come to the King's apartment.

He muses about how he will manage to see Imogen. He decides that gold offered to one of her ladies will get him admittance. While he and the lady chat, Imogen enters. After a greeting, he swears he loves her, but she has no regard for him. They banter until Imogen complains he is making her forget "a lady's manners." Cloten tries to make her rejection of him an act of disobedience to her father. He belittles Posthumus as a "base wretch" and "bred of alms." She can look forward to "beggary" married to such a "base slave." Imogen declares "his meanest garment" is worth more to her "than all the hairs above thee/ Were they all made such men." She calls for Pisanio.

Cloten keeps repeating the phrase, "His meanest garment." Imogen sends Pisanio to her woman, Dorothy, to search for her bracelet. She remembers kissing it, and hopes it is not gone "to tell my lord/ That I kiss aught but he." Again, Cloten repeats, "His meanest garment." Imogen, quietly amused, declares that indeed those were her words. He can "call witness to 't." Cloten will inform her father. Perhaps, Imogen suggests, her mother, too. He goes away, swearing revenge and muttering, "His meanest garment."

Act II: Scene 4

This scene takes place in Rome a few days later. Posthumus and Philario are in an apartment in the latter's house discussing the Italian Ambassador's trip to Britain to collect the tribute due Rome. As they talk, Iachimo enters. He gives Posthumus letters from Imogen and then proceeds to prove by circumstantial evidence —a description of her and of her room—that he seduced her.

Posthumus finally believes that Iachimo has seduced Imogen. In his anger he threatens to expose her at her father's court. Philario encourages him to be patient, but is of little use.

Act II: Scene 5

This short scene, later the same day, consists of a soliloquy by Posthumus. It shows that he now hates Imogen and that he will take revenge because she has betrayed his faith in her. He muses on the fickleness of women. He believes "there's no motion/ That tends to vice in man, but I affirm/ It is the woman's part!" After listing a catalogue of women's faults and weaknesses, he concludes, "all faults that may be named, nay that hell knows,/ Why, hers, in part or all; but rather all." He will pray that women have their will, for then the "very devils cannot plague them better."

Act III: Scene 1

This scene takes place in Britain the same day that Cloten had gone to Imogen's apartment. He had been told by Cymbeline that the latter would have need of him "toward this Roman." The ambassador Lucius from Rome and attendants, Cymbeline, the Queen, Cloten, lords, and attendants meet in a room of state in the palace. Asked by the King to present his business, the ambassador tells that he has been sent by Augustus Caesar to collect the tribute levied by Julius Caesar when he conquered the island. Britain owes "yearly three thousand pounds" that lately has not been paid.

The Queen interrupts to say that it never will be paid. Though not asked for his opinion, Cloten volunteers, "Britain is/ A world by itself; and we will nothing pay/ For wearing our own noses." Cymbeline is left out of the discussion. The Queen belittles Caesar's victory as a "kind of conquest." The "terrible seas" wrecked his boats. Cassibelan, the great King of the Britons, conquered Caesar. Cymbeline, finally, has a say and quickly turns British history to Mulmutius who "ordain'd" the nation's laws.

Act III: Scene 2

If he follows directions in Imogen's letter it will provide the "opportunity." A letter is enclosed to Imogen, telling her to go to the coast and that he (Posthumus) will meet her there.

The false accusations of the Italian greatly disturb Pisanio. He determines that no matter what the consequences, he will not murder her.

When he hears Imogen approaching, he pretends to be ignorant of any personal news from Posthumus. Imogen is happy to receive his letter and overjoyed that he will meet her in Milford-Haven. She is excited about the journey, though Pisanio bids her "consider." She decides to disguise herself to get away from the palace, and orders him to "provide" her with a "riding suit" like a "franklyn's" (farmer's) wife would wear.

Act III: Scene 3

This scene takes place in the mountainous country of Wales. A banished lord, Belarius, and two youths, Guiderius and Arviragus, the sons of Cymbeline, kidnapped in their infancy, live in a cave in the mountains. Belarius still harbors bitterness toward Cymbeline for banishing him unjustly. He kidnapped the youths and has brought them up to believe that they are his sons. Now they are beginning to resent the simple rustic lives they lead. They be-

come envious at Belarius' tales of his life at court and on the
battlefield. They ask what they will be able to talk about when they
grow up. It is not fair to stay hidden away in the mountains. They
declare, "We have seen nothing:/ We're beastly; subtle as the fox
for prey."

He tells them the world gives honors, but is full of hardships and
cruelty, too. Once Cymbeline loved him. And as a soldier, he was
highly praised. But "in one night," he was undone. Two men,
"villains, whose false oaths prevail'd/ Before my perfect honour,"
swore that he was a spy for the Romans. He was banished, and for
twenty years has lived in these mountains.

Belarius sits musing after he sends the youths up the mountain to
hunt a deer. He notes how they react to his tales. When he tells
of warlike feats the older one, Guiderius, struts like a warrior.
"The princely blood flows in his cheeks," and he "acts" Belarius'
words. The younger "strikes life" into a speech and is more original
in his reactions. Their nurse, Euriphile, they thought was their
mother. Now they keep flowers on her grave. They call Belarius,
Morgan.

Act III: Scene 4

This scene takes place several days later near Milford-Haven.
Imogen and Pisanio enter. Imogen is worried because she has not
found Posthumus as Pisanio had told her she would. He keeps looking at her and is seemingly distressed over something. Imogen
finally wheedles it out of him. He shows her Posthumus' letter
that orders him to murder her for being unfaithful to him. The
letter unnerves her. She declares life now will be unbearable for
her, and so she pleads with Pisanio to kill her. The more insistent
she is, the more he refuses.

Pisanio suggests that she not return to the court. She can stay in
the countryside. He will send some bloody sign "of her death"
to Posthumus. This will satisfy both him and the court. It pleases
Imogen. She will at least be rid of Cloten. Pisanio further suggests that she might follow the ambassador Lucius back to Rome
if she will disguise herself as a page and act the man's part. He
has brought "doubtlet, hat, hose," all she will need. She "must
forget to be a woman." He will send her money while she is in
Italy. Before he leaves, he gives her a box, which the Queen gave
him. It contains remedies for sea-sickness and "distemper." She
must hurry now and get into man's attire.

Act III: Scene 5

This scene takes place the following day in a room in Cymbeline's palace. The King, the Queen, and Cloten bid the Italian Ambassador farewell after his few days' visit. War is all but declared between the two countries over Britain's refusal to pay tribute. Cymbeline sends a friendly escort to take Lucius to Milford-Haven.

When the ambassador leaves, Cymbeline asks why Imogen has not "tender'd/ The duty of the day." The Queen declares she is still grieving for Posthumus. An attendant sent by Cymbeline to summon her returns with word that her "chambers are all lock'd." There is no answer to his loud knocking. The absence of Imogen disturbs Cymbeline. He hopes his fears "prove false." With Cloten he goes to her apartment. The Queen remains to muse over the seeming success of her plans—she has already given a death potion to Pisanio and he will soon take it, thinking it a simple curative. She feels despair has seized Imogen, and is happy she is gone "to death or dishonour." In either case she can bring it to a good end. With Imogen out of the way, she has "the placing of the British crown."

Cloten returns to confirm the King's fears that Imogen has fled. The Queen leaves to calm Cymbeline, who is in a rage over his daughter's disappearance. The Queen, in an aside, feels it may end him, too. That would be even better.

Left alone, Cloten muses that he both loves and hates Imogen. But she treats him so contemptuously that he is determined to have his revenge. When Pisanio enters, Cloten demands to know where Imogen is. The servant's hesitancy in replying infuriates Cloten, and he threatens to kill him unless he tells where she has gone. Pisanio gives Cloten a copy of the letter Posthumus wrote Imogen.

Cloten recognizes that the letter is from Posthumus. He will try to overtake Imogen before she arrives at Milford-Haven. But he needs the aid of Pisanio. In an aside, Pisanio declares he will never forsake Imogen or Posthumus. Feigning loyalty to Cloten, he helps him disguise himself as Posthumus by bringing him the "suit" Posthumus wore when he "took leave" of Imogen and helping him prepare to start for Milford-Haven. Cloten is determined to be "merry" in his revenge. When he leaves to don his disguise, Pisanio muses that Cloten cannot overtake Imogen because she will be on her way to Rome with Lucius. He wishes "heavenly blessings" on her.

Act III: Scene 6

The scene takes place a day or so after Pisanio left Imogen on her way to Milford-Haven. She gets lost in the mountains and is faint from hunger.

Imogen muses on her plight. Two beggars give her directions; maybe they, too, are false. But "falsehood is worse in kings, than beggars." When she notices a path to a cave, she stealthily enters. It is the home of Belarius and his two adopted sons, actually Imogen's brothers.

She is heartily welcomed. Asked her name, she replies, Fidele. She was on her way to Milford-Haven to see her cousin bound for Italy, but she missed meeting him. Belarius invites her to dine and spend the night with them.

One of the youths wishes she were "a woman" and he would "woo hard to be" her groom. The other is content that she is a man and will "love her as a brother." In an aside, Imogen praises them. She would change her sex "to be companion with them,/ Since Leonatus's false." After dinner they want to hear her story, "So far as thou wilt speak it."

Act III: Scene 7

This short scene is in a public place in Rome after the ambassador Lucius returns from Britain. Two senators discuss "the tenor of the Emperor's writ": Rome is at war against the Pannonians (inhabitants of modern Hungary and Yugoslavia) and the Dalmatians (inhabitants of a region of Yugoslavia on the Adriatic). Their armies in Gaul are not strong enough to fight the Britons. The "gentry" will have to be pressed into service. Lucius has been named proconsul. The tribunes are committed to provide ways and means to collect Britain's tribute.

One of the senators is ordered to find recruits to aid Lucius, now general of the army in Gallia (Gaul). The senator's commission will advise him regarding the size of the force "and the time/ Of their dispatch."

Act IV: Scene 1

The scene takes place in a forest in Wales near the cave of Belarius. Cloten, disguised as Posthumus, has come, he thinks, to the spot that Pisanio has marked as the trysting place of Posthumus and Imogen. He swaggers up and down, musing how well his disguise fits. Physically, and in every way, he is equal to Posthumus—especially in "single combat." He will have hacked off Posthumus' head within an hour; raped Imogen; and cut his "garments" to pieces before her face. Then he will take her back to her father. He may be disturbed, but the Queen will quiet him. He has tied up his horse. His sword drawn, he is ready to go.

Act IV: Scene 2

This scene follows immediately in front of Belarius' cave. He and his sons are worried that Fidele is ill. They insist she remain in the cave and rest. She admits she is "very sick," but begs them to go about their daily tasks and leave her by herself. They can trust her. She will rob none but herself. Both the boys love her as much as their father. If either Imogen or their father had to die, the younger brother would say, "My father, not this youth." In an aside, Belarius notes "the noble strain" in the boys—"the breed of greatness." When Belarius and the boys are preparing to leave, Imogen deplores their hopeless situation. She is more sick at heart than in body. She takes some of Pisanio's drug, thinking it will help. Belarius calls to her that she must not be sick, "For you must be our housewife." Imogen replies that, "well or ill" she is theirs forever. She enters the cave, and Belarius and the boys stay for a moment chatting about her. They fear some misfortune has happened in her life, but she never mentions it.

As they talk, Cloten arrives. He has lost his way and complains he cannot find those "runagates." Belarius recognizes him as son of the Queen and fears there is some "ambush," since he and his adopted sons are outlaws. Belarius and the younger son go to search for hidden troops. Guiderius talks with Cloten, and immediately they antagonize one another. Contemptuous of "villain mountaineers," Cloten belittles Guiderius. When Cloten brags he is the Queen's son, Guiderius is not impressed—were his name, "Toad, or Adder, Spider,/ 'Twould move" him sooner. In his anger Cloten threatens to kill him, his father, and his brother. He draws his sword, and they go off fighting.

When Belarius and his son return, they discuss the real reason for Cloten's visit. Belarius feels Cloten has never had good judgment, but rather foolhardy boldness. As they talk, the elder boy returns with Cloten's head. Belarius is worried that news of his murder will get to the court and Cymbeline will hunt for them as outlaws. Neither youth is sorry that Cloten is dead. Arviragus goes to talk with Imogen. His interest in her moves Belarius to muse over the hereditary traits of noble blood that create an "invisible instinct" in them.

After Guiderius returns, declaring he has sent Cloten's head downstream, an "ingenious instrument" is heard to play. Belarius thinks it is Arviragus who plays it. Not since his mother died has it played. As he talks, Arviragus enters, carrying Fidele (Imogen) as dead. He found her body on the floor, and thought she was asleep. Belarius and his sons are very sad. They decide to bury Fidele's body near their supposed mother, Euriphile.

Belarius reminds them that in their grief for Fidele, they must remember Cloten. He is the queen's son. Their "foe was princely" and must be buried as such. He goes to "fetch" Cloten's body and the youths sing a dirge over Imogen, covering her body with flowers: "Fear no more the heat o' the sun,/ Nor the furious Winter's rages."

Belarius and his sons place Cloten's body near Imogen. After strewing flowers, they kneel to pray and leave. As soon as they go, Fidele wakens in a daze, half dreaming. She sees the bloody headless corpse beside her, and recognizing Posthumus' clothes, believes that he has been murdered. She blames Pisanio and Cloten. In despair she throws herself on the corpse.

Lucius, now general of the Roman army, enters with a captain, a soothsayer and others. Word is brought to him that the troops from Gallia have arrived, and the legions from Rome, composed of the "gentlemen" of Italy under Iachimo, are on the way to Britain. The chances of Rome winning the war are good, according to the soothsayer, who in a dream saw the Roman eagle over Britain.

When they discover Fidele (who they think is a page) stretched over the headless corpse, they believe she is dead. On discovering she is alive, Lucius asks who it is that she mourns and why. Imogen says it is Richard du Champ, her master, and that her name is Fidele. The Roman finds out enough about her to ask her to

850

be his page. She readily accepts. They bury Cloten, Imogen believing it is Posthumus, in a "daisied plot." Lucius tells her to stop weeping, "Some falls are means the happier to arise."

Act IV: Scene 3

This scene takes place in a room in Cymbeline's palace. He asks an attendant to bring a report on the Queen's health. She has become very ill—"madness" over the absence of Cloten. Plagued by trouble—Imogen, the "great part of his comfort gone," his Queen ill, her son unheard from, and Rome threatening war—Cymbeline complains to the "heavens/ How deeply you at once do touch me." He has summoned Pisanio to find out what he knows about Imogen's disappearance. Threatened by torture to divulge his secrets, Pisanio pleads ignorance of Imogen's whereabouts. He begs the King to believe his loyalty. Cymbeline accepts his allegiance with reservations.

A lord in attendance gives the king word that the Roman troops from Gallia have landed on the "coast" with a supply "Of Roman gentlemen, by the Senate sent." Cymbeline longs for the counsel of his Queen and Cloten. The lord advises using the troops that are ready—"they long to go." The King is grateful for the advice. He can handle war, but his domestic problems are his greatest grief.

When the King and attendants leave, Pisanio stays and muses over the fact that he has not heard from Posthumus. He wrote him that he had "slain" Imogen. Nor has he had word from her. Of Cloten he has no knowledge. He is "perplex'd" by it all. But wherein he is "false," he is "honest; not true, to be true." In war the King will find him "loyal."

Act IV: Scene 4

This short scene takes place in front of Belarius' cave a few days later. With his two sons, Belarius discusses the several alternatives they have in escaping the Roman troops as well as the revenge of Cymbeline and the Queen if Cloten's death is traced to them. Tired of the inactive rustic life, the youths are anxious to join the King's army. They argue that no one will know them. Belarius is too well known to follow them into the army. He gives them his blessing. After they leave, he thinks that they are scornful of royalty now, but they will change their minds once they realize that they are "princes born."

Act V: Scene 1

This scene takes place a short time later in the Roman camp in Britain. Posthumus enters, carrying a bloody handkerchief. He is deeply remorseful over the supposed death of Imogen. He is not content in the Roman army, fighting against a country over which one day Imogen would have been Queen. He decides to disguise himself as a peasant and join Cymbeline's army. He prays to the gods to give him the strength of "the Leonati."

Act V: Scene 2

This scene takes place on a field between the British and Roman camps. On one side there is Lucius, Iachimo, and Imogen; opposing them are the troops of the British army. As the latter march to position in the field, Posthumus follows in peasant garb. There are alarms sounded. Both armies retreat and enter again. Iachimo and Posthumus are "in skirmish." The latter overcomes Iachimo, and, after disarming him, leaves.

Iachimo thinks about the wrong he has done to Imogen. He is humiliated at having lost the duel to Posthumus, whom he thinks is a simple "Carl" (countryman). The "knighthood and honors" that are his "are titles but of scorn" to the unlettered. Disheartened, he leaves the field.

The battle continues and Cymbeline is taken prisoner. Belarius and his sons attempt to rescue him. In the midst of the confusion, Posthumus enters and encourages the Britons. With his aid Cymbeline is freed. Lucius, Iachimo, and Imogen enter, the latter still in disguise. They urge her to save herself. The tide has turned against the Romans. They will all have to flee for their lives.

Act V: Scene 3

This scene takes place later the same day on the battlefield. Posthumus and a British Lord discuss how the Britons were able to overcome the Roman army. Posthumus explains that an old man (Belarius) and "two striplings" (Guiderius and Arviragus) erected an ambush at the side of a narrow mountain pass and shot the Roman soldiers as they passed through. Posthumus fought with them, but he does not identify himself in describing the victory.

After the lord leaves, Posthumus thinks that he is not interested in either side winning. He determines not to fight again but rather to yield to whichever side takes him—his "ransom's death." Two British captains enter and, believing he is a Roman, take him prisoner.

Act V: Scene 4

This scene follows immediately in a British prison. Posthumus enters with two jailers, who lock him in and leave. He muses on the great crime he has committed in ordering Imogen murdered. It has fettered his soul, and that is worse than the fetters he wears on his wrists. He wants to die; it will satisfy the gods and set his conscience free.

Soon Posthumus falls into a deep sleep. He has a vision of his father, mother, and two brothers killed in war. They sing to him, each chanting a stanza of a long song. The last stanza is sung by Jupiter, whom the brothers have begged to help Posthumus. He prophesies that Posthumus "shall be lord of Lady Imogen/ And happier much by his affliction made."

The jailer enters Posthumus' cell to tell him he is ordered to appear before Cymbeline. The King has ordered him to be hanged. Hanging is not so bad, the jailer says. It rids a man of his tavern debts. Posthumus is happy to die. But the jailer warns him that he does not know which "way" he is going (i.e., to heaven or to hell), but Posthumus insists he does.

A messenger arrives, demanding that the prisoner be brought at once to the King. Posthumus' readiness to die amazes the jailer. He wishes "we [all people] were all of one mind, and one mind good." It would do away with his job as hangman, but his "wish hath a preferment in 't."

Act V: Scene 5

This long scene follows immediately· in Cymbeline's tent. The King is seated with an array of Britons before him. They include

SHAKESPEARE'S BEST PLAYS

Belarius, Guiderius, Arviragus, Pisanio, and others. The King is
interested to learn the identity of the poor soldier (Posthumus)
who aided the old man [Belarius] and the two young soldiers to
rescue him and help to win the battle for the British. No one can
find him.

Cornelius, the physician, enters to report the Queen's death. She
died with "horror," raving madly as she lived. Her plan to
poison the King is revealed by the physician. Her deceit is hard
for Cymbeline to believe.

A contingent of Roman soldiers including Lucius, Iachimo, and
Posthumus file into the tent. Imogen, in disguise, is with Lucius
and is not recognized by Posthumus. Lucius pleads for the life of
his page. Cymbeline grants his request and, charmed by Imogen,
permits her to name any other prisoner and that man will be
spared. Taking Cymbeline aside, Imogen confides why she keeps
watching the Roman prisoner (Posthumus). Meanwhile, Belarius
and his sons are amazed to see "Fidele" alive.

At Imogen's request Iachimo steps forward and she questions
him regarding his treacherous slander. Iachimo relates the bedroom
scene in detail, accusing himself and completely exonerating Imogen. Posthumus then steps forward, identifies himself, and accuses
Iachimo in savage terms and berates himself for having believed
him. Imogen tries to intervene, and in his rage he strikes her.
She falls down. Pisanio hurries to help her. She repels him because of the "poison" drug he gave her. He pleads his innocence.
Cornelius speaks up to say that it was vile medicine he had given
the Queen, but not poison. It produced only a deep sleep. Belarius
and his adopted sons have recognized Imogen's (Fidele's) voice
and understand how they had mistaken her sleep for death.

Imogen turns to Posthumus and embraces him, asking why he is
so harsh with her. Both he and Cymbeline are overjoyed.

Cymbeline is astonished at the revelation of misdeeds and the
dropping of disguises. The last to reveal himself is Belarius. He
tells in detail of the kidnapping of the King's infant sons, his marriage to the nurse, Euriphile, who actually stole the children for
him, their rustic life, the arrival of Imogen, her supposed death,
and strange disappearance. Cymbeline is happy over the return
of his sons and pardons Belarius. There is great rejoicing by Imogen and her two brothers. Posthumus is presented to Cymbeline
by Imogen. The King's greeting, "We'll learn our freeness of a
son-in-law," is not so gracious as young Arviragus' joy over having

Posthumus for a "brother." He helped them when they needed him. Posthumus asks Cymbeline to request the soothsayer to interpret the "label" (i.e., a scroll) that the god Jupiter left on his bosom after his dream. The soothsayer explains that Cymbeline is the "lofty cedar," and the "lopp'd branches" (his sons) restored to him "are now revived." Their "issue/ Promises Britain peace and plenty."

Cymbeline is anxious to have peace in the realm. Though Rome lost the war, Britain will pay the tribute nevertheless. He grants pardon to all. The Britons will march through Lud's-town waving both Roman and British ensigns. He will ratify peace in the temple of Jupiter and "seal it with feasts."

Pericles

ANTIOCHUS, *King of Antioch.*
PERICLES, *Prince of Tyre.*
HELICANUS ⎫
ESCANES   ⎬ *two lords of Tyre.*
SIMONIDES, *King of Pentapolis.*
CLEON, *Governor of Tharsus.*
LYSIMACHUS, *Governor of Mytilene.*
CERIMON, *a lord of Ephesus.*
THALIARD, *a lord of Antioch.*
PHILEMON, *servant to Cerimon.*
LEONINE, *servant to Dionyza.*
MARSHAL.
PANDAR.
BOULT, *his servant.*
Another SERVANT.

DAUGHTER *of Antiochus.*
DIONYZA, *wife to Cleon.*
THAISA, *daughter to Simonides.*
MARINA, *daughter to Pericles and Thaisa.*
LYCHORIDA, *nurse to Marina.*
BAWD.

LORDS, LADIES, KNIGHTS, GENTLEMEN, SAILORS, PIRATES, FISHERMEN, *and* MESSENGERS.

The goddess DIANA.

GOWER, *as Chorus.*

Pericles

Act I: Prologue

The scene opens in Antioch in front of the King's palace. The "ghost" of John Gower stands in front of the gates, serving as a kind of chorus. He wishes to introduce a "song" that has been popular since early times. He tells how Antiochus built the city of Antioch, "the fairest of all Syria." When his wife died, he was left to rear their only child, Lucinda. Her beauty moved Antiochus to commit incest, which was not then considered sinful. However, Gower calls it "evil." Many young men came to woo the Princess Lucinda, and fearing to lose her, the King contrived a riddle that each suitor must solve or else lose his head. Many lost their heads, which were set up over the palace gate. To provide suspense, Gower gives no more of the story.

Act I: Scene 1

The scene opens in a room in Antiochus' palace. Pericles, the young Prince of Tyre and heir to the throne, is advised by King Antiochus of the danger that is entailed in seeking to marry his daughter. The Prince is not frightened. He is aware of the danger he risks in trying to solve the riddle.

Before Pericles begins the task, Lucinda enters to the strains of music and is dressed as a bride. Pericles is impressed by her beauty. He is again warned by Antiochus who points to the heads of the "martyrs" who have been slain in "Cupid's Wars." But Pericles will take a chance, and if he loses he bequeaths a "happy peace" to Antiochus. His "unspotted fire of love" for Lucinda enables him to accept "the sharpest blow."

Since Pericles persists in scorning advice, Antiochus bids him

Pericles

expound the riddle. Lucinda hopes he will have success. Though
he immediately senses the crime of Antiochus, he does not reveal
it. Sympathy is roused in him for her, and he could love her
still if the riddle were not "stored with ill."

He cautiously speaks of the evil inherent in incest and says that
no honest man will willingly become involved with it. He praises
Lucinda as a "fair viol" who, if "fingered" lawfully, "would draw
heaven down."

Antiochus pretends he is unable to comprehend Pericles' meaning
and demands that he be more plain-spoken. The Prince then boldly
remarks, "Few love to hear the sins they love to act," so he declines to explain the riddle further. Vice always brings evil in the
end. But since kings are all powerful, "in vice their law's their will."
Who dare reprove if "Jove doth ill?" Pericles begs to be let go
and keep his head. Antiochus, in an aside, admits Pericles has
solved the riddle. But he informs the Prince that he has misinterpreted it. In order to keep him at court, Antiochus extends his
time to solve the riddle to forty days. By then, perhaps, Pericles
can claim his daughter. In a long soliloquy, Pericles muses, "How
courtesy would seem to cover sin." He knows the King's respite
is only a ruse to keep him until he can be conveniently murdered,
since he could reveal the King's great sin. Pericles immediately
plans to escape from the country.

After Pericles leaves, Antiochus re-enters alone. He knows that
Pericles has discovered the secret, and so he must die. Thaliard,
lord of Antioch, is summoned and told to poison Pericles immediately. Gold is his reward for the task. A messenger interrupts
the king with word that Pericles has fled from Antioch. Thaliard
is sent to hunt for him, and he is not to return until he can say,
"Prince Pericles is dead."

Act I: Scene 2

This scene takes place a few days later in Tyre, Pericles' own seaport city in Phoenicia. Pericles is alone in a room of his palace.
Attendants have orders that he is not to be disturbed. He is despondent over the unfortunate incident at Antioch and realizes that the
king will wreak vengeance on him for fear his crime will become
known. Helicanus and several other lords enter and give Pericles
a cheerful greeting. They are scolded by Helicanus, who calls it
flattery; reproof, when needed, fits kings better. Pericles orders all

except Helicanus to leave. The others are to "ov'rlook" (i.e., oversee) the loading of ships in the harbor and report to him later. The remarks of Helicanus please Pericles because they show he is no flatterer. The prince trusts him and confides to him his personal danger because he has discovered that Antiochus is guilty of incest.

Pericles is advised by Helicanus to leave Phoenicia and travel on the sea for awhile. The incident will soon be forgotten or else Antiochus will die. Without more ado, Pericles turns over the welfare of the country to Helicanus, who promises to be faithful to his charge. Pericles prepares to set sail at once for Tarsus, a seaport of Cilicia.

Act I: Scene 3

This short scene takes place in Tyre in an antechamber of Pericles' palace. It is scarcely more than a conversation between Helicanus and Thaliard, who has just arrived in Tyre from the court of Antiochus to find Pericles. While he waits to speak to Helicanus, he muses on the murder he must perform or become a victim himself. It is a wise man, he thinks, who receives as a favor from a king the assurance that the latter would never tell him his secrets.

Thaliard overhears Helicanus and other lords of the court discussing Pericles' abrupt departure. He refuses to tell them more than that "he's gone to travel." The news surprises Thaliard. Then Helicanus elaborates a little, explaining that Pericles had gone on some business to Antioch and feels that the King is displeased with him about something. To show his sorrow, he has decided to risk his life by adopting the hazardous life of a seaman.

This news pleases Thaliard. He can tell Antiochus that Pericles " 'scaped the land, to perish at sea." He has learned all he needs to know. When Helicanus comes to greet him, Thaliard says he has come with a message to Pericles, but has learned that the Prince is away. So he will return with this word to Antiochus. Helicanus does not ask what message he has, but cordially invites Thaliard to dine with him.

Act I: Scene 4

This scene takes place at Tarsus in a room in the governor's house. Cleon, the governor, and his wife, Dionyza, are discussing the poverty and distress that has come to Tarsus after years of great abundance. Cleon moralizes on the haughty pride of the citizens who revelled in plenty; then there were no poor, so "the name of help grew odious to repeat." Dionyza does little more than agree with her husband. He considers the "change" that has come to Tarsus to be punishment from heaven. People who once scorned simple bread now "beg for it." He hopes other cities will heed the mistakes of Tarsus.

As he talks a messenger arrives with word that a ship is in the harbor. It displays white flags and thus is not an unfriendly vessel. Cleon is, nevertheless, suspicious. He sends word that he will see the "general" of the ship and wishes to know what business he has in Tarsus. If it is peace, he is welcome; if war, his nation has no arms to fight.

When Pericles enters, he relieves Cleon's fears that he means any harm. His ships are not like the Trojan horse "stuff'd within with bloody veins," but he has brought corn (i.e., wheat) to make bread for the poor of Tarsus. Cleon and his attendants kneel to thank Pericles. But he asks merely a friendly harbor to anchor his ships. He is welcomed by Cleon, who says that if anyone in Tarsus is not grateful for his help, that person shall be punished for "the curse of Heaven and men succeed their evils." Pericles accepts Cleon's hospitality and will stay until "our stars that frown lend us a smile."

Act II: Prologue

Gower enters and reviews the personalities of the first act of the play: Antiochus, the "mighty king" who has committed incest; and Pericles, who will later prove to be better, "both in deed and word." He remains at Tarsus, content to be with friends. A letter is brought to him that tells the news of his own court in Tyre.

A dumb show (pantomime) portrays Pericles talking with Cleon. A letter is brought to Pericles, who shows it to Cleon. He rewards the messenger and knights him.

Gower, serving as a chorus, explains the dumb show: the contents of the letter brought to Pericles recounts the scene between Helicanus and Thaliard. The former, careful of Pericles' interests, relates how Thaliard intended to murder him. Helicanus warns Pericles not to stay long in Tarsus.

Pericles then leaves and is shipwrecked. He is the only one saved
from the ship. He is washed ashore. Gower stops foretelling the
happenings of the play.

Act II: Scene 1

The scene takes place near Pentapolis on the coast of Greece.
Pericles enters bedraggled and wet, the lone survivor of his
ships wrecked by the storm. While he moralizes on his fate, he is
greeted by three fishermen. They discuss the wreck they have just
seen and are grieved that they were not able to rescue any of the
men who cried so pitifully for aid. They blame the porpoises, for
they always bring bad luck. The fishermen reflect on the curious
habits of men and fish. Both live by preying on others. Big fish
devour smaller ones, as rich misers devour the poor.

Pericles listens quietly. When they mention their King, Simonides,
he learns what country it is. Though Pericles is friendly to them,
the fishermen look askance at him and his request for aid. When
they find he has never begged and "never practised" fishing, they
are certain he will starve. In Pentapolis people earn more by
begging than by working.

Pericles feels his condition is hopeless; weakened by the storm, he
believes he will die. He asks the fishermen to see that he has a
decent burial. They become more friendly and give him a cloak to
keep him warm. If he will go home with them, they will care for
him. They describe King Simonides as "peaceable" and a good
governor. His palace is half a day's journey. Princes and knights
from "all parts of the world are coming to joust and tourney" for
his daughter's love on her birthday. Pericles wishes he might enter
the tourney, but fortune is against him.

As the fishermen draw up their nets and prepare to leave, one
fish is caught in a piece of rusty armor from the sea. It turns out
to be a small shield that Pericles lost in the shipwreck. His dead
father had given it to him as a lucky token. The fishermen give
it to Pericles. He quotes his father's words when he gave him the
token, begging the gods to defend him from harm. Pericles now
considers the shipwreck a good omen.

He decides to take part in the tourney, and he will wear the gown
the fishermen lend him and carry his good-luck shield. He will

purchase a "courser." One of the fishermen offers to provide a "pair of bases."

Act II: Scene 2

The scene is laid in Pentapolis. A platform to be used by the knights on horseback leads to the tournament field. There is a pavilion beside it where the King and his court are received.

Simonides and his daughter Thaisa, with their attendants, enter the pavilion. Thaisa is told by her father she has "to explain/ The labor of each knight in his devise." In succession, six knights enter and each passes his shield with its inscription written in Latin to the young princess. As she reads each motto, her father appraises the knight who offers it.

The sixth knight, Pericles, intrigues Simonides, and he praises his motto, "In hoc spe vivo," as a "pretty moral." The lords about Simonides and his daughter are not impressed by Pericles because of his poor dress. Simonides declares "opinion's but a fool, that makes us scan/ The outward habit by the inward man." They withdraw to the gallery to greet the knights.

Act II: Scene 3

This scene takes place the same day in the Hall of State of Simonides' palace. The King, his daughter, their attendants, and the knights who participated in the tourney are present at the banquet to honor the occasion. After Simonides welcomes them, Thaisa bestows the victor's wreath on Pericles. He receives it modestly. Everyone is glad that he won.

Simonides is pleased with Pericles' manner and personality, as is his daughter. To Thaisa, he "seems like diamond to glass." On Pericles' part, he sees a likeness to his own father in Simonides and reminds him "in that glory once he was." His father had princes around his throne like Simonides. All of them did "vail," or doff their crowns to his supremacy.

Pericles and Thaisa chat at the banquet. She tells him her father wishes to know his name, his parentage, and from where he comes. In the short sketch Pericles gives, he manages to tell enough of his parents and education "in arts and arms" and how shipwreck brought him to Pentapolis. Thaisa conveys the information to her father, who is highly pleased.

There is music, and Simonides invites the guests to dance. In asking Pericles to dance with his daughter, Simonides remarks that he has heard the knights of Tyre "are excellent in making ladies trip." When the dancing is over, Pericles is complimented by Simonides and his lodging will be next to the royal apartment.

Act II: Scene 4

This short scene takes place in Tyre in a room in the governor's house. Helicanus enters with another lord, Escanes. The whereabouts of Pericles have not been revealed to the court by Helicanus, and the lords have become suspicious that he has met with foul play. He tells Escanes that Antiochus is guilty of incest with his daughter. And, recently, it appears that "he was seated in a chariot" of great value with her when a fire came from heaven and burnt their bodies. The odor from their corpses was so great that none in the kingdom wishes to "give them burial." Helicanus declares, "sin had his reward."

Several lords join their conversation and question Helicanus concerning the disappearance of Pericles. If he is alive, they will find him; if he is dead, Helicanus must take over the rule of the country. They will be loyal to him. Helicanus persuades them to wait a year, and if Pericles does not return he will ascend the throne. He asks them to clasp hands with him: "When peers thus knit, a kingdom ever stands."

Act II: Scene 5

This scene takes place in a room, the next day, in Simonides' palace. The King enters, reading a letter. About him are knights who have taken part in the tourney.

Simonides puts away the letter and greets the knights. He tells them his daughter will not marry for a year. She refuses to give her reason to anyone. Thaisa has vowed to wear "Diana's livery" (i.e., remain a virgin) for that long. The knights, "loath to bid farewell," leave.

Simonides continues to read the letter, which he reveals is from his daughter. She has made up her mind to marry the stranger knight. Simonides muses that her "choice agrees" with his. But Simonides is surprised that she has not consulted him. At any rate, he approves of her choice. Pericles enters to express his thanks for the entertainment of the previous evening. Simonides is pleased and wishes to know whether Pericles likes his daughter. He is cautious in his praise of Thaisa. And when Simonides gives him her letter to read, Pericles fears it is a subtle way to trap him. Simonides teases Pericles, claiming he has "bewitched" his daughter and is a villain. Pericles takes him in earnest, and at one time in his fury at being called "traitor," turns on the King.

Thaisa enters and resolves the quarrel. She admits if he had "made love" to her, she would have been very glad. Her father, in an aside, declares he likes her independent way. Openly, he still pretends to scold her for falling in love, and with a "stranger," and without his sanction. Pretending to be stern, he declares, they must conform to his will or he will make them "man and wife." Simonides clasps their hands and asks that they seal their troth with a kiss. The King wishes them happiness and will "see" them wed.

Act III: Prologue

Gower enters and describes the details of the marriage feast. Then the palace quieted down. The couple went to their chamber, and he does not doubt "a babe is moulded."

The dumb show: Pericles and Simonides enter with attendants. A messenger gives Pericles a letter. He shows the letter to Simonides. Thaisa, who expects a child, enters with a nurse, Lychorida. Simonides gives the letter to Thaisa, who "rejoices." The couple, accompanied by Lychorida, bid her father goodbye and leave for Tyre.

Gower, as chorus, elaborates on the dumb show. The letters are from lords in Tyre. One tells the news of Antiochus' death. The lords want to make Helicanus King, but he demands they wait for "twice six moons," and if King Pericles "come not home," he will accept the crown. When the citizens of Pentapolis learn that Pericles is a king, they are greatly pleased.

Gower telescopes a description of the wedding, the arrival of the letters, and the departure for Tyre of Pericles and Thaisa, who is pregnant. He gives a description of the storm, and mentions Thaisa's fears, but refrains from telling the havoc caused by the storm.

Acts III, IV, and V are generally supposed to have been written by Shakespeare and (most likely) a collaborator.

Act III: Scene 1

This scene takes place some nine months later on a ship bound for Tyre. A storm is raging. Pericles enters and is worried that the storm will endanger the life of his wife during childbirth. While he is asking the gods to quiet the sea, the nurse, Lychorida, brings him the newborn infant. She tells Pericles that it is "all that is left living of your queen/ A little daughter: for the sake of it,/ Be manly, and take comfort."

The sailors inform Pericles that, according to an ancient superstition, a corpse must be immediately tossed into the sea, or else the storm will not cease. The sailors find a chest to hold Thaisa's body. Pericles places his jewels and "satin coffer" in the chest with her. Because the infant cannot survive a long voyage, he orders the mariners to "make" for Tarsus, where he will visit the governor, Cleon.

Act III: Scene 2

This scene takes place in Ephesus the morning after the storm. Cerimon, a lord of Ephesus, enters a room in his house with a servant and some persons who have been shipwrecked. He calls for Philemon, his personal servant, to "get fire and meat" for these poor men. He sends for medicine "to th' 'pothecary," and he wants a "report" on how it works. Cerimon is alone on the stage when two gentlemen enter. They, too, have felt the fury of the storm and have had to abandon their homes near the shore. They are surprised to find him up so early, but he explains that the life of a wealthy nobleman never appealed to him. He likes to study physics (medicine); and he has found how nature works and her cures. It gives him more delight than "to be thirsty and tottering after honor" or hiding his gold "in silken bags/ To please the Fool and Death."

While the gentlemen are talking with Cerimon and praising his great charity to the poor, several servants enter carrying a chest. They saw the waves wash it ashore. Cerimon orders the servants to open it. As the chest is "wrench't open," a sweet fragrance comes from it. Inside is a corpse, "Shrouded in cloth of state;

balmed and entreasured/ With bags of spice full! A passport too!" A scroll tells that the corpse is the wife of King Pericles. He begs that if her body is found, the finder will bury her. She was the daughter of a king. He asks, "The gods requite his charity!"

Cerimon thinks there is a possibility that the woman is still alive. He has heard of an Egyptian who had been dead nine hours and was revived by "good appliances."

The servants make a fire to warm her, and with the remedies from boxes in his closet and the sound of music from a viol, color returns to her cheeks. She slowly wakens and asks, "Where am I? Where's my lord? What world is this?"

Cerimon and his "gentle neighbors" carry her into an adjoining room. They must hurry, "For her relapse is mortal." He prays for Aesculapius to guide him.

Act III: Scene 3

Within a short time, Pericles arrives at Tarsus with the infant, whom he has named Marina, and the nurse, Lychorida. The three are in a room in the governor's house with Cleon and Dionyza. Pericles insists that he must return to Tyre. He is most grateful that Cleon and his wife will "give her princely training, that she may be/ Manner'd as she is born." For Pericles' bounty in sending corn to the hungry people of Tarsus, Cleon welcomes the chance to show his gratitude.

Before he leaves, Pericles vows never to cut his beard until Marina be married. He especially asks Dionyza to make him "blessed in your care/ In bringing up my child." Dionyza's own daughter will not be more dear to her than Marina. They offer to escort Pericles to the shore, and he leaves after a farewell to his daughter and Lychorida. He cautions the nurse, "O no tears,/ Lychorida, no tears!/ Look to your little mistress, on whose grace/ You may depend hereafter."

Act III: Scene 4

This scene is in Ephesus in a room in Cerimon's house. He is showing Thaisa the letter and jewels that were found in the "coffer." She recognizes the handwriting of the letter as that of her husband, Pericles. Since she will never see Pericles again, she has decided to live in Diana's temple. She will wear "vestal livery" and "never more have joy." The temple is close by and Cerimon offers to send his niece to accompany her there. Thaisa has only "thanks" to recompense her and though small, her good-will is great.

Act IV: Prologue

There is an interval of at least fourteen years between Acts III and IV. Marina is now a grown girl.

Gower enters and relates that Pericles is welcomed back to Tyre. He is unaware that his wife is a "votaress" in Diana's temple. From now on, Marina will dominate the play. Cleon has "trained" her in music and letters. Marina and Cleon's daughter, Philoten, are always seen together. But envy has gradually sprung up between them.

Marina has dainty, graceful fingers. She can play the lute and sing. She is always praised for her talents more highly than Philoten. Cleon's wife is envious of Marina and decides she must be killed. She has Lychorida murdered first; then she plans to murder Marina.

Act IV: Scenes 1-2

The scene takes place on the seashore in Tarsus. Dionyza is explaining to her servant Leonine that he must murder Marina as he has sworn. It will never be known. He must not listen to conscience or pity—the one is a cold law and the other, "even women have cast off." He must regard himself as a soldier doing his duty.

Leonine agrees to the murder, but he thinks Marina "is a goodly creature." Dionyza declares, "The fitter, then, the gods have her." They notice Marina walking toward them, crying over the death of her old nurse. Dionyza exacts a quick promise from Leonine that he will kill Marina. The girl pays no attention to them and walks along planning to strew flowers "purple violets and marigolds" on Lychorida's grave. She deplores the unhappy events that took away her parents. The world, to her, "is like a lasting storm."

Dionyza calls to her. She scolds her for being so somber. She has taken Lychorida's death too much to heart. A turn with Leonine "on the sea-margent walk" will sharpen her appetite. Marina refuses. Dionyza insists, because if her father arrives, as they expect, he will be distressed to see her so pale. He will blame her husband

and herself. Though Marina has "no desire for it," she will walk with Leonine. Pretending great sympathy for Marina, she gives final suggestions. "Pray you, walk softly, do not heat your blood."

With a final word to Leonine to "remember," Dionyza leaves. Marina and Leonine stroll along. Marina repeats all the nurse had told her about her father's valor and gallantry in the storm when she was born. Leonine interrupts and cautions her to say her prayers. But she must be quick. Marina at once asks if he will kill her, and why?

When she discovers it is the wish of Dionyza, she cannot understand it. She has never harmed her. She tells Leonine he has "a gentle heart." She once saw him separate two who were fighting. Now she begs him to save her. But Leonine declares, "I am sworn/ And will dispatch."

While Marina struggles with Leonine, three pirates enter. She is a "prize," and they go off with her aboard their ship. Leonine identifies the pirates as servants of the great pirate, Valdes.

He decides that Marina is as good as dead, and therefore he will swear to Dionyza that she was killed by pirates and thrown into the sea. But to be sure they do take her on board, he will stay and see. If they leave her on the shore, he will have to kill her.

Act IV: Scene 3

This scene takes place in a brothel in Mytilene near Lesbos, a Greek island in the Aegean sea. Pandar and his wife, Bawd, with the servant, Boult, discuss how they can improve their trade. Boult leaves to "search the market." There are too few women willing to enter the profession. If he had only "three or four thousant chequins" (Venetian gold coins) Pandar would get out of the traffic and live quietly. Moreover, they are "on sore terms" with the gods.

As they talk, Boult enters with Marina and the pirates. Because she "has a good face, speaks well and has excellent good clothes," they pay the pirates a thousand pieces of gold for her. Marina does not speak until the men are gone. She laments that Leonine was so slow to kill her or that the pirates had not thrown her overboard "to seek" her mother.

Bawd cannot understand why, pretty as she is, Marina begs the gods to defend her. Boult returns after having "cried her through the market place" and "drawn her picture" with his voice. He has stirred up trade for the night. But Marina's dignity and her determination not to surrender herself annoys Bawd, and especially the fact that she calls on Diana to defend her.

Act IV: Scene 4

The scene is laid in a room in Cleon's house in Tarsus. It is a few days after Marina's abduction. Dionyza is impatient at Cleon's distress over Marina's murder. His wife is callous about it. "Can it be undone?" she asks.

Cleon upbraids her for poisoning Leonine. He thinks it had been well if she "had drunk" the poison, too. He asks how they will tell Pericles that his daughter is dead. Dionyza has trumped up a story. She will insist that Marina "died by foul play." Dionyza calls Cleon childish and of a "coward spirit," and says that he has no love for his own child to see her "blurted at, and held a malkin/ Not worth the time of day" whenever Marina was with her. Dionyza has done "an enterprise of kindness" for their own daughter. But Cleon spurns her arguments, comparing her to a harpy who betrays with an "angel's face," and then "seize with thine eagle's talons."

Dumbshow

Gower stands in front of a monument that Dionyza has erected at Marina's "tomb" in Tarsus. He remarks that it does not tax the imagination that the story moves from "region to region," and yet only one language is used. To let the audience know "the stages of our story," he says that Pericles is on board ship and headed for Tarsus and is attended by many lords and ladies. Among them is Helicanus. Escanes has remained in Tyre to govern while Pericles brings his daughter back to Tyre.

Dumb Show: Pericles with his train enters from one side; Cleon and Dionyza from the other side. Cleon shows Pericles the tomb of Marina. According to the stage directions, Pericles makes great "lamentation, puts on sackcloth, and in a mighty passion departs."

Gower reads the inscription written on Marina's tomb. It begins, "The fairest, sweet'st and best lies here/ Who wither'd in her spring of year," and continues in the same sentimental vein. Though Pericles believes his daughter is dead, Lady Fortune will order things for the better. Meanwhile, it is necessary to follow Marina in her "unholy service." Gower requests patience, "And think you now are all in Mytilene."

Act IV: Scene 5

This short scene takes place on a street in front of the brothel in Mytilene. Two gentlemen have just left the place and one is astounded "to have divinity preach'd there!" The other declares he will patronize no more brothels and invites his friends "to go hear the vestals sing."

Act IV: Scene 6

Pander and his wife are unable to cope with Marina's aversion to their profession. Bawd insists that "she would make a puritan of the Devil, if he should cheapen [bargain for] a kiss of her." When Lysimachus, the governor of Mytilene, enters, Bawd tells Marina he is "an honorable man" and she "must use him kindly."

He is no more successful with Marina than others have been. He listens to her "sage" discourse sneering at first, but he leaves the brothel calling her a "piece of virtue" and "A curse upon him, die he like a thief,/ That robs thee of thy goodness!" If she hears from him again, it will be for her good.

Boult, desperate at Marina's virtuous ways, accuses her of making "our profession as it were to stink afore the face of the gods." At the suggestion of Pandar and Bawd, Boult tries to reason with Marina, but finds she is only amenable to things she likes. She "can sing, weave, sew, and dance." She begs that "the gods/ Would safely from this place deliver" her. Boult is won over by her, and promises to help her get away.

Act V: Prologue

Gower enters and relates that Marina leaves the brothel to go to an "honest house" where she can sew and sing, which she likes to do. Her art in embroidery "sisters the natural roses." She has many pupils who pay her well, "and her gain/ She gives the curs'd bawd." Her father, disconsolate over her supposed death, has gone to sea again. His boat is driven by the wind to Mytilene, and is anchored there. At the annual feast in honor of Neptune, Lysimachus notices Pericles' ship in the harbor, and he hurries out in a barge to welcome the owner. Gower describes the ship as "trimm'd with rich expense." What will happen now, the audience is asked, "please you, sit, and hark."

Act V: Scene 1

Three months have elapsed from the time Pericles left Cleon and Dionyza after learning of the death of his daughter. The scene is on board Pericles' ship. There is a pavilion on deck partitioned by a curtain, where Pericles is reclining on a couch. Lysimachus' barge is anchored close to the Tyrian ship.

A sailor from the ship and another from the barge enter. The sailor from the barge requests permission for Lysimachus to come aboard. He is referred to lord Helicanus who graciously receives him. Helicanus says that the king of Tyre is aboard the ship, but suffers from melancholia brought on by the death of his wife and daughter. He refuses to speak to anyone.

Lysimachus asks to be allowed to see him. When Helicanus draws aside the curtain, the governor greets Pericles, who does not answer. Immediately, Lysimachus remembers Marina and suggests that her beauty and charming manner would arouse the king. Though Helicanus is doubtful, he agrees that the young woman should be sent for.

When she arrives, Marina offers to do what she can, but none must be allowed to come near him except her "companion maid" and "herself."

Marina sings. But there is no response from Pericles. She tells him that her grief, perhaps, can equal his. Pericles asks her to repeat what she said about her "parentage—good parentage." She does, and a recognition scene follows, during which Marina tells her life story.

When Pericles realizes Marina is his daughter, he falls into a kind of ecstasy and insists he hears "most heavenly music." He wishes to sleep and everyone withdraws.

When he is left alone, the goddess Diana appears "as in a vision." She tells Pericles to go to her temple in Ephesus and offer sacrifice "Before the people all." And he must tell there how he lost his wife at sea. If Pericles fails to do her bidding, he will live "in woe"; if he does as she says, he will be happy. Pericles answers, "I will obey thee."

He recalls Helicanus, Lysimachus, Marina, and the others to tell them he intends to sail to Ephesus. He will disclose why, later. Meanwhile, he asks to go ashore with Lysimachus, and he will give him "gold for such provision" as his ship will need while in the harbor.

When Lysimachus agrees, he mentions that he has a request to make. Pericles tells him he may have all he wishes, even the hand of his daughter. They all go ashore.

Act V: Scene 2

Gower enters and stands in front of the temple of Diana in Ephesus. He describes the royal welcome with "pageantry" and "pretty din" that Lysimachus gives Pericles. The governor is assured that Marina will become his wife as soon as her father does Diana's bidding and make his "sacrifice" in her temple. Pericles and "all his company" shortly set sail for Ephesus.

Act V: Scene 3

The scene takes place some days later in the temple of Diana at Ephesus. A high priestess, Thaisa, is standing near the altar with a number of virgins on each side of her. Cerimon and other persons of Ephesus are in attendance.

Pericles enters with Lysimachus, Helicanus, Marina, and a lady in waiting. Pericles greets Thaisa, thinking she is Diana, and as she had told him to do, he reveals "how, at sea" he lost his wife in childbirth. Then, he relates how, years later, Cleon cruelly treated his daughter. Pericles describes how "her fortunes brought the maid aboard us."

On hearing Pericles' voice, Thaisa calls, "You are, you are—O royal Pericles!" and faints.

Pericles thinks the "nun" is dying and calls for help. He is told by Cerimon, if what he has just said is true, that "This is your wife." Pericles denies it is possible because he himself threw her body into the sea. The incidents connected with the finding of the "coffin," the jewels, how Cerimon "recover'd her" and placed her in Diana's Temple" are then quickly told.

A recognition scene follows between Pericles, Thaisa, and Marina. Pericles is anxious to know, "How this dead Queen re-lives," and Cerimon promises to tell him, later. Thaisa says she has word of her father's death in Pentapolis.

Pericles reveals that their daughter will marry Lysimachus in her father's city and will rule over Tyre. Thaisa and Pericles will remain in Pentapolis.

Gower re-enters and closes the scene and play with a quick review of the virtues and vices of the various characters. He includes Pericles' intent to burn Cleon's palace when he was deterred on the way by the unexpected reunion with his daughter in Mytilene. The gods "for murder seem'd so content to punish them, [Cleon and Dionyza]—although not done, but meant."

The Tempest

ALONSO, *King of Naples.*
SEBASTIAN, *his brother.*
PROSPERO, *the right Duke of Milan.*
ANTIONIO, *his brother, the usurping Duke of Milan.*
FERDINAND, *son to the King of Naples.*
GONZALO, *an honest old counselor.*
ADRIAN }
FRANCISCO } *Lords.*
CALIBAN, *a savage and deformed slave.*
TRINCULO, *a Jester.*
STEPHANO, *a drunken butler.*
MASTER *of a ship.*
BOATSWAIN.
MARINERS.

MIRANDA, *daughter to Prospero.*

ARIEL, *an airy Spirit.*
IRIS
CERES
JUNO } *Spirits.*
NYMPHS
REAPERS

Other SPIRITS *attending on Prospero.*

The Tempest

Act I: Scene 1

The play opens in the midst of a violent storm at sea, with thunder and lightning. In the midst of the storm there is a ship, furiously driven by the wind and rain, and the entire first scene takes place on the deck of this ship, which is in danger of sinking at any moment.

The Master of the ship calls his Boatswain, who as the subordinate officer in charge of the sails and rigging, is directly responsible for immediate action, to make every effort to save the ship. The fury of the storm is such that it might drive the ship onto a shore where it could be wrecked; therefore, the Boatswain calls upon the sailors of the crew to "fall to't yarely," that is to say: work as hard as you can to take in the sails. It should be remembered that this storm, which we learn later in the play is supernatural in origin, has come up very suddenly, and the sailors have not been prepared for it.

As the sailors do all they can to take in the sails and make the ship secure against the storm, Alonso, King of Naples, appears on deck with his son, Ferdinand, who is heir to the throne of Naples; they are accompanied by Antonio, Duke of Milan; Sebastian, the brother of Alonso; and Gonzalo, an honest adviser and councilor to Alonso.

Alonso advises the Boatswain to "Play the men." The word "play" here has been interpreted as "ply," which would mean that Alonso is ordering the Boatswain to make the men work; it is implied that Alonso and the other passengers are not prepared to trust the skill of the officers and sailors of the ship.

The furious activity of the crew in attempting to save the ship and the lives of all within it, at first does not impress Alonso and his friends. The Boatswain only wishes that they would get out of the way and go back to their cabins. "You mar our labors," he tells them. The Boatswain adds, speaking to Gonzalo: "What cares these roarers for the name of King?"

that is, the winds and waves of the storm will certainly not listen to the King if he should tell them to be quiet, and therefore the King and his party should go below and leave the sailors to do their proper work of fighting the storm. The conversation with the Boatswain makes this clear.

There is some ill feeling between the sailors of the crew and their passengers; thus, as the Boatswain shouts his orders and tells the King and his party to get out of the way, Antonio says to the Boatswain: "We are less afraid to be drowned than thou art." But Antonio does not trust the crew's skill, and shows it. On the other hand, Gonzalo seems to accept whatever happens philosophically; he is even mildly humorous in his reference to the Boatswain as having a complexion "of perfect gallows." That is, Gonzalo says at several points that it is obvious to him that the Boatswain looks like a man fated to die by hanging. Since the Boatswain will be hanged upon a gallows on dry land, he cannot die by drowning. In the circumstances, this is Gonzalo's idea of a joke.

Suddenly the sailors come in wet, shouting that all is lost and that the only thing anyone can do now is to pray. Antonio is angry; he believes that the crew has not done enough. "We are *merely* (that is, *simply*) cheated of our lives by drunkards," which means that Antonio believes that the crew has been drunk and not capable of doing its best. As Scene 1 ends, the sailors are shouting that the ship is about to split apart and sink. Gonzalo has the last word when he says: "The wills above be done! But I would fain die a dry death." "The wills above" refers to the will of God or of the divine powers who, in the terms of the play, watch over and are responsible for man's destiny. But at the same time, Gonzalo can wish that things might be different on board this ship which is evidently sinking.

Act I: Scene 2

The second Scene, which composes the rest of Act I, is very long; it takes place entirely in Prospero's cell, or small room and library where he practices his magic arts, on the enchanted island where most of the action of the play is set. The scene opens with an explanation of the origins of the storm. Miranda, daughter of Prospero, establishes her merciful character at the beginning as she asks her father, the creator of the tempest, to make the ship and all its people safe. She too is afraid all on the ship will be drowned. For Miranda has seen the ship, and as "O, I have suffered/ With those that I saw suffer . . ." she wishes those on the ship to be shown mercy.

Prospero reassures his daughter. Those on the ship will not be harmed;

nobody on the ship will suffer "so much perdition as an hair," that is, will not lose even a single hair from his head, so careful is Prospero of their safety as he works his magic on them.

Prospero then explains to Miranda who she is, and who he is. It becomes obvious that until this day she has not known their origins or how they had got to the enchanted island. He removes his magic garment, apparently a costume that Prospero wears when he is practicing his magic. Reassuring Miranda: "Wipe thou thine eyes; have comfort" he explains the mystery of their origin.

The explanation proceeds by question and answer, in such a way that the audience, as well as Miranda, becomes aware of the history of both Prospero and herself. They are also told of the history of Antonio, as well as that of Alonso, both of whom we saw on the ship.

Antonio is Prospero's brother, having taken the position of Duke of Milan away from Prospero, and having exiled both Prospero and Miranda to the island. Miranda makes it clear that in the past she has often wondered who she was and where she and her father had come from, but until this day her father had always put her off with excuses. Now Prospero will tell her.

He explains that twelve years previous to this day—the day of the tempest, that is—Prospero was the Duke of Milan and held the position now occupied by his brother Antonio. He recalls the days "in the dark backward and abysm of time" when Miranda, as she vaguely remembers, had many servants and attendants, as did he. Miranda would have been so young that she wouldn't remember much of what had happened. Prospero reassures her that he is in fact her father, and that he had been exiled to this lonely place with his daughter, by the treachery of Antonio.

Prospero recalls that among all the "signories" (the states of Northern Italy), the Duke of Milan, himself, had been the greatest and most powerful. But because he studied the liberal arts and became a master of many arts and sciences, he thereby took less and less interest in the governing of his Dukedom. He gradually turned over more and more of his power to his brother, Antonio. One day Antonio, this "false uncle" of Miranda, having secretly removed many of the men whom Prospero had appointed to positions of power in the government, took over the government himself in all but name. He acted as ruler while Prospero still had the title of Duke.

Antonio's ambition grew; "he needs will be/Absolute Milan," that is, he wanted to be the Duke. This meant that he began to plan a way to get rid of his brother. (A King or Duke is sometimes called by the place which he rules, thus, Antonio is sometimes referred to simply as "Milan" rather than as "Duke of Milan.") The exercise of power, then, gradually corrupts Antonio, as his ambition is not satisfied; he wants to have all of his brother's power.

For Prospero, as he himself says, his library "was dukedom large enough." He withdraws from the world of action and of the governing of men, into the world of ideas. His brother comes to despise Prospero's abilities as a ruler, and makes an arrangement with Alonso, the King of Naples, "so dry was he for sway" (meaning: How thirsty Antonio was for power), whereby Antonio, in return for help in taking over the Dukedom of Milan, will pay homage to the King of Naples and acknowledge his power.

Miranda, in asking her father whether Antonio could really be his brother since he has done such a terrible thing, implies that any brother capable of acting in such an unnatural way is no real brother. Here we see the idea of nature as opposed to the unnatural, which is developed further in the play.

One night, after the agreement between Antonio and Naples has been concluded, Antonio opens the gates of Milan to an invading army. Antonio, the King of Naples, and their soldiers dared not harm Prospero and Miranda, because the people of Milan all loved Prospero:

> . . . they durst not
> So dear the love my people bore me; nor set
> A mark so bloody on the business . . .

Instead, they put the father and daughter to sea, in "a rotten carcass of a butt." (The "butt" is apparently a small boat, without masts or sails, in such poor repair that it is leaking.) Antonio assumes that his brother will never be seen alive again. But Gonzalo, the noble courtier and adviser to Duke Prospero, had saved their lives by placing both food and water, as well as clothing, books, and other necessaries, on the fragile boat in which Prospero and Miranda were set adrift by their enemies. At this point, Prospero breaks off the story he is telling to Miranda. By his magic art, he puts Miranda to sleep, and then summons his attendant Spirit, Ariel.

Having made the above observations about the transition, in this scene, from reality to fantasy, we now proceed to meet the character of Ariel, who is pure fantasy.

Ariel appears at line 189, returning to his master, Prospero, in the latter's cell. This is also part of the exposition, and in this part of Scene 2, we learn through Ariel's report to his master that he, Ariel, under the orders of Prospero, has caused the tempest. Further, it is made clear that while Prospero and Ariel deliberately frightened the sailors into believing that the ship was sinking, yet none of them was harmed. Ariel, as a spirit, had leaped on to the ship and had "flamed amazement"; he had turned himself into flames, making eerie noises, and frightened the sailors so that some of them, believing that "all the devils are here," fell, or jumped overboard. One of the first to leave the ship was the King's son, Ferdinand.

We learn further that all of the men are safe: "Not a hair perished." Indeed, not even their clothing is wet. The ship itself has by magic power been safely docked in a sort of cove or harbor, with most of the crew "charmed . . . under hatches stowed." The rest of the fleet, believing the King's ship lost, has gone sadly home toward Naples.

The first mention of the "still vexed Bermoothes" is made at this point (line 229). We shall return to this later, but it is thought that *The Tempest* was partly inspired by the account of a voyage to Bermuda. "Still vexed" means "ever vexed, or troubled," "still" being an Elizabethan meaning for "always" or "ever." But whatever *places* are referred to in the play, one must remember that the actual place and its geography are not important. Shakespeare sets the action in an enchanted island, where the normal laws of Nature do not operate or, at any rate, seem to be modified by the enchantments and the magic arts of Prospero and those Spirits who assist him.

We realize, as Ariel makes his report to his master, that the time is "at least two glasses," that is, about two o'clock in the afternoon. Prospero, upon learning the time, says to Ariel that between the present and the time when his, Prospero's, work ends, he must have finished what it is his intention to finish. As Prospero says (lines 240-241)

> The Time 'twixt six and now
> Must by us both be spent most preciously.

At line 242 and following, the dialogue informs us that Ariel desires freedom from Prospero. Ariel is a servant of Prospero and is bound to serve him for a definite number of years. Prospero, Ariel reminds him, has promised to give Ariel his freedom early, if the present work they are doing is successful:

> Thou did promise
> To bate me a full year.

Ariel means by this that Prospero had promised to abate, or shorten, the term of his service by a year. Prospero reminds his servant that he, ruled by the darkest superstition. Part of the action of *The Tempest* involves the *education* of Caliban as well as of most of the other characters. But Caliban, as a semi-human serio-comic character, has farthest to go in the matter of education.

The scene changes to another part of the Island to reveal the shipwrecked son of the King of Naples; he has just come ashore from the wreck, and believes his father to be drowned. Suddenly hearing the strange and fantastic music, including the famous song "Full fathom five thy father lies. . ." Ferdinand is led by Ariel to a point where Prospero and Miranda meet him. Ferdinand realizes that he is in the midst of enchantment:

> This is no mortal business, nor no sound
> That the earth owes. (lines 407-408)

Ferdinand is the first man, other than her father, whom Miranda has ever seen. She believes him to be a god or a spirit, but Prospero reassures her that he is a man, who has human senses and qualities. But Miranda artlessly gives her heart to Ferdinand almost from the moment she sees him. This is exactly what Prospero intends:

> It goes on, I see,
> As my soul prompts it. (lines 419-420)

This statement by Prospero, spoken as an aside, is the first hint we have that everything that is to take place on the enchanted island, beginning with the meeting between Ferdinand and Miranda which Prospero intends shall end in their marriage, is at the will of Prospero, who is in perfect control of everything, and everybody: human, supernatural, and elemental, on the Island.

If Prospero intends Ferdinand to be his daughter's husband, one may reasonably observe that he does not show this in his initial treatment of Ferdinand. What is Prospero's motivation for his rough treatment of the young man who has already declared his wish to make Miranda the Queen of Naples?

Remember that Miranda herself is ignorant of men and of the world. She cannot, in order to be properly valued by her future husband, appear to be too easy a conquest. Ferdinand must win her, and Prospero intends that he do so by passing a kind of test. Therefore, he accuses Ferdinand of coming to the Island to spy, and in addition, of being an usurper:

> Thou dost here usurp
> The name thou ow'st ["ow'st" means "ownest"] not,
> and has put thyself
> Upon this island as a spy, to win it
> From me, the lord on't. (lines 453–456)

Prospero, had rescued Ariel from the enchantments of "the foul witch Sycorax." This reminder, and the retelling by Prospero of the story of Sycorax and her son, Caliban, is part of the exposition of the play. In speaking of the torment from which Prospero had rescued Ariel, he gives us much information that we must have if we are to understand the relationships among Prospero, Ariel, and Caliban. We also learn about Sycorax, who does not appear in the play. More important, we are given certain expectations as to what kind of a being Caliban is; he does not appear on the stage until he has been described and introduced by Prospero and Ariel as they discuss him.

Caliban's shape is not exactly human. Shakespeare leaves a good deal to our imagination, but apparently Caliban appears in part like a human being, in part like a fish, in part like a tortoise. Caliban is treated not as a valued servant by Prospero, but as a slave; this is contrast with Prospero's way of dealing with Ariel. Caliban is necessary in Prospero's service, but he is still a slave, "whom stripes may move, not kindness." That is to say, he can be made obedient only by the threat of stripes inflicted by a whip.

Prospero threatens Caliban with various punishments if he does not obey. At the same time, we learn much about Caliban's nature: he is resentful, and he believes that Prospero has taken away his rights:

> The island's mine by Sycorax my mother,
> Which thou tak'st from me. (lines 331-332)

Here Prospero loses his patience with Caliban, pointing out to him that he had treated Caliban well until he, Caliban, betrayed this kindness by attempting to attack Miranda, an attack that Prospero had prevented. Prospero had taught Caliban language and useful arts:

> I endowed thy purposes
> With words that made them known. (lines 356-357)

But Caliban does not appreciate this, and still struggles against his master.

Ariel gives us, as we are introduced to him in his scene and all through the play, an impression of lightness and lack of physical substance. He has many unusual qualities, which he uses in the service of his master, Prospero. The interchange between Prospero and Ariel, beginning at line 240 of this scene, is part of the exposition of Ariel's character. We learn that Ariel wishes his freedom; in this he is similar to Caliban, although in other respects he is quite different.

One of the abilities of Ariel, which we accept by this time, even though it is objectively fantastic, is his ability to travel anywhere almost instantaneously. Prospero makes this clear when he reproaches Ariel for his complaints:

> Dost thou forget
> From what a torment I did free thee? (lines 250-251)

Ariel answers, rhetorically, "no," whereupon Prospero continues to punish his servant verbally:

> Thou dost; and think'st it much to tread the ooze
> Of the salt deep,
> To run upon the sharp wind of the North,
> To do me business in the veins o'th' earth
> When it is baked with frost. (lines 253-257)

The purpose of this interchange is twofold: first, it provides additional exposition for the drama, so that we will know what the action has been prior to the actual chronological beginning of *The Tempest* with the shipwreck, and second, it builds up the character of Ariel so that we suspend our disbelief in such a fantastic creature.

It is best not to be too literal in one's analysis of Ariel. In the speech of Prospero quoted just above, we find that Ariel has the ability of traveling within three of the four "elements" or fundamental substances that Shakespeare and his Elizabethan contemporaries believed to constitute the material universe: Earth, Water, Air, and Fire. Ariel can move in the "salt deep"; he runs upon the "sharp wind of the North"; he serves Prospero "in the veins o'the'earth." The elements referred to are obviously Water, Air, and Earth. As to Fire, Ariel changed himself into fire to terrify the sailors in Scene 1, and as we shall see, that is the element which is most akin to Ariel's own nature.

In contrast to Ariel, Caliban is a creature of the earth, earthy. Remember that Prospero specifically addresses Caliban as "Slave! Caliban! Thou earth thou!" (Act I, Scene 2, lines 313-314). As one reads the entire second scene of Act I, the contrasting natures of Ariel and Caliban become more and more apparent. But both natures—and this is most important—need in some way to be guided, restrained, led or managed by Prospero. The threats that Prospero uses against Ariel are of a less menacing or physical nature than those he uses against Caliban, but in dealing with both of his servants the point is that Prospero must use threats. Prospero is, however, a kindly man, a beneficent authority-figure, and we are somehow not fully convinced that he would really put into action the threats he utters against Ariel and even Caliban.

The Tempest

Prospero once again reminds Ariel of "the damned witch Sycorax" from whom he, Prospero, had rescued Ariel—from her spell, that is, that caused Ariel to be confined in a pine tree. The reference to "Argier" (Algiers) from which Sycorax had been banished for her witchcraft, is one more geographical reference that shows the fantastic nature of the enchanted island. Algiers and Bermuda are not exactly close geographically, and yet the island where *The Tempest* is set seems to be in proximity to both —which is one more sign that you are not to take the geography in it seriously.

Having recalled Ariel to his duty—not that Ariel seriously contemplated defying his master—Prospero goes to Caliban, while Ariel departs in the shape of a water nymph. The entire dialogue between Prospero and Caliban, lines 321-376, is interesting in a number of ways. First, it establishes further the character of Prospero, and tends to confirm our view of him as one who is the master of everything and everyone on the enchanted island. Second, it gives something of Caliban's history and establishes his character so that we can see why Prospero treats him as he does. Caliban is at once a rather humorous creature, of indefinite shape, and a creature who has elements of pathos as well as comedy. He reproaches Prospero for having stolen his land: "This island's mine by Sycorax my mother. . . ." (line 331). The Elizabethan age was, of course, an age of discovery and exploration. English mariners such as Drake, Hawkins, Frobisher, had contributed their share to the explorations, and it was natural that reports of strange and wonderful lands and people, both real and exaggerated, should find their way back to England in Shakespeare's time. Caliban in part comes from these reports of exploration, and we shall discuss this aspect of his portrayal in additional comments on this scene.

Prospero reproaches Caliban for having attempted to "violate the honour of my child," that is, Caliban had attempted to attack Miranda. Prospero, of course, having total power on the Island, could foil this attempt. He says that Caliban was ungrateful because he had been taught language by Prospero, and had repaid evil for good. Caliban replies that the island was his by right of inheritance, and that Prospero had simply taken it from him by superior force and cunning. But Caliban recognizes, as we learn at the end of the dialogue between Prospero and his slave, that he has no choice but to obey—for he says of Prospero:

> His art is of such pow'r
> It would control my dam's god, Setebos,
> And make a vassal of him. (lines 373-375)

The god, Setebos, does not appear in the play, but the name and quality of this being have some importance as showing how Caliban is initially

The Tempest

Technically, Prospero would seem to be making up a story to test Ferdinand. But in a deeper level Prospero's charge contains an element of truth. Ferdinand is an usurper. He is the son of a man who had assisted in the usurpation of Prospero himself. And usurpation—the act of taking away the power of a lawful King or Prince—was considered not only a grave crime, amounting to treason, by the Elizabethans; it was also considered by many to be a religious offense, amounting to impiety or blasphemy. The whole question of the powers and duties of a King or Prince is examined in this play, and we shall have more to say about it hereafter. For the moment it should simply be pointed out, so that as you read the play you will pay particular attention to the speeches on government and Kingship, or the art of ruling well.

Ferdinand emphatically denies Prospero's charge that he is on the Island as a spy: "No, as I am a man!" (line 456). Here, in this short phrase, another opposition or contrast is set up by implication: man's nature and attributes. To put it another way, one of the pairs of contrasting values or qualities that the play stresses may be illustrated as

Man	against	The Non-human
		The Inanimate
		The Beast
		The Less-than-human
		The Supernatural

All of the qualities or kinds of beings opposite to man have slightly differing values. But it should be clear that when Ferdinand calls himself a Man he is assigning to the word values that are not all readily apparent. A Man—a true one—cannot be a spy or a traitor.*

Miranda tries to plead for Ferdinand:

> There's nothing ill can dwell in such a temple.
> If the ill spirit have so fair a house,
> Good things will strive to dwell with't. (lines 457–459)

But Prospero pretends to be hard and sternly resists his daughter's pleas. He proposes to manacle Ferdinand and to make him do hard labor like a common convict. When Miranda continues to intercede for Ferdinand, Prospero rebukes her:

> What, I say
> My foot my tutor? (lines 468–469)

---

* Theodore Spencer, *Shakespeare and the Nature of Man*, 2nd ed. (New York: Macmillan, 1958), is highly recommended as supplementary reading for *The Tempest*.

That is, Miranda, his daughter, is subordinate to Prospero in all things; he is her head and can tell her what to do, by the laws of relationship between parents and children. A relationship in which Miranda could prevail over her father and tell him what to do would not be natural, or according to what Shakespeare and his contemporaries would have called the Law of Nature. Prospero prevents Ferdinand from resisting by placing a "charm" on him, which prevents him from moving at all, so that he stands in a frozen position. He says that Ferdinand is so possessed with guilt, that is, a guilty conscience for being a "spy" and "traitor," that he does not dare to strike with his sword. Prospero further says to Miranda that she has been deceived by Ferdinand's appearance only because she has never seen other men; that Ferdinand is inferior to most:

> To th'most of men this is a Caliban,
> And they to him are angels. (lines 480–481)

Ferdinand has no choice but to give in and do what Prospero commands; he says in a brief soliloquy that he would sooner be imprisoned so long as he can see Miranda once a day than be free anywhere else in the world. To this, Prospero comments as an "aside" that "It works" (line 494). This means that the spell that Prospero has used—or rather, the "charm," is working—and also, the growing affection between Ferdinand and Miranda, which Prospero hopes will culminate in their marriage, is working as he wishes.

Ariel has been standing by, carrying out Prospero's commands, for he, Prospero, seems to work by the agency of his various servants, rather than directly. Prospero praises him and reminds him that if he does good work he shall be free. As the long scene ends, Miranda speaks to Ferdinand, excusing her father's apparent rudeness and lack of hospitality to a shipwrecked guest. Prospero orders Ferdinand to follow along, to the place where Prospero will put him to work, and once again, as the scene ends, cautions Miranda not to speak in behalf of Ferdinand.

Act II: Scene 1

The word-play at the beginning of this scene is interesting as a help to define further the various characters who are introduced here. Gonzalo, the old courtier, at the beginning of the scene counsels his king, Alonso, to be thankful for the escape of himself and his party from the shipwreck. This advice is in keeping with the cheerful and straightforward outlook manifested by Gonzalo in the brief first scene of Act I where he combines philosophical-religious acceptance of what cannot be changed, with a good practical streak of self-help: that the passengers and crew of the apparently sinking ship can and should do all in their power to save themselves and the ship.

The Tempest

Every day sees newly-ruined merchants and newly-widowed sailors' wives as a result of the sea's wrath, says Gonzalo to his master. Therefore, Alonso should be thankful for his preservation, for

> few in millions
> Can speak like us. Then wisely, good sir, weigh,
> Our sorrow with our comfort. (lines 7–9)

It is rare good fortune that any of the ship's passengers is still alive. But Alonso will not be comforted, because he believes his son, Ferdinand, to have been drowned. In the case of Alonso, the King of Naples, this is more than simply a personal grief, because what he manifests is deep grief for the loss of his heir, who was to inherit the throne of Naples from him. Gonzalo, whose function it is to serve and counsel his master, advises moderation, as well as submission to that which cannot be changed.

Sebastian and Antonio, on the other hand, establish themselves in a few words as rather sarcastic and cynical individuals who mock Gonzalo rather cruelly, although the old man is defenseless against their taunts and largely ignores them. The two are intent on baiting Gonzalo, but they seem to be striking beyond him at the King himself in the word-play at the beginning of Act II. Sebastian is, of course, the brother of Alonso and may be presumed to have a right to speak more familiarly to the King than anyone else could. Antonio is the brother of Prospero, the deposed Duke of Milan. At the beginning of the play, of course, Antonio is acting as the Duke of Milan, having usurped his brother's place as was recounted in the speech of Prospero to Miranda. Antonio has no idea that his brother is still alive, and indeed is the supreme ruler over the enchanted island upon which Antonio has been cast.

There is a certain balance or similarity between the situation of Sebastian and that of Antonio—with the difference that while Antonio is the present Duke of Milan (having usurped his brother), Sebastian is simply a nobleman, the brother of Alonso. But it becomes clear that what Sebastian wishes to do is to usurp the position of his brother—to depose and probably kill Alonso just as Antonio had usurped Prospero's place and had cast him adrift with Miranda.

The intentions of Sebastian and Antonio, then, are identical. The speeches that subtly attack Alonso depend on word-play: for example, in line 18 Sebastian and Gonzalo make a play on the different words "dollar" and "dolour," or sadness. It seems cruel of Sebastian to make fun of Gonzalo's comforting speech, spoken to the King with perfectly good intention. Sebastian mocks the old man, picturing him as a sort of cheap entertainer who ought to be thrown a dollar's worth of coins for his meager efforts. Alonso keeps asking the old courtier to be silent, for his grief over the supposed death of Ferdinand is too great to be borne.

Of Gonzalo, Sebastian and Antonio say:

> *Antonio:* He misses not much.
> *Sebastion:* No; he doth but mistake the truth totally.
> (lines 56-57)

This is because Gonzalo has been praising the island on which they have landed; he praises it as the means of their rescue and salvation:

> The air breathes upon us here most sweetly. (line 45)

So Adrian says.

Adrian is a neutral, and is thus the subject of attack by the cynical Sebastian and Antonio. The place is not good enough for them, they imply sneeringly, and this is their general attitude toward their surroundings. Therefore, they think Gonzalo an old fool, and Adrian as well, judging from the cutting remarks they make.

In a deeper sense, Gonzalo is right. "He misses not much." He is in harmony with the spirit of the enchanted island, which is a healing and educative spirit or temper, as we shall see further. Another thing that the "old fool," Gonzalo, picks up more quickly than anyone else is the fact that though all the men have been in a shipwreck, their garments are ". . . rather new-dyed than stained with salt water." (lines 62-63) Gonzalo, in short, is the first to perceive that the Island is a strange and enchanted place. His reaction is characteristic: he seems to accept his new circumstances cheerfully, just as he did on board the apparently sinking ship in the first scene of *The Tempest.*

The subject of the marriage of Alonso's daughter, Claribel, to the King of Tunis, is mentioned by Gonzalo. You will recall that the ship bearing the King of Naples home from the wedding of his daughter had been the one, out of a fleet, wrecked when the tempest sprang up suddenly. Therefore, it seems a bit rash for Gonzalo to refer to the marriage, for it simply reminds Alonso of his loss—both of his daughter, by marriage, and of his son, by drowning—

> Would I had never
> Married my daughter there! For, coming thence,
> My son is lost. . . . (lines 104-106)

Francisco, the other "neutral" character of the King's party, along with Adrian, reassures the King, in astonishingly vigorous poetic lines, that Ferdinand may still be alive, for he, Francisco, had seen Ferdinand strongly swimming toward the shore.

To Francisco's optimism about the fate of his son and heir, Alonso simply replies: "No, no, he's gone." (line 119) Alonso is a man bowed down by grief, and there is just a hint in this scene—confirmed later—that he is also troubled by secret guilt. In some way, he may regard Ferdinand's supposed drowning as a just punishment inflicted because of his, Alonso's, offense in assisting Antonio to usurp Prospero's rightful place as Duke of Milan. This is one of the reasons why Alonso seems prepared to believe the worst, and to assume that the waves have taken his son and heir.

Act II: Scene 2

The Scene begins with Caliban carrying a burden of firewood, as he has been ordered to do by his master. He curses Prospero, asking his, Caliban's, gods to inflict on Prospero various horrible diseases. He also tells of the tortures his master inflicts on him for his rebellious thoughts. Sometimes spirits appear to him in the form of apes, or snakes—both animals that Shakespeare's contemporaries regarded as peculiarly associated with magic and sorcery.

Trinculo, a jester, appears. His position at the court of Alonso, as the court jester, is to be a licensed Fool—he has affinities with the Fool in *King Lear* and similar characters in other plays of Shakespeare. But Trinculo is presented as a distinctly ordinary man, full of the ability to make petty mischief. It is significant for the meaning of the play that at first Caliban worships him as a god, first believing that he is a Spirit sent by Prospero to torment him. Trinculo humorously describes the fantastic half-human creature Caliban very vividly. This beginning of Scene 2 does possess genuine humor, in contrast to the forced humor and repartee of Sebastian and Antonio in the preceding scene; the humor inheres in the incredulity with which Trinculo and then Stephano, drunk, view Caliban, and the comments they make about him. Stephano, a butler at the court of Alonso, enters unsteadily waving a bottle and singing a tune, a sea-chantey.

Stephano and Trinculo, with the quickness of street rogues, understand that Caliban is more terrified of them than they of him. Caliban, most usually presented on stage as dressed in a bearskin (because Trinculo describes him as a fish does not necessarily mean he looks like one; he can take a number of forms as presented in the actual theatre) pleads with the two scapegrace characters and arouses their curiosity. They quickly realize that they may be able to turn the situation to their own profit. They both show a low form of cunning in this. Neither of the men knows whom Caliban is talking about, when he refers to his torments at the hands of Prospero. Their reckless courage—especially that of Stephano—is the wine talking in part. Trinculo assumes that Caliban is a devil. Stephano (line 96) alludes to the proverb: "He who sups with the Devil must needs have a long spoon," and he says with bravado that if Caliban is a devil and not a monster he will leave Caliban. But much of the "bravery" shown by the two rogues is clearly bravado. It will not stand any testing—and Stephano and Trinculo are, in a half-serious way, being tested even as Alonso and his party are being put to a test, and even as Ferdinand is tested. This is not to say that Stephano and Trinculo are "serious" characters; they are not. They provide comic relief from the lofty and compressed action of *The Tempest*, which teases us into thought. But here they, too, are tested.

Initially the two are successful in fooling Caliban. Like Miranda, although at a much more primitive level, Caliban is an innocent: he has no experience of the "outside." Thus, in an aside to the audience, Caliban indicates that he thinks Stephano and Trinculo to be "fine" creatures indeed. He decides that he will worship them, as long as they do not turn out to be spirits sent by Prospero to torment him. The "celestial liquor" that Stephano brings is a powerful inducement also to Caliban.

Stephano tells Trinculo that he has a "whole butt" of the liquor (line 130); the butt, or cask, of wine has apparently been washed ashore after being heaved overboard by the sailors to lighten the King's ship which had been thought to be sinking at the beginning of the play. This fact is important for the future action because it is on "firewater" that Stephano, Trinculo, and Caliban are going to obtain sufficient courage to attempt to kill Prospero and take over the island.

Caliban seeks a new master, then, and finds him in the rather unadmirable person of Stephano:

> I'll fish for thee, and get thee wood enough.
> A plague upon the tyrant that I serve!
> I'll bear him no more sticks, but follow thee,
> Thou wondrous man!
> (lines 157-60)

Trinculo himself perceives that Caliban's trust is misplaced, as he observes that Caliban is a—

> . . . most ridiculous monster, to make a wonder
> of a poor drunkard!
> (line 162)

Caliban, at the end of this Scene, exits with his new master, singing somewhat unsteadily of his new-found "freedom":

No more dams I'll make for fish,
  Nor fetch in firing
  At requiring,
Nor scrape trenchering, nor wash dish.
  'Ban, 'Ban, Ca—Caliban
  Has a new master. Get a new man.
Freedom, high-day! high-day, freedom! freedom, high-day,
freedom!

(lines 175-82)

Act III: Scene 1

At the conclusion of the preceding scene, Caliban has been deceived
into believing that Stephano and Trinculo, the lowest and most roguish
members of the ship's company cast up on the enchanted island, are
as gods; he has been led astray by what might be called his lack of
experience of mankind in general.

At a much more elevated level, in the present scene we see a process of
education taking place, in which Miranda, who has been entirely innocent previously, now begins to learn more about the world, under the
careful guidance of her father. In this, Miranda's state and Caliban's are
similar: they both need at this point to learn more about the "outside
world"; to recognize various types and characters of men, good and bad.
The scene, then, begins with Ferdinand; we see him undergoing his
test. This scene, in other words, forms a continuity with Act I, Scene 2
at the end, where we saw Prospero leading Ferdinand out to the place
where he is going to force him to do physical labor.

Ferdinand's task is to pile up thousands of heavy logs, and he must do
this under Prospero's "sore injunction"—if he does not complete the
work as he has been told to do, he will suffer for his neglect.

Miranda and Prospero enter; Miranda is visible to Ferdinand, while
Prospero is invisible. Her language is characterized by startling figures
of speech, quite in keeping with the romantic tone of the scene: thus
she says that the log that Ferdinand is at the moment lifting will itself
regret the effort it caused Ferdinand:

When this burns,
'Twill weep for having wearied you. (lines 18–19)

Ferdinand will not allow Miranda to help him with his task. It would
dishonor him to do so, as she is the lady he serves. He is, in a sense,

serving Miranda much as a knight-errant would serve his lady. A certain amount of comedy arises from the incongruity of the situation at the beginning of this scene: the high-flown, romantic language of Ferdinand, contrasted with his menial situation. But he is undergoing his test under the personal supervision of Prospero.

Prospero, unseen, contemplates the meeting of his daughter and his future son-in-law, and is very well satisfied. "Poor worm, thou art infected!" says Prospero of his daughter, but this is said in a tone of endearment. He means by this that Miranda has already fallen deeply in love with the Prince, which is exactly Prospero's intention, both from his concern for the personal happiness of his daughter and for reasons of state. A line from the charming short English opera *Dido and Aeneas,* composed by Henry Purcell in 1689, perfectly reveals the source of the special concern a King or Prince would have for the contracting of such a marriage alliance:

> When monarchs unite,
> How happy their state,
> They triumph at once
> O'er their foes and their fate!

So it will be with Prospero, for he too will triumph over his foes when the marriage is contracted.

Ferdinand, in this impossible romantic transport of his, suddenly asks Miranda her name; he has been so enthralled by this beautiful creature that he does not even know what she is called. She answers even though her father had told her not to disclose who she is:

> . . . Miranda. O my father,
> I have broke your hest to say so! (lines 35-6)

The name "Miranda" means a female who is "one to be admired" (Latin). Ferdinand does, of course, "admire" her, addressing her as "admired Miranda" (line 37).

Ferdinand goes on in extravagant praise of Miranda while continuing to pile up the logs. Miranda tells him in turn (line 48) that she scarcely knows what other men and other women look like because she cannot remember her early childhood.

Ferdinand announces his "condition," or social status, to Miranda at this point, in lines closely involved with the political meaning of this scene. He is a Prince, and since he believes that his father is dead, he thinks that he may have inherited the throne of Naples, although he wishes it were not so. This shows Ferdinand's soundness as both a son and a Prince: he is not too impatient for the supreme power of the throne, and demonstrates true filial affection for his father.

By doing the menial work demanded of him, he feels that he "serves" his lady, and this excuses the kind of labor he must perform at Prospero's order:

> I am in my condition
> A prince, Miranda—I do think a king
> (I would not so!)—and would no more endure
> This wooden slavery than to suffer
> The fleshfly blow my mouth. Hear my soul speak!
> The very instant that I saw you did
> My heart fly to your service, there resides . . . (lines 61-66)

This is, then, love at first sight between two royal persons who immediately recognize in each other their true mates.

Miranda asks very directly and artlessly: "Do you love me?" Normally, this is not a question that one in Miranda's position would ask, for natural innocence is, in the usual way of the world, obscured by guile and indirection. But remember that Miranda is in a state of innocence on the enchanted island, quite removed from ordinary life, and therefore she does not have the defenses and the devious ways one might expect such a beautiful woman to have in the world, in Shakespeare's presentation of her. Her lack of guile is charming rather than forward or offensive.

Within a few lines, the couple have exchanged vows of fidelity and are really engaged. A mutual promise to marry at some time in the future is, for the Elizabethans, a valid engagement, and would have been so understood by Shakespeare's audience.

Prospero is pleased to see this.

> Fair encounter
> Of two most rare affections! Heavens rain grace
> On that which breeds between 'em! (lines 73-75)

Prospero's observation can be understood in at least two senses. First, he signifies that he is pleased by the engagement, about which he has not been consulted, though he later ratifies it and gives the couple a proper betrothal (at the beginning of Act IV).

Second, and more important, he sees "that which breeds between 'em" as not only affection, but ultimately progeny. And to one of royal blood, this was most important. Prospero's line will inherit another throne, that of Naples, in addition to the one which is already Prospero's by right: the throne of Milan.

Miranda does not force herself on Ferdinand as his wife; her directness and lack of dissimulation are entirely natural to one who has had the isolated upbringing she has had. But her royal qualities manifest themselves, as do Ferdinand's.

Prospero cannot rejoice at the event as much as the actual participants, but the engagement represents the entire success of one portion of his master plan. He leaves, at the end of this scene, for he has much more to do before his plan can succeed entirely:

> I'll to my book;
> For yet ere supper time must I perform
> Much business appertaining. (lines 95-7)

Act III: Scene 2

On another part of the island, Caliban, Stephano, and Trinculo are wildly drunk; this is a continuation of Act II, Scene 2. The reader should note how the stories of Ferdinand and Miranda, the most ideal, innocent, and attractive types of man and woman, are alternated and contrasted with the comic relief provided by the drunken Stephano and Trinculo and the wild man or man-beast, Caliban. The two humans who are descending to the level of beasts, along with Caliban, are found at the beginning of this scene drinking from Stephano's butt of wine.

Caliban has taken Stephano as his lord and master; he asks if he may lick Stephano's shoe, and asserts that he will not serve Trinculo, for "he is not valiant." Trinculo mocks Caliban as a "deboshed fish." Caliban, offended, asks protection of his lord:

> Lo, how he mocks me! Wilt thou let him, my lord? (line 29)

In the above line, "let" means "stop."

Trinculo—and here Shakespeare—makes a play on the meaning of "natural" in line 30. Natural means "according to nature," or, in the case of Caliban, a "natural" being without any spirit or soul—merely a part of nature. "Natural" also, as a noun, means one who is an idiot or imbecile; a fool. But Caliban turns out to be more intelligent and more "human" than either of his two companions, so in this sense he proves himself to be not a "natural." A monster is by definition unnatural, so this is a play on words—the kind of play in which Trinculo and Stephano, as well as Antonio and Sebastian, engage in. It may be significant that Prospero, the lord and master of the island, does not engage in word-play of any sort; for him, what he says is what he means, if his hearers can understand his message. For most of the other characters, words can have various serious and comic meanings which are less than straight-forward, to fit in with the character of the speaker.

Stephano drunkenly threatens Trinculo, telling him to be respectful of his betters. There is here just a suggestion that even in a "state of nature," where men exist without laws or governments, a natural authority or chain of leadership will be established; if there are even two men, one will become the master and the other the subject. This could be an implied critique of Gonzalo's ideal commonwealth speech of Act II, Scene 1.

Ariel appears at this point, maintaining invisibility by magic arts, just as Caliban says to his new master:

> As I told thee before, I am subject to a tyrant,
> A sorcerer, that by his cunning hath cheated
> Me of the island. (Lines 40-42)

Ariel says to Caliban aloud: "Thou liest." Shakespeare uses this scene for comic relief, because while Ariel is invisible, his voice can be heard by the drunken pair as well as by Caliban. Stephano believes that it is Trinculo who says, "Thou liest." Accusing Trinculo of giving him the lie, he finally strikes him. Between gentlemen in Shakespeare's time, for one man *directly* to accuse another of calling him a liar was grounds for a duel. Here Stephano and Trinculo are presented as aping their betters, for both act as though they were kings and noblemen instead of ordinary rogues. They are examples of men acting under no restraint of lawful authority.

Ariel, then, says three times that Caliban has lied. The third time, Stephano mistakenly beats Trinculo for having said he, Stephano, has lied.

Act III: Scene 3

As Stephano, Trinculo and Caliban go crashing off through the woods, we find the party of the King wandering about on another part of the island. We know that this party too—certainly Sebastian and Antonio—represents the deterioration of man rather than his perfection. They plot murder and treason against their King, just as Caliban and his cohorts plot against Prospero.

Gonzalo and Alonso are, in the beginning of Scene 3, tired and disheartened. Alonso's spirit is dull, for the King is now certain that his
son is drowned. Antonio, again, viciously whispers in Sebastian's ear to
the effect that "he's so out of hope" that it makes Antonio glad; a most
unnatural statement:

> I am right glad that he's so out of hope.
> (line 11)

Antonio means by this that since the King is so beaten down by sorrow
for his lost son, he will be even easier to kill. But while this makes even
clearer the picture of Antonio as the instigator of the plot, and a most
cold-blooded villain, it still shows that neither Antonio nor Sebastian possesses the ruthlessness necessary to confront the King while he is awake
in order to kill him. If either of them did have such courage, *The Tempest*
would then have been a tragedy, not a tragi-comedy or dramatic romance.
Sebastian and Antonio agree to effect their treacherous plot that same
night. Suddenly, as they have concluded their agreement once again,
there is strange music. Prospero appears. As it would be staged in the
theatre, he stands on an upper stage, invisible to the members of the
King's party. He directs various strange shapes, who bring in a banquet
and dance about it, inviting the famished King and his companions to
eat.

Various fabulous monsters are mentioned by the members of the King's
party as they contemplate the banquet with the eyes of hunger. The
fabulous creature known as the unicorn, which has only one horn; the
phoenix, which regenerates itself periodically on its own funeral pyre,
and which was the subject of much mythological interpretation in the
middle ages and in Shakespeare's own age—these are talked of. The
King and his companions are amazed; they realize what Gonzalo, the
supposedly obtuse old courtier, has long since known: that a supernatural agency is at work on the island. Gonzalo stands his ground,
which is another piece of evidence that we should accept him as a kindly
and entirely wise old man rather than a garrulous fool. He points out
that the harpies and strange shapes have very gentle manners as they
go about setting the banquet:

> For certes these are people of the island,
> Who, though they are of monstrous shape, yet, note,
> Their manners are more gentle-kind than of
> Our human generation you shall find
> Many—nay almost any.
> (lines 30-34)

Prospero comments on this, from his perch of invisibility:

The Tempest

> Honest lord,
> Thou hast said well; for some of you there present
> Are worse than devils.
> > (lines 35-37)

He refers, of course, to those who had had a part in deposing him from his dukedom, as well as to the plotters who seek the life of the King. After further talk about the wonders of the little-known paths of the world, the party determines to taste the banquet. Alonso himself realizes that this may be a trap and that the banquet may be poisoned, but he is indifferent, "since I feel/The best is past" (lines 50-51). By this he means that he has little wish to live, so great is his sense of loss respecting his son.

As the party is in the very act of beginning the banquet, Ariel appears dressed like a harpy (a mythical creature possessing the face and body of a woman and the wings and claws of a bird), accompanied by thunder and lightning. Clapping his wings upon the table, he makes the banquet vanish with a "quaint device," or a trick of the stage.

Both Alonso and Sebastian draw their swords at this point. Ariel mocks them for doing so:

> You fools! I and my fellows
> Are ministers of Fate. . . .
> > (lines 60-61)

They have no material substance. How, then, can Ariel and his agents be hurt by the swords? Ariel casts here, by Prospero's power, a charm on the guilty men so that even if they could use the swords they are now unable to lift them. Ariel, at this point, recounts the specific crimes, primarily centering around the charge that the three:

> From Milan did supplant good Prospero. (line 70)

Here the loss of Ferdinand is tied up with the punishment for this offense of usurpation, as it has been earlier in the play. Alonso now knows what his guilt is, though he has sensed it earlier. During the time while Ariel is speaking, the party appears paralyzed, as in a trance.

The grammatical structure of this whole speech is complicated, but essentially it means that Ariel, as one of the ministers of fate, is called upon to be an avenger of Prospero, and that the fates have pronounced on the three "lingering perdition," meaning that the characters must undergo a purgation of their guilt leading to "a clear life ensuing"—a life free of guilt. At this point we are doubly sure that the play has as one of its important themes that of purgation and purification from guilt.

In the final portion of Scene 3, Ariel vanishes to the accompaniment of praise for him and his performance from his hidden master, who sees all. The shapes put on a dance with comic overtones: perhaps mocking the hungry men further as they remove the table on which the feast had been set.

Now Prospero has his enemies exactly where he wants them; as he says:

> My high charms work,
> And these, mine enemies, are all knit up
> In their distractions. They are now in my pow'r . . . (lines 88-90)

But it has been clear from the action of the play that Prospero has been in control of his enemies from the very beginning, when the ship was caught in the magical tempest. Prospero then leaves to visit his daughter and his prospective son-in-law.

Alonso, staring, still partly in a trance, seems to think that the thunder has spoken to him, for Prospero appears as a vision.

> . . . the thunder
> That deep and dreadful organ pipe, pronounced
> The name of Prosper; it did bass my trespass.
> Therefore my son i'th' ooze is bedded . . . (lines 97-100)

The tie-up between Alonso's sin against Prospero and the drowning, or supposed drowning, of Ferdinand, has been made earlier in the play in Alonso's mind: he has a conscience, and knows he has done wrong and must be punished for the wrong. Alonso is recalled to his sense of guilt. He is so overcome with remorse that he no longer wishes to live; he would prefer to join Ferdinand.

Alonso is suicidal, while Sebastian and Antonio, even more deeply marked with guilt since they have just been planning a murder, are defiant. They swear to fight all the "legions of fiends," as they exit in a frenzy of fear and defiance. Gonzalo speaks the final, and most significant lines here as the scene ends:

> All three of them are desperate. Their great guilt,
> Like poison given to work a great time after,
> Now gins to bite the spirits.
> (lines 106-108)

This is the first time that Gonzalo has even hinted at all he knows about the guilt of the three, but obviously he knows what they have done to Prospero. Remember that at the beginning of the play Prospero had mentioned that it was Gonzalo who provided the means to save his life and the life of Miranda. So it is clear that Gonzalo knows much, yet he forgives much.

Gonzalo has a parallel with the faithful and noble servant Kent, the follower who continues to safeguard and watch over King Lear even while the King banishes him in his anger. Gonzalo likewise will look after the best interests of his master, Alonso, and follows the distracted three along with Adrian and Francisco, to see that they do not harm themselves or others. With this high point of spiritual tension the scene ends.

Act IV: Scene 1

At the beginning of this scene Prospero abandons the stern posture that he has taken toward Ferdinand, who has successfully undergone his period of trial and testing. His trial, incidentally, is very mild compared to those undergone by all of the other guilty characters on the Island. This points up the fact that Ferdinand has been almost entirely guiltless; he is in every way a model young man, son, and Prince, and such guilt as he may have stems from his inheritance. He is, after all, the son of a King who has participated in usurpation, and in the King's guilt Ferdinand shares by birth, but not by his own actions or inclinations. Therefore his punishment is physical only.

> . . . all thy vexations
> Were but my trials of thy love, and thou
> Hast strangely stood the test: here, afore Heaven,
> I ratify this my rich gift.
> (lines 5-8)

Ferdinand here explicitly learns from Prospero that he has been subjected to a test, and that in Prospero's view he has passed it as a King's son should. ("Strangely" had, in Elizabethan times, the meaning of "care; respectful attention.") We have seen Ferdinand resisting the imposition of the menial task at first, until he was forced to do the work by Prospero's charm, and then gladly accepting the heavy physical burdens as he convinces himself that all he does is in the service of his lady, which is in keeping with the aristocratic code by which Shakespeare's audience would have expected a King's son to behave.

Prospero, then, ratifies the gift very formally: "a third of mine own life," which probably means that Prospero has devoted himself to Miranda's upbringing for a third of his 45 years (by the chronology of the play). Prospero does not have any children other than Miranda.*

---

* See W. A. Bacon, *Notes and Queries,* 9 August 1947, on this subject.

The betrothal of Ferdinand and Miranda is made quite formally. Prospero emphasizes several times the necessity for the full religious rites and cere-monies, the "full and holy rite" (line 17). Ferdinand and Miranda are sternly enjoined not to consider themselves as having the rights of married persons until they undergo the marriage ceremony. Ferdinand swears not to anticipate the delights of his appropriate wedding-day, whereupon Prospero praises him further and then calls his chief lieutenant, Ariel, to him. Ariel is to provide an entertainment for Prospero, Ferdinand, and Miranda, and therefore Prospero orders him to go and bring the "rabble" over whom he has power. These would be inferior Spirits whom Prospero can command by virtue of his white magic.

While Ariel goes away to do Prospero's bidding, the master of the Island once again warns Ferdinand that he and his bride must preserve the strictest chastity until their marriage.

Beginning with line 60, the Masque presented by Ariel for the amuse-ment of his master is acted. Iris, or a Spirit representing her, begins the entertainment. Iris is a personification of the rainbow and, according to some classicists, a messenger of the gods. She addresses Ceres, the god-dess of plenty, the protectress of agriculture and also the goddess of fer-tility. The poetry of the speech of Iris should not be overlooked, as it conjures up effortlessly an unimaginable picture of bounty—

> Of wheat, rye, barley, vetches, oats, and pease;
> Thy turfy mountains, where live nibbling sheep,
> And flat meads thatch'd with stover, them to keep;
> Thy banks with pioned and twilled brims,
> Which spongy April at thy hest betrims,
> To make cold nymphs chaste crowns. . . .
> (lines 60-66)

At the end of this speech, Juno descends. Juno was not only queen of the gods, she was also the patroness of childbirth and the protectress, as Juno Lucina, of women about to give birth.

Ceres has been summoned "a contract of true love to celebrate." Her speech, critical of Venus and of the son of Venus, Cupid, is critical be-cause of the theft of the daughter of Ceres, named Proserpina as a result of Cupid's machinations.

The climax of this scene of masque and festivity, making splendid the austere cell of Prospero, occurs as Juno and Ceres impart a marriage-blessing to Ferdinand and Miranda. Prospero explains, in answer to Ferdinand's question, that the performers are spirits—

The Tempest

> Spirits, which by mine Art
> I have from their confines call'd to enact
> My present fancies.
> (lines 120-22)

Ferdinand's answer is significant:

> Let me live here ever;
> So rare a wonder'd father and a wise
> Makes this place Paradise.

The Nymphs enter, and continue to celebrate the marriage festivities, accompanied by Reapers. Suddenly, Prospero remembers something: the plot of Caliban and the two drunkards against his life. He dismisses the Spirits rather abruptly, and seems distracted and "in some passion," as Ferdinand observes. In fact, his daughter says that never yet has she seen him so angry. The Spirits vanish in a "strange, hollow and confused noise." At this point Prospero begins what is certainly the most famous speech in the play, and one of the two or three best-loved pieces in all of Shakespeare's work.

Prospero realizes that the plot of Caliban has reached a critical point. Actually, this is an illusory statement, for Prospero has known all along what would happen and is at no time in any danger from Caliban's plot. Even his anger at the presumption of his slave in daring to plot against him seems not quite real, and not sufficiently motivated dramatically.

Speaking of dramatic motivation, Prospero's famous speech seems hardly motivated at all; it simply proceeds out of an excess of magnificent creative power on the part of the supreme English poet, and is quite beyond praise. But the question is: what is the special magic of these noble, austere, yet golden lines:

> You do look, my son, in a moved sort,
> As if you were dismayed. Be cheerful, sir.
> Our revels now are ended. These our actors,
> As I foretold you, were all spirits and
> Are melted into air, into thin air;
> And, like the baseless fabric of this vision,
> The cloud-capped towers, the gorgeous palaces,
> The solemn temples, the great globe itself,
> Yea, all which it inherit, shall dissolve,
> And, like this insubstantial pageant faded,
> Leave not a rack behind. We are such stuff
> As dreams are made on, and our little life
> Is rounded with a sleep.
> (lines 146-158)

What called this speech forth? On the surface, simply the disappearance at Prospero's command of the airy Spirits who have been putting on the entertainment. It asserts that life is a dream, that man himself is of little more substance than the Spirits who have so casually been called up for a few minutes of entertainment and who have so quickly vanished.

Further, it has long been known that Prospero's speech owes something to a stanza in the *Tragedie of Darius* (1603), by William Alexander, the Earl of Stirling:

> Let greatnesse of her glascie scepters vaunt;
> > Not scepters, no, but reeds, soone bruis'd, soone broken:
> And let this worldlie pomp our wits inchant,
> > All fades, and scarcelie leaves behind a token.
> Those golden pallaces, those gorgeous halles,
> > With fourniture superfluouslie faire:
> Those statelie courts, those sky-encountring walles
> > Evanish all like vapours in the aire.

The Earl of Stirling (1567-1640) was a distinctly minor Scottish poet who wrote several Senecan tragedies. Some of his lines including the aforementioned show considerable creativity, but by no stretch of the imagination could they be considered the equal of Shakespeare's verse. As a work of supreme genius, the speech of Prospero defies rational analysis. The ideas expressed in it are commonplace Elizabethan notions: that man's material life is not quite real, and that life may be described as a dream or a moment's interlude between the realities of birth and death—"the dreamcrossed twilight between birth and dying," as T. S. Eliot put in it in our own century. The idea of the evanescence of earthly things is an orthodox Christian idea: that at the Last Judgment the material world itself will come to an end. No doubt sermons on this topic were most familiar to the audience that saw *The Tempest*, and yet such sermons survive, if at all, in total obscurity. But Prospero's speech has outlasted and will outlast any sermon.

The notion that Prospero had "almost forgotten" the plot against his life is maintained. Prospero calls Ariel to him in order to arrange to foil Caliban's plot and to punish the man-monster and his two drunken associates. As Ariel describes his actions, it seems that he has led on the plotters, who have all sunk to the level of beasts:

> So I charmed their ears
> That calf-like they my lowing followed through . . .
> (lines 178-79)

The three have been led by Ariel until they have found themselves in the "filthy mantled" pool of stagnant water near Prospero's cell. At this point Prospero orders Ariel to bring various brightly-colored clothes for "stale" [a decoy] to catch the prospective thieves and murderers.

Prospero once again denounces Caliban as a "devil, a born devil," who can only be trained, or rather restrained and chastised, by hard punishment. But an interesting aspect of this scene, related to the thematic content of the play, is that Caliban's punishment, as it turns out, is astonishingly light.

As the three plotters approach the cell, Prospero and Ariel remain invisible, watching them. Suddenly they see the sort of clothesline upon which Ariel has hung the glistening apparel.

Caliban, showing more wisdom than his two sodden masters, tries to get them to proceed with the plot and not to be distracted by such "trash."

> Let it alone, thou fool! It is but trash.
> (line 223)

At this point, Caliban himself is beginning to realize that he has worshiped a fool and a dullard, for Trinculo and then Stephano are easily distracted from the plot to attempt to steal the clothing. Just as they are seizing the flimsy appearances of garments, a number of Spirits appear in the shapes of dogs and hounds, with Prospero and Ariel setting them on. Prospero orders that his "goblins" grind the joints of the plotters, and rack them with cramps and convulsions. The three run off, roaring with pain, while Prospero observes that all of his plans have come to fruition exactly on schedule. As Act IV ends Prospero, speaking to Ariel—even more so to himself—summarizes the state of the action when he says:

> At this hour
> Lie at my mercy all mine enemies.
> Shortly shall all my labors end, and thou
> Shalt have the air at freedom. For a little,
> Follow, and do me service.
> (lines 261-65)

Act V: Scene 1

This act, like Act IV, is not further divided into scenes; it consists only of the relatively short Scene 1, plus the Epilogue of twenty lines of tetrameter verse, spoken by Prospero, which is believed by some commentators on the play to be spurious—the later addition of someone other than Shakespeare.

At the end of Act IV, Prospero had announced that all of his enemies are

now completely at his mercy. However, as became clear almost at the
beginning of the play, Prospero always has been in control of events on
the enchanted island since the tempest began, so that nothing has changed
from beginning to end of the play as far as his absolute power is concerned.

In Act V, all of the characters in the play come together in the denouement—the "unknotting," or events following the major climax of the plot
of a play. In *The Tempest*, since Prospero's relative power has not changed
nor has he undergone any sudden reversal of fortune, good or bad, the
denouement of Act V is more in the nature of a final scene in which
mysteries are unraveled and misunderstandings, such as the mutual belief
of Alonso and Ferdinand that the other is dead, set straight.

At six o'clock—the sixth hour at which Prospero had predicted his work
would end—Prospero appears in his cell dressed in his magic garments.
The King and his followers are meanwhile confined in a grove near the
cell; the mariners of the King's ship sleeping the sleep of enchantment,
in the ship's hold. The two drunkards and Caliban are being "driven" like
wild animals in the direction of Prospero's cell; and Prospero's daughter
and new son-in-law, Miranda and Ferdinand, are playing at chess, oblivious to the world around them.

As Ariel describes the King, he and the two guilty lords, Antonio and
Sebastian, are "distracted" and unable to move, with Gonzalo, Adrian, and
Francisco watching over them. If Prospero could only see them, says his
servant, his affections, or disposition toward his enemies, "would become
tender." Ariel says that he would be tender toward them, were he human,
which of course he is not.

Prospero's answer to the observations of Ariel is quite important for the
meaning of the play, and might easily be overlooked in a quick reading:

> Hast thou, which art but air, a touch, a feeling
> Of their afflictions, and shall not myself,
> One of their kind, that relish all as sharply
> Passion as they, be kindlier moved than thou art?
> Though with their high wrongs I am struck to th' quick,
> Yet with my nobler reason 'gainst my fury
> Do I take part. The rarer action is
> In virtue than in vengeance. They being penitent,
> The sole drift of my purpose doth extend
> Not a frown further. Go, release them, Ariel.
> (lines 21–30)

In other words, Prospero's enemies have repented, and therefore the Duke
will not seek revenge. His reason—the faculty in man which alone he

shared with the angels and with the divine principle, in the belief of most of Shakespeare's contemporaries—bids Prospero practice forgiveness rather than take the stern revenge on his enemies, which he might well take otherwise.

His enemies, then, are completely helpless in his power. But Prospero masters himself. By an effort of will, based on Prospero's long study and teaching, he resists the entirely human tendency to take revenge on one's enemies. There is an apparent change in Prospero's outlook in this speech at the beginning of Act V: he turns from revenge to forgiveness. But actually he has been bent on this course from the very beginning of the play, so the change in his attitude is only apparent. For he has foreseen what will happen from the moment he first raised the tempest, and indeed seems to have foreseen everything even before putting his plan into operation. His change of heart is as much an illusion as anything else on the enchanted island, and is employed as a dramatic device by Shakespeare to heighten suspense. The audience of *The Tempest* is left wondering, until Act V, as to the extent of the revenge Prospero will take on his enemies. After all, those enemies are formidable, especially Antonio who, as we have observed earlier, has many of the qualities of an Iago.

As Ariel exits, Prospero utters the other great soliloquy of the play spoken by him—a speech almost equal in genius to the speech on the transitoriness of the "cloud-capped towers" in Act IV.

In this soliloquy, beginning as Prospero addresses

> Ye elves of hills, brooks, standing lakes, and groves,
> And ye that on the sands with printless foot
> Do chase the ebbing Neptune . . .
> (lines 33–34)

there is at once an invocation of the magic that Prospero has lived and acted by, and an abjuration of that magic:

> But this rough magic
> I here abjure; and when I have required
> Some heavenly music which even now I do
> To work mine end upon their senses that
> This airy charm is for, I'll break my staff,
> Bury it certain fathoms in the earth,
> And deeper than did ever plummet sound
> I'll drown my book.
> (lines 50–57)

Prospero ends with the requiring of "some heavenly music" that will soothe the troubled minds of Sebastian, Antonio, and the King and will awaken them free from the burden of that guilt for which they have repented.

At this point in Act V, Prospero now does what his servant Ariel had earlier done in Act III: he notifies the three guilty "men of sin" of their crimes. Alonso had "cruelly used" Prospero and his daughter; Sebastian and Antonio had been "furtherers in the act" and had behaved remorselessly; and, in the case of Antonio, had acted unnaturally toward his own brother, Prospero. Both are "unnatural," because both Antonio and Sebastian would have murdered the King, a peculiarly horrible and unnatural act for Shakespeare's age.

Remarking that of course the three noblemen would not recognize him in his magical garments, Prospero calls Ariel to him once again, promising him that before long he shall have his coveted freedom, and dresses himself once again in the garments of the Duke of Milan, perhaps symbolizing his imminent return to the world and his departure from the timelessness of the enchanted island.

Ariel's song (lines 88—94) is another of the entirely charming songs that surpass the songs of any other Shakespearean play. It is not just to say simply that they have little or no intellectual content; that is not their purpose. They are beyond the realm of the intellect.

The mariners, who have been sleeping a charmed sleep under the hatches of the King's ship, are ordered to be awakened by Ariel. Prospero presents himself to the awakening King and his company as the "wronged Duke of Milan," and embraces Alonso and Gonzalo.

Alonso, overcome, shows both disbelief at seeing Prospero and relief that Prospero is alive, for the guilt of his supposed death has weighed heavily on the King. Gonzalo, too, is overcome:

> Whether this be
> Or not be, I'll not swear.
> (lines 123–24)

Prospero turns to Antonio and Sebastian and tells them that were he so minded he could denounce the two conspirators to their King and "justify" them as traitors—that is, prove that they had intended to murder Alonso. But as treason would be punished by immediate execution, Prospero promises that at least for the moment he will tell no tales. "The devil speaks in him," observes Sebastian in an aside to Antonio. Prospero's answer is interesting and not without significance beyond its shortness, for he simply says: No. It is not the devil, but the principle of divinity which speaks through Prospero.

Prospero at this point peremptorily requires and demands his dukedom from his brother, "most wicked sir." It is significant that Antonio does not even answer, as he is so filled with shame and guilt. He is, after all, the deepest-dyed of the villians in *The Tempest,* and we are left with some doubt concerning the completeness of Antonio's reformation.

At this point, after Prospero's stern reproach directed at his brother (and it is significant that Prospero reserves his sternest words for that man who is clearly the most wicked among the sojourners on the enchanted island), the dramatic suspense is further built up by Shakespeare to a sort of minor climax where Prospero "discovers" Ferdinand and Miranda playing at chess.

This is, in the eyes of the beholders, "a most high miracle." The King is moved from despair to joy as he sees his son alive. Miranda exclaims—

> O, wonder!
> How many goodly creatures are there here!
> How beauteous mankind is! O brave new world
> That has such people in't.
> (lines 182–85)

To which Prospero replies simply—

> 'Tis new to thee.
> (line 186)

This has an implication that in Prospero's view his daughter will inevitably be somewhat disillusioned by the world, which is not characterized by the wise and humane control found on the enchanted island.

Gonzalo rejoices; "Was Milan thrust from Milan that his issue/Should become kings of Naples? O, rejoice . . ." (lines 206–7). This might seem superfluous; Prospero, having demonstrated great power over Nature herself, seems a bit silly settling for a mere dukedom again. But this signifies his rejoining of human society, strengthened by his sojourn on the enchanted island and by his studies. And his descendants will be Kings, not Princes. A cynic might observe that at the end of the play there occurs the Elizabethan equivalent of what our own age calls "upward mobility," as Prospero marries off his daughter to a King's son. But this ending would have seemed entirely fit, proper, and fortunate to Shakespeare's audience.

The ship, which "but three glasses since" appeared to be splitting—that is, three hourglasses previously—is bravely rigged and ready to go to sea again. Alonso observes that what he has witnessed must be supernatural, and Prospero promises to make clear to the assembled parties the "strangeness of this business." One practical consideration here might be simply that Prospero must demonstrate his use of white magic in his proceedings, rather than of black magic.

Prospero orders Ariel to set Caliban and his companions free, and they appear in their stolen clothing. Prospero reproaches Stephano for thinking that he could become King of the island. He orders Caliban to go to his, Prospero's, cell with his accomplices, and to "trim it handsomely." Caliban says that he will be wise hereafter:

> What a thrice-double ass
> Was I to take this drunkard for a god
> And worship this dull fool!
> (lines 295–97)

Caliban has learned, and has advanced one step towards humanity. As the short Act V ends, Prospero promises calm seas and favorable winds, so that the ship will not only reach Naples but even catch up on the rest of the fleet, which had proceeded on, believing the King's ship lost. He charges Ariel that he attend to this:

> Then to the elements
> Be free, and fare thou well!
> (lines 317–318)

As the play ends, the party enters Prospero's cell, there to hear the story of his life.

The Winter's Tale

LEONTES, *King of Sicilia.*
MAMILLIUS, *young prince of Sicilia.*
CAMILLO
ANTIGONUS   } *Lords of Sicilia.*
CLEOMENES
DION
POLIXENES, *King of Bohemia.*
FLORIZEL, *Prince of Bohemia.*
ARCHIDAMUS, *a lord of Bohemia.*
OLD SHEPHERD, *reputed father of Perdita.*
CLOWN, *his son.*
AUTOLYCUS, *a rogue.*
A MARINER.
A JAILER.

HERMIONE, *Queen to Leontes.*
PERDITA, *daughter to Leontes and Hermione.*
PAULINA, *wife to Antigonus.*
EMILIA, *a lady attending on Hermione.*

MOPSA   } *Shepherdesses.*
DORCAS
Other LORDS *and* GENTLEMEN, SERVANTS, SHEPHERDS, *and* SHEPHERDESSES.

The Winter's Tale

Act I: Scene 1

This opening scene takes place in the antechamber of the palace of Leontes, King of Sicilia, at a remote time in Greek history.

Camillo, a lord of Sicilia, and Archidamus, a lord of Bohemia, are discussing the current visit of Polixenes, King of Bohemia, to the court of Leontes. The two lords exchange pleasantries and Archidamus, who has had experience of both courts, remarks on the difference between them. According to him the court of Bohemia is much less magnificent than that of Sicilia, and he jocularly suggests that when the Sicilians arrive on their projected visit, the Bohemians will almost be forced into giving their visitors soporific drinks so that they will not notice the insufficiency of Bohemian hospitality.

Camillo then goes on to discuss the great friendship that exists between Leontes, King of Sicilia, and Polixenes, King of Bohemia. He tells how they were brought up together and how, despite their enforced absence from each other in ruling their respective countries, the monarchs have kept in close touch by means of gifts and letters. Archidamus also marvels at the constancy of the friendship, noting that there does not seem to be anything in the world capable of altering it.

The Bohemian lord then goes on to note the "unspeakable comfort" that the kingdom of Sicilia has in the person of the young prince, Mamillius. Camillo agrees and says that the older generation has the greatest hopes for his future as a monarch. Old men who were crippled before his birth now wish to live in order to see the prince fully grown. Archidamus rather humorously asks whether they would otherwise have preferred to die, to which Camillo replies that they would, had they no other reason to live. Archidamus suggests rather merrily that they might have wished to live on crutches until the King had a son.

Act I: Scene 2

This scene takes place in a room of state in Leontes' palace, with an assembled company consisting of Leontes, Hermione his wife, Mamillius, Polixenes, Camillo, and attendants. Polixenes opens the proceedings by noting that nine months have now gone by since he left his kingdom, Bohemia, and therefore he must return, though he could take another nine months in thanking Leontes and his Queen for their hospitality.

Leontes replies that he wishes his friend could remain longer. Polixenes, however, says that that would be impossible. He is concerned that something might have gone wrong at home. Further, he thinks he may have outstayed his welcome. Leontes protests that such certainly is not the case, and entreats his friend to stay at least a week longer. Polixenes is eventually persuaded to offer a compromise; he will leave tomorrow, not immediately. Leontes continues to press him to stay, but Polixenes is adamant. There are affairs at home which call for his attention, and a longer stay would cause too much trouble to Leontes. Therefore he must leave.

Convinced that he has failed in his persuasive techniques, Leontes turns to Hermione and bids her entreat Polixenes to stay. Hermione then breaks her womanly silence and addresses Polixenes, after first pointing out that Leontes has really been asking in a rather cold and abrupt manner.

Hermione then suggests that Leontes assure his friend that all goes well in Bohemia. This suggestion should do away with Polixenes' best argument for returning. Rather shrewdly Hermione surmises that the real reason is probably a desire to see his son at home. This of course would really be the best reason for Polixenes' desire to return. Jokingly, she says that if he will *swear* that this is his reason then she will hasten his departure, but if he merely *says* that she is right, then she will make him stay. Nevertheless Hermione begs Polixenes to lend Sicilia another week of his company, and in return she promises to permit Leontes to overstay the proposed date of his departure from Bohemia for an entire month, although she loves him dearly. Again she asks Polixenes to stay, and again he refuses. Then Hermione changes her tactics and resorts to the use of her sportive, merry wit. She simply refuses to let Polixenes go; and if he insists on departing she threatens to keep him as a prisoner in Sicilia rather than a guest. Merrily she offers Polixenes his choice between having her as a jailer or a hostess. Polixenes, amused by the turn of conversation, chooses Hermione the hostess, and the Queen goes on to ask about the nature of the friendship between the two Kings, begging Polixenes to tell her of the tricks they used to play.

Polixenes speaks eloquently of the joy of their youthful friendship which took every day as it came and believed that the next day would be just as pleasant as the preceding. Youth to them seemed to be something eternal and changeless.

In reply to Hermione's question whether Leontes was not the more sprightly trickster of the two of them, Polixenes uses the image of the two young lads frolicking and playing as innocently as twin lambs. They did not know evil, nor did they believe that anyone else did. Regretfully, he seems to wish that they had remained forever in that state of bliss; then they could be certain of their eternal salvation. Hermione continues with her merry questioning to ask if Polixenes has "tripped" since, if, in other words, he has succumbed to the temptations of evil. Taking up the challenge, Polixenes notes that indeed they have both met temptations, Leontes in the person of Hermione, and Polixenes in his own wife. Hermione appears mock angry and stops him right there before he takes the next step of insinuating that she and his queen are devils. The two of them will answer for any sexual offenses the gentlemen may have committed with their wives, if the so-called sin was first committed with them and continued only with them.

Leontes does not appear to have been listening very closely to this dialogue because he asks whether Polixenes is yet persuaded to stay, to which question Hermione replies unhesitatingly in the affirmative. Leontes mumbles suspiciously "At my request he would not," but then goes on to congratulate Hermione on the success of her eloquence, claiming that she had never used her tongue to better purpose. Hermione, now flushed with success, and in her wittiest mood, begins to flirt with Leontes, archly asking "Never?" In reply Leontes concedes that there was another occasion, and Hermione teasingly inquires when it was. Leontes says that it was when she accepted his proposal of marriage after a three months' courtship. Hermione then conjoins the two occasions and makes them of parallel importance: the first earned her "a royal husband," and the second "for some while a friend," a very delicate compliment to Polixenes.

But Leontes does not seem to consider this compliment quite so delicate. Immediately he mutters "Too hot, too hot!" and starts to give vent to his almost unspeakable suspicions of Hermione's virtue. Mingling friendship is "mingling bloods," he says, an image which has overtones of illicit sexual intercourse. Certainly he admits that

Hermione's sportive wit may have an innocence born of sincerity, but these two are going too far in holding hands too long, caressing rather than greeting or striking a bargain, smiling rather too knowingly at each other, each reflecting the gaze of the other. Their sighs seem more like the hunting note for the death of the deer, a hunting image which has overtones of cuckoldry, because the traditional figure of the cuckold, the betrayed husband, was that of a man with horns. Gradually Leontes' rage seems to increase, because he suddenly rounds on Mamillius with the unexpected question, "Art thou my boy?" which hints at the dishonesty of Hermione.

Mamillius, of course, cannot understand what his father is talking about and answers the query "Art thou my boy?" quite literally and says that he is. Leontes then starts looking at the child and speaking to him with terms of endearment, glad to note that the youngster's nose is a copy of his own. He calls the child his "bawcock," a corruption of the French *beau coq*, or fine fellow; then the child becomes his calf, and finally his collop, or piece of meat. The exchange between Mamillius and Leontes, however, is not all in terms of endearment. Leontes' jealousy is growing by the moment, and when he suggests that the child must be neat (as he wipes his son's nose) he recalls that "neat" was also a term for horned cattle, a remembrance that again raises the question of his own cuckoldry. So the words he uses concerning himself, Polixenes, and Hermione promptly become those taken from the raising of cattle: steer, heifer, calf. Continually, Leontes' mind shifts between the two topics, Mamillius' likeness to himself, and his own growing certainty that he has been cuckolded by his friend. He watches the way she is still "virginalling" or playing with Polixenes' hand—though Leontes probably exaggerates here. Nevertheless, the pun on the virginals (a pianolike instrument) and chastity is quite clear. And Leontes always comes back to the question of his brows, the "hardening" of his brows both literally, in terms of his frowning gaze, and figuratively, in terms of the cuckold's horns. Leontes' agitation is becoming manifest through Shakespeare's use of turbulent syntax and language.

Hermione does not help matters any when she looks at her distraught husband and speaks of his "brow of much distraction." Leontes covers up his real thoughts by saying how gazing on his child has made him look back on himself at the same age. He asks the child if he will "take eggs for money," take something worthless for something better, and Mamillius says that he would rather fight. Leontes is gratified by this aggressive instinct and asks Polixenes whether his friend is as fond of his son as he is of Mamillius.

Polixenes replies with a charming speech on the joys of fatherhood and the therapeutic value of playing with an innocent child who can cure in his father thoughts that would otherwise chill the blood.

Leontes then suggests that he walk with Mamillius, leaving Hermione to walk with Polixenes, and charging her to make provision for his friend's entertainment. Next to her and Mamillius, he says, Polixenes is the recipient of his affection.

Hermione, totally unaware of these suspicions, willingly agrees, and with a cheerful remark, "We are yours i' the garden," takes the arm of Polixenes and the two withdraw. Leontes, however, makes a cryptic reply which would be understood by the audience, but not by the participants in such a scene, "You'll be found,/ Be you beneath the sky."

Then, aside, he speaks of the way in which he is giving these two fish enough line to entrap themselves. He tortures himself by looking at the way Hermione holds up her *neb,* her nose, literally, but Leontes deliberately uses an archaic word for the bill of a bird. He is struck with horror to see how she puts her arm in the arm of his friend. Again he speaks of "a fork'd one," and the reference is unclear: it is either to Hermione as a double-dealing devil, or to himself who must, as he thinks, wear the forked horns. The bawdy metaphors now come thick and fast; and after Leontes sends Mamillius away to play he speaks rather crudely of the way in which a husband may not be suspicious that his wife has been "sluiced" and "his pond fish'd by his next neighbor." Both of these comments are obvious references to illicit sexual intercourse. Leontes takes cold comfort in the fact that many husbands are cuckolds, and there is no remedy for that disease, since unfaithful wives are like a bawdy planet that strikes when it is in the ascendancy.

Ironically, just after this bitter speech the young Mamillius tries to get his father's attention with the words "I am like you, they say," to which Leontes replies with even greater irony, "Why, that's some comfort."

Leontes then turns to Camillo, his councillor, and asks whether he had noted the way in which Polixenes had been persuaded to stay. Camillo remarks that indeed it had been a difficult task, and that Leontes himself had not been able to succeed. This comment arouses further anger in the breast of Leontes. He seethes inwardly, and in a short, bitter aside, he shows that he is firmly convinced that his subjects are even now whispering about his own disgrace. He twists the knife in his own wound and forces Camillo to say that Polixenes has stayed only because of Hermione's entreaty. Then he asks his councillor whether anyone else might have noted this circumstance—or are the lower classes blind. Note here the way in which Leontes' speech now shifts its rhythms, breaks the back of the lines, and seems full of rhetorical questions. Every remark seems to be packed with meaning and also with the horror of the situation, until Leontes finally rounds on the innocent Camillo and asks whether he is dishonest, negligent in his trust, or else a coward that he refuses to say precisely what he thinks about the situation. Camillo, astonished by this sudden attack on him, replies with dignity and skill, denying the truth of each of the three charges.

Leontes is finally forced into stating very specifically to Camillo exactly what he means. He accuses Hermione of dishonesty, speaking of her as a "hobby-horse," a loose woman, whom any man may ride. Camillo protests against such a cruel misreading of Hermione's behavior, and he takes on himself the office of a wise councillor in rebuking Leontes for even thinking such thoughts. But Leontes is convinced and he presents what he considers evidence: whispering, leaning towards each other so that their cheeks touch, kissing with the inside of the lip, hiding in corners, wishing that time would pass more quickly, and other such examples. It does not matter that the audience has seen no such behavior; in fact this detailing of offenses gives color to the belief that Leontes is in effect making everything up out of his own diseased mind. He also refers to his wife as a creature as hotly sexual as a common flaxworker who has illicit intercourse even before she has plighted her troth to the man concerned.

Camillo begs Leontes to have some sense and to rid himself of such diseased thoughts, but the monarch turns on him and calls him a liar, expressing hatred of him as "a gross lout, a mindless slave, . . . a hovering temporizer." He threatens that if Hermione's liver were as infected as her life she would not outlive the hour.

Camillo then asks the source of the infection which Leontes is talking about, and is appalled when Leontes names Polixenes. But he is totally shocked and horrified when the king finishes by proposing that Camillo, Polixenes' cupbearer, see to it that the visitor is poisoned. Camillo replies that indeed he could perform this service, and with a slow-working poison too, but for the fact that he is firmly convinced that Hermione is totally innocent. He attempts to soothe Leontes by a recollection of his own services, but the monarch turns on him and insists that he is not imagining things, but rather wishes to preserve the purity of his sheets. Camillo then says that he must believe his King, and that he will do away with Polixenes, but only on condition that Leontes again take Hermione as his wife, both for the sake of Mamillius and his international reputation. Leontes agrees, saying that that was in effect his plan, and Camillo seems to acquiesce in the entire arrangement. Left alone, however, Camillo reveals his doubts about his course of action. Certainly, if he kills Polixenes in obedience to a master who is temporarily not in command of himself, then he will gain promotion. But there is no future in slaying an anointed King. No one who has ever done so has flourished afterwards. For Camillo there seems to be only one alternative. He must disobey Leontes and then he must leave the court of Sicilia.

Just then Polixenes returns and seems puzzled to note that quite suddenly he no longer feels welcome in Sicilia. Naturally he questions Camillo and asks what is the meaning of Leontes' sudden change of behavior: the King has just treated his visitor with contempt and walked away. Camillo at first refuses to say, but then Polixenes charges him to tell the truth, saying that *his* changed attitude seems to indicate complicity with Leontes. Camillo starts out indirectly by speaking of the disease that is caught by those who are well, and finally, at Polixenes' insistence he blurts out quite bluntly, "I am appointed by him to murder you," and then to Polixenes' growing horror he tells him the reason—his alleged misconduct with Hermione. Polixenes is totally shocked and swears that he is innocent.

Camillo then believes Polixenes and offers himself to the service of Bohemia, since by revealing the mind of Leontes he has obviously forfeited his place at the court of Sicilia. The astounded Polixenes accepts Camillo's offer, but at the same time he cites extenuating circumstances which make Leontes' rage more comprehensible: since it is for such a rare creature as Hermione it must be violent; since Leontes is a royal person, it must also be mighty; since the alleged betrayer was a great friend, the rage must be increased. Polixenes then thinks of flight, and since Camillo is able to command the opening of any gate in the palace of Sicilia the departure of the fugitives is made easier.

Act II: Scene 1

This scene takes place a short time later in another room in Leontes' palace. Hermione, her ladies, and Mamillius are there. At first Hermione asks one of her ladies to take Mamillius from her because she finds his energy too much for her. Two of the ladies in turn offer to play with him and the child engages each in a merry, if somewhat precocious, wit combat with them. One, he claims, will treat him like a baby, while the other has black eyebrows.

The ladies gladly indulge him and one mentions that it will not be long before Mamillius will be very glad to have them offer to play with him when his mother gives birth to a second child. Throughout these speeches there is a great delight in the fact of Hermione's pregnancy, as can be seen from the comments made on the subject: "The queen your mother rounds apace"; and "She is spread of late/Into a goodly bulk: good time encounter her." This joy in fertility is one of the themes which will frequently be encountered in the play. Hermione then takes Mamillius back to her and asks him to tell her a story. He decides that his account will be sad, because "a sad tale's best for winter."

Suddenly Leontes, accompanied by Antigonus, some lords, and other attendants, rushes in on this scene of tranquillity, interrupting Mamillius' tale. He immediately asks whether anyone present has seen Polixenes and Camillo, and a lord replies that he met them as they were proceeding to the Bohemian ships. Leontes now flies into a fearful rage and says that now his suspicions are justified.

He then launches into a condemnation of Camillo, who has aided Polixenes in his flight. Suspiciously, he sees almost every happening as a plot against both his person and his crown.

Suddenly he turns to Hermione who has Mamillius in her arms and orders her to give the child to him, saying insultingly that he is glad she did not nurse him, but that he regrets every drop of blood in him that is hers. Hermione answers amazedly, and courteously inquires whether Leontes is joking. But Leontes' next speech leaves her in no doubt. He attacks her openly, looking with loathing upon her pregnant body, bidding her play "With that she's big with"; for " 'tis Polixenes/Has made thee swell thus."

Even at this point Hermione is most tolerant, and mildly indignant. She answers her enraged husband with consideration, spirit, and politeness, denying the truth of the charge. Leontes then turns to his lords and makes the charge more specific, telling his followers to look on his lady and say it is a pity she is not honest. This lengthy and insulting speech culminates in the final charge, "She's an adulteress." This last comment galvanizes Hermione into action and she denies the charge most vigorously, but again she shows respect for her beloved husband, saying that he is mistaken. Leontes now increases the tempo of his accusation; as well as claiming that she has "mistaken" Polixenes for Leontes, he accuses her of traitorous intentions, and of being in league against him with Camillo, whom he has already accused of being a procurer. Again Hermione replies fairly mildly, showing only pity for her husband. As her speeches increase in length so also does her queenly dignity. She never descends to the depths of insult, as does Leontes, and even when her husband orders her to be taken to prison she resigns herself to her lot, which will probably be unfortunate until the evil planet that is in the ascendancy shall have been replaced by another, more favorable one. She asks only that in view of her condition her ladies be permitted to accompany her in order to look after her. Courageously she tells her attendants not to weep; let them save their tears for an occasion on which their mistress has really deserved prison. She takes this imprisonment as a trial, a purification, and her only rebuke to her husband is loving, mild, and dignified: "I never wish'd to see you sorry; now/ I trust I shall."

So dignified is her appearance that one of the lords begs Leontes to call her back, and Antigonus suggests that Leontes ought to be quite certain of the rightness of his actions, because otherwise the King and Mamillius would also suffer the consequences, as well as Hermione. The lord says that he himself is prepared to wager his own life on the Queen's innocence, and Antigonus remarks that if Hermione is false, so too is his own wife, whom he will lock up, and so is every woman in the world; in fact if Hermione be dishonest, then he, Antigonus, will geld every one of his three daughters to prevent them from producing illegitimate children.

The lord and Antigonus continue to defend the honor of Hermione and they beg Leontes to be more patient, an action which takes considerable courage in face of the monarch's rage. Leontes, however, is quite certain of the rightness of his course and does not wish to listen to any of his councillors. He tries to show by means of circumstantial evidence that the flight of Polixenes and Camillo automatically indicates their guilt. Nevertheless, he has sent Cleomenes and Dion, two lords of the court, to "sacred Delphos, Apollo's temple," in order to get corroboration from the oracle. Leontes' reason is not, however, to confirm his own knowledge of the case; as far as he is concerned that needs no further evidence. He is merely concerned to convince the common and ignorant people of the rightness of his actions. Leontes throughout this scene is acting as a tyrant by refusing to listen to any advice and taking the law into his own hands.

Act II: Scene 2

This scene takes place a short time later in the prison where Hermione has been sent. Paulina, the wife of Antigonus, enters and sends in a gentleman to bring the jailer back with him. Paulina then asks to be conducted to the Queen, but the jailer says that he has strict orders not to do so. However, when Paulina asks if it is possible to see Emilia, one of Hermione's waiting women, the jailer agrees, as long as Paulina sees her under his surveillance.

Emilia announces to Paulina that Hermione has been prematurely delivered of a baby daughter, in whom she takes great comfort.

Paulina says that she will take it upon herself to inform the king of the birth of his child, and then she has an idea. She asks Emilia to see whether Hermione will entrust the child to her so that she may show it to Leontes in order to soften his hard heart. Emilia is a trifle doubtful whether the mission would be successful, and also whether Hermione would let the child out of her sight. The jailer, being a literal-minded soul, says that he is not sure whether he could sign a release for the infant, but Paulina blinds him with rather specious reasoning. She claims that the child entered the prison as the prisoner of the womb, and since it had itself no part of its mother's sin, then it has no reason to be imprisoned.

Act II: Scene 3

This scene takes place in a room in Leontes' palace with Antigonus and other lords and servants present. Leontes speaks first, saying that he cannot gain any rest since his violent action against both Polixenes and Hermione. He wishes to take vengeance on his former friend who is now out of his power. However, he does have possession of Hermione, and if he can get rid of her, give her to the fire, then perhaps he may again find peace.

A servant then enters and Leontes asks after the health of Mamillius, to be told that the child rested well this evening and there is hope that the worst of his sickness may be over. Leontes then muses aloud over the way the child took so to heart the dishonor of his mother that he immediately sickened, taking her shame upon himself, and started to decline.

As the servant departs, Leontes begins to think aloud about his revenges once more. Polixenes and Camillo are out of his grasp and he imagines that they are both laughing at him. Still, Hermione is still in his power and he can be revenged on her.

At this singularly inopportune moment Paulina enters with the child. One of the lords tries to prevent her from meeting with the king. Paulina, however, shows no fear, despite the fact that she is told that the King has forbidden all access to him since he has not been able to sleep. Undaunted, Paulina replies that she has come to bring sleep to the monarch. She comes with curative words aimed to purge him of the humor that prevents his sleeping.

Leontes, enraged, orders Paulina from his sight, turning on Antigonus to say that he has been told to keep his wife under control and away from the court. Antigonus rather weakly says that he has indeed informed his wife of that order, and Leontes caustically asks whether he cannot rule her. As the scene progresses it is difficult to see how anyone could fully control Paulina. The fact remains, however, that she is on the side of the angels, and therefore the audience should accept her not as a common shrew, but as a magnificent ranter, a crusader in the cause of righteousness.

Paulina then violently threatens to scratch out the eyes of any man who tries to prevent her from speaking and she announces that she has come from "the good queen." She then lays the innocent babe at Leontes' feet, while the King insults her as a bawd. Almost insane with anger, Leontes shouts to his lords to push her out, along with the bastard, and he insults Antigonus as a henpecked husband.

Paulina refuses to be put off by Leontes, even when he claims that she, Antigonus, and all the others are in effect a nest of traitors. Leontes swears that the "brat" that Paulina has brought is no true child of his, but rather the child of Polixenes, and calls for it to be taken away and burned, together with its mother. In reply, Paulina says that the child is so like Leontes that it is the worse for being so, and she shows the child to the lords, who are horrified at their master's violence. The only thing, she says, that the child lacks is yellow, that is, jealousy, to prove her parentage. Leontes again insults Paulina and demands that Antigonus take her out, under pain of being hanged himself. Antigonus rather ruefully says that if the King were to hang all husbands who were unable to control their wives he would hardly have a single subject left alive. Leontes now threatens to have Paulina burned, but that sturdy lady says that she is not afraid of the fire, only a heretic is, not a martyr. She castigates

Leontes for his cruelty toward Hermione and gets to the heart of the problem: Leontes really has no evidence of Hermione's guilt except his own imaginings. But the physical strength of one lord is too much, and in obedience to Leontes' command, Paulina is pushed from the room upbraiding Leontes and protesting to the last. She also takes care to leave the child behind, still rather innocently convinced that Leontes cannot fail to be softened by its helplessness.

With Paulina's departure, Leontes now turns on Antigonus and orders once more that the child be taken out and burned. He picks Antigonus for the task because his wife was the person who brought the child to him in the first place, and therefore he is responsible. But Antigonus and the other lords disclaim responsibility for Paulina's coming, while one lord in particular entreats Leontes to change his mind about the fate of the child. Leontes then claims that he is too soft-hearted for his own good and asks Antigonus what he would do in order to save the life of the "bastard." Antigonus replies that he would do anything, and so Leontes makes him swear that he will do as he is told. On receiving Antigonus' assurance, he tells him to take the child to the remotest possible corner outside the dominion of Sicilia and there expose it where it may either survive or die. Sadly, Antigonus takes up the child, saying that a swift death might have been a more merciful fate than this. He recalls mythological situations in which birds and animals of prey have befriended deserted children, and he hopes that something similar may happen here. But he is not optimistic.

The intransigent Leontes swears that he will not rear the child of another man. At this moment a servant enters to say that Cleomenes and Dion have returned with a message from the oracle. Leontes now gets everything in readiness for a public trial of Hermione. He says that she will have "a just and open trial," but in view of what we have already seen of Leontes' disposition it is obvious that as far as he is concerned the outcome is assured. Leontes as judge is convinced of Hermione's guilt and he intends to hold a public trial simply for the purpose of proving her guilt in public. He is determined to have her life because he will always be heavyhearted while she lives.

Act III: Scene 1

This scene takes place at a Sicilian seaport where Cleomenes and Dion have just landed after their visit to Delphos. They seem to have been struck with awe at the sacredness of the shrine, the beauty of the island, and the mildness of its climate. They recount in part the ceremonial of the Oracle and the solemnity with which the pronouncement was made. Dion hopes that the journey will be as successful for Hermione as it has been a moving experience for both of them. Both the councillors express sympathy for and belief in the innocence of Hermione. Obviously they do not believe Leontes' charges.

Act III: Scene 2

This scene is laid in a court of justice. Leontes, with his lords and officers in attendance, declares the session open; then Hermione, with Paulina and other ladies attending her, is brought in under guard. Leontes, in his opening speech before Hermione's entrance, expresses his grief that this trial should be necessary, and says that he wants to clear himself of the charge of tyranny, and therefore he will hold an open trial which will proceed according to the forms of justice and can end in either of two verdicts: guilty or innocent.

The indictment is then read by an officer of the court. It accuses Hermione of high treason in the form of adultery with Polixenes, King of Bohemia, conspiracy with Camillo to murder Leontes, and finally with conniving at the flight of the two guilty men.

Hermione then replies to the charges against her in a completely dignified manner. She is the wronged wife, and that is the attitude she adopts. She knows that Leontes has sent to the Oracle and she is as a result confident that she will be vindicated, since she is sure of her innocence, and also since she has implicit faith in the gods. She even states her belief quite openly:

> . . . if powers divine
> Behold our human actions, as they do,
> I doubt not then but innocence shall make
> False accusation blush, and tyranny
> Tremble at patience . . . (III.ii.29–33)

With this confidence born of security in faith and innocence, Hermione's speeches are in effect statements of her wrongs and of the purity of her past life. She recalls the favor in which Leontes held her before the arrival of Polixenes, and speaks of her performance of duty to Leontes. She claims that certainly she loved Polixenes, but only as far as honor required, with the kind of love that becomes a lady like herself; and further, Leontes himself had commanded that she show affection for his friend. As for the charge of conspiracy with Camillo, Hermione confesses herself ignorant of the reason for his departure from the court.

Leontes, however, sticks to his guns, despite everything that Hermione says. He merely repeats his accusations and offers no evidence to support them. With heavy irony he asks whether Hermione's evil actions have been his "dreams," the figments of his imagination. She had an illegitimate child by Polixenes, and he, Leontes, dreamed it? Surely not! Then he cruelly reveals to Hermione what has become of her daughter; the child has been cast out, and as for its mother, she can look for no easier fate than death.

Hermione, though appalled at the fate of her child, still has courage and refuses to be frightened by the threats of her husband. Life does not mean much to her now since she has lost the favor of Leontes, whom she loves, and since she has also been forbidden to see her son Mamillius. Thirdly, her baby daughter has been torn from her and in effect murdered. Lastly, she herself has been dragged from her prison without even being allowed "the child-bed privilege," a period of time to rest and regain her strength, while her good name has been besmirched by unwarranted accusations. She concludes by calling for the pronouncement of the Oracle to be read. The officer of the court declares that the request is in order and while the company is awaiting the arrival of Cleomenes and Dion, Hermione speaks of her lineage: "The Emperor of Russia was my father," and she wishes sadly that he were there to see his daughter's fate, not with eyes of vengeance, but with pity.

Cleomenes and Dion now enter and take the customary oath that they have not broken the seal of the Oracle's pronouncement. The text of the document is then read and it offers complete vindication of Hermione and Camillo while openly accusing Leontes of being a jealous tyrant. In addition, the Oracle declares that Hermione's child is no bastard and that Leontes will live without an heir "if that which is lost be not found."

The lords immediately rejoice that the Oracle has vindicated the Queen and they offer praise to the god, only to be dumbfounded by Leontes' next move. Quite bluntly he rejects the Oracle:

> There is no truth at all i' the oracle:
> The sessions shall proceed: this is mere falsehood.
>   (III.ii.141–142)

Immediately following this blasphemy, a servant enters to tell the king that Mamillius is dead, and with a suddenness that goes beyond the onset of his jealousy, Leontes realizes his own guilt, injustice, and blasphemy. Hermione faints, and Paulina gives the impression that the queen is dying. Leontes, however, says that she will recover, but he openly recants his charges and says that he has believed too much in his own mere suspicions. As the ladies depart, taking with them the unconscious Hermione, Leontes utters a long speech of repentance, asking pardon of Apollo for his blasphemy against the Oracle, for which he has been so speedily punished. In return for forgiveness he promises to be reconciled to Polixenes, to woo his queen once again, and to recall "the good Camillo" to the court. He goes even further, publicly flagellating himself for his jealousy and his suspicion, even confessing to the assemblage his desire to have Polixenes poisoned by Camillo, whom he now praises as a most virtuous and courageous man. The longer he speaks and the more he says, the blacker in his eyes do his deeds seem, and his repentance becomes more and more abject.

No sooner has Leontes finished his confession and repentance speech than Paulina enters weeping bitterly and full of anger. She tells Leontes that she does not fear his anger or his threats, but she will speak her mind. And indeed she does in a tirade against him for his suspicion, his jealousy, his folly, his betrayal of Polixenes, his plotting, his casting out of his baby daughter, and his contribution to the death of Mamillius. Then after a pause she reveals the ultimate horror: the death of Hermione. Paulina attacks Leontes further, telling him that he ought to repent for the rest of his life, and that he should do nothing but despair for the evil actions which have brought about these shocking results.

Leontes, however, replies in a manner which Paulina does not expect. She does not know of his repentance, but Leontes is now a changed man. He bids her go on with her scolding and ranting. He has deserved the worst she can say about him, and he willingly accepts the blame she lays upon him. Paulina herself is touched to see the manifest sorrow of Leontes and she regrets that she has been so hard on him, asking that she be punished for reminding him of things he would prefer to forget. From now on, she says, she will not remind him of his wife and children, or of her husband, Antigonus, who is apparently lost also.

Leontes then orders that Mamillius and Hermione be buried together and he promises to visit their chapel daily to weep for their loss.

Act III: Scene 3

This scene takes place in a desert area of Bohemia, near the sea. Antigonus, carrying a child, enters with a mariner who warns him to make haste with his business because a storm is imminent, and he thinks that this shows that the gods are angry over what Antigonus is about to do. The lord tells the sailor to return to the ship and he will hurry back himself. As he departs the sailor warns Antigonus that the storm looks like an unusually severe one, and in addition there are other dangers, because the place is famous for the beasts of prey that dwell there. Antigonus says that he will keep a careful lookout.

Left alone, Antigonus speaks pityingly to the child, saying that he dreamed last night that the spirit of Hermione appeared to him, weeping bitterly. She then addressed him and suggested that he leave the child in Bohemia, and further, that he call it Perdita, since the child is considered lost forever. Antigonus, however, must pay for his part in the exposure of the child and he will never see Paulina again. Obviously Antigonus is very shaken by this dream, and although he claims that dreams are toys, he decides to follow the instructions of his vision and leave Perdita on the seashore of Bohemia. He even considers that this is indeed the will of Apollo who wishes to see Polixenes' issue laid on the shore of its father's kingdom. The storm begins to threaten most ominously, and Antigonus fears for the safety of the child, pitying it that he has to leave it here because of its mother's sin. He regrets that he is bound to this action by oath, though the fact that he does fulfill what he takes to be the instructions of a true vision indicates some innate kindness in the man. The heavens get dimmer and dimmer; suddenly a bear appears and Antigonus rushes away pursued by the hungry animal.

A shepherd then enters. He is a middle-aged man and is complaining about the disgraceful behavior of the youth of the time, and in particular of its irresponsibility. Suddenly he sees the child, Perdita, lying on the ground and he comments that here undoubtedly is a bastard child, the product of some "behind-door work." Although his suspicions of the looseness of youth are hereby confirmed, he nevertheless takes up the infant out of pity and waits for his son. The son enters almost immediately and soon establishes himself as the common rustic clown. He tells of two strange sights that he has just seen: the foundering of a ship off the shore with the loss of all hands, and the devouring of a gentleman by a bear. In this way the audience is told what has happened to everyone who is involved in the exposure of Perdita to the elements. The clown tells of these two happenings with a certain comic glee which seems to mitigate the horror of their end, and at the same time may be meant to indicate what should be the attitude of the audience to the situation.

The shepherd is rather a simple soul in the best sense of the word. He is also superstitious, and therefore he sees the child as perhaps a changeling—this is a different approach from his earlier, earthier comment concerning its origin. He remembers that it was told him that he should become rich through the agency of fairies, and obviously this is going to be the case. The clown then sends his father home and says that he will go back to see if the bear has left anything of Antigonus worth the burying. This act is praised by the shepherd as a good deed.

Act IV: Scene 1

Time enters as a Chorus to recount all that has happened during the sixteen years which have intervened between these two acts. Leontes has retired from the world in grief. Prince Florizel, the son of Polixenes, is now well grown, as is Perdita. Time speaks in glowing terms of the grace of the young girl, but he abruptly ceases just when he seems about to reveal the conclusion of the plot. This part of the play, he says, concerns the fate of a shepherd's daughter, and Time suggests that the audience pay attention because the subject is most interesting.

Act IV: Scene 2

This scene takes place in the palace of Polixenes, where the King is trying to dissuade the trusted Camillo from returning to Sicilia. Quite naturally Camillo wishes to see his native land after such a long absence, and further, Leontes has sent for him asking him to return. Camillo, who has long ago forgiven his master, generously thinks that perhaps his presence in Sicilia might help to assuage the King's grief. Polixenes also pleads for Camillo to remain with him as his own highly trusted councillor—and one can well understand the desire of both princes for Camillo's company. An honest and fearless councillor is hard to find.

Then Polixenes changes the subject and asks when Camillo last saw the young prince Florizel, explaining that he is rather concerned over the conduct of the young man. Camillo says that he has not seen him for some three days, but he has noted that Florizel seems lately to have withdrawn himself from the court and to have been paying less attention to his princely duties than before. Polixenes in reply says that he has noted the same thing and therefore has had someone spy on the young man. Consequently the King has learned that he is spending a great deal of time at the house of a humble shepherd who has lately shown signs of considerable wealth. Camillo remarks that he also has heard of this shepherd, and what is more he believes that he has a daughter "of most rare note." Polixenes then suggests that he and Camillo disguise themselves in order to observe what is going on. Camillo agrees.

Act IV: Scene 3

In this scene, a road near the shepherd's cottage, the rogue Autolycus is introduced to the audience with a song. This song is a most interesting mixture of poetry and earthy reality, and in some ways it indicates the function of Autolycus in the play. He is the thievish rogue in the pastoral world, the astringent element which prevents the world of shepherds and shepherdesses from becoming too cloyingly sweet.

The opening song bears investigation for its meaning and for what it reveals about Autolycus. It begins conventionally enough with the praise of the flowers of spring: "When daffodils begin to peer," but then in the next line there is a sudden switch into what sounds like a refrain, "With heigh the doxy over the dale." Now a doxy is a beggar's mistress, and immediately we are taken out of the realm of flowers and love and into the world of beggary, knavery, and sensuality. The rest of the four-line first stanza carries out the same contrast between "the sweet of the year" and "the red blood [that] reigns in the winter's pale." Here we have the passion that rules winter's enclosure, or perhaps winter's paleness. In the second stanza the order is reversed, and the white sheets bleaching on the hedges are contrasted with the song of thrush and jay, which in turn is followed by the confession that Autolycus' pugging, or thievish, tooth is thereby set on edge. The third stanza operates as a kind of summation of the ideas that went before. The lark, the thrush, and the jay are all spoken of in the first two lines, to be followed by the contrast lines:

> Are summer songs for me and my aunts
> While we lie tumbling in the hay.

Here the word "aunts" has much the same meaning as "doxy" in the first stanza, and any attitude toward love which is expressed is obviously that of sensual passion.

Autolycus then interpolates a little autobiography, but he is such a congenital liar that we must always take what he says with a grain of salt. He claims that he was once a servant of Prince Florizel and wore velvet livery. But now he has been cast aside. Autolycus claims that he does not mourn for the loss of his place; instead he has gained a vagabond's freedom to wander wherever he pleases without having to answer to anybody. If he is put in the stocks he can say that he is a tinker and therefore has the right to wander. His business, he says, is sheets, and obviously the reference is to stolen sheets, perhaps those very sheets which were bleaching in the sunlight on the hedge, and the reference to the kite and smaller linen recalls the way in which the kite lines its nest with stolen scraps of cloth.

Merrily unrepentant, Autolycus goes on with his autobiography: he claims he was "littered under Mercury," a planet considered to confer cunning, and has come to his present state through gambling and women. He now makes his living by trickery, but since hanging and beating hold some terrors for him he is only a small-time operator and thief. As for the future, he does not care in the slightest; he will live each day as it comes.

At this moment the clown enters with a shopping list given him by his sister, Perdita, containing her grocery requirements for the sheep-shearing feast. The clown obviously has money with him because he opens by trying to calculate the proceeds of his wool. An examination of the grocery list reveals, incidentally, that Shakespeare is adhering very closely to reality.

Autolycus, seeing a chance for some villainy, promptly flings himself to the ground groaning, pretending that he has been robbed and left with the ragged clothes he is now wearing. He claims that his shoulder blade is out of joint and as the clown helps him up Autolycus deftly picks his pocket. When he is asked what kind of man robbed him, Autolycus gives a very specific account of the "robber"—and gives his own autobiography. He seems to be a kind of "carnival" character who has run a sideshow, led around an ape for exhibition, run a puppet show, and married a tinker's wife. All in all this robber knave seems to have gone through many dishonest professions, and his name is—Autolycus. By this time the audience should be enjoying the joke at the expense of the clown, who compounds it by claiming that he himself knows Autolycus very well; he then proceeds to give an account of Autolycus' alleged cowardice. The knave then thanks the clown who, ignorant that he himself has been robbed, goes off to the market to buy his spices.

Autolycus himself, always on the alert to turn a dishonest penny, decides that he will attend the sheep shearing; so with another song he departs.

Act IV: Scene 4

This scene, one of the longest in Shakespeare, takes place outside the shepherd's cottage where Prince Florizel and Perdita are walking together. She is in festive dress ready for the sheep-shearing feast, and is so bedecked with flowers that she seems to Florizel to be the goddess Flora herself. Perdita humbly turns aside such praise, saying that it does not become her, a lowly maiden, to chide the extremities of language in which the prince is indulging. She notes the way in which he has cast off his princely clothing and instead wears the garments of a mere countryman, while she is dressed like a goddess for the occasion. So humble is Perdita, and so conscious of her lowly rank as a shepherd's daughter, that she would not wish to be dressed as she is, except for the fact that the shepherds rather foolishly seem to want it so. She sees Florizel in his humble clothes as almost a looking glass to remind her of her own station. Florizel gives thanks for the happy accident whereby his falcon flew over the shepherd's land. Perdita, however, does not fully share his joy, because she is afraid of the consequences. Florizel, as a prince, is unused to fear of those in high places, but Perdita trembles in case Polixenes should chance to wander the same way and discover his son so poorly dressed, while she herself is "pranked up" in borrowed finery. Florizel speedily reassures her with examples drawn from the mythology of Greece: Jupiter himself became a bull, Neptune a ram, and Apollo a humble shepherd. Then Florizel adds another delicate compliment to Perdita in saying that they changed themselves into animals for women who were much less beautiful than Perdita. In addition, Florizel claims that his cause is a greater one, since his sexual desires are controlled and do not go beyond the bounds of honesty and honor.

Perdita is still afraid, however, and doubts whether the resolution of the young prince could be proof against the power of the King should the two ever be opposed, as indeed they someday must be concerning her. Either Florizel must choose, or Perdita must change her life. Florizel lovingly tells her to forget such dark thoughts and promises that he will be Perdita's forever, and will let his father disown him rather than give up Perdita. He then bids her be joyful and as merry as if this feast were the wedding feast they have both sworn will take place.

At this moment the shepherd enters with the clown, Mopsa and Dorcas, two country wenches, and Polixenes and Camillo in disguise. The shepherd rebukes his daughter, Perdita, for neglecting her duties as hostess at the feast, and recalls the way his own wife used to do everything much more efficiently. Perdita acts instead as if she were the guest of honor, not the hostess.

Perdita takes her father's rebuke as justified and she greets the disguised Polixenes and Camillo with the utmost humility and courtesy, offering them flowers as greeting. She presents them with rosemary and rue, herbs which keep their shape and savor throughout the whole winter. As she points out, these herbs offer grace (and also regret), and remembrance to them both.

Polixenes addresses the shepherdess kindly and notes her beauty, commenting wryly that she has chosen flowers of winter for them, well befitting their ages. Again Shakespeare introduces the opposition of youth and age. With the greatest of respect Perdita tells the gentlemen the reasons for her choice. The season is growing late; it is autumn, and in fact almost winter, and these are the only flowers in the garden since she does not care for the flowers that are usually in season at this time. These are carnations and gillyvors (gillyflowers, or clove-pinks, another kind of carnation), which some call "nature's bastards," because they are the result of artificial crossbreeding. Perdita objects to the art that is here used to improve on "great creating nature." Polixenes does not agree with the young girl and argues that the art which improves on nature still has its basis in nature itself and therefore should not be discriminated against. He speaks in glowing terms of grafting "A gentler scion to the wildest stock" in order to combine the best qualities of both "And make conceive a bark of baser kind/ By bud of nobler race." This practice, he claims, is an art which improves nature, but "the art itself is nature." He then exhorts her to fill her garden with carnations and gillyvors and not to call them bastards.

Fearlessly Perdita answers Polixenes, and flatly refuses to have such flowers in her garden, no more than she would wish, if she herself were artificially painted, that Florizel should wish to breed by her.

Perdita then turns to slightly younger men and offers them "Hot lavender, mints, savory, marjoram/ The marigold that goes to bed with the sun." These flowers, as she notes, are the flowers of "middle summer," and are therefore eminently suitable for men of middle age.

Finally Perdita turns to Florizel, the embodiment of youth in the play, to give him suitable flowers. But she must speak regretfully, because she really does not have anything for him. He merits only flowers of spring. The rest of this speech "is full of sexual significance" (Bethell, p. 97). She speaks of the young men and women as wearing their maidenheads on their virgin branches, but at the same time she speaks warmly of the joy that comes from sexual fulfillment. Daffodils "take the winds of March with beauty," and violets which are associated both with constancy and with the goddess Ceres (or Juno), the goddess of fertility, and Venus (Cytherea) the goddess supreme in beauty. She speaks sadly of the "pale primroses" because, like maids, they die unmarried before they see Phoebus, the sun, in his prime, or before they are fulfilled. Here there is certainly no ascetic praise of virginity. Then she goes on to praise the "bold oxlips" which stand up more straight and bold than cowslips, and the "crown imperial," a rather showy plant from the Levant, "lillies of all kinds," which are generally symbols of purity, and in particular the "flower-de-luce," or *fleur-de-lis*. Then, as Bethell notes (p. 97), she turns to an open declaration of love for the young man. She would wish to have such flowers in order to make him a garland, and to cover him with. Florizel asks, "What, like a corpse?" and Perdita speedily reassures him: "No, like a bank for love to lie and play on," and she wishes him "quick [alive] and in mine arms." Here there is an opposition of death and life, and Perdita passionately affirms life. The flower speech also contains a very specific reference to the same affirmation of life in its use of the Proserpine myth. It is Proserpine, the daughter of Cybele, who returns to earth every spring and is the patroness of fertility.

Florizel then turns to the beautiful shepherdess and speaks most lovingly to her, saying that whatever she does, it is the action of a queen, whether it be dancing, ordering her affairs, or even moving. She is in his eyes completely unique. Perdita replies most humbly to the words of her swain, who goes among the shepherds under the name of Doricles. She says that he overpraises her, and except for the fact that his youth and good breeding speak in his favor, she might almost consider that he was trying to woo her falsely with flattery. The two then dance, and Florizel takes her hand "as turtles pair/ That never mean to part." The clown and Mopsa also pair off, minding their manners in front of the nobility.

As the young couple move away, Polixenes and Camillo remark how impressed they are with the person of the "low-born lass." Polixenes says she is quite the prettiest one he has ever seen, and somehow she seems nobler than the station she occupies. Camillo, following the progress of the lovers with his eyes, says that she seems "the queen of curds and cream."

As the lovers dance on, Polixenes asks the shepherd the identity of the young man dancing with Perdita. The shepherd says that he is called Doricles and he has "a worthy feeding," in other words, a good farm with good livestock. The shepherd confides that the young man claims to be in love with Perdita, and in reply to Polixenes' compliment that she dances well, the shepherd more than agrees, saying that she does everything well. He also hints that she will bring the young Doricles something he does not even dream of should he marry her. Some secret surrounds the young girl.

At that moment a servant enters to announce the arrival of Autolycus. Immediately the clown and the servant fall into conversation, enquiring after the wares of the peddler, and the servant says that he has all sorts of wares suitable for men and women, as well as carrying a huge collection of ballads. The clown then orders the servant to send in the peddler, but Perdita modestly warns in advance that none of his ballads should be coarse or tasteless. Autolycus then enters singing merrily of his goods, and the clown remarks ruefully that since he is in love with Mopsa he will undoubtedly have to buy her something from the itinerant peddler.

The rustics in general cluster around Autolycus, who tells them all the ballads he has in his pack, and sings snatches of them in order to sell his wares. A set of country folk who specialize in a special kind of dance, "a gallimaufry of gambols," a collection of various steps, then arrives. They are "Saltiers," or "Satyrs," who specialize in leaping—even about twelve feet and a half—and have jumped before the King himself.

After the dance is finished Polixenes decides that it is time to part Perdita and Florizel because the affair has gone on too long and appears to be serious. He goes up to Florizel and reproaches him for not having bought his lady, Perdita, anything from the peddler. He himself, he claims, was accustomed to load his lady with gifts, and Perdita will probably take his failure to buy her something as a sign of his lack of love. Florizel replies with great dignity and sincerity, saying that he knows very well that Perdita does not value such trifles. The gifts she expects from him are instead gifts which arise from his heart, in other words, the gifts of love, honor, and fidelity.

Florizel then turns to Perdita and takes her hand, which he praises with exaggerated rhetoric. He declares his love for Perdita and says that he cannot live without her. Perdita replies that she cannot the King, Cleomenes, Dion, Paulina, and servants. Cleomenes, who had been one of the messengers to the Oracle, is trying to persuade Leontes to cease his mourning and repentance. He says that he has repented and sorrowed like a saint. In fact there does not seem to be any fault ever committed that Leontes' penance could not have redeemed, and since the heavens have obviously forgotten Leontes' evil, he should forgive himself.

Leontes in reply says that he can never forget Hermione, and while he remembers her and her virtue he can never forget the wrong he did to her, and also to the kingdom, since it has been left without an heir. In symbolic terms one should here note the sterility of anger and jealousy as passions. Paulina then speaks in praise of Hermione, claiming that she was more than the sum of all the virtues of every woman in the world. Paulina is as blunt-tongued as ever, and she does not hesitate to twist the knife in the wound in referring to Hermione as "she you kill'd." Leontes takes up the word and says that he knows his guilt only too well, and therefore he wishes that Paulina would mention it less frequently. Cleomenes also rebukes her for her continued insistence on Leontes' guilt. Paulina tartly remarks that Cleomenes is one of those courtiers who would wish Leontes to marry again, but Dion claims that Paulina is not thinking of the good of the state in insisting on Leontes' remaining unmarried. After all, the country needs an heir, because all sorts of civil dangers can befall a state when the succession is disputed.

Dion also says that remarriage would in effect be a compliment to the dead queen, because it would show that the King had indeed been happily married before, since he would so willingly enter again into that state of life. Paulina claims that there is no one worthy in comparison with Hermione; in fact the impossibility of finding such a lady is just as great as the impossibility of Hermione's arising from the grave. Further, did not the Oracle say that the King should not have an heir until his lost child be found? Therefore advice to remarry is really running counter to the will of the gods as stated by the Oracle. After all, Alexander the Great left the crown to the worthiest—why cannot Leontes do the same?

Leontes, obviously tortured by the memory of Hermione, wishes vainly that he had listened to advice in the past; then he could have enjoyed his Queen's presence for these past sixteen years. He realizes his unparalled loss and says he will not remarry because such an action would cause her ghost to walk again. Paulina agrees, and Leontes says that a ghost would even incite him to the murder of a second wife. Paulina then very dramatically acts out what the

speak as eloquently as her lover, but she endorses all his sentiments. The shepherd tells the two of them to join hands in a bargain, a betrothal, and he tells Polixenes and Camillo, the two witnesses, that he willingly gives his daughter to Doricles, and will make her portion equal to his. In reply, Florizel says that "one being dead," obviously his father, will bring him much more than the old shepherd could ever dream of. But then he asks the shepherd to contract them before these unknown witnesses.

Polixenes, however, interrupts the proceeding to ask the young man whether he has a father, and on receiving an affirmative answer, he asks whether he has been informed of this situation. Florizel replies that he neither knows nor shall know. To this surprising remark Polixenes comments that a father's place is at the nuptial of his son, unless of course he has grown totally senile, which Florizel denies. Polixenes then speaks in support of the filial duty by which a son should inform his father. Respectfully, Florizel says that he has very good reasons indeed for not acquainting his father with this business, and once more he asks the shepherd to ratify the contract. At this moment Polixenes reveals himself with "Mark your divorce, young sir." Then he flies into an almost uncontrollable rage directed first against his son, next against the old shepherd whom he threatens with hanging, and lastly against Perdita herself, whose beauty he threatens to destroy. Again he rages at his son and declares that he will bar his succession to the throne and disown him entirely. He temporarily excuses the shepherd but threatens Perdita with death if she does not keep away from Florizel.

Polixenes then departs, leaving everyone behind in a state of consternation. Perdita seems to be the first to recover her self-possession and she remarks that she was not really afraid, and more than once she was on the verge of telling Polixenes that the same sun that shines on the court also shines on the shepherd's cottage. By these words she seems to mean that Polixenes has no right to consider himself any better than a shepherd. Here we have the conflict between court and country, of civil and uncivil life.

The shepherd now turns to the lovers and blames both of them for conspiring against him. Florizel has ruined an old man of eighty-three who had hoped to die quietly, knowing that his daughter was well settled. Now he may very well be hanged and buried in unconsecrated ground. Perdita has deceived him also because she has known all along of Florizel's identity and yet she did not inform her father.

Camillo, however, has remained behind, and he plays substantially the same role that he had played in the first act. He shows sympathy with the fate of the lovers and says that it is best not to talk to Polixenes when he is in such a rage. Perdita then comments that she had always expected that something like this would happen. But Florizel gallantly asserts that he does not care whether his life itself will be destroyed, or whether his father will disown him. He considers himself as not belonging to his father any more, but solely to Perdita. Camillo, in his customary common sense manner, attempts to stop Florizel from saying anything rash, but Florizel declares that he knows quite well what he is doing and that nothing whatsoever will make him break his faith to Perdita.

Florizel then begs Camillo to try to assuage Polixenes' rage, because his plan is to fly on a vessel which happens to be in the harbor at the moment. Camillo then has a fine idea: perhaps he can manage to turn Florizel's flight to his own advantage. He can save Florizel from danger and help him achieve his desire, and as for himself, he can thereby "Purchase the sight again of dear Sicilia."

Camillo then makes his proposition to Florizel and assures the young man that he has nothing but the good of the lovers at heart. He suggests that they make for Sicilia and present themselves at the court. In the meantime he will remain in Bohemia and try to placate the King. He also refers to Perdita as "your fair princess," saying that indeed she appears to be of such noble rank. As a cover story for Leontes, Camillo suggests that Florizel say that he has been sent to bear greetings and gifts from his father; in addition, Camillo promises to write suitable instructions for Florizel. He says that at least the lovers will have a specific destination in mind, and it is better that they be safe because prosperity is "the bond of love," and affliction may waste the cheek and alter the course of love. Perdita, however, steadfastly disagrees, saying that the cheek may waste, but not the mind. Camillo is profoundly moved by her steadfastness. Again, the audience ought to remember the conduct of Hermione and see the resemblance between mother and daughter. Florizel says that despite her birth she seems to be noble, while Camillo comments with wonderment that she really seems a mistress to most of those who set themselves as teachers. Florizel is concerned about his dress when he arrives in Sicilia, but Camillo tells him not to be disturbed. He will make arrangements to have the lovers well received. The lovers then talk aside. (See Coghill, "Six Points . . .")

Autolycus now enters and speaks of the tricks he has been playing on the rustics. He has sold all his goods, most of which were quite worthless. He managed to distract the attention of the company by

means of his ballad singing and then was able to pick most of [their] pockets, which were full of money since the owners were [at the] festival.

The nobles and Perdita suddenly become aware of the presence [of] Autolycus, and Camillo says that they can make some use of [him.] Autolycus then becomes a trifle concerned, because if the w[rong] person has overheard his recent confession of trickery he i[s in] danger of hanging. Camillo suggests, however, that Autol[ycus] change clothes with Florizel in order to provide a disguise for [the] young prince. Autolycus congratulates himself on his excha[nge] because he has certainly got the better part of the bargain. [The] unjust man is indeed thriving.

Florizel, Perdita, and Camillo depart and the shepherd and [the] clown enter. The clown tries to convince his father that he sh[ould] go to the King. After all, the shepherd is not to blame for [the] situation with Florizel because Perdita is a changeling and none [of] his flesh and blood. The shepherd promptly determines to go to [the] King and tell him everything, and in particular inform him that [his] own son, Florizel, had taken the initiative in wooing Perd[ita.] Autolycus then decides to take a hand in the situation and pas[s] himself off in his new clothes as a courtier.

Autolycus identifies himself as a courtier, and his clothes procla[im] him so. He then offers himself as a suitable escort for the rusti[cs] who innocently answer all his leading questions and reveal that th[ey] are carrying secret information in their bundle which will be [of] great interest to the King, especially in view of Florizel's desire [to] marry Perdita. The rustics then even give him money in order [to] ensure that Autolycus will take them into the King's presence so th[at] they may speak to him. The rogue has managed to get the count[ry] folk entirely within his power because he has detailed at great leng[th] the appalling fate that will await them once the King gets hold [of] them. Autolycus then tells the shepherd and the clown to prece[de] him and he will follow. Left alone he regrets that Fortune simp[ly] will not permit him to be honest. Now he has been given gold wh[ere] he intended to rob. He will bring the rustics to the King, but n[ot] immediately. After all, there may be some profit in the business f[or] him. Therefore he later delays their visit to the King, but gets the[m] aboard the ship bound for Sicilia.

Act V: Scene 1

This scene takes place in a room in Leontes' palace, where we find

supposed ghost of Hermione might say, and Leontes reiterates his determination never to remarry. Paulina now asks him to swear to that resolution, which Leontes does, and the lady calls upon the lords present to act as witnesses, though Cleomenes says she is really pushing the repentant King too far. Paulina does, however, offer two glimmerings of hope. Leontes must swear not to remarry unless a woman who is in every possible physical manifestation the counterpart of Hermione appear, or until Paulina shall choose him a suitable queen, such that Hermione's ghost would rejoice to see. Leontes then swears that he will not remarry without Paulina's permission, which she says will not be forthcoming until Hermione lives again.

Just then a servant appears to announce the arrival of Prince Florizel and his princess, "the fairest I have yet beheld." The young couple desire an audience with Leontes. The King is a trifle puzzled because the visit is unannounced, and therefore it may be the result of necessity or accident. He is also surprised to learn that Prince Florizel has a very small and rather poorly accoutred company with him. Again the servant expatiates on the unparalleled beauty of the "princess" and Paulina laments that Hermione should be so soon forgotten. The servant politely disagrees with Paulina, saying that she too will certainly join in the praises of this young girl when she sees her, as will all other women. Leontes then sends Cleomenes and his friends to escort the prince and his lady to the court. But as the gentlemen of the court depart, Leontes begins to wonder at the way Florizel and his princess have arrived so unexpectedly and unannounced. Paulina, who never allows Leontes to forget anything, recalls that if Mamillius had lived he would have been precisely the age of the young Florizel. Again Leontes pleads with Paulina not to remind him of his irreparable losses, and at this instant Cleomenes and his company return, bringing with them Florizel and Perdita.

Leontes greets the young people joyfully and remarks on the striking likeness between Florizel and his father, Polixenes. But once more, as he looks on the pair he realizes the depth and the irreparable nature of his loss, all through his own doing. Florizel presents greetings from his father and says that Polixenes would have wished to come had he not been prevented from an infirmity of an unspecified nature which keeps him at home. However, he, Florizel, has come at his father's request to see Leontes. Again the King castigates himself for his suspicion of Polixenes those many years ago, and he welcomes the young people again as joyfully as one welcomes the spring to the earth.

Florizel says that Perdita is a princess from Libya and that they are both on their way home after he had won the hand of the King's daughter, the lady who is with him. He explains his lack of a suitable train by explaining that he himself has made a detour to Sicilia and has sent everyone else back to Bohemia to tell Polixenes of the success of the mission. Leontes again expresses his joy in seeing them and then recalls that if things had happened otherwise he too might have had such a son and daughter.

Just then a lord enters with the news that a ship bearing Polixenes has just arrived in harbor, and he begs Leontes to apprehend Florizel who has dared to fly from Bohemia with a mere shepherd's daughter. Apparently Polixenes has been somehow informed of the flight of the pair, and the clown and the shepherd are on board ship with him. Immediately Florizel jumps to the logical conclusion that the honest Camillo has betrayed them, but the newly arrived servant says that since Camillo is with Polixenes the prince can tax him with the falsehood. The news of Polixenes' arrival causes Leontes to rejoice.

Perdita expresses sorrow for her poor father, the shepherd, and mournfully says that the heavens seem to be against their ever celebrating their marriage in a proper manner. Leontes seizes on this piece of information and delivers a homily on filial obedience. Certainly Perdita is very beautiful, but at the same time the young man ought to realize his obligations as a prince and marry where he should, not where he wishes. Florizel, however, does not listen very hard. Instead he turns to Perdita and says that his love for her is unchangeable. Then he begs Leontes for help, asking him to act as advocate to Polixenes, and begging him to remember how he felt when he was their age. At the pleading of Leontes, Florizel is quite certain that Polixenes will grant even the most precious things as if they were mere trifles. Leontes, however, makes the surprising admission that in that case he would beg Perdita for himself. Paulina, quite shocked, tells Leontes to remember Hermione, who was more beautiful than this young girl. Leontes, somewhat chastened, says that he thought of Hermione with every look he directed toward Perdita. And partly because of this subconscious evocation of memory, he decides that he will speak in Florizel's behalf.

Act V: Scene 2

This scene takes place outside the palace of Leontes. Autolycus and a gentleman enter, and then two more arrive. All have just come from inside the palace and can talk of nothing but the astonishing scene they have just witnessed. The shepherd has brought with him a bundle containing proof of Perdita's identity as the daughter of Leontes who had been thought lost, but is now found. Luckily the shepherd had the foresight to keep Perdita's baby clothes against just such a possibility. Leontes and Camillo can hardly take their eyes from each other, so glad are they to meet again under such pleasant circumstances.

The entire action of the past sixteen years is then recounted, including the death of Antigonus and the drowning of the crew of the ship which had brought Perdita to Bohemia. The occasion was most merry and sorrowful at the court on this day, judging by the account of it.

Everyone tells Perdita that she is very like her mother, and we are informed that the lady Paulina has just had a lifelike statue of Hermione completed for her by the noted sculptor, Julio Romano. The moment Perdita hears of this, she begs to be allowed to see it, so that Paulina promises to take the company to an isolated house to see it. One of the gentlemen remarks that Paulina has often been observed visiting this house, but no one had known why.

The shepherd and the clown then enter, the young man rather foolishly rejoicing that the King has declared them both to be gentlemen. The clown makes comments at the expense of courtly morality, and in his behavior attempts to ape the manners of the noble folk. The shepherd, who is both more sensible and more discriminating, declares that he will stick to the honest usages of the country. In this attitude he is shown as typifying the honesty of ideal shepherds uncorrupted by civilization and the court. The clown, however, is feeling his power and now condescendingly offers to help Autolycus.

Act V: Scene 3

This scene takes place in a chapel in the house of Paulina. Leontes, Polixenes, Florizel, Perdita, Camillo, Paulina, and a crowd of lords and attendants have assembled. Paulina has taken the company on a tour of her other works of art, but Leontes is desperately impatient to see the statue and begs Paulina to show it to him.

Paulina says that the statue counterfeits life as superbly as death can sometimes counterfeit life. She then draws the curtain to disclose Hermione standing as if she were a sculptured figure. The likeness is greeted with astonished silence by everyone present, until

Leontes breaks the spell by expressing his amazement at the naturalness of the posture, and again he expresses his repentance. Yet he does note that the Hermione he remembers was less wrinkled than the statue before him. Paulina comments that that is simply part of the sculptor's skill, for he has carved Hermione's likeness not as she was sixteen years ago, but as she might have been now, had she lived. The sight pierces Leontes to the soul, and then Perdita speaks, begging to be allowed to kiss the hand of the statue, in lieu of the mother whom she never knew. Paulina, however, intervenes with the excuse that the colors are not yet dry and firmly set. Camillo and Polixenes also express their amazement at the statue, but Leontes seems profoundly depressed by his sad remembrance and expresses his repentance openly. Paulina therefore apologizes for reawakening old memories by this sight, but Leontes seems to live only by gazing on the statue, and finally determines to kiss the likeness. Once again Paulina warns that the colors are not dry, but tells Leontes that she is able to make the statue move from its pedestal, but not through wicked powers.

She then calls for music, and Hermione comes down to embrace her husband. Paulina tells the Queen that Perdita is her lost daughter, miraculously restored, and the entire company rejoices.

Paulina then speaks of her widowhood, and Leontes promptly offers her Camillo as a husband. The King admires both of them for their loyalty to the reputation of Hermione, and therefore he foresees a fine match. Actually this marriage looks rather like a contrivance to people the stage with happy couples and show that order has again been restored to the chaotic world of passions, confusions, disguises, and repentance. Symbolically, however, the three marriages represent a return to harmony and order. All evil has been purged away and joy now reigns.

Memorable Quotations

A horse! a horse! my kingdom for a horse!
(Richard III, Act V, Scene 4)

A lion among ladies is a most dreadful thing.
(A Midsummer Night's Dream, Act III, Scene 1)

A plague upon it when thieves cannot be true one to another!
(Henry IV Part I, Act II, Scene 2)

Age cannot wither her, nor custom stale
Her infinite variety.
(Antony and Cleopatra, Act II, Scene 2)

Alas, poor Yorick! I knew him, Horatio: a fellow of infinite jest, of most excellent fancy.
(Hamlet, Act V, Scene 1)

And thereby hangs a tale.
(The Taming of the Shrew, Act IV, Scene 1)

Are you good men and true?
(Much Ado About Nothing, Act III, Scene 3)

As full of spirit as the month of May.
(Henry IV Part I, Act IV, Scene 1)

A little more than kin, and less than kind.
(Hamlet, Act I, Scene 2)

Ay, every inch a king.
(King Lear, Act IV, Scene 6)

Beggar that I am, I am even poor in thanks.
(Hamlet, Act II, Scene 2)

Brevity is the soul of wit.
(Hamlet, Act II, Scene 2)

But, for my own part, it was Greek to me.

(Julius Caesar, Act I, Scene 2)

But I will wear my heart upon my sleeve
For daws to peck at: I am not what I am.

(Othello, Act I, Scene 1)

Costly thy habit as thy purse can buy,
But not express'd in fancy; rich, not gaudy;
For the apparel oft proclaims the man.

(Hamlet, Act I, Scene 3)

Death lies on her like an untimely frost
Upon the sweetest flower of all the field.

(Romeo and Juliet, Act IV, Scene 5)

Every why hath a wherefore.

(The Comedy of Errors, Act II, Scene 2)

Every one can master a grief but he that has it.

(Much Ado About Nothing, Act III, Scene 2)

For Brutus is an honourable man;
So are they all, all honourable men.

(Julius Caesar, Act III, Scene 2)

Forbear to judge, for we are sinners all.

(Henry VI Part II, Act III, Scene 3)

Foul whisp'rings are abroad.

(Macbeth, Act V, Scene 1)

Frailty, thy name is woman!

(Hamlet, Act I, Scene 2)

Friends, Romans, countrymen, lend me your ears.

(Julius Caesar, Act III, Scene 2)

Give me that man
That is not passion's slave.

(Hamlet, Act III, Scene 2)

God befriend us, as our cause is just!

(Henry IV Part I, Act V, Scene 1)

God hath given you one face, and you make yourselves another.

(Hamlet, Act III, Scene 1)

Good name in man and woman, dear my lord,
Is the immediate jewel of their souls.

(Othello, Act III, Scene 3)

Memorable Quotations

Goodnight, goodnight! parting is such sweet sorrow,
That I shall say good night till it be morrow.
(Romeo and Juliet, Act II, Scene 2)

Great men may jest with saints; 'tis wit in them;
But in the less foul profanation.
(Measure for Measure, Act II, Scene 2)

Have more than thou showest,
Speak less than thou knowest.
(King Lear, Act I, Scene 4)

He does it with a better grace, but I do it more natural.
(Twelfth Night, Act II, Scene 3)

He hath eaten me out of house and home.
(Henry IV Part II, Act II, Scene 1)

He that dies pays all debts.
(The Tempest, Act III, Scene 2)

He will give the devil his due.
(Henry IV Part I, Act I, Scene 2)

Help me Cassius, or I sink!
(Julius Caesar, Act I, Scene 2)

His life was gentle, and the elements
So mix'd in him that Nature might stand up,
And say to all the world, "This was a man!"
(Julius Caesar, Act V, Scene 5)

Her voice was ever soft,
Gentle and low, an excellent thing in woman.
(King Lear, Act V, Scene 3)

How sharper than a serpent's tooth it is
To have a thankless child.
(King Lear, Act I, Scene 4)

How use doth breed a habit in a man!
(Two Gentlemen of Verona, Act V, Scene 4)

I am a Jew: Hath not a Jew eyes? Hath not a Jew hands, organs,
dimensions, senses, affections, passions? fed with the same food, hurt with the
same weapons, subject to the same diseases, healed by the same means,
warmed and cooled by the same winter and summer, as a Christian is?
(The Merchant of Venice, Act III, Scene 1)

SHAKESPEARE'S BEST PLAYS

I am a man
More sinn'd against than sinning.

(King Lear, Act III, Scene 2)

I am as poor as Job, my lord, but not so patient.

(Henry IV Part II, Act I, Scene 2)

I am disgrac'd, impeach'd and baffled here,
Pierc'd to the soul with slander's venom'd spear.

(Richard II, Act I, Scene 1)

I am wealthy in my friends.

(Timon of Athens, Act II, Scene 2)

I earn that I eat, get that I wear, owe no man hate, envy no man's happiness,
glad of other men's good, content with my harm.

(As You Like It, Act III, Scene 2)

I have no other but a woman's reason;
I think him so because I think him so.

(Two Gentlemen of Verona, Act I, Scene 2)

I must be cruel, only to be kind.

(Hamlet, Act III, Scene 4)

I see that the fashion wears out more apparel than the man.

(Much Ado About Nothing, Act III, Scene 3)

I to myself am dearer than a friend.

(Two Gentlemen of Verona, Act II, Scene 6)

I wish you all the joy that you can wish.

(Merchant of Venice, Act III, Scene 2)

If all the year were playing holidays,
To sport would be as tedious as to work.

(Henry IV Part I, Act I, Scene 2)

If you have tears, prepare to shed them now.

(Julius Caesar, Act III, Scene 2)

I'll take thy word for faith, not ask thine oath:
Who shuns not to break one will sure crack them both.

(Pericles, Act I, Scene 2)

It is a wise father that knows his own child.

(The Merchant of Venice, Act II, Scene 2)

Jesters do oft prove prophets.

(King Lear, Act V, Scene 3)

Memorable Quotations

Let them obey that know not how to rule.
(Henry VI Part II, Act V, Scene 1)

Let your own discretion be your tutor: suit the action to the word,
the word to the action.
(Hamlet, Act III, Scene 2)

Lord, we know what we are, but know now what we may be.
(Hamlet, Act IV, Scene 5)

Lord, what fools these mortals be!
(A Midsummer Night's Dream, Act II, Scene 2)

Love sought is good, but given unsought is better.
(Twelfth Night, Act III, Scene 1)

Many a man's tongue shakes out his master's undoing.
(All's Well That Ends Well, Act II, Scene 4)

Men are April when they woo, December when they wed.
(As You Like It, Act IV, Scene 1)

Men have died from time to time and worms have eaten them, but not for love.
(As You Like It, Act IV, Scene 1)

Misery acquaints a man with strange bed-fellows.
(The Tempest, Act II, Scene 2)

Murder most foul, as in the best it is,
But this most foul, strange and unnatural.
(Hamlet, Act I, Scene 5)

My heart is ever at your service.
(Timon of Athens, Act I, Scene 2)

My man's as true as steel.
(Romeo and Juliet, Act II, Scene 4)

Neither a borrower nor a lender be;
For loan often loses both itself and friend,
And borrowing dulleth edge of husbandry.
(Hamlet, Act I, Scene 3)

Nothing in his life
Became him like the leaving it.
(Macbeth, Act I, Scene 4)

Now is the Winter of our discontent.
(Richard III, Act III, Scene 4)

O! call back yesterday, bid time return.
(Richard II, Act III, Scene 2)

SHAKESPEARE'S BEST PLAYS

O fortune, fortune! all men call thee fickle.

(Romeo and Juliet, Act III, Scene 5)

O God, that men should put an enemy in their mouths to steal away their brains; that we should, with joy, pleasance, revel and applause, transform ourselves into beasts!

(Othello, Act II, Scene 3)

O, it is excellent
To have a giant's strength, but it is tyrannous
To use it like a giant.

(Measure for Measure, Act II, Scene 2)

O judgement! thou art fled to brutish beasts,
And men have lost their reason.

(Julius Caesar, Act III, Scene 2)

O sleep, O gentle sleep,
Nature's soft nurse.

(Henry IV Part II, Act III, Scene 1)

Rich gifts wax poor when givers prove unkind.

(Hamlet, Act III, Scene 1)

Sermons in stones and good in every thing.

(As You Like It, Act II, Scene 1)

Ships are but boards, sailors but men.

(The Merchant of Venice, Act I, Scene 3)

Sigh no more, ladies, sigh no more.
Men were deceivers ever;
One foot in sea and one on shore,
To one thing constant never.

(Much Ado About Nothing, Act II, Scene 3)

Some are born great, some achieve greatness
and some have greatness thrust upon em.

(Twelfth Night, Act II, Scene 5)

Something is rotten in the state of Denmark.

(Hamlet, Act I, Scene 4)

Sweet are the uses of adversity,
Which, like the toad, ugly and venomous,
Wears yet a precious jewel in his head.

(As You Like It, Act II, Scene 1)

Memorable Quotations

Sweets to the sweet: farewell!

(Hamlet, Act V, Scene 1)

The better part of valour is discretion.

(Henry IV Part I, Act V, Scene 4)

The course of true love never did run smooth.

(A Midsummer Night's Dream, Act I, Scene 1)

The devil can cite Scripture for his purpose.

(The Merchant of Venice, Act I, Scene 3)

The empty vessel makes the greatest sound.

(Henry V, Act IV, Scene 4)

The evil that men do lives after them,
The good is oft interred with their bones.

(Julius Caesar, Act III, Scene 2)

The fool doth think he is wise, but the wise man knows himself to be a fool.

(As You Like It, Act V, Scene 1)

The jury, passing on the prisoner's life,
May in the sworn twelve have a thief or two
Guiltier than him they try.

(Measure for Measure, Act II, Scene 1)

The law hath not been dead, though it hath slept.

(Measure for Measure, Act II, Scene 2)

The man that hath no music in himself,
Nor is not moved with concord of sweet sounds,
Is fit for treasons, stratagems and spoils.

(The Merchant of Venice, Act V, Scene 1)

The play's the thing.

(Hamlet, Act II, Scene 2)

The prince of darkness is a gentleman.

(King Lear, Act III, Scene 4)

The purest treasure mortal times afford
Is spotless reputation: that away,
Men are gilded loam or painted clay.

(Richard II, Act I, Scene 1)

The ripest fruit first falls.

(Richard II, Act II, Scene 1)

SHAKESPEARE'S BEST PLAYS

The soul of this man is his clothes.
> *(All's Well That Ends Well, Act II, Scene 5)*

The worst is not
So long as we can say "This is the worst."
> *(King Lear, Act IV, Scene 1)*

There's a divinity that shapes our ends,
Rough-hew them how we will.
> *(Hamlet, Act V, Scene 2)*

There is a tide in the affairs of men,
Which, taken at the flood, leads on to fortune.
> *(Julius Caesar, Act IV, Scene 3)*

There is nothing either good or bad, but thinking makes it so.
> *(Hamlet, Act II, Scene 2)*

There was never yet philosopher,
That could endure the toothache patiently.
> *(Much Ado About Nothing, Act V, Scene 1)*

There's a time for all things.
> *(The Comedy of Errors, Act II, Scene 2)*

There's small choice in rotten apples.
> *(The Taming of the Shrew, Act I, Scene 1)*

There's villainous news abroad.
> *(Henry IV Part I, Act II, Scene 4)*

Thieves for their robbery have authority
When judges steal themselves.
> *(Measure for Measure, Act II, Scene 2)*

This royal throne of kings, this sceptr'd isle,
This earth of majesty, this seat of Mars,
This other Eden, demi-paradise,
This fortress built by nature for herself
Against infection and the hand of war;
This happy breed of men, this little world,
This precious stone set in the silver sea.
> *(Richard II, Act II, Scene 1)*

Memorable Quotations

This was the most unkindest cut of all;
For when the noble Caesar saw him stab,
Ingratitude, more strong than traitors' arms,
Quite vanquish'd him; then burst his mighty heart.

(Julius Caesar, Act III, Scene 2)

This was the noblest Roman of them all.

(Julius Caesar, Act V, Scene 5)

Though this be madness, yet there is method in't.

(Hamlet, Act II, Scene 2)

Thy wish was father, Harry, to that thought.

(Henry IV Part II, Act IV, Scene 5)

'Tis time to fear when tyrants seem to kiss.

(Pericles, Act I, Scene 2)

'Tis but a base, ignoble mind
That mounts no higher than a bird can soar.

(Henry V, Act IV, Scene 1)

'Tis not the many oaths that makes the truth,
But the plain single vow that is vow'd true.

(All's Well That Ends Well, Act IV, Scene 2)

To be, or not to be: that is the question:
Whether 'tis nobler in the mind to suffer
The slings and arrows of outrageous fortune,
Or to take arms against a sea of troubles,
And by opposing end them?

(Hamlet, Act III, Scene 1)

To die: to sleep;
No more; and, by a sleep to say we end
The heartache and the thousand natural shocks
That flesh is heir to, 'tis a consummation
Devoutly to be wish'd.

(Hamlet, Act III, Scene 1)

To sleep: perchance to dream.

(Hamlet, Act III, Scene 1)

Uneasy lies the head that wears a crown.

(Henry IV Part II, Act III, Scene 1)

SHAKESPEARE'S BEST PLAYS

We are such stuff
As dreams are made on, and our little life
Is rounded with a sleep.

(The Tempest, Act IV, Scene 1)

What is the city but the people?

(Coriolanus, Act III, Scene 1)

What's done cannot be undone.

(Macbeth, Act V, Scene 1)

What's gone and what's past help
Should be past grief.

(The Winter's Tale, Act III, Scene 2)

What's in a name? that which we call a rose
By any other name would smell as sweet.

(Romeo and Juliet, Act II, Scene 2)

What's mine is yours, and what is yours is mine.

(Measure for Measure, Act V, Scene 1)

When that the poor have cried, Caesar hath wept;
Ambition should be made of sterner stuff:
Yet Brutus says he was ambitious;
And Brutus is an honourable man.

(Julius Caesar, Act III, Scene 2)

Yet do I fear thy nature;
It is too full o' th' milk of human kindness.

(Macbeth, Act I, Scene 5)

Yond Cassius has a lean and hungry look;
He thinks too much: such men are dangerous.

(Julius Caesar, Act I, Scene 2)

Bibliography

General Criticism

Bradby, Anne, ed. *Shakespeare Criticism 1919–1935*. New York: Oxford University Press, 1936.

Coleridge, Samuel Taylor. *Lectures and Notes on Shakespeare*. London: Oxford University Press, 1931.

Dowden, Edward. *Shakespeare: His Mind and Art*. London: Oxford University Press, 1887.

Frye, Northrop. "The Argument of Comedy." English Institute Essays, 1948, 58-73.

Granville-Barker, Harley. *Prefaces to Shakespeare*. Princeton, N.J.: Princeton University Press, 1946.

Granville-Barker, Harley, and Harrison, George B. *Companion to Shakespeare Studies*. Cambridge, M.A.: Cambridge University Press, 1934.

Hazlitt, William. *Characters of Shakespeare's Plays*. New York: Dutton, 1870, and often reprinted.

Holzknecht, Karl J. *The Backgrounds of Shakespeare's Plays*. New York: American Book Co., 1950.

Spurgeon, Caroline. *Shakespeare's Imagery And What It Tells Us*. Cambridge, M.A.: Cambridge University Press, 1935.

Traversi, Derek A. *An Approach to Shakespeare*. New York: Doubleday Anchor, 1956.

Van Doren, Mark. *Shakespeare*. New York: Doubleday Anchor, 1953.

Life and Times

Chambers, Sir E.K. *William Shakespeare: A Study of Facts and Problems*. Oxford: Clarendon Press, 1930. 2 vols.

Chute, Marchette. *Shakespeare of London*. New York: E. P. Dutton, 1949.

Halliday, F. E. *The Life of Shakespeare*. London: Duckworth, 1961.

Parrott, Thoman Marc. *William Shakespeare: A Handbook*. Revised Edition. New York: Scribner's, 1955.

Tillyard, E.M.W. *The Elizabethan World Picture*. New York: Macmillan, 1944.

SHAKESPEARE'S BEST PLAYS

Shakespeare's Theatre

Adams, John Cranford. *The Globe Playhouse*. Cambridge, M.A.: Harvard University Press, 1943.

Chambers, E. K. *The Elizabethan Stage*. Oxford: Clarendon Press, 1923. 4 vols.

Harbage, Alfred. *Shakespeare and the Rival Traditions*. New York: Macmillan, 1952.

Nagler, Alois M. *Shakespeare's Stage*. New Haven, Connecticut: Yale University Press, 1958.

Sources and Text

Craig, Hardin. *The Enchanted Glass*. London: Basil Blackwell, 1960.

Lovejoy, A.O. *Essays in the History of Ideas*. New York: G. Braziller, 1955.

———— *The Great Chain of Being*. Cambridge, M.A.: Harvard University Press, 1936.

Spencer, Theodore. *Shakespeare and the Nature of Man*. New York: Macmillan, 1958.

Index